ACT®
Total Prep
2025

Lead Editor

Kathryn Sollenberger, M.Ed.

Contributing Editors

Dr. Brandon Deason, M.D.; M. Dominic Eggert; Paula L. Fleming, MA; Katy Haynicz-Smith, MA; Melissa McLaughlin; J. Scott Mullison; Glen Stohr; Alexandra Strelka, MA; Heather Waite

Special thanks to our writers and reviewers:

Laura Aitcheson, Michael Collins, Michael Cook, Maria Cuffe, Sterling Davenport, Boris Dvorkin, Mark Feery, Emily Graves, Jonathan Habermacher, Laurel Haines, Jack Hayes, Peter Haynicz-Smith, Stephanie Jolly, Samee Kirk, Jo L'Abbate, Melissa McLaughlin, Lauren Miller, Aishwarya Pillai, Gail Rivers, Anne Marie Salloum, Gordon Spector, Caroline Sykes, Heather Waite, Bonnie Wang, and Ethan Weber

Additional special thanks to

Deborah Becak, Isaac Botier, Megan Buckman, Brian Carlidge, Tim Eich, Joanna Graham, Rebecca Knauer, Camellia Mukherjee, Kristin Murner, Denise Pangia, Narender Patyal, Subitha R.K., Ashley Stussy, Oscar Velazquez, Michael Wolff, Amy Zarkos, and the countless others who made this project possible.

ACT® is a registered trademark of ACT, Inc., which is not affiliated with Kaplan and was not involved in the production of, and does not endorse, this product.

This publication is designed to provide accurate and authoritative information in regard to the subject matter covered. It is sold with the understanding that the publisher is not engaged in rendering legal, accounting, or other professional service. If legal advice or other expert assistance is required, the services of a competent professional should be sought.

Published by Kaplan North America, LLC dba Kaplan Publishing
1515 W. Cypress Creek Road
Fort Lauderdale, Florida 33309

ISBN: 978-1-5062-9042-3
10 9 8 7 6 5 4 3 2

Kaplan North America, LLC print books are available at special quantity discounts to use for sales promotions, employee premiums, or educational purposes. For more information or to purchase books, please call the Simon & Schuster Special Sales department at 866-506-1949.

TABLE OF CONTENTS

Three Tips for ACT Success

Colleges will consider your ACT score as part of your application, so it's no surprise that it's a pretty tough test. It can feel intimidating, like a barrier you need to climb over. At Kaplan, it's our goal to help you look at the ACT as an opportunity—a chance to demonstrate your knowledge, as well as your critical thinking skills, which will be key to your success as a college student. Looking at the ACT as an opportunity will help you do better on the test.

Besides committing to a positive attitude toward the test, give yourself a head start with these tips:

- The ACT is a standardized test, meaning that scores for every testing administration mean the same thing. To achieve this reliability, the test maker must always ask questions on the same topics and in the same way. This makes the test predictable and, therefore, easier to prepare for. We've distilled how high-scoring students approach each section into Kaplan Methods. In fact, each method gets its own chapter. Learn these simple, step-by-step methods, and you'll approach questions like an expert.

- The ACT is not like the tests you take in school. When colleges want to know how you do on tests in school, they look at your transcript. Acing the ACT requires different skills. This book highlights these skills, from taking math shortcuts to avoiding incorrect-answer "traps" to managing your time. By studying this book, you'll learn to think like the test.

- Your skill level now has nothing to do with your skill level on test day. Getting some questions incorrect? Having trouble with a specific topic? That just means you've found an opportunity to raise your score. Be patient with yourself! In your life so far, you've already learned thousands of things. You can learn a few more things to succeed on the ACT.

Read on to learn how your book and online resources are organized and how to make the best use of them. Good luck on the test—you're going to nail it!

Welcome to Kaplan!

Congratulations on taking this important step in your college admissions process! By studying with Kaplan, the official partner of live instruction for the ACT®, you'll maximize your score on the ACT, a major factor in your overall application.

Our experience shows that the greatest ACT score increases result from active engagement in the preparation process. Kaplan will give you direction, focus your preparation, and teach you the specific skills and effective test-taking strategies you need to know for the ACT. We will help you achieve your top performance on test day, but your effort is crucial. The more you invest in preparing for the ACT, the greater your chances of achieving your target score and getting into your top-choice college.

Are you registered for the ACT? Kaplan cannot register you for the official ACT. If you have not already registered for the upcoming ACT, visit the official website at **www.act.org** to register online and for information on registration deadlines, test sites, accommodations, fees, and test updates.

Chapter Organization

The chapters in this book follow a standard format to make this book as easy to use as possible.

How Much Do You Know?

At the beginning of most chapters, you have an opportunity to assess how much you already know about the topics by answering a set of test-like questions. If you answer most or all of the questions in a set correctly and in the most efficient way, you may want to skip one or more lessons in that chapter. If you answer some or all of the questions in a set incorrectly or in an inefficient way, you will want to review most or all of the lessons in that chapter. The answers and explanations for these sections are provided in the "Check Your Work" section immediately after the question set.

Try on Your Own

The lessons within each chapter start with a question (or passage) typical of the way the ACT tests a given topic and ends with a set of practice questions called "Try on Your Own." These sections are designed to provide immediate, targeted practice. Complete these questions and review their explanations at least once after reviewing the lesson. You might consider completing these questions multiple times if you are preparing for the ACT over an extended period of time. The answers and explanations for these sections are provided at the end of each chapter.

On Test Day

Most of the Math chapters include an "On Test Day" section that highlights one or more ways a question can be approached strategically. Complete these sections after you have reviewed the lessons but before you complete the "How Much Have You Learned?" question set.

How Much Have You Learned?

You need to reinforce what you learn in each chapter by practicing the Kaplan methods and strategies. Most chapters include a section called "How Much Have You Learned?" that features additional practice questions reinforcing the concepts explained in that chapter. The answers and explanations for these sections are provided at the end of each chapter.

Reflect

These sections can be completed during or after a chapter's completion. You might prefer to use the "Reflect" sections to evaluate your retention over time or reflect on the chapter as a whole when you complete all of the lessons. However you choose to reflect on your ACT studying, what's important is taking the time to do so.

Test Yourself

After all the chapters on each test—English, Math, Reading, Science, and Writing—you have an opportunity for full section practice. Apply what you've learned to a test-like mix of questions. Use your results to determine what you've mastered and which chapters, if any, you should review.

SmartPoints®

Different topics are worth different numbers of points on the ACT because they show up more or less frequently in questions. By studying the information released by the test maker, Kaplan has been able to determine how often certain topics are likely to appear on the ACT, and therefore, predict how many points these topics are worth on test day. This means that if you master a given topic and answer all of the questions from that category correctly on test day, then you can expect to earn approximately that number of SmartPoints® out of the overall 36 points total for that test.

The breakdown of SmartPoints® for English, Math, Reading, and Science are summarized in the following tables. You can also see how these topics align to chapters in this book.

English SmartPoints®

SmartPoints® Category	# of Points	Chapter
Sentence Structure	9	Ch. 3
Agreement	10	Ch. 3
Conciseness	4	Ch. 4
Organization	4	Ch. 4
Development	9	Ch. 4
TOTAL	**36**	

Math SmartPoints®

SmartPoints® Category	# of Points	Chapter(s)
Number and Quantity	8	Ch. 8 and 9
Algebra	7	Ch. 10
Statistics and Probability	6	Ch. 11
Functions	4	Ch. 12
Geometry	11	Ch. 13
TOTAL	**36**	

Reading SmartPoints®

SmartPoints® Category	# of Points	Chapters
Vocab-in-Context	3	
Function	6	
Inference	10	Ch. 17 and 18
Detail	13	
Global	4	
TOTAL	**36**	

Science SmartPoints®

SmartPoints® Category	# of Points	Chapter
Interpreting Data	7	Ch. 23
Using Data	9	Ch. 23
Experimental Design	6	Ch. 24
Synthesizing Data	6	Ch. 24
Applying Core Knowledge	2	Ch. 25
Supporting Hypotheses	6	Ch. 25
TOTAL	**36**	

Practice Tests

Kaplan's practice tests are designed to mimic the actual ACT. By taking practice exams, you will prepare yourself for the actual test day experience.

We recommend you complete your in-book and online practice tests as you make your way through the content of this book. You can score your in-book practice tests by hand using the score conversion tables in this book. Your online practice tests can be easily scored online, and Kaplan will provide you with a detailed score report. Use this summary to help you focus and review the content areas that comprise your greatest areas of improvement.

Online Resources

To access the online resources that accompany this book, follow the steps below.

1. Go to **kaptest.com/moreonline.**

2. Have this book available as you complete the on-screen instructions.

Then, whenever you want to use your online resources, go to **kaptest.com/login** and log in using the email address and password you used to register your book.

Your book's online resources include:

- A tool to make your own personalized study plan—answer three quick questions and download a detailed week-by-week prep calendar. If your plans change, no problem—just answer the questions again and make a new schedule.

- Over 40 videos—Kaplan teachers review key topics in English, Reading, Math, and Science.

- ACT Writing—a bonus chapter that will answer your questions about the optional ACT Writing test. The chapter covers the Kaplan Method for ACT Writing and provides a simple essay template that you can use on test day. You'll find this bonus chapter in the Review section of your online resources.

- Qbank—make custom quizzes from 500 practice questions.

- Practice tests—four more Kaplan practice tests, plus easy online scoring and detailed score reports. You can also use Kaplan's proctoring video for a more realistic practice test experience.

PART 1

THE ACT AND YOU

[CHAPTER 1]

INSIDE THE ACT

LEARNING OBJECTIVES

After completing this chapter, you will be able to:

- Recall the timing and scope of each ACT test in anticipation of section management
- State what the ACT scoring system means for you as a test taker

---

ACT Structure

The ACT, like any standardized test, is predictable. The more comfortable you are with the test structure, the more confidently you will approach each question type, thus maximizing your score.

The ACT is 2 hours and 55 minutes long, or 3 hours and 35 minutes long if you choose to complete the optional essay in the Writing Test. The ACT is made up of multiple-choice questions that test four subject areas: English, Math, Reading, and Science.

Test	Allotted time (minutes)	Question count
English	45	75
Math	60	60
Reading	35	40
Science	35	40
Writing (optional)	40	1
Total	175 OR 215 (w/writing)	215 OR 216 (w/writing)

When you take the ACT, you may take a fifth multiple-choice test. The results of this fifth test may not be reflected in your final score report, but you should treat this test as if it counts, just in case.

ACT Scoring

ACT scoring can seem a bit complex. You will receive one scaled score ranging from 1 to 36 for each required test, and these four scores will be averaged to calculate your composite score. You will receive a separate score for the Writing Test, if you choose to take it.

In addition to your overall scores, you will receive subscores that provide a deeper analysis of your ACT performance, including STEM and, if you take the optional Writing Test, ELA scores. The ACT also gives you a percentile ranking, which allows you to compare your scores with those of other test takers. For example, a student who scored in the 63rd percentile did better than 63 percent of all others who took that test.

The scores you need depend primarily on which colleges you are planning to apply to. For example, if you want to attend an engineering school, you'll typically need a higher math score than if you want to attend a liberal arts college. Research the colleges you are interested in, find out what scores they require, and structure your ACT studying accordingly.

Superscoring

The score reports sent to colleges for students who have taken the ACT more than once will include superscores. A superscore is like a composite score in that it is an average of your four subject scores, but for the superscore, ACT selects your best subject score from every test administration. Therefore, your superscore is never lower than any composite score, and it is often higher than each of your composite scores. Not all schools consider the superscore in admissions, but many do, so check out the superscore policies of the colleges to which you plan to apply.

Since you can only get a superscore after you've taken more than one ACT, it's important to study for the entire test the first time around and work through as much of this book as you can before test day. However, if you're focused on only one, two, or three sections in an effort to raise your superscore, just use those units of this book.

How to Maximize Your Score

What is most important to remember while taking the test is that maximizing all the various scores and subscores depends on getting the most points you can out of every section. You'll find advice on test-taking strategies below and in the section management chapters at the end of the English, Math, Reading, and Science sections of this book. However, if you still have a substantial amount of time to prepare for the ACT, the best advice we can give you is to improve the specific skills you need to answer math, verbal, and science questions correctly and efficiently. That's what this book is for. You can work through the chapters and sections in any order you like, and you can skip the lessons you don't need. You don't need to start with English or answer every single question; just use the book. Pick a lesson, read the instructional text, and work your way through the practice questions. There are hundreds of them in this book, and they are very similar to those that you will see on test day. Practice will not only improve your skills but also raise your confidence, and that's very important to test day success.

Interested in generating a personalized study schedule? If you've already registered your book, go online (**kaptest.com/login**) and log in, then click into Plan Your Path. To use Kaplan's study-planning tool, answer three quick questions and download a detailed week-by-week prep calendar. If your plans change, just answer the questions again to make a new schedule.

GO ONLINE

kaptest.com/login

When and Where to Take the ACT

For students testing in the United States or US territories, the ACT is offered each school year on seven Saturday test dates. Typically, exams are offered in September, October, December, February, April, June, and July. You can take the ACT up to 12 times. Some states offer special administrations of the ACT on different dates, and no test centers are scheduled in New York for the July test date. Non-Saturday testing is available by request for students requiring religious or other exemptions.

Though they had not done so at the time of this book's printing, ACT may introduce section retesting. This is how section retesting would work: once you have taken the four required sections of the ACT on one day, you will be able to retest one, two, or three sections at a time by testing online at an approved testing center on a national test date. If enacted by ACT, section retesting will offer several benefits, but you should be sure to take your first ACT test day seriously; if that's the only time you take the full ACT, it will show up on every score report you send to colleges.

The ACT is increasingly offering online testing options. The ACT is administered at schools around the country that serve as testing centers, some of which offer online testing. Your high school may or may not be a testing center, and the test center most convenient for you may not offer online testing. Check **www.actstudent.org** for a list of testing centers near you, and visit **www.act.org** for continued updates about online testing and any other upcoming test changes. Historically, students have needed to register for the ACT approximately one month in advance to avoid paying a late fee.

Students who are testing outside of the United States or US territories should visit the ACT website for test date and test center information.

The ACT English Test

The ACT English Test will focus on your ability to revise and edit text from a range of content areas.

ACT English Test Overview	
Timing	45 minutes
Questions	75 passage-based multiple-choice questions
Passages	5 single passages with 15 questions each
Passage length	300–400 words per passage

The ACT English Test will contain five single passages of different genres with a variety of rhetorical situations. A passage could be an argument, an informative or explanatory text, or a narrative.

The most prevalent question format on the ACT English Test will ask you to choose the best of three alternatives to an underlined portion of the passage or to decide that the current version is already the best option. You will be asked to improve the development, organization, and diction in the passages to ensure they conform to conventional standards of English grammar, usage, and style. There are three English Test reporting categories.

Skills Tested by English Test Questions	
Production of Writing (29%–32%)	Topic development and organization, unity, and cohesion
Knowledge of Language (15%–17%)	Precision and conciseness in word choice and consistency in style and tone
Conventions of Standard English (52%–55%)	Sentence structure and formation, punctuation, and usage

The ACT Math Test

The ACT Math Test will focus on mathematical skills typically learned in required math courses before the beginning of grade 12.

ACT Math Test Overview	
Timing	60 minutes
Questions	60 multiple-choice questions

All ACT math questions are multiple-choice questions with five answer choices, and some questions will be part of a set of multiple questions related to the same graph or chart. The Math Test is divided into three reporting categories.

Skills Tested by Math Test Questions	
Preparing for Higher Mathematics (57%–60%)	Using higher-level math to answer questions in five domains: • Number and Quantity (7%–10%) • Algebra (12%–15%) • Functions (12%–15%) • Geometry (12%–15%) • Statistics and Probability (8%–12%)
Integrating Essential Skills (40%–43%)	Using essential concepts and skills to solve more complex problems, including: • Rates and percentages • Area, surface area, and volume • Solving problems using a chain of steps
Modeling (all questions counted within one of the two categories above)	Producing, interpreting, evaluating, and improving models

The ACT Reading Test

The ACT Reading Test will focus on your comprehension and reasoning skills when you are presented with challenging extended passages taken from a variety of content areas.

ACT Reading Test Overview	
Timing	35 minutes
Questions	40 passage-based multiple-choice questions
Passages	3 independent passages and 1 set of paired passages or 4 independent passages
Passage length	750–1,000 words

Each passage is preceded by a heading that names the passage type, author, and source; this heading may also include important background information related to the passage.

The ACT Reading Test includes four types of passages: prose fiction or literary narrative, social science, humanities, and natural science. One of the four passages will consist of two shorter prose passages that are related in some way. There are three reporting categories for the Reading Test.

Skills Tested by Reading Test Questions	
Key Ideas and Details (52%–60%)	Determining central ideas and themes, summarizing information and ideas, understanding relationships between ideas, and drawing conclusions from facts stated in a passage
Craft and Structure (25%–30%)	Determining word and phrase meanings, analyzing rhetorical word choice, analyzing text structure, and understanding and analyzing purpose and point of view
Integration of Knowledge and Ideas (13%–23%)	Understanding author's claims, differentiating between facts and opinions, using evidence to make connections, analyzing how authors construct arguments, and evaluating reasoning and evidence from various sources

The ACT Science Test

The ACT Science Test will focus on your scientific reasoning ability, not your knowledge of scientific content.

ACT Science Test Overview	
Timing	35 minutes
Questions	40 passage-based multiple-choice questions
Passages	6 passages with 6–8 questions each
Passage length	100–300 words depending on passage type

There are three passage types on the ACT Science Test:

ACT Science Test Passage Types	
Data Representation (25%–35%)	2 passages, each with multiple figures and/or tables
Research Summaries (45%–60%)	3 passages, each with one or more experiments or studies and usually at least one figure and/or table
Conflicting Viewpoints (15%–20%)	1 passage with at least two viewpoints related to a theory or phenomenon

The ACT Science Test provides three reporting categories:

Skills Tested by Science Test Questions	
Interpretation of Data (40%–50%)	Manipulating and analyzing data in tables, graphs, and diagrams
Scientific Investigation (20%–30%)	Understanding experimental tools, procedures, and design and comparing, extending, and modifying experiments
Evaluation of Models, Inferences, and Experimental Results (25%–35%)	Judging the validity of scientific information and formulating conclusions and predictions based on that information

The ACT Writing Test (Optional)

The ACT Writing Test assesses your writing skills. The Writing Test includes one prompt describing a complex issue and three perspectives related to that prompt. Your goal is to write an essay in which you present your own reasoned perspective; this perspective might—but does not need to—relate to one or more of the three perspectives in the prompt, but your essay must include a discussion of both your own perspective and at least one other. The specific perspective you decide to take will not affect your final score.

The issue discussed in the prompt might be a familiar one, but it might also be completely new to you. The Writing Test will always include a paragraph providing background on the issue because prior knowledge is not required.

The ACT Writing Test will be broken down into four categories for scoring: Ideas and Analysis, Development and Support, Organization, and Language Use and Conventions. Each of these elements will be scored on a scale of 2 to 12, and you will receive a single subject-level writing score, also on a scale of 2 to 12.

To help you prepare for the ACT Writing Test, check out the bonus chapter "The Method for the ACT Writing Test" in the Review section of your online resources (**kaptest.com/login**). This chapter will help you decide whether to take this optional test. The chapter also covers the Kaplan Method for ACT Writing, provides a simple essay template that you can use on test day, and includes sample essay prompts and responses.

GO ONLINE

kaptest.com/login

Test-Taking Strategies

The ACT is different from the tests you are used to taking in school. For example, on a test given in school, you probably go through the questions in order. You spend more time on the harder questions than on the easier ones because harder questions are usually worth more points. You also probably show your work because your teacher tells you that how you approach a question is as important as getting the correct answer.

This approach is not optimal for the ACT. On the ACT, you benefit from moving around within a section if you come across tough questions because the harder questions are worth the same number of points as the easier questions. Similarly, showing your work is unimportant. It doesn't matter how you arrive at the correct answer—only that you bubble in the correct answer choice.

The good news is that you can use the ACT's particular structure to your advantage. You have already learned about the overall structure of the ACT as well as the structures of the five tests. The strategies outlined in this section can be applied to any of these tests.

Strategy #1: Triage the Test

You do not need to complete questions on the ACT in order. Every student has different strengths and should attack the test with those strengths in mind. Your main objective on the ACT should be to score as many points as you can. While approaching questions out of order may seem counterintuitive, it is a surefire way to achieve your best score.

Just remember, you can skip around within each test, but you cannot work on any test other than the one you've been instructed to work on.

To triage a test effectively, do the following:

1. Work through all the low-difficulty questions that you can do quickly. Skip questions that are hard or time-consuming.

    - For the Reading Test, start with the passage you find most manageable and work toward the one you find most challenging. You do not need to go in order.
    - For the Science Test, start with the passage type you find most manageable and work toward the one you find most challenging. You do not need to go in order.

2. Work through the questions that are doable but time-consuming.

3. Work through the high-difficulty questions.

Strategy #2: Eliminate

Even though there is no incorrect-answer penalty on the ACT, Elimination is still a crucial strategy. If you can determine that one or more answer choices are definitely incorrect, you can increase your chances of getting the correct answer by paring the selection down.

To eliminate answer choices, do the following:

- Read each answer choice.
- Cross out the answer choices that are incorrect.
- Remember: there is no incorrect-answer penalty, so take your best guess.

Strategy #3: Guess

The English, Reading, and Science multiple-choice questions on the ACT have four answer choices and no incorrect-answer penalty. That means if you have no idea how to approach a question, you have a 25 percent chance of randomly choosing the correct answer. Even though there's a 75 percent chance of selecting the incorrect answer, you won't lose any points for doing so. The worst that can happen on the ACT is that you'll earn zero points on a question, which means you should always at least take a guess, even when you have no idea what to do. While the probabilities are slightly different for the Math Test, which has five answer choices, the logic is the same.

When guessing on a question, do the following:

- Try to strategically eliminate answer choices before guessing.
- If you run out of time, or have no idea what a question is asking, pick a Letter of the Day.

A "Letter of the Day" is an answer choice letter [A/F, B/G, C/H, D/J, or (math only) E/K] that you choose before test day to select for questions you guess on. You can use the same Letter of the Day for the entire ACT or change it depending on the section, but you should always use the same Letter of the Day within an individual section.

[PART 2]

ACT ENGLISH

[CHAPTER 2]

THE METHOD FOR ACT ENGLISH

LEARNING OBJECTIVE

After completing this chapter, you will be able to:

- Effectively and efficiently apply the ACT English Method

How to Do ACT English

The English Test of the ACT tests a limited number of grammar errors and style or logic issues. You should feel empowered by familiarizing yourself with these recurring errors and issues and learn to spot them and address them quickly and efficiently. We'll describe the issues that you're likely to see on test day and how to deal with them in the next two chapters. In this chapter, we'll present a simple series of steps for tackling English questions.

Take a look at the passage and questions below and think about how you would approach them on test day. Then compare your approach to the recommendations that follow.

Gregory Hines, a Beloved Icon

During the last five decades of the 20th century; Gregory Hines enriched musical theater with his performances as a star of the Broadway stage. A multitalented artist, he was also employed as an actor, a director, and a producer in television and film. He

had the experience of earning and receiving numerous awards, including a Tony and a Daytime Emmy.

Hines began performing as a dancer when he was five, touring professionally in nightclubs across the country with his older brother, Maurice, as a duo. Hines found inspiration in watching fellow performers such as the Nicholas Brothers and Sandman Sims. At eight, he made his Broadway debut and remained a star of the stage in a variety of musicals, including *Eubie!*, *Sophisticated Ladies,* and *Jelly's Last Jam*.

1. A. NO CHANGE
    B. century, Gregory
    C. century. Gregory
    D. century, from the 1950s to the late 1990s,

2. F. NO CHANGE
    G. had the experience of earning
    H. had the experience of receiving
    J. earned

3. Which choice provides the most specific information regarding Hines's Broadway performances?

    A. NO CHANGE
    B. which debuted at various locations among the many venues of Broadway.
    C. which opened at different times throughout Hines's considerably long career.
    D. all of which were evaluated by the rotating group of dozens of theater professionals who are selected by the Tony Awards Administration Committee.

There is no need to read the entire passage before you start to answer questions. Instead, answer them as you read. When you see a number, finish the sentence you are reading and then look at the corresponding question. If you can answer the question based on what you've read so far, do so—this will likely be the case if the question is testing grammar. If you need more information—which may happen if the question is testing organization or relevance—keep reading until you have enough context to answer the question.

Sometimes the issue being tested will be obvious to you when you look at the underlined segment. If it isn't, glance at the answer choices to help you determine what the test maker is after. For instance, in question 1 above, a semicolon is underlined. A quick glance at the choices shows that most of them have the same words in the same order, and only the punctuation marks are different; this means that the question is testing punctuation. **Identifying the issue**, using the choices if necessary, is step 1 of the English method.

To determine the correct punctuation, use the surrounding text. "During the last five decades of the 20th century" is an introductory phrase and cannot stand on its own, so A and C are incorrect; what comes before and after either a period (choice C) or a semicolon (choice A) must be able to stand on its own as a complete sentence. **Eliminating answer choices that do not address the issue** is step 2 of the English method.

There may be more than one choice that addresses the issue. When that happens, you need to base your final response on three considerations: conciseness, relevance, and the potential of a given choice to introduce a new error. The two remaining choices are both grammatically correct and relevant to the surrounding context. However, (B) is more concise and therefore the correct answer. Choice D can be eliminated because "from the 1950s to the late 1990s" is redundant; the sentence already says "the last five decades of the 20th century." **Choosing the most concise and relevant response from those that are grammatically correct** is step 3 of the English method.

Here's what we did:

> ### ACT ENGLISH METHOD
>
> Step 1. Identify the issue (use the choices if need be)
>
> Step 2. Eliminate answer choices that do not address the issue
>
> Step 3. Plug in the remaining answer choices and select the most *correct*, *concise*, and *relevant* one

Some questions include errors that may not seem apparent. For example, the underlined segment in question 2 is grammatically correct but wordy. Start by **identifying the issue**, using the choices if necessary. The answer choices are shorter than the original text, so conciseness is likely the issue being tested. **Eliminating answer choices that do not address the issue** is next, and F can definitely be eliminated due to wordiness. **Finally, plugging in the remaining choices and choosing the most correct, concise, and relevant one** points you to (J): the single word *earned* expresses the same information as the much longer phrase "had the experience of earning and receiving." Choices G and H are shorter than the original, but they are not nearly as concise as (J).

Other questions may ask you to determine which answer choice provides the most specific description of a particular aspect of the passage. In those instances, **identifying the issue** is straightforward. **Eliminating answer choices that do not address the issue** is essential to answering this type of question. Question 3 requires you to determine which option provides the most specific information about Hines's Broadway performances. Eliminate B and C because they do not include specific details. **Plug in the remaining choices** and eliminate D because the process by which plays are evaluated by the Tony Awards Administration Committee is not relevant to the passage. Choice (A) is the correct answer.

Correct, **concise**, and **relevant** means that the answer choice you select:

- Has no grammatical errors
- Is as short as possible while retaining the writer's intended meaning
- Is relevant to the paragraph and the passage as a whole

Correct answers do NOT:

- Provide information that contradicts or is irrelevant to the ideas developed by the original sentence, paragraph, or passage
- Introduce new grammatical errors

How Much Have You Learned?

Directions: Take as much time as you need on these questions. Work carefully and methodically. Practice using the steps that you just learned.

Liberal Arts Education

[1]

The concept of liberal arts has existed since the time of ancient Greece, and the parameters of this discipline have remained largely <u>over the centuries</u> unchanged. [A]
1
In essence, liberal arts are defined as "any study given to reflection and free inquiry," which

1. The best placement for the underlined portion would be:

   A. where it is now.

   B. after the word *concept*.

   C. after the word *arts*.

   D. after the word *unchanged*.

is a <u>lengthy</u> category that has included various subjects
2
throughout its history.

2. Which choice best indicates that liberal arts include many disciplines?

   F. NO CHANGE

   G. broad

   H. challenging

   J. perplexing

[2]

In medieval times, the seven liberal arts were divided into two parts: the Trivium ("the three roads") and the Quadrivium ("the four roads").
[B] The Trivium consisted of grammar, rhetoric, and <u>logic, the Quadrivium</u> consisted of arithmetic, geometry,
3
astronomy, and music. However, the description of a liberal arts college is somewhat more limiting. A liberal arts college

3. A. NO CHANGE

   B. logic; while the Quadrivium

   C. logic, so the Quadrivium

   D. logic; the Quadrivium

generally <u>awarded</u> a Bachelor of Arts degree after four
4
years of study, primarily enrolls full-time students between the ages of 18 and 24, typically has between 800 and 1,800 students, and does not provide professional or vocational preparation.

4. F. NO CHANGE

   G. have awarded

   H. award

   J. awards

[3]

Liberal arts has been the primary focus of
undergraduate education in the United States <u>since</u>
                                               5
the United States was only a British colony. [C] The
number of liberal arts colleges in the United States

<u>steady increased</u> throughout the 20th century as private
      6
universities, state universities, and community

colleges all sought to <u>give their</u> undergraduates a broad
                         7
education. [D]

[4]

The content of liberal arts study still focuses on the
arts, humanities, and <u>sciences, and</u> the basic notion of
                     8
forming well-rounded students in these areas is still the
concept behind liberal arts education today. There

is some concern, however, that the philosophy behind
liberal arts education <u>does not reflect the current times</u>
                                     9
<u>in which today's students are living.</u> Responding to this
       9

5. A. NO CHANGE
    B. because
    C. even though
    D. while

6. F. NO CHANGE
    G. steadily increased
    H. increased in a steady fashion
    J. increased in a steadily fashion

7. A. NO CHANGE
    B. give its
    C. giving their
    D. gave its

8. F. NO CHANGE
    G. sciences; and
    H. sciences. And
    J. sciences: and

9. A. NO CHANGE
    B. does not reflect the latest trends in education and the current times in which today's students are living.
    C. does not reflect the times in which today's students are living or the times in which future students will live.
    D. does not reflect the times in which today's students are living.

concern, <u>courses in computer science and information</u>
                                              10
<u>technology have been added to the curricula of many</u>
                                              10
<u>colleges and universities.</u> Does this mean the end of
            10

liberal arts education as it has been practiced since the

days of Martianus Capella? <u>They don't</u> believe so.
                                  11

<u>Most liberal arts colleges award master's and doctoral</u>
                                              12
<u>degrees as well.</u> The study of liberal arts may have to
            12
evolve with the times, but its basic premise—that

well-rounded students are well-educated students—<u>remain</u>
                                                      13
as valid today as it was in medieval times.

10.　F.　NO CHANGE

　　　G.　computer science and information technol-
　　　　　ogy courses have been added to the curric-
　　　　　ula of many colleges and universities.

　　　H.　computer science and information tech-
　　　　　nology are the subject of courses that
　　　　　have been added to the curricula of many
　　　　　colleges and universities.

　　　J.　many colleges and universities have added
　　　　　courses in computer science and informa-
　　　　　tion technology to their curricula.

11.　A.　NO CHANGE

　　　B.　Many educators don't

　　　C.　You wouldn't

　　　D.　We don't

12.　The writer is considering deleting the under-
　　　lined sentence. Should the writer make this dele-
　　　tion?

　　　F.　Yes, because it contradicts information
　　　　　earlier in the paragraph.

　　　G.　Yes, because it interrupts the writer's dis-
　　　　　cussion of modern liberal arts education
　　　　　with irrelevant information.

　　　H.　No, because it provides an example show-
　　　　　ing how liberal arts education is still
　　　　　relevant.

　　　J.　No, because it makes a claim important to
　　　　　the writer's overall argument.

13.　A.　NO CHANGE

　　　B.　remaining

　　　C.　remains

　　　D.　remained

---

14. The writer wants to add the following sentence to the essay:

> The late 1800s saw an expansion of liberal arts colleges as the right to education began to include minorities and women.

If the writer were to add this sentence, it would most logically be placed at:

F.   Point A in Paragraph 1.

G.   Point B in Paragraph 2.

H.   Point C in Paragraph 3.

J.   Point D in Paragraph 3.

15. Suppose the writer's primary purpose had been to write an essay summarizing the history of higher education in the United States. Would this essay accomplish this purpose?

A.   Yes, because it discusses the natural evolution of liberal arts, which is taught only at the collegiate level.

B.   Yes, because it explains how most liberal arts colleges award master's and doctoral degrees as well.

C.   No, because it does not mention higher education anywhere.

D.   No, because it focuses exclusively on liberal arts education rather than higher education as a whole.

Reflect

Directions: Take a few minutes to recall what you've learned and what you've been practicing in this chapter. Consider the following questions, jot down your best answer for each one, and then compare your reflections to the expert responses on the following page. Use your level of confidence to determine what to do next.

1.   What does an ACT expert look for when answering an ACT English question?

_____

_____

_____

2.   Describe at least three types of issues that could be present in English questions.

_____

_____

_____

3.   How does eliminating choices that do not address the issue make it easier to identify the correct answer?

_____

_____

_____

4.   Why do correct answers need to be grammatically correct, concise, and relevant?

_____

_____

_____

Responses

1. What does an ACT expert look for when answering an ACT English question?

ACT experts look for clues in both the passage and answer choices—and question stem, if one is present—to help identify the issue and determine which choices are correct and which are incorrect. These include punctuation marks, answer choice lengths, and words such as "relevant" in the question stem.

2. Describe at least three types of issues that could be present in English questions.

Punctuation issues could involve commas, colons, parentheses, and other punctuation marks. Correct answers should be concise, so incorrect choices could use more words than necessary. Correct answers should not add information that contradicts or is irrelevant to the rest of the passage.

3. How does eliminating choices that do not address the issue make it easier to identify the correct answer?

When you identify choices that must be incorrect because they don't address the issue, you save time by eliminating them without plugging them in and checking for correctness, conciseness, and relevance.

4. Why do correct answers need to be grammatically correct, concise, and relevant?

It's not enough for an answer choice to be grammatically correct or concise or relevant. The correct answer to an ACT English question must be grammatically correct, concise, and relevant, and incorrect choices will often only meet one or two—but not all three!—of these criteria.

Next Steps

If you answered most questions correctly in the "How Much Have You Learned?" section, and if your responses to the Reflect questions were similar to those of the ACT expert, then consider the ACT English Method an area of strength and move on to the next chapter. Do keep using the method as you work on the questions in future chapters.

If you don't yet feel confident, review those parts of this chapter that you have not yet mastered and try the questions you missed again. As always, be sure to review the explanations closely. Also, go online (**kaptest.com/login**) to watch a video about the Method for ACT English questions and to use your Qbank for more practice. If you haven't already registered your book, do so at **kaptest.com/moreonline.**

GO ONLINE

kaptest.com/login

Answers and Explanations

How Much Have You Learned?

1. D
Difficulty: Medium
Category: Sentence Structure
Getting to the Answer: The phrase "over the centuries" must be placed logically and punctuated properly. Its original position interrupts the phrase "largely unchanged," so A is incorrect. Choices B and C are incorrect because placing the phrase at the beginning of the sentence is not logical; "over the centuries" is not referring to the concept of liberal arts but rather to the parameters of the discipline. Placing the phrase at the end of the sentence is logical and does not require additional punctuation, so (D) is correct.

2. G
Difficulty: Medium
Category: Development
Getting to the Answer: The word *broad* means "covering a large number of subjects or areas," so (G) is correct. Choices F, H, and J are incorrect because they do not clearly express the idea that liberal arts include a variety of subjects.

3. D
Difficulty: Medium
Category: Sentence Structure
Getting to the Answer: As written, the sentence is a run-on; a comma cannot connect two independent clauses without a FANBOYS (For, And, Nor, But, Or, Yet, So) coordinating conjunction, so A is incorrect. Although there are a number of ways to correct a run-on sentence, only one answer choice will do so without introducing additional errors. Choices B, C, and (D) all address the run-on error. However, B uses a semicolon while also making the second clause dependent. The conjunction *so* in C creates a cause-and-effect relationship between the clauses that is inappropriate in context. Only (D) corrects the run-on and does not introduce new errors.

4. J
Difficulty: Medium
Category: Agreement
Getting to the Answer: Items in a list must be in parallel form. As written, this list includes four verb phrases, but they are not parallel, so F is incorrect. Choice G is incorrect because it includes present perfect tense, which does not agree with the simple present tense verb phrases in the rest of the list. Choice H is in present tense, but the plural verb *award* does not match the singular subject *college*. The present-tense singular verb *awards* agrees with both the subject and the rest of the sentence, so (J) is correct.

5. A
Difficulty: Medium
Category: Organization
Getting to the Answer: When a transition word is underlined, check that it correctly represents the relationship between the ideas it connects. In this sentence, the transition needs to convey that liberal arts have been the focus of colleges in the United States "from the time when" the country was still a British colony. *Since* does exactly that, so choice (A) is correct. Choices B, C, and D all incorrectly change the relationship between the parts of the sentence.

6. G
Difficulty: Medium
Category: Agreement
Getting to the Answer: Adjectives can modify only nouns and pronouns; all other parts of speech are modified by adverbs. As written, the sentence uses the adjective *steady* to modify the verb *increased*, so F is incorrect. Both (G) and H correct the error, but H is unnecessarily wordy, so (G) is correct. Choice J incorrectly uses the adverb *steadily* to modify the noun *fashion*.

7. A
Difficulty: Medium
Category: Agreement
Getting to the Answer: Check underlined verbs and pronouns for agreement errors. The infinitive verb *to give* is idiomatically correct with *sought*, and *their* agrees with its plural antecedent *colleges*. (A) is correct. Choices B and D pair a singular pronoun with a plural antecedent; C and D do not properly construct the infinitive verb form.

8.   F
Difficulty: Medium
Category: Sentence Structure
Getting to the Answer: Carefully examine the different punctuation marks. Here, the comma is used together with a coordinating conjunction to join two independent clauses, so (F) is correct. Although the semicolon in G can join two independent clauses, it cannot be used together with a coordinating conjunction. The period in H creates a sentence fragment. Finally, J is incorrect because a colon should not be followed by a coordinating conjunction.

9.   D
Difficulty: Medium
Category: Conciseness
Getting to the Answer: As written, the underlined portion includes a redundancy with the words *current* and *today's*. Choice (D) corrects this error by omitting the word *current*. Choices B and C are incorrect because they are even wordier than the original.

10.   J
Difficulty: Medium
Category: Sentence Structure
Getting to the Answer: An introductory clause generally modifies the noun that immediately follows it. As written, this sentence says that "courses in computer science and information technology" are "Responding to this concern." Choice F is incorrect. Choice (J) correctly puts the noun phrase, "many colleges and universities," immediately after the modifying clause. Choices G and H do not address the error.

11.   B
Difficulty: Medium
Category: Agreement
Getting to the Answer: Choice A uses the pronoun "They," but the antecedent of this pronoun is not clear from context; eliminate A. The author does not address the audience directly or use the word *we*, so C and D are incorrect. Choice (B) correctly uses "Many educators" instead of a pronoun.

12.   G
Difficulty: Medium
Category: Development
Getting to the Answer: When deciding whether to delete a sentence, identify the purpose of the paragraph and determine whether the sentence supports it. This paragraph discusses concerns about liberal arts education in modern times. The sentence states that liberal arts schools also offer advanced degrees, which is not pertinent to the paragraph. Eliminate H and J. Choice (G) correctly identifies the sentence as an irrelevant interruption.

13.   C
Difficulty: Medium
Category: Agreement
Getting to the Answer: A verb must agree with its subject, which may not be the noun closest to it in the sentence. Although the plural noun *students* is the closest noun to the verb *remain*, the verb's subject is actually the singular noun *premise*, so A is incorrect. Choice (C) corrects the agreement error. Choice B creates a sentence fragment, and D uses a past-tense verb that does not match the surrounding verbs, which are in present tense.

14.   H
Difficulty: Medium
Category: Development
Getting to the Answer: Consider where in the essay a reference to "The late 1800s" would fit best. Choice (H) correctly places the sentence between a reference to "the United States since it was a British colony" and "the 20th century." Choices F, G, and J position the sentence illogically within the essay, either too early or too late in the history of liberal arts education.

15.   D
Difficulty: High
Category: Development
Getting to the Answer: First, answer the "yes" or "no" part of the question. While the author does outline the history of liberal arts, higher education encompasses more than just "arts, humanities, and sciences." Eliminate A and B. Choice C is incorrect because the author does mention higher education throughout the essay. Choice (D) is correct.

[CHAPTER 3]

SPOTTING AND FIXING ERRORS: SENTENCE STRUCTURE, PUNCTUATION, AND AGREEMENT

LEARNING OBJECTIVES

After completing this chapter, you will be able to:

- Determine the correct punctuation and/or conjunctions to form a complete sentence
- Identify and correct inappropriate uses of semicolons
- Set off simple parenthetical elements using punctuation
- Identify and correct inappropriate uses of commas, dashes, and colons
- Identify and correct verb agreement issues
- Identify and correct pronoun agreement issues
- Identify and correct modifier agreement issues
- Identify and correct inappropriate uses of apostrophes
- Identify and correct expressions that deviate from idiomatic English

Sentence Structure: 9/36 SmartPoints® (Very high yield)

Agreement: 10/36 SmartPoints® (Very high yield)

How Much Do You Know?

Directions: Try out the questions below. The "Category" heading in the explanation for each question gives the title of the lesson that covers how to answer it. If you answered the question(s) for a given lesson correctly, you may be able to move quickly through that lesson. If you answered incorrectly, you may want to take your time on that lesson.

The Bebop Movement

For a jazz musician in New York City in the 1940s. The most interesting place to spend the hours
1
between midnight and dawn was likely a Harlem nightclub called Minton's. After finishing their jobs at other clubs, young musicians like Charlie Parker, Dizzy Gillespie, Kenny Clarke, and Thelonious Monk would gather at Minton's and have "jam" sessions, or informal performances featuring lengthy group and solo improvisations, the all-night sessions resulted in the birth
2
of modern jazz as these African American artists together forged a new sound, known as bebop.

Unlike "swing," the enormously popular jazz played in the 1930s, bebop was not dance music. Often it had been blindingly fast, incorporated irregular rhythms,
3
and featured discordant sounds that jazz audiences
3
had never heard before. The harmonic complexity of bebop distinguished it from other forms of jazz at the time. Bebop, unlike other forms of jazz, was based on a 12-note scale, thereby opening up vast new harmonic opportunities for musicians.

The musicians who pioneered bebop shared,
4
two common elements, a vision of the new music's
4
possibilities and astonishing improvisational skill—the ability to play or compose a musical line on the spur of the

1. A. NO CHANGE
   B. 1940s; the
   C. 1940s, the
   D. 1940s, it was when the

2. F. NO CHANGE
   G. improvisations and the all-night sessions
   H. improvisations, the all-night sessions,
   J. improvisations. The all-night sessions

3. A. NO CHANGE
   B. was going to be blindingly fast, incorporated irregular rhythms, and featured discordant sounds
   C. was blindingly fast, incorporated irregular rhythms, and featured discordant sounds
   D. was blindingly fast, incorporated irregular rhythms, and featuring discordant sounds

4. F. NO CHANGE
   G. shared two common elements: a vision
   H. shared, two common elements a vision
   J. shared two common elements a vision

moment. As the essence of jazz, <u>providing the context of a</u>
<u>group setting for improvisation is paramount</u>.
₅

5. A. NO CHANGE
    B. improvisation within the context of a group setting is paramount.
    C. paramount is improvisation within the context of a group setting.
    D. paramount is the context of a group setting for improvisation.

Parker, perhaps the <u>most great</u> instrumental genius jazz has
₆
known, was a brilliant improviser. He often played twice as
fast as the rest of the band, but his solos, infused with

6. F. NO CHANGE
    G. most greatest
    H. greater
    J. greatest

creativity, <u>was</u> always in rhythm and exquisitely shaped,
₇
revealing a harmonic imagination that enthralled his
listeners.

7. A. NO CHANGE
    B. is
    C. are
    D. were

Unfortunately, the bebop movement, like many
revolutions that fought <u>its</u> way into mainstream culture,
₈
initially encountered heavy resistance. Opposition came

8. F. NO CHANGE
    G. it's
    H. their
    J. there

not only from older jazz musicians initially, <u>but also, later</u>
<u>and more lastingly</u> from a general public alienated
₉

9. A. NO CHANGE
    B. but, later and more lastingly
    C. but, later and more lastingly—
    D. but also—later and more lastingly—

by the music <u>genre's</u> complexity and sophistication.
₁₀
Furthermore, due to the significant drop in

10. F. NO CHANGE
    G. genres'
    H. genres's
    J. genres

music recordings during the musicians' <u>strike, that was,</u>
<u>in effect</u>, from 1942 through 1944, the
₁₁

11. A. NO CHANGE
    B. strike that was in effect
    C. strike that was; in effect
    D. strike—that was in effect

creative ferment that first produced bebop <u>most remains</u>
₁₂
undocumented today.

12. F. NO CHANGE
    G. remains most
    H. remains mostly
    J. remain mostly

Check Your Work

1.   C
Difficulty: Low
Category: Sentence Structure: The Basics
Getting to the Answer: As written, the phrase before the period is a sentence fragment, so A is incorrect. Replacing the period with a semicolon does not address this issue, so B is incorrect. Choice (C) fixes the fragment by joining the dependent clause "For a jazz musician in New York City in the 1940s" and the independent clause "the most interesting place to spend the hours between midnight and dawn was likely a Harlem nightclub called Minton's" with a comma. Choice D both creates an illogical sentence structure and is unnecessarily wordy. Choice (C) is correct.

2.   J
Difficulty: Low
Category: Sentence Structure: The Basics
Getting to the Answer: As written, the underlined portion creates a run-on sentence, so F is incorrect. Eliminate G because replacing the comma with a coordinating conjunction (in this case, the word *and*) does not fix the run-on. Adding a comma after *sessions* does not fix the run-on either, so H is also incorrect. Choice (J) correctly separates the two independent clauses with a period.

3.   C
Difficulty: Medium
Category: Agreement: Verbs
Getting to the Answer: As written, the sentence includes a list of three verbs that are not in parallel form. A is incorrect. Eliminate B and D, since their verbs are also not in parallel form. Choice (C) correctly uses three past-tense verb phrases.

4.   G
Difficulty: Medium
Category: Sentence Structure: Commas, Dashes, and Colons
Getting to the Answer: Colons are used to introduce lists or short phrases, so a colon is appropriate to use after *elements*. (G) is correct. Choice F is incorrect because the phrase "two common elements" is essential to the sentence, so it should not be surrounded by commas. Choice H incorrectly separates a verb from its object, and J incorrectly omits punctuation altogether.

5.   B
Difficulty: High
Category: Agreement: Modifiers
Getting to the Answer: "As the essence of jazz" is an introductory modifying phrase, so the word(s) that immediately follow the comma must be the item(s) being modified. The word *improvisation* must come after the comma because the passage indicates that "jam" sessions, or informal performances, are the essence of jazz. (B) is correct. Choices A, C, and D do not put the word *improvisation* after the comma, so they all display modification errors.

6.   J
Difficulty: Low
Category: Agreement: Modifiers
Getting to the Answer: Eliminate F and G because "most great" and "most greatest" are idiomatically incorrect. Choice H does not create an idiom error, but the comparative form of *great* should be used only when exactly two objects or individuals are being compared. Choice (J) correctly uses the superlative form.

7.   D
Difficulty: Medium
Category: Agreement: Verbs
Getting to the Answer: If a verb is underlined, make sure that it agrees with its subject. The subject, *solos*, is plural, and the verb *was* is singular, so A is incorrect. Eliminate B because it is also singular. Choice C is plural but in the present tense. Choice (D) is plural and correctly uses the past tense, which matches the tense of the rest of the paragraph.

8.   H
Difficulty: Medium
Category: Agreement: Pronouns
Getting to the Answer: When a pronoun is underlined, check that it agrees with its antecedent, the noun to which it refers. The antecedent is the plural noun *revolutions*, so the plural pronoun *their* is needed; (H) is correct. Choice F is incorrect because *its* is singular. Choices G and J do not make sense in context; *it's* means "it is," and *there* indicates location, not possession.

9. D
Difficulty: High
Category: Sentence Structure: Parenthetical Elements
Getting to the Answer: The phrase "later and more lastingly" is a parenthetical phrase that must be properly punctuated. Only (D) correctly sets it off from the rest of the sentence. In addition, B and C incorrectly omit the word *also*, which must be included because the sentence includes the first part of the idiomatic phrase "not only...but also."

10. F
Difficulty: Medium
Category: Agreement: Modifiers
Getting to the Answer: The word *genre's* is a singular possessive noun. It makes sense in context because the sentence is describing the "complexity and sophistication" of a single genre of music. (F) is correct. Choices G and H are possessive, but they are both plural. In addition, H incorrectly adds an extra *s* after the apostrophe; *genres's* is considered grammatically incorrect in any context. Finally, choice J does not show possession at all.

11. B
Difficulty: Medium
Category: Sentence Structure: Commas, Dashes, and Colons
Getting to the Answer: When a punctuation mark is underlined, make sure that it is actually necessary. Commas, semicolons, and dashes all separate elements of the sentence into different logical units. Since the phrase "strike that was in effect" is one cohesive phrase, no punctuation of any sort should be used. Choice (B) is correct.

12. H
Difficulty: Medium
Category: Agreement: Modifiers
Getting to the Answer: As written, the phrase *most remains* is in the wrong order. Additionally, it uses the adjective *most,* instead of the adverb *mostly,* to modify the adjective *undocumented.* Choice (H) is the only option that is in the correct order, uses an adverb, and does not introduce a new error. J incorrectly changes the singular verb *remains* to the plural verb *remain,* which does not agree with the singular subject *ferment.*

SENTENCE STRUCTURE: THE BASICS

LEARNING OBJECTIVES

After this lesson, you will be able to:

- Determine the correct punctuation and/or conjunctions to form a complete sentence
- Identify and correct inappropriate uses of semicolons

To answer a question like this:

Women's Suffrage

The struggle for women's suffrage in the United

States began several decades before national legislation

was <u>enacted and the</u> movement included a myriad of
₁

efforts that culminated in nationwide voting rights

nearly fifty years after the birth of the women's suffrage

movement.

1. A. NO CHANGE
    B. enacted, the
    C. enacted; the
    D. enacted but the

You need to know this:

Fragments and Run-ons

A complete sentence must express a complete thought and have both a subject and a verb. If any one of these elements is missing, the sentence is a **fragment**. You can recognize a fragment because the sentence will not make sense as written.

Missing element	Example	Corrected sentence
Subject	*Ran a marathon.*	*Lola ran a marathon.*
Verb	*Lola a marathon.*	
Complete thought	*While Lola ran a marathon.*	*While Lola ran a marathon, her friends cheered for her.*

The fragment "While Lola ran a marathon" is an example of a dependent clause: it has a subject (Lola) and a verb (ran), but it does not express a complete thought because it starts with a subordinating conjunction (while). Notice what the word *while* does to the meaning: While Lola ran a marathon, what happened? To fix this type of fragment, eliminate the subordinating conjunction or join the dependent clause to an independent clause using a comma. Subordinating conjunctions are words and phrases such as *since*, *because*, *therefore*, *unless*, *although*, and *due to*.

Unlike a dependent clause, an independent clause can stand on its own as a complete sentence. If a sentence has more than one independent clause, those clauses must be properly joined. If they are not, the sentence is a **run-on**: *Lucas enjoys hiking, he climbs a new mountain every summer.* There are several ways to correct a run-on:

To correct a run-on	Example
Use a period	*Lucas enjoys hiking. He climbs a new mountain every summer.*
Use a semicolon	*Lucas enjoys hiking; he climbs a new mountain every summer.*
Make one clause dependent	*Since Lucas enjoys hiking, he climbs a new mountain every summer.*
Use a comma and a FANBOYS conjunction: For, And, Nor, But, Or, Yet, So	*Lucas enjoys hiking, so he climbs a new mountain every summer.*
Use a colon or a dash	*Lucas enjoys hiking: he climbs a new mountain every summer.* *Lucas enjoys hiking—he climbs a new mountain every summer.*

Semicolons

Semicolons are used in one specific way on the ACT:

Use a semicolon to . . .	Example
Join two independent clauses that are not connected by a comma and a FANBOYS conjunction	*Gaby knew that her term paper would take at least four hours to write; she got started in study hall and then finished it at home.*

You need to do this:

To recognize and correct errors involving fragments, run-ons, and semicolons, familiarize yourself with the ways in which they are tested.

- Fragments
  - If a sentence is missing a subject, a verb, or a complete thought, it is a fragment.
  - Correct the fragment by adding the missing element.
- Run-ons
  - If a sentence includes two independent clauses, they must be properly joined:
    - Use a period
    - Use a semicolon
    - Make one clause dependent by using a subordinating conjunction (since, because, therefore, unless, although, due to, etc.)
    - Use a comma and a FANBOYS (For, And, Nor, But, Or, Yet, So) conjunction
    - Use a colon or a dash
- Semicolon Use
  - A semicolon is used to join two independent clauses that are not connected by a comma and a FANBOYS conjunction.

Explanation:

The clauses before and after the word *and* are independent clauses and must be punctuated properly. Choice (C) correctly uses a semicolon to join the two clauses. Choices A, B, and D include either a comma or a coordinating conjunction but not both, so they are incorrect.

Drills

If sentence formation or semicolons give you trouble, study the information above and try out these drill questions before completing the Try on Your Own questions below. Drill answers can be found in Answers and Explanations.

a. Correct the fragment by adding a subject: Volunteered to organize the upcoming fundraiser.

b. Correct the fragment by completing the thought: Upon finding the misplaced house keys.

c. Correct the run-on sentence by adding a punctuation mark: The historic center of town was restored it once again bustled with activity.

d. Correct the run-on sentence by adding a punctuation mark: Logical thinking is essential to scientific research the irony is that scientists who make important discoveries often do so on a hunch.

e. Make one clause dependent to correct the run-on sentence: The local farms had a poor harvest last year, the price of produce at the market has risen dramatically.

Try on Your Own

Directions: Take as much time as you need on these questions. Work carefully and methodically. There will be an opportunity for timed practice at the end of the chapter.

Espresso 89

For what seemed like <u>eons; people</u> in my
                              2
neighborhood complained about the lack of coffee shops in our community. The discussions at times became

<u>passionate, and it</u> seemed that my neighbors believed
          3
that a coffee shop would cure just about any problem our suburban neighborhood faced. Not a coffee drinker, I remained unconvinced that a venue to purchase coffee would make a significant difference. However, when a

2. F. NO CHANGE
    G. eons, people
    H. eons, and people
    J. eons. People

3. Which of the following replacements for the underlined segment of the sentence would NOT be acceptable?

    A. passionate it
    B. passionate; it
    C. passionate. It
    D. so passionate that it

coffee shop did open <u>nearby. I</u> discovered that it offered
4
much more than warm beverages and convenient
snacks. Ingrid and Gus, the owners of Espresso 89,

work diligently to create an inclusive <u>atmosphere thanks</u>
5
to their dedication, their shop serves as a community
center for the area.

    Espresso 89 began by inviting a local artist to display
her paintings on the walls of the shop and holding a
"gallery" opening for the occasion. Ingrid and Gus
encouraged other local artists to sign up for future
opportunities to share their work with the coffee-
drinking public. Two or three nights a week, Espresso 89
hosts music or literary events that provide entertainment
and the opportunity for local artists to showcase their
talent. A retired elementary school teacher conducts
a weekly children's story <u>hour she offers</u> storybook
6
after storybook to delighted children and their grateful
parents.

4. F. NO CHANGE
    G. nearby, I
    H. nearby and
    J. nearby, and also I

5. A. NO CHANGE
    B. atmosphere, thanks
    C. atmosphere—thanks
    D. atmosphere so thanks

6. E. NO CHANGE
    F. hour, she offers
    G. hour; offering
    J. hour, offering

SENTENCE STRUCTURE: PARENTHETICAL ELEMENTS

LEARNING OBJECTIVE

After this lesson, you will be able to:
- Set off simple parenthetical elements using punctuation

To answer a question like this:

    The Nineteenth <u>Amendment which granted all</u>
1
<u>American women the right to vote, was</u> passed by
1
Congress on June 4, 1919.

1. A. NO CHANGE
    B. Amendment, which granted all American women the right to vote, was
    C. Amendment which granted all American women the right to vote was
    D. Amendment which granted all American women the right to vote—was

You need to know this:

Answer choices often move punctuation marks around, replace them with other punctuation marks, or remove them altogether. When underlined portions include commas, dashes, or parentheses, check to make sure the punctuation is used correctly in context.

Parenthetical Elements

Parenthetical elements may appear at the beginning, in the middle, or at the end of a sentence. They must be properly punctuated with parentheses, commas, or dashes for the sentence to be grammatically correct. A phrase such as *the capital of France* is considered parenthetical if the rest of the sentence is grammatically correct when it is removed. Do not mix and match; a parenthetical element must begin and end with the same type of punctuation.

Parenthetical element placement	Parentheses	Comma(s)	Dash(es)
Beginning	N/A	The capital of France, Paris is a popular tourist destination.	N/A
Middle	Paris (the capital of France) is a popular tourist destination.	Paris, the capital of France, is a popular tourist destination.	Paris—the capital of France—is a popular tourist destination.
End	A popular tourist destination is Paris (the capital of France).	A popular tourist destination is Paris, the capital of France.	A popular tourist destination is Paris—the capital of France.

You need to do this:

If the underlined portion includes punctuation, ask yourself:

- Is the punctuation used correctly?

  The commas, dashes, or parentheses need to set off a parenthetical element, be used consistently, and be placed in the correct location.

- Is the punctuation necessary?

  If you cannot identify a reason why the punctuation is included, the punctuation should be removed.

Explanation:

The phrase "which granted all American women the right to vote" is a parenthetical element that must be set off from the rest of the sentence with either two commas or two dashes. Choice (B) is correct.

Drills

If parenthetical elements give you trouble, study the information above and try out these drill questions before completing the Try on Your Own questions below. Drill answers can be found in Answers and Explanations.

a. Use a comma to correctly punctuate the parenthetical element at the beginning of the sentence: Delayed for two hours due to a thunderstorm the baseball game started much later than fans had expected.

b. Use parentheses to correctly punctuate the parenthetical element in the middle of the sentence: *The Heart of a Woman* originally published in 1981 is one of Maya Angelou's most popular books.

c.   Use commas to correctly punctuate the parenthetical element in the middle of the sentence: The architect a keen observer known for her meticulous attention to detail gently pointed out the error in her coworker's design.

d.   Use dashes to correctly punctuate the parenthetical element in the middle of the sentence: Contemporary Hawaiian quilts which are often featured at the Mokupāpapa Discovery Center reflect an eclectic blend of Hawaiian tradition and modern vision.

e.   Use a comma to correctly punctuate the parenthetical element at the end of the sentence: A hurricane's strength is rated on a scale of 1 to 5 depending on the speed of sustained winds.

Try on Your Own

Directions: Take as much time as you need on these questions. Work carefully and methodically. There will be an opportunity for timed practice at the end of the chapter.

Medusa

For more than two thousand <u>years; Medusa</u> has been
₂
a prominent image in the world of art and the world of
myth. As far back as 200 BCE, images of

2.   F. NO CHANGE
      G. years, Medusa
      H. years Medusa
      J. years. Medusa

<u>Medusa—the defeated Gorgon, abounded</u>. The shield of
₃
Alexander the Great, for example, was graced with an
image of the mythical Medusa with her locks of

3.   A. NO CHANGE
      B. Medusa the defeated Gorgon, abounded.
      C. Medusa the defeated Gorgon abounded.
      D. Medusa—the defeated Gorgon— abounded.

live <u>serpents, and</u> a gaze that turned onlookers into
₄
stone.

4.   F. NO CHANGE
      G. serpents;
      H. serpents,
      J. serpents and

Medusa was surely one of the most threatening figures of ancient Greek mythology. One of the three Gorgon <u>sisters</u> Medusa had been known for her beauty.
5

5. A. NO CHANGE
   B. sisters,
   C. sisters because
   D. sisters was because

However, she aroused the anger of the goddess Athena, who turned <u>Medusa's, once lovely hair</u>, to snakes. With the power to turn anyone who looked upon her into stone, Medusa was feared and thought impossible to defeat.
6

6. F. NO CHANGE
   G. Medusa's once lovely hair
   H. Medusa's once, lovely hair
   J. Medusa's—once lovely hair

SENTENCE STRUCTURE: COMMAS, DASHES, AND COLONS

LEARNING OBJECTIVE

After this lesson, you will be able to:

- Identify and correct inappropriate uses of commas, dashes, and colons

To answer a question like this:

In 1848, suffragists at the Seneca Falls Convention developed a wide array of demands, many of which were eventually considered too radical to be feasible. As a way of gaining broader support, these suffragists found it necessary to streamline and slightly alter their positions. The process was <u>tedious, but</u> necessary.
1

1. A. NO CHANGE
   B. tedious: but
   C. tedious; but
   D. tedious but

You need to know this:

Answer choices often move punctuation marks around, replace them with other punctuation marks, or remove them altogether. When underlined portions include commas, dashes, or colons, check to make sure the punctuation is used correctly in context.

Commas

There are two situations in which commas are not interchangeable with any other punctuation: when listing a series of items and when separating introductory words or phrases from the rest of the sentence.

Use commas to...	Comma(s)
Set off three or more items in a series	*Jeremiah packed a sleeping bag, a raincoat, and a lantern for his upcoming camping trip.*
Separate an introductory word or phrase from the rest of the sentence	*For example, carrots are an excellent source of several vitamins and minerals.*

Commas and Dashes

In many cases, either a comma or a dash may be used to punctuate a sentence.

Use commas or dashes to . . .	Comma(s)	Dash(es)
Separate independent clauses connected by a FANBOYS conjunction (For, And, Nor, But, Or, Yet, So)	*Jess finished her homework earlier than expected, so she started an assignment that was due the following week.*	*Jess finished her homework earlier than expected—so she started an assignment that was due the following week.*
Separate an independent and dependent clause	*Tyson arrived at school a few minutes early, which gave him time to organize his locker before class.*	*Tyson arrived at school a few minutes early—which gave him time to organize his locker before class.*
Separate parenthetical elements from the rest of the sentence (use either two commas or two dashes, not one of each)	*Professor Mann, who is the head of the English department, is known for assigning extensive projects.*	*Professor Mann—who is the head of the English department—is known for assigning extensive projects.*

Colons and Dashes

Colons and dashes are used to include new ideas that introduce or explain something or that break the flow of the sentence. Note that the clause before the colon or dash must be able to stand on its own as a complete sentence.

Use colons and dashes to...	Colon	Dash
Introduce and/or emphasize a short phrase, quotation, explanation, example, or list that follows an independent clause	*Sanjay had two important tasks to complete: a science experiment and an expository essay.*	*Sanjay had two important tasks to complete—a science experiment and an expository essay.*
Separate two independent clauses when the second clause explains, illustrates, or expands on the first sentence	*Highway 1 in Australia is one of the longest national highways in the world: it circles the entirety of the continent and connects every mainland state capital.*	*Highway 1 in Australia is one of the longest national highways in the world—it circles the entirety of the continent and connects every mainland state capital.*

Unnecessary Punctuation

Knowing when punctuation should not be used is equally important. If an underlined portion includes punctuation, take time to consider whether it should be included at all.

Do NOT use punctuation to...	Incorrect	Correct
Separate a subject from its verb	*The diligent student council, meets every week.*	*The diligent student council meets every week.*
Separate a verb from its object or a preposition from its object	*The diligent student council meets, every week.*	*The diligent student council meets every week.*
Set off elements that are essential to a sentence's meaning	*The, diligent student, council meets every week.*	*The diligent student council meets every week.*
Separate adjectives that work together to modify a noun	*The diligent, student council meets every week.*	*The diligent student council meets every week.*

You need to do this:

If the underlined portion includes punctuation, ask yourself:

- Is the punctuation used correctly?

  The punctuation needs to be the correct type (comma, dash, or colon) and in the correct location.

- Is the punctuation necessary?

  If you cannot identify a reason why the punctuation is included, the punctuation should be removed.

Explanation:

A comma must be placed before *but* only if the words that follow form an independent clause. Here, only the word *necessary*, which is not an independent clause, appears after *but*, so no punctuation is needed. Choice (D) is correct.

Drills

If commas, colons, and dashes give you trouble, study the information above and try out these drill questions before completing the Try on Your Own questions below. Drill answers can be found in Answers and Explanations.

Edit each sentence to correct the punctuation issue.

a. The recipe includes my favorite fruit sweet red cherries.

b. Historically popular sayings are transferred by word of mouth and rarely found in written records so there is often no definite answer to the question of their origin.

c. Paradise tree snakes subsist mostly on lizards and bats which they immobilize with mild venom.

d. As a result the United States entered an isolationist period after World War I.

e. *Hamlet* begins with two of Shakespeare's favorite ways to grab an audience's attention a supernatural phenomenon and a murder plot.

Try on Your Own

Directions: Take as much time as you need on these questions. Work carefully and methodically. There will be an opportunity for timed practice at the end of the chapter.

Music in the Park

Some people think of classical music as

<u>tedious, and</u> unimaginative. They feel that music without
₂

lyrics is lacking in emotion or simply too complex to

fully appreciate. For many years, I was among those

who thought that listening to classical music was an

abysmal experience. <u>However</u> when a friend convinced
₃

me to attend the New York Philharmonic performance

in Central Park, a free event usually scheduled twice each

summer, my entire perception of orchestras and classical

music changed.

I knew that there would be a large audience for the

<u>performance, but</u> I didn't think the atmosphere would
₄

be festive. Thousands of people had spread out blankets

to relax and experience the music. By the end of the first

<u>piece: Mendelssohn's</u> Symphony No. 4 in A Major—I
₅

was enthralled. The second piece was Tchaikovsky's

1812 Overture, and the audience hushed their already

whispered conversations to hear the work's interplay

among the brass, strings, woodwinds, and percussion

instruments. The emotional ending, punctuated with

booming cannons and <u>lyrical, church</u> bells, provided the
₆

opportunity for me to genuinely enjoy classical music,

albeit for the very first time.

2. F. NO CHANGE
    G. tedious; and
    H. tedious, and,
    J. tedious and

3. A. NO CHANGE
    B. However,
    C. However;
    D. However:

4. F. NO CHANGE
    G. performance; but
    H. performance; so
    J. performance, so

5. A. NO CHANGE
    B. piece, Mendelssohn's
    C. piece—Mendelssohn's
    D. piece Mendelssohn's

6. F. NO CHANGE
    G. lyrical church
    H. lyrical—church
    J. lyrical: church

AGREEMENT: VERBS

To answer a question like this:

Instead of arguing for equality based on principle, suffragists insisted that the difference between the two genders <u>were</u> precisely why women must be allowed
¹
to participate in government. In an attempt to appease opponents, suffragists insisted that the female vote would aid in purifying politics, enacting reforms, and outweighing less-desirable votes. The positive outcome of a female voting bloc, suffragists posited, would be a government that reflected a woman's position as protector of the home, family, and society.

1. A. NO CHANGE
   B. was
   C. will be
   D. was exactly and

You need to know this:

Verb Tense

Verb tense indicates when an action or state of being took place: past, present, or future. The tense of the verb must fit the context of the passage. Each tense can express three different types of action.

Type of action	Past	Present	Future
Single action occurring only once	Connor **planted** vegetables in the community garden.	Connor **plants** vegetables in the community garden.	Connor **will plant** vegetables in the community garden.
Action that is ongoing at some point in time	Connor **was planting** vegetables in the community garden this morning before noon.	Connor **is planting** vegetables in the community garden this morning before noon.	Connor **will be planting** vegetables in the community garden this morning before noon.
Action that is completed before some other action	Connor **had planted** vegetables in the community garden every year until he gave his job to Jasmine.	Connor **has planted** vegetables in the community garden since it started five years ago.	Connor **will have planted** vegetables in the community garden by the time the growing season starts.

Subject-Verb Agreement

A verb must agree with its subject in person and number:

- Person (first, second, or third)
  - First: *I ask a question.*
  - Second: *You ask a question.*
  - Third: *She asks a question.*
- Number (singular or plural)
  - Singular: *The apple tastes delicious.*
  - Plural: *Apples taste delicious.*

The noun closest to the verb is not always the subject. Take the following sentence as an example: *The chair with the lion feet is an antique.* The singular verb in this sentence, *is*, is closest to the plural noun *feet*. However, the verb's actual subject is the singular noun *chair*, so the sentence is correct as written.

When a sentence includes two nouns, only the conjunction *and* forms a compound subject requiring a plural verb form:

- Plural: *Saliyah **and** Taylor **are** in the running club.*
- Singular: ***Either** Saliyah **or** Taylor **is** in the running club.*
- Singular: ***Neither** Saliyah **nor** Taylor **is** in the running club.*

Collective nouns are nouns that name entities with more than one member, such as *group*, *team*, and *family*. Even though these nouns represent more than one person, they are grammatically singular and require singular verb forms:

- ***The collection** of paintings **is** one of the most popular art exhibits in recent years.*
- ***The team looks** promising this year.*

Parallelism

Verbs in a list, a compound, or a comparison must be parallel in form:

Feature	Example	Parallel form
A list	*Chloe **formulated** a question, **conducted** background research, and **constructed** a hypothesis before starting the experiment.*	3 simple past verb phrases
A compound	***Hunting** and **fishing** were essential to the survival of Midwestern Native American tribes such as the Omaha.*	2 –ing verb forms
A comparison	*Garrett enjoys **sculpting** as much as **painting**.*	2 –ing verb forms

Note that parallelism may be tested using other parts of speech besides verbs. In general, any items in a list, compound, or comparison must be in parallel form. For example, if a list starts with a noun, the other items in the list must also be nouns; if it starts with an adjective, the other items must be adjectives, etc.:

Incorrect	Correct alternatives
*Naomi likes **pumpkin pie and to drink coffee** on chilly weekend afternoons.*	*Naomi likes **pumpkin pie and coffee** on chilly weekend afternoons.* *Naomi likes **to eat pumpkin pie and to drink coffee** on chilly weekend afternoons.*
Which of the dogs is the **most** docile and **better** behaved?	*Which of the dogs is the **most** docile and **best** behaved?* *Which of the dogs is the **more** docile and **better** behaved?*

You need to do this:

If the underlined portion includes a verb, check that the verb:

- Reflects the correct tense: Does it fit the context?
- Agrees with the subject in person and number
- Is parallel in form with other verbs in a series, list, or compound if there is one in the sentence

Explanation:

A verb must agree with its subject. In this case, the plural verb *were* does not agree with its singular subject *difference*; eliminate A. Eliminate C because the future tense does not make sense in context. The remaining choices both use the past-tense singular verb *was*, but D is unnecessarily wordy. Choice (B) is correct.

Drills

If verbs give you trouble, study the information above and try out these drill questions before completing the Try on Your Own questions below. Drill answers can be found in Answers and Explanations.

Edit each sentence to correct the verb issue.

a.   Pablo present his experiment at the science fair last week.

b.   The movie, with its complex plot and stirring themes, were critically acclaimed.

c.   Neither the director nor the lead actor are at rehearsal today.

d.   The park and wildlife refuge comprises more than 800 acres of mountains, lakes, and forests.

e.   In order to pass the foreign language proficiency exam, you must be both a fluent speaker and able to read it as well.

Try on Your Own

Directions: Take as much time as you need on these questions. Work carefully and methodically. There will be an opportunity for timed practice at the end of the chapter.

Mia's Attic

I thought the tour of my friend's new house was finished as we came to a halt outside her bedroom on the third floor. However, Mia had something else in mind. "Do you want to go up to the attic?" she asked me, her eyes sparkling with mischief. "When my mom inherited[2] the house from my grandmother last year, she told me that no one had gone up there for forty years!" In past situations, either Mia's mom or older brother were[3] available to help me convince Mia that her latest plan was inadvisable. Unfortunately, they were both at work and unavailable to assist me in pleading my case.

2. F. NO CHANGE
    G. inherits
    H. had inherited
    J. would have inherited

3. A. NO CHANGE
    B. was
    C. would be
    D. will have been

I wasn't thrilled about the idea of exploring the dark, musty space overhead. In the past, I'd hesitated whenever Mia suggested risky or dangerous activities, but this time I just nodded, trying to appear nonchalant. Mia yanked on the cord dangling from the wooden door; a staircase unfolded, the bottom step landing directly in front of my feet. I looked up, acknowledging that seemingly endless darkness, quite possibly replete with eight-legged monsters, often <u>teem</u> with a myriad of
4
unexpected unpleasantries.

Hoping Mia wouldn't notice, I took a deep breath and <u>grip</u> the ladder. As I placed my foot on the
5
bottom rung, I wondered how my best friend had failed to take my considerable fear of spiders into account. I like arachnids about as much as I enjoy watching gory movies, enduring frightening pranks, and <u>dental appointments</u>. "The sooner you get this over
6
with, the better," I whispered to myself, trying to exude as much courage as possible.

4. F. NO CHANGE
    G. will have teemed
    H. teems
    J. to teem

5. A. NO CHANGE
    B. grips
    C. would grip
    D. gripped

6. F. NO CHANGE
    G. going to the dentist.
    H. trips to the dentist.
    J. dental appointments for a root canal.

AGREEMENT: PRONOUNS

LEARNING OBJECTIVE

After this lesson, you will be able to:
* Identify and correct pronoun agreement issues

To answer a question like this:

Despite anti-suffragist objections, the suffrage movement finally achieved <u>its'</u> ultimate goal, but only
1
after offering its participants a political education and a sense of taking an active role in the nation's history, which in turn helped to convince the rest of the country of the worth of the woman's vote.

1. A. NO CHANGE
    B. their
    C. they're
    D. its

K   43

You need to know this:

Pronoun Forms

A pronoun is a word that takes the place of a noun. Pronouns can take three different forms, each of which is used based on the grammatical role it plays in the sentence.

Form	Pronouns	Example
Subjective: The pronoun is used as the subject	I, you, she, he, it, we, they, who	*Rivka is the student **who** will lead the presentation.*
Objective: The pronoun is used as the object of a verb or a preposition	me, you, her, him, it, us, them, whom	*With **whom** will Rivka present the scientific findings?*
Possessive: The pronoun expresses ownership	my, mine, your, yours, his, her, hers, its, our, ours, their, theirs, whose	*Rivka will likely choose a partner **whose** work is excellent.*

Note that a pronoun in subjective form can, logically, be the subject in a complete sentence. Pronouns that are in objective form cannot function as the subject.

When there are two pronouns or a noun and a pronoun in a compound structure, drop the other noun or pronoun to tell which form to use. For example: Leo and me walked into town. If you were talking about yourself only, you would say, "I walked into town," not "Me walked into town." Therefore, the correct form is subjective, and the original sentence should read: Leo and I walked into town.

Pronoun-Antecedent Agreement

A pronoun's antecedent is the noun it logically represents in a sentence. If the noun is singular, the pronoun must be singular; if the noun is plural, the pronoun must be plural.

Antecedent	Incorrect	Correct
selection	The selection of books was placed in **their** designated location.	The selection of books was placed in **its** designated location.
girls	The girls fed the giraffes all of the lettuce **she** had purchased.	The girls fed the giraffes all of the lettuce **they** had purchased.
sapling	The sapling, along with dozens of flowers, was relocated to where **they** would thrive.	The sapling, along with dozens of flowers, was relocated to where **it** would thrive.

You need to do this:

If the underlined portion includes a pronoun, find the logical antecedent. Check that the pronoun:

- Uses the correct form
  - If the pronoun is the subject of the sentence, use a subjective pronoun such as *I, you, she, he, it, we, they,* or *who.*
  - If the pronoun is an object within the sentence, use an objective pronoun such as *me, you, her, him, it, us, they,* or *whom.*
  - If the pronoun indicates possession, use a possessive pronoun such as *my, mine, your, yours, his, her, hers, its, our, ours, their, theirs,* or *whose.*

- Agrees with its antecedent
  - A singular antecedent requires a singular pronoun; a plural antecedent requires a plural pronoun.

Explanation:

Eliminate A immediately because the word *its'* is not correct in any context. The pronoun's antecedent, the noun to which the pronoun is referring, is "the suffrage movement," which is singular. Choice (D) correctly uses the singular possessive pronoun *its*. Choice B incorrectly uses a plural possessive pronoun, and C means *they are*, which does not make sense in context.

Drills

If pronouns give you trouble, study the information above and try out these drill questions before completing the Try on Your Own questions below. Drill answers can be found in Answers and Explanations.

Edit each sentence to correct the pronoun issue.

a. The scientist, about who I had read, was more charismatic in person than I had expected.

b. Between you and I, you are the better singer.

c. A jaguar, with its keen senses and sharp teeth and claws, is known for their ability to dominate prey.

d. The jar of olives is not in their regular location on the shelf.

e. One cannot help but be amazed by the scientific advances in the past century, especially if you study the history of science.

Try on Your Own

Directions: Take as much time as you need on these questions. Work carefully and methodically. There will be an opportunity for timed practice at the end of the chapter.

Galloping Gertie

For four months in the fall of 1940, citizens of the Puget Sound area of Washington used one of the most illustrious, and most dangerous, suspension bridges ever built; it had the opportunity to travel across the Tacoma Narrows Bridge, or "Galloping Gertie," which enjoyed a relatively short life compared to similar structures in the United States. "Gertie" taught important lessons on what to do—and what not to do—when building a suspension bridge.

2. F. NO CHANGE
    G. their
    H. them
    J. they

State officials in Washington were the ones <u>whom</u>
₃
identified a need for a bridge across Puget Sound.
The closest point was the Tacoma Narrows, a windy
2,800-foot gap. Construction began in November of
1938, and the bridge was officially opened on July 1,
1940. Although they knew about form and structure,
the bridge's engineers failed to take into account
aerodynamic components, particularly the wind, and <u>it's</u>
₄
effect on the roadway. Because the roadbed was

3. A. NO CHANGE
   B. who
   C. that
   D. that spoke up and

4. F. NO CHANGE
   G. its
   H. its'
   J. their

constructed with rigid plate girders, <u>it</u> could not absorb
₅
the winds of Puget Sound. Consequently, on any windy
day, the roadway buckled and contorted, or "galloped"—
hence, the nickname. The undulation became so severe
that the bridge, as <u>you</u> would hope, was eventually closed
₆
to traffic.

5. A. NO CHANGE
   B. they
   C. those
   D. these

6. F. NO CHANGE
   G. we
   H. it
   J. one

AGREEMENT: MODIFIERS

LEARNING OBJECTIVES

After this lesson, you will be able to:

• Identify and correct modifier agreement issues
• Identify and correct inappropriate uses of apostrophes

To answer a question like this:

Much to their surprise, <u>it was quickly apparent to</u>
₁
<u>anti-suffragists</u> that women, in fact, did not vote together
₁
as a bloc. Women voted as individuals and in smaller
proportions than men.

1. A. NO CHANGE
   B. it was quick apparent to
      anti-suffragists
   C. anti-suffragists quick found
   D. anti-suffragists quickly found

You need to know this:

A modifier is a word or phrase that describes, clarifies, or provides additional information about another part of the sentence. Modifier questions require you to identify the part of a sentence being modified and use the appropriate modifier in the proper place.

In order to be grammatically correct, the modifier must be placed as close to the word it describes as possible. Use context clues in the passage to identify the correct placement of a modifier; a misplaced modifier can cause confusion and is always incorrect on test day.

Note that a common way the ACT tests modifiers is with modifying phrases at the beginning of a sentence. Just like any other modifier, the modifying phrase grammatically modifies whatever is right next to it in the sentence. For example, consider the sentence, "While walking to the bus stop, the rain drenched Bob." The initial phrase, "While walking to the bus stop," grammatically modifies "the rain," creating a nonsense sentence; the rain can't walk to the bus stop. The writer meant that Bob was walking to the bus stop, so the sentence should read, "While walking to the bus stop, Bob was drenched by the rain."

Modifier/Modifying phrase	Incorrect	Correct
nearly	Andre **nearly** watched the play for four hours.	Andre watched the play for **nearly** four hours.
in individual containers	The art teacher handed out paints to students **in individual containers**.	The art teacher handed out paints **in individual containers** to students.
A scholar athlete	**A scholar athlete**, maintaining high grades in addition to playing soccer was expected of Maya.	**A scholar athlete**, Maya was expected to maintain high grades in addition to playing soccer.

Adjectives and Adverbs

Use adjectives only to modify nouns and pronouns. Use adverbs to modify everything else.

- Adjectives are single-word modifiers that describe nouns and pronouns: *Ian conducted an **efficient** lab experiment.*
- Adverbs are single-word modifiers that describe verbs, adjectives, or other adverbs: *Ian **efficiently** conducted a lab experiment.*

Note that nouns can sometimes be used as adjectives. For example, in the phrase "the fashion company's autumn line," the word *fashion* functions as an adjective modifying *company*, and the word *autumn* functions as an adjective modifying *line*.

Comparative/Superlative

When comparing similar things, use adjectives that match the number of items being compared. When comparing two items or people, use the comparative form of the adjective. When comparing three or more items or people, use the superlative form.

Comparative (two items)	Superlative (three or more items)
better, more, newer, older, shorter, taller, worse, younger	best, most, newest, oldest, shortest, tallest, worst, youngest

Possessive Nouns and Pronouns

Possessive nouns and pronouns indicate that something belongs to someone or something. In general, possessive nouns are written with an apostrophe, while possessive pronouns are not.

To spot errors in possessive noun or pronoun construction, look for...	Incorrect	Correct
Two nouns in a row	The **professors lectures** were both informative and entertaining.	The **professor's lectures** were both informative and entertaining.
Pronouns with apostrophes	The book is **her's**.	The book is **hers**.
Words that sound alike	The three friends decided to ride **there** bicycles to the park over **they're** where **their** going to enjoy a picnic lunch.	The three friends decided to ride **their** bicycles to the park over **there** where **they're** going to enjoy a picnic lunch.

Apostrophes

Use an apostrophe to...	Example
Indicate the possessive form of a single noun	My oldest **sister's soccer game** is on Saturday.
Indicate the possessive form of a plural noun	My **two** older **sisters' soccer games** are on Saturday.
Indicate a contraction (e.g., don't, can't)	**They've** won every soccer match this season.

Note that plural nouns are formed without an apostrophe.

Incorrect	Correct
Sting ray's are cartilaginous fish related to **shark's**.	**Sting rays** are cartilaginous fish related to **sharks**.
There are many **carnival's** in this area every summer.	There are many **carnivals** in this area every summer.

To check whether *it's* is appropriate, replace it in the sentence with *it is* or *it has*. If the sentence no longer makes sense, *it's* is incorrect. The following sentences are correct:

The tree frog blends perfectly into its surroundings. When it holds still, it's nearly invisible.

Note that *its'* and *its's* are never correct.

You need to do this:

If the underlined portion includes a modifier, determine whether the modifier:

- Is placed correctly
  - Is it as near as possible to the word it logically modifies?
  - If it is not in the correct place, where should it be moved?
- Agrees with the word or words it is describing
  - Does the sentence require an adjective or an adverb?
  - Does the noun or pronoun show proper possession?

If the underlined portion includes an apostrophe, make sure it correctly indicates either possession or a contraction. If an apostrophe is missing, select the answer choice that places it in the correct location.

Explanation:

"Much to their surprise" is an introductory modifying phrase, so the noun that the phrase is modifying must come immediately after the comma. Eliminate A and B because "much to their surprise" is not modifying "it." Choice C introduces a new error by changing the adverb *quickly* to *quick*, which cannot be used to modify the verb *found*. Choice (D) places the correct phrase after the comma and does not introduce any new errors.

Drills

If modifiers give you trouble, study the information above and try out these drill questions before completing the Try on Your Own questions below. Drill answers can be found in Answers and Explanations.

Edit each sentence to correct the modifier or apostrophe issue.

a. A more safely approach is to test the temperature of the water before entering.

b. Jonas had to run to the store real quick before it closed.

c. The new student is the better speller in the class.

d. It took the chameleon a few weeks to acclimate to its' new habitat.

Try on Your Own

Directions: Take as much time as you need on these questions. Work carefully and methodically. There will be an opportunity for timed practice at the end of the chapter.

Basketry

Basketry may be the world's oldest handicraft. The earlier examples of basketry are 10,000 years old. These
2

2. F. NO CHANGE
   G. more earlier
   H. most earliest
   J. earliest

ancient fragments, which have been preserved good by
3
the dry environment of Danger Cave, Utah, show that early Native Americans mastered the art of weaving semi-rigid materials into useful objects. Notably,

3. A. NO CHANGE
   B. very good
   C. quite well and thoroughly
   D. well

the <u>remains of baskets</u> like the ones discovered in Utah
₄
have been found on nearly every continent.

Materials, rather than technique or decoration, are
oftentimes most useful in identifying a basket's origin.
Willow, just pliant enough to be either woven or
plaited, is the favored basket-making material of
northern Europe. Opting for rigid materials, <u>bamboo</u>
₅
<u>and rattan have been used by basket makers to create</u>
₅
<u>sturdy baskets</u> in other regions. Africa has yielded many
₅
basket-making materials, including palm leaves, tree
roots, and grasses.

Not surprisingly, a basket's provenance truly
depends on <u>it's</u> composite materials.
₆

4. F.   NO CHANGE
    G.   remains' of baskets
    H.   remain's of baskets
    J.   remains of baskets'

5. A.   NO CHANGE
    B.   bamboo and rattan are used to cre-
         ate sturdy baskets by basket makers
    C.   basket makers use bamboo and
         rattan to create sturdy baskets
    D.   sturdy baskets are made by basket
         makers out of bamboo and rattan

6. F.   NO CHANGE
    G.   its
    H.   their
    J.   they're

AGREEMENT: IDIOMS

LEARNING OBJECTIVE

After this lesson, you will be able to:

- Identify and correct expressions that deviate from idiomatic English

To answer a question like this:

Early 20th-century women did not necessarily
vote as a united caucus, but they did feel a new sense
of empowerment. They were, by law, participants in a
democracy that <u>couldn't hardly</u> ignore them.
₁

1. A.   NO CHANGE
    B.   would not hardly
    C.   wouldn't hardly
    D.   could hardly

You need to know this:

An idiom is a combination of words that must be used together to convey either a figurative or literal meaning. Idioms are tested in three ways:

1. Proper preposition use in context: The preposition must reflect the writer's intended meaning.

   - *She waits **on** customers.*
   - *She waits **for** the bus.*
   - *She waits **with** her friends.*

2. Idiomatic expressions: Some words or phrases must be used together to be correct.

   - *Simone will **either** bike **or** run to the park.*
   - ***Neither** the principal **nor** the teachers will tolerate tardiness.*
   - *This fall, Shari is playing **not only** soccer **but also** field hockey.*

3. Implicit double negatives: Some words imply a negative and therefore cannot be paired with an explicit negative. The words *barely*, *hardly*, and *scarcely* fall into this category.

   - Incorrect: *Janie **can't hardly** wait for vacation.*
   - Correct: *Janie **can hardly** wait for vacation.*

Frequently tested prepositions	Idiomatic expressions	Words that can't pair with negative words
at	as…as	barely
by	between…and	hardly
for	both…and	scarcely
from	either…or	
of	neither…nor	
on	just as…so too	
to	not only…but also	
with	prefer…to	

You need to do this:

- If the underlined portion includes a preposition, a conjunction, or *barely/hardly/scarcely*, look for a common idiom error.
- If the underlined segment includes a commonly misused word, check the context to determine whether it is used properly.

Explanation:

Since *hardly* is implicitly negative, it cannot be paired with *not*; (D) is correct. Choices A and C include the words *couldn't* and *wouldn't*, respectively, which mean *could not* and *would not*. Choice B explicitly pairs the word *not* with *hardly*, so it is incorrect.

Drills

If idioms give you trouble, study the information above and try out these drill questions before completing the Try on Your Own questions below. Drill answers can be found in Answers and Explanations.

Edit each sentence to correct the idiomatic issue.

a. Straining to hear the bird perched in the tree, Jessa stood completely still, waiting with the sound to reach her.

b. The engineer examined the malfunctioning machine closely for evidence to missing components or worn elements.

c. The protestors' bold slogans not only angered the opposition, but elicited loud reactions from bystanders.

d. Given the cold climate, farmers quickly found that they could grow neither dates or figs.

e. The writing was nearly barely legible after the rain soaked through Tia's backpack and saturated her notebook.

Try on Your Own

Directions: Take as much time as you need on these questions. Work carefully and methodically. There will be an opportunity for timed practice at the end of the chapter.

Alfred Nobel

Given that few people have had the opportunity to read their own obituaries, scientist Alfred Nobel <u>couldn't scarcely</u> believe that, in 1888, his obituary was in the daily newspaper. Alfred surmised that the newspaper editor had been either grossly

2. F. NO CHANGE
    G. could scarcely
    H. could not scarcely
    J. not scarcely

<u>misinformed, and</u> confused by a misidentification. In actuality, Alfred's brother Ludvig had died, and Ludvig was mistaken for Alfred. While Alfred was primarily known as an inventor and one of the richest people

3. A. NO CHANGE
    B. misinformed and
    C. misinformed, or
    D. misinformed or

<u>in the world at the time</u>, the paper unapologetically gave him the moniker "Merchant of Death" because of the innumerable lives that his most notable invention, dynamite, had taken.

4. F. NO CHANGE
    G. in the world for the time being
    H. on the world for the time being
    J. on the world at the time

Unable to accept that dynamite—which was widely <u>used by</u> warfare—would be his enduring legacy,
5
Alfred crafted provisions in his will to create the Nobel Foundation upon his death. Nobel's foundation has not only acknowledged outstanding achievements in chemistry, economics, literature, medicine, peace, and physics, <u>but</u> raised awareness regarding crucial global
6
issues.

5. A. NO CHANGE
    B. used with
    C. used in
    D. used to

6. F. NO CHANGE
    G. it
    H. but it
    J. but also

How Much Have You Learned?

Directions: For test-like practice, give yourself 7 minutes to complete this question set. Note that this is not a test-like mix of questions; rather, these 12 questions cover the sentence structure, punctuation, and agreement issues covered in this chapter.

Be sure to study the explanations, even for questions you got correct. They can be found at the end of this chapter.

The History of Marbles

It is impossible to pinpoint the exact date when the first marble was constructed, most likely out of clay, it is a reasonable assumption to regard the concept of marbles as nearly as old as humankind. Marbles as we know them today, however, first originated in the middle of the 19th century when they were produced in mass quantities in Europe. Originating from their appearance, material, or use, an important identifying factor is often indicated by marbles' names.

"Alleys," for example were named for their composite material; the name indicates that they are made from alabaster. At least, that was the case for alleys produced at the turn of the last century. Nowadays, it's far more common for marbles to consist: of glass, baked clay, steel, onyx, plastic, or agate.

Regardless of the material with which they are made, marbles can be manipulated in a variety of ways.

1. A. NO CHANGE
   B. clay, nevertheless, it
   C. clay, but it
   D. clay; but it

2. F. NO CHANGE
   G. an important identifying factor is often indicated by the names of marbles.
   H. marble's names often indicate an important identifying factor.
   J. marbles' names often indicate an important identifying factor.

3. A. NO CHANGE
   B. "Alleys" for example, were
   C. "Alleys," for example: were
   D. "Alleys," for example, were

4. F. NO CHANGE
   G. consist of
   H. consist—of
   J. consist, of

5. A. NO CHANGE
   B. Regardless to
   C. Regardlessly of
   D. Regardlessly to

"Knuckling" is a <u>technique in which</u> the knuckles of the
₆
hand are balanced against the ground while a marble placed
against the forefinger is shot outward by the

thumb. Marbles may be thrown, rolled, and <u>players can</u>
₇
<u>even kick marbles</u>.
₇

Not surprisingly, there <u>is near</u> as many varieties of
₈
marble games as there are ways to manipulate marbles.
The most common American version involves winning
opponents' marbles by knocking them out of a designated
area with one's own marbles. Another popular game is
<u>taw—also known as ringtaw, or ringer, the object</u> of which
₉
is to shoot marbles arranged like a cross out of a large ring.
Players in a pot game such as moshie try to knock one
another's marbles into a hole.

In nineholes, or bridgeboard, players shoot <u>our</u> marbles
₁₀
through numbered arches on the board.

The popularity of marbles crosses cultural boundaries.
The first marble games took place in <u>antiquity. Were</u> played
₁₁
with nuts, fruit pits, or pebbles. Even the great Augustus
Caesar was known to have played marble games as a child.
During Passover, Jewish children have customarily used
filberts as marbles. Several traditional Chinese games are
also played with marbles. Indeed, while many people
consider the game of marbles to be simple, <u>they actually</u>
₁₂
<u>have</u> a complex history.
₁₂

6. F. NO CHANGE
   G. technique, in which,
   H. technique in, which
   J. technique in which;

7. A. NO CHANGE
   B. players can choose to kick marbles.
   C. kicked or punted.
   D. kicked.

8. F. NO CHANGE
   G. is nearly
   H. are near
   J. are nearly

9. A. NO CHANGE
   B. taw—also known as ringtaw—or ringer the object
   C. taw—also known as ringtaw or ringer—the object
   D. taw, also known as ringtaw, or ringer, the object

10. F. NO CHANGE
    G. your
    H. their
    J. its

11. A. NO CHANGE
    B. antiquity and were
    C. antiquity, and were
    D. antiquity; were

12. F. NO CHANGE
    G. they actually has
    H. it actually have
    J. it actually has

Reflect

Directions: Take a few minutes to recall what you've learned and what you've been practicing in this chapter. Consider the following questions, jot down your best answer for each one, and then compare your reflections to the expert responses on the following page. Use your level of confidence to determine what to do next.

1. Name at least three ways to correct a run-on sentence.

_____
_____
_____

2. How does the ACT test subject-verb agreement and parallelism?

_____
_____
_____

3. What are the three different pronoun forms? When do you use each one?

_____
_____
_____

4. What is the difference between an adjective and an adverb?

_____
_____
_____

5. What are the three ways that apostrophes are tested on the ACT?

_____
_____
_____

Responses

1.   Name at least three ways to correct a run-on sentence.

There are a number of ways to fix a run-on sentence on the ACT. The six ways that you are likely to see are: 1) use a period to create two separate sentences, 2) use a semicolon between the two independent clauses, 3) use a colon between the two independent clauses, 4) make one clause dependent, 5) add a FANBOYS conjunction after the comma, or 6) use a dash between the two independent clauses.

2.   How does the ACT test subject-verb agreement and parallelism?

A subject and a verb must always agree in person (first, second, or third) and number (singular or plural). You will need to be able to spot subject-verb mismatches and correct them. Parallelism requires that all items in a list, a compound, or a comparison be in parallel form. The ACT may test lists or comparisons in which one item is in the incorrect form.

3.   What are the three different pronoun forms? When do you use each one?

The three forms are subjective (when the pronoun is the subject), objective (when the pronoun is the object of a verb or preposition), and possessive (when the pronoun expresses ownership).

4.   What is the difference between an adjective and an adverb?

An adjective is a single word that modifies a noun or a pronoun, while an adverb is a single word that modifies a verb, an adjective, or another adverb.

5.   What are the three ways that apostrophes are tested on the ACT?

Apostrophes on the ACT are used to: 1) indicate the possessive form of a singular noun ('s), 2) indicate the possessive form of a plural noun (s'), or 3) indicate a contraction (don't = do not).

Next Steps

If you answered most questions correctly in the "How Much Have You Learned?" section, and if your responses to the Reflect questions were similar to those of the ACT expert, then consider sentence structure, punctuation, and agreement areas of strength and move on to the next chapter. Come back to these topics periodically to prevent yourself from getting rusty.

If you don't yet feel confident, review those parts of this chapter that you have not yet mastered. In particular, review punctuation usage in the Sentence Structure: The Basics and Sentence Structure: Commas, Dashes, and Colons lessons, as well as how to select the appropriate pronoun or modifier in the Agreement: Pronouns and Agreement: Modifiers lessons. Then, try the questions you missed again. As always, be sure to review the explanations closely. Then go online (**kaptest.com/login**) to watch video lessons about the highest-yield concepts in this chapter and to use your Qbank for more practice. If you haven't already registered your book, do so at **kaptest.com/moreonline**.

GO ONLINE

kaptest.com/login

Answers and Explanations

Sentence Structure: The Basics

1. Review the Explanation portion of the Sentence Structure: The Basics lesson.

Drill Answers

Note: These are not the only ways to correct the sentences; your answers may differ.

a. **The student** volunteered to organize the upcoming fundraiser.

b. Upon finding the misplaced house keys, **Hannah locked the front door.**

c. The historic center of town was restored. **It** once again bustled with activity.

d. Logical thinking is essential to scientific research**;** the irony is that scientists who make important discoveries often do so on a hunch.

e. The local farms had a poor harvest last year, **so** the price of produce at the market has risen dramatically.

2.   G
Difficulty: Medium
Category: Sentence Structure
Getting to the Answer: The phrase "For what seemed like eons" is a dependent clause that must be set off from the rest of the sentence with a comma, so (G) is correct. Choices F, H, and J all create sentence fragments, since the first part of the sentence cannot stand on its own.

3.   A
Difficulty: Low
Category: Sentence Structure
Getting to the Answer: If a sentence includes two independent clauses, they must be properly combined. The independent clauses can be separated by a coordinating conjunction and a comma, as they currently are in the passage; separated by a semicolon, as in B; separated into two sentences, as in C; or edited so that the first part of the sentence is a dependent clause, as in D. By omitting punctuation altogether, (A) creates a run-on sentence.

4.   G
Difficulty: Medium
Category: Sentence Structure
Getting to the Answer: Choice F is incorrect because placing a period after *nearby* creates a sentence fragment. Changing the period to a comma creates a grammatically correct sentence with an introductory phrase followed by an independent clause. Choice (G) is correct. Choices H and J incorrectly use the coordinating conjunction *and*, which makes the resulting sentence an incomplete thought.

5.   C
Difficulty: High
Category: Sentence Structure
Getting to the Answer: The sentence includes two independent clauses that must be properly combined. Choice A is incorrect because it includes no punctuation whatsoever. Choice (C) correctly uses a dash to join the two clauses. Choices B and D are incorrect because both a comma and a coordinating conjunction are required to join two independent clauses. Choice B omits the conjunction, while D omits the comma.

6.   J
Difficulty: Medium
Category: Sentence Structure
Getting to the Answer: The underlined portion contains parts of two independent clauses that must be properly combined. Choice F includes no punctuation at all, and choice G incorrectly uses a comma without a coordinating conjunction. Both choices create a run-on sentence. Finally, eliminate H because *offering* makes the part that follows the semicolon a dependent clause. A semicolon cannot be used to separate an independent clause and a dependent clause. Choice (J) is correct because the comma properly joins the independent clause at the beginning of the sentence with the dependent clause after the comma.

Sentence Structure: Parenthetical Elements

1. Review the Explanation portion of the Sentence Structure: Parenthetical Elements lesson.

Drill Answers

Note: These are not the only ways to correct the sentences; your answers may differ.

a. Delayed for two hours due to a thunderstorm, the baseball game started much later than fans had expected.

b. *The Heart of a Woman* (originally published in 1981) is one of Maya Angelou's most popular books.

c. The architect, a keen observer known for her meticulous attention to detail, gently pointed out the error in her coworker's design.

d. Contemporary Hawaiian quilts—which are often featured at the Mokupāpapa Discovery Center—reflect an eclectic blend of Hawaiian tradition and modern vision.

e. A hurricane's strength is rated on a scale of 1 to 5, depending on the speed of sustained winds.

2. G
Difficulty: Low
Category: Sentence Structure
Getting to the Answer: The first part of the sentence is an introductory phrase and must be set off from the sentence with a comma. Eliminate choices F and J because they use incorrect punctuation, and eliminate H because it removes punctuation altogether. Choice (G) is correct.

3. D
Difficulty: Medium
Category: Sentence Structure
Getting to the Answer: The underlined segment sets off the nonessential phrase "the defeated Gorgon" with one comma and one dash. Either two commas or two dashes must be used to set off this phrase; using one of each is not correct. Eliminate A. Choices B and C do not provide punctuation on both sides of the nonessential phrase, so they can be eliminated as well. Choice (D) is correct.

4. J
Difficulty: High
Category: Sentence Structure
Getting to the Answer: As written, the sentence includes an unnecessary comma before the word *and*. Choice (J) correctly eliminates this unneeded punctuation mark. The phrase "a gaze that turned onlookers into stone" is not an independent clause. Since semicolons are used to join two independent clauses, choice G is incorrect. Finally, choice H is incorrect because it both includes the unnecessary comma and omits the necessary word *and*.

5. B
Difficulty: Medium
Category: Sentence Structure
Getting to the Answer: "One of the three Gorgon sisters" is an introductory modifying phrase that must be followed by a comma; (B) is correct. Choice A omits the comma, and C and D add unnecessary words that do not fix the original error.

6. G
Difficulty: High
Category: Sentence Structure
Getting to the Answer: The phrase "once lovely hair" is essential to the meaning of the sentence, so it should not be separated from the surrounding text with commas or dashes, as in choices F and J. Choice (G) is correct because no punctuation is needed. Choice H incorrectly inserts a comma into the phrase "once lovely hair." Since this phrase is one logical unit, it should not be broken up by a punctuation mark.

Sentence Structure: Commas, Dashes, and Colons

1. Review the Explanation portion of the Sentence Structure: Commas, Dashes, and Colons lesson.

Drill Answers

Note: These are not the only ways to correct the sentences; your answers may differ.

a. The recipe includes my favorite fruit: sweet red cherries.

b. Historically popular sayings are transferred by word of mouth and are rarely found in written records, so there is often no definite answer to the question of their origin. OR Historically popular sayings are transferred by word of mouth and are rarely found in written records—so there is often no definite answer to the question of their origin.

c. Paradise tree snakes subsist mostly on lizards and bats, which they immobilize with mild venom.

d. As a result, the United States entered an isolationist period after World War I.

e. *Hamlet* begins with two of Shakespeare's favorite ways to grab an audience's attention—a supernatural phenomenon and a murder plot. OR *Hamlet* begins with two of Shakespeare's favorite ways to grab an audience's attention: a supernatural phenomenon and a murder plot.

2. J
Difficulty: Medium
Category: Sentence Structure
Getting to the Answer: When a comma is underlined, check to make sure it is necessary. The phrase "tedious and unimaginative" is one logical unit and should not be broken up by any sort of punctuation; (J) is correct.

3. B
Difficulty: Low
Category: Sentence Structure
Getting to the Answer: *However* is a transition word that needs to be separated from the rest of the sentence with a comma; (B) is correct.

4. F
Difficulty: Medium
Category: Sentence Structure
Getting to the Answer: The sentence includes two independent clauses properly joined with a comma and a FANBOYS (For, And, Nor, But, Or, Yet, So) conjunction, so no change is needed. Choice (F) is correct. Choice G incorrectly uses a semicolon to separate two independent clauses with a FANBOYS conjunction between them. Choices H and J are incorrect because the ideas in the two independent clauses contrast with each other. The transition word *so* indicates cause-and-effect, not contrast.

5. C
Difficulty: Medium
Category: Sentence Structure
Getting to the Answer: The phrase "Mendelssohn's Symphony No. 4 in A Major" is a parenthetical phrase that must be set off by either two commas or two dashes. Since a dash is used at the end of the phrase, (C) is correct.

6. G
Difficulty: High
Category: Sentence Structure
Getting to the Answer: When a comma is underlined, check to make sure it is necessary. The phrase "lyrical church bells" is one logical unit and should not be broken up by any sort of punctuation; (G) is correct.

Agreement: Verbs

1. Review the Explanation portion of the Agreement: Verbs lesson.

Drill Answers

Note: These are not the only ways to correct the sentences; your answers may differ.

a. Pablo present**ed** his experiment at the science fair last week.

b. The movie, with its complex plot and stirring themes, **was** critically acclaimed.

c. Neither the director nor the lead actor **is** at rehearsal today.

d. The park and wildlife refuge **comprise** more than 800 acres of mountains, lakes, and forests.

e. In order to pass the foreign language proficiency exam, you must be both a fluent speaker and **reader**.

2. F
Difficulty: Low
Category: Agreement
Getting to the Answer: When a verb is underlined, look for context clues that indicate which tense is needed. The sentence includes the phrase *last year*, so the simple past tense is appropriate; (F) is correct. Choice H is incorrect because it is in the past perfect form. This tense is used to indicate that one action happened *before* another action in the past. However, in this paragraph, the two verbs *inherited* and *told* occur at the same time. Finally, choice J contains the auxiliary verb *would*. This form is appropriate to use only when the sentence contains another clause starting with *if*.

3. B
Difficulty: High
Category: Agreement
Getting to the Answer: The idiomatic expressions *either…or* and *neither…nor* create singular subjects, and the phrase *past situations* indicates that past tense is required. Choice (B) is correct because it is the only option that uses the singular past-tense verb *was*.

4. H
Difficulty: High
Category: Agreement
Getting to the Answer: When a verb is underlined, identify its subject. The subject is *darkness*, which is singular. The singular present tense verb *teems* is needed; (H) is correct. Choice F is present tense but plural. Choices G and J are incorrect because the future perfect tense and the infinitive form of the verb *teem* do not make sense in context.

5. D
Difficulty: Medium
Category: Agreement
Getting to the Answer: Since the verb *grip* is part of the compound verb phrase "took a deep breath and grip the ladder," the verbs *took* and *grip* must match. As written, *took* is past tense and *grip* is present tense; eliminate A. Choice (D) corrects the error by changing *grip* to *gripped*.

6. G
Difficulty: High
Category: Agreement
Getting to the Answer: All items in a list must be parallel in structure. The first two items are verb phrases, so the last item must also be a verb phrase; (G) is correct. Choices F, H, and J are all noun phrases, not verb phrases.

Agreement: Pronouns

1. Review the Explanation portion of the Agreement: Pronouns lesson.

Drill Answers

Note: These are not the only ways to correct the sentences; your answers may differ.

a. The scientist, about **whom** I had read, was more charismatic in person than I had expected.

b. Between you and **me**, you are the better singer.

c. A jaguar, with its keen senses and sharp teeth and claws, is known for **its** ability to dominate prey.

d. The jar of olives is not in **its** regular location on the shelf.

e. One cannot help but be amazed by the scientific advances in the past century, especially if **one studies** the history of science.

2. J
Difficulty: Low
Category: Agreement
Getting to the Answer: When a pronoun is underlined, identify its antecedent, the noun to which it refers. The antecedent is *citizens*, so the subjective plural pronoun *they* is needed; (J) is correct. Choice F is incorrect because *it* is singular. Choices G and H are plural, but *their* is possessive and *them* is objective.

3. B
Difficulty: High
Category: Agreement
Getting to the Answer: When deciding between *who* and *whom*, see if there is a preposition in front of the word in question. If there is, then you need the objective case *whom*. In this sentence, there is no preposition, so the subjective case *who* is required; (B) is correct. The word *that* will not be used to refer to people on the ACT, so C and D are incorrect.

4. J
Difficulty: Medium
Category: Agreement
Getting to the Answer: The antecedent, the noun to which the pronoun refers, is *components*, so a plural pronoun is required; (J) is correct. Choice F means *it is* and H is not grammatically correct in any context. While G is a correctly written possessive pronoun, it is singular, not plural.

5. A
Difficulty: Medium
Category: Agreement
Getting to the Answer: The underlined pronoun refers to *the roadbed*, which is singular, so the singular pronoun *it* is correct as written.

6. J
Difficulty: Medium
Category: Agreement
Getting to the Answer: Throughout the passage, the writer does not address the reader directly, so F and G are incorrect. Choice H does not make sense

in context. Choice (J) correctly uses the more formal indefinite pronoun *one*, which is grammatically correct and matches the writer's tone.

Agreement: Modifiers

1.   Review the Explanation portion of the Agreement: Modifiers lesson.

Drill Answers

Note: These are not the only ways to correct the sentences; your answers may differ.

a.   A **safer** approach is to test the temperature of the water before entering.

b.   Jonas had to run to the store **really quickly** before it closed.

c.   The new student is the **best** speller in the class.

d.   It took the chameleon a few weeks to acclimate to **its** new habitat.

2.   **J**
Difficulty: Medium
Category: Agreement
Getting to the Answer: The underlined segment includes the comparative adjective *earlier*. The comparative form is used only when discussing exactly two items or people. This sentence is about all examples of basketry, so F is incorrect. Choices G and H are incorrect because the phrases *more early* and *most early* are not as concise as *earliest*. Choice (J) correctly uses the superlative adjective *earliest*.

3.   **D**
Difficulty: Low
Category: Agreement
Getting to the Answer: The verb phrase "have been preserved" must be modified by an adverb; eliminate A and B, which contain adjectives. Choice C is unnecessarily wordy. Choice (D) is both correct and concise.

4.   **F**
Difficulty: Medium
Category: Agreement
Getting to the Answer: If the sentence had used the phrase "baskets' remains," an apostrophe would be needed. However, the preposition *of* makes punctuation unnecessary; G, H, and J are incorrect. Choice (F) correctly omits all apostrophes.

5.   **C**
Difficulty: High
Category: Agreement
Getting to the Answer: "Opting for rigid materials" is an introductory modifying phrase, so the noun that the phrase is modifying must come immediately after the comma. Choice (C) correctly places *basket makers* after the comma. Choices A, B, and D do not feature the correct noun after the comma.

6.   **G**
Difficulty: Medium
Category: Agreement
Getting to the Answer: The sentence requires the possessive form of the word *it*, which is written without an apostrophe; (G) is correct. The word *it's* means *it is*, so F is incorrect. Choice H is incorrect because the antecedent (the word *basket*) is singular, while the pronoun *their* is plural. Finally, J is incorrect because *they're*, which means "they are," does not fit in the context of the sentence.

Agreement: Idioms

1.   Review the Explanation portion of the Agreement: Idioms lesson.

Drill Answers

Note: These are not the only ways to correct the sentences; your answers may differ.

a.   Straining to hear the bird perched in the tree, Jessa stood completely still, waiting **for** the sound to reach her.

b.   The engineer examined the malfunctioning machine closely for evidence **of** missing components or worn elements.

c.   The protestors' bold slogans not only angered the opposition, but **also** elicited loud reactions from bystanders.

d.   Given the cold climate, farmers quickly found that they could grow neither dates **nor** figs.

e.   The writing was **barely** legible after the rain soaked through Tia's backpack and saturated her notebook.

2. G
Difficulty: Medium
Category: Agreement
Getting to the Answer: Since *scarcely* is implicitly negative, it cannot be paired with *not*; (G) is correct. Choice F includes *couldn't*, which means *could not*. Choices H and J also pair the word *not* with *scarcely*, so they are incorrect.

3. D
Difficulty: Medium
Category: Agreement
Getting to the Answer: The word *either* must be paired with *or*, not *and*; eliminate A and B. The phrase "confused by a misidentification" is not an independent clause, so a comma is not needed before *or*; (D) is correct.

4. F
Difficulty: Medium
Category: Agreement
Getting to the Answer: When prepositions such as *in* and *at* are underlined, make sure they are idiomatically correct. The phrase "in the world" is correct because Alfred was a part of the world population rather than an object placed upon the Earth's surface. In addition, "at the time" is correct because the context indicates that Alfred was one of the richest people in the world during that time period. Choice (F) is correct. The phrase "for the time being" doesn't make sense because the passage is describing past events, so G and H are incorrect. While J correctly includes "at the time," it incorrectly uses the preposition *on* instead of *in*.

5. C
Difficulty: Medium
Category: Agreement
Getting to the Answer: When a preposition is underlined, make sure that it is idiomatically correct. Warfare is an abstract concept and cannot use dynamite, so eliminate A. People use dynamite *in* war, so (C) is correct. Choice B is incorrect because dynamite is used as part of war, not alongside it. Choice D is incorrect because *used to* must be followed by a verb, which does not happen in this sentence.

6. J
Difficulty: High
Category: Agreement
Getting to the Answer: When a sentence includes the words *not only*, it must include *but also* as well. Only (J) includes *also*, so it is correct.

How Much Have You Learned?

1. C
Difficulty: Medium
Category: Sentence Structure
Getting to the Answer: As written, the sentence is a run-on, so A is incorrect. Choices B, (C), and D all attempt to fix the run-on error. Choice B is incorrect because the word *nevertheless* is not a coordinating conjunction and cannot join two sentences unless a semicolon is used as well. Choice D suffers from the opposite problem; it uses a coordinating conjunction with a semicolon instead of a comma. Only (C) corrects the run-on and does not introduce new errors.

2. J
Difficulty: High
Category: Agreement
Getting to the Answer: "Originating from their appearance, material, or use," is an introductory modifying phrase, so the item(s) that the phrase is modifying must immediately follow the comma after *use*. Eliminate F and G because the phrase is describing marbles' names, not "an important identifying factor." Choice H is incorrect because it uses the singular possessive *marble's*, which does not match the plural noun *names*. Choice (J) correctly places *marbles' names* after the modifying phrase and does not introduce new errors.

3. D
Difficulty: Medium
Category: Sentence Structure
Getting to the Answer: Parenthetical information includes words or phrases that aren't essential to the sentence structure or content and must be set off with commas. Choices A and B are incorrect because they do not include commas on both sides of the parenthetical phrase *for example*. Choice C misuses the colon, which is used to introduce a short phrase, quotation, explanation, example, or list. Choice (D) correctly sets off the nonessential phrase *for example* with two commas.

4. G
Difficulty: Medium
Category: Sentence Structure
Getting to the Answer: Since the verb *consist* and the preposition *of* form one logical unit, they should not be separated by punctuation of any sort; (G) is correct.

5. A
Difficulty: Low
Category: Agreement
Getting to the Answer: The underlined segment contains an idiom, or a phrase that must have a certain combination of words in order to be correct. The phrase *Regardless of* is idiomatically correct, so (A) is correct. Choice B uses the incorrect preposition *to*. Choices C and D use the word *regardlessly*, which is not correct in any context.

6. F
Difficulty: Medium
Category: Sentence Structure
Getting to the Answer: Determine whether any of the tested comma rules apply to the underlined segment. Two commas are used to set off a nonessential phrase, so read the sentence without *in which* to see if the sentence still makes sense. Choice G is incorrect because the phrase *in which* is essential and thus should not be set off with commas. Choice H mistakenly places a comma between the preposition *in* and its object *which*. Finally, choice J is incorrect because the semicolon here is not joining two independent clauses. Choice (F) is correct.

7. D
Difficulty: Low
Category: Agreement
Getting to the Answer: The sentence includes items in a list that are not in parallel form, so A is incorrect. Eliminate B because it does not address the error. Choice (D) fixes the issue by using the past-tense *kicked*, which matches the other past-tense verbs in the list. Choice C includes the correct verb form but is unnecessarily wordy.

8. J
Difficulty: High
Category: Agreement
Getting to the Answer: The underlined portion has two issues. The verb *is* does not agree with its subject *varieties,* and the adverb *nearly*, not the adjective *near*, is needed. Choice (J) fixes both mistakes. None of the other options corrects both errors.

9. C
Difficulty: Medium
Category: Sentence Structure
Getting to the Answer: Although a parenthetical phrase may appear in the beginning, middle, or end of a sentence, punctuation will always separate it from the rest of the sentence. Because the sentence makes logical sense without the phrase "also known as ringtaw, or ringer," two commas or two dashes are needed to set it off from the rest of the sentence. Eliminate A because using one dash and one comma is not acceptable. Eliminate B because the second dash is incorrectly placed in the middle of the parenthetical phase. Choice D uses two commas correctly but includes an unnecessary comma after *ringtaw*. Choice (C) is correct, since it uses two dashes to offset the parenthetical phrase and excludes unnecessary punctuation.

10. H
Difficulty: Low
Category: Agreement
Getting to the Answer: Pronouns must agree with their antecedents in both person and number. The antecedent here is *players*, so a third-person plural pronoun is needed; (H) is correct. Choice F is incorrect because *our* is first-person. Choice G uses a second-person pronoun, and J uses a singular pronoun.

11. B
Difficulty: Low
Category: Agreement
Getting to the Answer: The sentence that appears after the underlined period is a fragment, so A is incorrect. Choice (B) fixes the fragment by using the conjunction *and* to join the verb phrase after the period with the independent clause before the period. Choices C and D are incorrect because a semicolon or a comma and a coordinating conjunction are used to join two independent clauses, not an independent clause and a verb phrase.

12. J
Difficulty: Medium
Category: Agreement
Getting to the Answer: The underlined portion includes a pronoun and a verb. The phrase is referring to *the game*, so a singular pronoun and a singular verb are needed; (J) is correct. None of the other choices includes singular forms of both the pronoun and the verb.

[CHAPTER 4]

SPOTTING AND FIXING ISSUES: CONCISENESS, ORGANIZATION, AND DEVELOPMENT

LEARNING OBJECTIVES

After completing this chapter, you will be able to:

- Revise wordy writing
- Determine the appropriate transition word or phrase to establish logical relationships within and between sentences
- Determine the appropriate transition sentence to establish logical relationships between paragraphs
- Determine the most logical place for a sentence in a paragraph or passage
- Identify the word that accomplishes the appropriate purpose within a sentence
- Provide an introduction or conclusion to a paragraph or passage
- Revise a sentence to accomplish a specific purpose
- Determine the relevance of a sentence within a passage
- Determine whether a passage has met a goal and state why or why not

---

Conciseness: 4/36 SmartPoints® (Medium yield)

Organization: 4/36 SmartPoints® (Medium yield)

Development: 9/36 SmartPoints® (Very high yield)

A Note About the Passages in This Chapter

Due to the more global nature of Organization and Development questions and the fact that ACT English passages include at least one Organization question and at least two Development questions, you will see the same passages intentionally used multiple times throughout this chapter. Each lesson will present the portion of the passage needed to answer the question(s). On test day, the various question types will be spaced throughout the passage, so you should prepare to review the entire passage, not just the underlined segments or only one or two paragraphs.

How Much Do You Know?

Directions: Try out the questions below. The "Category" heading in the explanation for each question gives the title of the lesson that covers how to answer it. If you answered the question(s) for a given lesson correctly, you may be able to move quickly through that lesson. If you answered incorrectly, you may want to take your time on that lesson.

Eva Salazar: Master Weaver

The Kumeyaay are a Native American people who have <u>developed</u> in the area now known as San Diego, California,
1
for 12,000 years. They have retained a rich cultural and social life despite a forced split in 1875, when many Kumeyaay were driven across the border into Mexico. Now resettled in small farming communities, such as San José de la Zorra, the families have preserved their traditional way of life.

It is in this remote valley that Eva Salazar learned the ancient art of basket weaving from her tribal elders. Traditionally, Kumeyaay women have the <u>crucially</u>
2
<u>necessary</u> responsibility of making baskets, which are
2
important artifacts of everyday life. Kumeyaay baskets are tightly woven with expressive designs. They are made mostly for utilitarian purposes: cooking, storing food products, and gathering ingredients. As traditional objects of art, they are also valued for their aesthetic beauty.

1. A. NO CHANGE
   B. blossomed
   C. thrived
   D. withered

2. F. NO CHANGE
   G. crucial
   H. necessary and crucial
   J. fundamentally crucial

<u>Following in her ancestors' footsteps</u>, Eva Salazar uses
₃ native materials to weave her intricate baskets, primarily the strong, sharp reed known as juncus, as well as yucca, sumac, and other native plants. She colors the reeds with black walnut, elderberry, and other natural dyes. Eva specializes in coiled baskets, and her shapes and decorations echo traditional forms.

<u>Though</u> she is best known for her baskets, Eva Salazar
₄ also makes dolls, willow bark skirts, nets, and shell necklaces. Her most ambitious work is a basket measuring almost three feet in diameter. The basket took her two years to weave and represents a masterpiece of Native American art.

Today, Eva is heralded as a master weaver. Now an American citizen living in San Diego, she remains focused on traditional tribal arts and teaches basket weaving at local reservations and colleges. <u>Her baskets continue to represent</u>
₅ <u>the height of Kumeyaay basket-weaving artistry</u>.
₅

3. If the author were to delete the underlined portion, the sentence would primarily lose:

   A. a counterargument regarding the authenticity of modern crafts.
   B. a key detail that explains Eva Salazar's relationship to the Kumeyaay.
   C. a claim that Eva Salazar will develop her own basket-weaving methods in the future.
   D. a suggestion that the Kumeyaay should place greater value on Eva Salazar's work.

4. F. NO CHANGE
   G. Because
   H. Nonetheless
   J. On the other hand

5. Which choice most effectively concludes the passage?

   A. NO CHANGE
   B. She is famous for not letting the Kumeyaay traditions be lost.
   C. Her work has inspired countless artists to follow in her footsteps, ensuring that Kumeyaay basket weaving continues to thrive.
   D. She will be remembered for her unique adaptations of the Kumeyaay traditions.

Sweat Lodges

The 21st century has seen a marked increase in the popularity of natural medicines and therapies. Among the most common of these is the sweat lodge, a practice established by some groups of indigenous peoples of the Americas. <u>Because of the benefits this practice offers, many cultures independently evolved similar traditions</u>, including the Finnish sauna and the Turkish steam room. The basic purpose of these therapies is to raise the body's core temperature to between 102 and 106 degrees Fahrenheit. At this temperature, bacterial and viral infections within the body cannot easily survive. The heat can also ease muscle tension and soreness, and the resulting perspiration flushes the system of toxins.

[1] In other designs, an altar barrier is positioned between the fire and the entrance to prevent participants from accidentally falling into the fire pit when they emerge from the lodge. [2] A traditional sweat lodge may be built from willow, as its bark is considered medicinal and, indeed, contains the same analgesic as aspirin. [3] Other lodges are made using a few different materials, including blankets, animal skins, and canvas. [4] In some traditions, the entrance of the sweat lodge faces east, with a clear and unobstructed view of a sacred fire pit where the stones are heated before being brought inside the lodge. [7]

6. Which choice provides the best transition from the start of the paragraph into the information that follows?

   F. NO CHANGE
   G. Nearly every culture has adopted this practice in some form,
   H. The benefits this practice offers have led many other cultures to adapt it in forms more suited to their own resources,
   J. The popularity of the practice is well-earned by the many health benefits it grants to participants,

7. For the sake of the logic and coherence of this paragraph, Sentence 1 should be placed:

   A. where it is now.
   B. after Sentence 2.
   C. after Sentence 3.
   D. after Sentence 4.

The exact ceremonial process will vary, but prior to entering the lodge, <u>participants usually change into simple, traditional clothing</u>. In some versions of the ceremony, the Stone People spirits are called upon and the sweat leader sounds the Water Drum once all participants have entered the lodge. A sweat might include more than one session, each lasting 30 to 45 minutes and focused on one of four distinct themes: the spirit world, cleanliness and honesty, individual prayer, and growth and healing.

Traditional sweat lodge ceremonies, which often included songs, prayers, and chants, were believed to purify not only the body <u>but also the mind as well</u>. "Healing comes on a spiritual level," wrote Dr. Lewis Mehl-Madrona in his book *Coyote Medicine*. "Ceremony and ritual provide the means of making ourselves available."

8. Which of the following details best empha-sizes the spiritual aspects of the sweat lodge tradition?

    F.   NO CHANGE

    G. the sweat leader must complete years of intense training to be entrusted with the role.

    H. it is important to ensure that all participants are healthy, since other-wise the intense conditions of a sweat can be harmful.

    J. participants are often smudged with the smoke of burning sage, sweetgrass, or cedar to signify ritual cleanliness.

9.   A. NO CHANGE

    B. but also the mind in addition.

    C. but also the mind.

    D. but also additionally the mind.

Question 10 asks about the preceding passage as a whole.

---

10. Suppose the author's main goal had been to write an essay describing a personal experi-ence with a sweat lodge. Would this passage accomplish the purpose?

    F. Yes, because the passage tells about the process a person goes through in a sweat.

    G. Yes, because the passage explains how Dr. Lewis Mehl-Madrona feels about the ceremony.

    H. No, because only the last two para-graphs discuss what happens at a sweat lodge.

    J. No, because the passage describes gen-eral information about sweat lodge cer-emonies, not one specific experience.

Check Your Work

1. C
Difficulty: Medium
Category: Development: Precision
Getting to the Answer: This question tests word choice. The sentence says that the Kumeyaay have lived in southern California for millennia; moreover, the sentence that follows says they maintained "a rich cultural and social life," so the correct answer must reflect that. Choices A and B both incorrectly suggest a process or change, and D is the opposite of the author's meaning. Only (C) correctly expresses the intended meaning.

2. G
Difficulty: Low
Category: Conciseness
Getting to the Answer: *Crucially necessary* is redundant. Choices F and H both include these words in different forms, so eliminate them. Choice J includes a word with a similar meaning in context, *fundamentally*, so it is also redundant. Only (G) eliminates the redundancy.

3. B
Difficulty: Medium
Category: Development: Revising Text
Getting to the Answer: The underlined portion details the relationship between Eva Salazar and the Kumeyaay. Deleting this would take away a key detail explaining her ties to the native community whose traditions she carries on through her art. Choice (B) is correct. Since the underlined segment does not provide a counterargument, claim, or suggestion, A, C, and D are incorrect.

4. F
Difficulty: Medium
Category: Organization: Transitions
Getting to the Answer: Transitions must accurately convey the relationship between ideas. The underlined transition correctly shows a contrast between what Eva is primarily known for and her other artistic creations. Choice (F) is correct. Choice G is not a contrast transition. The contrast transitions in H and J both make the first clause independent rather than dependent, turning the sentence into a run-on. Since they introduce a grammatical error, they are incorrect.

5. C
Difficulty: High
Category: Development: Introductions and Conclusions
Getting to the Answer: The final sentence must effectively conclude both the passage and the paragraph. The passage discusses Eva Salazar's dedication to preserving Kumeyaay traditions. According to the final paragraph, she has done this through learning her craft and passing her knowledge on to other artists. Choice (C) conveys how she has kept basket-weaving traditions alive through her own work and through teaching others. You may hesitate to choose this answer because it is noticeably less concise than the other options, but sometimes a long sentence is needed to convey complex ideas. Always think carefully about what a question asks to make sure the answer fulfills it. Choices B and D are incorrect because both bring up ideas outside the scope of the passage; Salazar's fame or unique adaptations of traditional art are never discussed. Choice A is factually correct but not a good conclusion because it does not emphasize the preservation of Kumeyaay artistic traditions.

6. F
Difficulty: High
Category: Organization: Transitions
Getting to the Answer: An effective transition must show the relationship between the ideas it connects. The beginning of this paragraph introduces the popularity of natural medicine, particularly sweat lodges. The information that follows briefly mentions similar practices elsewhere but primarily discusses the health benefits of such practices. Choice G does not connect sweat lodges to health benefits, so eliminate it. Choice H does connect the two, but it also brings up the topic of resources, which is not mentioned in the paragraph at all. Choice J may be tempting because it neatly connects the popularity of sweat lodges to their health benefits. However, when plugged into the sentence, it creates a modifier error in which the phrase "including the Finnish sauna and the Turkish steam room" describes *participants* instead of *examples* of similar practices. Only (F) connects sweat lodges with similar practices and with health benefits.

7.   D
Difficulty: Medium
Category: Organization: Sentence Placement
Getting to the Answer: Sentence 1 does not fit well where it is now, since it jumps right into the middle of an ongoing description with specific details that have not yet been discussed, like the fire and the entrance. The paragraph would be clearer and more logical if Sentence 1 were placed after those details have been introduced in Sentence 4. Thus, (D) is the correct answer.

8.   J
Difficulty: Medium
Category: Development: Revising Text
Getting to the Answer: This question asks for a detail emphasizing the spiritual aspects of the sweat lodge. Choice H discusses purely practical concerns and can be quickly eliminated. Choices F and G do not make clear whether the preparations they describe have spiritual significance or not. Choice (J) is the only answer that explicitly states that an action is undertaken for ritual, symbolic reasons, so (J) is correct.

9.   C
Difficulty: Low
Category: Conciseness
Getting to the Answer: Including both *also* and *as well* makes this phrase redundant. Choices A, B, and D all include similarly redundant transition words, so (C) is correct.

10.   J
Difficulty: Medium
Category: Development: Purpose
Getting to the Answer: To answer this type of question, first determine the primary purpose of the passage. This passage describes the physical and spiritual elements of Native American sweat lodge traditions. If the author's goal were to focus on an individual's experience, this passage would not be successful. Eliminate F and G. Choice H gives an incorrect reason why the passage does not fulfill the author's goal. Only (J) correctly identifies that the passage does not succeed because it gives a general description rather than tells an individual's story.

CONCISENESS

LEARNING OBJECTIVE

After this lesson, you will be able to:

- Revise wordy writing

To answer a question like this:

Sweat Lodges

Traditional Native American sweat lodges focus on both physical and spiritual healing. Sometimes, a sweat might include more than one session, each lasting 30 to 45 minutes and focused on one of four distinct themes: the spirit world, cleanliness and honesty, individual prayer, and growth and healing.

1. A. NO CHANGE
   B. More often,
   C. Occasionally,
   D. DELETE the underlined portion and capitalize the word *A*.

You need to know this:

Conciseness

A concise sentence does not include any unnecessary words. Phrasing that is wordy is considered stylistically incorrect on the ACT and needs to be revised. Each word must contribute to the meaning of the sentence; otherwise, it should be eliminated.

A *redundant* sentence says something twice: "The new policy precipitated a crisis situation." A crisis is a type of situation, so there is no need to include both *crisis* and *situation*. The sentence should be rephrased as, "The new policy precipitated a crisis." Redundancy is always incorrect on the ACT.

Wordy/Redundant sentence	Concise sentence
The superb musical score **added enhancement to the experience of** the play's development.	The superb musical score **enhanced** the play's development.
I **did not anticipate** the **surprising, unexpected** plot twist.	I **did not anticipate** the plot twist.
The students **increased some of their knowledge of** Tuscan architecture.	The students **learned about** Tuscan architecture.

You need to do this:

Choose the most concise grammatically correct option that conveys the writer's intended meaning. When answering questions about conciseness:

- Consider selecting the "DELETE the underlined portion" answer choice if there is one, according to the following guidelines:
  - If the underlined portion is wordy or redundant, delete it.
  - If the underlined portion does not enhance the intended meaning or clarity of the passage, delete it.
  - Each of the four answer choices is equally likely, so give this option the same weight as the others.
- Identify the shortest answer choice (it will not always be the correct answer, but it is an efficient place to start).
- Identify words and phrases that have the same meaning, e.g., *thoughtful* and *mindful* or *end result* and *final outcome*. Find a choice that deletes one of the redundant expressions.

Explanation:

When "DELETE the underlined portion" is an option, check whether the underlined portion contributes to the meaning of the passage. Eliminate A because the word *might* already shows that multi-session sweats do not occur all the time. *More often* and *occasionally* introduce information about frequency that is not supported by the passage, so B and C are incorrect. Because none of the other answer choices add to the meaning of the sentence, (D) is the correct answer.

Drills

If conciseness gives you trouble, study the information above and try out these drill questions before completing the Try on Your Own questions below. Drill answers can be found in Answers and Explanations.

Eliminate word(s) to make the sentences more concise without losing meaning.

a. The school was founded and established in 1906.

b. I felt a sense of nervous anxiety before the curtain rose.

c. We were in agreement with each other that Naomi should be captain.

d. After a job interview, make sure to send a note of gratitude expressing thanks to your interviewer.

e. Not long after he graduated from Oxford, Oscar Wilde moved to London, a place in which he embarked on his literary career in earnest.

Try on Your Own

Directions: Take as much time as you need on these questions. Work carefully and methodically. There will be an opportunity for timed practice at the end of the chapter.

International Model United Nations

For many years, the Hague has been the stage of The European International Model United Nations (TEIMUN), <u>which is a model of the United Nations</u>. ₂ TEIMUN started in 1987, when a group of American students on an exchange program in the Netherlands organized the first conference as a part of their focus on international relations. The organizers hoped to educate participants about the workings of an international organization in order to combat <u>a growing sense of</u> ₃ <u>isolationism</u> among European youth.
₃

There were many hurdles to overcome, for students' attitudes in Europe toward simulations of the United Nations were not favorable. Hence, drumming up interest was a struggle. The Americans also wanted to ensure that <u>this new model UN would have a plan to</u> ₄ <u>help students from less-developed European countries</u> ₄ <u>with their participation</u>. Through the American students' ₄ hard work, TEIMUN prospered and attracted more participants. Over the years, the TEIMUN conference has become one of the biggest and most important model United Nations on the European continent, with participants from over 65 countries.

2. F. NO CHANGE
   G. being a model of the United Nations.
   H. which is a model UN.
   J. DELETE the underlined portion and change comma after *(TEIMUN)* to a period.

3. A. NO CHANGE
   B. the increasing and growing isolationism
   C. a growing feeling of isolationism and separation
   D. the increasing isolationism and sense of alienation

4. F. NO CHANGE
   G. their new model United Nations had systems in place to help students from less-developed European countries participate.
   H. there were rules built in to the system with the purpose of helping students from less-developed countries in their participation.
   J. there were methods for helping students from less-developed countries to participate.

ORGANIZATION: TRANSITIONS

LEARNING OBJECTIVES

After this lesson, you will be able to:

- Determine the appropriate transition word or phrase to establish logical relationships within and between sentences
- Determine the appropriate transition sentence to establish logical relationships between paragraphs

To answer a question like this:

International Model United Nations

Students still direct and organize each yearly conference. They seek new ways to attract enthusiastic participants, <u>since students from less-developed nations</u>[1] <u>are still underrepresented</u>[1]. Countless alumni have gone on to pursue careers in international policy after first encountering the art of diplomacy during their years in TEIMUN.

1. Which choice most effectively concludes this sentence and leads into the information that follows in the paragraph?

   A. NO CHANGE

   B. and they strongly believe that TEIMUN is a powerful avenue for fostering an interest in diplomacy among Europe's youth.

   C. even working to expand recruitment outside of Europe.

   D. and they closely follow the policies of individual countries as well as international relations in order to keep the conference up to date.

You need to know this:

Writers use transitions to show relationships such as contrast, cause and effect, continuation, emphasis, and chronology (order of events). Knowing which words indicate which type of transition will help you choose the correct answer on test day.

Contrast transitions	Cause-and-effect transitions	Continuation transitions	Emphasis transitions	Chronology transitions
although, but, despite, even though, however, in contrast, nonetheless, on the other hand, rather than, though, unlike, while, yet	as a result, because, consequently, since, so, therefore, thus	also, furthermore, in addition, moreover	certainly, in fact, indeed, that is	before, after, first (second, etc.), then, finally

You need to do this:

If a transition word is underlined, you must determine the writer's intended meaning and find the transition that best conveys this meaning. Use the surrounding text to pinpoint the appropriate word.

Explanation:

The underlined portion needs to connect the beginning of the paragraph, which discusses student organizers recruiting participants, with the last sentence, which discusses TEIMUN alumni inspired to pursue diplomatic careers. The only answer choice that does so effectively is (B).

Drills

If transitions give you trouble, study the information above and try out these drill questions before completing the Try on Your Own questions below. Drill answers can be found in Answers and Explanations.

Choose the correct transition word for each sentence.

a. (Due to/Despite) its impressive technical innovations, the small startup thrived.

b. Cashew nuts are a popular snack worldwide; (however/moreover), they can be difficult to harvest because their shells contain a toxic resin.

c. Izdehar is the most level-headed of my friends—(in fact/next), I think she's more reliable than some adults I know.

d. After days of hard work, we (finally/nonetheless) finished our science fair project.

e. The actor won an award for best supporting role this year (consequently/in addition to) releasing her first pop music album.

Try on Your Own

Directions: Take as much time as you need on these questions. Work carefully and methodically. There will be an opportunity for timed practice at the end of the chapter.

The Victorian Way of Life

The Victorian Era stretched from the coronation of Queen Victoria in 1837 to her death in 1901. Over her 63-year reign, her influence on Britain was profound. Politics and international affairs aside, manners, morals, and even dress conformed to Victoria's straightlaced concepts of what was and was not acceptable. Despite the upper classes, propriety and reputation had to be spotlessly maintained.

2. F. NO CHANGE
    G. Especially for
    H. Regardless of
    J. Occasionally among

[3] In the 1840s, women's dresses were relatively simple, albeit with a number of stiff petticoats. Thirty years later, restricting corsets were worn to pull in the waist to the

smallest width possible <u>while</u> still leaving the wearer
4
room to breathe. Hats and gloves were expected for all occasions.

Most upper-class women were educated only to the point of literacy, with household management and domestic arts such as needlework heavily emphasized. <u>Because of this,</u> some women were quite well schooled,
5
depending on their fathers' opinion about the propriety of educated females. Queen Victoria herself, unsurprisingly, fell on the more educated end of the spectrum; she spoke multiple languages and studied law and ethics as a teenager. <u>However, her favorite subject</u>
6
<u>was history</u>.
6

It is a mark of the length, importance, and impact of Queen Victoria's reign that this period of British history is known as the Victorian Era. She left her indelible mark not only on society and culture but also on British influence throughout the world.

3. Which of the following provides the most effective transition from the previous paragraph to this paragraph?

  A. Victoria believed modesty was particularly important for women.

  B. Lower classes were less constrained.

  C. Fashion styles were among the prescribed customs.

  D. The period's fashion innovations remain famous to this day.

4. F. NO CHANGE

  G. rather than

  H. therefore

  J. thus

5. A. NO CHANGE

  B. Therefore,

  C. Indeed,

  D. On the other hand,

6. Given that all the choices are true, which one provides the best transition to the next paragraph?

  F. NO CHANGE

  G. This background both prepared her to be a world leader and influenced her royal policy.

  H. Her governess and varied tutors found her a bright but willful student.

  J. In fact, she was better educated than many of her prime ministers.

ORGANIZATION: SENTENCE PLACEMENT

LEARNING OBJECTIVE

After this lesson, you will be able to:

* Determine the most logical place for a sentence in a paragraph or passage

To answer a question like this:

Symbiotic Relationships

In the natural world, when two or more different organisms coexist, they are involved in a symbiotic relationship. Sometimes these relationships are beneficial to both organisms; other times, these relationships are beneficial to only one organism and either have no effect or are harmful to the other organism. When both organisms benefit, their relationship is known as mutualism.

[1] A classic symbiotic relationship of this kind takes place in the digestive tract of Florida wood-eating termites. [2] The protozoa provide the termite with a service necessary to its survival: they digest the cellulose in the wood that the termite consumes. [3] We think of a termite as being able to digest wood, but, in fact, it cannot. [4] The termite plays host to the protozoa, single-celled organisms that live in the termite's gut. ☐1

1. For the sake of the logic and coherence of this paragraph, Sentence 2 should be placed:

   A. where it is now.

   B. before Sentence 1.

   C. after Sentence 3.

   D. after Sentence 4.

You need to know this:

Some Organization questions will ask you to check and potentially fix the placement of a sentence within a paragraph (or a paragraph within a passage, though this is rare). Others will ask you for the best place to insert a new sentence. Your approach in both cases should be the same.

You need to do this:

Look for specific clues that indicate the best organization. Common clues include:

- Chronology: If the information is presented in order by the time when it occurred, place the sentence within the correct time frame.
- Explanation of a term or phrase: If the passage features a term, such as nuclear fusion, the writer will explain what it is (in this case, the joining of two or more nuclei to form a heavier nucleus) before using the term in other contexts.
- Introduction of a person: If the passage introduces someone, such as Grace Hopper, the writer will first refer to the person by first and last name before referring to the person by either first name (Grace) or last name (Hopper) only.
- Examples: A general statement is often followed by support in the form of examples.
- Logic: Transition words such as "however," "also," "furthermore," and "therefore" may signal the logic of the paragraph. For example, the word "therefore" indicates that a conclusion is being drawn from evidence that should logically come before it.

Explanation:

Sentence 2 discusses the function of the protozoa, but the protozoa haven't yet been introduced in the paragraph. Sentence 2 must be moved to follow the sentence that introduces the protozoa, which is Sentence 4. Choice (D) is correct.

Try on Your Own

Directions: Take as much time as you need on these questions. Work carefully and methodically. There will be an opportunity for timed practice at the end of the chapter.

Symbiotic Relationships

In the natural world, when two or more different organisms coexist, they are involved in a symbiotic relationship. Sometimes these relationships are beneficial to both organisms; other times, these relationships are beneficial to only one organism and either have no effect or are harmful to the other organism. [A] When both organisms benefit, their relationship is known as mutualism.

A classic symbiotic relationship of this kind takes place in the digestive tract of Florida wood-eating termites. We think of a termite as being able to digest wood, but, in fact, it cannot. The termite plays host to the protozoa, single-celled organisms that live in the termite's gut. The protozoa provide the termite with a service necessary to its survival: they digest the cellulose in the wood that the termite consumes.

That is far from the whole story, however. The only movement that protozoa are capable of on their own is spinning; they cannot move around inside the termite's intestine to reach the cellulose. This problem is solved by a third member of the partnership. [B] Each protozoan harbors a colony of thousands of bacteria attached to its surface. Whip-like tentacles on the bacteria (known as flagella) wave back and forth and propel each host protozoan forward. [C]

These bacteria may do more than just drive the protozoan around. Some bacteria can be found inside the protozoan and are thought to help with the digestion of tiny wood particles. [D] If this all sounds strange, consider the fact that humans have symbiotic relationships with bacteria of their own. [2]

Early 19th-Century Women in New England

In the early 19th century, the market economy expanded, and the home became a haven from the developing commercialism. [A] With men working in factories, women were responsible for housekeeping, providing religious education, and raising children.

> Question 2 asks about the preceding passage as a whole.

2. The writer would like to add the following sentence:

   > This allows the protozoan to move around and to continue consuming cellulose within the termite.

   The sentence would be most logically placed at:

   F. Point A in Paragraph 1.
   G. Point B in Paragraph 3.
   H. Point C in Paragraph 3.
   J. Point D in Paragraph 4.

[B] In addition to running their households, women also had opportunities for wage work. This included producing goods, such as palm-leaf hats and straw-braided items, for wider consumption. [C] Wage work provided women with the ability to live at home while earning money to supplement the family's income. [D]

[1] Shoemaking was another source of income for women, but their work was socially and physically isolated from the shoe binding that took place in cobblers' shops. [2] However, when increased demand for shoes required the use of sewing machines to speed up the pace of production, women organized a small-scale movement that trained young women to use sewing machines in their homes. [3] Despite this move, women who worked at home as shoe binders remained isolated and vulnerable to competition from the more lucrative and efficient factories. [4] Women were also denied craft status and admission into unions, which limited their influence. [3]

3. For the sake of logic, Sentence 4 should be placed:

   A. where it is now.

   B. before Sentence 1.

   C. before Sentence 2.

   D. before Sentence 3.

[F] Women who worked in factories were also prohibited from joining unions, allowing factories such as the Lowell Mills to exploit their labor. [G] However, female factory workers were offered a type of work outside of the home and away from their families, which provided them with a new level of independence. [H]

For many women, the changes in women's roles during the first half of the 19th century were part of a positive and liberating transformation. [J] For others, though, either their roles remained quite traditional, or their new endeavors, such as working in factories, were not as freeing as they had hoped. Women's experiences with and reactions to the changes they encountered varied, but many were eager for the journey ahead.

Questions 4–5 ask about the preceding passage as a whole.

---

4. The writer would like to add the following sentence:

   > During this time, middle-class wives and mothers in New England assumed the role of protectors and leaders of home life.

   The sentence would be most logically placed at:

   F. Point A in Paragraph 1.
   G. Point B in Paragraph 2.
   H. Point C in Paragraph 2.
   J. Point D in Paragraph 2.

5. The writer would like to add the following sentence:

   > For example, they were paid half the wages given to men.

   The sentence would be most logically placed at:

   A. Point F in Paragraph 4.
   B. Point G in Paragraph 4.
   C. Point H in Paragraph 4.
   D. Point J in Paragraph 5.

DEVELOPMENT: PRECISION

LEARNING OBJECTIVE

After this lesson, you will be able to:

• Identify the word that accomplishes the appropriate purpose within a sentence

To answer a question like this:

Humphrey Bogart

Although the screen appeal of Humphrey Bogart has grown immeasurably since his death in 1957, his early life was not filled with success. Born in New York City in 1899 as the son of a prominent surgeon, young Humphrey was quickly put on the track to medical school. After finishing his early schooling, he went to the prestigious Phillips Academy. Bogart, however, was not academically inclined, and during adolescence he was often described as a troublemaker. In 1918, Bogart entered the navy. It was during the service when he received an injury that partially paralyzed his upper lip, creating his <u>splendid</u> snarl.
1

1. Which of the following best conveys how the injury noticeably marked Bogart's appearance?

   A. NO CHANGE
   B. outrageous
   C. distinctive
   D. insignificant

You need to know this:

Some questions test your knowledge of the correct word to use in context. You must identify which word(s) best convey the writer's intended meaning.

Incorrect	Correct
The initial *reason the students gather in the auditorium is that it is the only location large enough for all of them.*	The primary *reason the students gather in the auditorium is that it is the only location large enough for all of them.*
It is common for children to perform *the actions of their parents.*	*It is common for children to* mimic *the actions of their parents.*
Zeke apologized for overstepping *when he walked into the crowded conference room.*	*Zeke apologized for* intruding *when he walked into the crowded conference room.*

You need to do this:

Read the surrounding text to deduce the author's intended meaning. Then evaluate all four answer choices. Eliminate the answer choices that:

- Create grammatical errors
- Do not make sense in context
- Do not convey the writer's intended meaning

If one or more of the words among the answer choices are unfamiliar, the process of elimination can still help you get to the correct answer. If you recognize any of the options, decide whether to keep or eliminate them. For the words that remain, use roots, prefixes and suffixes, and word charge (whether a word is positive, negative, or neutral in meaning) to make your decision. If all else fails, trust your instincts and guess; never leave a question blank.

Explanation:

The question asks for a word that approximately means *noticeably marked*. Choice D is the exact opposite, and A and B are too strongly charged—*splendid* has a strong positive charge and *outrageous* has a strong negative charge. Choice (C) is correct.

Try on Your Own

Directions: Take as much time as you need on these questions. Work carefully and methodically. There will be an opportunity for timed practice at the end of the chapter.

The History of Advertising

Over the past few decades, advertising has changed radically. In the 1990s, large companies hoped to reach their target markets through advertisements in national magazines and network television, while smaller companies <u>promoted</u> local newspapers, phone books, and radio stations. Of course, companies large and small still buy advertisements in mass media outlets that reach large numbers of consumers. However, with a new

2.   F.   NO CHANGE

       G.   appropriated

       H.   utilized

       J.   manipulated

millennium came new <u>competitors</u>, including a larger
₃
media outlet than previously imagined: the internet.

3. Which of the following best conveys the opportunity presented by the internet?

    A. NO CHANGE
    B. circumstances,
    C. occurrences,
    D. possibilities,

Thomas Paine

   As a young man, Paine worked as a corsetmaker, sailor, and minister, but he only found his true calling when he moved to the British colonies in America. Paine first gained recognition as the editor of *Pennsylvania Magazine*, and as political turmoil engulfed the colonies, he became more <u>vocal</u>. In 1776, Paine anonymously
₄
published a pamphlet titled "Common Sense" that argued forcefully for American independence from Britain. The pamphlet was tremendously popular; soon there were 200,000 copies in circulation. Many historians credit the pamphlet with helping to convince the American people to fight for self-rule.

4. Which choice best conveys Paine's increased fame?

    F. NO CHANGE
    G. prominent.
    H. understandable.
    J. divisive.

   Thomas Paine's influence continued far beyond sparking the Revolutionary War. Once the war began, Paine published a series of pamphlets called *The American Crisis*, which, in the midst of a bloody war, helped keep the morale of the troops up. In addition to his achievements as a writer, Thomas Paine is <u>credited</u>
₅
with conceiving the name "The United States of America."

5. A. NO CHANGE
    B. tasked
    C. helped
    D. noted

Because Thomas Paine was <u>a writer</u>, Thomas
₆
Jefferson and John Adams drew heavily on his work
when drafting the Declaration of Independence. Later in
life, Paine wrote other highly controversial works. In
1797, Paine did his part to inspire what would become
Social Security. He suggested a system of social
insurance for the young and the elderly in his last great
work, "Agrarian Justice."

6. Which of the following replacements most
effectively portrays Paine positively and
describes why Jefferson and Adams used his
work?

   F.   an extremely talented writer,

   G.   the best writer in the colonies,

   H.   an adequate author,

   J.   an author of controversial content,

DEVELOPMENT: INTRODUCTIONS AND CONCLUSIONS

LEARNING OBJECTIVE

After this lesson, you will be able to:

- Provide an introduction or conclusion to a paragraph or passage

To answer a question like this:

Early Writing Careers

Many well-known writers began their careers while
they were still teenagers. Stephen King, for example,
began submitting stories to science fiction magazines
when he was just thirteen years old. If you are serious
about a writing career, you can submit work to many
publications that accept unsolicited manuscripts. It is
best, however, to send a query letter first.

A query letter is a one-page document in which you
introduce yourself to the editors of the publication and
ask if they would like to read your work. Begin by telling
the editor a little bit about yourself. Include a paragraph
or two outlining the story you've written or would like
to write. If you've taken any creative writing courses,
won prizes for your writing, or had any work published,
tell the editor about that, too. Don't forget to thank the
editor for taking the time to read your letter.

You probably won't sell your first story, but don't get discouraged. Stephen King didn't sell his first submission either—or dozens after that. <u>Nevertheless, he persisted, and he became a best-selling author</u>.
[1]

1. Which choice best concludes the essay?

   A. NO CHANGE

   B. Eventually, he found an editor who liked his work, and the rest is history.

   C. Despite that, he didn't give up, and neither should you.

   D. Being a professional writer is a difficult career to break into.

You need to know this:

Some questions ask you to improve the beginning or ending of a paragraph or passage. These questions often have a question stem.

- An introduction should:
  - Explain the topic and purpose of a paragraph
  - Include information discussed later in the paragraph
  - When applicable, provide an appropriate transition from the previous paragraph or into the next paragraph
- A conclusion should:
  - Summarize the topic and purpose of a paragraph/passage
  - Include information discussed earlier in the paragraph/passage
  - When applicable, provide an appropriate transition from the previous paragraph or into the next paragraph

Note that when the question has a question stem, you are not being tested on conciseness, even when asked about deleting information. *When you see a question stem, focus on relevance rather than conciseness.* This means that you can focus on identifying the concise and relevant choice without spending time considering the grammar of each choice.

You need to do this:

- Determine the writer's intended purpose for the paragraph or essay as a whole.
- Read before and/or after the underlined segment, noting key transition words.
- Eliminate choices that do not provide an appropriate introduction or conclusion.
- For a question about the conclusion to the passage, eliminate choices that focus too much on the final paragraph and not enough on the passage as a whole or too much on the passage as a whole and not enough on the final paragraph.
- Choose the most relevant option.

Explanation:

This passage focuses on advising and encouraging aspiring young writers. The last paragraph in particular discusses the importance of not giving up and cites the example of Stephen King. Choice (C) is correct because it references both ideas and ties them together. Choice A may be tempting, but it is incorrect because it refers only to Stephen King. It does not address young writers in general.

Try on Your Own

Directions: Take as much time as you need on these questions. Work carefully and methodically. There will be an opportunity for timed practice at the end of the chapter.

Community-Supported Agriculture

This spring, my family joined our local community-supported agriculture, or CSA, association. We wanted to eat more locally grown foods, and the CSA provided the perfect opportunity. Like other members, we bought a year's "share" of the farm's crop before the growing season began. Once it did, the farm delivered a box filled with freshly harvested fruits and vegetables every week.

We immediately discovered that fresh, in-season food is delicious. I had disliked broccoli previously, but one bunch that arrived in our second June box convinced me I'd been wrong. My younger brother, who is normally resistant to new foods, ventured to try both kale and turnips from the CSA and enjoyed both. <u>Of the four people in my family, my mother is definitely the most accomplished cook.</u>
2

2. Given that all the choices are true, which one provides a conclusion to this paragraph that is most consistent with the other information in the paragraph?

F. NO CHANGE

G. Prior to our experience with the CSA, the most exotic vegetable he would willingly eat was a carrot—and only the orange kind.

H. The cardboard boxes are recycled each week, and the CSA even provides composting services on-site.

J. We pick up our vegetables from the farmer's delivery every Thursday afternoon.

Furthermore, we've been vexed by the outlandish
3
number of zucchini in our boxes. Each week in July, we
3
received at least six. At first, we just grilled the zucchini.
Then, we sautéed it with pasta. By the third week, when
we opened our box to find ten more zucchini, we had to
get inventive. We experimented with recipes for zucchini
soup, casserole, bread, pizza, and even brownies. Though
everything was tasty, we're all anticipating the end of
zucchini season with relief. Of course, by then tomato
season will have begun, and we'll be looking for ways to
prepare a new vegetable deluge. I foresee more delicious
experiments in the future.

Early 19th-Century Women in New England

In the early 19th century, the market economy
expanded, and the home became a haven from the
developing commercialism. During this time, middle-
class wives and mothers in New England assumed
the role of protectors and leaders of home life. With
men working in factories, women were responsible for
housekeeping, providing religious education, and raising
children.

In addition to running their households, women
4
became deeply involved in the labor movements of the
4
time. This included producing goods, such as palm-leaf
4
hats and straw-braided items, for wider consumption.
Wage work provided women with the ability to live at
home while earning money to supplement the family's
income.

3. Which of the following choices most effectively introduces this paragraph?

A. NO CHANGE

B. We have, however, found a minor
flaw in the CSA boxes: a profusion of
zucchini.

C. The CSA has also encouraged creative
cooking with unfamiliar produce.

D. Not all of the produce we've received
has been good, however.

4. Which choice best completes the sentence
and introduces this paragraph?

F. NO CHANGE

G. women became some of the most
important contributors to the industrial age.

H. women grew increasingly involved in
politics.

J. women also had opportunities for
wage work.

Shoemaking was another source of income for women, but their work was socially and physically isolated from the shoe binding that took place in cobblers' shops. However, when increased demand for shoes required the use of sewing machines to speed up the pace of production, women organized a small-scale movement that trained young women to use sewing machines in their homes. Despite this move, women who worked at home as shoe binders remained isolated and vulnerable to competition from the more lucrative and efficient factories. Women were also denied craft status and admission into unions, which limited their influence.

Francis Cabot Lowell employed women in a new kind of factory, where they were also prohibited from joining unions. This allowed factories such as the Lowell Mills to exploit women's labor. For example, they were usually paid half the wages given to men. However, female factory workers were offered a type of work outside of the home and away from their families, which provided them with a new level of independence.

For many women, the changes in women's roles during the first half of the 19th century were a part of a positive and liberating transformation. For others, though, either their roles remained quite traditional, or their new endeavors, such as working in factories, were not as freeing as they had hoped. Women's experiences with and reactions to the changes they encountered varied, but many were eager for the journey ahead.

5. Which choice provides the best introduction to this paragraph?

A. NO CHANGE
B. A similar tension marked women's employment in factories,
C. Women attempted to reform laws governing factories,
D. Some women abandoned their responsibilities at home for jobs in factories,

6. Which of the following provides the best conclusion to the essay?

F. NO CHANGE
G. Unfortunately, discrimination and unfair work practices continue to plague women in the workplace to this day.
H. Decades passed before the societal changes of the 19th century were widely accepted.
J. This divide led to an alienation that plagued the women's movement of New England throughout the 19th and 20th centuries.

DEVELOPMENT: REVISING TEXT

LEARNING OBJECTIVES

After this lesson, you will be able to:

- Revise a sentence to accomplish a specific purpose
- Determine the relevance of a sentence within a passage

To answer a question like this:

Humphrey Bogart

When Bogart was released from the navy in 1920, he turned his attention toward the theater. A family friend in the business hired him to work in a theater office in New York. Bogart eventually became a stage manager and finally procured some minor roles on the stage. His inexperience showed, however, and he struggled to
<u>_____1</u>
find any substantive parts. In the early 1930s, Bogart set out for Hollywood, and although he quickly signed a contract with Fox Pictures, he appeared, marginally, in only three films.

1. If the writer were to delete the underlined portion (adjusting capitalization as necessary), the sentence would primarily lose:

    A. details about Bogart's success.

    B. a warning against changing careers.

    C. an example illustrating Bogart's lack of expertise.

    D. a reason for Bogart's slow start in the theater.

You need to know this:

Some Development questions focus on revising text in a way that affects the meaning of the passage. Most questions with this focus ask you to select the choice that:

- Accomplishes a unique, specified goal,
- Describes what would be lost if the underlined segment were deleted, or
- States why a sentence should or should not be added or deleted.

For these questions, all of the answer choices are grammatically and stylistically correct. Given this fact, your task is to determine which option provides information that is most pertinent to the passage. The correct choice will relate directly to the surrounding text and could serve as support for a point, a transition to a new idea, or some other purpose.

You need to do this:

When a Development question focuses on revising text in a meaningful way, you should always consider both what information the question stem and/or underlined segment provides and whether that information (a) matches the writer's focus and (b) helps express the purpose of the sentence or paragraph. Then, refine your approach:

- When a question asks you which choice accomplishes a unique, specified goal, eliminate incorrect choices that do not accomplish this goal and confirm the correct choice using the passage. Incorrect choices:
  - Mention information that is beyond the scope of the writer's discussion,
  - Do not relate to the surrounding text, or
  - Do not help express the purpose of the sentence or paragraph.
- When a question describes what would be lost if the underlined segment were deleted, treat it like a Reading question: evaluate the passage and the underlined segment and predict the answer.
- When the answer choices state why a sentence should or should not be added or deleted, decide whether the answer should include Yes or No and eliminate the two choices that don't match; then, use the passage to determine the correct reasoning.

Be sure to plug the proposed revisions back into the passage and read the full sentence (or paragraph) to best assess the change in context.

Explanation:

When asked what would be lost if a phrase were deleted, consider what the phrase adds to the surrounding text. The second half of the sentence says that Bogart "struggled to find any substantive parts," and the underlined portion supports that claim by citing his inexperience. Eliminate A because the underlined portion is about Bogart's early struggles rather than his success. Eliminate B because the paragraph describes Bogart's life without giving any advice to the reader. Choice C is incorrect because the underlined portion does not provide a specific example of Bogart's inexperience. Only (D) correctly characterizes the underlined portion and its relationship to the rest of the sentence.

Try on Your Own

Directions: Take as much time as you need on these questions. Work carefully and methodically. There will be an opportunity for timed practice at the end of the chapter.

Community Supported Agriculture

This spring, my family joined our local community-supported agriculture, or CSA, association. We wanted to eat more healthy foods, and the CSA provided the perfect opportunity. Like other members, we bought a year's "share" of the farm's crop before the growing season began. Once it did, the farm delivered a box filled with freshly harvested fruits and vegetables every week.

2. Which choice offers the clearest and most precise information about how the family wanted to change their diet?

F.   NO CHANGE
G.   more fruits and vegetables,
H.   more locally grown foods,
J.   more unfamiliar fruits and vegetables,

We immediately discovered that fresh, in-season food is delicious. I had disliked broccoli previously, but one bunch that arrived in our second June box convinced me I'd been wrong. My younger brother, <u>who showed little interest in the CSA at first</u>, ventured

3
to try both kale and turnips from the CSA and enjoyed both. Prior to our experience with the CSA, the most exotic vegetable he would willingly eat was a carrot—and only the orange kind.

The History of Advertising

Over the past few decades, advertising has changed radically. In the 1990s, large companies hoped to reach their target markets through advertisements in national magazines and network television, while smaller companies utilized local newspapers, phone books, and radio stations. Of course, companies <u>large and small</u> still

4
buy advertisements in mass media outlets that reach large numbers of consumers. However, with a new millennium came new possibilities, including a larger media outlet than previously imagined: the internet.

3. Which choice best supports the paragraph's main point by showing a contrast with the information that follows in the sentence?

   A. NO CHANGE

   B. who is usually the most adventurous member of the family,

   C. who has never met a food he wasn't curious about,

   D. who is normally resistant to new foods,

4. The primary purpose of the underlined portion is to provide:

   F. a connection between the advertising methods of small and large companies.

   G. information about how companies can differ in size.

   H. a description of what makes a company large or small.

   J. an opinion about the importance of maintaining a variety of business sizes.

The internet allowed businesses to use targeted advertising, including company websites, banner advertisements, and ads generated by search engines, to reach more specific audiences. Small, local businesses in particular benefited greatly from these new marketing opportunities. ⑤

Thomas Paine

Compared to most of America's other Founding Fathers, Thomas Paine is not nearly as well known. In fact, there are many Americans who have either never even heard of him or cannot recall his significance in history. ⑥ Paine was born in 1737 as the son of a corsetmaker—a tailor specializing in corsets and other undergarments—and grew up in rural Thetford, England.

As a young man, Paine worked as a corsetmaker, sailor and minister, but he only found his true calling when he moved to the British colonies in America. Paine first gained recognition as the editor of *Pennsylvania Magazine*, and as political turmoil engulfed the colonies, he became more prominent. In 1776, Paine anonymously published a pamphlet titled "Common Sense" that argued forcefully for American independence from Britain. The pamphlet's popularity spread like wildfire; soon there were 200,000 copies in circulation. Many historians credit the pamphlet with helping to convince the American people to fight for self-rule. ⑦

Thomas Paine's influence continued far beyond sparking the Revolutionary War. Once the war began, Paine published a series of pamphlets called *The American Crisis*, which, in the midst of a bloody war,

5. The writer is considering adding the following sentence:

> Small specialty shops were once relatively limited to serving local populations of customers, but today those same shops can have customers from around the world.

Should the writer make this addition here?

A. Yes, because it clarifies the kind of advertising being discussed.

B. Yes, because it explains why small businesses benefited from internet advertising.

C. No, because it does not explain why small shops should use internet advertising.

D. No, because it is unnecessarily specific.

6. If the writer were to delete the preceding sentence, the paragraph would primarily lose:

F. an explanation for Paine's relative obscurity.

G. a statement supporting and elaborating on the previous sentence.

H. a claim the writer will prove in the rest of the paragraph.

J. an expression of the writer's disappointment in Americans' ignorance.

7. If the writer were to delete the preceding sentence, the paragraph would primarily lose:

A. a detail that demonstrates the impact of Paine's writings.

B. evidence that conflicts with information presented earlier in the passage.

C. a description of the contents of Paine's pamphlet.

D. an elaboration of Paine's goals in writing "Common Sense."

helped keep the morale of the troops up. In addition to his achievements as a writer, Thomas Paine is credited with conceiving the name "The United States of America." Because Thomas Paine was an extremely talented writer, Thomas Jefferson and John Adams drew heavily on his work when drafting the Declaration of Independence. Later in life, Paine wrote other highly controversial works. He was even exiled from England and imprisoned in France for his writings. 8 In 1797, Paine did his part to inspire what would become Social Security. He suggested a system of social insurance for the young and the elderly in his last great work, "Agrarian Justice."

Early 19th-Century Women in New England

In addition to running their households, women also had opportunities for wage work. This included producing goods, such as palm-leaf hats and straw-braided items, for wider consumption. Wage work provided women with the ability to live at home while earning money to supplement the family's income.

Shoemaking was another source of income for women, <u>and, like wage work, it allowed them to earn</u>
9
<u>money from home</u>. However, when increased demand
9
for shoes required the use of sewing machines to speed

8. The writer is considering deleting the previous sentence. Should the writer make this deletion?

   F. Yes, because it detracts from the focus on controversy.

   G. Yes, because it does not describe the writings.

   H. No, because it contributes to the focus on Paine's international relations.

   J. No, because it adds an interesting detail that contributes to the purpose of the paragraph.

9. Given that all the choices are accurate, which one best emphasizes the disadvantages experienced by women working from home?

   A. NO CHANGE

   B. though it required more specialized tools than other goods they could produce from home.

   C. but their work was socially and physically isolated from the shoe binding that took place in cobblers' shops.

   D. who often sought multiple sources of income they could fit around their household responsibilities.

up the pace of production, <u>many women had to turn to</u>
<u>other sources of work and revenue</u>. Despite this bold
move, women who worked at home as shoe binders
remained isolated and vulnerable to competition from
the more lucrative and efficient factories. Women were
also denied craft status and admission into unions,
which limited their influence.

Women who worked in factories were also
prohibited from joining unions, allowing factories such
as the Lowell Mills to exploit their labor. However,
female factory workers were offered <u>a type of work</u>
<u>outside of the home and away from their families</u>, which
provided them with a new level of independence.

10. Which of the following provides the most
relevant information at this point in the
essay?

F. NO CHANGE
G. few women could afford to make the
switch because of the high cost of
personal sewing machines.
H. women had a difficult time keeping up
in addition to their responsibilities at
home.
J. women organized a small-scale movement that trained young women to use
sewing machines in their homes.

11. Given that all are true, which choice
provides new information that helps
emphasize the opportunity factory work
offered for some women?

A. NO CHANGE
B. income in addition to that of their
families,
C. lower wages than their male
counterparts,
D. a part in the burgeoning Industrial
Revolution,

DEVELOPMENT: PURPOSE

LEARNING OBJECTIVE

After this lesson, you will be able to:

- Determine whether a passage has met a goal and state why or why not

To answer a question like this:

Humphrey Bogart

Although the screen appeal of Humphrey Bogart has grown immeasurably since his death in 1957, his early
life was not marked by success. Born in New York City in 1899 as the son of a prominent surgeon, young
Humphrey was quickly put on the track to medical school. After finishing his early schooling, he went to the
prestigious Phillips Academy. Bogart, however, was not academically inclined, and during adolescence he was
often described as a troublemaker. In 1918, Bogart entered the navy. It was in the service that he received an
injury that partially paralyzed his upper lip, creating his distinctive snarl.

When Bogart was released from the navy in 1920, he turned his attention toward the theater. A family friend in the business hired him to work in a theater office in New York. Bogart eventually became a stage manager and finally worked himself into some minor roles on the stage. His inexperience showed, however, and he struggled to find any substantive parts. In the early 1930s, Bogart set out for Hollywood, and although he quickly signed a contract with Fox Pictures, he appeared, marginally, in only three films.

Frustrated with his stagnant career, he returned to the Broadway stage and finally caught his break as Duke Mantee in the play *The Petrified Forest*. Bogart's performance as the quintessential tough guy soon catapulted his career. Bogart consistently created rich and complex screen images punctuated by his hangdog expressions, perennial five o'clock shadow, and world-weary attitude. From his early gangster roles to his consummate portrayal of the reluctant hero, Bogart's performances came to personify male elegance on the screen, and it is unlikely that his illustrious career will ever be forgotten.

> Question 1 asks about the preceding passage as a whole.

1. Suppose the writer's primary purpose had been to describe the life of someone who struggled before finding success. Would this essay accomplish that purpose?

    A. Yes, because it describes Bogart's perseverance in response to people who doubted his talent.

    B. Yes, because it depicts several setbacks Bogart experienced before he found a lasting career.

    C. No, because it focuses mainly on the reasons for Bogart's success.

    D. No, because it does not describe Bogart's troubles in detail.

You need to know this:

On the ACT, some Development questions will ask you to determine why an essay does or does not achieve a given purpose. Writers select particular wording and details to support the purpose of the passage while maintaining a consistent tone and focus, so determining why a given purpose is or is not appropriate will require use of the entire passage.

Only some passages will include these types of questions, but when one is present, it will be the last question in the set and preceded by a boxed-in instructional sentence:

> Question 15 asks about the preceding passage as a whole.

You need to do this:

- Determine the author's point of view and main topic and predict the purpose.
- Ask yourself whether the given purpose is close to your prediction (Yes, because...) or not (No, because...).
- Eliminate the two choices that do not match your Yes/No conclusion.
- Examine the reasoning in the two remaining answers and use the passage to determine which is correct.

Explanation:

To determine the essay's primary purpose, summarize the passage as a whole. The passage describes Bogart's slow rise to fame, detailing the challenges he faced before and during his attempts to become a successful actor. This matches the purpose in the question stem, so eliminate C and D. The passage does not mention anyone doubting Bogart's talent, so A is incorrect. Choice (B) is correct because it accurately connects the features of the passage to the stated purpose.

Try on Your Own

Directions: Take as much time as you need on these questions. Work carefully and methodically. There will be an opportunity for timed practice at the end of the chapter.

Early Writing Careers

Many well-known writers began their careers while they were still teenagers. Stephen King, for example, began submitting stories to science fiction magazines when he was just thirteen years old. If you are serious about a writing career, you can submit work to many publications that accept unsolicited manuscripts. It is best, however, to send a query letter first.

A query letter is a one-page document in which you introduce yourself to the editors of the publication and ask if they would like to read your work. Begin by telling the editor a little bit about yourself. Include a paragraph or two outlining the story you've written or would like to write. If you've taken any creative writing courses, won prizes for your writing, or had any work published, tell the editor about that, too. Don't forget to thank the editor for taking the time to read your letter.

You probably won't sell your first story, but don't get discouraged. Stephen King didn't sell his first submission either—or dozens after that. Despite that, he didn't give up, and neither should you.

> Question 2 asks about the preceding passage as a whole.

2. If the writer's primary goal were to write an essay about a well-known author's path to success, would this essay accomplish that purpose?

   F. Yes, because it discusses how Stephen King's career began.

   G. Yes, because it tells about the writer's path to success.

   H. No, because it doesn't give enough details about Stephen King's career path.

   J. No, because it focuses on giving advice to aspiring authors.

The History of Advertising

Over the past few decades, advertising has changed radically. In the 1990s, large companies hoped to reach their target markets through advertisements in national magazines and network television, while smaller companies utilized local newspapers, phone books, and radio stations. Of course, companies large and small still buy advertisements in mass media outlets that reach large numbers of consumers. However, with a new millennium came new possibilities, including a larger media outlet than previously imagined: the internet.

The internet allowed businesses to use targeted advertising, including company websites, banner advertisements, and ads generated by search engines, to reach more specific audiences. Small, local businesses in particular benefited greatly from these new marketing opportunities. Small specialty shops, previously limited to serving local populations of customers, were able to expand their clientele around the world.

Today, companies continue to develop ever more sophisticated methods to use the internet to reach their customers. Individually tailored advertisements appear on social media sites, in email inboxes, in the midst of streamed entertainment, and more. As internet use expands, so too will the ways businesses advertise through it.

Question 3 asks about the preceding passage as a whole.

---

3. Suppose the writer's goal had been to write an essay about how the internet has changed the world. Would this essay accomplish that goal?

   A. Yes, because it describes how businesses use the internet.

   B. Yes, because it emphasizes the broad impact the internet has had.

   C. No, because it focuses on advertising rather than the overall impact of the internet.

   D. No, because it suggests that companies would have changed without the internet.

Community-Supported Agriculture

This spring, my family joined our local community-supported agriculture, or CSA, association. We wanted to eat more locally grown foods, and the CSA provided the perfect opportunity. Like other members, we bought a year's "share" of the farm's crop before the growing season began. Once it did, the farm delivered a box filled with freshly harvested fruits and vegetables every week.

We immediately discovered that fresh, in-season food is delicious. I had disliked broccoli previously, but one bunch that arrived in our second June box convinced me I'd been wrong. My younger brother, who is normally resistant to new foods, ventured to try both kale and turnips from the CSA and enjoyed both. Prior to our experience with the CSA, the most exotic vegetable he would willingly eat was a carrot—and only the orange kind.

We have, however, found a minor flaw in the CSA boxes: a profusion of zucchini. Each week in July, we received at least six. At first, we just grilled the zucchini. Then, we sautéed it with pasta. By the third week, when we opened our box to find ten more zucchini, we had to get inventive. We experimented with recipes for zucchini soup, casserole, bread, pizza, and even brownies. Though everything was tasty, we're all anticipating the end of zucchini season with relief. Of course, by then tomato season will have begun, and we'll be looking for ways to prepare a new vegetable deluge. I foresee more delicious experiments in the future.

> Question 4 asks about the preceding passage as a whole.

4. If the writer's goal were to write a brief essay about the purpose and organization of community-supported agriculture, would this essay successfully accomplish that goal?

   F. Yes, because it explains how community-supported agriculture works.
   G. Yes, because it fully describes both the benefits and drawbacks of community-supported agriculture.
   H. No, because it focuses instead on one family's experience with community-supported agriculture.
   J. No, because it fails to provide an overview of how membership in a community-supported agriculture association works.

Thomas Paine

Compared to most of America's other Founding Fathers, Thomas Paine is not nearly as well known. In fact, there are many Americans who have either never even heard of him or cannot recall his significance in history. Paine was born in 1737 as the son of a corsetmaker—a tailor specializing in corsets and other undergarments—and grew up in rural Thetford, England.

As a young man, Paine worked as a corsetmaker, sailor and minister, but he only found his true calling when he moved to the British colonies in America. Paine first gained recognition as the editor of *Pennsylvania Magazine*, and as political turmoil engulfed the colonies, he became more vocal. In 1776, Paine anonymously published a pamphlet titled "Common Sense" that argued forcefully for American independence from Britain. The book's popularity spread like wildfire; soon there were 200,000 copies in circulation. Many historians credit the book with helping to convince the American people to fight for self-rule.

Thomas Paine's influence continued far beyond sparking the Revolutionary War. Once the war began, Paine published a series of pamphlets called *The American Crisis*, which, in the midst of a bloody war, helped keep the morale of the troops up. In addition to his achievements as a writer, Thomas Paine is credited with conceiving the name "The United States of America." Because Thomas Paine was an extremely talented writer, Thomas Jefferson and John Adams drew heavily on his work when drafting the Declaration of

Independence. Later in life, Paine wrote other highly controversial works. In 1797, Paine did his part to inspire what would become Social Security. He suggested a system of social insurance for the young and the elderly in his last great work, "Agrarian Justice."

Given Thomas Paine's contributions to America, he deserves recognition as one of our most important Founding Fathers. Whether you think of him as a patriot who named an entire nation or a controversial activist who lobbied for socialist ideas, he should at the very least be remembered as a seminal figure in the development of a new, autonomous nation.

> Question 5 asks about the preceding passage as a whole.

5. Suppose the writer's primary purpose had been to advocate placing a greater emphasis on Thomas Paine's contributions to American history. Would this essay accomplish that purpose?

   A. Yes, because it praises Paine's influence.

   B. Yes, because it is a thorough treatise on American history.

   C. No, because it does not establish that Paine's contributions were beneficial.

   D. No, because it focuses too much on the American Revolution.

How Much Have You Learned?

Directions: For test-like practice, give yourself 9 minutes to complete this question set. Be sure to study the explanations, even for questions you got correct. They can be found at the end of this chapter.

The Library System

Since the turn of the century, library systems have undergone increasing computerization, a trend that has led some people to speculate about the future of libraries. Some people believe that not only the card catalog but also the library stacks themselves will

1. A. NO CHANGE
    B. brought about speculative consideration on
    C. led to speculation about
    D. brought some people to make predictions about

eventually be rendered obsolete. Many today have never even used a card catalog and hardly know what one is.

2. Which choice best supports the paragraph's main idea by emphasizing the changes technology is bringing to libraries?

    F. NO CHANGE
    G. It is quite likely, they say, that in the very near future, electronic data will replace books as we know them.
    H. Along with decreases in funding, this may spell trouble for libraries in the future.
    J. Young people, they say, are less and less interested in reading books, even on electronic devices like tablets.

This thought presents an interesting picture of the future. Despite spending a cozy evening with a good

3. A. NO CHANGE
    B. While
    C. Since
    D. Instead of

book, we may be <u>looking at</u> a laptop computer. With all the
4
intriguing possibilities the future holds, we are

inclined to ignore the past. [A] <u>We should not ignore the</u>
5
<u>past because it helps make us who we are.</u>
5

Libraries may have originated as early as the third

millennium BCE in Babylonia. There, clay tablets were

used for record-keeping purposes and stored in <u>temples</u>
6
<u>in ancient Babylonia</u>. [B] In the seventh century BCE,
6
the King of Assyria organized an enormous collection of

records; approximately 20,000 tablets and fragments

4. Which choice best emphasizes the coziness
of reading while maintaining the essay's
positive tone?

    F.   NO CHANGE

    G.   next to

    H.   stuck with

    J.   curling up with

5. Given that all the choices are true, which
one provides the best transition to the rest
of the essay?

    A.   NO CHANGE

    B.   Libraries have a past as well as a future,
both of which are important to keep in
mind when thinking about them.

    C.   The future of libraries is something
perhaps none of us can fully predict,
and we shouldn't try.

    D.   While the future of libraries is an
interesting topic, the library system's
rich history is also quite intriguing.

6.   F.   NO CHANGE

    G.   temples millennia ago in a country
called Babylonia.

    H.   temples.

    J.   temples located in Babylonia.

have been recovered. ⁷ In the second century CE, libraries were founded in monasteries.

7. At this point, the writer is considering adding the following true statement:

> The first libraries to store books were fourth-century BCE Greek temples established in conjunction with the various schools of philosophy.

Should the writer make this addition here?

A. Yes, because it adds a relevant detail.

B. Yes, because it supports the main idea of religious contributions to libraries.

C. No, because it does not say where the temples were.

D. No, because it distracts from the emphasis on books.

[C] <u>One of the most influential of these schools was</u>
    8
<u>Neoplatonism.</u>
    8

8. Given that all the statements are true, which one provides the most relevant information at this point in the essay?

F. NO CHANGE

G. It was not until the 13th century that university libraries were created.

H. The Greeks also preserved knowledge through lengthy epics memorized and recited by poets.

J. At that time, it was rare for individuals to own books.

<u>The institution of the library continued to change over</u>
    9
<u>time</u>. The emergence of a middle class, a growth
    9
in literacy, and the invention of the printing
press all played a role. [D] However, wars and revolutions
served to hinder the development of the library system

9. Given that all the choices are true, which one provides the best introduction to this paragraph?

A. NO CHANGE

B. Many societal changes occurred in the Renaissance.

C. During the Renaissance, a series of societal changes began to transform the library system into the form we have today.

D. The Renaissance was a rebirth of classical ideas and artistic styles.

in England. ☐10 For example, Henry VIII ordered the destruction of countless manuscripts and disbanded some monastic libraries.

In the days of King Henry, many English citizens were pondering the fate of the <u>nascent</u> library system. Today's
₁₁
societal changes are likewise causing some of us

to <u>consider and think about</u> the same thing,
₁₂

<u>although</u> in ways that medieval readers could never
₁₃
have imagined. Have we progressed from clay tablets to paperbacks only to trade our paperbacks in for microchips?

10. If the writer were to delete the preceding sentence, the paragraph would primarily lose:

   F. details that support the second sentence of the paragraph.
   G. a link between Henry VIII's actions and libraries.
   H. an introduction to the details in the final sentence of the paragraph.
   J. an emphasis on library developments after the 13th century.

11. A. NO CHANGE
    B. futile
    C. delicate
    D. immature

12. F. NO CHANGE
    G. consider
    H. consider while thinking about
    J. consider and be thinking about

13. A. NO CHANGE
    B. despite
    C. also
    D. consequently

Questions 14–15 ask about the preceding passage as a whole.

---

14. The writer would like to add the following sentence:

    With the increased availability of books, patrons of scholarship founded libraries with accompanying academies of scholars in major cities throughout much of Europe.

    The sentence would most logically be placed at:

    F. Point A in Paragraph 2.
    G. Point B in Paragraph 3.
    H. Point C in Paragraph 3.
    J. Point D in Paragraph 4.

15. Suppose the writer's primary purpose had been to develop a prediction about the future of libraries. Would this essay accomplish that purpose?

    A. Yes, because it gives evidence in favor of thinking that libraries will change.
    B. Yes, because it treats the past as unimportant.
    C. No, because it focuses on the history of libraries.
    D. No, because it emphasizes the struggles of libraries throughout history.

Reflect

Directions: Take a few minutes to recall what you've learned and what you've been practicing in this chapter. Consider the following questions, jot down your best answer for each one, and then compare your reflections to the expert responses on the following page. Use your level of confidence to determine what to do next.

1. When should you consider selecting "DELETE the underlined portion"?

   _____

   _____

   _____

2. How can transition words help you determine the most logical placement for a sentence?

   _____

   _____

   _____

3. Why is relevance important in determining whether a sentence should be revised, added, or deleted?

   _____

   _____

   _____

4. Name one goal of the introduction to a paragraph/passage. Name one goal of the conclusion to a paragraph/passage.

   _____

   _____

   _____

Responses

1. When should you consider selecting "DELETE the underlined portion"?

If the underlined portion is wordy/redundant, does not enhance the meaning of the sentence, or does not provide clarity, select "DELETE the underlined portion." Remember that "DELETE the underlined portion" is just as likely as any of the other three choices.

2. How can transition words help you determine the most logical placement for a sentence?

The kind of transition word that a sentence begins with (contrast, cause-and-effect, continuation, emphasis, chronology) determines the purpose the sentence should serve within the context. If the sentence does serve that purpose within the context, it is logically placed.

3. Why is relevance important in determining whether a sentence should be revised, added, or deleted?

If a sentence is missing relevant information, it needs to be revised. If you are going to add a sentence, it should be relevant to the existing information in the passage. If information is not relevant to the passage, it should be deleted.

4. Name one goal of the introduction to a paragraph/passage. Name one goal of the conclusion to a paragraph/passage.

A good introduction should explain the topic and purpose and include information that will be discussed later in the paragraph/passage. A good conclusion should summarize the topic and purpose and include information that was discussed earlier in the paragraph/passage.

Next Steps

If you answered most questions correctly in the "How Much Have You Learned?" section, and if your responses to the Reflect questions were similar to those of the ACT expert, then consider conciseness, organization, and development areas of strength and move on to the next chapter. Come back to these topics periodically to prevent yourself from getting rusty.

If you don't yet feel confident, review those parts of this chapter that you have not yet mastered. Then, try the questions you missed again. As always, be sure to review the explanations closely. Then go online (**kaptest.com/login**) to watch video lessons about the highest-yield concepts in this chapter and to use your Qbank for more practice. If you haven't already registered your book, do so at **kaptest.com/moreonline**.

GO ONLINE

kaptest.com/login

Answers and Explanations

Conciseness

1. Review the Explanation portion of the Conciseness lesson.

Drill Answers

Note: These are not the only ways to correct the sentences; your answers may differ.

a. The school was founded ~~and established~~ in 1906.

b. I felt ~~a sense of~~ nervous ~~anxiety~~ before the curtain rose.

c. We ~~were in agreement with each other~~ **agreed** that Naomi should be captain.

d. After a job interview, make sure to send a note ~~of gratitude expressing thanks~~ to **thank** your interviewer.

e. Not long after he graduated from Oxford, Oscar Wilde moved to London, ~~a place in which~~ **where** he embarked on his literary career in earnest.

2. J
Difficulty: Low
Category: Conciseness
Getting to the Answer: The underlined portion in F repeats information that is already included in the name of TEIMUN. Choices G and H do so as well; (J) is the only choice that eliminates the redundancy.

3. A
Difficulty: Low
Category: Conciseness
Getting to the Answer: This question tests redundancy. Choices B, C, and D all introduce redundant language. Thus, (A) is the correct answer.

4. J
Difficulty: Medium
Category: Conciseness
Getting to the Answer: The underlined portion uses more words than is necessary to convey its meaning, as do G and H. Choice (J) is less wordy while still being clear, so it is correct.

Organization: Transitions

1. Review the Explanation portion of the Organization: Transitions lesson.

Drill Answers

a. **Due to** its impressive technical innovations, the small startup thrived.

b. Cashew nuts are a popular snack worldwide; **however**, they can be difficult to harvest because their shells contain a toxic resin.

c. Izdehar is the most level-headed of my friends—**in fact**, I think she's more reliable than some adults I know.

d. After days of hard work, we **finally** finished our science fair project.

e. The actor won an award for best supporting role this year **in addition to** releasing her first pop music album.

2. G
Difficulty: Medium
Category: Organization
Getting to the Answer: Transitions must accurately reflect the writer's purpose. Here, the writer's goal is to emphasize how important good manners were for the upper classes. The word *Despite* is a contrast transition, which is the opposite of the writer's intent. Eliminate F and H because they are both contrast transitions. Choice J is incorrect because good manners were important at all times, not just occasionally. Choice (G) is correct, since *Especially for* emphasizes the point the writer is making.

3. C
Difficulty: Medium
Category: Organization
Getting to the Answer: This question asks for a transition sentence connecting the first and second paragraphs. The first is about Queen Victoria's ideas of propriety impacting culture; the second is about period fashion. The correct answer will include both ideas, and only (C) does so.

4. F
Difficulty: Medium
Category: Organization
Getting to the Answer: This sentence presents a contrast between two ideas: the desire to cinch the waist as much as possible and the fact that women still needed to breathe. Therefore, a contrast transition word is needed. Choice (F) is correct. Choices H and J are incorrect because they are cause-and-effect transition words. Finally, G is incorrect because *rather than* indicates a substitution, not a contrast.

5. D
Difficulty: Medium
Category: Organization
Getting to the Answer: The preceding sentence discusses the limited education many women received during the Victorian Era. Then the paragraph states that a minority of women were educated more fully. The difference between the two requires a contrast transition, and the current transition word does not serve that purpose. Choices B and C do not provide the appropriate contrast, so the correct answer is (D).

6. G
Difficulty: High
Category: Organization
Getting to the Answer: This question asks for a transition sentence from the third paragraph into the fourth paragraph. The third paragraph discusses women's education in the Victorian era, including Victoria's own, while the fourth paragraph discusses Victoria's lasting impact. Choices F, H, and J are all focused on her education alone and offer specific details rather than showing a connection between ideas. Choice J may be tempting because it compares her education to her prime ministers', which indirectly suggests the topic of government policy. However, the final paragraph does not mention her prime ministers, so J does not actually show the connection between these two paragraphs. Choice (G), on the other hand, clearly states the relationship between Victoria's education and her reign, so it is correct.

Organization: Sentence Placement

1. Review the Explanation portion of the Organization: Sentence Placement lesson.

2. H
Difficulty: Medium
Category: Organization
Getting to the Answer: When looking for the correct location to add a sentence, first consider the contents of the sentence to be added. The pronoun *This* at the beginning of the sentence shows that the previous sentence must reference something that "allows the protozoan to move." Choice (H) would place the new sentence after one about flagella propelling the protozoan; thus, it is correct.

3. A
Difficulty: Medium
Category: Organization
Getting to the Answer: Sentence 4 contains the continuation transition *also*. This shows that it is a logical extension of the sentence that comes immediately before it. Since Sentence 4 references craft status and unions, the sentence before Sentence 4 must also discuss these or other closely related topics. Use this to determine where Sentence 4 should go. Choice B is clearly incorrect because then the transition word *also* would have nothing from which to transition. Choices C and D are incorrect because neither contains references to anything remotely similar to craft status and unions. Thus, (A) is correct.

4. F
Difficulty: High
Category: Organization
Getting to the Answer: The sentence the writer wants to add discusses women and home life. It also starts with the phrase "During this time," which needs to make sense as a transition from the previous sentence. Choice (F) places the sentence correctly in a paragraph discussing women and home life in the 19th century. Choices G, H, and J all place it in a paragraph about women and wage work, which doesn't fit the content of the sentence.

5. B
Difficulty: Medium
Category: Organization
Getting to the Answer: The new sentence provides an example of women being treated unfairly, so it must follow and support a sentence about problems women faced at work. Choice A is incorrect because it places the example at the very beginning of the paragraph where it would not follow or support any sentence. Choices C and D place the example after sentences that describe some of the benefits of women working outside of the home. The new sentence details some of the injustices that women faced, so the two ideas do not logically belong together. Choice (B) is the only option that places the new sentence after one about difficulties women encountered, so it is correct.

Development: Precision

1. Review the Explanation portion of the Development: Precision lesson.

2. H
Difficulty: Medium
Category: Development
Getting to the Answer: The sentence sets up a parallel between large companies using certain outlets to advertise and small companies using others, so the underlined word needs to mean *use*. Only (H) conveys this meaning.

3. D
Difficulty: Medium
Category: Development
Getting to the Answer: This question tests precision in conveying nuanced meaning. While all of the answers might seem as if they could fit in the context, the question asks for one that conveys opportunity, or positive potential. Choice A, *competitors*, is too negative, while B and C are both neutral. Choice (D) highlights the positive potential of the internet and is correct.

4. G
Difficulty: High
Category: Development
Getting to the Answer: While each answer choice is grammatically correct, only (G) conveys Paine's increased fame.

5. A
Difficulty: Low
Category: Development
Getting to the Answer: When the underlined portion is a single word, make sure the word fits in the context. Because Paine lived hundreds of years ago, it does not make sense to say that he is *tasked* or is *helped* with something, so eliminate B and C. Choice D creates the phrase *is noted with*. *With* is not the correct preposition to use with this verb, so D is incorrect. Choice (A) is correct.

6. F
Difficulty: Medium
Category: Development
Getting to the Answer: Consider both the surrounding details and the author's tone to determine which phrase fits the context of the essay. Throughout, the author describes increased recognition of Paine's achievements. Eliminate H and J because they are too neutral. While G is certainly positive in tone, it goes beyond what is stated in the passage. The author says that Paine was a good writer, but this does not necessarily mean that he was the best in the colonies. Choice (F) is correct because it perfectly matches the author's positive tone regarding Paine and accurately describes why Paine's work would be used by Jefferson and Adams.

Development: Introductions and Conclusions

1. Review the Explanation portion of the Development: Introductions and Conclusions lesson.

2. G
Difficulty: Medium
Category: Development
Getting to the Answer: On the ACT, a strong concluding sentence will not introduce a new topic. The correct answer choice will be clearly connected to the other details in the paragraph and function as an effective summary. The paragraph describes how the narrator's family reacted positively to the CSA. Choice (G) is correct; it follows naturally from the information about the new vegetables the brother has eaten because of the family's CSA membership. The other choices are not connected to the topic of the family's positive experience with the new food from the CSA.

3. B
Difficulty: High
Category: Development
Getting to the Answer: This paragraph describes a small problem the narrator's family has encountered with the CSA, although the narrator presents it with humor and maintains a positive tone. Choices A and D are both too negative, so eliminate them. Choice C is true but does not accurately capture the main point of the paragraph. The correct answer is (B).

4. J
Difficulty: Medium
Category: Development
Getting to the Answer: The paragraph is primarily about women's ability to earn money by producing goods from home. Choice F, while it is about women in the workforce, brings up a topic outside the scope of the paragraph. Likewise, G makes a claim much stronger than the paragraph can actually support. Finally, H isn't about labor at all. The correct answer is (J), which introduces wage work as an opportunity for women.

5. B
Difficulty: Medium
Category: Development
Getting to the Answer: This paragraph discusses both the negative and positive aspects of factory jobs for women. Choices A and C bring in ideas outside the scope of the paragraph and passage and are thus incorrect. Choice D, while it does discuss women working at factories, has a strong negative tone that is incompatible with the rest of the passage. On the other hand, (B) acknowledges that factory work was a mixed blessing for women, which fits well with the rest of the paragraph. The correct answer is (B).

6. F
Difficulty: High
Category: Development
Getting to the Answer: The concluding sentence must effectively summarize both the final paragraph and the passage as a whole. The main topic of the passage is the positive and negative changes in women's roles, and the final paragraph is a broad retrospective on those developments. Choice (F) provides the best conclusion by focusing on women's roles in the early 19th century. The other choices, G, H, and J, either bring up new ideas or look beyond the early 19th century.

Development: Revising Text

1. Review the Explanation portion of the Development: Revising Text lesson.

2. H
Difficulty: High
Category: Development
Getting to the Answer: This question asks for specific information about the dietary aims that the CSA helped the family fulfill. Choices F, G, and J all suggest general goals that could be easily addressed without using the CSA. Only (H) includes *locally grown foods*, which is a precise goal that would be most effectively achieved through the CSA.

3. D
Difficulty: High
Category: Development
Getting to the Answer: The paragraph's main point is that the produce from the CSA is especially delicious, and the latter part of the sentence supports this by saying that the narrator's brother tried and liked vegetables that the CSA supplied. The question asks for a contrast with the rest of the sentence that will support the paragraph as a whole, so the correct answer will provide information that conflicts with the brother liking the vegetables from the CSA. Choice (D) is correct.

4. F
Difficulty: Low
Category: Development
Getting to the Answer: In the previous sentence, the author discussed how large companies advertise differently than small companies. This sentence describes what is common to both, and the underlined portion makes the connection explicit. Choice (F) is correct.

5. B
Difficulty: Medium
Category: Development
Getting to the Answer: When a question asks about adding a sentence, consider what the sentence contributes to the paragraph as a whole. This paragraph describes the advantages of internet advertising, focusing particularly on the benefits for small businesses. The additional sentence illustrates this benefit, so it should be added. Eliminate C and D. Choice A advocates adding the sentence, but for the incorrect reason. The correct answer is (B).

6. G
Difficulty: High
Category: Development
Getting to the Answer: The first sentence in the paragraph says that Paine is not widely known. The sentence in question supports this claim by stating that few people today are aware of him. Choice (G) is correct. Choice F is incorrect because the sentence does not provide an explanation, only an elaboration. Choice H is incorrect because the rest of the paragraph is not devoted to proving this claim. Finally, J is incorrect because the author's tone is neutral, not judgmental.

7. A
Difficulty: Medium
Category: Development
Getting to the Answer: The sentence in question is preceded by a sentence describing the popularity of Paine's pamphlet "Common Sense"; the sentence being considered for deletion explains the importance of that popularity by describing its influence on historical events. The correct answer is (A).

8. J
Difficulty: High
Category: Development
Getting to the Answer: The preceding sentence mentions Paine's controversial works; additional information about his being exiled and imprisoned for his writings emphasizes this controversy. Thus, (J) is correct because it helps the paragraph achieve its purpose.

9. C
Difficulty: Medium
Category: Development
Getting to the Answer: The question specifically asks for a choice that emphasizes the disadvantages of working from home. Choice (C) describes how women were isolated as a result, whereas the other choices focus on positive or neutral aspects of such work. The correct answer is (C).

10. J
Difficulty: High
Category: Development
Getting to the Answer: This sentence starts out describing a change in the shoemaking industry that affected women. The following sentence begins with "Despite this bold move" and goes on to describe

how women still struggled to compete with factories. The underlined portion must describe a bold move intended to help women keep up with changes in the shoemaking industry. Choice (J) is correct.

11. A
Difficulty: High
Category: Development
Getting to the Answer: This question asks for new information that emphasizes how factory work was beneficial for women. Choices B and D both present information included earlier in the passage. Choice C gives new information, but it focuses on the downsides of factory work. Only (A) gives new information that shows how factory work could be an opportunity, so (A) is correct.

Development: Purpose

1. Review the Explanation portion of the Development: Purpose lesson.

2. J
Difficulty: Medium
Category: Development
Getting to the Answer: First determine the main idea of the passage. This passage is focused on giving advice to aspiring authors, occasionally using an established author as an example. This does not match the purpose described in the question stem, so eliminate F and G. Choice H does not accurately state why the passage does not match the described purpose. The correct answer is (J).

3. C
Difficulty: Medium
Category: Development
Getting to the Answer: This passage focuses on how advertising has changed over time, particularly with the arrival of the internet. The question's description of "how the internet has changed the world" is much more broad, so it does not match the passage. Eliminate A and B. The passage does not make the suggestion described in D, so choice (C) is correct.

4.   H
Difficulty: Medium
Category: Development
Getting to the Answer: Begin by identifying the main idea of the passage. The main idea is that one family has enjoyed its experience with a CSA membership but has also experienced some drawbacks. This main idea does not match the much more general purpose given in the question, so eliminate F and G. Choice J contradicts the essay, which does provide some information on membership. Choice (H) correctly identifies the focus of the essay.

5.   A
Difficulty: High
Category: Development
Getting to the Answer: When asked whether a passage accomplishes a particular purpose, consider the scope and tone of the passage. The passage focuses on Paine's influence on the founding of the United States, and the final paragraph says that he deserves more recognition. This matches the purpose in the question stem, so eliminate C and D. Eliminate B because it incorrectly describes the scope of the passage. Choice (A) accurately reflects the scope and tone of the passage and is therefore correct.

How Much Have You Learned?

1.   C
Difficulty: Low
Category: Conciseness
Getting to the Answer: The underlined portion is wordy, and B and D are even more so. Choice (C) conveys the same meaning without unnecessary words, so it is correct.

2.   G
Difficulty: High
Category: Development
Getting to the Answer: The question asks for a sentence that emphasizes the changes technology is bringing to libraries. Choice F is about a change that has already happened. Choice H refers to funding, not technology. Choice J mentions electronic devices and people reading less, but technology is not cited as the cause of the change. Choice (G) is correct because it discusses how electronic data may replace physical books.

3.   D
Difficulty: Medium
Category: Organization
Getting to the Answer: When a transition word is underlined, identify what ideas it connects and determine their relationship. In this sentence, the first part is about reading a book, and the second part is about using a laptop. Given the context of the passage so far, these two are likely meant to be in contrast. *Despite* and *While*, although contrast words, do not reflect the author's intended meaning that people are using laptops as an alternative to reading books, so eliminate A and B. *Instead of* is a contrast transition that makes sense in context, so (D) is correct.

4.   J
Difficulty: Low
Category: Development
Getting to the Answer: When asked which choice best maintains a particular tone, eliminate answer choices that are neutral or that convey the opposite tone. Choices F and G are neutral, and H is negative. Therefore, (J) is correct.

5.   D
Difficulty: Medium
Category: Development
Getting to the Answer: The current paragraph speculates about the future of libraries, and the following paragraph discusses the origin and development of libraries. The transition sentence should connect these two topics. Eliminate A because it does not discuss libraries. Choice B connects the past and the future, but it does not provide any reason to begin discussing the history of libraries. Choice C focuses only on the future, so it is not an appropriate transition. Choice (D) connects the future of libraries with their past, while giving the reader a reason to want to know more about their history, so it is correct.

6.   H
Difficulty: Medium
Category: Conciseness
Getting to the Answer: The underlined phrase includes information that is already stated earlier in the paragraph. The only answer choice that eliminates all redundancy is (H).

7. A
Difficulty: High
Category: Development
Getting to the Answer: A sentence should be added only if it is relevant to the main point of the paragraph and fits well in context. The additional sentence is relevant to the discussion about the history of libraries because it helps fill in the timeline of library development. Since it should be added, eliminate C and D. While B may be tempting, the paragraph does not emphasize religious contributions to libraries; it merely mentions that a few of the developments took place in temples and monasteries. Choice (A) correctly states the reason for adding the sentence.

8. G
Difficulty: High
Category: Development
Getting to the Answer: The paragraph is about the historical development of libraries, so the correct answer will supply more information about that topic. Choice (G) is correct.

9. C
Difficulty: Medium
Category: Development
Getting to the Answer: An introductory sentence should give the reader a broad idea of the paragraph's topic and flow well into the sentence that immediately follows it. Because the next sentence lists societal factors that "played a role," the introductory sentence should relate these factors to the history of libraries. Choice (C) is correct because it both introduces the societal changes and continues the timeline of library development from the preceding paragraph.

10. H
Difficulty: Medium
Category: Development
Getting to the Answer: Look for the answer choice that accurately describes how the sentence in question relates to the surrounding sentences. Because the sentence begins with *However*, it contrasts with the preceding sentence; therefore, F can be eliminated. Choice G is incorrect because the passage establishes the link between Henry VIII's actions and libraries in the

sentence *after* the one in question. Finally, the entire paragraph deals with library developments after the 13th century, so J is not specific enough. The correct answer is (H).

11. A
Difficulty: High
Category: Development
Getting to the Answer: This question tests word choice. The rest of the sentence states that the fate of the library system was in question, and the previous paragraph describes circumstances that hindered its growth and development. The correct answer will reflect this context. Choice B, *futile*, is too strongly negative. Choice C, *delicate*, does not capture the idea that the library system was growing and changing. Finally, D, *immature*, is used to describe a person's emotional state and cannot be meaningfully used to describe an inanimate object. *Nascent* captures the meaning that the library system was just beginning and the course of its development was still unknown; (A) is correct.

12. G
Difficulty: Low
Category: Conciseness
Getting to the Answer: When one answer choice is noticeably shorter than the others, the question may be testing conciseness. Since *consider* and *think about* mean the same thing, F, H, and J are all unnecessarily repetitive. Therefore, (G) is correct.

13. A
Difficulty: Medium
Category: Organization
Getting to the Answer: When a transition word is underlined, check that it is logically and grammatically correct. Logically, the connected ideas are in contrast. People may consider questions similar to those considered by English citizens under Henry VIII, but they think about these questions in very different ways. Eliminate C and D. Since the word *despite* can introduce only a noun phrase, B is incorrect. Choice (A) fits with both the logic and grammatical structure of the sentence, so it is correct.

14. J
Difficulty: Medium
Category: Organization
Getting to the Answer: When considering where to add a sentence, first examine its content. This sentence says that books became more available and patrons founded libraries throughout Europe, so it must go in one of the paragraphs about the history of libraries. Paragraph 2 does not discuss this topic, so eliminate F. Paragraph 3 is about the historical development of the first libraries, but Paragraph 4 describes their proliferation, so both G and H can be eliminated. Choice (J) correctly places the new sentence in the paragraph discussing the development of libraries in Europe, including the invention of the printing press.

15. C
Difficulty: Medium
Category: Development
Getting to the Answer: When asked whether the passage accomplishes a particular purpose, first check whether the stated purpose is too narrow or too broad. While the passage does discuss predictions about the future of libraries, it focuses mostly on the historical development of libraries. Thus, the stated purpose is too narrow. Eliminate A and B. The passage does not go into detail about the struggles of libraries, so D is incorrect. The correct answer is (C).

[CHAPTER 5]

ACT ENGLISH: TIMING AND SECTION MANAGEMENT STRATEGIES

LEARNING OBJECTIVE

After completing this chapter, you will be able to:

- Move quickly and efficiently through the English Test so that you have a fair chance at every question

Timing

You have 45 minutes to complete 5 passages with 15 questions each, so you need to complete each passage and accompanying questions in 9 minutes. This means that after about 20 minutes, you should be working through your third passage. When the proctor informs you that there are 5 minutes remaining, you should have a little more than half of a passage to finish.

Section Management

While you do want to spend approximately the same amount of time on each passage, you definitely do not need to spend the same amount of time on each question. Every question counts for the same number of points, so be sure to complete the questions you find easiest to answer first. If a particular question is challenging, take a guess and come back to it if you have time. The test rewards students for conciseness, so when you guess, choosing the shortest option is a good idea. It won't always be the correct answer, but it certainly is a good option.

Moving efficiently through this section is important, but that does not mean that you should skip over any text. Even if sections of a passage may not be underlined, you need an understanding of the passage as a whole to answer certain questions. Reading all of the text in the passage is essential to answering questions efficiently and accurately.

There is a full-length English passage in the "How Much Have You Learned?" section that comes next. Use it to practice timing: skip questions you find too time-consuming, return to them if you have time, and keep an eye on the clock. When you are finished, check your work—and reflect on how well you managed the timing. Then keep practicing these timing strategies when you take full-length tests, both in your book and online.

How Much Have You Learned?

Directions: For test-like practice, give yourself 9 minutes to complete this question set. Be sure to study the explanations, even for questions you got correct. They can be found at the end of this chapter.

Frankenstein

The character of Frankenstein did not originate in Hollywood. Rather, the legendary mad scientist <u>whom sought to reanimate</u> lifeless bodies was the creation of Mary Wollstonecraft Shelley, who was married to famed poet Percy Bysshe Shelley. *Frankenstein: The Modern Prometheus*, Mary Shelley's novel published in 1818, is considered <u>one of the greater</u> horror tales of all time.

1.
A. NO CHANGE
B. whom seeks to reanimate
C. who sought in reanimating
D. who sought to reanimate

2.
F. NO CHANGE
G. one of her greater
H. one of the greatest
J. the greatest

Mary Shelley created her <u>desperate</u> subject in response to a bet. [A] She, her husband—Lord Byron— and Byron's physician had a contest to see who could

3. Which choice best emphasizes that the work is a horror story?

A. NO CHANGE
B. offensive
C. nightmarish
D. dangerous

write the best ghost story. Although <u>the writing project began whimsical</u>, her tale became a serious examination of the fate of an individual who decides to overstep moral and social bounds. [B]

4.
F. NO CHANGE
G. the writing project was begun whimsical,
H. the writing project began whimsically, but
J. the writing project began whimsically,

Shelley's novel tells the story of a scientist, Dr. Victor

Frankenstein, who discovers the secret of
_____
5

bringing corpses back to life and creates a monster with
_____
6
material from graveyards, dissecting rooms, and
_____
6
slaughterhouses.
_____
6

Similar to his gruesome appearance, the monster is basically
_____
7
good. [C] After being rejected by Dr. Frankenstein and all

other people with whom he comes into contact, the monster

becomes violent.

One by one, the monster murders the people Dr.

Frankenstein cares for the most: his younger brother, and
_____
8
his best friend, and he even killed his wife. [D] The tale ends
_____
8
with Dr. Frankenstein

chasing the monster to the North Pole, where each of them
_____
9
eventually die.
_____
9

5. A. NO CHANGE
   B. Dr. Victor Frankenstein–who
   C. Dr. Victor Frankenstein: who
   D. Dr. Victor Frankenstein, he

6. If the writer were to delete the underlined portion, the paragraph would primarily lose:
   F. information that emphasizes the grisliness of how Frankenstein acquired his materials.
   G. details about the sources from which Mary Shelley drew inspiration for her story.
   H. an explanation of why Frankenstein's monster ultimately became dangerous.
   J. a description that shows Frankenstein's dedication to his work.

7. A. NO CHANGE
   B. Although
   C. Despite
   D. Because of

8. F. NO CHANGE
   G. his younger brother, and his best friend, and his wife.
   H. his younger brother, best friend, and his wife.
   J. his younger brother, his best friend, and his wife.

9. A. NO CHANGE
   B. where both of them eventually dies.
   C. where each of them eventually have died.
   D. where each of them eventually dies.

It is a horror story, Mary Shelley's *Frankenstein* is
10
respected by many as a literary classic. The critical acclaim
and continued popularity of the story are also evidenced by
the numerous films that have been based

on it. Some versions like *Young Frankenstein*, provide a
11
humorous retelling of the story. Other versions, like the
1994 *Mary Shelley's Frankenstein*, attempt to be

faithful and true to the original.
12

The many adaptations demonstrate that Mary Shelley's
13
story of overreach and its dark consequences remains
13
compelling to this day.
13

10. F. NO CHANGE

    G. Although it is a horror story,

    H. It is a horror story, for

    J. The horror story,

11. A. NO CHANGE

    B. Some versions, like *Young Frankenstein*, provide

    C. Some versions, like *Young Frankenstein*; provide

    D. Some versions–like *Young Frankenstein*, provide

12. F. NO CHANGE

    G. faithful to

    H. faithful and closely follow

    J. accurate and faithful reproductions of

13. Which choice provides the most effective conclusion to the paragraph and the passage?

    A. NO CHANGE

    B. Some film adaptations, however, bear little resemblance to the original book beyond sharing a title with it.

    C. Mary Shelley would be pleased by the lasting appeal of a book she wrote for a wager.

    D. Hollywood, it seems, never tires of creating new interpretations of this story.

Questions 14 and 15 ask about the preceding passage as a whole.

14. The writer wants to add the following sentence to the essay:

> The monster, who is nameless, only becomes evil when his creator refuses to accept and care for him.

The sentence would most logically be placed at:

F. Point A in Paragraph 2.

G. Point B in Paragraph 2.

H. Point C in Paragraph 3.

J. Point D in Paragraph 3.

15. Suppose the writer's primary purpose had been to write an essay analyzing the film adaptations of Mary Shelley's *Frankenstein*. Would this essay accomplish this purpose?

A. Yes, because it compares and contrasts various film versions of the story.

B. Yes, because it critiques how closely film versions follow the original story.

C. No, because it only focuses on one type of film adaptation of the story.

D. No, because the film adaptations are one point in an overall discussion of the story.

Answers and Explanations

1.   D
Difficulty: Medium
Category: Agreement
Getting to the Answer: A subjective pronoun performs the action in a sentence; an objective pronoun is the receiver of the action in a sentence. The pronoun in the underlined segment, *whom*, is an objective pronoun. However, the verbs in the answer choices require the subjective pronoun *who*. Eliminate A and B. Choice C introduces an idiom error, since "sought in reanimating" is not grammatically correct English. The correct answer is (D).

2.   H
Difficulty: Medium
Category: Agreement
Getting to the Answer: The adjective *greater* is used only when comparing two items or people. The passage compares Shelley's novel to all other horror tales. The superlative adjective form is needed, so F and G are incorrect. If J is plugged back into the sentence, it creates the illogical phrase "considered the greatest horror tales of all time." The correct answer is (H).

3.   C
Difficulty: Medium
Category: Development
Getting to the Answer: This question tests word choice. Although all of the answer choices are grammatically correct, the question asks for one that particularly emphasizes horror. *Desperate*, *offensive*, or *dangerous* subjects do not necessarily inspire horror, so A, B, and D are incorrect. Only *nightmarish* has connotations of horror, so the correct answer is (C).

4.   J
Difficulty: Medium
Category: Agreement
Getting to the Answer: Recall that adverbs modify verbs, while adjectives modify nouns. Since the word being modified is the verb *began*, it must be modified by an adverb. The word *whimsical* is an adjective, so eliminate F and G. Choice H correctly contains an adverb but disrupts the structure of the sentence with the extra conjunction *but*. The correct answer is (J).

5.   A
Difficulty: Medium
Category: Sentence Structure
Getting to the Answer: The underlined section includes a comma that sets off nonessential information—the name of the scientist. The punctuation at the beginning and end of the nonessential information must match. Since the opening punctuation is a comma, the closing punctuation must be a comma as well; eliminate B and C. Choice D keeps the comma, but introduces a new error by changing *who* to *he*, which makes the sentence a run-on. The sentence is correct as written, so (A) is the answer.

6.   F
Difficulty: High
Category: Development
Getting to the Answer: This question asks what would be lost if the underlined portion were deleted. The underlined portion is a list of places from which Dr. Frankenstein gathered body parts. Including these details emphasizes the morbid nature of the story. Choice (F) is correct. There is nothing in the passage that suggests that Mary Shelley was inspired by these locations or that the monster became dangerous because of his origins; in fact, evidence elsewhere in the passage contradicts both G and H. Choice J is incorrect because showing Frankenstein's dedication to his work is not the primary effect of the underlined portion.

7.   C
Difficulty: Medium
Category: Organization
Getting to the Answer: This sentence asks for a transition word that contrasts the monster's *gruesome appearance* with his good nature. The transitions *Similar to* and *Because of* do not convey this contrast, so eliminate A and D. Choice B contains the contrast word *Although*, but it creates a fragment when plugged back into the original sentence. The correct answer is (C).

8.   J
Difficulty: Low
Category: Sentence Structure
Getting to the Answer: When a list is underlined, ensure that all items of the list have parallel structure. Choices F and H both contain elements that do not match each other, so they are incorrect. The list items in choice G match, but the *and* before the phrase "his best friend" is unnecessary. The correct answer is (J).

9. D
Difficulty: High
Category: Agreement
Getting to the Answer: The subject of the verb *die* is *each*, which requires a singular verb. Eliminate A and C, which contain plural verbs. Choice B includes the singular verb *dies* but introduces a different subject, *both*, which is plural. Only (D) matches a singular subject with a singular verb. The correct answer is (D).

10. G
Difficulty: Medium
Category: Sentence Structure
Getting to the Answer: This sentence includes two independent clauses incorrectly joined with a comma, forming a run-on sentence. Eliminate F. Choice H correctly contains a coordinating conjunction that joins the two independent clauses, but it creates an incorrect logical relationship between the clauses—being a horror story is not a result of the book being viewed as a classic. Choice J changes the sentence structure completely and introduces a comma error. Choice (G) makes the first clause dependent by using a subordinating conjunction that correctly captures the logical relationship between the clauses. The correct answer is (G).

11. B
Difficulty: Low
Category: Sentence Structure
Getting to the Answer: The phrase "like *Young Frankenstein*" is nonessential information that must be set off from the rest of the sentence with either two commas or two dashes. Only (B) has the same punctuation mark at both the beginning and end of the phrase, so (B) is correct.

12. G
Difficulty: Low
Category: Conciseness
Getting to the Answer: The underlined phrase is redundant. Eliminate F. Choices H and J are also unnecessarily wordy, so eliminate them, too. Only (G) is free of redundancy, so (G) is correct.

13. A
Difficulty: High
Category: Development
Getting to the Answer: A concluding sentence must summarize both the entire passage and the last paragraph. The passage discusses Mary Shelley's *Frankenstein*, including its origin, substance, and critical reception. The last paragraph focuses on critical responses to and interpretations of the book. The closing sentence of the passage must incorporate both, which (A) does effectively. Choice B introduces new ideas, and D is too narrowly focused on the final paragraph. Choice C, while it returns to an earlier part of the passage, is also too narrowly focused on one particular detail. The correct answer is (A).

14. H
Difficulty: High
Category: Organization
Getting to the Answer: This sentence focuses on the monster's transition from good to evil. Paragraph 2 does not discuss the monster at all, so you can eliminate F and G. Choice J would put the sentence too late in Paragraph 3, after the monster has already committed evil acts. Choice (H) is the correct answer.

15. D
Difficulty: High
Category: Development
Getting to the Answer: While the passage does examine various film adaptations of *Frankenstein*, the essay focuses mostly on how the classic horror story was created and what it means. Eliminate A and B. Eliminate C because the reasoning is not correct; the essay does explore different types of films, even though discussing the films is not the author's main purpose. The correct answer is (D).

TEST YOURSELF: ACT ENGLISH

English

Directions: For test-like timing, give yourself 36 minutes to complete the following 60 questions.

Passage I

Television Displays

When most people watch their favorite shows, they probably don't stop to think about how the television set or computer screen works. All such displays, as well as film projectors, depend on an optical illusion called the phi phenomenon. If a human eye sees a series of related <u>snapshots quickly</u> enough, one after the other, the brain perceives motion. Flipping through pages of similar

doodles <u>offered</u> a simple demonstration of

<u>this thing</u>.

1. A. NO CHANGE
   B. snapshots, quickly
   C. snapshots quickly,
   D. snapshots; quickly

2. F. NO CHANGE
   G. offers
   H. offer
   J. has offered

3. A. NO CHANGE
   B. this effect.
   C. all that.
   D. DELETE the underlined portion and end the sentence with a period.

For television screens, the technical challenge

<u>is how to change images, quickly,</u> the display has to
    4

present each image, hold it for a split second, and then

replace it with the next image. To achieve the illusion of

motion, television shows are typically displayed at thirty

<u>images, or frames—per second.</u>
        5

For decades after the birth of television, a more

controversial event than many people realize, <u>the tool</u>
                                                      6
<u>with which these images were created was primarily</u> a
                4

beam of electrons, or cathode ray. ⃞7 In cathode ray

tubes, or CRTs, this beam sweeps over an

4. F. NO CHANGE
    G. is, how to change images quickly—
    H. is how to change images quickly:
    J. is, how to change images quickly

5. A. NO CHANGE
    B. images, or frames
    C. images or frames
    D. images—or frames—

6. F. NO CHANGE
    G. the tool primarily used to create these images was
    H. these images were primarily created using
    J. these images were primarily drawn by a device using

7. The writer is considering deleting the following phrase from the preceding sentence:

    a more controversial event than many people realize,

    Should the writer make this deletion?

    A. Yes, because the phrase is irrelevant to the paragraph's discussion of the technical details of how certain televisions work.
    B. Yes, because the phrase suggests that the controversy surrounding television contributed to the challenges of creating it.
    C. No, because the phrase offers additional information about the birth of television that gives context to the details that follow.
    D. No, because the phrase makes clear that people's views about television have changed alongside the physical challenges of making television.

array of dots that glow when the beam strikes <u>it.</u> The
                                                 8
television signal rapidly turns the beam on and off,

synchronizing the electrons to hit exactly the dots that

<u>making</u> up the proper picture. As the glow from one
  9
sweep fades, another sweep begins.

In consumer applications, cathode ray tubes have

been replaced by liquid crystal <u>displays (LCDs) and</u> are
                                              10
thinner, lighter, and potentially bigger. [A] Unlike CRTs,

LCDs work by selectively blocking light rather than

emitting it: the entire screen is backlit, with layers

of filters determining the quantity and color of <u>light that</u>
                                                       11
<u>reaches the screen</u>. [B] One of these filters, the liquid
   11
crystal from which the technology takes its name, can be

turned on or off electronically, allowing the image to

change <u>quick</u> as electricity passes through the screen.
       12
[C] However, as technology marches on, these displays

may <u>in turn be surpassed</u> by organic light-emitting
       13

8. F. NO CHANGE
    G. these.
    H. that.
    J. them.

9. A. NO CHANGE
    B. make
    C. made
    D. would make

10. F. NO CHANGE
    G. displays (LCDs) because
    H. displays (LCDs), which
    J. displays (LCDs), they

11. A. NO CHANGE
    B. light that reaches the screen
        through the filters.
    C. light that passes through and
        reaches the screen.
    D. light that is filtered out or allowed
        to reach the screen.

12. F. NO CHANGE
    G. quickly
    H. quickest
    J. more quickly

13. A. NO CHANGE
    B. in turn be surpassed,
    C. in turn, be surpassed,
    D. in turn, be surpassed

diodes or the more <u>mysteriously</u> named "quantum
14

dots." [D] CRTs dominated television for five decades; in

five more, who knows how we will watch TV? [15]

14. Which choice most clearly indicates that
the name "quantum dots" is of interest?

    F.   NO CHANGE

    G. confusingly

    H. secretively

    J.   intriguingly

15. The writer wants to divide this paragraph into two in order to separate
discussion of current television displays
from speculation about future television
displays. The best place to begin the new
paragraph would be at Point:

    A. [A]

    B. [B]

    C. [C]

    D. [D]

Passage II

A Prima Ballerina

[1]

Until the late 1940s, no ballerinas in the world were

as prominent <u>than</u> the best Europeans, particularly the
16

Russians. In 1949, however, American Maria Tallchief

danced the lead in *The Firebird*, staged by celebrated

choreographer George Balanchine for the New York

City Ballet. With this performance, Tallchief <u>vaulted</u> to
17

international stardom. [A]

[2]

Born in 1925 to a Native American father of the

Osage Nation and a Scots-Irish mother, Tallchief began

dancing ballet at the age of three. Elizabeth Marie

Tall Chief, as she was then named, also studied

16. F.   NO CHANGE

      G. as

      H. then

      J.   of

17. A. NO CHANGE

      B. vaults

      C. vaulting

      D. had vaulted

other subjects, while her grandmother took her to
18
traditional Osage dance ceremonies. These experiences

probably provided for Tallchief's later belief the basis
19
that ballet should be grounded in movement and
musicality.

[3]

Moving to Los Angeles to further her studies,
Tallchief resolved in her teenage years devoted her life to
20
the craft of ballet. She moved again in 1942, this time to

New York City. Soon despite her relative inexperience,
21
she was accepted into the prestigious Ballet Russe de
Monte Carlo. [B] As a newcomer, Tallchief resisted

pressure to "Russify" her name to "Tallchieva" and
22
appeared in seven different ballets within two months.
22

[4]

When Balanchine began to coach the company, he
and Tallchief clicked artistically. He designed ballets to
highlight her technical prowess, easy energy, and regal

18. Which choice provides the most specific
and relevant information at this point in the
passage?

F. NO CHANGE
G. gymnastics and piano,
H. reading and math,
J. academic topics,

19. The best placement for the underlined
portion would be:

A. where it is now.
B. after the word *experiences*.
C. after the word *basis*.
D. after the word *grounded*.

20. F. NO CHANGE
G. that would devote
H. to devote
J. devoting

21. A. NO CHANGE
B. Soon, despite her relative inexperience
C. Soon, despite her relative inexperience,
D. Soon—despite her relative inexperience,

22. Given that all the statements are true, which
answer choice best builds on the beginning
of the sentence to emphasize the pressure
Tallchief was under to imitate the contemporary stars of ballet?

F. NO CHANGE
G. but strove to match the skill of first
ballerina Nathalie Krassovska.
H. and lost weight due to poor nutrition
and stress.
J. but went by Maria and combined the
words Tall and Chief.

grace through his designs. [C] In response, she worked
relentlessly to improve her skills, actually lengthening
her limbs over time. When Balanchine left the
Ballet Russe in 1946 to found the New York City

23. A. NO CHANGE
    B. grace that she would show.
    C. grace, all qualities of hers.
    D. grace.

Ballet. Tallchief followed in order to continue their
artistic collaboration. This relationship continued for

24. F. NO CHANGE
    G. Ballet, Tallchief
    H. Ballet; Tallchief
    J. Ballet—Tallchief

over a decade, resulting in productions such as *The
Nutcracker*. [D]

25. Which choice most effectively suggests
    that Tallchief's artistic partnership with
    Balanchine led to success?

    A. NO CHANGE
    B. performances
    C. triumphs
    D. works

[5]

Tallchief retired as a ballerina in 1965, but she
went on to found ballet schools and companies in
Chicago and remained active in the ballet community

26. F. NO CHANGE
    G. 1965 but she went on—
    H. 1965: but she went on
    J. 1965, but she went on:

until her death. In contrast, she is remembered as a

27. A. NO CHANGE
    B. Therefore,
    C. At last,
    D. Today,

force in the history of dance, a woman whom shattered

28. F. NO CHANGE
    G. that
    H. who
    J. which

stereotypes and broadened the field of ballet. [29] [30]

29. The writer is considering adding the following sentence to the essay:

> Previously little-known, this ballet became a staple of the art form thanks to Tallchief's soaring performance in Balanchine's reinvented version.

If the writer were to add this sentence, it would most logically be placed at Point:

A. A in Paragraph 1.
B. B in Paragraph 3.
C. C in Paragraph 4.
D. D in Paragraph 4.

30. Suppose that the writer's primary purpose had been to describe an artist's rise to prominence. Would this essay accomplish that purpose?

F. Yes, because it focuses primarily on Tallchief's training and early career.
G. Yes, because it tells about how Tallchief gained international fame.
H. No, because it focuses on Tallchief's partnership with George Balanchine.
J. No, because it focuses on what made Tallchief unique rather than on her fame.

Passage III

Stax Records

[1]

In the 1960s, Stax Records stood at the forefront of new and evolving musical genres. It did not give its name to an entire trend in popular music, as its rival Motown Records did. However, Stax arguably influenced the development of rhythm and blues just as extensively. [A] There, luminaries such as Otis Redding

31. A. NO CHANGE
B. music. As
C. music; as
D. music, and as

and Isaac Hayes recorded numerous songs that <u>become</u>
                                                  32
radio sensations during Stax's heyday.

[2]

Many credit the session musicians at Stax with
the achievements of the record label. <u>However, these</u>
                                           33
musicians, several of whom formed the successful band
Booker T. & the M.G.'s, were renowned within the

industry for their skill. Regrettably, the <u>performers, who</u>
                                                     34
<u>were</u> underappreciated and underpaid, even as they
34

recorded <u>dozens and dozens of hits of the era.</u>
                            35

[3]

[B] Another reason Stax found success is that <u>partial</u>
                                                     36
<u>owner and entrepreneur</u>, Estelle Axton also ran a record
        36
store. Playing rough drafts of songs for her teenaged

customers and observing their reactions, Axton quickly
discovered what would sell and what would not. [37]

32. F. NO CHANGE
    G. have become
    H. became
    J. had become

33. A. NO CHANGE
    B. Thus, these
    C. At first, these
    D. These

34. F. NO CHANGE
    G. performers were
    H. performers,
    J. performers

35. A. NO CHANGE
    B. dozens of hits, maybe fifty or sixty,
       or even more.
    C. multiple dozen hits.
    D. dozens of hits.

36. F. NO CHANGE
    G. partial owner, and entrepreneur
    H. partial owner and entrepreneur
    J. partial owner, and entrepreneur,

37. If the writer were to delete the preceding
    sentence, the paragraph would primarily
    lose:

    A. an explanation of how the store
       added to the label's success.

    B. background information about one
       of the owners of Stax.

    C. an overview of typical leisure activi-
       ties of teenagers at the time.

    D. an observation that weighs against
       a claim made earlier.

[4]

Atlantic Records was another successful record
                                              38
label of the time. Stax had signed a distribution deal with
        38
Atlantic Records, but the arrangement ended bitterly in

1968. The legal rights for almost all the hits

went to Atlantic, leading to a gradual decline that led
                                          39
to a devastating downturn for Stax. In 1975, the label
        39
declared bankruptcy. Even after its corporate rebirth

shortly afterward, Stax struggled for decades, surviving

only by reissuing the few songs still under there
                                            40
control. [C]

[5]

In recent years, however, a floundering Stax Records
                               41
has signed new artists and begun recording hits again.

[D] In 2013, several Stax musicians even performed at

38. Which choice most effectively intro-
    duces the paragraph?

    F. NO CHANGE
    G. Unfortunately, this golden age did
        not last.
    H. Legal ownership of songs is a prime
        component of music law.
    J. Stax Record's business relationship
        with Atlantic Records also bene-
        fited Stax.

39. A. NO CHANGE
    B. downturn in its position in the
        music industry
    C. devastating decline
    D. bad time

40. F. NO CHANGE
    G. their
    H. its
    J. it's

41. Which choice most effectively indicates
    that Stax is making a comeback?

    A. NO CHANGE
    B. a fledgling
    C. an outdated
    D. a rejuvenated

the White House in an event that <u>showcased</u> Memphis
42

soul music. Back in Memphis, <u>dedicated to American</u>
43
<u>soul music, the site where the legendary recording</u>
43
<u>studio once stood is now occupied by a museum.</u>
43

42. F. NO CHANGE
G. supplied
H. uncovered
J. unified

43. A. NO CHANGE
B. a museum dedicated to American soul music now occupies the site where the legendary recording studio once stood.
C. dedicated to American soul music, the legendary recording studio once stood on a site now occupied by a museum.
D. an American soul music museum now occupies the dedicated site where the legendary recording studio once stood.

Questions 44 and 45 ask about the preceding passage as a whole.

44. The writer is considering adding the following sentence to the essay:

Indeed, the sound of Southern soul was largely born at the Stax studio in Memphis, Tennessee.

If the writer were to add this sentence, it would most logically be placed at:

F. Point A in Paragraph 1.
G. Point B in Paragraph 3.
H. Point C in Paragraph 4.
J. Point D in Paragraph 5.

45. Suppose the writer's primary purpose had been to describe Stax Records' unique contributions to American music styles. Would this essay accomplish that purpose?

A. Yes, because it lists several American music styles that were influenced by music recorded at Stax.
B. Yes, because it explains the specific ways in which music recorded at Stax impacted American rhythm and blues.
C. No, because the essay focuses on the history and characteristics of Stax Records.
D. No, because the essay does not catalog sufficient examples of specific hit songs recorded at Stax.

Passage IV

Dropping an Egg

<u>My freshman teacher, Ms. Windham, of physics,</u>
did not like sitting down. After greeting us at the door,

46. F. NO CHANGE
    G. Ms. Windham my freshman teacher of physics
    H. My freshman physics teacher, Ms. Windham,
    J. My physics teacher, Ms. Windham, for freshmen,

she <u>sprang</u> around the room, acting out the motion of a

47. Which choice best conveys the high level of energy with which Ms. Windham taught?

    A. NO CHANGE
    B. twitched
    C. sauntered
    D. tottered

projectile according to <u>Newton's laws or the behavior of
gas particles'</u> under pressure.

48. F. NO CHANGE
    G. Newton's laws or the behavior of gas particles
    H. Newtons laws or the behavior of gas particle's
    J. Newtons laws or the behavior of gas particles'

<u>We were taking a test</u>, she

49. A. NO CHANGE
    B. Although we were taking a test,
    C. As we were taking a test;
    D. Even when we were taking a test,

moved quietly and actively among our desks, as if eager

for the class to return to more energetic activities. [50]

50. In the preceding sentence, the writer is considering revising the phrase "and actively" to "but almost impatiently." Given that the revised phrase is accurate, should the writer make this revision?

F. Yes, because the revision better explains the teacher's behavior as described later in the sentence.

G. Yes, because the revision introduces a negative aspect of the teacher's habits that would not otherwise be discussed.

H. No, because the revision contradicts the teacher's typical teaching style as described elsewhere in the passage.

J. No, because the revision does not specify the speed at which the teacher moved in the classroom.

With her infectious enthusiasm that was contagious
                                              51
among the students, Ms. Windham did not want us
     51

51. A. NO CHANGE

B. infectious zeal that spread from person to person,

C. zealous, eager enthusiasm that infected us all,

D. contagious enthusiasm,

to be sitting for long, either. They themselves were
                                    52

52. F. NO CHANGE

G. You yourselves

H. We ourselves

J. They and I

often the gas particles or the projectiles—although not
                 53
literally, of course. We built various devices to accelerate
small steel balls, including painstakingly calibrated
catapults and cartoonishly twisted rolling tracks. In the
gymnasium, we floated on a noisy hovercraft that she

53. A. NO CHANGE

B. particles:

C. particles;

D. particles—

and the rest of the science department <u>had constructed a contraption</u> of plywood and garbage bags powered by leaf blowers. That occasion was one of the few times I saw Ms. Windham seated, smiling as she glided across the gym floor.

The highlight of the year was the springtime egg drop. Much prestige was associated at this contest, which involved building a capsule that, when dropped from the roof of the science wing, would protect a raw egg nestled inside it. As Ms. Windham explained, the top <u>prize was for a combination of speed and accuracy would</u> be awarded to the capsule that fell fastest and landed closest to the target while still preserving its egg.

Another prize <u>went</u> to the pod that took the longest to land. The Disaster Miracle trophy would be for the capsule that broke apart most dramatically—in Ms. Windham's judgment—but nevertheless kept the egg inside safe.

<u>Before this class, I had never operated power tools.</u> My lab partner and I ultimately chose to aim for the Disaster Miracle: we thought it would be the most fun to design and especially to deploy. On the day of the

54. F. NO CHANGE
    G. had constructed, a contraption
    H. had constructed a contraption,
    J. had constructed a contraption:

55. A. NO CHANGE
    B. prize was for a combination of speed and accuracy, would
    C. prize, for a combination of speed and accuracy, to
    D. prize, for a combination of speed and accuracy, would

56. F. NO CHANGE
    G. goes
    H. would go
    J. has gone

57. Given that all the choices are true, which one provides the best transition from the preceding paragraph to this paragraph?

    A. NO CHANGE
    B. On the day of the drop, the weather was gorgeous.
    C. Earlier in the spring, I had read my first book about engineering.
    D. Deciding which prize to strive for was far from straightforward.

drop, <u>my</u> "Egg-splorer" module shattered beautifully on
58

impact, and the egg survived. <u>Years later,</u> the photo of
59
my partner and me holding our trophy over our heads
still makes me smile, even as I prepare to pursue my
undergraduate degree in mechanical engineering.

<u>The photo has a special spot in my scrapbook of high</u>
60
<u>school memories.</u>
60

58. F.　NO CHANGE
　　G.　their
　　H.　whose
　　J.　our

59. A.　NO CHANGE
　　B.　Next,
　　C.　In the meantime,
　　D.　So far,

60. Which choice most effectively concludes
　　the paragraph and the essay?

　　F.　NO CHANGE
　　G.　I credit Ms. Windham and her
　　　　engaging approach to teaching
　　　　physics with sparking my passion
　　　　for science.
　　H.　Ms. Windham still conducts the
　　　　popular egg drop event, with its
　　　　humorous Disaster Miracle prize,
　　　　every spring.
　　J.　Ms. Windham, in her true ener-
　　　　getic style, would literally jump
　　　　with excitement when viewing
　　　　the egg drops.

Answers and Explanations

Passage I

1. A
Difficulty: Low
Category: Sentence Structure: Commas, Dashes, and Colons
Getting to the Answer: This question tests correct usage of commas and semicolons. *Snapshots* is part of the object of the verb *sees*, and *quickly* is an adverb describing the verb; neither of them should be separated from another part of the sentence, so no punctuation is needed here. The correct answer is (A).

For the record: putting a comma between *snapshots* and *quickly* separates *quickly* from the verb it describes, so B is incorrect. In C, the comma is separating the words *quickly* and *enough*, but since *enough* is describing *quickly*, the two words should not be separated, so C is incorrect. The semicolon in D does not separate two independent clauses, so D is incorrect.

2. G
Difficulty: High
Category: Agreement: Verbs
Getting to the Answer: Although this sentence may seem grammatically correct on its own, the underlined verb is in past tense while the rest of the paragraph is in simple present tense. Eliminate F and J since neither matches the tense of the rest of the paragraph. Choice H is in the correct tense, but it introduces a new error: *offer* is a plural verb, but the subject of the verb is the act of flipping, which is singular. Thus, it requires the singular present tense verb *offers*. Choice (G) is correct.

3. B
Difficulty: Medium
Category: Development: Precision
Getting to the Answer: The phrase *this thing* is vague; more specific wording is necessary. Eliminate A. Choice C is just as vague, so eliminate it as well. Choice D may be tempting, since deleting the phrase would fix the vagueness problem and make the sentence more concise, but when this option is plugged into the sentence, the result is "a simple demonstration of." Since *of* has no object, this is incorrect; eliminate it. Choice (B) clearly and specifically refers to the phi phenomenon, so it is the correct answer.

4. H
Difficulty: Medium
Category: Sentence Structure: The Basics
Getting to the Answer: As written, this sentence has two issues. First, the adjective *quickly* is not parenthetical information and thus should not be set off with commas. Second, two complete sentences cannot be joined with just a comma. Eliminate F. All of the answer choices remove the commas around *quickly*, but J puts no punctuation at all between the two independent clauses; eliminate it. Both dashes and colons can connect two sentences in which the first introduces an explanation in the second, as is the case here. However, G includes a comma after the verb *is*; this separates *is* from its object, which is incorrect. Choice (H) is correct because it fixes the original errors without creating any new ones.

5. D
Difficulty: Low
Category: Sentence Structure: Parenthetical Elements
Getting to the Answer: Parenthetical elements, like the phrase *or frames*, must be set off by matching punctuation, whether commas, dashes, or parentheses. Eliminate A because the punctuation does not match. Eliminate B because only one punctuation mark is present. Eliminate C because it has no punctuation at all. Choice (D) is the only answer to use matching punctuation to set off nonessential information, so it is correct.

6. H
Difficulty: Medium
Category: Conciseness
Getting to the Answer: If the issue in a question is unclear from the underlined portion in the passage, check the answer choices. Here, the original sentence is much wordier than it needs to be. All of the choices preserve the writer's meaning, but the most concise, and therefore correct, choice is (H).

7. A
Difficulty: Medium
Category: Development: Revising Text
Getting to the Answer: First, determine whether the line in question should be deleted. In this case, the phrase is unrelated to the sentence and paragraph it is in, so it should be deleted. Eliminate C and D. Then, check the "Yes" choices for the one that matches your reasoning. Choice (A) matches and is correct.

8. J
Difficulty: High
Category: Agreement: Pronouns
Getting to the Answer: When a pronoun is underlined, check that it is in the correct form and matches the noun it refers to. Here, the pronoun must be plural because it is the *dots* that are lighting up—you can tell because the verb *glow* is plural, so its subject must be the plural *dots* rather than the singular *array*. Eliminate F. *That* is also singular, so eliminate H. *These*, while plural, is not in the correct form to fit in the sentence, so eliminate G. *Them* is plural and in the right form, so (J) is correct.

9. B
Difficulty: Low
Category: Agreement: Verbs
Getting to the Answer: As written, the phrase "that making up the proper picture" is idiomatically incorrect. To fit in the sentence, the verb should be *make*; (B) is correct. Although both C and D would result in an idiomatically correct verb, neither matches the tense of the rest of the paragraph, so both are incorrect.

10. H
Difficulty: High
Category: Sentence Structure: The Basics
Getting to the Answer: As written, this sentence has distorted logic. CRTs are not lighter and thinner than LCDs; CRTs have been replaced by LCDs because *LCDs* are lighter and thinner. The wording of the sentence should reflect this, so eliminate F. Replacing *and* with *because* fixes the logical error but creates a new problem since the clause after *because* has no subject. Eliminate G. Similarly, J creates a run-on by joining two complete sentences with a comma, so eliminate it as well. Choice (H) makes clear that it is the *LCDs* that are thinner and lighter without introducing any new errors; (H) is correct.

11. A
Difficulty: Medium
Category: Conciseness
Getting to the Answer: When the underlined portion seems to be grammatically correct, check the choices to see if there is another issue. Here, the problem is wordiness. Since the sentence discusses filters earlier, B and D are redundant. Choice C is simply unnecessarily wordy. Choice (A) conveys the writer's meaning most concisely, so it is correct.

12. G
Difficulty: Low
Category: Agreement: Modifiers
Getting to the Answer: In this sentence, *quick* is describing the verb *change*, so it should be an adverb rather than an adjective. Eliminate F. *Quickly* is the correct form, so (G) is correct.

Choices H and J are incorrect because nothing is being compared.

13. A
Difficulty: Medium
Category: Sentence Structure: Commas, Dashes, and Colons
Getting to the Answer: This question tests correct comma usage. Eliminate B because the comma separates the verb from the rest of the predicate, which is incorrect. Eliminate D because the comma separates the verb *surpassed* from the subject *these displays*, which is also incorrect. Eliminate C because the main verb of the sentence is set off with commas as if it were unnecessary information, which is not correct. No commas are needed here, so (A) is correct.

14. J
Difficulty: High
Category: Development: Precision
Getting to the Answer: Since the question stem asks for a word that shows quantum dots are *of interest*, look for a choice that means *interesting*. Choice (J) fits well and is correct.

Mysteriously describes something that is unknown; *confusingly* describes something that is not understood; and *secretively* describes something that is deliberately hidden. These things do not necessarily have to be *interesting*, however, so F, G, and H are incorrect.

15. C
Difficulty: Medium
Category: Organization: Sentence Placement
Getting to the Answer: To answer a question like this, look for where the paragraph shifts its focus. The transition word *However* is a good clue, and the sentence continues with "as technology marches on." Furthermore, the sentence immediately before this one describes the liquid crystal filter in LCD televisions. Point C is where the paragraph changes from discussing current television displays to speculating about future ones, so (C) is correct.

Passage II

16. G
Difficulty: Low
Category: Agreement: Idioms
Getting to the Answer: As written, "as prominent than" is idiomatically incorrect. To complete the idiom, the underlined word should be *as*. Choice (G) is correct.

17. A
Difficulty: Low
Category: Agreement: Verbs
Getting to the Answer: To fit with the other verbs in this paragraph, the underlined word should be in simple past tense. It is correct as written, so the correct choice is (A).

Choices B and C are in present tense, so they are incorrect. Choice D may be more tempting, because it uses past tense. However, the helping verb *had* suggests that Tallchief had already achieved fame before some other past event occurred. Because the passage does not mention such an event, D is incorrect as well.

18. G
Difficulty: High
Category: Development: Revising Text
Getting to the Answer: The question asks for information that is both specific and relevant. Neither F nor J is specific, so eliminate them. Choice H, "reading and math," has little to do with Tallchief's dancing studies, so eliminate it. Additionally, the next sentence discusses Tallchief's belief in the importance of "movement and musicality," which parallels nicely with "gymnastics and piano." Choice (G) is correct.

19. C
Difficulty: Medium
Category: Agreement: Modifiers
Getting to the Answer: As written, this sentence has a modifier placement issue. The underlined phrase ought to immediately follow the word it is describing, so think about what word in the sentence "for Tallchief's later belief" logically modifies. Because Tallchief's experiences gave her a *basis for* her belief, (C) is correct. Choices A, B, and D all incorrectly place the underlined phrase so that it modifies a different word in the sentence.

20. H
Difficulty: Medium
Category: Agreement: Verbs
Getting to the Answer: As written, the underlined verb's tense is idiomatically incorrect. This is clear if you remove the phrase "in her teenage years": saying she "resolved *devoted* her life to ballet" is incorrect. Eliminate F. Plug in the remaining choices to see which results in an idiomatically correct tense. Choice J does not provide an acceptable verb form—"resolved *devoting* her life to ballet" is no better than F—so eliminate J. Choice G creates a subordinate clause by introducing the word *that*. The verb *would devote* is in an acceptable tense for this new clause, but it lacks a subject; therefore, G is also incorrect. Choice (H) fixes the tense problem without introducing any new errors, so it is correct.

21. C
Difficulty: Medium
Category: Sentence Structure: Parenthetical Elements
Getting to the Answer: *Soon* is nonessential information that must be set off from the rest of the sentence with punctuation. Because A lacks punctuation after *Soon*, eliminate it. Choice D inserts a dash, but parenthetical elements at the beginning of sentences cannot be set off with dashes, so eliminate D. Choice B correctly uses a comma after *Soon*, but it omits the comma after *inexperience*. Because "despite her relative inexperience" is also parenthetical information that should be separated from the rest of the sentence, B is incorrect. Choice (C) fixes the initial error by inserting a comma after *Soon* and does not create any new issues, so (C) is correct.

22. J
Difficulty: High
Category: Development: Revising Text
Getting to the Answer: Think carefully about which choice would best accomplish the purpose given in the question. The first paragraph states that the most famous ballerinas of the time were Russian, and the first half of this sentence describes how Tallchief refused to "Russify" her name. Dancing in many ballets does not show pressure to imitate Russian ballerinas, so eliminate F. Tallchief might easily have wished to be as skilled as the first ballerina without any external pressure, so eliminate G. Similarly, although the mention of *stress* in H may be tempting, there is no evidence that pressure to imitate others

caused the stress. Eliminate H. Choice (J) fits, showing that although Tallchief did not want to use a Russian version of her name, she did partially alter it when pressured to do so.

23. D
Difficulty: Low
Category: Conciseness
Getting to the Answer: The first part of the sentence states that Balanchine designed ballets with Tallchief in mind, so the phrase "through his designs" is redundant. Eliminate A. Choices B and C are also unnecessarily wordy, so eliminate them also. Choice (D) is the most concise choice and therefore correct.

24. G
Difficulty: Low
Category: Sentence Structure: The Basics
Getting to the Answer: The sentence before the period in the underlined portion is a fragment. It cannot stand alone and needs to be connected to the following sentence, so eliminate F. A semicolon connects two independent clauses, so eliminate H. When a dash is used between two clauses, both must be independent, so J is also incorrect. A comma is used to connect a dependent to an independent clause, so (G) is correct.

25. C
Difficulty: Medium
Category: Development: Precision
Getting to the Answer: While all of the choices could fit grammatically in the sentence, the question specifically asks for one that conveys a sense of success. Choices A, B, and D are all too neutral; *productions, performances,* and *works* can all be successes or failures. *Triumphs* clearly shows that Tallchief and Balanchine achieved success by working together, so (C) is correct.

26. F
Difficulty: Medium
Category: Sentence Structure: Commas, Dashes, and Colons
Getting to the Answer: If you have difficulty identifying the issue by reading the passage, check the choices. This question is focused on punctuation. As written, the sentence has two independent clauses separated by a comma and a FANBOYS conjunction (*but*). This is an acceptable way to join independent

clauses, and since there are no other clauses or parenthetical elements in the underlined portion, no further punctuation is needed. The correct choice is (F).

Choice G is incorrect because it uses a FANBOYS conjunction with no comma. Choice H is incorrect because it uses a FANBOYS conjunction with a colon. Choice J is incorrect because it inserts a colon where one is not needed.

27. D
Difficulty: High
Category: Organization: Transitions
Getting to the Answer: When a transition word or phrase is underlined, check that it accurately illustrates the relationship between the information on either side of it. The previous sentence discusses Tallchief's post-retirement contributions to ballet, and this one describes her as being remembered positively. *In contrast* does not describe this relationship, so eliminate A. *Therefore* may be tempting, but Tallchief is remembered positively for much more than her post-retirement contributions. Additionally, the second part of the sentence describes her as shattering stereotypes, which is the result of her earlier career, not her post-retirement work. Eliminate B. *At last* suggests that Tallchief was not previously appreciated, which contradicts the passage—she became famous in her lifetime, after all. Eliminate C. *Today* matches the chronological flow of the passage from Tallchief's career to her retirement to the present day and indicates that the passage is drawing to a close. The correct choice is (D).

28. H
Difficulty: High
Category: Agreement: Pronouns
Getting to the Answer: When a pronoun is underlined, make sure that it matches the noun it stands in for and that it is in the right form. This pronoun refers to *a woman*, so eliminate G and J, because *that* and *which* cannot be used for people. To distinguish between *who* and *whom*, remember that *whom* is in objective form, like *them* or *her*. Saying "her shattered stereotypes" is incorrect, therefore *whom* is not the correct form to use here. The correct choice is (H), *who.*

29. D
Difficulty: Medium
Category: Organization: Sentence Placement
Getting to the Answer: The words *this ballet* are a clue that this sentence must follow one that discusses a specific ballet. The rest of the sentence shows that it must be one that Tallchief and Balanchine both worked on. Point A in Paragraph 1 follows a sentence about Tallchief's fame, not a particular ballet, so eliminate A. Point B in Paragraph 3 follows a sentence discussing the ballet troupe Tallchief joined but not a specific ballet, so eliminate B. Point C in Paragraph 4 does discuss Balanchine designing ballets for Tallchief, but it does not name a specific one, so eliminate C. Point D in Paragraph 4 would place the new sentence directly after one describing how Tallchief and Balanchine's artistic collaboration resulted in successes like *The Nutcracker*, which fits perfectly; (D) is correct.

30. F
Difficulty: Medium
Category: Development: Purpose
Getting to the Answer: First, identify the main idea of the passage. This passage describes Maria Tallchief's early life and career, as well as how she became famous. This fits with the purpose in the question stem, so eliminate H and J. Although the passage tells about Tallchief achieving international fame as the lead in *The Firebird* (Paragraph 1), both the passage and the question are focused more broadly on her steadily increasing distinction; eliminate G. The correct choice is (F).

Passage III

31. A
Difficulty: Low
Category: Sentence Structure: The Basics
Getting to the Answer: The underlined portion connects two clauses. The word *as* subordinates the second clause, meaning that the clause cannot function as a stand-alone sentence. Eliminate B, which turns the second clause into a fragment. Also eliminate C and D, which are ways of joining two independent clauses. Choice (A) is correct because a comma should be used to join a subordinate clause to an independent clause.

32. H
Difficulty: Low
Category: Agreement: Verbs
Getting to the Answer: Use context to determine the appropriate tense for the underlined verb. In the same sentence as the underline, the verb *recorded* appears in past tense. Therefore, the action described by the underlined verb should also be in the past—something that occurred back in *Stax's heyday*. The simple past tense (H) is correct.

Choice F is incorrect because it is present tense. Choices G and J are incorrect because they use tenses that are too complex for this context. (For the record, G indicates a past action that is complete or continuing into the present time, and J indicates an action that occurred before another past action.)

33. D
Difficulty: Medium
Category: Organization: Transitions
Getting to the Answer: The underlined word *However* indicates a contrast, so determine whether this type of transition is appropriate in context. The previous sentence attributes the *achievements* of Stax to its *musicians*. The sentence with the underline builds on this idea by claiming the musicians were "renowned within the industry for their skill." These ideas do not contrast, so eliminate A. Eliminate the cause-and-effect transition in B because the achievements of the label are not the cause of the musicians' renown. The sentence is not part of a chronological narrative, so eliminate C. Eliminating the transition word, (D), is the only choice that maintains the appropriate logic between the ideas in the paragraph.

34. G
Difficulty: Medium
Category: Sentence Structure: The Basics
Getting to the Answer: As written, the sentence is a fragment. The pronoun *who* turns the phrase "who were underappreciated and underpaid" into a nonessential descriptive phrase. If you were to take out this supposedly nonessential information, the resulting sentence would lack a predicate verb and would not express a complete thought. Eliminate F. Choices H and J also create sentence fragments, since both produce phrases that lack a predicate verb. Choice (G) is correct because it eliminates *who*, thus

turning the verb *were* into the sentence's predicate verb and resulting in a complete sentence.

35. D
Difficulty: Low
Category: Conciseness
Getting to the Answer: The underlined portion repeats the word *dozens* and the answer choices are of varying lengths, so check to see if there is an issue with conciseness. Indeed, repeating *dozens* is unnecessary, as is specifying that the hits were during the era in which the performers recorded them. Eliminate A. Eliminate B, which is even wordier. The phrase *multiple dozen* in C is still redundant. Choice (D) is correct because it most concisely expresses the writer's intended meaning: the performers recorded *many* hits.

36. H
Difficulty: Medium
Category: Sentence Structure: Commas, Dashes, and Colons
Getting to the Answer: The name *Estelle Axton* is essential information that clarifies who is "partial owner and entrepreneur." Essential information should not be set off by commas, so eliminate F and J. There is no reason to include a comma between two nouns joined with an *and*, as in G, so (H) is correct.

37. A
Difficulty: Medium
Category: Development: Revising Text
Getting to the Answer: Consider the relevance of the sentence in the context of the paragraph. The first sentence of the paragraph identifies the topic: Axton running a record store was an additional reason for Stax's success. The sentence in question explains why this was the case: she was able to discover "what would sell and what would not." Choice (A) is correct because it accurately identifies the sentence as an explanation of how the store contributed to Stax's success.

The other choices are incorrect because they do not identify the sentence as support for the paragraph's topic. Furthermore, B and C are incorrect because the sentence provides little background about Axton or teenagers. Choice D is incorrect because the sentence does not counter any previous claim.

38. G
Difficulty: Hard
Category: Development: Introductions and Conclusions
Getting to the Answer: Read the paragraph and paraphrase its main idea before looking at the answer choices. The paragraph begins by mentioning a deal between Stax and Atlantic Records that ended badly. The remainder of the paragraph focuses on what happened to Stax afterward: losing the rights to hit songs, filing bankruptcy, and going through decades of struggle. The paragraph focuses on the decline of Stax, so (G) is correct.

Choice F is incorrect because the paragraph's main focus is Stax, not Atlantic Records. Choice H is incorrect because it focuses too broadly on overall music law. Choice J is incorrect because the paragraph is about Stax's decline, not its success.

39. C
Difficulty: Medium
Category: Conciseness
Getting to the Answer: The underlined phrase contains a redundancy because *downturn* and *decline* mean the same thing in this context. Eliminate A. Check to see which answer choice most concisely conveys the intended meaning. Eliminate B because it is also wordy and redundant in context: the passage has already well established that Stax is in the *music industry*. Choice (C) is correct because it concisely identifies Stax as *declining* using the single descriptive, relevant adjective *devastating*. Choice D is incorrect because it is too informal for the tone of the passage.

40. H
Difficulty: Medium
Category: Agreement: Pronouns
Getting to the Answer: When a pronoun (or sound-alike for a pronoun) is underlined, determine its antecedent to ensure that they match. The underlined word refers to Stax. The record company is a singular entity, so eliminate the plural pronoun *their*, G, and its sound-alike *there*, F. The pronoun should be possessive because the control of the songs belongs to Stax. Choice (H) is correct because it is a singular possessive pronoun. Choice J is the contraction for *it is*.

41. D
Difficulty: Medium
Category: Development: Precision
Getting to the Answer: Analyze the choices to determine which word best indicates that Stax is undergoing a *comeback*—a change from struggle to success. Eliminate A, *floundering*, which indicates struggle only. Choice B, *fledgling*, means something that is young and inexperienced, which does not describe a decades-old music label. Choice C, *outdated*, would mean that Stax is old-fashioned, not that it is achieving new success. Choice (D), *rejuvenated*, means to make new or fresh and thus correctly captures the essence of a comeback.

42. F
Difficulty: Medium
Category: Development: Precision
Getting to the Answer: When the answer choices contain various word choices, first make a prediction for the intended meaning of the underlined word. The sentence describes an *event* at the White House that did something to Memphis soul music. Predict that an event likely had the purpose of positively *featuring* or *celebrating* or *highlighting* the music style. This matches (F), *showcased*.

Music is not usually said to be *supplied*, so G is incorrect. Nothing in the context indicates that Memphis soul music was previously hidden or disunited, so H and J are incorrect.

43. B
Difficulty: Hard
Category: Agreement: Modifiers
Getting to the Answer: The answer choices place the modifying phrase "dedicated to American soul music" in various locations. The phrase describes *a museum*, therefore, it should be adjacent to *a museum*. Eliminate A, in which the phrase describes *the site*, and C, in which the phrase describes "the legendary recording studio." Choice D changes the meaning of the sentence by using *dedicated* to describe *site*. Choice (B) is correct because it places the modifying phrase next to *a museum*.

44. F
Difficulty: Medium
Category: Organization: Sentence Placement
Getting to the Answer: The new sentence begins with the transition word *Indeed,* indicating that the

detail about Southern soul developing at Stax should build upon a related idea in the previous sentence. The new sentence also identifies Stax studio's location in Memphis. Test the potential placements for the sentence to determine where these details logically fit. Choice (F) is correct because the new sentence ties together the ideas before and after Point A. The previous sentence identified Stax's strong influence on rhythm and blues, and the new sentence identifies this type of music as "the sound of Southern soul." The new sentence's detail that the studio was in Memphis identifies the *There* in the sentence that follows Point A.

Choices G and H are incorrect because the new sentence does not match the topics of Paragraphs 3 and 4, which discuss Estelle Axton's contribution to the success of Stax and Stax's decline, respectively. Choice J is incorrect because placing the sentence at Point D would interrupt the discussion of Stax's successes in recent years.

45. C
Difficulty: Hard
Category: Development: Purpose
Getting to the Answer: Paraphrase the main ideas of the essay. The essay begins by describing Stax's role in emerging music styles. The next two paragraphs explain two reasons for Stax's success, and the fourth paragraph describes the label's decline. The final paragraph identifies ways in which Stax has found success in recent years. Although the essay contains references to Stax's contributions to American music styles in the first and last paragraphs, the overall purpose of the essay is to describe the history of the record company; eliminate A and B. Choice (C) is correct because it identifies the actual purpose of the essay. Choice D is incorrect because it provides an incorrect reason; examples of hit songs would not match the purpose of describing Stax's unique contributions to American music styles.

Passage IV

46. H
Difficulty: Medium
Category: Sentence Structure: Parenthetical Elements
Getting to the Answer: Either *Ms. Windham* or some form of "my freshman physics teacher" could be the subject of the sentence. Either phrase by itself would sufficiently specify the person being described, so the

other phrase, if also included, would be parenthetical information added to the sentence to provide additional detail. Keeping in mind that parenthetical elements must be set off by commas, look for the choice that punctuates the phrases correctly. Choice F does set off the phrase *Ms. Windham* with commas, but it is incorrect because it inserts the phrase in the middle of "My freshman teacher of physics" and adds an unnecessary comma after *physics*, separating the subject and verb of the sentence. Choice G fails to use commas to set off the nonessential phrase "my freshman teacher of physics," so it is incorrect. Choice (H) is correct because it sets off the nonessential phrase *Ms. Windham* without adding unneeded punctuation. Choice J introduces the same issues as F, inserting the phrase *Ms. Windham* in an illogical spot and adding a comma between the sentence's subject and verb.

47. A
Difficulty: Medium
Category: Development: Precision
Getting to the Answer: Evaluate the word choices to see which conveys a high level of energy. As written, *sprang* can mean to move suddenly or quickly, which certainly conveys movement with a high level of energy; (A) is correct. Choice B, *twitched*, could describe sudden movement, but the word implies a jerking motion that does not necessarily convey the idea of moving energetically around a classroom. Choice C is incorrect because *sauntered* means to walk slowly, which is the opposite of the intended meaning. Choice D is incorrect because *tottered* means to move unsteadily, not energetically.

48. G
Difficulty: Medium
Category: Agreement: Modifiers
Getting to the Answer: This question is testing two instances of apostrophe usage in possessive modifiers. Evaluate each apostrophe usage separately. In the first instance, the *laws* are those developed by *Newton*, so a possessive apostrophe is appropriate; eliminate H and J. The *gas particles*, however, are not in possession of anything—the prepositional phrase *under pressure* describes the *gas particles*, but the *gas particles* are not in possession of *pressure*. No possessive apostrophe is needed, so (G) is correct.

49. D
Difficulty: Medium
Category: Sentence Structure: The Basics
Getting to the Answer: As written, the sentence is a run-on; two independent clauses (*We were…* and *she moved…*) are joined by only a comma. Eliminate A. Eliminate C as well, which correctly subordinates the first clause by adding the word *as* but incorrectly places a semicolon, which is used to separate independent clauses, between the clauses. Both B and (D) subordinate the first clause and use a comma to separate it from the independent clause, so determine which choice uses the most logical wording in context. B is incorrect because *although* creates a contrast; the writer is not contrasting test-taking and the teacher's actions. Choice (D) is correct because the phrase *even when* emphasizes that the teacher moved even when the students were taking a test.

50. F
Difficulty: Medium
Category: Development: Revising Text
Getting to the Answer: Analyze the context to determine whether "quietly and actively" or "quietly but almost impatiently" makes more sense in context. The topic of the paragraph concerns Ms. Windham and her tendency to keep in motion while teaching. This sentence describes her behavior while students are taking tests, concluding that she acted "as if eager for the class to return to more energetic activities." The paragraph has already established that the teacher is *active* in the classroom, which makes the adverb *actively* redundant. Further, the revision to *but almost impatiently* is in line with the description of the teacher's eagerness at the end of the sentence. The revision should be made, so eliminate H and J. Choice (F) matches the rationale for making the revision, so (F) is correct. Choice G is incorrect because the intent of the revision is not to introduce a negative trait of the teacher. The writer does not mention the teacher's impatience as a criticism, but as an indicator of her eagerness to get the class moving again.

51. D
Difficulty: Medium
Category: Conciseness
Getting to the Answer: When there are no grammatical errors in an underlined portion, consider whether there may be an issue with conciseness. In

context, *infectious* and *contagious* are redundant, so eliminate A. Choices B and C are also unnecessarily wordy ways to express the idea that Ms. Windham's enthusiasm spread to others. For B, *infectious* means the same as "spread from person to person," and for C, *zealous* and *eager* are redundant. Choice (D) is correct because it most concisely conveys the writer's intended meaning.

52. H
Difficulty: Medium
Category: Agreement: Pronouns
Getting to the Answer: When a pronoun is underlined, find its antecedent to determine whether they are in agreement. In this sentence, the pronoun refers to whoever were the "gas particles or the projectiles." The previous sentence provides the context: "Ms. Windham did not want *us* to be sitting for long." The pronoun refers to the group of students that includes the narrator, so eliminate the choices that do not include the narrator, F and G. In context, J is an unnecessarily wordy way of referring to *we*, so J is incorrect. Choice (H) is correct.

53. A
Difficulty: Medium
Category: Sentence Structure: Commas, Dashes, and Colons
Getting to the Answer: A punctuation mark always indicates some kind of break or pause in a sentence. In this example, the phrase "the gas particles or the projectiles" is the object of the verb *were*. There is no reason to insert punctuation within this phrase, so (A) is correct. Using a colon, B, is incorrect because a colon introduces or clarifies information that relates to the previous clause. Using a semicolon, C, is incorrect because a semicolon joins two independent clauses. A pair of dashes, D, may be used around parenthetical information. However, the phrase "or the projectiles" is not parenthetical to the sentence, but rather part of the *or* phrase.

54. G
Difficulty: Medium
Category: Sentence Structure: Parenthetical Elements
Getting to the Answer: As written, the parts of the sentence run together. The phrases "that she and the rest of the science department had constructed" and "a contraption of plywood..." both describe the hovercraft. The lack of punctuation seems to

make *a contraption* the object of *had constructed*, but this creates an illogical sentence. Eliminate F. Look for a choice that includes a comma between the two descriptive phrases; (G) is correct. Choices H and J both separate the phrases at the incorrect spot, inappropriately separating *a contraption* from the prepositional phrase "of plywood and garbage bags..." that follows.

55. D
Difficulty: High
Category: Sentence Structure: Parenthetical Elements
Getting to the Answer: As written, the parts of the sentence run together. Two verbs (*was...would be*) apply to the subject *the top prize*, but there isn't an *and* to correctly set up this compound predicate. Eliminate A. Eliminate B as well; merely placing a comma before the second verb does not correct the original error. Choice C is incorrect because it removes all predicate verbs from the sentence, resulting in a fragment. Choice (D) fixes the error by making the phrase "for a combination of speed and accuracy" parenthetical and deleting the verb *was*, resulting in a sentence with *would be* as the main verb. Choice (D) is correct.

56. H
Difficulty: Low
Category: Agreement: Verbs
Getting to the Answer: When a verb is underlined, always check that it both agrees with its subject and matches the surrounding verb tenses. The paragraph is describing prizes for the upcoming egg drop, so the conditional verbs *would* and *would be* are used in the second and last sentences of the paragraph. Only (H), *would go*, matches the tense of the rest of the paragraph, so (H) is correct.

The other choices do not match the conditional verbs used in the rest of the paragraph: F is past tense, G is present tense, and J is present perfect tense.

57. D
Difficulty: Medium
Category: Organization: Transitions
Getting to the Answer: Because you are asked to make a transition, consider both what was occurring at the end of the previous paragraph and what is happening in this paragraph. The previous paragraph describes the various possible prizes for the egg drop,

and this paragraph begins by stating that the narrator and her partner chose to try to win the *Disaster Miracle* prize. The correct choice should provide a link between the general description of the contest to the narrator's particular experience. This is best accomplished by (D).

None of the other choices provide this transition. Choice A is entirely off-topic. Choice B introduces the day of the egg drop but does not logically fit between sentences about making the choice of which prize to pursue. Choice C connects to ideas later in the last paragraph, but, like B, interrupts the flow of the ideas about the egg drop prizes.

58. J
Difficulty: Medium
Category: Agreement: Pronouns
Getting to the Answer: Make sure that an underlined pronoun both matches its antecedent and is in the correct form. The pronoun here should be possessive, because the "Egg-splorer" belongs to the pronoun. All of the choices are possessive, so now consider the pronoun's antecedent. The previous sentence makes it clear that the Egg-splorer belongs to "My lab partner and I" and uses the pronoun *we*. The underlined pronoun should include both the narrator and the lab partner, so (J) is correct.

Choice F is incorrect because *my* excludes the lab partner. Choice G is incorrect because *their* excludes the narrator. Choice H is incorrect because *whose* would change the structure of the sentence, indicating that the Egg-splorer belongs to the "day of the drop."

59. A
Difficulty: Medium
Category: Organization: Transitions
Getting to the Answer: Consider the sequence of events in the surrounding context to determine which transition phrase is appropriate. The previous sentence describes what happens "the day of the

drop." The sentence with the underline indicates that the photo *still* makes the narrator smile while preparing for college. The transition phrase should link this past event to the present, which is best accomplished by (A).

Choice B is incorrect because *Next* indicates sequential events, which is not appropriate for the timeline described in the passage. Choice C, *in the meantime*, describes two concurrent events. Choice D is incorrect because the author does not make any indication that the photo has only made her smile *so far* and will stop making her smile in the future.

60. G
Difficulty: High
Category: Development: Introductions and Conclusions
Getting to the Answer: Review the main ideas of the essay so you can determine the best conclusion. The first two paragraphs describe the active teaching style of the narrator's physics teacher. The third paragraph describes the annual spring egg drop. The focus of the last paragraph shifts to the narrator's particular experience of winning a prize at the egg drop, including the positive reaction the memory of the event continues to have on the narrator as she prepares for college. The last sentence should synthesize these ideas; (G) is correct because it connects Ms. Windham's teaching to its positive impact on the narrator.

Choice F is incorrect because it focuses too narrowly on photos, which are only referenced in a detail in the previous sentence. Choice H is incorrect because it omits any mention of Ms. Windham's teaching style in the first two paragraphs and any indication of her lasting impact on the narrator. Choice J is incorrect because Ms. Windham's immediate reaction to the egg drops does not logically fit after the narrator's reflection on the photo of the egg drop.

PART 3

ACT MATH

CHAPTER 6

PREREQUISITE SKILLS AND CALCULATOR USE

LEARNING OBJECTIVES

After completing this chapter, you will be able to:

- Identify skills you need to develop to obtain the full benefits of the math sections of this book

- Distinguish ACT questions on which a calculator will be helpful or unhelpful

---

MATH FUNDAMENTALS

LEARNING OBJECTIVE

After this lesson, you will be able to:

- Identify skills you need to develop to obtain the full benefits of the math sections of this book

---

Course Prerequisites

This course focuses on the skills that are tested on the ACT. It assumes a working knowledge of arithmetic, algebra, and geometry. Before you dive into the subsequent chapters, where you'll try test-like questions, there are a number of concepts—ranging from basic arithmetic to geometry—that you should master. The following sections contain a brief review of these concepts.

Order of Operations

The **order of operations** is one of the most fundamental of all arithmetic rules. A well-known mnemonic device for remembering this order is PEMDAS: Please Excuse My Dear Aunt Sally. This translates to Parentheses, Exponents, Multiplication/Division, Addition/Subtraction. Perform multiplication and division from left to right (even if it means division before multiplication) and treat addition and subtraction the same way.

$$(14 - 4 \div 2)^2 - 3 + (2 - 1)$$
$$= (14 - 2)^2 - 3 + (1)$$
$$= 12^2 - 3 + 1$$
$$= 144 - 3 + 1$$
$$= 141 + 1$$
$$= 142$$

Subtracting a positive number is the same as adding its negative. Likewise, subtracting a negative number is the same as adding its positive.

$$r - s = r + (-s) \rightarrow 22 - 15 = 7 \text{ and } 22 + (-15) = 7$$
$$r - (-s) = r + s \rightarrow 22 - (-15) = 37 \text{ and } 22 + 15 = 37$$

Commutative, Associative, and Distributive Properties

Three basic properties of number (and variable) manipulation—commutative, associative, and distributive—will assist you with algebra on test day.

- **Commutative:** Numbers can swap places and still provide the same mathematical result. This is valid only for addition and multiplication.

$$a + b = b + a \rightarrow 3 + 4 = 4 + 3$$
$$a \times b = b \times a \rightarrow 3 \times 4 = 4 \times 3$$

BUT: $3 - 4 \neq 4 - 3$ and $3 \div 4 \neq 4 \div 3$

- **Associative:** Different number groupings will provide the same mathematical result. This is valid only for addition and multiplication.

$$(a + b) + c = a + (b + c) \rightarrow (4 + 5) + 6 = 4 + (5 + 6)$$
$$(a \times b) \times c = a \times (b \times c) \rightarrow (4 \times 5) \times 6 = 4 \times (5 \times 6)$$

BUT: $(4 - 5) - 6 \neq 4 - (5 - 6)$ and $(4 \div 5) \div 6 \neq 4 \div (5 \div 6)$

- **Distributive:** A number that is multiplied by the sum or difference of two other numbers can be rewritten as the first number multiplied by the two others individually. This does not work with division.

$$a(b + c) = ab + ac \rightarrow 6(x + 3) = 6x + 6(3)$$
$$a(b - c) = ab - ac \rightarrow 3(y - 2) = 3y + 3(-2)$$

BUT: $12 \div (6 + 2) \neq 12 \div 6 + 12 \div 2$

Note: When subtracting an expression in parentheses, such as in $4 - (x + 3)$, distribute the negative sign outside the parentheses first: $4 + (-x - 3) \rightarrow 1 - x$.

Prime Factorization

A **prime number** is a positive integer that is divisible without a remainder by only 1 and itself. The number 2 is the smallest prime number and the only even prime number; 1 is not considered prime.

To find the prime factorization of an integer, use a factor tree to keep breaking the integer up into factors until all the factors are prime numbers. To find the prime factorization of 36, for example, you could begin by breaking it into 4×9. Then break 4 into 2×2 and break 9 into 3×3. The prime factorization of 36 is $2 \times 2 \times 3 \times 3$.

Manipulating Fractions

You should be comfortable manipulating both proper and improper fractions.

- To add and subtract fractions, first find a common denominator, then add the numerators together.

$$\frac{2}{3} + \frac{5}{4} \rightarrow \left(\frac{2}{3} \times \frac{4}{4}\right) + \left(\frac{5}{4} \times \frac{3}{3}\right) = \frac{8}{12} + \frac{15}{12} = \frac{23}{12}$$

- Multiplying fractions is straightforward: Multiply the numerators together, then repeat for the denominators. Cancel when possible to simplify the answer.

$$\frac{5}{8} \times \frac{8}{3} = \frac{5}{\overset{}{\underset{1}{8}}} \times \frac{\overset{1}{8}}{3} = \frac{5 \times 1}{1 \times 3} = \frac{5}{3}$$

- Dividing by a fraction is the same as multiplying by its reciprocal. Once you've rewritten a division question as multiplication, follow the rules for fraction multiplication to simplify.

$$\frac{3}{4} \div \frac{3}{2} = \frac{\overset{1}{\cancel{3}}}{\underset{2}{\cancel{4}}} \times \frac{\overset{1}{\cancel{2}}}{\underset{1}{\cancel{3}}} = \frac{1 \times 1}{2 \times 1} = \frac{1}{2}$$

Evaluating Expressions and Equations

Whatever you do to one side of an equation, you must do to the other. For instance, if you multiply one side by 3, you must multiply the other side by 3 as well.

The ability to solve straightforward, one-variable equations is critical on the ACT. Here's an example:

$$\frac{4x}{5} - 2 = 10$$
$$\frac{4x}{5} = 12$$
$$\frac{5}{4} \times \frac{4x}{5} = 12 \times \frac{5}{4}$$
$$x = 15$$

Number Lines

Absolute value refers to the distance a number is from 0 on a number line. Because absolute value is a distance, it is always positive or 0. Absolute value can never be negative.

$$|-17| = 17, |21| = 21, |0| = 0$$

Fraction/Decimal/Percent Conversion

Percent means "out of a hundred." For example, $27\% = \frac{27}{100}$. You can also write percents as decimals, e.g., $27\% = 0.27$.

The ability to recognize a few simple fractions masquerading in decimal or percent form will save you time on test day, as you won't have to turn to your calculator to convert them. Memorize the content of the following table.

Fraction	Decimal	Percent
$\frac{1}{10}$	0.1	10%
$\frac{1}{5}$	0.2	20%
$\frac{1}{4}$	0.25	25%
$\frac{1}{3}$	$0.333\overline{3}$	$33.3\overline{3}\%$
$\frac{1}{2}$	0.5	50%
$\frac{3}{4}$	0.75	75%

You will encounter **irrational numbers**, such as common radicals and π, on test day. You can carry an irrational number through your calculations as you would a variable (e.g., $4 \times \sqrt{2} = 4\sqrt{2}$). Only convert to a decimal when you have finished any intermediate steps and when the question asks you to provide an *approximate* value.

Graphing

Basic two-dimensional graphing is performed on a coordinate plane. There are two axes, x and y, that meet at a central point called the origin. Each axis has both positive and negative values that extend outward from the origin at evenly spaced intervals. The axes divide the space into four sections called quadrants, which are labeled I, II, III, and IV. Quadrant I is always the upper-right section, and the rest follow counterclockwise.

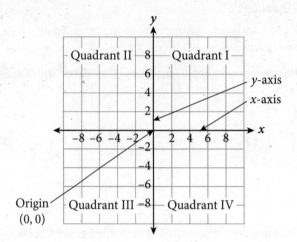

To plot points on the coordinate plane, you need their coordinates. The x-coordinate is where the point falls along the x-axis, and the y-coordinate is where the point falls along the y-axis. The two coordinates together make an ordered pair written as (x,y). When writing ordered pairs, the x-coordinate is always listed first (think alphabetical order). Four points are plotted in the following figure as examples.

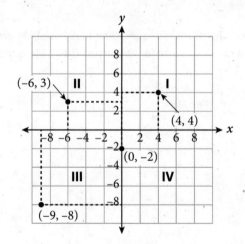

When two points are vertically or horizontally aligned, calculating the distance between them is easy. For a horizontal distance, only the *x*-value changes; for a vertical distance, only the *y*-value changes. Take the positive difference of the *x*-coordinates (or *y*-coordinates) to determine the distance—that is, subtract the smaller number from the larger number so that the difference is positive. Two examples are presented here:

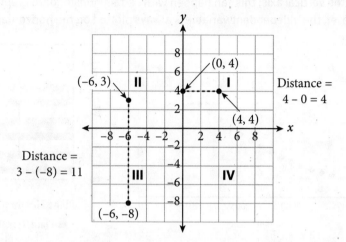

Two-variable equations have an independent variable (input) and a dependent variable (output). The dependent variable (often *y*), depends on the independent variable (often *x*). For example, in the equation $y = 3x + 4$, *x* is the independent variable; any *y*-value depends on what you plug in for *x*. You can construct a table of values for the equation, which can then be plotted.

x	y
−3	−5
−2	−2
−1	1
0	4
1	7
2	10

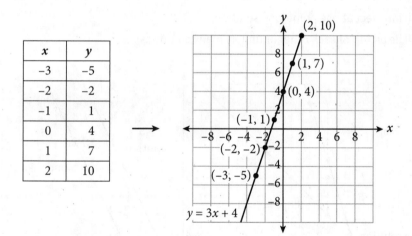

You may be asked to infer relationships from graphs. In the first of the following graphs, the two variables are time and population. Clearly the year does not depend on how many people live in the town; rather, the population increases over time and thus depends on the year. In the second graph, you can infer that plant height depends on the amount of rain; thus, rainfall is the independent variable. Note that the independent variable for the second graph is the vertical axis; this can happen with certain nonstandard graphs. On the standard coordinate plane, however, the independent variable is always plotted on the horizontal axis.

Lines and Angles

When two straight lines are graphed simultaneously, one of three possible scenarios will occur:

- The lines will not intersect at all (no solution).
- The lines will intersect at one point (one solution).
- The lines will lie on top of each other (infinitely many solutions).

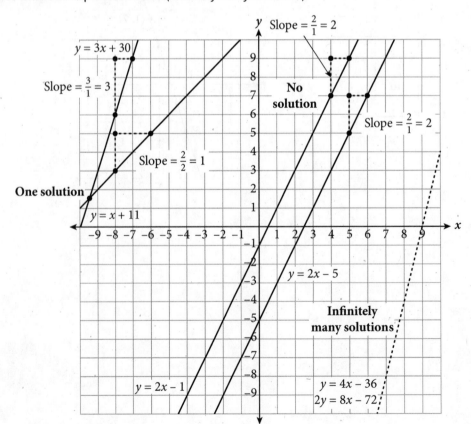

Adjacent angles can be added to find the measure of a larger angle. The following diagram demonstrates this:

Two angles that sum to 90° are called complementary angles. Two angles that sum to 180° are called supplementary angles.

Two distinct lines in a plane will either intersect at one point or extend indefinitely without intersecting. If two lines intersect at a right angle (90°), they are perpendicular and are denoted with ⊥. If the lines never intersect, they are parallel and are denoted with ||.

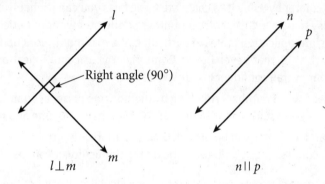

Radius and Diameter

A circle's perimeter is known as its circumference (C) and is found using $C = 2\pi r$, where r is the radius (distance from the center of the circle to its edge). The area of a circle is given by $A = \pi r^2$. The strange symbol is the lower-case Greek letter pi (π, pronounced "pie"), which is approximately 3.14. As mentioned in the algebra section, you should carry π throughout your calculations without rounding unless instructed otherwise.

A tangent line touches a circle at exactly one point and is perpendicular to a circle's radius at the point of contact.

The presence of a right angle opens up the opportunity to draw otherwise hidden shapes, so pay special attention to tangents when they're mentioned.

Simple Counting Techniques

Counting techniques are used to find how many arrangements of something are possible.

When dealing with groups of numbers, keep in mind the **Fundamental Counting Principle**: If an event has m possible outcomes, and another independent event has n possible outcomes, then there are mn ways for the two events to occur together (multiply). You'll know to use this principle when you see phrases like "how many different" or "how many distinct."

Here's a good general strategy to follow:

- Step 1: Draw a blank to represent each position.
- Step 2: Fill in the number of possibilities for each position.
- Step 3: Multiply.

Factorials (!) are sometimes used when counting is happening. A factorial is a term with an exclamation mark following it; the exclamation mark means that instead of just the term shown, you need to calculate the value of term $\times$ (term $-$ 1) $\times$ (term $-$ 2) $\times$ ... $\times$ 1. So, the value of 4! is $4 \times 3 \times 2 \times 1 = 24$. On the ACT, factorials within a fraction are a clue that you can cancel common terms before multiplying.

Mental Math

Even if you're a math whiz, you need to adjust your thought process in regard to the ACT to give yourself the biggest advantage you can. Knowing a few extra things will boost your speed on test day.

- Don't abuse your calculator by using it to calculate basic facts you can probably memorize, such as $15 \div 3$; it's far too easy to type in the incorrect number or operator without noticing. You can save time on test day by reviewing multiplication tables in particular. At a minimum, work up through the 10s. If you know them through 12 or 15, that's even better. Comfort with basic multiplication can go a long way toward improving your overall confidence on test day.

- You can save a few seconds of number crunching by memorizing perfect squares. Knowing perfect squares through 10 is a good start; go for 15 or even 20 if you have the time and motivation.

- Advanced formulas and identities will be provided, but memorizing certain relationships, such as $\cos^2(x) + \sin^2(x) = 1$, could save you valuable time on high-difficulty questions.

If you're comfortable with these concepts, read on for tips on calculator use. If not, frequently review this lesson and remember to refer to it for help if you get stuck in a later chapter.

CALCULATOR USE

LEARNING OBJECTIVE

After this lesson, you will be able to:

- Distinguish ACT questions on which a calculator will be helpful or unhelpful

Calculators and the ACT

Educators and parents believe that calculators serve a role in solving math questions, but they are sometimes concerned that students rely too heavily on calculators. They believe this dependence weakens students' overall ability to think mathematically. While the ACT does have a calculator policy that prohibits some models of calculators, they do allow you to have access to your permissible calculator during the entire ACT Math Test.

However, just because you can use your calculator doesn't mean you should. Many students never stop to ask whether using a calculator is the most efficient way to solve a question. This chapter will show you how the strongest test takers use their calculators strategically; that is, they carefully evaluate when to use the calculator and when to skip it in favor of a more streamlined approach. As you will see, even though you can use a calculator, sometimes it's more beneficial to save your energy by approaching a question more strategically. Work smarter, not harder.

Which Calculator Should You Use?

The ACT allows most four-function, scientific, and graphing calculators, but you should visit ACT's website to confirm your ability to use your usual calculator. Due to the wide range of mathematics topics you'll encounter on test day, we recommend using a graphing calculator, such as the TI-83/84, but remember to confirm that your favorite graphing calculator model isn't prohibited, such as the TI-89.

No matter which calculator you choose, start practicing with it now; you don't want to waste valuable time on test day looking for the exponent button or figuring out how to correctly graph equations. If you don't already own one, see if you can borrow one from your school's math department or a local library.

A graphing calculator's capabilities extend well beyond what you'll need for the test, so don't worry about memorizing every function. The next few pages will cover which calculator functions you'll want to know how to use for the ACT. If you're not already familiar with your graphing calculator, you'll want to get the user manual; you can find this on the internet by searching for your calculator's model number. Identify the calculator functions necessary to answer various ACT Math questions, then write down the directions for each to make yourself a handy study sheet.

When Should You Use a Calculator?

Some ACT question types are designed based on the idea that students will do some or all of the work using a calculator. As a master test taker, you want to know what to look for so you can identify when calculator use is advantageous. Questions involving statistics, determining roots of complicated quadratic equations, and other topics are generally designed with calculator use in mind.

Other questions aren't intentionally designed to involve calculator use. Solving some with a calculator can save you time and energy, but you'll waste both if you go for the calculator on others. You will have to decide which method is best when you encounter the following topics:

- Graphing quadratics and circles
- Simplifying exponents and radicals and calculating roots
- Plane and coordinate geometry

Practicing long computations by hand and with the calculator will not only boost your focus and mental math prowess, but it will also help you determine whether it's faster to do the work for a given question by hand or reach for the calculator on test day.

Graphing quadratic equations may be a big reason you got that fancy calculator in the first place; it makes answering these questions a snap! This is definitely an area where you need to have an in-depth knowledge of your calculator's functions. The key to making these questions easy using the calculator is being meticulous when entering the equation. Also, be aware that some equations, such as the equation of a circle, might be more time-consuming to graph on your calculator than to sketch on paper.

Another stressful area for many students is radicals, especially when the answer choices are written as decimals. Those two elements are big red flags that trigger a reach for the calculator. Beware: not all graphing calculators have a built-in radical simplification function, so consider familiarizing yourself with this process.

Geometry can also be a gray area for students when it comes to calculator use. Consider working by hand when dealing with angles and lines, specifically when filling in information on complementary, supplementary, and congruent angles. You should be able to work fluidly through those questions without using your calculator, but feel free to reach for your calculator when operating on large numbers.

If you choose to use trigonometric functions to get to the answer on triangle questions, make sure you have your calculator set to degrees or radians as required by the question.

To Use or Not to Use?

A calculator is a double-edged sword on the ACT: using one can be an asset for verifying your work if you struggle when doing math by hand, but turning to it for the simplest computations will cost you time that you could devote to more complex questions. Practice solving questions with and without a calculator to get a sense of your personal preference as well as your strengths and weaknesses with and without one. Think critically about when a calculator saves you time and when mental math is faster. Use the exercises in this book to practice your calculations so that by the time test day arrives, you'll be in the habit of using your calculator as effectively as possible!

[CHAPTER 7]

THE METHOD FOR ACT MATH QUESTIONS

LEARNING OBJECTIVE

After completing this chapter, you will be able to:

- Effectively and efficiently apply the ACT Math Method

How to Do ACT Math

ACT Math questions can seem more difficult than they actually are, especially when you are working under time pressure. The method we are about to describe will help you answer ACT Math questions, whether you are comfortable with the math content or not. This method is designed to give you the confidence you need to get the correct answers on the ACT by helping you think through a question logically, one piece at a time.

Take a look at this question and spend a minute thinking about how you would attack it if you saw it on test day.

> A certain television set is discounted 20% on Monday and then discounted another 25% on Tuesday. What is the total percent discount applied to the price of the television on Monday and Tuesday?
>
> A. 22.5%
>
> B. 40%
>
> C. 45%
>
> D. 50%
>
> E. 60%

Many test takers will see a question like this and panic. Others will waste a great deal of time reading and rereading without a clear goal. You want to avoid both of those outcomes.

Start by defining clearly for yourself **what the question is actually asking**. What do the answer choices represent? In this question, they represent total percent discount.

Next, **examine the information** that you have and organize it logically. The question asks about the total percent discount applied to the price of the television on Monday and Tuesday. You are given the percent discount on Monday (20%) and the discount on Tuesday (25%). However, you can't just add the two percents to get the total percent discount. Watch out for C, which is a distractor. You need to use the discounted price on Monday to calculate the discounted price on Tuesday in order to calculate the total percent change.

Now, **make a strategic decision** about how to proceed. You aren't given the original price of the television set, so this is a perfect question for Picking Numbers. When Picking Numbers for percents questions for which the initial value is unknown, you should usually start with 100 to make your calculations easier: pick $100 as the original cost. Then Monday's cost is 80% of that, or $100(0.8) = $80, and Tuesday's cost is 75% of the new amount, or $80(0.75) = $60. The total amount of the discount is $100 − $60 = $40. Now use the percent change formula:

$$\text{percent change} = \frac{\text{new price} - \text{original price}}{\text{original price}} \times 100\%$$

$$= \frac{\$60 - \$100}{\$100} \times 100\%$$

$$= \frac{-\$40}{\$100} \times 100\%$$

$$= -40\%$$

Finally, **confirm** that you answered the right question: you want the total percent discount applied to the price of the television on Monday and Tuesday. Great! You're done; the correct answer is (B).

Here's what we did:

ACT MATH METHOD
Step 1. State what the question is asking
Step 2. Examine the given information
Step 3. Choose your approach
Step 4. Confirm that you answered the right question

You can think of these steps as a series of questions to ask yourself:

1. What do they want?

2. What are they giving me to work with?

3. How should I approach this?

4. Did I answer the right question?

Not all ACT Math questions will require that you spend time on all the steps. The question above required a fair amount of analysis in steps 1 and 2 because it is a word problem. Other questions will require very little thought in steps 1 and 2. Carefully deciding on the appropriate strategy in step 3 will allow you to effectively answer questions. Step 4 is quick, but you should always do it: just make sure you answered the question that was actually asked before you bubble in your response. Doing so will save you from speed mistakes on questions that you know how to do and should be getting credit for.

There are several approaches you can choose from in step 3: Picking Numbers; Backsolving; doing the traditional math; eliminating; or taking a strategic guess.

Note that since the answer choices in the question above were numbers and did not contain variables, you were done once you found a match. However, when using the **Picking Numbers** strategy for questions with variables in the question stem *and* the answer choices, it is always possible that another answer choice can produce the same result, so check all the answer choices to be sure there isn't another match. Choose a number(s) to substitute for the variable(s) in the question and then substitute the same number(s) for the variable(s) in the choices to see which one matches. If there is more than one match, go back and pick another number to distinguish between the choices that match.

When Picking Numbers, use numbers that are permissible and manageable. That is, use numbers that are allowed by the stipulations of the question and that are easy to work with. A small positive integer is usually the best choice in this situation. Here is an example:

Which of the following expressions will produce an odd number for any integer a?

F. a^2

G. $a^2 + 1$

H. $a^2 + 2$

J. $2a^2 + 1$

K. $3a^2 + 1$

Step 1: What do they want? The choice that is always odd.

Step 2: What do they give you? a is any integer.

Step 3: What approach will you use?

Rather than trying to think this one through abstractly, it may be easier to Pick Numbers for a. The question states that a is any integer, so it could be even or odd. Try an even value for a. Let $a = 2$ and plug the value into the answer choices. Eliminate choices that are not odd:

Choice F: $a^2 = 2^2 = 4$ Eliminate.

Choice G: $a^2 + 1 = 2^2 + 1 = 5$ Keep.

Choice H: $a^2 + 2 = 2^2 + 2 = 6$ Eliminate.

Choice (J): $2a^2 + 1 = 2(2)^2 + 1 = 9$ Keep.

Choice K: $3a^2 + 1 = 3(2)^2 + 1 = 13$ Keep.

Choices G, (J), and K all give an odd result. Go back and try an odd value for a, like 3, for the remaining choices.

Choice G: $a^2 + 1 = 3^2 + 1 = 10$ Eliminate.

Choice (J): $2a^2 + 1 = 2(3)^2 + 1 = 19$ Keep.

Choice K: $3a^2 + 1 = 3(3)^2 + 1 = 28$ Eliminate.

Only (J) is odd for any integer a, so (J) is correct.

In the next example, you'll see Backsolving in action:

A physics midterm has 60 questions. The test is scored as follows: for each correct answer, 2 points are awarded; for each incorrect answer, $\frac{2}{3}$ of a point is subtracted; for unanswered questions, points are neither added nor subtracted. If Denise scored a 68 and did not answer 2 of the questions, how many questions did she answer correctly?

A. 34

B. 36

C. 38

D. 40

E. 42

Step 1: What do they want? The number of questions Denise answered correctly.

Step 2: What do they give you? The total number of questions answered ($60 - 2 = 58$), the number of points for correct (2) and incorrect $\left(-\frac{2}{3}\right)$ answers, and Denise's midterm score (68).

Step 3: What approach will you use?

Here's a chance to practice Backsolving: plug the choices in for the unknown and see which one works. It often makes sense to start with C/H when you can tell from the context whether you'll need a larger or smaller answer choice if the one you're testing fails. If the question asks for the smallest or largest value, start with A/F or E/K.

For this question, start with the middle answer choice, C. If Denise answered 38 of the questions correctly and skipped 2, then she answered $60 - 38 - 2 = 20$ questions incorrectly. She gets 2 points for every correct question and loses $\frac{2}{3}$ of a point for every incorrect question, so do the calculations to determine her total points:

$$38(2) - 20\left(\frac{2}{3}\right) = 76 - \frac{40}{3}$$
$$= \frac{228}{3} - \frac{40}{3}$$
$$= \frac{188}{3}$$
$$= 62\frac{2}{3}$$

This is too low, so eliminate both A and B, and try the next-largest choice: 40. If Denise answered 40 questions correctly, she earned $40(2) - 18\left(\frac{2}{3}\right) = 80 - 12 = 68$ points.

Step 4: Did you solve for the right thing? You found the number of questions Denise answered correctly to earn a score of 68 points, so yes. Choice (D) is the correct answer. You do not need to evaluate the other answer choices.

Here's an example using the Elimination strategy.

Suppose line *PQ* is perpendicular to line *RS* and *Q* is a point on line *RS*. If *L* is in the interior of ∠*PQS*, which of the following could be the measure of ∠*LQR* ?

F. 110°

G. 90°

H. 70°

J. 50°

K. 30°

Step 1: What do they want? The measure of ∠*LQR*.

Step 2: What do they give you? *PQ* is perpendicular to *RS* and *Q* is a point on *RS*. *L* is in the interior of ∠*PQS*.

Step 3: What approach will you use?

When the question does not provide a figure, draw one yourself.

Because lines *PQ* and *RS* are perpendicular, ∠*PQR* must form a 90° angle. If point *L* is in the interior of ∠*PQS*, the measure of ∠*LQR* must be greater than 90°. You can eliminate all choices that are less than or equal to 90°. Only (F) is greater than 90°, so it is correct.

Step 4: Did you solve for the right thing? You found the measure of ∠*LQR*, so yes. Choose (F) and move on.

Now it's your turn. Be deliberate with the questions in the next section. If there is analysis to do up front, do it. If there is more than one way to do a question, consider carefully before choosing your approach, and be sure to check whether you answered the right question. Forming good habits now, in slow and careful practice, will set you up for confidence on test day.

How Much Have You Learned?

Directions: Take as much time as you need on these questions. Work carefully and methodically. There will be opportunities for timed practice in future chapters.

1. Let z equal $3x - 2y + 1$. If the value of x is increased by 2 and the value of y is decreased by 3, what will happen to the value of z?

    A. It will decrease by -13.
    B. It will decrease by -12.
    C. It will be unchanged.
    D. It will increase by 12.
    E. It will increase by 13.

2. Deepa scored 150, 195, and 160 in 3 bowling games. What should she score on her next bowling game if she wants to have an average score of exactly 175 for the 4 games?

    F. 205
    G. 195
    H. 185
    J. 175
    K. 165

3. Which of the following is the graph for the function defined below?

    $$f(x) = \begin{cases} x^2 + 1 & \text{for} \quad x \leq 2 \\ x - 4 & \text{for} \quad 2 < x < 6 \\ 2 - x & \text{for} \quad x \geq 6 \end{cases}$$

    A.

    B.

    C.

    D.

    E.

Use the following information to answer questions 4–5.

A scientist measured all of the trees in an area that was once a waste dump and is now being returned to nature. The scientist made the following histogram to show the heights of the trees.

4. Which range of heights contains the median of the data?

F. 0–4

G. 5–9

H. 10–14

J. 15–19

K. Cannot be determined from the given information

5. The scientist decides to present the data in a circle graph (pie chart). To the nearest degree, what is the measure of the central angle of the sector for 15–19?

A. 16°

B. 31°

C. 47°

D. 94°

E. 157°

6. On the number line below, point G is the midpoint of FH and $HJ = JK$. If $HK = 18$, what is the length of GJ?

F. 13

G. 18

H. 22

J. 26

K. 31

7. What is the period of the function $f(x) = 2\sin(3x - \pi)$?

A. $\dfrac{\pi}{3}$

B. $\dfrac{\pi}{2}$

C. $\dfrac{2\pi}{3}$

D. $\dfrac{5\pi}{6}$

E. π

8. In 1992, the cost of a school lunch was \$1.20. In 2017, the cost of a school lunch was \$2.90. Assuming the cost increased linearly, what was the cost of a school lunch in 2002?

F. \$1.30

G. \$1.52

H. \$1.70

J. \$1.88

K. \$2.20

Math

9. Viktor owns a car dealership. The numbers of different types of vehicles on his car lot are given in the following table. If a vehicle is selected at random, what is the probability that it is NOT a luxury vehicle or SUV?

Vehicle type	Number on lot
Subcompact	64
Compact	35
Midsize	61
Full-size	58
Luxury	32
SUV	43
Truck	27
Total	320

A. $\dfrac{7}{32}$

B. $\dfrac{15}{64}$

C. $\dfrac{101}{320}$

D. $\dfrac{49}{64}$

E. $\dfrac{7}{8}$

10. If the sum of five consecutive even integers is equal to their product, what is the greatest of the five integers?

F. 4

G. 10

H. 14

J. 16

K. 20

Reflect

Directions: Take a few minutes to recall what you've learned and what you've been practicing in this chapter. Consider the following questions, jot down your best answer for each one, and then compare your reflections to the expert responses on the following page. Use your level of confidence to determine what to do next.

1. Think about your current habits when attacking ACT questions. Are you a strategic test taker? Do you take the time to think through what would be the fastest way to the answer?

    _____

    _____

    _____

2. Do word problems give you trouble? If so, what can you do?

    _____

    _____

3. What are the steps of the ACT Math Method, and why is each step important?

    _____

    _____

    _____

Responses

1. Think about your current habits when attacking ACT questions. Are you a strategic test taker? Do you take the time to think through what would be the fastest way to the answer?

If yes, good for you! If not, we recommend doing questions more than one way whenever possible as part of your ACT prep. If you can discover now, while you're still practicing, that Picking Numbers is faster for you on certain types of questions but not on others, you'll be that much more efficient on test day.

2. Do word problems give you trouble? If so, what can you do?

If word problems are difficult for you, get into the habit of taking an inventory, before you do any math, of what the question is asking for and what information you have.

3. What are the steps of the ACT Math Method, and why is each step important?

Here are the steps:

   Step 1. *State what the question is asking*

   Step 2. *Examine the given information*
   (Taking an inventory is especially important in word problems.)

   Step 3. *Choose your approach*
   (Taking a moment to decide what approach will be the fastest way to the answer will ultimately save you time.)

   Step 4. *Confirm that you answered the right question*
   (Making sure you solved for the right thing will save you from losing points to speed mistakes on questions that you know how to do and should be getting credit for.)

Next Steps

If you answered most questions correctly in the "How Much Have You Learned?" section, and if your responses to the Reflect questions were similar to those of the ACT expert, then consider the ACT Math Method an area of strength and move on to the next chapter. Do keep using the method as you work on the questions in future chapters.

If you don't yet feel confident, review those parts of this chapter that you have not yet mastered, and try the questions you missed again. As always, be sure to review the explanations closely. Then go online (**kaptest.com/login**) to watch a video about the Kaplan Method for ACT Math and use your Qbank for more practice. If you haven't already registered your book, do so at **kaptest.com/moreonline.**

GO ONLINE

kaptest.com/login

Answers and Explanations

1. D
Difficulty: Medium
Category: Number and Quantity
Getting to the Answer: The question asks for the value of z after x is increased by 2 and y is decreased by 3. You are given $z = 3x - 2y + 1$. The new value of x is $x + 2$ and the new value of y is $y - 3$. Substitute these new values into the expression, $3x - 2y + 1$, to find the new value of z: $3(x + 2) - 2(y - 3) + 1$. This gives $3x + 6 - 2y + 6 + 1$, which equals $3x - 2y + 13$. Since z is $3x - 2y + 1$, the expression in terms of z is $(3x - 2y + 1) + 12$. Thus, the value of z will increase by 12. You found the change in z. (D) is correct.

Alternatively, you could Pick Numbers for x and y. If $x = 1$ and $y = 2$, then $z = 3(1) - 2(2) + 1 = 0$. Increasing x by 2 and decreasing y by 3 gives $x + 2 = 1 + 2 = 3$ and $y - 3 = 2 - 3 = -1$. Thus, the new value of z is $3(3) - 2(-1) + 1 = 9 + 2 + 1 = 12$. The change is $12 - 0 = 12$. Since the change is positive, z will increase by 12. This matches (D).

2. G
Difficulty: Medium
Category: Statistics and Probability
Getting to the Answer: The question asks what score a bowler must get for her next game to attain an average score of 175 for 4 games, and gives the scores of her first 3 games. The average of a group of numbers is the sum of the values divided by the number of values. You can either set up an equation involving the missing score or use Backsolving to plug each of the possible scores into the question stem to see which one works.

Backsolving is often a great way to solve questions about averages, especially ones that give you the average and ask for a missing number. If you Backsolve, remember to start with the middle number:

Choice H: $\dfrac{150 + 195 + 160 + 185}{4} = \dfrac{690}{4} = 172.5$

Too low? Try the next-largest number:

Choice (G): $\dfrac{150 + 195 + 160 + 195}{4} = \dfrac{700}{4} = 175$

Choice (G) is correct.

To answer the question algebraically, call the missing score x and set up the average equation:

$$\dfrac{150 + 195 + 160 + x}{4} = 175$$
$$505 + x = 700$$
$$x = 195$$

This approach also shows that (G) is correct.

Alternatively, if you know how to use the balance approach for averages, you could determine that the 150 score was 25 less than the desired average, the 195 score was 20 greater, and the 160 score was 15 less, for a total of 20 less. Thus, the fourth score would need to be $175 + 20 = 195$ to raise the average to 175. Remember, step 3 is all about figuring out which approach works best for you, so be sure to practice approaching questions in multiple ways.

3. E
Difficulty: Medium
Category: Functions
Getting to the Answer: The question asks which of the graphs in the choices correctly shows the piecewise function given. To identify which graph matches the piecewise-defined function, evaluate each piece of the function for the given domain.

When $x \leq 2$, the function is $f(x) = x^2 + 1$. This is an upward-facing parabola since the coefficient of x^2 is positive. Eliminate A and B. An easy point to evaluate is $x = 0$, at which point $f(0) = 1$. Eliminate C.

Evaluate the next piece of the function, $f(x) = x - 4$. Note that the domain of this piece of the function is $2 < x < 6$, which matches (E). Graph D does not match since the domain of the line $x - 4$ is $-2 < x < 6$. There is no need to consider the third piece of the function.

4. G
Difficulty: Medium
Category: Statistics and Probability
Getting to the Answer: The question asks which range of the histogram contains the median value. The median of a set of data is the middle value when the data is written in ascending order. This means that half of the data is less than the median and half is greater.

The total number of data values is the sum of the number of trees in each group: $300 + 1,000 + 600 + 200 + 100 + 100 = 2,300$. Half of that is 1,150.

From left to right, the first bar contains 300 data values and the second bar contains 1,000 more, for a total of 1,300 data values. The middle value for all the data must therefore lie within the interval represented by the second bar, making (G) correct. Note that it is not possible to determine the exact median, only the interval within which it lies. Be certain that you used the correct total when determining the median.

5.   B
Difficulty: Medium
Category: Geometry
Getting to the Answer: The question asks what the central angle of the 15–19 range would be if the same data were shown as a circle graph. According to the histogram, approximately 200 trees are in the 15–19 group. The total number of trees is the sum of the number of trees in each group: $300 + 1,000 + 600 + 200 + 100 + 100 = 2,300$. Thus, the fraction of trees that is in the 15–19 group is $\frac{200}{2,300} = \frac{2}{23}$.

Since there are $360°$ in a circle, to find the measure of the central angle of the sector for the 15–19 group, multiply $360°$ by the fraction above: $360°\left(\frac{2}{23}\right) = 31.3°$. Choice (B) is correct; the number of values in the range is slightly more than $\frac{1}{12}$th of the total number of values, and $31°$ is slightly more than $\frac{1}{12}$th of $360°$.

6.   H
Difficulty: Medium
Category: Number and Quantity
Getting to the Answer: The question asks for the length of segment GJ on the line segment shown. Point G bisects segment FH and point J bisects segment HK. The length of FG is 13 and the length of HK is 18.

Since G is the midpoint of FH, $GH = FG = 13$. Also, since $HK = 18$ and $HJ = JK$, $HJ = JK = 9$. Line segment $GJ = GH + HJ$, which is $13 + 9 = 22$. The correct choice is (H). Check that you answered the question that was asked; G is HK, J is FH, and K is GK.

7.   C
Difficulty: High
Category: Functions
Getting to the Answer: The question asks for the period of the function $2\sin(3x - \pi)$. Recall that the period of sin, cos, sec, and csc graphs is 2π, which means that the function values repeat themselves every full rotation around a circle, which is 2π radians.

For the general function $a\sin(bx - c) + d$, a affects the amplitude or vertical stretch, b affects the period or horizontal stretch, b and c together affect the horizontal shift, and d affects the vertical shift.

Since only b affects the period, you can think of this function as just $\sin(3x)$. Multiplying the value inside the parentheses "speeds up" the process of completing the full circle, which shortens the period and results in a horizontal contraction. Thus, multiplying the x by 3 means that the function will cycle through its values 3 times as quickly as $\sin(x)$. The function will make three cycles every 2π radians, or one cycle every $\frac{2\pi}{3}$ radians. Choice (C) is correct.

8.   J
Difficulty: Medium
Category: Algebra
Getting to the Answer: The question asks for the cost of a school lunch in 2002. You are given the costs in 1992 and 2017 and the fact that the cost increased linearly during that time span. Since the cost increased linearly, determine the constant rate at which the cost of a school lunch increased per year. The constant rate, or slope, is $\frac{\$2.90 - \$1.20}{2017 - 1992} = \frac{\$1.70}{25} = \$0.068$ per year. Thus, the cost in 2002 (10 years after 1992) is $\$1.20 + \$0.068(10) = \$1.88$. Choice (J) is correct.

9.   D
Difficulty: Medium
Category: Statistics and Probability
Getting to the Answer: The question asks for the probability that a vehicle selected at random from the cars shown in the table will not be either a luxury vehicle or an SUV. Recall the fundamental probability formula: $\text{probability} = \frac{\#\,\text{desired outcomes}}{\#\,\text{total outcomes}}$. Also remember that the probability of an event NOT occurring is 1 minus the probability of that event occurring. Since calculating the probability of selecting a luxury vehicle or SUV involves less number-crunching, determine that probability and then subtract it from 1 to find the probability of NOT selecting a luxury vehicle or SUV:

Viktor has 320 cars in his lot. The probability of selecting a luxury vehicle or SUV is $\frac{32 + 43}{320} = \frac{75}{320} = \frac{15}{64}$.
Thus, the probability of NOT selecting a luxury vehicle or SUV is $1 - \frac{15}{64} = \frac{64}{64} - \frac{15}{64} = \frac{49}{64}$. Choice (D) is correct.

10. F

Difficulty: Medium

Category: Number and Quantity

Getting to the Answer: The question asks for the greatest of five consecutive even integers whose product is equal to their sum. First, put the question into words you can more easily understand. It says that when you add up the five consecutive even integers, you get the same thing as when you multiply them. The word *even* tells you that the difference between each integer in the sequence is 2. Finally, the answer choices themselves represent numbers that could be the final term of this sequence.

You could model the situation with an equation: $x + (x-2) + (x-4) + (x-6) + (x-8) = x(x-2)(x-4)(x-6)(x-8)$. However, that's a very difficult equation to solve algebraically; try Backsolving instead. The question asks for the greatest of the integers, so you have to start with the greatest answer choice, K. If you start with any other, you won't know whether it's the largest, even if it works.

Choice K: $20 + 18 + 16 + 14 + 12 = 80$. Unfortunately, $20 \times 18 \times 16 \times 14 \times 12$ is way too big. Try H. If H is too small, then J is correct.

Choice H: $14 + 12 + 10 + 8 + 6 = 50$. The product $14 \times 12 \times 10 \times 8 \times 6$ is still way too big! Jump to (F); if it is too small, then G must be the correct answer.

Choice (F): $4 + 2 + 0 + (-2) + (-4) = 0$ and the product $4 \times 2 \times 0 \times -2 \times -4 = 0$.

Choice (F) is correct.

CHAPTER 8

NUMBER AND QUANTITY

LEARNING OBJECTIVES

After completing this chapter, you will be able to:

- Apply exponent rules
- Add, subtract, multiply, and divide numbers written in scientific notation
- Apply radical rules
- Solve absolute value equations
- Identify a specific term in an arithmetic or geometric sequence
- Perform arithmetic operations on imaginary and complex numbers
- Perform arithmetic operations using matrices

Number and Quantity: 8/36 SmartPoints® (Very high yield)

How Much Do You Know?

Directions: Try out the questions below. Show your work so that you can compare your solutions to the ones found on the next page. The "Category" heading in the explanation for each question gives the title of the lesson that covers how to solve it. If you answered the question(s) for a given lesson correctly, and if your scratchwork looks like the explanations, you may be able to move quickly through that lesson. If you answered incorrectly or used a different approach, you may want to take your time on that lesson.

1. What is the value of $\dfrac{10^5 \times 100^7}{1{,}000^6}$?

   A.   1
   B.   10
   C.   100
   D.   1,000
   E.   10,000

2. Which of the following is equivalent to $\sqrt{24} + \sqrt{150}$?

   F. $\sqrt{174}$
   G. $7\sqrt{6}$
   H. $29\sqrt{6}$
   J. $36\sqrt{7}$
   K. $36\sqrt{29}$

3. If $x = 4$, evaluate $\left|\dfrac{x-8}{2x+2}\right|$.

   A. $-\dfrac{1}{2}$
   B. $-\dfrac{2}{5}$
   C. $\dfrac{2}{5}$
   D. $\dfrac{1}{2}$
   E. $\dfrac{3}{4}$

4. If the first term in a geometric sequence is 4 and the third term is 100, what is the common ratio (r)?

   F.   3
   G.   4
   H.   5
   J.   6
   K.   7

5. Write $(3i + 4) - (5i + 3)$ in $a + bi$ form.

   A. $1 - 2i$
   B. $7 - 2i$
   C. $7 + 8i$
   D. $5 + 2i$
   E. $4 - 5i$

Answers and explanations are on the next page. ▶ ▶ ▶

Check Your Work

1. B
Difficulty: Low
Category: Number and Quantity: Exponents
Getting to the Answer: To perform the arithmetic efficiently, begin by rewriting every term in the expression as 10 raised to some power:

$$\frac{10^5 \times (10^2)^7}{(10^3)^6}$$

Apply exponent rules and simplify. Remember that when you divide, you subtract the exponents, and when you raise one exponent to another, you multiply:

$$\frac{10^5 \times 10^{14}}{10^{18}} = \frac{10^{19}}{10^{18}} = 10^{19-18} = 10$$

Therefore, (B) is correct.

2. G
Difficulty: Low
Category: Number and Quantity: Radicals
Getting to the Answer: Simplify each radical by looking for two numbers that multiply to equal the radicand (the number under the radical sign). Numbers that are perfect squares are optimal. Then combine like terms:

$$\sqrt{24} + \sqrt{150}$$
$$\sqrt{4}\sqrt{6} + \sqrt{25}\sqrt{6}$$
$$2\sqrt{6} + 5\sqrt{6}$$
$$7\sqrt{6}$$

Choice (G) is correct.

3. C
Difficulty: Low
Category: Number and Quantity: Absolute Value
Getting to the Answer: You need to find the value of the expression. To do so, plug in the value for x and simplify.

Remember that the final answer is positive since the entire expression is inside absolute value brackets:

$$\left|\frac{(4)-8}{2(4)+2}\right| = \left|\frac{-4}{10}\right|$$
$$= \frac{4}{10}$$
$$= \frac{2}{5}$$

Choice (C) is correct.

4. H
Difficulty: Medium
Category: Number and Quantity: Sequences
Getting to the Answer: The question asks for the common ratio in a sequence. Since the sequence is geometric, you multiply each term by some constant (r) to get to the next term. The best way to solve this question is to plug in the answer. Since the first and third terms of the sequence are given, multiply the first term by the common ratios given in the answer choices twice. Whichever one results in 100 is the correct answer.

F) $4 \times 3 \times 3 = 36$
G) $4 \times 4 \times 4 = 64$
H) $4 \times 5 \times 5 = 100$

You can stop here: (H) is correct.

5. A
Difficulty: Low
Category: Number and Quantity: Imaginary Numbers
Getting to the Answer: Combine like terms, being careful to distribute the negative on the outside of the parentheses.

$$(3i + 4) - (5i + 3)$$
$$3i + 4 - 5i - 3$$
$$-2i + 1$$
$$1 - 2i$$

Choice (A) is correct.

EXPONENTS

To answer a question like this:

Which of the following is equivalent to $\dfrac{(3.0 \times 10^4)(8.0 \times 10^9)}{1.2 \times 10^6}$?

A. 2.0×10^5

B. 2.0×10^6

C. 2.0×10^7

D. 2.0×10^8

E. 2.0×10^9

You need to know this:

Exponents

Rule	Example
When multiplying two terms with the same base, add the exponents.	$a^b \times a^c = a^{(b+c)} \rightarrow 4^2 \times 4^3 = 4^{(2+3)} = 4^5$
When dividing two terms with the same base, subtract the exponents.	$\dfrac{a^b}{a^c} = a^{(b-c)} \rightarrow \dfrac{4^3}{4^2} = 4^{(3-2)} = 4^1$
When raising a power to another power, multiply the exponents.	$(a^b)^c = a^{(bc)} \rightarrow (4^3)^2 = 4^{(3\times2)} = 4^6;$ $(y^2)^3 = y^{(2\times3)} = y^6$
When raising a product to a power, apply the power to all factors in the product.	$(2m)^3 = 2^3 \times m^3 = 8m^3$
Any nonzero term raised to the zero power equals 1.	$a^0 = 1 \rightarrow 4^0 = 1$
A base raised to a negative exponent can be rewritten as the reciprocal raised to the positive of the original exponent.	$a^{-b} = \dfrac{1}{a^b} \rightarrow 4^{-2} = \dfrac{1}{4^2};$ $\dfrac{1}{a^{-b}} = a^b \rightarrow \dfrac{1}{5^{-3}} = 5^3$
A negative number raised to an even exponent will produce a positive result; a negative number raised to an odd exponent will produce a negative result.	$(-2)^4 = 16$, but $(-2)^3 = -8$

Math

Scientific Notation

Scientific notation is used to express very large or very small numbers.

- A number written in scientific notation is a number that is greater than or equal to 1, but less than 10, raised to a power of 10.
  - 3.64×10^8 is written in scientific notation, while 36.4×10^7 is not.
  - The two numbers are equivalent, but the second doesn't meet the definition of scientific notation because 36.4 is not between 1 and 10.
- To write a number in scientific notation, move the decimal point (to the right or to the left) until the number is between 1 and 10.
  - Count the number of places you moved the decimal point—this tells you the power of 10 that you'll need.
  - If the original number was a tiny decimal number (which means you had to move the decimal to the right), the exponent will be negative.
  - If the original number was a large number (which means you had to move the decimal point to the left), the exponent will be positive.
- You can add and subtract numbers written in scientific notation as long as the power of 10 in each term is the same; simply add (or subtract) the numbers and keep the same power of 10.
- You can multiply and divide numbers written in scientific notation using rules of exponents; simply multiply (or divide) the numbers and add (or subtract) the powers of 10.

You need to do this:

- Identify the appropriate rule by looking at the operation.
- Apply the rule.
- Repeat as necessary.

Straightforward ACT exponent questions should be quick points, but it's more likely you'll apply exponent rules as one step in solving a medium or high-difficulty question. Make sure you memorize the rules in the table on the previous page before test day.

Explanation:

You'll need several exponent rules to answer the scientific notation question at the beginning of this lesson. Work through this question slowly and methodically.

First, simplify the numerator by multiplying the 3.0 and 8.0: $3 \times 8 = 24.0$. Then, determine the product of 10^4 and 10^9 by adding the exponents: $10^4 \times 10^9 = 10^{(4+9)} = 10^{13}$. Now, the numerator has a value of 24.0×10^{13}.

Since the values in both the numerator and the denominator are being multiplied, you can simplify the fraction by dividing the similar terms. First, divide the first terms of the expressions: $24.0 \div 1.2 = 20.0$. To find the value of $10^{13} \div 10^6$, subtract the exponents: $10^{(13-6)} = 10^7$. Combine these terms: 20.0×10^7.

Finally, convert the result into standard scientific notation. All of the choices start with 2.0, so factor out 10 from the first term ($20.0 \div 10 = 2.0$) and multiply the second term (10^7) by that 10, which can also be written as 10^1:

$$\frac{(3.0 \times 10^4)(8.0 \times 10^9)}{1.2 \times 10^6} = \frac{24.0 \times 10^{13}}{1.2 \times 10^6}$$
$$= 20.0 \times 10^7$$
$$= 2.0 \times 10^7 \times 10^1$$
$$= 2.0 \times 10^8$$

Therefore, (D) is correct.

Drills

If exponents or scientific notation gives you trouble, study the information above and try out these drill questions before completing the Try on Your Own questions below. Simplify each expression, and if the answer involves numbers only, write your answer in scientific notation. Drill answers can be found in Answers and Explanations.

a. $820,000,000 + 500,000,000$

b. $(3.5 \times 10^5) \times (4.0 \times 10^3)$

c. $\dfrac{4.2 \times 10^8}{2.0 \times 10^5}$

d. $x^4 \times x^3$

e. $\dfrac{y^{10}}{y^4}$

Try on Your Own

Directions: Take as much time as you need on these questions. Work carefully and methodically. There will be an opportunity for timed practice at the end of the chapter.

1. What is the value of $\dfrac{3,200,000 - 2,300,000}{3,000}$?

   A. 3.0×10^2
   B. 3.0×10^3
   C. 3.0×10^4
   D. 3.0×10^5
   E. 3.0×10^6

2. Simplify $\dfrac{z^9 y^4 x^6}{x y^6 z^3}$.

   F. $\dfrac{y^2}{xz^6}$
   G. $\dfrac{x^5 z^6}{y^2}$
   H. $\dfrac{z^8 x^3}{y^2}$
   J. $\dfrac{y^2}{z^8 x^3}$
   K. $z^8 y^2 x^3$

3. Evaluate $\dfrac{(2.0 \times 10^4)(6.0 \times 10^7)}{4.0 \times 10^2}$ and write in scientific notation.

   A. 3.0×10^8
   B. 3.0×10^9
   C. 3.5×10^8
   D. 4.0×10^8
   E. 4.0×10^9

4. Which of the following is equivalent to $\dfrac{a^{-7} c^2 b^{-4}}{b^2 c^{-3} a^{-3}}$?

   F. $\dfrac{c^5}{a^4 b^6}$
   G. $\dfrac{a^{-10} b^{-4}}{c^5}$
   H. $\dfrac{a^{10} b^6}{c^5}$
   J. $\dfrac{c^{-5}}{a^{-10} b^{-6}}$
   K. $\dfrac{a^5 b}{c}$

HINT: For Q5, remember the definition of scientific notation. What must be true about the first part?

5. Write $\dfrac{2.1 \times 10^{-12}}{(2.0 \times 10^4)(5.0 \times 10^3)}$ in scientific notation.

   A. 0.21×10^{-4}
   B. 0.21×10^{-5}
   C. 2.1×10^{-6}
   D. 2.1×10^{-19}
   E. 2.1×10^{-20}

RADICALS

LEARNING OBJECTIVE

After this lesson, you will be able to:

- Apply radical rules

To answer a question like this:

Which of the following expressions is equivalent to $\dfrac{4x}{10 - \sqrt{5}}$?

A. $\dfrac{40x + 4x\sqrt{5}}{95}$

B. $\dfrac{40x + 4x\sqrt{5}}{105}$

C. $\dfrac{44x - 77}{95}$

D. $\dfrac{44x - 77}{105}$

E. $\dfrac{4x - 7}{10 + \sqrt{5}}$

You need to know this:

Rule	Example
When a fraction is under a radical, you can rewrite it using two radicals: one containing the numerator and the other containing the denominator.	$\sqrt{\dfrac{a}{b}} = \dfrac{\sqrt{a}}{\sqrt{b}} \rightarrow \sqrt{\dfrac{4}{9}} = \dfrac{\sqrt{4}}{\sqrt{9}} = \dfrac{2}{3}$
Two factors under a single radical can be rewritten as separate radicals multiplied together.	$\sqrt{ab} = \sqrt{a} \times \sqrt{b} \rightarrow \sqrt{75} = \sqrt{3 \times 25}$ $= \sqrt{3} \times 5$ $= 5\sqrt{3}$
A radical can be written using a fractional exponent.	$\sqrt{a} = a^{\frac{1}{2}} \rightarrow \sqrt{289} = 289^{\frac{1}{2}}$ $\quad \sqrt[3]{a} = a^{\frac{1}{3}} \rightarrow \sqrt[3]{729} = 729^{\frac{1}{3}}$
When you have a fractional exponent, the numerator is the power to which the base is raised, and the denominator is the root to be taken.	$a^{\frac{b}{c}} = \sqrt[c]{a^b} \rightarrow 5^{\frac{2}{3}} = \sqrt[3]{5^2}$
When a number is squared, the original number can be positive or negative, but the square root of a number can only be positive.	If $a^2 = 81$, then $a = \pm 9$, BUT $\sqrt{81} = 9$ only.
Cube roots of negative numbers are negative.	$\sqrt[3]{-27} = -3$

To rationalize a fraction containing a radical combined with a number or variable in the denominator, multiply both the numerator and the denominator by the conjugate of the denominator. (The conjugate of a binomial uses the same terms but the opposite sign between them.)

$\dfrac{3}{2+\sqrt5} \to$ the conjugate of $(2+\sqrt5)$ is $(2-\sqrt5)$

$$\dfrac{3}{2+\sqrt5} \times \dfrac{2-\sqrt5}{2-\sqrt5} = \dfrac{3(2-\sqrt5)}{(2+\sqrt5)(2-\sqrt5)}$$

$$= \dfrac{6-3\sqrt5}{4-2\sqrt5+2\sqrt5-\sqrt5\times5}$$

$$= \dfrac{6-3\sqrt5}{4-\sqrt{25}}$$

$$= \dfrac{6-3\sqrt5}{4-5}$$

$$= \dfrac{6-3\sqrt5}{-1}$$

$$= -6+3\sqrt5$$

You need to do this:

- Identify the appropriate rule by looking at the answer choices. What form do you need to get the expression into? What rule do you need to apply to get there?
- Apply the rule.
- Repeat as necessary.

Straightforward ACT radicals questions should be quick points. Make sure you memorize the rules in the table on the previous page before test day.

Explanation:

Notice that four of the answer choices have no radicals in the denominator; this suggests that the denominator most likely needs to be rationalized. Multiply both the numerator and denominator by the conjugate of the denominator since this will eliminate any radicals in the denominator.

$$\dfrac{(4x)(10+\sqrt5)}{(10-\sqrt5)(10+\sqrt5)} = \dfrac{40x+4x\sqrt5}{100-5} = \dfrac{40x+4x\sqrt5}{95}$$

Choice (A) is correct.

Drills

If radicals give you trouble, study the information above and try out these drill questions before completing the Try on Your Own questions below. Drill answers can be found in Answers and Explanations.

a. $\dfrac{1}{\sqrt3}+\dfrac{8}{\sqrt2}$

b. $9^{-\frac{3}{2}}$

c. $\sqrt{0.0016x^2}$

d. $(5\sqrt3)^2$

e. $13x\sqrt5-4x\sqrt5$

Math

Try on Your Own

Directions: Take as much time as you need on these questions. Work carefully and methodically. There will be an opportunity for timed practice at the end of the chapter.

1. What is the greatest integer smaller than $\sqrt{160}$?

   A. 12
   B. 13
   C. 14
   D. 15
   E. 16

2. Which of the following is equivalent to $(\sqrt{8} + \sqrt{6})(\sqrt{8} - \sqrt{6})$?

   F. 1
   G. 2
   H. $\sqrt{7}$
   J. $\sqrt{14}$
   K. 7

3. Which of the following is equivalent to the product $\sqrt{3} \times \sqrt[6]{3}$?

   A. $\sqrt[9]{3}$
   B. $\sqrt[3]{3}$
   C. $\sqrt[6]{6}$
   D. $\sqrt[3]{9}$
   E. Cannot be determined from the given information

4. Which of the following values of n satisfies the inequality $\frac{4}{5} < n < 1$?

   F. $\frac{\sqrt{10}}{5}$
   G. $\frac{\sqrt{14}}{5}$
   H. $\frac{\sqrt{18}}{5}$
   J. $\frac{\sqrt{26}}{5}$
   K. $\frac{\sqrt{30}}{5}$

HINT: For Q5, is there an alternative to the radicals presented in the question stem and answer choices that could make the algebra easier to manage?

---

5. Which of the following is equivalent to $\dfrac{\sqrt[5]{x^3}\sqrt{z^5}\sqrt[3]{y^4}}{z^2\sqrt[3]{y}\sqrt[5]{x^2}}$?

   A. $\sqrt[3]{x^2}\sqrt[5]{y^3}\sqrt[5]{z^4}$
   B. $\dfrac{x^5}{zy^2\sqrt[4]{z}\sqrt[5]{y^3}}$
   C. $\dfrac{zy^2\sqrt[4]{z}\sqrt[5]{y^3}}{x^5}$
   D. $\dfrac{x\sqrt[6]{y^{17}}}{\sqrt[3]{z^{10}}}$
   E. $y\sqrt[5]{x}\sqrt{z}$

ABSOLUTE VALUE

To answer a question like this:

Evaluate $\left|\dfrac{5-9}{8-6}\right| - |4-8|$.

A. -4

B. -2

C. 0

D. 2

E. 4

You need to know this:

- Absolute value means the distance a number is from 0 on a number line.
- Because absolute value is a distance, it is always positive or 0.
- Absolute value symbols function as grouping symbols (like parentheses or brackets) in the order of operations.

You need to do this:

- Follow the order of operations and simplify the expression from the inside set of parentheses or absolute value brackets out.
- Collect and combine like terms.
- Be careful with your positive and negative signs.

Explanation:

There are two sets of absolute value brackets, but they are not nested, so you can calculate them independently. First, simplify the terms within the grouping symbols; then, determine the absolute value and complete the subtraction. To account for the absolute value brackets, make each term positive after you simplify it.

$$\left|\frac{5-9}{8-6}\right| - |4-8| = \left|\frac{-4}{2}\right| - |-4|$$
$$= |-2| - 4$$
$$= 2 - 4$$
$$= -2$$

Hence, (B) is correct.

Drills

If absolute values give you trouble, study the information above and try out these drill questions before completing the Try on Your Own questions below. Drill answers can be found in Answers and Explanations.

a. $||-4+3|-|7-10||$

b. $\left|\dfrac{-7 \times 4}{6 \times 2}\right|$

c.   Given $x = -2$, evaluate $-|x - 4| + 5x$.

d.   Given $x = 3$, evaluate $-\left|\dfrac{4x - 10}{-x - 2}\right|$.

e.   Given $x = -3$ and $y = 4$, evaluate
$|xy + 5| - \left|\dfrac{y}{2} - 1\right|$.

Try on Your Own

Directions: Take as much time as you need on these questions. Work carefully and methodically. There will be an opportunity for timed practice at the end of the chapter.

1.   What is the value of $\dfrac{|5 - 2x| - 13}{-x}$ when $x = 3$?

   A.   3

   B.   4

   C. $\dfrac{14}{3}$

   D.   6

   E. $\dfrac{19}{3}$

2.   If $a = -2$, then which of the following is equivalent to $-2|5a - 4|$?

   F. -28

   G. -12

   H.   0

   J.   12

   K.   28

3.   When $t = 8$, what is the value of $-4\left|\dfrac{t}{2} - 4\right| + 4$?

   A. -8

   B. -4

   C.   0

   D.   4

   E.   8

4.   Which of the following is equivalent to $-\left|\dfrac{-4 \times 10}{3 \times 5}\right|$?

   F. $-\dfrac{8}{3}$

   G. $-\dfrac{4}{3}$

   H.   1

   J. $\dfrac{4}{3}$

   K. $\dfrac{8}{3}$

HINT: For Q5, take the time to familiarize yourself with both the question and the information provided. Which two answer choices can be marked incorrect without doing any substitution or algebra?

---

5.   Given that $b = 3$ and $d = 1$, which of the following is equivalent to $\left|\dfrac{2b - 3}{-4d + 1}\right|$?

   A. -2

   B. -1

   C.   0

   D.   1

   E.   2

SEQUENCES

To answer a question like this:

If the first term in a geometric sequence is 3, the third term is 48, and all the terms are positive integers, what is the ELEVENTH term?

A.   228

B.   528

C.   110,592

D. 3,145,728

E. 12,582,912

You need to know this:

A **sequence** is a list of numbers or expressions in which there is a pattern.

- Each number in a sequence is called a term and is named by, or is a function of, its position in the sequence.
- The first term in a sequence is called a_1, the nth term is called a_n, the term right after the nth term is called a_{n+1}, and so on. So a general sequence looks like $a_1, a_2, a_3, \ldots a_{n-1}, a_n, a_{n+1}, \ldots$.
- You can also write a sequence using function notation: $f(1), f(2), f(3), \ldots, f(n-1), f(n), f(n+1), \ldots$.
- A sequence can be arithmetic, geometric, or neither. For example, the sequence $1, 8, 27, 64, 125, \ldots$ has a pattern (perfect cubes) but is neither arithmetic nor geometric.

An **arithmetic sequence** is a sequence in which the same number is added to get from one term to the next.

- The difference between any two terms is called the common difference and is usually represented by the variable d.
- You can find the nth term in an arithmetic sequence using this formula: $a_n = a_1 + (n-1)d$.

A **geometric sequence** is a sequence in which the same number is multiplied to get from one term to the next.

- The number that you're multiplying by is called the common ratio and is usually represented by the variable r.
- You can find the nth term in a geometric sequence using this formula: $a_n = a_1 r^{(n-1)}$.

You need to do this:

- Look for clues in the question stem to help you determine the type of sequence.
- Use any given terms to calculate the common difference or common ratio.
- Use Backsolving or the appropriate formula as needed to calculate the missing value.

Explanation:

To find the next term in a geometric sequence, multiply the current term by a constant r. You are told that $a_1 = 3$ and $a_3 = 48$, so find r by creating the equation $a_1 \times r \times r = a_3$. Plugging in the given values yields $3 \times r \times r = 48$. Thus, $r^2 = 16$ and $r = 4$. Finally, use the general form of a geometric sequence, $a_n = a_1 r^{(n-1)}$, to solve for a_{11}.

$$a_{11} = a_1 (r)^{(11-1)}$$
$$= 3(4^{10})$$
$$= 3{,}145{,}728$$

Choice (D) is correct.

Try on Your Own

Directions: Take as much time as you need on these questions. Work carefully and methodically. There will be an opportunity for timed practice at the end of the chapter.

1. Four numbers are in a sequence with 8 as the first term and 36 as the last term. The first three numbers form an arithmetic sequence with a common difference of -7. The last three numbers form a geometric sequence. What is the common ratio of the last three terms of the sequence?

   A. -10
   B. -6
   C. 0
   D. 10
   E. 32

   HINT: For Q2, how can you determine the common difference without consecutive terms?

   ---

2. What three numbers should be placed in the blanks below so that the difference between consecutive numbers is the same?

   $$12, \_\_, \_\_, \_\_, 32$$

   F. 16, 22, 28
   G. 17, 22, 27
   H. 20, 22, 30
   J. 22, 24, 30
   K. 23, 29, 31

3. If the first and second terms of a geometric sequence are 3 and 12, what is an expression for the value of the TWENTY-FOURTH (24th) term of the sequence?

   A. $a_{24} = 3^4 \times 12$
   B. $a_{24} = 3^4 \times 23$
   C. $a_{24} = 4^3 \times 12$
   D. $a_{24} = 4^{23} \times 3$
   E. $a_{24} = 4^{24} \times 3$

4. If the first four terms of an arithmetic sequence are 25, 21, 17, and 13 respectively, what is the TWENTIETH (20th) term of the sequence?

   F. -55
   G. -51
   H. -47
   J. -43
   K. -39

5. If the fifth and the sixth terms of a geometric sequence are 3 and 1, respectively, what is the FIRST term of the sequence?

   A. -5
   B. $\dfrac{1}{27}$
   C. 11
   D. 27
   E. 243

IMAGINARY NUMBERS

LEARNING OBJECTIVE

After this lesson, you will be able to:

- Perform arithmetic operations on imaginary and complex numbers

To answer a question like this:

Given a positive integer n such that $i^n = -1$, which of the following statements about n must be true? (Note: $i^2 = -1$)

A. When n is divided by 4, the result is a multiple of 0.

B. When n is divided by 4, the result is a multiple of $\frac{1}{3}$.

C. When n is divided by 4, the result is a multiple of $\frac{1}{2}$.

D. When n is divided by 4, the result is a multiple of 1.

E. When n is divided by 4, the result is a multiple of 2.

You need to know this:

The square root of a negative number is not a real number but an **imaginary number**.

To take the square root of a negative number, use i, which is defined as $i = \sqrt{-1}$. For example, to simplify $\sqrt{-49}$, rewrite $\sqrt{-49}$ as $\sqrt{-1 \times 49}$, take the square root of -1 (which is by definition i), and then take the square root of 49, which is 7. The end result is $7i$.

When a number is written in the form $a + bi$, where a is the real component and b is the imaginary component (and i is $\sqrt{-1}$), it is referred to as a **complex number**.

Solving ACT questions that involve complex numbers in the denominator of a fraction will require the use of a conjugate number. Complex numbers and the conjugates that go with them are binomials, so you can use FOIL to multiply complex numbers by their conjugate numbers. Review this skill in chapter 10 if needed.

The powers of i follow a predictable pattern that can help you work more efficiently on the ACT.

When you have ...	... it becomes ...
i^1	i
i^2	$\sqrt{-1} \times \sqrt{-1} = -1$
i^3	$i^2 \times i = -1 \times i = -i$
i^4	$i^2 \times i^2 = -1 \times -1 = 1$

So, the cycles of i are i, -1, $-i$, 1, then repeat (try a few more if you're not convinced). When you have i raised to an exponent greater than 4, divide the exponent by 4. The remainder will dictate the final answer.

- Take i^{63} as an example.
- Divide 63 by 4 to get 15 with a remainder of 3.
- This means that $i^{63} = (i^4)^{15} \times i^3 = 1^{15} \times i^3$.
- Because $i^3 = -i$, i^{63} becomes $-i$.

Math

You need to do this:

Add, subtract, multiply, and divide complex numbers just as you do real numbers.

- To add (or subtract) complex numbers, simply add (or subtract) the real parts and then add (or subtract) the imaginary parts.
- To multiply complex numbers, treat them as binomials and use FOIL. To simplify the product, use the simplification $i^2 = -1$ and combine like terms.
- To divide complex numbers, write them in fraction form and multiply the numerator and denominator by the **conjugate** of the complex number in the denominator. To form the conjugate, change the sign in the complex number. For example, the conjugate of $2 + i$ is $2 - i$.
- Use FOIL as needed to multiply complex numbers by their conjugates.

Explanation:

The statement $i^n = -1$ will be satisfied when $n = 2, 6, 10, 14, \ldots$ because there are four stages in the cycle of i and the definition of i is that $i^2 = -1$. Every answer asks what happens when n is divided by 4. Divide each of the values of n above by 4 and see if you can spot a pattern.

$\frac{n}{4} = \frac{1}{2}, \frac{3}{2}, \frac{5}{2}, \frac{7}{2}, \ldots$ All of these numbers are multiples of $\frac{1}{2}$, so (C) is correct.

Try on Your Own

Directions: Take as much time as you need on these questions. Work carefully and methodically. There will be an opportunity for timed practice at the end of the chapter.

HINT: For Q1, what quadratic process can help you multiply the complex numbers in the question?

---

1. Given that $i = \sqrt{-1}$, which of the following is equal to $(11 + 4i)(2 - 5i)$?

   A. 2

   B. 42

   C. $2 - 75i$

   D. $22 - 20i$

   E. $42 - 47i$

2. Which of the following is the correct simplification of the expression $(2 + 7i) - (4 - 3i)$?

   F. $-2 - 10i$

   G. $-2 - 4i$

   H. $-2 + 10i$

   J. $2 - 4i$

   K. $2 + 10i$

3. The complex number i is defined such that $i^2 = -1$. What is the value of $(2i - 3)^2$?

   A. -13

   B. 5

   C. $-3 - 4i$

   D. $9 + 4i$

   E. $5 - 12i$

4. If $i^2 = -1$, which of the following is a square root of $8 - 6i$?

   F. $3 + i$

   G. $3 - i$

   H. $3 - 4i$

   J. $4 + 3i$

   K. $4 - 3i$

5. Which of the following numbers is NOT a real number?

   A. $-\sqrt{9}$

   B. 3^{-2}

   C. $\sqrt{-9}$

   D. $\sqrt{3}$

   E. $(-3)^2$

MATRICES

LEARNING OBJECTIVE

After this lesson, you will be able to:

• Perform arithmetic operations using matrices

To answer a question like this:

If $\begin{bmatrix} 1 & 2 & 3 \end{bmatrix} \begin{bmatrix} x \\ 2x \\ 3x \end{bmatrix} = 42$, what is the value of x?

   A. 2

   B. 3

   C. 4

   D. 6

   E. 7

You need to know this:

A **matrix** (*plural: matrices*) is a rectangular arrangement of numbers, symbols, or expressions, formatted in rows and columns.

• You can think of matrices as tables with no borders around the cells.

• The ACT tests matrices mostly in basic ways—addition, subtraction, and perhaps a multiplication question here or there.

• To add (or subtract) matrices, the matrices must be exactly the same size. Add (or subtract) the corresponding entries (the numbers that sit in the same spots).

• You can multiply an entire matrix by a number by multiplying each entry in the matrix by that number.

• Often, a high-difficulty matrix question will appear as one of the final 10 questions.

  • These questions are more difficult because they typically require algebraic and critical thinking skills as opposed to straightforward calculations.

  • The definition of the determinant of matrix $\begin{bmatrix} a & b \\ c & d \end{bmatrix}$ (which is equal to $ad - bc$) will be provided when needed.

You need to do this:

Carefully determine whether the question is asking for:

- a missing value within a matrix?
- the sum or difference of two or more matrices?
- the product of a matrix and a number?
- something else, potentially unfamiliar?

Examine the given information:

- How many matrices are there?
- Are you given a specified piece of information, such as the definition of the discriminant, to use in some way?
- How many variables are there? How many do you need?

Choose your approach:

- Can you Backsolve using the answer choices?
- Can you use algebra to find a requested combination?
- If so, what equation can you set up to find a missing value?
- If you're stuck or know the approach will take a long time, mark the question to return to later if you have time remaining.

Explanation:

When multiplying matrices, the number of columns in the first matrix must match the number of rows in the second matrix. Here, you are multiplying a 1×3 matrix and 3×1 matrix. These match up, so multiply the rows of the first matrix by the columns of the second matrix. This creates a simple equation in x.

$$(1)(x) + (2)(2x) + (3)(3x) = 42$$
$$x + 4x + 9x = 42$$
$$14x = 42$$
$$x = 3$$

Choice (B) is correct.

Try on Your Own

Directions: Take as much time as you need on these questions. Work carefully and methodically. There will be an opportunity for timed practice at the end of the chapter.

1. If $A = \begin{bmatrix} 4 & 0 & 3 \\ 0 & -2 & 1 \end{bmatrix}$ and $B = \begin{bmatrix} 1 & 5 & -2 \\ 0 & 0 & 4 \end{bmatrix}$, then $2A + B = ?$

   A. $\begin{bmatrix} 9 & 5 & 4 \\ 0 & -4 & 6 \end{bmatrix}$

   B. $\begin{bmatrix} 9 & 5 & 4 \\ 0 & 0 & 4 \end{bmatrix}$

   C. $\begin{bmatrix} 9 & 5 & 4 \\ 0 & -2 & 4 \end{bmatrix}$

   D. $\begin{bmatrix} 8 & 0 & 6 \\ 0 & -4 & 2 \end{bmatrix}$

   E. $\begin{bmatrix} 5 & 5 & 1 \\ 0 & -2 & 5 \end{bmatrix}$

2. From the four matrices shown below, which of the following products is NOT possible?

   $A = \begin{bmatrix} 1 & 2 \\ 3 & 4 \end{bmatrix}$ $B = \begin{bmatrix} 5 & 6 & 7 \\ 8 & 9 & 0 \end{bmatrix}$ $C = \begin{bmatrix} 2 \\ 4 \end{bmatrix}$ $D = \begin{bmatrix} 3 & 5 \end{bmatrix}$

   F. AB

   G. AC

   H. BC

   J. CD

   K. DA

3. The product of $\begin{bmatrix} 1 & 2 & 3 \end{bmatrix} \begin{bmatrix} -1 \\ -2 \\ -3 \end{bmatrix}$ is

   A. -14

   B. 0

   C. 14

   D. $\begin{bmatrix} -1 & 0 & 0 \\ 0 & -4 & 0 \\ 0 & 0 & -9 \end{bmatrix}$

   E. $\begin{bmatrix} 0 & 1 & -1 \\ 2 & 0 & -2 \\ 3 & -3 & 0 \end{bmatrix}$

4. Evaluate $2x + y + 4z$, given $\begin{bmatrix} 4 & y & 8 \end{bmatrix} \begin{bmatrix} x \\ 2 \\ z \end{bmatrix} = 10$.

   F. 1

   G. 2

   H. 3

   J. 4

   K. 5

HINT: For Q5, how can you calculate the values of the four variables?

---

5. What is the value of $zy - xw$, given $\begin{bmatrix} 3x & 3 \\ 2w & 2z \end{bmatrix} + \begin{bmatrix} 6 & -2y \\ -4 & -6 \end{bmatrix} = \begin{bmatrix} 9 & 4 \\ 6 & 10 \end{bmatrix}$?

   A. -9

   B. -1

   C. 3

   D. 6

   E. 7

On Test Day

Remember that the ACT doesn't ask you to show your work. If you find the math in a question challenging, there may be another way to get to the answer.

Try out this question first using straightforward math and then using the Backsolving strategy from earlier in this chapter. Which approach do you find easier? There's no right or wrong answer—just remember your preferred approach and try it first if you see a question like this on test day.

1. What is the greatest integer smaller than $\sqrt{250}$?

    A. 15
    B. 16
    C. 17
    D. 19
    E. 20

The correct answer and both ways of solving can be found at the end of this chapter.

How Much Have You Learned?

Directions: For test-like practice, give yourself 10 minutes to complete this question set. Be sure to study the explanations, even for questions you got correct. They can be found at the end of this chapter.

1. The number $5^{\frac{5}{2}}$ is equal to which of the following?

   A. 5
   B. 12.5
   C. 25
   D. $\sqrt[5]{25}$
   E. $\sqrt{5^5}$

2. If $i^2 = -1$, which of the following represents $\dfrac{1}{3-i}$ written in $a + bi$ form?

   F. $\dfrac{3}{10} + \dfrac{1}{10}i$
   G. $\dfrac{1}{3} - \dfrac{1}{i}$
   H. $\dfrac{3}{8} + \dfrac{1}{8}i$
   J. $3 + i$
   K. $3 - i$

3. Evaluate $\dfrac{|14 + |2x - 4||}{5x + 6}$ when $x = -2$.

   A. -12
   B. $-\dfrac{11}{2}$
   C. -2
   D. $\dfrac{9}{4}$
   E. $\dfrac{11}{2}$

4. The first four terms of a geometric sequence are $-2, 4, -8$, and 16. What is the NINTH term of the geometric sequence?

   F. -512
   G. -256
   H. 128
   J. 256
   K. 512

5. If $m = 2n$, then for what positive value of n does the determinant of $\begin{bmatrix} m & 8 \\ 4 & n \end{bmatrix}$ equal 0?
   (Note: The determinant of matrix $\begin{bmatrix} a & b \\ c & d \end{bmatrix}$ equals $ad - bc$.)

   A. 4
   B. $4\sqrt{2}$
   C. 8
   D. $8\sqrt{2}$
   E. There is no such value of n.

6. Which of the following is equivalent to $\dfrac{10}{7 - 2\sqrt{5}}$?

   F. $\dfrac{70 - 47\sqrt{55}}{29}$
   G. $\dfrac{70 + 47\sqrt{71}}{69}$
   H. $\dfrac{70 + 20\sqrt{5}}{29}$
   J. $\dfrac{27 + \sqrt{5}}{45}$
   K. $\dfrac{25 - \sqrt{55}}{45}$

7. Which of the following is equivalent to

$$\dfrac{\left(xy^2\right)^{-4}z^3}{z^{-1}y^2x^{-3}}?$$

A. z^4

B. $\dfrac{1}{z^4}$

C. $\dfrac{x^3y^2}{z^4}$

D. $\dfrac{z^2}{x^4y^3}$

E. $\dfrac{z^4}{xy^{10}}$

8. When the imaginary number i is defined as $i = \sqrt{-1}$, it follows that $i^2 = -1$. Based on this information, which of the following is equivalent to $\dfrac{i^3 + 4i}{\sqrt{-9}}$?

F. -1

G. 1

H. 3

J. i

K. $3i$

9. Which of the following expresses the value of $530{,}000{,}000 - 442{,}000{,}000$ in scientific notation?

A. 8.8×10^5

B. 8.8×10^6

C. 8.8×10^7

D. 8.8×10^8

E. 88×10^6

10. If $\begin{bmatrix} x & 6 \\ 13 & x \end{bmatrix} + \begin{bmatrix} 2 & 3y \\ 5 & y \end{bmatrix} = \begin{bmatrix} 6 & 12 \\ 18 & z \end{bmatrix}$, what is the value of z?

F. -6

G. 6

H. 8

J. 22

K. 24

Reflect

Directions: Take a few minutes to recall what you've learned and what you've been practicing in this chapter. Consider the following questions, jot down your best answer for each one, and then compare your reflections to the expert responses on the following page. Use your level of confidence to determine what to do next.

1. How do you add, subtract, multiply, and divide terms that involve exponents? What must be true in order to complete these operations?

_____

_____

_____

2. How are exponents and radicals related?

_____

_____

_____

3. When you answer questions involving absolute value, what is the most important thing to pay attention to?

_____

_____

_____

4. How can the algebraic skill FOIL help you answer tough imaginary number questions?

_____

_____

_____

Responses

1. How do you add, subtract, multiply, and divide terms that involve exponents? What must be true in order to complete these operations?

To combine terms that involve exponents, the terms must have the same base. To add or subtract, keep the base and the exponent the same and add or subtract the coefficients (e.g., $2x^2 + 3x^2 = 5x^2$). To multiply, keep the base the same and add the exponents (e.g., $x^2x^3 = x^5$). To divide, keep the base the same and subtract the exponents (e.g., $x^8 \div x^2 = x^6$).

2. How are exponents and radicals related?

Radicals are fractional, or inverse, exponents.

3. When you answer questions involving absolute value, what is the most important thing to pay attention to?

When solving an equation like $|x| = 8$, there are two possibilities for x: 8 and -8. Do not forget that the answer could be negative!

4. How can the algebraic skill FOIL help you answer tough imaginary number questions?

To multiply two imaginary numbers in a $+$ bi form, you must FOIL. Simplify, collect like terms, and remember that $i^2 = -1$.

Next Steps

If you answered most questions correctly in the "How Much Have You Learned?" section, and if your responses to the Reflect questions were similar to those of the ACT expert, then consider Number and Quantity an area of strength and move on to the next chapter. Come back to this topic periodically to prevent yourself from getting rusty.

If you don't yet feel confident, review those parts of this chapter that you have not yet mastered. Then, try the questions you missed again. As always, be sure to review the explanations closely. Then go online (**kaptest.com/login**) to watch video lessons about the highest-yield concepts in this chapter and to use your Qbank for more practice. If you haven't already registered your book, do so at **kaptest.com/moreonline.**

GO ONLINE

kaptest.com/login

Answers and Explanations

Exponents

Drill Answers

a. 1.32×10^9

b. 1.4×10^9

c. 2.1×10^3

d. x^7

e. y^6

1. A
Difficulty: Low
Category: Number and Quantity
Getting to the Answer: Simplify the numerator and divide. Then convert into scientific notation.

$$\frac{3,200,000 - 2,300,000}{3,000} = \frac{900,000}{3,000}$$
$$300 = 3.0 \times 10^2$$

Choice (A) is correct.

2. G
Difficulty: Medium
Category: Number and Quantity
Getting to the Answer: Combine like terms and apply exponent rules to simplify. Remember that when you divide, you subtract the exponents.

$$\frac{x^6 \, y^4 \, z^9}{x \, y^6 \, z^3} = x^5 y^{-2} z^6 = \frac{x^5 z^6}{y^2}$$

Choice (G) is correct.

3. B
Difficulty: Low
Category: Number and Quantity
Getting to the Answer: First, simplify the numerator. Divide the numbers without exponents (12.0 and 4.0) first. Then, apply exponent rules to determine the correct power of 10: add the exponents when multiplying the same bases and subtract the exponents when dividing the same bases.

$$\frac{(2.0 \times 10^4)(6.0 \times 10^7)}{4.0 \times 10^2} = \frac{12.0 \times 10^{11}}{4.0 \times 10^2} = 3.0 \times 10^9$$

Choice (B) is correct.

4. F
Difficulty: Medium
Category: Number and Quantity
Getting to the Answer: Remember that you can make a term with a negative exponent have a positive exponent by taking the reciprocal of the term. To make this expression easier to understand, begin by making all the exponents positive. Then apply exponent rules to simplify.

$$\frac{a^{-7}c^2b^{-4}}{b^2c^{-3}a^{-3}} = \frac{a^3c^2c^3}{a^7b^2b^4} = \frac{c^5}{a^4b^6}$$

Choice (F) is correct.

5. E
Difficulty: Medium
Category: Number and Quantity
Getting to the Answer: Simplify the denominator and divide. Make sure that the answer is written in correct scientific notation.

$$\frac{2.1 \times 10^{-12}}{(2.0 \times 10^4)(5.0 \times 10^3)} = \frac{2.1 \times 10^{-12}}{10.0 \times 10^7}$$
$$\frac{2.1 \times 10^{-12}}{10^8} = 2.1 \times 10^{-20}$$

Thus, (E) is correct.

Radicals

Drill Answers

a. $\dfrac{\sqrt{2} + 8\sqrt{3}}{\sqrt{6}}$

b. $\dfrac{1}{27}$

c. $\pm 0.04x$

d. 75

e. $9x\sqrt{5}$

1. A
Difficulty: Low
Category: Number and Quantity
Getting to the Answer: The best way to find the biggest integer smaller than $\sqrt{160}$ is to square each answer choice. The largest one that, when squared, is still smaller than 160 is correct.

$$A)\ 12^2 = 144$$
$$B)\ 13^2 = 169$$

Since the answer choices are listed in increasing order, all other choices will be even larger than 169. Thus, (A) is correct.

2. G

Difficulty: Medium
Category: Number and Quantity
Getting to the Answer: Use the FOIL method to simplify. Notice that the terms being multiplied are conjugates, which means that the cross terms will cancel out. If you observe this, you can save some time by multiplying only the first and last terms.

$$(\sqrt{8} + \sqrt{6})(\sqrt{8} - \sqrt{6}) = 8 - \sqrt{48} + \sqrt{48} - 6 = 2$$

Choice (G) is correct.

3. D
Difficulty: Medium
Category: Number and Quantity
Getting to the Answer: Because the radicals have different roots, you can't use the basic radical properties. Instead, change each radical into exponent form. Since you are multiplying two terms with the same base, add the exponents. Finally, change the expression back into radical form.

$$\sqrt{3} \times \sqrt[6]{3} = 3^{\frac{1}{2}} \times 3^{\frac{1}{6}}$$
$$= 3^{\frac{3}{6}} \times 3^{\frac{1}{6}}$$
$$= 3^{\frac{4}{6}}$$
$$= 3^{\frac{2}{3}}$$
$$= \sqrt[3]{3^2}$$
$$= \sqrt[3]{9}$$

Choice (D) is correct.

4. H
Difficulty: Low
Category: Number and Quantity
Getting to the Answer: Your task is to find the fraction between $\frac{4}{5}$ and 1. Notice that all the answer choices have radicals in the numerator and 5 in the denominator. Manipulate the given inequality to get it into the same form.

$$\frac{4}{5} < n < 1$$
$$\frac{4}{5} < n < \frac{5}{5}$$
$$\frac{\sqrt{16}}{5} < n < \frac{\sqrt{25}}{5}$$

Since 18 is between 16 and 25, (H) is correct.

5. E
Difficulty: High
Category: Number and Quantity
Getting to the Answer: First, change the radicals into exponent form. Next, apply exponent rules to simplify, adding exponents when multiplying and subtracting exponents when dividing. Remember that you need common denominators to add or subtract fractions. Finally, convert the exponents back into radical form.

$$\frac{\sqrt[5]{x^3} \ \sqrt{z^5} \ \sqrt[3]{y^4}}{z^2 \ \sqrt[3]{y} \ \sqrt[5]{x^2}} = \frac{x^{\frac{3}{5}} z^{\frac{5}{2}} y^{\frac{4}{3}}}{z^2 y^{\frac{1}{3}} x^{\frac{2}{5}}}$$
$$\frac{x^{\frac{3}{5}} y^{\frac{4}{3}} z^{\frac{5}{2}}}{x^{\frac{2}{5}} y^{\frac{1}{3}} z^{\frac{4}{2}}} = x^{\frac{1}{5}} y z^{\frac{1}{2}}$$
$$x^{\frac{1}{5}} y z^{\frac{1}{2}} = y \sqrt[5]{x} \sqrt{z}$$

Choice (E) is correct.

Absolute Value

Drill Answers

a. 2

b. $\frac{7}{3}$

c. -16

d. $-\frac{2}{5}$

e. 6

1. B
Difficulty: Low
Category: Number and Quantity
Getting to the Answer: Plug in 3, the value given for x, and simplify. Remember that absolute-value brackets change negative numbers into positive numbers.

$$\frac{|5-2x|-13}{-x}=\frac{|5-6|-13}{-3}$$
$$=\frac{|-1|-13}{-3}$$
$$=\frac{1-13}{-3}$$
$$=\frac{-12}{-3}$$
$$=4$$

Choice (B) is correct.

2. F
Difficulty: Medium
Category: Number and Quantity
Getting to the Answer: Start by plugging in -2, the given value. Simplify and make sure to utilize the absolute value.

$$-2|5a-4|=-2|5(-2)-4|$$
$$=-2|-14|$$
$$=-28$$

Thus, (F) is correct. Do not be tricked by choice K: this would be the answer without using the absolute value.

3. D
Difficulty: Medium
Category: Number and Quantity
Getting to the Answer: First, plug in the given value of 8 and simplify inside of the absolute value. Make sure the number inside the absolute value is not negative before moving on to the next simplifying steps.

$$-4\left|\frac{t}{2}-4\right|+4=-4\left|\frac{(8)}{2}-4\right|+4$$
$$=-4|0|+4$$
$$=4$$

Choice (D) is correct.

4. F
Difficulty: Medium
Category: Number and Quantity
Getting to the Answer: First simplify the numerator and denominator, then reduce the resulting fraction. The fraction inside the absolute value will be positive. Then multiply the negative outside of the absolute value.

$$-\left|\frac{40}{15}\right|=-\left|\frac{8}{3}\right|=-\frac{8}{3}$$

Choice (F) is correct. K is a trap answer; it is the expression's result if the absolute value were absent.

5. D
Difficulty: Medium
Category: Number and Quantity
Getting to the Answer: Plug in the given values ($b=3$ and $d=1$) and simplify the numerator and denominator. After you divide, make sure that the resulting number is positive because of the absolute value.

$$\left|\frac{2b-3}{-4d+1}\right|=\left|\frac{2(3)-3}{-4(1)+1}\right|$$
$$=\left|\frac{3}{-3}\right|$$
$$=|-1|$$
$$=1$$

Choice (D) is correct. Be careful; B would be the answer if there were no absolute value brackets.

Sequences

1. B
Difficulty: Medium
Category: Number and Quantity
Getting to the Answer: Your task is to find r, the common ratio of a geometric sequence. Since you are told that the first three terms form an arithmetic sequence with a common difference of -7, you can find the second and third term in the sequence by subtracting 7. So, $a_1=8$, $a_2=1$, and $a_3=-6$. You are also told that $a_4=36$ and that the last three terms form a geometric sequence. $1\times r=-6$ and $-6\times r=36$, so the ratio is -6. Choice (B) is correct.

2. G

Difficulty: Medium

Category: Number and Quantity

Getting to the Answer: The question gives you the first and fifth terms of an arithmetic sequence. The task is to figure out the middle three terms. Use the arithmetic sequence formula with $n = 5$ and $a_1 = 12$ to solve for the common difference.

$$a_5 = a_1 + (n - 1)d$$
$$32 = 12 + (5 - 1)d$$
$$32 = 12 + 4d$$
$$4d = 20$$
$$5 = d$$

Starting at 12 and repeatedly adding 5 yields 12, 17, 22, 27, 32.

Hence, (G) is correct. Note that you can also solve this question by Backsolving. Choices H, J, and K are themselves not arithmetic sequences, so they're incorrect. Choice F doesn't work because the difference between 12 and 16 is 4, whereas the difference between 16 and 22 is 6. This leaves (G) as the only choice that works.

3. D

Difficulty: Low

Category: Number and Quantity

Getting to the Answer: Since the first and second terms are given, find the common ratio r by setting $3r = 12$. This yields $r = 4$. The question asks for the 24th term, so plug $r = 4$, $n = 24$, and $a_1 = 3$ into the geometric sequence formula.

$$a_n = a_1 r^{(n-1)}$$
$$a_{24} = 3 \times 4^{(24-1)}$$
$$a_{24} = 3 \times 4^{23}$$

Terms can be multiplied in any order, so $a_{24} = 3 \times 4^{23} = 4^{23} \times 3$. Therefore, (D) is correct.

4. G

Difficulty: Low

Category: Number and Quantity

Getting to the Answer: It is too laborious to calculate the 20th term of this sequence by hand, so plug

$d = -4$, $n = 20$, and $a_1 = 25$ into the arithmetic sequence formula.

$$a_n = a_1 + (n - 1)d$$
$$a_{20} = 25 + (20 - 1)(-4)$$
$$a_{20} = 25 - 76$$
$$a_{20} = -51$$

Therefore, (G) is correct.

5. E

Difficulty: Low

Category: Number and Quantity

Getting to the Answer: Since the fifth and sixth terms of the sequence are given, you can find the common ratio r by setting $3r = 1$. This yields $r = \frac{1}{3}$. Now plug $r = \frac{1}{3}$, $a_6 = 1$, and $n = 6$ into the geometric sequence formula and solve for a_1.

$$a_n = a_1 r^{(n-1)}$$
$$a_6 = a_1 \left(\frac{1}{3}\right)^{(6-1)}$$
$$1 = a_1 \left(\frac{1}{3}\right)^5$$
$$1 = a_1 \left(\frac{1}{243}\right)$$
$$243 = a_1$$

Therefore, (E) is correct.

Imaginary Numbers

1. E

Difficulty: Medium

Category: Number and Quantity

Getting to the Answer: FOIL the given expression and remember that $i^2 = -1$. Simplify by combining like terms. Finally, make sure that your answer is in $a + bi$ form.

$$(11 + 4i)(2 - 5i) = 22 - 55i + 8i - 20i^2$$
$$= 22 - 47i - 20(-1)$$
$$= 22 - 47i + 20$$
$$= 42 - 47i$$

Choice (E) is correct.

2. H
Difficulty: Low
Category: Number and Quantity
Getting to the Answer: Combine like terms, being careful to distribute the negative outside the parentheses.

$$2 + 7i - (4 - 3i)$$
$$2 + 7i - 4 + 3i$$
$$-2 + 10i$$

Choice (H) is correct.

3. E
Difficulty: Medium
Category: Number and Quantity
Getting to the Answer: Since the term in parentheses is squared, write out both terms and FOIL. Remember that $i^2 = -1$.

$$(2i - 3)(2i - 3)$$
$$4i^2 - 6i - 6i + 9$$
$$4i^2 - 12i + 9$$
$$4(-1) - 12i + 9$$
$$-4 - 12i + 9$$
$$5 - 12i$$

Choice (E) is correct.

4. G
Difficulty: Medium
Category: Number and Quantity
Getting to the Answer: The square root of n is a number that yields n when it is multiplied by itself. It is difficult to take the square root of $8 - 6i$ directly because the number has both a real and an imaginary component, so approach the question strategically. Square each answer choice: the one that equals $8 - 6i$ is the square root.

$$(3 + i)(3 + i) = 8 + 6i$$
$$(3 - i)(3 - i) = 8 - 6i$$
$$(3 - 4i)(3 - 4i) = -7 - 24i$$
$$(4 + 3i)(4 + 3i) = 7 + 24i$$
$$(4 - 3i)(4 - 3i) = 7 - 24i$$

Therefore, (G) is correct. Note that if you go in order, you can stop after you see that (G) is correct: there is no need to waste time doing math on test day if you've already found the answer.

5. C
Difficulty: Low
Category: Number and Quantity
Getting to the Answer: The imaginary number i is defined as $i = \sqrt{-1}$. The only answer that has a negative number under a radical sign is (C).

Matrices

1. A
Difficulty: Medium
Category: Number and Quantity
Getting to the Answer: To add or subtract matrices, both matrices need to have the same dimensions. Both A and B are 2×3 matrices, so they are compatible. To compute $2A$, multiply each entry in A by 2. To add A and B, add each corresponding component in A and B.

$$2\begin{bmatrix} 4 & 0 & 3 \\ 0 & -2 & 1 \end{bmatrix} + \begin{bmatrix} 1 & 5 & -2 \\ 0 & 0 & 4 \end{bmatrix}$$
$$\begin{bmatrix} 8 & 0 & 6 \\ 0 & -4 & 2 \end{bmatrix} + \begin{bmatrix} 1 & 5 & -2 \\ 0 & 0 & 4 \end{bmatrix}$$
$$\begin{bmatrix} 9 & 5 & 4 \\ 0 & -4 & 6 \end{bmatrix}$$

Thus, (A) is correct.

2. H
Difficulty: Low
Category: Number and Quantity
Getting to the Answer: When multiplying matrices, the number of columns of the first matrix must match the number of rows in the second matrix. BC is not possible because the 3 columns in B do not match the 2 rows in C.

Choice (H) is correct.

3. A
Difficulty: Low
Category: Number and Quantity
Getting to the Answer: When multiplying matrices, the number of columns in the first matrix must match the number of rows in the second matrix. Here, you are multiplying a 1×3 matrix and 3×1 matrix. The product matrix will have the same number of rows as the first matrix and the same number of columns as the second matrix. This means that the resulting matrix is 1×1.

Eliminate D and E immediately. Finally, multiply the two matrices by multiplying the rows of the first matrix by the columns of the second matrix.

$$\begin{bmatrix} 1 & 2 & 3 \end{bmatrix} \begin{bmatrix} -1 \\ -2 \\ -3 \end{bmatrix}$$

$$1(-1) + 2(-2) + 3(-3)$$

$$-1 - 4 - 9$$

$$-14$$

Choice (A) is correct.

4.   K
Difficulty: Medium
Category: Number and Quantity
Getting to the Answer: Remember that you multiply two matrices by multiplying the columns of the first matrix by the rows of the second matrix.

$$\begin{bmatrix} 4 & y & 8 \end{bmatrix} \begin{bmatrix} x \\ 2 \\ z \end{bmatrix} = 10$$

$$4(x) + 2(y) + 8(z) = 10$$

$$4x + 2y + 8z = 10$$

Notice that your end goal is very similar to the equation above. Divide both sides by 2 to obtain $2x + y + 4z = 5$.

Thus, (K) is correct.

5.   A
Difficulty: High
Category: Number and Quantity
Getting to the Answer: Matrices can be added only if their dimensions are the same. Here, all the matrices are 2 × 2, so add the matrices component-wise.

$$\begin{bmatrix} 3x + 6 & 3 - 2y \\ 2w - 4 & 2z + -6 \end{bmatrix} = \begin{bmatrix} 9 & 4 \\ 6 & 10 \end{bmatrix}$$

Next, write out four equations and solve for each variable.

$$3x + 6 = 9 \Rightarrow x = 1$$

$$2w - 4 = 6 \Rightarrow w = 5$$

$$3 - 2y = 4 \Rightarrow y = -\frac{1}{2}$$

$$2z + -6 = 10 \Rightarrow z = 8$$

Finally, plug these values into $zy - xw$.

$$zy - xw$$

$$8\left(-\frac{1}{2}\right) - 1(5)$$

$$-4 - 5$$

$$-9$$

Choice (A) is correct.

On Test Day

1.   A
Difficulty: Low
Category: Number and Quantity
Getting to the Answer: Using straightforward math, you will use your calculator to approximate the square root of 250: 15.8114. This is between the integers 15 and 16, and 16 is not smaller than 15.8114, so (A) is correct.

Another way to find the biggest number smaller than $\sqrt{250}$ is to Backsolve and square each answer choice. The largest one that is still smaller than $\sqrt{250}$ is correct:

$$A) \ 15^2 = 225$$

$$B) \ 16^2 = 256$$

Since the answer choices are listed in increasing order, all other choices will be even larger than 256. Thus, (A) is correct.

How Much Have You Learned?

1.   E
Difficulty: Medium
Category: Number and Quantity
Getting to the Answer: Recall that with a fractional exponent, the top number represents the power, while the bottom number represents the root. Thus, an exponent of $\frac{5}{2}$ involves raising a number to the 5th power and taking a square root. The base of the exponent is 5, so raise it to the 5th power and take the square root. The only choice that does this is (E), so (E) is correct.

2. F
Difficulty: Medium
Category: Number and Quantity
Getting to the Answer: For this question, you need to rearrange an expression, not solve an equation. When there are imaginary numbers in the denominator of a fraction, multiply both the numerator and denominator by the conjugate of the denominator to make sure all imaginary numbers are eliminated in the denominator.

$$\frac{1}{3-i} \cdot \frac{(3+i)}{(3+i)} = \frac{3+i}{9-i^2}$$

$$\frac{3+i}{10} = \frac{3}{10} + \frac{1}{10}i$$

Choice (F) is correct.

3. B
Difficulty: Medium
Category: Number and Quantity
Getting to the Answer: Plug in -2, the value for x, and simplify. Make sure that any number that comes out of an absolute value is positive.

$$\frac{|14 + |2x - 4||}{5x + 6} = \frac{|14 + |2(-2) - 4||}{5(-2) + 6}$$

$$= \frac{|14 + |-4 - 4||}{-10 + 6}$$

$$= \frac{|14 + 8|}{-4}$$

$$= \frac{22}{-4}$$

$$= -\frac{11}{2}$$

Choice (B) is correct. Be wary of E; the numerator has absolute value symbols, but the full fraction does not.

4. F
Difficulty: Medium
Category: Number and Quantity
Getting to the Answer: Since you are working with a geometric sequence, first find r by comparing the first and second terms.

$$-2r = 4$$

$$r = -2$$

Then plug $r = -2$ and $n = 9$ into the geometric sequence formula to solve for the ninth term, a_9.

$$a_n = -2r^{(n-1)}$$

$$a_9 = -2(-2)^{(9-1)}$$

$$= -2(-2)^8$$

$$= -2^9$$

$$= -512$$

Choice (F) is correct.

5. A
Difficulty: High
Category: Number and Quantity
Getting to the Answer: The question asks for the value of n that makes the determinant of the given matrix equal 0. You are given the formula for calculating the determinant. Substitute m for a, 8 for b, 4 for c, and n for d, and set the resulting expression equal to 0.

$$ad - bc = 0$$

$$mn - 8(4) = 0$$

$$mn - 32 = 0$$

$$mn = 32$$

The question states that $m = 2n$. Substitute $2n$ for m and solve for n:

$$(2n)n = 32$$

$$2n^2 = 32$$

$$n^2 = 16$$

$$n = \pm 4$$

The question asks for the positive value of n, so (A) is correct.

6. H
Difficulty: Medium
Category: Number and Quantity
Getting to the Answer: On the ACT, square roots normally do not appear in the denominators of fractions in answer choices. Rationalize the denominator by multiplying the top and bottom by the conjugate.

$$\frac{(10)}{(7 - 2\sqrt{5})} \times \frac{(7 + 2\sqrt{5})}{(7 + 2\sqrt{5})} = \frac{70 + 20\sqrt{5}}{49 - 4(5)}$$

$$= \frac{70 + 20\sqrt{5}}{29}$$

Choice (H) is correct.

7. E
Difficulty: Medium
Category: Number and Quantity
Getting to the Answer: Remember that when an exponent is raised to another exponent, the exponents are multiplied. Simplify and combine like terms.

$$\frac{(xy^2)^{-4}z^3}{z^{-1}y^2x^{-3}} = \frac{x^{-4}y^{-8}z^3}{z^{-1}y^2x^{-3}} = \frac{x^{-1}y^{-10}z^4}{1} = \frac{z^4}{xy^{10}}$$

Choice (E) is correct.

8. G
Difficulty: High
Category: Number and Quantity
Getting to the Answer: Rather than solving an equation, you are manipulating an expression using properties of i. Simplify the expression using the information given in the question stem.

$$\frac{i^3 + 4i}{\sqrt{-9}} = \frac{i^2(i) + 4i}{\sqrt{9}\sqrt{-1}} = \frac{-i + 4i}{3i} = \frac{3i}{3i} = 1$$

Choice (G) is correct.

9. C
Difficulty: High
Category: Number and Quantity
Getting to the Answer: Your task is to select the answer choice that expresses the difference in scientific notation. Write each number in scientific notation, then solve.

$$530{,}000{,}000 = 5.3 \times 10^8$$
$$442{,}000{,}000 = 4.42 \times 10^8$$
$$5.3 \times 10^8 - 4.42 \times 10^8 = 0.88 \times 10^8$$

However, this is not the final answer. To be in scientific notation, the number before the multiplication sign must be between 1 and 10. Adjust the value to 8.8×10^7, and you find that the answer is (C).

10. G
Difficulty: Medium
Category: Number and Quantity
Getting to the Answer: Your task is to find z. Although writing an equation for z only involves the bottom right numbers in the matrices, doing so will give you $x + y = z$, so you will need the rest of the matrix to determine the missing variables.

First, add the two matrices. Remember that matrix addition is performed component-wise—add the numbers that sit in the same spots:

$$\begin{bmatrix} x & 6 \\ 13 & x \end{bmatrix} + \begin{bmatrix} 2 & 3y \\ 5 & y \end{bmatrix} = \begin{bmatrix} x+2 & 6+3y \\ 13+5 & x+y \end{bmatrix}$$

Next, set the matrix sum equal to the third matrix:

$$\begin{bmatrix} x+2 & 6+3y \\ 18 & x+y \end{bmatrix} = \begin{bmatrix} 6 & 12 \\ 18 & z \end{bmatrix}$$

You can now write out three equations and solve for each variable:

$$x + 2 = 6 \Rightarrow x = 4$$
$$6 + 3y = 12 \Rightarrow y = 2$$
$$x + y = z \Rightarrow z = 6$$

Choice (G) is correct.

CHAPTER 9

RATES, RATIOS, PROPORTIONS, AND PERCENTS

Math

LEARNING OBJECTIVES

After completing this chapter, you will be able to:

- Solve math questions with real-world scenarios using one or more rates
- Create a ratio to represent the relationship between two numbers
- Set up a proportion and solve to find a missing value
- Calculate percents
- Calculate percent change

Number and Quantity: 8/36 SmartPoints® (Very high yield)

How Much Do You Know?

Directions: Try out the questions below. Show your work so that you can compare your solutions to the ones found on the next page. The "Category" heading in the explanation for each question gives the title of the lesson that covers how to solve it. If you answered the question(s) for a given lesson correctly, and if your scratchwork looks like ours, you may be able to move quickly through that lesson. If you answered incorrectly or used a different approach, you may want to take your time on that lesson.

1. Muna bikes to school every morning. It takes her 20 minutes to travel 3 miles. What is Muna's average rate of speed, in miles per hour, on her trip to school?

    A.   7
    B.   8
    C.   9
    D.   10
    E.   11

2. The ratio of seniors to juniors in a class is 3:5. If the class has 32 total students who are exclusively juniors and seniors, how many more juniors are there than seniors?

    F.   2
    G.   5
    H.   8
    J.   12
    K.   20

3. Tyrone is reading a road map. On the map, $\frac{1}{4}$ inch represents 12 miles. Approximately how many miles apart are two cities that are $3\frac{1}{2}$ inches apart on Tyrone's map?

    A.   12
    B.   48
    C.   96
    D.   132
    E.   168

4. If 125% of a number is 470, what is 50% of the number?

    F.   168
    G.   188
    H.   208
    J.   228
    K.   248

5. There are green, red, and blue marbles in a bag in a ratio of 1:2:3. The total number of marbles in the bag is 42. All the red marbles are taken and moved into a new bag with different marbles. After the addition of the red marbles, the second bag contains 52 marbles. How many marbles were in the second bag before the addition of the red marbles?

    A.   17
    B.   24
    C.   31
    D.   38
    E.   45

Answers and explanations are on the next page. ▶ ▶ ▶

Check Your Work

1. C
Difficulty: Low
Category: Number and Quantity: Rates, Ratios, and Proportions
Getting to the Answer: The question asks for a bicyclist's average speed and provides distance in miles and time in minutes. Notice that all of the answer choices are in miles per hour, so start by converting the time from minutes into hours:

$$20 \text{ minutes} \times \frac{1 \text{ hour}}{60 \text{ minutes}} = \frac{20}{60} \text{ hours} = \frac{1}{3} \text{ hours}$$

Now use the formula $d = rt$ to solve for r.

$$d = rt$$
$$3 = r\left(\frac{1}{3}\right)$$
$$9 = r$$

The question asks for r, so (C) is correct.

2. H
Difficulty: Medium
Category: Number and Quantity: Rates, Ratios, and Proportions
Getting to the Answer: Read carefully; the question asks how many more juniors than seniors are in a class. The stem provides the number of *total* students and the ratio of seniors to juniors. Convert the part-to-part ratio to a part-to-whole ratio of seniors to total students: $\frac{3}{3+5} = \frac{3}{8}$. Then, set up a proportion and cross-multiply to solve for the number of seniors:

$$\frac{3}{8} = \frac{s}{32}$$
$$3(32) = 8s$$
$$96 = 8s$$
$$12 = s$$

Since there are 12 seniors in a class of 32 total students, there must be $32 - 12 = 20$ juniors. The question asks how many more juniors there are than seniors, so the correct answer is $20 - 12 = 8$, (H).

3. E
Difficulty: Medium
Category: Number and Quantity: Rates, Ratios, and Proportions
Getting to the Answer: The question asks you to determine the mileage between two cities. You are given their distance apart on a road map and the scale used for the map. Set up a proportion and cross-multiply. Convert $3\frac{1}{2}$ into the improper fraction $\frac{7}{2}$ to make the calculations easier.

$$\frac{\frac{1}{4}\text{inch}}{12 \text{ miles}} = \frac{\frac{7}{2}\text{inch}}{x \text{ miles}}$$
$$\frac{1}{4}x = 12\left(\frac{7}{2}\right)$$
$$\frac{1}{4}x = 42$$
$$x = 168$$

The question asks for x, so (E) is correct.

4. G
Difficulty: Medium
Category: Number and Quantity: Percents
Getting to the Answer: This question asks for the value of 50% of a number given the value of 125% of that number. Translate carefully from English into math. In a word problem, "of" means multiply, "a number" means a variable, and "is" means equals. Translate the first part of the question and solve for x. Remember that $125\% = 1.25$.

$$1.25x = 470$$
$$x = 376$$

Finally, because it's what the question asks for, take 50% of x.

$$(0.50)x = (0.50)(376)$$
$$= 188$$

Choice (G) is correct.

5. D

Difficulty: Medium

Category: Number and Quantity: Rates, Ratios, and Proportions

Getting to the Answer: The question asks for the original number of marbles in the second bag. You are given the final number of marbles in that bag, the ratio of different colors of marbles, and the total number of marbles in the first bag from which the red marbles were taken. Use the ratio to find the number of red marbles and subtract that from the total number of marbles in the second bag.

Since the ratio of green to red to blue marbles in the first bag is 1:2:3, the ratio of red marbles to total marbles is 2:6. Set up a proportion and cross-multiply to solve for the number of red marbles in the first bag:

$$\frac{2}{6} = \frac{r}{42}$$

$$\frac{1}{3} = \frac{r}{42}$$

$$42 = 3r$$

$$14 = r$$

Since there are 52 marbles in the second bag after the addition of the red marbles from the first bag, there must have been $52 - 14 = 38$ marbles originally in the second bag. This is the value you need, so (D) is correct.

Math

RATES, RATIOS, AND PROPORTIONS

To answer a question like this:

A construction team is building a house from blueprints that are made to scale. Every 0.5 inch on the blueprint corresponds to 5 feet that the construction team needs to build. One wall the team is currently working on is 4.5 inches tall in the blueprint. Approximately how many *feet* tall does the wall need to be?

A. 15

B. 27

C. 38

D. 45

E. 63

You need to know this:

A **rate** is any "something per something"—days per week, miles per hour, dollars per gallon, etc.

• Pay close attention to the units of measurement; the rate could be given in one measurement in the question and a different measurement in the answer choices.

  • This means you would need to convert the units in the first rate to the units in the desired rate before you answer the question.

  • On the ACT, unit conversion is usually tested in conjunction with geometry, so you should review chapter 13 for instruction on this skill.

• Rate questions will often use the DIRT formula: Distance Is Rate × Time, or $d = rt$. The rate will always be the something per something, the distance value will match the units in the first part of the rate ("something per . . . "), and the time value will match the units in the second part of the rate (" . . . per something").

A **ratio** is a comparison of one quantity to another.

• When writing ratios, you can compare one part of a group to another part of that group, or you can compare a part of the group to the whole group.

  • If you have a bowl of apples and oranges, you can write ratios that compare apples to oranges (part to part), apples to total fruit (part to whole), and oranges to total fruit (part to whole).

• Ratios can be expressed using colons (3:5), fractions $\left(\frac{3}{5}\right)$, or words (3 to 5).

• Ratios are typically expressed in lowest terms and convey relative amounts—not necessarily actual amounts.

  • If there are 10 apples and 6 bananas in a bowl, the ratio of apples to bananas would likely be expressed as $\frac{5}{3}$ on the ACT rather than as $\frac{10}{6}$.

  • If you know the ratio of apples to bananas and either the actual number of apples or the total number of pieces of fruit, you can find the actual number of bananas by setting up a proportion, but if you only know ratios and no actual numbers, you cannot calculate any actual numbers.

- If the ratio of apples to bananas is $\frac{5}{3}$ and there are 10 apples, then you can use the common multiplier 2 (because $5 \times 2 = 10$) to determine that there must be $3 \times 2 = 6$ bananas.
- If the ratio of apples to bananas is $\frac{5}{3}$ and there are 16 pieces of fruit, you can set up a proportion to find the number of bananas:

$$\frac{3 \text{ bananas}}{5 \text{ apples}} \rightarrow \frac{3 \text{ bananas}}{8 \text{ total fruit}}$$

$$\frac{3 \text{ bananas}}{8 \text{ total fruit}} = \frac{b \text{ bananas}}{16 \text{ total fruit}}$$

$$3(16) = 8b$$

$$48 = 8b$$

$$6 = b$$

- If the only information provided is that the ratio of apples to bananas is $\frac{5}{3}$ and the ratio of apples to total fruit is $\frac{5}{8}$, then there is not enough information to determine the actual numbers of apples or bananas or the total number of fruit.

A **proportion** is simply two ratios set equal to each other, e.g., $\frac{a}{b} = \frac{c}{d}$.

- Proportions are an efficient way to solve certain questions, but you must exercise caution when setting them up.
- Noting the units of each piece of the proportion will help you put each piece of the proportion in the right place.
- Cross-multiplication allows you to easily convert a proportion into an often easy-to-solve equation:

$$\frac{a}{b} \times \frac{c}{d} \rightarrow ad = bc$$

- If you know any three numerical values in a proportion, you can solve for the fourth.
  - For example: say a fruit stand sells 3 peaches for every 5 apricots, and you need to calculate the number of peaches sold on a day when 20 apricots were sold.
  - You could use this information to set up a proportion and solve for the unknown:

$$\frac{3}{5} = \frac{p}{20}$$

  - You can now solve for the number of peaches sold, p, by cross-multiplying:

$$60 = 5p$$

$$p = 12$$

  - Alternatively, you could use the common multiplier to solve for p: the numerator and denominator in the original ratio must be multiplied by the same value to arrive at their respective terms in the new ratio.
  - To get from 5 to 20 in the denominator, you multiply by 4, so you also have to multiply the 3 in the numerator by 4 to arrive at the actual number of peaches sold: $4(3) = 12$.

You need to do this:

- Identify the quantities and units used in any rates, ratios, or proportions in the question stem or answer choices.
- When needed, convert between part:part and part:whole ratios.
- When helpful, convert ratios that use colons into ratios that use fractions.

- Use common multipliers to calculate common ratios.
- Set up a proportion using two ratios and solve for the unknown either by cross-multiplying or by using the common multiplier.

Explanation:

The question asks how many feet tall a wall must be and gives the blueprint scale in inches. Use the given information to set up a proportion to solve for the actual height of the wall. Make sure that the units on both sides of the equal sign match up:

$$\frac{0.5 \text{ inch}}{5 \text{ feet}} = \frac{4.5 \text{ inch}}{x \text{ feet}}$$

$$0.5x = 4.5(5)$$
$$0.5x = 22.5$$
$$x = 45$$

Thus, the wall must be 45 feet tall, and choice (D) is correct.

Drills

If rates, ratios, and proportions give you trouble, study the information above and try out these drill questions before completing the Try on Your Own questions below. Determine the value of the variable for each part. Drill answers can be found in Answers and Explanations.

a. $\frac{2}{10} = \frac{x}{15}$

b. $\frac{7}{2} = \frac{7}{x}$

c. $\frac{a}{12} = \frac{6}{8}$

d. $\frac{\frac{1}{2}}{w} = \frac{\frac{1}{4}}{\frac{5}{2}}$

e. $\frac{2.5}{5} = \frac{z}{4}$

Try on Your Own

Directions: Take as much time as you need on these questions. Work carefully and methodically. There will be an opportunity for timed practice at the end of the chapter.

1. Which of the following values of x satisfies the proportion $\frac{5(x-2)}{9} = \frac{4}{3}$?

   A. $\frac{18}{15}$
   B. $\frac{33}{15}$
   C. $\frac{42}{15}$
   D. $\frac{51}{15}$
   E. $\frac{66}{15}$

HINT: For Q2, fractions inside of fractions can look confusing, but the cross-multiplication still works the same way. Which terms should you multiply together?

2. What is the value of $x - y$ if $y = 4$ and $\frac{\frac{3}{5}}{\frac{1}{2}} = \frac{x}{10}$?

   F. 4
   G. 8
   H. 10
   J. 12
   K. 16

3. At the end of the season, a team's ratio of wins to losses was 3:5. If there were no ties, what percentage of its games did the team win?

   A. $33\frac{1}{3}$%

   B. $37\frac{1}{2}$%

   C. 40%

   D. $62\frac{1}{2}$%

   E. 75%

4. Four liters of water are mixed with 6 juiced lemons to make lemonade. How many liters of water should be mixed with 10 juiced lemons to obtain the same result?

   F. $4\frac{2}{3}$

   G. $5\frac{1}{3}$

   H. $6\frac{1}{3}$

   J. $6\frac{2}{3}$

   K. $8\frac{1}{3}$

5. For a certain company, a train coming from New York to Washington, D.C., takes 3 hours to travel 228 miles. A new train company is able to complete the same journey in only 2.5 hours. How much faster is the new company's train in terms of miles per hour (mph)?

   A. 7.5

   B. 11.7

   C. 15.2

   D. 17.3

   E. 21.4

6. Two packages of strawberries are sold for $10. How many packages could you buy with $25?

   F. 3

   G. 4

   H. 5

   J. 6

   K. 7

7. Which of the following is equivalent to $\dfrac{x^2y}{2zw} = \dfrac{4xy^2}{3z^3w}$?

   A. $y = \dfrac{3xz^2}{8}$

   B. $x = \dfrac{3yz^2}{8}$

   C. $z = \dfrac{3xy^2}{8}$

   D. $w = \dfrac{3xz^2}{8}$

   E. $\dfrac{3}{8} = yxz^2$

HINT: For Q8, do you have part:part or part:whole ratios? What actual numbers are you given? What are you trying to find?

---

8. The ratio of students to faculty on the First Year College Experience Committee at a certain university is 1.2:1. If there are 22 people on the committee, how many faculty are on the committee?

   F. 3

   G. 7

   H. 10

   J. 15

   K. 19

9. The school newspaper staff is selling cookies to raise money for the next school year. The first student who sells 252 boxes earns a laptop. Eva sells on average 7 boxes per hour, while Sylvia sells on average 3 boxes every 30 minutes. How much time, in hours, will pass until at least one of the students sells enough boxes to earn a laptop?

   A. 10
   B. 15
   C. 23
   D. 36
   E. 42

10. Carmen and Eduardo are building a tree house. Their mother constructs a drawing to scale that uses only two different lengths of wood pieces. The ratio, in inches, of the wood pieces is 2:3. If the longer wood piece is 5.5 feet, then how long is the shorter wood piece? (12 inches = 1 foot)

    F. 3 feet, 8 inches
    G. 3 feet, 10 inches
    H. 4 feet
    J. 4 feet, 2 inches
    K. 8 feet, 3 inches

PERCENTS

LEARNING OBJECTIVES

After this lesson, you will be able to:

- Calculate percents
- Calculate percent change

To answer a question like this:

In 1960, scientists estimated a certain animal population in a particular geographical area to be 6,400. In 2000, the population had risen to 7,200. If this animal population experiences the same percent increase over the next 40 years, what will the approximate population be in 2040?

A. 7,200
B. 8,000
C. 8,100
D. 8,500
E. 9,000

You need to know this:

To calculate percents, use this basic equation:

$$\text{percent} = \frac{\text{part}}{\text{whole}} \times 100\%$$

Alternatively, use this statement: [blank] percent of [blank] is [blank]. Translating from English into math, you get [blank]% × [blank] = [blank].

You may sometimes need to calculate percent change on the ACT. You can determine the percent change in a given situation by applying this formula:

$$\text{percent change} = \frac{\text{amount of change}}{\text{original amount}} \times 100\%$$

If the change is positive, the amount of change will be positive. If the change is negative, the amount of change will be negative. So, a change in population might be a 3% change, while the change in a sales price might be −40%.

Sometimes more than one change will occur. Be careful here, as it can be tempting to take a "shortcut" by just adding two percent changes together (which will almost always lead to an incorrect answer). Instead, you'll need to find the total amount of the increase or decrease and then apply the formula.

You need to do this:

To use the basic percents equation:

- Plug in the values for any two parts of the formula and solve for the third.
- In some calculations, it may be more convenient to express percents as decimals. To do this, use the formula above, but stop before you multiply by 100% at the end.

To calculate a percent change:

- Calculate the actual increase or decrease.
- Divide by the original amount (not the new amount!).
- Multiply by 100%.

Explanation:

Use the percent change formula to find the percent change from 1960 to 2000.

$$\text{percent change} = \frac{\text{amount of change}}{\text{original amount}} \times 100\%$$

Plug in the values given in the question stem.

$$\frac{7,200 - 6,400}{6,400} = \frac{800}{6,400} = 0.125 \times 100\% = 12.5\%$$

Finally, apply this same percent increase to the population in the year 2000. Remember that 12.5% = 0.125.

$7,200 + 7,200(0.125) = 8,100$. Hence, (C) is correct.

Drills

If percents give you trouble, study the information above and try out these drill questions before completing the Try on Your Own questions below. Drill answers can be found in Answers and Explanations.

a. Calculate 25% of 200.

b. Calculate $1.8 \times 75\%$.

c. Express $\frac{11}{15}$ as a percent.

d. Express 1.3×0.4 as a percent.

e. Express 150% of 60% as a percent.

Try on Your Own

Directions: Take as much time as you need on these questions. Work carefully and methodically. There will be an opportunity for timed practice at the end of the chapter.

1. A school admits applicants only if they are able to pass a written and oral exam. Past records have shown that 60% of the applicants pass the written exam, and 80% of the applicants who pass the written exam go on to pass the oral exam. If there are 1,500 applicants, how many students will be admitted?

   A.   500
   B.   720
   C.   900
   D.   1,000
   E.   1,200

2. The managers of a restaurant calculated their business expenditures for the previous month. Overhead cost was $4,800, food cost was $8,000, and wages paid to employees were $6,500. What percent of the total expenditures did the greatest expense comprise? Round your answer to the nearest whole percent.

   F.   25%
   G.   29%
   H.   35%
   J.   41%
   K.   46%

3. 12% of 50 is $\frac{3}{5}$ of what number?

   A.   7
   B.   8
   C.   9
   D.   10
   E.   11

4. What number is 16% of 25?

   F.   4
   G.   5
   H.   6
   J.   7
   K.   8

HINT: Questions like Q5 can be quick and easy to solve if you translate carefully from English to math.

---

5. 40% of 24 is $\frac{5}{2}$ of what number?

   A.   2.76
   B.   3.35
   C.   3.84
   D.   4.52
   E.   5.12

On Test Day

When a question features multiple percentages, you have to make a key strategic decision: Can you do the arithmetic on the percentages themselves and get the answer right away, or do you have to calculate each percentage individually and do the arithmetic on the actual values?

For example, suppose a car traveling 50 miles per hour increases its speed by 20 percent and then decreases its speed by 20 percent. Can you just say that its final speed is 50 miles per hour since $+20\% - 20\% = 0$? No, because after a 20% increase, the car's speed becomes 120% of the original: $1.2(50) = 60$. When the car "decreases its speed by 20 percent," that 20 percent is calculated based on the new speed, 60, not the original speed, and 20 percent of 60 is greater than 20 percent of 50. Thus, the car's final speed is lower than its starting speed: $50(1.2)(0.8) = 48$ miles per hour.

By contrast, suppose you have to find how many more pet owners than non-pet owners live in a certain region where there are 13,450 residents, 32 percent of whom don't own a pet and 68 percent of whom do. It may be tempting to find 32 percent of 13,450 ($0.32 \times 13,450 = 4,304$), then find 68 percent of 13,450 ($0.68 \times 13,450 = 9,146$), and finally subtract those two numbers to get the answer ($9,146 - 4,304 = 4,842$). This is a waste of time, even though it will give you the correct answer. Instead, you can quickly find the difference between the two percentages ($68 - 32 = 36$) and take 36 percent of the total to get the answer in one step: $13,450 \times 0.36 = 4,842$, which is the same answer because the totals are the same.

If you can do arithmetic using the percentages but choose to do arithmetic on the raw numbers instead, you'll waste time doing unnecessary work. But if you can't do arithmetic on the percentages (as in the first example) but try anyway, you'll get the incorrect answer. Being able to tell whether you can or can't do the arithmetic on the percentages is a useful skill.

Luckily, the fundamental principle is simple: you can do arithmetic on the percentages as long as the percentages are out of the same total. If the totals are different, then you must convert the percentages into actual values. Practice applying this principle to this question from earlier in this chapter:

1. A school admits applicants only if they are able to pass a written and oral exam. Past records have shown that 60% of the applicants pass the written exam, and 80% of the applicants who pass the written exam go on to pass the oral exam. If there are 1,500 applicants, how many students will be admitted?

    A. 500
    B. 720
    C. 900
    D. 1,050
    E. 1,200

The answer and explanation can be found at the end of this chapter.

How Much Have You Learned?

Directions: For test-like practice, give yourself 10 minutes to complete this question set. Be sure to study the explanations, even for questions you got correct. They can be found at the end of this chapter.

1. Which of the following will result in an odd integer for any integer n?

   A. n^2

   B. $3n^2$

   C. $4n^2$

   D. $3n^2 + 1$

   E. $4n^2 + 1$

2. Yeong-Ho owns two dogs. Each day, one dog eats $1\frac{1}{2}$ scoops of dog food, and the other eats $2\frac{3}{4}$ scoops of the same dog food. If one bag of this dog food contains about 340 scoops, how many days should it last the two dogs?

   F. 80

   G. 85

   H. 92

   J. 100

   K. 120

3. If $a:b = 2:5$ and $b:c = 4:3$, what is the ratio of $a:c$?

   A. 4:1

   B. 2:3

   C. 5:3

   D. 8:15

   E. 15:8

4. If 12 inches equal 30.48 centimeters, how many centimeters are in 36 inches?

   F. 91.44

   G. 92.33

   H. 93.48

   J. 93.89

   K. 94.52

5. A construction company is building a group of houses that all have the same ratio of length to width. If one house has a ratio of 10:3 and another house has a ratio of 5:a, then what is the value of $2a + 4$?

   A. -4

   B. $\frac{3}{2}$

   C. 7

   D. 8

   E. 12

6. At a factory, Taj produces 23 toys per hour and Rosa produces 47 toys per hour. How many hours will it take for Taj and Rosa to produce 490 toys?

   F. 4

   G. 5

   H. 6

   J. 7

   K. 8

7. Ernesto is shopping at a store that is having a clearance sale. The price of everything in the store is discounted by 25%. If Ernesto buys a shirt originally priced at $22.00 and a 6% sales tax is added, what will be the total price of the shirt?

   A. $29.15

   B. $23.10

   C. $18.66

   D. $17.49

   E. $16.50

8. Atiya bought pants that were on clearance for 40% off the original price. She paid the cashier a total of $29.70 after sales tax. If sales tax is 10%, what was the original price of the pants?

    F. $39.52

    G. $41.80

    H. $45

    J. $48

    K. $52.18

9. Ryan and Kamini can make 30 gallons of chocolate milk in 5 hours. Ryan can make 2 gallons of chocolate milk every hour. How many gallons of chocolate milk can Kamini make every hour?

    A. 1

    B. 2

    C. 3

    D. 4

    E. 5

10. A 12 foot metal alloy bar weighs 114 pounds. What is the weight in pounds of a bar made out of the same alloy, with the same width and height, that is 3 feet 8 inches long?

    F. $27\frac{1}{2}$

    G. $34\frac{5}{6}$

    H. $41\frac{2}{3}$

    J. $49\frac{1}{6}$

    K. $58\frac{1}{4}$

Reflect

Directions: Take a few minutes to recall what you've learned and what you've been practicing in this chapter. Consider the following questions, jot down your best answer for each one, and then compare your reflections to the expert responses on the following page. Use your level of confidence to determine what to do next.

1. What is a ratio, and how is it different from a proportion?

    _____

    _____

    _____

2. If you're given a ratio of one quantity to another, what can you say about the total number of quantities?

    _____

    _____

    _____

3. Suppose the value of something increases by 20 percent. How can you calculate the final value in the fewest number of steps? What if the value decreases by 20 percent?

    _____

    _____

    _____

4. What is the percent change formula, and what is the biggest pitfall to avoid when using it?

    _____

    _____

    _____

Responses

1. What is a ratio, and how is it different from a proportion?

A ratio is the relative comparison of one quantity to another. For example, if the ratio of dogs to cats in an animal shelter is 3 to 5, then there are 3 dogs for every 5 cats. A proportion is two ratios set equal to each other.

2. If you're given a ratio of one quantity to another, what can you say about the total number of quantities?

Given a ratio, you know that the total must be a multiple of the sum of the ratio's parts. For example, if the ratio of dogs to cats is 3 to 5, then the total number of dogs and cats must be a multiple of 3 + 5, or 8. This means that when the ACT gives you one ratio, it's actually giving you several. If you're told that dogs:cats = 3:5, then you also know that dogs:total = 3:8 and cats:total = 5:8. You can use this "hidden" knowledge to your advantage.

3. Suppose the value of something increases by 20 percent. How can you calculate the final value in the fewest number of steps? What if the value decreases by 20 percent?

The fastest way to increase a value by 20 percent is to multiply it by 1.2, which is 100% + 20% = 120%. Similarly, to decrease something by 20 percent, you multiply it by 0.8, as that is 100% − 20% = 80%.

4. What is the percent change formula, and what is the biggest pitfall to avoid when using it?

The percent change formula is:

$$\text{percent change} = \frac{\text{amount of change}}{\text{original amount}} \times 100\%$$

A common mistake is to put the new amount on the bottom of the fraction rather than the original amount.

Next Steps

If you answered most questions correctly in the "How Much Have You Learned?" section, and if your responses to the Reflect questions were similar to those of the ACT expert, then consider ratios and the related topics in this chapter an area of strength and move on to the next chapter. Come back to this topic periodically to prevent yourself from getting rusty.

If you don't yet feel confident, review those parts of this chapter that you have not yet mastered, and try the questions you missed again. As always, be sure to review the explanations closely. Then go online (**kaptest.com/login**) to watch video lessons about the highest-yield concepts in this chapter and to use your Qbank for more practice. If you haven't already registered your book, do so at **kaptest.com/moreonline.**

GO ONLINE

kaptest.com/login

Answers and Explanations

Rates, Ratios, and Proportions

Drill Answers

a. 3

b. 2

c. 9

d. 5

e. 2

1.   E
Difficulty: Medium
Category: Number and Quantity
Getting to the Answer: The question asks for the value of x and provides a proportion in which one term is x. Cross-multiply and simplify to solve for x:

$$\frac{5(x-2)}{9} = \frac{4}{3}$$
$$15(x-2) = 36$$
$$x - 2 = \frac{36}{15}$$
$$x = \frac{36}{15} + 2$$
$$x = \frac{36}{15} + \frac{30}{15}$$
$$x = \frac{66}{15}$$

You don't need to do anything with x, so (E) is correct.

2.   G
Difficulty: High
Category: Number and Quantity
Getting to the Answer: The question asks for the value of $x - y$. The value of y is provided, and x is part of a proportion with stacked fractions. Fractions inside of fractions can look confusing, but the cross-multiplication still works the same way:

$$\frac{\frac{3}{5}}{\frac{1}{2}} = \frac{x}{10}$$
$$\frac{3}{5}(10) = \frac{1}{2}x$$
$$6 = \frac{1}{2}x$$
$$12 = x$$

Remember that you need to find $x - y$. Since $x = 12$ and $y = 4$, $x - y = 8$, choice (G) is the correct answer.

3.   B
Difficulty: Low
Category: Number and Quantity
Getting to the Answer: The question gives you a team's win-loss ratio and asks for the percentage of games that the team won. Since there were no ties, you can convert the given part-to-part ratio of 3:5 to the part-to-whole ratio of 3:8. (Note that the 8 comes from the fact that $3 + 5 = 8$.) To find the percentage of games won, convert that ratio to a percentage: $\frac{3}{8} \times 100\% = 37.5\%$.

This is the percentage of games won, so (B) is correct. Be careful; D is the percentage of games *lost* and is therefore incorrect.

4.   J
Difficulty: Low
Category: Number and Quantity
Getting to the Answer: The question asks how many liters of water should be mixed with the juice from 10 lemons to create lemonade with the same concentration as mixing 4 liters of water with the juice from 6 lemons. Set up a proportion using the given information and designate the number of liters of water as w. Cross-multiply and solve for w:

$$\frac{w \text{ liters of water}}{10 \text{ lemons}} = \frac{4 \text{ liters of water}}{6 \text{ lemons}}$$
$$6w = 40$$
$$w = \frac{40}{6}$$
$$w = \frac{20}{3} = 6\frac{2}{3}$$

The question asks for w, so (J) is correct.

5.   C
Difficulty: Medium
Category: Number and Quantity
Getting to the Answer: The question asks how much faster one train is than another. The choices are stated in terms of mph. You are given the distance of a certain trip and the time it takes each train to complete the journey. Calculate each rate separately

by plugging the given distance and time into the $d = rt$ equation.

$$d_1 = r_1 t_1 \qquad d_2 = r_2 t_2$$
$$228 = r_1(3) \qquad 228 = r_2(2.5)$$
$$76 = r_1 \qquad 91.2 = r_2$$

The question asks for the difference between the rates, which is $91.2 - 76 = 15.2$ mph, (C).

6.   H
Difficulty: Low
Category: Number and Quantity
Getting to the Answer: The question asks how many packages of strawberries can be bought for $25 and gives the price for 2 packages of strawberries. Set up a proportion using the given information. Cross-multiply and solve for p.

$$\frac{2 \text{ packages}}{10 \text{ dollars}} = \frac{p \text{ packages}}{25 \text{ dollars}}$$
$$10p = 50$$
$$p = 5$$

This is the number of packages that you could buy with $25, so (H) is correct.

7.   A
Difficulty: High
Category: Number and Quantity
Getting to the Answer: The question asks which choice is equivalent to the given proportion. Since the choices are stated in terms of different variables, your strategy is to cross-multiply and isolate for one variable at a time, then compare your results to the corresponding choice. You may have to do this multiple times until you find something that matches an answer choice.

$$\frac{x^2 y}{2zw} = \frac{4xy^2}{3z^3 w}$$
$$3x^2 y z^3 w = 8xy^2 zw$$
$$3xz^2 = 8y$$
$$\frac{3xz^2}{8} = y$$

This question relies on trial and error, so you may not arrive at this answer immediately. When you isolate y, the resulting expression matches choice (A), so that is the correct answer.

8.   H
Difficulty: High
Category: Number and Quantity
Getting to the Answer: The question asks how many faculty are on a committee. You are given the total number of committee members and the ratio of students to faculty, which is 1.2:1.

Convert the part-to-part ratio to a part-to-whole ratio and use this ratio to solve for the number of faculty.

$$\frac{1 \text{ faculty}}{1 + 1.2 \text{ total}} = \frac{f \text{ faculty}}{22 \text{ total}}$$
$$(22)(1) = 2.2f$$
$$22 = 2.2f$$
$$10 = f$$

There are 10 faculty on the committee. Hence, (H) is correct.

9.   D
Difficulty: Medium
Category: Number and Quantity
Getting to the Answer: The question asks how long it will take the more efficient of the two students selling cookies to reach a specific sales goal. You are given the rates at which both students are selling, but these rates are in different units. First, check to see which student is selling boxes at a faster rate. Sylvia sells 3 boxes every 30 minutes, or 6 boxes every hour. Eva sells 7 boxes per hour, so she will reach the goal first.

Now use the $d = rt$ equation to solve for t to determine how long it will take her to sell 252 boxes:

$$d = rt$$
$$252 = 7t$$
$$36 = t$$

This is how long it will take the faster student to sell the cookies, so (D) is correct. Note that E is how many hours it would take Sylvia, the student who sells at a slower rate, to sell the 252 boxes.

10. F

Difficulty: Medium
Category: Number and Quantity
Getting to the Answer: The question gives you the ratio of the lengths of two pieces of wood and asks for the length of the shorter piece. Set up a proportion and cross-multiply to solve.

$$\frac{2 \text{ in}}{3 \text{ in}} = \frac{x \text{ ft}}{5.5 \text{ ft}}$$

$$2(5.5) = 3x$$

$$\frac{11}{3} = x$$

Finally, convert $\frac{11}{3}$ into a mixed number of feet and inches.

$$\frac{11}{3} \text{ ft} = 3\frac{2}{3} \text{ ft}$$

$$\frac{2}{3} \text{ ft} \times \frac{12 \text{ in}}{\text{ft}} = 8 \text{ in}$$

This is the length of the shorter piece, so (F) is correct. Choice K is a strong distractor that you would choose if you reversed the ratio.

Percents

Drill Answers

a. 50

b. 1.35

c. 73.33%

d. 52%

e. 90%

1. B

Difficulty: Medium
Category: Number and Quantity
Getting to the Answer: The question asks how many students will be admitted to a certain school. You're given the total number of applicants, the percent who pass the written exam, and the percent (of those who pass the written exam) who pass the oral exam. Start by multiplying the total number of applicants by the percent of applicants who pass the written exam.

$$1,500\,(0.60) = 900$$

Then multiply by the percent of applicants who pass the oral exam.

$$900\,(0.80) = 720$$

This gives the number of admitted applicants, so (B) is correct.

2. J

Difficulty: Low
Category: Number and Quantity
Getting to the Answer: The question asks you to find the greatest expenditure and calculate what percent of the total it was. Recall that percent $= \dfrac{\text{part}}{\text{whole}} \times 100\%$. The question asks about the highest expenditure, which is food cost. The total expenditure is $4,800 + $8,000 + $6,500 = $19,300. Plug these numbers into the percent formula.

$$\text{percent} = \frac{8,000}{19,300} \times 100\%$$

$$= 0.41451 \times 100\%$$

$$= 41.451\%$$

Round to the nearest whole number to get 41%, choice (J).

3. D

Difficulty: Medium
Category: Number and Quantity
Getting to the Answer: To understand what the question asks, translate carefully from English into math. Recall that "of" means multiply, "is" means equals, and "what number" means x. First convert 12% to 0.12.

$$0.12(50) = \frac{3}{5}x$$

$$6 = \frac{3}{5}x$$

$$6\left(\frac{5}{3}\right) = x$$

$$10 = x$$

You chose x to represent the number the question asked for, so (D) is correct.

4. F

Difficulty: Low
Category: Number and Quantity
Getting to the Answer: To understand what the question asks, translate carefully from English into math. Recall that "what number" means x, "is" means equals, and "of" means multiply. Convert 16% to 0.16.

$$x = (0.16)(25)$$

$$x = 4$$

This is the number that was asked for, so (F) is correct.

5.   C

Difficulty: Medium

Category: Number and Quantity

Getting to the Answer: To understand what the question asks, translate carefully from English into math. Recall that "of" means multiply, "is" means equals, and "what number" means x.

$$0.40 \times 24 = \frac{5}{2}x$$

$$9.6 = \frac{5}{2}x$$

$$9.6\left(\frac{2}{5}\right) = x$$

$$3.84 = x$$

This is the value you need, so (C) is correct.

On Test Day

1.   B

Difficulty: Medium

Category: Number and Quantity

Getting to the Answer: The question asks how many students will be admitted to a certain school. You're given the total number of applicants, the percent who pass the written exam, and the percent (of those who pass the written exam) who pass the oral exam. Start by multiplying the total number of applicants by the percent of applicants who pass the written exam:

$$1,500\,(0.60) = 900$$

Then multiply by the percent of applicants who pass the oral exam:

$$900\,(0.80) = 720$$

This gives the number of admitted applicants, so (B) is correct.

The students who pass the written exam and the students who pass the oral exam are separate groups, but the number of students who pass the oral exam is a subset of the number of students who pass the written exam. This means that the totals are different, and thus, you must calculate each percent independently. Someone who chooses to average the percents will end up with $1,500(0.7) = 1,050$, D, which is incorrect. Skipping the first percent and directly finding 80% of the original total (instead of 80% of those who pass the written exam) will also yield an incorrect answer, E: $1,500(0.8) = 1,200$.

How Much Have You Learned?

1.   E

Difficulty: High

Category: Number and Quantity

Getting to the Answer: You need to find the expression that will always yield an odd integer. The question states that n is an integer, but it could be positive or negative or zero, and it could be even or odd. The answers contain variables, so Picking Numbers is an option.

Each choice contains an n^2, so start with that. Remember, n can be any integer, so you may as well pick an easy nu mber to start with.

If $n = 2$, then:

$n^2 = 2^2 = 4$, even. Eliminate A.

$3n^2 = 3(4) = 12$, even. Eliminate B.

$4n^2 = 4(4) = 16$, even. Eliminate C.

$3n^2 + 1 = 12 + 1 = 13$, odd. Keep D.

$4n^2 + 1 = 16 + 1 = 17$, odd. Keep E.

To decide between D and E, pick another value for n. This time, try an odd value. (You can then try negative numbers if using an odd number doesn't help you narrow it down to the correct answer.)

If $n = 3$, then:

$3n^2 + 1 = 3(9) + 1 = 28$, even. Eliminate D.

Choice (E) is correct.

2.   F

Difficulty: Medium

Category: Number and Quantity

Getting to the Answer: The question asks how many days it will take two dogs to consume a dog food bag of a certain size. You are told how much food each dog eats every day and how much food is in the bag. Since the dogs are eating out of the same bag of food, add the number of scoops each dog eats per day to find how many total scoops per day are being eaten.

$$1\frac{1}{2} + 2\frac{3}{4}$$

$$\frac{3}{2} + \frac{11}{4}$$

$$\frac{6}{4} + \frac{11}{4}$$

$$\frac{17}{4}$$

Since you are given a rate and asked to solve for time, use the $d = rt$ equation.

$$340 = \frac{17}{4}t$$

$$340\left(\frac{4}{17}\right) = t$$

$$80 = t$$

Because t represents the number of days the food will last, (F) is correct.

3.   D
Difficulty: Medium
Category: Number and Quantity
Getting to the Answer: The question asks for the ratio of a to c and provides the ratios of a to b and b to c. Notice that $\left(\frac{a}{b}\right)\left(\frac{b}{c}\right) = \frac{a}{c}$. To find $\frac{a}{c}$, simply multiply the two given ratios together.

$$\left(\frac{2}{5}\right)\left(\frac{4}{3}\right) = \frac{8}{15}$$

This is the ratio of a to c, so (D) is correct. Be certain that you answered the question that was asked. Choice E is the ratio of c to a.

4.   F
Difficulty: Low
Category: Number and Quantity
Getting to the Answer: The question asks how many centimeters are equivalent to 36 inches. You are given the number of centimeters in 12 inches. Set up a proportion and cross-multiply to solve for c, the number of centimeters in 36 inches.

$$\frac{12 \text{ inches}}{30.48 \text{ centimeters}} = \frac{36 \text{ inches}}{c \text{ centimeters}}$$

$$12c = (30.48)36$$

$$12c = 1{,}097.28$$

$$c = 91.44$$

Because c is the variable you chose to represent the answer, (F) is correct.

5.   C
Difficulty: Medium
Category: Number and Quantity
Getting to the Answer: The question asks for the value of $2a + 4$ and provides two equivalent ratios, one of which contains a. Begin by solving for a. Set up a proportion and cross-multiply:

$$\frac{10}{3} = \frac{5}{a}$$

$$10a = 15$$

$$a = \frac{3}{2}$$

You're not done yet, though. The question asks for $2a + 4$, so plug in $a = \frac{3}{2}$ to find the value of this expression.

$$2a + 4 = 2\left(\frac{3}{2}\right) + 4$$

$$= 3 + 4$$

$$= 7$$

This is the final answer, so (C) is correct. Be certain that you answered the question that was asked; choice B is the value of a.

6.   J
Difficulty: Medium
Category: Number and Quantity
Getting to the Answer: The question asks how long, in hours, it will take for two workers to produce 490 toys. You are given the rates at which each worker produces toys. Since both workers' rates are given in toys per hour, you can add the two rates together to find how many toys both workers make per hour: $23 + 47 = 70$. Plug this rate and the total number of toys needed into the $d = rt$ equation.

$$490 = 70t$$

$$7 = t$$

This is how long it will take the workers to produce 490 toys, so (J) is correct.

7.   D
Difficulty: Medium
Category: Number and Quantity
Getting to the Answer: The question asks what price Ernesto paid for a shirt. You are given the original price, a discount percentage, and a sales tax percentage. First determine the price of the shirt after the 25% discount. Recall that $22 - 22(0.25) = 22(0.75)$.

$$22(0.75) = 16.50$$

Now add the 6% sales tax by multiplying the price of the shirt by 1.06 (again, note that $100\% + 6\% = 106\% = 1.06$):

$$16.50\,(1.06) = 17.49$$

This is the final price of the shirt, so (D) is correct. Be certain that you considered everything stated in the question; E is the price without the sales tax added.

8.   H
Difficulty: High
Category: Number and Quantity
Getting to the Answer: The question asks for the original price of a pair of pants for which Atiya paid $29.70. You are given the discount rate and the sales tax rate in percents. If Atiya bought her pants at a 40% discount, then she must have paid 60% of what the original price was. Call the original price P:

$$0.60P$$

Additionally, Atiya was taxed 10% on this purchase. Recall that $0.60P + 0.60P(0.10) = 1.10(0.60P)$:

$$1.10(0.60P)$$

Finally, you are told that she paid the cashier $29.70. Create an equation and solve for P:

$$1.10\,(0.60P) = 29.70$$
$$0.66P = 29.70$$
$$P = 45$$

The original price of the pants was $45, so (H) is correct.

9.   D
Difficulty: Medium
Category: Number and Quantity
Getting to the Answer: The question asks how much chocolate milk Kamini can make per hour. You are given the rate at which Ryan makes chocolate milk and told that Ryan and Kamini working together

can make 30 gallons in 5 hours. Since both rates are given as gallons per hour, the rates can be added. Kamini's rate is not known, so call it k. Plug the given information into to the $d = rt$ equation. Simplify and solve for k.

$$30 = (2 + k)5$$
$$6 = 2 + k$$
$$4 = k$$

This is Kamini's rate, so (D) is correct.

10.   G
Difficulty: Medium
Category: Number and Quantity
Getting to the Answer: The question asks for the weight of a metal bar that is 3 feet 8 inches long. You are given the weight of the same type of bar that is 12 feet long. Before setting up a proportion, convert the 8 inches of the 3 feet 8 inch bar into feet.

$$8 \text{ inches} \left(\frac{1 \text{ foot}}{12 \text{ inches}}\right)$$
$$\frac{8}{12} \text{ foot}$$
$$\frac{2}{3} \text{ foot}$$

Thus, $3 \text{ feet} + 8 \text{ inches} = 3 \text{ feet} + \frac{2}{3} \text{ feet} = 3\frac{2}{3} \text{ feet} = \frac{11}{3}$ feet. Now set up the proportion and cross-multiply to solve for the weight of the bar.

$$\frac{12 \text{ feet}}{114 \text{ lbs}} = \frac{\frac{11}{3} \text{ feet}}{w \text{ lbs}}$$
$$12\,w = 114\left(\frac{11}{3}\right)$$
$$12\,w = 38(11)$$
$$w = \frac{38(11)}{12}$$
$$w = \frac{209}{6}$$

This is the final answer, but unfortunately, none of the answer choices are improper fractions. Convert into a mixed number to match the format of the choices: $\frac{209}{6} = 34\frac{5}{6}$. The answer is (G).

[CHAPTER 10]

ALGEBRA

LEARNING OBJECTIVES

After completing this chapter, you will be able to:

- Add, subtract, multiply, and factor polynomials
- Isolate a variable
- Calculate the slope or midpoint of a line given two points
- Write the equation of a line in slope-intercept form
- Solve an inequality for a range of values
- Identify the graph of an inequality
- Determine the inequality given a graph
- Identify solutions to quadratic equations
- Solve systems of equations
- Translate word problems into equations and/or inequalities and solve

Algebra: 7/36 SmartPoints® (High yield)

How Much Do You Know?

Directions: Try out the questions below. Show your work so that you can compare your solutions to the ones found on the next page. The "Category" heading in the explanation for each question gives the title of the lesson that covers how to solve it. If you answered the question(s) for a given lesson correctly, and if your scratchwork looks like ours, you may be able to move quickly through that lesson. If you answered incorrectly or used a different approach, you may want to take your time on that lesson.

1. What is the slope of the line given by the equation $-12x - 2y = 14$?

   A. -7
   B. -6
   C. $-\dfrac{1}{6}$
   D. $\dfrac{1}{6}$
   E. 6

2. At a certain toy store, tiny stuffed zebras cost $3 and giant stuffed zebras cost $14. The store doesn't sell any other sizes of stuffed zebras. If the store sold 29 stuffed zebras and made $208 in revenue in one week, how many tiny stuffed zebras were sold?

   F. 8
   G. 11
   H. 14
   J. 18
   K. 21

3. Which of the following expressions is equivalent to $\dfrac{2}{3}a(12a - 6b - 6a + 9b)$?

   A. $6a^2b$
   B. $9ab$
   C. $2a^2 + ab$
   D. $4a^2 + 2ab$
   E. $8a^2 - 4ab - 4a + 6b$

4. What is the midpoint of a line segment with endpoints $(4,-4)$ and $(-2,6)$?

   F. $(-1,5)$
   G. $(0,4)$
   H. $(1,1)$
   J. $(\sqrt{5}, \sqrt{13})$
   K. $(2\sqrt{5}, 2\sqrt{13})$

5. Brandy has a collection of comic books. If she adds 15 to the number of comic books in her collection and multiplies the sum by 3, the result will be 65 less than 4 times the number of comic books in her collection. How many comic books are in her collection?

   A. 50
   B. 85
   C. 100
   D. 110
   E. 145

6. Which of the following graphs represents the solution set for $5x - 10y > 6$?

    F.

    G.

    H.

    J.

    K.

7. What is the solution for x in the system of equations below?

    $$\begin{cases} 3x + 4y = 31 \\ 3x - 4y = -1 \end{cases}$$

    A. 4
    B. 5
    C. 6
    D. 9
    E. 10

8. Which of the following are solutions to the quadratic equation $(x + 1)^2 = \dfrac{1}{25}$?

    F. $x = -6, x = 4$
    G. $x = -\dfrac{24}{25}$
    H. $x = -\dfrac{6}{5}, x = -\dfrac{4}{5}$
    J. $x = -\dfrac{4}{5}, x = \dfrac{6}{5}$
    K. $x = \dfrac{4}{5}, x = \dfrac{6}{5}$

9. Which of the following inequalities is equivalent to $-2 - 4x \le -6x$?

    A. $x \ge -2$
    B. $x \ge 1$
    C. $x \ge 2$
    D. $x \le -1$
    E. $x \le 1$

10. Which value(s) of x satisfies the equation $5|2x - 6| + 3 = 13$?

    F. -2
    G. 2
    H. 4
    J. -2 and 4
    K. 2 and 4

Check Your Work

1.   B

Difficulty: Low
Category: Algebra: Linear Graphs
Getting to the Answer: To find the slope of a line given by an equation in standard form, rewrite the equation in slope-intercept form: $y = mx + b$. In this form, the coefficient of x gives you the slope, so manipulate the equation in the question to put it in slope-intercept form:

$$-12x - 2y = 14$$
$$-2y = 12x + 14$$
$$y = \frac{12x}{-2} + \frac{14}{-2}$$
$$y = -6x - 7$$

The slope of the equation is -6, which is (B).

2.   J

Difficulty: Medium
Category: Algebra: Systems of Equations
Getting to the Answer: The question asks how many tiny stuffed zebras were sold. Carefully translate from English into math. Because both toys are zebras, z is likely to be a confusing choice for a variable. Instead, use t for tiny and g for giant.

$$t + g = 29$$
$$3t + 14g = 208$$

You now have a system of equations. You want to find t, so use combination to eliminate g. Multiply the first equation by -14 and add the result to the second equation. Then solve for t.

$$-14t - 14g = -406$$
$$+ \quad 3t + 14g = \quad 208$$
$$\overline{\qquad\qquad -11t = -198}$$
$$t = \quad 18$$

Don't waste time finding the value of g. The question asks only for the number of tiny stuffed zebras, so you're done. Choice (J) is correct.

3.   D

Difficulty: Low
Category: Algebra: Polynomials
Getting to the Answer: The question asks you to simplify the expression. Resist the urge to distribute the $\frac{2}{3}a$ to each term inside the parentheses immediately; instead, first use PEMDAS to combine like terms inside the parentheses: $\frac{2}{3}a(6a + 3b)$. Then, distribute the $\frac{2}{3}a$: $4a^2 + 2ab$. Choice (D) is correct.

4.   H

Difficulty: Low
Category: Algebra: Linear Graphs
Getting to the Answer: The question asks for the midpoint of the two given points. The coordinates of the midpoint of a line segment with endpoints (x_1, y_1) and (x_2, y_2) are $\left(\frac{x_1 + x_2}{2}, \frac{y_1 + y_2}{2}\right)$. Plug the points $(4, -4)$ and $(-2, 6)$ into the midpoint equation: $\left(\frac{4 + -2}{2}, \frac{-4 + 6}{2}\right) = (1, 1)$. Choice (H) is correct.

5.   D

Difficulty: Medium
Category: Algebra: Word Problems
Getting to the Answer: The question asks how many comic books are in Brandy's collection. Call the number of comic books in Brandy's collection c. Then, translate methodically from English into math. First, "she adds 15 to the number" means $c + 15$. Then she "multiplies the sum by 3," so you have $3(c + 15)$. "The result will be" indicates an equal sign, and "65 less than 4 times the number" is $4c - 65$. So this scenario can be modeled by the equation $3(c + 15) = 4c - 65$. Now solve for c:

$$3(c + 15) = 4c - 65$$
$$3c + 45 = 4c - 65$$
$$45 = c - 65$$
$$110 = c$$

Brandy has 110 comic books in her collection. Choice (D) is correct.

Math

6. H
Difficulty: Medium
Category: Algebra: Graphing Inequalities
Getting to the Answer: The question asks you to match the given inequality to the correct graph. Start with straightforward math by rewriting the inequality in slope-intercept form. Remember that the inequality symbol flips when you divide by a negative:

$$5x - 10y > 6$$
$$-10y > -5x + 6$$
$$\frac{-10y}{-10} < \frac{-5x}{-10} + \frac{6}{-10}$$
$$y < \frac{1}{2}x - \frac{3}{5}$$

The y-intercept is $-\frac{3}{5}$, so you can eliminate F, J, and K immediately. The "less than" symbol indicates that the shading should be below the dashed line (use the y-axis values to determine what's "less than" as needed), so (H) must be correct.

7. B
Difficulty: Low
Category: Algebra: Systems of Equations
Getting to the Answer: The question asks you to solve for the x-value in the system of equations. Any system of equations with the same number of equations as variables can be solved with either combination or substitution, but one approach will often be easier than the other. Because this system already has $+4y$ and $-4y$, combination is the better choice here:

$$3x + 4y = 31$$
$$+ \ 3x - 4y = -1$$
$$6x = 30$$
$$x = 5$$

The question asks for the value of x, so (B) is correct. There is no need to find the value of y.

8. H
Difficulty: Medium
Category: Algebra: Quadratics
Getting to the Answer: The question asks you to solve for the solutions of the given quadratic. Both sides of this equation are already perfect squares, so take the square roots of both sides instead of FOILing the left side. Then, solve the resulting equations. Remember that there will be two equations to solve as a result of the square root step, both a positive case and a negative case:

$$(x + 1)^2 = \frac{1}{25}$$
$$\sqrt{(x + 1)^2} = \sqrt{\frac{1}{25}}$$
$$x + 1 = \frac{1}{5}$$
$$x = -\frac{4}{5}$$

Now simplify each equation:

$$x = -1 + \frac{1}{5} = -\frac{5}{5} + \frac{1}{5} = -\frac{4}{5}$$

and

$$x = -1 - \frac{1}{5} = -\frac{5}{5} - \frac{1}{5} = -\frac{6}{5}$$

The solutions are $x = -\frac{6}{5}$ and $-\frac{4}{5}$. Choice (H) is correct.

9. E

Difficulty: Low
Category: Algebra: Solving Inequalities
Getting to the Answer: The question asks you to solve for the given inequality. You solve an inequality the same way you solve an equation, but with one difference: if you multiply or divide by a negative number, you must reverse the direction of the inequality symbol. To keep things simple, try to move the terms in such a way that you don't end up with negatives:

$$-2 - 4x \le -6x$$
$$-2 + 2x \le 0$$
$$2x \le 2$$
$$x \le 1$$

The values of x are less than or equal to 1. Choice (E) is correct.

10. K

Difficulty: Medium
Category: Algebra: Solving Equations
Getting to the Answer: The question asks you to solve for the values of x. Isolate x by first subtracting 3 from both sides and then dividing by 5:

$$5|2x - 6| + 3 = 13$$
$$5|2x - 6| = 10$$
$$|2x - 6| = \frac{10}{5}$$
$$|2x - 6| = 2$$

Recall that if $|x| = a$, then $x = a$ and $x = -a$. Therefore, you must split the absolute value equation into two separate equations and solve for x:

$$2x - 6 = 2$$
$$2x = 8$$
$$x = 4$$

and

$$2x - 6 = -2$$
$$2x = 4$$
$$x = 2$$

Therefore, $x = 2$ and $x = 4$. Choice (K) is correct.

POLYNOMIALS

LEARNING OBJECTIVE

After this lesson, you will be able to:

- Add, subtract, multiply, and factor polynomials

To answer a question like this:

Which of the following expressions is equivalent to $x(x - 6) - 8(2 - x)$?

A. $3x - 16$

B. $6x - 16$

C. $x^2 - 14x - 16$

D. $x^2 + 2x - 16$

E. $2x^2 - 4x - 16$

You need to know this:

A **polynomial** is an expression composed of variables, exponents, and coefficients. By definition, a polynomial cannot have a variable in a denominator, and all exponents must be integers. Here are some examples of polynomial and non-polynomial expressions:

Polynomials	Non-Polynomials
$23x^2$	$\frac{10}{z} + 13$
$\frac{x}{5} - 6$	$x^3 y^{-6}$
$y^{11} - 2y^6 + \frac{2}{3}xy^3 - 4x^2$	$x^{\frac{1}{2}}$
$z + 6$	$\frac{4}{y - 3}$

You need to do this:

To add and subtract polynomials, start by identifying like terms—that is, terms in which both the types of variables and their exponents match. For example, x^2 and $3x^2$ are like terms; adding them would give $4x^2$ and subtracting them would give $x^2 - 3x^2 = -2x^2$. Note that you cannot add or subtract unlike terms. For example, there is no way to simplify $x^2 + y$. You can, however, multiply unlike terms: $x^2 \cdot y = x^2 y$.

To multiply two polynomials, multiply each term in the first factor by each term in the second factor, then combine like terms.

To factor a polynomial, find a value or variable that divides evenly into each term. For example: $2x^3 + 2x^2 + 2x = 2x(x^2 + x + 1)$.

Explanation:

The question asks you to simplify the given expression. First, distribute the x and -8: $x^2 - 6x - 16 + 8x$. Then combine like terms: $x^2 + 2x - 16$. Choice (D) is correct.

Try on Your Own

Directions: Take as much time as you need on these questions. Work carefully and methodically. There will be an opportunity for timed practice at the end of the chapter.

1. The expression $3(x + 4) - 7(2x - 5)$ is equivalent to:

   A. $-6x - 5$

   B. $-6x + 19$

   C. $-6x - 23$

   D. $-11x - 23$

   E. $-11x + 47$

2. Which of the following expressions is equivalent to $\frac{1}{4}x(-8x - 12y + 4x + 4y)$?

   F. $-x + 2xy$

   G. $-4x - 8xy$

   H. $-x^2 - 2y$

   J. $-x^2 - 2xy$

   K. $-2x^2 + x - 2xy$

3. $(x^2 - 3x + 2) - (3x^2 - 3x - 2)$ is equivalent to:

   A. $-2x^2$

   B. $-2x^2 - 6$

   C. $-2x^2 + 4$

   D. $-2x^2 - 6x + 4$

   E. $-2x \, 2 + 6x - 4$

HINT: For Q4, is there anything you can factor out to make the algebra easier?

---

4. For $x \neq 0$, $\dfrac{8x^6 - 16x^2}{2x^2} = ?$

   F. $4x^3 - 8$

   G. $4x^3 - 16x^2$

   H. $4x^4 - 8$

   J. $4x^4 - 8x$

   K. $4x^4 - 16x^2$

HINT: For Q5, what is the most efficient way to approach this question?

---

5. If $a = 4$, what is the value of $\dfrac{4a^4 + 64b}{16}$?

   A. $\frac{1}{4} + 4b$

   B. $4 + 16b$

   C. $64 + 4b$

   D. $32 + 16b$

   E. $16 + 64ba$

SOLVING EQUATIONS

LEARNING OBJECTIVE

After this lesson, you will be able to:

- Isolate a variable

To answer a question like this:

If $5x = -17(3 - x)$, then $x = $?

A. $-4\frac{1}{4}$

B. $-4\frac{1}{12}$

C. $-2\frac{7}{22}$

D. $4\frac{1}{3}$

E. $4\frac{1}{4}$

You need to know this:

Isolating a variable means getting that variable by itself on one side of the equation. To do this, use inverse operations to manipulate the equation, remembering that whatever you do to one side of the equation, you must do to *both* sides.

If needed, review the order of operations information in chapter 7 before continuing on with this lesson.

You need to do this:

It usually makes sense to proceed in this order:

- Eliminate any fractions.
- Collect and combine like terms.
- Divide to leave the desired variable by itself.

Explanation:

The question asks you to solve for the given equation. First, distribute the -17 to each term inside the parentheses: $-51 + 17x$. Then solve for x:

$$5x = -51 + 17x$$

$$-12x = -51$$

$$x = \frac{51}{12}$$

Convert the improper fraction to a mixed fraction: $\frac{51}{12} = 4\frac{3}{12}$, which reduces to $4\frac{1}{4}$. Choice (E) is correct.

Math

Drills

If you find isolating a variable to be challenging, try out these drills before proceeding to the Try on Your Own set. Isolate the variable in each equation. Drill answers can be found in Answers and Explanations.

a. $2(a + 5) = 11 - (3 - 6a)$

b. $4(3 - r) = 2r + 18$

c. $\dfrac{2t}{3} - \dfrac{5t}{2} = \dfrac{5}{6}$

d.   Isolate F: $C = \dfrac{5}{9}(F - 32)$

e.   Isolate b: $A = \dfrac{1}{2}bh$

Try on Your Own

Directions: Take as much time as you need on these questions. Work carefully and methodically. There will be an opportunity for timed practice at the end of the chapter.

1.   What is the value of x that satisfies the equation $15(x + 9) = -21$?

   A. $-\dfrac{52}{5}$

   B. -2

   C. 2

   D. $\dfrac{114}{15}$

   E. $\dfrac{52}{5}$

2.   If $9(a - 3) = 15a$, then $a = ?$

   F. $-4\dfrac{1}{2}$

   G. $-1\dfrac{1}{8}$

   H. $-\dfrac{2}{9}$

   J. $\dfrac{8}{9}$

   K. $6\dfrac{3}{4}$

3.   The two solutions to $|7x - 1| + 2 = 4$ are equal to which of the following pairs of equations?

   A. $7x + 1 = 4$
         $7x + 1 = -4$

   B. $7x - 1 = 2$
         $-(7x - 1) = 2$

   C. $7x + 1 = 2$
         $-7x + 1 = 4$

   D. $7x - 1 = 6$
         $-(7x - 1) = 6$

   E. $7x - 1 = 2$
         $-(7x - 1) = 6$

K

HINT: For Q4, when absolute value is involved, what must be true?

---

4. Which of the following values of x satisfy the equation $|-x + 3| = -2$?

   F. -1

   G. 1

   H. 5

   J. 1 and 5

   K. There are no values of x for which the equation is true.

5. If $8(x - 2y) = 16x$, then what is x in terms of y?

   A. $-8y$

   B. $-2y$

   C. $-\dfrac{2}{3}y$

   D. $2y$

   E. $4y$

LINEAR GRAPHS

LEARNING OBJECTIVES

After this lesson, you will be able to:

- Calculate the slope or midpoint of a line given two points
- Write the equation of a line in slope-intercept form

To answer a question like this:

Which of the following is an equation of the line that crosses through $(-3,4)$ and $(3,6)$?

A. $x + 3y = -15$

B. $x - 3y = -15$

C. $\dfrac{1}{3}x - y = 5$

D. $3x + y = 5$

E. $-3x + y = 5$

You need to know this:

The answer choices in this question are written in standard form and need to be written in slope-intercept form: $y = mx + b$. In this form of a linear equation, m represents the slope of the line and b represents the y-intercept. You can think of the slope of a line as how steep it is. The y-intercept is the point at which the line crosses the y-axis and can be written as the ordered pair $(0,y)$.

You can calculate the slope of a line if you know any two points on the line. The formula is $m = \dfrac{y_2 - y_1}{x_2 - x_1}$, where (x_1,y_1) and (x_2,y_2) are the coordinates of the two points on the line.

A line that moves from the bottom left to the top right has a positive slope. A line that moves from the top left to the bottom right has a negative slope. A horizontal line has a slope of zero, and a vertical line has an undefined slope.

Some ACT questions ask about parallel or perpendicular lines. Parallel lines have the same slope, while perpendicular lines have negative reciprocal slopes.

You need to do this:

- Find the slope of the line.
- Write the equation in slope-intercept form, substituting the value of the slope you found and one of the known points for x and y.
- Solve for the y-intercept.

Explanation:

The question asks you to solve for the given equation. The equation of a line is given by $y = mx + b$, where m is the slope of the line and b is the y-intercept. First, use the two points to find the slope:

$$m = \frac{y_2 - y_1}{x_2 - x_1}$$

$$= \frac{6 - 4}{3 - (-3)}$$

$$= \frac{2}{6} = \frac{1}{3}$$

Then use the slope to find the y-intercept. Plug in $m = \frac{1}{3}$ and either of the given points for x and y:

$$y = mx + b$$

$$4 = \frac{1}{3}(-3) + b$$

$$4 = -1 + b$$

$$5 = b$$

The slope-intercept form of the line is $y = \frac{1}{3}x + 5$. The answer choices are written in standard form, so rewrite the equation:

$$y = \frac{1}{3}x + 5$$

$$3(y) = 3\left(\frac{1}{3}x + 5\right)$$

$$3y = x + 15$$

$$-x + 3y = 15$$

$$x - 3y = -15$$

The line that goes through the given points is $x - 3y = -15$. This matches (B).

Try on Your Own

Directions: Take as much time as you need on these questions. Work carefully and methodically. There will be an opportunity for timed practice at the end of the chapter.

1. If the equation of a line is $4x - 7y = 14$, what is the slope of the line?

    A. -7

    B. $-\dfrac{4}{7}$

    C. $\dfrac{4}{7}$

    D. $\dfrac{7}{4}$

    E. 7

HINT: For Q2, what equation can you create that will help you easily identify the y-intercept?

---

2. What is the y-intercept of the line that passes through the points $(1,-13)$ and $(-10,31)$?

    F. -9

    G. -4

    H. 0

    J. 4

    K. 9

3. Given point $A(-3,-8)$, if the midpoint of segment AB is $(1,-5)$, what are the coordinates of point B?

    A. $(5,-2)$

    B. $(4,-2)$

    C. $(-1,-6.5)$

    D. $(-2,-2)$

    E. $(-1,-1.5)$

4. The following graph represents which of the following equations?

    F. $y = -3x + 4$

    G. $y = -3x - 4$

    H. $y = -\dfrac{1}{3}x + 4$

    J. $y = \dfrac{1}{3}x - 4$

    K. $y = 3x - 4$

HINT: For Q5, how can the format of the answer choices help you decide how to answer this question?

---

5. Which of the following equations best describes the linear relationship shown in the table, where r represents the number of pounds of rice sold and d represents the price in dollars of one pound of rice?

Price of one pound	Projected number of pounds sold
$1.20	15,000
$1.40	12,500
$1.60	10,000
$1.80	7,500
$2.00	5,000
$2.20	2,500

    A. $r = 1.2d + 12{,}500$

    B. $r = 12{,}500d + 15{,}000$

    C. $r = -12{,}500d + 17{,}500$

    D. $r = 12{,}500d + 30{,}000$

    E. $r = -12{,}500d + 30{,}000$

SOLVING INEQUALITIES

LEARNING OBJECTIVE

After this lesson, you will be able to:

- Solve an inequality for a range of values

To answer a question like this:

Which of the following represents all the values of x that satisfy the inequality $2 \leq 3 - \frac{x}{4} \leq 4$?

A. $x \leq -16$

B. $x \geq 4$

C. $x \geq 16$

D. $-4 \leq x \leq 4$

E. $x \leq -4$ or $x \geq 4$

You need to know this:

Linear inequalities are similar to linear equations but have two differences:

- You are solving for a **range of values** rather than a single value.
- If you multiply or divide both sides of the inequality by a negative, you must **reverse the inequality sign**.

You need to do this:

- Eliminate any fractions.
- Collect and combine like terms.
- Divide to leave the desired variable by itself.
  - If you multiply or divide both sides of the inequality by a negative, reverse the inequality sign.
  - If possible, avoid moving the variable terms in such a way that the coefficients become negative.

Explanation:

The question asks you to solve for the given inequality. This is a compound inequality, so whatever you do to one piece, you must do to all three pieces. First add 3, and then multiply all three parts by −4.

$$2 \leq 3 - \frac{x}{4} \leq 4$$

$$-1 \leq -\frac{x}{4} \leq 1$$

$$-4(-1) \geq -4\left(-\frac{x}{4}\right) \geq -4(1)$$

$$4 \geq x \geq -4$$

Don't forget to flip the entire inequality to more easily match it with the correct answer: $-4 \leq x \leq 4$. Choice (D) is correct.

Try on Your Own

Directions: Take as much time as you need on these questions. Work carefully and methodically. There will be an opportunity for timed practice at the end of the chapter.

1. Which of the following is equivalent to the inequality $-8x + 2y \leq 14$?

    A. $y \geq -4x - 7$
    B. $y \geq -4x + 7$
    C. $y \leq -4x + 7$
    D. $y \geq 4x - 7$
    E. $y \leq 4x + 7$

2. Which of the following represents the solution set for $-15 \leq 2x - 13 < 3$?

    F. $-1 \leq x < 8$
    G. $-2 \leq x < 16$
    H. $-5 \leq x < -1$
    J. $-14 \leq x < 8$
    K. $-28 \leq x < 16$

3. If $-3x + 7y \leq 4y + 6$ and x is an integer, which of the following statements must be true?

    A. $x \geq -y - 2$
    B. $x \geq -y + 2$
    C. $x \leq y - 2$
    D. $x \geq y - 2$
    E. $x \leq y + 2$

HINT: For Q4, if $|x| = a$, then what are the possible values for x?

4. Which of the following values of x satisfies the inequality $|2x + 5| < 11$?

    F. $-8 < x < 3$
    G. $-8 > x > 3$
    H. $-3 < x < -8$
    J. $-3 < x < 8$
    K. $-3 > x > 8$

5. Which of the following is the set of x such that $x + 2 > x + 1$?

    A. The empty set
    B. The set containing all real numbers
    C. The set containing all negative real numbers
    D. The set containing all positive real numbers
    E. The set containing only zero

GRAPHING INEQUALITIES

LEARNING OBJECTIVES

After this lesson, you will be able to:

- Identify the graph of an inequality
- Determine the inequality given a graph

To answer a question like this:

The solution to which inequality is represented in the graph shown?

A. $x + 4y < -12$

B. $x + 4y > -12$

C. $x - 4y < 12$

D. $x - 4y > 12$

E. $4x + y < -3$

You need to know this:

Linear inequalities in one variable are graphed on a number line as a point that is or is not filled in ("closed" or "open," respectively), with an arrow representing the location of the solutions as either less than or greater than the point.

- Use a closed circle (●) for inequalities with ≤ or ≥ signs because the point itself is included in the solution set.
- Use an open circle (○) for inequalities with < or > signs because the point itself is not included in the solution set.

While linear equations in two variables graph as simple lines, inequalities in two variables are graphed as shaded regions.

- Use solid lines for inequalities with ≤ or ≥ signs because the line itself is included in the solution set.
- Use dashed lines for inequalities with < or > signs because, in these cases, the line itself is not included in the solution set.
- The shaded region represents all points that make up the solution set for the inequality.

You need to do this:

To graph a linear inequality in one variable, start by isolating the variable.

- For $x \leq a$ and $x \geq a$, use a closed circle ($\bullet$).
- For $x < a$ and $x > a$, use an open circle ($\circ$).
- For $x < a$ and $x \leq a$, draw an arrow pointing to the left of the circle.
- For $x > a$ and $x \geq a$, draw an arrow pointing to the right of the circle.

To graph an inequality in two variables, start by writing the inequality in slope-intercept form, then graph the solid or dashed line.

- For $y > mx + b$ and $y \geq mx + b$, shade the region above the line.
- For $y < mx + b$ and $y \leq mx + b$, shade the region below the line.

If it's hard to tell which region is above/below the line (which can happen when the line is steep), compare the y-values on both sides of the line.

Explanation:

The question asks you to match the correct inequality with the given graph. Don't answer this question too quickly! The shading is below the line, but that does not necessarily mean that the symbol in the equation will be the less than symbol ($<$). Start by writing the equation of the dashed line shown in the graph in slope-intercept form. Then use the shading to determine the correct inequality symbol.

The slope of the line shown in the graph is $\frac{1}{4}$ and the y-intercept is -3, so the equation of the dashed line is $y = \frac{1}{4}x - 3$. The graph is shaded below the boundary line, so use the $<$ symbol. When written in slope-intercept form, the inequality is $y < \frac{1}{4}x - 3$. The inequalities in the answer choices are written in standard form $(Ax + By = C)$, so rewrite your answer in this form.

$$y < \frac{1}{4}x - 3$$

$$-\frac{1}{4}x + y < -3$$

Multiply everything by -4 to get integer coefficients, and don't forget to reverse the inequality symbol: $x - 4y > 12$. Choice (D) is correct.

Drills

If graphing inequalities gives you trouble, study the information above and try out these drill questions before completing the Try on Your Own questions below. Drill answers can be found in Answers and Explanations.

Graph the following inequalities.

a. $-1 < x \leq 3$

b. $|x + 1| \leq 3$

c. $y > 2x$

d. $y + 2 \leq x$

e. $x - 1 < y \leq x + 1$

Try on Your Own

Directions: Take as much time as you need on these questions. Work carefully and methodically. There will be an opportunity for timed practice at the end of the chapter.

HINT: For Q1, how do you solve an inequality that includes absolute value?

---

1. Which of the following represents the solution to the inequality $|2x - 5| > 11$?

2. For the number line shown, which of the following inequalities describes the range of possible values for some number w?

    F. $|w - 2| \leq 2$

    G. $|w - 2| \leq 4$

    H. $|w + 2| \leq -4$

    J. $|w + 2| \leq 2$

    K. $|w + 2| \leq 4$

3. Which of the following systems of inequalities includes the shaded region in the graph below?

    A. $\begin{cases} x < -2 \\ y \leq -\frac{1}{2}x + 1 \end{cases}$

    B. $\begin{cases} x > -2 \\ y \leq -2x + 1 \end{cases}$

    C. $\begin{cases} x > -2 \\ y \leq -\frac{1}{2}x + 1 \end{cases}$

    D. $\begin{cases} y > -2 \\ y \leq -2x + 1 \end{cases}$

    E. $\begin{cases} y > -2 \\ y \geq -2x + 1 \end{cases}$

4. Which of the following graphs represents the region $2 < y - x < 3$ in the standard (x,y) coordinate plane?

F.

G.

H.

J.

K.

HINT: For Q5, how can thinking about absolute value as a distance help you approach this question more efficiently?

5. If the following number line shows the range of possible values for some number b, which of the following inequalities shows the same possible values for b?

A. $|b - 5| \leq 1$

B. $|b - 5| \leq 2$

C. $|b - 2| \leq 5$

D. $|b - 2| \leq 3$

E. $|b - 1| \leq 5$

Math

K 249

QUADRATICS

LEARNING OBJECTIVE

After this lesson, you will be able to:

- Identify solutions to quadratic equations

To answer a question like this:

If $x^2 + 8x = 48$ and $x > 0$, what is the value of $x - 5$?

   A. -9

   B. -1

   C. 4

   D. 7

   E. 9

You need to know this:

A **quadratic** expression is a second-degree polynomial—that is, a polynomial containing a squared variable. You can write a quadratic expression as $ax^2 + bx + c$.

The **FOIL** acronym (which stands for First, Outer, Inner, Last) will help you remember how to multiply two binomials to create a quadratic expression: multiply the first terms together (ac), then the outer terms (ad), then the inner terms (bc), and finally the last terms (bd):

$$(a + b)(c + d) = ac + ad + bc + bd$$

FOIL can also be done in reverse if you need to go from a quadratic expression to its factors. To solve a quadratic equation by factoring, the quadratic expression must be set equal to zero. For example:

$$x^2 + x - 56 = 0$$
$$(x + 8)(x - 7) = 0$$

From the binomial factors, you can find the solutions, also called roots or zeros, of the equation. For two factors to be multiplied together and produce zero as the result, one or both of those factors must be zero. In the example above, either $x + 8 = 0$ or $x - 7 = 0$, which means that $x = -8$ or $x = 7$.

The quadratic formula can be used to solve any quadratic equation. It yields solutions to any quadratic equation that is written in standard form, $ax^2 + bx + c = 0$:

$$x = \frac{-b \pm \sqrt{b^2 - 4ac}}{2a}$$

The term under the square root, $b^2 - 4ac$, can help you determine how many real solutions there are. When the term is negative, there are no real solutions for x because negative numbers have no real square roots. When the term is 0, then the value of x will be $\frac{-b}{2a}$, which yields only one solution. Finally, when the term is positive, x will have two solutions because of the $\pm$ symbol.

Memorizing the following classic quadratic equations may save you time on test day:

- $x^2 - y^2 = (x + y)(x - y)$
- $x^2 + 2xy + y^2 = (x + y)^2$
- $x^2 - 2xy + y^2 = (x - y)^2$

You need to do this:

Here are the steps for solving a quadratic equation by factoring:

- Set the quadratic expression equal to zero.
- Factor the squared term. For factoring, it's easiest when a, the coefficient in front of x^2, is equal to 1.
- Make a list of the factors of c. Remember to include negatives.
- Find the factor pair that, when added, equals b, the coefficient in front of x.
- Write the quadratic as the product of two binomials.
- Set each binomial equal to zero and solve.

To solve a quadratic using the quadratic formula, start by getting the quadratic equation into the form $ax^2 + bx + c = 0$. Then substitute a, b, and c into the quadratic formula and simplify.

When you see a pattern that matches the left or the right side of a classic quadratic equation, simplify by substituting its equivalent form. For example, say you need to simplify the following:

$$\frac{a^2 - 2ab + b^2}{a - b}$$

You would substitute $(a - b)(a - b)$ for the numerator and cancel to find that the expression simplifies to $a - b$:

$$\frac{a^2 - 2ab + b^2}{a - b} = \frac{(a - b)(a - b)}{a - b} = \frac{a - b}{1} = a - b$$

Explanation:

The question asks you to first solve for x and then evaluate $x - 5$. When solving a quadratic equation, always start by rewriting the equation to make it equal to 0 (unless both sides of the equation are already perfect squares). Then, take a peek at the choices. If they are all integers, then factoring is probably the quickest method for solving the equation. If the answers include messy fractions or square roots, then the quadratic formula may be a better choice.

To make the original equation equal to 0, subtract 48 from both sides to get $x^2 + 8x - 48 = 0$. The choices are all integers, so try to factor the equation. Look for two numbers whose product is -48 and whose sum is 8: -4 and 12. This means the factors are $(x - 4)$ and $(x + 12)$.

Now, set each factor equal to 0 and solve to obtain $x = 4$ and $x = -12$. The question states that $x > 0$, so x must equal 4. Before selecting an answer, check that you answered the right question! The question asks for the value of $x - 5$, not just x, so the correct answer is $4 - 5 = -1$. (B) is correct.

Try on Your Own

Directions: Take as much time as you need on these questions. Work carefully and methodically. There will be an opportunity for timed practice at the end of the chapter.

1. If $x^2 - 4x - 6 = 6$, what are the possible values for x?

   A. -6 and -2

   B. -6 and 2

   C. 6 and -2

   D. 4 and 12

   E. 6 and 2

2. For all a and b, what is the product of $(b - a)$ and $(a + b)$?

   F. $-a^2 + b^2$

   G. $a^2 - b^2$

   H. $a^2 + b^2$

   J. $a^2 - 2ab + b^2$

   K. $-a^2 - 2ab + b^2$

HINT: For Q3, how are the answer choices formatted?
---

3. Which of the following are the roots of the equation $x^2 + 8x - 3 = 0$?

   A. $-8 \pm \sqrt{19}$

   B. $-4 \pm \sqrt{19}$

   C. $-4 \pm \sqrt{3}$

   D. $4 \pm \sqrt{19}$

   E. $8 \pm \sqrt{19}$

4. Which of the following is the simplified form of $\dfrac{x^2 - 4x + 4}{2x^2 + 4x - 16}$?

   F. $\dfrac{1}{2}$

   G. $\dfrac{x}{x + 4}$

   H. $\dfrac{x - 2}{2(x + 4)}$

   J. $\dfrac{x + 2}{2(x - 8)}$

   K. $\dfrac{x^2 - 4x + 1}{x^2 + 2x - 4}$

HINT: For Q5, what does "how long will it take the projectile to hit the ground" mean in terms of h and t?
---

5. A projectile is launched from a cannon on top of a building. The height of the projectile in feet can be modeled using the quadratic equation $h = -16t^2 + 128t + 320$, where h represents the height and t represents the number of seconds after the projectile was launched. After it is launched, how long will it take the projectile to hit the ground?

   A. 2 seconds

   B. 4 seconds

   C. 8 seconds

   D. 10 seconds

   E. 12 seconds

SYSTEMS OF EQUATIONS

LEARNING OBJECTIVE

After this lesson, you will be able to:

• Solve systems of equations

To answer a question like this:

Which of the following pairs is a solution to the following system of equations:

$$\begin{cases} -x + 3y = 9 \\ 2x + 5y = 4 \end{cases}$$

A. $(-15,-2)$

B. $(-15,2)$

C. $(-3,2)$

D. $(3,-2)$

E. $(15,2)$

You need to know this:

A **system** of two linear equations is the set of equations of two lines. "Solving" a system of two linear equations usually means finding the point where the two lines intersect.

• A system of linear equations may have one solution, infinitely many solutions, or no solution.

• If a system of equations represents two lines that intersect, then the system will have exactly one solution (in which the x- and y-values correspond to the point of intersection).

• If a system of equations has infinitely many solutions, the two equations actually represent the same line. For example, $2x + y = 15$ and $4x + 2y = 30$ represent the same line. If you divide the second equation by 2, you arrive at the first equation. Every point along this line is a solution.

• If a system of equations has no solution, the lines are parallel: there is no point of intersection.

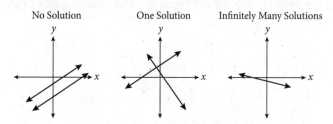

There are two algebraic ways to solve a system of linear equations: substitution and combination, a strategy fundamentally the same as elimination. For some ACT questions, substitution is faster; for others, combination is faster.

Substitution involves substituting the value for one variable into that variable's location in a second equation. Combining two equations means adding or subtracting them, usually with the goal of either eliminating one of the variables or solving for a combination of variables, e.g., $5n + 5m$.

You need to do this:

To solve a system of two linear equations by substitution:

- Isolate a variable (ideally, one whose coefficient is 1) in one of the equations.
- Substitute the result into the other equation.

To solve a system of two linear equations by combination:

- Make sure that the coefficients for one variable have the same absolute value. (If they don't, multiply one equation by an appropriate constant. Sometimes, you'll have to multiply both equations by constants.)
- Either add or subtract the equations to eliminate one variable.
- Solve for the remaining variable, then substitute its value into either equation to solve for the other variable.

Explanation:

The question asks you to solve for the given system of equations. You can solve this system by either substitution or combination. To use combination, multiply the first equation by 2 and then add it to the second equation to cancel out the x terms:

$$\begin{array}{r} -2x + 6y = 18 \\ \underline{2x + 5y = 4} \\ 11y = 22 \\ y = 2 \end{array}$$

Then substitute $y = 2$ into one of the original equations to solve for x:

$$-x + 3(2) = 9$$
$$-x = 9 - 6$$
$$-x = 3$$
$$x = -3$$

Therefore, $(-3, 2)$ is a solution for the system of equations. Choice (C) is correct.

To use substitution, solve the first equation for x in terms of y and then plug that expression into the second equation:

$$-x + 3y = 9$$
$$-x = 9 - 3y$$
$$x = -9 + 3y$$

$$2(-9 + 3y) + 5y = 4$$
$$-18 + 6y + 5y = 4$$
$$11y = 22$$
$$y = 2$$

Finally, substitute $y = 2$ into one of the original equations to get $x = -3$.

Math

Try on Your Own

Directions: Take as much time as you need on these questions. Work carefully and methodically. There will be an opportunity for timed practice at the end of the chapter.

1. What is the sum of the solutions for the following system of equations?

$$\begin{cases} 6x = 20 \\ 3y + 7 = 14 \end{cases}$$

    A. 1
    B. $2\frac{5}{6}$
    C. 3
    D. $5\frac{2}{3}$
    E. $7\frac{7}{9}$

2. If A and B are polynomial expressions such that $A = 24xy + 13$ and $B = 8xy + 1$, how much greater is A than B?

    F. $32xy - 14$
    G. $16xy - 14$
    H. $16xy + 12$
    J. $32xy + 12$
    K. $32xy + 14$

3. If $2x + 5y = 49$ and $5x + 3y = 94$, then the product of x and $y = ?$

    A. 17
    B. 34
    C. 42
    D. 48
    E. 51

HINT: For Q4, which is likely to be more efficient: substitution or combination? Why?

---

4. You are given the following system of equations:

$$\begin{cases} x + 9y = 11 \\ 2x - 7y = -3 \end{cases}$$

    What is the value of $4x - 5y$?

    F. -6
    G. 1
    H. 2
    J. 3
    K. 13

HINT: For Q5, what part of the quadratic formula provides information about the number of roots for a quadratic equation or function?

---

5. You are given the following system of equations:

$$\begin{cases} y = x \\ -py + qx^2 = r \end{cases}$$

    where p, q, and r are integers. For which of the following expressions will there be more than one real solution?

    A. $p^2 - 4qr < 0$
    B. $p^2 + 4qr < 0$
    C. $p^2 + 4qr > 0$
    D. $q^2 - 4pr > 0$
    E. $q^2 + 4pr > 0$

WORD PROBLEMS

LEARNING OBJECTIVE

After this lesson, you will be able to:

- Translate word problems into equations and/or inequalities and solve

To answer a question like this:

At a school trivia competition, contestants can answer two kinds of questions: easy questions and hard questions. Easy questions are worth 3 points, and hard questions are worth 5 points. Chantrea knows that she correctly answered 21 questions and that she had a total of 79 points. How many hard questions did she answer correctly?

A.   7

B.   8

C.   12

D.   13

E.   15

You need to know this:

The ACT likes to test your understanding of how to describe real-world situations using math equations. For some questions, it will be up to you to extract and solve an equation; for others, you'll have to interpret an equation in a real-life context. The following table shows some of the most common phrases and mathematical equivalents you're likely to see on the ACT.

Word Problems Translation Table	
English	**Math**
equals, is, equivalent to, was, will be, has, costs, adds up to, the same as, as much as	$=$
times, of, multiplied by, product of, twice, double	$\times$
divided by, out of, ratio	$\div$
plus, added to, sum, combined, increased by	$+$
minus, subtracted from, smaller than, less than, fewer, decreased by, difference between	$-$
a number, how much, how many, what	x, n, etc.

You need to do this:

When translating from English to math, start by *defining the variables*, choosing letters that make sense. Then, *break the question down into small pieces*, writing down the translation for one phrase at a time.

Explanation:

The question asks you to solve for how many hard questions Chantrea answered correctly. Both Backsolving and straightforward algebra work well here.

To solve algebraically, set up a system of equations with one equation that represents the number of questions of each type (e for easy and h for hard) and another that represents the number of points that Chantrea earned. Because she correctly answered 21 questions, $e + h = 21$. The number of points that she earned is $3e + 5h = 79$. Substitute $e = 21 - h$ into the second equation and solve for h:

$$3(21 - h) + 5h = 79$$
$$63 - 3h + 5h = 79$$
$$2h = 16$$
$$h = 8$$

To Backsolve, start with C. Remember that the choices represent the number of *hard* questions, not the number of *easy* questions. If Chantrea got 12 hard questions right, then she got $21 - 12 = 9$ easy questions right for a total of $9(3) + 12(5) = 27 + 60 = 87$ points. This is too many points, so she must have gotten fewer hard questions right.

Try (B). If she got 8 hard questions right, then she got $21 - 8 = 13$ easy questions right. This would give her a total of $13(3) + 8(5) = 39 + 40 = 79$ points, so (B) is correct.

Drills

If word problems give you trouble, study the information above and try out these drill questions before completing the Try on Your Own questions below. Drill answers can be found in Answers and Explanations.

Translate the following into math.

a.   If n is greater than m, the positive difference between twice n and m

b.   A quarter of the sum of a and b is 4 less than a.

c.   The product of y and 9 decreased by the sum of x and 7 is the same as dividing x decreased by z by 7 decreased by x.

d.   The ratio of $4q$ to $7p$ is 5 to 2.

e.   If $500 is taken from F's salary, then the combined salaries of F and G will be double what F's salary would be if it were increased by 50%.

Try on Your Own

Directions: Take as much time as you need on these questions. Work carefully and methodically. There will be an opportunity for timed practice at the end of the chapter.

1. An aquarium contains dolphins, sharks, and whales. There are twice as many dolphins as whales and 8 fewer sharks than dolphins and whales combined. If there are w whales, which of the following represents the number of sharks?

   A. $5w$
   B. $3w - 8$
   C. $10 + w$
   D. $3w^2 - 8w$
   E. $3\sqrt{2w} - 8$

2. If paintbrushes cost $1.50 each and canvases cost 6 times that much, which of the following represents the cost, in dollars, of p paintbrushes and c canvases?

   F. $7.5pc$
   G. $10.5pc$
   H. $7.5(p + c)$
   J. $9c + 1.5p$
   K. $10.5(p + c)$

3. The toll for driving a segment of a certain freeway is $1.50 plus 25 cents for each mile traveled. Joy paid a $25.00 toll for driving a segment of the freeway. How many miles did she travel?

   A. 75
   B. 94
   C. 96
   D. 100
   E. 106

4. At a local theater, adult tickets cost $8 and student tickets cost $5. At a recent show, 500 tickets were sold for a total of $3,475. How many adult tickets were sold?

   F. 125
   G. 200
   H. 325
   J. 400
   K. 450

HINT: For Q5, what do the 20 pints of glaze represent in relation to v?

5. A ceramist uses $(v^2 + v)$ pints of glaze for v porcelain vases. What is the maximum number of vases the ceramist can glaze with 20 pints of glaze?

   A. 2
   B. 4
   C. 5
   D. 10
   E. 20

On Test Day

Remember that the ACT doesn't ask you to show your work; if you find the algebra in a question challenging, there is often another way to get to the answer.

Try out this new question, first using algebra and then using the Backsolving strategy you learned in chapter 7. Time yourself both times. Which approach do you find easier? Which one was faster? Did you get the correct answer both times? Remember your preferred approach and try it first if you see a question like this on test day.

1. Which of the following values of x satisfies the equation $|2x - 6| = -4$?

    A. -1

    B. 1

    C. 5

    D. 1 and 5

    E. There are no values of x for which the equation is true.

The correct answer and both ways of solving can be found at the end of this chapter.

How Much Have You Learned?

Directions: For test-like practice, give yourself 10 minutes to complete this question set. Be sure to study the explanations, even for questions you got correct. They can be found at the end of this chapter.

1. How many distinct real roots does the equation $3x^3 + 30x^2 + 75x = 0$ have?

   A. 0
   B. 1
   C. 2
   D. 3
   E. 5

2. Point P $(-3,5)$ and point Q $(0,1)$ are points on the (x,y) coordinate plane. What is the midpoint between points P and Q?

   F. $(-3,1)$
   G. $\left(-\frac{3}{2},1\right)$
   H. $\left(-\frac{3}{2},3\right)$
   J. $(1,3)$
   K. $\left(1,\frac{1}{2}\right)$

3. What is the y-intercept of the line that passes through the points $(1,21)$ and $(4,42)$?

   A. 0
   B. 7
   C. 9
   D. 14
   E. 19

4. What is the solution set for the equation $|2x - 3| = 13$?

   F. $\{-8\}$
   G. $\{-8, 8\}$
   H. $\{-5\}$
   J. $\{-5, 8\}$
   K. $\{5, -8\}$

5. Bye Bye Bugs charges a $275 annual fee for quarterly service plus $20 per additional visit. Pest Be Gone charges a $200 annual fee for quarterly service plus $25 per additional visit. For how many additional visits in a year would the total charges from each exterminator be equal?

   A. 2
   B. 5
   C. 15
   D. 50
   E. 95

6. Which of the following systems of inequalities includes the shaded region in the graph shown?

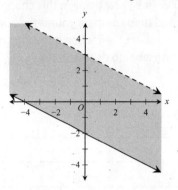

   F. $-\frac{1}{2}x - 2 \le y < -\frac{1}{2}x + 3$

   G. $-\frac{1}{2}x - 2 < y \le -\frac{1}{2}x + 3$

   H. $-\frac{1}{2}x - 2 \ge y > -\frac{1}{2}x + 3$

   J. $-2x - 2 \le y < -2x + 3$

   K. $-2x - 2 < y \le -2x + 3$

7. Which of the following expressions is equivalent to $\frac{1}{5}p(7q - p + 8q + 11p)$?

   A. $5p^2q$

   B. $25pq$

   C. $3pq + 2p^2$

   D. $15pq + 10p$

   E. $\frac{7}{5}pq - \frac{1}{5}p + \frac{8}{5}q^2 + \frac{11}{5}p^2$

8. For the system of equations below, which of the following gives the solutions for x?

$$\begin{cases} y = x^2 \\ 24 + y = 10x \end{cases}$$

   F. -12 and 2

   G. -6 and -4

   H. -2 and 12

   J. 3 and 8

   K. 4 and 6

9. The 2 solutions to $|4x + 3| - 1 < 8$ are equal to which of the following pairs of inequalities?

   A. $4x + 3 < 7$

         $4x + 3 > -7$

   B. $4x + 3 < 7$

         $4x + 3 < -9$

   C. $4x + 3 < 9$

         $4x + 3 < -9$

   D. $4x + 3 < 9$

         $4x + 3 < 7$

   E. $4x + 3 < 9$

         $4x + 3 > -9$

10. Rasheed is contemplating whether to buy a membership for a trampoline park, which is $50 a year. As a member, Rasheed receives a 15% discount on jump tickets. If the non-membership price for a jump ticket is $12 per hour, for how many hours does Rasheed need to jump in order for the cost of the membership to be less than the total cost of buying jump tickets at the non-membership price?

   F.   22

   G.   23

   H.   25

   J.   27

   K.   28

Reflect

Directions: Take a few minutes to recall what you've learned and what you've been practicing in this chapter. Consider the following questions, jot down your best answer for each one, and then compare your reflections to the expert responses on the following page. Don't be intimidated by the number of reflection questions here. Answer them at your own pace, then use your level of confidence to determine what to do next.

1. How do you multiply two polynomials?

2. What should you do to isolate a particular variable in an equation?

3. What is the most useful equation for a line in the coordinate plane? Why?

4. When the ACT gives you two points on a line, what can you figure out?

5. How are parallel and perpendicular lines related to each other?

6. What types of keywords should you look for when translating English into math?

7. What is the difference between a linear inequality and a linear equation?

    _____

    _____

    _____

8. The rules for manipulating an inequality are very similar to those for manipulating an equation. What is the major difference?

    _____

    _____

    _____

9. Which form of a quadratic equation gives its *y*-intercept?

    _____

    _____

    _____

10. When is substitution a good choice for solving a system of equations?

    _____

    _____

    _____

11. When is combination a good choice for solving a system of equations?

    _____

    _____

    _____

12. What does it mean if a system of equations has no solution? Infinitely many solutions?

    _____

    _____

    _____

13. How do you solve a system of one linear and one quadratic equation?

    _____

    _____

    _____

Responses

1. How do you multiply two polynomials?

Distribute each term in the first set of parentheses to each term in the second set, then combine like terms.

2. What should you do to isolate a particular variable in an equation?

Perform inverse operations until the variable is by itself on one side of the equal sign. If the equation has fractions, make them disappear by multiplying both sides of the equation by the denominator(s). If like terms appear on different sides of the equation, collect them on the same side so that you can combine them.

3. What is the most useful equation for a line in the coordinate plane? Why?

The best equation is slope-intercept form, $y = mx + b$, because it tells you the slope (m) and the y-intercept (b). Conversely, if you need to derive an equation yourself, you can plug the slope and y-intercept into slope-intercept form and you're done.

4. When the ACT gives you two points on a line, what can you figure out?

If you know two points, you can figure out the slope of the line with the equation $m = \dfrac{y_2 - y_1}{x_2 - x_1}$. From there, you can plug one of the points and the slope into slope-intercept form and find the y-intercept.

5. How are parallel and perpendicular lines related to each other?

Parallel lines never intersect, and they have equal slopes. Perpendicular lines intersect at a 90° angle, and they have negative reciprocal slopes.

6. What types of keywords should you look for when translating English into math?

Look for keywords that signal equality ("is," "has," "was"), variable names ("Marina's age," "the cost of one bathtub"), or one of the four arithmetic operations (addition, subtraction, multiplication, and division).

7. What is the difference between a linear inequality and a linear equation?

A linear equation is solved for a single value, whereas a linear inequality is solved for a range of values.

8. The rules for manipulating an inequality are very similar to those for manipulating an equation. What is the major difference?

When solving an inequality, you can do the same thing to both sides, just as you can for an equation. The big difference is that if you divide or multiply both sides of an inequality by a negative number, you have to flip the inequality sign.

9. Which form of a quadratic equation gives its y-intercept?

The vertex form is $y = a(x - h)^2 + k$. The constant k is the y-value at the vertex, which occurs at the maximum or minimum.

10. When is substitution a good choice for solving a system of equations?

Substitution works best when at least one of the variables has a coefficient of 1, making the variable easy to isolate. This system, for example, is well suited for substitution:

$$a + 3b = 5$$
$$4a - 6b = 21$$

That's because in the first equation, you can easily isolate the a as $a = 5 - 3b$ and plug that result in for a in the other equation. By contrast, substitution would not be a great choice for solving this system:

$$2a + 3b = 5$$
$$4a - 6b = 21$$

If you used substitution now, you'd have to work with fractions, which is messy.

11. When is combination a good choice for solving a system of equations?

Combination is often a good choice. It is at its worst in systems such as this one:

$$2a + 3b = 5$$
$$3a + 5b = 7$$

Neither a-coefficient is a multiple of the other, and neither b-coefficient is a multiple of the other, so to solve this system with combination, you'd have to multiply both equations by a constant (for example, multiplying the first equation by 3 and the second equation by 2 to create a 6a term in both equations). But substitution wouldn't be stellar in this situation, either.

Note that combination may be particularly effective when the ACT asks for a combination of variables. For example, if a question based on the previous system of equations asked for the value of $5a + 8b$, then you could find the answer instantly by adding the equations together because $2a + 3a = 5a$ and $3b + 5b = 8b$.

12. What does it mean if a system of equations has no solution? Infinitely many solutions?

A system of equations with no solution represents two parallel lines, which never cross. The coefficient of a variable in one equation will match the coefficient of the same variable in the other equation, but the constants will be different. For example, this system has no solution:

$$2x + 3y = 4$$
$$2x + 3y = 5$$

Subtracting one equation from the other yields the equation $0 = -1$, which makes no sense.

If a system of equations has infinitely many solutions, then the two equations represent the same line. For example, this system has infinitely many solutions:

$$2x + 3y = 4$$
$$4x + 6y = 8$$

Dividing the second equation by 2 yields $2x + 3y = 4$, so while the two equations look different, they are actually the same.

13. How do you solve a system of one linear and one quadratic equation?

Put the linear equation in the form $y = mx + b$ *and the quadratic equation in the form* $y = ax^2 + bx + c$. *Set the right sides of the equations equal to each other, and solve.*

Next Steps

If you answered most questions correctly in the "How Much Have You Learned?" section, and if your responses to the Reflect questions were similar to those of the ACT expert, then consider Algebra an area of strength and move on to the next chapter. Come back to this topic periodically to prevent yourself from getting rusty.

If you don't yet feel confident, review those parts of this chapter that you have not yet mastered. Then, try the questions you missed again. As always, be sure to review the explanations closely. Then go online (**kaptest.com/login**) to watch video lessons about the highest-yield concepts in this chapter and to use your Qbank for more practice. If you haven't already registered your book, do so at **kaptest.com/moreonline.**

GO ONLINE

kaptest.com/login

Answers and Explanations

Polynomials

1. E

Difficulty: Low
Category: Algebra
Getting to the Answer: The question asks you to simplify the given expression. First, distribute the 3 and -7: $3x + 12 - 14x + 35$. Then combine the like terms: $-11x + 47$. Choice (E) is correct.

2. J

Difficulty: Low
Category: Algebra
Getting to the Answer: The question asks you to simplify the given expression. Before distributing $\frac{1}{4}x$ to each term inside the parentheses, combine like terms inside the parentheses: $\frac{1}{4}x(-4x - 8y)$. Then distribute the $\frac{1}{4}x$: $-x^2 - 2xy$. Choice (J) is correct.

3. C

Difficulty: Low
Category: Algebra
Getting to the Answer: The question asks you to simplify the given expression. First, distribute the -1 to each of the terms in the second set of parentheses: $-3x^2 + 3x + 2$. Now combine like terms: $x^2 - 3x + 2 - 3x^2 + 3x + 2 = -2x^2 + 4$. Choice (C) is correct.

4. H

Difficulty: Medium
Category: Algebra
Getting to the Answer: The question asks you to simplify the given expression. Notice that you can factor out a $2x^2$ from each term in the numerator:

$$\frac{2x^2(4x^4 - 8)}{2x^2}$$

Then cancel the $2x^2$, since it appears in both the numerator and denominator:

$$\frac{2\cancel{x^2}(4x^4 - 8)}{2\cancel{x^2}}$$
$$4x^4 - 8$$

$4x^4 - 8$ is equivalent to the given expression; (H) is correct.

5. C

Difficulty: Medium
Category: Algebra
Getting to the Answer: The question asks you to simplify the given expression with the known value of a. Simplifying before plugging in $a = 4$ will save you valuable time on test day. Notice that you can factor out 4 from each term in the numerator:

$$\frac{4(a^4 + 16b)}{16}$$

Then cancel the 4, since it appears in both the numerator and the denominator:

$$\frac{a^4 + 16b}{4}$$

Now plug in $a = 4$ and simplify:

$$\frac{4^4 + 16b}{4} = \frac{256 + 16b}{4}$$
$$= \frac{256}{4} + \frac{16b}{4}$$
$$= 64 + 4b$$

The given expression simplifies to $64 + 4b$. Choice (C) is correct.

Solving Equations

Drill Answers

a. $2(a + 5) = 11 - (3 - 6a)$
$2a + 10 = 11 - 3 + 6a$
$2a + 10 = 8 + 6a$
$2 = 4a$
$\frac{1}{2} = a$

b. $4(3 - r) = 2r + 18$
$12 - 4r = 2r + 18$
$-6 = 6r$
$-1 = r$

c. $\left(\dfrac{2}{2}\right)\dfrac{2t}{3} - \left(\dfrac{3}{3}\right)\dfrac{5t}{2} = \dfrac{5}{6}$

$$\dfrac{4t}{6} - \dfrac{15t}{6} = \dfrac{5}{6}$$

$$-\dfrac{11t}{6} = \dfrac{5}{6}$$

$$6\left(-\dfrac{11t}{6}\right) = 6\left(\dfrac{5}{6}\right)$$

$$-11t = 5$$

$$t = -\dfrac{5}{11}$$

d. $\dfrac{9}{5} \times C = \dfrac{9}{5} \times \dfrac{5}{9}(F - 32)$

$$\dfrac{9}{5}C = F - 32$$

$$\dfrac{9}{5}C + 32 = F$$

e. $A = \dfrac{1}{2}bh$

$$2(A) = 2\left(\dfrac{1}{2}bh\right)$$

$$2A = bh$$

$$\dfrac{2A}{h} = b$$

1. A

Difficulty: Low

Category: Algebra

Getting to the Answer: The question asks you to solve for the given equation. Distribute the 15 to each term in the parentheses: $15x + 135$. Then solve for x:

$$15x + 135 = -21$$

$$15x = -156$$

$$x = -\dfrac{156}{15}$$

Reduce $-\dfrac{156}{15}$ to $-\dfrac{52}{5}$. Choice (A) is correct.

2. F

Difficulty: Low

Category: Algebra

Getting to the Answer: The question asks you to solve for the given equation. First, distribute the 9 to the two terms inside the parentheses: $9a - 27$. Then solve for a:

$$9a - 27 = 15a$$

$$-27 = 6a$$

$$-\dfrac{27}{6} = a$$

Since $-\dfrac{27}{6}$ is not an answer, reduce it to $-\dfrac{9}{2}$. Then, write it as a mixed number: $-\dfrac{9}{2} = -4\dfrac{1}{2}$. This matches (F).

3. B

Difficulty: Medium

Category: Algebra

Getting to the Answer: The question asks you to solve for the given equation. Recall that if $|x| = a, x = a$ and $-x = a$. In this question, $|7x - 1| + 2 = 4$ simplifies to $|7x - 1| = 2$. Therefore, $7x - 1 = 2$ and $-(7x - 1) = 2$. This matches (B).

4. K

Difficulty: Medium

Category: Algebra

Getting to the Answer: The question asks you to solve for the given equation, so there is no math necessary here! If you remember that absolute value represents distance on a number line and therefore cannot be negative, you'll immediately see that there are no values of x for which the equation is true because the right-hand side is -2. Choice (K) is correct.

5. B

Difficulty: Low

Category: Algebra

Getting to the Answer: The question asks you to solve for x. First, distribute the 8 to each of the terms in the parentheses: $8x - 16y$. Then isolate x:

$$8x - 16y = 16x$$

$$-16y = 8x$$

$$-2y = x$$

x in terms of y is $x = -2y$. The correct answer is (B).

Linear Graphs

1. C

Difficulty: Low
Category: Algebra
Getting to the Answer: The question asks for the slope of the given line equation. The equation of a line is $y = mx + b$, where m is the slope and b is the y-intercept. Rewrite the given equation to get y in terms of x.

$$4x - 7y = 14$$
$$-7y = -4x + 14$$
$$y = \frac{4}{7}x - 2$$

The slope of the line given by this equation is the coefficient of x, which is $\frac{4}{7}$. Choice (C) is correct.

2. F

Difficulty: Medium
Category: Algebra
Getting to the Answer: The question asks for the y-intercept of the line that passes through the given points. Here is another type of question in which you need to use the slope-intercept form of a line, $y = mx + b$. First, use the two given points and the slope formula to find the slope of the line:

$$m = \frac{y_2 - y_1}{x_2 - x_1} = \frac{31 - (-13)}{-10 - 1} = \frac{44}{-11} = -4$$

Now, plug this slope and the values of either point into $y = mx + b$ to find b (the y-intercept). Using $(1, -13)$, the result is $-13 = -4(1) + b$. Simplify the equation to get $b = -9$, which is (F).

Notice that G is a distractor; it's the slope of the line, not the y-intercept. Double-check that you're answering the right question before you make your selection.

3. A

Difficulty: Low
Category: Algebra
Getting to the Answer: The question asks for the endpoint of the line with the given endpoint and midpoint. The coordinates of the midpoint of a line segment with endpoints (x_1, y_1) and (x_2, y_2) are $\left(\frac{x_1 + x_2}{2}, \frac{y_1 + y_2}{2}\right)$. Setting $x_1 = -3$ and $y_1 = -8$, solve for x_2 and y_2.

First, $1 = \frac{-3 + x_2}{2}$, or $2 = -3 + x_2$. Add 3 to both sides to get $x_2 = 5$. You can already select (A) based on this because none of the other x-coordinates are correct.

If you have extra time to confirm your choice or have more than one choice remaining, find y_2 using the same process: $-5 = \frac{-8 + y_2}{2}$, or $-10 = -8 + y_2$. Add 8 to both sides to get $y_2 = -2$. Choice (A) is correct.

4. J

Difficulty: Low
Category: Algebra
Getting to the Answer: The question asks you to match one of the given line equations with the given graph. Use the graph to determine the y-intercept and the slope of the line. Then write an equation in slope-intercept form: $y = mx + b$. Once you have your equation, look for the answer choice that matches. The line crosses the y-axis at $(0, -4)$, so the y-intercept (b) is -4. The line rises 1 unit for every 3 units that it runs to the right, so the slope (m) is $\frac{1}{3}$. The equation of the line is thus $y = \frac{1}{3}x - 4$, which matches (J).

5. E

Difficulty: High
Category: Algebra
Getting to the Answer: The question asks you to solve for the line equation that models the given table; start by looking at the answer choices. The equations are given in slope-intercept form, so start by finding the slope. Substitute two pairs of values from the table (pick small numbers if possible) into the slope formula, $m = \frac{y_2 - y_1}{x_2 - x_1}$.

Keep in mind that the projected number of pounds sold depends on the price, so the price is the independent variable (x) and the projected number of pounds is the dependent variable (y). Using the points $(1.2, 15000)$ and $(2, 5000)$, the slope is calculated as follows:

$$m = \frac{5,000 - 15,000}{2 - 1.20}$$
$$= \frac{-10,000}{0.8}$$
$$= -12,500$$

Eliminate A, B, and D because the slope is not correct. To choose between C and (E), you could find the

y-intercept of the line, but this is a fairly time-consuming process. Instead, choose the simplest pair of values from the table, (2,5000), and substitute them into both C and (E). Choice (E) is correct because the equation $5,000 = -12,500(2) + 30,000$ is true.

Solving Inequalities

1.   E

Difficulty: Low
Category: Algebra
Getting to the Answer: The question asks you to solve for the given inequality. Since all of the choices are y in terms of x, solve for y:

$$-8x + 2y \leq 14$$
$$2y \leq 14 + 8x$$
$$y \leq 7 + 4x$$

The inequality simplifies to $y \leq 4x + 7$. Choice (E) is correct.

2.   F

Difficulty: Medium
Category: Algebra
Getting to the Answer: The question asks you to solve for the solution set of the given inequality. Straightforward algebra is the best approach here. Don't forget—whatever you do to one piece, you must do to all three pieces:

$$-15 \leq 2x - 13 < 3$$
$$-2 \leq 2x < 16$$
$$\frac{-2}{2} \leq \frac{2x}{2} < \frac{16}{2}$$
$$-1 \leq x < 8$$

The solution set is numbers greater than or equal to -1 but less than 8. Choice (F) is correct.

3.   D

Difficulty: Medium
Category: Algebra
Getting to the Answer: The question asks you to solve for the given inequality. Since all of the choices are x in

terms of y, solve for x. Remember that you need to flip the inequality when multiplying or dividing by a negative number:

$$-3x + 7y \leq 4y + 6$$
$$-3x \leq -3y + 6$$
$$x \geq y - 2$$

The inequality solved for x in terms of y is $x \geq y - 2$. Choice (D) is correct.

4.   F

Difficulty: High
Category: Algebra
Getting to the Answer: The question asks you to solve for the given inequality. If $|x| = a$, then $x = a$ and $x = -a$. Accordingly, if $|x| < a$, $x < a$ and $x > -a$ because the direction of the inequality flips when multiplying or dividing by a negative. Therefore, $|2x + 5| < 11$ can be written as $2x + 5 < 11$ and $2x + 5 > -11$. Solve each inequality for x:

$$2x + 5 < 11$$
$$2x < 6$$
$$x < 3$$

$$2x + 5 > -11$$
$$2x > -16$$
$$x > -8$$

Thus, $-8 < x < 3$. Choice (F) is correct.

5.   B

Difficulty: Medium
Category: Algebra
Getting to the Answer: The question asks you to solve for the given inequality. To find x such that $x + 2 > x + 1$, subtract x from both sides to obtain $2 > 1$. This inequality is true for any value of x, so the set of x is the set of all real numbers. Choice (B) is correct.

Graphing Inequalities

Drill Answers

a.

b.

c.

d.

e.

1.   A

Difficulty: High
Category: Algebra
Getting to the Answer: The question asks you to solve for the given inequality. Whenever you encounter an absolute value inequality, you must rewrite it without the absolute value signs. The symbol here is $>$, so this will become two inequalities separated by an "or." Split $|2x - 5| > 11$ into $2x - 5 > 11$ or $2x - 5 < -11$ and solve each inequality separately.

$$2x - 5 > 11$$
$$2x > 16$$
$$x > 8$$

or

$$2x - 5 < -11$$
$$2x < -6$$
$$x < -3$$

Find the number line that matches. Choice (A) is correct.

2.   K

Difficulty: Medium
Category: Algebra
Getting to the Answer: The question asks you to choose the correct inequality that matches the given number line. The shaded region in the number line shows a range from -6 to 2. The center is $\frac{-6 + 2}{2} = -2$, with -6 and 2 each 4 units away from the center. Recall that $|x - b| \leq a$ represents all numbers up to and including a units away from the center b. Thus, the absolute value inequality is $|w - (-2)| \leq 4$ or $|w + 2| \leq 4$. This matches choice (K).

You can check your choice by solving for w algebraically:

$$w + 2 \leq 4$$
$$w \leq 2$$

$$w + 2 \geq -4$$
$$w \geq -6$$

The range of w is $-6 \leq w \leq 2$, which exactly matches the number line.

3.   B

Difficulty: Medium
Category: Algebra
Getting to the Answer: The question asks you to match the correct system of inequalities with the given graph. First, determine the equations of the lines in the graph. Then, determine the signs of the inequalities. The vertical line is dashed and passes through $x = -2$. The area to the right of the line is shaded, so the inequality is $x > -2$. Eliminate A, D, and E. The other line is solid and has a slope of -2 (it moves down 2 units for every increase of 1 unit to the right) and a y-intercept of 1. The area below the line is shaded, so the inequality is $y \leq -2x + 1$. Choice (B) is correct.

Math

4. F
Difficulty: Medium
Category: Algebra
Getting to the Answer: The question asks you to match the correct graph with the given inequality. Start by rewriting the compound inequality as two separate inequalities. Then write the inequalities in slope-intercept form, $y = mx + b$, where m is the slope and b is the y-intercept. Solving each one for y yields:

$$2 < y - x$$
$$y > x + 2$$
$$y - x < 3$$
$$y < x + 3$$

The two lines are parallel lines with a positive slope of 1. Thus, the lines must be increasing (going up) from left to right. Eliminate H and J. To decide between the remaining choices, consider the y-intercepts of the lines. One line has a y-intercept of 2, and the other has a y-intercept of 3. This matches (F).

5. D
Difficulty: High
Category: Algebra
Getting to the Answer: The question asks you to solve for the possible values of b. One approach to this question is to solve each of the answer choices algebraically to get a range of values for b and then see which one gives you the same range as that shown in the figure. However, a faster method is to think of absolute value as a distance. The center of the shaded region is $\frac{-1 + 5}{2} = 2$, with -1 and 5 each 3 units away from the center. Therefore, the distance between b and 2 must be less than or equal to 3, so $|b - 2| \leq 3$. Choice (D) is correct.

You can confirm your choice by rewriting the absolute value inequality as a compound inequality and solving for b:

$$|b - 2| \leq 3$$
$$-3 \leq b - 2 \leq 3$$
$$-1 \leq b \leq 5$$

This inequality matches the number line exactly.

Quadratics

1. C
Difficulty: Low
Category: Algebra
Getting to the Answer: The question asks you to solve for the given quadratic equation. All of the choices are integers, so factoring is likely the quickest route to the answer. Start by setting the equation equal to 0.

$$x^2 - 4x - 6 = 6$$
$$x^2 - 4x - 12 = 0$$

Now find two numbers whose product is -12 and whose sum is -4. That's -6 and 2: $(x - 6)(x + 2) = 0$. Solving for x yields:

$$(x - 6) = 0 \rightarrow x = 6$$
$$(x + 2) = 0 \rightarrow x = -2$$

The possible values of x are -2 and 6. Choice (C) is correct.

2. F
Difficulty: Low
Category: Algebra
Getting to the Answer: The question asks you to multiply two expressions and simplify. Although there are variables in the question stem and the choices, using the Picking Numbers strategy will be laborious. The more straightforward route is to use FOIL:

$$(b - a)(a + b) = ba + b^2 - a^2 - ab$$
$$= b^2 - a^2$$

Note that the ab terms cancel out. Rearranging $b^2 - a^2$ gives you $-a^2 + b^2$, which is (F).

3. B
Difficulty: High
Category: Algebra
Getting to the Answer: The question asks you to solve for the given quadratic equation. The choices contain radicals, so use the quadratic formula. First, jot down the values for a, b, and c. You should also write down the formula itself so you're not trying to remember it and plug in values at the same time.

$$x = \frac{-b \pm \sqrt{b^2 - 4ac}}{2a}$$
$$a = 1, b = 8, c = -3$$

Carefully substitute the values into the formula and simplify.

$$x = \frac{-(8) \pm \sqrt{(8)^2 - 4(1)(-3)}}{2(1)}$$

$$= \frac{-8 \pm \sqrt{64 + 12}}{2}$$

$$= \frac{-8 \pm \sqrt{76}}{2}$$

This is not one of the choices, which tells you that you need to simplify the radical. To simplify the radical, look for a perfect square that divides evenly into 76.

$$x = \frac{-8 \pm \sqrt{4}\sqrt{19}}{2}$$

$$= \frac{-8 \pm 2\sqrt{19}}{2}$$

$$= -4 \pm \sqrt{19}$$

The roots of the given quadratic are $-4 \pm \sqrt{19}$, so (B) is correct.

4. H
Difficulty: Medium
Category: Algebra
Getting to the Answer: The question asks you to simplify the given expression. Factor the numerator and denominator. For the denominator, first factor out a 2 to get 1 for the x^2 coefficient. Then factor the quadratic as usual. If the numerator and denominator have any factors in common, cancel those factors.

$$\frac{x^2 - 4x + 4}{2x^2 + 4x - 16} = \frac{(x-2)(x-2)}{2(x^2 + 2x - 8)}$$

$$= \frac{(x-2)(x-2)}{2(x+4)(x-2)}$$

$$= \frac{x-2}{2(x+4)}$$

This is the most simplified form of the given expression; (H) is correct.

5. D
Difficulty: High
Category: Algebra
Getting to the Answer: The question asks how long it will take for the projectile to hit the ground after launch. To find the amount of time it takes for the

projectile to hit the ground, find the value of t for which $h = 0$. The fact that 16 divides evenly into 32 (and therefore into 320) is a big hint that you'll be able to factor.

$$0 = -16t^2 + 128t + 320$$
$$0 = -16(t^2 - 8t - 20)$$
$$0 = t^2 - 8t - 20$$
$$0 = (t - 10)(t + 2)$$

Setting each factor equal to 0 gives $t = 10$ or $t = -2$. However, because time cannot be negative, the answer is $t = 10$ seconds. Choice (D) is correct.

Systems of Equations

1. D
Difficulty: Low
Category: Algebra
Getting to the Answer: The question asks you to solve for the sum of the given system of equations. Solve for x and y individually, and then add them together to find the final answer.

$$6x = 20$$
$$x = \frac{20}{6}$$
$$x = \frac{10}{3}$$
$$3y + 7 = 14$$
$$3y = 7$$
$$y = \frac{7}{3}$$

The sum is $x + y = \frac{10}{3} + \frac{7}{3} = \frac{17}{3}$. Writing $\frac{17}{3}$ as a mixed number yields $5\frac{2}{3}$, which matches (D).

2. H
Difficulty: Low
Category: Algebra
Getting to the Answer: The question asks how much greater A is than B. Determining how much greater A is than B means finding the difference between the two, $A - B$:

$$(24xy + 13) - (8xy + 1)$$
$$24xy + 13 - 8xy - 1$$
$$16xy + 12$$

A is $16xy + 12$ greater than B. Choice (H) is correct.

3. E

Difficulty: Medium

Category: Algebra

Getting to the Answer: The question asks you to solve for the product of x and y. First, solve for x and y individually. Then multiply them together to find their product.

To solve using combination, you will need to multiply each equation by a constant. Suppose you want to eliminate x. The coefficients of the x terms are 2 and 5, so you need to multiply the equations by numbers that will give you -10 and 10 as your new x term coefficients. To do this, multiply the first equation by -5 and the second equation by 2:

$$-5(2x + 5y = 49)$$
$$2(5x + 3y = 94)$$

Now add the resulting equations:

$$-10x - 25y = -245$$
$$+10x + 6y = 188$$
$$-19y = -57$$
$$y = 3$$

Next, plug $y = 3$ back into either equation and solve for x. This yields $x = 17$. Finally, multiply x and y together to obtain 51, which is (E).

4. J

Difficulty: High

Category: Algebra

Getting to the Answer: The question asks you to solve for the value of $4x - 5y$. To determine the value of $4x - 5y$, first find the solution to the system of equations. You can solve by either substitution or combination/elimination. However, since it is easy to isolate x in the first equation, substitution is preferred. Solve the first equation for x and then substitute it into the second equation to solve for y:

$$x = 11 - 9y$$
$$2(11 - 9y) - 7y = -3$$
$$22 - 18y - 7y = -3$$
$$-25y = -25$$
$$y = 1$$

Then plug $y = 1$ into $x = 11 - 9y$ to find x: $x = 11 - 9(1) = 2$. Thus, $4x - 5y = 4(2) - 5(1) = 8 - 5 = 3$. Choice (J) is correct.

5. C

Difficulty: High

Category: Algebra

Getting to the Answer: The question asks you to choose the inequality that will have more than one real solution. Substitute $y = x$ into the second equation and set the equation equal to 0:

$$-py + qx^2 = r$$
$$-px + qx^2 - r = 0$$
$$qx^2 - px - r = 0$$

Recall that the quadratic formula for a quadratic equation in the form $ax^2 + bx + c = 0$ is $x = \dfrac{-b \pm \sqrt{b^2 - 4ac}}{2a}$. The term under the square root, $b^2 - 4ac$, determines how many real solutions there are. When the term is negative, there are no real solutions for x because negative numbers have no real square roots. When the term is 0, then the value of x will be $\dfrac{-b}{2a}$, which yields only one solution. Finally, when the term is positive, x will have two solutions because of the $\pm$ symbol.

Thus, there will be more than one solution if the term under the square root is greater than 0. Here $a = q$, $b = -p$ and $c = -r$. Substitute accordingly and solve:

$$b^2 - 4ac > 0$$
$$(-p)^2 - 4q(-r) > 0$$
$$p^2 + 4qr > 0$$

$p^2 + 4qr$ will produce more than one real solution. Choice (C) is correct.

Word Problems

Drill Answers

a. $2n - m$

b. $\dfrac{1}{4}(a + b) = a - 4$

c. $9y - (x + 7) = \dfrac{(x - z)}{7 - x}$

d. $\dfrac{4q}{7p} = \dfrac{5}{2}$

e. $F - 500 + G = 2(F + 0.50F)$

1. B
Difficulty: Medium
Category: Algebra
Getting to the Answer: The question asks for the correct expression of the number of sharks in terms of whales and dolphins. If w represents the number of whales, then the phrase "twice as many dolphins as whales" means that there are $2w$ dolphins. Therefore, "dolphins and whales combined" is $2w + w$, or $3w$. Because there are 8 fewer sharks than dolphins and whales combined, you need to subtract 8 from $3w$, which makes (B) correct.

You can also answer this question by using the Picking Numbers strategy. Pick a small, positive number, like 5, for the number of whales. If there are 5 whales and "twice as many dolphins as whales," then there must be 10 dolphins. Combine the number of whales and dolphins and subtract 8 from that sum to find the number of sharks: $(5 + 10) - 8 = 15 - 8 = 7$. Plug in $w = 5$ to determine which answer choice gives you a value of 7:

Choice A: $5(5) = 25$ Eliminate.

Choice (B): $3(5) - 8 = 15 - 8 = 7$ Keep.

Choice C: $10 + 5 = 15$ Eliminate.

Choice D: $3(5)^2 - 8(5) = 75 - 40 = 35$ Eliminate.

Choice E: $3\sqrt{2(5)} - 8 = 3\sqrt{2} \neq 7$ Eliminate.

Choice (B) is the only answer that works.

2. J
Difficulty: Low
Category: Algebra
Getting to the Answer: The question asks for the expression that represents the cost, in dollars, of p paintbrushes and c canvases. The total cost of the two kinds of items is the cost of the paintbrushes multiplied by the number of paintbrushes purchased plus the cost of the canvases multiplied by the number of canvases purchased. Because a canvas costs "6 times" the cost of a paintbrush, a canvas costs $6(\$1.50) = \$9$.

Total cost of paintbrushes: $1.50 \times p = 1.5p$
Total cost of canvases: $9 \times c = 9c$
Sum of both: $9c + 1.5p$

$9c + 1.5p$ represents the expression for costs in dollars. Therefore, (J) is correct.

3. B
Difficulty: Medium
Category: Algebra
Getting to the Answer: The question asks you to determine how many miles Joy traveled. Backsolving works well on many word problems with integers in the choices. Start with the middle choice, C. If Joy drove 96 miles, she would have paid $\$1.50 + \$0.25(96) = \$25.50$. This is too much, so try (B). If she drove 94 miles, she would have paid $\$1.50 + \$0.25(94) = \$25.00$. Choice (B) is correct.

You could also set up an equation and solve algebraically. If m is the number of miles traveled, then the toll is $\$1.50 + \$0.25m$. Joy paid a total of $\$25.00$, so solve this equation:

$$\$1.50 + \$0.25m = \$25.00$$
$$\$0.25m = \$23.50$$
$$m = 94$$

This confirms that (B) is correct.

4. H
Difficulty: Medium
Category: Algebra
Getting to the Answer: The question asks how many adult tickets were sold. Algebra and Backsolving both work well on word problems like this one. Use the method with which you are more comfortable.

To solve this question algebraically, first translate it into a system of equations. At $8 per adult ticket and $5 per student ticket, the total amount of money collected can be written as $8a + 5s = 3,475$. Because there were 500 tickets total, $a + s = 500$. Plug $s = 500 - a$ into the first equation and solve for a:

$$8a + 5(500 - a) = 3,475$$
$$8a + 2,500 - 5a = 3,475$$
$$3a = 975$$
$$a = 325$$

Choice (H) is correct.

To Backsolve, start with (H). If there are 325 adult tickets, then there are $500 - 325 = 175$ student tickets. The total amount of money collected would be $\$325(8) + \$175(5)$, or $\$2,600 + \$875 = \$3,475$. Because this is the total given in the question stem, (H) is correct.

Math

5. B

Difficulty: High

Category: Algebra

Getting to the Answer: The question asks for the maximum number of vases the ceramist can glaze with 20 pints of glaze. Because you want to know the value of v when the given expression is at most 20, set up an inequality and solve for v:

$$v^2 + v \leq 20$$
$$v^2 + v - 20 \leq 0$$
$$(v + 5)(v - 4) \leq 0$$
$$v \leq -5 \text{ and } 4$$

Thus, the maximum number of vases the ceramist can glaze is 4. (B) is correct.

On Test Day

1. E

Difficulty: Medium

Category: Algebra

Getting to the Answer: A strategic "guess" is actually the best approach for this question; the question asks you to solve for the given equation, so there is no math actually necessary here. If you remember that absolute value represents distance on a number line and therefore cannot be negative, you'll immediately see that there are no values of x for which the equation is true because the right-hand side is -4. Choice (E) is correct.

However, you might not spot this shortcut, or the question might not provide such an easy way to eliminate 4 out of 5 choices. In that case, you'll want to consider algebra or Backsolving as alternative approaches.

To solve this equation algebraically, follow the order of operations, making sure you create two equations when you account for the absolute value symbols:

$$|2x - 6| = -4$$

$2x - 6 = +(-4)$	or	$2x - 6 = -(-4)$
$2x = 6 + (-4)$		$2x = 6 + 4$
$2x = 2$		$2x = 10$
$x = 1$		$x = 5$

Be careful! Plug these values back into the equation to ensure success. At this point, you'll notice that neither value works:

$$|2x - 6| = -4$$

$|2(1) - 6| = -4$	or	$|2(5) - 6| = -4$
$|3 - 6| = -4$		$|10 - 6| = -4$
$|-3| = -4$		$|4| = -4$
$3 \neq -4$		$4 \neq -4$

If you choose to solve this question by Backsolving, consider the answer choices carefully. If you start with B and prove that $x \neq 1$, then you can eliminate both B and D:

$$|2(1) - 6| = -4$$
$$|3 - 6| = -4$$
$$|-3| = -4$$
$$3 = -4$$

Then, plug in both A and C:

A: $|2(-1) - 6| = -4$	C: $|2(5) - 6| = -4$
$|-2 - 6| = -4$	$|10 - 6| = -4$
$|-8| = -4$	$|4| = -4$
$8 \neq -4$	$4 \neq -4$

Since neither value is a solution, (E) must be correct.

How Much Have You Learned?

1. C

Difficulty: High

Category: Algebra

Getting to the Answer: The question asks how many distinct roots the given equation has. The equation is a polynomial in one variable, so the greatest number of roots (solutions) it can have is equal to the highest power of the variable, which is 3. This means that you can eliminate E right away. That doesn't mean the answer is 3, however, because you are counting the number of *distinct* real solutions. To solve the equation, start by factoring out the GCF, which is $3x$. Then factor:

$$3x^3 + 30x^2 + 75x = 0$$
$$3x(x^2 + 10x + 25) = 0$$
$$3x(x + 5)(x + 5) = 0$$

Setting each factor equal to 0 and solving for x yields $x = 0$, $x = -5$, and $x = -5$. There are only two distinct real solutions, 0 and -5, so (C) is correct.

2. H
Difficulty: Low
Category: Algebra
Getting to the Answer: The question asks for the coordinate of the midpoint between the two points given. The coordinates of the midpoint of a line segment with endpoints (x_1, y_1) and (x_2, y_2) are $\left(\dfrac{x_1 + x_2}{2}, \dfrac{y_1 + y_2}{2}\right)$. Plug the points $(-3,5)$ and $(0,1)$ into the formula:
$\left(\dfrac{-3 + 0}{2}, \dfrac{5 + 1}{2}\right) = \left(-\dfrac{3}{2}, 3\right)$. Choice (H) is correct.

3. D
Difficulty: Low
Category: Algebra
Getting to the Answer: The question asks for the y-intercept of the line that passes through the given points. You are looking for the y-intercept, so use the slope-intercept form, $y = mx + b$. Unfortunately, you must find m before you can find b.

$$m = \frac{y_2 - y_1}{x_2 - x_1} = \frac{42 - 21}{4 - 1} = \frac{21}{3} = 7$$

Plug in $m = 7$ and the (x,y) values of either point to find b. It's typically easier to work with smaller numbers, so use $(1,21)$.

$$y = mx + b$$
$$21 = 7(1) + b$$
$$21 = 7 + b$$
$$14 = b$$

You don't need to write out the full equation of the line, since you are interested in b only. Choice (D) is correct.

4. J
Difficulty: Medium
Category: Algebra
Getting to the Answer: The question asks for the solution set for the given equation. To solve an absolute value equation, you must always consider the two possibilities: If $|2x - 3| = 13$, then the expression inside the absolute value signs could equal either 13 or -13:

$$2x - 3 = 13$$
$$2x = 16$$
$$x = 8$$

and
$$2x - 3 = -13$$
$$2x = -10$$
$$x = -5$$

Together, the two solutions form the solution set $\{-5, 8\}$, which is (J).

5. C
Difficulty: Medium
Category: Algebra
Getting to the Answer: The question asks for the number of additional visits in a year that that would yield the same cost for both exterminators. Carefully translate from English into math.

Bye Bye Bugs: $\$275 + \$20 \times$ number of additional visits

Pest Be Gone: $\$200 + \$25 \times$ number of additional visits

Call v the number of additional visits and set the two equations equal to each other:

$$275 + 20v = 200 + 25v$$
$$75 = 5v$$
$$15 = v$$

It will take 15 additional visits for the cost of both exterminators to be equal. Choice (C) is correct.

6. F
Difficulty: Medium
Category: Algebra
Getting to the Answer: The question asks you to choose the inequality that matches the given graph. First, determine the equations of the lines in the graph. Then, determine the sign of the inequality. The dashed line has a slope of $-\dfrac{1}{2}$ and a y-intercept of 3. The area below the dashed line is shaded, so $y < -\dfrac{1}{2}x + 3$. The solid line also has a slope of $-\dfrac{1}{2}$ and a y-intercept of -2. The area above the solid line is shaded, so $y \geq -\dfrac{1}{2}x - 2$. Thus, $-\dfrac{1}{2}x - 2 \leq y < -\dfrac{1}{2}x + 3$. Choice (F) is correct.

7. C

Difficulty: Low

Category: Algebra

Getting to the Answer: The question asks you to simplify the given expression. Before distributing the $\frac{1}{5}p$, combine like terms inside the parentheses: $\frac{1}{5}p(15q + 10p)$. Then distribute the $\frac{1}{5}p$: $3pq + 2p^2$. Choice (C) is correct.

8. K

Difficulty: High

Category: Algebra

Getting to the Answer: The question asks for the solutions of x. First, substitute $y = x^2$ into the second equation.

$$24 + x^2 = 10x$$

You now have a quadratic equation. Set it equal to 0, factor, and solve for x.

$$24 + x^2 = 10x$$
$$x^2 - 10x + 24 = 0$$
$$(x - 4)(x - 6) = 0$$

Thus, $x = 4$ and $x = 6$. Choice (K) is correct.

9. E

Difficulty: Medium

Category: Algebra

Getting to the Answer: The question asks for the two solutions of the given inequality. If $|x| = a$, then $x = a$ and $x = -a$. Similarly, for $|x| < a$, $x < a$ and $x > -a$. Recall that the direction of the inequality sign flips when you multiply or divide by a negative. Therefore, $|4x + 3| - 1 < 8$ can be written as $4x + 3 < 9$ and $4x + 3 > -9$. This matches (E).

10. K

Difficulty: High

Category: Algebra

Getting to the Answer: The question asks you to determine how many hours Rasheed needs to jump in order for the cost of the membership to be less than the total cost of buying jump tickets at the non-membership price. An individual non-membership ticket costs $12, so if Rasheed jumps for h hours, the total cost will be $12h.

If Rasheed buys the membership, then the total cost will be the membership fee plus the discounted rate of the jump ticket per hour. The discounted ticket is $12 - (0.15 \times 12)$, or $12 \times 0.85 = 10.2$.

Set up an inequality to solve for the minimum number of hours, h, Rasheed needs to jump in order for the cost of the membership to be less than the total cost of buying jump tickets at the non-membership price.

$$50 + 10.2h < 12h$$
$$50 < 1.8h$$
$$27.8 < h$$

The smallest whole number greater than 27.8 is 28, so the answer is (K).

CHAPTER 11

TABLES, GRAPHS, STATISTICS, AND PROBABILITY

LEARNING OBJECTIVES

After completing this chapter, you will be able to:

- Draw inferences about data presented in a variety of graphical formats
- Calculate mean, median, mode, range, and expected value
- Calculate probabilities based on data sets

Statistics and Probability: 6/36 SmartPoints® (High yield)

How Much Do You Know?

Directions: Try out the questions below. Show your work so that you can compare your solutions to the ones found on the next page. The "Category" heading in the explanation for each question gives the title of the lesson that covers how to solve it. If you answered the question(s) for a given lesson correctly, and if your scratchwork looks like the explanations, you may be able to move quickly through that lesson. If you answered incorrectly or used a different approach, you may want to take your time on that lesson.

1. Jamal has a suitcase that contains 2 white socks (and no other socks). He wants to add enough black socks so that the probability of randomly selecting a white sock is $\frac{1}{5}$. How many black socks should Jamal add to the suitcase?

   A. 6
   B. 7
   C. 8
   D. 9
   E. 10

2. What is the distance, on a number line, between the median and the range of the set $\{-9, -6, -2, 0, 4, 9\}$?

   F. -1
   G. 0
   H. 1
   J. 18
   K. 19

3. Jasmin's goal is to collect 200 cans of food during a food drive. During her first 4 days, she averages 10 cans per day. With 10 days remaining, Jasmin must average how many cans per day to meet her goal?

   A. 12
   B. 14
   C. 16
   D. 18
   E. 20

4. The following frequency chart shows the number of Ms. Kirkham's English students whose test scores fell within certain score ranges. All test scores are whole numbers. How many students have a test score in the interval 71–75?

Score range	Cumulative number of students
60–65	1
60–70	3
60–75	8
60–85	9
60–100	12

   F. 1
   G. 3
   H. 4
   J. 5
   K. 8

5. A certain baseball stadium has 12,000 seats. Based on several previous years' attendance rates, the owners of the stadium constructed the following table showing the daily attendance rates, expressed as decimals, and their probabilities of occurring for the coming baseball season. Based on the probability distribution in the table below, what is the expected number of seats that will be occupied on any given day during the coming baseball season?

Attendance rate	Probability
0.40	0.15
0.50	0.25
0.60	0.35
0.70	0.15
0.80	0.10

A. 5,400
B. 6,240
C. 6,960
D. 7,080
E. 7,200

6. The data set $\{1, 3, -8, x, 10\}$ has a mean of 7. What is the median of this data set?

F. −8
G. 1
H. 3
J. 10
K. 29

7. Zaina's bookshelf contains 10 horror novels, 10 romance novels, 10 true crime books, and no other books. If Zaina chooses 2 books from the shelf at random to take with her on vacation, what is the probability that the two books she chooses will belong to the same genre?

A. $\frac{9}{87}$

B. $\frac{1}{6}$

C. $\frac{9}{29}$

D. $\frac{56}{87}$

E. $\frac{2}{3}$

8. The average of a list of 4 numbers is 100. If the first number is increased by 4, the second number decreased by 5, the third number increased by 6, and the fourth number increased by 1, what will the average be?

F. 95
G. 97.5
H. 100
J. 101.5
K. 102

9. Janelle is planning to go out of town for 2 consec-
    utive days and needs to create a watering schedule
    for her garden. During her time out of town, there
    is a 50% chance of rain each day. Assuming that
    the chance of rain is independent of the day, what
    is the probability that it will rain both days that
    she is gone?

    A.   0.20
    B.   0.25
    C.   0.50
    D.   0.75
    E.   1.00

10. A researcher is looking to evaluate the impact on
    blood pressure levels of stroking various types of
    pets. Her 120 research participants were grouped
    by the one type of pet they would be interacting
    with during the study.

    If 1 person from this research group is randomly
    selected, what is the probability that this person
    will interact with a dog or a cat?

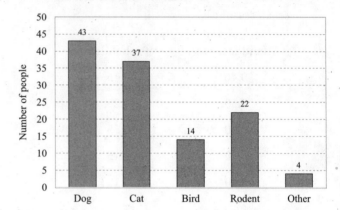

    F. $\dfrac{37}{120}$

    G. $\dfrac{40}{120}$

    H. $\dfrac{43}{120}$

    J. $\dfrac{37}{43}$

    K. $\dfrac{80}{120}$

Check Your Work

1. C
Difficulty: Low
Category: Statistics and Probability: Probability
Getting to the Answer: The question asks how many black socks Jamal should add to a suitcase so that the probability of randomly selecting a white sock is $\frac{1}{5}$. In order for the probability of selecting one of the 2 white socks to be $\frac{1}{5}$, there must be 10 total socks in the suitcase, since $\frac{1}{5}=\frac{2}{10}$. Currently, the only socks in the suitcase are the 2 white socks, so Jamal must add $10-2=8$ black socks to the suitcase to bring the total to 10. Choice (C) is correct.

2. K
Difficulty: Medium
Category: Statistics and Probability: Statistics
Getting to the Answer: The question asks for the distance between the median and the range of the given set. In a set with an even number of values, the median is the average of the two middle numbers. The values are already in ascending order, so the two middle numbers are -2 and 0. The median is thus -1. This is not the answer to the question, though.

The range of a set of numbers is the biggest number minus the smallest number. The range is thus $9-(-9)=9+9=18$. This still is not the answer to the question; keep going.

The distance between -1 and 18 on a number line is $18-(-1)$, or $18+1=19$. Choice (K) is correct.

3. C
Difficulty: Medium
Category: Statistics and Probability: Statistics
Getting to the Answer: The question asks how many cans per day Jasmin must collect in her remaining 10 days to meet her goal. Use the average formula:

$$\text{average}=\frac{\text{sum of terms}}{\text{number of terms}}$$

You are told that the average for the first 4 days is 10. Plug these values into the formula:

$$10=\frac{\text{sum of terms}}{4}$$

The total number of cans that Jasmin collected in the first 4 days is therefore $10\times4=40$. Jasmin wants to collect 200 cans in all, so she needs to collect another $200-40=160$ cans. There are 10 days left, so use the average formula a second time:

$$\text{average}=\frac{160}{10}$$

Jasmin needs to average $\frac{160}{10}=16$ cans per day to reach her goal. Choice (C) is correct.

4. J
Difficulty: Medium
Category: Statistics and Probability: Tables and Graphs
Getting to the Answer: The question asks how many students have a test score in the interval 71–75, but the interval 71–75 does not appear in the frequency chart. However, you can deduce the number of students in this interval by comparing the number of students in the 60–70 and 60–75 intervals.

According to the chart, there are 3 students in the 60–70 interval, and there are 8 students in the 60–75 interval. Since both intervals have the 60–70 range in common, the 5 additional students must have come from the 71–75 range.

Choice (J) is correct.

5. C
Difficulty: High
Category: Statistics and Probability: Probability
Getting to the Answer: The question asks for the expected number of seats that will be occupied on any given day during the coming baseball season. To calculate the expected value, multiply each value by its probability and add up the results:

$$(0.40\times0.15) \qquad 0.060$$
$$(0.50\times0.25) \qquad 0.125$$
$$(0.60\times0.35) \longrightarrow 0.210$$
$$(0.70\times0.15) \qquad 0.105$$
$$+(0.80\times0.10) \qquad +0.080$$
$$\qquad\qquad\qquad 0.580$$

Be careful! This value represents the expected *attendance rate*, but the question asks for the expected number of *seats*. To find the expected number of seats, multiply the expected attendance rate by the total number of seats in the stadium, 12,000:

$$12,000(0.58) = 6,960$$

Choice (C) is correct.

6. H
Difficulty: Low
Category: Statistics and Probability: Statistics
Getting to the Answer: The question asks for the median of the given data set. To find the median, you must first find *x*. Apply the average formula to solve for *x*.

$$\text{average} = \frac{\text{sum of terms}}{\text{number of terms}}$$

$$7 = \frac{1 + 3 - 8 + x + 10}{5}$$

$$7 = \frac{6 + x}{5}$$

$$35 = 6 + x$$

$$29 = x$$

The median is the middle number when the data set is arranged in increasing order:

$$\{-8, 1, 3, 10, 29\}$$

3 is the median, and (H) is correct.

7. C
Difficulty: High
Category: Statistics and Probability: Probability
Getting to the Answer: The question asks for the probability that Zaina picks two books of the same genre. Use the probability formula:

$$\text{probability} = \frac{\text{\# of desired outcomes}}{\text{\# of possible outcomes}}$$

After Zaina chooses her first book, there will be $10 - 1 = 9$ books of that type left. Thus, the "desired" number of books is 9. There are $10 + 10 + 10 = 30$ total books to start with. After Zaina takes one, 29 books remain. Thus, the total number of possibilities is 29. Plugging these values into the probability formula yields $\frac{9}{29}$.

Answer choice (C) is correct.

8. J
Difficulty: Medium
Category: Statistics and Probability: Statistics
Getting to the Answer: The question asks for the average of a list of 4 numbers after some changes are made. This scenario may look intimidating, but start with what you know: "the average of a list of 4 numbers is 100" can be written mathematically as:

$$\frac{a + b + c + d}{4} = 100$$

You don't know the individual variables' values, but that information is not necessary to answer this question. If you multiply both sides of the equation by 4, you can determine the sum of the four variables: $a + b + c + d = 400$. Then, use the numbers in the question stem to calculate the new sum: $400 + 4 - 5 + 6 + 1 = 406$. The new average, then, will be this new sum divided by the number of values: $406 \div 4 = 101.5$. Choice (J) is correct.

9. B
Difficulty: Medium
Category: Statistics and Probability: Probability
Getting to the Answer: Your task is to calculate the probability that it will rain two days in a row. The probability that multiple independent events will all occur is the product of their individual probabilities. The probability of rain each day is 50%, or 0.5. The probability of getting rain on both days is therefore $0.5 \times 0.5 = 0.25$, choice (B).

10. K
Difficulty: Low
Category: Statistics and Probability: Probability
Getting to the Answer: Probability is the ratio of the number of desired outcomes to the number of possible outcomes. Here, the desired outcome is that a participant has a dog or a cat. According to the graph, this is $43 + 37 = 80$ participants. The question states that there are 120 participants, which is the number of possible outcomes. So the probability that one randomly selected person will have either a dog or a cat is 80 out of 120, or $\frac{80}{120}$, which is (K).

TABLES AND GRAPHS

To answer a question like this:

Callum is playing a game in which he draws cards out of a standard 52-card deck. If he draws an odd number, he awards himself 2 points. If he draws an even number, he awards himself 3 points. If he draws a face card (jack, queen, king, or ace) he awards himself 4 points. Let the random variable x represent the total number of points awarded on any draw from the deck. What is the expected value of x? (Note: A standard deck of cards contains four copies of the numbers 2 through 10 and four copies of each of the face cards.)

A. 2

B. 2.85

C. 3

D. 3.57

E. 4

You need to know this:

The ACT uses some straightforward methods of representing data sets that you are probably already familiar with, such as **tables** and **bar graphs**. There are, however, some less common types of tables or graphs that show up from time to time that can be confusing at first glance.

Histograms, piecewise graphs, and circle graphs could all show up on the Math Test. They shouldn't be difficult to interpret, but it's helpful to keep in mind that the test maker often includes more information than you actually need. It's important to consider what the question asks for so that you find only the information that you need.

• **Histograms** look a lot like bar charts and can be read in the same way, but they show how many times a certain value shows up in a number range (as opposed to showing counts of various groups).

  • The numbers on the x-axis provide the boundaries for each bar's range.

- **Piecewise graphs** are graphs created from functions that are defined, literally, by multiple pieces.
  - The domain, the set of *x*-values, is what determines the breaks between pieces.
  - The pieces can be similar or vastly different. All of the pieces could be horizontal segments of the same length that "jump" *y*-coordinates at designated *x*-values. Alternatively, one piece could be part of a linear function, one piece could be part of a quadratic function, one piece could be a single *y*-value, etc.

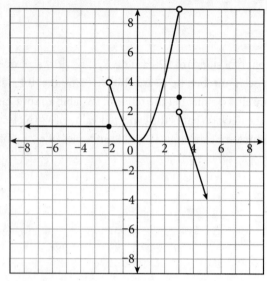

$$f(x) = \begin{cases} 1, & \text{if } x \le -2 \\ x^2, & \text{if } -2 < x < 3 \\ 3, & \text{if } x = 3 \\ -3x + 11, & \text{if } x > 3 \end{cases}$$

- **Circle graphs** (also called **pie graphs**) represent data as parts of a circle where relative percentages dictate the portions of the circle.
  - When displaying data in a circle graph, find the measures of the central angles for each sector of the circle. To do this, multiply each percent by 360°.
  - For example, a sector that represents 35% of the data should have a central angle that measures approximately $0.35(360°) \doteq 126°$.
  - When you're done, the percentages should sum to 100%, and the angle measures should sum to 360°.

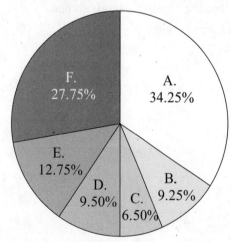

A. inert, mild or no side effects

B. inert, moderate side effects

C. inert, severe side effects

D. drug, mild or no side effects

E. drug, moderate side effects

F. drug, severe side effects

You need to do this:

When presented with a question that uses a graph or table to present information, first inspect the format of the graph or table. What kind of graph or table is it? What information is presented on each axis? What information do you need to find in order to answer the question?

Find the information you need from the table or graph, and then use the information for any calculation the question might require, such as taking the average, finding the median, or determining the expected value.

Explanation:

The question asks for the expected value of x. There is a lot of information in this question, so make a table to organize it:

Draw	Points
Odd	2
Even	3
Face	4

Next, determine the probability of drawing an odd, even, or face card. Remember that there are 4 odd numbers and 5 even numbers in each of the 4 suits:

Draw	Probability
Odd	$\frac{16}{52}$
Even	$\frac{20}{52}$
Face	$\frac{16}{52}$

Next, update the first table with the probabilities you found in the second table:

Draw	Probability	Points
Odd	$\frac{16}{52}$	2
Even	$\frac{20}{52}$	3
Face	$\frac{16}{52}$	4

Finally, calculate the expected value. Think of expected value as a weighted average: multiply the number of points Callum earns by the probability of getting these points and then adding those products together. Expected value is designed to give an idea of the "long term" behavior of the probability distribution: how many points Callum would expect to earn per card if he kept drawing cards for years and years.

$$\frac{16}{52}(2) + \frac{20}{52}(3) + \frac{16}{52}(4)$$

$$\frac{32}{52} + \frac{60}{52} + \frac{64}{52}$$

$$\frac{156}{52}$$

$$3$$

The expected value of x is 3, so (C) is correct. This makes intuitive sense, since 3 points is the midpoint between 2 and 4.

Try on Your Own

Directions: Take as much time as you need on these questions. Work carefully and methodically. There will be an opportunity for timed practice at the end of the chapter.

HINT: Expected value is really just a weighted average. Review the first question and associated explanation from earlier in this lesson if needed to answer Q1.

---

1. Dr. Li has taught 1,520 university students over the past 10 years. The grade points (0–4) earned by past students and their corresponding probabilities are recorded in the table shown. Based on this probability distribution, what is the expected number of grade points that a randomly selected student in her class this semester can expect to earn?

Grade points	Probability
4	0.20
3	0.35
2	0.30
1	0.10
0	0.05

A. 1.85

B. 2.0

C. 2.25

D. 2.55

E. 3

Use the following information to answer questions 2 and 3.

The following table shows the number of infants born in a certain hospital in August 2016. The table categorizes the births by gender and whether the infant was below, above, or within the healthy weight range, as defined by the World Health Organization.

	Below range	Within range	Above range	Total
Male	1	56	10	67
Female	8	48	5	61
Total	9	104	15	128

2. Approximately what percent of the infants born at this hospital in August 2016 were below the healthy weight range?

F. 7%

G. 8%

H. 9%

J. 12%

K. 15%

3.   A neonatal care company conducted a study on the female infants born at this hospital in August 2016 who were either below or above the healthy weight range. If an infant is randomly selected from females born at this hospital in August 2016, what is the probability that the infant is one of those who were included in the study?

A. $\dfrac{5}{128}$

B. $\dfrac{5}{61}$

C. $\dfrac{13}{128}$

D. $\dfrac{13}{61}$

E. $\dfrac{61}{128}$

Use the following information to answer questions 4 and 5.

Phase I clinical trials are run to determine the safety of an investigational drug. Dr. Gibbons is overseeing a treatment-resistant influence Phase I trial with 400 healthy participants. Half are given the drug, and half are given an inert pill. The circle graph below shows a distribution of the severity of common side effects.

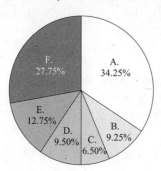

A. inert, mild or no side effects
B. inert, moderate side effects
C. inert, severe side effects
D. drug, mild or no side effects
E. drug, moderate side effects
F. drug, severe side effects

4.   What percent of the participants experienced severe side effects?

F.   6.50%

G.   21.25%

H.   27.75%

J.   34.25%

K.   65.75%

5.   How many more participants experienced mild or no side effects than severe side effects?

A.   10

B.   38

C.   42

D.   50

E.   64

STATISTICS

LEARNING OBJECTIVE

After this lesson, you will be able to:

• Calculate mean, median, mode, range, and expected value

To answer a question like this:

The average of a list of 3 distinct numbers is 20. A new list of 3 distinct numbers has the same median as the original list and the same largest number as the original list. The range of the new list is 3 greater than the range of the original list. What is the average of this new list of numbers?

A. 19

B. 20

C. 21

D. 22

E. 23

You need to know this:

Suppose a nurse took a patient's pulse at different times of day and found it to be 75, 78, 71, 71, and 68. Here are four fundamental statistics figures you can determine for this data set:

• **Mean** (also called arithmetic mean or average): The sum of the values divided by the number of values. For this data set, the mean pulse is $\dfrac{75 + 78 + 71 + 71 + 68}{5} = \dfrac{363}{5} = 72.6$.

   • When a question involves the mean, or average, it is often helpful to write out the average formula and use it to determine the missing piece(s):

$$\text{average} = \frac{\text{sum of values}}{\text{\# of values}}$$

• **Median:** The value that is in the middle of the set when the values are arranged in ascending order. The pulse values in ascending order are 68, 71, 71, 75, and 78. The middle term is the third term, making the median 71. (If the list consists of an even number of values, the median is the average of the middle two values.)

• **Mode:** The value that occurs most frequently. The value that appears more than any other is 71, which appears twice (while all other numbers appear only once), so it is the mode.

   • If more than one value appears the most often, that's okay; a set of data can have multiple modes. For example, if the nurse took the patient's pulse a sixth time and it was 68, then both 71 and 68 would be modes for this data set.

   • A set of data can also have no mode. For example, if the nurse had accidentally written down the 71 twice and removed one, the new data set would not have any number that occurs the most frequently, and therefore, there would not be a mode.

• **Range:** The difference between the highest and lowest values. In this data set, the lowest and highest values are 68 and 78, respectively; so the range is $78 - 68 = 10$.

You need to do this:

When a question involves averages or modes, the order of the values does not matter. To determine a missing value, write out the sum in the average formula as shown below:

$$\text{average} = \frac{\text{value 1} + \text{value 2} + \text{value 3} + \text{value 4}}{4}$$

Then, fill in the information given in the question stem and use algebra to solve.

To find the median, arrange all values in order. In a histogram, that means finding the group with the middle value.

Explanation:

The question asks for the average of the new list after changes are made to the original list of numbers. Recall that $\text{average} = \frac{\text{sum of terms}}{\text{number of terms}}$. "The average of a list of 3 numbers is 20" can therefore be written as:

$$\frac{a + b + c}{3} = 20$$
$$a + b + c = 60$$

The new list contains the same median and the same largest number as the original list, so it also contains b and c. However, you are told that the range of the new list is 3 greater than the original list. This means that the smallest element of the new list is 3 smaller than a:

$$x = a - 3$$

Plug these numbers into the average formula and simplify. Remember that $a + b + c = 60$:

$$\begin{aligned}
\text{average} &= \frac{x + b + c}{3} \\
&= \frac{(a - 3) + b + c}{3} \\
&= \frac{(a + b + c) - 3}{3} \\
&= \frac{60 - 3}{3} \\
&= \frac{57}{3} \\
&= 19
\end{aligned}$$

The average of the new list is 19, so choice (A) is correct.

Try on Your Own

Directions: Take as much time as you need on these questions. Work carefully and methodically. There will be an opportunity for timed practice at the end of the chapter.

1. What is the average of the expressions $2x + 5$, $5x - 6$, and $-4x + 2$?

    A. $x - \dfrac{1}{3}$

    B. $x + \dfrac{1}{4}$

    C. $x + \dfrac{1}{3}$

    D. $3x + 3$

    E. $3x - 3$

HINT: For Q2, what information do you need to determine the range of a data set?

---

2. The list of numbers 21, 31, 5, x, y, 12 has a median of 14. What is the range of the list?

    F. 5

    G. 26

    H. 27.25

    J. 31

    K. Cannot be determined from the given information

3. The following table gives the frequency of grades in certain grade intervals for 25 test grades in an AP Statistics class. Which interval contains the median of the grades?

Grade interval	Frequency
A (91–100)	5
B (81–90)	7
C (71–80)	7
D (61–70)	4
F (60 and below)	2

    A. A (91–100)

    B. B (81–90)

    C. C (71–80)

    D. D (61–70)

    E. F (60 and below)

4. Lunenburg County has 4 public parks. The following pictograph shows the number of trees in each park. What is the average number of trees per park in Lunenburg County?

    Number of Trees in Public Parks in Lunenburg County

    = 50 trees

    F. 50

    G. 75

    H. 125

    J. 150

    K. 200

5. The list of numbers 3, 6, 7, $2x + 1$, $x - 12$ has an arithmetic mean of 1.6. What is the mode of this list of numbers?

    A. -9

    B. 1

    C. 3

    D. 4

    E. 7

PROBABILITY

LEARNING OBJECTIVE

After this lesson, you will be able to:

- Calculate probabilities based on data sets

To answer a question like this:

Alicia is playing a game in which she draws marbles from a box. There are 50 marbles, numbered 1 through 50. Alicia draws one marble from the box and sets it aside, then draws a second marble. If both marbles have the same units digit, then Alicia wins. If the first marble she draws is numbered 25, what is the probability that Alicia will win on her next draw?

A. $\dfrac{1}{50}$

B. $\dfrac{1}{49}$

C. $\dfrac{2}{25}$

D. $\dfrac{4}{49}$

E. $\dfrac{9}{49}$

You need to know this:

Probability is a fraction or decimal between 0 and 1 comparing the number of desired outcomes to the number of total possible outcomes.

- The formula is:

$$\text{probability} = \frac{\text{number of desired outcomes}}{\text{number of total possible outcomes}}$$

- A probability of 0 means that an event will not occur; a probability of 1 means that it definitely will occur.
  - For instance, if you roll a six-sided die, each side showing a different number from 1 to 6, the probability of rolling a number higher than 4 is $\dfrac{2}{6} = \dfrac{1}{3}$ because there are two numbers higher than 4 (5 and 6) and six numbers total (1, 2, 3, 4, 5, and 6).
  - To find the probability that an event will not happen, subtract the probability that the event will happen from 1.
  - Continuing the previous example, the probability of not rolling a number higher than 4 would be $1 - \dfrac{1}{3} = \dfrac{2}{3}$.
- The ACT tests probability in the context of data tables. Using a table, you can find the probability that a randomly selected data value (be it a person, object, etc.) will fit a certain profile.

Math

- Expected value is the weighted average of all possible values that the variable can take on; for the ACT, you will need to have a basic understanding of what expected value is and a strong understanding of how to calculate it based on a probability distribution table.

  - Calculating expected value from a probability distribution table is very straightforward: simply multiply each outcome by its corresponding probability and add the results.

  - Word problems that involve expected value will often call it something different, so look out for questions involving weighted averages and follow this process when needed.

You need to do this:

- Determine the number of desired and total possible outcomes by looking at the table.

- Read the question carefully when determining the number of possible outcomes: Do you need the entire set or a subset?

- Calculate probabilities and expected values based on the data in the table(s).

Explanation:

The question outlines a game scenario and asks for the probability that Alicia wins on her next draw. Recall that probability $= \frac{\text{desired}}{\text{total}}$. Since Alicia has already drawn a 25, there are 49 marbles left in the box. She needs a 5, 15, 35, or 45 to match the units digit of 5 and win, so there are 4 desired numbers.

$$\text{probability} = \frac{\text{desired}}{\text{total}} = \frac{4}{49}$$

Choice (D) is correct.

Try on Your Own

Directions: Take as much time as you need on these questions. Work carefully and methodically. There will be an opportunity for timed practice at the end of the chapter.

HINT: For Q1, are the probabilities dependent or independent? What does that mean for your calculations?

---

1. In 3 fair coin tosses, what is the probability of obtaining at least 2 heads? (Note: In a fair coin toss, the 2 outcomes of heads and tails are equally likely.)

   A. $\frac{1}{8}$

   B. $\frac{3}{8}$

   C. $\frac{1}{2}$

   D. $\frac{2}{3}$

   E. $\frac{7}{8}$

2. Two events are *dependent* if the outcome of one event affects the outcome of the other event. One of the following statements describes dependent events. Which one?

   F. A king is drawn from a deck of cards and set aside. Then a coin lands heads up.

   G. A coin lands heads up. Then an ace is drawn from a deck of cards.

   H. A coin lands tails up. Then a 6-sided die lies with a 5 face up.

   J. A 6-sided die lies with a 3 face up. Then a queen is drawn from a deck of cards.

   K. A king is drawn from a deck of cards and set aside. Then a queen is drawn from the same deck.

3. The following figure shows the number of people enrolled in different divisions in a local power-lifting meet. If 1 person is randomly selected out of the 150 total lifters, what is the probability that this person is a member of either the Class I or the Elite division?

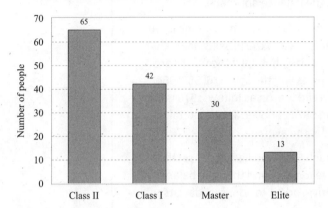

A. $\dfrac{13}{150}$

B. $\dfrac{31}{150}$

C. $\dfrac{42}{150}$

D. $\dfrac{55}{150}$

E. $\dfrac{95}{150}$

4. To be admitted into the Springfield Technological Academy, applicants must pass both a written and an oral test. Academy records show that 50% of applicants pass the written test, and 20% of the applicants who pass the written test pass the oral test. Based on these figures, how many persons in a random group of 800 applicants would you expect to be admitted to Springfield Technological Academy?

F. 80

G. 120

H. 240

J. 400

K. 560

HINT: For Q5, don't stop too soon. Completing all of the steps for this question will take some time and careful calculator use.

---

5. In a darts tournament, Lorena and her friends use a scoring system that awards points only when the player hits the same number that is announced before throwing. Landing a dart anywhere within a number's "wedge" counts as a hit and earns a score of that number. No points are awarded for hitting a different number. The following table shows the probability of hitting the announced number and how many throws Lorena attempted. What is Lorena's expected total score from the tournament?

Number, n, announced	Probability of hitting n in a throw	Number of throws Lorena attempted
15	0.25	12
16	0.70	20
17	0.80	15
18	0.75	24
19	0.80	30
20	0.85	60

A. 122

B. 161

C. 1,020

D. 2,273

E. 2,983

Math

On Test Day

The ACT tests the concept of average fairly heavily. The average formula will serve you well on questions that ask about a sum of values or the average of a set of values, but for questions that give you the average and ask for a missing value in the data set, there is an alternative that can be faster: the balance approach.

The balance approach is based on the idea that if you know what the average is, you can find the totals on both sides of the average and then add the missing value that makes both sides balance out. This approach is especially helpful if the values are large and closely spaced. Imagine that a question gives you the set $\{976, 980, 964, 987, x\}$ and tells you that the average is 970. You would reason as follows: 976 is 6 over the average, 980 is 10 over, 964 is 6 under, and 987 is 17 over. That's a total of $6 + 10 - 6 + 17 = 27$ over, so x needs to be 27 under the average, or $970 - 27 = 943$.

Try solving this question from chapter 7's "How Much Have You Learned?" section (reprinted below) both ways, using first the average formula and then the balance approach. If you find the latter to be fast and intuitive, add it to your test day arsenal.

1. Deepa scored 150, 195, and 160 in 3 bowling games. What should she score on her next bowling game if she wants to have an average score of exactly 175 for the 4 games?

    A. 205
    B. 195
    C. 185
    D. 175
    E. 165

The correct answer and both ways of solving can be found at the end of the chapter.

How Much Have You Learned?

Directions: For test-like practice, give yourself 10 minutes to complete this question set. Be sure to study the explanations, even for questions you got right. They can be found at the end of this chapter.

Use the table below to answer questions 1 and 2.

The following table shows the number of students in Jordan High School. The table categorizes students by grade level and whether or not they are taking Driver's Education.

	Freshman	Sophomore	Junior	Senior	Total
Enrolled in Driver's Ed	98	381	200	85	764
Not Enrolled in Driver's Ed	491	118	251	355	1,215
Total	589	499	451	440	1,979

1. Approximately what percent of juniors are NOT enrolled in Driver's Ed?

   A. 10%
   B. 13%
   C. 26%
   D. 44%
   E. 56%

2. A research group is conducting a study about freshmen and seniors who choose not to enroll in Driver's Ed. If two students are randomly selected one at a time from the students not enrolled in Driver's Ed, what is the approximate probability that the first student will be a senior and the second student will be a freshman?

   F. 0.06
   G. 0.12
   H. 0.43
   J. 0.70
   K. 0.82

3. Laisha works as a software salesperson. The following graph shows Laisha's sales for the year 2018. What is her median number of sales per month?

   A. 22
   B. 23
   C. 23.5
   D. 24.5
   E. 25

4. The average of a list of 5 numbers is 110. A new list of 5 numbers has the same first 3 numbers as the original list. The average of the last two numbers in the original list is 70, and the average of the last two numbers in the new list is 75. What is the average of this new list of numbers?

   F. 111
   G. 112
   H. 112.5
   J. 113.5
   K. 115

5. If you randomly pick an integer between 1 and 25, inclusive, what is the probability that it is both odd and prime?

   A. $\dfrac{1}{5}$

   B. $\dfrac{7}{25}$

   C. $\dfrac{8}{25}$

   D. $\dfrac{9}{25}$

   E. $\dfrac{17}{25}$

6. The list of integers 15, 20, 26, x, y, 32 has a mode of 26 and an arithmetic mean of 27. What is the median of the list of numbers?

   F. 15

   G. 23

   H. 23.5

   J. 26

   K. 32

7. Roman is playing a game in which he draws cards from a standard 52-card deck. Roman draws one card from the deck, sets it aside, then draws a second card. Roman wins if the color of the first card is the same as the color of the second card. If the first card that Roman draws is red, what is the probability that he will win on his next draw? (Note: A standard deck of cards contains 26 red cards and 26 black cards.)

   A. $\dfrac{25}{104}$

   B. $\dfrac{25}{52}$

   C. $\dfrac{25}{51}$

   D. $\dfrac{1}{2}$

   E. $\dfrac{50}{51}$

8. At the state fair, Mai plays a game in which she rolls a pair of fair 6-sided dice. She is awarded 10 points if the sum of the numbers on the dice is either 2 or 12. She is awarded 5 points if the sum of the numbers on the dice is between 3 and 5, inclusive, or 9 and 11, inclusive. Finally, she is awarded 3 points if the sum of the numbers on the dice is between 6 and 8, inclusive. Let the random variable x represent the total number of points awarded on any given roll of the dice. What is the approximate expected value of x? (Note: A fair 6-sided die has six sides numbered 1 through 6. When a fair die is rolled, each of the six outcomes is equally likely.)

   F. 3.55

   G. 4.39

   H. 5

   J. 6.79

   K. 9.27

9. Jin's Xtreme Xscape Rooms includes 3 keys to the doors out of the room. To make the puzzle more challenging, Jin adds 5 other keys that do not open any door. Jin puts all of the keys together in a bag. If you walk into the escape room and select a key at random, what is the probability that it will NOT open any door?

   A. $\dfrac{3}{8}$

   B. $\dfrac{1}{2}$

   C. $\dfrac{3}{5}$

   D. $\dfrac{5}{8}$

   E. $\dfrac{7}{8}$

10. Consider the data set $\{1, 6, -1, 9, -5\}$. What is the positive difference between its range and its median?

   F. 1

   G. 5

   H. 8

   J. 13

   K. 15

Reflect

Directions: Take a few minutes to recall what you've learned and what you've been practicing in this chapter. Consider the following questions, jot down your best answer for each one, and then compare your reflections to the expert responses on the following page. Use your level of confidence to determine what to do next.

1. What are some common ways the ACT may present data?

    _____

    _____

    _____

2. What is the difference between median, mode, and range?

    _____

    _____

    _____

3. What is expected value?

    _____

    _____

    _____

4. What are two ways to calculate the probability of a single event?

    _____

    _____

    _____

Math

Responses

1. What are some common ways the ACT may present data?

The ACT may present data in tables, bar graphs, histograms, pie graphs, and piecewise graphs.

2. What is the difference between median, mode, and range?

The median of a set is the middle value, whereas the mode is the most common value. The range of a set is the distance between the smallest value and the largest one.

3. What is expected value?

Expected value is the weighted average of all possible values that the variable can take on.

4. What are two ways to calculate the probability of a single event?

The fundamental probability formula is:

$$\text{probability} = \frac{\text{\# desired}}{\text{\# total}}$$

Alternatively, the probability that an event happens is 1 minus the probability that it doesn't happen.

Next Steps

If you answered most questions correctly in the "How Much Have You Learned?" section, and if your responses to the Reflect questions were similar to those of the ACT expert, then consider tables and graphs, statistics, and probability an area of strength and move on to the next chapter. Come back to this topic periodically to prevent yourself from getting rusty.

If you don't yet feel confident, review those parts of this chapter that you have not yet mastered, then try the questions you missed again. As always, be sure to review the explanations closely. Then go online (**kaptest.com/login**) to watch video lessons about the highest-yield concepts in this chapter and to use your Qbank for more practice. If you haven't already registered your book, do so at **kaptest.com/moreonline.**

GO ONLINE

kaptest.com/login

Answers and Explanations

Tables and Graphs

1.   D
Difficulty: High
Category: Statistics and Probability
Getting to the Answer: The question asks for the expected number of grade points that a random student in Dr. Li's class will earn. Recall from the first question in this lesson that expected value is really a weighted average: calculate it by multiplying the grade points by the probability of getting these points and then adding everything together at the end.

$$4(0.20) + 3(0.35) + 2(0.30) + 1(0.10)$$
$$= 0.80 + 1.05 + 0.60 + 0.10$$
$$= 2.55$$

Choice (D) is correct.

2.   F
Difficulty: Low
Category: Statistics and Probability
Getting to the Answer: The question asks for the percent of infants who were born below the healthy weight range. According to the table, 9 infants were born below the healthy weight range in August 2016. The table also shows that a total of 128 infants were born in August 2016. Plug these two numbers into the percent formula.

$$percent = \frac{part}{whole} \times 100\%$$
$$= \frac{9}{128} \times 100\%$$
$$\approx 0.07 \times 100\%$$
$$\approx 7\%$$

Choice (F) is correct.

3.   D
Difficulty: Medium
Category: Statistics and Probability
Getting to the Answer: Read the question carefully! An infant is being randomly selected, not from the *total* number of infants, but from the *females* only. This means that you should look only at the second row of the table and ignore everything else.

According to the table, 8 females were below the healthy weight range and 5 females were above the healthy weight range. There were a total of 61 females born in this hospital in August 2016. Plug these numbers into the probability formula and simplify.

$$probability = \frac{desired\ \#}{total\ \#}$$
$$= \frac{8 + 5}{61}$$
$$= \frac{13}{61}$$

Choice (D) is correct.

Be sure that you answered the question that was being asked; C is the probability of selecting an infant from *all* of the infants, not the females alone.

4.   J
Difficulty: Low
Category: Statistics and Probability
Getting to the Answer: Look carefully at the graph's legend. Categories C and F are both marked as severe side effects. Add these two percents together to get the total percentage of participants with severe side effects: $6.5\% + 27.75\% = 34.25\%$.

Choice (J) is correct.

5.   B
Difficulty: Medium
Category: Statistics and Probability
Getting to the Answer: The question asks how many more participants experienced mild or no side effects than severe side effects. According to the graph, 34.25% + $9.5\% = 43.75\%$ of participants experienced mild or no side effects. Since there were 400 total participants in the study, $400(0.4375) = 175$ participants experienced mild or no side effects.

Similarly, $6.5\% + 27.75\% = 34.25\%$ of participants experienced severe side effects. Therefore, $400(0.3425)$ $= 137$ participants experienced severe side effects.

Don't stop too soon, though. The question asks how many more participants experienced mild or no side effects than severe side effects, so subtract these two numbers: $175 - 137 = 38$.

Choice (B) is correct.

Math

Statistics

1.   C
Difficulty: Medium
Category: Statistics and Probability
Getting to the Answer: The question asks for the average of the given expressions, and all of the choices contain the variable x. Don't let this intimidate you, though. Just apply the average formula and simplify:

$$\text{average} = \frac{\text{sum of terms}}{\text{number of terms}}$$

$$= \frac{(2x + 5) + (5x - 6) + (-4x + 2)}{3}$$

$$= \frac{3x + 1}{3}$$

$$= \frac{3x}{3} + \frac{1}{3}$$

$$= x + \frac{1}{3}$$

Choice (C) is correct.

2.   K
Difficulty: High
Category: Statistics and Probability
Getting to the Answer: The question asks you to calculate the range of the given list, which includes two variables. Recall that the range is the biggest number in the list minus the smallest number in the list. The median is the middle number when the data set is arranged in increasing order. Since there are an even number of terms, the median is the average of the two middle terms.

In a question like this that allows for many possibilities for x and y, try Picking Numbers to see if you can find values that yield a median of 14.

One way is to let $x = 7$ and $y = 16$. This gives a median of 14 because $\frac{12 + 16}{2} = 4$. When the data set is arranged in increasing order, it looks like:

$$5, 7, 12, 16, 21, 31$$

The range of this data set is $31 - 5 = 26$.

Notice that letting $y = 16$ gives you considerable freedom for what you can pick for x. As long as x is less than 12, the median will still be 14. There is thus the possibility of obtaining a different value for the range. With this in mind, let $x = 3$ and $y = 16$. When the data set is arranged in increasing order, it looks like:

$$3, 7, 12, 16, 21, 31$$

The range of this data set is $31 - 3 = 28$.

Since there at least two possibilities for the range, it cannot be determined from the information given. Choice (K) is correct.

3.   C
Difficulty: Medium
Category: Statistics and Probability
Getting to the Answer: The question asks which interval contains the median of the grades. Recall that the median is the middle number when the data set is arranged in increasing order. Since there are 25 total terms, the median is the 13th term. Working upward from the lowest grades, there are 2 F's, 4 D's, and 7 C's, so the 13th term is in the C interval.

Choice (C) is correct.

4.   H
Difficulty: Low
Category: Statistics and Probability
Getting to the Answer: The question asks for the average number of trees in the parks based on the pictograph. Since each tree in the pictograph represents 50 real trees, East Side contains 150 trees, West Side 200 trees, Town Center 100 trees, and Court House 50 trees. Plug these numbers into the average formula.

$$\text{average} = \frac{150 + 200 + 100 + 50}{4}$$

$$= \frac{500}{4}$$

$$= 125$$

Choice (H) is correct.

5.   C
Difficulty: Medium
Category: Statistics and Probability
Getting to the Answer: The question asks for the mode of the given list of numbers. Don't let the variables intimidate you; just apply the average formula and solve for x:

$$\frac{3 + 6 + 7 + (2x + 1) + (x - 12)}{5} = 1.6$$

$$3 + 6 + 7 + 2x + 1 + x - 12 = 8$$

$$5 + 3x = 8$$

$$3x = 3$$

$$x = 1$$

K

Next, plug $x = 1$ back in to see what the data set looks like.

$$3, 6, 7, 3, -11$$

Finally, recall that the mode is the most frequently occurring number in the data set. The mode is thus 3, and (C) is correct.

Probability

6.   C
Difficulty: High
Category: Statistics and Probability
Getting to the Answer: The question asks for the probability of obtaining at least 2 heads when a coin is flipped 3 times. Since the coin is being flipped 3 times, the phrase "at least 2 heads" means either 2 heads or 3 heads. Consider each situation separately:

First, think about the different ways in which you could get 2 heads. It is helpful to write down the different possibilities for each coin:

$$HHT$$
$$HTH$$
$$THH$$

Now think about the ways in which you could get 3 heads. This is much simpler:

$$HHH$$

All together, there are $3 + 1 = 4$ different ways to obtain at least 2 heads.

Next, calculate the total number of possible outcomes of flipping a coin 3 times. Since each flip has exactly 2 possibilities (heads or tails), there are $(2)(2)(2) = 8$ possible outcomes.

Finally, plug these numbers into the probability formula:

$$\text{probability} = \frac{\#\text{ of desired outcomes}}{\#\text{ of total possible outcomes}}$$
$$= \frac{1 + 3}{8}$$
$$= \frac{4}{8}$$
$$= \frac{1}{2}$$

Choice (C) is correct.

Be certain that you answered the question that was being asked. Choice B is the probability of obtaining exactly 2 heads rather than 2 or more heads.

7.   K
Difficulty: Low
Category: Statistics and Probability
Getting to the Answer: The question defines dependent events and then asks you to find an example. Work through each answer choice systematically.

Drawing a card and flipping a coin are two completely separate processes and do not affect each other in any way. Therefore, F and G are incorrect.

Similarly, flipping a coin and rolling a die are independent events. Eliminate H.

Finally, rolling a die and drawing a card are also independent. Choice J is incorrect.

By process of elimination, (K) must be correct.

8.   D
Difficulty: Low
Category: Statistics and Probability
Getting to the Answer: The question asks for the probability of randomly selecting a person who is competing in either the Class I or the Elite division. Recall that probability $= \frac{\#\text{ of desired outcomes}}{\#\text{ of total possible outcomes}}$. Since there are 150 lifters in the competition, the total is 150. There are 42 lifters in the Class I division and 13 lifters in the Elite division, so the number of desired lifters is $42 + 13 = 55$. Plug these numbers into the probability formula.

$$\text{probability} = \frac{\text{desired}}{\text{total}} = \frac{55}{150}$$

Choice (D) is correct.

Be certain that you answered the question that was asked. Choice E is the probability that the selected contestant is in the Class II or Master division.

9.   F
Difficulty: Low
Category: Statistics and Probability
Getting to the Answer: You are being asked for the total number of students who will be admitted from a group of 800 applicants. First, calculate the number who pass the written test. Then determine the number who pass the oral test as well.

The number of applicants who pass the written test is $800(0.50) = 400$. Out of these 400, only 20% pass the oral test. Thus, $400(0.20) = 80$ pass both the written and oral tests.

Choice (F) is correct.

Be certain that you correctly interpreted the question. If you added the percentages to get a 70% pass rate, you would have incorrectly chosen K.

10. D
Difficulty: High
Category: Statistics and Probability
Getting to the Answer: Lorena's expected total score can be calculated by multiplying the number, n, by the probability of hitting n by the number of attempted throws:

- $0.25 \times 12 \times 15 = 45$
- $0.70 \times 20 \times 16 = 224$
- $0.80 \times 15 \times 17 = 204$
- $0.75 \times 24 \times 18 = 324$
- $0.80 \times 30 \times 19 = 456$
- $0.85 \times 60 \times 20 = 1,020$

These values represent Lorena's expected score based on the number announced. Lorena's expected total score, then, is the sum of these values: $45 + 224 + 204 + 324 + 456 + 1,020 = 2,273$ points, (D).

On Test Day

1. B
Difficulty: Medium
Category: Statistics and Probability
Getting to the Answer: The question asks what score a bowler must get for her next game to attain an average score of 175 for 4 games and gives the scores of her first 3 games. The average of a group of numbers is the sum of the values divided by the number of values. You can either set up and solve an equation involving the missing score or use the balance approach.

To answer the question algebraically, call the missing score x and set up the average equation:

$$\frac{150 + 195 + 160 + x}{4} = 175$$

$$505 + x = 700$$

$$x = 195$$

Choice (B) is correct.

Using the balance approach for averages, you could determine that the 150 score was 25 less than the desired average, the 195 score was 20 greater, and the 160 score was 15 less, for a total of 20 less. Thus, the fourth score would need to be $175 + 20 = 195$ to raise the average to 175. This approach also shows that (B) is correct.

How Much Have You Learned?

1. E
Difficulty: Low
Category: Statistics and Probability
Getting to the Answer: The question asks what percent of juniors are not enrolled in Driver's Ed. Recall that $\text{Percent} = \frac{\text{part}}{\text{whole}} \times 100\%$. Since the question asks "what percent of juniors," the total number of juniors, 451, is the needed whole. According to the table, 251 juniors are not enrolled in Driver's Ed. Plug these numbers into the percent formula and simplify.

$$\text{Percent} = \frac{\text{part}}{\text{whole}} \times 100\%$$

$$= \frac{251}{451} \times 100\%$$

$$\approx 0.557 \times 100\%$$

$$\approx 55.7\%$$

Choice (E) is correct.

Be certain that you answered the question that was asked! Choice D is the percentage of juniors that *are* enrolled in Driver's Ed.

2. G
Difficulty: Medium
Category: Statistics and Probability
Getting to the Answer: The question asks for the probability of selecting a senior and then a freshman from the students who are not enrolled in Driver's Ed. First, find the probability of selecting a senior from the students who are not enrolled in Driver's Ed.

$$\text{Probability} = \frac{\text{desired}}{\text{total}} = \frac{355}{1,215} = 0.292$$

Now find the probability that the second student selected will be a freshman. Since you already picked out one senior, you must reduce the denominator by 1.

$$\text{Probability} = \frac{\text{desired}}{\text{total}} = \frac{491}{1,214} = 0.404$$

In probability questions involving multiple events, the word "and" means to multiply. To find the probability of the first student being a senior *and* the second student being a freshman, multiply the two individual probabilities together.

$$(0.292)(0.404) = 0.118$$

Since the question asks for the approximate probability, (G) is correct.

3.   C
Difficulty: Low
Category: Statistics and Probability
Getting to the Answer: The question asks for the median of Laisha's sales in 2018. Recall that the median is the middle number when the data are arranged in increasing order. Since this data set is not in order, put it in order:

10, 19, 20, 21, 21, 22, 25, 27, 28, 30, 31, 36

This data set contains an even number of terms, so there are actually two middle numbers: 22 and 25. The median is the average of these two numbers.

$$\frac{22 + 25}{2} = \frac{47}{2} = 23.5$$

The median of Laisha's sales from 2018 is 23.5. Choice (C) is correct.

4.   G
Difficulty: High
Category: Statistics and Probability
Getting to the Answer: The question asks for the average of the new list after changes are made to the original list. At its heart, this question is nothing more than a repeated application of the average formula:

$$\text{Average} = \frac{\text{sum of terms}}{\text{number of terms}}$$

Methodically translate from English into math. "The average of a list of 5 numbers is 110" can be written as:

$$\frac{a + b + c + d + e}{5} = 110$$

This statement allows you to conclude that the sum of the variables $a + b + c + d + e$ is 550.

"A new list of 5 numbers has the same first 3 numbers as the original list" means that the new list includes a, b, and c. To avoid confusion, call the fourth and fifth numbers in the new list x and y.

Now, compare the averages of the last two numbers in each list. In the original list, the average of these two numbers is 70; this can be translated from English to math:

$$\frac{d + e}{2} = 70$$

This means the sum of $d + e = 140$, so the sum of $a + b + c = 550 - 140 = 410$.

Next, calculate the sum of the last two numbers in the new list. Fill in the average formula:

$$\frac{x + y}{2} = 75$$

This means that $x + y = 150$. Finally, "What is the average of this new list of numbers?" tells you what the question is asking for:

$$\frac{a + b + c + x + y}{5} = \text{average}$$

Since you determined that $a + b + c = 410$ and $x + y = 150$, you can plug these values into the formula:

$$\frac{410 + 150}{5} = \frac{560}{5} = 112$$

The average of the new list is 112. Choice (G) is correct.

5.   C
Difficulty: Medium
Category: Statistics and Probability
Getting to the Answer: The question asks for the probability that a randomly selected integer between 1 to 25 inclusive will be both prime and odd. Recall that probability $= \frac{\text{desired}}{\text{total}}$. You are choosing out of a group of 25 numbers, so "total" is 25. To find "desired," simply write down all of the odd numbers between 1 and 25 and cross out the ones that are not prime, which leaves: 3, 5, 7, 11, 13, 17, 19, and 23. "Desired" is thus 8. Finally, plug these numbers into the probability formula.

$$\text{probability} = \frac{\text{desired}}{\text{total}} = \frac{8}{25}$$

Choice (C) is correct.

Be sure that you answered the correct question! You are asked about the numbers that are both odd and prime. You would arrive at D if you simply counted the number of primes between 1 and 25, not specifically the odd primes.

6.   J
Difficulty: High
Category: Statistics and Probability
Getting to the Answer: The question asks for the median of the list of numbers. Recall that the mode of a data set is the number that occurs the most frequently. Thus, either $x = 26$, $y = 26$, or $x = y = 26$. At this point, you cannot tell.

Fortunately, you are also given that the arithmetic mean is 27. Set up an equation to obtain more information about x and y.

$$\frac{15 + 20 + 26 + x + y + 32}{6} = 27$$
$$15 + 20 + 26 + x + y + 32 = 162$$
$$93 + x + y = 162$$
$$x + y = 69$$

Since $26 + 26 = 52$, there is no way that x and y could *both* be 26. If $x = 26$, then $y = 69 - 26 = 43$. Thus, the list looks like:

$$15, 20, 26, 26, 32, 43$$

Recall that the median is the middle number when the data are arranged in increasing order. This data set contains an even number of terms, so there are actually two middle numbers: 26 and 26. The median is the average of these two numbers, which is just 26.

Thus, (J) is correct.

7.   C
Difficulty: Medium
Category: Statistics and Probability
Getting to the Answer: The question asks for the probability that Roman will draw another red card, assuming that his first draw was also a red card. Recall that probability $= \frac{\text{desired}}{\text{total}}$. Since Roman has already picked out one card, there are 51 cards left in the deck. Similarly, since he has already set aside a red card, there are 25 red cards left. Plug these two numbers into the probability formula.

$$\text{probability} = \frac{\text{desired}}{\text{total}} = \frac{25}{51}$$

Choice (C) is correct.

Be sure to read the question carefully! If you didn't remember that the first card drawn was not replaced in the deck, you would have picked B.

8.   G
Difficulty: High
Category: Statistics and Probability
Getting to the Answer: This question outlines a game scenario and asks for the expected value. There is a lot of information here, so make a table to organize it:

Roll Total	Points
2 or 12	10
3, 4, 5, 9, 10, or 11	5
6, 7, or 8	3

Next, determine the probability of actually getting these rolls. Since there are two dice to keep track of, this is also best visualized with a table:

Roll Total	(Die 1, Die 2)	Probability
2	(1, 1)	$\frac{1}{36}$
3	(1, 2) (2, 1)	$\frac{2}{36}$
4	(1, 3) (2, 2) (3, 1)	$\frac{3}{36}$
5	(1, 4) (2, 3) (3, 2) (4, 1)	$\frac{4}{36}$
6	(1, 5) (2, 4) (3, 3) (4, 2) (5, 1)	$\frac{5}{36}$
7	(1, 6) (2, 5) (3, 4) (4, 3) (5, 2) (1, 6)	$\frac{6}{36}$
8	(2, 6) (3, 5) (4, 4) (5, 3) (6, 2)	$\frac{5}{36}$

Roll Total	(Die 1, Die 2)	Probability
9	(3, 6) (4, 5) (5, 4) (6, 3)	$\frac{4}{36}$
10	(4, 6) (5, 5) (6, 4)	$\frac{3}{36}$
11	(5, 6) (6, 5)	$\frac{2}{36}$
12	(6, 6)	$\frac{1}{36}$

Next, update the first table with the probabilities you found in the second table. Remember that if you want to find the probability of rolling a 3, 4, or 5, you must add these individual probabilities together:

Roll Total	Probability	Points
2 or 12	$\frac{2}{36}$	10
3, 4, 5, 9, 10, or 11	$\frac{18}{36}$	5
6, 7, or 8	$\frac{16}{36}$	3

Finally, calculate the expected value. Think of this as a weighted average: multiply the number of points Mai earns by the probability of getting these points and then add those products together.

$$10\left(\frac{2}{36}\right) + 5\left(\frac{18}{36}\right) + 3\left(\frac{16}{36}\right)$$

$$\frac{20}{36} + \frac{90}{36} + \frac{48}{36}$$

$$\frac{158}{36}$$

$$4.388$$

The expected value of x is 4.388, so (G) is correct. This makes sense since half of the results are 5 points, but there are more 3-point outcomes than 10-point outcomes. You would thus expect the result to be less than 5.

9. D
Difficulty: Low
Category: Statistics and Probability
Getting to the Answer: The question asks for the probability that a randomly selected key will not open any door. Recall that probability $= \frac{\text{desired}}{\text{total}}$. Since there were 3 keys originally and Jin added another 5, there are now 8 total. You are asked for the probability that a key does *not* open a door, so the desired number of keys is 5. Plug these numbers into the probability formula.

$$\text{probability} = \frac{\text{desired}}{\text{total}} = \frac{5}{8}$$

Choice (D) is correct.

Double-check that you answered the question that was asked. Choice A is the probability that the key *will* open a door.

10. J
Difficulty: Medium
Category: Statistics and Probability
Getting to the Answer: The question asks for the difference between the range and median of the given data set. The range is the difference between the highest and lowest values of the data set.

$$\text{range} = 9 - (-5) = 14$$

The median is the middle number when the numbers are arranged in increasing order.

$$\{-5, -1, 1, 6, 9\}$$

The median is 1.

The question asks for the difference between the range and the median, so subtract the two: $14 - 1 = 13$. Choice (J) is correct.

Be sure that you subtract the two values when finding the range. If you added 14 and 1, you would have picked K.

CHAPTER 12

FUNCTIONS

LEARNING OBJECTIVES

After completing this chapter, you will be able to:

- Apply function notation
- Define the domain and range of a function
- Evaluate the output of a function for a given input
- Interpret the graph of a function
- Write a function to describe a rule or data set
- Find coordinates of a point that is translated, reflected over an axis, or rotated about the origin
- Match graphs of basic trigonometric functions with their equations
- Use trigonometric concepts and basic identities to solve questions
- Given an equation or function, find an equation or function whose graph is a translation

Functions: 4/36 SmartPoints® (Medium yield)

How Much Do You Know?

Directions: Try out the questions below. Show your work so that you can compare your solutions to the ones found on the next page. The "Category" heading in the explanation for each question gives the title of the lesson that covers how to solve it. If you answered the question(s) for a given lesson correctly, and if your scratchwork looks like ours, you may be able to move quickly through that lesson. If you answered incorrectly or used a different approach, you may want to take your time on that lesson.

1. In the figure shown, what is the approximate value of $f(0) + g\left(\frac{1}{2}\right)$?

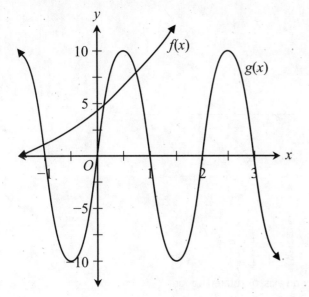

A. -4
B. 4
C. 6
D. 10
E. 14

2. The following graph shows a transformation of the absolute value function, $f(x) = |x|$. Which equation best describes the transformation?

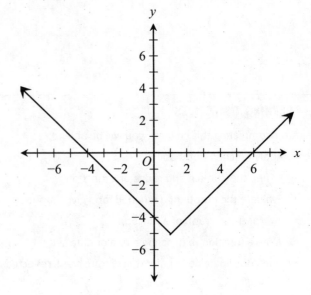

F. $y = f(x + 1) - 5$
G. $y = f(x - 1) - 5$
H. $y = f(x - 1) + 5$
J. $y = -f(x + 1) - 5$
K. $y = -f(x - 1) - 5$

3. If $a(x) = \sqrt{x^2 + 7}$ and $b(x) = x^3 - 7$, then what is the value of $\dfrac{a(3)}{b(2)}$?

A. $\dfrac{\sqrt{11}}{20}$

B. $\dfrac{1}{4}$

C. $\sqrt{11}$

D. 4

E. $4\sqrt{11}$

4. The following graph of $f(x)$ is a quadratic equation. Which of the following represents the domain and range of the function?

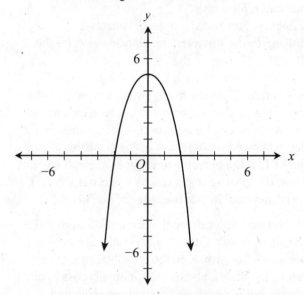

F. Domain: $f(x) \geq 5$; range: all real numbers
G. Domain: $f(x) \leq 5$; range: all real numbers
H. Domain: all real numbers; range: $f(x) \geq 5$
J. Domain: all real numbers; range: $f(x) \leq 5$
K. Domain: all real numbers; range: all real numbers

5. Which of the following correctly describes the range of the function $h(x) = 4x^2 - 9$?

A. All real numbers
B. All real numbers greater than $-3/2$
C. All real numbers greater than or equal to -9
D. All real numbers between $-3/2$ and $3/2$
E. All real numbers between and including -9 and 9

6. If $p(x) = x^2 - 4x + 8$ and $q(x) = x - 3$, what is the value of $\dfrac{q(p(5))}{p(q(5))}$?

F. 0
G. 0.4
H. 1
J. 2.5
K. 10

7. What is the amplitude of the function $f(x) = 4 \sin(2x + \pi)$?

A. $\dfrac{1}{4}$
B. $\dfrac{1}{2}$
C. 2
D. π
E. 4

8. If $-2 \leq x \leq 2$, the maximum value of $f(x) = 1 - x^2$ is which of the following?

F. 2
G. 1
H. 0
J. -1
K. -2

9. For the function $g(x) = 3x^2 - 5x - 7$, what is the value of $g(-2)$?

A. -29
B. -9
C. -5
D. 15
E. 39

10. Suppose a polynomial function $p(x)$ has roots of -4 and 7. If $q(x)$ is a translation of $p(x)$ such that $q(x) = p(x - 2)$, through which two points must the graph of $q(x)$ pass?

F. $(-4,0)$ and $(7,0)$
G. $(-4,2)$ and $(7,2)$
H. $(-4,-2)$ and $(7,-2)$
J. $(-2,0)$ and $(9,0)$
K. $(-6,0)$ and $(5,0)$

Check Your Work

1.   E
Difficulty: Low
Category: Functions: Graphs of Functions
Getting to the Answer: The question asks for the approximate sum of the values of the two functions on the graph at two specified points. Use the graph to find the y-values for the given x-values. For the graph f, when $x = 0$, $y = 4$. For the graph g, when $x = \frac{1}{2}$, $y = 10$. So, $f(0) + g\left(\frac{1}{2}\right) = 4 + 10 = 14$.

Thus, (E) is correct. Be certain that you answered the question that was asked. Choice C is $f\left(\frac{1}{2}\right) + g(0)$.

2.   G
Difficulty: Medium
Category: Functions: Transformations
Getting to the Answer: The question asks for the choice that represents the transformation shown in the graph. Adding or subtracting inside of the function parentheses moves the function left or right. If you subtract 1 from x, the function shifts 1 to the right. The way the function moves is actually opposite of the sign; eliminate F and J.

Moving the function up or down is much more straightforward. The addition or subtraction *outside* of the parentheses moves the function vertically in the direction of the sign. In the above example, the function shifts down by 5 so the function should have −5 in the equation. Eliminate H.

The last difference is the positive or negative sign in front of the $f(x - 1)$. A negative sign reflects, or flips, the function around the x-axis. Since the absolute value graph is opening upward, the sign should be positive. Eliminate J.

Therefore, (G) is correct.

3.   D
Difficulty: Low
Category: Functions: Function Notation
Getting to the Answer: This question asks for the value of the function $a(3)$ divided by the function $b(2)$. The question defines the two functions, so merely plug in the values:

$$\frac{a(3)}{b(2)} = \frac{\sqrt{(3)^2 + 7}}{(2)^3 - 7} = \frac{\sqrt{16}}{1} = 4$$

Hence, (D) is correct. Be certain that you answered the correct question; B is the reciprocal of the correct value.

4.   J
Difficulty: Medium
Category: Functions: Graphs of Functions
Getting to the Answer: The question asks for the domain and range of the function shown in the graph. Domain refers to the x-values on the graph, and range refers to the y-values on the graph. It is easy to find the range a quadratic equation because its minimum or maximum value always occurs at its vertex. In the figure above, the parabola's vertex is located at (0,5). Notice that the parabola never goes above the vertex. Thus, the greatest that y can be is 5. Since $y = f(x)$, you can conclude that the range of f is $f(x) \leq 5$.

At this point, you can see that the answer must be (J). But, just to confirm, the domain is all real numbers because of the arrows on the parabola. These lines extend infinitely and thus will eventually pass through every x-value. Be certain that you correctly used domain and range since G reverses these.

5.   C
Difficulty: Medium
Category: Functions: Function Notation
Getting to the Answer: The question asks which choice correctly describes the range of a given function. Range refers to the y-values on the graph (the "output" of the function). The function $4x^2 - 9$ is simply a transformed version of the more basic function x^2, an upward-opening parabola whose vertex is (0,0). Thinking about this more elementary function can help you understand the graph of $4x^2 - 9$.

Since the parabola x^2 opens upward, its minimum value is $y = 0$. Multiplying the x^2 by 4 makes the parabola "skinnier," but it will not affect its range. The −9 represents a downward shift. Thus, the minimum value is no longer 0, but −9. This means that the range is greater than or equal to −9.

Choice (C) is correct. Since you didn't have to do much calculating, be certain that your logic is correct.

6.   J
Difficulty: Medium
Category: Functions: Function Notation
Getting to the Answer: The question asks for the value of dividing one nested combination of two functions by another and provides the equations for

the functions. When evaluating nested functions, start with the innermost parentheses and work your way out. First, find $p(5)$ and $q(5)$.

$$p(5) = (5)^2 - 4(5) + 8 \quad q(5) = (5) - 3$$
$$p(5) = 25 - 20 + 8 \quad\quad q(5) = 2$$
$$p(5) = 13$$

Now plug these values into the given expression and simplify.

$$\frac{q(p(5))}{p(q(5))} = \frac{q(13)}{p(2)} = \frac{(13) - 3}{(2)^2 - 4(2) + 8}$$

$$= \frac{10}{4 - 8 + 8}$$

$$= \frac{10}{4}$$

$$= 2.5$$

Choice (J) is correct. Be certain that you answered the exact question that was asked; G is the reciprocal of the correct value.

7. E
Difficulty: Medium
Category: Functions: Trigonometry on the Coordinate Plane
Getting to the Answer: The question asks for the amplitude of a given sine function. Think of the amplitude as the "height" of the sine function—the maximum difference from 0. The maximum value of $\sin(x)$ is 1, so its amplitude is 1. However, this question asks us to consider $4\sin(2x + \pi)$.

Think about the rules of translation: expressions inside the function parentheses affect horizontal shifts, while expressions outside the function parentheses affect vertical shifts. Since you are interested in the height of the sine function, the terms inside the function parentheses are irrelevant. The 4 on the outside vertically stretches the sine function by a factor of 4. Thus, the amplitude is $4(1) = 4$.

Choice (E) is correct.

8. G
Difficulty: Medium
Category: Functions: Function Notation
Getting to the Answer: The question asks for the maximum value of $f(x) = 1 - x^2$. You are given the

allowable domain of x. The function $1 - x^2$ is simply a transformed version of the more basic function x^2, an upward-opening parabola whose vertex is $(0,0)$. Thinking about this more elementary function can help you understand the graph of $1 - x^2$.

The negative sign in front of the x^2 term means that the parabola opens downward. Since the parabola x^2 opens downward, its maximum value is $y = 0$. The $+1$ shifts the function up by 1. Thus, the vertex is now at $(0,1)$, and the maximum value is 1.

Choice (G) is correct.

9. D
Difficulty: Low
Category: Functions: Function Notation
Getting to the Answer: The question asks for the value of $g(x)$ when $x = 2$ and provides the equation for the function. Plug in $x = -2$ and simplify.

$$g(-2) = 3(-2)^2 - 5(-2) - 7$$
$$g(-2) = 3(4) - (-10) - 7$$
$$g(-2) = 12 + 10 - 7$$
$$g(-2) = 15$$

Hence, (D) is correct. Be certain that you used the correct value for x. Using $x = 2$ rather than $x = -2$ would result in choosing C.

10. J
Difficulty: High
Category: Functions: Transformations
Getting to the Answer: The question asks through which two points in the choices the graph of $q(x)$ passes. You are given that $q(x) = p(x - 2)$ and that $p(x)$ has roots of -4 and 7. Thus, the points $(-4,0)$ and $(7,0)$ lie on its graph.

Adding or subtracting inside of the function parentheses moves the function left or right. If you subtract 2 from x, the function shifts 2 to the right. Moving 2 to the right corresponds to *adding* 2 to the x-coordinate of every point on the graph of $p(x)$.

$$(-4 + 2, 0) = (-2,0)$$
$$(7 + 2, 0) = (9,0)$$

Thus, (J) is correct. K is a distractor as these points would result from shifting the graph 2 units to the left instead of 2 units to the right.

FUNCTION NOTATION

LEARNING OBJECTIVES

After this lesson, you will be able to:

- Apply function notation
- Define the domain and range of a function
- Evaluate the output of a function for a given input

To answer a question like this:

If $f(x) = x^2 + \frac{x}{2}$, then $f(a + 2) =$

A. $a^2 + \frac{a}{2}$

B. $a^2 + \frac{5a}{2} + 2$

C. $a^2 + \frac{5a}{2} + 5$

D. $a^2 + \frac{9a}{2} + 2$

E. $a^2 + \frac{9a}{2} + 5$

You need to know this:

A **function** is a rule that generates one unique output for a given input. In function notation, the x-value is the input and the y-value, designated by $f(x)$, is the output. Be sure to note that other letters besides x and f may be used.

A linear function has the same form as the slope-intercept form of a line; just think of $f(x)$ as y:

$$f(x) = mx + b$$

In questions that describe real-life situations, the y-intercept will often be the starting point for the function. You can think of it as $f(0)$, or the value of the function where $x = 0$.

The set of all possible x-values is called the **domain** of the function, while the set of all possible y-values is called the **range**.

You need to do this:

- To find $f(x)$ for some value of x, substitute the concrete value in for the variable and do the arithmetic.
- For questions that ask about the domain of a function, check whether any inputs are not allowed, such as those that would cause division by zero.
- For questions that ask about a function of a function, e.g., $g(f(x))$, start on the inside and work your way out.

Explanation:

The notation $f(a+2)$ means that you should plug in $a+2$ everywhere you see an x in the expression $x^2 + \frac{x}{2}$.

$$f(a+2) = (a+2)^2 + \frac{(a+2)}{2}$$

Simplify and collect like terms.

$$(a+2)(a+2) + \frac{(a+2)}{2} = a^2 + 4a + 4 + \frac{(a+2)}{2}$$

$$= a^2 + 4a + 4 + \frac{a}{2} + \frac{2}{2}$$

$$= a^2 + 4a + 4 + \frac{a}{2} + 1$$

$$= a^2 + \frac{8a}{2} + 4 + \frac{a}{2} + 1$$

$$= a^2 + \frac{9a}{2} + 5$$

Choice (E) is correct.

Try on Your Own

Directions: Take as much time as you need on these questions. Work carefully and methodically. There will be an opportunity for timed practice at the end of the chapter.

1. What is $f(g(x+2))$ if $f(x) = x^2 - 4x + 7$ and $g(x) = 7x - 3$?

    A. $49x^2 + 126x + 84$
    B. $63x^2 - 80x + 52$
    C. $25x^2 + 75x - 33$
    D. $-16x^2 - 22x + 5$
    E. $-17x^2 + 61x - 10$

2. Doctors use the function shown below to calculate the concentration, in parts per million, of a certain drug in a patient's bloodstream after t hours. How many more parts per million of the drug are in the bloodstream after 20 hours than after 10 hours?

    $$c(t) = -0.05t^2 + 2t + 2$$

    F. 5
    G. 7
    H. 12
    J. 17
    K. 22

HINT: For Q3, what do the numbers in the answer choices represent? What could cause you to stop too soon or go too far when calculating the answer to this question?

3. A company uses the function below to determine how much profit the company will make when it sells 150 units of a certain product that sells for x dollars per unit. How much more profit per unit will the company make if it charges \$25 for the product than if it charges \$20?

    $$p(x) = 150x - x^2$$

    A. \$3.50
    B. \$35
    C. \$52.50
    D. \$350
    E. \$525

4. If $h(x) = 3x - 1$, what is the value of $h(5) - h(2)$?

    F.   5

    G.   8

    H.   9

    J.   12

    K.   14

5. If $f(x) = 3\sqrt{x^2 + 3x + 4}$, what is the value of $f(4)$?

    A.   4

    B. $3\sqrt{2}$

    C. $4\sqrt{2}$

    D.   12

    E. $12\sqrt{2}$

GRAPHS OF FUNCTIONS

LEARNING OBJECTIVES

After this lesson, you will be able to:

- Interpret the graph of a function
- Write a function to describe a rule or data set

To answer a question like this:

A pep club is keeping track of how many students show up to home football games wearing their school colors. To encourage participation, there is a prize giveaway at each game. As the prizes get more exciting, participation begins to increase.

If x represents the game number and $f(x)$ represents the number of students wearing school colors at game x, which of the following functions best models the information in the table below?

Game	1	2	3	4	5	6	7	8
Number of students	5	11	21	35	53	75	101	131

    A. $f(x) = x + 4$

    B. $f(x) = 2x + 3$

    C. $f(x) = 6x - 1$

    D. $f(x) = x^2 + 4$

    E. $f(x) = 2x^2 + 3$

You need to know this:

Interpreting graphs of functions is similar to interpreting graphs of equations. For example:

Say the graph above represents the function $f(x)$, and you're asked to find the value of x for which $f(x) = 6$. Because $f(x)$ represents the output value, or range, you can translate this to, "When does the y value equal 6?" To answer the question, find 6 on the y-axis, then trace over to the function (the line). Read the corresponding x value: It's -2, so when $f(x) = 6$, x must be -2.

The ACT may sometimes ask about a function's **maximum** or **minimum**. These terms mean the greatest and least value of the function, respectively. This graph of $f(x)$ does not have a maximum or minimum, as the arrows on the line indicate that it continues infinitely in both directions.

Modeling real-life situations using functions is the same as modeling them using equations; the only difference is the function notation and the rule that each input has only one output.

You need to do this:

- Treat $f(x)$ as the y-coordinate on a graph.
- The maximum and minimum refer to a function's greatest and least y-coordinates, respectively.
- In word problems involving function notation, translate the math equations exactly as you learned in chapter 10 in the Word Problems lesson, but substitute $f(x)$ for y.

Explanation:

This is not a linear expression because the y-values, or number of students, do not increase by the same number for each individual game. Eliminate A, B, and C. Since only two answer choices are left, start plugging in x values and eliminate the equation that is not true. When $x = 1$, both equations equal 5. However, when $x = 2$, D equals 8 and (E) equals 11. Since 11 matches the data in the table, (E) is correct.

Try on Your Own

Directions: Take as much time as you need on these questions. Work carefully and methodically. There will be an opportunity for timed practice at the end of the chapter.

1. What is the domain of the following function?

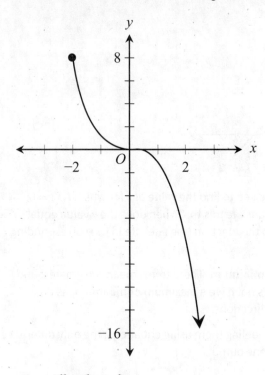

The graph that follows shows $h(x)$, which represents a portion of a polynomial function.

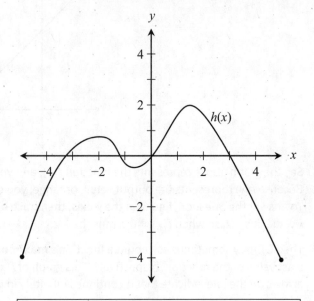

Use the graph for questions 2−3.

A. All real numbers

B. All real numbers less than or equal to 8

C. All real numbers greater than or equal to −2

D. All real numbers between −2 and 2

E. All real numbers between and including 2 and 8

2. What is the range of $h(x)$?

F. All real numbers

G. All real numbers greater than or equal to −5

H. All real numbers greater than or equal to −4

J. All real numbers between and including −5 and 5

K. All real numbers between and including −4 and 2

HINT: For Q3, what does $h(x) = 0$ mean in terms of the graph?

3. Given that $-5 \le x \le 5$, for how many values of x does $h(x) = 0$?

A. 0

B. 1

C. 2

D. 3

E. 4

4. The following graph shows two functions, $f(x)$ and $g(x)$. Which of the following statements is true?

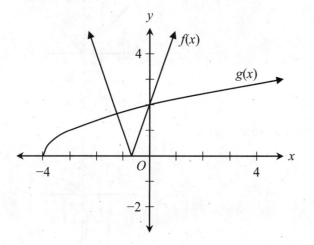

5. Which of the following is the equation that represents the data given in the table shown here?

x	−3	−2	−1	0	1	2	3	4
$f(x)$	−11	−7	−3	1	5	9	13	17

   A. $y = -2x - 11$

   B. $y = 4x + 1$

   C. $y = x + 5$

   D. $y = 2x^2 + 9$

   E. $y = 3x^2 - 7$

   F. $f(0) = -4$

   G. $g(2) = 0$

   H. $f(x) > g(x)$ for all values of x

   J. $(0,2)$ is a solution for $f(x) = g(x)$

   K. $f(x) = 0$ has exactly two solutions

TRANSFORMATIONS

LEARNING OBJECTIVE

After this lesson, you will be able to:

- Find coordinates of a point that is translated, reflected over an axis, or rotated about the origin

To answer a question like this:

Which of the following transformations, when applied to the parent function $y = |x|$, results in the graphs of $y = |x + 4| - 2$?

   A.   Translation to the right 4 coordinate units and up 2 coordinate units

   B.   Translation to the left 4 coordinate units and down 2 coordinate units

   C.   Translation down 4 coordinate units and to the right 2 coordinate units

   D.   Translation up 4 coordinate units and to the left 2 coordinate units

   E.   Reflection across the line $x = -2$

You need to know this:

A **family of functions** is a group of functions that have the same basic shape and characteristics.

- The simplest function in a family is called the parent function.
- Learning the basic shapes of these parent functions can help you to recognize or write equations for more complex functions in the same family.

Math

Equation family	Graph	Equation family	Graph
linear: $f(x) = x$		absolute value: $f(x) = |x|$	
quadratic: $f(x) = x^2$		square root: $f(x) = \sqrt{x}$	
cubic: $f(x) = x^3$		cube root: $f(x) = \sqrt[3]{x}$	
exponential: $f(x) = b^x$		logarithmic: $f(x) = \log_b x$	

A **transformation** occurs when a change is made to the function's equation or graph. The most commonly tested transformations are translations (moving a graph up/down, left/right) and reflections (flips about an axis or other line). How do you know which is occurring? The table on the following page provides some rules for altering the cubic function $f(x) = x^3$.

Algebraic change	Corresponding graphical change	Graph
$f(x + a)$ $f(x - a)$	$f(x)$ moves left a units $f(x)$ moves right a units	
$f(x) + a$ $f(x) - a$	$f(x)$ moves up a units $f(x)$ moves down a units	
$f(-x)$ $-f(x)$	$f(x)$ is reflected over the y-axis (left to right) $f(x)$ is reflected over the x-axis (top to bottom)	
$af(x)$	$f(x)$ is stretched or compressed vertically (the y-values are multiplied by a)	

Math

- Adding or subtracting inside the parentheses of a function results in a horizontal translation. If the alteration is outside the parentheses, the result is a vertical translation.
- The same is true for reflections. When the negative is inside the parentheses (with the x), the reflection is horizontal; when the negative is outside the parentheses (away from the x), the reflection is vertical.
- Pay careful attention to horizontal translations—they are opposite of what they look like: $+a$ shifts to the left, while $-a$ shifts to the right.
- If you forget what a particular transformation looks like, you can always plug in a few values for x and plot the points to determine the effect on the function's graph.

You need to do this:

Evaluate the function to be transformed:

- Is there addition or subtraction within grouping symbols (parentheses, absolute value, etc.)? If so, move horizontally the opposite way of the sign/operator.
- Is there addition or subtraction outside of grouping symbols? If so, move vertically the same way as the sign/operator.
- Is there a negative inside of the grouping symbols? If so, reflect horizontally.
- Is there a negative outside of the grouping symbols? If so, reflect vertically.
- Are the y-values being multiplied by another number? If so, the function is either being stretched or compressed.

Perform the transformations needed, choosing one point to follow at a time instead of trying to focus on the entire function.

Explanation:

Look at the horizontal and vertical translations separately. Addition or subtraction inside of the absolute value sign will shift the graph horizontally in the *opposite* direction of the sign. Thus, $|x+4|$ shifts the graph 4 units to the left. Addition or subtraction outside the absolute value sign will shift the graph vertically in the same direction as the sign. So $|x+4|-2$ shifts the graph 2 units down.

Hence, (B) is correct.

Try on Your Own

Directions: Take as much time as you need on these questions. Work carefully and methodically. There will be an opportunity for timed practice at the end of the chapter.

1. The vertex of an upward-facing parabola is at $(-3,4)$. Which of the following represents the coordinates of the vertex after the parabola has been reflected about the x-axis?

   A. $(-3,-4)$
   B. $(-3,4)$
   C. $(0,0)$
   D. $(3,-4)$
   E. $(3,4)$

2. The graph of $f(x) = 2x^3$ is translated 3 units to the right and 2 units down. Which of the following represents the equation of the graph after this translation?

   F. $(x-3)^3 - 2$
   G. $2(x+3)^3 + 2$
   H. $(x-3)^3 + 2$
   J. $(x+3)^3 - 2$
   K. $2(x-3)^3 - 2$

3. The function $f(x)$ passes through the point (x,y). The function $g(x)$ is obtained by translating $f(x)$ 3 units to the left and 4 units up. Through which one of the following points must $g(x)$ pass?

   A. $(x-4, y+3)$
   B. $(x-3, y-4)$
   C. $(x-3, y+4)$
   D. $(x+3, y-4)$
   E. $(x+4, y+3)$

4. The function $g(x)$ is translated 4 units to the right and 1 unit down to form $f(x)$. If $g(x) = \sqrt{x-5} + 3$, which of the following represents $f(x)$?

   F. $f(x) = \sqrt{x-6} + 7$
   G. $f(x) = \sqrt{x-1} + 4$
   H. $f(x) = \sqrt{x-4} - 1$
   J. $f(x) = \sqrt{x-9} + 2$
   K. $f(x) = \sqrt{x-5} + 8$

HINT: For Q5, the functions may look more complicated than usual, but the standard transformation rules apply.

5. If $f(x) = e^x$ and $g(x) = e^{(x+3)} - 2$, which of the following describes the translation from $f(x)$ to $g(x)$?

   A. Translation to the left 3 coordinate units and down 2 coordinate units
   B. Translation to the left 2 coordinate units and down 3 coordinate units
   C. Translation to the right 2 coordinate units and down 3 coordinate units
   D. Translation to the left 3 coordinate units and up 2 coordinate units
   E. Translation to the right 3 coordinate units and up 2 coordinate units

TRIGONOMETRY ON THE COORDINATE PLANE

LEARNING OBJECTIVES

After this lesson, you will be able to:

- Match graphs of basic trigonometric functions with their equations
- Use trigonometric concepts and basic identities to solve questions
- Given an equation or function, find an equation or function whose graph is a translation

To answer a question like this:

The graph of $g(x) = \cos(3x)$ is shown below. Which of the following lists represents the values of x for which $g(x) = 0$?

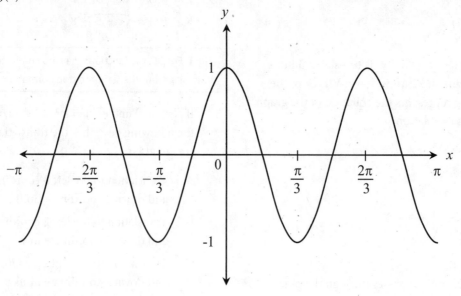

A. $-180°, -120°, -60°, 60°, 120°, 180°$

B. $-165°, -105°, -45°, 45°, 105°, 165°$

C. $-150°, -90°, -30°, 30°, 90°, 150°$

D. $-120°, -80°, -40°, 40°, 80°, 120°$

E. $-105°, -90°, -75°, 75°, 90°, 105°$

You need to know this:

The ACT may ask you to recognize the graphs of the **sine**, **cosine**, and **tangent functions**, which are presented in the table below. You may also be asked to apply transformations to these graphs.

Sine	Cosine	Tangent

The domain of the sine and cosine functions is all real numbers, but notice that their graphs oscillate (bounce back and forth) between $y = -1$ and 1.

- This means the range of $y = \sin x$, and also $y = \cos x$ is $-1 \leq y \leq 1$.
- This is not true for tangent, which has a range of all real numbers.
- In other words, the maximum value of a standard sine or cosine function is 1 and the minimum value is -1, while the tangent function has no maximum or minimum.

When trigonometric functions are graphed, the horizontal axis is almost always measured in **radians**.

- The conversion rate is simple: $180° = \pi$ radians.
- Use this relationship as a conversion factor to convert degrees into radians: $90° \times \dfrac{\pi \text{ radians}}{180°} = \dfrac{\pi}{2}$ radians.
- You can also use this relationship to convert radians into degrees: $\dfrac{\pi}{2} \times \dfrac{180°}{\pi \text{ radians}} = 90°$.

You are also likely to see words such as **amplitude** and **period** in questions about trig functions.

- The amplitude of a wave function (such as sine or cosine) is the vertical distance from the center line (the horizontal at rest line) to the maximum or minimum value.
- For the standard sine and cosine functions, the amplitude is 1.
- The period of the standard sine and cosine functions is 2π because their graphs repeat every 2π units.
- The period of the standard tangent function is π.

There are three reciprocal trig functions: secant (sec), cosecant (csc), and cotangent (cot). Their values are the reciprocals of the sine, cosine, and tangent functions:

$$\csc x = \frac{1}{\sin x}$$

$$\sec x = \frac{1}{\cos x}$$

$$\cot x = \frac{1}{\tan x}$$

To find the value of one of these functions, flip the relationships given by SOHCAHTOA (which are covered in the Geometry chapter):

$$\csc x = \frac{\text{hypotenuse}}{\text{opposite}}$$

$$\sec x = \frac{\text{hypotenuse}}{\text{adjacent}}$$

$$\cot x = \frac{\text{adjacent}}{\text{opposite}}$$

Two other particularly useful trigonometric relationships include $\tan x = \dfrac{\sin x}{\cos x}$ and the Pythagorean identity: $\sin^2 x + \cos^2 x = 1$ (notice that it resembles the Pythagorean theorem).

You need to do this:

- Identify the trigonometric information needed to answer the question.
- Use transformation rules or trig properties and relationships to determine unknown values.
- Use the x- and y-intercepts strategically to help eliminate choices or determine the correct answer.

Explanation:

The question asks you to find the *x*-intercepts of the graph. Notice that the *x*-intercepts are already marked by dots on the graph. The graph is in radians while the answer choices are in degrees, so you must convert from radians to degrees. Begin with the smallest *x*-intercept.

$$\frac{-5\pi \text{ radians}}{6}\left(\frac{180 \text{ degrees}}{\pi \text{ radians}}\right) = \frac{-900 \text{ degrees}}{6} = -150 \text{ degrees}$$

Since all of the answer choices begin with different values, you can conclude that (C) is correct.

Try on Your Own

Directions: Take as much time as you need on these questions. Work carefully and methodically. There will be an opportunity for timed practice at the end of the chapter.

1. What is the period of the function
    $f(x) = 2\sin\left(\frac{x}{4} - \pi\right) + 3$?

    A. $-\pi$

    B. $\frac{\pi}{4}$

    C. $\frac{\pi}{2}$

    D. 4π

    E. 8π

2. The functions $f(x) = \cos(x)$ and $g(x) = a\cos(x + b)$ have the same minimum value and are graphed in the standard (x,y) coordinate plane as shown. Which one of the following statements could be true?

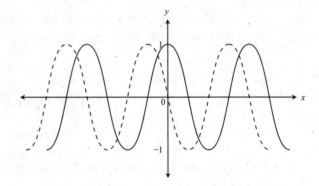

    F. $a = 1$ and $b = 0$

    G. $a < 1$ and $b > 0$

    H. $a = 1$ and $b > 0$

    J. $a < 1$ and $b = 0$

    K. Cannot be determined from the given information

HINT: Some trigonometry on the coordinate plane questions can be answered using basic function transformation rules. Use what you know about translations, reflections, and scaling on the coordinate plane to answer a question like Q3.

3. One of the following graphs is the graph of $y = \frac{1}{2}\sin(2x) + 4$. Which one?

    A.

    B.

    C.

    D.

    E.

4. What is the amplitude of the function $f(x) = 2\cos(4x - \pi)$?

    F. 1

    G. $\frac{\pi}{2}$

    H. 2

    J. π

    K. $\frac{3\pi}{2}$

5. The graph of $y = a\cos(bx)$ is shown. One of the following values is equal to b. Which one?

    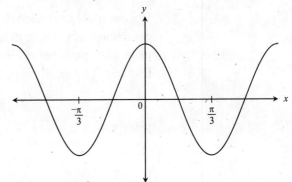

    A. $\frac{1}{6}$

    B. $\frac{1}{3}$

    C. 1

    D. 3

    E. 6

On Test Day

The ACT likes to test the modeling of real-life situations. Get comfortable with function notation in these questions. Remember that you can write the equation of a line as $y = mx + b$ or as $f(x) = mx + b$, where m is the slope and b is the y-intercept. Both mean the same thing.

In a formula using function notation, the slope indicates rate of change. Often, in questions asking about real-life situations, the x-variable indicates time. In that case, the y-intercept (that is, the value of the function at $x = 0$, or $f(0)$) indicates the starting point. Practice interpreting this principle using this question from earlier in this chapter.

1. Doctors use the function shown below to calculate the concentration, in parts per million, of a certain drug in a patient's bloodstream after t hours. How many more parts per million of the drug are in the bloodstream after 20 hours than after 10 hours?

$$c(t) = -0.05t^2 + 2t + 2$$

   F.   5
   G.   7
   H.   12
   I.   17
   J.   22

The correct answer and an explanation can be found at the end of this chapter.

How Much Have You Learned?

Directions: For test-like practice, give yourself 10 minutes to complete this question set. Be sure to study the explanations, even for questions you got right. They can be found at the end of this chapter.

1. Which of the following functions represents the data given below?

x	0	1	2	3	4	5	6	7
$f(x)$	-19	-11	-3	5	13	21	29	37

    A. $f(x) = 8x - 19$
    B. $f(x) = x^2 - 4$
    C. $f(x) = -8x + 19$
    D. $f(x) = (x-4)^2 - 19$
    E. $f(x) = 4x + 2$

2. The graph of a function $h(x)$ is found by translating the graph of the function $g(x)$ up 4 units and left 3 units. If $g(x) = (x-1)^2$, then $h(x) = $?

    F. x^2
    G. $(x-3)^2 + 4$
    H. $(x+2)^2 + 4$
    J. $(x+3)^2 + 4$
    K. $(x+4)^2 - 3$

3. Several values for the functions $g(x)$ and $h(x)$ are shown in the following table. What is the value of $g(h(3))$?

x	$g(x)$	x	$h(x)$
-6	-3	0	6
-3	-2	1	-4
0	-1	2	2
3	0	3	0
6	1	4	-2

    A. -1
    B. 0
    C. 1
    D. 3
    E. 6

4. If $f(x) = x^2 + 1$ and $g(x) = 3x + 1$, which of the following expressions represents $f(g(x))$?

    F. $3x^2 + 2$
    G. $3x^2 + 4$
    H. $9x^2 + 2$
    J. $9x^2 + 3x + 4$
    K. $9x^2 + 6x + 2$

5. If $f(x) = x^2 + 3x - 5$, what is the value of $f(x+h)$?

    A. $x^2 + 3x - 5 - h$
    B. $x^2 + 3x - 5 + h$
    C. $x^2 + 3x - 5 + 2h$
    D. $x^2h^2 + 2xh + 3x + 3h - 5$
    E. $x^2 + 2xh + 3x + h^2 + 3h - 5$

6. The rule of translation from $f(x)$ to $g(x)$ is $(x,y) \rightarrow (x - 1.5, y + 2.8)$. If $f(x)$ passes through $(-2.3, -1.2)$, which coordinate pair must $g(x)$ pass through?

    F. $(-0.8, -3.8)$
    G. $(0.8, 1.6)$
    H. $(2.7, -3.8)$
    J. $(-3.8, 1.6)$
    K. $(3.8, 1.6)$

7. If $x > 0$, $a = x \cos \theta$, and $b = x \sin \theta$, then which of the following is equivalent to $\sqrt{a^2 + b^2}$?

    A. 1
    B. x
    C. $2x$
    D. $x(\cos \theta + \sin \theta)$
    E. $x \cos \theta \sin \theta$

8. If $f(x) = -4x + 1$ and $g(x) = \sqrt{x} + 2.5$, what is the value of $f\left(g\left(\frac{1}{4}\right)\right)$?

    F. -11

    G. -2

    H. 0

    J. 2.5

    K. 3

9. What is the range of the function shown here?

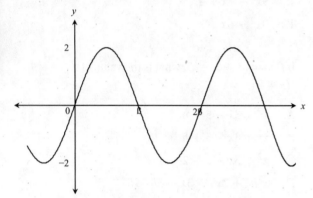

    A.   All real numbers between and including -2 and 2

    B.   All real numbers less than or equal to 2

    C.   All real numbers greater than or equal to -2

    D.   All real numbers between 0 and 2π

    E.   All real numbers

10. Which trigonometric function could be represented by the following graph?

    F. $g(x) = \sin(x - \pi)$

    G. $g(x) = \sin(x + \pi)$

    H. $g(x) = \sin(x + 2\pi)$

    J. $g(x) = \sin\left(x - \frac{\pi}{2}\right)$

    K. $g(x) = \sin\left(x + \frac{\pi}{2}\right)$

Reflect

Directions: Take a few minutes to recall what you've learned and what you've been practicing in this chapter. Consider the following questions, jot down your best answer for each one, and then compare your reflections to the expert responses on the following page. Use your level of confidence to determine what to do next.

1. What are the domain and range of a function?

    _____

    _____

    _____

2. What is another way to write the function $f(x) = x + 4$?

    _____

    _____

    _____

3. In the function above, what does x represent? What does $f(x)$ represent?

    _____

    _____

    _____

4. What will the above function look like when graphed?

    _____

    _____

    _____

5. In a function whose x-value represents time, what does the y-intercept represent?

    _____

    _____

    _____

Responses

1. What are the domain and range of a function?

The domain of a function indicates the possible x-values, and the range of a function indicates the possible y-values. For example, in the function $f(x) = x^2$, the domain is all real numbers because any number can be squared, and the range is any number greater than or equal to 0, because x^2 can't be negative.

2. What is another way to write the function $f(x) = x + 4$?

When you graph the function on the xy-coordinate plane, you can replace $f(x)$ with y. This function is equivalent to $y = x + 4$.

3. In the function above, what does *x* represent? What does $f(x)$ represent?

In this function, x is the input and $f(x)$ is the output.

4. What will the above function look like when graphed?

The slope of the line is 1 and its y-intercept is 4, so it will move from the lower left to the upper right and cross the y-axis at $y = 4$.

5. In a function whose *x*-value represents time, what does the *y*-intercept represent?

The y-intercept represents the initial quantity when $t = 0$. Say a function represents the progress of a machine manufacturing widgets at a rate of 6 widgets per hour. The machine adds the widgets it makes to a growing pile that consisted of 12 widgets when the machine started working. If this function were graphed as a function of time, the y-intercept would be 12—the pile of 12 widgets that was there when the machine started its task.

Next Steps

If you answered most questions correctly in the "How Much Have You Learned?" section, and if your responses to the Reflect questions were similar to those of the ACT expert, then consider Functions an area of strength and move on to the next chapter. Come back to this topic periodically to prevent yourself from getting rusty.

If you don't yet feel confident, review those parts of this chapter that you have not yet mastered. All four lessons in this chapter cover question types that are fairly common on the ACT, and it is to your advantage to have a firm grasp on this material, so go back over it until you feel more confident. Then, try the questions you missed again. As always, be sure to review the explanations closely. Then go online (**kaptest.com/login**) to watch video lessons about high-yield ACT Math concepts and to use your Qbank for more practice. If you haven't already registered your book, do so at **kaptest.com/moreonline.**

GO ONLINE

kaptest.com/login

Answers and Explanations

Function Notation

1. A
Difficulty: Medium
Category: Functions
Getting to the Answer: The question asks for the value of two nested functions in terms of the variable x. Calculate this from the inside out, just like you would for any set of nested parentheses. First, calculate $g(x + 2)$ by substituting $x + 2$ wherever you see an x in the g function:

$$g(x + 2) = 7(x + 2) - 3$$
$$g(x + 2) = 7x + 14 - 3$$
$$g(x + 2) = 7x + 11$$

Then, plug this value of $g(x + 2)$ into the f function, $f(x) = x^2 - 4x + 7$:

$$f(g(x + 2)) = f(7x + 11)$$
$$= (7x + 11)^2 - 4(7x + 11) + 7$$
$$= (7x + 11)(7x + 11) - 28x - 44 + 7$$
$$= 49x^2 + 77x + 77x + 121 - 28x - 37$$
$$= 49x^2 + 126x + 84$$

Thus, (A) is correct.

2. F
Difficulty: Medium
Category: Functions
Getting to the Answer: The question is asking you to calculate $c(20) - c(10)$ for the given function since, in word problems, the phrase "how many more" indicates subtraction. Calculate $c(20)$ and $c(10)$ individually and then subtract:

$$c(20) = -0.05(20^2) + 2(20) + 2$$
$$= -0.05(400) + 40 + 2$$
$$= -20 + 40 + 2$$
$$= 22$$

$$c(10) = -0.05(10^2) + 2(10) + 2$$
$$= -0.05(100) + 20 + 2$$
$$= -5 + 20 + 2$$
$$= 17$$

Since $c(20) - c(10) = 22 - 17 = 5$, (F) is correct. Be certain that you answered the question that was asked since J and K are the individual values for $c(20)$ and $c(10)$.

3. A
Difficulty: High
Category: Functions
Getting to the Answer: Pay careful attention to the wording of this question. You are being asked NOT for the difference in profit but for the difference in profit *per unit*.

Begin by calculating $p(25)$ and $p(20)$ individually.

$$p(25) = 150(25) - (25)^2$$
$$= 3{,}750 - 625$$
$$= 3{,}125$$

$$p(20) = 150(20) - (20)^2$$
$$= 3{,}000 - 400$$
$$= 2{,}600$$

However, the question is asking for profit *per unit*, so you must divide 525 by 150:

$$\frac{525}{150} = 3.5$$

Choice (A) is correct. Confirm that you answered the question that was asked. Since $p(25) - p(20) = 3{,}125 - 2{,}600 = 525$, it may be tempting to select E.

4. H
Difficulty: Low
Category: Functions
Getting to the Answer: The question asks for the difference between the two outputs of the function $h(x)$ when the given values of x are used as inputs. First, calculate $h(5)$ and $h(2)$ individually:

$$h(5) = 3(5) - 1$$
$$= 15 - 1$$
$$= 14$$

$$h(2) = 3(2) - 1$$
$$= 6 - 1$$
$$= 5$$

Since $h(5) - h(2) = 14 - 5 = 9$, (H) is correct. Confirm that you answered the question that was asked; F and K are the individual values of the function.

5. E
Difficulty: Low
Category: Functions
Getting to the Answer: The question asks for the value of $f(4)$ given that $f(x) = 3\sqrt{x^2 + 3x + 4}$. The notation $f(4)$ means that you should plug in a 4 everywhere there is an x in the equation $3\sqrt{x^2 + 3x + 4}$.

$$f(4) = 3\sqrt{(4)^2 + 3(4) + 4}$$
$$= 3\sqrt{16 + 12 + 4}$$
$$= 3\sqrt{32}$$
$$= 3\sqrt{16}\sqrt{2}$$
$$= 3(4)\sqrt{2}$$
$$= 12\sqrt{2}$$

Choice (E) is correct. Confirm that you used the correct values given in the question.

Graphs of Functions

1. C
Difficulty: Low
Category: Functions
Getting to the Answer: The question asks for the values of the domain of the function shown on the graph. Remember that domain is another word for x-values, which are shown on the horizontal axis of the graph. The leftmost point on the graph is the minimum value of the domain. This occurs at $x = -2$. Eliminate choices A and B.

Now find the maximum value of the domain by looking for the rightmost point. The arrow on the point $(2, -8)$ indicates that the graph keeps going toward infinity. Eliminate D and E.

Thus, choice (C) is correct.

2. K
Difficulty: Medium
Category: Functions
Getting to the Answer: The question asks for the range of the function shown on the graph. Remember that range is another word for y-values, which are

shown on the vertical axis of the graph. The lowest y-value occurs at $y = 4$ because the dots indicate that the curve terminates at those points. The highest y-value is 2. Thus, the range of $h(x)$ is from -4 to 2.

Choice (K) is correct. Be certain that you determined the range; the domain is J.

3. E
Difficulty: Low
Category: Functions
Getting to the Answer: The question asks for the number of points on the graph at which the function equals 0. Remember that $y = h(x)$. Thus, the question is asking how many times $y = 0$. Look at the graph and see that this occurs 4 times. Therefore, (E) is correct. Be certain that you answered the question that was asked. Choice B is the number of points where $x = 0$.

4. J
Difficulty: Medium
Category: Functions
Getting to the Answer: The question asks which of the choices is true based on the graph of the two functions. Work through each choice systematically.

Eliminate F, since $f(0) = 2$.

Eliminate G, since $g(2) \approx 2.5$.

Eliminate H, since $g(x) > f(x)$ roughly between $x = -1.2$ and $x = 0$.

Recall that a solution for $f(x) = g(x)$ occurs when the graphs of the functions touch or cross each other. Since one of the points where the two functions cross is at $(0,2)$, (J) is correct.

For the record, K is incorrect because $f(x)$ has only one solution, at approximately $(-0.75, 0)$. Confirm that you answered the question that was asked.

5. B
Difficulty: Medium
Category: Functions
Getting to the Answer: The question asks which of the choices is the equation for the data given in the table. First, determine whether the data are in a linear or non-linear relationship. Since all the x-values increase by 1, the y-values should increase or decrease proportionally. Notice that the y-values always increase by 4 throughout the table, so this is indeed a linear relationship. Eliminate D and E.

The slope of the line is the coefficient of x in the linear equation. Since y increases by 4 for every 1 unit increase in x, that value is 4, and (B) is correct. You can confirm this by plugging 4 into the equation to obtain the y-value of 17.

Transformations

1.   A
Difficulty: Medium
Category: Functions
Getting to the Answer: The question asks for the coordinates of the vertex of the given parabola after it is reflected about the x-axis. Reflecting about the x-axis will not change the x-coordinate but will reverse the sign of the y-coordinate. So, $(-3,4)$ becomes $(-3,-4)$.

Therefore, (A) is correct. Be certain that you answered the question that was asked. Reflection about the y-axis would result in the vertex being E.

2.   K
Difficulty: Low
Category: Functions
Getting to the Answer: The question asks which of the choices is the expression for $f(x)$ after performing the given horizontal and vertical translation. Addition or subtraction inside of the function parentheses will shift the graph horizontally in the *opposite* direction of the sign. Thus, a translation of 3 units to the right is obtained by subtracting 3 from inside the function parentheses so the function becomes $2(x-3)^3$.

Addition or subtraction outside of the function parentheses will shift the graph vertically in the same direction of the sign. Thus, a translation of 2 units down is obtained by subtracting 2 from outside the function parentheses: $2(x-3)^3 - 2$.

Choice (K) is correct. Be certain that you followed the correct procedures for translation; J shifts the function 3 units to the left.

3.   C
Difficulty: Medium
Category: Functions
Getting to the Answer: The question asks which of the choices is a point through which $f(x)$ must pass

after performing the given horizontal and vertical translation. Translating 3 units to the left means subtracting 3 from the x-coordinate: $x - 3$. Translating 4 units up means adding 4 to the y-coordinate: $y + 4$. Thus, (C) is correct. You can readily verify this by noticing that (C) is the only choice with the term $y + 4$.

4.   J
Difficulty: Medium
Category: Functions
Getting to the Answer: The question asks which of the choices is the given function translated 4 units to the right and 1 unit down. Translate the square root sign to the $\frac{1}{2}$ power. Addition or subtraction inside of the function parentheses will shift the graph horizontally in the *opposite* direction of the sign. Thus, a translation of 4 units to the right is obtained by subtracting 4 inside the parentheses. Translating 1 unit down subtracts 1 from the constant outside the radical.

So, $\sqrt{x-5} + 3 = (x-5)^{\frac{1}{2}} + 3$. After translation, this becomes $(x-5-4)^{\frac{1}{2}} + 3 - 1 = (x-9)^{\frac{1}{2}} + 2$. When returned to radical format, this matches (J). Ensure that you translated in the correct direction; G is a translation 4 units right and 1 unit up.

5.   A
Difficulty: Medium
Category: Functions
Getting to the Answer: The question asks which of the choices describes the transformation of $f(x)$ to $g(x)$ and provides the exponential expressions for each function. Do not be intimidated by the exponential function! The same translation rules still apply.

Addition or subtraction inside of the function parentheses will shift the graph horizontally in the *opposite* direction of the sign. Here, the exponential function e acts like function parentheses. Thus, $e^{(x+3)}$ represents a translation of 3 units to the left. Eliminate B, C, and E.

Addition or subtraction outside of the function parentheses will shift the graph vertically in the same direction of the sign. Thus, $e^{(x+3)} - 2$ represents a translation of 2 units down. Eliminate D.

Thus, (A) is correct. Be certain that you correctly applied the translation rules and used the proper signs.

Trigonometry on the Coordinate Plane

1. E
Difficulty: Medium
Category: Functions
Getting to the Answer: To answer this question, use function transformation rules. The period of a sine function is determined by the coefficient of x, so you can ignore the 2, π, and 3 values. When the coefficient of x is 1, the period of a sine function is 2π. When the coefficient of x is larger than 1, the graph is horizontally compressed, so the period of a sine function gets smaller. When the coefficient is smaller than 1, the graph is horizontally expanded, so the period of a sine function gets larger. In this function, the coefficient of x is $\frac{1}{4}$, so the period will be 4 times as big: $2\pi \times 4 = 8\pi$. Choice (E) is correct.

You could also use a trigonometry rule to answer this question. When a sine function has the setup $a\sin(bx)$, the period is $\frac{2\pi}{b}$. In this equation, $b = \frac{1}{4}$, so the period of the function is $\frac{2\pi}{\frac{1}{4}} = 8\pi$.

2. H
Difficulty: Medium
Category: Functions
Getting to the Answer: The question asks which of the choices could be true and refers to the given graph of two functions of $\cos(x)$, one of which appears to be the other shifted horizontally. The most basic form of the cosine function is $f(x) = \cos(x)$. Since the minimum and maximum values of both functions are the same, there is no scaling from $f(x)$ to $g(x)$. You can therefore deduce that $a = 1$. Since the graph does shift horizontally, $b \neq 0$. With the given information, b could be either positive or negative, but not 0. Hence, (H) is correct.

3. B
Difficulty: High
Category: Functions
Getting to the Answer: Use function transformation rules to answer this question. The graph of a basic sine function crosses both the x- and y-axes at $(0,0)$ and has a period of 2π and an amplitude of 1. The sine function in the question has a vertical compression $\left(\text{from the } \frac{1}{2}\right)$, a horizontal compression (from the 2), and a vertical shift (from the 4).

Eliminate E because it does not include a vertical shift. Eliminate C and D because they involve a vertical expansion (the amplitude is bigger than 1) instead of a vertical compression (the amplitude is smaller than 1). Choice (B) is correct because it has a horizontal compression (the period is smaller than 2π), whereas A has a horizontal expansion (the period is bigger than 2π).

4. H
Difficulty: Medium
Category: Functions
Getting to the Answer: The question asks for the amplitude of the given function. Think of the amplitude as the "height" of the cosine function. The maximum value of $\cos(x)$ is 1, so its amplitude is 1. However, this question asks for the value of $2\cos(4x - \pi)$.

Think back to the rules of translation. Expressions inside the function parentheses affect horizontal shifts, while expressions outside the function parentheses affect vertical shifts. Since you are interested in the height of the cosine function, the terms inside the function parentheses are irrelevant. The 2 on the outside vertically stretches the cosine function by a factor of 2. Thus, the amplitude is $2(1) = 2$.

Choice (H) is correct. Since the question asks for amplitude, be certain that you considered only the y-value of the function.

5. D
Difficulty: Medium
Category: Functions
Getting to the Answer: The question asks about the value of b in the graph $y = a\cos(bx)$ based on the graph. The coefficient in front of x indicates a horizontal compression or expansion. The graph of a basic cosine function crosses the y-axis at $(0,1)$ and has a period of 2π and an amplitude of 1. The period of this graph is $\frac{2\pi}{3}$, which means that this graph has undergone a horizontal compression as the period is smaller than 2π. Thus, b is greater than 1. Eliminate A, B, and C.

As b is the coefficient in front of x, the period of the function can be calculated as $\frac{2\pi}{b}$. Set up the equation $\frac{2\pi}{3} = \frac{2\pi}{b}$, and recognize that $b = 3$. Choice (D) is correct.

On Test Day

1. A
Difficulty: Medium
Category: Functions
Getting to the Answer: The question is asking you to calculate $c(20) - c(10)$ for the given function since, in word problems, the phrase "how many more" indicates subtraction. Calculate $c(20)$ and $c(10)$ individually and then subtract:

$$c(20) = -0.05(20^2) + 2(20) + 2$$
$$= -0.05(400) + 40 + 2$$
$$= -20 + 40 = 2$$
$$= 22$$

$$c(10) = -0.05(10^2) + 2(10) + 2$$
$$= -0.05(100) + 20 + 2$$
$$= -5 + 20 + 2$$
$$= 17$$

Since $c(20) - c(10) = 22 - 17 = 5$, (A) is correct. Be certain that you answered the question that was asked since D and E are the individual values for $c(20)$ and $c(10)$.

So what does $c(0)$ represent? Since $c(t)$ represents the amount of the drug in parts per million present in the bloodstream after t hours, $c(0)$ represents the amount of the drug in parts per million present in the bloodstream after 0 hours—at the beginning of the treatment.

How Much Have You Learned?

1. A
Difficulty: Medium
Category: Functions
Getting to the Answer: The question asks for the function that creates the values shown in the table. First, determine whether the data are in a linear or a non-linear relationship. Since all the x-values increase by 1, the changes in the y-values will be consistent if it is a linear relationship. Notice that the y-values always increase by 8 throughout the table, so this is indeed a linear relationship. Eliminate B and D.

Since the y-values increase by 8 and the x-values increase by 1 at every point, the slope is 8. This is the value of the x-coefficient, so you can eliminate C and E. Thus, (A) is correct. You can plug any of the x-values into that equation to get the matching y-value in order to verify that it is the correct choice.

2. H
Difficulty: Medium
Category: Functions
Getting to the Answer: The question asks for the translation of $g(x)$ 4 units upward and 3 units to the left. Addition or subtraction inside of the function parentheses will shift the graph horizontally in the *opposite* direction of the sign. Thus, a translation of 3 units to the left is obtained by adding 3 inside the function parentheses. This means $(x - 1)^2$ becomes $(x + 2)^2$.

On test day, you could stop here since only (H) has the correct expression inside the parentheses. However, for the sake of completeness, recall that addition or subtraction outside of the function parentheses will shift the graph vertically in the same direction of the sign. Thus, a translation of 4 units up is obtained by adding 4 outside the parentheses.

Therefore, (H) is correct. Be certain that you used the correct values for the original function; using x rather than $x - 1$ would result in the expression in J.

3. A
Difficulty: Low
Category: Functions
Getting to the Answer: The question asks for the value of nested functions for $x = 3$, and you are given tables showing various x- and y-values for the two functions. Work from the inside out. Before trying to determine the equations for the functions, see if the tables already contain the values that you require. Find the y-value of the h function when $x = 3$. The table indicates that $h(3) = 0$.

Now evaluate $g(0)$ in the same way. The y-value when $x = 0$ is -1.

Choice (A) is correct. Be certain that you answered the question that was asked; reversing the functions would result in the value in E.

4.   K
Difficulty: Medium
Category: Functions
Getting to the Answer: The question asks for the value of $f(g(x))$ in terms of x and provides both expressions. Calculate $f(g(x))$ by plugging $g(x) = 3x + 1$ into the f function.

$$f(g(x)) = (3x + 1)^2 + 1$$
$$= (3x + 1)(3x + 1) + 1$$
$$= 9x^2 + 3x + 3x + 1 + 1$$
$$= 9x^2 + 6x + 2$$

Therefore, (K) is correct. Be certain that you evaluated the correct expression; $g(f(x))$ is G.

5.   E
Difficulty: Medium
Category: Functions
Getting to the Answer: The question asks for the value of $f(x + h)$ given that $f(x) = x^2 + 3x - 5$. Calculate $f(x + h)$ by plugging in $x + h$ everywhere you see an x in the f function.

$$f(x + h) = (x + h)^2 + 3(x + h) - 5$$
$$= (x + h)(x + h) + 3x + 3h - 5$$
$$= x^2 + xh + xh + h^2 + 3x + 3h - 5$$
$$= x^2 + 2xh + 3x + h^2 + 3h - 5$$

Thus, (E) is correct.

6.   J
Difficulty: Medium
Category: Functions
Getting to the Answer: The question asks which of the coordinate pairs is a valid value of $g(x)$. You are given the translation operations from $f(x)$ to $g(x)$ in terms of x- and y-coordinates, and the coordinates of a point through which $f(x)$ passes. Take the given point, subtract 1.5 from the x-coordinate, and add 2.8 to the y-coordinate:

$$(-2.3, -1.2)$$
$$(-2.3 - 1.5, -1.2 + 2.8)$$
$$(-3.8, 1.6)$$

Choice (J) is correct. Be certain that you used the correct values given in the question.

7.   B
Difficulty: Medium
Category: Functions
Getting to the Answer: The question asks which of the choices is equivalent to $\sqrt{a^2 + b^2}$ and gives you the equations for a and b. Plug in the given values and simplify. Remember the Pythagorean identity: $\cos^2\theta + \sin^2\theta = 1$.

$$\sqrt{a^2 + b^2} = \sqrt{(x\cos\theta)^2 + (x\sin\theta)^2}$$
$$= \sqrt{x^2\cos^2\theta + x^2\sin^2\theta}$$
$$= \sqrt{x^2(\cos^2\theta + \sin^2\theta)}$$
$$= \sqrt{x^2(1)}$$
$$= x$$

Choice (B) is correct. Be certain that you used all the given values; omitting the x term results in choice A.

8.   F
Difficulty: Medium
Category: Functions
Getting to the Answer: The question asks for the value of nested functions when $x = \frac{1}{4}$ and provides the equations for both functions. Start by evaluating $g\left(\frac{1}{4}\right)$:

$$g\left(\frac{1}{4}\right) = \sqrt{\frac{1}{4}} + 2.5$$
$$= \frac{1}{2} + 2.5$$
$$= 3$$

Now evaluate $f(3)$:

$$f(3) = -4(3) + 1$$
$$= -12 + 1$$
$$= -11$$

Thus, (F) is correct. Be certain that you answered the question that was asked. Determining $g\left(f\left(\frac{1}{4}\right)\right)$ results in the value in J.

9.   A
Difficulty: Medium
Category: Functions
Getting to the Answer: The question asks for the range of the function shown in the graph. Range refers to the maximum and minimum of the y-values of a

function. Notice that the function never goes above 2 or below −2. Since the minimum value is −2 and the maximum value is 2, the range is all real numbers between −2 and 2, including those endpoints. Choice (A) is correct. Be certain that you found the range rather than the domain.

10. K
Difficulty: Medium
Category: Functions
Getting to the Answer: The question asks which trigonometric function could be shown on the graph. Notice that all the answer choices are of the form

$\sin(x + k)$. Compare the parent function, $\sin(x)$, to the given graph and solve for the horizontal shift k.

Observe that the y-intercept of the graph is 1. Since the y-intercept occurs when $x = 0$, plug $x = 0$ into the equation $\sin(x + k) = 1$ and solve for k.

$$\sin(x + k) = 1$$
$$\sin(0 + k) = 1$$
$$\sin(k) = 1$$

Since $\sin\left(\frac{\pi}{2}\right) = 1$, you can conclude that $k = \frac{\pi}{2}$.

Therefore, (K) is correct.

[CHAPTER 13]

GEOMETRY

LEARNING OBJECTIVES

After completing this chapter, you will be able to:

- Identify equal angles when two parallel lines are crossed by a transversal
- Identify supplementary and vertical angles and determine missing angle measures
- Determine an unknown angle measure in a polygon using line and angle properties
- Calculate the value of the third angle in a triangle given the other two angle measures
- Identify similar triangles and apply their properties
- Apply relationships between side lengths and angle measures in a triangle
- Calculate the length of the third side of a right triangle given the other two side lengths
- Given one side length of a 45–45–90 or 30–60–90 triangle, calculate the other two
- Calculate the area or perimeter of a polygon or complex figure
- Perform unit conversions
- Answer math questions about circles using relationships among angles, arcs, distances, and area
- Relate properties of a quadratic function to its graph and vice versa
- Identify and calculate measurements within a complex figure
- Transfer information among multiple figures
- Calculate the volume and surface area of common three-dimensional (3D) figures
- Apply basic trigonometric ratios and formulas to answer questions involving right triangles

Geometry: 11/36 SmartPoints® (Very high yield)

How Much Do You Know?

Directions: Try out the questions below. Show your work so that you can compare your solutions to the ones found on the next page. The "Category" heading in the explanation for each question gives the title of the lesson that covers how to solve it. If you answered the question(s) for a given lesson correctly, and if your scratchwork looks like the explanations, you may be able to move quickly through that lesson. If you answered incorrectly or used a different approach, you may want to take your time on that lesson.

Math

1. In the figures shown, $\triangle ABC$ is similar to $\triangle DEF$. $\angle A$ corresponds to $\angle D$, $\angle B$ corresponds to $\angle E$, and $\angle C$ corresponds to $\angle F$. If the given lengths are of the same unit of measure, what is the value of x?

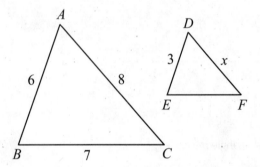

    A.   3

    B.   3.5

    C.   4

    D.   5

    E.   6

2. What is the area, in square centimeters, of the polygon in the figure shown here?

    F.   100

    G.   225

    H.   300

    J.   550

    K.   600

3. In the following figure, *O* is the center of the circle, and the ratio of the area of sector *OABC* to the area of sector *OCDA* is 3 to 5. What is the value of *x*?

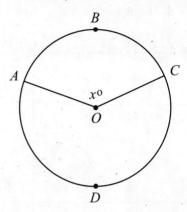

A. 120°

B. 135°

C. 144°

D. 150°

E. 216°

4. In the following figure, line *t* crosses parallel lines *m* and *n*. What is the degree measure of ∠*x*?

F. 40

G. 50

H. 60

J. 130

K. 140

5. In the figure shown, *ABCD* is a square, and $\overline{AB}$ is a diameter of the circle centered at *O*. If $\overline{AD}$ is 10 units long, what is the area, in square units, of the shaded region?

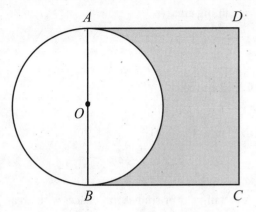

A. $100 - 50\pi$

B. $100 - 25\pi$

C. $100 - \dfrac{25}{2}\pi$

D. $100 - 10\pi$

E. $100 - \dfrac{5}{2}\pi$

6. If an isosceles right triangle has a hypotenuse of 4 inches, what is the perimeter, in inches, of the triangle?

F. $4\sqrt{2}$

G. $4 + 4\sqrt{2}$

H. $4 + 8\sqrt{2}$

J. 8

K. $8 + 4\sqrt{2}$

7. A certain rectangle is $(x + 3)$ units long and $(x + 7)$ units wide. If a square with sides of length x is removed from the interior of the rectangle, which of the following is an expression for the remaining area?

   A. 10

   B. 21

   C. $2x + 10$

   D. $10x + 21$

   E. $x^2 + 10x + 21$

8. A rectangular prism has three faces with areas of 28, 20, and 35 square centimeters. What is the volume of this solid in cubic centimeters?

   F. 83

   G. 140

   H. 166

   J. 196

   K. 19,600

9. Elizabeth plans to install artificial grass around the patio and fountain in her backyard as shown in the following figure. How many square feet of artificial grass does she need?

   A. $4,140 - 6\pi$

   B. $4,140 - 12\pi$

   C. $4,140 - 36\pi$

   D. $4,224 - 12\pi$

   E. $4,224 - 36\pi$

10. Armando wants to determine the height of a flagpole. He stands 100 feet from the base of the flagpole and measures the angle of elevation to be 40°, as shown in the following figure. Which of the following is the best approximation of the height of the flagpole, in feet? Note: sin 40° = 0.643, cos 40° = 0.766, and tan 40° = 0.839.

   F. 40

   G. 50

   H. 64

   J. 77

   K. 84

Check Your Work

1.   C

Difficulty: Low

Category: Geometry: Triangle Properties

Getting to the Answer: You need to find the value of x. You are told that the triangles are similar and are given a figure with labeled side lengths. In similar triangles, corresponding sides are proportional. $\overline{DE}$ corresponds to $\overline{AB}$, and $\overline{DF}$ corresponds to $\overline{AC}$. Use this relationship to set up a proportion. Cross-multiply to solve for x.

$$\frac{\overline{AB}}{\overline{DE}} = \frac{\overline{AC}}{\overline{DF}}$$

$$\frac{6}{3} = \frac{8}{x}$$

$$6x = 3(8)$$

$$6x = 24$$

$$x = 4$$

You found the value of x, so you are done. Choice (C) is correct.

2.   H

Difficulty: Medium

Category: Geometry: Complex Two-Dimensional Figures

Getting to the Answer: The area of the polygon can be found by dividing the polygon into two 5 cm × 20 cm rectangles and one 10 cm × 10 cm square. The area of the polygon is thus the sum of the areas of the rectangles and square: $2(5 \times 20) + (10 \times 10) = 300$ square centimeters. Choice (H) is correct.

Alternatively, the area of the polygon can be found by subtracting the two 10 cm × 15 cm rectangles from the larger 30 cm × 20 cm rectangle: $20 \times 30 - 2(10 \times 15) = 300$ square centimeters.

3.   B

Difficulty: Medium

Category: Geometry: Circles and Parabolas

Getting to the Answer: You need to find the value of x. You are given a circle that is divided into two sectors. You are also given the ratio of the areas of the sectors: $\frac{OABC}{OCDA} = \frac{3}{5}$. Because the only angle measure you know is the whole circle (360°), you need to rewrite the given part-to-part ratio as a part-to-whole ratio:

$$\frac{OABC}{OABC + OCDA} = \frac{3}{3+5} = \frac{3}{8}.$$

Now use what you know about the parts of a circle: the ratio between the interior angle of a sector and 360° is the same as the ratio between the area of a sector and the area of the whole circle. This means that you can use the part-to-whole ratio from the areas to find the missing angle measure by setting up a proportion.

$$\frac{\text{area of sector}}{\text{area of circle}} = \frac{\text{central angle}}{360°}$$

$$\frac{3}{8} = \frac{x}{360°}$$

$$360(3) = 8x$$

$$1080 = 8x$$

$$135 = x$$

You found the value of x. Choice (B) is correct.

4.   K

Difficulty: Low

Category: Geometry: Lines and Angles

Getting to the Answer: When a transversal crosses parallel lines, the four acute angles formed are all equal, the four obtuse angles formed are all equal, and any angles that are not equal are supplementary. The angle marked x is obtuse, so it is supplementary to the given 40° angle. Since $180 - 40 = 140$, the answer is (K).

5.   C

Difficulty: Medium

Category: Geometry: Complex Two-Dimensional Figures

Getting to the Answer: You are looking for the area of the shaded region. You are given a figure and told that $\overline{AB}$ is a diameter of the circle and that $\overline{AD}$ (one side of the square) is 10 units long.

First, determine which area you are actually looking for. Describe it in words first, and then apply the correct formulas. Finally, fill in the dimensions given in the question stem. The side of the square is 10 units. The radius of the circle is half the diameter, or 5.

$$\text{shaded region} = \text{square} - \text{semicircle}$$

$$A_{shaded} = s^2 - \frac{1}{2}\pi r^2$$

$$A_{shaded} = 10^2 - \frac{1}{2}\pi(5)^2$$

$$= 100 - \frac{1}{2}(25\pi)$$

$$= 100 - \frac{25}{2}\pi$$

Stop! Look back at the answer choices before you waste time trying to simplify. You already have a match. Choice (C) is correct.

6. G
Difficulty: Medium
Category: Geometry: Right Triangles
Getting to the Answer: An isosceles right triangle is a 45-45-90 triangle, which has sides in the ratio $x:x:x\sqrt{2}$.

If the hypotenuse has a length of 4 inches, then the sides are each $\frac{4}{\sqrt{2}}$ or $2\sqrt{2}$ inches long. This means that the perimeter of the triangle is $2\sqrt{2} + 2\sqrt{2} + 4 = 4 + 4\sqrt{2}$, which is (G).

7. D
Difficulty: Medium
Category: Geometry: Polygons
Getting to the Answer: If you have trouble keeping track of the variables, you can Pick Numbers. However, many students find it slightly faster to work with variables in a question like this.

Use FOIL to find that the rectangle has an area of $(x+3)(x+7) = x^2 + 10x + 21$. The square that is being removed has an area of x^2, so the area after removing the square is $x^2 + 10x + 21 - x^2 = 10x + 21$, which is (D).

8. G
Difficulty: High
Category: Geometry: Three-Dimensional Figures
Getting to the Answer: To answer this question, sketch an "unfolded" drawing of the solid and add dimensions to your sketch as you reason through the information provided in the question:

Opposite faces of a rectangular solid are congruent, so there are six faces with the corresponding areas shown above. Look for factors that will produce the given areas. These factors are the dimensions of the solid. Since $7 \times 4 = 28$, $7 \times 5 = 35$, and $4 \times 5 = 20$, the dimensions are 7 cm, 4 cm, and 5 cm. Finally, use the volume formula to arrive at the correct answer: $V = lwh = 7 \times 5 \times 4 = 140$ cubic centimeters, which is (G).

9. E
Difficulty: High
Category: Geometry: Complex Two-Dimensional Figures
Getting to the Answer: To determine the amount of artificial grass Elizabeth needs, subtract the area of the patio and the area of the fountain from the total area of the backyard. The total area of the backyard is 60 ft $\times$ 90 ft $= 5,400$ ft^2. The patio is in the shape of a trapezoid, so its area is $\frac{1}{2}(b_1 + b_2)h = \frac{1}{2}(52 + 60)21 = 1,176$ square feet. The area of the fountain represented by a circle is $\pi r^2 = \pi 6^2 = 36\pi$ square feet. Thus, the amount of artificial grass Elizabeth needs is $5,400 - 1,176 - 36\pi = 4,224 - 36\pi$ square feet. Choice (E) is correct.

10. K
Difficulty: High
Category: Geometry: Triangles and Trigonometry
Getting to the Answer: Don't try to do questions like these in your head. Set up an equation that relates the thing you're looking for to the things that you know and then solve.

You know the angle of elevation and the distance from the base of the flagpole, and you're looking for the height of the flagpole. In other words, you know one angle and the length of the side adjacent to it, and you're looking for the length of the side opposite it. Which trig function describes the relationship between an angle and the opposite and adjacent sides? Tangent does: $\tan 40° = \frac{h}{100}$, where h is the height of the flagpole.

Therefore, $100 \tan 40° = h$. The question tells you that $\tan 40°$ is approximately 0.839, so h is approximately $100(0.839) = 83.9$. The best approximation of this is (K).

LINES AND ANGLES

LEARNING OBJECTIVES

After this lesson, you will be able to:

- Identify equal angles when two parallel lines are crossed by a transversal
- Identify supplementary and vertical angles and determine missing angle measures
- Determine an unknown angle measure in a polygon using line and angle properties

To answer a question like this:

Lines E, F, and G are parallel lines cut by transversal H as shown. What is the value of $a + b + c + d$?

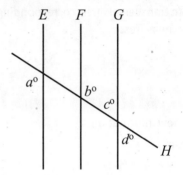

A. $180°$

B. $270°$

C. $360°$

D. $540°$

E. Cannot be determined from the given information

You need to know this:

Adjacent angles can be added to find the measure of a larger angle. The following diagram demonstrates this.

Total angle measure = $63° + 93° = 156°$

Two angles that sum to $90°$ are called **complementary angles**. Two angles that sum to $180°$ are called **supplementary angles**.

Two distinct lines in a plane will either intersect at one point or extend indefinitely without intersecting. If two lines intersect at a right angle (90°), they are **perpendicular** and are denoted with ⊥. If the lines never intersect, they are **parallel** and are denoted with ||.

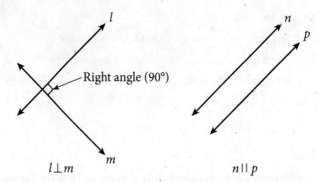

When a third line crosses two parallel lines, it creates two points of intersection and eight angles. This line is called a transversal. When a question involves parallel lines and one or more transversal lines, corresponding and supplementary angle relationships will help you identify missing angle measures.

You need to do this:

- If the question does not include an image, draw one.
- Label the figure.
- Look for line and angle relationships that will allow you to determine new information.
- Add more information to the figure(s) as needed to answer the question.

Explanation:

The question asks for the value of $a + b + c + d$. You are told that line H is a transversal through the parallel lines E, F, and G. There are no angle measures given, so you need to think about properties of parallel lines. The angles labeled a and b are obtuse angles; the angles labeled c and d are acute angles. Thus, angle a must be supplementary to angle d, and angle b must be supplementary to angle c. In other words, $a + d = 180$ and $b + c = 180$. Thus, $a + b + c + d = 180 + 180 = 360$. You found the sum of the four angle measures, so you are done. Choice (C) is correct.

Drills

If lines and angles give you trouble, study the information above and try out these drill questions before completing the Try on Your Own questions below. Drill answers can be found in Answers and Explanations.

Solve for the variable.

a.

b. For the following figure, lines l and m are parallel and lines n and o are parallel.

c.

e.

d.

Try on Your Own

Directions: Take as much time as you need on these questions. Work carefully and methodically. There will be an opportunity for timed practice at the end of the chapter.

1. In the following figure, $\overline{CD}$ is parallel to $\overline{AB}$, and $\overline{PQ}$ intersects $\overline{CD}$ at R and $\overline{AB}$ at T. If the measure of $\angle CRP$ is 110°, what is the measure of $\angle ATQ$?

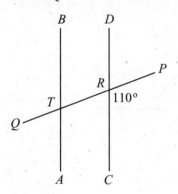

A. 30°

B. 50°

C. 70°

D. 90°

E. 110°

2. In the following figure, lines a and b are perpendicular, and line c passes through their point of intersection. What is the measure of y in terms of x?

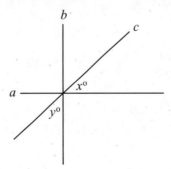

F. $x°$

G. $(45 + x)°$

H. $(90 - x)°$

J. $(90 + x)°$

K. $(180 - x)°$

HINT: For Q3, start by adding the information from the question to the figure: label the equalities. What do you notice?

HINT: For Q4, you will need to know the total interior angle measure of a polygon: when $n =$ the number of sides, the interior angle measure is $(n - 2) \times 180°$.

---

3. What is the value of $b - c$ in the figure shown given the equalities listed here?
    $\overline{LM} = \overline{MN} = \overline{NO} = \overline{OL} = \overline{LN}$

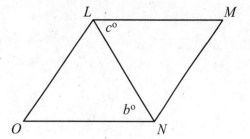

   A. $-30°$
   B. $-10°$
   C. $0°$
   D. $10°$
   E. $30°$

4. The following figure shows quadrilateral $ABCD$. The measure of $\angle B$ is $2x°$ and the measure of $\angle D$ is $3x°$. What is the measure of $\angle A$ in terms of x?

   F. $(90 + 5x)°$
   G. $(180 - 5x)°$
   H. $(180 + 5x)°$
   J. $(270 - 5x)°$
   K. $(270 - 5x)°$

5. In the following figure, $\angle ABC = 45°$ and $\angle CDE = 155°$. What is $\angle BCD$?

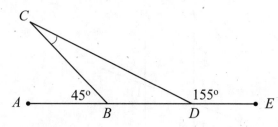

   A. $15°$
   B. $20°$
   C. $25°$
   D. $30°$
   E. $35°$

TRIANGLE PROPERTIES

LEARNING OBJECTIVES

After this lesson, you will be able to:

- Calculate the value of the third angle in a triangle given the other two angle measures
- Identify similar triangles and apply their properties
- Apply relationships between side lengths and angle measures in a triangle

To answer a question like this:

In the following figure, K, L, N, and O lie on the same line. If $\overline{LM} = \overline{MN}$ and $\angle NOP$ and $\angle OPN$ are as marked, what is the measure of $\angle KLM$?

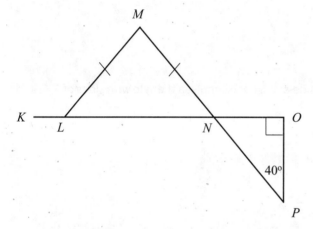

A. 125°

B. 130°

C. 135°

D. 140°

E. 150°

You need to know this:

The **interior angles** of a triangle sum to 180°. If you know any two interior angles, you can calculate the third.

The corresponding angles and side lengths of **congruent triangles** are equal. **Similar triangles** have the same angle measurements and proportional sides. In the figure below, $\triangle ABC$ and $\triangle DEF$ have the same angle measurements, so the side lengths can be set up as the following proportion: $\frac{A}{D} = \frac{B}{E} = \frac{C}{F}$.

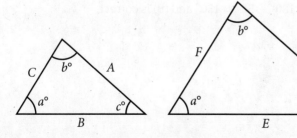

Two triangles are similar if three specific conditions are met:

- Two of their three angles are congruent (angle-angle). For example, two triangles that each have one 40° and one 55° angle are similar.

- Two of their three sides are in the same proportion and the intervening angle is congruent (side-angle-side). For example, a triangle with sides of 10 and 12 and an intervening angle of 40° and another triangle with sides of 20 and 24 and an intervening angle of 40° are similar.

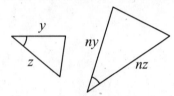

- Their three sides are in the same proportion (side-side-side). For example, a triangle with sides of 5, 6, and 8 and a triangle with sides 15, 18, and 24 are similar.

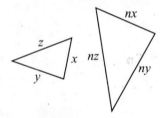

You need to do this:

- Use line and angle properties to determine missing triangle angle measures.
- Determine whether two triangles are similar by checking for angle-angle, side-angle-side, or side-side-side relationships.
- Find a missing side length by setting up a proportion.

Explanation:

You are trying to find $\angle KLM$, but you have very little information about this part of the figure. However, you do have a lot of information about $\triangle NOP$, so start there. Since there are 180 degrees in a triangle, $\angle ONP$ is $180° - 40° - 90° = 50°$. Angles ONP and MNL are vertical, so they are equal. Recall that angles that are opposite equal sides in a triangle are equal. Thus, $\angle MLN$ is also 50°. Finally, since $\angle MLN$ and $\angle KLM$ lie on a straight line, they are supplementary. Thus, $\angle KLM = 180° - 50° = 130°$ and (B) is correct.

Try on Your Own

Directions: Take as much time as you need on these questions. Work carefully and methodically. There will be an opportunity for timed practice at the end of the chapter.

1. In the following figure, $\overline{DE}$ is parallel to $\overline{AC}$. If $\overline{DF} = \overline{DE} = \overline{FE}$, then what is the measure of $\angle DAB$?

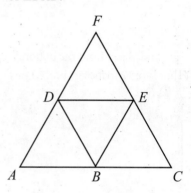

   A. 20°

   B. 30°

   C. 45°

   D. 60°

   E. 70°

2. In isosceles triangle ABC, $\overline{AB}$ and $\overline{BC}$ are congruent. If $m\angle CAB = 27°$, what is the measure of $\angle ABC$?

   F. 27°

   G. 54°

   H. 90°

   J. 126°

   K. 153°

3. If the measures of the angles of a triangle are in the ratio 2:3:7, what is the measure of the largest angle?

   A. 15°

   B. 30°

   C. 45°

   D. 84°

   E. 105°

4. In the figure shown, what is the length of the altitude that passes through vertex X in $\triangle YXZ$?

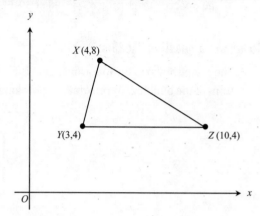

   F. $\sqrt{5}$

   G. 4

   H. $2\sqrt{5}$

   J. $2\sqrt{13}$

   K. 7

HINT: For Q5, how does the dotted line segment d help you answer this question?

---

5. $\triangle PQR$ has side lengths a, b, and c, as shown in the following figure. A dotted line segment, d, originates at point P and is perpendicular to $\overline{QR}$. What is the ratio of the length of d to the length of $\overline{PQ}$?

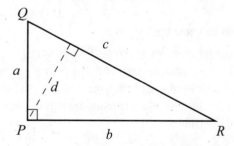

   A. $\dfrac{a}{c}$

   B. $\dfrac{b}{c}$

   C. 1

   D. $\dfrac{a}{b}$

   E. $\dfrac{b}{a}$

RIGHT TRIANGLES

LEARNING OBJECTIVES

After this lesson, you will be able to:

- Calculate the length of the third side of a right triangle given the other two side lengths
- Given one side length of a 45–45–90 or 30–60–90 triangle, calculate the other two

To answer a question like this:

The ramp shown in the following figure is placed at a 30° angle with the ground, 8 feet from the bottom step in front of the building. Approximately how long, in inches, is the ramp? (There are 12 inches in 1 foot.)

A.   67

B.   84

C.   116

D.   128

E.   134

You need to know this:

The Pythagorean theorem states that in any right triangle (and only in right triangles), the square of the hypotenuse (the longest side) is equal to the sum of the squares of the legs (the shorter sides). If you know the lengths of any two sides of a right triangle, you can use the Pythagorean equation, $a^2 + b^2 = c^2$, to find the length of the third. In this equation, a and b are the legs of the triangle and c is the hypotenuse, the side across from the right angle of the triangle.

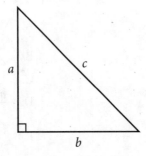

Consider an example: a right triangle has a leg of length 9 and a hypotenuse of length 14. To find the missing leg, plug the known values into the Pythagorean equation: $9^2 + b^2 = 14^2$. This simplifies to $81 + b^2 = 196$, which becomes $b^2 = 115$. Take the square root of both sides to find that $b = 10.7$.

Some right triangles have side lengths that are all integers. These sets of integer side lengths are called Pythagorean triples. The two most common Pythagorean triples on the ACT are 3-4-5 and 5-12-13. Look for multiples of these (for example, 6-8-10 and 10-24-26) as well. Memorizing these triples now can save you valuable calculation time on test day.

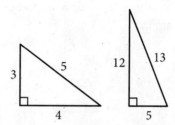

Special right triangles are defined by their angles. As a result, the ratios of their side lengths are always the same.

- If you know the length of any one of the three sides of a special right triangle, you can find the lengths of the other two.
- The ratio of the sides of a 45-45-90 triangle is $x{:}x{:}x\sqrt{2}$, where x is the length of each leg and $x\sqrt{2}$ is the length of the hypotenuse.
- The ratio of the sides of a 30-60-90 triangle is $x{:}x\sqrt{3}{:}2x$, where x is the shorter leg, $x\sqrt{3}$ is the longer leg, and $2x$ is the hypotenuse.
- These side length ratios are not provided to you on the ACT, so you should memorize them, especially if you are working to earn a top score.

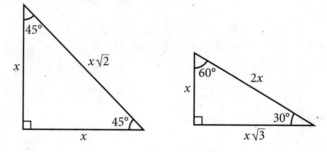

You need to do this:

- Keep in mind that the Pythagorean theorem applies only to right triangles.
- When you need to find a side length of a right triangle, look first for the common Pythagorean triples or their multiples.
- If you cannot identify any Pythagorean triples, substitute any two known side lengths into the equation $a^2 + b^2 = c^2$, where c represents the hypotenuse, to find the third.
- Look for hidden special right triangles within other shapes. For example, an equilateral triangle can be bisected (cut in half) to form two congruent 30-60-90 triangles, and a square can be divided with a diagonal into two congruent 45-45-90 triangles.
- Use one known side length to deduce the other two in a special right triangle. For example, if the shorter leg of a 30-60-90 triangle has a length of 5, then the longer leg has a length of $5\sqrt{3}$, and the hypotenuse has a length of $5(2) = 10$.

Explanation:

Two of the angles in the triangle have degree measures of 30 and 90, which means that the third angle must measure 60 degrees. Thus, you can use the properties of 30-60-90 triangles to help you. In a 30-60-90 triangle, the sides are always in the ratio $x:x\sqrt{3}:2x$ (short leg:long leg:hypotenuse). The only length that you know is the long leg, the side represented by the ground and the width of the bottom two steps. Convert feet into inches so that the units are the same. The ramp is to be placed 8 feet $\times \dfrac{12 \text{ inches}}{1 \text{ foot}} = 96$ inches from the bottom step, and the steps themselves account for an additional 20 inches. This means that this leg of the triangle is $96 + 20 = 116$ inches long. Use the ratio of the sides given above to set up a proportion to find the length of the hypotenuse, which corresponds to the length of the ramp, r.

$$\frac{\sqrt{3}}{2} = \frac{116}{r}$$

$$\sqrt{3}r = 232$$

$$r \approx 133.95$$

The result is approximately 134 inches, which matches (E).

Try on Your Own

Directions: Take as much time as you need on these questions. Work carefully and methodically. There will be an opportunity for timed practice at the end of the chapter.

1. The hypotenuse of $\triangle ABC$ is 20 meters and $\angle ABC$ is 30°. What is the length, in meters, of AB?

    A. 10
    B. $10\sqrt{2}$
    C. $10\sqrt{3}$
    D. 20
    E. $20\sqrt{3}$

2. The diagonal measure of a square tile is 18 inches. What is the side length, in inches, of the tile?

    F. $6\sqrt{3}$
    G. 9
    H. $9\sqrt{2}$
    J. $9\sqrt{3}$
    K. $18\sqrt{2}$

3. The longer leg of a right triangle is twice the length of the shorter leg. If the length of the shorter leg is 6 inches, what is the length, in inches, of the hypotenuse?

    A. $3\sqrt{5}$
    B. 12
    C. $6\sqrt{5}$
    D. $9\sqrt{2}$
    E. 18

4. A playground slide is 10 feet long, and the base of the slide is 8 feet from the base of a ladder, as shown in the following figure. If the ladder is perpendicular to the ground, what is the height, in feet, of the ladder?

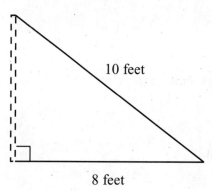

8 feet

F. 3
G. 4
H. 5
J. 6
K. 7

HINT: There are two approaches you can take to answer Q5. Which one is more efficient for you?

5. What is the length, in units, of side *AB* in the following diagram?

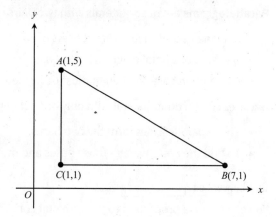

A. $\sqrt{13}$
B. 4
C. 6
D. $2\sqrt{13}$
E. 8

POLYGONS

LEARNING OBJECTIVES

After this lesson, you will be able to:

- Calculate the area or perimeter of a polygon or complex figure
- Perform unit conversions

To answer a question like this:

Jayden plans to order a rectangular rug for his dorm room. His roommate wants a rug that has a perimeter of 14 yards and covers an area of 12 square yards. What are the dimensions of the rug, in feet? (Note: 1 yard = 3 feet)

A. 3 by 36
B. 4 by 27
C. 6 by 18
D. 7 by 14
E. 9 by 12

You need to know this:

Perimeter and area are basic properties that all two-dimensional shapes have.

- The **perimeter** of a polygon can easily be calculated by adding the lengths of all its sides.
- **Area** is the amount of two-dimensional space a shape occupies.

Parallelograms are quadrilaterals with two pairs of parallel sides.

- Rectangles and squares are subsets of parallelograms.
- The area of a parallelogram is $A = bh$.
- Remember, base and height must be perpendicular when using geometric formulas.

A **trapezoid** is a quadrilateral with only one set of parallel sides.

- Those parallel sides form the two bases.
- To find the area, average those bases and multiply by the height.

Unit Conversion

You can set up a proportion to perform unit conversions. This is especially useful when there are multiple conversions or when the units are unfamiliar. On the ACT, you may see unit conversion involve scale factors related to maps or blueprints.

For example, though these units of measurement are no longer commonly used, there are 8 furlongs in a mile and 3 miles in a league. Say you're asked to convert 4 leagues to furlongs. A convenient way to do this is to set up a proportion so that equivalent units cancel:

$$4 \text{ leagues} \times \frac{3 \text{ miles}}{1 \text{ league}} \times \frac{8 \text{ furlongs}}{1 \text{ mile}} = 4 \times 3 \times 8 = 96 \text{ furlongs}$$

Notice that all the units cancel out except the furlongs, which is the unit you want.

You need to do this:

- If a figure is not provided as part of the question, draw one.
- Label the figure with given information.
- Use angle and line properties to determine missing values, such as base or height.
- Double-check the units in the question and the units in the choices to plan for any necessary unit conversion.
- When unit conversion is necessary, set up a proportion to make equivalent units cancel.
  - Keep track of the units by writing them down next to the numbers in the proportion.
  - You should be left with the units you're converting into.

Explanation:

You can approach this question by setting up a system of equations using the formulas for the area and perimeter of a rectangle. The area is $l \times w$, and the perimeter is $l + l + w + w$ or $2l + 2w$.

$$l \times w = 12$$
$$2l + 2w = 14$$

Solve the second equation for l: $l = 7 - w$. Then substitute it into the first equation to solve for w:

$$(7 - w)w = 12$$
$$7w - w^2 = 12$$
$$0 = w^2 - 7w + 12$$
$$0 = (w - 3)(w - 4)$$
$$3 \text{ and } 4 = w$$

Thus, $l = 4$ and 3, respectively. Finally, use the 1 yard = 3 feet conversion factor to convert 3 and 4 yards into feet:

$$3 \text{ yards} \times \frac{3 \text{ feet}}{1 \text{ yard}} = 9 \text{ feet}$$

and

$$4 \text{ yards} \times \frac{3 \text{ feet}}{1 \text{ yard}} = 12 \text{ feet}$$

Choice (E) is correct.

Alternatively, you could Backsolve. All of the choices except D yield an area of length (feet) × width (feet) = area (square feet) = 108 ft^2, and $108 \text{ ft}^2 \times \frac{1 \text{ yd}}{3 \text{ ft}} \times \frac{1 \text{ yd}}{3 \text{ ft}} = 12 \text{ yd}^2$, so D is incorrect. The perimeters in choices A, B, and C are larger than $14 \text{ yards} \times \frac{3 \text{ feet}}{1 \text{ yard}} = 42 \text{ feet}$. Only (E) works.

Drills

If polygons and unit conversion gives you trouble, study the information above and try out these drill questions before completing the Try on Your Own questions below. Drill answers can be found in Answers and Explanations.

Solve the following.

a.   What is the perimeter?

b.   If the perimeter is 48, $x =$?

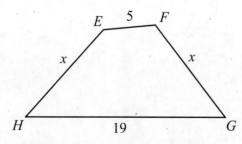

c.   What is the area?

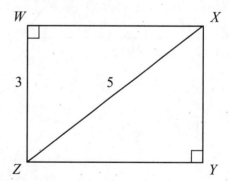

d. What is the area?

e. What is the area?

Try on Your Own

Directions: Take as much time as you need on these questions. Work carefully and methodically. There will be an opportunity for timed practice at the end of the chapter.

1. Triangle *PQR* has a base of 16 centimeters and an altitude of 10 centimeters. If the area of square *ABCD* is twice the area of Δ*PQR*, what is the length, in centimeters, of a side of the square *ABCD*?

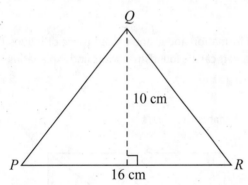

A. 4
B. $4\sqrt{5}$
C. $4\sqrt{10}$
D. $8\sqrt{5}$
E. 8

2. As shown in the following figure, points $(-2,2)$, $(4,2)$, $(0,5)$, and $(6,5)$ are the vertices of a parallelogram. What is the area, in square units, of the parallelogram?

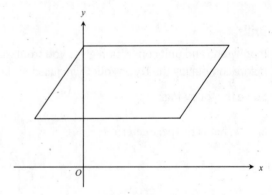

F. 12
G. 18
H. $6\sqrt{13}$
J. 24
K. 30

HINT: For Q3, how can you calculate the missing
side lengths?

---

3. In the polygon shown, all angles are right
    angles. What is the perimeter, in centimeters?

A. 3,000
B. 4,500
C. 6,000
D. 9,700
E. 12,500

4. In the figure shown, $\overline{BE}$ is perpendicular to $\overline{AD}$,
    and the lengths of $\overline{AB}$, $\overline{BC}$, $\overline{CD}$, and $\overline{BE}$ are
    given in inches. What is the area, in square
    inches, of trapezoid ABCD?

F. 24
G. 30
H. 32
J. 34
K. 36

5. For the area of a square to triple, the new side
    lengths must be the old side lengths multiplied
    by which of the following?

A. $\sqrt{3}$
B. 3
C. 9
D. $\sqrt{27}$
E. 27

CIRCLES AND PARABOLAS

LEARNING OBJECTIVES

After this lesson, you will be able to:

*   Answer math questions about circles using relationships among angles, arcs, distances, and area
*   Relate properties of a quadratic function to its graph and vice versa

To answer a question like this:

A circle centered at (2,2) has a radius of 5. A parabola on the same coordinate plane has a vertex at (0,3)
and passes through (−2,7). At how many points do the circle and parabola intersect?

A. 0
B. 1
C. 2
D. 3
E. 4

You need to know this:

On the ACT, you might see a question with a system of equations that involves one parabola and one circle. This system is usually solved using a coordinate plane. Use the information in the following sections to graph and interpret circles and parabolas.

Circles

The equation of a circle in the coordinate plane is as follows:

$$(x - h)^2 + (y - k)^2 = r^2$$

In this equation, called **standard form**, r is the radius of the circle, and h and k are the x- and y-coordinates of the circle's center, respectively: (h, k).

You might also see what is referred to as **general form**:

$$x^2 + y^2 + Cx + Dy + E = 0$$

In the general form, the fact that there are x^2 and y^2 terms with coefficients of 1 is an indicator that the equation does indeed graph as a circle. To convert to standard form, complete the square for the x terms, then repeat for the y terms. Refer to chapter 10 for a quadratics review if needed.

The ACT may also ask you about the following parts of circles: arcs, central angles, and sectors. The ability to set up ratios and proportions correctly is essential for these questions. Review chapter 9 for more information on rates, ratios, proportions, and percents.

- An **arc** is part of a circle's circumference. If the circumference is divided into exactly two arcs, the smaller one is called the minor arc, and the larger one is called the major arc. If a diameter cuts the circle in half, the two arcs formed are called semicircles. An arc length can never be greater than the circle's circumference.
- An angle formed by two radii is called a **central angle**. Because a full circle contains 360°, a central angle measure cannot be greater than this.
- The part of a circle's area defined by a central angle is called a **sector**. The area of a sector cannot be greater than the circle's total area.

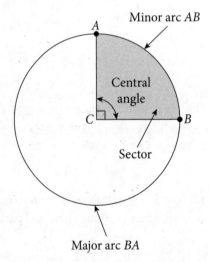

Here's a summary of the ratios formed by these three parts and their whole counterparts:

$$\frac{\text{central angle}}{360°} = \frac{\text{arc length}}{\text{circumference}} = \frac{\text{sector area}}{\text{circle area}}$$

Notice that all of these ratios are equal. Intuitively, this should make sense: when you slice a pizza into four equal slices, each piece should have $\frac{1}{4}$ of the cheese, crust, and sauce. If you slice a circle into four equal pieces, the same principle applies: each piece should have $\frac{1}{4}$ of the degrees, circumference, and area.

Parabolas

As defined in the Functions chapter, a quadratic function is a quadratic equation set equal to y or $f(x)$ instead of 0.

- Remember that the solutions (also called "roots" or "zeros") of any polynomial function are the same as the x-intercepts.
- To solve a quadratic function, substitute 0 for y, or $f(x)$, then solve algebraically.
- Alternatively, you can plug the equation into your graphing calculator and read the x-intercepts from the graph.

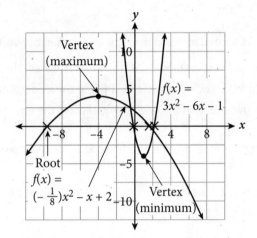

The graph of every quadratic equation (or function) is a **parabola**, which is a symmetric U-shaped graph that opens either upward or downward.

- To determine which way a parabola will open, examine the value of a in the equation.
- If a is positive, the parabola will open upward.
- If a is negative, it will open downward.
- Take a look at the examples above to see this graphically.

Like quadratic equations, quadratic functions will have zero, one, or two real solutions, corresponding to the number of times the parabola crosses the x-axis. Graphing is a powerful way to determine the number of solutions a quadratic function has:

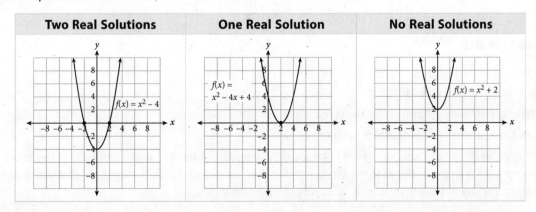

There are three algebraic forms that a quadratic equation can take: standard, factored, and vertex. Each is provided in the following table along with the graphical features that are revealed by writing the equation in that particular form:

Standard	Factored	Vertex
$y = ax^2 + bx + c$	$y = a(x - m)(x - n)$	$y = a(x - h)^2 + k$
y-intercept is c	Solutions are m and n	Vertex is (h,k)
In real-world contexts, starting quantity is c	x-intercepts are m and n	Minimum/maximum of function is k
Format needed to solve via quadratic formula	Vertex is halfway between m and n	Axis of symmetry is given by $x = h$

You've already seen standard and factored forms in the Algebra chapter, but vertex form might be new to you.

- In vertex form, a is the same as the a in standard form, and h and k are the coordinates of the **vertex** (h,k).
- If a quadratic function is not in vertex form, you can still find the x-coordinate of the vertex by plugging the appropriate values into the equation $h = -\dfrac{b}{2a}$, which is also the equation for the axis of symmetry (see graph that follows).
- Once you determine h, plug this value into the quadratic function and solve for y to determine k, the y-coordinate of the vertex.

The equation of the **axis of symmetry** of a parabola is $x = h$, where h is the x-coordinate of the vertex.

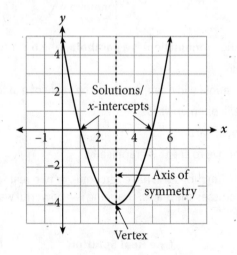

You need to do this:

Circles

- Get the circle into standard form.
- Determine the center and radius using the standard form equation.
- Use the center and/or radius to answer the question.
- To find the length of an arc or the area of a sector, you need to know the angle that defines the arc or sector as well as the radius of the circle. Questions that are especially tricky might not give you those values directly but will instead give you a way of calculating them.

Parabolas

- To find the vertex of a parabola, get the function into vertex form: $y = a(x - h)^2 + k$, or use the formula $h = \dfrac{-b}{2a}$.
- To find the y-intercept of a quadratic function, plug in 0 for x.
- To determine whether a parabola opens upward or downward, look at the coefficient of a.
  - If a is positive, it opens upward.
  - If a is negative, it opens downward.
- To determine the number of x-intercepts, set the quadratic function equal to 0 and solve or examine its graph.

To answer a question involving a system of equations with a parabola and a circle, take it one figure at a time until you find the point(s) of intersection and/or gather the information you need to answer the question.

Explanation:

Sketch the circle and parabola to visualize the situation and make the question easier to answer. Since the circle is centered at $(2,2)$ and has a radius of 5, the vertex of the parabola $(0,3)$ lies within the circle. Since the parabola passes through $(-2,7)$, it opens upward and intersects the circle at two distinct points:

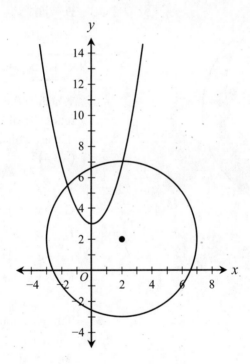

Choice (C) is correct.

Try on Your Own

Directions: Take as much time as you need on these questions. Work carefully and methodically. There will be an opportunity for timed practice at the end of the chapter.

1. What is the area, in square inches, of a circle that has a circumference of 8π inches?

    A. 4π
    B. 8π
    C. 16π
    D. 32π
    E. 64π

2. The two circles shown are tangent to each other. The radius of the larger circle is 75% greater than that of the smaller circle. What is the area, in square feet, of the shaded region?

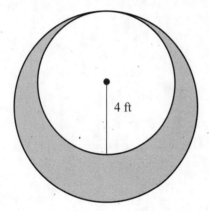

4 ft

    F. 6π
    G. 9π
    H. 10π
    J. 16π
    K. 33π

HINT: What information in the question stem for Q3 is useful in determining the correct answer?

---

3. Earth makes one complete rotation about its axis every 24 hours, at a fairly constant rate. Assuming the Earth is a perfect sphere, through how many degrees would Quito, Ecuador, which lies on the Earth's equator, rotate from 12:00 noon on January 1 to 3:00 p.m. on January 2?

    A. $340°$
    B. $370°$
    C. $385°$
    D. $405°$
    E. $415°$

HINT: For Q4, what does the distance of 5 represent?

---

4. Which of the following equations describes the set of all points (x,y) in the coordinate plane that are a distance of 5 units from the point $(-3,4)$?

    F. $(x+3) + (y-4) = 5$
    G. $(x-3) + (y+4) = 5$
    H. $(x+3)^2 + (y-4)^2 = 5$
    J. $(x+3)^2 + (y-4)^2 = 25$
    K. $(x-3)^2 + (y+4)^2 = 25$

5. If the equation for a parabola is $y = (x+3)^2 - 1$, which of the following best describes the solutions for x?

    A. 2 distinct negative real solutions
    B. 2 distinct positive real solutions
    C. 1 positive real solution and 1 negative real solution
    D. 2 real solutions that are not distinct
    E. 2 distinct solutions that are not real

COMPLEX TWO-DIMENSIONAL FIGURES

LEARNING OBJECTIVES

After this lesson, you will be able to:

- Identify and calculate measurements within a complex figure
- Transfer information among multiple figures

To answer a question like this:

The following figure shows a rectangular basketball court that is symmetric about the mid-court line (the vertical line with a shaded circle located in the middle of the figure). The shaded area is approximately what percent of the full court?

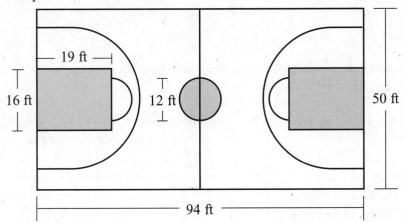

A. 13.7

B. 15.3

C. 22.6

D. 37.4

E. 61.7

You need to know this:

Some ACT math questions will combine multiple 2D figures, especially quadrilaterals, circles, and triangles.

- These questions can involve multiple formulas or steps.
- They can require other math skills, such as percent calculations.

You need to do this:

- If a figure is not provided as part of the question, draw one.
- Label the figure with the given information.
- Use angle and line properties to determine missing values, such as base or height.
- Share information among figures when permissible.
- Double-check the units in the question and the units in the choices to plan for any necessary unit conversion.
- When unit conversion is necessary, set up a proportion to make equivalent units cancel.
- Pause for an extra moment before selecting your answer to confirm you really did answer the right question.
- Look out for other math skills needed to answer these questions.

Math

Explanation:

You are asked to find approximately what percent of the full court is constituted by the shaded regions. To do so, you need to use the percent formula, $\% = \dfrac{\text{part}}{\text{whole}} \times 100\%$. First, determine the area of the shaded regions. Next, find the area of the full basketball court. Finally, plug these numbers into the formula.

The shaded areas include the two equal rectangles that are 16 by 19 feet and the center circle that has a diameter of 12 feet. Use $2 \times l \times w$ to calculate the area of the 2 rectangles: $2 \times 16 \times 19 = 608$ square feet. Use $A = \pi r^2$ to calculate the area of the center circle: $\pi (6)^2 \approx 113$ square feet. The sum of the areas is thus approximately $608 + 113 = 721$ feet. The total area of the rectangular basketball court is $50 \times 94 = 4{,}700$ square feet.

Now plug these numbers into the $\% = \dfrac{\text{part}}{\text{whole}} \times 100\%$ formula to calculate approximately what percent the shaded region is of the full court: $\dfrac{721}{4{,}700} \times 100\% = 15.3\%$. Choice (B) is correct.

Try on Your Own

Directions: Take as much time as you need on these questions. Work carefully and methodically. There will be an opportunity for timed practice at the end of the chapter.

1. Lorenzo is deciding between two examination room layouts for his new clinic. The cross-sectional area of each square chair is 2 square feet, and the cross-sectional areas of the circle chair and exam table are π and 4.9 square feet, respectively. What is the difference in the areas, in square feet, of the shaded portion between the two layouts?

   A. 2
   B. 4
   C. 6
   D. 8
   E. 10

2. The following figure shows a scale drawing of the table layout for Yan's upcoming graduation party $\left(\dfrac{3}{4}\text{ inch} = 9\text{ feet}\right)$. What is the area, in square inches, of each table in the scale drawing?

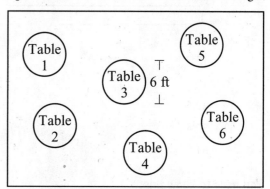

   F. $\dfrac{1}{16}\pi$

   G. $\dfrac{1}{4}\pi$

   H. $\dfrac{4}{9}\pi$

   J. $\dfrac{1}{2}\pi$

   K. 2π

3. A circle with radius 5 is inscribed in a square. What is the difference between the area of the square and the area of the circle?

    A. 25π

    B. 50π

    C. $50 - 25\pi$

    D. $100 - 25\pi$

    E. 100

4. In the figure shown, the shaded region is a square with an area of 12 square units, inscribed inside equilateral triangle ABC. What is the perimeter of $\triangle ABC$?

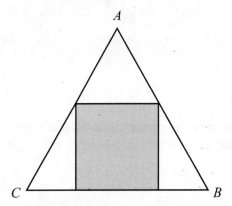

    F. $18\sqrt{3}$
    G. $4 + \sqrt{3}$
    H. $4 + 6\sqrt{3}$
    J. $8 + 6\sqrt{3}$
    K. $12 + 6\sqrt{3}$

HINT: For Q5, what additional line segments can you add to the figure to help you get closer to determining the distance between $\overline{YZ}$ and $\overline{WX}$?

5. The semicircle shown has a radius of r inches, and chord $\overline{YZ}$ is parallel to diameter $\overline{WX}$. If the length of $\overline{YZ}$ is 25% shorter than the length of $\overline{WX}$, what is the shortest distance between $\overline{YZ}$ and $\overline{WX}$ in terms of r?

Note: Figure not drawn to scale

    A. $\frac{1}{4}\pi r$

    B. $\frac{3}{4}\pi r$

    C. $\frac{5}{4}\pi r$

    D. $\frac{\sqrt{2}}{4}r$

    E. $\frac{\sqrt{7}}{4}r$

THREE-DIMENSIONAL FIGURES

LEARNING OBJECTIVE

After this lesson, you will be able to:

• Calculate the volume and surface area of common three-dimensional (3D) figures

To answer a question like this:

A rectangular box with an open top is constructed from cardboard to have a square base of area x^2 and height h. If the volume of this box is 50 cubic units, how many square units of cardboard, in terms of x, are needed to build the box?

A. $5x^2$

B. $6x^2$

C. $\dfrac{200}{x} + x^2$

D. $\dfrac{200}{x} + 2x^2$

E. $\dfrac{250}{x} + 2x^2$

You need to know this:

Three-dimensional (3D) shapes are also called solids. There are several different types of solids that might appear on test day—rectangular solids, cubes, cylinders, prisms, spheres, cones, and pyramids—and knowing their structures will help you on test day.

The following diagram shows the basic anatomy of a 3D shape:

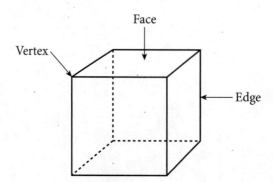

A **face** (or **surface**) is a two-dimensional (2D) shape that acts as one of the sides of the solid. Two faces meet at a line segment called an **edge**, and three faces meet at a single point called a **vertex**.

Volume

Volume is the amount of 3D space occupied by a solid. Volume is analogous to the area of a 2D shape. You can find the volume of many 3D shapes by finding the area of the base and multiplying it by the height: $(V = A_{\text{base}} \times h)$. In the table of formulas, the pieces that represent the areas of the bases are enclosed in parentheses.

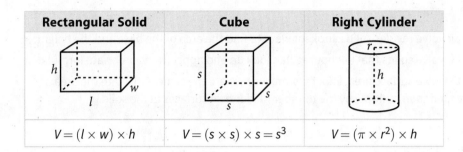

Rectangular Solid	Cube	Right Cylinder
$V = (l \times w) \times h$	$V = (s \times s) \times s = s^3$	$V = (\pi \times r^2) \times h$

These three 3D shapes are **prisms**. Almost all prisms on the ACT are right prisms; that is, all faces are perpendicular to those with which they share edges. You might see less common prisms, such as a triangular or a hexagonal prism, but don't worry: the volume of any right prism can be calculated by finding the area of the base and multiplying it by the height.

When you are not explicitly given the area of the base of a prism, you'll need to rely on your two-dimensional geometry knowledge to find it before calculating the volume of the prism.

More complicated 3D shapes include the right pyramid, right cone, and sphere. The vertex of a right pyramid or right cone will always be centered above the middle of the base. Their volume formulas are similar to those of prisms, albeit with different coefficients.

Some of these formulas might look daunting, but you won't have to memorize them for test day; they'll be provided in the question stem if they are needed.

Right Rectangular Pyramid	Right Cone	Sphere
$V = \frac{1}{3} \times (l \times w) \times h$	$V = \frac{1}{3} \times (\pi \times r^2) \times h$	$V = \frac{4}{3} \times \pi \times r^3$

A right pyramid can have any polygon as its base, but the square variety is the one you're most likely to see on the ACT. Also note that the vertex above the base of a right pyramid or cone is not necessarily formed by an intersection of exactly three faces, as in prisms, but it is still a single point and is still called a vertex.

Surface Area

Surface area is the sum of the areas of all faces of a solid. To calculate the surface area of a solid, simply find the area of each face using your 2D geometry skills, then add them all together.

You won't be expected to know the surface area formulas for right pyramids, right cones, and spheres. They'll be provided at the beginning of each Math section. However, you could be asked to find the surface area of a prism, in which case you'll be given enough information to find the area of each surface of the solid.

You might think that finding the surface area of a solid with many sides, such as a right hexagonal prism, is a tall order. However, you can save time by noticing a vital trait: this prism has two identical hexagonal faces and six identical rectangular faces. Don't waste time finding the area of each of the eight surfaces. Find the area of one hexagonal face and one rectangular face only. Then multiply the area of the hexagonal face by 2 and the area of the rectangular face by 6, add the products together, and you're done. The same is true for other 3D shapes such as rectangular solids (including cubes), other right prisms, and certain pyramids.

You need to do this:

- To answer questions that involve regular solids, look for ways to find the area of the base and the height.
- To answer questions that involve solids that are not regular, look up and apply the appropriate formula.
- To answer questions that involve surface area, look for surfaces that are the same. Calculate the area of each kind of surface once, and then multiply by the number of identical surfaces in the solid.

Explanation:

Use the given volume, 50, to get h in terms of x:

$$\text{volume} = \text{length} \times \text{width} \times \text{height}$$
$$50 = x^2 h$$
$$\frac{50}{x^2} = h$$

Since the box has an open top, the area you're looking for is equal to four lateral faces and one bottom face.

Each lateral face has area $xh = x\left(\frac{50}{x^2}\right) = \frac{50}{x}$ square units, and the base has area x^2 square units. Thus, the total area you're looking for is:

$$4\left(\frac{50}{x}\right) + x^2 = \frac{200}{x} + x^2$$

Choice (C) is correct.

Try on Your Own

Directions: Take as much time as you need on these questions. Work carefully and methodically. There will be an opportunity for timed practice at the end of the chapter.

1. In the figure that follows, a wooden plank is shown with its dimensions in inches. If Hawanatu wants to spray-paint every surface of the plank, how much paint, in square inches, will Hawanatu need?

A. 38
B. 76
C. 240
D. 450
E. 510

HINT: How can the fact that the figure in Q2 is half of a cube help you determine the answer more efficiently?

2. If the solid shown is half of a cube that has been cut in half along the diagonal, from one edge to the opposite edge, what is its volume?

F. 4
G. $4\sqrt{2}$
H. 8
J. $8\sqrt{2}$
K. 12

3. What is the volume, in cubic inches, of the cylinder shown?

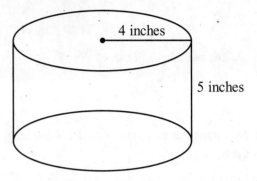

4 inches

5 inches

    A. 20π

    B. 40π

    C. 60π

    D. 80π

    E. 100π

HINT: For Q4, which surfaces will you actually be covering with wrapping paper?

---

4. Mali bought several right cylindrical candles as party favors and plans to wrap them such that the gift paper wraps around the candle exactly once with no overlap. She wants to leave an extra 3 inches of wrapping paper past each end of the candles so she can tie both ends with a bit of ribbon. If each candle has a diameter of 4 inches and is 8 inches tall, how many square inches of wrapping paper will Mali need to wrap one candle?

Candle

Gift wrap

    F. 32π

    G. 40π

    H. 44π

    J. 56π

    K. 64π

5. Noelle submerges a figurine into a tank of water to determine the volume of the figurine. The tank is 10 inches by 13 inches, and the water is filled to a depth of 5 inches. If the water level rises 0.4 inches when the figurine is submerged, what is the volume, in cubic inches, of the object?

    A.   4

    B.   52

    C.   130

    D.   650

    E.   702

TRIANGLES AND TRIGONOMETRY

LEARNING OBJECTIVE

After this lesson, you will be able to:

- Apply basic trigonometric ratios and formulas to answer questions involving right triangles

To answer a question like this:

In the following figure, a surfboard is propped up against a rectangular box. If the board is 7 feet long, which of the following is closest to the height, in feet, of the box?

(Note: sin 23° ≈ 0.3907, cos 23° ≈ 0.9205, tan 23° ≈ 0.4245)

A. 2.7

B. 3.0

C. 4.3

D. 5.6

E. 6.4

You need to know this:

The ACT tests three trigonometric functions: **sine**, **cosine**, and **tangent**.

- All three are simply the ratios of side lengths within a right triangle.
- The notation for sine, cosine, and tangent functions always includes a reference angle; for example, cos x or cos θ. That's because you'll need to refer to the given angle within a right triangle to determine the appropriate side ratios.

There is a common mnemonic device for the sine, cosine, and tangent ratios: SOHCAHTOA (commonly pronounced: sew-kuh-TOE-uh). Here's what it represents:

- **S**ine is **O**pposite over **H**ypotenuse.
- **C**osine is **A**djacent over **H**ypotenuse.
- **T**angent is **O**pposite over **A**djacent.

See the triangle and the table below for a summary of the ratios and what each equals for $\angle A$ in $\triangle CAB$:

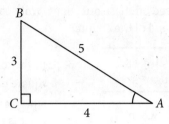

Sine (sin)	Cosine (cos)	Tangent (tan)
$\dfrac{\text{opposite}}{\text{hypotenuse}}$	$\dfrac{\text{adjacent}}{\text{hypotenuse}}$	$\dfrac{\text{opposite}}{\text{adjacent}}$
$\dfrac{3}{5}$	$\dfrac{4}{5}$	$\dfrac{3}{4}$

Complementary angles have a special relationship relative to sine and cosine:

- $\sin x° = \cos(90° - x°)$
- $\cos x° = \sin(90° - x°)$
- In other words, the sine of an acute angle is equal to the cosine of the angle's complement and vice versa. For example, $\cos 30° = \sin 60°$, $\cos 45° = \sin 45°$, and $\cos 60° = \sin 30°$.

You need to do this:

Apply the appropriate trigonometric ratio to a right triangle, or use the relationship between the sine and cosine of complementary angles.

Explanation:

You need to find the height of the box. You are given a figure that includes a right triangle and an angle measure, as well as the length of the surfboard. You are also given three trig values, which you may or may not need. Let x equal the height of the triangle (which is also the height of the box). Now, look at the triangle. You know the length of the hypotenuse, and you're looking for the side opposite the given angle. This tells you which trig function to use: $\sin x = \dfrac{\text{opp}}{\text{hyp}}$. The question states that $\sin 23° \approx 0.3907$. Use this information to solve for x:

$$\sin 23° = \frac{x}{7}$$
$$0.3907 = \frac{x}{7}$$
$$0.3907 \times 7 = x$$
$$2.7349 = x$$

The height of the box is approximately 2.7 feet, so choice (A) is correct.

Try on Your Own

Directions: Take as much time as you need on these questions. Work carefully and methodically. There will be an opportunity for timed practice at the end of the chapter.

HINT: The unit circle will help you answer Q1, a high-difficulty question, more confidently.

---

1. If $0 \leq \theta \leq \pi$, what are the values of θ when $\sin\theta = \frac{1}{2}$?

    A. $\frac{\pi}{6}$ and $\frac{2\pi}{3}$

    B. $\frac{\pi}{6}$ and $\frac{5\pi}{6}$

    C. $\frac{\pi}{4}$ and $\frac{3\pi}{4}$

    D. $\frac{\pi}{3}$ and $\frac{4\pi}{3}$

    E. $\frac{7\pi}{6}$ and $\frac{11\pi}{6}$

2. In a right triangle with angle measure β, $\cos\beta = \frac{36}{39}$ and $\sin\beta = \frac{15}{39}$. What is the value of $\tan\beta$?

    F. $\frac{15}{36}$

    G. $\frac{36}{15}$

    H. $\frac{39}{36}$

    J. $\frac{39}{15}$

    K. Cannot be determined from the given information

3. In the following figure, $\triangle ABC$ has an area of 60 square centimeters. If $\angle ABC$ is reduced to $45°$ and the length of $\overline{AC}$ is shortened accordingly, what is the new area, in square centimeters, of $\triangle ABC$? (Note: The area of a triangle is $\frac{1}{2}ab \sin x$, where a and b are the lengths of the sides and x is the angle between them.)

    A. 20

    B. 30

    C. 40

    D. 50

    E. 60

4. Eric is a glass collector. The following figure is one of the triangular glass fragments that Eric collected. Which of the following expressions is the value of z? (Note: The law of sines states that for a triangle with sides of lengths a, b, and c and opposite angles of measure A, B, and C, respectively, $\dfrac{\sin A}{a} = \dfrac{\sin B}{b} = \dfrac{\sin C}{c}$.)

F. $\dfrac{7 \sin 35°}{\sin 45°}$

G. $\dfrac{7 \sin 35°}{\sin 100°}$

H. $\dfrac{7 \sin 45°}{\sin 100°}$

J. $\dfrac{7 \sin 100°}{\sin 35°}$

K. $\dfrac{7 \sin 100°}{\sin 45°}$

HINT: Q5 looks complicated, but the question stem gives you the formulas you need to answer the question correctly.

5. Triangle *EFG* is shown in the following figure. What is the length, in inches, of $\overline{FG}$? (Note: For a triangle with side lengths a, b, and c and opposite angles A, B and C, respectively, $\dfrac{\sin A}{a} = \dfrac{\sin B}{b} = \dfrac{\sin C}{c}$, and $c^2 = a^2 + b^2 - 2ab \cos C$.)

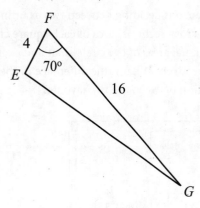

A. $4 \sin 70°$

B. $16 \sin 70°$

C. $\sqrt{16^2 - 4^2 - 2(16)(4)\cos 70°}$

D. $\sqrt{16^2 + 4^2 - 2(16)(4)\cos 70°}$

E. $\sqrt{16^2 + 4^2 + 2(16)(4)\cos 70°}$

On Test Day

Occasionally, a question will give you more information than you need to determine the correct answer. Think about what information you really need to arrive at the answer before you begin your calculations so that you don't get sidetracked and spend time doing unnecessary work.

As you read through this question from earlier in this chapter, plan your strategy to get the correct value and identify what information you need to carry out that strategy. Note if there is any unnecessary information that you can ignore.

1. Lorenzo is deciding between two examination room layouts for his new clinic. The cross-sectional area of each square chair is 2 square feet, and the cross-sectional areas of the circle chair and exam table are π and 4.9 square feet, respectively. What is the difference in the areas, in square feet, of the shaded portion between the two layouts?

A. 2

B. 4

C. 6

D. 8

E. 10

The explanation appears at the end of this chapter.

How Much Have You Learned?

Directions: For test-like practice, give yourself 10 minutes to complete this question set. Be sure to study the explanations, even for questions you got right. They can be found at the end of this chapter. Note that this question set includes foundational topics in geometry covered in Math Fundamentals in chapter 6.

1. In the following figure, N is the intersection of segments $\overline{MO}$ and $\overline{LP}$. If $\overline{LM} = \overline{MN} = \overline{NL}$, what is the measure of $\angle NPO$?

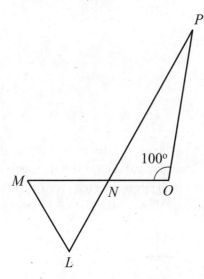

A. 10°

B. 15°

C. 20°

D. 25°

E. 30°

2. The ratio of the perimeters of two similar triangles is 4:7. The sides of the larger triangle are 10, 12, and 13 cm, respectively. What is the perimeter, in centimeters, of the smaller triangle?

F. 7

G. 11

H. 12

J. 20

K. 26

3. During a hiking trip, Keesha and Dwayne decide to climb a mountain using two different routes to the top. Keesha takes the hiking route that travels 5 miles south, 6 miles east, 7 miles south, and 2 miles west to the summit; Dwayne uses the climbing route that starts at the same point as the hiking route but goes directly from there to the summit. Approximately how many miles in all will the two hike on the way to the summit?

A. 12.65

B. 29.42

C. 32.65

D. 33.42

E. 34.00

4. The following figure shows $\triangle WXY$ in which Z is the midpoint of $\overline{WY}$ and $\overline{WX}$ is perpendicular to $\overline{YX}$. What is the length, in inches, of $\overline{WZ}$?

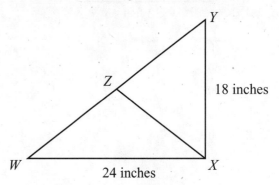

F. 13

G. 15

H. 21

J. 30

K. 32

5. In the following figure, $\overline{CD} = \overline{BD}$ and $\angle BED$ is 17°. What is the measure, in degrees, of $\angle ABC$?

A.   30

B.   45

C.   54

D.   62

E.   107

6. The following figure shows the floor dimensions of Akanksha's living room. She wants to install floor molding along the perimeter of the floor. How many feet of molding does she need?

F.   76

G.   86

H.   90

J.   96

K.   100

7. Yesenia has a rectangular orchard that she would like to divide into two triangular fields—one for planting orange trees and one for planting grapefruit trees—by building a fence from one corner of the field to the opposite corner. If the area of the field is 540 square feet and the length of the field is 36 feet, how many feet of fence will Yesenia need to create the divider?

A.   39

B.   51

C.   60

D.   81

E.   102

8. In the following figure, the diameter of the smallest circle is 2 inches, and each of the other circles has a radius 1 inch larger than the previous. What percent of the total area is the area of the shaded region?

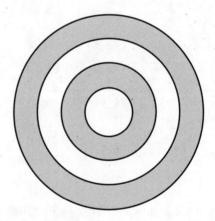

F.   25

G.   37.5

H.   50

J.   62.5

K.   75

9. The opening of a perfectly cylindrical sewer tunnel has a circumference of 8π. The tunnel has a volume of $2{,}048\pi$ cubic feet. How many feet long is the tunnel?

   A.   44

   B.   62

   C.   84

   D.   128

   E.   156

10. In the following figure, point C is the center of the circle, and the measure of angle D is $37°$. Which of the following expresses the length of the radius?

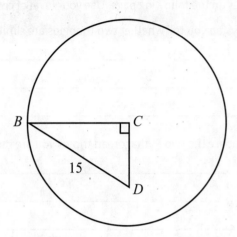

   F. $15 \sin 53°$

   G. $15 \sin 37°$

   H. $15 \cos 37°$

   J. $15 \tan 53°$

   K. $15 \tan 37°$

Reflect

Directions: Take a few minutes to recall what you've learned and what you've been practicing in this chapter. Consider the following questions, jot down your best answer for each one, and then compare your reflections to the expert responses on the following page. Use your level of confidence to determine what to do next.

1. How can you tell whether two triangles are similar?

   _____

   _____

   _____

2. What are the two Pythagorean triples you are most likely to see on test day?

   _____

   _____

   _____

3. What are the ratios of the side lengths of a 45-45-90 triangle? Of a 30-60-90 triangle?

   _____

   _____

   _____

4. When doing unit conversions, how can you make sure you're doing them correctly?

   _____

   _____

   _____

5. What is the standard form for the equation of a circle?

   _____

   _____

   _____

6. What is the relationship of a circle's central angle to the arc and sector the angle defines?

   _____

   _____

   _____

7. How would you find the surface area of a right triangular prism with equilateral triangles as its bases?

   _____

   _____

   _____

Responses

1. How can you tell whether two triangles are similar?

There are three ways to tell:

- *Two of their three angles are congruent (angle-angle).*
- *Two of their three sides are in the same proportion and the intervening angle is congruent (side-angle-side).*
- *Their three sides are in the same proportion (side-side-side).*

2. What are the two Pythagorean triples you are most likely to see on test day?

The two most common Pythagorean triples on the ACT are 3:4:5 and 5:12:13. You may also see multiples of these, e.g., 6:8:10 or 10:24:26.

3. What are the ratios of the side lengths of a 45-45-90 triangle? Of a 30-60-90 triangle?

The side lengths of a 45-45-90 triangle are always in the ratio of $x:x:x\sqrt{2}$. The side lengths of a 30-60-90 triangle are always in the ratio of $x:x\sqrt{3}:2x$. Remember that the shortest side of any triangle is across from the smallest angle, and the longest side is across from the greatest angle.

4. When doing unit conversions, how can you make sure you're doing them correctly?

To do unit conversions correctly, set up the conversion in whichever way makes units cancel. For example, to convert 3 feet into inches, you multiply 3 feet by 12 inches per foot, because it cancels out the feet unit. If instead you multiplied 3 feet by 1 foot per 12 inches, then the resulting units would be "feet squared per inch," which makes no sense.

5. What is the standard form for the equation of a circle?

The equation of a circle in the coordinate plane is $(x - h)^2 + (y - k)^2 = r^2$, where r is the radius of the circle, and (h,k) is the ordered pair representing its center.

6. What is the relationship of a circle's central angle to the arc and sector the angle defines?

The central angle, the arc, and the sector are all in proportion to the full circle:

$$\text{central angle} = \frac{\text{arc length}}{\text{circumference}} = \frac{\text{sector area}}{\text{circle area}}$$

7. How would you find the surface area of a right triangular prism with equilateral triangles as its bases?

Calculate the area of one of the equilateral triangles and multiply by 2. Calculate the area of one of the rectangular faces and multiply by 3. Then add the results.

Next Steps

If you answered most questions correctly in the "How Much Have You Learned?" section, and if your responses to the Reflect questions were similar to those of the ACT expert, then consider Geometry an area of strength and move on to the next chapter. Come back to this topic periodically to prevent yourself from getting rusty.

If you don't yet feel confident, review those parts of this chapter that you have not yet mastered. In particular, review the lessons on triangles, as these are important shapes on the ACT. Then, try the questions you missed again. As always, be sure to review the explanations closely. Then go online (**kaptest.com/login**) to watch video lessons about the highest-yield concepts in this chapter and to use your Qbank for more practice. If you haven't already registered your book, do so at **kaptest.com/moreonline**.

GO ONLINE

kaptest.com/login

Math

Answers and Explanations

Lines and Angles

Drill Answers

a. 36°

b. 120°

c. 50°

d. 70°

e. 65°

1. C

Difficulty: Low

Category: Geometry

Getting to the Answer: To answer questions about angles formed when a transversal cuts parallel lines, figure out which angles are equal and which are supplementary. Remember that when a transversal crosses two parallel lines, all the acute angles are equal and all the obtuse angles are equal. Here, $\angle CRP = \angle ATR$ because $\overline{CD}$ and $\overline{AB}$ are parallel. $\angle ATR$ and $\angle ATQ$ are supplementary, so the measure of $\angle ATQ = 180° - 110° = 70°$. Choice (C) is correct.

2. H

Difficulty: Low

Category: Geometry

Getting to the Answer: Because lines a and b are perpendicular, the lines form four 90° angles. Line c, which passes through the intersection of lines a and b, creates two sets of vertical angles. The angle across from the angle that is $y°$ also equals $y°$, and the angle across from the angle that is $x°$ equals $x°$. Thus, $x° + y° = 90°$. Solving for y in terms of x gives $y = (90 - x)°$. Choice (H) is correct.

3. C

Difficulty: Medium

Category: Geometry

Getting to the Answer: Because $\overline{OL} = \overline{NM}$ and $\overline{LM} = \overline{ON}$, $\overline{LM}$ and $\overline{ON}$ must be parallel lines, making $\overline{LN}$ a transversal. Angles b and c are opposite interior angles, which means that they have congruent angle measures. Although you can calculate the actual values of b and c, the fact that $b = c$ means that $b - c$ will always equal 0, regardless of the actual angle measures. Choice (C) is correct.

4. J

Difficulty: Low

Category: Geometry

Getting to the Answer: In a quadrilateral, the sum of the interior angles is 360°. Thus, $\angle A + 2x° + 90° + 3x° = 360°$. Solving for $\angle A$ in terms of x gives $\angle A = 360° - 90° - 2x° - 3x°$. Thus, $\angle A = 270° - 5x°$, and (J) is correct.

5. B

Difficulty: Low

Category: Geometry

Getting to the Answer: Use the properties of supplementary angles to find the measures of $\angle DBC$ and $\angle BDC$: $\angle DBC = 180° - 45° = 135°$ and $\angle BDC = 180° - 155° = 25°$. The sum of the interior angles in a triangle equals 180°, so $\angle BCD = 180° - (135° + 25°) = 20°$. Choice (B) is correct.

Triangle Properties

1. D

Difficulty: Medium

Category: Geometry

Getting to the Answer: Since $\overline{DF} = \overline{DE} = \overline{FE}$, $\triangle DFE$ is an equilateral triangle and all the interior angles are 60°. $\overline{DE}$ is parallel to $\overline{AC}$, so $\angle FDE$ and $\angle DAB$ are corresponding angles. Thus, $\angle DAB$ is also 60°. Choice (D) is correct.

2. J

Difficulty: Low

Category: Geometry

Getting to the Answer: The question asks for the measure of $\angle ABC$. You know that $\overline{AB}$ and $\overline{BC}$ are congruent sides of $\triangle ABC$ and that $m\angle CAB = 27°$. Sketch out $\triangle ABC$ to visualize this information.

Because $\overline{AB}$ and $\overline{BC}$ are congruent, $m\angle ACB$ must also equal 27°. The sum of the measures of the interior angles of a triangle is 180°. Therefore, find $m\angle ACB$ by subtracting $2 \times 27°$ from 180°: $m\angle ABC = 180° - 54° = 126°$. You found the measure of $\angle ABC$, so you are done. Choice (J) is correct.

3. E
Difficulty: Medium
Category: Geometry
Getting to the Answer: The measures of the angles of a triangle sum to 180°. You can use the given ratio to represent the relative sizes of the angles. For example, if x equals one "part," the measures of the angles can be represented by $2x$, $3x$, and $7x$. To find the size of one part, solve the equation $2x + 3x + 7x = 180°$. This simplifies to $12x = 180°$, or $x = 15°$. Be careful; this is not the answer. The question asks for the measure of the largest angle, which is $7x = 7(15) = 105°$. Choice (E) is correct.

4. G
Difficulty: Low
Category: Geometry
Getting to the Answer: The altitude is the perpendicular line from a vertex to the opposite side of the triangle. Thus, the length of the altitude from X to $\overline{YZ}$ is 4. Choice (G) is correct.

5. B
Difficulty: High
Category: Geometry
Getting to the Answer: When two triangles have two equal angles, they are similar triangles. When you notice a triangle within a triangle, like the one in this figure, pay special attention to the angles that are shared by both triangles.

The triangle with hypotenuse b that is formed by the dotted line is similar to $\triangle PQR$. This is because they both contain a right angle and both have angle R in common. The sides of this smaller triangle, therefore, will be in proportion to the sides of $\triangle PQR$. Your job is to evaluate the answer choices to find which ratio describes the ratio of the smaller triangle to $\triangle PQR$.

Side d is the shortest side of the smaller triangle, and a is the shortest side of $\triangle PQR$. Side c is the longer leg of the smaller triangle, and b is the longer leg of $\triangle PQR$. Therefore, the ratio between the two pairs of sides is the same, and $\dfrac{d}{a} = \dfrac{b}{c}$. Choice (B) is correct.

Right Triangles

1. C
Difficulty: Medium
Category: Geometry
Getting to the Answer: Triangle ABC is a 30-60-90 triangle, and side AB is across from the 60° angle. Set up a proportion using the ratio of the sides in a 30-60-90 triangle, $x{:}x\sqrt{3}{:}2x$, to find the length of AB:

$$\frac{\sqrt{3}}{2} = \frac{AB}{20}$$
$$20\sqrt{3} = 2AB$$
$$10\sqrt{3} = AB$$

Choice (C) is correct.

2. H
Difficulty: Medium
Category: Geometry
Getting to the Answer: The diagonal of the square tile is also the hypotenuse of two 45-45-90 triangles.

Use the ratio of the sides in a 45-45-90 triangle, $x{:}x{:}x\sqrt{2}$, to set up a proportion to determine the side length of the square. Let s be the side of the square:

$$\frac{s}{18} = \frac{1}{\sqrt{2}}$$
$$\sqrt{2}s = 18$$
$$s = \frac{18}{\sqrt{2}}$$

Rationalize this expression by multiplying the numerator and denominator by $\sqrt{2}$: $\dfrac{18}{\sqrt{2}} \times \dfrac{\sqrt{2}}{\sqrt{2}} = \dfrac{18\sqrt{2}}{2} = 9\sqrt{2}$. Choice (H) is correct.

Math

3. C
Difficulty: Low
Category: Geometry
Getting to the Answer: Since the length of the shorter leg is 6 inches and the length of the longer leg is twice the length of the shorter leg, the length of the longer leg is $2 \times 6 = 12$. Use the Pythagorean theorem, $a^2 + b^2 = c^2$, to find the hypotenuse c:
$c = \sqrt{6^2 + 12^2} = \sqrt{36 + 144} = \sqrt{180} = 6\sqrt{5}$. Choice (C) is correct.

4. J
Difficulty: Low
Category: Geometry
Getting to the Answer: The figure shown is a right triangle. The length of the hypotenuse equals the length of the slide, which is 10 feet, and the length of the long leg equals the distance between the base of the slide and the ladder, which is 8 feet. Since you are given two of the sides, you can use the Pythagorean theorem, $a^2 + b^2 = c^2$, to determine the third side. Let a equal the height of the ladder:

$$a = \sqrt{c^2 - b^2}$$
$$= \sqrt{10^2 - 8^2}$$
$$= \sqrt{36}$$
$$= 6$$

Choice (J) is correct.

If you recognized that the sides were a multiple of the Pythagorean triple 3:4:5, then you could avoid using the Pythagorean theorem and quickly see that the third side must be $3 \times 2 = 6$.

5. D
Difficulty: Medium
Category: Geometry
Getting to the Answer: In the figure above, $\overline{AB}$ is the hypotenuse of a right triangle. $\overline{AC}$ is 4 units and $\overline{CB}$ is 6 units, so use the Pythagorean theorem, $a^2 + b^2 = c^2$, to find the length of $\overline{AB}$:

$$c = \sqrt{a^2 + b^2}$$
$$= \sqrt{4^2 + 6^2}$$
$$= \sqrt{52}$$
$$= \sqrt{4}\sqrt{13}$$
$$= 2\sqrt{13}$$

Choice (D) is correct.

Alternatively, you could use the distance formula, which is derived from the Pythagorean theorem: $d = \sqrt{(y_2 - y_1)^2 + (x_2 - x_1)^2}$. The distance between points A and B is therefore $d = \sqrt{(1-5)^2 + (7-1)^2} = 2\sqrt{13}$.

Polygons

Drill Answers

a. 14
b. 12
c. 12
d. 14
e. 14

1. C
Difficulty: Medium
Category: Geometry
Getting to the Answer: First, use $A_{triangle} = \frac{1}{2}bh$ to calculate the area of $\triangle PQR$: $A_{PQR} = \frac{1}{2}(16)(10) = 80$. Then, determine the area of the square. Since the area of square $ABCD$ is twice the area of $\triangle PQR$, the area of square $ABCD$ is $2 \times 80 = 160$. Use $A_{square} = s^2$ to determine the length of a side: $s = \sqrt{160} = \sqrt{16}\sqrt{10} = 4\sqrt{10}$, which is (C).

2. G
Difficulty: Low
Category: Geometry
Getting to the Answer: Use the formula $A = bh$ to determine the area of the parallelogram. The length of the base, b, is the distance between -2 and 4, which is 6. The height, h, is the perpendicular distance from the base to the top of the parallelogram, which is the change in the y-coordinate values: $5 - 2 = 3$. Thus, the area is $6 \times 3 = 18$ square units, which matches (G).

3. C
Difficulty: Low
Category: Geometry
Getting to the Answer: Imagine moving the short horizontal side to the top of the polygon to form a rectangle that is 10 meters by 12.5 meters. Then, add the perimeter of that rectangle to the two sides that are 7.5 meters to get the perimeter of the polygon:

$2(10) + 2(12.5) + 2(7.5) = 60$ m. Finally, use 1 meter = 100 centimeters to convert 60 meters to centimeters: $60 \text{ m} \times \dfrac{100 \text{ cm}}{1 \text{ m}} = 6{,}000$ cm. Choice (C) is correct.

4.   K
Difficulty: Medium
Category: Geometry
Getting to the Answer: The formula for the area of a trapezoid is $A = \left(\dfrac{b_1 + b_2}{2}\right)h$, where b_1 and b_2 are the lengths of the parallel sides. You could also think of this formula as the height times the average of the bases.

You are given the height (3 inches), one base (8 inches), and enough information to determine the other base. Notice that $\triangle ABE$ is a 3-4-5 triangle, so $AE = 4$ inches. And if you were to drop an altitude down from point C, you'd get another 3-4-5 triangle on the right:

Now you can see that the bottom base is 16 inches. Plug these numbers into the area formula:

$$A = \left(\dfrac{b_1 + b_2}{2}\right)h$$
$$= \left(\dfrac{8 + 16}{2}\right) \times 3$$
$$= 12 \times 3$$
$$= 36$$

The answer is (K).

If you don't remember the area formula on test day, you can also just find the areas of the two side triangles and the rectangle in the middle and add them all up.

5.   A
Difficulty: Medium
Category: Geometry
Getting to the Answer: Picking Numbers can make a theoretical question like this much more concrete. If you are not sure which answer choice makes the most sense, assume that each side starts with length 1 and try each answer choice out. The area starts as $1 \times 1 = 1$, so triple the area is 3. Begin testing with the middle answer choice:

C: area $= (1 \times 9)(1 \times 9) = 81$. This is too big, so try a smaller choice.

B: area $= (1 \times 3)(1 \times 3) = 9$. Still too big.

(A): area $= (1 \times \sqrt{3})(1 \times \sqrt{3}) = \sqrt{3} \times \sqrt{3} = 3$.

Choice (A) is correct.

Circles and Parabolas

1.   C
Difficulty: Medium
Category: Geometry
Getting to the Answer: You need to find the area of the circle, and you are given the circumference of the circle. As with most circle questions, the first thing you need to do is find the radius. Use the given circumference and the circumference formula to find r.

$$C = 2\pi r$$
$$8\pi = 2\pi r$$
$$4 = r$$

Now you can use the radius to find the area: $A = \pi r^2 = \pi(4)^2 = 16\pi$. You found the area, 16π, so you are done. Choice (C) is correct.

2.   K
Difficulty: Medium
Category: Geometry
Getting to the Answer: The area of the shaded region can be determined by subtracting the area of the smaller circle from the area of the larger circle. First, find the radius of the larger circle. Then, use $A = \pi r^2$ to calculate the area of each circle. Finally, find the difference in areas.

Since the radius of the larger circle is 75% greater than that of the smaller circle, the radius of the larger circle is $4 + 4 \times 0.75 = 7$. The area of the smaller circle is $\pi(4)^2 = 16\pi$, and the area of the larger circle is $\pi(7)^2 = 49\pi$. This means the area of the shaded region is $49\pi - 16\pi = 33\pi$ square feet. Choice (K) is correct.

3.   D
Difficulty: High
Category: Geometry
Getting to the Answer: Think logically to answer this question. Because Earth makes a complete rotation about its axis in 24 hours, any point on the equator must rotate through $360°$ during that time.

Quito rotates 360° in the 24 hours from noon on January 1 to noon on January 2. There are 3 hours between noon on January 2 and 3:00 p.m. on January 2, so it rotates an additional $\frac{3}{24} \times 360° = 45°$, for a total of $360° + 45° = 405°$. Choice (D) is correct.

4. J
Difficulty: High
Category: Geometry
Getting to the Answer: The set of points described in the question stem form a circle centered at $(-3,4)$. The distance of 5 represents the length of its radius. This means that you have everything you need to use the standard equation for a circle with center (h,k) and radius r. The equation is:

$$(x - h)^2 + (y - k)^2 = r^2$$
$$(x - (-3))^2 + (y - 4)^2 = 5^2$$
$$(x + 3)^2 + (y - 4)^2 = 25$$

The answer is (J).

5. A
Difficulty: Medium
Category: Geometry
Getting to the Answer: To find the solutions for x, set the equation equal to 0 and solve for x.

$$0 = (x + 3)^2 - 1$$
$$1 = (x + 3)^2$$
$$\sqrt{1} = x + 3$$
$$\pm 1 = x + 3$$
$$-4 \text{ and } -2 = x$$

Both values of x are negative, so (A) is correct.

Alternatively, you could graph the equation. The solutions for x are the x-intercepts of the graph. In this graph, the parabola intersects the x-axis in two places, both to the left of the origin. This means that the equation has two different negative real solutions:

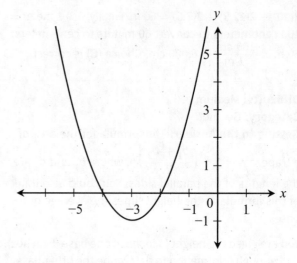

Choice (A) is correct.

Complex Two-Dimensional Figures

1. A
Difficulty: High
Category: Geometry
Getting to the Answer: The difference in areas of the shaded portion between the two layouts arises solely from the different desk shapes. Thus, you need to calculate the difference in the cross-sectional area of the desks only. The triangular desk in Layout 1 has an area of $\frac{1}{2}bh = \frac{1}{2}(4)(4) = 8$ square feet. The rectangular desk in Layout 2 has an area of $l \times w = 5 \times 2 = 10$ square feet. The difference in the areas of the desks, and therefore of the shaded portions between the layouts, is $10 - 8 = 2$ square feet, which matches (A).

2. F
Difficulty: Medium
Category: Geometry
Getting to the Answer: A scale can be written in the form of a fraction. The question states that the scale here is $\frac{3}{4}$ inches to 9 feet, which can be written as $\frac{\frac{3}{4}}{9}$.

To find the area, in square inches, of each table in the scale drawing, first set up a proportion to solve for the diameter of the table in the scale drawing.

$$\frac{\frac{3}{4} \text{ inch}}{9 \text{ feet}} = \frac{x \text{ inch}}{6 \text{ feet}}$$

$$\frac{18}{4} = 9x$$

$$\frac{1}{2} = x$$

The diameter is x, so the radius is $\frac{1}{2} \div 2 = \frac{1}{4}$. Finally, calculate the area of a table using πr^2:

$A = \pi \left(\frac{1}{4}\right)^2 = \frac{1}{16}\pi$. Choice (F) is correct.

3. D
Difficulty: Medium
Category: Geometry
Getting to the Answer: Because the question does not provide you with a figure, draw one to visualize what you are being asked.

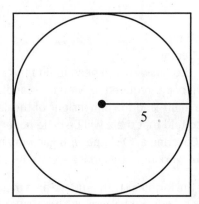

The circle is inscribed within the square, so its radius is half the side of the square. The circle has a radius of 5, so the square has a side of $2 \times 5 = 10$. Therefore, the area of the circle is $5^2\pi = 25\pi$, and the area of the square is $10^2 = 100$. The difference between the area of the square and the area of the circle is thus $100 - 25\pi$, which is (D).

4. K
Difficulty: High
Category: Geometry
Getting to the Answer: You want to find the perimeter of the triangle. Unfortunately, you do not have much concrete information about it yet. Instead, start with what you know about the shaded square. Because its area is 12, each side must be $\sqrt{12} = \sqrt{4}\sqrt{3} = 2\sqrt{3}$. Jot this down because you'll need it later.

Triangle ABC is an equilateral triangle, so each of its interior angles measures $60°$. This means that the two vertical sides of the square each represent the longer leg of a 30-60-90 triangle (the small white triangles on the sides).

Use the ratio of the sides, $x{:}x\sqrt{3}{:}2x$, to determine the length of the short leg. Since the length of the long leg is $2\sqrt{3}$, the short legs are each 2. You now have the length of the base of the large equilateral triangle: $2 + 2\sqrt{3} + 2 = 4 + 2\sqrt{3}$.

Because the triangle is equilateral, each side of the triangle has length $4 + 2\sqrt{3}$. The perimeter is the sum of all three sides, so multiply the side length by 3 to get $12 + 6\sqrt{3}$. Choice (K) is correct.

5. E
Difficulty: High
Category: Geometry
Getting to the Answer: You need to determine the shortest distance between the two chords in terms of r. You are told that $\overline{WX}$ is the diameter and that $\overline{YZ}$ is 25% smaller than $\overline{WX}$. One of the simplest ways to discover new information in tough geometry questions is to draw additional lines. Start with an additional radius (call it r) that extends from the center of the diameter of the semicircle to $\overline{YZ}$. Then add a line that represents the shortest distance between the two chords. This creates a right triangle.

You know that $\overline{YZ}$ is 25% shorter than $\overline{WX}$, so $\overline{YZ} = \frac{3}{4}\overline{WX}$. Since $\overline{WX}$ is the diameter of the circle, $\overline{WX} = 2r$. Combine these two equations to determine the other side of the right triangle, $\frac{1}{2}\overline{YZ}$:

$$\overline{YZ} = \frac{3}{4}\overline{WZ}$$

$$\overline{YZ} = \frac{3}{4}(2r)$$

$$\overline{YZ} = \frac{3}{2}r$$

$$\frac{1}{2}\overline{YZ} = \frac{3}{4}r$$

You now have two of the three sides of the right triangle and can solve for the third using the Pythagorean theorem.

$$\left(\frac{3}{4}r\right)^2 + s^2 = r^2$$

$$\frac{9}{16}r^2 + s^2 = r^2$$

$$s^2 = \frac{16}{16}r^2 - \frac{9}{16}r^2$$

$$s^2 = \frac{7}{16}r^2$$

$$s = \pm\frac{\sqrt{7}}{4}r$$

Distance can't be negative, so (E) is the correct answer.

Three-Dimensional Figures

1. E
Difficulty: Medium
Category: Geometry
Getting to the Answer: You need to determine the amount of paint that Hawanatu needs in square inches. You are given a rectangular prism with several dimensions. Jot these down: $l = 30$, $w = 3$, $h = 5$. The amount of paint needed to cover the surface is the same as the total surface area of the solid. Use $SA = 2(wl + hl + hw)$ to find the amount of paint needed: $2[3(30) + 5(30) + 5(3)] = 2(90 + 150 + 15) = 510$ square inches. Choice (E) is correct.

2. F
Difficulty: High
Category: Geometry
Getting to the Answer: You need to find the volume of the solid. You are told that the solid is half a cube, and you are given the length of one part. Since the shape is half a cube, the perpendicular edges are equal and form the legs of a 45-45-90 triangle. Use the ratio of the sides, $x{:}x{:}x\sqrt{2}$, to determine the length of the legs (and the edges of the half cube). Since the hypotenuse is $2\sqrt{2}$, the length of the leg is 2.

The volume of the whole cube is $V_{cube} = s^3 = (2)^3 = 8$. Thus, the volume of the half-cube figure is 4. Choice (F) is correct.

3. D
Difficulty: Medium
Category: Geometry
Getting to the Answer: Your task is straightforward: find the volume of the cylinder. You are given a figure that includes the dimensions $r = 4$ and $h = 5$. The volume of a cylinder is the area of its base (a circle) times its height. Jot down the formula and fill in the given dimensions: $V = \pi r^2 h = \pi(4)^2(5)$. This expression simplifies to $V = 80\pi$ cubic inches. Choice (D) is correct.

4. J
Difficulty: High
Category: Geometry
Getting to the Answer: You need to find the amount of wrapping paper required to wrap one candle. You are given a figure and the dimensions of the candle. You are also told that there will be extra paper on each end. Covering a 3D shape with gift wrap means that you are working with surface area.

Recall that the formula for the surface area of a cylinder is $2\pi r^2 + 2\pi rh$, but be careful. The circular top and bottom of the candle will not be covered, so the surface area of the gift wrap is just $2\pi rh$. You are given that the diameter of the candle is 4 inches, so assuming the thickness of the gift wrap is negligible, $r = 2$ inches. Since Mali wants the gift wrap to be 3 inches past the top and bottom of the candle, the height of the gift wrap is $h = 3 + 8 + 3 = 14$ inches. Plug these numbers into $2\pi rh$ and simplify: $2\pi(2)(14) = 56\pi$ square inches. Check that your answer is in the correct units. Choice (J) is correct.

5. B

Difficulty: Medium

Category: Geometry

Getting to the Answer: To find the volume of the figurine, you need to find the change in the volume of the water after placing the figurine in the water. After the figurine is submerged, the height of the water rises 0.4 inches, but the length and width do not change. You can multiply these dimensions by a height of 0.4 to find the volume of the figurine: $10 \times 13 \times 0.4 = 52$ cubic inches. Choice (B) is correct.

Alternatively, you could determine the volume before and after the figurine is submerged and then calculate the difference:

$$V_{before} = 10(13)(5)$$
$$= 650$$
$$V_{after} = 10(13)(5.4)$$
$$= 702$$
$$V_{after} - V_{before} = 702 - 650$$
$$= 52$$

As expected, this matches (B).

Triangles and Trigonometry

1. B

Difficulty: High

Category: Geometry

Getting to the Answer: The question asks you to find the values of θ when $\sin \theta = \frac{1}{2}$. Use the unit circle to determine that for θ between 0 and π, $\sin \theta = \frac{1}{2}$ occurs when $\theta = \frac{\pi}{6}$ and $\frac{5\pi}{6}$. This matches (B).

If you do not know the unit circle by memory, draw a sketch. Since θ is between 0 and π, draw θ in Quadrants I and II.

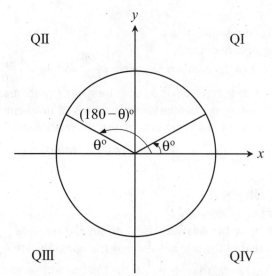

Recall that the definition of sine is $\frac{\text{opposite}}{\text{hypotenuse}}$. Form a right triangle using θ and label the opposite side 1 and the hypotenuse 2. Note that these sides correspond to those of a 30-60-90 triangle. Use the ratio of the sides, $x:x\sqrt{3}:2x$, to determine θ. The angle opposite 1 is 30°. Thus, $\theta = 30°$ and $180° - 30° = 150°$.

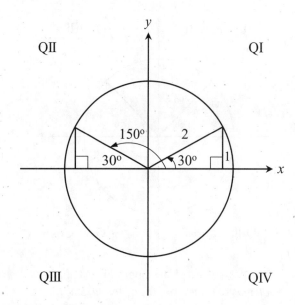

Convert your answer into radians using the conversion factor $180° = \pi$ radians: $30° = \frac{\pi}{6}$ and $150° = \frac{5\pi}{6}$. Finally, double-check that you used the correct interval for θ. Choice (B) is correct.

2.   F
Difficulty: Medium
Category: Geometry
Getting to the Answer: Since $\cos = \dfrac{adj}{hyp}$ and $\sin = \dfrac{opp}{hyp}$, the side adjacent to β is 36 units long, the hypotenuse is 39 units long, and the side opposite is 15 units long. To determine the value of tanβ, use the relationship $\tan = \dfrac{opp}{adj}$: $\tan\beta = \dfrac{15}{36}$, so choice (F) is correct.

3.   E
Difficulty: High
Category: Geometry
Getting to the Answer: Use $\frac{1}{2}ab\sin x$ to compare the areas of the original and new triangles. The area of the original triangle is $\frac{1}{2}fg\sin 135°$, and the area of the new triangle is $\frac{1}{2}fg\sin 45°$. The only difference is the angle.

On the unit circle, 45°, which is between 0° and 90°, is in Quadrant I, and 135°, which is between 90° and 180°, is in Quadrant II. Note that 180° − 135° = 45°.

You might have heard of the mnemonic *All Students Take Calculus* to remember the order *All, Sin, Tan, Cos* as you move counter-clockwise around the unit circle; like PEMDAS, there are multiple mnemonics that can be used to remember this information. In Quadrants I and II, sin is positive. Therefore, $\sin(135°) = \sin(45°)$, and the areas are equal. The new area is also 60 square centimeters, so (E) is correct.

4.   K
Difficulty: High
Category: Geometry
Getting to the Answer: On test day, be on the lookout for questions that simply ask you to plug values into a given formula. They may look tough, but they don't require you to do much thinking.

Here, the question is asking for the expression that represents the value of z. Since you know the values of two of the three angles in the triangle, you can deduce that the unmarked angle has a measure of 180° − 35° − 45° = 100°. You are given the length of $\overline{DS}$ along with its opposite angle, so plug that information into the law of sines to solve for z:

$$\frac{\sin 45°}{7} = \frac{\sin 100°}{z}$$
$$z\sin 45° = 7\sin 100°$$
$$z = \frac{7\sin 100°}{\sin 45°}$$

Choice (K) is correct.

5.   D
Difficulty: High
Category: Geometry
Getting to the Answer: For $\triangle EFG$, $\overline{FG} = 16$, $\overline{EF} = 4$, and $\angle F = 70°$. Use the second formula, $c^2 = a^2 + b^2 - 2ab\cos C$, to find $\overline{EG}$:

$$\overline{EG} = \sqrt{e^2 + g^2 - 2eg\cos F}$$
$$= \sqrt{16^2 + 4^2 - 2(16)(4)\cos 70°}$$

This matches (D).

On Test Day

1.   A
Difficulty: High
Category: Geometry
Getting to the Answer: The difference in the areas of the shaded portion between the two layouts arises solely from the different desk shapes. Thus, you need to calculate the difference in the cross-sectional area of the desks only; ignore the other furniture. The triangular desk in Layout 1 has an area of $\frac{1}{2}bh = (4)(4) = 8$ square feet. The rectangular desk in Layout 2

has an area of $l \times w = 5 \times 2 = 10$ square feet. The difference in the areas of the desks, and therefore of the shaded portions between the layouts, is $10 - 8 = 2$ square feet, which matches (A).

How Much Have You Learned?

1. C
Difficulty: Medium
Category: Geometry
Getting to the Answer: Since $\overline{LM} = \overline{MN} = \overline{NL}$, $\triangle MNL$ is an equilateral triangle. Thus, each interior angle is 60°. Vertical angles are congruent, so $\angle PNO$, which is opposite $\angle MNL$, also has a measure of 60°. The sum of the measures of the interior angles of a triangle is always 180°. Therefore, $\angle NOP = 180° - 60° - 100° = 20°$, which is (C).

2. J
Difficulty: Low
Category: Geometry
Getting to the Answer: The corresponding sides in similar triangles are proportional. Since the perimeter is the sum of all the sides, the perimeters are proportional as well. Set up the following equation to solve for the perimeter of the smaller triangle, denoted by

x: $\dfrac{\text{perimeter smaller}}{\text{perimeter larger}} = \dfrac{4}{7} = \dfrac{x}{10 + 12 + 13}$.

$$\frac{4}{7} = \frac{x}{35}$$
$$140 = 7x$$
$$20 = x$$

The correct answer is (J).

3. C
Difficulty: Medium
Category: Geometry
Getting to the Answer: You are asked to find the number of miles that Keesha and Dwayne will hike on their way to the summit. You are given verbal descriptions of the hikers' paths to the summit, but it is much easier to understand the situation if you draw a diagram of Keesha and Dwayne's routes. After drawing and labeling the diagram with the information given, look for a way to create a right triangle by drawing in additional lines. Then, fill in the lengths of any new segments that you draw.

Use the Pythagorean theorem to calculate the distance that Dwayne hikes.

$$c^2 = (5 + 7)^2 + 4^2$$
$$c^2 = 144 + 16$$
$$c^2 = 160$$
$$c = \sqrt{160}$$

You're not done yet! The question asks you to find the total distance the two hikers travel. Keesha traveled $5 + 6 + 7 + 2 = 20$ miles. So, the total distance is $\sqrt{160} + 20 = 32.65$ miles. Choice (C) is correct.

4. G
Difficulty: Medium
Category: Geometry
Getting to the Answer: Before you rush to the Pythagorean theorem, note that 18 and 24 fit the pattern of a 3:4:5 Pythagorean triple that has been multiplied by 6: $(3:4:5) \times 6 = 18:24:30$. This means that $\overline{WY}$ is 30, but the question asks for the length of $\overline{WZ}$. Since Z is the midpoint of $\overline{WY}$, $\overline{WZ}$ is half of 30, or 15. Choice (G) is correct.

5. D
Difficulty: Medium
Category: Geometry
Getting to the Answer: Since $\angle CDB$ and $\angle BDE$ are on a straight line, they are supplementary. Because $\angle CDB$ is 90°, $\angle BDE$ is also 90°. The sum of the interior angles of a triangle equals 180°, so $\angle EBD$ is $180° - 90° - 17° = 73°$. Because $\overline{CD} = \overline{BD}$, $\triangle CDB$ is a 45-45-90 triangle. Thus, $\angle DBC = 45°$. Angles ABC, DBC, and EBD are supplementary, so $\angle ABC = 180° - 73° - 45° = 62°$. This matches (D).

6. G
Difficulty: Low
Category: Geometry
Getting to the Answer: To determine the total amount of molding needed, find the perimeter of the floor. Notice that the diagonal is the hypotenuse of a triangle that has a height of $15 - 9 = 6$ feet and a base of $30 - 22 = 8$ feet.

If you do not recognize the Pythagorean triple $(3:4:5) \times 2 = 6:8:10$, use the Pythagorean theorem $(a^2 + b^2 = c^2)$ to calculate the hypotenuse.

$$c^2 = 8^2 + 6^2$$
$$c^2 = 100$$
$$c = 10$$

Add up all the sides to calculate the total length of molding Akanksha needs: $15 + 9 + 30 + 22 + 10 = 86$ feet. Choice (G) is correct.

7. A
Difficulty: Low
Category: Geometry
Getting to the Answer: You need to find the length of the fence. You are told that the orchard is rectangular and that Yesenia will split it diagonally into two triangles. You're also given some dimensions: $A = 540$ square feet and $l = 36$ feet.

Draw and label a figure to visualize the situation.

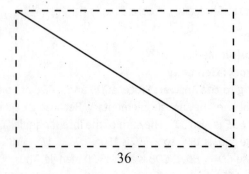

The area of a rectangle is the product of its length and width. Because you know the length and the area, you can find the width:

$$A = lw$$
$$540 = 36w$$
$$15 = w$$

Add the width to the diagram. Now you know that the fence is the hypotenuse of a right triangle with legs of lengths 15 and 36. Before turning to the Pythagorean theorem, look for a Pythagorean triplet to save time. Indeed, this is a 5-12-13 triangle multiplied by 3. Therefore, the hypotenuse—and the amount of fence needed—is $13 \times 3 = 39$ feet, which is (A).

If you didn't recognize this fact, you could also have plugged these numbers into the Pythagorean theorem, $a^2 + b^2 = c^2$.

$$c^2 = 15^2 + 36^2$$
$$c^2 = 225 + 1,296$$
$$c = \sqrt{1,521}$$
$$= 39$$

8. J
Difficulty: High
Category: Geometry
Getting to the Answer: First, determine the radius of each circle. Starting from the innermost circle, the radii for the circles are 1, 2, 3, and 4 inches, respectively.

The area of the smaller shaded ring is the area of the small shaded circle minus the small white circle: $4\pi - \pi = 3\pi$ square inches. The area of the larger shaded ring is the area of the larger shaded circle minus the larger white circle: $16\pi - 9\pi = 7\pi$ square inches.

The total area of the shaded region is therefore the sum of the shaded areas: $3\pi + 7\pi = 10\pi$ square inches.

Finally, calculate the percent of the total area the shaded area represents using the formula $\frac{\text{part}}{\text{whole}} \times 100\%$. Thus, the percent is $\frac{10\pi}{16\pi} \times 100\% = \frac{5}{8} \times 100\% = 62.5\%$. Choice (J) is correct.

9. D
Difficulty: Medium
Category: Geometry
Getting to the Answer: The question tells you that the circumference of the opening (which is a circle) is 8π, so substitute this value into the formula for circumference and solve for r:

$$C = 2\pi r$$
$$8\pi = 2\pi r$$
$$4 = r$$

You can now find h, which represents the length of the tunnel. Use the formula $V = \pi r^2 h$:

$$2{,}048\pi = \pi(4)^2(h)$$
$$2{,}048 = 16h$$
$$128 = h$$

The tunnel is 128 feet long, which is (D).

10. G
Difficulty: High
Category: Geometry
Getting to the Answer: Remembering the acronym SOHCAHTOA can get you through a lot of trig questions. This question is asking for the length of $\overline{BC}$. The only length you are given is that of the hypotenuse of the triangle, so start by checking for either a cosine or sine relationship (since the tangent part of the acronym, TOA, does not involve the hypotenuse). Since $\overline{BC}$ is opposite $\angle D$, the 37° angle, you can set up an equation involving sin 37°:

$$\sin = \frac{\text{opp}}{\text{hyp}}$$
$$\sin(37°) = \frac{BC}{15}$$
$$15 \sin(37°) = BC$$

Choice (G) is correct.

[CHAPTER 14]

ACT MATH: TIMING AND SECTION MANAGEMENT STRATEGIES

LEARNING OBJECTIVE

After this lesson, you will be able to:

- Triage the ACT Math section by making quick decisions about which questions to do and which to skip

ACT Math: Timing and Section Management Strategies

The Math Test has 60 questions to be completed in 60 minutes, which means you'll have one minute per question. This is an average, though. Some questions will be straightforward, meaning that you can get the correct answer in 30 seconds or less. Others will be more difficult and time-consuming. Test takers who start at the beginning of the section, attempt the questions in order, and only move on to the next question when the previous one is complete often find that they get bogged down and don't make it to the end of the section, potentially missing questions that they could have answered correctly. Flexibility can earn you more points.

A better approach is to make your way through the section with a plan to deal with each question. Each time you read a new question, take a moment to gauge your gut reaction:

- Does this question seem quick and easy? Do it immediately.
- Does this question seem time-consuming but manageable? Skip it for now. Put a circle around it, and try it on a second pass through the section.
- Does this question look confusing or difficult? Skip it. Don't worry about circling or marking questions like this. You'll approach them only after you have worked on the other questions in the section, and only if you have time.

Try to make this decision quickly. The more you practice, the easier it will be to recognize which questions are easier and which are more challenging for you.

When you approach a test section this way, you'll end up taking two or three passes through it. This technique ensures that you'll get all of the easy points first, and if you run out of time, you'll know that the questions you didn't attempt were the hardest in the section and would have been tougher to get right anyway.

Before the end of the section, make sure you have something bubbled in for every question since there is no penalty for guessing. Also, be very careful when bubbling your answers. It's easy to skip a question but then forget to skip a line on the grid and bubble your answer to the next question in the incorrect place.

The questions in the Math Test will be in approximate order of difficulty, with the easiest questions at the beginning of the section and the most difficult questions at the end of the section.

If you tend to finish the Math sections early but find that you are making speed mistakes, you may consider pausing at the confirmation step to check your logic and calculations before bubbling your response to each question.

How Much Have You Learned?

Directions: Use this question set to practice effective question triage. Skip those questions that you feel will take too long; come back to them if you have time. Try to get as many questions correct as you can in 15 minutes. As always, be sure to study the explanations, even for questions you got right. They can be found at the end of this chapter.

1. What are the roots of $3x^2 + 5x - 3$?

   A. $\dfrac{5 \pm \sqrt{11}}{3}$

   B. $\dfrac{3 \pm \sqrt{51}}{6}$

   C. $\dfrac{-3 \pm \sqrt{61}}{6}$

   D. $\dfrac{-5 \pm \sqrt{11}}{3}$

   E. $\dfrac{-5 \pm \sqrt{61}}{6}$

2. $\triangle XYZ$ is similar to $\triangle UVW$. If $\overline{XY} = 10$, $\overline{YZ} = 6$, and $\overline{UV} = 15$, then what is the length of $\overline{VW}$?

   F. 3

   G. 6

   H. 9

   J. 17

   K. 25

3. Which of the following is equivalent to $(3 - 8i)(5 + 3i)$?

   A. $39 - 31i$

   B. $-9 - 31i$

   C. $39 + 49i$

   D. $-9 + 49i$

   E. $11 + 3i$

4. A customer of a retail store purchases an item for $23.10 after the 10% tax. If the item was discounted by 30%, what was the original price of the item in dollars?

   F. 24

   G. 26

   H. 28

   J. 30

   K. 33

5. Which of the following is equivalent to tan E?

   A. $\dfrac{4}{7}$

   B. $\dfrac{4}{\sqrt{33}}$

   C. $\dfrac{7}{4}$

   D. $\dfrac{7}{\sqrt{33}}$

   E. $\dfrac{\sqrt{33}}{4}$

6. If the first term of an arithmetic sequence is 3 and the 32nd term is 127, what is the 17th term?

   F. 59

   G. 63

   H. 67

   J. 71

   K. 75

7. A circle has a diameter of 8 feet. If the circle's area were tripled, what would its new radius be in feet?

   A. 5

   B. 6

   C. $4\sqrt{3}$

   D. $8\sqrt{3}$

   E. $\sqrt{30}$

8. Kareem is learning about a standard deck of 52 cards. What is the likelihood that he will pick a red face card after one has already been picked and not replaced back in the deck? (A face card is classified as a Jack, Queen, King, or Ace. There are four of each face card in a standard deck: two black and two red.)

   F. $\dfrac{7}{51}$

   G. $\dfrac{7}{52}$

   H. $\dfrac{8}{51}$

   J. $\dfrac{2}{13}$

   K. $\dfrac{4}{51}$

9. If $a{:}b = 3{:}7$ and $c{:}b = 4{:}5$, what is the ratio of a to c?

   A. 3:4

   B. 3:5

   C. 15:20

   D. 15:28

   E. 28:15

| Use the table below for questions 10–12. |

x	-2	-1	0	1	2
$f(x)$	-6	-2	2	6	10
$g(x)$	4	2	0	-2	-4

10. Which of the following equations describes $f(x)$?

   F. $f(x) = -2x^2 + 5x - 2$

   G. $f(x) = 4x + 2$

   H. $f(x) = 3x^2 - 2x + 4$

   J. $f(x) = -2x - 2$

   K. $f(x) = 3x$

11. What is the value of $f(g(1))$?

   A. -6

   B. -2

   C. 0

   D. 4

   E. 6

12. If the equation for function g is $g(x) = -2x$, then what is the solution that satisfies both $f(x)$ and $g(x)$?

    F. $\left(-\frac{4}{3}, -\frac{2}{3}\right)$

    G. $\left(-\frac{2}{3}, -\frac{1}{3}\right)$

    H. $\left(-\frac{1}{3}, \frac{2}{3}\right)$

    J. $\left(\frac{1}{3}, -\frac{2}{3}\right)$

    K. $\left(\frac{2}{3}, \frac{1}{3}\right)$

13. Suppose $f(x) = x^2$ and $g(x) = (x+4)^2 - 2$. Which of the following points lies on $g(x)$ if $(-2,4)$ lies on $f(x)$?

    A. $(-6,-2)$

    B. $(-6,2)$

    C. $(-4,0)$

    D. $(0,8)$

    E. $(2,6)$

14. Given the data set $\{-5, 8, 6, -3, -1\}$, what is the positive difference between the arithmetic mean and median?

    F. 1

    G. 2

    H. 3

    J. 4

    K. 5

15. If the base of a scale model is 12 inches by 18 inches and the shorter side of the real object is 14 feet, then how long in feet is the longer side of the real object?

    A. 9

    B. 14

    C. 18

    D. 21

    E. 26

Answers and Explanations

How Much Have You Learned?

1.   E
Difficulty: Medium
Category: Algebra
Getting to the Answer: The question asks you to find the roots, or solutions, of the given quadratic equation. Because all the answer choices are in quadratic formula form, the best strategy is to use the quadratic formula. Write down that $a = 3$, $b = 5$, and $c = -3$, and plug into the quadratic formula.

$$x = \frac{-(5) \pm \sqrt{(5)^2 - 4(3)(-3)}}{2(3)}$$
$$= \frac{-5 \pm \sqrt{25 + 36}}{6}$$
$$= \frac{-5 \pm \sqrt{61}}{6}$$

Hence, (E) is correct. Be very careful and keep track of all negative signs when plugging in: the other choices could be correct if values were incorrectly plugged in.

2.   H
Difficulty: Medium
Category: Geometry
Getting to the Answer: This question asks for the length of the segment $\overline{VW}$ in the second triangle given certain lengths of two similar triangles. Look carefully at the order in which the vertices of the similar triangles are stated, as that will tell you which segments correspond to each other. With the given segments, $\overline{XY}$ corresponds to $\overline{UV}$ while $\overline{YZ}$ corresponds to $\overline{VW}$. Create an equation with proportions to solve for $\overline{VW}$.

$$\frac{6}{10} = \frac{x}{15}$$
$$10x = 90$$
$$x = 9$$

$\overline{VW} = 9$, so (H) is correct. Be careful of K, as this could be an answer if the proportions were set up incorrectly.

3.   A
Difficulty: Medium
Category: Number and Quantity
Getting to the Answer: This question asks you to evaluate an expression that contains imaginary numbers. Use FOIL, and take care to keep track of the negative signs while multiplying. Plug in the value $i^2 = -1$ when appropriate.

$$(3 - 8i)(5 + 3i) = 15 + 9i - 40i - 24i^2$$
$$= 15 - 31i + 24$$
$$= 39 - 31i$$

Choice (A) is correct. Notice that B is the answer you would get if you plugged in 1 for i^2 instead of -1.

4.   J
Difficulty: High
Category: Number and Probability
Getting to the Answer: The question asks for the original price of an item before a 30% discount and a 10% tax. First, calculate the discounted price before the tax by using the equation $x + 0.1x = 23.10 \rightarrow 1.1x = 23.10 \rightarrow x = 21$. Set up another equation that shows that when the original price is reduced by 30%, it equals $21. Use the complement of 30%, which is 70%, to get $0.7x = 21 \rightarrow x = 30$. The original price of the item is $30, which matches (J).

5.   B
Difficulty: Medium
Category: Geometry
Getting to the Answer: The question asks you to solve for tan E. Because tangent = opposite over adjacent, use the Pythagorean theorem to solve for the adjacent side: $a^2 + (4)^2 = (7)^2 \rightarrow a^2 = 33 \rightarrow a = \sqrt{33}$. So, $\tan E = \frac{4}{\sqrt{33}}$, and (B) is correct.

Another way to find the answer is to use Elimination. The side opposite angle E is 4, so 4, or one of its factors, should be in the numerator of the answer. This eliminates C, D, and E. The adjacent side can't be 7, because that's the hypotenuse. Thus, A is incorrect. Only (B) is left, so it must be the answer.

6. H
Difficulty: High
Category: Number and Quantity
Getting to the Answer: The question asks you to solve for a_{17} given information about the arithmetic sequence. Use the arithmetic sequence equation $a_n = a_1 + (n-1)d$ and plug in all the given information to solve for d, the common difference between each term:

$$a_{32} = a_1 + (32-1)d$$
$$(127) = (3) + 31d$$
$$124 = 31d$$
$$4 = d$$

Now use the same equation to solve for a_{17}:

$$a_{17} = (3) + (17-1)(4)$$
$$= 3 + (16)(4)$$
$$= 3 + 64$$
$$= 67$$

The 17th term in the arithmetic sequence is 67. Thus, (H) is correct. Be certain that you used $n-1$ rather than n in your calculations.

7. C
Difficulty: Medium
Category: Geometry
Getting to the Answer: The question asks what the radius of a circle with an 8-foot diameter would become if its area were tripled. First, use the diameter given to calculate the radius of the circle: $d = 2r \rightarrow 8 = 2r \rightarrow 4 = r$. Next, use the area formula for a circle, $A = \pi r^2$, to find the area: $A = \pi (4)^2 = 16\pi$. The question states that the circle's area is tripled, so its new area is $(3)16\pi = 48\pi$. Use the area of the larger circle to calculate the radius: $(48\pi) = \pi r^2 \rightarrow 48 = r^2 \rightarrow \sqrt{48} = 4\sqrt{3} = r$. Therefore, (C) is correct. Notice that D is a trap since this is the calculation using the diameter.

8. F
Difficulty: High
Category: Statistics and Probability
Getting to the Answer: The question asks how likely it is to pick a red face card after one has already been picked with no replacement. Use the probability formula: $\text{probability} = \frac{\text{desired}}{\text{total}}$. There are 8 red face cards in a standard deck of 52 cards. After one is picked,

only 7 red face cards and 51 total cards remain, so the probability is $\frac{7}{51}$. Hence, (F) is correct. If you did not remember to decrease the denominator by the card that was already drawn, you would have answered G.

9. D
Difficulty: High
Category: Statistics and Probability
Getting to the Answer: Between the two ratios, there are three variables, which means this is a three-part ratio. If you have two ratios, $a{:}b$ and $c{:}b$, you can derive $a{:}c$ by finding a common multiple of the b terms to make them the same. Here, a common multiple is 35. Multiply each ratio by the factor that will get you to $b = 35$. Use 5 for $a{:}b$ and 7 for $c{:}b$. The result is $5(3{:}7) = 15{:}35$ and $7(4{:}5) = 28{:}35$. Now that the b terms are the same, $a{:}b = 15{:}35$ and $c{:}b = 28{:}35$, you can rewrite the ratio $a{:}b{:}c$ as $15{:}35{:}28$. This means the ratio of $a{:}c$ is $15{:}28$, which is (D).

Alternatively, you can recognize that $\frac{a}{b} \times \frac{b}{c} = \frac{a}{c}$ and plug in the given values (inverting $c{:}b$ to get $b{:}c$) to determine that $\frac{a}{c} = \frac{3}{7} \times \frac{5}{4} = \frac{15}{28}$.

10. G
Difficulty: Medium
Category: Algebra
Getting to the Answer: This question asks for the definition of $f(x)$ that is consistent with the data in the table. Notice that all the choices are either quadratic or linear, so check the table to see which relationship fits $f(x)$. All the x-values increase by one, while all the y-values increase by 4. This means that the table represents a linear equation, so eliminate the quadratic choices F and H. Calculate the slope or y-intercept to eliminate further choices: the point $(0,2)$ is the y-intercept, which eliminates choices J and K. Thus, (G) is correct. The slope can be calculated by choosing two points, such as $(0,2)$ and $(1,6)$, and plugging them into the slope formula:

$$m = \frac{y_2 - y_1}{x_2 - x_1}$$
$$= \frac{6 - 2}{1 - 0}$$
$$= \frac{4}{1}$$
$$= 4$$

Only (G) has a slope of 4.

11. A

Difficulty: Low

Category: Algebra

Getting to the Answer: This question asks you to solve for the composite function using the given data table. Use the table and make sure to work from the inside out, starting with solving for $g(1)$: for function g, when $x = 1$, $f(x) = -2$. Now you can solve for $f(-2)$: for function f, when $x = -2$, $f(x) = -6$. Therefore, (A) is correct. Note that if you had incorrectly used the value of $g(-2)$, you would have selected D.

12. H

Difficulty: Low

Category: Algebra

Getting to the Answer: This question asks for the solution to the system of equations $f(x)$ and $g(x)$. Use the given equation and the equation for $f(x)$ that you figured out earlier. Substitution is the easiest method.

$$-2x = 4x + 2$$
$$-6x = 2$$
$$x = -\frac{1}{3}$$

This means that the lines intersect when $x = -\frac{1}{3}$. Note that (H) is correct since it is the only choice with that x-value. If you needed to calculate the y-value, you could plug in $x = -\frac{1}{3}$ to either equation and simplify.

13. B

Difficulty: Medium

Category: Algebra

Getting to the Answer: The question asks which of the choices lies on the graph $g(x)$. You could plug the x-coordinate of each choice into $g(x)$ and see which one produces the matching y-coordinate, but you will find the answer more quickly if you apply the properties of function transformations. Notice that, compared to $f(x)$, $g(x)$ translates 4 units to the left and 2 units down. You can confirm this by setting the inside of what is being squared to zero and solving: $x + 4 = 0 \rightarrow x = -4$. This is reason for the horizontal shift of 4 units to the left. The term on the right side is the vertical shift, which is more straightforward: the function shifts 2 units down because of the subtraction of 2. Take the given point on f, subtract 4 from the x-coordinate, and subtract 2 from the y-coordinate: $(-2 - (4), 4 - (2)) = (-6, 2)$. Thus, (B) is correct.

14. G

Difficulty: Medium

Category: Statistics and Probability

Getting to the Answer: The question asks for the positive difference between the arithmetic mean and median of the given data set. First, calculate the mean by adding all the given numbers and dividing by the total amount of numbers.

$$\frac{-5 + 8 + 6 - 3 - 1}{5} = \frac{5}{5} = 1$$

Next, find the median by arranging the list in ascending order and locating the middle number. $\{-5, 8, 6, -3, -1\} \rightarrow \{-5, -3, -1, 6, 8\}$, so -1 is the median. Remember that the question asks for the positive difference between the two values, which is $1 - (-1) = 1 + 1 = 2$. Thus, (G) is correct.

15. D

Difficulty: Medium

Category: Number and Quantity

Getting to the Answer: The question asks for the length of the longer side of the real object given information about the scale model. Notice that the scale model is given in inches, while the choices are given in feet. However, because units often cancel when you set up a proportion, don't waste time converting everything into feet. Immediately set up a proportion and solve:

$$\frac{12}{18} = \frac{14}{x}$$
$$12x = 14 \times 18$$
$$x = \frac{14 \times 18}{12}$$
$$x = 21$$

The longer side of the real object is 21 feet. Therefore, (D) is correct. Choice A would be the answer if the proportion were set up incorrectly.

TEST YOURSELF: ACT MATH

Directions: For test-like timing, give yourself 64 minutes to complete the following 64 questions.

$$||4 - 7| - |-10 + 2||$$

1. Which of the following is the value for the given expression?

    A. -11
    B. -5
    C. 0
    D. 5
    E. 11

2. What is the slope of the line that corresponds to the equation $6x - 5y = 4$ in the standard (x,y) coordinate plane?

    F. $-\dfrac{6}{5}$
    G. $-\dfrac{5}{6}$
    H. $-\dfrac{4}{5}$
    J. $\dfrac{5}{6}$
    K. $\dfrac{6}{5}$

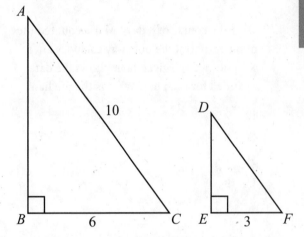

3. In the given figure, $\triangle ABC$ and $\triangle DEF$ are similar triangles with the given side lengths in meters. What is the perimeter of $\triangle DEF$, in meters?

    A. 8
    B. 11
    C. 12
    D. 16
    E. 24

	Number of Toys Put Away
Day 1	10
Day 2	8
Day 3	12
Day 4	7
Day 5	5
Day 6	12
Day 7	5
Day 8	9

4. Over the course of 8 days, Marie counted the number of toys she put away each day after babysitting. The given table shows the data recorded for each day. What is the median?

    F. 7.5
    G. 8
    H. 8.5
    J. 9
    K. 9.5

5. Which of the expressions below is equivalent to $9x^2\left(-\frac{1}{3}y + 3x - 21x\right)$?

    A. $8x^3$
    B. $18y^2$
    C. $6x^2y - 8x^3$
    D. $-3x^2y - 162x^3$
    E. $-3x^2y - x^3 + 6y - 21x$

6. For the polygon shown in the given figure, all adjacent line segments are perpendicular to one another. The dimensions given are in feet. What is the perimeter of the object, in feet?

    F. 27
    G. 36
    H. 39
    J. 40
    K. 42

7. A wooden rod length of $12\frac{2}{3}$ feet is cut into 3 pieces, with nothing left over (and with no loss of wood in the cuts themselves). If the lengths of two of the pieces are $6\frac{5}{9}$ feet and $3\frac{13}{18}$ feet, what is the length of the third piece, in feet?

    A. $2\frac{7}{18}$
    B. $2\frac{11}{18}$
    C. 3
    D. $3\frac{7}{18}$
    E. $4\frac{11}{50}$

8. If $y = -4$, what is $\dfrac{(y-4)^2}{y}$?

   F.   −16

   G.   −4

   H.   0

   J.   4

   K.   16

9. A cable of unknown length, x, stretches from the ground to the top of a pole in a straight line. The pole is 12 feet tall and the distance from the base of the pole to the base of the cable measures 9 feet. How many feet, in length, is the cable?

   A.   5

   B.   15

   C.   18

   D. $\sqrt{30}$

   E. $10\sqrt{3}$

10. A linear relationship is drawn in the standard (x,y) coordinate graph given. Which of the following equations correctly reflects the relationship?

    F. $y = -\dfrac{3}{4}x - 4$

    G. $y = -\dfrac{3}{4}x + 4$

    H. $y = \dfrac{3}{4}x - 4$

    J. $y = \dfrac{4}{3}x - 4$

    K. $y = \dfrac{4}{3}x + 4$

11. $\dfrac{6.4 \times 10^{-3}}{2.0 \times 10^4}$ is equal to which of the following?

    A. 3.4×10^{-12}

    B. 3.2×10^{-7}

    C. 3.2×10^{-1}

    D. 3.1×10^1

    E. 3.1×10^{12}

$$f(x) = 7x - (3x^2 - 2)$$

12. What is the value of $f(-3)$ for the given equation?

    F. -46

    G. -4

    H. 4

    J. 8

    K. 46

13. At 12:00 p.m., Ming sat down on a merry-go-round that was facing due west. By 12:30 p.m., heavy winds had rotated the merry-go-round $270°$ clockwise. If the rate of rotation was kept constant, how many degrees clockwise would the merry-go-round rotate in 45 minutes?

    A. $305°$

    B. $335°$

    C. $360°$

    D. $405°$

    E. $675°$

14. What is the midpoint of the line segment in the (x,y) coordinate plane that begins at $(-2,-4)$ and ends at $(1,2)$?

    F. $\left(-\frac{1}{2},-1\right)$

    G. $\left(-\frac{1}{2},1\right)$

    H. $\left(\frac{1}{2},-2\right)$

    J. $\left(\frac{1}{2},-1\right)$

    K. $\left(\frac{1}{2},1\right)$

15. A math teacher owns 10 pairs of pants, 2 pairs of shoes, and 6 shirts. Each outfit the teacher wears includes a combination of 1 shirt, 1 pair of shoes, and 1 pair of pants. How many possible outfits could the math teacher wear?

    A. 120

    B. 112

    C. 62

    D. 26

    E. 18

16. If $9 - 3(y - 3) \leq 0$, which of the following correctly characterizes the range of possible values for y?

    F. $y \leq -6$

    G. $y \leq 3$

    H. $y = 3$

    J. $y \geq -6$

    K. $y \geq 6$

17. If 1,024 is the first term, what is the eighth term in the geometric sequence 1,024, 512, 256, 128, . . . ?

    A. 8

    B. 16

    C. 32

    D. 64

    E. 96

18. What is the *y*-intercept of the line in the standard (x,y) coordinate plane that goes through the points $(-1,2)$ and $(5,-2)$?

    F. $-\dfrac{2}{3}$

    G. 0

    H. 1

    J. $\dfrac{4}{3}$

    K. 2

19. In the given figure, point *F* is on *EG*, and points *B* and *C* are on *AD*. *AD* is parallel to *EB*. What is the measure of $\angle ABF$?

    A. $30°$

    B. $45°$

    C. $90°$

    D. $120°$

    E. $135°$

20. In the standard (x,y) coordinate plane, what is the distance, in coordinate units, between $(7,-3)$ and $(-2,5)$?

    F. 7

    G. 17

    H. $\sqrt{17}$

    J. $\sqrt{85}$

    K. $\sqrt{145}$

21. If *a* is an even integer and *b* is an odd integer, which of the following must be an even integer?

    A. $2a + b$

    B. $4a - b$

    C. $a^2 b$

    D. $\dfrac{7b}{a}$

    E. $\dfrac{b}{a^2}$

22. What is the value of $q(p(-3))$ given that $p(x) = 7 - x^2$ and $q(x) = 4 - x$?

    F. -42

    G. -12

    H. 2

    J. 6

    K. 20

23. The time it takes to complete a certain job is directly proportional to the number of units produced. If it takes 22 minutes to produce 18 units, how many units are produced in 33 minutes?

    A. 12

    B. 27

    C. 29

    D. 40

    E. 54

Math

24. Deja is playing with building blocks and has a landscape that is 2 feet by 1.5 feet where the blocks snap in. Each building block is 2 inches by 1 inch by 0.5 inches. What is the minimum number of building blocks Deja needs to cover the entire landscape, in a single layer, if the building blocks are all oriented in the same direction?

   F.   108
   G.   216
   H.   432
   J.   864
   K.   1,728

25. Fifty students went on a camping trip: 14 are freshman, 14 are sophomores, 24% are juniors, and the rest are seniors. If one of the students is chosen at random, what is the probability that the person chosen will NOT be a senior?

   A. $\dfrac{1}{5}$
   B. $\dfrac{7}{25}$
   C. $\dfrac{3}{10}$
   D. $\dfrac{7}{10}$
   E. $\dfrac{4}{5}$

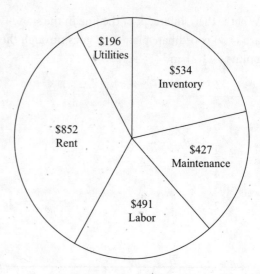

26. A business made a pie chart, by category, for its total expenditures for the previous month. Based on the given pie chart, what percent of the total expenditures came from the category with the least amount spent, rounded to the nearest percent?

   F.   8%
   G.   17%
   H.   20%
   J.   21%
   K.   34%

27. The given figure shows that points F and G are on the segment $\overline{EH}$, where $\overline{EH}$ is 35 units long. How many units long, if it can be determined, is $\overline{FG}$ given that $\overline{EG}$ is 15 units long and $\overline{FH}$ is 25 units long?

   A.   3
   B.   5
   C.   10
   D.   15
   E.   Cannot be determined from the given information

Use the following information to answer questions 28–29.

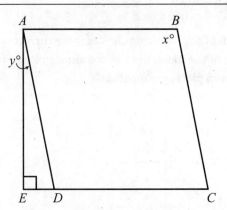

28. What is the value of x, in terms of y, in the given parallelogram $ABCD$?

    F. $y°$
    G. $(y + 30)°$
    H. $(y + 60)°$
    J. $(y + 90)°$
    K. $(y + 120)°$

29. If $\overline{EC}$ is 2 more units than $\overline{AB}$, $\overline{AE}$ is 10 units long, and the area of the given trapezoid $ABCE$ is 110 square units, what is the length of $\overline{EC}$?

    A. 10
    B. 11
    C. 12
    D. 13
    E. 14

30. The price of a stock increased by 40 percent in Year 1, and then increased by 30 percent in Year 2. By what percent did the price of the stock increase over the 2-year period?

    F. 93%
    G. 82%
    H. 77%
    J. 70%
    K. 35%

31. A charity raffle ticket costs $4.00 for pre-sales and $5.00 at the door. Amelie buys 7 pre-sale raffle tickets and then buys 2 raffle tickets at the door. What is the average cost per ticket, in dollars, for Amelie's 9 raffle tickets? Round your answer to the nearest penny.

    A. $3.11
    B. $4.00
    C. $4.22
    D. $4.68
    E. $5.21

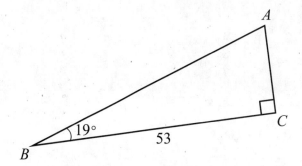

32. In the given diagram, which of the following expressions gives the correct length of $\overline{AC}$ in $\triangle ABC$?

    F. $\dfrac{53}{\cos 71°}$
    G. $\dfrac{53}{\tan 19°}$
    H. $53 \tan 19°$
    J. $53 \cos 19°$
    K. $53 \cos 71°$

33. What is the sum of the (x,y) coordinates at which the lines $2y - 3x = 9$ and $3y = 9$ intersect?

    A. −1
    B. 0
    C. 2
    D. 3
    E. 4

34. Given the expression $x^2 - 7x + 12$, which of the following is the factored form?

    F. $(x-3)(x-4)$

    G. $(x+3)(x-4)$

    H. $(x+3)(x+4)$

    J. $(x-6)(x-2)$

    K. $(x+6)(x+2)$

35. Which of the following expressions is equivalent to $x^4 \sqrt[5]{x^2} \cdot y^3 \sqrt{y^7}$?

    A. $x^2 y^3 \sqrt[6]{x^3 y^2}$

    B. $x^3 y^4 \sqrt{xy}$

    C. $x^4 y^5 \sqrt[10]{x^2 y^8}$

    D. $x^4 y^6 \sqrt[10]{x^4 y^5}$

    E. $x^6 y^6$

Department	Month			
	Jan	Feb	Mar	Apr
Clothing	$1,150	$1,220	$1,080	$1,240
Shoes	$1,000	$1,050	$1,350	$830
Accessories	$750	$720	$950	$810

36. A department store's sales are shown in the table. Approximately what percentage of the department store's sales in the month of January did Accessories account for? (Assume that the department store only generates sales in the 3 departments listed.)

    F. 23%

    G. 26%

    H. 29%

    J. 31%

    K. 33%

$$y = \begin{cases} x \text{ when } x \le -2 \\ |x| \text{ when } -2 < x < 2 \\ -x \text{ when } x \ge 2 \end{cases}$$

37. Which of the following choices is the correct graph in the standard (x,y) coordinate plane for the given piecewise function?

    A.

    B.

    C.

    D.

    E.

Hours of Labor (*h*)	Price at Carl's Shop (*c*)	Price at Sherri's Shop (*s*)
1	$20	$15
3	$40	$30
5	$60	$45
7	$80	$60
9	$100	$75
11	$120	$90

38. The given table shows two different auto shops and the prices they charge for the hours of labor worked. Which of the following equations represents the relationship between the price at Carl's shop and the hours of labor worked?

F. $c = 0.1h + 19.9$

G. $c = 0.1h + 15$

H. $c = 5h + 15$

J. $c = 10h + 10$

K. $c = 10h + 20$

39. A solvent manufacturing company is producing toluene and storing it in two different vats with 10,000 gallons of capacity each. Vat *A* currently contains 450 gallons of toluene, and its contents are increasing at a rate of 40 gallons per minute. Vat *B* currently contains 1,250 gallons of toluene, and its contents are increasing at a rate of 15 gallons per minute. In how many minutes will the two vats contain equal amounts of toluene?

A. 30

B. 32

C. 48

D. 50

E. 60

Use the following information to answer questions 40 and 41.

The coach of a basketball team documented the number of free throws that his team of 19 made during their final game of the season. The bar graph shows the results.

40. What fraction of the players made fewer than 2 free throws?

F. $\dfrac{7}{100}$

G. $\dfrac{1}{5}$

H. $\dfrac{7}{19}$

J. $\dfrac{15}{19}$

K. $\dfrac{4}{5}$

41. What was the average number of free throws, to the nearest tenth, made during the game?

A. 2.0

B. 2.1

C. 2.2

D. 2.3

E. 2.4

42. If $\log_2 16^2 = x$, what is the value of x?

    F. -8

    G. -6

    H.   6

    J.   8

    K.   16

43. A circle in the standard (x,y) coordinate plane is tangent to both the x-axis and the line $y = 6$. Which of the following could be the equation of the circle?

    A. $x^2 + y^2 = 36$

    B. $x^2 + (y - 3)^2 = 36$

    C. $(x - 3)^2 + y^2 = 36$

    D. $(x - 3)^2 + (y + 3)^2 = 9$

    E. $(x + 3)^2 + (y - 3)^2 = 9$

44. To sterilize an insect-infected building, workers emptied out the building completely. Then 2,700 cubic feet of chlorine gas, which is heavier than air, was pumped inside. If the chlorine gas forms a layer along the floor that is uniformly 0.4 feet thick, about how many square feet of floor space does the building contain?

    F.   Less than 1,000

    G.   Between 1,000 and 2,000

    H.   Between 2,000 and 3,000

    J.   Between 3,000 and 4,000

    K.   More than 4,000

45. Two friends, Bill and Todd, have finished having dinner together and are now trying to figure out how to split the check. If the total cost of the check is $52, and Bill ordered items costing $14 more than what Todd had ordered, how much does Bill owe for the check? (Ignore all tax and tip considerations.)

    A. $19

    B. $26

    C. $33

    D. $36

    E. $40

46. Which of the following expressions is equal to $\dfrac{i}{3 - i}$?

    F. i

    G. $3i$

    H. $-\dfrac{1}{8} + \dfrac{3i}{10}$

    J. $\dfrac{1}{10} - \dfrac{3i}{10}$

    K. $-\dfrac{1}{10} + \dfrac{3i}{10}$

Number, n, of typing mistakes made	Probability that n typing mistakes were made in a day
0	0.10
1	0.40
2	0.30
3	0.20

47. Each day at work, for 4 weeks, Lena recorded how many typing mistakes she made. Based on the distribution given, what is the expected value of typing mistakes made in one day?

    A.   0.00

    B.   0.55

    C.   0.85

    D.   1.20

    E.   1.60

48. The graph of $y = f(x)$ is given in the standard (x,y) coordinate plane. Which of the following is the set of its domain?

    F. $\{-2, -1, 0, 1, 2\}$
    G. $\{-1, 0, 1, 2, 3\}$
    H. $\{0, 1, 2, 3, 4\}$
    J. $\{x \mid -2 \leq x < 2\}$
    K. $\{x \mid -1 \leq x < 2\}$

Weekly Hours	Number of Volunteers
10	8
11	3
12	6
13	3
14	2

49. A soup kitchen logs the number of weekly hours volunteers work by creating the frequency table given. Which of the following values is the median number of weekly hours?

    A. 10
    B. 11.5
    C. 12
    D. 13.5
    E. 14

Use the following information to answer questions 50 and 51.

In the given figure, *ABCD* is a square with a circle centered at *E* inscribed inside of it. A right triangle is inscribed inside of the circle; its hypotenuse forms a diameter of the circle.

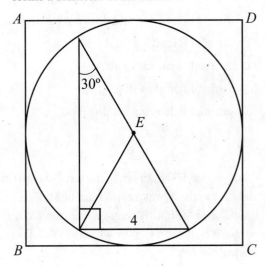

50. What is the ratio of the area of the square to the area of the right triangle?

    F. 2:1
    G. 4:1
    H. 4:$\sqrt{3}$
    J. 8:$\sqrt{3}$
    K. 16:$\sqrt{3}$

51. What is the circumference of the circle?

    A. 2π
    B. 4π
    C. 8π
    D. 16π
    E. 32π

52. Consider the following 3 statements to be true:

    - All animals that eat dog food are dogs.
    - Animal E is not a dog.
    - Animal F eats dog food.

    Which of the following statements is necessarily true?

    F. Animal E is a dog and does not eat dog food.
    G. Animal E eats dog food.
    H. Animal F eats cat food.
    J. Animal F is not a dog.
    K. Animal E does not eat dog food.

53. Frank worked 70 hours over the last 7-day period, and his paycheck was a minimum of $1,470. Frank's average hourly wage, h, over the 7-day period is best expressed by which of the following inequalities?

    A. $h \leq \$3$
    B. $h \geq \$3$
    C. $h \leq \$21$
    D. $h \geq \$21$
    E. $h \geq \$147$

54. The graph of the parabola $y = x^2$ is shown in the standard (x,y) coordinate plane. For which of the following equations is the graph of the parabola shifted 2 units to the left and 3 units down?

    F. $y = (x - 2)^2 - 3$
    G. $y = (x - 2)^2 + 3$
    H. $y = (x + 2)^2 - 3$
    J. $y = (x + 2)^2 + 3$
    K. $y = (x + 3)^2 - 2$

55. The number of trees in a certain park can be shown in the given matrix:

$$\begin{array}{cccc} \text{Oak} & \text{Elm} & \text{Pine} & \text{Birch} \\ [70 & 30 & 40 & 50] \end{array}$$

A park ranger estimates the ratios of the number of healthy trees to the total number of trees for each kind of tree and constructs the following matrix using the ratios:

$$\begin{array}{c} \text{Oak} \\ \text{Elm} \\ \text{Pine} \\ \text{Birch} \end{array} \begin{bmatrix} 0.4 \\ 0.6 \\ 0.8 \\ 0.7 \end{bmatrix}$$

Given these matrices, what is the park ranger's estimate for the number of healthy trees in the park?

A. 113
B. 115
C. 117
D. 118
E. 119

56. The height of a right circular cylinder is 10 inches with a radius of 9 inches. What is the volume, in cubic inches, of this cylinder?

F. 405π
G. 480π
H. 640π
J. 810π
K. $1,620\pi$

57. A company wants to get feedback from its employees about their experience working for the company. Out of 1,000 employees, 200 are selected at random to take the survey. Which of the following best describes the company's testing?

A. Non-randomized experiment
B. Non-randomized sample survey
C. Randomized census
D. Randomized experiment
E. Randomized sample survey

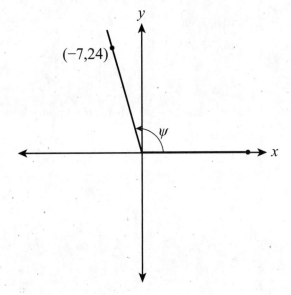

58. In the standard (x,y) coordinate plane drawn, the angle ψ is shown; its vertex is the origin. One side of the angle is located on the positive x-axis, while the other side of the angle passes through the point $(-7,24)$. What is the value of $\sin \psi$?

F. $-\dfrac{7}{24}$

G. $-\dfrac{7}{25}$

H. $-\dfrac{24}{25}$

J. $\dfrac{7}{25}$

K. $\dfrac{24}{25}$

Math

59. The growth of a particular bacterial colony, P, in a Petri dish can be modeled by the equation $P = \dfrac{3^{2t-1}}{h} + 200$, where t is time measured in days, such that $t > 0$. The variable h represents a growth coefficient, such that $0 < h \leq 10$. In ideal heat and moisture conditions, $h = 0.5$. Which of the following values represents the population of the bacterial colony after 5 days of growth under ideal heat and moisture conditions?

A.   10,041.5

B.   39,566

C.   354,494

D.   10,077,896

E.   10,077,696

60. If $f(x) = \dfrac{3}{4} \sin(2x - \pi)$, what is the amplitude of the function $f(x)$?

F. $\dfrac{1}{2}$

G. $\dfrac{3}{4}$

H. $\dfrac{4}{3}$

J.   2

K.   3

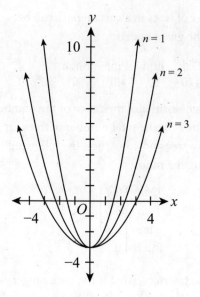

61. The given graph in the standard (x,y) coordinate plane shows parabolas from a shared family. What is the general equation that describes this family of parabolas for all $n \geq 1$?

A. $y = -\dfrac{1}{n}x^2 - 3$

B. $y = -nx^2 - 3$

C. $y = x^2 - n$

D. $y = \dfrac{1}{n}x^2 - 3$

E. $y = nx^2 - 3$

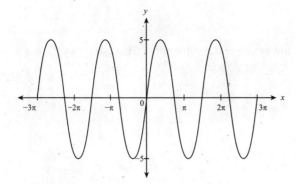

x	Probability $P(X = x)$
0	$\frac{1}{3}$
1	$\frac{1}{12}$
2	$\frac{1}{24}$
3	0
4	0
5	$\frac{7}{24}$
6	$\frac{1}{4}$

62. The trigonometric function shown is graphed in the standard (x,y) coordinate plane. The equation of the function is of the form $f(x) = y = a\cos(bx + c)$, where a, b, and c are constants. The graph regularly repeats itself. The period of the function is defined as the smallest positive number r such that $f(x + r) = f(x)$. Which of the following is the period of the function graphed above?

F. $\dfrac{3\pi}{4}$

G. $\dfrac{3\pi}{2}$

H. $\dfrac{\pi}{2}$

J. 3π

K. 6π

63. What is the expected value of X, a discrete random variable, based on the given probability distribution table?

A. $\dfrac{1}{12}$

B. $\dfrac{1}{4}$

C. $\dfrac{2}{3}$

D. $\dfrac{19}{8}$

E. $\dfrac{25}{8}$

64. The sides of an obtuse triangle measure 8 inches, 12 inches, and 15 inches, respectively. Which of the following equations, when solved for θ, gives the measure of the largest angle of the triangle? (Note: For any triangle with sides of length a, b, and c that are opposite angles A, B, and C, respectively, $\dfrac{\sin A}{a} = \dfrac{\sin B}{b} = \dfrac{\sin C}{c}$ and $c^2 = a^2 + b^2 - 2ab\cos C$.)

F. $\dfrac{\sin\theta}{15} = \dfrac{1}{12}$

G. $\dfrac{\sin\theta}{15} = \dfrac{1}{8}$

H. $\dfrac{\sin\theta}{8} = \dfrac{1}{15}$

J. $(8)^2 = (12)^2 + (15)^2 - 2(12)(15)\cos\theta$

K. $(15)^2 = (8)^2 + (12)^2 - 2(8)(12)\cos\theta$

Answers and Explanations

1.   D
Difficulty: Low
Category: Number and Quantity
Getting to the Answer: The question asks for the value of the expression, so follow the order of operations to simplify. Solve the arithmetic, taking care not to make careless mistakes with the absolute value bars or negative signs:

$$||4 - 7| - |-10 + 2||$$
$$= ||-3| - |-8||$$
$$= |3 - 8|$$
$$= |-5|$$
$$= 5$$

The expression simplifies to 5, so (D) is correct.

2.   K
Difficulty: Low
Category: Algebra
Getting to the Answer: The question asks for the slope of the given line, so convert the equation into slope-intercept form ($y = mx + b$) by solving for y. First, subtract $6x$ from both sides and then divide by -5. Make sure to change the signs when dividing or multiplying by a negative.

$$6x - 5y = 4$$
$$-5y = -6x + 4$$
$$\frac{-5}{-5}y = \frac{-6}{-5}x + \frac{4}{-5}$$
$$y = \frac{6}{5}x - \frac{4}{5}$$

In slope-intercept form, m represents the slope of the line. Therefore, the slope of this line is $\frac{6}{5}$, and (K) is correct.

3.   C
Difficulty: Medium
Category: Geometry
Getting to the Answer: The question asks for the perimeter of $\triangle DEF$, but you are only given the length of one side, so you need to solve for the remaining side lengths. Because $\triangle ABC$ and $\triangle DEF$ are similar triangles, the corresponding sides between the two triangles will

always have the same ratio. Set up a proportion and solve for side $\overline{DF}$:

$$\frac{\overline{BC}}{\overline{EF}} = \frac{\overline{AC}}{\overline{DF}}$$
$$\frac{6}{3} = \frac{10}{\overline{DF}}$$
$$6\overline{DF} = 3 \times 10$$
$$\overline{DF} = \frac{3 \times 10}{6} = 5$$

Now, two sides of $\triangle DEF$ are known.

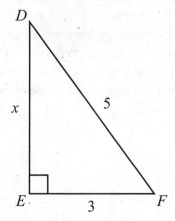

Because two sides are known and it is a right triangle, use the Pythagorean theorem, $a^2 + b^2 = c^2$, to solve for the unknown side:

$$3^2 + x^2 = 5^2$$
$$9 + x^2 = 25$$
$$x^2 = 25 - 9 = 16$$

Take the square root of both sides to find x:

$$x^2 = 16$$
$$\sqrt{x^2} = \sqrt{16}$$
$$x = 4$$

Alternatively, you might have recognized that this triangle was a 3:4:5 right triangle. Perimeter is the sum of all the side lengths, so the perimeter of $\triangle DEF$ is $3 + 4 + 5 = 12$. Hence, (C) is correct.

Another way to solve this is to first use the Pythagorean theorem to show that side $\overline{AB} = 8$, which makes the perimeter of $\triangle ABC = 24$. The ratio of the similar triangles is 2:1, so the perimeter of $\triangle DEF$ is half of that of $\triangle ABC$ or $24 \div 2 = 12$. This matches (C).

4. H
Difficulty: Low
Category: Statistics and Probability
Getting to the Answer: The question asks for the median of the given data set. The median of a data set is the middle value when the values are arranged in ascending or descending order. If the data set contains an even number of values, as is the case here, then the median can be found by averaging the middle two numbers in the data set. Start by rearranging the values in order: 5, 5, 7, 8, 9, 10, 12, 12. Now select the two middle values and average them: $\frac{8+9}{2} = 8.5$, so (H) is correct.

5. D
Difficulty: Low
Category: Algebra
Getting to the Answer: The question asks for an equivalent expression, so use the order of operations to simplify. Resist the urge to immediately distribute the $9x^2$. Instead, combine like terms in the parentheses and then distribute. Remember, when you multiply exponents with the same base, add the exponents.

$$9x^2\left(-\frac{1}{3}y + 3x - 21x\right)$$
$$= 9x^2\left(-\frac{1}{3}y - 18x\right)$$
$$= -3x^2y - 162x^3$$

The expression simplifies to $-3x^2y - 162x^3$, so (D) is correct.

6. K
Difficulty: Medium
Category: Geometry
Getting to the Answer: The question asks you to determine the perimeter based on an incomplete listing of the lengths of all the sides of the 10-sided polygon. However, it is given in the question that all of the line segments are perpendicular to one another. Therefore, all of the line segments are either horizontal or vertical. The sum of the horizontal line segments at the top must equal the sum of the horizontal line segments at the bottom. Likewise, the sum of the vertical line segments at the left must equal the sum of the vertical line segments at the right. This can be thought of as a rectangle in this case. The perimeter is then $2w + 2l$ or $2(w + l)$, where w is the width and l is the length.

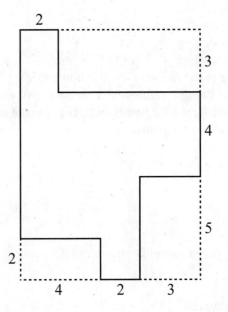

In this case, the bottom base (w) is $4 + 2 + 3 = 9$ and the right side (l) is $3 + 4 + 5 = 12$. Plugging these values into the perimeter formula, $2(w + l)$, gives $2(9 + 12) = 2(21) = 42$. Since 42 is the perimeter, (K) is correct.

7. A
Difficulty: Medium
Category: Number and Quantity
Getting to the Answer: The question asks for the length of the third wooden piece, so set up an equation to represent the situation. Let the length of the unknown piece be x. Because the lengths of the three pieces of wood must equal the length of the original wooden rod, set up the following equation: $6\frac{5}{9} + 3\frac{13}{18} + x = 12\frac{2}{3}$.

Now solve for x by converting the mixed fractions to improper fractions and finding a common denominator to combine the terms. Then express your answer as a mixed fraction to match the form of the choices.

$$\frac{59}{9} + \frac{67}{18} + x = \frac{38}{3}$$
$$x = \frac{38}{3} - \frac{59}{9} - \frac{67}{18}$$
$$x = \frac{228}{18} - \frac{118}{18} - \frac{67}{18}$$
$$x = \frac{43}{18}$$
$$x = 2\frac{7}{18}$$

Since x is the length of the third wood piece, (A) is correct.

8.   F

Difficulty: Low
Category: Algebra
Getting to the Answer: The question asks you to evaluate the given expression with the known value of y. Substitute -4 for every instance of y in the given expression and simplify:

$$\frac{(-4-4)^2}{-4} = \frac{(-8)^2}{-4}$$

$$= \frac{64}{-4}$$

$$= -16$$

The expression simplifies to -16, so (F) is correct.

9.   B

Difficulty: Low
Category: Geometry
Getting to the Answer: The question asks for the length, in feet, of the cable that stretches from the ground to the top of the pole. Notice that this is the hypotenuse of the triangle in the diagram. When given two sides of a right triangle, use the Pythagorean theorem to solve for the unknown value:

$$a^2 + b^2 = x^2$$

$$(9)^2 + (12)^2 = x^2$$

$$81 + 144 = x^2$$

$$\sqrt{225} = \sqrt{x^2}$$

$$15 = x$$

Since x is 15 feet long, (B) is correct. Alternatively, if you noticed that the triangle was a 3-4-5 right triangle multiplied by 3, you could solve for the missing side by calculating $5 \times 3 = 15$.

10.   J

Difficulty: Medium
Category: Algebra
Getting to the Answer: The question asks for the linear equation that represents the given graph. Notice that in the graph, the line passes through the points $(3,0)$ and $(0,-4)$. Recall that a line, in slope-intercept form, is defined by $y = mx + b$, where m is the slope

and b is the y-intercept. Use the slope formula, $\frac{y_2 - y_1}{x_2 - x_1}$, to solve for m:

$$m = \frac{(-4) - (0)}{(0) - (3)} = \frac{-4}{-3} = \frac{4}{3}$$

Eliminate F, G, and H. To solve for b, look at the graph. The line crosses the y-axis at -4, so the y-intercept b is -4. Therefore, the equation is $y = \frac{4}{3}x - 4$, and (J) is correct.

11.   B

Difficulty: Low
Category: Number and Quantity
Getting to the Answer: The question asks you to determine which of the given choices are equivalent to the given expressions. When dealing with scientific notation, it is important to separate the digit terms (in this case 6.4 and 2.0) from the exponential terms. Then work on each piece separately and bring the results together at the end. Remember, when you divide exponents with the same base, subtract the exponents:

$$\frac{6.4 \times 10^{-3}}{2.0 \times 10^4} = \frac{6.4}{2.0} \times \frac{10^{-3}}{10^4}$$

$$= 3.2 \times 10^{-3-4}$$

$$= 3.2 \times 10^{-7}$$

Since 3.2×10^{-7} is equivalent to one of the given expressions, (B) is correct.

12.   F

Difficulty: Medium
Category: Function
Getting to the Answer: The question asks you to find $f(-3)$ for the given function. For every instance of x, substitute -3 and evaluate:

$$f(x) = 7x - (3x^2 - 2)$$

$$f(-3) = 7(-3) - (3(-3)^2 - 2)$$

$$f(-3) = -21 - (27 - 2)$$

$$f(-3) = -21 - 25$$

$$f(-3) = -46$$

Since $f(-3) = -46$, (F) is correct.

13. D

Difficulty: Medium

Category: Number and Quantity

Getting to the Answer: The merry-go-round is rotating 270° in 30 minutes. That is 9° per minute. So, 9° × 45 minutes = 405°. Thus, (D) is correct. Alternatively, if you prefer an algebraic approach, set up a proportion and solve:

$$\frac{270}{30} = \frac{x}{45}$$

$$12,150 = 30x$$

$$405 = x$$

$x = 405°$, which confirms (D) is correct.

14. F

Difficulty: Medium

Category: Algebra

Getting to the Answer: The question asks for the midpoint of the two points given. Visualizing this may help:

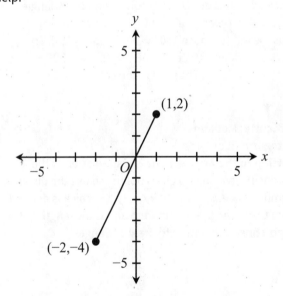

By drawing the diagram, you can see that the solution should be in the third quadrant, where both coordinates will be negative. This means (F) is correct.

The algebraic approach is to use the midpoint formula, $\left(\frac{x_1 + x_2}{2}, \frac{y_1 + y_2}{2}\right)$, which is the average of the x- and y-coordinates from the tail ends of the line.

$$\left(\frac{x_1 + x_2}{2}, \frac{y_1 + y_2}{2}\right)$$

$$\left(\frac{-2 + 1}{2}, \frac{-4 + 2}{2}\right)$$

$$\left(-\frac{1}{2}, -1\right)$$

This proves that (F) must be correct as previously thought.

15. A

Difficulty: Low

Category: Number and Quantity

Getting to the Answer: The question asks you to determine how many possible outfits the math teacher can wear with the given numbers of pants, shoes, and shirts. For each of the 10 pairs of pants, the teacher can wear either of 2 pairs of shoes. The number of combinations of pants and shoes is represented by 2 × 10 = 20. For each of these 20 combinations of pants and shoes, the teacher can also wear any of the 6 shirts. The number of combinations of pants and shoes together with shirts is therefore represented by 20 × 6 = 120. The number of unique combinations of all three items is therefore 120, and (A) is correct. Remember, a simple formula for combination questions is to multiply all the options together.

16. K

Difficulty: Medium

Category: Algebra

Getting to the Answer: The question asks for the range of possible values for y given the inequality. Solve the inequality for y as you would an equation, but make sure that you flip the inequality sign any time you multiply or divide both sides of the inequality by a negative number.

$$9 - 3(y - 3) \leq 0$$

$$-3(y - 3) \leq -9$$

$$y - 3 \geq 3$$

$$y \geq 6$$

This means that for all values of y greater than or equal to 6, $9 - 3(y - 3) \leq 0$. Thus, (K) is correct.

17. A
Difficulty: Low
Category: Number and Quantity
Getting to the Answer: The question asks for the eighth term in the given geometric sequence. In a geometric sequence, each term is multiplied by the same number, called the common ratio, to get to the next term. In this sequence, each term is multiplied by $\frac{1}{2}$ or divided by 2. Use the geometric formula, $a_n = a_1 r^{n-1}$, where a_1 is the first number of the sequence, r is the common ratio, and a_n is the nth term of the sequence, to solve for a_8:

$$a_n = a_1 r^{n-1}$$
$$a_8 = 1{,}024\left(\frac{1}{2}\right)^{8-1}$$
$$a_8 = 1{,}024\left(\frac{1}{128}\right)$$
$$a_8 = 8$$

Another way to solve is to divide by 2 until you get to the 8th term:

$$\frac{128}{2} = 64$$
$$\frac{64}{2} = 32$$
$$\frac{32}{2} = 16$$
$$\frac{16}{2} = 8$$

The eighth term in the sequence is 8, so (A) is correct.

18. J
Difficulty: Medium
Category: Algebra
Getting to the Answer: The question asks for the y-intercept of a line that passes through the two given points. The slope-intercept equation is $y = mx + b$, where m is the slope and b is the y-intercept. First solve for m by using the slope formula, $\frac{y_2 - y_1}{x_2 - x_1}$:

$$\frac{(-2) - (2)}{(5) - (-1)} = \frac{-4}{6} = -\frac{2}{3}$$

Then solve for b by plugging the slope and one of the points into the slope-intercept equation. Using $(-1,2)$:

$$y = -\frac{2}{3}x + b$$
$$2 = -\frac{2}{3}(-1) + b$$
$$2 - \frac{2}{3} = b$$
$$\frac{6}{3} - \frac{2}{3} = b$$
$$\frac{4}{3} = b$$

The y-intercept of the line is $\frac{4}{3}$, and (J) is correct.

19. E
Difficulty: Medium
Category: Geometry
Getting to the Answer: The question asks for the measure of $\angle ABF$ in the given diagram. Note that $\angle ABF$ and $\angle CBF$ are supplementary angles (make a straight line), so $\angle ABF = 180° - \angle CBF$.

Since two sides of $\triangle BCF$ are congruent, this triangle is isosceles. Given $\angle BFC$ is 90°, the other two angles must be 45° (because $180° = 90° + 45° + 45°$). Thus, $\angle CBF = \angle BCF = 45°$, and $\angle ABF = 180° - \angle CBF = 180° - 45° = 135°$. Thus, (E) is correct.

20. K
Difficulty: Medium
Category: Geometry
Getting to the Answer: The question asks for the distance between two given points, so use the distance formula $d = \sqrt{(x_2 - x_1)^2 + (y_2 - y_1)^2}$, which is derived from the Pythagorean theorem and is the length of the hypotenuse if you were to draw a triangle:

$$\sqrt{(x_2 - x_1)^2 + (y_2 - y_1)^2}$$
$$= \sqrt{(-2 - 7)^2 + (5 - (-3))^2}$$
$$= \sqrt{(-9)^2 + (8)^2}$$
$$= \sqrt{81 + 64}$$
$$= \sqrt{145}$$

The distance between the given points is $\sqrt{145}$, so (K) is correct.

21. C
Difficulty: Medium
Category: Number and Quantity
Getting to the Answer: The question asks for the choice that is always even. Pick Numbers for a and b to eliminate the incorrect choices.

Let $a = 2$ and $b = 3$:

Choice A: $2(2) + (3) = 7 =$ odd, eliminate.

Choice B: $4(2) - (3) = 5 =$ odd, eliminate.

Choice (C): $(2)^2(3) = 12 =$ even, keep.

Choice D: $\frac{7(3)}{2} =$ not an integer, eliminate.

Choice E: $\frac{3}{2^2} =$ not an integer, eliminate.

The answer is (C). Alternatively, you may have recognized the number property, even × odd = even, and selected (C) without having to Pick Numbers.

22. J
Difficulty: Medium
Category: Function
Getting to the Answer: The question asks for the value of $q(p(-3))$. For nested functions, evaluate the inside function first, and then work your way out. Start by substituting -3 for x in the p function:

$$p(x) = 7 - x^2$$
$$p(-3) = 7 - (-3)^2$$
$$p(-3) = 7 - 9$$
$$p(-3) = -2$$

Since $p(-3) = -2$, now evaluate $q(-2)$ by substituting -2 for x in the q function:

$$q(x) = 4 - x$$
$$q(-2) = 4 - (-2)$$
$$q(-2) = 6$$

This means that $q(p(-3)) = 6$, and (J) is correct.

23. B
Difficulty: Low
Category: Number and Quantity
Getting to the Answer: The question asks how many units are produced in 33 minutes. The statement that "the time it takes to complete a certain job is directly proportional to the number of units produced" implies that the ratio $\dfrac{\text{time to complete the job, in minutes}}{\text{units produced}}$ must be equal for all instances of the job. Therefore, you can set up a proportion and solve (let u be the unknown number of units produced):

$$\frac{22}{18} = \frac{33}{u}$$
$$22u = 18(33)$$
$$u = \frac{594}{22}$$
$$u = 27$$

In 33 minutes, 27 units can be produced, and (B) is correct.

24. G
Difficulty: Medium
Category: Geometry
Getting to the Answer: The question asks for the minimum number of building blocks needed to cover the entire landscape. To determine the minimum number, you need to calculate the area of the largest face of one block and the area of the landscape. The largest face of one block has a length of 2 inches and a width of 1 inch, which yields an area of $2 \times 1 = 2$ square inches. Note that the height (0.5 in.) is irrelevant.

Since the dimensions of the block are in inches, first convert the units of the landscape from feet to inches: (2 by 1.5 feet) $\times 12 \dfrac{\text{inches}}{\text{feet}} = 24$ by 18 inches. The total area is thus, $24 \times 18 = 432$ square inches. Therefore, the minimum number of building blocks needed to fill up the entire landscape is the total area of the landscape divided by the area of the largest face of one block: $432 \div 2 = 216$. (G) is correct.

25. E

Difficulty: Medium
Category: Statistics and Probability
Getting to the Answer: The question asks for the probability that a student selected at random will *not* be a senior. The probability of not selecting a senior is the total number of non-seniors (freshman + sophomores + juniors) divided by the total number of students (50). Since the number of juniors is given as a percent, calculate the number of juniors: $50 \times 0.24 = 12$. Thus, the number of non-seniors is 14 freshman + 14 sophomores + 12 juniors = 40. So the probability of choosing a non-senior is $\frac{40}{50} = \frac{4}{5}$. Thus, (E) is correct.

Remember that the probability of something not happening equals 1 minus the probability of it happening. Therefore, alternatively, you could subtract the probability of selecting a senior from 1 to determine the probability of not selecting a senior: $1 - \frac{10}{50} = \frac{40}{50} = \frac{4}{5}$. This matches (E).

26. F

Difficulty: Low
Category: Statistics and Probability
Getting to the Answer: Start by identifying the category of the smallest slice of the pie chart since the question asks for the percent of the total from the least expenditure category. The utilities category is the smallest at \$196, and the total spent is $196 + \$427 + \$491 + \$534 + \$852 = \$2,500$. Use the percent formula, percent $= \frac{\text{part}}{\text{whole}} \times 100\%$, where \$196 is the part and \$2,500 is the whole. Don't forget to multiply by 100 to convert your answer into a percent.

$$\frac{196}{2500} = 0.0784 \times 100\% = 7.84\%$$

Rounded to the nearest percent, 7.84% is 8%. Thus, the business's utilities expenditure was 8% of the previous month's total expenditures. (F) is correct.

27. B

Difficulty: Medium
Category: Number and Quantity
Getting to the Answer: The question asks for the length of segment $\overline{FG}$. Notice that from the segment lengths given, $\overline{FG}$ is the intersection because $\overline{FG}$ is in both $\overline{EFG}$ and $\overline{FGH}$.

This means that you can find $\overline{FG}$ by subtracting the length of $\overline{EH}$ (35) from the sum of $\overline{EG}$ (15) and $\overline{FH}$ (25), which is 40. So, $40 - 35 = 5$. Hence, (B) is correct.

To solve this algebraically, let x be the length of $\overline{FG}$. Thus, $\overline{EF} = 15 - x$ and $\overline{GH} = 25 - x$. Create an equation for the total length of $\overline{EH}$ and solve for x.

$$(15 - x) + x + (25 - x) = 35$$
$$40 - x = 35$$
$$5 = x$$

28. J

Difficulty: Medium
Category: Geometry
Getting to the Answer: The question asks for the value of x in terms of y. Recall that in a parallelogram, opposite angles are congruent while adjacent angles are supplementary. Thus, $\angle ADC = \angle ABC$ and $\angle DAB$ is supplementary to $\angle ABC$ because they are same side interior angles. $\angle ADE$ is congruent to $\angle DAB$ because they are alternate interior angles. From the rules of substitution, $\angle ABC$ is supplementary to $\angle ADE$. Remember that all angles in a triangle add up to $180°$. This means that $\angle ADE + 90° + y = 180°$. Hence, $\angle ABC = y + 90°$, and (J) is correct.

Alternatively, since the exterior angle of a triangle is equal to the sum of the opposite interior angles, $\angle ADC = (y + 90)°$. Thus, because $\angle ADC = \angle ABC$, $x = \angle ADC = (y + 90)°$, which matches (J).

29. C

Difficulty: High
Category: Geometry
Getting to the Answer: The question asks for the length of $\overline{EC}$. Note that the formula for the area of a trapezoid is $\frac{b_1 + b_2}{2}h$, where h is the height of the trapezoid and b_1 and b_2 are the lengths of the bases. Since $\overline{AB}$ and $\overline{EC}$ are parallel, they must be the bases. Let the length of $\overline{AB}$ be w, so the length of $\overline{EC}$ is $w + 2$. Since $\overline{AE}$ is perpendicular to one of the bases ($\overline{EC}$), it must be the height. Plug all of these into the area formula and solve for w.

$$\frac{w+(w+2)}{2}(10)=110$$

$$\frac{w+(w+2)}{2}=11$$

$$w+(w+2)=22$$

$$2w+2=22$$

$$2w=20$$

$$w=10$$

Remember that $\overline{EC}=w+2$, so $\overline{EC}=12$. Thus, (C) is correct.

30. G

Difficulty: Medium
Category: Number and Quantity
Getting to the Answer: The question asks for the percent increase of the stock over a 2-year period. Since the original price of the stock is not given, picking a number will be helpful. Usually, the easiest number to work with when dealing with percent change is 100. So, let the price of the stock be $100 at the beginning of Year 1. In Year 1, it increased by 40% × $100 = $40, to $140. In Year 2, it increased another 30%, or 30% × 140 = $42, to $140 + $42 = $182. Plugging these values into the percent change formula, $\frac{\text{Final amount} - \text{Initial amount}}{\text{Initial amount}} \times 100\%$, gives:

$$\frac{\$182-\$100}{\$100}\times100\%=\frac{\$82}{\$100}\times100\%=82\%$$

Therefore, the price of the stock increased by 82%, and (G) is correct.

31. C

Difficulty: Medium
Category: Statistics and Probability
Getting to the Answer: The question asks for the average cost per ticket for the 9 raffle tickets. First, calculate the sum total of the 9 tickets Amelie paid. Since Amelie bought 7 pre-sale tickets and 2 tickets at the door, she paid a total of 7 × $4.00 + 2 × $5.00 = $28 + $10 = $38. Therefore, the average cost of each ticket is given by:

$$\text{average}=\frac{\text{sum of items}}{\text{number of items}}=\frac{\$38.00}{9}\approx\$4.22$$

Thus, (C) is correct.

32. H

Difficulty: Medium
Category: Geometry
Getting to the Answer: The question asks for the length of $\overline{AC}$. Little information is given about this triangle, so trigonometry is the best method, as the formatting of the answer choice options hints. Remember SOHCAHTOA and relate all sides to the given angle. $\overline{AC}$ is the opposite side and $\overline{BC}$ is the adjacent side of $\angle ABC$; this describes tangent.

$$\tan19°=\frac{\overline{AC}}{53}$$

$$53\tan19°=\overline{AC}$$

Hence, (H) is correct.

33. C

Difficulty: Medium
Category: Algebra
Getting to the Answer: The question asks for the sum of the (x,y) coordinates of the solution of the given system of equations. Begin by isolating y in the second equation to obtain $y=3$. Substitute $y=3$ into $2y-3x=9$ and solve for x.

$$2y-3x=9$$

$$2(3)-3x=9$$

$$6-3x=9$$

$$-3x=3$$

$$x=-1$$

The solution for the given system of equations is $(-1,3)$. However, the question asks for the sum of the coordinates: $-1+3=2$. (C) is correct.

34. F

Difficulty: Medium
Category: Algebra
Getting to the Answer: To factor, you need two numbers that multiply to equal +12 and add to equal −7. These are −3 and −4, so $x^2-7x+12=(x-3)(x-4)$. Choice (F) is correct. To double check, you can always FOIL and get back to the original expression.

35. D

Difficulty: High

Category: Number and Quantity

Getting to the Answer: Convert from radical form into exponential form and combine like terms:

$$x^4\sqrt[5]{x^2} \cdot y^3\sqrt{y^7} = x^{\frac{4}{1}}x^{\frac{2}{5}} \cdot y^{\frac{3}{1}}y^{\frac{7}{2}}$$

$$= x^{\frac{20}{5}}x^{\frac{2}{5}} \cdot y^{\frac{6}{2}}y^{\frac{7}{2}}$$

$$= x^{\frac{20}{5}+\frac{2}{5}} \cdot y^{\frac{6}{2}+\frac{7}{2}}$$

$$= x^{\frac{22}{5}} \cdot y^{\frac{13}{2}}$$

Notice that the answers are in radical form, so now reverse this process by converting the improper fractions into mixed fractions. The leftover fractions will require a common denominator when they are converted back into radical form.

$$x^{\frac{22}{5}}y^{\frac{13}{2}} = x^4 x^{\frac{2}{5}}y^6 y^{\frac{1}{2}}$$

$$= x^4 y^6 x^{\frac{2}{5}}y^{\frac{1}{2}}$$

$$= x^4 y^6 x^{\frac{4}{10}}y^{\frac{5}{10}}$$

$$= x^4 y^6 \sqrt[10]{x^4 y^5}$$

The given expression is equivalent to $x^4 y^6 \sqrt[10]{x^4 y^5}$. Choice (D) is correct.

36. G

Difficulty: Medium

Category: Statistics and Probability

Getting to the Answer: The question asks for the approximate percentage of sales in January that were from Accessories. This is equal to January Accessories sales ($750), divided by the total sales in January for all 3 departments ($1,150 + $1,000 + $750):

$$\frac{\$750}{\$1,150 + \$1,000 + \$750} = \frac{\$750}{\$2,900} = \frac{\$15}{\$58}$$

Therefore, $\frac{15}{58} \approx 0.2586$ and $0.2586 \times 100 = 25.86\%$. This means that Accessories sales is approximately 26% of the January sales, so (G) is correct.

37. A

Difficulty: Medium

Category: Functions

Getting to the Answer: The question asks you to match the graph to the given piecewise function. The best strategy is process of elimination, starting with the top equation and working your way down. The top equation is $y = x$ but is only graphed when $x \le -2$. This is a simple linear equation with a slope of 1. Eliminate B, C, and D because when $x \le -2$, the lines have a negative slope.

Now notice that when $x \ge 2$, the remaining choices, A and E, have a line with either a positive or negative slope. When $x \ge 2$, $y = -x$, which is a negative slope. This means that (A) is correct.

38. J

Difficulty: Medium

Category: Algebra

Getting to the Answer: The question asks for the relationship between the price at Carl's shop and the hours of labor worked. Do not use the third column since the question does not mention Sherri's shop. Notice that all the choices are in slope-intercept form, $y = mx + b$ (or $c = mh + b$ in this case), so it must be a linear relationship. Any data point (h,c) from the table should satisfy the equation.

Plug a data point, for example $(3,40)$, into the answer choices to determine which equation is satisfied:

F: $40 \ne 0.1(3) + 19.9$. Eliminate it.

G: $40 \ne 0.1(3) + 15$. Eliminate it.

H: $40 \ne 5(3) + 15$. Eliminate it.

J: $40 = 10(3) + 10$. This is true, so (J) is correct.

Note that a data point may satisfy more than one equation. In that case, choose another data point and evaluate the remaining choices. For the record, K: $40 \ne 10(3) + 20$.

Alternatively, you could solve for the equation algebraically. The table shows that the price increases $20 for every 2 hours of labor worked. Apply the slope formula: $m = \frac{\text{change in } c}{\text{change in } h} = \frac{20}{2} = 10$. Since the slope is 10, eliminate choices F, G, and H.

Next, plug in a point from the table and solve for b. $(1, 20)$ should yield the easiest numbers to work with:

$$c = 10h + b$$
$$20 = 10(1) + b$$
$$20 = 10 + b$$
$$10 = b$$

Since $c = 10h + 10$ describes the relationship between the price at Carl's shop and the hours of labor worked, (J) is correct.

39. B

Difficulty: High
Category: Number and Quantity
Getting to the Answer: Write an equation that sets the volume of Vat A equal to the volume of Vat B after x minutes. Since the volume of Vat A, which initially was 450 gallons, is increasing at a rate of 40 gallons per minute, the volume of Vat A after x minutes equals $450 + 40x$. Similarly, since the volume of Vat B, which initially was 1,250 gallons, is increasing at a rate of 15 gallons per minute, the volume of Vat B after x minutes is $1,250 + 15x$. Set the two equal to each other and solve for x:

$$450 + 40x = 1,250 + 15x$$
$$40x = 800 + 15x$$
$$25x = 800$$
$$x = 32$$

Therefore, it will take 32 minutes before the vats contain equal amounts of toluene. (B) is correct.

40. H

Difficulty: Medium
Category: Statistics and Probability
Getting to the Answer: The question asks what fraction of players made fewer than 2 free throws. The total number of players was already given as 19, so find how many players made fewer than 2 free throws. The bar graph shows that 5 players scored 0 free throws and that 2 players scored 1 free throw. This means that 7 players scored fewer than 2 free throws. The fraction of players that scored fewer than 2 free throws is therefore $\frac{7}{19}$, and (H) is correct.

41. E

Difficulty: Medium
Category: Statistics and Probability
Getting to the Answer: The question asks for the average number of free throws made. Apply the average formula, calculating the sum of the terms by multiplying the number of free throws made by the number of players for each bar in the bar graph:

$$\text{average} = \frac{\text{sum of terms}}{\text{number of terms}}$$

$$\text{average} = \frac{5(0) + 2(1) + 4(2) + 1(3) + 4(4) + 2(5) + 1(6)}{19}$$

$$= \frac{45}{19}$$

$$\approx 2.4$$

Since the average of free throws made is about 2.4, (E) is correct.

42. J

Difficulty: High
Category: Number and Quantity
Getting to the Answer: The question asks for the value of x in the given logarithmic equation. Convert the equation into exponential form using the fact that $\log_b a = x$ is the same as $b^x = a$ (which you might remember by thinking that *the base is the base* and *the edge is the exponent*):

$$\log_2 16^2 = x$$
$$2^x = 16^2$$

When the variable that you are solving for is in an exponent, try to make both bases equal. Rewrite 16^2 as $(2^4)^2 = 2^8$. Now that both bases are the same, set the exponents equal to each other and solve:

$$2^x = 2^8$$
$$x = 8$$

Thus, the value of x equals 8, and (J) is correct.

43. E

Difficulty: High
Category: Geometry
Getting to the Answer: The question asks for the equation of the circle described. Recall that the standard equation of a circle is $(x - h)^2 + (y - k)^2 = r^2$, where (h,k) is the center of the circle and r is its radius.

Since the circle is tangent to both the *x*-axis and the line $y = 6$, the circle must lie in quadrants I and/or II. It cannot be centered at or below $y = 0$. Eliminate A and C, for which the *y*-value of the center is 0, and eliminate D since the center of D, $(3, -3)$, has a negative *y*-value. The circle occupies all the points from $y = 0$ to $y = 6$ inclusive, so its diameter is 6 and its radius is 3. Since, $r^2 = 3^2 = 9$, (E) is correct.

44. K
Difficulty: Medium
Category: Geometry
Getting to the Answer: The question asks how many square feet of floor space are inside the building described. Use the fact that the volume of a rectangular object is equal to length × width × height. The question tells you that a volume of 2,700 cubic feet of chlorine gas is pumped into the building, and since the gas is heavier than air, it lies on the floor with the height given at 0.4 ft. To calculate the area of the floor, solve for length × width:

$$l \times w \times (0.4) = 2,700$$
$$l \times w = 6,750$$

The area of the floor of the building is 6,750 square feet, which is more than 4,000. Choice (K) is correct.

45. C
Difficulty: Medium
Category: Algebra
Getting to the Answer: The question asks how much Bill owes, given the total amount of the check and the fact that Bill owes $14 more than Todd. Let Bill's amount owed equal B and let Todd's amount owed equal T. The combined amount owed is $52, so $B + T = $52. Additionally, Bill owes $14 more than Todd does, so $B = T + \$14$. Therefore, $T = B - \$14$. Substitute this into the first equation and solve for B:

$$B + (B - 14) = 52$$
$$2B - 14 = 52$$
$$2B = 66$$
$$B = 33$$

Since Bill owes $33, (C) is correct.

46. K
Difficulty: High
Category: Number and Quantity
Getting to the Answer: The question asks for an equivalent expression. When imaginary numbers are in the denominator of a fraction, the denominator must be rationalized by multiplying by its conjugate.

$$\frac{i}{(3-i)} \times \frac{(3+i)}{(3+i)} = \frac{3i + i^2}{9 - i^2}$$
$$= \frac{3i - 1}{9 - (-1)}$$
$$= \frac{-1 + 3i}{10}$$
$$= -\frac{1}{10} + \frac{3i}{10}$$

Choice (K) is correct.

47. E
Difficulty: High
Category: Statistics and Probability
Getting to the Answer: The question asks for the expected value of typing mistakes made in a day. Multiply each number of typing mistakes by its associated probability. Then add up all the terms. $EV(n) = 0(0.10) + 1(0.40) + 2(0.30) + 3(0.20) = 1.60$. The expected value of typing mistakes made in a day is 1.60, so (E) is correct.

48. J
Difficulty: Medium
Category: Function
Getting to the Answer: The question asks for the domain of the given function. Remember that domain refers to the *x*-values that are mapped by the function. Looking at the graph, you can see that the *x*-values range from -2 to 2. Even though there are open dots, notice how the dots along the *y*-axis overlap with one another, leaving no gaps in the domain. This means the domain is unbroken between -2 and 2. So, the domain can be written as $-2 \leq x < 2$. Choice (J) is correct.

49. B

Difficulty: Medium

Category: Statistics and Probability

Getting to the Answer: The question asks for the median of the given frequency table. Remember that the median is the middle number when the data are arranged in increasing order. Rewrite the numbers in ascending order as 10, 10, 10, 10, 10, 10, 10, 10, 11, 11, 11, 12, 12, 12, 12, 12, 12, 13, 13, 13, 14, 14. There are a total of 22 data values, so the middle number is the average of the 11th and 12th number, which is 11.5. Since the median value of this data set is 11.5, (B) is correct.

50. J

Difficulty: High

Category: Geometry

Getting to the Answer: The question asks for the ratio of the area of the square to the area of the right triangle. The given information is that the right triangle has angles of 90° and 30°, so the third angle must be 60°. Recall that for a 30-60-90 right triangle, the sides are related by the ratio $x : x\sqrt{3} : 2x$. The smaller leg of the triangle is 4, so the longer leg is $4\sqrt{3}$, and the hypotenuse is $4(2) = 8$. Finally, note that the hypotenuse is the diameter of the circle, which is also the side of the square. You now have all you need to calculate the areas. The triangle's area is:

$$\frac{bh}{2} = \frac{4(4\sqrt{3})}{2} = 8\sqrt{3}$$

The square's area is $s^2 = (8)^2 = 64$. The ratio of the area of the square to the area of the right triangle is therefore $64 : 8\sqrt{3}$, which reduces to $8 : \sqrt{3}$. (J) is correct.

51. C

Difficulty: Low

Category: Geometry

Getting to the Answer: The question asks for the circumference of the circle. Remember that the equation for a circle's circumference is $C = 2\pi r$ or $C = \pi d$. The diameter was calculated to be 8, so $C = 8\pi$. Choice (C) is correct.

52. K

Difficulty: High

Category: Number and Quantity

Getting to the Answer: The first statement is that "all animals that eat dog food are dogs." You can therefore deduce that because Animal F eats dog food, it must be a dog. The flip side of the premise is that if an animal is *not* a dog, then it *doesn't* eat dog food. (This must be true because if the animal *did* eat dog food, then it would, according to the premise, be a dog.) Consequently, since you know that Animal E is not a dog, you can deduce that it does not eat dog food.

Examine each choice, looking for the one that matches one of the deductions you've made. Only (K) does, so it's correct. For the record: F contradicts the fact that Animal E is a dog, G and J contradict your deductions, and H is off topic (for all you know, dogs may or may not eat cat food).

53. D

Difficulty: Low

Category: Algebra

Getting to the Answer: Frank's total paycheck is his number of hours worked times the average hourly wage ($70 \times h$). Since \$1,470 is the minimum paycheck, $70h \geq \$1,470$, or $h \geq \$21$. Choice (D) is correct.

54. H

Difficulty: Medium

Category: Functions

Getting to the Answer: The question asks for the equation that represents a shift 2 units to the left and 3 units down. Recall that to shift a function n units to the left, you add n inside the parentheses; to shift a function m units down, you subtract m outside the parentheses. Thus, you want the equation that adds 2 inside the parentheses and subtracts 3 outside of them. The only choice that does this is (H), so it is correct.

55. A

Difficulty: Medium
Category: Number and Quantity
Getting to the Answer: The question asks for the park ranger's estimate for the number of healthy trees in the park. The second matrix indicates the percentage of each type of tree that is healthy (represented as decimals). Multiply the number of each type of tree by its corresponding decimal and add all of these values together to get the total number of healthy trees: $70(0.4) + 30(0.6) + 40(0.8) + 50(0.7) = 28 + 18 + 32 + 35 = 113$. Thus, (A) is correct.

56. J

Difficulty: Medium
Category: Geometry
Getting to the Answer: The question asks for the volume of the described cylinder. Use the volume formula $V = \pi r^2 h$:

$$V = \pi r^2 h$$
$$= \pi (9^2)(10)$$
$$= \pi (81)(10)$$
$$= 810\pi$$

Choice (J) is correct.

57. E

Difficulty: Low
Category: Statistics and Probability
Getting to the Answer: The question asks for the method that describes the company's testing. First, check whether the testing is non-randomized or randomized. The question states that the employees selected to take the survey were chosen at random, so eliminate A and B. Next, use process of elimination on the remaining choices. There is no control group, so this is not an experiment; eliminate D. A census is a survey conducted on the entire population, so eliminate C. Choice (E) must be correct because a smaller group, or sample, of all the employees was chosen to complete the survey.

58. K

Difficulty: Medium
Category: Geometry
Getting to the Answer: The question asks for $\sin \psi$—and it's okay if you aren't familiar with the ψ symbol, which represents the Greek letter *psi*. If it makes this question easier to think through, you can always substitute a θ or even just an x. To remember which quadrants are positive, you might recall a mnemonic, such as *All Students Take Calculus*, which signifies which trigonometric functions are positive in the order of the quadrants, starting in Quadrant 1 (top right) and moving counterclockwise: All, Sine, Tangent, Cosine. Sine is always positive in the first two quadrants, so eliminate F, G, and H. Draw a right triangle from the given coordinate to the x-axis and label the known lengths.

Use the Pythagorean theorem to solve for the hypotenuse of the right triangle.

$$a^2 + b^2 = c^2$$
$$(7)^2 + (24)^2 = c^2$$
$$625 = c^2$$
$$25 = c$$

Recall that $\sin = \dfrac{\text{opposite}}{\text{hypotenuse}}$. The opposite side is 24 and the hypotenuse is 25, so $\sin\psi = \sin\dfrac{24}{25}$. Choice (K) is correct.

59. B
Difficulty: Medium
Category: Algebra
Getting to the Answer: The question asks for the value of the bacteria population after 5 days under ideal heat and moisture conditions. Plug the given values, $h = 0.5$ and $t = 5$, into the given formula.

$$P = \frac{3^{2t-1}}{h} + 200$$

$$P = \frac{3^{2(5)-1}}{(0.5)} + 200$$

$$P = 39,566$$

The population of the bacteria colony is 39,566 after 5 days in ideal heat and moisture conditions, so (B) is correct.

60. G
Difficulty: High
Category: Functions
Getting to the Answer: The question asks for the amplitude of the given function. Recall that the amplitude of a function in the form $A\sin(Bx + C)$ is $|A|$. This means that $\frac{3}{4}$ is the amplitude, and (G) is correct.

61. D
Difficulty: High
Category: Functions
Getting to the Answer: The question asks for the general equation that describes the family of parabolas graphed. Notice that the vertex of each parabola is at $(0, -3)$, so eliminate C. All of the parabolas open upwards, so the coefficient of the x^2 term must be positive; eliminate A and B. The only difference between the remaining choices is the coefficient of the x^2 term. The larger the coefficient is, the slimmer the parabola will be. The smaller the coefficient is, the wider the parabola becomes. The graph indicates that as n gets larger, the parabola widens, meaning the coefficient of the x^2 term becomes smaller, so (D) is correct.

62. G
Difficulty: High
Category: Functions
Getting to the Answer: The question asks for the period of the graphed function. The period is the distance that passes along the x-axis until the graph repeats itself. At the origin, the graph is heading upwards; the next time that the graph crosses the x-axis and is heading upwards is in between π and 2π at $\frac{3\pi}{2}$. Choice (G) is correct.

63. E
Difficulty: High
Category: Statistics and Probability
Getting to the Answer: The question asks for the expected value from the given probability distribution table. Use the formula $E(X) = x_1 p_1 + x_2 p_2 + \ldots + x_i p_i$.

$$E(X) = 0\left(\frac{1}{3}\right) + 1\left(\frac{1}{12}\right) + 2\left(\frac{1}{24}\right) + 3(0) + 4(0)$$

$$+ 5\left(\frac{7}{24}\right) + 6\left(\frac{1}{4}\right)$$

$$E(X) = \frac{1}{12} + \frac{2}{24} + \frac{35}{24} + \frac{6}{4}$$

$$E(X) = \frac{2}{24} + \frac{2}{24} + \frac{35}{24} + \frac{36}{24}$$

$$E(X) = \frac{75}{24}$$

Because $\frac{75}{24}$ is not a choice, simplify the fraction: $\frac{75}{24} = \frac{25}{8}$. Hence, (E) is correct.

64. K
Difficulty: High
Category: Geometry
Getting to the Answer: The question asks for the expression that represents the measure of the largest angle of the triangle. The question stem reminds you that the law of sines is $\frac{\sin A}{a} = \frac{\sin B}{b} = \frac{\sin C}{c}$ and the law of cosines is $c^2 = a^2 + b^2 - 2ab \cos C$. To use the law of sines, you have to know at least one of the angles. This is not the case, so eliminate F, G, and H. To distinguish between J and (K), consider the fact that the question asks about the largest angle. Recall that in a triangle, the largest angle is always across from the largest side. The largest side of the given triangle is 15, so the c term in the law of cosines must be 15, and (K) is correct.

ACT READING

CHAPTER 15

THE METHOD FOR ACT READING

LEARNING OBJECTIVES

After completing this chapter, you will be able to:

- Read passages strategically by applying the ACT Reading Passage Strategy
- Effectively and efficiently apply the Method for ACT Reading Questions

---

How to Do ACT Reading

The ACT Reading Test is usually made up of three independent passages and one set of paired passages, each approximately 750–1,000 words long and accompanied by 10 questions, for a total of 40 questions in the section. To tackle all of this effectively in 35 minutes, the most successful test takers:

- Read the passages strategically to zero in on the text that leads to points.

- Approach the questions with a method that minimizes rereading and leads directly to correct answers.

The key to maximizing correct answers on the ACT Reading Test is learning in advance the kinds of questions that the test asks. ACT Reading questions focus more on the author's purpose (*why* she wrote the passage) and the passage's structure (*how* the author makes and supports her points) than on the details or facts of the subject matter (*what* the passage is about). You can answer these predictable questions more confidently by reading more effectively, and paying attention to *how* and *why* the author wrote the passage or chose to include certain words or examples.

In this chapter, we'll give you an overview of how to tackle Reading passages and questions. The other chapters in this unit will help you become a stronger reader and present the five ACT Reading question types, as well as tips for improving your approach to literature and paired passages.

Try the passage and questions that follow on your own. Then, keep reading to compare your approach to our recommendations for how to approach ACT Reading.

SOCIAL SCIENCE: The following passage is adapted from an article in a travel journal on tourism in Mexico.

Before tourism became a mainstay of the economy, the value of terrain in Mexico was defined by the arability of the land. To many Americans, tropical tourist-oriented beach towns
5   such as Acapulco and Puerto Vallarta characterize Mexico. These may be the most common sorts of destinations for foreign travelers, but they certainly are not the most representative areas of the country itself. These cities, and others
10 like them, are set up to be attractive to the tourist trade, for better or worse. But the land and culture are vastly different from those of the *altiplano*, or high plain. The function and appearance of each type of terrain dictate this
15 divergence.

A tropical beach is a specialized area, not only because it cannot be found outside of specific latitude measurements; any living thing must be highly specialized to survive there or else must
20 acclimate quickly. This is the least livable area: the closer a land dweller moves to the ocean, the fewer the resources necessary to sustain life, and vice versa. Specialized areas in nature are analogous to the settlements of indigenous
25 people in forbidding environments, untouched by modern society. Surroundings dictate the life of a consumer—human or otherwise—and, through adaptation, one is nearly defined by the other. In sharp contrast is the tourist in the tropics,
30 who has likely settled upon a destination by how different it looks from home. In order to appeal to such tourists, the beach towns often contain deliberate marks of earlier civilizations, but these contrivances do not characterize the history or
35 culture of the portions of the country inhabited for function rather than beauty.

Mexico's beach towns import resources to accommodate a great number of people, but the terrain itself generally lacks certain basic human
40 necessities: soil suitable for plant cultivation and sufficient reserves of drinking water, both

of which occur naturally in the temperate and fertile *altiplano* region. A traveler in Acapulco would learn no more about the foundations of
45 Mexican agriculture than a visitor to Yellowstone Park would learn about New York City. While the tourist often delights in the year-round heat and humidity of the coast, the Mayan people, the first known to flourish in coastal Mexico,
50 are considered to have been brilliant in their eschewing of the natural hazards and barrenness of tropical beaches rather than reveling in this environment. The Mayans relied on the discovery and utilization of *cenotes*, natural springs that
55 provided fresh water. Without a *cenote* nearby, the Mayans would not settle in a locale, no matter how picturesque.

The tropical coast is uniformly regulated by the ocean, but the *altiplano* is a tapestry of
60 microclimates that vary from one mile to the next. The coast extends laterally, breaking only for the mouth of a river or the edge of a mountain range, where cliffs are slowly eroding into future beaches. The *altiplano*, on the other hand,
65 expands in all directions and gradually fades into the mountains. The coast presents a border; the *altiplano* is expansive and indefinite. The difference is akin to that between a gymnasium and an open market. A gymnasium is set up to
70 provide a basic range of functions, and because of this, a person familiar with one gymnasium will find similar equipment and be able to obtain a similar experience at another. The gymnasium is equipped to sustain its patrons for a short
75 period of time. It presents a widely understood and repeatable experience to visitors. Any great variance would do customers a disservice. The market, conversely, represents the surroundings through products and vendors. When there
80 are avocados at a market, there are avocados in fields nearby. If one product is found in a disproportionately large number of vendors' stands, it is likely well suited for cultivation or popular with local consumers. The local

85 residents set the tone for both what is available
and what is popular. A different market keeps
only the conventions of the seller and buyer; the
local residents and agricultural terrain dictate
price, product, and appearance. The traveler's
90 preferences are not addressed. An unseasoned cut
of meat may not be available, and its replacement
may include an array of flavors completely new to
a foreign palate. A desired apple could be a rare
and exotic indulgence and may give way to the
95 ubiquitous guava.

The best way to experience foreign lands,
therefore, is a less conventional way: through areas
defined by local culture rather than by tourists,
avoiding both the prepared environments and the
100 artificial familiarity that defines them.

1. Which of the following best states the main idea
    of the passage?

    A. More people ought to visit the *altiplano*
        regions of Mexico instead of its tropical
        beaches.

    B. Without the contributions of the *altiplano*,
        Mexico's beach resort towns would not be
        able to sustain themselves or their visitors.

    C. The *altiplano* is more diverse and rich in life
        than tropical beaches.

    D. Although tropical beaches are popular tour-
        ist destinations, the *altiplano* provides a truer
        experience of Mexican culture.

2. According to the passage, what makes a tropical
    beach a specialized area?

    F. It cannot exist outside of particular
        longitudes.

    G. It resembles a gymnasium.

    H. Land-based life has difficulty finding the
        resources to survive there.

    J. One tropical beach is much like any other
        tropical beach.

3. As it is used in line 26, the word *dictate* most
    nearly means:

    A. command action.

    B. speak for recording.

    C. forbid response.

    D. shape development.

4. The passage most strongly suggests that the
    Mayan people were the first to flourish in coastal
    Mexico because they:

    F. adapted to thrive in the year-round heat and
        humidity.

    G. successfully discovered enough *cenotes* to
        support the population.

    H. conveniently avoided the risks of living on
        the coastline.

    J. avoided confrontations with others by using
        the coast as a border.

5. The comparison between a gymnasium and an
    open market in paragraph 4 is meant to:

    A. contrast tourists who visit the coast with
        those who visit the *altiplano*.

    B. show that inland areas are better equipped
        than beach towns to accommodate the needs
        of visitors.

    C. emphasize that beach resorts are set up to
        cater to visitors in a way that the *altiplano* is
        not.

    D. indicate that consumer goods are less
        available on the coast than inland.

Strategic Reading

The ACT Reading Test is an open-book test: the passage is right there for you to reference. Because of the way the test is constructed, it is in your best interest to read fairly quickly, noting the outline of the passage as you go and writing notes in the margins as you read. Your goal is to get a solid understanding of the main idea without wasting time memorizing details. You can think of this process of outlining the passage as **mapping** it: you are taking note of its major features but letting go of the minor details.

Be sure to read the pre-passage blurb, the short introduction that comes before the passage. Identify any information that helps you to understand the topic of the passage or to anticipate what the author will discuss. For the passage above, the blurb states the topic (tourism) and announces that the passage is an excerpt from "a travel journal on tourism in Mexico." That's an invitation to keep your eye out for a perspective on tourism in Mexico as you read.

You'll learn all the skills you need to **read strategically** in chapter 16, but for now, here's an example of an expert's strategic thinking and passage map notes. Don't worry if your notes don't look exactly like this (or even anything like this, yet). Follow the expert's thought process in the discussion that follows the passage to see what he was thinking and asking as he read the passage.

SOCIAL SCIENCE: The following passage is adapted from an article in a travel journal on tourism in Mexico.

Before tourism became a mainstay of the economy, the value of terrain in Mexico was defined by the arability of the land. To many Americans, tropical tourist-oriented beach towns
5 such as Acapulco and Puerto Vallarta characterize Mexico. These may be the most common sorts of destinations for foreign travelers, but they certainly are not the most representative areas of the country itself. These cities, and others
10 like them, are set up to be attractive to the tourist trade, for better or worse. But the land and culture are vastly different from those of the *altiplano*, or high plain. The function and appearance of each type of terrain dictate this
15 divergence.

beach towns vs. altiplano; beaches = tourism

ANALYSIS

Pre-passage blurb: The passage will address tourism in Mexico.

¶1 This paragraph introduces a contrast in how land in Mexico is valued, based on tourism or arability. The author connects tourism with tropical beach cities but says these areas are not "representative" of Mexico. The author then contrasts this with the *altiplano* (note the "But" at the beginning of the sentence in line 11). It seems like coming paragraphs will discuss how "function and appearance" lead to this contrast.

A tropical beach is a specialized area, not only because it cannot be found outside of specific latitude measurements; any living thing must be highly specialized to survive there or else must
20 acclimate quickly. This is the least livable area: the closer a land dweller moves to the ocean, the fewer the resources necessary to sustain life, and vice versa. Specialized areas in nature are analogous to the settlements of indigenous
25 people in forbidding environments, untouched by modern society. Surroundings dictate the life of a consumer—human or otherwise—and, through adaptation, one is nearly defined by the other. In sharp contrast is the tourist in the tropics,
30 who has likely settled upon a destination by how different it looks from home. In order to appeal to such tourists, the beach towns often contain deliberate marks of earlier civilizations, but these contrivances do not characterize the history or
35 culture of the portions of the country inhabited for function rather than beauty.

Mexico's beach towns import resources to accommodate a great number of people, but the terrain itself generally lacks certain basic human
40 necessities: soil suitable for plant cultivation and sufficient reserves of drinking water, both of which occur naturally in the temperate and fertile *altiplano* region. A traveler in Acapulco would learn no more about the foundations of
45 Mexican agriculture than a visitor to Yellowstone Park would learn about New York City. While the tourist often delights in the year-round heat and humidity of the coast, the Mayan people, the first known to flourish in coastal Mexico,
50 are considered to have been brilliant in their eschewing of the natural hazards and barrenness of tropical beaches rather than reveling in this environment. The Mayans relied on the discovery and utilization of *cenotes*, natural springs that
55 provided fresh water. Without a *cenote* nearby, the Mayans would not settle in a locale, no matter how picturesque.

beaches require adaptation; tourists just want good looks

¶2 The author discusses the function and appearance of tropical beaches. They are "specialized" environments; organisms must adapt to survive. "In sharp contrast"—the author wants to make a point—tourists are attracted by appearance, not function.

altiplano has better resources than beach; Maya smart for avoiding beach

¶3 This paragraph emphasizes the necessity of basic resources. The author again contrasts beaches and *altiplano*, saying that the beach lacks resources available in the "temperate and fertile" *altiplano*. The author clearly favors the *altiplano*. The second part of the paragraph contains another contrast ("While," line 46), this time between the tourists and the Maya, "brilliant" for settling only where they could find resources.

Reading

The tropical coast is uniformly regulated
by the ocean, but the *altiplano* is a tapestry of
60 microclimates that vary from one mile to the
next. The coast extends laterally, breaking only
for the mouth of a river or the edge of a mountain
range, where cliffs are slowly eroding into future
beaches. The *altiplano*, on the other hand,
65 expands in all directions and gradually fades
into the mountains. The coast presents a border;
the *altiplano* is expansive and indefinite. The
difference is akin to that between a gymnasium
and an open market. A gymnasium is set up to
70 provide a basic range of functions, and because
of this, a person familiar with one gymnasium
will find similar equipment and be able to obtain
a similar experience at another. The gymnasium
is equipped to sustain its patrons for a short
75 period of time. It presents a widely understood
and repeatable experience to visitors. Any great
variance would do customers a disservice. The
market, conversely, represents the surroundings
through products and vendors. When there
80 are avocados at a market, there are avocados
in fields nearby. If one product is found in a
disproportionately large number of vendors'
stands, it is likely well suited for cultivation
or popular with local consumers. The local
85 residents set the tone for both what is available
and what is popular. A different market keeps
only the conventions of the seller and buyer; the
local residents and agricultural terrain dictate
price, product, and appearance. The traveler's
90 preferences are not addressed. An unseasoned cut
of meat may not be available, and its replacement
may include an array of flavors completely new to
a foreign palate. A desired apple could be a rare
and exotic indulgence and may give way to the
95 ubiquitous guava.

The best way to experience foreign lands,
therefore, is a less conventional way: through areas
defined by local culture rather than by tourists,
avoiding both the prepared environments and the
100 artificial familiarity that defines them.

*altiplano is
varied and
extensive;
gym/market
analogy*

*author:
altiplano
better
to visit*

¶4 This paragraph expands on the contrast
between beach and *altiplano*. There's more
information about the *altiplano*, shown as a
series of contrasts with the beach. Again, the
author's language choices favor the *altiplano*,
describing it as a "tapestry" that "expands in
all directions." Then, the author presents an
extended analogy comparing the beach to
a gym—limited and uniform, catering to its
customers—and the *altiplano* to a market—
varied and expansive, a product of many local
factors.

¶5 The last paragraph states the author's opinion: that foreign visitors should seek out local
culture, not artificial sculpted environments.

To sum up **the big picture**, pause for a moment after reading to consider the passage's main idea and the author's purpose for writing it.

BIG PICTURE SUMMARY

Main idea: Although most tourists opt to visit Mexico's resort towns, the author argues that these towns are not representative of the country as a whole.

Author's purpose: To compare the experiences of tourists who visit the Mexican coast and those who visit the *altiplano*

Notice that the ACT expert reads actively, consistently paraphrasing what the author has said, identifying the author's viewpoint, asking what must come next, and never getting too caught up in details.

Think about how the ACT expert used the ACT Reading Passage Strategy to read this passage strategically:

- Extract everything you can from the pre-passage blurb
- Read each paragraph actively
- Summarize the passage's big picture

Don't worry if your notes don't look exactly like the ones in this book. When you review a set of strategic thinking notes, focus on comparing your overall thought process and main takeaways to those of a strategic test taker and determine at least one way you can read more effectively and efficiently next time. When you take the time to read strategically first, you are more likely to answer questions both efficiently and correctly.

The Method for ACT Reading Questions

Once you've read the passage strategically, you're ready for the questions. ACT experts use a simple four-step method to tackle each question quickly and confidently.

ACT READING QUESTION METHOD

Step 1. Unpack the question stem

Step 2. Research the answer

Step 3. Predict the answer

Step 4. Find the one correct answer

Because different question types require different strategies, start by **unpacking the information in the question stem** and identifying the question type while ignoring the answer choices. There are only five types of questions in the Reading Test, so knowing what type of question you're answering will help you decide where to look for your answer. You'll learn how to do this important step in chapter 17.

Next, based on the type of question, **research the passage** or your passage map to get the information you need. The incorrect answer choices on a multiple-choice test actually have a name: distractors. Distractors are carefully crafted to sound correct and take your attention away from the correct choice, so if you read all of the answer choices as soon as you finish examining the question stem, you risk getting distracted from what's actually supported by the passage. With the relevant part of the passage in mind, **predict** what the correct answer will say before you look at the answer choices.

Finally, check your prediction against the choices and **find the one correct answer** that matches. Because ACT experts arm themselves with strong predictions in step 3, they can often zero in on the correct response without wasting time by rereading or hunting around in the passage to check each answer. You'll go over the strategies and tactics that experts use for steps 2–4 in chapter 18.

Take a look at our expert's application of the Method for ACT Reading Questions to the questions from the Mexico tourism passage.

Question	Explanation
1. Which of the following best states the main idea of the passage? A. More people ought to visit the *altiplano* regions of Mexico instead of its tropical beaches. B. Without the contributions of the *altiplano*, Mexico's beach resort towns would not be able to sustain themselves or their visitors. C. The *altiplano* is more diverse and rich in life than tropical beaches. D. Although tropical beaches are popular tourist destinations, the *altiplano* provides a truer experience of Mexican culture.	**Step 1: Unpack the question stem.** The question stem includes the phrase "main idea," which indicates that it is a Global question. **Step 2: Research the answer.** To answer this type of question, you should review the main idea summary in your notes. **Step 3: Predict the answer.** Predict that the correct answer will involve a contrast between the tropical beach, which is specialized to cater to tourism, and the *altiplano*, which displays the diversity of the local population. **Step 4: Find the one correct answer.** Choice (D) matches this prediction and is correct. Choices B and C, while factually accurate, do not fully capture the main idea of the whole passage. Choice A is too extreme, making a stronger statement than the passage does.

Question	Explanation
2. According to the passage, what makes a tropical beach a specialized area? F. It cannot exist outside of particular longitudes. G. It resembles a gymnasium. H. Land-based life has difficulty finding the resources to survive there. J. One tropical beach is much like any other tropical beach.	**Step 1: Unpack the question stem.** The question stem includes the phrase "According to the passage," which indicates that it is a Detail question. **Step 2: Research the answer.** The tropical beach as a specialized area is discussed in paragraph 2, which describes the beach as "the least livable area: the closer a land dweller moves to the ocean, the fewer the resources necessary to sustain life." **Step 3: Predict the answer.** Predict that these regions are specialized because it is hard to live there due to the lack of resources. **Step 4: Find the one correct answer.** Choice (H) matches the prediction and is correct. Choice F is a distortion; the passage states that tropical beaches cannot exist outside of certain *latitudes*, not *longitudes*. Choice G is a misused detail; while the author does compare tropical beach towns to gymnasiums, the resemblance is not the reason why such locations are specialized. Finally, choice J does not address what makes these areas specialized.
3. As it is used in line 26, the word *dictate* most nearly means: A. command action. B. speak for recording. C. forbid response. D. shape development.	**Step 1: Unpack the question stem.** The question stem includes the clues "As used in line" and "the word . . . most nearly means," which indicate that it is a Vocab-in-Context question. **Step 2: Research the answer.** To answer a question like this, read a little bit above and below line 26 and think about what the word *dictate* means here. **Step 3: Predict the answer.** Predict that the environment *impacts* or *molds* the living things that dwell there. **Step 4: Find the one correct answer.** Choice (D) matches the prediction and is correct. Choices A, B, and C are all other meanings of *dictate* that do not fit the context of the sentence: surroundings cannot *command, speak*, or *forbid*.

Reading

Question	Explanation
4. The passage most strongly suggests that the Mayan people were the first to flourish in coastal Mexico because they: F. adapted to thrive in the year-round heat and humidity. G. successfully discovered enough *cenotes* to support the population. H. conveniently avoided the risks of living on the coastline. J. avoided confrontations with others by using the coast as a border.	**Step 1: Unpack the question stem.** The question stem includes the phrase "most strongly suggests," indicating that it is an Inference question. Use the strong keyword clue "Mayan" and your passage map to lead you to paragraph 3. **Step 2: Research the answer.** Tropical beaches' inhospitable nature is discussed in paragraph 3, which states that tropical beaches usually lack basic necessities like drinking water. Lines 48–49 mention the Maya as the "first known to flourish," so read around those lines for the reason. The rest of the paragraph discusses the brilliance of the Maya in avoiding barren tropical coasts in favor of *cenotes*, which provided the fresh water they needed. **Step 3: Predict the answer.** Predict that the *cenotes* were likely the reason why the Maya flourished in coastal regions where others had not. **Step 4: Find the one correct answer.** Choice (G) matches the prediction and is correct. Choice F is a distortion; the passage says that tourists enjoy the heat and humidity in order to contrast them with the Maya. Choice H is vague and does not specifically explain how the Mayans succeeded. Finally, choice J is out of scope; the passage does not mention any potential conflicts with others.

Question	Explanation
5. The comparison between a gymnasium and an open market in paragraph 4 is meant to: A. contrast tourists who visit the coast with those who visit the *altiplano*. B. show that inland areas are better equipped than beach towns to accommodate the needs of visitors. C. emphasize that beach resorts are set up to cater to visitors in a way that the *altiplano* is not. D. indicate that consumer goods are less available on the coast than inland.	**Step 1: Unpack the question stem.** The question stem includes the clue "is meant to," indicating that it is a Function question. **Step 2: Research the answer.** Use your passage map to predict how the comparison contributes to the main idea of the passage. The fourth paragraph compares beach areas to the *altiplano*. The comparison between a predictable gymnasium experience and the unique experience of an open-air market is used as an analogy for the tourist-centered beach compared to the local-focused *altiplano*. **Step 3: Predict the answer.** Predict that the reference is meant to show that the beach resort towns are set up more specifically for the needs of visitors than the *altiplano* is. **Step 4: Find the one correct answer.** Choice (C) matches the prediction and is correct. Choice A is out of scope; there is no comparison between different types of tourists. Choice B is opposite; the author says that the beach towns, not the *altiplano*, are set up for tourists. Finally, choice D is out of scope; the passage never compares the quantities of consumer goods in the different areas.

Putting It All Together

To recap, to efficiently tackle the ACT Reading Test, make sure you:

- Never skip the pre-passage blurb. Quickly assess it to gather any information that provides context for the passage or that helps you anticipate what the author will cover.

- Read *actively*, asking what the author's purpose is in writing each paragraph. Anticipate where the passage will go. "Map" the passage by jotting down a short summary of each paragraph. You might also circle or underline keywords that indicate the author's opinion, details the author emphasized, and comparisons and contrasts made in the text.

- Pause for a moment after reading the passage to summarize the big picture: quickly note the main idea and the author's purpose for writing the passage.

- Once you have strategically read the passage, use the Method for ACT Reading Questions to attack the question set.

ACT READING QUESTION METHOD

Step 1. Unpack the question stem

Step 2. Research the answer

Step 3. Predict the answer

Step 4. Find the one correct answer

By reading strategically and using the Method for ACT Reading Questions every time you practice, you'll internalize the steps. By test day, you'll be attacking this section efficiently and accurately without even thinking about it.

In the next section, you'll see another ACT Reading passage, this time with 10 questions. Try to apply the ACT Reading Passage Strategy and the ACT Reading Question Method presented in this lesson to read and answer the questions as quickly and confidently as possible.

How Much Have You Learned?

Directions: Take as much time as you need on these questions. Assess your work by comparing it to the expert responses at the end of the chapter.

SOCIAL SCIENCE: This passage is adapted from a 2018 article.

The history of the New York City subway system, quickly told: the first stations opened in 1904, and over the next century, it expanded to 472 stations, more than any other subway system
5   in the world, with 850 miles of track. Operating 24 hours a day, seven days a week, with an average weekday ridership of approximately 5.7 million, it is the planet's 7th-busiest rapid transit system. While the system is, on many levels, an amazing
10 achievement, it is also beset by a problem that harms both quality of life and economic activity. Such a large system must inevitably suffer from service interruptions and delays; normal wear and tear combined with the sheer age of the system
15 necessitates regular maintenance. However, there is no consensus as to the best way to accomplish the required repairs.

The current maintenance scheme is designed to minimize service interruptions. A subway line in
20 need of repair will be taken out of service during a comparatively less busy time, such as nights or weekends, while another line is re-routed to cover as many as possible of the missing line's stops. The main advantage to this approach is that trains
25 are not taken out of service during rush hour, when most subway trips occur; subway service generally remains predictable and commuters are, for the most part, able to use the system to get to their destinations on time.

30 But critics are quick to point out the disadvantages to this approach. Perhaps most obvious is the confusion caused by trains switching lines. The labyrinthine system is hard enough to navigate at the best of times, especially
35 for tourists. A subway rider on the A train naturally expects the train to make stops on the A line. If, instead, it is diverted temporarily to the F line, the rider may find herself miles from her intended destination.

40 While annoying, the confusion arising from route switching is hardly the most serious problem with the current approach to repairs. Because the system runs 24 hours a day, routine maintenance can generally be done only during
45 the temporary closures on nights and weekends. This means that more serious repair and crucial preventative maintenance are often neglected. Problems that could have been fixed or prevented reasonably expeditiously given a slightly longer
50 closure wind up leading to major breakdowns and service interruptions later on.

On rare occasions, such breakdowns have resulted in entire subway lines being shut down for months or even a year. Beginning in 2019, for
55 example, the L train connecting lower Manhattan to parts of Brooklyn was scheduled to close for as much as 15 months for long overdue service and upgrades. In a city fewer than half of whose households own a car, this can have serious
60 economic impacts. Residents of the affected area may face a much longer commute via an alternate subway line if one is available; or, if there is no alternate subway service, they may need to take other, potentially more expensive, modes of
65 transportation, such as taxis or ferries. Moreover, studies indicate that increased stress from the commute to work can lead to lower productivity, and that businesses near the impacted lines may see decreased revenue as potential customers have
70 a harder time getting to them.

One controversial proposal for reducing breakdowns and the resulting transit interruptions is to end the subway's 24-hour service and to shut down for several hours each night. Proponents
75 of this plan argue that this would allow time, on a regular rather than sporadic basis, for more preventative maintenance. This, they claim, would ultimately lead to more consistent service; rather than shutting down entire lines for long periods
80 of a time, there would merely be shorter service

outages overnight, when fewer people use the
subway system. While this may seem a preferable
outcome to the economic consequences of a total
shutdown resulting from a breakdown, it has its
85 liabilities as well. While most subway trips may
occur during rush hour, not everyone works
during the daytime. New York is famously known
as the "the city that never sleeps." Doctors, nurses,
bartenders, police officers, and firefighters are
90 just a few examples of occupations whose workers
need transportation at all hours of the day and
night. Rather than be subjected to a relatively
short period of inconvenience, these workers
would find their commutes irrevocably altered.
95 One thing, at least, is clear: the city must carefully
consider many economic and social factors in
designing a subway maintenance plan.

1. The main purpose of the passage is to:

    A. argue that the New York City subway system
        maintenance plan should be altered.

    B. explain the effects of the current New York
        City subway system maintenance plan and a
        proposed alternative.

    C. discuss the economic and social importance
        of the New York City subway system.

    D. show how the history of the New York City
        subway system has resulted in the current
        maintenance crisis.

2. According to the passage, which of the following
    is true of the New York City subway system?

    F. It is the oldest subway system in the world.

    G. It is the busiest mass transit system in the
        world.

    H. It has more stations than any other subway
        system.

    J. A majority of city residents rely on the sub-
        way to get to work.

3. Based on the passage, advocates of the current
    New York City subway maintenance plan would
    most likely agree that:

    A. given its size, the city's subway system is one
        of the most well maintained in the world.

    B. avoiding service interruptions during rush
        hour is a paramount consideration when
        designing a maintenance schedule.

    C. confusion caused by route switching is a
        minor inconvenience for commuters and
        tourists.

    D. operating the subway system 24 hours a day,
        seven days a week is untenable given the
        wear and tear it causes.

4. Based on the passage, which choice best describes
    a claim that critics of the current subway mainte-
    nance plan would likely make?

    F. The negative impacts that arise from neglect-
        ing preventative maintenance outweigh
        the benefits of minimizing subway service
        interruptions.

    G. When devising a subway maintenance plan,
        no factor is more important than avoiding
        rush hour service interruptions.

    H. The negative impact from subway line clo-
        sures is greater on commuters than it is on
        businesses near the affected lines.

    J. Slightly longer periods of scheduled mainte-
        nance would help the subway system mini-
        mize rush hour service interruptions.

5. As it is used in line 33, the word *labyrinthine* most
    nearly means:

    A. subterranean.

    B. mythological.

    C. meandering.

    D. complicated.

6. In the third paragraph, the discussion of two specific subway lines (lines 35–39) primarily serves to:

    F. support the contention that line switching has a negative impact on tourism.

    G. illustrate one problem created by the current subway maintenance plan.

    H. underline the importance of minimizing subway service interruptions.

    J. quantify the social costs that arise from extended subway repair schedules.

7. In the passage, the primary purpose of the fifth paragraph (lines 52–70) is to:

    A. illustrate the impact of the current maintenance plan on one subway line.

    B. advocate for increased funding for subway repair and maintenance.

    C. provide support for a proposal to curtail 24-hour subway service.

    D. outline the negative impacts of extended subway line outages.

8. The passage indicates that non–rush hour commuters:

    F. would risk losing public transportation options if 24-hour subway service were suspended.

    G. would face only minor inconveniences if 24-hour subway service were suspended.

    H. work primarily in health care and its related fields.

    J. are among the strongest advocates for a change to the current subway maintenance plan.

9. The reference to New York City as the "city that never sleeps" (lines 87–88) primarily serves to:

    A. highlight an example of one of the ways in which the city is depicted in popular culture.

    B. provide support to a counterargument to the proposal to close the subway for a portion of the night.

    C. identify the anticipated economic and social benefits of nightly subway shutdowns for maintenance.

    D. advocate for the importance of residents in noisy urban environments being able to get an adequate amount of rest.

10. Based on the passage, with which of the following statements would the author most likely agree?

    F. The controversy surrounding New York City's subway system reflects similar issues for mass transit in many American cities.

    G. Without major changes to its subway maintenance plan, New York City will be unable to provide regular service to its 5.7 million weekly riders.

    H. Any plan for maintaining New York City's subway system will entail advantages and disadvantages for commuters.

    J. The social and economic costs resulting from New York City's current subway maintenance schedule justify an end to 24-hour, seven-day subway service.

Reading

K   451

Reflect

Directions: Take a few minutes to recall what you've learned and what you've been practicing in this chapter. Consider the following questions, jot down your best answer for each one, and then compare your reflections to the expert responses on the following page. Use your level of confidence to determine what to do next.

1. Describe active, or strategic, reading on ACT passages.

_____

_____

_____

2. What do ACT experts mean by summarizing the big picture of a passage?

_____

_____

_____

3. How can writing brief "margin notes" help you answer ACT Reading questions more effectively?

_____

_____

_____

4. What does an ACT expert look for in the question stem of an ACT Reading question?

_____

_____

_____

5. Why do expert test takers predict or characterize the correct answer to each ACT Reading question before assessing the answer choices?

_____

_____

_____

6. What will you do differently on future passages and their questions?

_____

_____

_____

Responses

1. Describe active, or strategic, reading on ACT passages.

Because the ACT asks many questions about why an author has written the passage or about how the author makes a point, expert test takers read for the author's purpose and main idea. Noting keywords that indicate a shift or contrast in points of view or that indicate opinions and emphases helps keep ACT experts on point as they anticipate where the passage will go.

2. What do ACT experts mean by summarizing the big picture of a passage?

To read for the big picture means to be able to accurately summarize the main idea of a passage and note the author's purpose for writing it. The big picture summary helps you answer Global questions and questions that ask about the author's opinion or point of view.

3. How can writing brief "margin notes" help you answer ACT Reading questions more effectively?

Jotting down margin notes provides a reference "map" to the subject or purpose of each paragraph in the passage. It helps you locate specific subjects or opinions expressed in the passage when they are called out in the questions.

4. What does an ACT expert look for in the question stem of an ACT Reading question?

Each question stem indicates the type of question and contains clues as to whether the answer will come from researching the passage text or from the big picture summary. Many question stems have specific clues (for example, line numbers or references to details from the passage) that tell you precisely where to research.

5. Why do expert test takers predict or characterize the correct answer to each ACT Reading question before assessing the answer choices?

Predicting or characterizing the correct answer allows you to evaluate each answer choice one time and avoid rereading for every answer choice. Incorrect answers often distort what the passage said or misuse details from the passage, so it's best to research the passage once to know what the correct answer must say before diving into the choices.

6. What will you do differently on future passages and their questions?

There is no one-size-fits-all answer to this question. Each student has individual initial strengths and opportunities in the Reading section. What's important here is that you're honestly self-reflective. Take what you need from the expert's examples and strive to apply it to your own performance. Many test takers convince themselves that they'll never get faster or more confident in ACT Reading, but the truth is, many test takers who now routinely ace the Reading section were much slower and more hesitant before they learned to approach this section systematically and strategically.

Next Steps

If you answered most questions correctly in the "How Much Have You Learned?" section, and if your responses to the Reflect questions were similar to those of the ACT expert, then consider the ACT Reading Question Method an area of strength and move on to the next chapter. Come back to this topic periodically to prevent yourself from getting rusty.

If you don't yet feel confident, review the material in this chapter, and then try the questions you missed again. As always, be sure to review the explanations closely. Then go online (**kaptest.com/login**) to watch a video lesson about the Kaplan Method for ACT Reading and use your Qbank for more practice. If you haven't already registered your book, do so at **kaptest.com/moreonline.**

GO ONLINE

kaptest.com/login

Answers and Explanations

How Much Have You Learned?

SOCIAL SCIENCE: This passage is adapted from a 2018 article.

The history of the New York City subway system, quickly told: the first stations opened in 1904, and over the next century, it expanded to 472 stations, more than any other subway system

5 in the world, with 850 miles of track. Operating 24 hours a day, seven days a week, with an average weekday ridership of approximately 5.7 million, it is the planet's 7th-busiest rapid transit system. While the system is, on many levels, an amazing

10 achievement, it is also beset by a problem that harms both quality of life and economic activity. Such a large system must inevitably suffer from service interruptions and delays; normal wear and tear combined with the sheer age of the system

15 necessitates regular maintenance. However, there is no consensus as to the best way to accomplish the required repairs.

The current maintenance scheme is designed to minimize service interruptions. A subway line in

20 need of repair will be taken out of service during a comparatively less busy time, such as nights or weekends, while another line is re-routed to cover as many as possible of the missing line's stops. The main advantage to this approach is that trains

25 are not taken out of service during rush hour, when most subway trips occur; subway service generally remains predictable and commuters are, for the most part, able to use the system to get to their destinations on time.

30 But critics are quick to point out the disadvantages to this approach. Perhaps most obvious is the confusion caused by trains switching lines. The labyrinthine system is hard enough to navigate at the best of times, especially

35 for tourists. A subway rider on the A train naturally expects the train to make stops on the A line. If, instead, it is diverted temporarily to the F line, the rider may find herself miles from her intended destination.

NYC subway: how to repair? diff. views

Current approach: night and weekend repairs

Critics: line switch confusion

ANALYSIS

Pre-passage blurb: Though the passage blurb does not give many details, it does identify that the passage is from an "article"; expect an academic tone.

¶1 The first few sentences introduce the New York subway system with its history and various facts. The contrast word "While" signals a transition to a discussion of problems with maintenance and service interruptions. The author previews that the article will discuss the lack of "consensus" about addressing these issues.

¶2 The first sentence indicates that this paragraph discusses the current maintenance plan. Its goal is to "minimize service interruptions." The author describes this plan and its "main advantage."

¶3 The contrast keyword "But" shows the transition to a discussion of the "disadvantages" pointed out by "critics" of the current plan.

40   While annoying, the confusion arising from
route switching is hardly the most serious
problem with the current approach to repairs.
Because the system runs 24 hours a day, routine
maintenance can generally be done only during
45   the temporary closures on nights and weekends.
This means that more serious repair and crucial
preventative maintenance are often neglected.
Problems that could have been fixed or prevented
reasonably expeditiously given a slightly longer
50   closure wind up leading to major breakdowns and
service interruptions later on.

    On rare occasions, such breakdowns have
resulted in entire subway lines being shut down
for months or even a year. Beginning in 2019, for
55   example, the L train connecting lower Manhattan
to parts of Brooklyn was scheduled to close for
as much as 15 months for long overdue service
and upgrades. In a city fewer than half of whose
households own a car, this can have serious
60   economic impacts. Residents of the affected area
may face a much longer commute via an alternate
subway line if one is available; or, if there is no
alternate subway service, they may need to take
other, potentially more expensive, modes of
65   transportation, such as taxis or ferries. Moreover,
studies indicate that increased stress from the
commute to work can lead to lower productivity,
and that businesses near the impacted lines may
see decreased revenue as potential customers have
70   a harder time getting to them.

    One controversial proposal for reducing
breakdowns and the resulting transit interruptions
is to end the subway's 24-hour service and to shut
down for several hours each night. Proponents
75   of this plan argue that this would allow time, on
a regular rather than sporadic basis, for more
preventative maintenance. This, they claim, would
ultimately lead to more consistent service; rather
than shutting down entire lines for long periods
80   of a time, there would merely be shorter service
outages overnight, when fewer people use the
subway system. While this may seem a preferable
outcome to the economic consequences of a total
shutdown resulting from a breakdown, it has its

Even worse: major breakdowns

¶4 This paragraph discusses an even more
"serious problem" with the current plan:
required maintenance may not be done and
breakdowns may occur.

Eco. & soc. harms of shutdowns

¶5 This paragraph provides more details about
the problems caused by the "major breakdowns"
mentioned in the previous paragraph. The phrase
"for example" indicates a specific instance of a
major breakdown, and the keyword "Moreover"
introduces another problem.

Alt. proposal: stop 24-hour service Pros

¶6 The final paragraph discusses an alternate,
"controversial proposal" for maintaining the
subways. The author includes arguments from
both "Proponents" and critics (signaled by the
contrast word "While") of the plan. The author
doesn't pick a side, but concludes with the
neutral viewpoint that any plan must be carefully considered.

Cons

85 liabilities as well. While most subway trips may occur during rush hour, not everyone works during the daytime. New York is famously known as the "the city that never sleeps." Doctors, nurses, bartenders, police officers, and firefighters are

90 just a few examples of occupations whose workers need transportation at all hours of the day and night. Rather than be subjected to a relatively short period of inconvenience, these workers would find their commutes irrevocably altered.

95 One thing, at least, is clear: the city must carefully consider many economic and social factors in designing a subway maintenance plan.

BIG PICTURE SUMMARY

Main idea: There are different views about the best way to perform repairs and maintenance on the extensive New York subway system.

Author's purpose: To objectively describe the pros and cons of various approaches to maintaining the New York subway system

---

1. B
Difficulty: Medium
Category: Global
Getting to the Answer: Consult your big picture summary, and find the one answer that matches the passage's scope and the author's purpose. Here, the author does not take a side. He lays out advantages and disadvantages to both the current maintenance plan and one proposal offered by critics of the current plan. That matches (B).

Choice A distorts the author's position. He doesn't advocate for the critics of the current plan. Choice C is too broad. It misses the key subject of subway maintenance. Choice D is too narrow. This answer describes only the first paragraph.

2. H
Difficulty: Medium
Category: Detail
Getting to the Answer: The phrase "According to the passage" in the question stem shows that this is a Detail question. The correct answer will be something explicitly stated in the passage. Start by checking

the answers against paragraph 1, where the author provides general facts about the New York City subway. Doing so will lead you to the correct answer, (H).

Choice F is unsupported. You're told that the subway opened in 1904, but not whether other subway systems already existed at that time. Choice G contradicts the details in the passage, which states that New York City's subway system is the seventh busiest in the world. Choice J distorts a fact from the passage. The fifth paragraph states that fewer than half of the households in the city own a car, but that doesn't mean that everyone in the majority of households that do not own cars takes the subway.

3. B
Difficulty: Hard
Category: Inference
Getting to the Answer: The phrases "Based on the passage" and "most likely agree" in the question stem indicate that this is an Inference question since what it asks for is not directly stated in the passage. The current maintenance plan is outlined in paragraph 2. You're told that its goal is to "minimize service

interruptions" and that its main advantage is that trains operate during rush hour. Combining those statements leads to the correct answer, (B).

Choice A is too extreme. Everyone seems to agree that maintaining the system is a huge challenge. The debate is over how best to implement the necessary repairs. Choice C misuses a detail from the passage. The author says critics think route switching is a problem, but he says nothing about how serious a problem those who support the current plan consider route switching to be. They might understand that it causes a major inconvenience but still be willing to reroute trains in order to keep the subway open during rush hour. Choice D states a position taken by critics, not advocates, of the current plan.

4.   F
Difficulty: Hard
Category: Inference
Getting to the Answer: The phrases "Based on the passage" and "would likely" indicate an Inference question. Note that this question asks specifically for the position of the *critics* of the current plan. The correct answer will be implied by the passage text. The critics' objections to the current plan are laid out primarily in paragraphs 3 and 4. Quick research shows that they make two arguments. First, line switching for routine maintenance can be confusing and frustrating for riders (paragraph 3). Second, and worse, the limited time allowed for routine maintenance prevents important preventative maintenance from taking place (paragraph 4). That leads to severe service outages that can last for weeks or months. This second criticism accords with the correct answer, (F).

Choice G is something that advocates, not opponents, of the current plan might say. See paragraph 2 for this argument. Choice H is an irrelevant comparison. Paragraph 5 lays out the social and economic impacts of extended subway line closures to both riders and businesses, but it doesn't assert that the impacts are worse for one group or the other. Choice J distorts the critics' argument. They contend that slightly longer periods of scheduled maintenance would allow time for preventative maintenance, not that it would reduce rush hour interruptions.

5.   D
Difficulty: Easy
Category: Vocab-in-Context
Getting to the Answer: Check the sentence in which the word was used to determine the author's intended meaning. The correct answer can be substituted for the word without changing the meaning of the sentence. Here, the author uses *labyrinthine* to describe the New York subway system's complexity, given the "confusion" that could be caused by line switching and the assertion that the system is "hard enough to navigate at the best of times." Choice (D) fits perfectly.

Choice A means *underground*. That is true of the subway system, of course, but it would be redundant for the author to use *labyrinthine* in this way. Choice B plays off the famous labyrinth from Greek mythology, but this definition does not fit the word *labyrinthine* or the context of the sentence. Choice C suggests that the subway system is random or wandering. While the huge system may be difficult to navigate at times, it isn't random.

6.   G
Difficulty: Hard
Category: Function
Getting to the Answer: The phrase "serves to" tags this as a Function question, asking for the role a specific detail plays in the passage. Research the lines cited in the question stem to see why the author has included this example. The third paragraph introduces the first disadvantage cited by critics of the current subway maintenance schedule. The detail referenced in the question stem provides an example. That purpose is accurately described in the correct answer, (G).

Choice F misuses a detail from the passage. You're told that line switching—the problem being discussed—is particularly difficult for tourists, but that's not the reason the author included this example. Choice H refers to the rationale provided by supporters of the current maintenance plan in paragraph 2. In J, the word "quantify" suggests that the example provides numbers to show the impact of the current maintenance plan. That's something the author never does in this passage.

7.   D
Difficulty: Easy
Category: Function
Getting to the Answer: On this Function question, you're asked for the author's purpose for including an entire paragraph. Consult your passage notes to see the role of paragraph 5 in the passage. Paragraph 5 details some of the social and economic harms caused by shutting down subway lines. That matches (D).

Choice A distorts the purpose of the paragraph. The specific line—the L train—is given as an example of an extended shutdown, but the harms described in the paragraph apply to all similar extended service outages. Choice B is outside the scope of the passage. The author does not discuss the need for increased funding. Choice C refers to a proposal from paragraph 6. The author never endorses that proposal and does not use paragraph 5 to support it.

8.   F
Difficulty: Medium
Category: Detail
Getting to the Answer: The phrase "[t]he passage indicates" shows this to be a Detail question. The correct answer will paraphrase a statement made explicitly in the text. The author discusses non–rush hour commuters in paragraph 6. He lists some examples of these commuters—"doctors, nurses, bartenders, police officers, and firefighters"—and explains that a cessation of 24-hour subway service could permanently alter their commutes. That matches choice (F), the correct answer here.

Choice G is the opposite of what the passage says. The current system creates minor inconveniences for these workers when their subway lines are rerouted or closed for repair, but a suspension of 24-hour service would entail a permanent disruption. Choice H distorts the paragraph. Doctors and nurses are among the non–rush hour commuters, but that doesn't mean they are the majority of them. Choice J is outside the scope of the passage. The author does not discuss which occupations show the strongest support for a change in subway maintenance.

9.   B
Difficulty: Medium
Category: Function
Getting to the Answer: The phrase "serves to" signals that this is a Function question, so examine the context of the cited lines and ask yourself why the author chose to mention that New York is called the "city that never sleeps." The phrase appears in a paragraph about a "controversial proposal" for closing the subway for a few hours at night to do maintenance. The author provides the reasoning of the "Proponents" of this proposal, and the word "While" in line 82 transitions to a discussion of reasons why the proposal might be a bad idea: people who work at night would be negatively impacted. The phrase supports this counterargument by emphasizing that New York is known for its high level of activity at night; this matches (B).

Choices A and D are incorrect because the author's focus is on subway maintenance plans, not on depictions of New York City or getting enough sleep. Choice C is opposite; the phrase is used in the argument *against* nightly shutdowns.

10.   H
Difficulty: Hard
Category: Inference
Getting to the Answer: For an open-ended Inference question like this one, predict the correct answer based on your big picture summary. Consider also any thesis statement or conclusion that sums up the author's point of view. This author outlines both sides of a debate and discusses the advantages and disadvantages to both the current subway maintenance plan and proposed alternatives. The author's conclusion at the end of the passage is neutral, encouraging the city to carefully consider all factors without advocating for a specific outcome. This matches up with the correct answer, (H).

Choice F strays beyond the scope of the passage. Be careful not to bring in bigger issues if the author has not discussed them in the passage. Choice G is too extreme. To be sure, the author considers subway maintenance a major issue but stops short of dire predictions like the one stated in this answer choice. Choice J matches the position of one side in the debate, but not that of the author, who remains neutral throughout.

CHAPTER 16

ACT READING PASSAGE STRATEGIES

LEARNING OBJECTIVES

After completing this chapter, you will be able to:

- Identify keywords that promote active reading and relate the passage text to the questions
- Create short, accurate margin notes that help you research the text efficiently
- Summarize the big picture of the passage

How Much Do You Know?

Directions: In this chapter, you'll learn how ACT experts actively read the passage, take notes, and summarize the main idea to prepare themselves to answer all of the passage's questions quickly and confidently. You saw this kind of reading modeled in the previous chapter. To get ready for the current chapter, take five minutes to actively read the following passage by:

1.   noting the keywords that indicate the author's point of view and the passage's structure

2.   jotting down a quick summary next to each paragraph

3.   summarizing the big picture (the passage's main idea and the author's purpose for writing it)

When you're done, compare your work to the passage notes that follow.

HUMANITIES: This passage explores the relationship between the immigrant experience and one person's career choice.

My grandfather was born in a turbulent time in Russia. His non-communist lineage made him unwelcome before he had left the womb. His father, an officer in the Russian army, was
5   considered an enemy of the communist Bolsheviks, so my grandfather lived less than a year in what was his native Moscow and spent most of his younger years moving across Asia. Despite this, he had pride in being Russian, associated with
10   Russians throughout his life, and would frequently quiz me on Russian history. This all in tribute to a country that ended up under hostile rule during the time his mother was pregnant with him.

As a child, exiled to Siberia, my grandfather
15   heard his father tell of the greatness that existed within the country that had forced the family into exile. It was known that, first with his parents, and later as an adult, my grandfather was going to have to seek a new place to call home.
20   Despite this foregone conclusion, Russia was still romanticized, and my grandfather learned to treat the country with reverence. This was in contrast to the sentiments found in other recently exiled Russians, who would not simply lament the actions
25   taken by the country but disparage all eight million square miles. In my family's search for a place to settle, attempting to forge a consistent identity was nearly impossible, as no one knew whether the next location would hold for a month, let alone a year.
30   All hoped for an unattainable "new Moscow."

The first long-term refuge was found, ironically, in China, which would have its own communist revolution. After several years of relative stability, this revolution precipitated the move to the
35   United States. Upon arrival in San Francisco, my grandfather, along with my grandmother and their young son, my father, found other Russian immigrants who were also new to the country. "*Ya amerikanets*," people would say, and despite the fact
40   that they were recent immigrants who associated primarily with those of shared ethnicity and circumstance, they would play the role they desired and repeat "*ya amerikanets*"—"I am American." They would share many stories about their native
45   land, but did not repeat "*ya russkiy*," because being Russian went without saying. While it was clear that this would be the last country my grandfather would reside in and that he wished to become more American, it was perhaps the most confusing
50   of times. It was less a problem of acclimating to an adopted setting and more of dealing with a permanent setting at all. The only consistency throughout the first thirty years of my grandfather's life was the knowledge that every "home" was
55   temporary, and now this was no longer the case. I often wonder if his successful career in the real estate business had anything to do with what must have been a rare transformation of circumstance.

Not only was my grandfather interested in
60   real estate, he was ardent about the importance of ownership, a naturally discordant view to that of the then Soviet Union. Thus, selling homes became a purpose in addition to an occupation.

Part of his success in real estate was owed to
strategic compromise. Considering American
sentiments regarding Russia during the Cold War,
there were times that he was sure he lost certain
house sales due to his last name and accent.
However, to those willing to listen, he found
advantages to informing people that he was an
exiled Russian who ardently disagreed with the
communist government. He would also point out
his pride in being a new American and allow a
potential buyer to degrade Russia without blinking.

Fortunately, the 1950s were a time of settling
across the country, and this made real estate a
very lucrative profession. It wasn't just this that
attracted my grandfather, though; he also saw it as
an opportunity to give tiny parts of the country to
other people—returning the favor, in a way.

Yet, it always seemed that something vital
still rested in the opposite hemisphere. Once
communism fell, he began returning to Russia
yearly. He and my grandmother never showed the
family pictures from Russia the way they would
from the various cruise ships they traveled on; it
could be deduced that returning to Russia was a
journey of personal necessity for him rather than

pleasure, and the encounter elucidated his existence
in a way that being solely American could not. In
selling real estate, my grandfather had worked to
make this unnecessary. I believe that he wished for
people to keep those houses and pass them down
to later generations, giving the space a sort of
familial permanence rather than a fleeting stay.

For most, the thought of real estate agents
conjures up images of smiling advertisements
on benches and buses and the skill of selling
something so important. Many are wary of
salespeople in general, questioning the practice
of convincing people something is in their
best interest when the salesperson stands to
personally benefit. My grandfather did financially
benefit from sales, but there was more to it: his
realization of the American dream only made him
want to be a part of others reaching for the same
thing, whether their native home was around the
block or thousands of miles away.

Check Your Work

HUMANITIES: This passage explores the relationship between the immigrant experience and one person's career choice.

My grandfather was born in a turbulent time in Russia. His non-communist lineage made him unwelcome before he had left the womb. His father, an officer in the Russian army, was
5 considered an enemy of the communist Bolsheviks, so my grandfather lived less than a year in what was his native Moscow and spent most of his younger years moving across Asia. Despite this, he had pride in being Russian, associated with
10 Russians throughout his life, and would frequently quiz me on Russian history. This all in tribute to a country that ended up under hostile rule during the time his mother was pregnant with him.

As a child, exiled to Siberia, my grandfather
15 heard his father tell of the greatness that existed within the country that had forced the family into exile. It was known that, first with his parents, and later as an adult, my grandfather was going to have to seek a new place to call home.
20 Despite this foregone conclusion, Russia was still romanticized, and my grandfather learned to treat the country with reverence. This was in contrast to the sentiments found in other recently exiled Russians, who would not simply lament the actions
25 taken by the country but disparage all eight million square miles. In my family's search for a place to settle, attempting to forge a consistent identity was nearly impossible, as no one knew whether the next location would hold for a month, let alone a year.
30 All hoped for an unattainable "new Moscow."

The first long-term refuge was found, ironically, in China, which would have its own communist revolution. After several years of relative stability, this revolution precipitated the move to the
35 United States. Upon arrival in San Francisco, my grandfather, along with my grandmother and their young son, my father, found other Russian immigrants who were also new to the country. "*Ya amerikanets,*" people would say, and despite the fact
40 that they were recent immigrants who associated primarily with those of shared ethnicity and

grandfather, chaotic childhood

still loves Russia

ANALYSIS

Pre-passage blurb: From this blurb, you learn that the passage will focus on one person's career choice and, in particular, how that person's career choice is impacted by being an immigrant.

¶1 The author introduces his grandfather and gives some background, focusing in particular on his grandfather's chaotic and unstable childhood.

¶2 This paragraph provides additional context about why the author's grandfather still feels positively toward Russia, despite his unstable, chaotic childhood.

circumstance, they would play the role they desired
and repeat "*ya amerikanets*"—"I am American."
They would share many stories about their native
45 land, but did not repeat "*ya russkiy,*" because being
Russian went without saying. While it was clear
that this would be the last country my grandfather
would reside in and that he wished to become
more American, it was perhaps the most confusing
50 of times. It was less a problem of acclimating to
an adopted setting and more of dealing with a
permanent setting at all. The only consistency
throughout the first thirty years of my grandfather's
life was the knowledge that every "home" was
55 temporary, and now this was no longer the case.
I often wonder if his successful career in the real
estate business had anything to do with what must
have been a rare transformation of circumstance.

Not only was my grandfather interested in
60 real estate, he was ardent about the importance
of ownership, a naturally discordant view to that
of the then Soviet Union. Thus, selling homes
became a purpose in addition to an occupation.

Part of his success in real estate was owed to
65 strategic compromise. Considering American
sentiments regarding Russia during the Cold War,
there were times that he was sure he lost certain
house sales due to his last name and accent.
However, to those willing to listen, he found
70 advantages to informing people that he was an
exiled Russian who ardently disagreed with the
communist government. He would also point out
his pride in being a new American and allow a
potential buyer to degrade Russia without blinking.

75 Fortunately, the 1950s were a time of settling
across the country, and this made real estate a
very lucrative profession. It wasn't just this that
attracted my grandfather, though; he also saw it as
an opportunity to give tiny parts of the country to
80 other people—returning the favor, in a way.

Yet, it always seemed that something vital
still rested in the opposite hemisphere. Once
communism fell, he began returning to Russia
yearly. He and my grandmother never showed the
85 family pictures from Russia the way they would
from the various cruise ships they traveled on; it

*moves
to US,
becomes
real estate
agent*

¶3 In this paragraph, the author's grandfather
starts to find stability: first in China, then in
the United States. There, the author's grandfather finds a group of immigrants like him, and
the author reflects on his grandfather's journey. At the end of this paragraph, it's revealed
that his grandfather is a real estate agent.

*real estate
is his
vocation*

¶4 The author expands on his grandfather's
career choice, adding a deeper meaning
behind the choice.

*allows
people
to insult
Russia*

¶5 The author opens by discussing his grandfather's willingness to strategically compromise, even if it meant degrading the home
country he felt so positively about.

*wants to
give back*

¶6 Selling homes was not just a career or a
source of income for the author's grandfather;
rather, it was a way for him to help others in
the way he felt he had been helped.

Reading

could be deduced that returning to Russia was a journey of personal necessity for him rather than pleasure, and the encounter elucidated his existence
90 in a way that being solely American could not. In selling real estate, my grandfather had worked to make this unnecessary. I believe that he wished for people to keep those houses and pass them down to later generations, giving the space a sort of
95 familial permanence rather than a fleeting stay.

For most, the thought of real estate agents conjures up images of smiling advertisements on benches and buses and the skill of selling something so important. Many are wary of
100 salespeople in general, questioning the practice of convincing people something is in their best interest when the salesperson stands to personally benefit. My grandfather did financially benefit from sales, but there was more to it: his
105 realization of the American dream only made him want to be a part of others reaching for the same thing, whether their native home was around the block or thousands of miles away.

visits Russia every year

¶7 Now that Russia is more open than it was in the author's grandfather's past, he makes a point to visit yearly but does not share these journeys with his family. The author has a sense that his grandfather uses this annual trip to remind himself of his motivations.

wants to give people a home

¶8 Real estate agent may not have seemed like an obvious career choice for the author's grandfather, but his motivation to help others find their own *native homes*, wherever that may be, resulted in both his own financial success and his success in an unexpected career.

BIG PICTURE SUMMARY

Main idea: A Russian immigrant attempts to make a life and find a purpose in his new homeland through real estate.

Author's purpose: To reminisce about his grandfather's life experiences, memories, and impact

ACT READING STRATEGIES: KEYWORDS, MARGIN NOTES, AND THE BIG PICTURE SUMMARY

LEARNING OBJECTIVES

After this lesson, you will be able to:

- Identify keywords that promote active reading and relate the passage text to the questions
- Create short, accurate margin notes that help you research the text efficiently
- Summarize the big picture of the passage

To read and map a passage like this:

NATURAL SCIENCE: This passage is adapted from an essay about astrobiology.

Astrobiology, also known as exobiology, is a complex, multidisciplinary science dedicated to studying the possibility of life outside the confines of Earth. Humanity has speculated for centuries
5 about whether or not we are alone in the universe, but with the advent of space exploration in the 1950s and 1960s, for the first time in human history there was the possibility of actually exploring the surface of alien planets. Scientists
10 and engineers worked together to build what they called landers, spacecraft capable not only of landing on other planets, but also of exploring and photographing them.

When the first of the two Viking landers touched
15 down on Martian soil on July 20, 1976, and began to send camera images back to Earth, the scientists at the Jet Propulsion Laboratory could not suppress a certain nervous anticipation. Like people who hold a ticket to a lottery, they had a one-in-a-million
20 chance of winning. The first photographs that arrived, however, did not contain any evidence of life. They revealed merely a barren landscape littered with rocks and boulders. The view resembled nothing so much as a flat section of desert. In
25 fact, the winning entry in a contest at J.P.L. for the photograph most accurately predicting what Mars would look like was a snapshot taken from a particularly arid section of the Mojave Desert.

The scientists were soon ready to turn their
30 attention from visible life to microorganisms. The twin Viking landers carried out experiments

designed to detect organic compounds. Researchers thought it possible that life had developed on early Mars just as it is thought to have developed on
35 Earth, through the gradual chemical evolution of complex organic molecules. To detect biological activity, Martian soil samples were treated with various nutrients that would produce characteristic by-products if life forms were active in the soil.
40 The results from all three experiments were inconclusive. The fourth experiment heated a soil sample to look for signs of organic material but found none—an unexpected result because organic compounds were thought to have been present due
45 to the steady bombardment of the Martian surface by meteorites.

The absence of organic materials, some scientists speculated, was the result of intense ultraviolet radiation penetrating the atmosphere
50 of Mars and destroying organic compounds in the soil. Although Mars' atmosphere was at one time rich in carbon dioxide and thus thick enough to protect its surface from the harmful rays of the sun, the carbon dioxide had gradually left the
55 atmosphere and been converted into rocks. This means that even if life had gotten a start on early Mars, it could not have survived the exposure to ultraviolet radiation that occurred when the atmosphere thinned. Mars never developed a
60 protective layer of ozone as Earth did.

Despite the disappointing Viking results, there are those who still keep open the possibility of life on Mars. They point out that the Viking data cannot be considered the final word on
65 Martian life because the two landers sampled only

limited—and uninteresting—sites. The Viking
landing sites were not chosen for what they might
tell of the planet's biology. They were chosen
primarily because they appeared to be safe for
70 landing a spacecraft. The landing sites were on
parts of the Martian plains that appeared relatively
featureless according to orbital photographs.

The type of terrain that these researchers
suggest may be a possible hiding place for active
75 life has an Earthly parallel: the ice-free region of
southern Victoria Land, Antarctica, where the
temperatures in some dry valleys average below
zero. Organisms known as endoliths, a form of
blue-green algae that has adapted to this harsh
80 environment, were found living inside certain
translucent, porous rocks in these Antarctic valleys.
The argument based on this discovery is that if life
did exist on early Mars, it is possible that it escaped
worsening conditions by similarly seeking refuge
85 in rocks. Skeptics object, however, that Mars in its
present state is simply too dry, even compared with
Antarctic valleys, to sustain any life whatsoever.

Should Mars eventually prove barren of life,
as some suspect, then this finding would have
90 a significant impact on the current view of the
chemical origins of life. It could be much more
difficult to get life started on a planet than
scientists thought before the Viking landings.

The possibility exists, of course, that our
95 definition of what constitutes life may not hold true
throughout the universe. It has long been speculated
that our current belief that all life must contain
carbon, oxygen, calcium, chlorine, potassium, and
phosphorous simply because this holds true on our
100 planet might be too narrow a view. In 2010, NASA
scientists believed they had discovered a bacterium
that used arsenic in place of phosphorous, though
these exciting findings later proved to be incorrect.
The possibility remains, however, that future
105 astrobiologists exploring the Martian surface from
140 million miles away might be able to make use
of a more advanced definition of what we call "life."

You need to know this:

- ACT Reading passages are preceded by short blurbs that tell you about the author and source of the passage.
- There are three categories of keywords that reveal an author's purpose and point of view and that unlock the passage's structure:
  - **opinion and emphasis**—words that signal that the author finds a detail noteworthy (e.g., *especially, crucial, important, above all*) or has an opinion about it (e.g., *fortunately, disappointing, I suggest, it seems likely*)
  - **connection and contrast**—words that suggest that a subsequent detail continues the same point (e.g., *moreover, in addition, also, further*) or that indicate a change in direction or point of difference (e.g., *but, yet, despite, on the other hand*)
    - In some passages, these keywords may show steps in a process or developments over time (e.g., *traditionally, in the past, recently, today, first, second, finally, earlier, since*)
  - **evidence and example**—words that indicate an argument (the use of evidence to support a conclusion), either the author's or someone else's (e.g., *thus, therefore, because*), or that introduce an example to clarify or support another point (e.g., *for example, this shows, to illustrate*)

You need to do this:

Apply the ACT Reading Passage Strategy to every Reading passage:

- Extract everything you can from the pre-passage blurb
- Read each paragraph actively
- Summarize the passage's big picture

Extract everything you can from the pre-passage blurb

Quickly prepare for the passage by unpacking the pre-passage blurb.

- What do the title and date of the original book or article tell you about the author and her purpose for writing?
- What information can you glean from the source (nonfiction book, novel, academic journal, etc.)?
- Is there any other information that provides context for the passage?

Read each paragraph actively

Note keywords (circling or underlining them may help) and use them to focus your reading on:

- The author's purpose and point of view
- The relationships between ideas
- The examples or other support provided for passage claims

WHY PAY ATTENTION TO KEYWORDS?

Keywords indicate opinions and signal structure that make the difference between correct and incorrect answers on ACT questions. Consider this test-like question and two potential choices:

The passage makes clear that coffee beans that grow at high altitudes typically produce:

A. dark, mellow coffee when brewed.

B. light, acidic coffee when brewed.

To answer that based on an ACT passage, you will need to determine whether the author said:

Type X coffee beans grow at very high altitudes, *so* they produce a dark, mellow coffee when brewed.

That would make choice (A) correct. But if the author instead said:

Type X coffee beans grow at very high altitudes, *but* they produce a *surprisingly* dark, mellow coffee when brewed.

Then choice (B) would be correct. The facts in the statements did not change at all, but the correct answer to the ACT question would be different in each case because of the keywords the author chose to include.

As you read, jot down brief, accurate margin notes. These notes can be referred to as a **passage map** because they will guide you as you research your answers.

- Paraphrase the text (put it into your own words) as you go.
- Ask, "What's the author's point and purpose?" for each paragraph.

Summarize the passage's big picture

At the end of the passage, pause for a few seconds to summarize the passage's big picture. Doing so will help you understand the passage as a whole and prepare you to answer Global questions. Ask yourself:

- "What is the main idea of the entire passage?" (If the author had only a few seconds to state what she thinks is most important, what would she say?)
- "Why did the author write it?" (State the purpose as a verb, e.g., *to explain, to explore, to argue, to rebut,* etc.)

Explanation

NATURAL SCIENCE: This passage is adapted from an essay about astrobiology.

Astrobiology, also known as exobiology, is a complex, multidisciplinary science dedicated to studying the possibility of life outside the confines of Earth. Humanity has speculated for centuries
5 about whether or not we are alone in the universe, but with the advent of space exploration in the 1950s and 1960s, for the first time in human history there was the possibility of actually exploring the surface of alien planets. Scientists
10 and engineers worked together to build what they called landers, spacecraft capable not only of landing on other planets, but also of exploring and photographing them.

When the first of the two Viking landers touched
15 down on Martian soil on July 20, 1976, and began to send camera images back to Earth, the scientists at the Jet Propulsion Laboratory could not suppress a certain nervous anticipation. Like people who hold a ticket to a lottery, they had a one-in-a-million
20 chance of winning. The first photographs that arrived, however, did not contain any evidence of life. They revealed merely a barren landscape littered with rocks and boulders. The view resembled nothing so much as a flat section of desert. In
25 fact, the winning entry in a contest at J.P.L. for the photograph most accurately predicting what Mars would look like was a snapshot taken from a particularly arid section of the Mojave Desert.

The scientists were soon ready to turn their
30 attention from visible life to microorganisms. The twin Viking landers carried out experiments designed to detect organic compounds. Researchers thought it possible that life had developed on early Mars just as it is thought to have developed on
35 Earth, through the gradual chemical evolution of complex organic molecules. To detect biological activity, Martian soil samples were treated with various nutrients that would produce characteristic by-products if life forms were active in the soil.
40 The results from all three experiments were inconclusive. The fourth experiment heated a soil sample to look for signs of organic material but

astrobiology: finding non-Earth life

Mars landing no signs of life

inconclusive tests for micro-organisms

ANALYSIS

Pre-passage blurb: In the pre-passage blurb, you learn the topic of the essay: astrobiology.

¶1 The author defines astrobiology and provides a brief explanation for why it is a field of study.

¶2 The author changes tone in the second paragraph, prompting excitement, only to shift back into a more neutral voice for the second half of the paragraph as she describes the disappointing results of the Viking landers in 1976.

¶3 This paragraph transitions from what was expected out of the initial landing to what happened next, describing the next set of efforts undertaken to better study life beyond Earth, this time with a focus on micro-organisms. Unfortunately, the results from these experiments were inconclusive.

found none—an unexpected result because organic compounds were thought to have been present due to the steady bombardment of the Martian surface by meteorites.

The absence of organic materials, some scientists speculated, was the result of intense ultraviolet radiation penetrating the atmosphere of Mars and destroying organic compounds in the soil. Although Mars' atmosphere was at one time rich in carbon dioxide and thus thick enough to protect its surface from the harmful rays of the sun, the carbon dioxide had gradually left the atmosphere and been converted into rocks. This means that even if life had gotten a start on early Mars, it could not have survived the exposure to ultraviolet radiation that occurred when the atmosphere thinned. Mars never developed a protective layer of ozone as Earth did.

Despite the disappointing Viking results, there are those who still keep open the possibility of life on Mars. They point out that the Viking data cannot be considered the final word on Martian life because the two landers sampled only limited—and uninteresting—sites. The Viking landing sites were not chosen for what they might tell of the planet's biology. They were chosen primarily because they appeared to be safe for landing a spacecraft. The landing sites were on parts of the Martian plains that appeared relatively featureless according to orbital photographs.

The type of terrain that these researchers suggest may be a possible hiding place for active life has an Earthly parallel: the ice-free region of southern Victoria Land, Antarctica, where the temperatures in some dry valleys average below zero. Organisms known as endoliths, a form of blue-green algae that has adapted to this harsh environment, were found living inside certain translucent, porous rocks in these Antarctic valleys. The argument based on this discovery is that if life did exist on early Mars, it is possible that it escaped worsening conditions by similarly seeking refuge in rocks. Skeptics object, however, that Mars in its present state is simply too dry, even compared with Antarctic valleys, to sustain any life whatsoever.

no organic material b/c UV?

¶4 There is some speculation around why organic materials are absent; some scientists believe it was the result of intense UV light.

may be life elsewhere, testing locations limited

¶5 Scientists haven't given up; more research is needed, and they have suggestions about how this research can be better conducted.

how life could exist in rocks

¶6 Although Earth and Mars are very different planets, there is one place in Antarctica that might allow us to study the development of life in very dry places without leaving the planet; there are skeptics, though.

469

Should Mars eventually prove barren of life, as some suspect, then this finding would have
90 a significant impact on the current view of the chemical origins of life. It could be much more difficult to get life started on a planet than scientists thought before the Viking landings.

impact if no life

¶7 If Mars does prove to be completely free of life, this finding could be just as impactful on our collective scientific knowledge.

The possibility exists, of course, that our
95 definition of what constitutes life may not hold true throughout the universe. It has long been speculated that our current belief that all life must contain carbon, oxygen, calcium, chlorine, potassium, and phosphorous simply because this holds true on our
100 planet might be too narrow a view. In 2010, NASA scientists believed they had discovered a bacterium that used arsenic in place of phosphorous, though these exciting findings later proved to be incorrect. The possibility remains, however, that future
105 astrobiologists exploring the Martian surface from 140 million miles away might be able to make use of a more advanced definition of what we call "life."

definition of life may change

¶8 Our very definition of life may be incorrect. There is still much more to learn in the field of astrobiology!

BIG PICTURE SUMMARY

Main idea: Despite initial tests for Martian life yielding inconclusive results, the continued search for possible lifeforms could yield valuable information.

Author's purpose: To inform the reader about both a brief history of and the predicted future of astrobiology discoveries

---

Now, try another passage on your own. Use the ACT Reading strategies and tactics you've been learning to read and map this passage as quickly and accurately as you can.

Try on Your Own

Directions: Actively read and map the following passage by:

1.   circling or underlining keywords (opinion and emphasis, connection and contrast, or evidence and example)

2.   jotting down brief, accurate margin notes that reflect good paraphrases of each paragraph

3.   summarizing the big picture

When you're done, compare your work to that of an expert in the explanations found at the end of the chapter.

HUMANITIES: This passage is adapted from an article about modern architecture.

Fallingwater, a small country house constructed in 1936, stands as perhaps the greatest residential building achievement of the American architect Frank Lloyd Wright.
5 In designing the dwelling for the Pittsburgh millionaire Edgar J. Kaufmann, Wright was confronted with an unusually challenging site beside a waterfall deep in a Pennsylvania ravine. However, Wright viewed this difficult location
10 not as an obstacle but as a unique opportunity to put his architectural ideas into concrete form.

In the early 1930s, Edgar J. Kaufmann's son, Edgar J. Kaufmann Jr., studied with Wright as an apprentice at Wright's Taliesin Studio in Spring
15 Green, Wisconsin. At the time, architecture critics deemed Wright's style anachronistic and assumed that his career was coming to an end. Kaufmann Jr., on the other hand, greatly admired Wright's work and was delighted to introduce his parents
20 to the esteemed architect. Shortly thereafter, the Kaufmanns asked Wright to design Fallingwater.

The site Kaufmann chose for his country getaway was originally the location of a cabin in Mill Run, Pennsylvania, that he offered as a vacation
25 retreat for the numerous employees he oversaw at Kaufmann's Department Store, located in downtown Pittsburgh. When the Great Depression struck, Kaufmann's employees could no longer afford the cost of traveling more than 60 miles to Mill Run,
30 and Kaufmann decided that the land, a wooded area nestled along the banks of a mountain stream called Bear Run, was an ideal location for a vacation home. Kaufmann had assumed that the home would stand

at the bottom of a nearby waterfall, where it would
35 provide a perfect venue from which to appreciate the view. However, Wright had other ideas. When Wright showed Kaufmann his plans, Kaufmann initially balked, but Wright convinced him that incorporating the falls into the design of the house
40 was far preferable. In the end, Wright was able to turn Fallingwater into an artistic link between untamed nature and domestic tranquility—and a masterpiece in his brilliant career.

Edgar J. Kaufmann's original plan to build
45 his house on the ample flat land at the bottom of the waterfall would indisputably have proven less challenging. Wright's more daring response to the site required builders to construct the house on a small stone precipice atop the falls. Wright
50 further proposed extending the living room of the house out over the rushing water and making use of modern building techniques so that no vertical supports would be needed to hold up the room. Wright brilliantly utilized the "cantilever"
55 technique, in which steel rods are laid inside a shelf of concrete, eliminating the need for external supports. Unfortunately, however, the builders did not employ an adequate amount of reinforcing steel to support the first floor. Kaufmann had hired
60 consulting engineers to review Wright's design prior to Fallingwater's construction, but Wright dismissed the engineers' claims that the main floor girders needed additional support. Over time, the first floor cantilever began to sag, and in 2002, a technique
65 called post-tensioning was used to permanently repair the gradual collapse.

Despite Wright's miscalculation, Fallingwater, as a whole, is an impressive structure. Rather

than allowing the environment to determine the
70 placement and shape of the house, Wright sought
to construct a home that intentionally confronted
and interacted with the landscape. Each bedroom
has its own terrace, and cornerless windows open
outward so that window panes do not obstruct
75 the spectacular view. In addition, Fallingwater
contains a great many traditional and natural
building materials. The home's 5,300-square foot
expanse includes custom-designed black walnut
wood furniture and walls and floors constructed
80 of locally sourced sandstone. The boulders that
provide the foundation for the house also extend
up through the floor and form part of the
fireplace. A staircase in the living room extends
down to an enclosed bathing pool at the top of
85 the waterfall. To Wright, the ideal dwelling in
this spot was not simply a modern extravaganza
or a direct extension of natural surroundings;
rather, it was a little of both.

Architecture enthusiasts have taken a wide
90 range of approaches to understanding this unique
building. Some have asserted that the house
exalts the artist's triumph over untamed nature.

Others have compared Wright's building to a
cave, providing a psychological and physical safe
95 haven from a harsh, violent world. The members
of the American Institute of Architects named
Fallingwater the "best all-time work of American
architecture," and the Western Pennsylvania
Conservancy, which has owned and preserved
100 Fallingwater since 1963, hails the building as
an inspiration.

Edgar Kaufmann Jr. may have summed up the
innovation and awe of Fallingwater best when
he said, "Wright understood that people were
105 creatures of nature; hence, an architecture which
conformed to nature would conform to what
was basic in people. . . . Sociability and privacy
are both available, as are the comforts of home
and the adventures of the seasons." This, then, is
110 Frank Lloyd Wright's achievement in Fallingwater:
a home that connects the human and the natural
for the invigoration and exaltation of both.

How Much Have You Learned?

Directions: Take five minutes to actively read the following passage by:

1.   noting the keywords

2.   jotting down margin notes next to each paragraph

3.   summarizing the big picture

When you're done, compare your work to the explanations at the end of the chapter.

SOCIAL SCIENCE: This passage is adapted from an article about how humans develop language.

The influential theory of universal grammar (UG) postulates that all humans have an innate, genetic understanding of certain grammatical "rules," which are universal across all languages
5   and absolutely not affected by environment. The idea of such a universal grammar has a long history, starting with Roger Bacon's thirteenth-century book *Overview of Grammar* and continuing through the Renaissance with attempts to construct
10   an ideal language. In the eighteenth century, the first edition of the Encyclopedia Britannica included a section dedicated to universal grammar. In modern times, however, the linguistic theory of universal grammar is most closely associated
15   with Noam Chomsky, who did much to codify and popularize it in the 1950s–1970s. According to Chomsky, we are all born with a knowledge of "deep structure," basic linguistic constructions that allow us, if not to understand all languages, at least
20   to understand how they are put together. From there, we have only to learn how the parameters are set in our particular language in order to create an unlimited number of "correct" utterances.

For example, he suggests that structure
25   dependency—a rule that says that sentences are defined by phrase structure, not linear structure—is inherent to all languages, with minor variations. Thus, the meaning of a sentence is really dependent on the meaning of its phrases, rather than each
30   individual word. In addition, the head parameter rule stipulates that each phrase contains a "head" (main) word, and all languages have the head word in essentially the same position within the phrase.

Chomsky's famous sentence "Colorless green ideas
35   sleep furiously" exemplifies this theory of universal grammar—while the sentence itself is meaningless, it is easily recognizable as a grammatical sentence that fits a basic but higher level of organization. "Furiously sleep ideas green colorless," on the other
40   hand, is obviously not a grammatical sentence, and it is difficult to discern any kind of meaning in it. For other evidence to support this theory, Chomsky points to our relative ease in translating one language to another; again, while we may
45   not necessarily recognize individual words in an unfamiliar language, we can certainly recognize and engage with sentences that are grammatical.

This evidence is still fairly theoretical, receiving play mostly in the linguistic sphere rather than in
50   the biological sciences. Most of those researching the theory seem more concerned with attempting to draw universal parallels across languages than with searching for biological evidence of such phenomena. We might ask: Where exactly are
55   these universal grammar constraints located in our genetic code? How and when are they altered by natural evolutionary processes—or do they remain relatively unaltered and non-mutated from generation to generation? As both languages and
60   human beings evolve over time, does UG also evolve or stay relatively stable?

Even within the linguistic sphere, Chomsky's theory has drawn criticism. Some scientists suggest that by ignoring the role of environment
65   in language development, Chomsky completely discredits the possibly important effect our surroundings could have on language development. Still other researchers say that universal grammar

is not nearly as ordered and absolute as Chomsky
70 and other linguists make it out to be—that merely
identifying similarities in different languages does
not prove that a universal grammar underlies
them. They suggest that since the universal
grammar theory is not falsifiable, it is in fact
75 pseudoscientific rather than scientific, the result
of our flawed human tendency to impose order
where there is none.

More recent researchers have begun to
advocate that, rather than focusing on explaining
80 linguistic similarities among various languages,
we instead acknowledge the evolutionary roots of
language and look specifically for neurobiological
explanations. Claiming that the humanistic
exploration of universal grammar is too abstract,
85 they recommend that we instead view language
(and grammar) as a function of the brain.
Some progress has been made in studying the
neurobiology of language; for instance, scientists
have identified specific regions of the brain that
90 handle language. However, these findings are
simple and preliminary, offering little insight into
the vast intricacy of human language use.

Neither linguistics nor biology alone is sufficient
to understand the foundations of language.
95 Language is unbelievably complex: even a single
word can offer several definitions and associations.
Thus, any single connection between, say, two
languages causes those myriad associations to
become oversimplified and sterile. For example,
100 simply pointing out that the subject of a sentence is
in the same position in Turkish and English as an
illustration of UG merely acknowledges that single
linguistic association, while failing to consider any
social circumstances that may cause the mind to
105 modify that grammar. In short, say scientists, not
until we create a better marriage between biology
and linguistics—and a better understanding of the
human brain—can we even begin to address the
complexities of human language development.

Reflect

Directions: Take a few minutes to recall what you've learned and what you've been practicing in this chapter. Consider the following questions, jot down your best answer for each one, and then compare your reflections to the expert responses on the following page. Use your level of confidence to determine what to do next.

1. Why do ACT experts note keywords as they read?

    _____

2. What are the three categories of keywords? Provide some examples from each category.

    1. _____

        - Examples:
            - _____
            - _____
            - _____

    2. _____

        - Examples:
            - _____
            - _____
            - _____

    3. _____

        - Examples:
            - _____
            - _____
            - _____

3. Why do ACT experts jot down margin notes next to the text?

    _____

4. What are the elements of a strong big picture summary?

    _____

Responses

1. Why do ACT experts note keywords as they read?

Keywords indicate what the author finds important, express his point of view about the subject and details of the passage, and signal key points in the passage structure. Keywords are the pieces of text that help test takers see which parts of the passage are likely to be mentioned in questions and help the test taker to distinguish between correct and incorrect answer choices about those parts of the passage.

2. What are the three categories of keywords? Provide some examples from each category.

    1. *Opinion and emphasis*
       - Examples:
         - *indeed*
         - *quite*
         - *masterfully*
         - *inadequate*
    2. *Connection and contrast*
       - Examples:
         - *furthermore*
         - *plus*
         - *however*
         - *on the contrary*
    3. *Evidence and example*
       - Examples:
         - *consequently*
         - *since*
         - *for instance*
         - *such as*

3. Why do ACT experts jot down margin notes next to the text?

Margin notes help the test taker research questions that ask about details, examples, and arguments mentioned in the passage by providing a "map" to their location in the text. Margin notes can also help students answer questions about the passage structure and the purpose of a specific paragraph.

4. What are the elements of a strong big picture summary?

A strong big picture summary prepares a test taker to answer any question about the main idea of the passage or the author's primary or overall purpose in writing it. After reading the passage, ACT experts pause to ask, "What is the main idea of the entire passage?" and "Why did the author write it?"

Next Steps

If you answered most questions correctly in the "How Much Have You Learned?" section, and if your responses to the Reflect questions were similar to those of the ACT expert, then consider strategic reading and passage mapping an area of strength and move on to the next chapter. Come back to this topic periodically to prevent yourself from getting rusty.

If you don't yet feel confident, review the material in this chapter, and then try the questions you missed again. As always, be sure to review the explanations closely. Then go online (**kaptest.com/login**) to use your Qbank for more practice. If you haven't already registered your book, do so at **kaptest.com/moreonline.**

GO ONLINE

kaptest.com/login

Answers and Explanations

Try on Your Own

HUMANITIES: This passage is adapted from an article about modern architecture.

Fallingwater, a small country house constructed in 1936, stands as perhaps the greatest residential building achievement of the American architect Frank Lloyd Wright.

5 In designing the dwelling for the Pittsburgh millionaire Edgar J. Kaufmann, Wright was confronted with an unusually challenging site beside a waterfall deep in a Pennsylvania ravine. However, Wright viewed this difficult location

10 not as an obstacle but as a unique opportunity to put his architectural ideas into concrete form.

In the early 1930s, Edgar J. Kaufmann's son, Edgar J. Kaufmann Jr., studied with Wright as an apprentice at Wright's Taliesin Studio in Spring

15 Green, Wisconsin. At the time, architecture critics deemed Wright's style anachronistic and assumed that his career was coming to an end. Kaufmann Jr., on the other hand, greatly admired Wright's work and was delighted to introduce his parents

20 to the esteemed architect. Shortly thereafter, the Kaufmanns asked Wright to design Fallingwater.

The site Kaufmann chose for his country getaway was originally the location of a cabin in Mill Run, Pennsylvania, that he offered as a vacation

25 retreat for the numerous employees he oversaw at Kaufmann's Department Store, located in downtown Pittsburgh. When the Great Depression struck, Kaufmann's employees could no longer afford the cost of traveling more than 60 miles to Mill Run,

30 and Kaufmann decided that the land, a wooded area nestled along the banks of a mountain stream called Bear Run, was an ideal location for a vacation home. Kaufmann had assumed that the home would stand at the bottom of a nearby waterfall, where it would

35 provide a perfect venue from which to appreciate the view. However, Wright had other ideas. When Wright showed Kaufmann his plans, Kaufmann initially balked, but Wright convinced him that incorporating the falls into the design of the house

ANALYSIS

Pre-passage blurb: The blurb tells you that the topic of this passage is modern architecture.

Fallingwater: architectural achievement by FLW ¶1 This paragraph introduces you to both Fallingwater and Frank Lloyd Wright. Fallingwater is significant not because of its difficult location but because of how Wright used it as an opportunity to showcase his unique architectural ideas.

how FLW came to design Fallingwater ¶2 Despite the opinion of critics that his career was coming to an end, Wright was commissioned to build Fallingwater after the Kaufmann family was introduced to him by their son.

location; below vs. on falls ¶3 Kaufmann chose an ideal location for his vacation home: the bottom of a waterfall. Wright was able to convince him to build the home around the falls, which linked both nature and domestic life.

40 was far preferable. In the end, Wright was able
to turn Fallingwater into an artistic link between
untamed nature and domestic tranquility—and a
masterpiece in his brilliant career.

Edgar J. Kaufmann's original plan to build
45 his house on the ample flat land at the bottom of
the waterfall would indisputably have proven less
challenging. Wright's more daring response to
the site required builders to construct the house
on a small stone precipice atop the falls. Wright
50 further proposed extending the living room of
the house out over the rushing water and making
use of modern building techniques so that no
vertical supports would be needed to hold up the
room. Wright brilliantly utilized the "cantilever"
55 technique, in which steel rods are laid inside a
shelf of concrete, eliminating the need for external
supports. Unfortunately, however, the builders did
not employ an adequate amount of reinforcing steel
to support the first floor. Kaufmann had hired
60 consulting engineers to review Wright's design prior
to Fallingwater's construction, but Wright dismissed
the engineers' claims that the main floor girders
needed additional support. Over time, the first floor
cantilever began to sag, and in 2002, a technique
65 called post-tensioning was used to permanently
repair the gradual collapse.

Despite Wright's miscalculation, Fallingwater,
as a whole, is an impressive structure. Rather
than allowing the environment to determine the
70 placement and shape of the house, Wright sought
to construct a home that intentionally confronted
and interacted with the landscape. Each bedroom
has its own terrace, and cornerless windows open
outward so that window panes do not obstruct
75 the spectacular view. In addition, Fallingwater
contains a great many traditional and natural
building materials. The home's 5,300-square foot
expanse includes custom-designed black walnut
wood furniture and walls and floors constructed
80 of locally sourced sandstone. The boulders that
provide the foundation for the house also extend
up through the floor and form part of the
fireplace. A staircase in the living room extends
down to an enclosed bathing pool at the top of

challenges

¶4 Kaufmann had a safer plan to build his home at the bottom of the falls, but Wright was more daring. He utilized a technique that allowed the living room to extend over the falls. Although this design was brilliant (even though it ignored the engineers' recommendation for more support), it did need repairs in 2002.

house interacts w/ nature

¶5 This paragraph lists several examples of how Wright was able to turn Fallingwater into a masterpiece that combined modern design with nature.

85 the waterfall. To Wright, the ideal dwelling in
    this spot was not simply a modern extravaganza
    or a direct extension of natural surroundings;
    rather, it was a little of both.

       Architecture enthusiasts have taken a wide
90 range of approaches to understanding this unique
    building. Some have asserted that the house
    exalts the artist's triumph over untamed nature.
    Others have compared Wright's building to a
    cave, providing a psychological and physical safe
95 haven from a harsh, violent world. The members
    of the American Institute of Architects named
    Fallingwater the "best all-time work of American
    architecture," and the Western Pennsylvania
    Conservancy, which has owned and preserved
100 Fallingwater since 1963, hails the building as
    an inspiration.

       Edgar Kaufmann Jr. may have summed up the
    innovation and awe of Fallingwater best when
    he said, "Wright understood that people were
105 creatures of nature; hence, an architecture which
    conformed to nature would conform to what
    was basic in people. . . . Sociability and privacy
    are both available, as are the comforts of home
    and the adventures of the seasons." This, then, is
110 Frank Lloyd Wright's achievement in Fallingwater:
    a home that connects the human and the natural
    for the invigoration and exaltation of both.

critical responses

¶6 Paragraph 6 gives you insight into the opinion of other architects, which was overwhelmingly positive.

connects human and nature

¶7 The conclusion to the passage sums up by revealing Kaufmann's thoughts on Fallingwater: a home that connects humans with nature for the benefit of both.

BIG PICTURE SUMMARY

Main idea: Fallingwater, an unusual and impressive building, was an architectural achievement by Frank Lloyd Wright.

Author's purpose: To inform the reader about the history of a unique piece of architecture

As with the other passages in this chapter, don't worry about whether you used the exact language found in the expert's passage map and big picture summary. Instead, focus on how the expert used the skills and strategies outlined here to prepare herself to tackle the question set with speed and confidence.

How Much Have You Learned?

SOCIAL SCIENCE: This passage is adapted from an article about how humans develop language.

The influential theory of universal grammar (UG) postulates that all humans have an innate, genetic understanding of certain grammatical "rules," which are universal across all languages
5 and absolutely not affected by environment. The idea of such a universal grammar has a long history, starting with Roger Bacon's thirteenth-century book *Overview of Grammar* and continuing through the Renaissance with attempts to construct
10 an ideal language. In the eighteenth century, the first edition of the Encyclopedia Britannica included a section dedicated to universal grammar. In modern times, however, the linguistic theory of universal grammar is most closely associated
15 with Noam Chomsky, who did much to codify and popularize it in the 1950s–1970s. According to Chomsky, we are all born with a knowledge of "deep structure," basic linguistic constructions that allow us, if not to understand all languages, at least
20 to understand how they are put together. From there, we have only to learn how the parameters are set in our particular language in order to create an unlimited number of "correct" utterances.

For example, he suggests that structure
25 dependency—a rule that says that sentences are defined by phrase structure, not linear structure— is inherent to all languages, with minor variations. Thus, the meaning of a sentence is really dependent on the meaning of its phrases, rather than each
30 individual word. In addition, the head parameter rule stipulates that each phrase contains a "head" (main) word, and all languages have the head word in essentially the same position within the phrase. Chomsky's famous sentence "Colorless green ideas
35 sleep furiously" exemplifies this theory of universal grammar—while the sentence itself is meaningless, it is easily recognizable as a grammatical sentence that fits a basic but higher level of organization. "Furiously sleep ideas green colorless," on the other
40 hand, is obviously not a grammatical sentence, and it is difficult to discern any kind of meaning in it. For other evidence to support this theory,

ANALYSIS

Pre-passage blurb: The blurb tells you that the article is about how humans develop language.

theory of UG through history

¶1 The theory of UG has been prevalent throughout history. It states that all humans have an innate understanding of universal grammar rules. These rules are not affected by environment and are universal across all languages.

ex. of rules that support UG

¶2 This paragraph gives two specific examples of rules that support Chomsky's theory of UG. The structure dependency rule says that sentences are defined by phrases, and the head parameter rule states that each phrase has a main word that is in the same position across languages. Chomsky also points to the ease by which we can translate from one language to another as further evidence to support his theory.

Chomsky points to our relative ease in translating one language to another; again, while we may
45 not necessarily recognize individual words in an unfamiliar language, we can certainly recognize and engage with sentences that are grammatical.

This evidence is still fairly theoretical, receiving play mostly in the linguistic sphere rather than in
50 the biological sciences. Most of those researching the theory seem more concerned with attempting to draw universal parallels across languages than with searching for biological evidence of such phenomena. We might ask: Where exactly are
55 these universal grammar constraints located in our genetic code? How and when are they altered by natural evolutionary processes—or do they remain relatively unaltered and non-mutated from generation to generation? As both languages and
60 human beings evolve over time, does UG also evolve or stay relatively stable?

Even within the linguistic sphere, Chomsky's theory has drawn criticism. Some scientists suggest that by ignoring the role of environment
65 in language development, Chomsky completely discredits the possibly important effect our surroundings could have on language development. Still other researchers say that universal grammar is not nearly as ordered and absolute as Chomsky
70 and other linguists make it out to be—that merely identifying similarities in different languages does not prove that a universal grammar underlies them. They suggest that since the universal grammar theory is not falsifiable, it is in fact
75 pseudoscientific rather than scientific, the result of our flawed human tendency to impose order where there is none.

More recent researchers have begun to advocate that, rather than focusing on explaining
80 linguistic similarities among various languages, we instead acknowledge the evolutionary roots of language and look specifically for neurobiological explanations. Claiming that the humanistic exploration of universal grammar is too abstract,
85 they recommend that we instead view language (and grammar) as a function of the brain. Some progress has been made in studying the

ev. =
theoretical,
biological ?

criticism

lang. and
brain

¶3 This paragraph tells you that the theory of UG is prominent mostly in the area of linguistics and not in biology. There are genetic questions relating to the theory: is UG evolving or stable over time?

¶4 Paragraph 4 gives you insight into what critics think. Some say Chomsky's theory ignores the influence environment could have on language. Others say that similarities and differences among languages do not mean that a universal theory ties them together. There is a question as to whether the theory is science at all.

¶5 Recently, researchers have looked for neurobiological explanations for language. So far, this brain research has offered little insight into the intricacies of human language.

neurobiology of language; for instance, scientists
have identified specific regions of the brain that

90 handle language. However, these findings are
simple and preliminary, offering little insight into
the vast intricacy of human language use.

Neither linguistics nor biology alone is sufficient
to understand the foundations of language.

95 Language is unbelievably complex: even a single
word can offer several definitions and associations.
Thus, any single connection between, say, two
languages causes those myriad associations to
become oversimplified and sterile. For example,

100 simply pointing out that the subject of a sentence is
in the same position in Turkish and English as an
illustration of UG merely acknowledges that single
linguistic association, while failing to consider any
social circumstances that may cause the mind to

105 modify that grammar. In short, say scientists, not
until we create a better marriage between biology
and linguistics—and a better understanding of the
human brain—can we even begin to address the
complexities of human language development.

*biology &
linguistics
both needed*

¶6 In this concluding paragraph, you learn
that it is necessary to better merge biology
and linguistics to understand the complexities
of human language; anything less would be
an oversimplification of a complex process.

Reading

BIG PICTURE SUMMARY

Main idea: Chomsky's theory of innate linguistic structure is popular among linguists but does not address biological influences on language development.

Author's purpose: To inform the reader about the limitations and possibilities of universal grammar

IDENTIFYING QUESTION TYPES

LEARNING OBJECTIVES

After completing this chapter, you will be able to:

- Unpack ACT Reading question stems by
  - distinguishing among the five ACT Reading question types
  - determining if the correct answer is best found by researching the passage text or by consulting your big picture summary

---

Vocab-in-Context: 3/36 SmartPoints® (Medium yield)

Function: 6/36 SmartPoints® (High yield)

Inference: 10/36 SmartPoints® (Very high yield)

Detail: 13/36 SmartPoints® (Very high yield)

Global: 4/36 SmartPoints® (Medium yield)

How Much Do You Know?

Directions: In this chapter, you'll learn to unpack ACT Reading question stems (step 1 of the ACT Reading Question Method). Unpacking a question stem means pinpointing your task (as identified by the question type) and noting where the answer will be found (a specific reference within the passage text or in your big picture summary). For your reference as you complete this quiz, here are the ACT Reading question types:

- **Global**—asks about big picture ideas, including both main idea and tone
- **Detail**—asks about explicitly stated facts or details
- **Inference**—asks about points that are unstated but strongly suggested
- **Function**—asks why or how the author wrote specific parts of the text
- **Vocab-in-Context**—asks for the intended meaning of a word as it is used in the passage

For each of the following question stems, identify the question type, cite the language in the stem that helped you identify that type, and indicate where you would begin to research the question: either your big picture summary or a specific part of the text.

Example

The author most strongly suggests that public transportation options in rural locations:

Question type: *Inference*

Identifying language: *"most strongly suggests"*

Research where? *passage, where author discusses public transportation in rural areas*

1. Which of the following statements best expresses the main idea of the passage?

   Question type:
   Identifying language:
   Research where?

2. According to the passage, the author's grandfather's birth happened:

   Question type:
   Identifying language:
   Research where?

3. The final sentence of the second paragraph (line 30) most directly serves to emphasize that the exiles:

   Question type:
   Identifying language:
   Research where?

4. Why did the narrator's grandfather and other recent immigrants say "*ya amerikanets*"?

   Question type:
   Identifying language:
   Research where?

5. According to the third paragraph, what made settling in America a difficult time for the narrator's grandfather?

   Question type:
   Identifying language:
   Research where?

6. What "advantage" did the narrator's grandfather most likely find in telling people about his relationship with Russia?

   Question type:
   Identifying language:
   Research where?

7. In the seventh paragraph, the passage states that the speaker's grandfather traveled to Russia because:

    Question type:
    Identifying language:
    Research where?

8. The speaker describes the typical view people have of real estate agents (lines 96–99) primarily in order to:

    Question type:
    Identifying language:
    Research where?

9. As it is used in line 105, the word *realization* most nearly means:

    Question type:
    Identifying language:
    Research where?

10. Based on the passage, why was the speaker's grandfather attracted to real estate as a profession?

    Question type:
    Identifying language:
    Research where?

Check Your Work

1. Which of the following statements best expresses the main idea of the passage?

   Question type: Global
   Identifying language: "main idea"
   Research where? big picture summary

2. According to the passage, the author's grandfather's birth happened:

   Question type: Detail
   Identifying language: "According to the passage"
   Research where? passage, where author discusses grandfather's birth (first paragraph)

3. The final sentence of the second paragraph (line 30) most directly serves to emphasize that the exiles:

   Question type: Function
   Identifying language: "most directly serves to emphasize"
   Research where? passage map, second paragraph

4. Why did the narrator's grandfather and other recent immigrants say *"ya amerikanets"*?

   Question type: Detail
   Identifying language: "Why did [people] say [phrase]?"
   Research where? passage, the line numbers and paragraph where the narrator's grandfather and other immigrants say this

5. According to the third paragraph, what made settling in America a difficult time for the narrator's grandfather?

   Question type: Detail
   Identifying language: "According to the third paragraph"
   Research where? passage, third paragraph

6. What "advantage" did the narrator's grandfather most likely find in telling people about his relationship with Russia?

   Question type: Inference
   Identifying language: "most likely"
   Research where? passage, line numbers and paragraph where the grandfather is telling people about his relationship with Russia

7. In the seventh paragraph, the passage states that the speaker's grandfather traveled to Russia because:

   Question type: Detail
   Identifying language: "the passage states"
   Research where? passage, seventh paragraph

8. The speaker describes the typical view people have of real estate agents (lines 96–99) primarily in order to:

   Question type: Function
   Identifying language: "the speaker describes . . . in order to"
   Research where? passage, lines 96–99

9. As it is used in line 105, the word *realization* most nearly means:

   Question type: Vocab-in-Context
   Identifying language: "the word . . . most nearly means"
   Research where? passage, line 105

10. Based on the passage, why was the speaker's grandfather attracted to real estate as a profession?

    Question type: Global
    Identifying language: "Based on the passage"
    Research where? passage map and big picture summary

HOW TO UNPACK ACT READING QUESTION STEMS

To unpack question stems like these:

1. One of the main points of the second paragraph (lines 14–28) is that:

2. The passage suggests that an important difference between Mars and Earth is that, unlike Earth, Mars:

3. According to the passage, which of the following describes the atmosphere of Mars?

4. The passage suggests that Mars is void of organic compounds because:

5. The passage states that the Viking landing sites were chosen because of their:

6. As it is used in line 88, the word *barren* most nearly means:

7. The researchers' argument that life may exist in Martian rocks rests on the idea that:

8. The author mentions blue-green algae in the sixth paragraph primarily in order to:

9. It can be inferred from the passage that the possibility mentioned in line 94 refers to:

10. In the final paragraph, which of the following is listed as a compound that is necessary for life?

You need to know this:

There are five question types, each of which defines a specific task:

- **Global**—asks about big picture ideas, including both main idea and tone
  - Which of the following best states the main idea of the passage?
  - The main purpose of the passage is to:
  - The passage as a whole can best be described as:
- **Detail**—asks about explicitly stated facts or details
  - According to the passage, what makes a tropical beach a specialized area?
  - According to the passage, which of the following is true of the New York City subway system?
  - The passage indicates that non-rush hour commuters:
- **Inference**—asks about points that are unstated but supported by the passage
  - The passage most strongly suggests that the Mayan people were the first to flourish in coastal Mexico because they:
  - Based on the passage, which choice best describes a claim that critics of the current subway mainte-nance plan would likely make?

- **Function**—asks why or how the author wrote specific parts of the text
  - The comparison between a gymnasium and an open market in paragraph 4 is meant to:
  - In the third paragraph, the discussion of two specific subway lines (lines 35–39) primarily serves to:
  - The narrator describes what she is seeing as she travels in lines 54–60 primarily in order to:
- **Vocab-in-Context**—asks for the intended meaning of a word as it is used in the passage
  - As it is used in line 26, the word *dictate* most nearly means:
  - As it is used in line 33, the word *labyrinthine* most nearly means:

There are specific types of clues in ACT Reading question stems that can help you answer questions more accurately and efficiently:

- **Line numbers**—Mentions of "line 53" or "lines 37–40," often in parentheses, tend to stand out and give you a clear place to start your research.
- **Paragraph numbers**—A reference to "paragraph 5," "the third paragraph," or "the last two paragraphs" is not as precise as a line reference but will still give you an idea of where to look. Start with your margin notes for the paragraph.
- **Quoted text** (often accompanied by line numbers)—Check the context of the quoted term or phrase to see what the author meant by it in the passage.
- **Proper nouns**—Names like "Professor James," "World War II," and "Baltimore" will likely stand out in question stems due to the capitalization. If a particular proper noun is discussed in only part of the passage, it narrows the range of text you have to research.
- **Specific content clues**—Sometimes a question stem will repeat terminology used in part of the passage, like "federalism" or "action potentials." Use your passage map to direct your research to the right part of the passage.
- **Whole passage clues**—If a question lacks specific content clues but refers to the passage as a whole or to the author in general, you are likely dealing with a Global question or an open-ended Inference question, which should lead you to your big picture summary rather than to rereading parts of the text.

You need to do this:

ACT READING QUESTION METHOD

Step 1. Unpack the question stem

Step 2. Research the answer

Step 3. Predict the answer

Step 4. Find the one correct answer

Step 1. Unpack the question stem.

- Identify the question type and anticipate how it will need to be answered.
- Note research clues that indicate how best to research the correct answer.

You will complete Steps 2, 3, and 4 in chapter 18.

Why distinguish question types in ACT Reading?

Unpacking the question stem puts you in control. You'll know exactly what the question is asking, where to find the correct answer, and what form the correct answer will take.

- **Global:** The correct answer must take the entire passage into account. A choice that reflects only part of the passage is incorrect.
- **Detail:** The correct answer must be stated in the passage explicitly. A choice that is not directly stated in the passage is incorrect.
- **Inference:** The correct answer will be a conclusion that can be drawn from the passage. A choice that draws too strong of a conclusion from the evidence available in the passage is incorrect.
- **Function:** The correct answer will say *why* a certain detail is included. Look up the detail, then ask yourself what the author was trying to accomplish by putting it there.
- **Vocab-in-Context:** The correct answer will give the meaning of a word as it is used in the context of the passage. Choices that give common meanings of the word are often incorrect.

Correct answers to Reading questions are never random or vague. They are tailored to the precise language of the stem, so being able to distinguish the question types will save you time and eliminate confusion during the test.

Explanations

1. This is a Global question. The identifying language in the question stem is "the main points." You can locate support for the correct answer in your big picture summary and passage map notes.

2. This is an Inference question. The identifying language in the question stem is "The passage suggests." You can locate support for the correct answer in the passage, using your passage map notes to help guide you to the answer more efficiently.

3. This is a Detail question. The identifying language in the question stem is "According to the passage." You can locate the correct answer in the passage, using your passage map notes to guide you to the correct paragraph more efficiently.

4. This is an Inference question. The identifying language in the question stem is "The passage suggests." You can locate support for the correct answer in the passage, using your passage map notes to guide you to the correct paragraph more efficiently.

5. This is a Detail question. The identifying language in the question stem is "The passage states." You can locate the correct answer in the passage, using your passage map notes to guide you to the correct paragraph more efficiently.

6. This is a Vocab-in-Context question. The identifying language in the question stem is "as it is used in line 88" and "most nearly means." You can locate support for the correct answer by reading the entire sentence that includes the word and more, if needed.

7. This is an Inference question. The identifying language in the question stem is not as clear, but the more open-ended phrasing is a clue that it might be Inference rather than Detail. You can locate support for the correct answer in the passage, using your passage map to figure out where the researchers talked about life in Martian rocks.

8. This is a Function question. The identifying language in the question stem is "The author mentions . . . in order to." You can locate support for the correct answer by going back to the cited example and rereading the entire paragraph.

9. This is an Inference question. The identifying language in the question stem is the word *inferred*. You can locate support for the correct answer in the passage by going to line 94, rereading the sentence, and reviewing your big picture summary for a reminder of the passage as a whole if needed.

10. This is a Detail question. The identifying language in the question stem is that the question asks for something *listed* in the paragraph. You can locate the correct answer by going back to the final paragraph and figuring out what is listed as a necessary component for life.

Try on Your Own

Directions: Analyze each of the following question stems by:

1. naming the question type

2. identifying the word or phrase that describes your task

3. noting how best to research the correct answer (research the text or consult the big picture summary)

Answers are found at the end of the chapter.

1. The overall organization of the passage is best described as a:

    Question type:
    Identifying language:
    Research where?

2. Based on the passage, architecture critics regarded Frank Lloyd Wright's career prior to Fallingwater's construction (lines 15–17) as:

    Question type:
    Identifying language:
    Research where?

3. It can be reasonably inferred that the site chosen for Fallingwater was:

    Question type:
    Identifying language:
    Research where?

4. The passage indicates that Edgar J. Kaufmann's original plans for the site were:

    Question type:
    Identifying language:
    Research where?

5. The author's use of the phrases "black walnut wood" and "locally sourced sandstone" (lines 78–80) most nearly serves to emphasize which of the following points?

    Question type:
    Identifying language:
    Research where?

6. According to the passage, a cantilever is designed to include:

    Question type:
    Identifying language:
    Research where?

7. It can reasonably be inferred that the miscalculation the author mentions in line 67 refers to:

    Question type:
    Identifying language:
    Research where?

8. One of the main purposes of the information in lines 72–85 is to:

    Question type:
    Identifying language:
    Research where?

9. Architecture enthusiasts' comparisons of Fallingwater to a cave (lines 93–95) most strongly suggest that the house provides a sense of:

   Question type:

   Identifying language:

   Research where?

10. As it is used in line 112, the phrase *invigoration and exaltation* most nearly means:

    Question type:

    Identifying language:

    Research where?

For any question types that you misidentified, return to the definitions and question stem examples before you try the "How Much Have you Learned?" questions in this chapter.

How Much Have You Learned?

Directions: For practice identifying reading question types, analyze each of the following question stems by:

1. naming the question type

2. identifying the word or phrase that describes your task

3. noting how best to research the correct answer (research the text or consult the big picture summary)

Answers are found at the end of the chapter.

1. Throughout the passage, the character's reaction to the narrator is to:

   Question type:
   Identifying language:
   Research where?

2. Based on the passage, how do Renaissance efforts to design a language relate to Chomsky's theory of universal grammar?

   Question type:
   Identifying language:
   Research where?

3. In the first paragraph, Chomsky claimed that an "innate, genetic understanding":

   Question type:
   Identifying language:
   Research where?

4. According to the passage, universal grammar's structure dependency rule states that:

   Question type:
   Identifying language:
   Research where?

5. The author includes the quotes "Colorless green ideas sleep furiously" and "Furiously sleep ideas green colorless" primarily in order to:

   Question type:
   Identifying language:
   Research where?

6. The questions in paragraph 3 primarily serve to:

   Question type:
   Identifying language:
   Research where?

7. The passage suggests that the researchers mentioned in line 68 believe which of the following?

   Question type:
   Identifying language:
   Research where?

8. One of the main purposes of the fifth paragraph is to:

   Question type:
   Identifying language:
   Research where?

9. As it is used in line 99, the word *sterile* most nearly means:

   Question type:
   Identifying language:
   Research where?

10. As it is used in line 106, the phrase *a better marriage* most nearly means:

    Question type:
    Identifying language:
    Research where?

Reading

Reflect

Directions: Take a few minutes to recall what you've learned and what you've been practicing in this chapter. Consider the following questions, jot down your best answer for each one, and then compare your reflections to the expert responses on the following page. Use your level of confidence to determine what to do next.

1. Why is it important to always unpack the question stem before proceeding?

_____

_____

_____

2. Can you name the five ACT Reading question types and cite words or phrases that identify each one?

   1. _____

     • Identifying language: _____

     _____

   2. _____

     • Identifying language: _____

     _____

   3. _____

     • Identifying language: _____

     _____

   4. _____

     • Identifying language: _____

     _____

   5. _____

     • Identifying language: _____

     _____

3. How will you approach ACT Reading question stems differently as you continue to practice and improve your performance in the Reading section? What are the main differences you see between ACT Reading questions and those you're used to from tests in school?

_____

_____

_____

Responses

1. Why is it important to always unpack the question stem before proceeding?

Knowing the ACT Reading question types makes you a more strategic and efficient reader because the test maker uses the same question types on every test. Fully analyzing each question stem helps you research the text more effectively, predict the correct answer in a way that fits the question stem, and avoid incorrect answers made from misreading the question.

2. Can you name the five ACT Reading question types and cite words or phrases that identify each one? (*answers in no particular order*)

    1. Global
        *   Identifying language: *the author's attitude*, *main idea*
    2. Detail
        *   Identifying language: *according to [line/paragraph/passage]*, *states that*, *claims*
    3. Inference
        *   Identifying language: *most strongly suggests*, *most strongly implies*
    4. Function
        *   Identifying language: *the primary function of*, *in order to*
    5. Vocab-in-Context
        *   Identifying language: *as used in line [number]*, *the word most nearly means*

3. How will you approach ACT Reading question stems differently as you continue to practice and improve your performance in the Reading section? What are the main differences you see between ACT Reading questions and those you're used to from tests in school?

There is no one-size-fits-all answer here. Reflect on your own strengths and weaknesses as you consider how to best improve your performance in the ACT Reading section. Depending on the kinds of classes and teachers you've had in high school, the skills rewarded on ACT Reading questions may be more or less familiar, but almost every test taker needs to be aware of her own instincts as a reader, and needs to break certain reading habits, to master this section of the test. The more you give yourself an honest self-assessment, the better prepared you'll be to handle all of the ACT Reading question types confidently.

Next Steps

If you answered most questions correctly in the "How Much Have You Learned?" section, and if your responses to the Reflect questions were similar to those of the ACT expert, then consider identifying Reading question types an area of strength and move on to the next chapter. Come back to this topic periodically to prevent yourself from getting rusty.

If you don't yet feel confident, review the material in this chapter, and then try the questions you missed again. As always, be sure to review the explanations closely. Then go online (**kaptest.com/login**) to watch video lessons about how to handle each ACT Reading question type and use your Qbank for more practice. If you haven't already registered your book, do so at **kaptest.com/moreonline.**

GO ONLINE

kaptest.com/login

Answers and Explanations

Try on Your Own

1. The overall organization of the passage is best described as a:

   Question type: Global
   Identifying language: "overall organization"
   Research where? passage map

2. Based on the passage, architecture critics regarded Frank Lloyd Wright's career prior to Fallingwater's construction (lines 15–17) as:

   Question type: Detail
   Identifying language: "Based on the passage"
   Research where? lines 15–17

3. It can be reasonably inferred that the site chosen for Fallingwater was:

   Question type: Inference
   Identifying language: "It can be reasonably inferred"
   Research where? the paragraph that talks about Fallingwater's location

4. The passage indicates that Edgar J. Kaufmann's original plans for the site were:

   Question type: Inference
   Identifying language: *indicates*
   Research where? Likely near the beginning of the passage; use your passage map to identify the correct location to review

5. The author's use of the phrases "black walnut wood" and "locally sourced sandstone" (lines 78–80) most nearly serves to emphasize which of the following points?

   Question type: Function
   Identifying language: "most nearly serves to emphasize"
   Research where? around the cited lines

6. According to the passage, a cantilever is designed to include:

   Question type: Detail
   Identifying language: "According to the passage"
   Research where? the paragraph that discusses how Fallingwater was built

7. It can reasonably be inferred that the miscalculation the author mentions in line 67 refers to:

   Question type: Inference
   Identifying language: "It can reasonably be inferred"
   Research where? line 67 and the surrounding lines

8. One of the main purposes of the information in lines 72–85 is to:

   Question type: Function
   Identifying language: "one of the main purposes"
   Research where? the cited lines and the passage map to determine how the cited lines fit within the whole

9. Architecture enthusiasts' comparisons of Fallingwater to a cave (lines 93–95) most strongly suggest that the house provides a sense of:

   Question type: Inference
   Identifying language: "most strongly suggests"
   Research where? the cited lines

10. As it is used in line 112, the phrase *invigoration and exaltation* most nearly means:

    Question type: Vocab-in-Context
    Identifying language: "as it is used in line 112 . . . most nearly means"
    Research where? at least the entire sentence that includes the cited phrase

How Much Have You Learned?

1. Throughout the passage, the character's reaction to the narrator is to:

   Question type: Global
   Identifying language: "Throughout the passage"
   Research where? big picture summary, passage map

2. Based on the passage, how do Renaissance efforts to design a language relate to Chomsky's theory of universal grammar?

   Question type: Inference
   Identifying language: "Based on the passage"
   Research where? passage, where author discusses Renaissance efforts to design a language

3. In the first paragraph, Chomsky claimed that an "innate, genetic understanding":

   Question type: Detail
   Identifying language: "Chomsky claimed"
   Research where? passage, paragraph 1

4. According to the passage, universal grammar's structure dependency rule states that:

   Question type: Detail
   Identifying language: "According to the passage"
   Research where? passage, where author discusses structure dependency rule

5. The author includes the quotes "Colorless green ideas sleep furiously" and "Furiously sleep ideas green colorless" primarily in order to:

   Question type: Function
   Identifying language: "author includes . . . in order to"
   Research where? passage, where author references the quotes "Colorless green ideas sleep furiously" and "Furiously sleep ideas green colorless"

6. The questions in paragraph 3 primarily serve to:

   Question type: Function
   Identifying language: "serve to"
   Research where? passage, paragraph 3

7. The passage suggests that the researchers mentioned in line 68 believe which of the following?

   Question type: Inference
   Identifying language: "passage suggests"
   Research where? passage, around line 68

8. One of the main purposes of the fifth paragraph is to:

   Question type: Function
   Identifying language: "main purposes"
   Research where? passage, paragraph 5

9. As it is used in line 99, the word *sterile* most nearly means:

   Question type: Vocab-in-Context
   Identifying language: "most nearly means"
   Research where? passage, line 99

10. As it is used in line 106, the phrase *a better marriage* most nearly means:

    Question type: Vocab-in-Context
    Identifying language: "most nearly means"
    Research where? passage, line 106

CHAPTER 18

ANSWERING READING QUESTIONS

LEARNING OBJECTIVES

After completing this chapter, you will be able to:

- Research the answer in the passage text or your big picture summary
- Predict the correct answer
- Identify the one correct answer choice

Vocab-in-Context: 3/36 SmartPoints® (Medium yield)

Function: 6/36 SmartPoints® (High yield)

Inference: 10/36 SmartPoints® (Very high yield)

Detail: 13/36 SmartPoints® (Very high yield)

Global: 4/36 SmartPoints® (Medium yield)

How Much Do You Know?

Directions: In this chapter, you'll learn how best to research, predict, and find the correct answers to ACT Reading questions. For this quiz, first take a couple of minutes to refresh your memory of the passage, which you first saw in chapter 16. Then, for each question:

1. research the answer in the passage text or from your big picture summary

2. predict the correct answer in your own words

3. identify the one correct answer

HUMANITIES: This passage explores the relationship between the immigrant experience and one person's career choice.

My grandfather was born in a turbulent time in Russia. His non-communist lineage made him unwelcome before he had left the womb. His father, an officer in the Russian army, was
5 considered an enemy of the communist Bolsheviks, so my grandfather lived less than a year in what was his native Moscow and spent most of his younger years moving across Asia. Despite this, he had pride in being Russian, associated with
10 Russians throughout his life, and would frequently quiz me on Russian history. This all in tribute to a country that ended up under hostile rule during the time his mother was pregnant with him.

As a child, exiled to Siberia, my grandfather
15 heard his father tell of the greatness that existed within the country that had forced the family into exile. It was known that, first with his parents, and later as an adult, my grandfather was going to have to seek a new place to call home.
20 Despite this foregone conclusion, Russia was still romanticized, and my grandfather learned to treat the country with reverence. This was in contrast to the sentiments found in other recently exiled Russians, who would not simply lament the actions
25 taken by the country but disparage all eight million square miles. In my family's search for a place to settle, attempting to forge a consistent identity was nearly impossible, as no one knew whether the next location would hold for a month, let alone a year.
30 All hoped for an unattainable "new Moscow."

The first long-term refuge was found, ironically, in China, which would have its own communist revolution. After several years of relative stability,

this revolution precipitated the move to the
35 United States. Upon arrival in San Francisco, my grandfather, along with my grandmother and their young son, my father, found other Russian immigrants who were also new to the country. "*Ya amerikanets*," people would say, and despite the fact
40 that they were recent immigrants who associated primarily with those of shared ethnicity and circumstance, they would play the role they desired and repeat "*ya amerikanets*"—"I am American." They would share many stories about their native
45 land, but did not repeat "*ya russkiy*," because being Russian went without saying. While it was clear that this would be the last country my grandfather would reside in and that he wished to become more American, it was perhaps the most confusing
50 of times. It was less a problem of acclimating to an adopted setting and more of dealing with a permanent setting at all. The only consistency throughout the first thirty years of my grandfather's life was the knowledge that every "home" was
55 temporary, and now this was no longer the case. I often wonder if his successful career in the real estate business had anything to do with what must have been a rare transformation of circumstance.

Not only was my grandfather interested in
60 real estate, he was ardent about the importance of ownership, a naturally discordant view to that of the then Soviet Union. Thus, selling homes became a purpose in addition to an occupation.

Part of his success in real estate was owed to
65 strategic compromise. Considering American sentiments regarding Russia during the Cold War, there were times that he was sure he lost certain house sales due to his last name and accent.

However, to those willing to listen, he found
70   advantages to informing people that he was an
exiled Russian who ardently disagreed with the
communist government. He would also point out
his pride in being a new American and allow a
potential buyer to degrade Russia without blinking.

75   Fortunately, the 1950s were a time of settling
across the country, and this made real estate a
very lucrative profession. It wasn't just this that
attracted my grandfather, though; he also saw it as
an opportunity to give tiny parts of the country to
80   other people—returning the favor, in a way.

Yet, it always seemed that something vital
still rested in the opposite hemisphere. Once
communism fell, he began returning to Russia
yearly. He and my grandmother never showed the
85   family pictures from Russia the way they would
from the various cruise ships they traveled on; it
could be deduced that returning to Russia was a
journey of personal necessity for him rather than
pleasure, and the encounter elucidated his existence
90   in a way that being solely American could not. In
selling real estate, my grandfather had worked to
make this unnecessary. I believe that he wished for
people to keep those houses and pass them down
to later generations, giving the space a sort of
95   familial permanence rather than a fleeting stay.

For most, the thought of real estate agents
conjures up images of smiling advertisements
on benches and buses and the skill of selling
something so important. Many are wary of
100   salespeople in general, questioning the practice
of convincing people something is in their
best interest when the salesperson stands to
personally benefit. My grandfather did financially
benefit from sales, but there was more to it: his
105   realization of the American dream only made him
want to be a part of others reaching for the same
thing, whether their native home was around the
block or thousands of miles away.

1.   Which of the following statements best expresses
the main idea of the passage?

   A.   Immigrants would often rather live in their
native land.

   B.   American-born people tend not to understand
how displacement affects immigrants.

   C.   Immigrants who acclimate well to America
may still have indelible ties to their native land.

   D.   Immigrants are sometimes surprised by the
stability offered to them in America.

2.   According to the passage, the author's grandfather's
birth happened:

   F.   during the communist revolution.

   G.   under communist rule.

   H.   prior to the communist revolution.

   J.   after the fall of communism.

3.   The final sentence of the second paragraph (line 30)
most directly serves to emphasize that the exiles:

   A.   wished for a counter-revolution led by
opponents to communism.

   B.   yearned for a home that they had lost.

   C.   longed to rebuild and revitalize Moscow.

   D.   preferred to settle near other Russians.

4.   Why did the narrator's grandfather and other
recent immigrants say "*ya amerikanets*"?

   F.   They wanted to become American.

   G.   They were worried about anti-Russian
sentiment.

   H.   It reinforced the immigrant community.

   J.   It distanced them from their origins.

5. According to the third paragraph, what made settling in America difficult for the narrator's grandfather?

    A. San Francisco was different from any place he'd been before.

    B. He had to adjust to the idea of having a permanent home.

    C. He did not speak the language when he first arrived.

    D. He knew he would never be able to live in Russia again.

6. What "advantage" did the narrator's grandfather most likely find in telling people about his relationship with Russia?

    F. It gave him an edge over competitors because it was a gimmick they could not match.

    G. It made potential customers more inclined to buy from him because they felt pity for him.

    H. It gave him an edge over competitors because customers viewed him as more honest.

    I. It made potential customers more inclined to buy from him because he catered to their worldview.

7. In the seventh paragraph, the passage states that the speaker's grandfather traveled to Russia because:

    A. it was an enjoyable vacation.

    B. the communist government fell.

    C. he felt a personal need to go.

    D. the cruise ships stopped there.

8. The speaker describes the typical view people have of real estate agents (lines 96–99) primarily in order to:

    F. express discomfort with the profession.

    G. undermine the validity of this view.

    H. set up a contrast with his grandfather.

    J. make a personal connection with readers.

9. As it is used in line 105, the word *realization* most nearly means:

    A. the fruition of a desire.

    B. full understanding of an idea.

    C. a sudden epiphany.

    D. profit from a transaction.

10. Based on the passage, why was the speaker's grandfather attracted to real estate as a profession?

    F. It was extremely lucrative at the time he joined the profession.

    G. The profession would not have been available to him in Russia.

    H. It was among the better professional opportunities open to immigrants.

    J. He wanted to give to others what America had given to him.

Check Your Work

Suggested Passage Map Notes:

¶1: grandfather, chaotic childhood

¶2: still loves Russia

¶3: moves to US, becomes real estate agent

¶4: real estate is his vocation

¶5: allows people to insult Russia

¶6: wants to give back

¶7: visits Russia every year

¶8: wants to give people a home

BIG PICTURE SUMMARY

Main idea: A Russian immigrant attempts to make a life and find a purpose in his new homeland through real estate.

Author's purpose: To reminisce about his grandfather's life experiences, memories, and impact

---

1. C
Difficulty: High
Category: Global
Getting to the Answer: Since this question asks for the main idea, it is a Global question. Refer to your passage notes in order to answer it. The passage makes it clear throughout that both Russia and America are extremely important to the identity of the speaker's grandfather. The correct answer is (C).

Choice A does not fit the passage, since the author's grandfather is clearly pleased to be American. The passage does not discuss how American-born people view displacement, so B is out of scope. Choice D, while discussed in the passage, is far too narrowly focused to be the main idea.

2. G
Difficulty: Medium
Category: Detail
Getting to the Answer: The clue "According to the passage" shows that this is a Detail question. The last sentence in the first paragraph (lines 11–13) states that the country came under new rule while the grandfather's mother was pregnant with him. Therefore, you can predict that he was born after the revolution and under communist rule. Choice (G) is correct. Choices F, H, and J contradict that statement.

3. B
Difficulty: Medium
Category: Function
Getting to the Answer: The phrase "most directly serves to emphasize" in the question stem identifies this as a Function question. For context, read the surrounding lines in addition to the one cited. The passage states that, in searching for a place to settle, the exiles hoped for a place like the one they left. However, the author calls this *unattainable*. Predict that this line emphasizes the exiles' homesickness and pain. Choice (B) is correct.

Choice A is out of scope; the passage never discusses a counter-revolution. Choice C contradicts the passage; the "new Moscow" that the author cites refers not to a new version of the old city but to a new city that is like the one they left. Finally, choice D is incorrect because settling near other Russians is not *unattainable*.

4. F
Difficulty: Medium
Category: Detail
Getting to the Answer: Sometimes you will see questions, like this one, for which the question type is difficult to determine based on the wording alone. Here, it might be either Detail or Inference, depending on whether the passage directly tells you why the phrase was used. Either way, you will need to research in the passage. According to the passage, "*ya amerikanets*" means "I am American," and the immigrants said it in order to "play the role" they wanted. You can predict that they aspired to be American, which matches (F).

While the passage does state that the author's grandfather was the victim of some anti-Russian sentiments, this is not mentioned until the fifth paragraph. This makes choice G outside the scope of this question. The passage never mentions reinforcing the community, so H is incorrect. Finally, J contradicts the passage, which says that "being Russian went without saying."

5. B
Difficulty: Low
Category: Detail
Getting to the Answer: The clue "According to the third paragraph" shows that this is a Detail question. Lines 46–55 state that this period was confusing because the grandfather had never settled anywhere permanently. Predict that the narrator's grandfather

had to accustom himself to staying in one place. Choice (B) is correct.

While A and D may be true, a new, non-Russian place was not what caused the difficulty, according to the passage. It is not clear in the passage whether the grandfather spoke English upon arrival, so C is incorrect.

6.   J
Difficulty: Medium
Category: Inference
Getting to the Answer: The phrase "most likely" in this question stem is a clue that it is an Inference question. Since the stem does not provide a line or paragraph number, use your passage notes to locate the relevant text in paragraph 5. Here, the passage states that the grandfather lost sales because of anti-Russian bias from some customers, but he gained standing with others by telling them that he was an anti-communist exile and allowing them to insult Russia. You can predict that indulging his customers' bias allowed him to make more sales. Choice (J) is correct.

The passage does not compare him with competitors in any way, so F and H are out of scope. There is no evidence in the passage that customers pitied him, so G is also incorrect.

7.   C
Difficulty: Medium
Category: Detail
Getting to the Answer: The phrase "the passage states" shows that this is a Detail question. Paragraph 7 calls the trip "a journey of personal necessity." Predict that the speaker's grandfather felt compelled to go. The correct answer is (C).

Choice A is the exact opposite of what the passage says. The fall of communism in Russia allowed him to go, but is not the reason he decided to go, so B is incorrect. Finally, choice D is a distortion; while the passage mentions trips on cruise ships, it suggests they were separate from the trips to Russia.

8.   H
Difficulty: Medium
Category: Function
Getting to the Answer: The wording "The speaker describes . . . in order to" indicates that this is a Function question. After describing a typical view of real estate agents in the final paragraph, the speaker immediately goes on to say that the grandfather does not fit this

depiction. You can predict that the description is necessary background information to show the contrast with the narrator's grandfather. This matches (H).

Choice F is a distortion; while the speaker acknowledges that some people feel discomfort with salespeople, that is not the purpose of the description. Choice G is extreme; the speaker merely wants to say that the grandfather is not like this. Choice J is incorrect because the speaker goes on to contradict the image described, so there is no personal connection with readers.

9.   A
Difficulty: High
Category: Vocab-in-Context
Getting to the Answer: This question displays the wording characteristic of a Vocab-in-Context question: "the word . . . most nearly means." The sentence indicated discusses the "realization of the American dream" and the desire to help others trying to do the same, so you can predict that in this context *realization* means achievement or gain. Choice (A) is correct.

Choices B and C both describe the most common meanings of the word, which are rarely correct for this type of question. Choice D refers to a transaction, which does not fit with the discussion of the American dream.

10.   J
Difficulty: High
Category: Global
Getting to the Answer: This question includes the phrase "Based on the passage," which can indicate an Inference question. However, it asks for the grandfather's professional motivations, which are discussed through much of the passage—and even parts of the passage that do not directly discuss them provide information relevant to understanding them. Thus, this is a Global question. The passage makes clear that having a home and continuity in America was important to the grandfather, as was offering these benefits to others. Choice (J) is therefore correct.

Choice F is a misused detail; although the profession was lucrative, the speaker says that money was not the grandfather's primary motivation. Similarly, while metaphorically thumbing his nose at the Soviet Union may have been a perk of the job (since ownership conflicted with the Soviet Union's views), there is no evidence that the grandfather was motivated to become a realtor specifically because it was impossible in Russia. Thus, G is also incorrect. Finally, H introduces ideas not mentioned in the passage at all, so it is out of scope.

HOW TO ANSWER ACT READING QUESTIONS

LEARNING OBJECTIVES

After this lesson, you will be able to:

- Research the answer in the passage text or your big picture summary
- Predict the correct answer
- Identify the one correct answer choice

To answer questions like these:

NATURAL SCIENCE: This passage is adapted from an essay about astrobiology.

Astrobiology, also known as exobiology, is a complex, multidisciplinary science dedicated to studying the possibility of life outside the confines of Earth. Humanity has speculated for centuries
5 about whether or not we are alone in the universe, but with the advent of space exploration in the 1950s and 1960s, for the first time in human history there was the possibility of actually exploring the surface of alien planets. Scientists
10 and engineers worked together to build what they called landers, spacecraft capable not only of landing on other planets, but also of exploring and photographing them.

When the first of the two Viking landers touched
15 down on Martian soil on July 20, 1976, and began to send camera images back to Earth, the scientists at the Jet Propulsion Laboratory could not suppress a certain nervous anticipation. Like people who hold a ticket to a lottery, they had a one-in-a-million
20 chance of winning. The first photographs that arrived, however, did not contain any evidence of life. They revealed merely a barren landscape littered with rocks and boulders. The view resembled nothing so much as a flat section of desert. In
25 fact, the winning entry in a contest at J.P.L. for the photograph most accurately predicting what Mars would look like was a snapshot taken from a particularly arid section of the Mojave Desert.

The scientists were soon ready to turn their
30 attention from visible life to microorganisms. The twin Viking landers carried out experiments designed to detect organic compounds. Researchers thought it possible that life had developed on early

Mars just as it is thought to have developed on
35 Earth, through the gradual chemical evolution of complex organic molecules. To detect biological activity, Martian soil samples were treated with various nutrients that would produce characteristic by-products if life forms were active in the soil.
40 The results from all three experiments were inconclusive. The fourth experiment heated a soil sample to look for signs of organic material but found none—an unexpected result because organic compounds were thought to have been present due
45 to the steady bombardment of the Martian surface by meteorites.

The absence of organic materials, some scientists speculated, was the result of intense ultraviolet radiation penetrating the atmosphere
50 of Mars and destroying organic compounds in the soil. Although Mars' atmosphere was at one time rich in carbon dioxide and thus thick enough to protect its surface from the harmful rays of the sun, the carbon dioxide had gradually left the
55 atmosphere and been converted into rocks. This means that even if life had gotten a start on early Mars, it could not have survived the exposure to ultraviolet radiation that occurred when the atmosphere thinned. Mars never developed a
60 protective layer of ozone as Earth did.

Despite the disappointing Viking results, there are those who still keep open the possibility of life on Mars. They point out that the Viking data cannot be considered the final word on
65 Martian life because the two landers sampled only limited—and uninteresting—sites. The Viking landing sites were not chosen for what they might tell of the planet's biology. They were chosen primarily because they appeared to be safe for

70 landing a spacecraft. The landing sites were on
parts of the Martian plains that appeared relatively
featureless according to orbital photographs.

The type of terrain that these researchers
suggest may be a possible hiding place for active
75 life has an Earthly parallel: the ice-free region of
southern Victoria Land, Antarctica, where the
temperatures in some dry valleys average below
zero. Organisms known as endoliths, a form of
blue-green algae that has adapted to this harsh
80 environment, were found living inside certain
translucent, porous rocks in these Antarctic valleys.
The argument based on this discovery is that if life
did exist on early Mars, it is possible that it escaped
worsening conditions by similarly seeking refuge
85 in rocks. Skeptics object, however, that Mars in its
present state is simply too dry, even compared with
Antarctic valleys, to sustain any life whatsoever.

Should Mars eventually prove barren of life,
as some suspect, then this finding would have
90 a significant impact on the current view of the
chemical origins of life. It could be much more
difficult to get life started on a planet than
scientists thought before the Viking landings.

The possibility exists, of course, that our
95 definition of what constitutes life may not hold true
throughout the universe. It has long been speculated
that our current belief that all life must contain
carbon, oxygen, calcium, chlorine, potassium, and
phosphorous simply because this holds true on our
100 planet might be too narrow a view. In 2010, NASA
scientists believed they had discovered a bacterium
that used arsenic in place of phosphorous, though
these exciting findings later proved to be incorrect.
The possibility remains, however, that future
105 astrobiologists exploring the Martian surface from
140 million miles away might be able to make use
of a more advanced definition of what we call "life."

1. One of the main points of the second paragraph
(lines 14–28) is that:

A. scientists were disappointed by the inconclusive results of their experiments.

B. theories about how life developed on Earth
were shown to be flawed.

C. there was no experimental confirmation that
life existed on Mars.

D. meteorite bombardment of the Martian surface is less constant than scientists predicted.

2. The passage suggests that an important difference
between Mars and Earth is that, unlike Earth, Mars:

F. accumulated organic compounds in its soil.

G. lies in the path of harmful rays of ultraviolet
radiation.

H. once possessed an atmosphere rich in carbon
dioxide.

J. could not sustain any life that developed.

3. According to the passage, which of the following
describes the atmosphere of Mars?

A. Rich in carbon dioxide

B. Lacks a protective ozone layer

C. Contains rocks converted from organic
compounds

D. Not susceptible to ultraviolet radiation

4. The passage suggests that Mars is void of organic
compounds because:

F. the lack of an ozone layer did not allow life
to proliferate on Mars.

G. they were destroyed by constant meteorite
bombardment.

H. carbon dioxide left the atmosphere and was
converted to rocks.

J. endoliths were found living in hidden areas.

5. The passage states that the Viking landing sites were chosen because of their:

    A. scientific value.
    B. safety.
    C. biology.
    D. diversity.

6. As it is used in line 88, the word *barren* most nearly means:

    F. full of rocks.
    G. abundantly productive.
    H. with a reddish hue.
    J. void of life.

7. The researchers' argument that life may exist in Martian rocks rests on the idea that:

    A. organisms usually adopt identical survival strategies in similar environments.
    B. life developed in the form of blue-green algae on Mars.
    C. life could have evolved in the same way on two different planets.
    D. organisms that survived in Antarctica could survive on Mars.

8. The author mentions blue-green algae in the sixth paragraph primarily in order to:

    F. give an example of a translucent organism that existed on Earth and Mars.
    G. draw a similarity between survival mechanisms of terrestrial and, potentially, Martian organisms.
    H. show how Martian organisms escaped harsh environments by seeking out shelter in rocks.
    J. draw a parallel between the harsh conditions in Martian valleys and Antarctic valleys.

9. It can be inferred from the passage that the possibility mentioned in line 94 refers to:

    A. a chance for scientists to prove our current definition of life definitively correct.
    B. the opportunity to open up new possibilities for what we call life.
    C. a deeper understanding of bacteria that survive on arsenic.
    D. the development of new technology that would allow scientists to study foreign atmospheres directly.

10. In the final paragraph, which of the following is listed as a compound that is necessary for life?

    F. Arsenic
    G. Sodium
    H. Potassium
    J. Magnesium

You need to know this:

Use clues to direct your research to a specific part of the passage or to your big picture summary.

- **Line numbers**—Reread the indicated text and possibly the lines before and after; look for keywords indicating why the referenced text has been included or how it's used.

- **Paragraph numbers**—Consult your margin notes to see the paragraph's purpose and scope before rereading the text. Sometimes your passage map alone is enough to find an answer.

- **Quoted text**—Go back to the passage to read the entire quote if the stem or answer choices use ellipses (. . .). Then check the surrounding context of the quoted term or phrase to see what the author meant by it in the passage.

- **Proper nouns**—Use your passage map or look for capital letters in the text to find the term, and then check the context to see why the author included it in the passage; note whether the author had a positive, negative, or neutral evaluation of it.

- **Specific content clues**—Use your margin notes to help you search the passage for terms or ideas mentioned in the question stem; these clues will usually refer to something the author offered an opinion about or emphasized.

- **Whole passage clues**—Begin by reviewing your big picture summary, and only go back to the passage if you can't find the information you need. If you do get stuck, the first and last paragraphs are typically the best places to go for global takeaways.

Predicting what you're looking for in the correct answer saves time and reduces confusion as you read each choice.

ACT Reading questions always have one correct answer and three incorrect choices.

- The correct answer will match what the passage says in a way that responds to the task set out in the question stem.

- Incorrect choices often fall into one of five categories. Not every incorrect choice matches one of these types exactly, but learning to spot them can help you eliminate some incorrect choices more quickly.

  - **Out of scope**—contains a statement that is too broad, too narrow, or beyond what the passage discusses

  - **Extreme**—contains language that is too strong (*all, never, every, none*) to be supported by the passage

  - **Distortion**—based on details or ideas from the passage, but distorts or misstates what the author says or implies

  - **Opposite**—directly contradicts what the correct answer must say

  - **Misused detail**—accurately states something from the passage, but in a manner that incorrectly answers the question

You need to do this:

ACT READING QUESTION METHOD
Step 1. Unpack the question stem
Step 2. Research the answer
Step 3. Predict the answer
Step 4. Find the one correct answer

Step 1. Unpack the question stem.

- This step is covered in chapter 17. Make sure you have completed that lesson before continuing through this one.

Step 2. Research the answer.

- When clues point to a specific part of the passage (line or paragraph numbers, quotations, content discussed only in particular paragraphs), begin by rereading the specified text and immediate context.

  - If the immediate context does not provide enough information to answer the question, gradually expand outward, rereading sentences that come before and after.

- With whole passage clues or questions that seem to lack clear content clues, begin by reviewing your big picture summary.

- If you can't figure out where to research the question and your big picture summary doesn't help either, consider using process of elimination, skipping the question and coming back to it later, or just making a guess.

Step 3. Predict or characterize what the correct answer will say or suggest.

- Don't worry about phrasing your prediction as a complete sentence or about repeating exactly the language used in the passage. Just try to answer the question in your own words based on your research.

- If you struggle to predict, use your active reading of the passage to characterize the correct answer, setting expectations about characteristics it must possess.

  - For example, if the author has a negative view of a topic in the question, expect a correct answer with negative language and eliminate choices that suggest a positive or neutral view.

Step 4. Find the one correct answer.

- Identify the choice that matches your prediction, if possible.

  - Don't expect a word-for-word match, but look for a correspondence of ideas. For example, if you predict that the function of a detail is to "provide support for the main idea," an answer choice that says it "supplies evidence for the author's thesis" would likely be correct.

- If there is no clear match, use process of elimination.

  - Eliminate any choice that contradicts your prediction or that clearly falls into one of the five incorrect choice categories.

  - Choose the only answer remaining, or guess among those you were unable to eliminate.

Explanations

Suggested Passage Map Notes:

¶1: astrobiology: finding non-Earth life

¶2: Mars landing no signs of life

¶3: inconclusive tests for microorganisms

¶4: no organic material b/c UV?

¶5: may be life elsewhere, testing locations limited

¶6: how life could exist in rocks

¶7: impact if no life

¶8: definition of life may change

BIG PICTURE SUMMARY

Main idea: Despite initial tests for Martian life yielding inconclusive results, the continued search for possible lifeforms could yield valuable information.

Author's purpose: To inform the reader about both a brief history of and the predicted future of astrobiology discoveries

---

Question	Explanation

1. One of the main points of the second paragraph (lines 14–28) is that:

   A. scientists were disappointed by the inconclusive results of their experiments.

   B. theories about how life developed on Earth were shown to be flawed.

   C. there was no experimental confirmation that life existed on Mars.

   D. meteorite bombardment of the Martian surface is less constant than scientists predicted.

1. C
Difficulty: Medium
Category: Global
Getting to the Answer: A question asking for "The main point" of a passage or paragraph is a Global question. Use your passage notes to answer these questions. Your notes should indicate that paragraph 2 discusses four experiments carried out by the Viking landers. These experiments were designed to detect signs of life but were inconclusive. Look for a match for this general prediction. The correct answer is (C).

Choice A is a distortion; while it is reasonable to think that the scientists would be disappointed by the results, this is not mentioned in this paragraph. Choice B is out of scope; no such conclusions are suggested about Earth. Choice D both contradicts information in the passage—which describes the bombardment as steady—and isn't part of this paragraph, so it is also incorrect.

2. The passage suggests that an important difference between Mars and Earth is that, unlike Earth, Mars:

   F. accumulated organic compounds in its soil.

   G. lies in the path of harmful rays of ultraviolet radiation.

   H. once possessed an atmosphere rich in carbon dioxide.

   J. could not sustain any life that developed.

2. J
Difficulty: High
Category: Inference
Getting to the Answer: The clue "The passage suggests" indicates that this is an Inference question, but the question stem does not point to any one paragraph definitively. When you receive limited help from the question stem, use your passage notes to help you confirm or rule out choices. Eliminate F because, according to paragraph 2, no organic compounds were found in Martian soil. Choice G is incorrect because the question asks for a difference between Earth and Mars. Both Earth and Mars lie in the path of ultraviolet radiation; the crucial distinction is that Earth is shielded by ozone. Choice H is also a distortion because the passage does not mention the amount of carbon dioxide in Earth's atmosphere. In paragraph 4, the passage tells us that even if life had begun on Mars, it could not have survived. The correct answer, then, is (J).

3. According to the passage, which of the following describes the atmosphere of Mars?

   A. Rich in carbon dioxide

   B. Lacks a protective ozone layer

   C. Contains rocks converted from organic compounds

   D. Not susceptible to ultraviolet radiation

3. B
Difficulty: Low
Category: Detail
Getting to the Answer: You can recognize this as a Detail question because of the phrase "According to the passage." Check your passage notes and go back to the fourth paragraph to form your prediction. Paragraph 4 says that the Martian atmosphere did not develop a protective ozone layer. Choice (B) is correct.

Choices A, C, and D all contradict information in paragraph 4.

Question	Explanation
4. The passage suggests that Mars is void of organic compounds because: F. the lack of an ozone layer did not allow life to proliferate on Mars. G. they were destroyed by constant meteorite bombardment. H. carbon dioxide left the atmosphere and was converted to rocks. J. endoliths were found living in hidden areas.	**4. F** **Difficulty:** Medium **Category:** Inference **Getting to the Answer:** You can tell this is an Inference question because of the phrase "the passage suggests." Paragraph 4 gives details about why Mars lacks organic compounds. Ultraviolet radiation penetrated the atmosphere and destroyed organic compounds in the soil; this occurred because Mars did not develop a protective ozone layer. Put these pieces together to get answer choice (F). Choice G distorts what the passage says; meteorite bombardment was not mentioned in relation to the destruction of organic compounds. Choice H is another distortion because, while true, this is not why Mars is void of organic compounds. Choice J is a misused detail; endoliths are mentioned in reference to Antarctic valleys on Earth, not Mars.
5. The passage states that the Viking landing sites were chosen because of their: A. scientific value. B. safety. C. biology. D. diversity.	**5. B** **Difficulty:** Low **Category:** Detail **Getting to the Answer:** The wording "The passage states" identifies this as a Detail question. While the question stem does not contain a line reference, the answer to a Detail question will be stated directly in the passage. Your notes should help direct you to paragraph 5. In lines 68–70, the passage says, "They were chosen primarily because they appeared to be safe for landing a spacecraft." This matches (B) exactly. None of the other choices match this statement.
6. As it is used in line 88, the word *barren* most nearly means: F. full of rocks. G. abundantly productive. H. with a reddish hue. J. void of life.	**6. J** **Difficulty:** Medium **Category:** Vocab-in-Context **Getting to the Answer:** This question has the distinctive phrasing of a Vocab-in-Context question, including "As it is used" and "most nearly means." Use the context of the passage to help answer this question. Pretend that the word *barren* is a blank, read around the cited line for clues, and make a prediction. The clues from the passage include: "did not contain any evidence of life." A good prediction for this word is "empty." Choice (J) is correct. Be careful with F! Even though the passage mentions that the area is littered with rocks, *barren* refers to the fact that there was no evidence of life. Choice G is opposite of what the passage suggests, and H references ideas from elsewhere in the passage.

Reading

Question	Explanation
7. The researchers' argument that life may exist in Martian rocks rests on the idea that: A. organisms usually adopt identical survival strategies in similar environments. B. life developed in the form of blue-green algae on Mars. C. life could have evolved in the same way on two different planets. D. organisms that survived in Antarctica could survive on Mars.	**7. C** **Difficulty:** High **Category:** Inference **Getting to the Answer:** With generally worded Inference questions, skim your notes to help you find the location of the relevant details in the passage. Martian rocks are discussed in paragraph 6: the author states that some scientists hypothesize that life on Mars may have "escaped worsening conditions by . . . seeking refuge in rocks" (lines 83–85), as happened on Earth. Predict that a way in which organisms may adapt to harsh conditions is similar on Earth and on Mars. Choice (C) is correct. Choice A is a distortion of the facts in the passage. This passage only discusses potential similarities between harsh environments on Earth and Mars, not in any other locations, and the author's statement that Mars is much drier than even the driest part of Antarctica proves that the two environments are not actually similar, only that they have some potential similarities. Additionally, the only organism discussed is blue-green algae. Choice B is incorrect because blue-green algae developed on Earth, not Mars. Choice D is incorrect because it suggests that the same organisms that survive in Antarctica could also survive on Mars, but there is no evidence to support that; the author uses the example of Antarctic life only to illustrate a theory of how Martian life might have adapted.
8. The author mentions blue-green algae in the sixth paragraph primarily in order to: F. give an example of a translucent organism that existed on Earth and Mars. G. draw a similarity between survival mechanisms of terrestrial and, potentially, Martian organisms. H. show how Martian organisms escaped harsh environments by seeking out shelter in rocks. J. draw a parallel between the harsh conditions in Martian valleys and Antarctic valleys.	**8. G** **Difficulty:** Medium **Category:** Function **Getting to the Answer:** "The author mentions . . . in order to" is a clue that this is a Function question. Paragraph 6 discusses a terrestrial organism that has adapted to harsh conditions: blue-green algae. The passage further states that this argument is based on the idea that an organism on Mars could have escaped harsh conditions by seeking refuge in rocks, like the blue-green algae have done on Earth. The author discusses how blue-green algae have survived and how it could be possible for Martian organisms to adapt and survive in a similar way. Choice (G) is correct. Choice F is a distortion; the rocks were translucent, not the blue-green algae. Choice H also twists the facts in the passage, which merely suggests that this is a possibility, not a certainty. Finally, choice J is out of scope; Martian valleys are not mentioned.

Question	Explanation
9. It can be inferred from the passage that the possibility mentioned in line 94 refers to: A. a chance for scientists to prove our current definition of life definitively correct. B. the opportunity to open up new possibilities for what we call life. C. a deeper understanding of bacteria that survive on arsenic. D. the development of new technology that would allow scientists to study foreign atmospheres directly.	**9. B** **Difficulty:** Medium **Category:** Inference **Getting to the Answer:** The word "inferred" in the question is a clear indicator that this is an Inference question! The final paragraph of this passage includes speculation about what could happen in the future regarding human understanding of life. The correct answer will reflect the idea that something might happen (not that it will or has already happened). Choice (B) is correct. Choice A is too definitive for something that *could* happen. Choice C is a distortion; scientists have not found bacteria that survive on arsenic. Choice D is out of scope, as technology to study foreign atmospheres directly is not mentioned.
10. In the final paragraph, which of the following is listed as a compound that is necessary for life? F. Arsenic G. Sodium H. Potassium J. Magnesium	**10. H** **Difficulty:** Low **Category:** Detail **Getting to the Answer:** This question asks for something listed in the final paragraph, so it is a Detail question. When answering a question like this, take a moment to go back to the passage to research your answer. Here, you should eliminate all answer choices that are not listed as compounds that are necessary for life. The last paragraph does not mention G or J at all, so they are not correct. Choice F is incorrect because, while arsenic is mentioned in the final paragraph, it is not among the compounds that are believed to be necessary for life. Potassium, (H), is part of the list and is correct.

Try on Your Own

Directions: Put the expert question strategies to work on the following passage. First, take a few minutes to refresh your memory of the passage below, which you first saw in chapter 16. Then, for each question:

1. identify the question type

2. note where/how you will research the answer

3. jot down your prediction of the correct answer

4. find the one correct answer

Answers are found at the end of the chapter.

HUMANITIES: This passage is adapted from an article about modern architecture.

Fallingwater, a small country house constructed in 1936, stands as perhaps the greatest residential building achievement of the American architect Frank Lloyd Wright.
5 In designing the dwelling for the Pittsburgh millionaire Edgar J. Kaufmann, Wright was confronted with an unusually challenging site beside a waterfall deep in a Pennsylvania ravine. However, Wright viewed this difficult location
10 not as an obstacle but as a unique opportunity to put his architectural ideas into concrete form.

In the early 1930s, Edgar J. Kaufmann's son, Edgar J. Kaufmann Jr., studied with Wright as an apprentice at Wright's Taliesin Studio in Spring
15 Green, Wisconsin. At the time, architecture critics deemed Wright's style anachronistic and assumed that his career was coming to an end. Kaufmann Jr., on the other hand, greatly admired Wright's work and was delighted to introduce his parents
20 to the esteemed architect. Shortly thereafter, the Kaufmanns asked Wright to design Fallingwater.

The site Kaufmann chose for his country getaway was originally the location of a cabin in Mill Run, Pennsylvania, that he offered as a vacation
25 retreat for the numerous employees he oversaw at Kaufmann's Department Store, located in downtown Pittsburgh. When the Great Depression struck, Kaufmann's employees could no longer afford the cost of traveling more than 60 miles to Mill Run,
30 and Kaufmann decided that the land, a wooded area nestled along the banks of a mountain stream called Bear Run, was an ideal location for a vacation home. Kaufmann had assumed that the home would stand

at the bottom of a nearby waterfall, where it would
35 provide a perfect venue from which to appreciate the view. However, Wright had other ideas. When Wright showed Kaufmann his plans, Kaufmann initially balked, but Wright convinced him that incorporating the falls into the design of the house
40 was far preferable. In the end, Wright was able to turn Fallingwater into an artistic link between untamed nature and domestic tranquility—and a masterpiece in his brilliant career.

Edgar J. Kaufmann's original plan to build
45 his house on the ample flat land at the bottom of the waterfall would indisputably have proven less challenging. Wright's more daring response to the site required builders to construct the house on a small stone precipice atop the falls. Wright
50 further proposed extending the living room of the house out over the rushing water and making use of modern building techniques so that no vertical supports would be needed to hold up the room. Wright brilliantly utilized the "cantilever"
55 technique, in which steel rods are laid inside a shelf of concrete, eliminating the need for external supports. Unfortunately, however, the builders did not employ an adequate amount of reinforcing steel to support the first floor. Kaufmann had hired
60 consulting engineers to review Wright's design prior to Fallingwater's construction, but Wright dismissed the engineers' claims that the main floor girders needed additional support. Over time, the first floor cantilever began to sag, and in 2002, a technique
65 called post-tensioning was used to permanently repair the gradual collapse.

Despite Wright's miscalculation, Fallingwater, as a whole, is an impressive structure. Rather

than allowing the environment to determine the
70 placement and shape of the house, Wright sought
to construct a home that intentionally confronted
and interacted with the landscape. Each bedroom
has its own terrace, and cornerless windows open
outward so that window panes do not obstruct
75 the spectacular view. In addition, Fallingwater
contains a great many traditional and natural
building materials. The home's 5,300-square foot
expanse includes custom-designed black walnut
wood furniture and walls and floors constructed
80 of locally sourced sandstone. The boulders that
provide the foundation for the house also extend
up through the floor and form part of the
fireplace. A staircase in the living room extends
down to an enclosed bathing pool at the top of
85 the waterfall. To Wright, the ideal dwelling in
this spot was not simply a modern extravaganza
or a direct extension of natural surroundings;
rather, it was a little of both.

Architecture enthusiasts have taken a wide
90 range of approaches to understanding this unique
building. Some have asserted that the house
exalts the artist's triumph over untamed nature.
Others have compared Wright's building to a
cave, providing a psychological and physical safe
95 haven from a harsh, violent world. The members
of the American Institute of Architects named
Fallingwater the "best all-time work of American
architecture," and the Western Pennsylvania
Conservancy, which has owned and preserved
100 Fallingwater since 1963, hails the building as
an inspiration.

Edgar Kaufmann Jr. may have summed up the
innovation and awe of Fallingwater best when
he said, "Wright understood that people were
105 creatures of nature; hence, an architecture which
conformed to nature would conform to what
was basic in people. . . . Sociability and privacy
are both available, as are the comforts of home
and the adventures of the seasons." This, then, is
110 Frank Lloyd Wright's achievement in Fallingwater:
a home that connects the human and the natural
for the invigoration and exaltation of both.

1. Which of the following statements best expresses
the main idea of the passage?

   A. Fallingwater's designs were heavily influ-
      enced by its owner's wealth, social position,
      and political opinions.

   B. Fallingwater proved to be only as durable as
      construction techniques available at the time
      would allow.

   C. Wright designed Kaufmann's home to be
      both impressive and in harmony with its
      natural surroundings.

   D. Wright proved that humans can triumph
      over the natural, untamed landscape and
      claim it as their own.

2. Based on the passage, architecture critics regarded
Frank Lloyd Wright's career prior to Fallingwater's
construction (lines 15–17) as:

   F. antiquated but likely to rebound.

   G. out of date and declining.

   H. admirable and well-regarded.

   J. requiring additional support.

3. It can be reasonably inferred that the site chosen
for Fallingwater was:

   A. the location of a cabin that Kaufmann
      banned his employees from using after they
      failed to properly care for the property.

   B. unlikely to have been selected if Kaufmann's
      employees had continued to use it as a refuge
      from the urban atmosphere of Pittsburgh.

   C. postponed for several years due to the
      difficulty of constructing a house on a small
      stone precipice atop the falls.

   D. strategically chosen based on the location of
      the waterfall in proximity to wildlife such as
      white-tailed deer.

4. The passage indicates that Edgar J. Kaufmann's original plans for the site were:

   F. straightforward and conventional.

   G. daring and bold.

   H. idealistic and whimsical.

   J. socially outlandish and culturally unorthodox.

5. The author's use of the phrases "black walnut wood" and "locally sourced sandstone" (lines 78–80) most nearly serves to emphasize which of the following points?

   A. Black walnut trees should be used sparingly to prevent deforestation.

   B. Sandstone is a preferable building material because of its stability.

   C. Fallingwater features multiple types of organic building materials.

   D. Natural elements are essential to creating a cave-like environment.

6. According to the passage, a cantilever is designed to include:

   F. vertical supports that hold up a room.

   G. concrete-encased steel rods.

   H. reinforcing steel to support the first floor.

   J. post-tensioning to correct sagging.

7. It can reasonably be inferred that the miscalculation the author mentions in line 67 refers to:

   A. an issue that might have been prevented if Wright had heeded engineers' warnings.

   B. a suboptimal structure plagued by gravitational forces that led to a complete collapse.

   C. cornerless windows that open outward to offer an unobstructed view of the landscape.

   D. a staircase that extends down to an enclosed bathing pool at the top of the waterfall.

8. One of the main purposes of the information in lines 72–85 is to:

   F. argue that Fallingwater would not have suffered from gradual collapse if it had been built during a time of advanced engineering.

   G. describe the intricacies of Wright's "cantilever" technique and its subsequent consequences.

   H. explain specific ways in which Fallingwater and the surrounding natural beauty enhance one another.

   J. show how architecture enthusiasts have generated a myriad of theories regarding the significance of Fallingwater.

9. Architecture enthusiasts' comparisons of Fallingwater to a cave (lines 93–95) most strongly suggest that the house provides a sense of:

   A. familial warmth accompanied by a sense of belonging.

   B. murkiness that is exacerbated by the dampness of the structure.

   C. inescapable claustrophobia that could lead one to panic.

   D. security and safety that is both literal and emotional.

10. As it is used in line 112, the phrase "invigoration and exaltation" most nearly means:

   F. robustness and jubilation.

   G. renewing and superiority.

   H. briskness and blessing.

   J. inspiration and glorification.

How Much Have You Learned?

Directions: Take a few minutes to refresh your memory of the passage below, which you first saw in chapter 16, and then answer the associated questions. Try to use the various ACT Reading question strategies you learned in this chapter. Be sure to study the explanations, even for questions you got correct. They can be found at the end of this chapter.

SOCIAL SCIENCE: This passage is adapted from an article about how humans develop language.

The influential theory of universal grammar (UG) postulates that all humans have an innate, genetic understanding of certain grammatical "rules," which are universal across all languages
5 and absolutely not affected by environment. The idea of such a universal grammar has a long history, starting with Roger Bacon's thirteenth-century book *Overview of Grammar* and continuing through the Renaissance with attempts to construct
10 an ideal language. In the eighteenth century, the first edition of the Encyclopedia Britannica included a section dedicated to universal grammar. In modern times, however, the linguistic theory of universal grammar is most closely associated
15 with Noam Chomsky, who did much to codify and popularize it in the 1950s–1970s. According to Chomsky, we are all born with a knowledge of "deep structure," basic linguistic constructions that allow us, if not to understand all languages, at least
20 to understand how they are put together. From there, we have only to learn how the parameters are set in our particular language in order to create an unlimited number of "correct" utterances.

For example, he suggests that structure
25 dependency—a rule that says that sentences are defined by phrase structure, not linear structure— is inherent to all languages, with minor variations. Thus, the meaning of a sentence is really dependent on the meaning of its phrases, rather than each
30 individual word. In addition, the head parameter rule stipulates that each phrase contains a "head" (main) word, and all languages have the head word in essentially the same position within the phrase. Chomsky's famous sentence "Colorless green ideas
35 sleep furiously" exemplifies this theory of universal grammar—while the sentence itself is meaningless, it is easily recognizable as a grammatical sentence that fits a basic but higher level of organization.

"Furiously sleep ideas green colorless," on the other
40 hand, is obviously not a grammatical sentence, and it is difficult to discern any kind of meaning in it. For other evidence to support this theory, Chomsky points to our relative ease in translating one language to another; again, while we may
45 not necessarily recognize individual words in an unfamiliar language, we can certainly recognize and engage with sentences that are grammatical.

This evidence is still fairly theoretical, receiving play mostly in the linguistic sphere rather than in
50 the biological sciences. Most of those researching the theory seem more concerned with attempting to draw universal parallels across languages than with searching for biological evidence of such phenomena. We might ask: Where exactly are
55 these universal grammar constraints located in our genetic code? How and when are they altered by natural evolutionary processes—or do they remain relatively unaltered and non-mutated from generation to generation? As both languages and
60 human beings evolve over time, does UG also evolve or stay relatively stable?

Even within the linguistic sphere, Chomsky's theory has drawn criticism. Some scientists suggest that by ignoring the role of environment
65 in language development, Chomsky completely discredits the possibly important effect our surroundings could have on language development. Still other researchers say that universal grammar is not nearly as ordered and absolute as Chomsky
70 and other linguists make it out to be—that merely identifying similarities in different languages does not prove that a universal grammar underlies them. They suggest that since the universal grammar theory is not falsifiable, it is in fact
75 pseudoscientific rather than scientific, the result of our flawed human tendency to impose order where there is none.

Reading

More recent researchers have begun to
advocate that, rather than focusing on explaining
80 linguistic similarities among various languages,
we instead acknowledge the evolutionary roots of
language and look specifically for neurobiological
explanations. Claiming that the humanistic
exploration of universal grammar is too abstract,
85 they recommend that we instead view language
(and grammar) as a function of the brain.
Some progress has been made in studying the
neurobiology of language; for instance, scientists
have identified specific regions of the brain that
90 handle language. However, these findings are
simple and preliminary, offering little insight into
the vast intricacy of human language use.

Neither linguistics nor biology alone is sufficient
to understand the foundations of language.
95 Language is unbelievably complex: even a single
word can offer several definitions and associations.
Thus, any single connection between, say, two
languages causes those myriad associations to
become oversimplified and sterile. For example,
100 simply pointing out that the subject of a sentence is
in the same position in Turkish and English as an
illustration of UG merely acknowledges that single
linguistic association, while failing to consider any
social circumstances that may cause the mind to
105 modify that grammar. In short, say scientists, not
until we create a better marriage between biology
and linguistics—and a better understanding of the
human brain—can we even begin to address the
complexities of human language development.

1. The passage as a whole can best be described as:

A. an argument against the validity of an
outdated theory.

B. a description of how scientific understanding
of a topic has evolved historically.

C. an examination of a well-known theory and
how it might be improved.

D. a defense of the contributions of a theory in
spite of its imperfections.

2. Based on the passage, how do Renaissance efforts
to design a language relate to Chomsky's theory of
universal grammar?

F. Renaissance linguists based their undertak-
ing on Chomsky's theory.

G. Both believed in the possibility of perfecting
language.

H. Chomsky's theory was inspired in part by
that constructed language.

J. They share underlying assumptions about
human language.

3. In the first paragraph, Chomsky claimed that an
"innate, genetic understanding":

A. allows humans to understand all language.

B. allows humans to understand all language
structure.

C. allows humans to easily speak in multiple
languages.

D. explains that grammar is a natural function
of the human brain.

4. According to the passage, universal grammar's structure dependency rule states that:

   F. the linear arrangement of words defines the meaning of sentences.

   G. a sentence's grammatical structure is dependent upon its meaning.

   H. a sentence's meaning relies on the meaning of the phrases that compose it.

   J. head words are the most critical to understanding the meaning of sentences.

5. The author includes the quotes "Colorless green ideas sleep furiously" and "Furiously sleep ideas green colorless" primarily in order to:

   A. support the idea that humans can recognize grammatical and ungrammatical structures regardless of content.

   B. show the importance of word order in determining whether a statement is grammatical or not.

   C. identify the correct position of the head word in two different phrase structures.

   D. demonstrate why it is easy to translate from one language to another even when dealing with unfamiliar vocabulary.

6. The questions in paragraph 3 primarily serve to:

   F. demonstrate that biology is a better lens for examining language.

   G. suggest potential theoretical weaknesses of universal grammar.

   H. list topics universal grammar seeks to elucidate.

   J. dismiss the possibility of an evolutionary basis for language.

7. The passage suggests that the researchers mentioned in line 68 believe which of the following?

   A. Identifying similarities across all known languages is the only way to prove universal grammar correct.

   B. Universal grammar is not chaotic enough to be a scientific theory.

   C. For a theory to be truly scientific, it must be possible to prove it wrong.

   D. Pseudoscience is a major problem in the field of linguistics.

8. One of the main purposes of the fifth paragraph is to:

   F. introduce the idea of examining language through neurobiology.

   G. describe the evolutionary development of language.

   H. outline the strides made in studying how the brain produces language.

   J. identify criticisms of the theory of universal grammar.

9. As it is used in line 99, the word *sterile* most nearly means:

   A. cold and sanitary.

   B. formal and meaningless.

   C. frigid and barren.

   D. dry and musty.

10. As it is used in line 106, the phrase *a better marriage* most nearly means:

   F. a more equitable partnership.

   G. a more effective synthesis.

   H. stronger communication.

   J. a permanent relationship.

Reflect

Directions: Take a few minutes to recall what you've learned and what you've been practicing in this chapter. Consider the following questions, jot down your best answer for each one, and then compare your reflections to the expert responses on the following page. Use your level of confidence to determine what to do next.

1. Why do ACT experts research and predict the correct answer to Reading questions before reading the answer choices?

    _____

    _____

    _____

2. What are the types of research clues contained in ACT Reading question stems?

    _____

    _____

    _____

3. What are the five common incorrect answer choice types associated with ACT Reading questions?

    - _____

    - _____

    - _____

    - _____

    - _____

4. How will you approach the process of answering ACT Reading questions more strategically going forward? Are there any specific habits you will practice to make your approach to ACT Reading more effective and efficient?

    _____

    _____

    _____

Responses

1. Why do ACT experts research and predict the correct answer to Reading questions before reading the answer choices?

Expert test takers know that the correct answer to each ACT Reading question is based on the text of the passage. They research to avoid answering based on memory or on a whim. Predicting the correct answer before reading the choices increases accuracy and speed by helping the test taker avoid rereading, confusion, and comparing answer choices to one another.

2. What are the types of research clues contained in ACT Reading question stems?

Line numbers, paragraph numbers, quoted text, proper nouns, specific content clues, and whole passage clues.

3. What are the five common incorrect answer choice types associated with ACT Reading questions?

    - *Out of scope*
    - *Extreme*
    - *Distortion*
    - *Opposite*
    - *Misused detail*

4. How will you approach the process of answering ACT Reading questions more strategically going forward? Are there any specific habits you will practice to make your approach to ACT Reading more effective and efficient?

There is no one-size-fits-all answer here. Reflect on your own habits in answering ACT Reading questions and give yourself an honest assessment of your strengths and weaknesses. Consider the strategies you've seen experts use in this chapter, and put them to work in your own practice to increase your accuracy, speed, and confidence.

Next Steps

If you answered most questions correctly in the "How Much Have You Learned?" section, and if your responses to the Reflect questions were similar to those of the ACT expert, then consider answering Reading questions an area of strength and move on to the next chapter. Come back to this topic periodically to prevent yourself from getting rusty.

If you don't yet feel confident, review the material in this chapter, and then try the questions you missed again. As always, be sure to review the explanations closely. Then go online (**kaptest.com/login**) to use your Qbank for more practice. If you haven't already registered your book, do so at **kaptest.com/moreonline.**

GO ONLINE

kaptest.com/login

Answers and Explanations

Try on Your Own

Suggested Passage Map Notes:

¶1: Fallingwater: architectural achievement by FLW

¶2: how FLW came to design Fallingwater

¶3: location; below vs. on falls

¶4: challenges

¶5: house interacts w/nature

¶6: critical responses

¶7: connects human and nature

BIG PICTURE SUMMARY

Main idea: Fallingwater, an unusual and impressive building, was an architectural achievement by Frank Lloyd Wright.

Author's purpose: To inform the reader about the history of a unique piece of architecture

---

1. C
Difficulty: Low
Category: Global
Getting to the Answer: This is a Global question because it is asking for the main idea of the passage. Use your passage notes to answer this question. Your notes should indicate that paragraph 1 introduces Fallingwater as one of Wright's greatest achievements and paragraph 7 concludes that Fallingwater interconnects humans and nature. Predict that Fallingwater is amazing and reflects nature, which matches (C).

The passage offers no evidence that Kaufmann's money, social status, or political beliefs influenced Wright's designs; A is incorrect. Choice B is out of scope; durability refers to a specific aspect of Fallingwater's construction, but Global questions are concerned with the passage as a whole. In addition, it was Wright's dismissal of the engineers' recommendation to provide additional support for the main floor girders that led to durability issues, not the limitations of the available construction techniques. Choice D is a distortion; Wright wanted the house to be an "extension of natural surroundings," not a triumph over them.

2. G
Difficulty: Medium
Category: Detail
Getting to the Answer: The phrase "Based on the passage" indicates that this is a Detail question. Paragraph 2 discusses Wright's career before Kaufman asked him to design Fallingwater. Lines 15–17 state that "architecture critics deemed Wright's style anachronistic and assumed that his career was coming to an end." *Anachronistic* refers to something that is not in its correct time period, so predict that critics thought that Wright's designs were too old to be relevant and that his career was deteriorating. Choice (G) is correct.

The critics did think that Wright's technique was antiquated, but they did not think it was likely to rebound; F is incorrect. Choices H and J are misused details. Edgar J. Kaufmann Jr., not the critics, admired Wright and held him in high regard, and Fallingwater's main floor girders, not Wright, required additional support.

3. B
Difficulty: Medium
Category: Inference
Getting to the Answer: The clue "It can be reasonably inferred" shows that this is an Inference question. Lines 23–27 state that the site was "originally the location of a cabin . . . that he offered as a vacation retreat for the numerous employees he oversaw at Kaufmann's Department Store, located in downtown Pittsburgh." However, "When the Great Depression struck, Kaufmann's employees could no longer afford the cost of traveling more than 60 miles to Mill Run" (lines 27–29). Since Kaufmann decided to build a new home only after his employees ceased traveling to the cabin, it can be inferred that if his employees had not stopped using the cabin, Kaufmann may not have decided to build a new home. Choice (B) is correct.

Choices A and D are out of scope; the passage does not mention how well (or poorly) Kaufmann's employees cared for the property or what type of wildlife existed near the waterfall. Choice C is a distortion; it took some convincing for Kaufmann to agree to build Fallingwater at the top of the waterfall, but the passage does not state that construction was postponed.

4. F
Difficulty: Medium
Category: Inference
Getting to the Answer: This is an Inference question because the question stem includes the word *indicates*. The correct answer to an Inference question will always be directly supported by the text. Your passage notes should point you to the fourth paragraph. The author writes that Kaufmann had originally planned to put the house on a flat site near the bottom of the waterfall, but Wright convinced him to accept a more daring location right over the waterfall. Predict that Kaufmann's original plans were not daring but traditional; the correct answer is (F).

Choices G and H are the opposite of your prediction; Wright's design, not Kaufmann's plan, was daring, bold, idealistic, and whimsical. Choice J is out of scope; the passage never indicates how the plans were considered within a social or cultural context.

5. C
Difficulty: Medium
Category: Function
Getting to the Answer: The phrase "most nearly serves to emphasize" indicates that this is a Function question. For more context, read the surrounding lines in addition to the one cited. The passage states that "Fallingwater contains a great many traditional and natural building materials" (lines 75–77). Predict that the phrases emphasize the natural materials that Wright used. Choice (C) is correct.

Choices A and B are out of scope; the passage does not mention deforestation or the stability of sandstone. The author doesn't mention the idea of a cave until the next paragraph, so D is incorrect.

6. G
Difficulty: Low
Category: Detail
Getting to the Answer: "According to the passage" indicates that this is a Detail question. Lines 55–56 state that "steel rods are laid inside a shelf of concrete," which matches (G).

Choice F is opposite because a cantilever eliminates the need for vertical supports. Choices H and J are misused details. Wright disregarded the engineers' recommendation to include additional reinforcing steel to support the first floor, and post-tensioning wasn't used until 2002, well after the initial design.

7. A
Difficulty: High
Category: Inference
Getting to the Answer: This is an Inference question because it asks for what "can reasonably be inferred." The line reference provided is at the very beginning of paragraph 5, and it refers to the miscalculation discussed in the previous paragraph. Your passage notes should indicate that paragraph 4 is about Wright's decision to use the "cantilever" technique. Lines 57–59 state that "the builders did not employ an adequate amount of reinforcing steel to support the first floor." Furthermore, "Wright dismissed the engineers' claims that the main floor girders needed additional support. Over time, the first floor cantilever began to sag, and in 2002, a technique called post-tensioning was used to permanently repair the gradual collapse" (lines 61–66). This information indicates that if Wright had listened to the engineers and included additional reinforcing steel, the cantilever may not have started to sag. Choice (A) is correct.

Choice B is extreme; the passage says that the collapse was gradual, not complete. Choices C and D are misused details; both answer choices are mentioned in the passage, but they are notable features that demonstrate how Fallingwater's design embraces nature, not examples of miscalculations.

8. H
Difficulty: Medium
Category: Function
Getting to the Answer: The phrase "One of the main purposes" shows that this is a Function question. Use your passage notes to review the main purpose of the paragraph that contains the sentences indicated by the question stem. Your notes should show that paragraph 5 discusses the ways in which Fallingwater intertwines impressive architecture with natural beauty. Predict that lines 72–85 provide details about this connection; (H) is correct.

Choice F is out of scope because the passage does not discuss whether Fallingwater would have proven more durable if it had been built during a period of more advanced engineering. Choices G and J are incorrect because they reflect the purposes of the fourth and sixth paragraphs, respectively, not the fifth paragraph.

9. D

Difficulty: Medium
Category: Inference
Getting to the Answer: When an Inference question asks for a characterization of an opinion, be sure to keep in mind whose opinion it is. Here, it is the architecture enthusiasts' notions of a cave that are important. According to the cited sentence, architecture enthusiasts compared Fallingwater to a cave because the house provided "a psychological and physical safe haven from a harsh, violent world" (lines 94–95). The critics' use of cave imagery suggests a feeling of safety, which matches (D).

Choices A, B, and C are distortions of what the architecture enthusiasts alluded to in their characterization. Eliminate these choices because the passage does not provide support for a sense of familial warmth, murkiness, or claustrophobia.

10. J

Difficulty: High
Category: Vocab-in-Context
Getting to the Answer: This question includes wording characteristic of a Vocab-in-Context question: "the phrase . . . most nearly means." The sentence indicated is the final sentence in a paragraph that begins with the statement "Edgar Kaufmann Jr. may have summed up the innovation and awe of Fallingwater best," so you can predict that in this context *invigoration and exaltation* means "innovation and awe." Choice (J) is correct.

Choice F includes definitions of *vigor* and *exultation*, which sound similar to *invigoration* and *exaltation* but have different meanings. Choices G and H are distortions; they represent other possible definitions of these words, but they do not make sense when plugged back into the sentence.

How Much Have You Learned?

Suggested Passage Map Notes:

¶1: theory of UG through history

¶2: ex. of rules that support UG

¶3: ev. = theoretical, biological?

¶4: criticism

¶5: lang. and brain

¶6: biology & linguistics both needed

BIG PICTURE SUMMARY

Main idea: Chomsky's theory of innate linguistic structure is popular among linguists but does not address biological influences on language development.

Author's purpose: To inform the reader about the limitations and possibilities of universal grammar

1. C

Difficulty: Medium
Category: Global
Getting to the Answer: The phrasing "The passage as a whole" shows that this is a Global question. Consult your notes for an overview. The passage is fairly neutral; it describes universal grammar and then discusses criticisms of the theory and how to resolve them. The correct answer is (C).

Choice A is extreme; the passage does not argue that universal grammar is invalid or outdated, only that it has flaws. The passage is not focused on the history of universal grammar, despite a brief outline in the first paragraph, so B is incorrect as well. Choice D is a distortion; the passage does not defend universal grammar.

2. J

Difficulty: High
Category: Inference
Getting to the Answer: The clue words "Based on the passage" identify this as an Inference question. The first paragraph states that universal grammar proposes that all humans have an inherent understanding of universal language principles. It then goes on to say, "The idea of such a universal grammar has a long history," including Renaissance linguists attempting to design an ideal language. You can predict that universal grammar and Renaissance linguists had similar beliefs about humans' innate understanding of grammar. This matches (J).

Choice F is incorrect because Chomsky's work came after that of the Renaissance linguists. Choice G is a distortion; while the Renaissance linguists believed this, there is no evidence that Chomsky did. Choice H is out of scope; the passage gives no information about what inspired Chomsky's theory.

3.   B
Difficulty: Medium
Category: Detail
Getting to the Answer: The clue words "Chomsky claimed" in the question stem show that the answer must have been directly stated in the passage. Thus, this is a Detail question. Go back to the first paragraph to find out what Chomsky said. According to Chomsky, we can innately perceive how languages "are put together." Predict that the correct answer should have something to do with how humans can intuitively understand the deep structure of languages. Answer choice (B) is correct.

Choices A and C are extreme; while humans can grasp the structure of all languages, they cannot necessarily understand or speak all languages. Choice D is mentioned in the passage, but it is given as a possible direction for future research. There is no evidence that Chomsky himself is concerned with human biology.

4.   H
Difficulty: Low
Category: Detail
Getting to the Answer: This question stem includes the phrase "According to the passage," showing that it is a Detail question. The passage discusses the structure dependency rule in the second paragraph; predict that a sentence's structure and meaning depend on its phrases. Choice (H) is correct.

Choice F is opposite; the passage says that neither linear structure nor individual words define sentence meanings. Choice G is also opposite; meaning depends on structure, not vice versa. Finally, the passage does not discuss how head words relate to meaning, so J is incorrect.

5.   A
Difficulty: Medium
Category: Function
Getting to the Answer: The wording "the author includes . . . in order to" marks this as a Function question. Research the context of these quotes to determine why the author included them. In the passage, they are offered as examples of unmistakably grammatical and ungrammatical sentences. Choice (A) is correct.

Choice B is a distortion; although the word order changes, the passage explicitly states that grammar is defined by phrases, not linear structure. Choice C is

incorrect because the passage does not identify any head words. Choice D is incorrect because the example sentences are not translated.

6.   G
Difficulty: Medium
Category: Function
Getting to the Answer: The phrase "primarily serve to" indicates that this is a Function question. Go back to paragraph 3 to determine the purpose of the cited questions. The first part of the paragraph contrasts the purely linguistic investigations of universal grammar with its lack of biological inquiry. Since the cited questions all relate to the biological implications of the theory, you can predict that they are included to point out possible oversights in universal grammar. Choice (G) is correct.

Choice F is extreme; the author is merely suggesting that biology should be considered, not that it is better. Choice H is opposite; the point of the questions is that universal grammar has not addressed these topics. Finally, the author is not dismissing any theory here, so J is incorrect.

7.   C
Difficulty: Medium
Category: Inference
Getting to the Answer: The clue word *suggests* indicates that this is an Inference question. The researchers from the cited line have multiple opinions listed in the passage, which makes a precise prediction difficult here. Instead, read lines 62–77 to get a general idea of what they think, and then go through the answer choices one by one, eliminating until you find a match.

Choice A is incorrect because the researchers do not offer a way to prove universal grammar correct. Choice B is a distortion; while the researches do say universal grammar is too ordered, they do not suggest that increased chaos would make it more scientific. However, they do say that being impossible to disprove makes universal grammar pseudoscientific; therefore, you can infer that they believe a legitimately scientific theory must be possible to disprove. Choice (C) is correct.

Once you have found an answer that fits the passage, you can move on without checking any remaining choices. However, if you are unsure, you can check all four. Choice D is out of scope; the passage does not discuss whether pseudoscience is a major problem in linguistic studies.

8. F
Difficulty: Medium
Category: Function
Getting to the Answer: The phrase "One of the main purposes" shows that this is a Function question. Consult your notes to determine the function of the fifth paragraph and predict that it discusses neurobiological investigations of language. The correct answer is (F).

Choice G is out of scope; the passage does not explain how language evolved. Choices H and J are misused details; although the paragraph mentions some discoveries and one criticism, neither is one of its overall purposes.

9. B
Difficulty: Medium
Category: Vocab-in-Context
Getting to the Answer: This question has the characteristic phrasing of a Vocab-in-Context question: "the word . . . most nearly means." Read the sentence that includes the cited line to get a feel for how this word is being used. The passage states that language is incredibly complex, so focusing too much on any one connection between words leads to an understanding that is rigid and lacking in nuance. Choice (B) is correct.

Choice A matches a common definition of *sterile*, but remember that the test rarely asks for the usual meanings of word. Choices C and D both reflect physical descriptions, but the context of this sentence is metaphorical.

10. G
Difficulty: Medium
Category: Vocab-in-Context
Getting to the Answer: This question has the distinctive wording of a vocab-in-context question: "the phrase . . . most nearly means." Read the sentence that includes the cited line to determine what this phrase means in context. The passage suggests that both linguistics and biology, working together, are needed to understand language. Predict that the phrase means "improved integration." The correct answer is (G).

Choice F is incorrect because the passage does not suggest that the current relationship between the disciplines is unfair. Choice H is incorrect because the disciplines need to integrate, not just communicate. Choice J is incorrect because the passage does not suggest a permanent relationship.

CHAPTER 19

LITERATURE PASSAGES

Reading

LEARNING OBJECTIVES

After completing this chapter, you will be able to:

- Draw inferences about characters' motivations and relationships
- Identify the tone of a literature passage

How Much Do You Know?

Directions: In this chapter, you'll learn to apply the ACT Reading strategies you've learned to literature passages. Take 9 minutes to actively read this passage and answer the 10 accompanying questions. Pay close attention to the relationships between characters as you read. When you're finished, compare your work to the explanations on the following pages.

LITERARY NARRATIVE: This passage is adapted from a short essay within a memoir.

The liminal state of being somewhere entirely new, entirely alien: is there any feeling like it? Heavy with potential, exciting, but always, just beneath the surface, there is the fluttery-
5 heart feeling of fear of the unknown. There was supposed to be a shopping center, and in it a department store, for all those things that somehow, between being taken from the cabinets and drawers of the past and arriving in cardboard
10 boxes to the present, managed to disappear. But how to find it?

Now, I suppose, it is as simple as plugging information into a phone, but this was before the days of such ubiquitous magic. Imagine, if you
15 can, not having satellites and geocached location data, the word "googol" still referring only to a number. There were maps, but I had no map. There were people, but they were strangers, all of them strangers, and the fluttery dread was enough to
20 prevent my asking them for help.

But there was also something quixotic about it all—a quest! An adventure! Standing on the front steps of this house where the bed was against the wrong wall, and the hot water took so much longer
25 to gush from the tap, and the backyard smelled of fresh-cut grass rather than the turned earth of my old garden. This had been the right decision. Surely, it must have been. The warm air, the breeze, the smell of fried food from the restaurant at the end
30 of the street, with its OPEN "24/7" sign and dirty windows. The restaurant owners, and all those who lived in the tall, narrow houses around me—they had made a home here. I could do the same.

So, shoulders set and deep breath taken, I set
35 off to see the unknown vanquished, turning right, reciting to myself the vague directions from the landlord: take a right, look for the bridge with

the red railing, and then it's on the left, just past Crane Street, you can't miss it. (I probably could, I
40 remember thinking at the time. I was, and am, quite talented at missing things, to be completely honest.) My determination was a thin, delicate veneer that I pretended was armor-strong as my familiar old boots began their journey down a new sidewalk
45 (new to me only, though, judging by the cracks and the stubborn late blooms pushing through them; the tree roots forcing concrete into tiny, craggy mountains).

And there was something, too, to realizing that
50 one day, and probably sooner than now seemed possible, I would sigh to think of having to walk this way, bored of it all, wondering if I could get by without trash bags or coffee filters or lemon juice for one more day. I wouldn't even notice
55 anymore the blue mailbox of the house two doors down from mine, nor the crooked little pine tree across the street, nor the way the street sign at the intersection was bent in the middle. I wouldn't need to look at that sign anymore to know the road
60 that I was crossing. (That street was Hawthorn, by the way, and my own street was Oak, despite the aforementioned pine. There were oaks as well, as I recall, though they might have been something else; my knowledge of trees generally extends to
65 "conifer" versus "deciduous" and no further.)

I would walk one day, then, with my head down, but with much less hesitation, no more wondering if I'd gone too far without noticing the bridge with the red railing or Crane Street,
70 because I'd know where the bridge was, and Crane Street, and everything else in this sprawling maze of a city. I'd know which buses to take, which stores had better prices than the one where I was going, which restaurants had the best
75 desserts, which houses had a cat who liked to sit on the porch and watch me pass.

And how mundane it would all be! How easy, how *dull*. There was dread in that, too, when I realized. Because there was beauty in
80 the unfamiliar, though it was fragile, easy as an eggshell to shatter into a million pieces when one stopped noticing it and no longer felt the need to be so cautious. This quest of mine was one to savor for as long as it lasted.

85 And there, as promised, was the bridge with the red railing, and the creek beneath was rocky and quick, shimmering, and beyond it, the boxy-brick, pocked-and-pitted walls of what must be my destination. Just a generic shopping center,
90 like so many hundreds of others. But still, who knew what awaited me inside? More unknown magic: perhaps a book of spells, or a genie's lamp, or a gateway to a new world. There was only one way to find out. And I had made it this far—I
95 would make it to the end.

1. The narrator's attitude in the passage as a whole can best be described as:

   A. desperate, but tentatively hopeful.

   B. uncertain, but ultimately upbeat.

   C. excited, but initially dour.

   D. cynical, but nonetheless determined.

2. The narrator describes what she is seeing as she travels in lines 54–60 primarily in order to:

   F. share with the reader more information to help paint a mental picture of the new place in which the narrator lives.

   G. contrast these details with the place where the narrator lived before she moved and describe what is different about the two places.

   H. compare what she sees to what she remembers from several other places she has lived.

   J. give examples of things that the narrator will no longer notice when the same trip becomes tedious and dull.

3. As it is used in the first paragraph, the word *alien* most nearly means something that is:

   A. sinister and threatening.

   B. unfamiliar and strange.

   C. out-of-place but exciting.

   D. unwelcoming but peaceful.

4. The narrator uses the phrase "I set off to see the unknown vanquished" in the fourth paragraph in order to:

   F. continue the mental theme of seeing the trip to the store as a fantastical quest.

   G. show the difficulty of overcoming fear of the unknown when in a new place.

   H. describe the way in which the narrator chose to travel to her new home.

   J. convey to the reader the dangers of not knowing where you're going.

5. It can reasonably be inferred from the passage that the narrator is writing about a time period:

   A. in the present day.

   B. in the distant past.

   C. in the near future.

   D. in the recent past.

6. In lines 79–83, the narrator compares finding beauty in the unknown to an eggshell primarily in order to emphasize:

   F. how much stronger she will be when she knows her surroundings better.

   G. how difficult it is to know one's own strength when faced with being in a new place.

   H. how delicate her current viewpoint is compared to how she will feel later.

   J. how mentally fragile she is feeling after she has come to a new place to live.

7. According to the passage, the narrator was given directions to the shopping center by:

    A. her landlord.

    B. restaurant owners.

    C. her real estate agent.

    D. the neighbors.

8. In lines 71–72, the narrator describes the new city in which she lives as a "sprawling maze" primarily in order to emphasize:

    F. the lack of planning that went into the city.

    G. the difference between her old home and her new one.

    H. her own dislike of using a map to find the shopping center.

    J. her current lack of knowledge of the city.

9. What do the narrator's fanciful ideas regarding what she may find at the shopping center (lines 90–93) suggest about her?

    A. She truly believes she will find something magical inside the shopping center.

    B. She wants to prolong the sense of adventure after completing her initial "quest."

    C. She is not certain of what types of items the shopping center might sell.

    D. She is fighting the potential for shopping trips to become mundane and tedious.

10. In lines 4–5, the narrator employs which of the following literary devices in order to describe what she will know about the city in future?

    F. Personification

    G. Symbolism

    H. Alliteration

    J. Metaphor

Check Your Work

Suggested Passage Map Notes:

¶1: narrator just moved, excited & nervous

¶2: needs store, lacks tools to find it

¶3–4: changing feelings about new home and "quest" – excitement, uncertainty, determination

¶5–6: narr. will be familiar and bored in future

¶7: narr. wants to keep sense of adventure

¶8: finds store, thinks about future adventures

BIG PICTURE SUMMARY

Main idea: The narrator is recounting how it feels to navigate a new location for the first time.

Author's purpose: To describe her current feelings and anticipate how those feelings might change in the future

---

1. B
Difficulty: Medium
Category: Global
Getting to the Answer: The clue words "passage as a whole" indicate this is a Global question. Consult your notes to refresh your memory on the whole passage and ask yourself how you might describe the narrator's attitude: while the narrator questions her decision to move to a new area, she ultimately chooses to try to see exploring her new environment as an enjoyable adventure. This matches (B).

The other answer choices all contain one part that is too extreme. While *tentatively hopeful* might accurately describe the narrator's attitude, *desperate* is too strong a word for how she feels, so A is incorrect. In C, while the narrator is indeed *excited*, there is nothing *dour*, or gloomy, about her attitude at the beginning of the passage. And finally, in D, the narrator could be said to be *nonetheless determined*, but her attitude is not *cynical*.

2. J
Difficulty: Low
Category: Function
Getting to the Answer: "Primarily in order to" in the question stem tells you this is a Function question. Review these lines in the passage. The narrator uses all the details of what she is seeing in her new neighborhood as a contrast to what will happen in the future, when she no longer notices those things because the familiar trip to the store will have lost its luster. This matches (J).

In F, while the narrator is in fact helping paint a mental picture of the new area, that is not why those details are included. Choice G might be a tempting choice if you did not refer back to the passage—the narrator does compare the house she lives in now to where she lived before, but that comparison was earlier in the passage. Multiple past residences are not discussed in the passage, making H incorrect.

3. B
Difficulty: Medium
Category: Vocab-in-Context
Getting to the Answer: The phrase "most nearly means" indicates this is a Vocab-in-Context question. Refer back to the first paragraph to see how the narrator uses the word *alien*. It appears in the first line, alongside being in a place that is "entirely new." Predict that *alien* relates to that, referring to a place in which the narrator is not yet entirely comfortable. This matches (B), which is the correct answer.

While the narrator is not yet comfortable with her new location, nothing implies that she finds it either sinister or threatening; A is too extreme and thus incorrect. Choice C might be tempting, but while it describes the narrator's overall feeling over the course of the passage, it isn't what is meant by the word *alien* specifically; C is incorrect. Choice D is out of scope; nothing is said about the narrator's new location being unwelcoming or peaceful.

4. F
Difficulty: Medium
Category: Function
Getting to the Answer: Since the question asks how a particular phrase is used, this is a Function question. Ask yourself how that particular phrase functions in relation to the rest of the passage. The narrator is trying to see her trip as "a quest! An adventure!" and you could predict that this phrase continues to use the kind of language you might associate with such a viewpoint. This matches (F), which is the correct answer.

While the narrator does discuss the fear of being in a new place, she is not referring to that fear when using the phrase quoted, making G incorrect. The narrator is describing going to the department store, not her home, which means H is out. Finally, the narrator does not discuss any true dangers at all (if anything, she seems to realize her fears are unfounded) which means you can eliminate J.

5. D
Difficulty: Low
Category: Inference
Getting to the Answer: The question asks what "can reasonably be inferred," making this an Inference question. Look at your passage notes to get a feel for when the narrator might be writing, and eliminate answer choices as you go. In the second paragraph, the narrator discusses cell phones that can be used to look up where something is located not yet existing, which eliminates A. Throughout the passage, the narrator is looking for a shopping center, a relatively modern invention, which eliminates B. There is nothing at all in the passage implying it might be set in the near future, so C is out. This leaves (D); based on the passage, it does appear likely the narrator is writing of a time in the recent past, so (D) is correct.

6. H
Difficulty: Medium
Category: Function
Getting to the Answer: Here, you are asked why the narrator makes a particular comparison, making this a Function question. Why does the narrator compare her current feeling to an eggshell? Review the lines in question. Predict that the narrator is emphasizing how easy that feeling is to crush with the passing of time. Now review the answer choices: the match to the prediction is (H).

Choices F, G, and J are all out of scope. They may or may not be true of the narrator, but none of them are why the narrator compared finding beauty in the unknown to an eggshell.

7. A
Difficulty: Low
Category: Detail
Getting to the Answer: "According to the passage" indicates that this is a Detail question. Refer back to the paragraph in which the narrator discusses being given directions. The landlord gave her the directions—this matches (A). The narrator does not mention speaking to the restaurant owners, a real estate agent, or her neighbors, eliminating B, C, and D.

8. J
Difficulty: Medium
Category: Function
Getting to the Answer: "Primarily in order to emphasize" tells you this is a Function question. It wants to know why the narrator describes the city

the way she did. Refer back to the line as well as the lines immediately around it. Predict that the narrator is emphasizing how little she knows now about the city compared to what she will know once it has grown familiar to her. This matches (J)—she calls the city a "sprawling maze" because it is currently unfamiliar.

Nothing is said about whether or not the city was planned, so F is incorrect. While the narrator does discuss differences between her old home and her new home, this isn't why she called the city a "sprawling maze," making G incorrect. Finally, while the narrator mentions maps, all she says is that she has none, not that she dislikes using them, so H is incorrect.

9. B
Difficulty: Medium
Category: Inference
Getting to the Answer: "Suggest" indicates that this is an Inference question. Refer back to the final paragraph, and predict that the narrator means that she will continue to imagine herself on an adventure despite having found what she was looking for originally (the shopping center). Choice (B) matches the prediction and is the correct answer.

There is nothing to indicate that the narrator truly believes she will find magical items in the shopping center, eliminating A. She may or may not be certain of what the shopping center sells, but this isn't why she mentions finding magical things inside, eliminating C. And while she does believe going shopping in this new place will eventually become boring, she does not reference magical items in relation to that, eliminating D.

10. H
Difficulty: High
Category: Function
Getting to the Answer: This is a rare question type, but don't let it trip you up! Tackle it just as you would any other question in the reading section. Because it asks you what the narrator is doing with a particular literary device, this is a Function question. Refer back to the referenced paragraph. The narrator uses alliteration, the occurrence of the same letter or sound at the beginning of closely connected words, in the phrase "fluttery-heart feeling of fear," so (H) is correct. The referenced lines do not contain personification, symbolism, or metaphor, eliminating F, G, and J.

HOW TO READ ACT LITERATURE PASSAGES

Exactly one passage in each ACT Reading section is a literature passage: an excerpt from a novel or short story. The ACT literature passage will be labeled **PROSE FICTION** or **LITERARY NARRATIVE**, and it will always be the first passage in the Reading Test. That doesn't mean you have to tackle it first, though. Some test takers may find fiction more engaging and feel comfortable reading dialogue and interpreting an author's descriptions of characters and settings. Others may find their strengths lie in more concrete, nonfiction passages on science and social studies. Don't make a snap judgment based on how you feel now, though. Practice all of the passage types to give yourself an honest, informed assessment. You'll find more tips and strategies on how best to approach the section in the chapter on ACT Reading section management.

To read passages and answer questions like these:

PROSE FICTION: This passage is adapted from a collection of short stories.

She had a little ball she liked to bounce, until one day she didn't. One minute it was there, the next—it wasn't. Even at six years old, she knew bouncy balls didn't just . . . just *disappear*. But
5   it was only her, and the empty hallway, and no bouncy ball.

She crawled around looking for it, even though it hadn't fallen, because it had vanished in mid-air. But it was nowhere. It hadn't slipped into one of the
10 floor vents (it was too big, anyway), it hadn't rolled under a door. It was just gone.

She didn't tell anyone about it; she knew they wouldn't believe her. "You always lose things. Stop being so *careless*." The same things they said
15 when she really had misplaced one of her schoolbooks, or her hairbrush, or half of a pair of socks. But this was different.

And it wasn't the only time it happened.

Things around her had a perplexing, marvelous
20 habit of disappearing. Never when anyone was around, and never when she might have predicted it. Sometimes those mysteriously purloined items came back, though. Like the doorknob. It once vanished as she was turning it, only to
25 reappear as she backed away, startled, her hand

still outstretched and curved around something that was no longer there. She remembered the feeling in the moment, a vertiginous swoop of discomfort. But a few seconds later, there it was
30 again. She wasn't just seeing things—she'd felt it go, the cold metal against her palm, and then nothing. Or there was the time she put her pencil down on her desk and when she reached for it again, it wasn't there. Instead, she found it later,
35 on the middle of her bed.

She grew up, as children will do, and got used to the experience. Nothing important ever disappeared permanently, thankfully—or at least, not in *that* way. She *wished* sometimes she could
40 blame her odd, thieving ghost for her missing homework.

And was it a ghost? Or something else? There was no way to know. It never bothered anyone else in the house—not her mother, or father, or
45 her little sister, or even the various pets they had over the years. As she grew older, she sometimes asked for things back, and usually, they would eventually show up, though in odd places. Once, she demanded her favorite hair clip back, and it
50 appeared on top of her head. "Oh, *very funny*."

But it was friendly, for the most part. It didn't pinch, or rattle the cupboards menacingly, or make things go bump in the night. It merely took things. Perhaps, she reasoned, it was the ghostly

55 equivalent of a magpie. She read up about ghosts, and apparently, what hers did was not all that unusual. Sometimes, she read aloud, in case her ghost was also curious about others of its kind and what they did. "But no pulling the covers off my
60 bed at night, ghost. That's just creepy."

She wondered if it had a name. She simply thought of it as her ghost, no greater eponymity required. It followed her away from home, to college, where it thieved the thumbtacks from her
65 corkboard and pens from the cup on her desk. It followed her to her first apartment, taking spoons and refrigerator magnets and, once, the charger for her phone. She demanded that one back, too. She found it behind a bookcase in the spare
70 bedroom, a room she did not use unless she had visitors. There were no visitors at the time.

It never left wherever she was living. She could go to work, and anything that disappeared was her own fault, or at best the fault of her coworker who
75 seemed to believe the snacks and drinks in the fridge were intended to be shared by anyone too penny-pinching to bother to bring their own. She could go out with friends, and not have to worry about disappearing French fries. It was a home
80 ghost.

Eventually, she married and had children, and they, like others, were not bothered by the ghost, though her children teased her about her inability to keep track of things; what had been
85 exasperating to her parents was a joke to the kids. But she knew the ghost approved of them, because one day, her six-year-old daughter came running to find her, grinning with excitement and delight:

"Mommy, look! It just appeared out of
90 nowhere! Like *magic*!"

A bouncy ball.

1. The point of view from which the passage is told is best described as that of:

   A. a first-person narrator who tells a story that continues throughout her life.

   B. a first-person narrator who offers insights into the thoughts of other characters as she chronicles the events in her life.

   C. a limited third-person narrator who relates events from the perspective of the main character.

   D. an omniscient third-person narrator who relates the thoughts and actions of the characters.

2. According to the passage, the first time an object disappeared, the girl:

   F. thought she had lost or misplaced it.

   G. found it later in an unexpected place.

   H. was afraid to tell her parents.

   J. saw it vanish before her eyes.

3. The narrator mentions the episode with the doorknob primarily in order to:

   A. illustrate that the girl is not hallucinating.

   B. support the idea that the ghost is friendly.

   C. demonstrate that any objects that disappear are later returned.

   D. question whether the objects are actually disappearing.

4. The use of italics on the words "very funny" in line 50 is most likely intended to convey a tone of:

   F. hilarity.

   G. impatience.

   H. sarcasm.

   J. importance.

5. According to the passage, when the girl first starts to notice items disappearing, she feels:

    A. concerned.
    B. delighted.
    C. frightened.
    D. worried.

6. Which of the following statements best captures the reason the girl reads aloud from books about ghosts?

    F. Reading aloud makes the girl more confident and calms her fears.
    G. The girl wants to help the ghost learn about other ghosts.
    H. The girl hopes her parents will overhear her and learn about the ghost.
    J. The girl is learning to read, and she is interested in ghosts.

7. The narrator describes the main character as responsible when objects disappear from:

    A. her childhood bedroom.
    B. her college apartment.
    C. her workplace.
    D. her home as an adult.

8. The statement "There were no visitors at the time" (line 71) primarily serves to suggest that:

    F. the ghost put the phone charger behind the bookcase.
    G. the phone charger had disappeared much earlier than the girl thought.
    H. earlier visitors may have borrowed the phone charger.
    J. the ghost would not return the charger.

9. According to the passage, the frequent disappearance of objects caused the girl's parents to:

    A. demand the objects be returned.
    B. scold her for carelessness.
    C. spend money to replace the missing objects.
    D. become annoyed.

10. It can reasonably be inferred from the passage that the girl believes that the ghost approves of her children because:

    F. the children were never bothered by the ghost.
    G. the ghost returned the first object taken from the girl.
    H. the children thought the ghost was a joke.
    J. objects stopped disappearing once the children were born.

You need to know this:

The ACT does not generally test symbolism, but it does test your ability to draw inferences about characters' relationships and attitudes and to recognize how the author creates a specific tone or effect.

Unpack the Pre-Passage "Blurb"

Be sure to read the little blurb that precedes an ACT Reading passage; this can be especially helpful on literature passages. The blurb may give you the author's name, the title of the book or short story from which the passage was adapted, and the original publication date. When necessary, it may provide information about the main characters and setting.

Author. If you happen to know the author, great, but don't expect to. If the name rings a bell that helps you identify the time frame or setting of the passage, take advantage of that, but otherwise, let it go. No questions will ask about the author's identity or biographical information.

Title. A book's title may help you identify its genre—tragedy, romance, coming-of-age stories, etc. It may also give you clues about the setting or theme of the passage.

Publication date. The ACT has used literature passages drawn from various time periods over the last 200 years or so. Obviously, language use and references will be different in passages from the 1850s than in those from the 1950s, and you can use that information to provide context about social conditions and historical events, or even about unusual vocabulary.

Characters and setting. When the test adds any information beyond author, title, and date, pay close attention. The people writing the test questions felt this information was essential for test takers to know, and it will always give you a head start in interpreting the passage and anticipating where the story is likely to go. Knowing, for example, that the main character is an adolescent or a mother, or knowing that a story takes place in a coal-mining town or an aristocratic palace, will change your understanding of the passage from the outset.

Tune In to the Narrator's "Voice"

Within the first few lines, you will be able to distinguish a passage written in first person (the narrator as the main character, knowing only what that character knows) from one written in third person (the narrator is separate from the characters). Keeping this in mind as you read will help you spot the purpose of each paragraph and will help you later with Inference questions ("With which of the following would the narrator/character most likely agree?").

In addition, take note of language that indicates the narrator's or a character's point of view. In a standard science or social studies passage, opinion and emphasis keywords help you keep track of an author's ideas about a topic. In literature passages, the author may put these ideas in the mind or the mouth of a character or in the way a scene or object is described. Take note of the passage's tone (e.g., joyful, nostalgic, anxious, angry, hopeful, ironic, satirical, etc.), especially if an event or conversation brings about a change in tone. Typically, one or more of the questions will reward your attention to the passage's tone and characters' points of view.

Track What Happens and the Main Character's Reaction or Response

In a standard ACT Reading passage on science or social studies, you can use an author's purpose to anticipate where the passage will go. When the author says there is a debate over a recent theory, you expect the next couple of paragraphs to lay out one side and then the other. If the author introduces a new idea, there will probably be an example to illustrate it. Literature passages unfold a little differently, but if you are reading actively, you can still anticipate and track the development of the story. Use what you know about a character to anticipate the action and to interpret the character's reactions. If an older worker who is concerned about having enough money for retirement has a conversation with her boss, you can understand what she's after, even if she is using language that talks around the subject. If a studious young man absorbed in a book is interrupted by a boisterous group of revelers, you can expect some annoyance or judgment in his reaction, even if he doesn't say anything to the newcomers. Keeping track of these things will help you jot down good paragraph summaries, just as you would in nonfiction passages.

When a character's reaction or response to an event surprises you, consider whether this signals a change in the tone of the passage or indicates that you've glossed over or misunderstood something about the character or situation. In either case, it's always valuable to track not only the plot but also the character's reactions to and interpretations of what is happening.

Use What You Already Know About ACT Reading Strategies and Question Types

While literature passages have a distinct look and feel, the questions that accompany them are of the same types as those that follow standard science and social studies passages. Thus, while the best test takers apply a few unique reading strategies tailored to literature, their overall approach remains similar to what they use for all passages. In every case, ACT experts read actively to prepare themselves for the question set. To do that, they read for the big picture, for the author's (or in this case, narrator's or characters') opinions and point of view, and for the passage's structure by noting the purpose and main idea of each paragraph.

For the most part, the questions that accompany literature passages are worded similarly to those for science or social studies passages. However, in literature passages, you may also see questions asking:

- for the passage's theme (which corresponds to its main idea)
- about a shift in the narrator's focus
- how the author creates a certain effect
- what is going on in a character's mind

As long as you read actively for tone and characters' motivations, you'll be ready for questions like these.

You need to do this:

- Use the pre-passage blurb to identify all that you can about:
  - The author's identity
  - The time frame and location
  - The passage's main character or characters
- Quickly recognize whether the passage is in first person or third person.
- Focus on the main character's defining characteristics: demographics (such as age, social position, occupation, race, and gender) and mental traits (attitudes, opinions, desires, and conflicts).
- Anticipate the character's responses to events or interactions with other characters.
- Note the purpose of each paragraph as you read.

Explanations

Suggested Passage Map Notes:

¶1–2: girl, 6 yrs old, ball disappears

¶3: doesn't tell anyone

¶4–6: objects really disappear, not seeing things

¶7–9: ghost? description

¶10: "home" ghost

¶11–13: adult, ghost still with her

BIG PICTURE SUMMARY

Main idea: The author shares instances when a "home ghost" has taken and replaced items over the years.

Author's purpose: To describe the author's interactions with a ghost over time

1.   C
Difficulty: Medium
Category: Global
Getting to the Answer: There will be several types of questions on the ACT that will test your knowledge of basic literary concepts. This passage has a narrator who describes the events and tells the story from the point of view of the girl, so (C) is correct.

A good clue that the passage does not have a first-person narrator is the lack of the word "I" in the text. A first-person narrator tells the story from the narrator's own perspective. Eliminate A and B. An omniscient narrator knows everything, but this narrator questions whether there's really a ghost, or something else; an omniscient narrator would know the answer to that question. Eliminate D as well.

2.   J
Difficulty: Medium
Category: Detail
Getting to the Answer: The phrase "According to the passage" tells you that this is a Detail question. The first time an object disappears is mentioned in the first two paragraphs, so return there and read carefully. Line 8 states, "it had vanished in mid-air," which matches (J), the correct answer.

Choice F is a subtle distortion of information in the passage. Although the girl looked for the ball, she knew

that it hadn't fallen and was too big to fall into a floor vent. At the end of the text, the girl's daughter finds the ball, so G is incorrect. Choice H is also incorrect. The girl chooses not to tell her parents, but she is never described as being afraid to do so.

3.   A
Difficulty: High
Category: Function
Getting to the Answer: "The author mentions . . . in order to" is a clue that this is a Function question. The doorknob anecdote appears in the fifth paragraph. The sample passage map notes tell you that section is explaining that the girl is not just seeing things disappear, but that the objects actually do vanish. The doorknob story emphasizes that by noting that the girl was able to feel the object until it disappeared. This story brings in the sense of touch to show that the girl's eyes are not deceiving her. This matches (A), the correct answer.

Choices B is a misused detail; the ghost is friendly, but that is not why the author describes the incident with the doorknob. Choice C is extreme; the passage only says that some objects are returned, not all of them. Choice D is an opposite choice. The anecdote is supporting, not questioning, the fact that the objects are actually disappearing.

4.   H
Difficulty: Medium
Category: Function
Getting to the Answer: The phrase "intended to convey" demonstrates that this is a Function question. Italics are used to emphasize the words, so imagine the girl's tone when she says them. Her favorite hair clip has disappeared, and when it returns, it's on top of her head . . . where it will be used, but not in that way. It's as if her ghost is teasing her, so she teases right back. Choice (H), *sarcasm*, is the best match.

Choice F, *hilarity*, is too literal. If the girl were amused, she would have laughed or smiled, but this is not mentioned in the text. Similarly, G and J do not have any support in the passage and are incorrect. There is no evidence that the girl has lost patience or that she thinks this is an important event.

5.   B
Difficulty: Medium
Category: Detail
Getting to the Answer: Because this question includes the phrase "According to the passage," you can identify

Reading

it as a Detail question. Whenever you are asked about an emotion, there will be a keyword in the passage that will support the correct choice. The context clue in the question tells you to identify the girl's feelings when she first starts to notice objects disappearing, so return to the beginning of the passage and scan for a keyword. The first sentence of the fifth paragraph describes the disappearances as "perplexing and marvelous," so the girl may be confused by them, but she also enjoys them. Choice (B) is correct.

Choices A, C, and D all have negative connotations not supported by the passage and so are incorrect.

6. G
Difficulty: Medium
Category: Detail
Getting to the Answer: This question includes few clues as to question type; it might be either Detail or Inference, depending on whether the passage states the reason or you need to infer it. Your first step to answering it, however, is the same: find the part of the passage that discusses the girl reading aloud and research there. The passage map directs you to the middle of the passage, paragraphs 7–9, for the description of the ghost. Reading aloud, the detail mentioned in the question, is found in the eighth paragraph, when the girl reads aloud "in case her ghost was also curious about others of its kind." This matches (G), the correct answer.

None of the other choices are mentioned in the passage, so they are all incorrect.

7. C
Difficulty: Medium
Category: Detail
Getting to the Answer: The clue word "describes" shows this is a Detail question. The passage map indicates that the tenth paragraph describes the ghost as a "home" ghost. The second sentence of that paragraph states that when things go missing at the girl's workplace it is either her fault or the fault of one of her coworkers. Choice (C) is correct.

The incorrect choices are all the opposite of what's in the passage. These are all places where objects have disappeared because of the ghost.

8. F
Difficulty: Medium
Category: Function
Getting to the Answer: The wording "The statement . . . serves to" marks this as a Function question. The lines

cited in the question appear in the ninth paragraph, where the sample passage map indicates there is a discussion of characteristics of the ghost. Review the paragraph. The anecdote about the missing phone charger is described, the girl requests the return of the charger, and she later finds it in the guest room. The narrator states "there were no visitors at the time" to emphasize that the disappearance and reappearance of the charger was due to the ghost, not anyone else. Choice (F) is correct.

Choices G and H are not mentioned in the text, and so are incorrect. Choice J contradicts the passage; the ghost did return the charger in this case.

9. D
Difficulty: High
Category: Detail
Getting to the Answer: You can identify this as a Detail question because of the clue "According to the passage." The girl's parents are mentioned twice in the passage: once in the third paragraph and once in the last paragraph. In the third paragraph, her parents chide her for being careless, but the text states they are doing so "when she really had misplaced" one of her things, not because the ghost had made some object disappear. Eliminate B. In the last paragraph, the girl's parents are described as "exasperated," and this matches (D), the correct answer. Choices A and C are not mentioned in the passage, so they are incorrect.

10. G
Difficulty: Medium
Category: Inference
Getting to the Answer: The girl's children are only mentioned in the final paragraphs, so review that section to identify why the girl believes her ghost approves of her children. That context clue is mentioned in line 83, followed by an anecdote of the girl's own six-year-old daughter "magically" finding the same ball that was the first object of the girl's to disappear. The implication is that the ghost showed its approval of the child by returning the ball. Choice (G) is correct.

Choice F is a misused detail; it accurately describes the relationship of the ghost and the children, but it is not mentioned as the sign of the ghost's approval and is thus incorrect. Choice H is a subtle distortion of information in the passage. The children thought the disappearing objects were lost by their mother; her "carelessness" was the joke, not the ghost. Choice J contradicts the passage; it is clear that disappearances continued after the narrator's children were born.

Try on Your Own

Directions: Actively read this literature passage and answer the questions that follow. Remember to note the tone of the story as you read and pay close attention to characters' attitudes and relationships.

Answers are found at the end of the chapter.

LITERARY NARRATIVE: This passage is excerpted from a series of short biographical stories.

There was a smoothness to the rhythm of her days. She was an old, old woman, and her name was Betty, and each of her days was just like the last. First thing, the careful way she had to
5 move, when it was early and everything about her seemed to have turned stiff and cold in the night. Easing into it, sitting up, joints slowly remembering how to do their creaky old job, but not happy about it—no, not happy about it at all.

10 She made coffee with a percolator, filling it from the sink, knowing just how long it would take. Her son had gotten her one of those coffee machines with the little plastic cups the year before, for her birthday, but she just couldn't
15 take to using it. It was alien. She no longer knew how to deal with alien. So she put it away in the cabinet, where it wouldn't take up all her counter space, and got it out when her son visited, so he wouldn't know she didn't appreciate his
20 thoughtfulness, and he was the one who filled it up, him or his wife or his daughter, who drank coffee at only thirteen. But for Betty herself, the percolator.

She drank her coffee slowly, with honey
25 and milk in it. Sometimes she sat on the porch, when the weather was nice, and watched the sun rise over the old crackerbox houses, houses older even than she was. But more often she sat at her worn kitchen table, still linoleum-surfaced,
30 aluminum-legged, perhaps not the style anyone would choose in the now, but things had been different in the then. She made breakfast with her second cup of coffee: a slice of toast, sometimes with jam, others with more of the honey. She did
35 have a sweet tooth, did Betty. And she knew her doctor wouldn't like that second cup of coffee (and probably not the first, either), but she had lived long enough for such indulgences. Besides,

if she didn't tell him, who was going to? Nobody,
40 that was who.

After breakfast, she dressed: another slow process. Rolling up her stockings, her fingers shaky as they buttoned up her dress. Then she saw to her hair, combing it, all that fluffy white
45 where once there had been smooth chestnut brown. Makeup, as her mother had taught her to do it, not too much, just enough to bring some color to her cheeks.

Most days, after she was dressed it was time
50 for her stories on the TV. That was the rest of her morning, one show giving way to the next, the usual commercials for Metamucil and heart medicine and walk-in bathtubs. They knew who was watching those shows. She supposed there
55 were people who studied that kind of thing, who was watching what and when. So it was this stuff during the weekdays, and ads for cars in the evenings, and sugary breakfast cereals and McDonalds toys on Saturday mornings. Although
60 her granddaughter didn't watch much TV—she was always on her phone, watching stuff that way.

(Betty also had a cell phone, and like the coffee machine it was a gift from her son, and like the coffee machine it mostly sat unused. It wasn't one
65 of the fancy ones like her granddaughter had, just a little black box that flipped open, but still, she didn't see the point. She had a perfectly good phone on the wall in the kitchen, and one by her recliner in the living room, and that was good
70 enough.)

For lunch she might have a sandwich, sometimes a bowl of soup if the day was cold or rainy. And with her lunch a glass of milk, because she had heard that it was good for older women
75 to get plenty of calcium, it helped prevent that bone disease where they broke too easily. She read magazines with her lunch, or worked in her

crossword puzzle book—she picked one up a few
times a month from the market. She was good at
80 them, though by now, there were some clues she
knew they used over and over, and she wished
they'd come up with new ones instead.

After lunch, it was time for chores. She liked to
sweep; it reminded her of doing it in her father's
85 store, hardly as tall then as the broom handle.
He'd had a tobacco shop, back when everyone and
their dog seemed to smoke, and she remembered
the lovely smell of it, all those jars of smoky-sweet
brown-and-red shreds of tobacco. She'd swept and
90 danced and pretended she was a princess forced
into penury, like in the movies. Now, she dusted,
and mopped when she needed to see a little shine
to the floors, and washed up her dishes from
breakfast and lunch, leaving them to dry in the
95 sun from the little window above the sink.

In the evening, she watched the news while she
ate dinner, though it sometimes made her sad to
see all the things people did to each other. It was
all just so terrible; it hadn't been like that when
100 she was a child. Sometimes, after, she watched a
movie, if there was anything good on. If not, she
might read a book; she did like those stories about
people living in villages in Ireland or Scotland,
with their sweet little romances and the exotic-
105 sounding ways of spelling words so you could
hear their accents in your head. And then the
day was over—just like the day before, and it was
time to undo all that she had done, return to her
nightgown and slip beneath her quilt, sleeping in
110 the safe knowledge that tomorrow would be just
the same as today.

1. Betty's attitude toward technology throughout the
passage could best be described as reluctance to:

A. have any modern technology at all in her home.

B. understand any modern technology
purchased for her by others.

C. use modern technology developed after she
grew old.

D. admit there is modern technology she
doesn't understand.

2. Based on lines 49–56, it can be reasonably
inferred that Betty believes the products in the
commercials shown during the day:

F. are marketed to older people like herself.

G. are marketed to those who are retired.

H. are things she should consider purchasing.

J. are things her granddaughter would not
want.

3. In the first paragraph, the author describes the
way Betty moves slowly when she wakes up in the
morning in order to:

A. contrast it with the way she later moves
when she is getting dressed and brushing
her hair.

B. reinforce with supporting details the idea
that Betty is elderly, as was stated at the very
beginning.

C. provide the reader with additional information about what waking up is like for all
older people.

D. set up a parallel with the later descriptions
of how Betty goes to bed again at the end of
the night.

4. What can most reasonably be inferred based
on the reference to "still linoleum-surfaced,
aluminum-legged" in lines 29–30?

F. Betty's home has some furniture that could
be considered an outdated style.

G. Furniture that was made in the past was
made to last longer than furniture made in
the present.

H. Betty's son will likely buy her a new kitchen
table and chairs for her next birthday.

J. Tables are no longer made with the surface
and the legs being of two different types of
material.

5. Which of the following statements most accurately describes Betty's attitude toward her doctor and his opinion on her drinking coffee?

    A. She feels some guilt for having the second cup of coffee, but not about having the first, even though he would approve of neither.

    B. She chooses not to think about it, because she knows she is not supposed to be drinking coffee at her age.

    C. She believes it is acceptable because her son bought her a coffee maker, even though she knows the doctor would not approve of it.

    D. Because he does not know she drinks it, she is dismissive of his potential disapproval of her drinking coffee.

6. One of the primary purposes of the sixth paragraph is to:

    F. emphasize the differences between Betty's life and her granddaughter's life.

    G. provide a factual example of why Betty would be better off without a cell phone.

    H. further reinforce Betty's dislike of technology she seems to consider superfluous.

    J. show that Betty believes technology should progress no further than it already has.

7. The author uses the word *safe* in the final paragraph to emphasize that:

    A. the area where Betty lives does not have crime problems.

    B. Betty finds comfort in following the same routine each day.

    C. Betty knows nothing bad will happen while she's asleep.

    D. going to bed is easier for Betty than getting up in the morning.

8. Chronologically, which of the following events happened first?

    F. Betty receiving the coffee maker as a gift from her son.

    G. Betty helping to sweep out her father's tobacco shop.

    H. Betty putting her makeup on the way that her mother taught her.

    J. Betty sitting outside on the porch on days when the weather is nice.

9. Based on the information in lines 83–100, what can most reasonably be inferred about Betty's memories of childhood?

    A. She has fond memories of childhood, but she might view them with somewhat rose-colored glasses.

    B. She does not like to reflect on her childhood because she had to work too young and the world is even less kind now.

    C. She looks back on her childhood as a time when nothing ever went wrong and the world was a safer, better place.

    D. She does not remember her childhood well, but she believes the world is a better place now than then.

10. In the first paragraph, the word *rhythm* most nearly means:

    F. ups and downs.

    G. a series of sounds.

    H. a poetic feeling.

    J. recurring events.

How Much Have You Learned?

Directions: For test-like practice, give yourself 9 minutes to complete this question set. Be sure to study the explanations, even for questions you got correct. They can be found at the end of this chapter.

LITERARY NARRATIVE: This passage is adapted from an essay about family pets.

I have wondered, sometimes, about how my cats view their world. Do they have any means to appreciate the warm air that blows from the vents, the bowl of food that is always full, the
5   blanket left on the bay window for them to curl up in as they watch life outside? They are always comfortable, but they have known no other life. Do they understand that it could be very different?

10   I knew a cat once named Reginald. (Reginald, of all things to name a cat!) Reginald had known the harshness of life. He should have been a mean old thing, with his torn-up ears, fur patchy and matted, scars on the pale skin beneath, his tail
15   crooked from a break that had healed badly. Ugly as sin, was Reginald; big and orange-furred. And he would have had every right to trust no one and no thing, because just looking at him, you could tell that very few ones or things had ever
20   treated him well until he found his way to our neighborhood.

But I've never met a sweeter cat. He would come looking for a little love, purring up a storm, and he'd happily take a bowl of food,
25   though he never wanted to come inside. He was an outdoorsman; it was where he had always been. Everyone in the neighborhood knew Reginald. I don't know who named him, but we all knew that was his name. He was a collective cat.
30   Where he came from, I don't know either, but he was already old when he showed up. A cat like Reginald seemed the type who was born old, old and weary, but happy for any taste of affection.

I had three cats of my own at the time,
35   and they were fat old things, spoiled rotten. They'd see Reginald out the window sometimes and hiss and spit and puff up, but Reginald paid them no mind. He knew his place in the world. And I guess he was smart enough to understand

40   that glass stood between him and them, and there was nothing they could do about it, no matter how much they postured. He'd sit outside to wash his uneven orange fur, taking pride in what he had, keeping himself clean as well as he could.

45   Some of the children in the neighborhood liked to pretend he was as mean as he looked, and it almost seemed like he could understand them—they'd run and shriek and hide, and he'd come after them, not getting too close, just looking at
50   them with his big golden eyes, and they'd run again, laughing and shouting at one another to *be careful, be careful, there he is!* He'd do it as long as they continued. They weren't *really* scared; the same children would be out the next day with a
55   slice of ham or turkey, feeding it to him bit by bit as he purred and purred and purred.

In winter, I would leave my garage door cracked, so he had somewhere to go, and I wasn't the only one. As I said, he wasn't interested in
60   coming inside, but a place out of the cold, with an old blanket or towels to lay on, seemed to be acceptable to him. On snowy days, I'd warm up a can of food for him, and he accepted that too. Meanwhile, my own pudgy beasts batted at the
65   snow through the windows, and I wondered how quickly they'd retreat if they were to feel the actual bite of it.

Reginald disappeared late in the spring five or six years after he first appeared in our
70   neighborhood. Someone said that cats went off by themselves to die. There was a field that disappeared into the woods, and people swore they had seen him heading that way, slow and arthritic by then. I don't know if that's true, but if
75   there was any cat who would have wanted to die with dignity, on his own terms, it was Reginald. I hope that whatever happened to him, it was painless. He deserved at least that much blessing in his difficult life.

80   My own cats have vet care, howling through
     it, fighting me about going into their carriers.
     Reginald probably never saw a vet in his life. I
     don't know how old he was. No one did. My cats
     have every amenity provided them and certainly
85   expect to continue to be catered to. Reginald
     asked for nothing, but we gave him what we
     could. He was an old fighter, that one. He had
     earned a little pampering.

     But I sometimes find myself wondering
90   how different my own cats would be, if they had
     been through what Reginald did: would they still
     know how to be affectionate? Would they be like
     Reginald, purring and head-butting, appreciative
     of every scrap? Do they understand that things
95   could be very different for them?

     I suspect they don't, but I do. When I fill
     their food bowls, or scoop out their litter box,
     or wash their blankets, I think of Reginald,
     even now, when many years have passed since
100 he disappeared. I make sure their every whim
     is satisfied, because they might have been in
     Reginald's place, and it breaks my heart to think
     of them going through what he went through.
     But I also like to think that, spoiled as they are in
105 their present life, they might, like Reginald, still
     know how to appreciate a little human kindness.
     They might play games with kids, unconcerned
     about their status as the designated monster. They
     might accept a place to sleep in the garage on cold
110 nights. I hope someone would give them those
     things, if I could not.

     And I also hope that wherever Reginald is now,
     he's okay. I hope he's warm, and dry, and well-fed.
     I hope his ears and his fur are whole. I hope there
115 are games to play.

     I hope he is at peace.

1. The passage as a whole might be characterized as
    the author's:

    A.   attempt to come to terms with the hardship
         of life for stray animals.

    B.   explanation of how and why her cats are
         different from Reginald.

    C.   reminiscence about a friendly neighborhood
         stray and her own cats.

    D.   exploration of human nature when a
         neighborhood cares for a cat.

2. The author seems to believe that Reginald viewed
    his place in the world:

    F.   with affable acceptance; he took what was
         offered to him and appreciated it, but saw no
         need to ask for more.

    G.   with begrudging amiability; he knew that
         what he needed was only offered as long as
         he acted in an expected way.

    H.   with necessary wariness; he was aware that
         the people around him might turn on him as
         it seemed had happened in the past.

    J.   with unnecessary greed; rather than choose
         to live with one person, he wanted to take
         from the whole neighborhood.

3. In the passage, the primary purpose of lines
    34–38 is to:

    A.   provide an explanation for why the author's
         cats are different from Reginald.

    B.   juxtapose Reginald and the author's cats.

    C.   explore the similarities between the author's
         cats and Reginald.

    D.   attempt to explain why Reginald behaved as
         he did when he saw the author's cats.

4. In the third-to-last paragraph, it is reasonable to conclude that one of the reasons the author cares for her cats as she does is because:

   F. she worries that she won't be able to take care of them in the future.

   G. she is required to take good care of them since she owns them.

   H. she feels some sense of guilt that she couldn't do more for Reginald.

   J. she thinks that they would not be able to care for themselves like Reginald.

5. As it is used in line 78, *blessing* most nearly means:

   A. a small gift.

   B. a source of protection.

   C. a peaceful prayer.

   D. an act of acceptance.

6. The author physically describes Reginald in lines 12–16 primarily in order to:

   F. establish why Reginald behaved as he did.

   G. contrast Reginald's appearance with his demeanor.

   H. show that Reginald had lived a hard life.

   J. indicate that Reginald's appearance was deserved.

7. The author calls Reginald an "outdoorsman" in line 26 in order to:

   A. reinforce his behavior outside as opposed to inside.

   B. anthropomorphize Reginald's choice to stay outside.

   C. identify why Reginald became a cat for the neighborhood.

   D. provide a reason why Reginald was not allowed inside the house.

8. The passage as a whole strongly suggests that Reginald:

   F. was able to appreciate whatever was offered to him.

   G. had often gotten into fights as a younger cat.

   H. was able to understand the rules of the games children played.

   J. had always understood he was not a house cat.

9. Within the context of the passage, the primary purpose of lines 53–56 is to:

   A. show that Reginald's outward appearance ultimately matched his demeanor.

   B. provide evidence that Reginald could sometimes be a friendly cat around children.

   C. show that children can behave differently in different circumstances.

   D. provide evidence that the children were just pretending that Reginald was monstrous.

10. Based on the passage, how did Reginald's personality affect his later life?

   F. He was begrudgingly cared for by people who felt sorry for him.

   G. He became reluctantly affectionate as he learned to trust people.

   H. He was readily helped out by people in the neighborhood.

   J. He was a favorite of neighborhood children but not adults.

Reflect

Directions: Take a few minutes to recall what you've learned and what you've been practicing in this chapter. Consider the following questions, jot down your best answer for each one, and then compare your reflections to the expert responses on the following page. Use your level of confidence to determine what to do next.

1. What are ACT Reading literature passages? How do expert test takers adjust their active reading to tackle literature passages most effectively?

    _____

    _____

    _____

2. How are the questions that accompany literature passages different than those accompanying standard science and social studies passages?

    _____

    _____

    _____

3. How confident do you feel with literature passages? What can you do in practice to improve your performance and gain even more confidence with these types of passages?

    _____

    _____

    _____

Responses

1. What are ACT Reading literature passages? How do expert test takers adjust their active reading to tackle literature passages most effectively?

On each ACT test, one reading stimulus is taken from a work of fiction, such as a novel or short story. Expert test takers actively read literature passages by paying attention to what happens to the main character and how he or she responds to these events.

2. How are the questions that accompany literature passages different than those accompanying standard science and social studies passages?

For the most part, questions accompanying literature passages are similar to those from standard nonfiction passages, but in literature, you may see:

1. *Global questions that focus on a change in the passage's tone*

2. *Inference questions that ask what the passage's narrator (as opposed to its author) would agree with*

3. *Function questions that ask how or why a character (as opposed to the author) used a detail or reference from the text*

3. How confident do you feel with literature passages? What can you do in practice to improve your performance and gain even more confidence with these types of passages?

There is no one-size-fits-all answer for this question. Give yourself honest self-assessment. If you feel that literature passages are a strength, that's great! Continue to practice them so that you'll be able to rack up the points associated with these passages on test day. If you feel less confident about literature passages, review the strategies in this chapter, and try to consistently apply the expert approaches outlined here whenever you practice passages in this format.

Next Steps

If you answered most questions correctly in the "How Much Have You Learned?" section, and if your responses to the Reflect questions were similar to those of the ACT expert, then consider Literature passages an area of strength and move on to the next chapter. Come back to this topic periodically to prevent yourself from getting rusty.

If you don't yet feel confident, review the material in this chapter, especially the sections on characters' responses and points of view. Then try the questions you missed again. As always, be sure to review the explanations closely. Then go online (**kaptest.com/login**) to use your Qbank for more practice. If you haven't already registered your book, do so at **kaptest.com/ moreonline.**

GO ONLINE

kaptest.com/login

Answers and Explanations

Try on Your Own

Suggested Passage Map Notes:

¶1: Betty: old woman waking up

¶2: B prefers old coffee machine, not new; son wants to help

¶3–5: morning routine; B likes her way, but aware of others'

¶6: B sees no use for cell phone

¶7: lunch

¶8: cleaning, childhood memories

¶9: end of day, next day will be same

BIG PICTURE SUMMARY

Main idea: Betty is an older woman with a routine who generally feels times were better before technology and other "new" things took over.

Author's purpose: To recount a typical day in Betty's life

---

1. C
Difficulty: Medium
Category: Global
Getting to the Answer: The phrase "throughout the passage" indicates this is a Global question (albeit one that also asks you to infer something). Because it is difficult to make a prediction about the correct answer in broad cases like this one, review your passage notes before looking at the answer choices. Knock them out one by one:

Choice A is too extreme. The passage says Betty allows modern technology in her home, she just doesn't necessarily use all of it. Choice B is a distortion. While the passage says that Betty is reluctant to use the coffee maker and the cell phone her son purchased for her, it doesn't say she won't use them because they were purchased by him.

Now look at (C). In the second paragraph, it says, "She no longer knew how to deal with alien." However, she can turn on a TV, implying that she was able to learn how to use technology earlier in life—this is a change for her. Choice (C) is a reasonable inference based on the passage as a whole, and is correct. Choice D

is incorrect because the passage does not include anything to support or refute Betty's willingness to admit when she's struggling to understand modern technology.

2. F
Difficulty: Low
Category: Inference
Getting to the Answer: The clue words "it can be reasonably inferred" indicate that this is an Inference question. Review the referenced lines and those immediately around them. Based on the paragraph, you might predict that Betty believes the target market for those things shown on daytime TV commercials are older people who might be more likely to have health or mobility issues. This matches (F).

Choice G is too extreme; there is nothing to indicate Betty believes people who are retired are the marketing demographic of the commercials. Choices H and J are out of scope; there is no way to know whether Betty has considered buying any of the things advertised or whether her granddaughter would want them.

3. B
Difficulty: Medium
Category: Function
Getting to the Answer: "Describes . . . in order to" should stand out as a clue that this is a Function question. Review your passage notes. Predict that the correct answer will show that Betty's waking-up process is slow because she's so very old. Choice (B) is correct.

Choice A can be eliminated because the two situations are not set up in contrast to one another. Choice C is too extreme; while this is true of Betty, you can't say for sure that the same is true of all older people. Choice D has the same problem as A. While both waking up and returning to bed are described, they are not presented as parallels to one another.

4. F
Difficulty: Low
Category: Inference
Getting to the Answer: The word *inferred* in the question makes it pretty straightforward to identify the question type: it's Inference! Look back to the

referenced lines. Predict that the correct answer will address the fact that tables with linoleum surfaces and aluminum legs are no longer popular. Choice (F) is correct.

There is no information in the passage to support the other answer choices. Just because Betty has an old table does not mean all furniture from the past was made to last longer, so G is out. While Betty's son might get her a new table and chairs, there's nothing to indicate it is likely, so you can eliminate H. Finally, while the passage says Betty's table is made of two different materials that seem to no longer be a popular choice, that does not prevent modern tables from being made of two different materials, as J says.

5.   D
Difficulty: Low
Category: Inference
Getting to the Answer: "Most accurately describes" indicates that this is an Inference question. Refer to your notes to find out where the doctor is mentioned: in the third paragraph. Predict that the correct answer will indicate that Betty considered what the doctor might say, but then decided it didn't matter because she wasn't going to tell him and neither was anyone else. That matches (D).

Choice A might be tempting if you consider that she thinks about what her doctor would say at the same point in the passage where the second cup is mentioned, but there is no indication that she feels guilty while having that second cup. Choice B is not supported by the passage, because clearly she is thinking of it. Finally, C is not supported because no link is made between the coffee maker her son got her and her attitude toward the doctor.

6.   H
Difficulty: High
Category: Function
Getting to the Answer: The phrase "One of the primary purposes" should serve as a clue that this is a Function question. The question wants to know why a particular paragraph was included in the passage. Review your notes on the sixth paragraph and predict that the paragraph was included to show another example of something, like the coffee maker described earlier, that Betty considers unnecessary in her life because she already has something that serves the same purpose. Choice (H) is correct.

Be careful of the incorrect choices on this one, though! They might all be tempting in different ways. The paragraph does highlight a difference between Betty's life and that of her granddaughter: they have different types of cell phones. That's not the reason why the paragraph was included, however, so F is out. For G, while Betty herself seems to believe there's no reason to have a cell phone, this would not be considered a factual reason—it's just her opinion. Finally, in J, while Betty doesn't see the need to change her own technology, there is nothing to indicate she opposes it progressing for the rest of the world.

7.   B
Difficulty: Low
Category: Function
Getting to the Answer: "The author uses" indicates this is a Function question. Refer back to the final paragraph. The word *safe* comes before *knowledge*—the knowledge that tomorrow will be the same as the day Betty has just experienced. Predict that the word is used to emphasize that she likes each day being the same. This matches (B).

Both A and C are out of scope; nothing is said in the passage about crime or about what Betty thinks will happen while she's asleep. And while D is implied to be true, that isn't the reason why the author uses the word *safe*.

8.   G
Difficulty: Medium
Category: Detail
Getting to the Answer: Since this question asks about particular events, it is a Detail question. Review your notes to make sure you remember the order in which things occurred in Betty's life. There's no way to predict, so review the answer choices and figure out which came first.

Choice F happened while Betty was an adult, but we don't know exactly when. Choice (G) came before F (as it happened during Betty's childhood), so F must be incorrect. Choice H happened in the passage, so it came after both F and (G) and must therefore be incorrect. J does not happen at any particular time in the passage, but definitely happened after the author's childhood, so (G) is the correct choice.

9. A
Difficulty: Medium
Category: Inference
Getting to the Answer: The clue words "what can reasonably be inferred" tell you this is an Inference question. Review the lines listed to make your prediction: Betty seems to have enjoyed helping out in her father's shop, and she believes, based on the news, that things are different now than they were when she was young, though no evidence is given to support this. Choice (A) is correct.

There is nothing in the passage to support the idea that Betty feels she was forced to work too young; if anything, as mentioned above, she seems to have enjoyed the work. So, B is incorrect. In C, while she does seem to believe the world was a safer and better place when she was young, there's nothing in the passage to indicate nothing ever went wrong for her then. Finally, in D, nothing in the passage supports the idea that she doesn't remember her childhood well.

10. J
Difficulty: Low
Category: Vocab-in-Context
Getting to the Answer: "Most nearly means" should tell you this is a Vocab-in-Context question. How is the word *rhythm* used in this passage? In the first paragraph, the *rhythm* is each day being like the last. This matches (J). While F, G, and H might also be described as a rhythm, they don't fit in with the way the word is used in the context of the passage.

How Much Have You Learned?

Suggested Passage Map Notes:

¶1: narrator's cats comfortable, narr. wonders if they know it

¶2: Reginald: stray cat who had hard life

¶3: R sweet anyway, neighborhood cares for him

¶4: narr. cats vs. R

¶5: children play w/ R

¶6: winter care

¶7: R disappears; narr. hopes he had easy death

¶8–10: narr. compares own cats' lives to R's life, hopes they would still be happy

¶11–12: narr. hopes for happy afterlife for R

BIG PICTURE SUMMARY

Main idea: Reginald is a beloved neighborhood cat whose life is very different from the narrator's own pets.

Author's purpose: To compare the life experiences of a friendly neighborhood cat with the lives of the narrator's house cats

1. C
Difficulty: Medium
Category: Global
Getting to the Answer: "The passage as a whole" indicates that this is a Global question. Review your notes and predict that the correct answer will be something that includes the author discussing both Reginald and the author's cats. That matches (C).

While the author does consider how hard it is for stray cats, as well as how her cats are different from Reginald, neither A nor B encompasses the passage as a whole. Finally, while the author does say that Reginald was cared for by the neighborhood, there is no exploration of human nature, knocking out D.

2. F
Difficulty: Medium
Category: Inference
Getting to the Answer: The clue words "seems to believe" signal that this is an Inference question. Review your notes: the author seems to believe Reginald was content with his way of life. Choice (F) is the best match for this.

There is nothing to indicate that Reginald was *begrudging*, or that he was acting as he did in order to gain something for himself, which eliminates G. He seems to have been the opposite of wary, which eliminates H. And he wasn't greedy, he was just, as the author says, "an outdoorsman" who preferred not to choose one place to call home, which eliminates J.

3. B
Difficulty: Low
Category: Function
Getting to the Answer: "Primary purpose" serves as a clue that this is a Function question. Refer back to those lines in the passage. Predict that the author describes her own cats to show how different they were from Reginald. This matches (B).

While the author is writing about how different her cats are from Reginald, she doesn't explain why in the referenced lines, which eliminates A. The author is highlighting differences, not similarities, which eliminates C. Finally, you can eliminate D because while the author does go on to describe how Reginald behaved when her cats were posturing and offers a potential explanation why, she is not yet discussing that explanation in the referenced lines.

4.   H
Difficulty: Medium
Category: Inference
Getting to the Answer: The words "reasonable to conclude" should clue you in that this is an Inference question. The author says that "it breaks my heart to think of them going through what he went through," so predict that the correct answer is related to that. The best match for the prediction is (H).

While the author does mention in that paragraph the possibility of not being able to care for her cats, she doesn't say that she expects this to happen, as in F. There is nothing in the passage to indicate she feels it is an obligation to care for them, as in G. Finally, while she worries that they would potentially struggle to care for themselves, this is not the reason why she cares for them, as in J.

5.   A
Difficulty: Low
Category: Vocab-in-Context
Getting to the Answer: The phrase "most nearly means" indicates that this is a Vocab-in-Context question. Refer back to the line in question. The author is discussing a painless death for Reginald, so predict that *blessing* is used to mean something like "favor." This matches (A).

While B, C, and D are all acceptable definitions of *blessing*, none of them match the way in which the author of the passage uses the word.

6.   G
Difficulty: Low
Category: Function
Getting to the Answer: "Primarily in order to" indicates this is a Function question. Refer back to the referenced lines and those around them. Predict that the author describes Reginald's appearance in order to contrast it with his friendly personality. This matches (G).

Choice F is a distortion; rather than his appearance matching his behavior, Reginald's appearance was in contrast to how he behaved. In H, while Reginald's appearance does indicate he had not lived an easy life, this isn't *why* the author described his appearance. Choice J is not supported by the passage at all; the author, if anything, seems to believe that Reginald deserved better than what he had gotten from life.

7.   B
Difficulty: Medium
Category: Function
Getting to the Answer: "In order to" signals that this is a Function question. Why does the author describe Reginald as an *outdoorsman*? This is a word that would normally be used to describe a person, but it is in this case used to describe a cat. This matches (B).

Choice A is not supported because the passage says nothing about Reginald's behavior when inside as opposed to outside. While Reginald is described as a neighborhood cat, this is not why the author uses the term *outdoorsman*, eliminating choice C. And in choice D, the author never indicates that Reginald would not have been welcomed into the house, just that he chose to remain outdoors.

8.   F
Difficulty: Medium
Category: Global
Getting to the Answer: The clue words "passage as a whole" indicate this is a Global question. It is often difficult to make specific predictions about Global questions, so go choice by choice, eliminating as you go.

Choice (F) is supported by the passage: the author mentions several times how much Reginald seemed to appreciate anything that was given to him. Choice G might or might not be true; though the author discusses Reginald having scars, she does not provide evidence that he got into fights. Choice H is too extreme. While the author says Reginald seemed to play a monster for the children, there is nothing to indicate he understood the games they played generally. Choice J, like G, might or might not be true. The author says nothing about Reginald's ability to understand he was not a house cat.

Reading

9. D
Difficulty: Low
Category: Function
Getting to the Answer: The clue words "the primary purpose" indicate this is a Function question. Refer back to the lines referenced in the passage. Predict that the correct answer will indicate that the children did not truly believe they needed to run away from Reginald. This matches (D), the correct answer.

The author makes it clear that Reginald's appearance did not match his demeanor, eliminating A. The idea that Reginald was only sometimes friendly around children is not supported by the passage, eliminating B. And the author did not discuss the children's behavior in order to show that it changes in different circumstances, eliminating C.

10. H
Difficulty: Low
Category: Inference
Getting to the Answer: The phrase "based on the passage" indicates this is an Inference question. Refer to your notes to get an idea of how Reginald's personality impacted his life, and predict that his affectionate nature meant he became a cat everyone in the neighborhood helped care for. This matches (H), the correct answer.

There is nothing to indicate people "begrudgingly" cared for him out of sympathy, which eliminates F. Similarly, nothing in the passage supports the idea that he became affectionate only reluctantly, eliminating G. Finally, while the passage supports that Reginald was popular with the neighborhood children, nothing indicates that he wasn't also popular with the adults (the passage author seems to be an adult), eliminating J.

PAIRED PASSAGES

How Much Do You Know?

Directions: In this chapter, you'll learn to apply the ACT Reading strategies you've learned to paired passages. Take 9 minutes to read the following paired passages and answer the 10 accompanying questions. When you're finished, compare your work to that of an ACT expert on the following pages. Identify ways in which the expert reads these paired passages differently than she would an independent passage.

HUMANITIES: Passage A is adapted from an online article about the difficulty women have historically had being successfully published using their own names. Passage B is adapted from an essay about the history of anonymous works.

Passage A

In 1913, modernist author Virginia Woolf wrote an essay for the *Times Literary Supplement*, originally published anonymously. In this essay, she discusses a particular phenomenon suffered by
5 female writers of the past: a lack of respect within their lifetimes for their talents. She frames this essay around Jane Austen, who was, during Woolf's lifetime, in the midst of a resurgence of popularity.

It is difficult to imagine two writers more
10 different from one another than Woolf, who lived from 1886 to 1941, and Austen, who died in 1817, more than half a century before Woolf was born; Woolf's labyrinthine, stream-of-consciousness style and arduous prose stands in sharp contrast
15 to Austen's witty social commentaries masked as lighthearted novels. In the essay, while Woolf clearly respects Austen as a writer, she does criticize what she perceives as timidity in Austen's writing. Woolf refers at one point to Austen removing a
20 hedge from one of her novels when she found out they didn't grow where the story is set, "rather than run the risk of inventing one which could not exist." Austen, Woolf believed, was too afraid to test boundaries.

25 But consider this belief in light of another essay by Woolf. In 1929's "A Room of One's Own," she discusses a proverbial sister of William Shakespeare, equal in genius and equal in desire to make her living as a playwright but prevented from doing
30 so because she is a woman. Until the nineteenth century, Woolf says, it was almost impossible for a woman to become a successful writer. This was because, "unless her parents were exceptionally rich or very noble" and gave their blessing, she was

35 unlikely to have the opportunities necessary to develop her craft.

This second essay potentially sheds light on Austen and her writing style. In "A Room of One's Own," Woolf discusses how limited life must have
40 been for women in the past. Jane Austen, who began her professional writing career in 1811 and died in 1817, never married, and while she was educated, it would have been a far more limited education than a wealthy man would have received
45 at the same time. She was forced to publish her works anonymously, even when they proved popular. As Woolf herself famously wrote, "I would venture to guess that Anon . . . was often a woman."

Should it come as a surprise, then, under the
50 conditions of Austen's upbringing and career, that she was rather rigid and conservative in the way she told her stories? It was hard enough for her to be published at all. She did not have the wealth or the increased freedoms of Woolf, writing a
55 century later. Whether Woolf is right or wrong in her criticism of Austen as a timid writer, it is surely easily understood why, based on Woolf's own 1929 essay, Austen chose to write as she did.

Passage B

In 1967, Roland Barthes, a French literary critic,
60 wrote an essay entitled "La mort de l'auteur," "The Death of the Author." In the essay, Barthes makes the argument that authors and their works should be considered entirely separately from one another: a text should be interpreted on its own terms, rather
65 than through a lens of biographical scrutiny.

But what of the other form of "death of the author": the infamous Anonymous, authors who published with no credit given to them for their craft? Books now considered to be classics that were
70 originally published anonymously include Mary Shelley's *Frankenstein* and the works of Jane Austen.

And who is Mary Ann Evans? Likely, few would immediately recognize her name, but many would be able to come up with at least one work written by
75 George Eliot. This was Evans' pen name, employed because she wanted her works to be taken seriously rather than dismissed as the light romances that were then believed to be the sole purview of female writers. When the Brontë sisters sought publication,
80 they too did so under anonymity; Charlotte, Emily, and Anne Brontë became in print the masculine-sounding Currer, Ellis, and Acton Bell.

Now certainly, authorial anonymity is not limited to women. While many women published
85 anonymous works because use of their own names might result in dismissal of the seriousness of their work or even outright rejection from publishers, some men, including such well-known figures as Edgar Allan Poe, Thomas Paine, Alexander
90 Hamilton, and James Madison, published anonymously at various points in their careers to avoid the risk of personal consequences or concerns. It is even true that women could, in rare, lucky circumstances, find success under their own
95 names: Ann Radcliffe, for instance, was one of the most successful authors of the late 1700s, writing wildly popular Gothic fiction.

Regardless of Radcliffe's unusual success, however, it is clear that many women who
100 sought a career in writing in the Georgian and Victorian eras felt the need to disguise who they truly were, or were compelled to do so by publishers afraid of public reception. "Death of the author," in these cases, often meant that
105 women in writing only had their true identities, and the associated respect they might earn from their talent, revealed after their own quite literal deaths.

1. In Passage A, Woolf's choice to publish her 1913 essay anonymously while criticizing Austen as a timid writer could best be described as:

A. hypocritical; Austen had a choice and still chose anonymity, while Woolf did not.

B. ironic; Woolf was criticizing behavior that could be called very similar to her own.

C. symbolic; Woolf likely chose anonymity as a point of solidarity with women in Austen's time.

D. modernistic; Woolf used her own novel-writing techniques to showcase Austen's.

2. Which of the following statements best explains why the author chose, in lines 40–47 of Passage A, to showcase particular aspects of Austen's personal life and education?

F. The author is attempting to convey why Austen might have written in a manner that could be called "timid."

G. The author uses details to evoke feelings of sympathy in the reader in order to make them appreciate Austen's work as superior to Woolf's.

H. The author is trying to make Austen appear to be a better writer than she might seem merely from her "rigid and conservative" novels.

J. The author provides details in order to later compare and contrast Austen's life with Woolf's.

3. As it is used in line 14, the word *sharp* most nearly means:

A. raised and pitchy.

B. razor-like and dangerous.

C. abrupt and unexpected.

D. notable and different.

4. In the third paragraph of Passage B, the author mentions other reasons some authors have chosen to publish anonymously primarily in order to:

   F. establish the notion that women have never chosen to publish anonymously, but some men have chosen to do so.

   G. set up a contrast between the common reasons men and women were published anonymously in the past.

   H. entertain the idea that while both men and women have published anonymously, more men do it than women.

   J. showcase the possibility that there are better reasons to choose to publish anonymously than public reaction.

5. In Passage B, it can most reasonably be inferred that Ann Radcliffe's success as an author might best be attributed to:

   A. being a female author at a time when those were rare.

   B. having her real name attached to her works.

   C. writing in a genre that was then very popular.

   D. publishing under a pen name everyone at the time recognized.

6. Based on the information in the first paragraph of Passage B, it can be most reasonably inferred that Roland Barthes believed:

   F. women were not given enough credit for their writing talent in past centuries.

   G. knowing the details of a writer's life is not necessary for literary criticism.

   H. only after an author dies can someone truly criticize their written works.

   J. men and women often published anonymously for different reasons.

7. The purpose of the information in lines 72–82 of Passage B is to:

   A. provide additional information on why women might be forced to publish anonymously.

   B. offer a contrast between women who publish as Anonymous and those who use pen names.

   C. set up a comparison between women and men who publish anonymously.

   D. show that in some cases women adopted male pen names in order to be more commercially successful writers.

8. Compared to Passage B, Passage A is more directly focused on:

   F. literary essays about an author who is discussed in the passage.

   G. the similarities between the works of two anonymous authors.

   H. an overarching theory that explains all anonymous texts.

   J. the importance of considering authors apart from their life context.

9. Passage B expands upon which of the following details from Passage A?

    A. men in the past might publish anonymously for the same reasons women often did.

    B. women in the past sometimes published anonymously.

    C. Jane Austen chose to remain an anonymous author during her lifetime.

    D. women in the past often chose masculine-sounding pen names.

10. In 1818, Jane Austen's *Northanger Abbey* was published. It parodied Gothic fiction like that of Ann Radcliffe. In light of the passages, it can most reasonably be inferred that this work:

    F. is one example of the "resurgence of popularity" (line 8) that Austen enjoyed before her death in 1817.

    G. was published with Austen's name attached since it was published posthumously.

    H. is further evidence that Gothic fiction was very popular during Austen's lifetime.

    J. is further evidence that women might choose to publish anonymously if writing subversively.

Reading

Check Your Work

Suggested Passage Map Notes:

Passage A:

¶1: VW essay about disrespected female writers and JA

¶2: contrasts between VW & JA, VW criticism of JA

¶3: 2nd VW essay: hard for past female writers

¶4–5: 2nd essay relates to JA

Passage B:

¶1: RB: "death of the author" – separate writer & text

¶2: author: "death of the author" – female writers stuck w/ anonymity

¶3: men sometimes anon, but not b/c had to be

¶4: female writers only get credit after death

BIG PICTURE SUMMARY

Passage A:

Main idea: The limited social approval of female writers may explain why Jane Austen did not take many risks in her writing.

Author's purpose: To defend Jane Austen against Woolf's earlier criticism using Woolf's argument in "A Room of One's Own"

Passage B:

Main idea: Many female authors wrote under male pseudonyms because they would not have been taken seriously otherwise.

Author's purpose: To explain why some authors, especially female authors, published anonymously

---

1. B
Difficulty: High
Category: Inference
Getting to the Answer: The phrase "could best be described as" gives you the clues necessary to identify this as an Inference question. Predict that the correct answer will recognize that Woolf was also being a "timid" writer in choosing anonymity even as she criticized the same in Austen. This matches (B).

While Woolf's behavior might be called hypocritical, as in A, the second part flips the situation: it was Woolf who had a choice, not Austen. In C, there is no evidence given for symbolism in Woolf's essay or in her choice to remain anonymous when it was published. Finally, in D, while Woolf's novel-writing techniques are discussed, the passage does not say she used those particular techniques in showcasing Austen's.

2. F
Difficulty: Medium
Category: Function
Getting to the Answer: The phrase "why the author chose . . . to showcase" indicates this is a Function question. Refer back to that part of the passage to refresh your memory. Predict that the correct answer will show that these details were included to support the idea that it was very difficult for women who wrote in Austen's time, which might help explain the style that Woolf criticizes. This matches (F).

In G, while the author could be said to be attempting to evoke sympathy, she is not trying to make one writer appear superior to the other. Nor does the author attempt to prove that Austen is a better writer than her novels make her appear, which eliminates H. Finally, in J, while the author does point out some of the differences for women in Austen's time and in Woolf's in the passage, that was not why the author included the details referenced in the question.

3. D
Difficulty: Low
Category: Vocab-in-Context
Getting to the Answer: "Most nearly means" tells you that this is a Vocab-in-Context question. Refer back to the line referenced. *Sharp* here refers to contrast—the author of the passage is discussing how different Woolf and Austen's writing is from one another. This matches (D), which is correct.

Note, however, that all the incorrect answer choices are acceptable definitions of *sharp*. Always make sure it is clear in your mind how the author is using a word with multiple definitions before you start looking at the answer choices!

4.   G
Difficulty: Medium
Category: Function
Getting to the Answer: Use the clue words "primarily in order to" to establish that this is a Function question. Refer back to the paragraph referenced, and read paragraph 3 for additional context. Predict that the correct answer will show that the author of the passage was acknowledging that men were also published anonymously, but it was by choice, whereas women were either forced into anonymity by publishers or chose it in order for their work to be taken seriously. Choice (G) matches this prediction, and is correct.

Choice F is too extreme. There is nothing to indicate that women have never made the choice to publish anonymously. Choice H is out of scope; the passage does not discuss whether more men or women publish anonymously. Finally, J is a distortion. The author's intent is to create a contrast between reasons to publish anonymously, not to prove that reasons other than public reaction are preferable.

5.   C
Difficulty: Low
Category: Inference
Getting to the Answer: The phrase "most reasonably be inferred" indicates that this is an Inference question. Refer to the third paragraph of Passage B, where Radcliffe is discussed. Predict that the correct answer will show that Radcliffe's success can be attributed to her writing popular Gothic fiction. This matches (C), which is correct.

Choices A and B are both distortions; female authors *were* rare at the time, and Radcliffe's choice to have her real name attached to her works was unusual, but her success came despite those things, not because of them. Choice D is simply factually incorrect, based on the information in the passage: Radcliffe was the rare exception, a successful female writer in the 1700s despite not using a pen name or publishing anonymously.

6.   G
Difficulty: Low
Category: Inference
Getting to the Answer: The phrase "most reasonably inferred" offers you clues to identify this as an Inference question. Refer back to the first paragraph to refresh your memory on Barthes's beliefs. Predict that the

correct answer will show that Barthes believed an author's work and their biography should be kept separate. This matches (G).

While F is part of the passage, it is not something Barthes necessarily believed. For H, Barthes was referring to "death" in a metaphorical sense, not a literal one. And J, like F, is in the passage, but the information in the passage does not suggest that Barthes believed this.

7.   D
Difficulty: Medium
Category: Function
Getting to the Answer: "The purpose of the information" tells you that this is a Function question. The author initially discusses women who published anonymously, but in the lines referenced, goes on to list some who adopted masculine-sounding pen names instead. Predict the correct answer will reflect this. The correct answer, then, is (D).

Choice A is incorrect because the lines referenced do not discuss why women might be forced to publish anonymously. It specifically mentions that in these cases, women chose to use male-sounding pen names. Choice B is incorrect because no contrast was given between the two groups. Choice C is incorrect because the information was not given in order to set up a comparison.

8.   F
Difficulty: High
Category: Global
Getting to the Answer: Since the question asks you to compare the focuses of the two passages, this is a Global question. Consult your big picture summaries of both passages, and think about how they compare. Passage A is concerned with responding to Woolf's literary criticism of Jane Austen using another of Woolf's own essays about the difficulty of being a woman writer in the past. Passage B discusses how common it was, especially for women authors, to write anonymously; the passage also explains various reasons for anonymity. Analyze the choices to find the one that reflects the focus of Passage A. Choice (F) is correct; Passage A uses Woolf's literary essays to discuss Austen.

Choice G is incorrect because it distorts the details in Passage A; although the passage identifies that both Woolf (at least for her essay in the *Times Literary Supplement*) and Austen wrote anonymously, the passage only emphasizes the differences between their works. Choices H and J are incorrect because they better reflect Passage B. For H, Passage B discusses anonymous writing, though not an overarching theory about the practice. Choice J refers to Barthes's "death of the author" argument that is mentioned in Passage B.

9.   B
Difficulty: Medium
Category: Detail
Getting to the Answer: The phrase "which of the following details" signals that this is a Detail question. It is difficult to make a prediction based on such a broad question, so review each answer choice, knocking out incorrect answers as you go.

While Passage B does discuss men publishing anonymously, this is not discussed at all in Passage A. Choice A is incorrect. Choice (B) is supported by the passages: Passage A mentions that Woolf wrote an essay anonymously and that Austen was forced into anonymous publication. Passage B gives information on some of the potential reasons why women wrote anonymously.

So (B) is correct. Choice C is not supported at all by Passage A, which specifically mentions that Austen was forced to publish anonymously, not that she chose to do so. Choice D, like A, is discussed in Passage B but is not mentioned at all In Passage A.

10.   H
Difficulty: Medium
Category: Inference
Getting to the Answer: The clue words "most reasonably be inferred" indicate that this is an Inference question. In Passage B, Radcliffe is discussed as a rare example of a successful female author who wrote under her own name. She was successful because the genre she was writing in was very popular. Predict that Austen's writing a parody of that genre is further evidence of its popularity. This matches (H).

Choice F is a distortion; there was a "resurgence of popularity" during Woolf's lifetime, which was well after Austen died. While both passages say Austen was published anonymously, no information is given about when her name began to be associated with her works; G is incorrect. There is also no mention in either passage of women writing subversively, so J is also incorrect.

HOW TO APPROACH ACT PAIRED PASSAGES

LEARNING OBJECTIVES

After this lesson, you will be able to:

- Apply unique strategies to effectively read ACT Reading paired passages in preparation for their question sets
- Identify the variations on common ACT Reading questions as they are used in paired passages

What are paired passages?

Typically, one pair of shorter passages take the place of a single longer passage in the ACT Reading section. Occasionally, all four passages on an ACT Reading Test will be independent passages, but you should be prepared to encounter a paired passage set on test day.

The two passages share the same topic (although each will usually have its own take on the subject matter). The combined length of the paired passages is approximately the length of most single passages, so you don't have much, if any, extra reading to do.

In this chapter, you'll learn how ACT experts actively read paired passages a little differently than they read single passages, and you'll see how the test uses variations of standard ACT Reading questions to test your comprehension of both passages.

To read passages and answer questions like these:

NATURAL SCIENCE: Passage A is adapted from a magazine article about recent technological efforts in conservation. Passage B is adapted from an online article about the success of using artificial intelligence to stop poachers.

Passage A

Conservationists are struggling to address the decimation of a growing number of plant and animal species due to environmental and human-made circumstances. Protecting the Earth's
5 biodiversity requires a better understanding of the behavior of animals in their natural habitats and the factors leading to their decline; this is one aspect of conservation where technology can lend a hand. Artificial intelligence, commonly referred
10 to as AI, has proved to be an important resource in the fight to protect species that already are, or might soon qualify as, endangered. The ability of AI to rapidly process large quantities of data makes it ideal for analyzing the decades
15 of extensive tracking information researchers have gathered. More importantly, AI may reveal patterns that might not be readily discernible solely through human analysis.

The cheetah population in sub-Saharan Africa
20 is a specific example of a species that has faced severe threats on several fronts. From 1900 to 2015, cheetahs saw an estimated 93% decline in population. This same time period also saw a 76% reduction in land that was formerly classified
25 as cheetah habitat. Additionally, smuggling and common misperceptions about the dangers of cheetahs to livestock exacerbated the population decline. Initially, as conservationists began to realize the need to protect cheetahs in their native
30 habitat, they focused on centuries-old tracking techniques. More recently, however, researchers have recognized how effective AI can be in conservation efforts.

Starting in 2001, the WildTrack team of
researchers worked with statistical analysis software
development companies JMP and SAS to create
the Footprint Identification Technique, or FIT.
Conservationists collected several high-quality
digital images—footprints in the sand, snow, mud,
and other natural substrates—and uploaded these
images into the JMP software. The researchers then
selected landmark points to form a basic outline of
each footprint. AI extrapolates more details from
the footprint, which is then assigned as a unique
identifier for that specific cheetah. This non-
invasive "digital tag" is then used in combination
with GPS to precisely track individual cheetahs in
their natural habitat.

This same technology can be used to identify
and track a variety of endangered or vulnerable
species (the WildTrack team has developed
algorithms for more than 15 species). Progressive
learning algorithms, which allow the AI to use
mathematical models to identify species, sex, and
age-class, become more accurate as the amount of
established data grows. Conservation experts can
use the collected data to predict the movements of
isolated populations, track births and deaths within
the population, and determine the best locations
for reintroducing species to their native habitat.
With so much work still to be done to protect the
Earth's endangered species, conservationists are
embracing the power of AI and looking for even
more sophisticated applications in the future.

Passage B

For years, wildlife reserves and the animals
who live there have been under attack. Poaching,
the illegal hunting and capturing of wild animals,
is the leading human cause of the severe decline
in numbers of certain species. Many poachers use
technology to aid them in their illegal activity. For
example, some poachers track elephants and rhinos
using GPS and night-vision goggles and kill them
for their tusks and horns. Conservation officials
are working to counter these attacks by applying
AI-modeling; the sheer size of most wildlife reserves

requires a technologically advanced approach to
most effectively protect the animals from poachers.

The Protection Assistant for Wildlife Security
(PAWS) program employs machine learning and
behavior modeling to aid wildlife reserve patrols.
By combining data about previous poaching
activity and patrol routes, the system can predict
where future poaching will likely take place and
design continuously changing patrol routes using
game-theory modeling. The constant variations of
the routes prevent poachers from picking up on
patterns, which in turn increases the chance of
catching poachers in the act. PAWS manages to
seamlessly blend machine learning with human
knowledge: the algorithm provides a few different
routes, and patrollers can choose the best one
based on their years of experience working to
prevent poaching.

Another aspect of the patrols that benefits from
technology is route optimization that accounts
for the terrain. While a substantial quantity of
data, gathered over years of conservation work,
exists about the most trafficked routes of animals
frequently targeted by poachers, past patrol routes
often involved climbs or descents that greatly
limited the amount of land secured by regular
patrols. Now AI can calculate the best routes
for both the human patrollers and the drones
in order to maximize the patrolled area. During
an eight-month trial of the program at Uganda's
Queen Elizabeth National Park, rangers found
approximately 10 times as many poachers in
areas designated as high-probability versus low-
probability by the algorithm.

Those taking the lead in the efforts to end
poaching for good sincerely hope that the
AI-enhanced patrol routes will serve as a significant
deterrent for poachers. As AI systems continue to
find more effective solutions through data analysis,
conservation experts feel confident that, with the
help of technology, they can win the battle against
poachers.

1. According to Passage A, AI is a valuable conservation resource because:

    A. it allows conservation officials to thwart attacks by poachers.

    B. it can allow researchers to uncover norms that human analysis might miss.

    C. it can calculate patrol routes for human and drone patrollers.

    D. it is the best way for researchers to protect endangered species.

2. The author of Passage A most likely mentions the statistics referenced in lines 21–25 in order to show:

    F. how AI has helped the cheetah population recover.

    G. how soon cheetahs will become extinct.

    H. how AI has helped prevent cheetahs from being attacked by poachers.

    J. how serious the threat facing the cheetah population is.

3. In Passage A, it can most reasonably be inferred that the decline in cheetah populations is due largely to:

    A. poachers attacking the cheetahs at an unprecedented rate.

    B. loss of land in natural cheetah habitats.

    C. tracking cheetahs using the Footprint Identification Technique.

    D. famine and drought, resulting in a lack of food for cheetah populations.

4. Passage A most strongly suggests that the Footprint Identification Technique:

    F. could be used to help other vulnerable species.

    G. will be used to save all species from extinction.

    H. will combine machine learning and human expertise.

    J. could be used to calculate future algorithms to track poachers.

5. As it is used in line 74, the word *counter* most nearly means:

    A. to oppose.

    B. to promote.

    C. to ignore.

    D. to tally.

6. According to Passage B, which of the following techniques does PAWS utilize to aid conservation officials in protecting animals from poachers?

    F. It uses centuries-old tracking techniques to find poachers.

    G. It uses an algorithm to provide only the best route to track poachers.

    H. It combines human knowledge with computer learning to give patrollers options.

    J. It uses a non-invasive digital tag to track animals.

7. It can most reasonably be inferred that the author of Passage B uses the phrase "win the battle" (line 116) to refer to the hope that wildlife reserves will eventually be:

    A. ignored by both poachers and conservation officials alike.

    B. emptied of wild animals after being overrun by poachers.

    C. completely protected with the help of AI.

    D. managed in a way that balances the needs of all groups.

8. Passage A and Passage B are similar in that they both support the use of AI to:

    F. limit the negative effect poachers are having on certain wildlife populations.

    G. preserve the natural habitats of species that are experiencing population decline.

    H. eliminate the need for human intervention in the protection of wildlife.

    J. protect wildlife species from the threats causing population decline.

9. Compared to the author of Passage A, the author of Passage B provides more information about:

   A. using AI to track species in their native habitats.

   B. using AI-enhanced technology against poachers.

   C. using machine learning to aid in conservation education.

   D. using AI to calculate large quantities of data.

10. It can be reasonably inferred that after learning about AI capabilities such as the Footprint Identification Technique, the conservationists described in Passage B would likely:

   F. utilize these capabilities to aid in catching poachers.

   G. dismiss these capabilities as unnecessary.

   H. praise these capabilities as revolutionary.

   J. question the ethical nature of these capabilities.

You need to know this:

Paired passages always address the same topic but will likely have different purposes and may reflect different opinions. Common relationships between the passages include:

- (Passage A) An excerpt from a piece of literature, and (Passage B) a related essay by the same author
- (Passage A) A history of an issue and/or a person, and (Passage B) a commentary on or evaluation of the same issue or person
- (Passage A) A report on an event or conflict, and (Passage B) a report on a different-but-related event or conflict
- (Passage A) Commentary on an issue as reflected through one context, and (Passage B) commentary on the same issue reflected through a different context

The authors of paired passages may disagree with each other but do not have to.

When paired passages refer to the same detail, each author may have a different reason for including the detail and a different point of view toward it.

The question set accompanying paired passages addresses the passages in order: roughly, the first third of the questions are about Passage A, the next third are about Passage B, and the final third are about the relationships between the two passages.

The questions that address single passages are just like those from standard science and social science passages.

Some questions that address the relationships between the passages are variations on standard ACT Reading question types.

You need to do this:

Unpack the blurb to discover all that you can about each passage and author; anticipate the possible relationships between the passages.

Manage your active reading and the question set strategically by completing the following steps:

- Actively read Passage A as you would a standard passage—note keywords, jot down the purpose of each paragraph, and summarize the big picture.
- Answer the questions associated exclusively with Passage A (roughly, the first third of the question set).

- Actively read Passage B as you would a standard passage—note keywords, jot down the purpose of each paragraph, and summarize the big picture.
- Answer the questions associated exclusively with Passage B (roughly, the next third of the question set).
- Answer the questions that ask about both passages in relationship to each other (the final third of the question set).

Research, predict, and answer questions exclusively addressing one of the passages as you would any standard ACT Reading question.

When answering questions that address the relationships between the passages, keep the following strategies in mind:

- To predict and answer Global questions comparing or contrasting both passages, consider your big picture summaries.
- To research, predict, and answer Inference questions comparing or contrasting both passages:
  - Locate the piece of text at issue in the question stem.
  - Consider the other author's likely reaction to or opinion of that piece of text. Locate the piece of text that supplies the other author's likely response.

Explanations

Suggested Passage Map Notes:

Passage A:

¶1: AI helpful for conservation

¶2: cheetah conservation situation

¶3: FIT: AI used to track cheetah footprints

¶4: FIT helpful for other species also

Passage B:

¶1: using AI to counter poachers

¶2: PAWS: AI helps suggest varied patrol routes

¶3: AI considers terrain, plans patrols for max effectiveness

¶4: conservationists hopeful

BIG PICTURE SUMMARY

Passage A:

Main idea: AI technology helps environmentalists preserve endangered animal species by gathering data about their movements.

Author's purpose: To describe how AI technology aids in tracking endangered animals

Passage B:

Main idea: AI technology makes anti-poaching wildlife patrols more effective by generating unpredictable patrol routes using game theory and by optimizing patrol routes for the given terrain.

Author's purpose: To describe how AI technology can assist environmentalists in countering poachers

1. B
Difficulty: Medium
Category: Detail
Getting to the Answer: The phrase "according to Passage A" shows that this is a Detail question, so it is important to check the passage for support. The end of the first paragraph tells us that AI can process large quantities of data, but, more importantly, it may reveal patterns that human analysis may miss. This matches (B) nicely.

Choices A and C reference information from Passage B. Choice D is extreme; beware of words like "best" or "worst." The passage talks about the benefits of AI but never states that it is the best way to protect endangered species.

2. J
Difficulty: Medium
Category: Function
Getting to the Answer: The wording "the author . . . in order to" tells us that this is a Function question. Paragraph 2 begins by stating that the cheetah population has faced severe threats. It tells us that from 1900–2015, the cheetah population saw a 93% decline in population and a 76% reduction in habitat. These statistics, then, serve to demonstrate the severity of the threat to the cheetah population. Choice (J) is correct.

Choice F is the opposite of what the statistics show; the cheetah population is in decline, not recovery. Choice G is extreme, as the passage never states that the cheetah will become extinct. Choice H refers to information from Passage B.

3. B
Difficulty: Medium
Category: Inference
Getting to the Answer: "It can most reasonably be inferred" is a phrase that indicates an Inference question. The correct answer will require you to link together facts in the passage to form a conclusion. The passage tells you that the cheetah population is in decline due to several factors, but, at the same time that the 93% population decline occurred, there was a 76% loss of cheetah habitat—a significant statistic. You can conclude, then, that the decline is largely due to the loss of land, which matches (B).

Choice A refers to information in Passage B. Choice C does as well, and it is a misused detail; the Footprint Identification Technique was used to help the cheetah population, not hurt it. Choice D is out of scope; drought and famine were not discussed in this passage.

4. F
Difficulty: Medium
Category: Inference
Getting to the Answer: Inference questions often contain the phrase "most strongly suggests." Paragraph

3 explains the Footprint Identification Technique, and paragraph 4 begins by referencing "the same technology," which can be used to track a variety of species. You can conclude that this technology can be used to help other species, choice (F).

Choice G is extreme; beware of words like "all." Choices H and J refer to information from Passage B.

5.   A
Difficulty: Medium
Category: Vocab-in-Context
Getting to the Answer: This question, like all Vocab-in-Context questions, asks you to identify what a word "most nearly means." Reread the sentence for context and predict a new word by pretending that "counter" is a blank in the sentence. A good prediction here would be something similar to "go against" the attacks by poachers. Choice (A) matches.

Choice B is the opposite of what the passage suggests. Choice C is incorrect because conservation officials do not want to ignore the attacks of poachers. Choice D refers to the action of counting, which also does not describe conservationists' intentions toward poachers.

6.   H
Difficulty: Medium
Category: Detail
Getting to the Answer: This question begins with, "According to Passage B," which indicates that it is a Detail question. Your strategy here should be to go back to the passage where PAWS is mentioned to get the correct answer. Paragraph 2 states that the system blends machine learning with human knowledge that patrollers can use to track poachers. This matches (H).

Choices F and J are misused details; they refer to cheetah-tracking methods discussed in Passage A. Choice G is extreme, as the passage states that the algorithm provides patrollers with options, not just the best route.

7.   C
Difficulty: Medium
Category: Inference
Getting to the Answer: Inference questions require you to use facts in the passage to determine something that is not stated directly. Here you are tasked with

figuring out what the unstated hope is. Refer to the final paragraph of Passage B to help you predict that the hope is that AI will help conservationists win the fight against poachers. This matches (C).

Answer choice A is the opposite of what you are looking for, as it contradicts the information in the passage. B also contradicts what the passage states; this passage is about preservation, not poachers overrunning natural habitats. D might be tempting, but it distorts the facts; conservationists are not interested in protecting the needs of poachers.

8.   J
Difficulty: Medium
Category: Global
Getting to the Answer: This question is Global in nature because it asks about a similarity between the two passages. Both passages deal with AI being used in wildlife conservation efforts. This matches (J).

Choice F refers to Passage B only. Choice G refers to Passage A. Answer choice H is out of scope; this passage does not discuss AI replacing humans.

9.   B
Difficulty: Medium
Category: Global
Getting to the Answer: Read this question carefully. It asks what the author "provides more information about," but it is difficult to determine the scope of the question, so it might be either Global or Detail. However, since an open-ended question like this is difficult to predict an answer for whether it is a Global or a Detail question, your approach will be the same: work through the choices one by one to find the correct answer. Note that the question is focused on Passage B, so you can immediately eliminate any choice not mentioned in Passage B. Choice A refers to the Footprint Identification Technique mentioned in Passage A; eliminate it. Choice (B) is correct; Passage A does not discuss poachers, whereas techniques to address poaching are the main idea of Passage B.

You can move on after finding the correct answer, but if you want to, check the others: neither passage discusses education, so C is incorrect. Choice D refers to information mentioned in Passage A, not Passage B.

Part 4
ACT READING

10. F
Difficulty: High
Category: Inference
Getting to the Answer: This question uses the phrase "it can be reasonably inferred" to ask us what one group might do with new information. The facts presented in each passage will help. The conservationists described by the author of Passage B are focused on stopping poachers. The Footprint Identification Technique is currently used to track cheetahs, but it can be used to track other species. It is reasonable to conclude that the conservationists described in Passage B would use this technique to help track poachers, so (F) is correct.

Choice G is the opposite of the correct answer; both authors deem it necessary to help wildlife. Choice H is extreme; while the author of Passage B would likely see the positive side of using the Footprint Identification Technique, the words *praise* and *revolutionary* do not match the tone of the passage. Choice J is out of scope, as ethics are not mentioned.

Reading

568 K

Try on Your Own

Directions: Actively read this paired passage set and answer its accompanying questions. Take note of any question stems that are specifically tailored to fit paired passages so that you can research, predict, and answer them strategically.

SOCIAL STUDIES: Passage A was adapted from a speech given by a prominent city planner. Passage B was adapted from a speech given by a community organizer promoting the inclusion of a new community center in a Chicago suburb.

Passage A

The North American suburb is an architectural and civic phenomenon that arose in response to the need to "get away" from the city and all the noise, pollution, and stress that went along with

5 it. Suburban communities, however, were not sufficient by themselves to support a full life. The people who lived in them needed to work, shop, and socialize, and most of the active part of their lives remained fixed in urban centers. Therefore,

10 suburbs were clustered around their parent cities, with all the suburban inhabitants commuting daily to the city center for work and play.

All of this seems perfectly logical and inevitable. The suburb should be the perfect

15 halfway point between city and country—away from the noise, congestion, and pollution, but not so far away that there's no access to culture, to income, to all the exciting benefits of urban life. In reality, though, few suburbs have actually

20 approached this ideal. Some critics have charged that, as suburbs have grown to the size of sprawling towns themselves, they are revealed as communities somehow devoid of community necessities. They lack local stores, community

25 centers, and places for kids to hang out; instead, they offer parking lots, chain stores, and strip malls.

The structure of the modern suburb, while offering a respite from city pollution, has created

30 health and environmental risks of its own. Because of the separation of living and commercial spaces imposed by many suburban zoning laws, nearly every activity, aside from visiting adjacent houses or the occasional neighborhood park, requires

35 an automobile trip. All of this driving creates pollution. Of course, America has had a long

love affair with the car, and any city planner who thinks he can single-handedly change that is in for a rude surprise. Surely, though, we must begin

40 to balance the appeal and freedom of the car with ecological and civic responsibility.

This does not mean, however, that we need to abandon suburbs altogether, as some have suggested. Instead, we need to more knowingly

45 pursue that ideal of the best of city and country. Suburbs could be fascinating and beautiful places; we need only exercise our power to determine the nature of the places in which we live.

Passage B

"America doesn't need any more!" is a common

50 refrain for those who see suburbs merely as a means to line construction companies' pockets without contributing much to the value and diversity of American culture. I, however, see the problem of suburbs as one of degree rather than

55 kind. I haven't given up yet on the possibility of infusing the suburbs with public spaces that we can be proud of, that are rewarding to the human spirit. What can be done to bring diversity and character into these respites from the hustle and

60 bustle of the city?

A crucial starting point is reshaping the narrative of what the suburbs are intended to be a respite from. As young people form family units and those families grow, naturally they desire more

65 space. In most major cities the desire for more space comes at a significant premium, one which all too often middle-income families are unable to afford. The suburbs have the potential to serve as a happy medium: an affordable neighborhood with space for

70 families to grow, all of the more robust amenities of a major city in close proximity, and a pace of life less frenetic than traditionally expected in the city.

For these public spaces to truly be representative, more is needed. We need community engagement

75 that will help us explore our identity, discover

what we value, and determine what makes us
different from the surrounding areas. In turn,
this will allow us to celebrate the character of our
unique community in our public spaces. I, for
80 one, do believe that the developers that we work
with are invested in our community beyond just
their financial bottom line. The proposed projects
each reflect thoughtful attempts to appeal to our
entire community; now, we have an opportunity to
85 determine which one resonates the most with us.

The suburbs still have the potential to deliver on
the core principles that led to their development.
Space to spread out need not mean distancing
ourselves from our neighbors. The cities do not
90 hold a monopoly on character; we are the architects
of the character of our community, and that is what
America needs more of: community architects,
ready to go to work.

1. In Passage A, the discussion in the final paragraph
implies that the author:

A. blames poor city planning for the existence
of the suburb.

B. thinks today's suburbs are actually fascinating and beautiful.

C. believes most people take too little interest in
their surroundings

D. is optimistic about the possibilities of the
American suburb.

2. Passage A most strongly suggests that "many
suburban zoning laws" (line 32):

F. ban parks from suburban neighborhoods.

G. make it difficult to sustain successful
business.

H. contribute to adverse environmental effects.

J. address environmental concerns at the cost
of cultural diversity.

3. According to the third paragraph of Passage A,
city planners need to consider:

A. accepting suburban residents' reluctance to
give up driving.

B. minimizing every boundary between residential and retail space.

C. placing more local stores and kids' hangouts
across the street from houses.

D. moving the local parks to safer and more
accessible neighborhoods.

4. The main purpose of Passage A is to:

F. bemoan the detrimental effect suburbs have
had on individual quality of life.

G. discourage the suburb dweller's dependence
on the automobile.

H. encourage a different, more effective vision
of the place of suburbs in communities.

J. call for a return to the type of suburb that
prevailed before World War II.

5. As it is used in line 66 in Passage B, the word
premium most nearly refers to a living space
that is:

A. a prize that might be won.

B. part of an insurance policy.

C. a high price.

D. higher quality.

6. In Passage B, lines 68–72 function as examples of
reasons why:

F. suburbs have the potential to be compara-
ble to or even potentially preferable to city
living.

G. diversity might naturally come to suburban
living spaces.

H. suburban living is inherently superior to
urban living in all situations.

J. families usually choose to move from
urban areas to suburban areas as they
have children.

7. Based on the first paragraph of Passage B, it can reasonably be inferred that the author of the passage believes:

    A. more needs to be done to make urban living spaces affordable to families as they grow.

    B. construction companies charge too much for projects that do not serve communities.

    C. suburban communities are currently harmful to the spirits of people living there.

    D. many who decry suburbs are basing their beliefs on things that are possible to change.

8. The authors of both Passage A and Passage B would most likely agree with which of the following statements?

    F. Urban spaces should be seen as less desirable places to live for the majority of the population.

    G. While suburban spaces have not always lived up to their potential, there are ways to continue to improve them.

    H. Research would probably show that living in an urban area is more affordable for most families.

    J. Nobody who currently lives in a suburban area feels the sense of community that urban areas provide.

9. Compared to the author of Passage B, the author of Passage A discusses in more detail:

    A. specific criticisms of suburban spaces.

    B. reasons why suburban living is more affordable.

    C. specific ways to improve suburban living.

    D. the need for more diversity in suburban spaces.

10. How would the author of Passage A likely respond to Passage B's assertion that "developers that we work with are invested in our community beyond just their financial bottom line"?

    F. The author of Passage A is likely to agree with it because suburban areas are designed to be affordable.

    G. The author of Passage A is likely to agree with it because developers are now supporting local stores and community centers.

    H. The author of Passage A is likely to disagree with it because suburbs currently seem to be designed without community in mind.

    J. The author of Passage A is likely to disagree with it because suburban areas are rarely profitable for anyone.

Reading

How Much Have You Learned?

Directions: For test-like practice, give yourself 9 minutes to complete this question set. Be sure to study the explanations, even for questions you got correct. They can be found at the end of this chapter.

LITERARY NARRATIVE: Passage A is adapted from the essay "The Language Barrier or Silence" by Joseph Fellows. Passage B is adapted from the essay "The First and Last Time" by Randy Benson.

Passage A by Joseph Fellows

I hadn't slept the night before I left, nor could I even doze on the plane. Piqued and red-eyed is not how I had envisioned my first day abroad. I had also hoped to have a little bit of the German
5 language under my belt before mingling with locals.

Unfortunately, the absurdly unpredictable nature of the *der/die/das* articles frustrated me so much that I never really got past the general salutations and simple, commonly used phrases. I was
10 therefore stubbornly determined to get as much mileage out of *danke* and *bitte* as I could. Every German person in Tegel Airport must have thought me incredibly gracious but dimwitted. I tried saying *freut mich, Sie kennenzulernen* (nice to meet you)
15 to the cab driver that I hailed, and after three tries, each receiving a quizzical stare in return, I gave up and simply told him my destination in English. I then squeezed myself into the tiny Peugeot; evidently, SUVs are not fashionable in Europe.

20 The bed-and-breakfast I had booked was nice—very quaint, but obviously a tourist spot. The owner was a scowling old woman who said little and waddled around, pointing and grunting, rightfully assuming I was linguistically stunted.
25 Thoroughly intimidated by the locals and their language, I decided to take a walk through historic Berlin in hopes of bonding with the nature and architecture, rather than the people. I was immediately glad that I did. Despite being
30 exhausted and surly, I found myself awestruck and humbled by the ubiquitous artistry of the city.

Despite knowing little about World War II and having been born forty years after, I was profoundly affected by my first view of the Kaiser
35 Wilhelm Gedächtniskirche (Memorial Church),

with its crushed steeple and bomb-ravaged stone walls, existing in jarring juxtaposition to the surrounding modern architecture.

Further east near the Berlin Zoo, I found
40 a lovely park along the murky water of the Landwehrkanal, and eventually, I came to a massive traffic circle. In the midst of this automotive maelstrom of Berlin rush hour stood the magnificent Siegessäule (Victory Column).
45 The immaculate craftsmanship against the verdant horizon and cerulean sky—there are no words in any language to describe it. So I sat on a stone bench, smiled contentedly, and said nothing.

Passage B by Randy Benson

My room was gray and windowless, with a
50 cement floor painted blood-red. The mattress had no sheets, but I was too disoriented to care. Bad way to start the semester. Why had I decided to follow Greg here anyway?

After we stored our bags in a locker at Termini,
55 Greg marched me to a trattoria where we feasted on pasta, fish, veal, salad, cheese, and fruit. After the meal, Greg took me on a bistro-and-basilica tour. "C'mon, Paisan'. I'm gonna show you how to do Rome right."

60 After two churches and two restaurants, I said to Greg, "I understand loving the food here. But what's your thing with churches?"

Greg looked at me like I had a trinity of heads. "I know you're not really that clueless, Paisan'. Quit
65 being such a middle-class American sophomore and ask me a real question, like 'Gee, Greg, that bone church we just went through makes me wonder whatever would possess a herd of Capuchin monks to make artistic masterpieces out
70 of their own skeletal remains.'"

Actually, the thought of the bone church made the hunk of Fontinella cheese I'd just wolfed

down twist in my stomach. "No. I don't wanna
talk about the bones. I wanna know why you're
75 dragging me through churches. Is it just a scenic
way to pace ourselves between bistros?"

"You mean to tell me, Paisan', that you really
got nothing out of St. Peter's?"

I wasn't going to admit it to Greg, but St. Peter's
80 really was kind of awesome. Made my jaw drop,
actually.

"Eh. It's a big church. Who cares?"

"You should, Paisan'. This is Rome, man. The
Republic. The Empire. The Church. In a place
85 like this, I shouldn't have to agitate you into an
outburst of culture. Up 'til now, everything about
life has numbed you. This place is gonna wake up
your soul." At this, he pushed another hunk of
Fontinella at me, and I had no confidence that it
90 would sit any better than the last after one more
church full of bones.

After seven more churches and three more
bistros, we finally ground to a halt at the Cafe
Montespiné. The locals gawked at the Americani
95 and engaged Greg in conversations that mixed
French, Greek, Italian, and Martian. We dragged
ourselves out of Montespiné at 4:30 in the
morning, with half of our newfound friends still
acting like the night was just starting.

100 Which is why I woke up this morning, bleary-
eyed, in the previous night's clothes, my head
heavy as a crushed Italian moon-rock breakfast
roll. Maybe not the best way to start the semester.
But I have to admit—it was quite a start.

1. The narrator includes the interaction with the cab
driver (lines 13–17) primarily in order to:

A. explain how the narrator got from the
airport to the bed-and-breakfast.

B. provide an example of the narrator's aggrava-
tion with the German language.

C. show the affinity that the narrator has for the
German language.

D. explain how to greet someone unfamiliar in
German.

2. In the third paragraph of Passage A (lines
20–31), the narrator's decision to go for a walk is
prompted by:

F. his insecurity that had developed as a result
of his frustration with the German language.

G. his anger toward the owner of the bed-and-
breakfast.

H. his eagerness to sightsee and experience the
culture of the city.

J. his stubborn determination to succeed at
speaking the German language.

3. The narrator states that "there are no words"
(lines 46–47) to describe the view at the
Siegessäule because the narrator:

A. can't speak German well enough to translate
the description thoroughly.

B. is too frustrated with the German language
to take the time to depict the scene's beauty.

C. feels that any explanation of the beauty of the
scene could not do it justice.

D. chose to sit quietly on the stone bench rather
than say anything.

4. In Passage B, the narrator's descriptions of Greg suggest that the narrator sees Greg as:

    F. too daring and bold to be a traveling companion in the future.

    G. compelling enough to follow and see what happens next.

    H. too numb to experience any pleasure in Rome.

    J. a fanatic driven by passion for churches.

5. In Passage B, the narrator uses line 79 ("I wasn't going to admit it to Greg") in order to:

    A. illustrate the narrator's unwillingness to follow Greg's scheme.

    B. argue that admiration of Roman churches is a more private matter.

    C. call attention to the jaw-dropping nature of St. Peter's.

    D. suggest the favorable influence that Greg's tour is having on the narrator.

6. In the last paragraph of Passage B (lines 100–104), the narrator summarizes his:

    F. transition from sleep to regret for staying out the previous night.

    G. transition from sleep to a celebratory embrace of new life circumstances.

    H. recognition of the previous night as a unique way to begin the stay in Rome.

    J. return to a reality made much happier by the absence of Greg.

7. Compared to Passage B's narrator, Passage A's narrator spends more time discussing:

    A. the history of the city he is visiting.

    B. his interactions with the local people.

    C. the various religious landmarks he encounters.

    D. his inability to speak the foreign language fluently.

8. Which of the following statements best describes the difference in the tone of the two passages?

    F. Passage A is impersonal and historical, whereas Passage B is thoughtfully nostalgic.

    G. Passage A is animated and comical, whereas Passage B is serious and introspective.

    H. Both passages begin with a sense of trepidation but end with an air of equability and calm.

    J. Both passages begin humorously and end on a note of introspection.

9. Both Passage A and Passage B highlight the narrators':

    A. individual reactions to novel surroundings and non-native languages.

    B. emotional shortcomings in response to stressful stimuli.

    C. determination to impress others with recently honed language skills.

    D. decisions to return home after unsuccessful attempts to acclimate.

10. Which of the following best describes the narrators' reactions to the architecture in the cities they visited?

    F. Passage A's narrator appreciates the architecture, whereas Passage B's narrator is indifferent.

    G. Passage A's narrator does not notice the architecture, whereas Passage B's narrator is wholly captivated by it.

    H. Passage A's narrator and Passage B's narrator both begin by appreciating the architecture and then grow tired of it.

    J. Passage A's narrator finds peace by looking at the architecture, whereas Passage B's narrator has a more complicated response to it.

Reading

Reflect

Directions: Take a few minutes to recall what you've learned and what you've been practicing in this chapter. Consider the following questions, jot down your best answer for each one, and then compare your reflections to the expert responses on the following page. Use your level of confidence to determine what to do next.

1. What are ACT Reading paired passages? How do expert test takers adjust their active reading to tackle paired passages most effectively?

    _____

    _____

    _____

2. How are the question sets that accompany paired passages different from those accompanying standard independent passages?

    _____

    _____

    _____

3. How confident do you feel with paired passages? What can you do in practice to improve your performance and gain even more confidence with this type of passage?

    _____

    _____

    _____

Reading

Responses

1. What are ACT Reading paired passages? How do expert test takers adjust their active reading to tackle paired passages most effectively?

On most ACT tests, one Reading stimulus is a pair of shorter passages instead of a single, long passage. Expert test takers actively read each passage and answer the questions exclusively associated with each. Then, experts compare and contrast the passages' big pictures and details and answer questions associated with both.

2. How are the question sets that accompany paired passages different from those accompanying standard independent passages?

Roughly, the first third of the question set exclusively addresses Passage A; the next third exclusively addresses Passage B; and the final third addresses comparisons and contrasts between the passages. The questions that address both passages reward students who accurately summarize the big picture of each passage and who can determine how one author would likely respond to something argued or proposed by the other author.

3. How confident do you feel with paired passages? What can you do in practice to improve your performance and gain even more confidence with this type of passage?

There is no one-size-fits-all answer for this question. Give yourself honest self-assessment. If you feel that paired passages are a strength, congratulations! Continue to practice them so that you'll be able to rack up the points associated with these passages on test day. If you feel less confident about the paired passage format, review the strategies in this chapter and try to consistently apply the expert approaches outlined here whenever you practice passages in this format.

Next Steps

If you answered most questions correctly in the "How Much Have You Learned?" section, and if your responses to the Reflect questions were similar to those of the ACT expert, then consider paired passages an area of strength and move on to the next chapter. Come back to this topic periodically to prevent yourself from getting rusty.

If you don't yet feel confident, review the material in this chapter, and then try the questions you missed again. As always, be sure to review the explanations closely. Then go online (**kaptest.com/login**) to use your Qbank for more practice. If you haven't already registered your book, do so at **kaptest.com/moreonline.**

GO ONLINE

kaptest.com/login

Answers and Explanations

Try on Your Own

Suggested Passage Map Notes:

Passage A:

¶1: suburb origins

¶2: ideal vs. actual

¶3: necessity of cars leads to pollution

¶4: need to improve suburbs

Passage B:

¶1: we can & should improve suburbs

¶2: what suburbs ought to be

¶3: community engagement → uniqueness → improvement

¶4: author sees potential, calls on audience

BIG PICTURE SUMMARY

Passage A:

Main idea: Suburbs often lack the necessities of everyday life and their reliance upon cars creates pollution.

Author's purpose: To describe the ways in which suburbs are less than perfect and suggest that they could be improved

Passage B:

Main idea: Suburbs can be made to have character with thoughtful planning.

Author's purpose: To argue that suburbs have the potential to allow residents more than they would have in cities without sacrificing community identity

---

1.   D
Difficulty: Low
Category: Inference
Getting to the Answer: The clue word *implies* shows that this is an Inference question. Do not rely on your memory; go back to the last paragraph of Passage A and research what was said. The author claims that we do not "need to abandon suburbs altogether"

and that "suburbs could be fascinating and beautiful places." Choice (D) matches these sentiments and is thus correct.

Choice A is incorrect because the author never casts *blame.* Choice B may be tempting, but it goes beyond what is actually stated in the text. The author says that suburbs have the potential to be beautiful, not that they already are. Finally, choice C is incorrect because the passage never discusses people taking interest in their surroundings.

2.   H
Difficulty: High
Category: Inference
Getting to the Answer: The word *suggests* identifies this as an Inference question. Read a little bit before and a little bit after the cited line. This research will help shape your prediction. Here, the reference to "suburban zoning laws" is used to show the separation between living and commercial spaces in the suburbs, causing almost everything to require an automobile trip. Finally, the author says that "all of this driving creates pollution." This matches answer choice (H).

Choice F contradicts the passage; in lines 32–35, the author describes how one of the few places that a suburbanite can actually walk to is a neighborhood park. If suburban zoning laws banned parks from neighborhoods, even this would be impossible. Choices G and J are out of scope, since *successful businesses* and *cultural diversity* are not mentioned anywhere in this passage.

3.   A
Difficulty: Low
Category: Detail
Getting to the Answer: The phrase *According to* is a clue that this is a Detail question. It directs you to the third paragraph, so go back and do some research. The author says that Americans love their cars and that "any city planner who thinks he can single-handedly change that is in for a rude surprise." Predict that the correct answer must therefore have something to do with how people love driving. Choice (A) is correct.

Choice B is extreme; the author does not advocate minimizing *every* boundary. Choice C is a misused detail; while the author suggests that more local stores and places for young people are needed, they are not the focus of this paragraph. Finally, D is incorrect because there is no mention of "safer and more accessible neighborhoods" in this paragraph.

4.   H
Difficulty: Medium
Category: Global
Getting to the Answer: You can tell this is a Global question because it asks for "The main purpose" of the passage. When answering Global questions, look back at your notes for each paragraph, think of the big picture, and do not be distracted by details. The passage begins by explaining how suburbs naturally developed out of cities and then moves into a discussion of some of the negative aspects of suburban living. However, the passage ends on a note of optimism, with the author claiming that "we need to more knowingly pursue that ideal of the best of city and country." Predict that the correct answer should say something about how the suburbs are by and large a sensible idea but could be better still. Choice (H) is correct.

Choice F is too extreme; since the author concludes optimistically, he is not *bemoaning* the effects of suburbs throughout the whole passage. Choice G is too narrow to be the answer to a Global question; automobiles are mentioned in the fourth paragraph only. Finally, choice J is out of scope; the passage never discusses suburbs before World War II.

5.   C
Difficulty: Low
Category: Vocab-in-Context
Getting to the Answer: "As it is used" should serve as a clue that this is a Vocab-in-Context question. Refer back to the second paragraph of Passage B, where a larger living space in the city is described as something many families will be "unable to afford." Predict that *premium* in this case means "expensive." This matches (C).

The other answer choices are all acceptable meanings for the word *premium*, but none of them match the way that the word is used within the context of the passage.

6.   F
Difficulty: High
Category: Function
Getting to the Answer: The keyword *function* tells you that this is, yes, a Function question! Refer back to the

lines in question, which are immediately preceded by "The suburbs have the potential to serve as a happy medium." Predict that the correct answer will reflect this. This matches (F), which is the correct answer.

While the author does encourage increased diversity in suburban areas, he is not specifically addressing this need in the lines referenced, eliminating G. Choice H is too extreme; while the author does encourage suburban living, he implies it could be roughly equal to living in an urban environment, not automatically better. Choice J is too extreme. The author is giving reasons why suburbs might be appealing to growing families, but does not say anything about whether or not families *usually* choose to move to suburbs as a result.

7.   D
Difficulty: Medium
Category: Inference
Getting to the Answer: The clue words "can reasonably be inferred" indicate this is an Inference question. The question asks for something the author might believe, so it is difficult to make a specific prediction. Instead, look at each answer choice, eliminating them one by one.

For A, while the author does discuss the higher cost of living in urban areas, that is not part of this paragraph; eliminate it. Choice B is a distortion; the passage suggests that other people believe this, not that the author does. Choice C is extreme; while the author does say that suburbs could be more rewarding, the paragraph does not imply that they are actively harmful. Finally, (D) is supported by the passage—the author discusses how some believe that suburban areas are just a way for construction companies to make money, but the author believes they do not have to be that way. (D) is correct.

8.   G
Difficulty: Medium
Category: Inference
Getting to the Answer: The keywords "most likely agree" signal that this is an Inference question. It asks for a statement with which both authors would most likely agree, so review your notes on both passages. This is too broad a question to make a prediction, so eliminate answer choices one by one until you find one that fits.

Choice F is too broad: both authors discuss some of the advantages that come from urban living. Choice (G) would be supported by both authors: they both discuss some of the problems in suburbs, but believe these can be fixed with better planning and effort. You can stop at this point, but if you did look at H or J: H is not supported by the author of Passage B, who specifically discusses the higher cost of living in urban areas for families needing more space. Choice J is too extreme to be supported by the author of Passage A, who does criticize the lack of community in suburban areas, but never says that absolutely nobody in a suburban area feels a sense of community.

9. A

Difficulty: Low

Category: Detail

Getting to the Answer: As the word *detail* is mentioned, this is, of course, a Detail question. Review your notes on both passages. What does Passage A focus on that Passage B does not? Passage A focuses more on what people specifically complain about regarding suburbs, so predict that the correct answer will reflect this. And it does—choice (A) matches the prediction, and is correct.

Affordability, as in B, and a need for diversity, as in D, are actually things discussed in Passage B. Neither passage discusses specific ways to improve suburbs, though both say they believe it is possible, which means you can eliminate C.

10. H

Difficulty: High

Category: Inference

Getting to the Answer: Asking how the author would "likely respond" signals that this is an Inference question. Predict that while the two authors agree that suburban areas are a good idea theoretically, the author of Passage A would be unlikely to agree that current developers are invested in the community, as the author of Passage B suggests here, because all the evidence in suburbs as they currently exist points to the contrary. This matches (H).

The author of Passage A does not discuss affordability at all, so you have no frame of reference as to whether he would agree that current developers are designing affordable locations or not, which eliminates F. Though Passage A does cite lack of local stores and community centers as a criticism some have made of suburbs,

there is nothing to support the idea that developers are focusing more on building them now, which eliminates G. Similarly, the author of Passage A does not discuss the profitability of suburbs, which eliminates J.

How Much Have You Learned?

Suggested Passage Map Notes

Passage A:

¶1: Horrible flight; trouble speaking German

¶2: More language trouble

¶3: Intimidated but goes for walk

¶4: Beautiful Berlin has impressive architecture

¶5: Content with trip in silence

Passage B:

¶1: Bare room, disoriented

¶2: Greg (G) takes lead, Paisan' = Narrator (N)

¶3: Why churches?

¶4: Bone churches

¶5: N doesn't understand

¶6–8: N impressed by St. Peter's / acts unimpressed

¶9: G enthusiastic about Rome

¶10: Late night with locals

¶11: N has rough morning but interesting experience

BIG PICTURE SUMMARY

Passage A:

Main idea: The narrator is feeling frustrated with the language of a foreign country, but finds pleasure in the aesthetics of his new surroundings.

Author's purpose: To relate a story about feeling out of place in a foreign environment

Passage B:

Main idea: Despite initial reservations, the narrator has an intense first night studying abroad after following Greg.

Author's purpose: To recount his first night in a new foreign city while studying abroad

1.   B
Difficulty: High
Category: Function
Getting to the Answer: The wording "The narrator includes . . . in order to" identifies this as a Function question. Every part of a passage contributes to the purpose of the larger section. According to the sample passage map for Passage A, the interaction between the narrator and the cab driver shows the narrator having language troubles, which is a theme throughout the passage. Choice (B) is correct.

Although A and D describe features of paragraph 1, they do not reflect the reason the narrator included the interaction. It's clear that the narrator does NOT have an affinity, or natural talent, for the German language, so C is incorrect.

2.   F
Difficulty: Medium
Category: Detail
Getting to the Answer: This question stem provides few clues as to question type; it might be either Detail or Inference, depending on whether the passage states directly what prompted the narrator's walk. However, your first step to answering it will be the same regardless: find the appropriate section of the passage and research the answer. In the third paragraph, the narrator mentions being "Thoroughly intimidated by the locals and their language" when describing his decision to go for a walk. Choice (F) is correct.

Although the narrator pointed out that the owner was *scowling*, there is no evidence that he is actually angry with her, so G is incorrect. The narrator did express his desire to "bond with nature and architecture," but "the culture of a city" includes the people in it as well, so H is incorrect. Choice J might be tempting because of the narrator's self-professed stubborn determination in line 10, but that detail is not connected to the narrator's reason for taking a walk.

3.   C
Difficulty: Medium
Category: Inference
Getting to the Answer: Although this question does not contain typical clue words, you can conclude that it is an Inference question because it asks about something the narrator has already said that will not be stated outright. Like other Inference questions, however, it will be supported by specific details that are in the passage. Immediately after the cited line,

the narrator says he smiled contentedly, so he must mean "there are no words" in a positive way. Only (C) matches this positive tone, and it is therefore correct.

Choice A is a misused detail; even though the narrator couldn't describe the scene well in German, he would choose not to even in English. The tone of the final paragraph is one of contentment, which suggests that the narrator is no longer frustrated with his inability to speak German, so B is incorrect. Choice D merely repeats that the narrator sat quietly, without explaining why.

4.   G
Difficulty: Medium
Category: Inference
Getting to the Answer: The clue word *suggest* marks this as an Inference question. For an Inference question that asks about a relationship, use the information provided about that relationship to form a prediction. The narrator expresses mixed feelings about going along with Greg. In the first paragraph, the narrator conveys some ambivalence when he wonders, "Why had I decided to follow Greg here anyway?" (lines 52–53). However, the narrator follows Greg all day and half the night, and he admits to enjoying St. Peter's. Choice (G) is correct. The narrator is compelled by Greg's behavior and tour-guide tendencies, and he thereby remains curious enough to stay with Greg through the entire night's tour.

When a character has mixed feelings, watch out for answer choices that are too extreme, such as F. Choice H is the opposite of how the narrator sees Greg; Greg seems to enjoy Rome immensely. It more closely resembles how Greg describes the narrator. Choice J is not supported by the passage; although Greg does want to tour historical churches, nothing about his stated reasons for doing so suggests fanaticism.

5.   D
Difficulty: Medium
Category: Function
Getting to the Answer: The phrasing "the narrator uses . . . in order to" shows that this is a Function question. It asks about the purpose of a particular part of Passage B in relation to the whole. In short, why does the narrator reveal that he is unwilling to admit to Greg an admiration of St. Peter's? The function of a part of a literary narrative passage often has to do with the characters' feelings, values, and relationships. The fact that the narrator isn't going to admit his enjoyment to Greg shows that the narrator is enjoying himself in spite of his protests, so (D) is correct.

When answering Function questions, watch out for answer choices that describe the passage without revealing the cited text's function within the passage. Because the narrator is willing to follow Greg all day, A is incorrect. While the narrator's attitude may call attention to St. Peter's, the point of the passage is not to praise St. Peter's; it is to describe two characters and their interaction. Thus, C is incorrect. Choice B is out of scope because nothing in the text indicates that the narrator sees admiration of churches as a private matter.

6. H
Difficulty: Medium
Category: Detail
Getting to the Answer: The words *author summarizes* show this question is asking about something the passage states directly, so it is a Detail question. Use your passage map notes for the final paragraph as a prediction. The sample passage map states that the narrator had a rough morning but viewed the previous day as an interesting experience. Only (H) accurately expresses that the previous night was an interesting experience without adding an extreme emotion.

Choices F, G, and J do not align with the narrator's tone: F is too negative, whereas G and J are too positive.

7. D
Difficulty: Medium
Category: Global
Getting to the Answer: When asked to compare two passages as a whole, use the main focus of each passage to form a prediction. Passage A focuses on the narrator's frustrations with the language barrier in Berlin, whereas Passage B describes a whirlwind tour through Rome. While the narrator of Passage B mentions "conversations that mixed French, Greek, Italian, and Martian" (lines 95–96), language is not a major theme in Passage B as it is in Passage A. The correct answer is (D).

Although both narrators mention some historical facts, interactions with locals, and the names of religious landmarks they've encountered, these topics are presented as supporting details in both texts rather than central points of each passage as a whole. Choices A, B, and C are incorrect.

8. H
Difficulty: High
Category: Global
Getting to the Answer: The tone of a passage includes the narrator's attitudes toward the subject matter.

Pay attention to shifts in attitude. Both narrators are anxious at the start of their respective passages, but both come to appreciate their individual experiences in a foreign country. Thus, (H) is correct.

Choice F is a distortion; Passage A has a more polished quality, but that does not mean it is impersonal or historical. Nothing about Passage B makes it more nostalgic, or sentimental, than Passage A. Choice G mixes up the passages; Passage A is more serious and introspective than Passage B, while Passage B is more animated and comical. Choice J is a distortion; while Passage B is humorous in the beginning, Passage A has a more serious tone.

9. A
Difficulty: Medium
Category: Global
Getting to the Answer: The question stem asks for what both passages prominently feature. Each passage describes the experience of visiting a foreign country from the personal perspective of the narrator, which matches (A).

Choice B is extreme; both narrators feel frustration, but the passages do not portray that emotion as a shortcoming. Passage A's narrator does discuss speaking a foreign language, but he admits that he was not fluent, and Passage B does not mention the narrator speaking Italian at all, so C is incorrect. The narrators do not mention returning home, so D is out of scope.

10. J
Difficulty: High
Category: Inference
Getting to the Answer: Since you are asked to describe feelings that are not directly stated, this is an Inference question. When asked to compare two passages in this way, use your passage maps to form a prediction. According to the map for Passage A, the narrator is impressed by Berlin's architecture and feels content. According to the map for Passage B, its narrator questions why he and his companion are visiting so many churches, and he hides his appreciation for St. Peter's. Choice (J) is correct because it describes Narrator A's contentment and Narrator B's more complicated response.

Choice F is incorrect because Narrator B is secretly in awe of St. Peter's, which shows that he is not indifferent. Choice G is incorrect because Narrator A does notice the architecture and Narrator B is not entirely captivated by it. Choice H is incorrect because Narrator A does not grow tired of the architecture.

CHAPTER 21

ACT READING: TIMING AND SECTION MANAGEMENT STRATEGIES

> **LEARNING OBJECTIVE**
>
> After completing this chapter, you will be able to:
>
> - Recognize at a glance which passages in a section are likely to be easiest for you

Timing

You have 35 minutes to complete 4 passages with 10 questions each, so you need to complete each passage and its accompanying questions in an average of 9 minutes to finish on time. (Note that passages are not all the same length or difficulty, so some will take longer than others.) After 17 minutes, you should be about halfway done with the Reading questions. When the proctor informs you that there are 5 minutes remaining, you should ideally be working on the fourth set of questions.

Note that this is a brisk pace. Reading strategically can help, as can triaging questions and skipping those that you can see at a glance will be time-consuming. Your real task is not actually to attempt all the questions in 35 minutes but to get as many points from the section as you can.

Section Management

You may want to triage entire passages on the Reading section, not just questions. Some test takers have a hard time with literature or natural science, while others struggle more with humanities or social science passages; if you have distinct preferences about subject matter, you might consider leaving a particular passage type for last. For example, the Reading Test always opens with the literature passage. If that's the passage you feel least confident about, it makes sense to skip it and do it last. (Just be careful with your answer bubbling.)

Moving efficiently through this section is important, but that does not mean that you should skip over any text. Reading all of the text in the passage is essential to answering questions efficiently and accurately.

Remember that you probably won't spend the same amount of time on each question. Every question counts for the same number of points, so be sure to complete the questions you find easiest to answer first.

There is one exception to the "read the passage first" rule: when you have only five minutes remaining in the Reading Test and at least one passage left to start. In this case, skip the passage and look for the questions that could be researched quickly. Vocab-in-Context questions, for example, can usually be answered using only the full sentence containing the word or phrase, and Detail questions might provide line references to tell you exactly where to look. Finally, remember not to leave anything blank; when you have one minute left, do a final answer grid check to confirm you didn't miss anything.

When considering the structure of the entire test, keep in mind that you will have a break right before this section. If you start to feel tired, remember that you are more than halfway done with the test. If you start reading the same sentence over and over, put your pencil down, close your eyes, and take three slow, deep breaths. The more focused you can remain, the easier it will be for you to determine each correct answer.

There is a half-length Reading section in the "How Much Have You Learned?" section of this chapter. Use it to practice timing: skip questions you find too time-consuming, return to them if you have time, and keep an eye on the clock. When you are finished, check your work—and reflect on how well you managed the pacing.

How Much Have You Learned?

Directions: Use this question set to practice effective question triage. Skip those questions that you feel will take too long; come back to them if you have time. Try to get as many questions correct as you can in 18 minutes. As always, be sure to study the explanations, even for questions you got right. They can be found at the end of this chapter.

LITERARY NARRATIVE: This passage is adapted from a short story about summertime in the author's hometown.

Ivan Pavlov was a physiologist who researched learned behaviors and the ways in which repeat exposure to specific stimuli can result in behaviors that occur without intention.

At the sound of the whistle, Pavlovian, we'd all push up from the sides of the pool. (We never used the ladders or the steps in the shallow end. It was a point of pride to have the strength to
5 push up from the sides.) For the next 20 minutes, we had to be out, all the kids; let the adults have some time without us splashing and screaming and generally creating pandemonium. We all went to the same place, compelled, drawn like flies: the
10 snack bar. Jiang first, because he was the oldest, his legs were longer. He was bossy, sometimes. Aisha came next, pretending like she didn't even care anymore, even though we all knew she did, or she would have stayed by the side of the pool, on one
15 of those lounge chairs that had the long vinyl slats that always stuck to your skin. Then Faiyaz and Neerav, who only we could tell apart besides their parents. Wolf—he was Wolfgang, named for his grandfather, but he hated the name—was usually
20 last, because he was never in the same hurry the rest of us always seemed to be in. It didn't matter, because there were a thousand kids, all in clumps, pushing and shouting, as if the bored teenage girl doling out ice cream was going to suddenly decide
25 to close up shop.

We pushed and shouted, too. Pushing and shouting just seemed to be part of what you were supposed to do, and so we did it. Neerav sometimes seemed to be shouting just for the enjoyment of
30 adding his voice to the cacophonous mess. The bored teenage girl probably took a lot of aspirin. When we finally got our turn at the counter, we all got the same thing, ignoring the bags of chips and the M&Ms and the cans of soda. Each and every
35 time, all of us in it together: ice cream. We were there to buy ice cream.

It wasn't even *good* ice cream—the stuff we had in our freezers at home was better by far. But we were all dropped off at the pool to spend our
40 summer mornings, and ice cream was our shared snack of choice. Little bits of memory come back with the scent of chlorine or hot pavement, even now: Wolf counting quarters because he never remembered to bring much money; the rest of us
45 had crumpled dollar bills we kept rolled up in our towels. The way the paper peeled off the top of the ice cream, the little stick to push it up. The ice cream was usually on the stale side, freezer-burnt. But it was the best-tasting ice cream in all the
50 world, because we could buy it ourselves. Kids don't have a whole lot of power, but we bought ice cream from the bored teenage girl at the snack bar by our own choice.

We'd go back to the lounge chairs to eat, sitting
55 there watching the kids still waiting to get theirs, or the adults who swam laps, smooth and steady. Wolf would be covered in ice cream before the end of it, his face and arms sticky and streaked orange; for some reason he could never keep it from dripping.
60 We'd be back in the water soon enough anyway, and it would all wash away again. Aisha ate hers slowly, while Faiyaz and Neerav competed to see who could finish first. Jiang sat on the edge of one of the round metal tables, one long leg swinging,
65 staring off at nothing in particular.

Long, slow summer days. It was too hot to run except for ice cream, when we were out of the water. Sometimes, we played with the other kids at the pool—Marco Polo, the normal sort of thing—but
70 more often, it was just us. We were together, and that was enough.

At some point, we must have begun to outgrow it. Did Jiang give up ice cream at the pool first, or Aisha? Aisha seems more likely. There came a
75 day when we were too old to care. By then we had money, allowances we earned doing chores at home.

We saved up for less ephemeral things—books, or clothes, or Neerav's endless supply of comic books. But we couldn't say when, precisely, it happened,
80 though we must have been aware of it at the time.

We all still talk on the phone now, and of course we can go out together anytime we like, but summer days at the neighborhood pool seem to have gone the same way as the sticky orange ice cream—just
85 not around anymore. The world changed, it seems, between the time of our childhood summers and now, and the disappearance of those pools, of the snack bars and adult swim time, was part of that change. Or maybe we just no longer notice them,
90 because there's no one to blow the whistle, nowhere to run for ice cream?

1. The passage as a whole is characterized by the author's sense of:

   A. cynicism, in light of her changed perception of the world as an adult.

   B. nostalgia, looking back on what seem to be fond memories of childhood.

   C. heartlessness, considering her jaded memories of the past.

   D. wonder, as seen in her knowledge that ice cream tasted better as a child.

2. The final paragraph most strongly implies that the author is:

   F. an adult.

   G. a child.

   H. an elderly person.

   J. a college student.

3. The author uses the word *Pavlovian* in line 1 primarily in order to describe:

   A. the way that the whistle sounded to the kids in the pool.

   B. the reaction of the kids to the whistle when pushing out of the pool.

   C. the pandemonium created by all the kids being in the pool together.

   D. the rush of the kids all running to the snack bar.

4. In the context of the passage, the primary function of lines 77–78 is to give an example of something that:

   F. stands in contrast to going to the pool.

   G. was a worse use of money than ice cream.

   H. stands in contrast to buying ice cream.

   J. was a better use of money than going to the pool.

5. The author describes the taste of the ice cream in lines 47–48 primarily in order to:

   A. contrast with the later assertion that it was the best-tasting ice cream in the world.

   B. show that buying the ice cream was actually a waste of everyone's money.

   C. offer an explanation as to why everyone eventually quit buying the ice cream.

   D. indicate why everyone chose ice cream over M&Ms or bags of chips.

6. The author in lines 10–14 most strongly implies that:

   F. she remembered that Jiang always liked the ice cream more than Aisha did.

   G. ice cream consumption is only for kids who are spending the day at the pool.

   H. deciding not to go to the pool and eat ice cream is a normal part of growing up.

   J. Aisha wants to appear to be more mature than the other kids at the pool.

7. As it is used in line 30, *mess* most nearly means:

   A. a dirty area.

   B. a difficult situation.

   C. a disordered state.

   D. a place to eat.

8. According to the final paragraph, the author of the passage believes that:

   F. community pools were built for children, not adults.

   G. adults were not allowed at the snack bar at the pool.

   H. there are not as many community pools now.

   J. childhood friends should always keep in touch.

9. One of the main purposes of the information in lines 5–8 is to explain:

   A. what the kids chose to get to eat.

   B. when it was time to go to the snack bar.

   C. why the kids were all forced to leave the pool at once.

   D. how the kids chose to always get ice cream.

10. The author mentions "the scent of chlorine or hot pavement" in the third paragraph primarily in order to:

    F. indicate what stood out most strongly to her while at she and her friends were at the pool.

    G. show that pools smelled the same way in the past that they do in the present.

    H. imply that smells of chlorine and hot pavement are often associated with one another.

    J. share particular smells that still remind her of the times that she and her friends ate ice cream at the pool.

HUMANITIES: This passage was adapted from an article about land art in a small art newspaper.

Humans have always bent their imaginations
to aesthetically reshape the world around them.
However, a particular problem for early artists
seems to have been finding ways to make artwork
5 last. It was not an easy task to create artwork with
natural and often perishable materials. Despite
these difficulties, countless examples of ancient art
fill museums throughout the world, from the cave
drawings in Lascaux to Egyptian hieroglyphics to
10 Greek sculpture. However, a modern movement
called land art, which embraces this difficulty, has
gained recognition around the world. Land art is
defined as art that either naturally deteriorates or is
deliberately dismantled after it is constructed.

15 Land or earth art was first developed during
the mid-1960s as a backlash in the art community
against the increasing commercialization of art
and seclusion of art from the natural world. Artists
like Alan Sonfist sought to incorporate nature in
20 their work as well as return to the fundamental
principles upon which they believed art was based.
The pioneers of land art rejected museums and art
galleries as the rightful settings for creative work.
They sought to remove the "plastic" influences and
25 what they viewed as the corrosive influence on pure
aesthetics. Thus, land art began with a mission to
create three-dimensional works set in and wrought
from the natural world.

The dawn of the movement coincided with
30 an emerging ecological movement. Land artists
typically prefer the rural to the urban, sometimes
searching for a spiritual connection with the earth.
Land artworks from the movement's inception
recall much older land works like Stonehenge, the
35 Nazca Lines of Peru, or the Great Pyramids of Giza.
Constructed in remote locations such as the deserts
of the American West, they experiment with
perceptions of light, space, and even the passage of
time. In so doing, they evoke the spirituality of far
40 more ancient works.

Above all, land artists utilize simple materials.
Unlike other minimalist artists, land artists use
only natural media such as rocks, soil, sand, wood,
water, and even plant matter in the creation of
45 their masterpieces. Land art icon Robert Smithson
constructed his work *Spiral Jetty* using nothing
more than stones, mud, algae, and water. Created
in the Great Salt Lake in 1970 during a severe
drought, *Spiral Jetty* was a 1,500-meter spiral of
50 rocks that projected from the lake shore and was
allowed to deteriorate without intervention. The
Jetty was covered by the lake within a few years
and remained underwater until 2004 when, to the
delight of contemporary artists, another drought
55 revealed the 30-year-old sculpture.

Another feature of land art is its massive scale,
which typically prevents it from being displayed
in any museum or gallery. Since land art makes
extensive use of landscape, entire vistas can be
60 said to be part of a work. The sheer size of land art
thus requires collaboration between artists and
engineers, as well as the employment of laborers
and volunteers, in order to complete a project. For
example, Australian artist Andrew Rogers's piece
65 *Rhythms of Life* was constructed in twelve different
sites around the world, making the work the largest
piece of aesthetic art to date—a feat reminiscent of
Christo and Jeanne-Claude's 1991 *Umbrellas* project,
which placed massive blue and yellow umbrellas in
70 selected stretches of the Japanese countryside and
the California mountains. Christo, however, denies
the label of "land artist," claiming that his and his
wife's work does not share the common principles
of land art, since it neither rejects gallery art nor
75 eschews the use of synthetic building materials.

Despite the artists' ideological differences,
Christo and Jeanne-Claude's work does share other
similarities to the work of land artists in that both
are intentionally short-lived. Land art is extensively
80 photographed during exhibition but afterward
exists only on film or in memory. Some critics and
art lovers decry limiting public access to a work
of art by deliberately creating it to be temporary.
Because creating land art often requires substantial
85 funding, allowing the finished product to fall
into ruin or even purposefully dismantling it is
considered by critics of the movement to be a waste
of resources. Land artists counter such indictments

by pointing out that they only borrow the elements
90 of nature to produce their work, and once a piece
has been exhibited, they feel justified in returning
the materials to their rightful owner. Moreover, they
assert that the very ephemeral nature of their works
is an integral part of those works. Land artworks
95 that capture the imagination can live on in memory
and appear even greater to the public consciousness
than they really were. As Christo once stated,
"Do you know that I don't have any artworks that
exist? They all go away when they're finished . . .
100 giving my works an almost legendary character. I
think it takes much greater courage to create things
to be gone than to create things that will remain."

The same could be said of the land art movement
itself. Because of their massive scale, land artworks
105 are costly to produce. Land artists frequently rely on
wealthy private patrons, foundations, or government
grants in order to create their masterpieces. With
economic downturns came a loss of funding, and in
recent years the movement has faded. Or, perhaps, it
110 has transformed—as all movements must once they
have done their work to change and inspire others.

11. According to the passage, why did ancient artists
have a difficult time creating lasting artworks?

    A. Such works were not popular among land
    artists of the time.

    B. The media available to ancient artists were
    prone to decay.

    C. Patrons refused to pay the necessary expense
    for such work.

    D. The elements of nature succumbed to
    human-made endeavors.

12. According to the passage, which of the following
is true of the land art movement's inception?

    F. The movement originated with the creation
    of *Spiral Jetty* by Robert Smithson.

    G. The movement began as a backlash against
    the creation of permanent artworks.

    H. The movement was primarily motivated by a
    desire to use natural materials in art.

    J. The movement was a negative reaction to
    attributes of modern art during the 1960s.

13. The passage most strongly suggests that some
ancient land works were concerned with:

    A. the natural world.

    B. the rural/urban divide.

    C. time and space.

    D. permanence.

14. It can be inferred from the fourth paragraph that
one distinction between other minimalist artists
and land artists is that other minimalist artists:

    F. create works that are extremely small.

    G. prefer exotic components over ordinary
    ones.

    H. are uninterested in spiritual aspects of art.

    J. make use of synthetic materials in their
    work.

15. As it is used in line 45, the word *icon* most nearly
means:

    A. religious idol.

    B. small graphic symbol.

    C. revered person.

    D. representative image.

16. The author mentions *Rhythms of Life* in line 65 primarily in order to:

    F.   provide an example of how large land artworks can be.

    G.   compare *Rhythms of Life* to the *Umbrellas* project.

    H.   emphasize the diminutive scale of land artworks.

    J.   describe the largest work of aesthetic art in human history.

17. One of the main purposes of the sixth paragraph is to:

    A.   examine the implications of creating artworks that exist for a brief period of time.

    B.   refute criticism of land art and the work of Christo and Jeanne-Claude.

    C.   analyze the difference between land art and Christo and Jeanne-Claude's work.

    D.   provide examples of legendary pieces of land art.

18. The author quotes Christo in lines 98–102 primarily in order to:

    F.   argue that none of the preeminent works of modern art still exist.

    G.   demonstrate that when Christo and Jeanne-Claude dismantle their artwork, they exhibit a courage entirely lacking in land artists.

    H.   show that the destruction of a piece of artwork can enhance that work's reputation in the minds of critics and admirers.

    J.   provide information about how artists care very little about wasting natural resources when they allow their artwork to be destroyed.

19. According to the passage, what happens to the building materials of land artwork after it is taken apart?

    A.   They are recycled.

    B.   They revert to nature.

    C.   They pass to a new owner.

    D.   They are used in future art.

20. The author's attitude toward the passage's main topic can best be described as:

    F.   critical and dismissive.

    G.   skeptical and disappointed.

    H.   passionate and dedicated.

    J.   interested and supportive.

Answers and Explanations

Suggested Passage Map Notes:

¶1: kids at pool getting snacks, friends introduced

¶2: always rowdy, get the same thing

¶3: narrator looks back as adult: memories, reflection

¶4: how friends ate differently

¶5: how things used to be

¶6–7: narr. reflects: outgrew it, sense of loss

BIG PICTURE SUMMARY

Main idea: The narrator reminisces about her summer days at the pool and reflects on how life has changed since her childhood.

Author's purpose: To evoke a sense of nostalgia

---

1. B
Difficulty: Low
Category: Global
Getting to the Answer: "The passage as a whole" signals that this is a Global question. Review your notes and predict that the author is looking back on a happy time in her life. This matches (B).

A and C can be eliminated because there is no cynicism nor heartlessness displayed by the author. D is not supported by the passage; though the author says that the ice cream she bought at the pool tasted good, she never says that ice cream as a whole tasted better when she was a child.

2. F
Difficulty: Low
Category: Inference
Getting to the Answer: The phrase "most strongly implies" tells you that this is an Inference question. In the final paragraph, the author mentions "between the time of our childhood summers and now"—predict that they have grown up since the time she is writing about. This matches (F).

This same phrase eliminates G because the author discusses childhood as being in the past. Choices H and J are not supported by the passage; the author may or may not be either elderly or a college student.

3. B
Difficulty: High
Category: Function
Getting to the Answer: The clue words "primarily in order to describe" indicate that this is a Function question. Refer to the line in question, and predict that *Pavlovian* is used here to describe how the kids all leave the pool when the whistle sounds. That matches (B).

A is incorrect because it is the kids' reaction that is described as *Pavlovian*, not the sound of the whistle itself. Neither the pandemonium nor the snack bar are referenced as *Pavlovian*, eliminating C and D.

4. H
Difficulty: Medium
Category: Function
Getting to the Answer: The phrase "primary function" lets you identify this as a Function question. Review the cited lines and predict that the correct answer will identify that books, clothes, and comic books were bought instead of ice cream. This matches (H).

Choices F and J can be eliminated because the author is contrasting what she and the others bought later to ice cream; there is no indication in the passage of whether they had to pay to use the pool at all. Choice G may or may not be true; while the author says this is what everyone later chose to spend their money on, she doesn't say that those things are a worse use of money than ice cream. (If anything, she implies that they were a better use because they lasted longer!)

5. A
Difficulty: Low
Category: Function
Getting to the Answer: The clue words "primarily in order to" tell you that this is a Function question. Refer back to the lines referenced and predict that the author describes the ice cream as "on the stale side, freezer-burnt" to show that it really wasn't all that good. Nonetheless, it was "the best-tasting ice cream in all the world" because the kids bought it themselves. This matches (A).

Choice B might be tempting since the author does go on to say that the kids eventually chose to spend their money on other things, but this isn't the reason why the narrator describes the taste of the ice cream.

Choice C is incorrect because, while the taste is described earlier in a relatively negative fashion, there is nothing to indicate that this is why the kids eventually quit buying it. Finally, D is not supported by the passage, since the ice cream is not described as being superior to either M&Ms or bags of chips.

6. J
Difficulty: High
Category: Inference
Getting to the Answer: "Most strongly implies" indicates that this is an Inference question. Refer back to the lines in question and review what's stated about Aisha: "Jiang . . . was the oldest . . . Aisha came next, pretending like she didn't even care anymore, even though we all knew she did, or she would have stayed by the side of the pool." The author's assertion that Aisha pretended not to care and was *more likely* to be the first one to outgrow it supports a prediction that Aisha tries to act older than her age. This matches (J).

Although the author describes the way the ice cream is consumed, there's nothing to support the statement that Jiang liked the ice cream *more* than Aisha, so F is incorrect. Choice G is extreme; although the ice cream seems like an essential part of the pool-day experience, the author explicitly states that not only was there ice cream at home, it was better than the ice cream at the pool. Although the author talks about outgrowing it, there is no evidence that the author believes one outgrows pools and ice cream entirely, especially given her observation of adults at the pool while she was there as a child.

7. C
Difficulty: Medium
Category: Vocab-in-Context
Getting to the Answer: The phrase "most nearly means" tells you that this is a Vocab-in-Context question. Refer back to the line in question, and predict that *mess* here means something like "unruly." The best match for this is (C).

While A, B, and D are all other definitions of *mess*, none of them matches the way the word is used within the passage.

8. H
Difficulty: Medium
Category: Inference
Getting to the Answer: "According to the final paragraph" indicates that this could be either a Detail or an Inference question, depending on the information in

the correct choice. Refer to your notes for the final paragraph, but realize it is hard to make a firm prediction from such a broad question. Instead, check each answer choice, eliminating them out one by one until you find the choice supported by the paragraph in question.

While the author does describe going to the community pool as a child, there is nothing to support the idea that she thinks such pools are just for children, which eliminates F. There is also nothing to support the idea that she thinks snack bars are just for children, which eliminates G. The author states that "The world changed, it seems, between the time of our childhood summers and now, and the disappearance of those pools, the snack bars and adult swim time, was part of that change." She does follow this by saying, "maybe we just no longer notice them," but this is presented as speculation, not counter-evidence, so (H) is correct. (If you're curious, note that J is too extreme—while the author says that she has kept up with the childhood friends from the passage, she never says that all childhood friends should stay in touch.)

9. C
Difficulty: Low
Category: Function
Getting to the Answer: The phrase "purposes of the information" means that this is a Function question. Refer back to the paragraph and predict that the referenced lines tell you why the kids all got out of the pool. This matches (C).

Nothing in the referenced lines gives any information about what foods the kids chose to get, eliminating A and D. While it is true that this was the time when the kids went to the snack bar, that wasn't what the referenced lines explained.

10. J
Difficulty: Medium
Category: Function
Getting to the Answer: "Primarily in order to" tells you that this is a Function question. Look back to the third paragraph to remind yourself why the author mentioned the chlorine and hot pavement. Predict that the correct answer will show that these smells bring up memories of eating ice cream at the pool. This matches (J).

Choice F may or may not be true; just because those particular smells bring back memories doesn't mean they stood out most strongly when she was a child.

Nothing is said about how pools smell now versus then, nor about an association between chlorine and hot pavement, which eliminates G and H.

Suggested Passage Map Notes:

¶1: land art embraces impermanent art

¶2: reacted against contemporary art

¶3: connection to natural world

¶4: use natural materials

¶5: massive scale

¶6: impermanence; critics vs. artists

¶7: movement faded/changed

BIG PICTURE SUMMARY

Main idea: Land art is a modern art style and movement based on art that is designed to be impermanent and steeped in nature.

Author's purpose: To inform the reader about the land art movement

---

11. B
Difficulty: Low
Category: Detail
Getting to the Answer: The phrase "According to the passage" indicates that this is a Detail question. The first paragraph describes materials available to ancient artists as "perishable" (line 6). Choice (B) matches this prediction.

Choice A is a misused detail; the passage describes land art as a contemporary movement. Choice C is also a misused detail; there is no mention of patrons for ancient art, only modern works. Finally, choice D is a distortion; while the passage does describe ancient media as perishable, it does not suggest that "human-made endeavors" themselves caused the natural materials to deteriorate.

12. J
Difficulty: Medium
Category: Detail
Getting to the Answer: "According to the passage" is a clue that this is a Detail question. The second paragraph discusses the influences that led to the land

art movement as a "backlash . . . against the increasing commercialization of art and seclusion of art from the natural world" (lines 16–18). Predict that land art opposed these trends. Choice (J) matches this prediction and is correct.

Choice F is a misused detail; the passage never states that *Spiral Jetty* was the first land artwork. Choice G is a distortion; the first paragraph discusses the impermanence of land art, but the author never suggests that land art was a direct reaction against permanent art. Choice H is extreme; the passage does discuss the use of natural materials in land art but never suggests that land art originated specifically from a desire to use such materials.

13. C
Difficulty: Medium
Category: Inference
Getting to the Answer: The phrase "most strongly suggests" shows that this is an Inference question. In paragraph 3, the passage states that land art works evoke ancient works through their interest in light, space, and time. Predict that ancient art will share these same concerns. This matches choice (C).

Choice A is a concern of land art, but not one that the passage connects to ancient land works. Choice B is out of scope; while the passage states that land artists prefer rural to urban, it does not mention the divide between them. Finally, choice D is a misused detail; the passage discusses the problem of permanence for ancient artists but not for ancient land works.

14. J
Difficulty: Medium
Category: Inference
Getting to the Answer: The clue word *inferred* shows that this is an Inference question. The fourth paragraph contrasts other minimalists with land artists by stating that land artists prefer to use natural materials. You can infer that other minimalists at least sometimes use non-natural materials to create art. The correct answer is (J).

Choice F is out of scope; the passage does not discuss the typical size of minimalist works. Choice G is a distortion; although the passage states that land artists prefer simple materials, the phrasing "other minimalist artists" suggests that minimalists in general may prefer them as well. The contrast is between natural and synthetic, not simple and exotic. Similarly, while the passage states that some land artists were concerned with spiritual aspects of nature, the passage does not discuss this with regard to other minimalists, so H is incorrect.

15. C
Difficulty: Medium
Category: Vocab-in-Context
Getting to the Answer: This stem has the characteristic wording of a Vocab-in-Context question. Read the sentence to determine how the word is being used in the passage. Here, *icon* refers to a specific, important artist. Choice (C) matches this prediction.

Choices A, B, and D all represent other meanings of the word *icon*. The sentence uses the phrase "Land art icon" to describe a person (Robert Smithson), and it is not logical to describe a person as either a "land art small graphic symbol" or a "land art representative image," so B and D are incorrect. While a person can be described as a religious idol, the sentence and paragraph do not contain any support for the idea that Robert Smithson is a religious idol, so A is incorrect.

16. F
Difficulty: Medium
Category: Function
Getting to the Answer: The phrasing "author mentions . . . in order to" indicates this is a Function question. Consider the cited line and surrounding sentences in the context of the paragraph as a whole. The purpose of the paragraph is to discuss the massive scale of land art works, and the cited line begins with "For example." Thus, you can predict that the author mentions *Rhythms of Life* as an example supporting the paragraph's main idea. Choice (F) is correct.

Choice G is a misused detail; the two works are compared, but that is not the author's main purpose for including this detail. Choice H is opposite; the passage describes *Rhythms of Life* as massive, not diminutive. Choice J is a misused detail; the passage does state that this work is the largest to date, but that is not the author's purpose for mentioning *Rhythms of Life*.

17. A
Difficulty: Medium
Category: Function
Getting to the Answer: The phrase "main purposes" is a clue that this is a Function question. Review your notes to determine what the author wants to communicate in the sixth paragraph. This paragraph describes the consequences of creating short-lived artwork, so (A) is correct.

Choice B is out of scope; the author does address criticism, just not for the entire paragraph. Choice C is out of scope; this comparison is made, but that is not one of the primary purposes of the whole paragraph. Finally, choice D is out of scope; the author does not provide any examples in this paragraph.

18. H
Difficulty: High
Category: Function
Getting to the Answer: The wording "author quotes . . . in order to" identifies this as a Function question. Examine the context in the paragraph to determine the author's purpose. The author quotes Christo, who uses words like *legendary* and *courage*, to support the explanation of artists' reasons for allowing their work to be destroyed. You can predict that this quote reinforces the idea that impermanence can raise the stature of art. Choice (H) captures this sentiment.

Choice F is extreme; the passage never states that no successful artworks still exist. Choice G is opposite; the paragraph cites similarities between land artists and Christo and Jeanne-Claude, not differences. Choice J is a distortion of the information in the passage; critics say that land artists waste resources, but land artists argue that they only borrow materials. It's possible that some land artists do waste resources, but the cited Christo quote does not support the idea that artists in general care very little about waste.

19. B
Difficulty: Medium
Category: Detail
Getting to the Answer: The phrase "According to the passage" shows that this is a Detail question. Lines 88–92 state that the materials from land art are taken from nature and returned to nature. Choice (B) is correct.

Choice A is out of scope; the passage does not discuss recycling. Choice C is opposite; the passage describes nature as the rightful owner of the materials, so the materials are returned to a previous owner, not passed to a new one. Choice D is out of scope; the passage does not describe the reuse of land art materials.

20. J

Difficulty: Medium

Category: Global

Getting to the Answer: The clues "author's attitude" and "main topic" indicate this is a Global question; consult your notes to determine the author's view of land art. The passage is mostly descriptive in tone, but it does present land art as unusual and interesting. Moreover, the author's positive view of the movement comes through in some places: in the sixth paragraph, the author defends land art, and in the final paragraph, the author refers to land art inspiring others. Choice (J) is therefore correct.

Choice F is opposite; the passage does not dismiss land art but explores it thoroughly. While it mentions some criticisms of the movement, it immediately offers counters to these criticisms. Choice G is also opposite; the author is interested in and enthusiastic about land art, not skeptical or dismissive. Choice H is extreme; while the tone is generally positive, "passionate and dedicated" goes too far.

TEST YOURSELF: ACT READING

Directions: For test-like timing, give yourself about 44 minutes to complete the following 50 questions.

Passage I

LITERARY NARRATIVE: This passage, which is set in the late 1990s, is adapted from a memoir by a Nicaraguan-American author.

My mother knew immediately what the old man was referring to when he told her to turn right *donde fue la farmacia Ixchen*—where the Ixchen pharmacy used to be. Directions in this
5 country are for those who knew all that had happened here, not for outsiders. Street addresses may exist on a government map, but no one uses them. Instead, everyone describes a path using landmarks, and you had better know that "toward
10 the lake" means north, and that the pharmacy used to be on that corner, where now only grass and trees grow amid the rubble.

We trudged forward under the blazing sun. "Mom, when was the last time it rained here?" I
15 asked. She made no response; her pace slowed, as she stared at a high concrete wall across the dirt road.

"Mom! Does it ever rain in Nicaragua?" I repeated insistently.

20 "Look," she said, pulling my hand. As we crossed over to the wall, I kicked pebbles, annoyed that she was ignoring my inquiries. She knelt down and traced her forefinger across the uneven concrete. "See these marks, Yesenia?" she
25 murmured. I remained silent, just as she had.

"These were made by bullets. There was a lot of fighting along this street. A lot of people…" Her voice trailed off, lost in mourning.

With that, it was as if someone else was
30 resentful, someone else was hot and tired and hungry. I tried to think of a man I had never met, who had died in this fighting just before I was born. My memories of him were not even my
own; I could only picture a worn photograph that
35 my mother always carried, its edges tattered from being touched over and over. In it, my father smiles conspiratorially, as if he has just told a joke but is trying to look serious for the camera. Next to him, my mother's head is turned, both indignant and
40 amused. I had always wondered what joke he told at that moment but never dared to ask, sensing that the memory would be too private.

This was our first trip back to the country since we left just after the war. My father had
45 fought on the victorious side, so with speeches and ceremonies we were honored, alongside other bereft families, for our sacrifice, but the hole in my mother was too big to fill with speeches. Her brother, my uncle Carlos, was living in the United
50 States and invited her north to start over again.

I was too young to remember the journey, which was not in an air-conditioned plane but rather on the roof of a freight train chugging precariously up the map. I never learned the details of our crossing
55 or of the first several years after we arrived. What most evokes my early childhood is a smell: the scent of pine trees artificially replicated by air fresheners. My mother would religiously hang those dark green pine trees from the rear-view
60 mirror of the unpleasantly pungent station wagon we shared with Uncle Carlos. This all-American aroma surrounded us protectively at all times.

A decade, then almost another, passed. Now we were back to visit, and our first stop was to see Don
65 Lorenzo, my father's uncle and my oldest living relative, a modest, stately man who was very ill.

"You found this new house okay?" he asked in a light, raspy Spanish like fine sandpaper, as we sat on his porch.

70　"Yes, they told me to turn where the pharmacy used to be. What happened to it?" my mother replied.

　　They continued to talk. My Spanish was not quite good enough for me to participate fully. Lost
75　in my own thoughts, I sipped my soda and watched the one-eyed cat skulk along the wall behind Don Lorenzo, stalking some kind of massive spindly bug. Meanwhile, Necio, the slavering pit bull, never took its menacing eyes off the cat.

80　　Out of nowhere, a cottontail rabbit, all fluff and enormous ears, crossed nonchalantly in front of the pit bull. What is this, a zoo? Why isn't that thing being eaten? I snorted at the absurdity of the scene, only to suppress a laugh with a blush as
85　Don Lorenzo and my mother turned.

　　"There it is," said Don Lorenzo, looking right at me. "The smile. The same as your father had." I froze. My childish reactions were suddenly infinitesimal compared to something enormous
90　and foreign as a planet inside me. I watched my mother's hand slip into her purse unconsciously; I knew she was touching the photograph.

　　At that moment, I felt more connected to my father than ever before or since. I no longer
95　needed to know the joke; in fact, I knew that I would probably not understand it. At the same time, I somehow knew the joke completely. It was not an arbitrary rabbit, but something else equally ridiculous and touching that had provoked my
100　father's sense of humor—a sense likely amplified in "serious" situations, as I realized with another leap. Like me, he laughed inappropriately and was reprimanded frequently, or so I imagined.

　　Later, we visited the cemetery; there were
105　plenty of carved letters in stone, but no picture, no new information about the man and his secret smile. Before long a rain shower burst from the sky, sending us running for cover and turning the dusty roads into streams of mud.

1.　It can reasonably be inferred that the narrator's mother doesn't finish her sentence when they are at the concrete wall because:

　　A.　she forgets what she was going to say.
　　B.　she is overcome by her recollections.
　　C.　she changes her mind about sharing her thoughts.
　　D.　she is tired and hungry.

2.　The narrator employs which of the following literary devices in line 68?

　　F.　Allusion
　　G.　Simile
　　H.　Euphemism
　　J.　Juxtaposition

3.　According to the passage, the narrator moved to the United States to live with:

　　A.　her father's brother.
　　B.　her mother's brother.
　　C.　her father's uncle.
　　D.　her mother's uncle.

4.　The author's use of the words "worn" and "its edges tattered" (lines 34–35) most nearly serves to emphasize which of the following points?

　　F.　The photograph is very important to the narrator's mother and has been damaged by how frequently she touches it.
　　G.　The narrator's mother has not been careful with the photograph, leading to it being damaged.
　　H.　The narrator used to want to see the photograph frequently but was too young to be careful with it, damaging it.
　　J.　Despite it being damaged, the photograph is very important to Don Lorenzo, who has no photographs of his own of his late nephew.

5. Which of the following statements best describes the narrator's view of Nicaragua?

   A. It feels shockingly familiar to her, though she has no memories of having lived there as a young child.

   B. It feels alien and strange to her, and she feels more like a visitor than someone returning home.

   C. It feels overwhelming to her, as she wants desperately to get to know better who her father really was.

   D. It feels hot and uncomfortable, and she hopes that the weather will improve so she can enjoy it.

6. The "hole" (line 47) the narrator describes as being left in her mother most nearly refers to:

   F. the injuries that her mother sustained during the war in Nicaragua.

   G. the difficulty her mother had in choosing to leave Nicaragua.

   H. the emotional injury caused by the death of the narrator's father.

   J. the marks in the high concrete wall that were made by bullets.

7. It can reasonably be inferred from the passage that the all-American aroma of the air fresheners referred to in lines 55–58 is mentioned to:

   A. emphasize that her early memories are not of the war-torn Nicaragua where she was born.

   B. contrast her early childhood memories with her mother's early childhood memories.

   C. juxtapose her vague memories of her father with a clear memory from childhood.

   D. compare what she wishes she could remember of childhood with what she actually remembers.

8. The narrator describes Don Lorenzo as a man who is:

   F. conspiratorial, inappropriate, and silly.

   G. rough, menacing, and frightening.

   H. modest, stately, and very ill.

   J. skulking, impatient, and quiet.

9. The narrator uses the phrase "or so I imagined" (line 103) most likely to convey how:

   A. the narrator and her father had a similar sense of humor.

   B. the narrator's father was often reprimanded for laughing inappropriately.

   C. the narrator felt, rather than knew, her father had certain traits.

   D. the narrator realized that the specific content of the joke was unimportant.

10. It can most reasonably be inferred from the passage that the narrator comes to the conclusion that:

   F. while the government viewed her father as a war hero, his family did not.

   G. her father loved her mother more than her mother loved her father.

   H. her mother has a contentious and difficult relationship with her late husband's family.

   J. it is possible to understand her father without being able to remember him.

Reading

Passage II

SOCIAL STUDIES: This passage is adapted from an article about architecture and democracy.

The physical arrangement of the courtroom is a far cry from the apolitical, public-spirited space it was once idealized to be. Centuries ago, courtrooms were designed to welcome the public, who would
5 attend proceedings in droves, depending on the case. The layout did not give any one party, including the judge, a positional advantage, and security measures were nominal, if included at all.

Today, court officers flank the courtroom
10 entrance in the back and stand at the front as well, monitoring the room for rule violations, and invariably, the proceedings are separated from the viewing area by a low wall or divider. The topography of the space, which includes a raised
15 platform for the judge, allows the judge to observe the room's activity from an elevated position, clearly a calculated architectural choice. It often feels more like a theater than anything else—a performance rather than a truth-seeking enterprise.

20 Members of the public who choose to attend courtroom proceedings must submit to stringent security measures, and they are given intractable courtroom conduct rules. If audience members do not adhere to the rules, they can be charged
25 with contempt of court. If found guilty of being disobedient or disrespectful toward a court of law and its officers, a person can be fined, jailed, or both.

It's not just the security measures, architectural
30 features, and strict attendance policies that leave courtrooms feeling less than welcoming to the public. All these are coupled with the "legalese" used by lawyers—most of which many lay people have not heard, let alone fully understand—the
35 adversarial, sometimes hostile, nature of the litigation process; and the general attitude of resentment and reluctance that pervades juries.

In 2003, Bexar County, Texas took on the challenge of changing all this with an innovative,
40 pioneering project aimed at meeting the needs of children who are requested to testify in front of a judge: the county designed court accommodations that enable children to testify in the courtroom in a non-threatening and comforting environment. It
45 was a radical departure from the typical modern approach to courtroom design and renovation, and it sprang from consensus in the county that a special courtroom to accommodate the high number of children who are asked to testify was
50 critical.

A design team was formed that included architectural, electrical, and mechanical engineers; a child psychologist; and the local deputy director of court technology. The design team, working with
55 county officials, determined that two courtrooms were needed, along with two hearing rooms and two interview rooms.

The creation of dual rooms made clear the significant role that technology would play.
60 According to the Center for Legal and Court Technology, "Each courtroom would need all technological tools available to present a case. The extensive use of video would be expected to allow a participant in any location within the complex to
65 communicate with another participant anywhere else. For example, a judge might need to interview a child in chambers with other participants viewing from the hearing room or courtroom."

The design even included a special waiting
70 room, created for the protection and entertainment of children. In addition to adhering to strict security measures, the waiting room is replete with games and books for children of all ages. Staff members are accustomed to welcoming
75 children who are initially perplexed, if not anxious. The comfortable room and the assurances from those around them help to assuage children's apprehension.

Unfortunately, endeavors like this remain rare
80 and are, as in the case of Bexar County, typically restricted to individuals with specific needs, such as children, and it is unlikely that a redesign of standard courtrooms will follow suit. Law is a highly traditional profession that pays, by its nature,
85 great respect to authority. Statutes and sacred, guiding documents, such as both state and federal

constitutions, are given the utmost respect, and
violations of them are taken seriously, involving law
enforcement if necessary. Architecture has reflected
90 that somber, inherently hierarchical model.

   Perhaps the most striking example of
hierarchical American courthouse architecture
is the Supreme Court itself. Forty-four steps rise
up to meet its ingress; massive red curtains hang
95 among intricate molding to adorn the front of
the courtroom; the elevation of the justices is
striking; and spectators are cabined by rank and
admission standards. Considering the high-stakes
decisions made in the walls of the building, one
100 might think these features are not only expected
but also appropriate. Few would dispute the
importance of the single branch of government
that has the authority to strike down laws deemed
unconstitutional.

105   Yet, law can be respected while still being made
accessible, understandable and, in courtrooms,
comfortable enough for witnesses to participate.
If witnesses are too intimidated to testify, the
courtroom fails to fulfill its fundamental purpose.

11. Which of the following statements best expresses
the main idea of the passage?

   A.   Courtrooms should be centers of spirited
        debate.

   B.   Courtroom architecture should reflect an
        appropriate respect for authority.

   C.   It is important to examine how courtroom
        architecture reflects American values and
        facilitates justice.

   D.   Prior to 2003, the discrepancy between
        American legal ideals and the realities of
        courtrooms had not been addressed.

12. The author mentions that a courtroom "often feels
more like a theater" in lines 17–18 primarily in
order to:

   F.   point out that legal proceedings are often
        scripted.

   G.   provide an example of an alternative court-
        room design.

   H.   underscore how current courtrooms may not
        feel open and welcoming.

   J.   emphasize how judges must consider viewers
        throughout legal proceedings.

13. It can reasonably be inferred that the "legalese"
the author mentions in line 32 refers to:

   A.   authority and tradition in the courtroom.

   B.   phrases that are often unfamiliar to the general
        public.

   C.   incendiary language that provokes anger and
        resentment.

   D.   architectural terms such as *ingress* and *molding*.

14. Which of the following statements best describes
the author's attitude toward the specialized
courtrooms in Bexar County, Texas?

   F.   They are appropriate for children but may
        not be relevant to all standard courtrooms.

   G.   They do not properly respect the authority of
        legal proceedings.

   H.   They are an example of how innovations can
        create accessible and inviting courtrooms.

   J.   The redesign may not be sufficiently
        public-spirited and apolitical.

15. The author describes the use of video in the Bexar
County courtrooms as instrumental in:

   A.   allowing participants to view proceedings
        and testify while in physically separate places.

   B.   accommodating a special waiting room for
        children's ease, protection, and entertainment.

   C.   preventing incarcerated defendants from
        traveling to the courthouse.

   D.   assisting the judge in observing proceedings
        both during and after court sessions.

16. According to the passage, Bexar County, Texas undertook the challenge of redesigning local courtrooms because:

    F. local residents felt intimidated by the previous courtroom architecture.

    G. local residents wanted to take on an innovative project.

    H. the number of incarcerated citizens made cases difficult to prosecute, which hindered legal processes.

    J. local residents believed that addressing the needs of children asked to testify was necessary.

17. The author uses the phrase "within the complex" (line 64) most likely to describe:

    A. intricacies of designing buildings that successfully address legal and psychological needs.

    B. complications of communicating with people via video rather than in person.

    C. ornate architecture features that reflect the staid model of courtrooms.

    D. multiple buildings that comprise the Bexar County courtrooms.

18. The author uses the word "unlikely" (line 82) to refer to how it is unrealistic to expect:

    F. standard courtrooms to adopt a less hierarchical style in the near future.

    G. court officers to become even more authoritarian.

    H. the law to be considered a traditional profession.

    J. residents of Bexar County, Texas to utilize their specialized courtrooms.

19. The author's use of the words and phrases "striking," "Forty-four steps," and "massive" (lines 91–94) most nearly serves to emphasize which of the following points?

    A. The law, as well as courtroom proceedings, must be given the utmost respect.

    B. Stratified architecture in courtrooms is strongly ingrained in the United States.

    C. The Supreme Court is designed to look like the most prestigious court in the United States.

    D. The elevation of the Supreme Court Justices is extreme and striking, even by American standards.

20. According to the author, most standard courtrooms today are characterized by:

    F. a raised platform for the judge and a waiting room for children.

    G. forty-four steps in front of the entrance and a considerable elevation of the justices.

    H. court officers at the entrance in the back and red curtains in the front.

    J. a raised platform for the judge and a divider separating the viewing area from the proceedings.

Passage III

HUMANITIES: This passage is adapted from an essay by a linguist on the power of words.

In 1940, Benjamin Lee Whorf wrote an article in *M.I.T.'s Technology Review* called "Science and Linguistics," in which he argued, among other things, that people's native language constrains

5 their minds and prevents them from being able to understand certain concepts. Whorf believed that if a language is missing the word for a particular idea, then its speakers should not be able to understand that particular principle.

10 In particular, Whorf's article discusses the Hopi language and the way it assigns verbs such as *wari*, which means to run, to both present and past tense. In addition, rather than saying, "the rain lasted five days," a Hopi language speaker

15 would state the fact as "the rain stopped on the fifth day" because the language does not include plural nouns such as days.

Whorf concluded that without knowledge of a language that is temporal—such as English or

20 Spanish—a Hopi language speaker would be unable to understand scientific concepts such as velocity because it hinges on the ability to distinguish and quantify changes in time. Whorf does not dismiss the idea of being able to incorporate some type of

25 scientific understanding of physics, but he does state that an evaluation of the physical world would be vastly different within the Hopi language than within a temporal language and may even require different mathematics.

30 Whorf's contentions, while clearly stated and well reasoned, weren't fully embraced at the time. People throughout the world are quite capable of thinking about the future and past, even if they lack the terminology for it. Think, for instance,

35 about a young child telling a teacher that a toy fell off a shelf, but not yet aware of the past tense: "Toy fall down," the child says, clearly referring to a past event and with apparent full understanding that the event has already happened.

40 Twenty years after Whorf's claim was published, renowned linguist Roman Jakobson arrived at a

related but more nuanced conclusion. "Languages," Jakobson argued, "differ essentially in what they must convey and not in what they may convey."

45 Therefore, if language shapes how we think, it does so by determining what we're obligated to think about rather than conveying all that it is possible to think about.

Consider this example offered by linguist

50 Guy Deutscher in *The New York Times* in 2010, reflecting on the difference between English and Mandarin: "If I want to tell you in English about a dinner with my neighbor, I have to tell you something about the timing of the event: I have

55 to decide whether we dined, have been dining, are dining, will be dining, and so on. Mandarin, on the other hand, does not oblige its speakers to specify the exact time of the action in this way because the same verb form can be used for past,

60 present or future actions." In other words, two languages may convey shared concepts such as time in vastly different ways.

Deutscher stressed that this does not mean that someone who speaks Mandarin exclusively would

65 be unable to understand the concept of time, rather that the person wouldn't have to articulate timing every time they wanted to tell a story about a meal. Could this mean Mandarin speakers think less about time than English speakers? Perhaps.

70 A very intriguing illustration of "linguistic obligation" is among speakers of the Australian Aboriginal language Guugu Yimithirr, which lacks coordinates related to the self, such as "in front of," "behind," "left of," "right of," and so on. The

75 language strictly uses geographical coordinates to describe directions—that is, north, south, east, and west. But what happens when they don't know where north is?

This is the fascinating part...because *it doesn't*

80 *happen*. Native Guugu Yimithirr speakers do not have that problem—they *always* know where north is, even without a compass, and accordingly, they know where the other cardinal directions are as well. While a native English speaker, reliant

85 on self-focused directional terminology, will most certainly not develop the same intuitive sense of

cardinal direction as one who was raised to rely solely on the geographical coordinates from birth, Guugu Yimithirr speakers are raised to be aware
90 of cardinal directions at all times. As a result, they're as aware of cardinal directions as English speakers might be that their toes are "in front" and their heels are "at the back" of their feet.

   To an extent, then, Whorf was right. He may
95 have missed the mark in positing that we cannot imagine or feel what we cannot say, but clearly, what we must say can leave us with modes of thinking and seeing that are far more influenced by language than we realize. It is important to note
100 that Whorf concluded his article with the sentiment that there is a great deal of diversity among linguistic systems throughout the globe and no one language should be considered the pinnacle. Rather, Whorf called for further research to be conducted
105 in the spirit of both curiosity and humility.

21. As it is used in line 19, the word *temporal* most nearly means to be:

   A. concerned with nonreligious affairs.

   B. capable of acknowledging time.

   C. easier to understand.

   D. exhibiting secular attitudes.

22. In the fourth paragraph (lines 30–39), the author provides an example of a child communicating with a teacher in order to:

   F. indicate that conceptual misunderstandings derive from poorly constructed phrases and sentences.

   G. show how a person may fully comprehend a concept without knowing how to properly convey it.

   H. illustrate the importance of early childhood education in developing effective language skills.

   J. make clear that the incorrect use of grammar may lead to confusion and frustration.

23. It can reasonably be inferred from the passage that the "nuanced conclusion" referred to in line 42 is:

   A. Whorf's clear but incomplete theory regarding the Hopi language.

   B. the deduction that cultural context is necessary when interpreting languages.

   C. an example Deutscher provides to support a new argument.

   D. the idea that language influences what speakers are obligated to consider.

24. The author states "two languages may convey shared concepts such as time in vastly different ways" primarily in order to:

   F. undermine Whorf's contentions.

   G. establish the principal foundation of linguistics.

   H. summarize one linguist's perspective.

   J. show how the concept of time affects understanding.

25. According to the passage, compared to English speakers, Mandarin speakers:

   A. spend fewer minutes each day thinking about time.

   B. dine with friends and neighbors more frequently.

   C. are less adept at event planning and scheduling.

   D. do not have to specify the exact time of an action.

26. Based on the passage, which of the following statements best describes how linguist Roman Jakobson is generally regarded?

   F. Jakobson was originally criticized but is now revered.

   G. Current scholars feel largely indifferent toward Jakobson.

   H. Jakobson and his scholarship are regarded in high esteem.

   J. Jakobson's theories are well-respected but his character has been called into question.

27. The author refers to Guugu Yimithirr primarily in order to:

A. emphasize the point that Guugu Yimithirr speakers think less about coordinates related to the self than English speakers.

B. argue that it is unlikely that a non-native speaker would be able to successfully navigate the Australian countryside.

C. help explain why the terms "in front of," "behind," "left of," and "right of," should be included in languages.

D. support the point that native speakers of certain languages demonstrate inherent knowledge, such as cardinal direction.

28. The passage describes "linguistic obligation" (lines 70–71) as the way in which language:

F. requires speakers to apply specific concepts that they presumably understand.

G. forces non-native speakers to identify information gaps within their own vocabulary.

H. urges scholars to conduct additional studies that focus solely on social constructs.

J. engenders feelings of disorientation when fundamental terms are not clearly defined.

29. The author asks, "But what happens when one doesn't know where north is?" (lines 77–78) most likely to:

A. raise a dilemma that current research is unable to solve.

B. point out a difficulty that many people face.

C. introduce an important attribute of a key example.

D. propose a caveat to a theory.

30. In the last paragraph (lines 94–105), the author revisits Whorf's thesis in order to:

F. acknowledge his contribution to linguistics.

G. reveal that his original theory was actually correct.

H. continue to point out the shortcomings in his findings.

J. credit him with new discoveries.

Passage IV

NATURAL SCIENCE: This passage is adapted from an article about the magnetic field of the Earth.

The Earth's magnetic field is an invisible force that affects many aspects of the natural world. Migratory animals, such as birds, use the magnetic field to guide their trajectory—without it, they

5 likely would be unable to return so precisely to the same area each season. Humans similarly benefit from the effects of the magnetic field. For example, the sun's radiation is severe enough to cause significant damage to humans, but the combination

10 of the filtering effects of the atmosphere and the protective barrier from the magnetic field make it possible for humans to live on Earth's surface without suffering from immediate radiation damage when exposed to sunlight. This powerful

15 natural force has gradually revealed a surprisingly complex history—with not entirely reassuring implications for the future.

How did this magnetic field originate? Its genesis is unclear, but the prominent theory is called the

20 dynamo effect, which posits that the iron core in the center of the Earth generates the field. Heat from radioactive decay compels the outermost part of the Earth's iron core to move. Iron is a conductive material, and its movement engenders an

25 electric current that interacts with magnetic forces, which creates a self-sustaining magnetic field.

Other forces also significantly influence the Earth's magnetic field. For example, Venus has an iron core similar to that of Earth. If the core

30 were the sole source of the magnetic field, Venus should experience similar magnetic effects, but there is no magnetic field surrounding Venus. It is likely that the planet's rotation affects the field generation; Earth rotates on its axis once every

35 24 hours, while Venus completes a rotation every 116 Earth days.

If Earth's magnetic field were unvarying, it would be an interesting geological feature but would have relatively little immediate impact. Studies of

40 iron deposits in rocks, however, indicate that the field has undergone both significant and ongoing

changes. Iron is a magnetic substance, so it will align with nearby magnetic fields—this effect can be seen on a small scale by watching iron filings

45 attracted to a simple magnet. On a larger scale, iron is present in volcanic lava. When the lava is liquefied, the iron is free to move and orient in a natural position. After the lava hardens, the iron particles are unable to move; a lava rock that

50 solidified at a particular point in time will therefore have iron particles oriented in the direction of magnetic north at that time.

By studying lava rocks from various periods, scientists have determined that magnetic north

55 has moved. Over the course of thousands of years, magnetic north shifted not only around the north pole, but also around the south pole: the field has been shown to completely reverse itself. Thus while today compass needles point toward

60 the north pole, several thousand years ago, they would have been drawn south.

It was assumed that shifting the Earth's magnetic field from one pole to another took thousands of years. Since scientists have been observing the field,

65 however, there has been substantial movement from the geographic North Pole. Magnetic north is slowly drifting toward Siberia at an increasingly rapid pace. Since 1831, magnetic north has moved 600 miles. Interestingly, the magnetic field is

70 also significantly weakening. It is approximately 15% weaker than it was 200 years ago. This rapid movement combined with the reduced strength is prompting scientists to reevaluate their original timeline. Instead of several thousand years, it is

75 entirely possible that magnetic north can switch poles after only a few hundred years. Some scientists believe that in the future, it could reverse in as few as 75 years.

If this is the case, magnetic north may move to

80 the geographic south pole in the very near future. While the hypothesis is not wholly embraced by the scientific community, the effects of a reversed magnetic north are worth discussing, especially given that this switch could have profound effects

85 on everyday life. Electrical grids use the Earth's magnetic field to function, and could become

inoperable as the field weakens. The field would
be likely to continue to weaken until it reversed
completely and remain weak for some time after.
90 Through this entire period, electrical systems
would be at risk.

Another important point to consider is that
people's health could be directly affected because
the magnetic field protects us from radiation, so a
95 weaker magnetic field creates more exposure risk.
The development of abnormal cells and mutations,
two results of increased radiation, could rise.
However, there is no evidence that any mass
extinctions or cataclysmic events occurred during
100 past field reversals, so the true extent of a reversed
magnetic north cannot yet be known.

31. The author's attitude toward the potential effects
of a global magnetic field reversal can best be
described as:

 A. skepticism and resignation.

 B. concern and attentiveness.

 C. hope and fascination.

 D. relief and ease.

32. According to the passage, iron can be used to
analyze the Earth's magnetic field because iron is:

 F. a magnetic substance.

 G. the primary component of volcanic lava.

 H. found near the magnetic north pole.

 J. relatively difficult to extract from solidified
lava.

33. The passage describes the dynamo effect as:

 A. a widely accepted fact.

 B. a hypothesis that is unlikely to be proven.

 C. a mistaken conception scientists used to
have.

 D. unclear, but a leading theory.

34. It can reasonably be inferred from the passage
that the occurrence of abnormal human cells
could increase as a result of:

 F. a weaker magnetic field on Earth.

 G. risky electrical systems.

 H. radiation from Earth's magnetic field.

 J. mutations that cause mass extinctions.

35. The passage points to which of the following as a
component of the dynamo effect that is thought
to be critical in generating Earth's magnetic field?

 A. Radioactive decay

 B. The rotation of the Earth

 C. Volcanic activity

 D. The periodic reversal of magnetic north

36. The author compares Earth and Venus primarily
in order to:

 F. explain why Venus's magnetic field is different
from Earth's magnetic field.

 G. provide evidence that factors other than
Earth's iron core impact its magnetic field.

 H. highlight the significant difference between
the rotation times of the planets.

 J. argue against the importance of Earth's iron
core in generating a magnetic field.

37. In the sixth paragraph (lines 62–78) the author
discusses support for the general hypothesis that:

 A. the Earth's magnetic field is produced via the
dynamo effect.

 B. a weak magnetic field could have devastating
effects on our way of life.

 C. a reversal of the Earth's magnetic poles in the
next few centuries is possible.

 D. magnetic north is not where scientists would
expect it to be.

38. According to the passage, which of the following would impact the position of iron filings in a lava rock?

    F. The location of magnetic north when the lava rock solidified

    G. The strength of the magnet that attracted the iron filings

    H. The length of time the lava rock was liquefied

    J. The amount of electric current generated by the iron

39. The passage identifies which of the following as a scientific hypothesis that scientists once accepted but is now being questioned?

    A. The Earth's magnetic field is a stable phenomenon.

    B. Venus has an Earth-like magnetic field.

    C. The movement of the Earth's iron core contributes to the Earth's magnetic field.

    D. The reversal of Earth's magnetic field takes thousands of years.

40. The primary purpose of the passage is to:

    F. inform the public about an impending disaster.

    G. describe a natural phenomenon and its potential effects.

    H. promote the dynamo effect as the most likely source of the Earth's magnetic field.

    J. discuss the importance of iron in scientific study.

Passage V

SOCIAL STUDIES: Passage A is an excerpt from an American history textbook. Passage B is adapted from a book on the history of nursing.

Passage A

The Battle of Normandy was not a battle that lasted a day or even a few days; it lasted three months, from June 1944 to August 1944. The invasion continued into Germany and directly
5   contributed to both Germany's surrender and the liberation of Europe from Nazi control.

The battle itself, code-named "Operation Overlord," was launched on June 6th, 1944, also known as D-Day. The visual of the launch of
10 Overlord has become iconic. More than 5,000 ships and landing craft carrying troops and supplies from England traversed the English Channel to France, while more than 11,000 aircraft descended upon five beaches that ran along a 50-mile stretch of
15 heavily fortified coast in France's Normandy region. Altogether, approximately 150,000 soldiers were transported—these Allied Forces were composed of American, British and Canadian forces, constituting one of the largest amphibious military assaults in
20 modern history.

To prepare an attack of such magnitude was a feat in itself and required planning for unexpected obstacles, such as the weather. Perhaps it should come as no surprise that D-Day was not originally
25 planned for June 6th: General Dwight D. Eisenhower had selected the date for the invasion as June 5th, but the weather from England over the English Channel was poor in the week leading up to it, and on the afternoon of the 4th, it remained so.

30 "The weather in this country is practically unpredictable," Eisenhower wrote. "For some days our experts have been meeting almost hourly and I have been holding Commander-in-Chief meetings once or twice a day to consider the
35 reports and tentative predictions." Fair predictions for the following day, however, led him to order the invasion on the 6th. He told the troops, "You are about to embark upon the Great Crusade,

toward which we have striven these many months.
40 The eyes of the world are upon you."

Prior to D-Day, the Allies had conducted a large-scale deception campaign designed to mislead the Germans about the intended invasion target. As a result, the German response to the invasion
45 was weak, and, by late August 1944, all of northern France had been liberated, and, by the spring of 1945, the Allies had defeated the Germans.

Passage B

Vera Hay, a British nurse during World War II, was one of the first nurses to land at Normandy
50 shortly after D-Day. Hay was stationed at the Chateau de Beaussy, a field hospital for British troops where major surgeries were performed in order to stabilize patients so that they were safe to travel back to England. There, Hay cared for up
55 to 200 injured soldiers a day, conducting triage on patients as they arrived—those with more serious injuries were rushed straight through to surgery.

Fifty years later, at age 92, Hay reflected on what stood out in her memory of that time. "The
60 pain of the casualties, both our own troops and the German prisoners of war," she told the British newspaper The Telegraph. "They all were patients to us. They needed rehydration, rest, morphine to keep them comfortable, and we were using the
65 new penicillin."

As soon as Hay had completed her nursing training in August 1943, she promptly volunteered for the Queen Alexandra's Imperial Military Nursing Service. Less than a year later, not even
70 a week after D-Day, she found herself landing on Normandy's Gold Beach and traveling sixteen kilometers to the hospital. The journey took about twenty-four hours, as she and the other nurses had to steer clear of pockets of German resistance
75 along the way. At the hospital, the nurses were not able to rotate out because there simply were not enough nurses to cover separate shifts. Everyone was required to work around the clock, sleeping only when they had the chance, which meant that
80 Hay usually slept for no more than one or two hours at a time.

On the other side of the English Channel, nurses such as Mary Virginia Desmarais were waiting. "We received our first casualties on D plus 4,"
85 she recollects. "They were fresh battle casualties in great pain that had been given only first aid in France and aboard the [boats] that brought them into Southampton, England." When the buses arrived with patients, an announcement would be
90 called over the loudspeaker: "Man your stations until further notice." Desmarais recalled that there was no time for meals or rest because the line of casualties seemed endless.

The English Channel, only 20 miles wide at its
95 narrowest point, separated Hay and Desmarais. On both sides of it, in the field hospitals of France and the city hospitals of England, both nurses worked tirelessly to save as many as they could of hundreds of thousands of injured men. Hay and Desmarais,
100 along with thousands of other dedicated nurses, were true heroes behind the front lines.

41. Passage A most strongly implies that which of the following was an unusual feature of the Battle of Normandy?

A. The number of countries involved

B. The severity of the casualties' injuries

C. The number of the troops deployed

D. The iconic status of General Eisenhower

42. The author of Passage A includes the quotes from Eisenhower (lines 30–40) primarily in order to:

F. explain the nature of the typical weather patterns in the regions bordering the English Channel.

G. demonstrate General Eisenhower's remarkable attention to detail.

H. argue that the weather conditions made the Battle of Normandy difficult for both soldiers and medical staff.

J. highlight the high difficulty of planning for the Normandy invasion.

43. Passage A most strongly suggests that the Allies' success in the Battle of Normandy was due in part to:

A. the quality of the medical care provided by the nurses and doctors at the front lines.

B. the significant number of British troops, ships, and landing craft that were involved in the battle.

C. the turn of the weather in early June 1944 that delayed the invasion until a time that was more favorable for the Allies.

D. the degree to which the Germans were misdirected by the deception campaign leading up to D-Day.

44. Passage B most strongly implies which of the following about nurses who served during World War II?

F. Even nurses who did not serve at field hospitals sometimes faced challenging work conditions.

G. The nurses of World War II have received inadequate praise for their tireless service.

H. Nurses who served near the front lines of battle typically performed surgeries on severely injured soldiers.

J. If not for nurses like Hay and Desmarais, the Allies could not have succeeded at Normandy.

45. The author of Passage B most likely includes Hay's quote, "'They all were patients to us'" (lines 62–63) in order to:

A. recognize that the nurses of Chateau de Beaussy treated soldiers from both sides of the battle.

B. demonstrate the high number of patients that required treatment after D-Day.

C. criticize the Allies for their practice of taking prisoners of war throughout World War II.

D. argue that the nurses at Chateau de Beaussy had more concern for their patients than the nurses in England demonstrated.

46. Based on Passage B, it can reasonably be inferred that hospitals in England:

    F. did not follow the practice of triaging patients for treatment according to the severity of their injuries.

    G. treated injured soldiers who had only been given first aid and injured soldiers who had undergone stabilizing surgeries in France.

    H. were staffed by nurses who did not have to work as many hours as nurses who worked in France.

    J. were primarily located near the port of Southampton.

47. As it is used in line 76, the word *rotate* most nearly means to:

    A. spin slowly in a circle.

    B. abruptly shift position.

    C. take turns working.

    D. move to different locations.

48. Compared to the author of Passage B, the author of Passage A provides more information about the:

    F. reasoning behind maneuvers made during the course of a battle.

    G. executive levels of wartime decision making.

    H. personal state of those enlisted in a battle.

    J. wartime contributions of non-combatants.

49. The description in Passage B of Hay's journey to the Chateau de Beaussy field hospital (lines 69–75) suggests further information about Passage A's description of:

    A. the extent to which German troops were driven from the area around Normandy.

    B. the number of boats, planes, and other vehicles that the Allies deployed to northern France.

    C. the goals of Allied leadership after the completion of the Battle of Normandy.

    D. the impact of selecting June 6th rather than June 5th as the date of D-Day.

50. Which of the following statements best describes the difference in the tone of the two passages?

    F. Passage A is inspirational, whereas Passage B is neutral.

    G. Passage A is informative, whereas Passage B is admiring.

    H. Passage A is confrontational, whereas Passage B is pessimistic.

    J. Passage A is conflicted, whereas Passage B is assertive.

Answers and Explanations

Passage I
Suggested Passage Map Notes:

¶1: mother (M) understood directions

¶2–3: narrator (N) impatient

¶4–5: M shows N bullet holes

¶6: N thinks of father (F)

¶7: first trip back

¶8: N came to US as kid

¶9: 15+ yrs later, visit Don Lorenzo (DL)

¶10–12: M and DL talk

¶13–14: N smile reminds DL of F

¶15–16: N finally feels connected to F

BIG PICTURE SUMMARY:

Main idea: The narrator explains her feelings toward a father who passed away before she was born and a country she left as a young child.

Author's purpose: To describe how her feelings change from impatience and resentment to an acknowledgement of her mother's grief to an unexpected sense of connection with her father

---

1. B
Difficulty: Medium
Category: Inference
Getting to the Answer: "It can reasonably be inferred" signals that this is an Inference question. In paragraph 5, the narrator states, "Her voice trailed off, lost in mourning." The word *mourning* indicates that the narrator's mother was very sad about what had happened years ago, which matches (B).

Choices A and C are incorrect because the passage does not give any indication that the narrator's mother forgot what she was going to say or changes her mind about sharing her thoughts; instead, the clues lead to the conclusion that she is too sad to continue her sentence. Choice D is a misused detail; it is the narrator, not her mother, who is described as tired and hungry.

2. G
Difficulty: Medium
Category: Function
Getting to the Answer: There will be several types of questions on the ACT that will test your knowledge of literary devices, such as metaphors and personification. The phrase "raspy Spanish like fine sandpaper," is a simile because it uses the word *like* to compare Don Lorenzo's speech to sandpaper; (G) is correct.

An allusion is an indirect reference to a person, event, or literary work, so F is incorrect. Choice H is incorrect because a euphemism is a word or phrase that describes graphic or offensive content in a milder way. Choice J is incorrect because a juxtaposition is the placement of two elements close together to highlight their similarities or differences.

3. B
Difficulty: Low
Category: Detail
Getting to the Answer: "According to the passage" indicates that this is a Detail question. Research the answer in the passage and match it to the correct choice. Paragraph 7 states, "Her brother, my uncle Carlos, was living in the United States and invited her north to start over again," which matches (B).

Choices A, C, and D are incorrect because they misidentify who invited the narrator and her mother to move north.

4. F
Difficulty: High
Category: Function
Getting to the Answer: The clue words "serve to emphasize" signal that this is a Function question. Use the information in the passage to predict the importance of the photograph and its description. The narrator states, "I could only picture a worn photograph that my mother always carried, its edges tattered from being touched over and over." The narrator's mother always carried the photograph, which indicates that it was important to her, and the tattered edges are from her mother handling it frequently, which matches (F).

Choice G is a distortion; the narrator's mother did cause the photograph to become worn, but she wouldn't be careless with something so important to her. Eliminate H and J because the passage does not provide information about the narrator handling the photograph as a young child or Don Lorenzo's feelings about the photograph.

5. B
Difficulty: Medium
Category: Global
Getting to the Answer: This question is asking about the narrator's view of Nicaragua, so this is a Global question. The passage begins with the narrator feeling impatient and resentful, and then ashamed of those feelings when she is reminded of the war. She states that she and her mother were "back to visit" and admits that her "Spanish was not quite good enough for me to participate fully," which indicates that she is somewhat reluctantly visiting and does not feel like she fits in perfectly, which matches (B).

Eliminate A because it is opposite; she does not feel it is familiar. Choices C and D are distortions; the narrator does want to feel a connection to her father but does not mention feeling overwhelmed, and while she is hot and uncomfortable, she doesn't talk about hoping that the weather will get better.

6. H
Difficulty: Medium
Category: Function
Getting to the Answer: The phrase "narrator describes" indicates that this is a Function question, so consider the purpose of the word within the context of the surrounding text. Paragraph 7 states, "My father had fought on the victorious side, so with speeches and ceremonies we were honored, along with other bereft families, for our sacrifice, but the hole in my mother was too big to fill with speeches." The speeches were for families who lost loved ones in the war, but they did not help to heal the narrator's mother profound grief over losing her husband, which matches (H).

Choices F and G are distortions; the injuries were emotional, not physical, and the passage indicates that the mother had difficulty grieving her husband, not difficulty choosing to leave Nicaragua. Choice J is a misused detail; the damage to the high concrete wall is mentioned at the beginning of the passage, but it is not connected to the discussion about the grief the mother experienced immediately following her husband's death.

7. A
Difficulty: High
Category: Inference
Getting to the Answer: "It can reasonably be inferred" shows that this is an Inference question. The narrator refers to the air fresheners in Uncle Carlos's car as "what most evokes my early childhood," so her earliest childhood memories were of the United States, not Nicaragua. The passage states that the narrator was "too young to remember the journey" to the United States, so she wouldn't have any memories of her life in Nicaragua before she relocated, which matches (A).

Choice B is out of scope because the passage does not include information about her mother's childhood memories. Eliminate C because the narrator does not have vague memories of her father—she does not have any memories of her father. Choice D is tempting because it is possible that the narrator wishes she could remember more of her childhood, but the passage does not provide direct evidence to support this idea; the passage focuses on the narrator's feelings toward a father who died before she was born.

8. H
Difficulty: Low
Category: Detail
Getting to the Answer: "The narrator describes" signals that this is a Detail question. Based on the passage map notes, paragraph 9 is the place to look. Here the narrator describes Don Lorenzo as old, modest, stately, and very ill; (H) is correct.

Eliminate F, G, and J because the passage does not attribute those characteristics to Don Lorenzo.

9. C
Difficulty: High
Category: Function
Getting to the Answer: The phrase "most likely to convey" indicates that this is a Function question. Consider how the sentence's meaning would change if that phrase were removed. Without the phrase "or so I imagined," the narrator would be asserting that her father definitely laughed inappropriately and was reprimanded frequently. By including the phrase, she conveys that she does not know these facts for sure, which matches (C).

Choices A, B, and D are tempting because they are all mentioned in paragraph 15, but they do not correctly explain the specific function of the phrase "or so I imagined."

10. J
Difficulty: Medium
Category: Inference
Getting to the Answer: The phrase "most reasonably be inferred" means that this is an Inference question, and it is asking about the passage as a whole. Use the passage map notes to consider how the narrator feels at the end of the passage compared to the beginning. In paragraphs 2 and 3, the narrator is impatient and resentful but in paragraphs 15 and 16, the narrator finally feels connected to her father, which matches (J).

Choices F and G are out of scope because the passage does not provide direct evidence to support either choice. Choice H is also not supported because the conversation between the narrator's mother and Don Lorenzo, the narrator's father's uncle, does not show any signs of conflict.

Passage II

Suggested Passage Map Notes:

¶1: modern courtrooms different from ancient, description of ancient

¶2: description of modern, author (au) critical

¶3: strict security rules

¶4: other inhospitable things

¶5: attempt to change for children, Bexar county

¶6: how they changed

¶7: what changed: tech/video

¶8: what changed: comfy waiting room

¶9: au POV: good start but limited

¶10: example: Supreme Court

¶11: au POV: change still possible

BIG PICTURE SUMMARY:

Main idea: Unlike those of ancient courts, the architecture and security procedures of modern courtrooms are inhospitable for visitors and intimidating for witnesses.

Author's purpose: To argue that the physical arrangements of modern courtrooms should be reevaluated to make courts more accessible to the public

11. C
Difficulty: Low
Category: Global
Getting to the Answer: Since this question asks for the main idea, it is a Global question. Refer to your passage notes in order to answer it. The author opens by claiming that the architecture of modern courtrooms is inhospitable to the public, provides an example of an alternative arrangement, and closes by stating that the current architecture may even undermine the purpose of the court. Choice (C) correctly matches this summary and is correct.

Choice A is not discussed in the text and is therefore incorrect. The extended example of the Bexar county court redesign focused on making the child witnesses comfortable and did not intend to accommodate "spirited debate." Choice B is a misused detail. Although the author agrees that respect for the authority of the court is an important consideration, the first sentence of the final paragraph of the passage indicates that the author believes the comfort of witnesses and the accessibility of the courts are more important. Choice D is an extreme choice. The Bexar county court redesign did occur in 2003, but the passage never states that this was the first attempt to resolve the discrepancy.

12. H
Difficulty: Medium
Category: Function
Getting to the Answer: The phrase in the question, "in order to," identifies this as a Function question. Return to the lines 17–18, but read above and below these lines to find the reason the author used those words. Immediately following the words cited in the question, the author says courtrooms may feel more like "a performance rather than a truth-seeking enterprise," and this criticism sums up the second paragraph's comparison of modern courtrooms with those of ancient times. The author continues in the remainder of the passage to develop the idea that modern courtrooms should be comfortable for witnesses and accessible to the public. Choice (H) is correct.

Choice F is not mentioned in the passage, so it is incorrect. Choice G is a distortion of information presented in the text; although a theater-style arrangement may meet the author's goal, this idea is not discussed in the passage and is not the reason the author used the cited words. Choice J is also a distortion of a detail from the passage. The author does state in the previous lines that the judge's elevated position enables the judge to see the viewers but does not emphasize this as an important consideration for courtroom design.

13. B
Difficulty: Low
Category: Inference
Getting to the Answer: The keyword *inferred* in the question tells you that the passage will support the correct answer. Since you are asked about an unusual word, the passage will have to provide enough context for you to understand its meaning. Go back to the cited line references and read above and below them to find the definition. Lines 32–34 state that *legalese* is something used by lawyers and that most non-lawyers "have not heard, let alone fully understand" it. Put your finger on these lines in the passage, and match them to the choices. Choice (B) is correct.

Choices A and D are misused details from the passage. Although the author addresses the need for authority and tradition in the courtroom and uses the architectural terms *ingress* and *molding*, legalese is not a word used to describe either of these concepts. Choice C is never mentioned in the passage, so it is incorrect.

14. H
Difficulty: High
Category: Inference
Getting to the Answer: The qualified language "best describes" identifies this as an Inference question. The correct answer will be supported by the passage, but will likely not be directly stated. It may also be necessary to support the correct answer by putting information together from different parts of the passage. This question asks about the author's attitude, so begin by identifying that attitude as positive, negative, or neutral. The author uses many positive adjectives to describe the Bexar county specialized courtrooms, such as "protection and entertainment of children," "replete with games and books," "Staff members are . . . welcoming," and "comfortable." Although the author does state that these changes are "unlikely" to extend to standard courtrooms, the first sentence in the final paragraph indicates that the author believes that changes like these are needed. Choice (H) is correct.

The negative tone of G and J does not match the author's positive view. Eliminate these choices. Choice F

is a subtle distortion of the author's concession. The author does state that the special needs of children drove the Bexar County reforms, but the author uses the extended example to illustrate how modern courtrooms can be improved, even if these changes may not be implemented in standard courtrooms. This makes F incorrect.

15. A
Difficulty: High
Category: Detail
Getting to the Answer: The keyword *describes* identifies this most likely as a Detail question, so look for the answer to be stated directly in the passage. Before returning to the text, though, try to put the question into your own words to focus your research. Here you might think, "I need to identify the reason the use of video was important." The passage map identifies paragraph 7 as the place to research, so reread that paragraph, looking for the answer to the question. Lines 62–66 provide the answer: "The extensive use of video would be expected to allow a participant in any location within the complex to communicate with another participant anywhere else." Match this to the choices: (A) is correct.

Choice B is a misused detail. The special, comfortable waiting room for children is discussed in the text, but it is not a reason the use of video was important. Choices C and D are not mentioned in the passage, so they are incorrect.

16. J
Difficulty: Low
Category: Detail
Getting to the Answer: The phrase "According to the passage" is a clue that this might be a Detail question, so look for the answer to be stated directly in the passage. Before returning to the text, put the question into your own words to focus your research. Here you might think, "Why did Bexar County redesign its courtrooms?" The passage map indicates the discussion of these changes starts in paragraph 5. Return to that section of the passage and look up the answer to the question: lines 47–50 state that there was a "consensus in the county that a special courtroom to accommodate the high number of children who are asked to testify was critical." This matches (J), the correct answer.

Choice F is a distortion of information in the passage, and is incorrect. Although the author does believe it is possible for visitors and witnesses to be intimidated by the courtroom, the author does not say that the citizens of Bexar County felt this way. Choices G and H are not mentioned in the passage, and so are incorrect.

17. D
Difficulty: Medium
Category: Inference
Getting to the Answer: The qualified keyword phrase "most likely" identifies this as an Inference question. Prove your answer from the passage but do not expect the answer to be directly stated. Return to line 64, and read a little before and after the cited line, looking for an explanation of "within the complex." The sentence that immediately follows the line reference gives the example of a judge using video to transmit the interview of a child from the judge's chambers to other participants in the trial in different locations. Choice (D) is correct.

Choices A and C are misused details from the passage. Both are mentioned in the passage but have no connection to "within the complex." Choice B is not discussed in the passage, so it is also incorrect.

18. F
Difficulty: Medium
Category: Function
Getting to the Answer: The phrase "the author uses" identifies this as a Function question. Refer back to the cited line and read above and below that line researching the idea that the author believes is "unlikely." The answer is found in the phrase immediately following the cited word: "it is unlikely that the design of standard courtrooms will follow suit." This matches (F), the correct answer.

Choices G and J are not mentioned in the passage and are therefore incorrect. Choice H is the opposite of what's stated in the passage; the author states that one of the issues hindering the redesign of courtrooms is the traditions surrounding the profession. The author would believe this idea to be likely, not unlikely.

19. B
Difficulty: High
Category: Function
Getting to the Answer: The keyword phrase "serves to" identifies this as a Function question. Return to the cited lines, read around them, and identify the author's point in that section of the passage. The

sentence immediately preceding the context clues identifies the Supreme Court as "the most striking example of hierarchical American courthouse architecture." Unfortunately, this doesn't match any of the choices. Continue to research further up in the passage and identify why the author is using the Supreme Court as an example. From the passage map, the main idea of the previous paragraph is that courts will likely not be redesigned soon because of the traditions and hierarchy of the law. This matches (B), the correct answer.

Choice A is incorrect because instilling respect for the institution is part of the reason the Supreme Court contains these features, but that is not the reason the author mentions them. Choice C is a subtle distortion of information in the passage. Although the passage identifies the Supreme Court as the most prestigious court in the United States, the author does not state that the reason these features were used was to establish that prestige. Choice D is an irrelevant comparison; the text never compares the design of the Supreme Court to that of other American courts.

20. J
Difficulty: Low
Category: Detail
Getting to the Answer: The definite phrase, "According to the author," identifies this as a Detail question. You'll be able to look up the answer in the passage. In the passage map, "most standard courtrooms" are described in the second paragraph, so return to that paragraph and compare the information there to the choices. The "low wall or divider" is mentioned in the second sentence, and the "raised platform for the judge" is mentioned in the third sentence. Choice (J) is correct.

Choice F is half-correct and half-incorrect. Although the platform is mentioned, the children's waiting room is a feature of the Bexar County courtroom, not "most standard courtrooms." Choice G is a misused detail. The forty-four steps and considerable elevation of the justices are features of the Supreme Court, not "most standard courtrooms." Choice H is also half-correct and half-incorrect. The court officers are a feature of "most standard courtrooms," but the red curtains are only mentioned as a feature of the Supreme Court.

Passage III

Suggested Passage Map Notes:

¶1: Whorf POV: limits of native language constrain thinking

¶2: Ex: Hopi language

¶3: Whorf: Hopis & English speakers would have different descriptions of physical world

¶4: Whorf's views not well received

¶5: Jakobson (20 yrs later): what must be said important vs what can be said

¶6: Deutscher example: English vs Mandarin

¶7: Deutscher POV: can understand concept w/o needing to include in conversation

¶8: Example 2: aboriginal language (GY) uses directions to describe location

¶9: Result: always know directions

¶10: author POV: essence of Whorf's thinking correct

BIG PICTURE SUMMARY:

Main idea: It is possible that native languages influence the ways humans perceive and describe the world.

Author's purpose: To discuss Whorf's theory and later developments

21. B
Difficulty: Low
Category: Vocab-in-Context
Getting to the Answer: The phrase "most nearly means" identifies this as a Vocab-in-Context question. Return to the line reference, reread the sentence, and predict a word or phrase that could replace the word *temporal*. If you don't know the meaning of *temporal*, the last phrase describes a language that can "distinguish and quantify changes in time." This description matches (B), the correct choice. Note that when substituted for *temporal* in the original sentence, the answer retains the identical meaning of the sentence.

Choice A is incorrect because *temporal* refers to how the language uses the concept of time, not to the time the language has been in existence. The passage never discusses the ease of understanding a language, so C

is incorrect. Choice D is the opposite of what's stated in the passage; the passage discusses how languages express time, not perpetuity or timelessness.

22. G
Difficulty: Medium
Category: Function
Getting to the Answer: The phrase "in order to" identifies this as a Function question. Return to the fourth paragraph and determine how the example contributes to the main idea of the passage. The sentence immediately preceding the example provides the reason: to show how "People throughout the world are quite capable of thinking about the future and past even if they lack the terminology for it." This matches (G), the correct choice.

The remaining choices are all incorrect because the author's intention is to make the point that the use of incorrect grammar does not mean that the speaker does not understand the concept being discussed.

23. D
Difficulty: High
Category: Inference
Getting to the Answer: The keyword "inferred" identifies this as an Inference question. The correct choice will be supported by the passage, but may not be directly stated. Here, the "nuanced conclusion" refers to Jakobson's point of view. Match this information to the choices; choice (D) is correct.

Choice A is a misused detail from the previous paragraph, and is incorrect. The "nuanced conclusion" is that of Jakobson, not Whorf. Choice B is not mentioned in the text and is therefore incorrect. The author never discusses "interpreting languages." Choice C is incorrect because Deutscher is not introduced until the following paragraph, so the "nuanced conclusion" cannot be his.

24. H
Difficulty: High
Category: Function
Getting to the Answer: The phrase "in order to" identifies this as a Function question. Find the citation in the passage, and read around it to determine how the author uses the idea to develop the purpose of the passage. The context clue is found at the end of the sixth paragraph. The passage map identifies

Reading

that paragraph as containing an example illustrating Deutscher's point of view. Choice (H) is correct.

Choice F is incorrect because, although the author does correct some aspects of Whorf's thinking, that is not the primary function of the cited detail. The first sentence of the final paragraph concedes, "To an extent, then, Whorf was right." Choice G is not discussed in the passage and is incorrect. There is never any attempt to identify "the principal foundation of linguistics." Choice J is incorrect because it is the content of the citation, not the reason the author used it. The purpose of the passage is not to review different concepts of time but to illustrate the different linguistic theories through the examples of statements involving time.

25. D
Difficulty: Medium
Category: Detail
Getting to the Answer: The phrase "According to the passage" is a clue that this might be a Detail question. The answer will be stated directly in the passage, so go back to the text and research. The passage map identifies the sixth and seventh paragraphs as the place to start, so skim them quickly looking for the comparison between English and Mandarin speakers. Lines 66–67 state, "the person [who speaks Mandarin] wouldn't have to articulate timing every time they wanted to tell a story." This matches (D), the correct choice.

Choice A is subtly extreme. The author does present the possibility that Mandarin speakers might think less about time than English speakers but does not definitely state that this is the case. Choice B is not discussed in the text and is therefore incorrect. Choice C is not mentioned in the passage and is incorrect.

26. H
Difficulty: Medium
Category: Detail
Getting to the Answer: "Based on the passage" indicates that this is likely a Detail question. The passage map indicates Jakobson is discussed in the fifth paragraph, so return to that paragraph and skim, looking for an emphasis keyword that describes how most people view his theories. In the first sentence, the adjective *renowned* indicates that Jakobson is famous in his field. Choice (H) is correct.

Choice F is half-incorrect and half-extreme. There is no mention in the passage of Jakobson ever being

criticized, and *revered* is too strong. *Revered* has a connotation of adoration, and although Jakobson was famous, there is no evidence in the passage that he was adored. Choice G is the opposite of what's stated in the passage. If Jakobson is *renowned*, he is famous for his work, and other linguists are not indifferent. Choice J is half-correct, half-incorrect. Jakobson's theories are well-respected, but his character is not discussed in the text.

27. D
Difficulty: Medium
Category: Function
Getting to the Answer: The phrase "in order to" identifies this as a Function question. Locate the discussion of Guugu Yimithirr in the passage, and determine how the author used it to build toward the purpose of the passage. The passage map identifies this discussion in the eighth and ninth paragraphs. Guugu Yimithirr is the third example the author provides to support the main idea of the passage: different native languages may affect how different peoples interpret the physical world, so (D) is correct.

Choice A is incorrect because it summarizes the "facts" presented about Guugu Yimithirr, but this summary is not the reason the author included the language in the text. Choice B is not discussed in the passage and is therefore incorrect. Choice C is a misused detail. Those terms are mentioned in the author's description of the way an English-speaker would usually think about direction but not to argue that those concepts should be included in other languages.

28. F
Difficulty: High
Category: Detail
Getting to the Answer: The keyword *describes* identifies this as a Detail question. The correct choice will be stated directly in the passage, so start at the line reference, but skim the lines above and below for the definition of "linguistic obligation." The beginning of the first sentence in paragraph 8 states that the paragraph will present an example of "linguistic obligation," so skim upward looking for the definition. The sixth and seventh paragraphs are Deutscher's example and opinion, so continue looking earlier in the passage. In lines 46–48, Jakobson describes the way language shapes our thinking as "determining what we're obligated to think about rather than all that it is possible to think about." This matches (F), the correct choice.

The remaining incorrect choices are not discussed in the text. For G, there is no mention of vocabulary or the issues facing non-native speakers. The author makes no recommendations for further studies as mentioned in H. There is no discussion of "fundamental terms" much less the effect of their poor definition, so J is also incorrect.

29. C
Difficulty: Medium
Category: Function
Getting to the Answer: The phrase "most likely to" identifies this as a Function question. Start at the lines cited in the question, but since the context clue is a rhetorical question, expect that the author's explanation of the purpose of the question will follow those lines. The answer to the question comes in the following line, "…*it doesn't happen*. Native Guugu Yimithirr speakers…*always* know where north is…" As noted in the passage map, this is another example of language affecting native speakers' understanding of the physical world. Choice (C) is correct.

Choice A is incorrect because the explanation is provided in the text. Choice B is incorrect because, according to the passage, the Guugu Yimithirr do not experience this problem. Choice D is incorrect because the question is used to illustrate an example, not to modify a theory.

30. F
Difficulty: Low
Category: Function
Getting to the Answer: The phrase "in order to" identifies this as a Function question. Since the question is asking about the final paragraph, start by reviewing the passage map and answering the question, "Why did the author return to Whorf's thesis?" Since the purpose of the passage is to discuss Whorf's theory and later developments, the last paragraph, as noted in the passage map, provides the author's summary: Whorf was fundamentally correct. This matches (F), the correct choice.

Choice G is a subtle distortion of information in the paragraph. The author does not state that Whorf's original theory was completely correct; the second sentence of the final paragraph acknowledges a correction of his view. Similarly, H is too extreme. The author recognizes the weakness in Whorf's theory, but opens the paragraph with "To an extent…Whorf was right." Choice J is

not mentioned in the passage and is incorrect. No new discoveries are credited to Whorf.

Passage IV

Suggested Passage Map Notes:

¶1: Earth's magnetic field—why important

¶2: Origin? dynamo effect

¶3: Venus—iron core, but no mag field

¶4: mag field changes, iron in volcanic rocks

¶5: mag field reversed in past

¶6: now, mag field may reverse w/in a few hundred yrs

¶7: effect of weakened field—elec grid

¶8: effect of weakened field—human health

BIG PICTURE SUMMARY:

Main idea: The Earth's magnetic field may reverse, so this possibility must be considered.

Author's purpose: To discuss the Earth's magnetic field and its changes

---

31. B
Difficulty: Medium
Category: Global
Getting to the Answer: When a question asks for the author's attitude, consider if you read any emphasis or emotional keywords such as "unfortunately," "remarkable," or "critical concern." This passage did not, and the author's neutral tone is captured in the purpose in the passage map. Choice (B), the correct choice, is the only choice that reflects the author's factual approach. In addition, the author's statement in lines 82–85 that "the effects of a reversed magnetic north are worth discussing, especially given that this switch could have profound effects on everyday life" supports the answer, "concern and attentiveness."

Although some scientists are skeptical that the magnetic field will reverse quickly, this is not the author's opinion, so A is incorrect. There are no positive keywords in the passage that indicate the author is hopeful, so C is incorrect. Finally, the author is concerned, not relieved, making D incorrect.

32. F
Difficulty: Low
Category: Detail
Getting to the Answer: Changes in the Earth's magnetic field and iron are mentioned in paragraph 4 of the passage map. Returning to that paragraph to research, line 42 states "iron is a magnetic substance." Later in the paragraph, the direction of the iron found in solidified lava is used to determine the direction of the magnetic field. Choice (F) is correct.

Choice G is an extreme choice; iron is mentioned as being present in lava, but not as "the primary component." Choices H and J are not mentioned in the passage and are incorrect. Neither the location of the lava nor the difficulty of extracting the iron is discussed.

33. D
Difficulty: Low
Category: Detail
Getting to the Answer: The keyword *describes* identifies this as a Detail question, so look up the answer in the passage. The dynamo effect is found in paragraph 2 of the passage map. The map states that this paragraph is discussing the origin of the magnetic field, and line 19 identifies the origin as *unclear*, and the dynamo effect as "the prominent theory." Choice (D) is correct.

Although the dynamo effect may be *widely accepted* because it is "the prominent theory," it is described as a theory, not a fact, so A is incorrect. The likelihood of the proof of the dynamo theory is never discussed, so B is also incorrect. As "the prominent theory," the dynamo effect is not described as a "mistaken conception" of the past, and C is incorrect.

34. F
Difficulty: Low
Category: Inference
Getting to the Answer: The passage map identifies paragraph 8 as containing the effects of a weaker magnetic field on human health, so research there to find out if the "abnormal human cells" mentioned in the question are one of those effects. Lines 96–97 mention the abnormal cells as a result of increased radiation, and the previous line identifies the cause of the increased radiation to be the weakening of Earth's magnetic field. Choice (F) is correct.

Although the danger to electrical systems from the weakened magnetic field is discussed in the previous paragraph, they are never described as "risky"

or connected to any effect on human health. Choice G is incorrect. Choice H is a distortion of information in the passage, and is incorrect. Although radioactive decay is mentioned in connection with the origin of the magnetic field, the text never discussed radiation from the magnetic field. Choice J is incorrect because it is another distortion of information in the text. "Mass extinctions" are only mentioned as something that has not been seen in conjunction with magnetic field reversals in the past.

35. A
Difficulty: Medium
Category: Detail
Getting to the Answer: The definite keyword phrase "points to" identifies this as a Detail question. In addition, the emphasis keyword "critical" indicates that you're looking for a one of the most important aspects of the dynamo effect. The passage map locates the discussion of the dynamo effect in paragraph 2, so return there to research the answer. In line 22, the keyword *compels* identifies a critical component: heat from radioactive decay. This matches (A), the correct choice.

Choice B is a faulty use of a detail from the next paragraph. Although the rotation of the Earth may affect the magnetic field, rotation is not mentioned as a component of the dynamo effect. Choice C is a distortion of information in the passage. The iron in rocks after volcanic activity is used to determine past movement of the magnetic field, but volcanic activity is not a component of the dynamo effect. Choice D is another faulty use of a detail from the passage. Although the passage goes on to discuss the periodic reversal of magnetic north (and this may be a result of the dynamo effect), this reversal is not a component of the generation of the magnetic field. These choices are all incorrect.

36. G
Difficulty: High
Category: Function
Getting to the Answer: The keyword phrase "in order to" identifies this as a Function question. Consider how the comparison between Earth and Venus contributed to the author's purpose: to discuss the Earth's magnetic field and its changes. According to the passage map, Venus is discussed in paragraph 3 because, like Earth, it has an iron core, but, unlike Earth, it does NOT have a magnetic field. Notice that the first sentence of

Paragraph 3 provides the author's reason for including the paragraph: "Other forces also significantly influence the Earth's magnetic field" and that the Earth/Venus comparison will provide an example of one of these forces. Choice (G) is correct.

Choices F and H are a type of common trap choice for Function questions: they relate to the content of the comparison, but not the reason the author included the comparison. Choice F also includes a subtle error: Venus' magnetic field is different from that of Earth because Venus does NOT have a magnetic field. Although the author does highlight the significant difference between the planets' rotation times, the reason the author does so is to indicate a possible influence on Earth's magnetic field, which makes H incorrect. Choice J is the opposite of true: the passage argues for the importance of Earth's iron core in generating the magnetic field, not against it.

37. C
Difficulty: Medium
Category: Inference
Getting to the Answer: This question is essentially asking for the main idea of the sixth paragraph. Questions on the content or purpose of an entire paragraph are usually quickly (and correctly!) answered from the passage map. The passage map notes for paragraph 6 read "now, mag field may reverse w/in a few hundred yrs." This matches (C), the correct choice.

For the incorrect choices, A and B are correct details from the passage, but they are not a part of the sixth paragraph since the dynamo effect is discussed in paragraph 2 and the effects of the weakening magnetic field are discussed in the final two paragraphs. Choice D is a distortion of the information presented in paragraph 6. Although the movement of magnetic north is accelerating, the text never suggests that scientists might be wrong about the location of magnetic north.

38. F
Difficulty: Low
Category: Detail
Getting to the Answer: The phrase "According to the passage" provides a clue that this might be a Detail question. Use the passage map to find the location of the information in the passage and look up the answer. In the passage map, "iron in volcanic rock" is discussed in paragraph 4. Return there, and find the discussion of the position of iron particles. Lines 49–52 state that

"…a lava rock that solidified at a particular point in time will therefore have iron particles oriented in the direction of magnetic north at that time." This matches (F), the correct choice.

Choice G is a distortion of information in the paragraph. The discussion of the magnet and iron filings was an example to illustrate that iron will align with a magnetic field, not a statement that a magnet could be or was used to affect the iron in lava rock. Choices H and J are not mentioned in the passage and are therefore incorrect.

39. D
Difficulty: Medium
Category: Detail
Getting to the Answer: "The passage identifies" indicates that this is likely a Detail question. This question can be approached in two different ways. If you noticed that paragraph 6 started with the contrast of an old view with a new one ("It was assumed…however…") and noted that in your passage map, a quick look at either the map or lines 62–66 is enough to lead you to (D), the correct choice. If that information is missing from your passage map, you can also take each choice back to the passage and eliminate the incorrect ones.

Choice A is mentioned in paragraph 4, but it is a hypothetical statement by the author, not a scientific hypothesis that has been revised. Choice B is the opposite of what's stated in the passage; the discussion of Venus in paragraph 3 indicated that unlike Earth, Venus does NOT have a magnetic field. Choice C is an aspect of the dynamo effect discussed in paragraph 2, and although it is a theory, it is well-accepted and has not been questioned.

40. G
Difficulty: Medium
Category: Global
Getting to the Answer: The keywords "primary purpose of the passage" identify this as a Global question. Use the purpose you identified in preparing your passage map as your prediction: to discuss the Earth's magnetic field and its changes. This matches (G), the correct choice.

For the incorrect choices, F is extreme. Although the author is concerned about the potential ill effects of a weakened/reversed magnetic field, the choice's strong language, "impending disaster," does not match the author's more neutral tone. Choice H is both too extreme and too narrow. The author is not "promoting" the dynamo effect; the dynamo effect is presented factually as the most prominent theory for the origin of the magnetic field. Also, this choice does not include any aspects of the magnetic field reversal discussed in paragraphs 4 through 8. Choice J misstates the author's intention in the frequent references to iron in the passage. Iron is always discussed in relation to the Earth's magnetic field, not to its importance in general scientific study.

Passage V

Suggested Passage Map Notes:

Passage A

¶1: Battle of Normandy—long, important

¶2: details of force, huge

¶3: problem—weather

¶4: E—weather difficult, but battle crucial

¶5: deception contributed to success

Passage B

¶1: V Hay, Brit nurse in field hosp in France

¶2: H's memories—severity of casualties

¶3: difficult conditions in France

¶4: MV Desmarais, Brit nurse in Eng, diff conds in Eng

¶5: author POV—nurses heroic

BIG PICTURE SUMMARY:

Passage A

Main idea: The Battle of Normandy was difficult but decisive.

Author's purpose: To describe the difficulties and some of the factors that led to the success of Battle of Normandy

Passage B

Main idea: Nurses were heroic caring for Battle of Normandy casualties.

Author's purpose: To describe the difficult conditions, and heroic actions, of nurses in Battle of Normandy

---

41. C
Difficulty: Medium
Category: Inference
Getting to the Answer: This question asks what the passage *implies*, so the correct choice will be supported by the passage but may not be directly stated. Use the context keyword *unusual*, go back to Passage A, and research which aspect of the Battle of Normandy is described as *unusual*. The last sentence of the second paragraph identifies "150,000 soldiers" as "one of the largest amphibious military assaults in modern history," so (C) is correct.

Choice A is a distortion of information in the passage and is incorrect. Although several nations contributed troops to the assault, this feature is not described as *unusual* in the passage. Neither B nor D are mentioned in the text, so both are incorrect. You might believe one (or both) of these choices to be true from your study of history, but neither is discussed in the passage. Remember: you must be able to prove your answer from the passage itself.

42. J
Difficulty: Medium
Category: Function
Getting to the Answer: This question asks why the author included particular information, so it's a Function question. The context clue is all of the fourth paragraph, so refer to your passage map to determine why the author included the paragraph. The passage map notes indicate that Eisenhower's quotations support the earlier statements on the difficulty of planning the exact day of the attack. The final sentence, addressed to the troops, emphasizes the battle's importance. This matches (J), the correct choice.

Choice F is a distortion of the information in the passage and is incorrect. Although Eisenhower comments on the weather, there is no attempt to "explain...the typical weather patterns." Choice G is a misused detail from the passage. The nearly constant meetings with advisers and the planned deception indicate Eisenhower's attention to detail, but the quotations are used to support the difficulty of the battle, not to highlight Eisenhower's planning skills. Choice H is a common type of tempting choice for those who read both passages before answering the questions on only one passage; medical staff are never mentioned in Passage A, so Eisenhower's quotations do not refer to them, and H is incorrect.

43. D

Difficulty: High

Category: Inference

Getting to the Answer: The keyword *suggests* identifies this as an Inference question. The correct choice will always be supported by the passage, but it may not always be directly stated. There are two approaches to this question. If you noticed that the main idea of the final paragraph was that the deception contributed to the success of the battle and included this information in your passage map, then you likely easily identified (D) as the correct choice. If you didn't, you can also reach the correct choice by elimination.

Choice A is a typical incorrect choice that is often chosen by those who read both passages without answering the questions about Passage A first. Passage A never mentions medical care. Choice B is a subtle distortion of information in the passage. The significant number of troops were from three countries, not just Britain. More importantly though, the passage never attributes the success of the assault to the large number of troops. Choice C is a distortion of the discussion of the weather. The weather affected the date of the invasion, but the passage never states that the specific time of the battle contributed to the invasion's success.

44. F

Difficulty: Medium

Category: Inference

Getting to the Answer: The keyword *implies* identifies this as an Inference question. The correct choice will be supported by the passage, but may not be directly stated. If you noted in your passage map that nurses in the field hospitals, close to the front lines, and those in England worked long hours with no opportunity for meals or rest because of the huge number of casualties, you can support (F), the correct choice, from your passage map. If you did not have these notes, you can also answer by elimination.

Choice G is extreme. Although the author praises the nurses' heroic efforts, the text never says their efforts were not praised by others. Choice H distorts information presented in the first paragraph. Nurses "rushed" seriously injured casualties "straight through to surgery;" nurses did not perform the surgeries themselves. Choice J is extreme. The author praises nurses who served during the Battle of Normandy, but the text never states that their contribution was a decisive factor in the battle's success.

45. A

Difficulty: Medium

Category: Function

Getting to the Answer: This question asks why the author included a quote, so it's a Function question. Identify how the quote contributes to the author's purpose. The quotation is found in paragraph 2, where Hay is recounting the number and severity of the casualties she treated. "'They all were patients to us'" indicates that Hay was treating both Allied and German casualties, so (A) is correct.

Choice B is incorrect because, although this choice captures the main idea of the entire paragraph, there is no stated connection between the high number of patients and the quotation. Choices C and D misstate the tone of the passage and are incorrect; the author never criticizes or compares the compassion of the two groups of nurses.

46. G

Difficulty: Medium

Category: Inference

Getting to the Answer: The keyword *inferred* identifies this as an Inference question. Support your choice from the passage, but the answer may not be stated directly. This question is very general, and the answer will be difficult to predict from the passage map, so proceed to the choices and work by elimination.

For F, triage is discussed in the field hospitals in the first paragraph, but never mentioned in connection with the English hospitals. Choice (G) is correct. The first paragraph states that "surgeries were performed in order to stabilize patients so that they were safe to travel back to England" and the fourth paragraph states English hospitals received "casualties…that had been given only first aid in France." Choice H is the opposite of what's stated in the passage: nurses in both locations worked long hours under difficult conditions. Choice J is a misused detail. The boats carrying the casualties arrived in Southampton, but the locations of the hospitals are never identified.

47. C

Difficulty: Medium

Category: Vocab-in-Context

Getting to the Answer: The phrase "most nearly means" identifies this as a Vocab-in-Context question. Return to the sentence that includes the line reference, and predict a word or phrase that would give the sentence the same meaning. The passage states, "the nurses were not able to *rotate* because there simply were not enough nurses to cover separate shifts" and then goes on to explain: "Everyone was required to work around the clock." If the nurses worked around the clock, they were not able to take time off. Choice (C) matches this prediction and is the correct choice.

Choice A is the most common definition of rotate, but this has no connection to working around the clock and is therefore incorrect. Choices B and D are incorrect because the sentence that includes the cited word is describing the working hours, not the positions the nurses may have been in (choice B) or their locations (choice D).

48. G
Difficulty: Medium
Category: Detail
Getting to the Answer: The definite keyword *provides* identifies this as a Detail question, so you'll likely be able to find the answer directly in the passage. Before reading the choices, consider the relationship between the two passages: Passage A describes the planning, difficulties, and success of the Battle of Normandy, and Passage B describes the heroic contributions of nurses who treated the casualties. Choice (G) is correct.

Choice F distorts information presented in the passage: the basic plan for the battle is described, but the specific decisions that were made during the battle are not. Choice H, the personal state of combatants, is not mentioned in either passage. Choice J incorrectly refers to Passage B, but the question requires that the correct choice includes information from Passage A.

49. A
Difficulty: Medium
Category: Inference
Getting to the Answer: The keyword *suggests* identifies this as an Inference question. Return to the sentence mentioned in the line reference, and consider how Hay's journey connects to Passage A. Refer to the passage map to recall the purpose of Passage A: to describe the difficulties and some of the factors that led to the success of the Battle of Normandy. Next, read the lines in Passage B and consider the description of Hay's journey: it was about a week after D-Day, it was a fairly short distance, but it took a very long time because there were pockets of the German army on the way. If there were still enough German troops to disrupt travel a week after the invasion, this underscores the difficulties faced by the Allies. Choice (A) is correct.

Choices B and D are incorrect because the travel difficulties are not related to the number of vehicles used in the invasion (choice B) or the date of the invasion (choice D). Choice C is never discussed in either passage and is also incorrect.

50. G
Difficulty: Easy
Category: Global
Getting to the Answer: Questions asking about the tone of a passage involve the passage as a whole, and so are Global questions. Use your summary of the main idea and the author's purpose of each passage to predict your answer. Passage A was a factual description, and the emphasis keyword *heroic* indicates that the author of Passage B had a positive attitude toward the nurses. Choice (G) matches this prediction, and is correct.

Because you can eliminate a choice if any part of that choice is incorrect and you've recognized the positive tone of Passage B, you can eliminate F, H, and J. Similarly, the neutral tone of Passage A can be used to eliminate those choices.

PART 5

ACT SCIENCE

CHAPTER 22

THE METHOD FOR ACT SCIENCE

LEARNING OBJECTIVE

After completing this chapter, you will be able to:

- Effectively and efficiently apply the ACT Science Method

How to Do ACT Science

The ACT Science Test is a test of your scientific reasoning ability, not a test of your knowledge of scientific content. While you do need to have knowledge of basic scientific concepts and terminology to answer some of the questions, you do NOT need to understand advanced concepts or memorize equations.

If you've completed high-school-level courses covering topics in biology, chemistry, earth/space science, and physics, then you should already know everything you'll need to know for test day. In fact, you can still do quite well on the ACT Science Test even if you've never studied or you're still taking classes on some of these subjects.

If you run across a question that requires background knowledge you don't have, eliminate as many answer choices as possible and then make an educated guess from the remaining choices. Most importantly, you should avoid wasting time by focusing your attention on the vast majority of questions that don't require outside knowledge.

In this chapter, we'll give you an overview of how to tackle Science passages and questions. The other chapters in this unit will help you improve your approach for the six ACT Science question types.

To see the ACT Science Method in action, try the passage and questions that follow on your own. Then, compare your approach to our recommendations for how to approach ACT Science. Finally, reflect on how you can become a more efficient test taker.

Passage I

Researchers compared the characteristics of grassland prescribed fires during the growing and dormant season to three experimental small-scale fire approaches. In all experiments, thermocouples 10 cm above the soil were used to determine time-temperature profiles.

Experiment 1

Two dormant-season and two growing-season prescribed burns, ignited via a ring-fire technique, were performed within a tallgrass prairie. The average fuel loads for the dormant-season and growing-season fires were 5,036 kg ha^{-1} and 5,545 kg ha^{-1}, respectively. The results are shown in Figure 1.

This data is from *Fire Ecology*, Vol. 11, Iss. 3, December 2015, pp. 34-44.

Figure 1

Experiment 2

Four 2 m × 2 m aluminum sheets were used to form a burn box around *in situ* vegetation of a prairie similar in composition to the prairie burned in Experiment 1. A propane torch was used to ignite the fire, and additional timothy hay was added to adjust the fuel load to 3,000 kg ha^{-1}. The experiment was repeated 4 times. The average results are shown in Figure 2.

Experiment 3

Grass species were grown in 15-cm plastic pots. The pots were placed below a metal burn table that was 1.2 m × 2.4 m with five 16.5-cm diameter circles. A drip torch was used to ignite the fire, and timothy hay was added at a rate of 3,000 kg ha^{-1}. The experiment was repeated 4 times. The average results are shown in Figure 2.

Experiment 4

A propane prong composed of a pipe, tube, and propane tank was shaped into a U with two 30-cm arms with holes (as shown in the diagram). Five pots, like those in Experiment 3, were each burned for 60 sec between the prongs inside a closed structure with ventilation. The average results are shown in Figure 2.

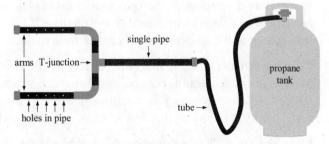

Adapted from Katherin Kral, *et al*., "Simulating Grassland Prescribed Fires Using Experimental Approaches." © 2015 by Fire Ecology.

Diagram

Key

——— burn box

– – – burn table

· · · · · propane prong

This data is from *Fire Ecology*, Vol. 11, Iss. 3, December 2015, pp. 34-44.

Figure 2

1. Experiment 2 differed from Experiment 3 in which of the following ways?

   A. In Experiment 2, timothy hay was added to adjust the fuel load, whereas in Experiment 3, greenhouse-grown plants were added to adjust the fuel load.

   B. In Experiment 2, natural habitat plants were burned, whereas in Experiment 3, greenhouse-grown plants were burned.

   C. A propane torch was used to ignite the fire in Experiment 2, whereas a ring-fire technique was used to ignite the fire in Experiment 3.

   D. The average fuel load in Experiment 2 was 5,036 kg ha^{-1}, whereas the average fuel load in Experiment 3 was 3,000 kg ha^{-1}.

2. Bends in a pipe and variations in pipe diameter create pressure differentials that cause fluids to undergo mixing. According to the diagram, where would mixing of air and propane most likely occur to support combustion?

   F. Arms

   G. T-junction

   H. Single pipe

   J. Tube

3. The researchers had predicted that the burn-box approach would best simulate the temperature profile of growing-season prescribed fires. Are the results of the study consistent with this prediction?

   A. Yes; the maximum mean temperatures for both growing-season and burn-box fires was around 350°C.

   B. Yes; the maximum mean temperatures for both growing-season and burn-box fires was around 650°C.

   C. No; the maximum mean temperature for growing-season fires was 650°C, whereas the maximum mean temperature for burn box was 350°C.

   D. No; the maximum mean temperature for growing-season fires was 350°C, whereas the maximum mean temperature for burn box was 650°C.

4. Suppose the maximum mean temperature and heat duration of an additional trial were 300°C and 175 sec, respectively. The time-temperature profile for this trial would most likely have been for a:

   F. dormant-season prescribed fire.

   G. burn-box fire.

   H. burn-table fire.

   J. propane-prong fire.

5. The scientists further calculated heat dosage, the product of heat duration and temperature, to predict plant mortality. Based on the results, which of the following fires had the highest heat dosage?

    A. Growing-season
    B. Burn-box
    C. Burn-table
    D. Propane-prong

6. During dormancy, grasses enter a state of temporary metabolic inactivity to conserve water and nutrients. In Experiment 1, what is the most likely reason the average maximum temperature for the dormant-season prescribed fire was almost twice that of the growing-season prescribed fire?

    F. The temperature of the dormant season is greater than that of the growing season, so the dormant-season fires burned hotter.
    G. More wind during the dormant season spread the fires at a faster rate.
    H. The fuel for the dormant-season fires had lower moisture content, so they produced hotter maximum temperatures.
    J. The average fuel load was greater for the dormant-season than for the growing-season fires.

Many test takers will see a diagram like the one in Experiment 4 and panic. Others will waste a great deal of time looking at all the data without a clear goal. You want to avoid both those outcomes. Before diving into how to tackle *this* passage, it's important first to understand the passage *types* you'll see in ACT Science, as the passage type will dictate your approach.

Passage Types

Passages in ACT Science fall into three passage types:

- Data Representation
- Research Summaries
- Conflicting Viewpoints

While the passage order varies, you can always expect to see three Research Summaries passages, two Data Representation passages, and one Conflicting Viewpoints passage. Regardless of type, passages in the ACT Science Test are taken from a variety of natural science subjects. These include topics in:

- Earth and Space Science—astronomy, geology, meteorology, etc.
- Biology—botany, genetics, zoology, etc.
- Chemistry—acids/bases, kinetics/equilibria, organic chemistry, etc.
- Physics—electromagnetism, mechanics, thermodynamics, etc.

While the text of Science passages is considerably shorter than what is found in the English and Reading tests, most Science passages are accompanied by graphs, tables, and/or diagrams, which you will have to interpret and analyze.

The ACT Science Method

Your first step for any ACT Science passage will be to **identify the passage type**. Recall that there are three types of passages; let the passage type guide your approach to the question set:

- Data Representation passages tend to be light on text but heavy on data presented in graphs or tables.

- Research Summaries passages tend to contain more text, consisting largely of descriptions of multiple experimental procedures, and often feature their own graphs or tables filled with results.

- Conflicting Viewpoints passages contain accounts of two or more competing theories/hypotheses on a particular phenomenon, typically featuring more text and fewer figures than the other two passage types.

Your next step is based on the type of passage. You need to **analyze the passage and figures strategically**, and this analysis will be different for each passage type. Chapter 23 will focus on the question types most common in Data Representation passages, chapter 24 will focus on the question types most common in Research Summaries passages, and chapter 25 will focus on the question types most common in Conflicting Viewpoints passages. However, it's important to note that question types are not exclusive to one passage type.

After you have analyzed the passage, you will **examine each question stem**. The specific information an individual question wants you to consider will be unique to your ACT exam, but the way in which the questions ask for that information—and the approaches required to answer them—fall into consistent patterns, or question types. The six question types fall into three categories:

- Data
  - Interpreting Data
  - Using Data
- Experiments
  - Experimental Design
  - Synthesizing Data
- Thinking Like a Scientist
  - Applying Core Knowledge
  - Supporting Hypotheses

Chapters 23–25 will provide additional information about how to more efficiently and effectively examine question stems. While each question type will be unique in the skills and approach required, it's important on *every question* to identify information in the question stem and answer choices like variables, units, or figure headings to help you hone in on the specific parts of the passage that apply to the question (for example, "mass," "kg," or "Figure 1").

Now that you've analyzed the passage and the question stem, you're ready to **predict and answer**:

- Locate the corresponding data in the passage and circle the parts of the figure or text that directly relate to the question.

- Based on what you discover in the passage, formulate a prediction about what the correct answer should say.

- Match your prediction to the correct answer choice.

Chapters 23–25 will provide additional information about how improve predictions based on passage and question type.

Here's what we did:

ACT SCIENCE METHOD

Step 1. Identify the passage type

Step 2. Analyze the passage and figures strategically

Step 3. Examine the question stem

Step 4. Predict and answer

Take a look at a strategic approach to Passage I. Look for at least one way per question that your original approach could have been faster and more confident.

Step 1: Identify the passage type

The passage provided at the start of this section has clearly labeled headers for Experiments 1 through 4, indicating that it is a Research Summaries passage.

Step 2: Analyze the passage and figures strategically

Central idea: The first paragraph indicates the experiments are comparing the burn characteristics of prescribed fires to grasslands during dormant and growing seasons to three smaller-scale experimental approaches. Note: *When* the experimenters measure the burn (growing vs. dormant season) and the burn method used are factors under their control; thus, they are independent variables. The paragraph also mentions that experimenters will be collecting time-temperature profiles; therefore, time and temperature are both dependent variables, as they will change depending on the burn type and season.

Experiment 1 and Figure 1: The details within the text are likely irrelevant to the majority of the questions. The figure, however, provides lots of key info in a quick glance:

- The x-axis is heat duration; the y-axis is mean temperature
- Dormant-season burns are several hundred degrees hotter and last ~40–50 seconds longer than growing-season burns

Experiments 2–4 and Figure 2: Skim the details within the text about the methods of each experiment quickly; these can easily be returned to if there is a specific question about them. Instead, focus your attention on Figure 2, which shows:

- The same axes and variables that were in Figure 1
- In both max temperature and duration, burn box > burn table > propane prong

Diagram: Don't spend time on this now. There will likely be a question on the experimental apparatus of Experiment 4 since the diagram is included, but wait to see what the question is first.

Steps 3 and 4: Examine the question stem, predict, and answer

Question	Explanation
1. Experiment 2 differed from Experiment 3 in which of the following ways? A. In Experiment 2, timothy hay was added to adjust the fuel load, whereas in Experiment 3, greenhouse-grown plants were added to adjust the fuel load. B. In Experiment 2, natural habitat plants were burned, whereas in Experiment 3, greenhouse-grown plants were burned. C. A propane torch was used to ignite the fire in Experiment 2, whereas a ring-fire technique was used to ignite the fire in Experiment 3. D. The average fuel load in Experiment 2 was 5,036 kg ha^{-1}, whereas the average fuel load in Experiment 3 was 3,000 kg ha^{-1}.	Methodology questions are not common, but they can come up from time to time. Step 2 in the ACT Science Method recommends skimming the text of the experiments during your first pass; now is the time to return to that text with the specific question in mind: "What's different between Experiments 2 and 3?" A quick return to the text reveals that Experiment 2 used "*in situ* vegetation," whereas in Experiment 3, "grass species were grown in 15-cm plastic pots." The correct answer won't necessarily be an exact match to the language of the passage; rather, it may use synonyms to some of the key terms. Notice how (B) correctly matches the described difference without mirroring the passage word for word. Both experiments added timothy hay to adjust the fuel load, eliminating A. While C correctly notes a propane torch was used in Experiment 2, a drip torch was used in Experiment 3, not a ring-fire technique. Lastly, D is incorrect because the average fuel load in both experiments was 3,000 kg ha^{-1}.
2. Bends in a pipe and variations in pipe diameter create pressure differentials that cause fluids to undergo mixing. According to the diagram, where would mixing of air and propane most likely occur to support combustion? F. Arms G. T-junction H. Single pipe J. Tube	The key to answering this question comes from the question stem itself, which can become clearer if you paraphrase what the question is stating: combustion takes place where air and propane mixes, which happens when there are bends in a pipe and variations in pipe diameter. Examine the diagram with this in mind, and note that this best describes a T-junction where the two wider arms combine with the single pipe at 90° angles. This prediction matches (G).

Question	Explanation
3. The researchers had predicted that the burn-box approach would best simulate the temperature profile of growing-season prescribed fires. Are the results of the study consistent with this prediction? A. Yes; the maximum mean temperatures for both growing-season and burn-box fires was around 350°C. B. Yes; the maximum mean temperatures for both growing-season and burn-box fires was around 650°C. C. No; the maximum mean temperature for growing-season fires was 650°C, whereas the maximum mean temperature for burn box was 350°C. D. No; the maximum mean temperature for growing-season fires was 350°C, whereas the maximum mean temperature for burn box was 650°C.	When asking if the results are consistent with the prediction, the question is really saying that you need to compare the growing-season fire to the burn-box fire. To compare their results, you will need to examine both Figure 1 and Figure 2 for the maximum mean temperature of each. Growing-season fires had a max temp of 350°C, whereas the burn box had a max temp of 600°C, matching (D). Note: the difference between their max temps makes the results not consistent with the prediction.
4. Suppose the maximum mean temperature and heat duration of an additional trial were 300°C and 175 sec, respectively. The time-temperature profile for this trial would most likely have been for a: F. dormant-season prescribed fire. G. burn-box fire. H. burn-table fire. J. propane-prong fire.	Paraphrase the question, including the new information provided in it: which burn profile is most similar to the temperature (300°C) and time (175 sec) of the new trial? These parameters match the profile of the propane-prong fire from Figure 2, making (J) correct.

Question	Explanation
5. The scientists further calculated heat dosage, the product of heat duration and temperature, to predict plant mortality. Based on the results, which of the following fires had the highest heat dosage? A. Growing-season B. Burn-box C. Burn-table D. Propane-prong	Heat dosage is a new concept, but it is simply heat duration × temperature, the two variables from Figures 1 and 2. The question stem thus indicates that you'll need to compare the heat durations and temperatures of four of the fires. From Figure 2, note that the burn box > the burn table > the propane prong in both duration and max temperature, so the burn box must also have a greater heat dosage than either the burn table or the propane prong. To determine whether the growing-season burn or the burn box has the higher heat dosage, their respective data must be compared from Figures 1 and 2. Growing-season burns had a max temp of ~350°C and duration of ~130 seconds; the burn box had a max temp of ~600°C and duration of ~210 seconds. Again, without performing any calculations, you can predict that the burn box will have the greater heat dosage since it has both higher temp and duration. Lastly, match the prediction with the correct answer choice, (B).
6. During dormancy, grasses enter a state of temporary metabolic inactivity to conserve water and nutrients. In Experiment 1, what is the most likely reason the average maximum temperature for the dormant-season prescribed fire was almost twice that of the growing-season prescribed fire? F. The temperature of the dormant season is greater than that of the growing season, so the dormant-season fires burned hotter. G. More wind during the dormant season spread the fires at a faster rate. H. The fuel for the dormant-season fires had lower moisture content, so they produced hotter maximum temperatures. J. The average fuel load was greater for the dormant-season than for the growing-season fires.	The question is asking you to infer *why* dormant-season fires burn twice as hot as growing-season fires. This may seem like a difficult question at first, and you may be tempted to go back and pore over the passage for helpful details. Resist that time-wasting approach and focus on the new information provided: dormant grasses are metabolically inactive due to *fewer nutrients* and *less water*. The only answer choice to highlight one of these differences is (H) by explaining that the hotter temperatures were due to "lower moisture content."

In the next section, you'll see another ACT Science passage. Try to apply the ACT Science Method presented in this lesson to read and answer the questions as quickly and confidently as possible.

How Much Have You Learned?

Directions: Take as much time as you need on these questions. Work carefully and methodically. There will be opportunities for timed practice in future chapters.

Passage II

A snowmobile's total braking distance, D, is the distance a snowmobile travels from the moment a driver first sees a "stop" signal until the snowmobile comes to a complete stop.

Students used 2 methods to calculate D using equations from physics. Method 1 calculated D using S and T and assuming a driver reaction time of 0.8 sec. S is the distance traveled after a driver sees a "stop" signal but before a driver begins the braking process; T is the average distance traveled after the brakes are applied. Method 2 maintains that D is simply the initial speed in ft/sec multiplied by 2 sec, based on the hypothesis that D is the distance the snowmobile would have traveled over 2 sec if the brakes had not been applied. Table 1 shows the results of both methods given various initial speeds, and Figure 1 graphs D from both methods versus initial speed.

Figure 1

Table 1					
Initial speed (mi/hr)	Initial speed (ft/sec)	Method 1			Method 2
		S(ft)	T(ft)	D(ft)	D(ft)
25	37	29	28	57	73
35	51	41	75	116	102
45	66	53	144	197	132
55	81	65	245	310	162

1. Based on Table 1, what is the approximate value of D according to Method 1 when the initial speed is 58 ft/sec?

   A. 70 ft

   B. 150 ft

   C. 250 ft

   D. 320 ft

2. According to Figure 1, at approximately which of the following initial speeds is the value of D from Method 1 equal to that from Method 2?

   F. 20 mi/hr

   G. 30 mi/hr

   H. 40 mi/hr

   J. 50 mi/hr

3. Suppose that a snowmobile was traveling at an initial speed of 75 mi/hr. Its D, according to Method 2, would most likely have been:

   A. less than 100 ft.

   B. between 100 and 200 ft.

   C. between 200 and 300 ft.

   D. greater than 300 ft.

4. Based on the results of the study, the S for an initial speed of 25 mi/hr, compared to S for an initial speed of 55 mi/hr, is approximately:

   F. $\frac{1}{4}$ as large.

   G. $\frac{1}{2}$ as large.

   H. 2 times as large.

   J. 4 times as large.

5. The average distance traveled after the brakes are applied (T) plotted against the distance traveled after a driver sees a stop sign (S) for Method 1 is best represented by which of the following graphs?

A.

B.

C.

D.

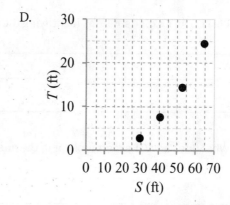

6. Which of the following describes a difference between Method 1 and Method 2? In Method 1:

   F. speeds were measured in mi/hr, but in Method 2, speeds were measured in ft/sec.

   G. distance was calculated based on a reaction speed of 0.8 sec, but in Method 2, distance was calculated based on a reaction speed of 2.0 sec.

   H. distance was calculated from the sum of two factors, but in Method 2, distance was calculated as the product of two factors.

   J. multiple trials were conducted at each speed, but in Method 2, only one trial was conducted at each speed.

Reflect

Directions: Take a few minutes to recall what you've learned and what you've been practicing in this chapter. Consider the following questions, jot down your best answer for each one, and then compare your reflections to the expert responses on the following page. Use your level of confidence to determine what to do next.

1. Name the three Science passage types.

    _____

    _____

    _____

2. Why do ACT experts start by identifying the passage type before analyzing the passage and figures?

    _____

    _____

    _____

3. What does an ACT expert look for in the question stem of an ACT Science question?

    _____

    _____

    _____

4. Why do expert test takers predict or characterize the correct answer to each ACT Science question before assessing the answer choices?

    _____

    _____

    _____

5. What will you do differently on future passages and their questions?

    _____

    _____

    _____

Responses

1. Name the three Science passage types.

The three Science passage types are Data Representation, Research Summaries, and Conflicting Viewpoints.

2. Why do ACT experts start by identifying the passage type before analyzing the passage and figures?

The approach you take to analyzing the text and figures depends on the type of passage you have, which is why taking the time to identify the passage type before reading is so crucial.

3. What does an ACT expert look for in the question stem of an ACT Science question?

Each question stem indicates the type of question and contains clues as to whether the answer will come from researching the passage text or from a particular figure or table. Many question stems have specific clues (for example, asking for a comparison of particular experimental methods) that tell us precisely where to research.

4. Why do expert test takers predict or characterize the correct answer to each ACT Science question before assessing the answer choices?

Predicting or characterizing the correct answer allows us to evaluate each answer choice one time and to avoid rereading for every answer choice. Incorrect answers often distort what the passage said or misuse details from the passage; they might mix methodologies between experiments or what was said with each hypothesis. Thus, it's best to have your own prediction of what the correct answer must say before diving into the choices.

5. What will you do differently on future passages and their questions?

There is no one correct answer to this question as you bring your own strengths and opportunities to the Science Test. Start by becoming more familiar with the ACT Science Method and the expert analysis and explanations in Part V. As you review, keep track of your mistakes and repeat lessons that are related to these areas of opportunity. Practice makes permanent!

Some test takers are overwhelmed by the unfamiliarity of the passage topics; if that's you, remember that Applying Core Knowledge questions are worth only 2/36 Science SmartPoints while the other question types are all worth at least 6/36. That means the points you can earn using your core science knowledge are minuscule compared to those you can earn by approaching this section systematically and strategically. It also means that your answer to this reflection question should almost certainly NOT include "memorize more science facts."

Next Steps

If you answered most questions correctly in the "How Much Have You Learned?" section, and if your responses to the Reflect questions were similar to those of the ACT expert, then consider the ACT Science Method an area of strength and move on to the next chapter. Come back to this topic periodically to prevent yourself from getting rusty.

If you don't yet feel confident, review the material in "How to Do ACT Science" and then try the questions you missed again. As always, be sure to review the explanations closely. Then go online (**kaptest.com/login**) to watch a video about the Kaplan Method for ACT Science and use your Qbank for more practice. If you haven't already registered your book, do so at **kaptest.com/moreonline**.

GO ONLINE

kaptest.com/login

Answers and Explanations

How Much Have You Learned?

1. B
Difficulty: Low
Category: Using Data
Getting to the Answer: The initial speed given in the question is in ft/sec (column 2) and not mi/hr (column 1). Fifty-eight ft/sec is not listed in Table 1, so you need to interpolate, or read between known data points: 51 ft/sec and 66 ft/sec. At 51 ft/sec, D from Method 1 is 116 ft, and at 66 ft/sec, D from Method 1 is 197 ft. Therefore, D at 58 ft/sec should fall between 116 and 197 ft. The only choice within that range is 150 ft, so (B) is correct.

Watch out for choice D, which gives a value that you might estimate if you looked at the mi/hr column instead of the ft/sec column.

2. G
Difficulty: Low
Category: Interpreting Data
Getting to the Answer: The value of D from Method 1 is equal to that from Method 2 where the two lines intersect on Figure 1. Draw a line down from where the two lines cross to the x-axis to find the corresponding initial speed of approximately 30 mi/hr. The correct choice is (G).

3. C
Difficulty: Low
Category: Using Data
Getting to the Answer: Since 75 mi/hr is beyond the range of the presented data, you need to extrapolate. Either continue the straight line that represents Method 2 to 75 mi/hr on Figure 1 or use Table 1 to estimate D. The straight line from Figure 1, if extended, gives a D of about 225 ft. Looking at Table 1, you can see that each 10 mi/hr increase in initial speed increases D by about 30 ft. Hence, an initial speed of 75 mi/hr would have a D that's about 60 ft greater than the D at 55 mi/hr: 60 ft + 162 ft = 222 ft. Either way, the answer lies between 200 and 300 ft, so the correct choice is (C). Choice D would be the result if you were looking at Method 1 instead of Method 2.

4. G
Difficulty: Low
Category: Using Data
Getting to the Answer: According to Table 1, S for an initial speed of 25 mi/hr is 29 ft, and S for an initial speed of 55 mi/hr is 65 ft. Since 29 is less than 65, eliminate H and J (which would indicate that 29 is larger than 65). Twenty-nine is a bit less than half of 65, so (G) is correct.

5. B
Difficulty: Medium
Category: Synthesizing Data
Getting to the Answer: According to Table 1, as the values for S increase, the values for T also increase. Hence, the relationship is direct. Eliminate choices A and C, which show an inverse relationship. Check values from Table 1 on the remaining two graphs. According to the table, for S = 29, T = 28. Choice (B) plots the data as given in the table, so the correct answer is (B).

Choice D has the appropriate shape, but the vertical axis is incorrect (it runs from 0 to 30 ft, rather than 0 to 300 ft).

6. H
Difficulty: Medium
Category: Experimental Design
Getting to the Answer: According to the passage, Method 1 calculates distance using S and T. In Table 1, the sum of S and T is D. Method 2 is calculated by taking "the initial speed in ft/sec multiplied by 2 sec." Thus, choice (H) is correct.

Both Method 1 and Method 2 had initial speeds given in both mi/hr and ft/sec, so F is incorrect. While the reaction speed rate of Method 1 was 0.8 sec, Method 1 was not calculated based on this or any specified reaction rate, so G is incorrect. Choice J is also incorrect because both methods were used to obtain calculations from the same four speeds.

DATA

Interpreting Data: 7/36 SmartPoints® (Very high yield)

Using Data: 9/36 SmartPoints® (Very high yield)

Science

How Much Do You Know?

Directions: Try out the questions below. Show your work so that you can compare your solutions to the ones found on the next page. The "Category" heading in the explanation for each question gives the title of the lesson that covers how to solve it. If you answered the question(s) for a given lesson correctly, and if your scratchwork looks like ours, you may be able to move quickly through that lesson. If you answered incorrectly or used a different approach, you may want to take your time on that lesson.

Passage I

The extent to which a solute will dissolve in a given solvent is dependent on several factors, including conditions of temperature and pressure and the electrochemical natures of the solute and solvent.

Students measured the solubilities in distilled water of several pairs of common sodium (Na) and potassium (K) salts at various temperatures. The pairs were NaCl and KCl, $NaNO_3$ and KNO_3, and $NaClO_3$ and $KClO_3$. All measurements were conducted at 1 atmosphere of pressure. After pooling and averaging all the data, the students plotted solubility curves to produce Figure 1.

Figure 1

1. For the given salts, what is the relationship, if any, between solubility and temperature?

   A. As the temperature increases, the solubility increases.

   B. As the temperature increases, the solubility decreases.

   C. As the temperature increases, the solubility remains the same.

   D. Solubility and temperature are unrelated.

2. Based on Figure 1, which solute exhibits the *greatest* variation in solubility between 0°C and 60°C?

   F. KNO_3

   G. NaCl

   H. KCl

   J. $KClO_3$

3. According to Figure 1, for which of the following salts would it be possible to dissolve more than 0.65 g/mL at 55°C?

   A. Any of the Na salts

   B. Any of the K salts

   C. Either of the NO_3 salts

   D. Either of the ClO_3 salts

4. According to the data, how many more grams of KNO_3 in 1 L of distilled water are dissolved at 50°C and normal atmospheric pressure than of $KClO_3$ under the same conditions?

   F. 0.18 g

   G. 0.66 g

   H. 180 g

   J. 660 g

5. Based on Figure 1, what is the order of the given solutes from least solubility to greatest solubility, at 90°C?

   A. $KClO_3$, KCl, NaCl

   B. NaCl, $KClO_3$, KCl

   C. KCl, $KClO_3$, NaCl

   D. $KClO_3$, KCl, NaCl

6. Based on Figure 1, if the temperature of KCl had been increased to 135°C, the solubility would most likely have been:

   F. 0.38 mg/mL

   G. 0.56 mg/mL

   H. 0.65 mg/mL

   J. 0.95 mg/mL

7. Consider the statement "When a solution is cooled, the amount of solute dissolved in excess of the lower solubility will precipitate out." If a 100-mL solution into which 0.3 g/mL of $KClO_3$ has been dissolved is cooled from 70°C to 30°C, approximately how many grams of $KClO_3$ would precipitate out?

   A. 0.2 g

   B. 2 g

   C. 20 g

   D. 40 g

Check Your Work

1.　A
Difficulty: Low
Category: Interpreting Data
Getting to the Answer: When you're looking for the relationship between two variables in a line graph, check to see if they go up or down together, if one remains constant as the other changes, or if one goes down as the other goes up. All six lines rise from left to right across the graph, indicating that solubility goes up as temperature goes up. Choice (A) is correct.

2.　F
Difficulty: Low
Category: Interpreting Data
Getting to the Answer: Unless the question stem specifically tells you to make guesses about what might happen beyond the range of a figure, consider only the given data when answering questions. The question stem limits you to the range between 0°C and 60°C. The phrase "exhibits the greatest variation in solubility" means "has the biggest change in solubility." KNO_3 starts very low (about 0.15 g/mL at 0°C) and comes close to 1.1 g/mL at 60°C, so it shows the greatest increase in solubility over the specified range. The solutes in G, H, and J have much smaller changes in solubility over the given temperature range. The correct answer is (F).

3.　C
Difficulty: Medium
Category: Interpreting Data
Getting to the Answer: When a question gives you a specific range of values for the x- or y-axis, make sure you focus your attention within that range. To find the solubility of the different salts at 55°C, draw a vertical line up from the x-axis. To find solubilities greater than 0.65 g/mL, draw a horizontal line across the graph from the y-axis. Only three of the solubility curves ever rise above 0.65 g/mL: those for $NaClO_3$, $NaNO_3$, and KNO_3. None of the answer choices include all three of those salts, but (C) lists two of the three, so (C) is the correct answer.

The other three answer choices contain at least one salt with a solubility below 0.65 g/mL at 55°C.

4.　J
Difficulty: High
Category: Using Data
Getting to the Answer: The question stem tells you where in the figure you'll find your answer. This question asks about a solution at 50°C, so start there. Trace the vertical

line up from the x-axis at 50°C until it crosses the curve for KNO_3. Find the solubility of KNO_3 by drawing a horizontal line from the point of intersection to the y-axis. The solubility is about 0.84 g/mL. For $KClO_3$, repeat the process to find that the solubility is about 0.18 g/mL. The difference is $0.84 - 0.18 = 0.66$ g/mL. Note, however, that the volume given in the question stem is not 1 mL, but 1 L (or 1,000 mL), so you'll need to multiply the difference by 1,000: 0.66 g/mL × 1,000 mL = 660 g. Choice (J) is correct.

Choice G is a trap that you might fall into if you forget to check your units. Choices F and H are incorrect because they represent the amount of $KClO_3$ dissolved in 1 mL and in 1 L, respectively.

5.　B
Difficulty: Medium
Category: Interpreting Data
Getting to the Answer: To determine solubility at 90°C, draw a vertical line up 90°C on the x-axis. At 90°C, NaCl has a solubility of ~0.38 g/mL, $KClO_3$ has a solubility of ~0.47 g/mL, and KCl has a solubility of ~0.54 g/mL. The correct answer is therefore (B).

Answer choice C reverses the order and lists from greatest to least.

6.　H
Difficulty: Medium
Category: Using Data
Getting to the Answer: To determine a value beyond the given graph, extend the line of KCl. At 100°C, the solubility of KCl is ~0.56 mg/mL; since it increases as temperature increases, eliminate A and B. For every 35° increase in temperature, the solubility of KCl increases 0.1 mg/mL. Therefore, the expected solubility at 135°C would be 0.1 mg/mL greater than the solubility at 100°C, or ~0.66 mg/mL. Thus, (H) is correct.

7.　C
Difficulty: High
Category: Using Data
Getting to the Answer: To determine the mass that will precipitate out, first determine the mass of solute dissolved at the higher temperature. At 70°C, $KClO_3$ has a solubility of 0.3 g/mL, so 100 mL × 0.3 g/mL = 30 g $KClO_3$. At 30°C, $KClO_3$ has a solubility of 0.1 g/mL, so 100 mL × 0.1 g/mL = 10 g $KClO_3$. The difference is 30 g − 10 g = 20 g, so (C) is correct.

Choice A incorrectly calculates the difference in solubility per 1-mL solution, not for a 100-mL solution.

DATA REPRESENTATION PASSAGES

To read passages and answer questions like these:

Passage II

To investigate the suitability of magnesium alloys for bone repair, four identical ingots were prepared of alloys A, B, C, and D, respectively. Five mechanical properties—grain size (μm), yield tensile strength (MPa), ultimate tensile strength (MPa), yield compressive strength (MPa), and ultimate compressive strength (MPa)—of each ingot were tested, with the results shown in Table 1. The ingots were then immersed in simulated body fluid for a period of 15 days, and the pH level was tested at the same time each day. The results are shown in Figure 1.

This data is from *Crystals*, Vol. 8, No. 7, June 2018, p. 271.

Figure 1

	Average grain size (μm)	Yield tensile strength (MPa)	Ultimate tensile strength (MPa)	Yield compressive strength (MPa)	Ultimate compressive strength (MPa)
			Table 1		
A	3.2	262.67	298.17	256.7	361.32
B	2.5	246	293.26	296.49	342.62
C	2	301.33	334.61	315.69	359.78
D	1.5	315.33	315.33	279.16	354.45

1. For each of the alloys measured in Table 1, as the grain size of the ingot increased, the ultimate compressive strength:

   A. increased only.

   B. decreased only.

   C. varied, but with no general trend.

   D. remained the same.

2. Suppose the duration of the study had been extended and additional measurements were taken on the following days. Based on Figure 1, on day 16, the pH of Ingot D would most likely have been:

   F. <10.

   G. between 10 and 10.5.

   H. between 10.5 and 11.

   J. >11.

You need to know this:

Two of the six passages you will see on test day will be Data Representation passages. In order to identify Data Representation passages as part of step 1, look for these typical characteristics:

- More figures than the other two passage types and a short 1–2 paragraph passage
- Multiple charts, tables, graphs, and diagrams

The majority of questions in Data Representation passages are either Interpreting Data questions or Using Data questions that can usually be answered based on the data in the figures.

Rarely, a question in a Data Representation set will be categorized as an Experiments question type (Experimental Design or Synthesizing Data) that might require support from the short passage. It is more common for the questions about a Research Summaries passage to include an Interpreting Data or a Using Data question. Review the "Research Summaries and Experimental Design Questions" lesson in chapter 24 for more information on how to strategically approach Research Summaries.

You need to do this:

Identifying the variables and units of each figure before moving straight to the questions. The "Interpreting Data Questions" and "Using Data Questions" lessons in this chapter describe the data interpretation skills needed to answer most ACT Science Data questions:

- Identifying features of figures (headings, units, axis labels, etc.)
- Determining how the value of one variable changes as the value of another changes
- Identifying mathematical relationships among data (linear, exponential, etc.)
- Reading values from figures with two or three variables
- Interpolating and extrapolating from data points
- Translating information into a table, graph, or diagram
- Analyzing given information when presented with new information

When presented with a complex figure:

- Focus on the variables, units, axes, and legend (if applicable) during your initial review and block out the rest.
- When returning to the figure after reading a question, check the figure key or table headings to ensure you are referring to the correct variable(s).
- Circle relevant points to avoid distractions when comparing data from multiple curves in a graph or multiple rows/columns in a table.

Explanation

Identify

The small section of introductory text followed only by a table and a figure indicate that this is a Data Representation passage.

Analyze

Skip the text in this Data Representation passage and move straight to the figures. You can go back for more information if needed.

Table 1: The rows indicate that four samples (A–D) are being tested; the columns indicate that five measurements (grain size, yield tensile strength, ultimate tensile strength, yield compressive strength, and ultimate compressive strength) are being taken.

Figure 1: The *x*-axis is time in days. The *y*-axis is pH. Note that for all four samples, pH increases as the number of days increases (positive correlation).

Examine, predict, and answer

Question	Explanation
1. For each of the alloys measured in Table 1, as the grain size of the ingot increased, the ultimate compressive strength: A. increased only. B. decreased only. C. varied, but with no general trend. D. remained the same.	**Answer: C** **Difficulty:** Low **Category:** Interpreting Data **Getting to the Answer:** This question asks if there's a correlation between grain size and ultimate compressive strength. Fortunately, the grain sizes are listed in the table in descending order, so to find the trend as they increase, examine what happens to the ultimate compressive strength starting at the bottom row, Ingot D, and moving to the top row, Ingot A. From Ingot D to Ingot C, there's an increase, but there's a decrease from Ingot C to Ingot B, and then there's another increase from Ingot B to Ingot A. Thus, there is no general trend, which means that (C) is correct. Choices A and B are incorrect because the ultimate compressive strength both increased and decreased as grain size increased; similarly, D is incorrect because the compressive strength did not remain the same as grain size increased.
2. Suppose the duration of the study had been extended and additional measurements were taken on the following days. Based on Figure 1, on day 16, the pH of Ingot D would most likely have been: F. <10. G. between 10 and 10.5. H. between 10.5 and 11. J. >11.	**Answer: G** **Difficulty:** Medium **Category:** Using Data **Getting to the Answer:** In order to find out what the pH level of Ingot D would likely have been on day 16, inspect the line representing that ingot in Figure 1 to see the trend in the last few days of the study. On day 13, the pH of Ingot D was approximately 9.6. On day 14, it had increased to around 9.8, and on day 15, it was approximately 10. Thus, if it continues this trend, on day 16, the pH level would have been approximately 10.2, making (G) the correct answer.

Try on Your Own

Directions: Take as much time as you need on the remaining questions in this set. Work carefully and methodically. There will be an opportunity for timed practice at the end of the chapter.

Answers are found at the end of the chapter.

3. According to Table 1, the yield compressive strength of Ingot C was closest to which of the following values?

    A.   296 MPa

    B.   316 MPa

    C.   343 MPa

    D.   360 MPa

4. Ultimate tensile strength is a measure of the maximum amount of force a material can withstand before breaking. Suppose the researchers exerted a force of 295 MPa on an unlabeled ingot, under which stress the ingot shattered. The unlabeled ingot was most likely composed of the same alloy as:

    F.   Ingot A.

    G.   Ingot B.

    H.   Ingot C.

    J.   Ingot D.

5. A *biocompatible* material is one capable of being implanted into the body without causing any harm to the surrounding tissues. Suppose that a pH above 9 is potentially harmful to human bone and tissue growth. According to Figure 1, Ingot A would be biocompatible for:

    A.   5 days.

    B.   6 days.

    C.   7 days.

    D.   8 days.

Science

INTERPRETING DATA QUESTIONS

To answer a question like this:

Figure 1

Based on Figure 1, if a colony of *Dactylococcopsis salina*, a type of algae, covered a pond floor with a density of 400 algae per square centimeter, approximately how long would its generation time most likely be?

A.   20 min

B.   50 min

C.   100 min

D.   200 min

You need to know this:

When you read from a graph or table, don't make an uninformed guess about the value. Instead, use your pencil to track what you are looking for:

- In a graph, find the value of a data point by tracing or drawing a line up from the *x*-axis and over to the *y*-axis or vice versa.
- In a table, circle data to keep your eyes from reading the incorrect row or column.

You can use your answer grid as a straightedge to help determine values, but be careful not to write on it unintentionally.

Data in tables may not always be in ascending or descending order.

- When the data is not in order, use your pencil and the margin space to reorder the data for one variable from least to greatest or greatest to least.
- Then, reorder the other variable and match the data of the other variable to the reordered data to identify the trend(s).

Some Interpreting Data questions will ask you to determine a trend in the data; that is, how one variable changes in response to another.

Sometimes these data will form a linear relationship.

- A linear relationship is one where a specific change in the independent variable will cause the dependent variable to change by the same amount each time.
- When plotted on a graph, the data form a straight line.
- The variables may be directly or inversely related.

Other times, data will form an exponential relationship.

- An exponential relationship is one where a specific change in the independent variable will cause the dependent variable to change by the same percent each time.
- When plotted on a graph, the data forms a nonlinear relationship, the exact shape of which depends on the power of the exponent.
- Exponential relationships also can be direct or inverse.

You need to do this:

- Determine the type of relationship(s), if any, formed by the data
  - If the dependent variable changes at a constant rate as the independent variable is changed, the relationship is linear.
  - If the dependent variable changes at an exponential rate as the independent variable is changed, the relationship is exponential.
- Identify whether the relationship between variables is direct or inverse or note that there is not a clear relationship between variables.
  - If, as one variable increases, the other also increases (or, as one variable decreases, the other decreases), the relationship is direct (positive slope).
  - If, as one variable increases, the other decreases, or vice versa, the relationship is inverse (negative slope).
  - If, as one variable doubles, the other quadruples, then the relationship is direct.
  - If, instead, as one variable doubles, the other is quartered, then the relationship is inverse.

Explanation

Identify

This question may appear to be missing a passage, but all ACT Science questions are associated with a passage; the fact that the question can be answered using only Figure I is an indication that this question is likely associated with a Data Representation passage.

Analyze

Identify the key information in the figure:

Figure 1: axes are algae density vs. generation time; units are algae/cm^2 and min, respectively; there is an exponential, direct relationship

Examine, predict, and answer

The question stem directly references Figure 1 and asks for the generation time that would be associated with a density of 400 algae/cm^2.

Using Figure 1, look to where the graph intersects with the x-value of 400. The y-value that corresponds with this time is 50. Thus, an algae with a density of 400 algae/cm^2 would have a generation time of 50 min. Now, look at the answer choices and see that this is a match for (B).

Drills

If Interpreting Data questions give you trouble, study the information above and try out these drill questions before completing the Try on Your Own questions below. Drill answers can be found in Answers and Explanations.

a.   Identify the trend in Figure A:

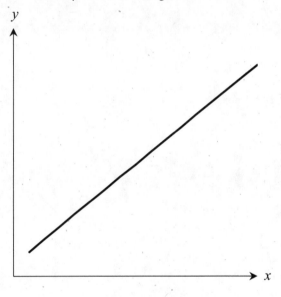

Figure A

b.   Identify the trend in Figure B:

Figure B

c. Identify the relationship between A and B in Figure C:

e. Identify the relationship between pH and [H$^+$] in Table E:

Figure C

Table E	
pH	**[H$^+$] (μmol/L)**
3	1,000
4	100
5	10
6	1
7	0.1
8	0.01

d. Identify the relationship between minutes walking and energy consumed in Table D:

Table D	
Time walking (min)	**Energy used (Cal)**
2	10
4	20
6	30
8	40
10	50

Try on Your Own

Directions: Take as much time as you need on these questions. Work carefully and methodically. There will be an opportunity for timed practice at the end of the chapter.

Answers are found at the end of the chapter.

Passage III

Gravitational acceleration, g, is the acceleration of an object due to gravity. The conventional standard value of g at the Earth's surface is exactly 9.80665 m/sec^2. Scientists wished to study variations in g at various latitudes, altitudes, and depths. They measured the gravitational acceleration of a 5-kg block in a vacuum as a function of (north) latitude at sea level and of altitude at 15°N latitude. The results are plotted in Figure 1.

To calculate gravitational acceleration as a function of depth in the Earth's interior, they used $g(d) = 2.8 \times 10^{-7}(R - d)\rho$, where R is the Earth's radius of 6,371 km, d is the Earth's depth, and ρ is the density at depth d (see Figure 2).

Figure 2

Figure 1

1. According to Figure 1, at approximately what latitude is the gravitational acceleration at 9.81 m/s^2 at sea level?

   A. 0°N
   B. 20°N
   C. 50°N
   D. 90°N

2. According to Figure 1, as altitude increases, gravitational acceleration:

   F. increases only.
   G. decreases only.
   H. increases and then decreases.
   J. decreases and then increases.

3. Based on Figure 1, the gravitational acceleration when a block is at an altitude of 500 meters above sea level is approximately:

   A. 9.60 m/s^2.

   B. 9.65 m/s^2.

   C. 9.76 m/s^2.

   D. 9.80 m/s^2.

4. At the center of the Earth, $d = R$. Based on Figure 2, what is the acceleration due to gravity, in meters per second squared, at the Earth's center?

   F. 0

   G. 4.9

   H. 9.8

   J. 10.3

5. The core of the Earth is between 2,900 and 6,371 kilometers deep. According to Figure 2, as core depth increases, gravitational acceleration:

   A. increases only.

   B. decreases only.

   C. increases and then decreases.

   D. decreases and then increases.

6. Assume the Earth is a sphere; the radius of the Earth's interior layers is measured from the Earth's center, whereas the depth of the interior layers is measured from the surface. Based on Figure 2 and the passage, at approximately what radius is the gravitational acceleration 4 m/s^2?

   F. 1,300 km

   G. 2,000 km

   H. 5,100 km

   J. 6,300 km

USING DATA QUESTIONS

LEARNING OBJECTIVES

After this lesson, you will be able to:

- Perform basic calculations using data
- Infer values not directly provided using interpolation, extrapolation, and lines of best fit
- Draw conclusions about data based on new information

To answer a question like this:

The utilization and replenishment of Earth's carbon supply is a cyclic process involving all living matter. This cycle is shown in the following diagram.

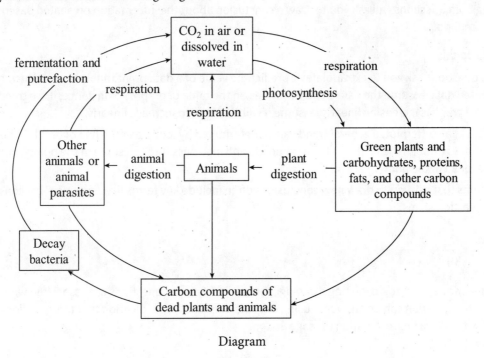

Diagram

Consider the carbon cycle illustrated in the diagram. What effect would a sudden drop in the amount of Earth's decay bacteria have on the amount of carbon dioxide in the atmosphere?

A. The CO_2 level would drop to a life-threatening level since bacteria are the sole source of CO_2.

B. The CO_2 level would rise because bacteria usually consume CO_2.

C. The CO_2 level would decrease but not completely drop because bacteria are not the only source of CO_2.

D. The CO_2 level would increase slightly due to an imbalance in the carbon cycle.

You need to know this:

The ACT Science section does NOT allow for the use of a calculator. This means any calculations required by these questions are readily solvable in your head or with paper and pencil.

Keeping track of the units in the passage and the figures as well as in the question stem and the choices requires close attention and careful scratchwork. Calculations could involve numbers presented in scientific notation.

Some Using Data questions will ask you to solve for a value that isn't given directly in the table or figure and may require **interpolation**, **extrapolation**, or determination of a **line of best fit**.

- Interpolation means estimating a value between known data points.
- Extrapolation means estimating a value outside the known range.
- A line of best fit is the line that most closely matches the pattern in the data.

Other Using Data questions will ask you to draw a conclusion about the information presented based on data and a new scenario.

You need to do this:

- When questions ask you to extrapolate or predict the value of a data point that is beyond the range of the presented data, assume the data trend continues on the table or graph. For instance, if the trend of the data in a graph is increasing linearly, assume it will continue to increase linearly.
- For data in a scatterplot, a general trend can be determined by looking at the line of best fit. This line should pass through the center of the data points and may pass through some of the points, none of the points, or all of the points.
- Questions that ask you to draw new conclusions often include key terms like "suppose" or "consider" in their question stems.

Explanation

Identify

This question may appear to be missing a passage, but all ACT Science questions are associated with a passage; the fact that the question can be answered using only the diagram is an indication that this question is likely associated with a Data Representation passage.

Analyze

Identify the key information in the diagram:

- **Diagram:** don't get bogged down in the details before getting to the associated question; the big picture is that carbon cycles between the air/water and plants/animals/bacteria through various forms of ingestion and respiration.

Examine, predict, and answer

The question stem directly refers you to the diagram and asks you to determine the impact that decreasing the number of decay bacteria would have on the amount of carbon dioxide in the atmosphere.

Predict the expected effect on carbon dioxide:

- The arrow from "Decay bacteria" to "CO_2 in air or dissolved in water" indicates that these bacteria produce CO_2 through fermentation and putrefaction.
- Thus, decreasing the amount of decay bacteria will reduce the amount of CO_2 in the air/water.
- However, animals and animal parasites also produce CO_2 through respiration, so a decrease in the decay bacteria would not completely deplete CO_2 levels.

Choice (C) is correct.

Drills

If Using Data questions give you trouble, study the information above and try out these drill questions before completing the Try on Your Own questions below. Drill answers can be found in Answers and Explanations.

a.   Based on Figure A, what is the approximate amount of dissolved oxygen, in milligrams per liter, at a water temperature of 5°C ?

Figure A

b. According to Figure B, the temperature at which the rate of oxygen consumption is 4 mL/g h is approximately how many times greater than the temperature at which carbon dioxide production is at the same rate?

Figure B

c. According to Figure C, what is the approximate mean surface temperature, in degrees Fahrenheit, at a distance of 250 million miles from the sun?

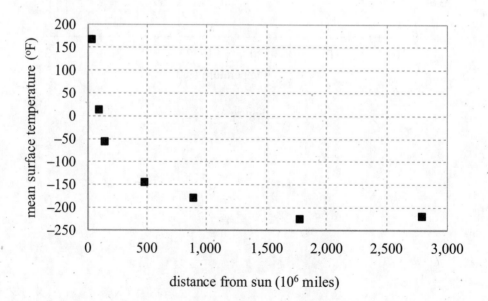

Figure C

d. Based on the diagram, if the gas pressure is increased, will h increase, stay the same, or decrease?

atmospheric pressure

h

gas pressure

mercury

Diagram

e. According to Table E, what is the velocity of sound in water, in meters per second, at a density of 990 kg/m³?

Table E	
Density (kg/m³)	Velocity of sound in water (m/s)
1,000	1,447
998	1,482
996	1,509
992	1,529
988	1,543
983	1,552

f. Based on Table F, what is the force, in Newtons, for a mass of 290 g?

Table F	
Mass (g)	Force (N)
70	0.15
110	0.65
150	1.15
190	1.65
230	2.15
270	2.65

Science

K 659

Try on Your Own

Directions: Take as much time as you need on these questions. Work carefully and methodically. There will be an opportunity for timed practice at the end of the chapter.

Answers are found at the end of the chapter.

Passage IV

A solution is a mixture composed of a solute (usually solid or gas) dissolved in a solvent (usually liquid). Solutions that can conduct an electrical current are called electrolytes. A study was conducted to examine the conditions that affect solute conductivity.

Various solutes were dissolved in 100 ml of water at 25°C in quantities of 10 mg and 30 mg. Table 1 shows the conductivity of each solution measured in millisiemens per centimeter (mS/cm). Figure 1 shows the conductivity of the solutions with the 30 mg solute concentrations at various temperatures (C).

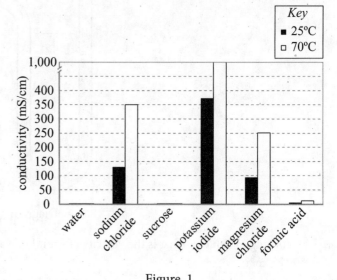

Figure 1

Table 1

Solute	Conductivity measurement (mS/cm) of 10 mg	Conductivity measurement (mS/cm) of 30 mg
Water (H$_2$O)	0.0	0.0
Sodium chloride (NaCl)	73.6	129.7
Sucrose (C$_{12}$H$_{22}$O$_{11}$)	0.0	0.0
Potassium iodide (KI)	119.2	371.8
Magnesium chloride (MgCl$_2$)	102.8	93.3
Formic acid (HCOOH)	3.6	4.8

1. Based on the results, which of the following solutions of NaCl should conduct the most electricity?

    A. 10 g in 100 mL of H$_2$O at 10°C
    B. 20 g in 100 mL of H$_2$O at 20°C
    C. 20 g in 100 mL of H$_2$O at 70°C
    D. 30 g in 100 mL of H$_2$O at 80°C

2. Suppose that when a solute reaches saturation, the conductivity of the solution decreases. Which of the following solutes most likely has a saturation point of 20 mg per 100 ml H$_2$O?

    F. NaCl
    G. KI
    H. MgCl$_2$
    J. HCOOH

Science

3. Consider the data presented in Figure 1. As the temperature of the electrolytic solutions was increased, the conductivity:

   A. increased only.

   B. increased for some solutions but was unchanged for others.

   C. decreased for $MgCl_2$ but increased for all others.

   D. decreased only.

4. Consider the statement, "Electrolytes dissociate into ions, whereas non-electrolytes do not." In a solution with which solute would ions most likely NOT be present?

   F. Magnesium chloride

   G. Potassium iodide

   H. Sucrose

   J. Sodium chloride

5. Consider the statement, "Strong electrolytes are good conductors of electricity; weak electrolytes are poor conductors of electricity." According to the results of the study, which of the following is most likely to be a poor electrolyte?

   A. H_2O

   B. NaCl

   C. KI

   D. HCOOH

6. Suppose a solution of potassium iodide (KI) was created using 20 mg of solute at 25°C. According to Table 1, the conductivity of this solution would most likely be:

   F. less than 119 mS/cm.

   G. between 119 mS/cm and 371.8 mS/cm.

   H. between 371.8 mS/cm and 1,000.9 mS/cm.

   J. greater than 1,000.9 mS/cm.

How Much Have You Learned?

Directions: For test-like practice, give yourself 6 minutes to complete this question set. Be sure to study the explanations, even for questions you got correct. They can be found at the end of this chapter.

Passage V

When a spring of L cm in length having a spring constant k is hung vertically with a mass of m attached, the downward force of gravity (g) displaces the spring x cm to its equilibrium position. Pulling further than x cm downward and then releasing will cause the spring to oscillate up and down. The time it takes to complete one cycle is called "period of oscillation (T)."

Diagram

To examine the effect of gravity on displacement, x was calculated for a spring for different m on the surface of Earth, Titan (Saturn's largest moon), and Jupiter (see Figure 1). For the same spring on Earth, Figure 2 shows T plotted against m.

Figure 1

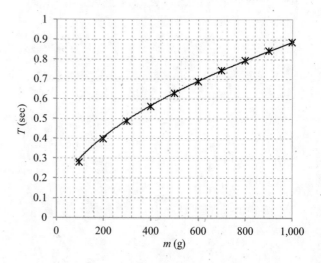

Figure 2

1. Based on Figure 1, what is the expected displacement of the spring on Earth's surface with a block of 0.8 kg attached?

   A. 1 cm

   B. 10 cm

   C. 15 cm

   D. 40 cm

2. Suppose a spring on Earth has a period of oscillation of 1 sec. Based on Figure 2, the mass of the attached block would most likely be:

   F. 5 g.

   G. 20 g.

   H. 400 g.

   J. 1,300 g.

3. The table below lists the gravitational acceleration (in m/sec^2) for four different astronomical bodies. Based on Figure 1, would the displacement for a given mass on Earth be greater or less than the displacement for that same mass on Mercury?

Planet or moon	Gravitational acceleration at surface (m/sec^2)
Jupiter	24.9
Earth	9.8
Mercury	3.7
Titan	1.4

   A. Greater than; as gravitational acceleration increases, displacement increases.

   B. Greater than; as gravitational acceleration increases, displacement decreases.

   C. Less than; as gravitational acceleration increases, displacement increases.

   D. Less than; as gravitational acceleration increases, displacement decreases.

4. Suppose the spring in Figure 1 has a displacement of 10 cm on Jupiter's surface. For the spring to have the same displacement on Earth's surface, m would have to be approximately:

   F. 2.5 times greater than that on Jupiter's surface.

   G. 2.5 times less than that on Jupiter's surface.

   H. 250 times greater than that on Jupiter's surface.

   J. 250 times less than that on Jupiter's surface.

5. Consider the relationship between m, g, x, and k in Figure 1. If two springs having the same spring constant k are attached with different masses m and $2m$ respectively, in order for displacement x to be the same, the spring with the heavier mass must be:

   A. half as long as the spring attached to the lighter mass.

   B. twice as long as the spring attached to the lighter mass.

   C. on a planet with a half as much gravitational acceleration.

   D. on a planet with two times as much gravitational acceleration.

6. The *frequency* of motion for a mass on a spring is defined as the number of oscillations per unit of time. Based on Figure 2, the spring with the highest frequency would have an attached mass of:

   F. 100 g.

   G. 200 g.

   H. 1,000 g.

   J. 1,200 g.

Science

Reflect

Directions: Take a few minutes to recall what you've learned and what you've been practicing in this chapter. Consider the following questions, jot down your best answer for each one, and then compare your reflections to the expert responses on the following page. Use your level of confidence to determine what to do next.

1. When presented with a complex figure that has no clear trends, what key features will an ACT expert focus on?

   _____

   _____

   _____

2. When might an ACT expert find it useful to make marks or circles on a figure or table?

   _____

   _____

   _____

3. What does an ACT expert do when data in a table aren't presented in ascending or descending order?

   _____

   _____

   _____

4. Why is it that both linear and exponential relationships can be either direct or inverse?

   _____

   _____

   _____

5. When drawing a line of best fit, does it need to pass through all the data points?

   _____

   _____

   _____

6. How will you approach Data Representation passages differently as you continue to practice and improve your performance in the ACT Science section?

   _____

   _____

   _____

Responses

1. When presented with a complex figure that has no clear trends, what key features will an ACT expert focus on?

In figures that are overwhelming at first glance or contain no clear pattern, it is best to revert to focusing on the variables, units, axes, and any legends that are present and save any analysis of the data for when you're answering a specific question.

2. When might an ACT expert find it useful to make marks or circles on a figure or table?

ACT experts often find it useful to circle relevant points to avoid distractions, especially when comparing data from multiple curves in a graph or multiple rows/columns in a table.

3. What does an ACT expert do when data in a table aren't presented in ascending or descending order?

Use your pencil to rewrite the data to order one variable from least to greatest or vice versa. Then, match the data of the other variable to the reordered data to identify the trend.

4. Why is it that both linear and exponential relationships can be either direct or inverse?

Direct and inverse refer to the direction of the effect that changing the independent variable has on the dependent variable, while linear and exponential refer to whether a specific change in the independent variable will cause the dependent variable to change by the same amount each time (linear) or by the same percent each time (exponential). These concepts overlap, as a positive increase in the independent variable could cause the dependent variable to change by a positive amount (direct, linear), a positive percent (direct, exponential), a negative amount (inverse, linear), or a negative percent (inverse, exponential).

5. When drawing a line of best fit, does it need to pass through all the data points?

The line of best fit is the line that most closely matches the pattern in the data. This line should pass through the center of the data points and may pass through some of the points, none of the points, or all of the points.

6. How will you approach Data Representation passages differently as you continue to practice and improve your performance in the ACT Science section?

There is no one-size-fits-all answer here. Reflect on your own habits in interpreting data presented in tables and figures as well as answering ACT Science questions and give yourself an honest assessment of your strengths and weaknesses. Consider the strategies you've seen experts use in this chapter, and put them to work in your own practice to increase your accuracy, speed, and confidence.

Next Steps

If you answered most questions correctly in the "How Much Have You Learned?" section, and if your responses to the Reflect questions were similar to those of the ACT expert, then consider Data Representation passages an area of strength and move on to the next chapter. Come back to this topic periodically to prevent yourself from getting rusty.

If you don't yet feel confident, review the material in this chapter, then try the questions you missed again. As always, be sure to review the explanations closely. Then go online (**kaptest.com/login**) to use your Qbank for more practice. If you haven't already registered your book, do so at **kaptest.com/moreonline**.

GO ONLINE

kaptest.com/login

Answers and Explanations

Data Representation Passages

1. Review the Explanation portion of the Data Representation Passages lesson.

2. Review the Explanation portion of the Data Representation Passages lesson.

3. **B**
Difficulty: Low
Category: Interpreting Data
Getting to the Answer: Find the row in Table 1 for Ingot C, then look for the column representing yield compressive strength. Doing so shows this strength to be 315.69, which means that (B) is correct.

4. **G**
Difficulty: Low
Category: Using Data
Getting to the Answer: If a force of 295 MPa broke an ingot, that must mean that the ingot's ultimate tensile strength was less than 295 MPa. This type of strength is detailed in the fourth column of Table 1. The only ingot with an ultimate tensile strength less than 295 MPa was Ingot B; therefore, (G) is correct.

5. **B**
Difficulty: Medium
Category: Interpreting Data
Getting to the Answer: Find the line for Ingot A in Figure 1 and see how long it stayed below a pH level of 9. On day 6, the pH level was around 8.75, which would mean it was still biocompatible. On day 7, the pH level jumped to 9.25, which would mean that it was no longer biocompatible. Choice (B) is correct because Ingot A would be biocompatible for 6 days.

Interpreting Data Questions

Drill Answers

a. linear, positive
b. exponential, negative
c. direct
d. direct
e. inverse

1. **C**
Difficulty: Low
Category: Interpreting Data
Getting to the Answer: On Figure 1, draw a horizontal line from 9.81 m/s^2 over to the data for latitude and draw a vertical line from the point of intersection down to the x-axis to determine the degrees of latitude. At 9.81 m/s^2, the latitude falls somewhere between 40°N and 60°N. The only answer choice in that range is (C).

2. **G**
Difficulty: Low
Category: Interpreting Data
Getting to the Answer: To determine the relationship between two variables on a graph, check the trend of the data. Do the variables go up or down together, does one stay constant as the other changes, does one go down as the other goes up, or is there a more complex pattern? According to Figure 1, as altitude increases, gravitational acceleration always decreases, so the correct answer is (G).

3. **C**
Difficulty: Low
Category: Interpreting Data
Getting to the Answer: Pay attention to which data points go with which axis—altitude is on the top x-axis. The question asks for gravitational acceleration at 500 m above sea level. On Figure 1, locate 500 m on the top x-axis and trace the vertical line down to the data point that represents altitude (represented by a solid triangle). Then from that point, draw a horizontal line to the y-axis to determine the gravitational acceleration. The gravitational acceleration is 9.76 m/s^2, as in (C).

4. **F**
Difficulty: Medium
Category: Interpreting Data
Getting to the Answer: According to the stimulus, R, the Earth's radius, is equal to 6,371 km. Look at Figure 2 to see what the gravitational acceleration would be at that depth; at that point on the graph, the curve reaches the x-axis. This means that the acceleration due to gravity at the center of the Earth is 0, and (F) is correct.

5. B
Difficulty: Medium
Category: Interpreting Data
Getting to the Answer: Find 2,900 km and 637 km in Figure 2 and determine the trend between those points. At just before 3,000 km, or approximately 2,900 km, the curve starts trending downward, and it keeps going down until it hits 0 at 6,371 km. Since the data trends downward between these two points, (B) is correct.

6. F
Difficulty: Hard
Category: Interpreting Data
Getting to the Answer: First, use Figure 2 to determine at what depth the gravitational acceleration is 4 m/s^2: at a depth of approximately 5,000 km. Next, subtract this depth from the radius of the Earth (6,371 km, according to the passage) to see how far this point is from the Earth's center: approximately 1,300 km. Choice (F) is correct.

Using Data Questions

Drill Answers

a. 12

b. $15 \div 5 = 3$

c. -100

d. increases

e. between 1,529 and 1,543

f. 2.9

1. D
Difficulty: Medium
Category: Using Data
Getting to the Answer: This question requires you to extrapolate from the results in Table 1 and Figure 1. You know from comparing the NaCl values that the conductivity is higher for 30.0 g of NaCl than for 10.0 g. You also know from comparing values in Figure 1 that higher temperatures result in higher conductivity measurements. Thus, to find the NaCl solution that conducts the most electricity (in other words, the one with the highest conductivity), you should look for the choice with the most solute and the highest temperature. Choice (D) is thus correct.

2. H
Difficulty: Medium
Category: Using Data
Getting to the Answer: To determine which solute reached saturation at 20 mg per 100 ml, you need to determine which solution exhibited a decrease in conductivity when the level of solute was increased from 10 mg per 100 ml to 30 mg per 100 ml. Compare the values in Table 1. The only solute whose conductivity decreased is $MgCl_2$, so the correct answer is (H).

3. A
Difficulty: Medium
Category: Using Data
Getting to the Answer: The passage describes an electrolytic solution as one that conducts electric current; thus, only the solutions with a conductivity greater than 0 (NaCl, KI, $MgCl_2$ and HCOOH) should be considered. For each of the four electrolytes, the conductivity at 70°C was greater than at 25°C. The correct answer is (A).

Choice B incorrectly describes a trend for non-electrolyte solutions. Conductivity of $MgCl_2$ decreased (choice C) when more solute was added, not when the temperature was increased.

4. H
Difficulty: Medium
Category: Using Data
Getting to the Answer: The passage describes an electrolyte as a solution that conducts electric current. The information in the question stem indicates that non-electrolytes do not dissociate into ions; therefore, ions would not be present in a non-electrolyte solution. Sucrose had a conductivity of zero and is thus a non-electrolyte. The correct answer is (H).

5. D
Difficulty: Medium
Category: Using Data
Getting to the Answer: According to the passage, an electrolyte can conduct electric current, so H_2O (choice A) can be eliminated. Of the remaining electrolytes, NaCl and KI are both good conductors of electricity; their conductivity measurements are more than 10 times larger than HCOOH at any given concentration or temperature. The weak electrolyte is therefore HCOOH. Choice (D) is correct.

6.   G
Difficulty: Low
Category: Using Data
Getting to the Answer: In order to find the most likely conductivity of a solute concentration that lies between two known concentrations, first identify the conductivity of the known concentrations. The conductivity of the new concentration is most likely to fall between these known values. According to Table 1, a 10 g KI solution had a conductivity of 119 mS/cm, and a 30 g KI solution had a conductivity of 371.8 mS/cm. Therefore, a 20 g KI solution will have a conductivity in between those values. Choice (G) is correct.

Choice H describes the conductivity of a KI solution with 30 g that has been heated above 25°C but less than 70°C.

How Much Have You Learned?

1.   C
Difficulty: Low
Category: Interpreting Data
Getting to the Answer: Trace the vertical line in Figure 1 up from 800 g, which equals 0.8 kg, on the x-axis to the diamond-marked line that represents Earth. Then from the point of intersection, draw a horizontal line to the y-axis to determine the expected displacement. The displacement is approximately 15 cm, so (C) is the correct answer.

Choice A would be the displacement for a spring on Titan, and D would be the displacement for a spring on Jupiter.

2.   J
Difficulty: Medium
Category: Using Data
Getting to the Answer: Use your pencil to extend the lines in graphs when required. This question directs you to Figure 2. What are the patterns in that data? For Earth, mass (m) increases as the period of oscillation (T) increases. When you extend the data curve following that trend, it's clear that the mass must be greater than 1,000 g. Only one answer, choice (J), has a mass that fits, so (J) is correct.

3.   A
Difficulty: Medium
Category: Using Data
Getting to the Answer: To determine the relationship between g and x, you have to combine the information from Figure 1 with the table provided in the question stem, which lists g for each planet or moon. For any given m greater than 0 in Figure 1, the spring's displacement is the highest for Jupiter, in the middle for Earth, and the lowest for Titan. According to the table, Jupiter has the highest gravitational acceleration at 24.9 m/sec^2, followed by Earth at 9.8 m/sec^2, followed by Titan at 1.4 m/sec^2. Thus, as gravitational acceleration increases, the spring's displacement increases. Because Earth has a greater gravitational acceleration than Mercury, the displacement on Earth would be greater than on Mercury. The correct answer is (A).

4.   F
Difficulty: Medium
Category: Using Data
Getting to the Answer: Approach questions methodically and you'll eliminate careless mistakes. According to Figure 1, a spring will have a displacement of 10 cm on Jupiter's surface when a mass (m) of 200 g is attached. What m would give the same spring on Earth a displacement of 10 cm? Trace the horizontal line that corresponds to 10 cm until it intersects the diamond-marked line that represents data for Earth. The intersection occurs around an m of 500 g. 500 g divided by 200 g is 2.5. Thus, to give the same displacement on Earth, m would have to be 2.5 times greater than the m for Jupiter. The correct answer is (F).

Watch out for G, which suggests that m would be 2.5 times *less*.

5.   C
Difficulty: High
Category: Using Data
Getting to the Answer: The equations in Figure 1 provide the relationships between the variables m, g, x, and k: $F = mg$ and $F = kx$. Therefore, $mg = kx$. Since the spring constant and displacement are the same for each of the two springs, kx is the same value for both springs. Therefore, if mass is doubled in one spring, the gravitational acceleration must be halved in order for the equation to continue equaling kx. Answer (C) is correct.

Choices A and B are incorrect because the length of the spring is not shown to be a factor in the diagram.

6.   F
Difficulty: Medium
Category: Interpreting Data
Getting to the Answer: According to the passage, the "time it takes to complete one cycle is called 'period of oscillation (T).'" Since frequency is defined as the number of oscillations per unit of time, the shorter the period of oscillation, the more oscillations are able to be completed, and thus, the higher the frequency. The fastest period of oscillation in Figure 2 is 0.29 secs and occurs when the attached mass is 100 g. Therefore, the correct choice is (F).

CHAPTER 24

EXPERIMENTS

LEARNING OBJECTIVES

After completing this chapter, you will be able to:

- Identify Research Summaries passages
- Describe the steps of the scientific method
- Identify the hypotheses, variables, and control(s) of an experiment
- Evaluate the purpose, methods, and results of an experiment
- Synthesize multiple tables, graphs, and/or diagrams to draw conclusions
- Synthesize information from multiple formats (text, tables, graphs, and/or diagrams)

Experimental Design: 6/36 SmartPoints® (High yield)

Synthesizing Data: 6/36 SmartPoints® (High yield)

How Much Do You Know?

Directions: Try out the questions below. Show your work so that you can compare your solutions to the ones found on the next page. The "Category" heading in the explanation for each question gives the title of the lesson that covers how to solve it. If you answered the question(s) for a given lesson correctly, and if your scratchwork looks like ours, you may be able to move quickly through that lesson. If you answered incorrectly or used a different approach, you may want to take your time on that lesson.

Passage I

As part of an ecological impact study, two experiments examined the factors affecting the rate of algae growth produced under various conditions. Experimenters utilized a constructed reservoir known as Lake Eight that has two basins of equal size connected by a strait.

Experiment 1

The two basins of Lake Eight were separated by an impermeable partition (see Diagram). Basin A was fertilized with phosphorus, carbon, and nitrogen, whereas Basin B received only carbon and nitrogen. The researchers also varied the temperature of different regions within each basin. Two months after fertilization, the number of algal blooms per square meter of water surface area was measured, yielding the data in Table 1.

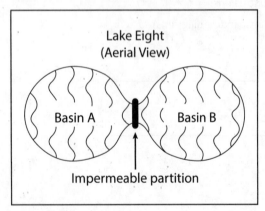

Lake Eight
(Aerial View)

Basin A   Basin B

Impermeable partition

Diagram

Table 1			
Basin	Additives	Temperature (°C)	Algal blooms per square meter
Basin A	phosphorus, carbon, and nitrogen	10	0.18
		25	0.48
		35	0.56
Basin B	carbon and nitrogen	10	0.04
		25	0.07
		35	0.08

Experiment 2

One year later, Experiment 1 was repeated, except that sodium bicarbonate ($NaHCO_3$) was added in place of phosphorus. The results are shown in Table 2.

Table 2			
Basin	Additives	Temperature (°C)	Algal blooms per square meter
Basin A	sodium bicarbonate, carbon, and nitrogen	10	0.26
		25	0.56
		35	0.78
Basin B	carbon and nitrogen	10	0.04
		25	0.07
		35	0.08

1. Which factor was varied in Experiment 1?

   A. Basin surface area

   B. Algae growth rate

   C. Algal blooms per square meter

   D. Water temperature

2. Experiment 1 differed from Experiment 2 in that Experiment 2:

   F. did not fertilize Basin B with phosphorus.

   G. did not fertilize Basin A with phosphorus.

   H. did not fertilize Basin A with sodium bicarbonate.

   J. fertilized Basin B with carbon and nitrogen only.

HINT: For Q3, remember that Research Summaries passages like this one will include mostly Experiments questions, but sometimes the question set will include one or more Data questions. To learn about answering questions like this one, review the "Using Data Questions" lesson in chapter 23.

---

3. Suppose that extensive algal blooms cause pollution problems and that detergents are a major source of phosphorus in fresh water. To reduce the pollution associated with algal blooms, it would be most useful to:

   A. increase the amount of detergent present in fresh water.

   B. decrease the amount of detergent present in fresh water.

   C. replace the phosphorus in detergents with sodium bicarbonate.

   D. balance the phosphorus added to detergents with equal amounts of sodium bicarbonate.

4. Based on the results of Experiments 1 and 2, which of the following bodies of water is likely to produce the greatest number of algal blooms per square meter?

   F. A 45°C pond fertilized with sodium bicarbonate

   G. A 5°C pond fertilized with sodium bicarbonate

   H. A 45°C pond fertilized with phosphorus

   J. A 5°C pond fertilized with a mixture that is equal parts phosphorus and sodium bicarbonate

5. The experimenters chose to modify the fertilizers added to Basin A between the two experiments without changing those added to Basin B. Which of the following statements gives the most likely reason the experimenters made that choice? The experimenters:

   A. wanted to use the same control for both experiments.

   B. wanted to test variations in the amount of fertilizer used.

   C. wanted to confirm the results from Experiment 1.

   D. did not have another fertilizer to test.

6. Suppose that Basin A had not been fertilized with carbon and nitrogen in Experiment 2. At the conclusion of their two years of testing, the experimenters would NOT have been able to:

   F. measure the effect of sodium bicarbonate on algae growth.

   G. measure the effect of phosphorus on algae growth.

   H. measure the effect of carbon and nitrogen alone on algae growth.

   J. measure the effect of temperature on algae growth.

Check Your Work

1. D
Difficulty: Low
Category: Experimental Design
Getting to the Answer: Understanding the scientific method will help you score points on questions like these. An independent variable is one that is altered directly by the researchers. The description of Experiment 1 states that the researchers "varied the temperature," so (D) is correct.

Choice A is incorrect because the surface area of each basin is constant. Choice B is incorrect because the rate of algal growth was not directly manipulated by the researchers, although it certainly had an impact on their results. Choice C is incorrect because the number of algal blooms was the dependent variable: the one the researchers measured, not the one they varied.

2. G
Difficulty: Medium
Category: Experimental Design
Getting to the Answer: In the description of Experiment 2, the only difference between it and Experiment 1 is said to be that sodium bicarbonate was used in place of phosphorus. In Experiment 1, the phosphorus was added to Basin A, so the difference between the two experiments is whether phosphorus or sodium bicarbonate was used in Basin A. Thus, (G) is correct.

Choice F is incorrect because neither experiment used phosphorus in Basin B. Experiment 2 is the experiment in which sodium bicarbonate was used in Basin B, so H is incorrect. Basin B was fertilized with only carbon and nitrogen in both experiments, so J is incorrect.

3. B
Difficulty: Medium
Category: Using Data
Getting to the Answer: You're looking for a choice that would decrease algal bloom density. Decreasing the amount of detergent would decrease the amount of phosphorus in the water, which would in turn reduce algal blooms (based on the results of Experiment 1) and the associated pollution. Choice (B), then, is correct.

Based on the results of Experiment 1, A would likely increase algal blooms; and based on the results of

Experiment 2, C would also probably increase the growth of algal blooms. Choice D might also increase the growth, though the combination of phosphorus and sodium bicarbonate was not directly studied in the experiments from the passage.

4. F
Difficulty: Low
Category: Synthesizing Data
Getting to the Answer: First, identify the trends that exist in the data; then you can extrapolate those trends to evaluate the choices and determine which body of water would have the most algal blooms. As temperatures increased in both experiments, algal blooms increased, so the correct answer will be one of the choices with a higher temperature; eliminate G and J. In Experiment 2, at every temperature, sodium bicarbonate produced more algal blooms than phosphorus did at the same temperatures in Experiment 1. Thus, (F) is correct.

It should be noted that J is incorrect because the effects of using both phosphorus and sodium bicarbonate were not studied, so no conclusions can be made about how it would affect algal blooms.

5. A
Difficulty: High
Category: Experimental Design
Getting to the Answer: What role did Basin B play in Experiment 1? It acted as the control, or the baseline case, which allowed researchers to isolate the effects of phosphorus on algal bloom density. In Experiment 2, the experimenters wanted to be able to isolate the effect of adding sodium bicarbonate instead of phosphorus. Therefore, they used the same fertilizers in Basin B to allow for the same kind of comparison as in the first experiment. The correct answer is (A).

The passage does not mention how much fertilizer is used, so B is incorrect. Choice C might be tempting because the results of Experiment 2 for Basin B are the same as those of Experiment 1 for Basin B, but this is not the main reason the experimenters repeated the conditions. Choice D is incorrect since it is never suggested in the passage.

6. F
Difficulty: Low
Category: Experimental Design
Getting to the Answer: Note that the question is asking what the experiments would have been able to measure at the conclusion of their *two* years of study, meaning that this includes the results of both Experiment 1 and Experiment 2. If Basin A was not fertilized with carbon and nitrogen, then no algae growth would occur, and the effect of the added fertilizer ingredient, sodium bicarbonate, could not be measured. Thus, (F) is correct. The remaining choices were all answered by Experiment 1 and Basin B of Experiment 2.

RESEARCH SUMMARIES AND EXPERIMENTAL DESIGN QUESTIONS

LEARNING OBJECTIVES

After this lesson, you will be able to:

- Identify Research Summaries passages
- Describe the steps of the scientific method
- Identify the hypotheses, variables, and control(s) of an experiment
- Evaluate the purpose, methods, and results of an experiment

To read passages and answer questions like these:

Passage II

The Brazilian tree frog (*Hyla faber*) exchanges gases through both its skin and its lungs. The exchange rate depends on the temperature of the frogs' environment. A pair of experiments was performed to investigate this dependence.

Experiment 1

Fifty frogs were placed in a controlled atmosphere that, with the exception of temperature, was designed to simulate the frogs' native habitat. The temperature was varied from 5°C to 25°C, and equilibrium was attained before each successive temperature change. The amount of oxygen absorbed by the frogs' lungs and skin per hour was measured, and the results for all the frogs were averaged. These results are shown in Table 1.

Temperature (°C)	Moles O_2 absorbed/hr	
	Skin	Lungs
5	15.4	8.3
10	22.7	35.1
15	43.6	64.9
20	42.1	73.5
25	40.4	78.7

Table 1

Experiment 2

The same frogs were placed under the same conditions as in Experiment 1. For this experiment, the amount of carbon dioxide eliminated through the frogs' skin and lungs was measured. The results were averaged and are shown below in Table 2.

Temperature (°C)	Moles O_2 eliminated/hr	
	Skin	Lungs
5	18.9	2.1
10	43.8	12.7
15	79.2	21.3
20	91.6	21.9
25	96.5	21.4

Table 2

1. Which of the following factors did the researchers intentionally vary?

   A. The number of frogs studied
   B. The humidity of the frogs' simulated habitat
   C. The temperature of the frogs' simulated habitat
   D. The amount of oxygen in the frogs' simulated habitat

2. Which of the following statements about gas exchange in *Hyla faber* is consistent with the results of Experiments 1 and 2? The Brazilian tree frog:

F. exchanges oxygen and carbon dioxide primarily through the skin.

G. absorbs oxygen primarily in the lungs but eliminates carbon dioxide primarily through the skin.

H. absorbs more oxygen in the lungs than carbon dioxide eliminated through the skin.

J. exchanges oxygen and carbon dioxide through both the skin and lungs equally.

3. Which of the following statements describes a difference between Experiments 1 and 2? In Experiment 2:

A. a different species of tree frog was used.

B. a broader range of temperatures was studied.

C. only oxygen absorption through the skin was measured.

D. carbon-dioxide elimination was measured.

4. Why was the study designed so that the frogs were placed in a controlled atmosphere designed to simulate their native habitat? These conditions ensured that the researchers could:

F. manipulate some variables but leave other elements as they were naturally.

G. prevent the predation of frogs by their natural predators.

H. control the frogs' food supply.

J. control the frogs' oxygen intake.

5. Which of the following best explains why the researchers allowed the temperature in the simulated habitat to achieve equilibrium before each temperature change? The researchers wanted to allow:

A. time for additional oxygen to be removed from the habitat.

B. time for the frogs to adjust their gas exchange rate to the new temperature.

C. time for the researchers to increase or decrease carbon dioxide levels in the habitat.

D. time for the habitat's humidity level to adjust with the new temperature.

6. The amount of oxygen absorbed through the skin at various temperatures is best represented by which of the following graphs?

F.

G.

H.

J.

You need to know this:

Experimental Design questions most often appear as part of a Research Summaries passage question set.

Research Summaries

Three of the six passages you will see on test day will be Research Summaries. In order to identify a Research Summaries passage as part of step 1, look for these typical characteristics:

- an introductory paragraph or two providing background information about a scientific phenomenon and/or some additional details on an experimental setup
- a series of experiments, differentiated with helpful labels like "Study 1" and "Experiment 2"
- details about each experiment, typically focusing on method
- at least one graph or table with experimental results

Research Summaries passages can feature the question types discussed in chapter 23 that are about the results of the experiments. However, these passages will focus on questions related to experimental design and the scientific method.

Experimental Design Questions

Approximately 20%–30% of the questions in the ACT Science Test fall into this category, and they appear more often within Research Summaries passages than with any other passage type. These questions involve:

- evaluating experimental tools and procedures
- interpreting experimental design by identifying variables and controls
- analyzing experimental designs and results
- predicting results of additional trials or experiments
- identifying the expected impact of modifying an experiment's design

The scientific method is a well-known process for conducting scientific research, but the specific steps and terminology used to describe the method can vary. For the ACT Science Test, you might find it helpful to think of the scientific method as the following set of steps:

1. Ask a question based on observations and initial research.

    Observation and Research: All scientific investigation begins by noticing a phenomenon that is interesting and posing a question about it.

2. Formulate a hypothesis that answers the question.

    Hypothesis: Based on initial observations and research, scientists form hypotheses. A hypothesis is an attempt to explain a particular observation and often indicates the independent and dependent variables.

3. Design an experiment to test the hypothesis.

    Experimental Design: A good experimental design will isolate the effect of one or more independent variables (manipulated quantities) on one or more dependent variables (measured quantities).

    Independent Variable: The variable being manipulated by the experimenters, typically the basis of the groups in the experiment

    Dependent Variable: The variable being measured by the experimenters, typically the "results" of the study

4. Conduct the experiment and record data.

    Control: A control group serves as a baseline within an experiment that allows for effective comparison. A control group is a group that does not receive any treatment or manipulation by the independent variable.

5.   Analyze the data and draw conclusions.

Analysis and Conclusion: Once data is obtained, scientists will look at that data and interpret it. Using trends in the results, scientists can conclude whether or not their hypothesis is supported.

6.   Communicate the results.

Publish: As a final step, scientists will often publish their results to share them with the scientific community.

Experimental Design questions will require you to:

- recognize and define hypotheses, variables, and control group
- describe and apply information from one or more experiments in terms of the scientific method

You need to do this:

When working through step 2, analyzing the passage and figures strategically, for Research Summaries passages in particular, you should NOT spend time trying to understand or analyze everything, and you should NOT be intimidated by technical terminology. You *should*:

- examine the introductory text for the central idea and purpose of the experiments
- move quickly though the text of the experiments and their methods, only pausing to underline keywords
- locate variables in the figures and, if applicable, identify whether the variables are independent or dependent
- locate units of measurement
- identify noticeable trends

Again, do NOT spend time trying to understand or analyze everything; you will return to examine the text and figures in more detail when questions reference them.

As you complete step 2 for Research Summaries, identify these mentally or in the margins:

- the hypothesis for each experiment: What is the researcher attempting to prove or disprove?
- the independent variable(s) for each experiment: What is the researcher manipulating?
- the dependent variable(s) for each experiment: What is the researcher measuring?
- the control group for each experiment: What will the researcher use as a baseline for the final results?

Some Experimental Design questions will test your ability to determine:

- the purpose of an experiment: What is the researcher testing?
- the methods of an experiment: look to the experimental design. What group is serving as the control and what group is being tested/treated?
- the results of an experiment: What form did the researcher use to share the results? What do the results mean in terms of a real-world situation?

Identifying the hypotheses, variables, and control group make it easier to determine the purpose of an experiment, evaluate its methods, and interpret its results, so considering all six steps of the scientific method while analyzing the passage and figures will help you work through Research Summaries more efficiently and effectively.

Explanation

Identify

Passage II includes a short introductory paragraph followed by sections with clearly labeled headings of Experiment 1 and Experiment 2, so this is a Research Summaries passage.

Analyze

Central idea: The first paragraph indicates there will be two experiments examining the relationship between the tree frog's gas exchange through its skin/lungs and atmospheric temperature.

Experiment 1 and Table 1: Quickly skim the methodology described in the text and describe the important information in the table:

- Oxygen absorption in the skin and lungs (dependent variables) is being measured at five different temperatures: 5, 10, 15, 20, and 25°C (independent variable)
- Trend in skin absorption: increases dramatically from 5 to 15, decreases slightly from 15 to 25
- Trend in lung absorption: increases dramatically from 5 to 15, then continues to increase from 15 to 25

Experiment 2 and Table 2: Again, skim the text and describe the important information in the table:

- Same table setup and independent variable, except carbon dioxide elimination (dependent variable) is being measured instead of oxygen absorption
- Trend in skin elimination: increases dramatically from 5 to 15, then continues to increase from 15 to 25
- Trend in lung elimination: increases dramatically from 5 to 15, then is fairly constant from 15 to 25

Examine, predict, and answer

Question	Explanation
1. Which of the following factors did the researchers intentionally vary? A. The number of frogs studied B. The humidity of the frogs' simulated habitat C. The temperature of the frogs' simulated habitat D. The amount of oxygen in the frogs' simulated habitat	**1. C** **Difficulty:** Low **Category:** Experimental Design **Getting to the Answer:** The phrase *intentionally vary* indicates that this question is asking for the independent variable. The passage explains that, for both experiments, "temperature was varied from 5°C to 25°C," so choice (C) is correct. Choice A is incorrect because the passage states that the number of frogs studied was constant (50 total). Choice B is incorrect because the passage does not mention humidity. Watch out for D, which is a common trap for these kinds of questions. The amount of oxygen that the frogs *absorbed* (not the amount in the habitat) varied according to temperature, but that was the dependent variable in Experiment 1, not the independent variable.

Question	Explanation
2. Which of the following statements about gas exchange in *Hyla faber* is consistent with the results of Experiments 1 and 2? The Brazilian tree frog: F. exchanges oxygen and carbon dioxide primarily through the skin. G. absorbs oxygen primarily in the lungs but eliminates carbon dioxide primarily through the skin. H. absorbs more oxygen in the lungs than carbon dioxide eliminated through the skin. J. exchanges oxygen and carbon dioxide through both the skin and lungs equally.	**2. G** **Difficulty:** Medium **Category:** Synthesizing Data **Getting to the Answer:** This question requires synthesizing data in both Tables 1 and 2 and is asking about the primary location of gas exchange. Table 1 indicates that the frogs absorb more oxygen in the lungs than in the skin, except at the lowest temperature. Choice F is therefore incorrect. Table 2 indicates that the frogs eliminate carbon dioxide primarily through the skin, as the moles eliminated through the skin are always higher than the moles eliminated by the lungs. The findings are therefore consistent with (G). The amount of carbon dioxide eliminated through the skin is greater than the amount of oxygen absorbed at any given temperature, so H is incorrect. The gas exchange rates are not equal, so J is incorrect.
3. Which of the following statements describes a difference between Experiments 1 and 2? In Experiment 2: A. a different species of tree frog was used. B. a broader range of temperatures was studied. C. only oxygen absorption through the skin was measured. D. carbon-dioxide elimination was measured.	**3. D** **Difficulty:** Low **Category:** Experimental Design **Getting to the Answer:** According to the description of Experiment 2, the frogs studied and the conditions of the habitat were the same as in Experiment 1. The only difference was that "the amount of carbon dioxide eliminated through the frogs' skin and lungs was measured" instead of the amount of oxygen absorbed. Choice (D) is thus correct.

Question	Explanation

4. Why was the study designed so that the frogs were placed in a controlled atmosphere designed to simulate their native habitat? These conditions ensured that the researchers could:
 	
   F. manipulate some variables but leave other elements as they were naturally.
 	
   G. prevent the predation of frogs by their natural predators.
 	
   H. control the frogs' food supply.
 	
   J. control the frogs' oxygen intake.
	4. F
	Difficulty: Low
	Category: Experimental Design
	Getting to the Answer: According to the introduction of the passage, the researchers wanted to investigate the dependence of gas exchange on temperature in the Brazilian tree frog. If the researchers had constructed an artificial environment that greatly differed from the frogs' natural habitat, then it would be impossible to tell whether temperature alone was responsible for changes in oxygen absorption and carbon dioxide elimination, or whether there was some other environmental difference or combination of differences that caused these changes. Making sure that the only differences are those that occur in the independent variable ensures more accurate results. Choice (F) is correct.
	
	Choices G and H are incorrect because predators and food supply are factors outside the scope of the experiment that are unrelated to the variables in question. Choice J is incorrect because oxygen intake was not directly controlled by the experimenters; rather, it was one of the dependent variables that was measured.

Question	Explanation
5. Which of the following best explains why the researchers allowed the temperature in the simulated habitat to achieve equilibrium before each temperature change? The researchers wanted to allow: A. time for additional oxygen to be removed from the habitat. B. time for the frogs to adjust their gas exchange rate to the new temperature. C. time for the researchers to increase or decrease carbon dioxide levels in the habitat. D. time for the habitat's humidity level to adjust with the new temperature.	**5. B** **Difficulty:** Medium **Category:** Experimental Design **Getting to the Answer:** According to the first paragraph of the passage, the researchers were interested in investigating the dependence of the frogs' gas exchange rate on the temperature of their environment. The description of the first experiment also indicates that the researchers simulated the frogs' native habitat "with the exception of temperature." Thus, the researchers did not remove oxygen from the habitat or modify its carbon dioxide levels, meaning A and C can be eliminated. Similarly, there is no suggestion in the passage that the humidity level changed, so D is also incorrect. This leaves only (B). And indeed, to achieve their stated purpose, the researchers had to allow the frogs' rate of gas exchange to adjust to each new temperature. Otherwise, the data they collected would not actually demonstrate a connection between the independent variable and the dependent variable. Choice (B) is correct.

Question	Explanation

6. The amount of oxygen absorbed through the skin at various temperatures is best represented by which of the following graphs?

F.

G.

H.

J.

6. J
Difficulty: Low
Category: Synthesizing Data
Getting to the Answer: Because the answer choices do not have scales on their y-axes, you should compare the data table to the answer choice graphs by identifying the trend of the data. Moles of oxygen absorbed through the skin are lowest at 5°C, increase to a peak at 15°C, and then slightly decrease at 25°C. That matches (J).

Choice F also shows an increase followed by a decrease. However, the values for 20°C and 25°C are lower than the values at 5°C and 10°C; this is inconsistent with the data table, so this graph is incorrect.

Drills

If Experimental Design questions give you trouble, study the information above and try out these drill questions before completing the Try on Your Own questions below. Drill answers can be found in Answers and Explanations.

a. What is the independent variable in Experiment A?

Experiment A

Cotton cultivars were grown in 25 plots under greenhouse conditions. The plots were divided into five sections, and each section was irrigated daily with different levels of water salinity for 20 minutes. Growth was measured every 10 days over a 2-month period.

b. What is the dependent variable in Experiment B?

Experiment B

Four different batches of iodized salt were sampled. For each sample, 40 g of salt were dissolved in 200 mL of water along with 2–5 drops of starch solution in a beaker. Sodium thiosulfate was added dropwise until the purple color disappeared. The equivalent volume was used to calculate the iodine content in parts per million.

c. What is the control in Experiment C?

Experiment C

Petroleum-tolerant and non-petroleum-tolerant fungal isolates were cultured in flasks enriched with crude oil at room temperature for 10 days. The researchers varied the amount of crude oil in each flask and monitored the degree of turbidity over a 10-day period to measure the capacity of hydrocarbon degradation by the fungi.

d. What is/are the independent variable(s) in Figure D?

Figure D

e.   What is/are the dependent variable(s) in Table E?

	Table E	
Tree species	Ambient temperature (°C)	Shade temperature (°C)
A. chinensis	38.9	32.5
F. benjamina	38.5	33.8
L. floribunda	38.7	34.3
M. indica	38.3	32.9
P. africanum	38.0	33.7

Try on Your Own

Directions: Take as much time as you need on these questions. Work carefully and methodically. There will be an opportunity for timed practice at the end of the chapter.

Answers are found at the end of the chapter.

Passage III

When a pure hydrocarbon-based fuel combusts under ideal circumstances, a reaction that produces carbon dioxide, water, and heat occurs:

$$CH_4 + 2O_2 \rightarrow CO_2 + H_2O + heat$$

When gasoline, a hydrocarbon-based fuel, is combusted in vehicle engines, the reaction often produces other by-products released in the vehicle exhaust, including carbon monoxide, nitric acid, sulfuric acid, soot, and/or smoke. This contamination can occur through the refinement process of gasoline itself or from the atmosphere in which a reaction occurs.

Students conducted a series of experiments to learn more about the conditions that affect vehicle emissions.

Experiment 1

Students connected a collection bag to the exhaust pipe of three of their school buses. The buses' engines were started, and the exhausts were captured by collection bags. A syringe was then used to extract a 5-mL sample of each exhaust. The exhaust was injected into a gas chromatograph, which separates mixtures of gases into their individual components. Students compared the exhaust to mixtures of known hydrocarbon concentration samples to determine what percentage

of the sample (by volume) was composed of unburned hydrocarbons.

Each bus was started on a 70°F day, and samples of the exhausts were collected and extracted at 30-second intervals for 3 minutes. The buses were then allowed to idle for 15 minutes and samples were again collected. The results are reproduced in Table 1.

Time after starting (min)	Percentage of hydrocarbons in the exhaust		
	Bus 1 1994 Model X	Bus 2 1992 Model X	Bus 3 2006 Model X
0.5	10.3	9.0	5.4
1	11.2	9.8	4.9
1.5	12.0	13.2	6.0
2	10.5	22.9	4.9
2.5	9.6	21.0	4.5
3	9.5	20.1	4.2
18	5.6	6.3	1.8
18.5	5.6	6.3	1.8

Table 1 caption: Table 1

Experiment 2

The students hypothesized that temperature would also affect the efficiency of the combustion reaction. The buses were tested again at different external temperatures after being allowed to idle for 15 minutes, using the same procedure as Experiment 1. The results are reproduced in Figure 1.

Figure 1

1. Which of the following factors did the students vary in Experiment 1?

   A. The time of day at which the samples were taken

   B. The instruments used to collect the exhaust samples

   C. The age of the buses tested

   D. The amount of exhaust used in the gas chromatograph

2. Consider that many states require buses to undergo emissions testing to ensure that peak hydrocarbon levels remain below a required threshold in order to pass an annual inspection. Based on the results of the students' experiments, approximately how long after starting should the exhaust be tested during the inspection process?

   F. Less than 75 seconds

   G. Between 75 and 150 seconds

   H. Between 150 and 240 seconds

   J. More than 15 minutes

3. Which of the following best explains why the students collected exhaust samples in a collection bag?

   A. To keep air and other gases from contaminating the exhaust samples

   B. To allow outside air and gases to mix with the exhaust samples equally

   C. To capture only the hydrocarbons in the exhaust

   D. To filter out sediments from the exhaust

4. How many temperatures were tested in Experiment 1, and how many temperatures were tested in Experiment 2?

	Experiment 1	Experiment 2
F.	1	1
G.	1	5
H.	5	5
J.	7	5

5. Which of the following statements best describes why Experiment 2 was designed so that the buses idled for 15 minutes prior to the exhaust measurements being taken?

    A. More exhaust is needed for analysis at warmer temperatures, so the buses needed to run for a longer period of time.

    B. The percentage of hydrocarbon emissions for each bus fluctuated immediately after startup, so any change could be attributed solely to the age of the bus.

    C. After idling, the percentage of hydrocarbon emissions for each bus stabilized, so any change could be attributed solely to temperature.

    D. It took longer for the buses to start in cold weather.

6. The students hypothesized that a sample taken from their school buses' exhaust after a period of idling would contain more hydrocarbons than one taken after the engines had been turned off and restarted. Do the results of Experiment 1 support this hypothesis?

    F. Yes; the highest percentage of hydrocarbons was found in the exhaust of the bus after idling.

    G. Yes; the lowest percentage of hydrocarbons was found in the exhaust of the bus after idling.

    H. No; the highest percentage of hydrocarbons was found in the exhaust of the bus shortly after restarting.

    J. No; the lowest percentage of hydrocarbons was found in the exhaust of the bus shortly after restarting.

Science

SYNTHESIZING DATA QUESTIONS

After this lesson, you will be able to:

- Synthesize multiple tables, graphs, and/or diagrams to draw conclusions
- Synthesize information from multiple formats (text, tables, graphs, and/or diagrams)

To answer a question like this:

Passage IV

The half-life of a radioactive isotope is the amount of time necessary for one-half of the initial number of its nuclei to decay. The decay curves of two radioactive thorium isotopes (^{231}Th and ^{234}Th) are graphed below as functions of the ratio of N, the number of nuclei remaining after a given time period, to N_0, the initial number of nuclei. The results are recorded in Figure 1 and Figure 2, respectively.

Figure 1

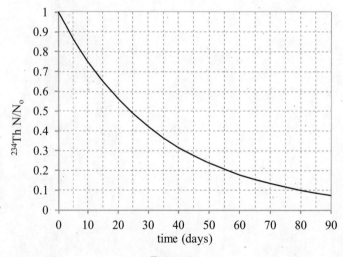

Figure 2

According to Figures 1 and 2, the half-life of ^{234}Th is approximately how many times longer than the half-life of ^{231}Th?

A. 1

B. 12

C. 24

D. 48

You need to know this:

Synthesizing Data questions require you to—you guessed it—synthesize information from multiple figures (tables, graphs, and diagrams only) or multiple formats (text from the passage or question stem and one or more figures).

- Synthesizing information means combining or piecing together a number of elements into a coherent whole.

- Synthesizing Data questions appear more commonly in connection with Research Summaries than Data Interpretation passages.

- These questions are usually a little more complicated than other Data or Experiments questions, and answering them will usually require more steps.

For Research Summaries, the steps you take to answer individual Synthesizing Data questions will likely overlap with the steps you take to answer the other questions about the passage. Identifying the steps of the scientific method when reading this type of passage will help you answer the accompanying Synthesizing Data questions more efficiently.

Some Synthesizing Data questions will ask you to combine information from multiple figures. Others will ask you to synthesize written information and one or more figures.

You need to do this:

When examining the question stem, step 3, determine which text and/or figures will be needed to answer the question. Look for clues like a reference to a particular figure or a hypothetical situation presented in the question stem.

These questions can be asked in many different ways. You may need to:

- use information from one figure to look up information from another figure

- perform basic mathematical operations, such as adding, subtracting, multiplying, or dividing

- apply patterns in the data to new variables in order to predict how they will behave

- apply or manipulate information from multiple figures in some other way

After completing step 3, remember to repeat step 2 (strategically analyzing the figures) using the clues from the question stem to focus your second analysis and locate the information needed to answer the question. Use this information to make a prediction before choosing an answer.

When asked to identify the correct figure that matches the presented data:

- check the trend of the data: is it increasing, decreasing, or constant?

- match the shape of the trend to the answer choices: is it linear, exponential, or something else?

- check specific values at one or more given points to confirm the correct answer

Science

Explanation

Examine the text, figures, and question stem for key information:

- **Intro:** the *half-life* of an isotope is defined as the amount of time needed for one-half of the initial number of nuclei to decay
- **Figures 1/2:** the decay curves of two radioactive thorium isotopes (^{231}Th and ^{234}Th, respectively)
- **Question stem:** the half-life of each isotope needs to be determined to see by what factor they differ

Predict and answer:

- To figure out the half-life of ^{231}Th, look at the first graph (when half of the nuclei have decayed, the N/N_0 ratio will be ½ or 0.5).
- Draw a horizontal line across the graph from 0.5 on the *y*-axis and, where that line intersects the curve, draw a vertical line down to the *x*-axis.
- This line intersects the *x*-axis slightly above 1.0, which means the amount of time it takes for half of the nuclei to decay is about 1 day.
- Repeat the process to determine the half-life for ^{234}Th (its half-life is about 24 days).
- Determine that the half-life of ^{234}Th is approximately 24 times the half-life of ^{231}Th.

Choice (C) is correct.

Try on Your Own

Directions: Take as much time as you need on these questions. Work carefully and methodically. There will be an opportunity for timed practice at the end of the chapter.

Answers are found at the end of the chapter.

Passage V

During anaerobic fermentation, the conversion of pyruvate to acetic acid and CO_2 is catalyzed by the enzyme pyruvate decarboxylase (PDC). PDC is prone to *point mutations* (the replacement of one nucleotide with another) at specific locations in its gene sequence. These mutations can have wide-ranging impacts on the enzyme's function.

Study 1

Table 1 lists nucleotide sequences for the wild-type PDC gene along with three different mutant variants. Table 2 provides the amino acids coded for by each three-nucleotide codon.

Table 1		
Enzyme	Codon	
	Location 1	Location 2
Wild-type	CAA	GAT
Mutant 1	CAA	AAT
Mutant 2	GAA	GAT
Mutant 3	CAA	GAC

Table 2	
Codon	Amino Acid
AAT	Asparagine
CAA	Glutamine
GAA	Glutamic Acid
GAC	Aspartic Acid
GAT	Aspartic Acid

Study 2

To determine the efficiency of the enzyme and its mutated forms, researchers ran several trials using the wild-type of the enzyme as well as three mutant types. Each was reacted with 1.5 mL of 0.08 M pyruvate, and decarboxylation of pyruvate was measured in number of molecules converted over time. Results are shown in Figure 1.

This data is from *Natural Science*, Vol. 4, No. 11, October 2012, pp. 881–893.

Figure 1

1. According to Tables 1 and 2, which enzyme contains a molecule of glutamic acid?

   A. Wild-type

   B. Mutant 1

   C. Mutant 2

   D. Mutant 3

2. Suppose that after introducing an unlabeled enzyme to a quantity of pyruvate, the researchers measure the concentration at 2 seconds to be 60 μ mol/L. Which of the following is most likely the nucleotide sequence of the unlabeled enzyme?

   F. CAA GAT

   G. CAA AAT

   H. CAA GAC

   J. GAA GAT

3. Based on Tables 1 and 2, what is the amino-acid sequence of Mutant 1?

	First Location	Second Location
A.	Asparagine	Glutamine
B.	Glutamine	Asparagine
C.	Glutamine	Aspartic Acid
D.	Glutamic Acid	Asparagine

4. *Silent mutations* are changes to the sequence of nucleotide bases in the DNA that do not result in a change of amino acid or affect the function of the protein. Which of the following mutated enzymes, if any, most likely contains only silent mutations?

   F. Mutant 1

   G. Mutant 2

   H. Mutant 3

   J. None of the mutated enzymes

5. The researchers had predicted that the nucleotide sequence in the first location was more directly responsible for the decarboxylation activity of the enzyme than the sequence in the second location. Are the results of the study consistent with this hypothesis?

   A. Yes; Mutant 2 shows the least enzymatic activity.

   B. Yes; Mutant 2 shows the most enzymatic activity.

   C. No; both the wild-type and Mutant 3 show similar enzymatic activity.

   D. No; Mutants 1 and 3 show less enzymatic activity than Mutant 2.

How Much Have You Learned?

Directions: For test-like practice, give yourself 7 minutes to complete this question set. Be sure to study the explanations, even for questions you got correct. They can be found at the end of this chapter.

Passage VI

Crop output can be stunted in areas with longer winters, persistent cloudy weather, or smog. Even in optimal growth conditions, production efficiency is less than optimal because lower leaves on tightly packed plants receive less light than those closer to the top. As a result, there is an interest in using artificial light to increase production.

Experiment 1

Researchers grew 100 tomato plants in a greenhouse under several conditions. To simulate cloudy weather, they used a shade cloth that blocked out some of the incoming light. Forty plants were placed under the shade cloth for 4 out of every 10 days. Another 40 were placed under the same cloth for 6 out of 10 days. Within each of these groups, half of the plants were grown with white LED lights illuminating the lower two-thirds of the leaves, while half were not. The final 20 plants were grown uncovered as a control group. After two months, plant growth and tomato yield were compared for all groups. Results are shown in Figure 1.

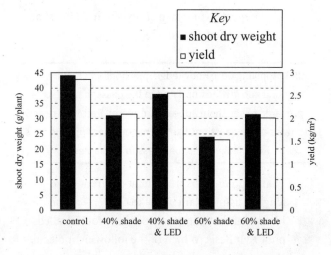

Figure 1

Experiment 2

To determine the optimal lighting conditions for growth, researchers repeated the procedure in Experiment 1 for 40% shade and an LED, this time using fluorescent light bulbs and several varieties of LED bulbs: white, blue, green, and two varieties of red—far-red (FR) and high-light (HL). The results are shown in Figure 2.

This data is from *PLOS ONE*, Vol. 13, No. 11, November 2018.

Figure 2

1. Which of the following variables remained constant throughout both experiments?

    A.   Light coverage

    B.   Light source

    C.   Plant species

    D.   Dry weight

Science

2. The researchers conducting the study chose to grow 20 of the tomato plants in a greenhouse outside of the shade cloth in Experiment 1. Which of the following statements gives the most likely reason for this decision? The researchers wanted:

    F. to determine if fluorescent lighting was more optimal for tomato yield.

    G. to ensure that at least one group of tomato plants would survive.

    H. to simulate the cloudy conditions tomato plants experience in areas with long winters.

    J. to compare the results of those grown under the shade cloth to those that weren't.

3. According to the results of the study, did the addition of LED lights increase or decrease the crop yield of the plants under a shade cover, and did the use of colored LED lighting increase or decrease the crop yield compared to white LED lighting?

	LED Under Shade Cover	**Colored LED Lighting**
A.	Increase	Increase
B.	Increase	Decrease
C.	Decrease	Increase
D.	Decrease	Decrease

4. The colors of visible light vary depending on their wavelengths; lights on the red end of the visible-light spectrum contain longer wavelengths than those on the violet end of the spectrum. Do the results of Experiment 2 support the hypothesis that increasing the wavelength of an LED light source leads to increased growth?

    F. Yes; the highest growth was observed in the plants exposed to red LED light.

    G. Yes; plants exposed to red LED light grew more than plants exposed to blue LED light.

    H. No; the lowest growth was observed in plants exposed to blue LED light.

    J. No; there is no correlation between wavelength and growth.

HINT: Research Summaries passages like this one will include mostly Experiments questions, but sometimes the question set will include one or more Data questions. To learn about answering questions like Q5, review the "Using Data Questions" lesson in chapter 23.

5. Suppose that an additional trial in Experiment 1 had been performed using 60% shade cover and fluorescent bulbs on the lower two-thirds of leaves. The approximate dry weight would most likely have been:

    A. less than 20 g/plant.

    B. between 20 g/plant and 30 g/plant.

    C. between 30 g/plant and 40 g/plant.

    D. greater than 40 g/plant.

6. Suppose the researchers wanted to determine whether percent shade impacts the effect of colored LED bulbs on growth. Which of the following experiments should be performed?

    F. Repeat Experiment 1, except use a fluorescent light bulb instead of a white LED light.

    G. Repeat Experiment 1, except use 80% shade instead of 60% shade.

    H. Repeat Experiment 2, except use black light instead of white.

    J. Repeat Experiment 2, except use 60% shade instead of 40% shade.

HINT: Applying Core Knowledge questions will require background knowledge unrelated to the passage type, so be prepared to see them appear throughout Part V. To review strategies for questions like Q7, review the "Applying Core Knowledge Questions" lesson in chapter 25.

7. Plant pigments absorb light at different wavelengths, using solar energy to convert carbon dioxide into carbohydrates through a process called photosynthesis. Which of the following molecules is produced as a direct result of photosynthesis?

    A. Fructose

    B. Galactose

    C. Glucose

    D. Sucrose

Reflect

Directions: Take a few minutes to recall what you've learned and what you've been practicing in this chapter. Consider the following questions, jot down your best answer for each one, and then compare your reflections to the expert responses on the following page. Use your level of confidence to determine what to do next.

1. When presented with a Research Summaries passage, how much should the ACT expert try to understand in depth before moving on to the questions?

    _____

    _____

    _____

2. How does an ACT expert use scientific method concepts when answering ACT Science questions?

    _____

    _____

    _____

3. How would not having a control group impact the results of a study?

    _____

    _____

    _____

4. What key features does an ACT expert focus on when asked to synthesize multiple figures or formats?

    _____

    _____

    _____

5. How will you approach Research Summaries passages differently as you continue to practice and improve your performance in the ACT Science section?

    _____

    _____

    _____

Responses

1. When presented with a Research Summaries passage, how much should the ACT expert try to understand in depth before moving on to the questions?

Not much! Move quickly though the text of the experiments and their methods, only pausing to underline keywords. Do not be intimated by technical terminology, as it will have little impact on answering questions.

2. How does an ACT expert use scientific method concepts when answering ACT Science questions?

An ACT expert uses scientific method concepts to find the key components (hypotheses, independent and dependent variables, and controls) of each experiment, making it easier to recognize the purpose of an experiment, understand its methods, and interpret its results.

3. How would not having a control group impact the results of a study?

A control group is a group that does not receive any treatment or manipulation by the independent variable. Without a control group, a manipulation to the independent variable has no baseline within the experiment that allows for effective comparison. In other words, no conclusions can be drawn about the impact of the independent variable on the dependent variable.

4. What key features does an ACT expert focus on when asked to synthesize multiple figures or formats?

When synthesizing information from multiple figures or formats, an ACT expert focuses on the trend of the data (positive, negative, or constant) and the shape in the trend (linear, exponential, or something else). An ACT expert also makes sure to check specific values at a given point.

5. How will you approach Research Summaries passages differently as you continue to practice and improve your performance in the ACT Science section?

There is no one-size-fits-all answer here. Reflect on your own habits in identifying the key features of experiments and interpreting their results and give yourself an honest assessment of your strengths and weaknesses. Consider the strategies you've seen experts use in this chapter, and put them to work in your own practice to increase your accuracy, speed, and confidence.

Next Steps

If you answered most questions correctly in the "How Much Have You Learned?" section, and if your responses to the Reflect questions were similar to those of the ACT expert, then consider Research Summaries passages an area of strength and move on to the next chapter. Come back to this topic periodically to prevent yourself from getting rusty.

If you don't yet feel confident, review the material in this chapter, then try the questions you missed again. As always, be sure to review the explanations closely. Then go online (**kaptest.com/login**) to use your Qbank for more practice. If you haven't already registered your book, do so at **kaptest.com/moreonline.**

GO ONLINE

kaptest.com/login

Answers and Explanations

Research Summaries and Experimental Design Questions

Drill Answers

a. levels of water salinity

b. iodine content

c. non-petroleum-tolerant fungal cultures

d. fuel type and time

e. shade temperature

1. C
Difficulty: Low
Category: Experimental Design
Getting to the Answer: This question is asking for an independent variable from Experiment 1. In that experiment, students took exhaust samples at intervals of 30 seconds from buses of the same model that were built in different years. So, time after starting and age of bus are the two independent variables. Only (C) mentions either of these variables, so it is correct.

Choice A may be tempting because it mentions time, but it does so incorrectly: the exhaust samples were collected at 30-second intervals, but the time of day at which they were collected wasn't mentioned. Choice B is incorrect because the same method of collection was used for each sample with each bus. Choice D is incorrect because you are told that 5 mL of each exhaust sample were injected into the gas chromatograph.

2. G
Difficulty: Low
Category: Using Data
Getting to the Answer: The goal is to test emissions when hydrocarbons are at their peak, so check Table 1 and Table 2 and determine the time at which each bus emits the highest percentage of hydrocarbons. Bus 1 emits peak hydrocarbons (12%) at 90 seconds, Bus 2 at 120 seconds (22.9%), and Bus 3 at 90 seconds (6%). This matches (G).

3. A
Difficulty: Medium
Category: Experimental Design
Getting to the Answer: The students were collecting exhaust samples to determine what percentage of the exhaust was composed of hydrocarbons, so they'd want to keep each exhaust sample as pure as possible. A bag attached to the tailpipe would collect the exhaust before it mixed with, and was diluted by, the outside air. Therefore, (A) is correct.

Choice B goes against the students' purpose. They wanted to compare the percentages of hydrocarbons in the exhaust, but adding air and other gases would make their results unreliable. Choice C is incorrect because you know that the collection bag captures all of the exhaust, not only hydrocarbons. Choice D is incorrect because you are given no reason to assume the bag filters anything from the exhaust.

4. G
Difficulty: Medium
Category: Experimental Design
Getting to the Answer: According to the description, in the first experiment, all of the testing was done on a 70°F day, which means there was only one temperature tested in that experiment. Thus, you can eliminate H and J, which both claim more than one temperature was tested in Experiment 1. The point of Experiment 2 was to test the effect of temperature on engine efficiency. It's helpful to notice, however, that you don't need to actually count the number of temperatures that were tested. Of the remaining choices, F and (G), only (G) correctly indicates that multiple temperatures were tested in Experiment 2. Therefore (G) is correct.

5. C
Difficulty: High
Category: Experimental Design
Getting to the Answer: To see the effect of idling, take a look at Table 1 to see what happened to the results after the buses idled. For each bus, the results held steady across consecutive measurements after idling, which indicates that the percentage of hydrocarbons in the emissions stabilizes after the engine has been running for a while. This is likely why they let the engines idle in the second experiment, so (C) is correct.

Science

Choice A is incorrect because there's no indication that more exhaust is needed at higher temperatures; furthermore, since the students collected samples in Experiment 2 in the same manner as in Experiment 1, the same amount was collected in each sample. Choice B may be tempting, as the hydrocarbon levels in the exhaust did fluctuate after the engines started up; however, it doesn't explain how idling for 15 minutes would solve the issue of the age of the bus affecting the results. Choice D is irrelevant; while it may be true that engines take longer to start in cold weather, no measurements were taken until the engines actually started.

6.   H
Difficulty: Low
Category: Synthesizing Data
Getting to the Answer: Look at Table 1 to see the levels of hydrocarbons in the exhaust after an engine start and after idling. For all three buses, the hydrocarbon levels were highest in the few minutes after start and lowest after a period of idling. This disproves the hypothesis that there would be more hydrocarbons after idling, so (H) is correct.

Choices F and G can both be eliminated because they state that the results supported the hypothesis. Even though J states that the hypothesis was not supported, it misstates the facts that support that result, so it is incorrect.

Synthesizing Data Questions

1.   C
Difficulty: Low
Category: Synthesizing Data
Getting to the Answer: First, look at Table 2 to determine which codon codes for glutamic acid. The only one that does is GAA. Now, use Table 1 to determine which of the enzyme types contains a GAA sequence at one of the two locations. Only Mutant 2 does, so (C) is correct.

2.   G
Difficulty: Medium
Category: Synthesizing Data
Getting to the Answer: First, look at the graph to see which type of enzyme resulted in a concentration of 60 µ mol/L of pyruvate after 2 seconds; a line drawn up from 2 seconds on the *x*-axis intersects with the curve for Mutant 1 at 60 µ mol/L. Next, look at Table 1 to get the nucleotide sequence of Mutant 1: it has CAA at the first position and AAT at the second. Choice (G) is correct.

3.   B
Difficulty: Medium
Category: Synthesizing Data
Getting to the Answer: According to Table 1, Mutant 1 has a CAA codon at the first position and an AAT codon at the second position. According to Table 2, CAA codes for glutamine and AAT codes for asparagine. Therefore, (B) is correct.

4.   H
Difficulty: Medium
Category: Synthesizing Data
Getting to the Answer: None of the given data relates to the function of PDC, so in determining whether any of the mutant variations of PDC are the result of silent mutations, you only need to consider whether the mutant strains code for the same amino acids in the two locations. A quick scan of Table 1 shows that none of the mutant variants have the same codons as the wild-type. However, according to Table 2, there's one pair of codons that code for the same amino acid; GAC and GAT both code for aspartic acid. Looking back at Table 1, Mutant 3 has the same codon in the first position as does the wild-type, and at the second position, Mutant 3 has GAC while the wild-type has GAT. Thus, Mutant 3 is the only mutant strain that codes for the same amino acids as the wild-type, which means it's the one most likely to be a silent mutation. Choice (H) is correct.

5.   A
Difficulty: Hard
Category: Synthesizing Data
Getting to the Answer: To see if there's a correlation between decarboxylation activity and the nucleotide sequence at the first location, first look at Figure 1, which shows the decarboxylation rates of the various enzymes. There are three enzymes (wild-type, Mutant 1, and Mutant 3) that show very similar trends in decarboxylation activity, while Mutant 2 has a much lower rate. Looking at Table 1, Mutant 2 has GAA at the first position, while the other three enzymes all have CAA. Since the three types with similar decarboxylation rates have the same nucleotide sequence at the first location and the enzyme with a much lower rate has a different nucleotide sequence, that's consistent with the hypothesis that the sequence at the first location is more responsible for decarboxylation activity, and (A) is correct.

Choice B is incorrect because it comes to the correct conclusion for an incorrect reason: Mutant 2 has the least decarboxylation activity, not the most. Choice C uses a correct fact—that Mutants 1 and 3 show similar levels of activity—to support an incorrect conclusion. Choice D both comes to incorrect conclusions and misstates the facts: Mutants 1 and 3 have higher levels of enzymatic activity, not lower.

How Much Have You Learned?

1.   C
Difficulty: Low
Category: Experimental Design
Getting to the Answer: Evaluate the choices one by one to find the one that was constant in both experiments. In Experiment 1, only some plants were exposed to artificial light, so this was an independent variable and A can be eliminated. Choice B is incorrect because the light sources were intentionally varied as an independent variable in Experiment 2. In both experiments, only tomato plants were used to test the hypothesis, so (C) is correct. The dry weight was measured in both experiments as a dependent variable, so D is incorrect.

2.   J
Difficulty: Low
Category: Experimental Design
Getting to the Answer: In the description of Experiment 1, it's stated that 80 of the tomato plants were grown under a shade cloth, while the other 20 were grown as a control group. This means that they were grown to compare the results of plants grown with a cloth to those without; (J) is correct.

Choice F may have been tempting. Some of the plants under the cloth were lit artificially, so in part, the control group was intended to measure the effects of artificial light. However, in Experiment 1, only LED lights, not fluorescent lights, were used, so F can be eliminated. Choice G is incorrect because there's no indication that the researchers wanted only one group to survive. Choice H is incorrect because it's the plants under the cloth that were meant to simulate growth under shady conditions, not the plants outside of the cloth.

3.   A
Difficulty: Low
Category: Synthesizing Data
Getting to the Answer: Figure 2 compares crop yield to the type of lighting used. All LED lighting resulted in a higher crop yield than fluorescent lighting, and the yields from colored LED lights were higher than the yield from white LED lighting. Thus, (A) is correct.

4.   J
Difficulty: Hard
Category: Synthesizing Data
Getting to the Answer: In Figure 2, the colors are already arranged in order of increasing wavelength; the colors toward the red end of the spectrum are on the right, while those toward the violet end are on the left. If there were a correlation between increased wavelengths, the four bars representing colored light (blue, green, red FR, red HL) would increase in height from left to right, but they do not. In fact, as the light changed from blue to green, the light wavelength increased but the dry weight decreased. Thus, the answer is (J).

While it is true that the plants with the highest yield were those exposed to red light, this fact on its own is not enough to indicate a correlation, so F is incorrect. Choice G is incorrect for similar reasons; plants with red light did grow more than plants with blue light, but plants with green light break the trend. Choice H comes to the correct conclusion based on an incorrect fact; the plants with the lowest growth were those exposed to green light.

5.   B
Difficulty: Low
Category: Using Data
Getting to the Answer: Look at Figure 2 to get an idea of the relationship between the dry weight of plants grown under 40% shade cover and white LED and fluorescent bulbs. In that experiment, plants grown under fluorescent bulbs appear to have approximately three-quarters of the yield and dry weight as those grown under white LED light. Thus, if a new trial in Experiment 1 had been done with 60% shade and fluorescent bulbs, the plants getting the fluorescent light would have had approximately three-quarters of the dry weight that the plants grown in 60% shade under white LEDs had. That dry weight was approximately 32 g/plant, so under fluorescent bulbs, the dry weight would likely be roughly 24 g/plant. That means (B) is correct.

6.　J
Difficulty: Medium
Category: Experimental Design
Getting to the Answer: Experiment 2 examines the effect of different colored LED bulbs on growth. Eliminate F and G. To determine the effect of percent shade, the researchers should repeat Experiment 2 using a different percent shade. Choice (J) is correct. Using a black light instead of white would test another color LED but not a different percent shade.

7.　C
Difficulty: Medium
Category: Applying Core Knowledge
Getting to the Answer: This question is testing your knowledge of photosynthesis. Glucose is produced in plants as a result of photosynthesis, so (C) is correct.

The three incorrect choices are all types of sugar molecules, but they are not produced during photosynthesis.

CHAPTER 25

THINKING LIKE A SCIENTIST

LEARNING OBJECTIVES

After completing this chapter, you will be able to:

- Apply knowledge of core science concepts in earth and space science, biology, chemistry, and physics to interpret data
- Identify Conflicting Viewpoints passages
- Identify the central claim of each viewpoint
- Determine how various viewpoints are connected (or not)
- Determine which hypothesis is supported given the data
- Determine how data and information from the passage or question stem relates to a particular viewpoint

---

Applying Core Knowledge: 2/36 SmartPoints® (Very low yield)

Supporting Hypotheses: 6/36 SmartPoints® (High yield)

How Much Do You Know?

Directions: Try out the questions below. Show your work so that you can compare your solutions to the ones found on the next page. The "Category" heading in the explanation for each question gives the title of the lesson that covers how to solve it. If you answered the question(s) for a given lesson correctly, and if your scratchwork looks like ours, you may be able to move quickly through that lesson. If you answered incorrectly or used a different approach, you may want to take your time on that lesson.

Passage I

The Himalayan blackberry, *Rubus armeniacus*, is a thorny shrub native to Eurasia. However, while not native to the state of Washington, it spreads aggressively and forms impenetrable thickets that negatively impact the local ecosystem. Thus, it is considered invasive. Consider these three hypotheses regarding how to control the spread of *R. armeniacus*.

Hypothesis 1

Without competition, the Himalayan blackberry will quickly dominate a landscape and alter the soil to suit its own propagation. The decomposition of blackberry leaf litter at the end of autumn replenishes soil nitrogen, which the blackberry canes use to grow in the spring. One way to control the spread of the invasive canes is to deplete the source of soil nitrogen by removing the leaf litter, which also improves soil conditions for native species.

Hypothesis 2

Blackberry leaves have high concentrations of 2-heptanol, a compound that decreases herbivory of the leaves by native Washington species. Without this predation, the blackberry is able to expand unchecked. Goats, however, will eat the blackberry bushes down to the soil and trample the residual canes. Clear plastic soil covers can then be applied to kill the root crown and prevent seed germination.

Hypothesis 3

The Himalayan blackberry releases thousands of seeds per square meter and is thus able to crowd out native species through rapid reproduction. Harvesting blackberries will reduce seed banks and prevent birds and pollinators from spreading the species. Fewer blackberry seedlings will mean more room for native trees to germinate and grow, which will eventually generate so much shade that blackberries will be unable to survive.

1. Which hypothesis, if any, asserts that the control of available soil nutrients will help to stop the spread of the Himalayan blackberry?

   A. Hypothesis 1
   B. Hypothesis 2
   C. Hypothesis 3
   D. None of the hypotheses

2. Which hypothesis, if any, asserts that consuming the fruit of the Himalayan blackberry is necessary in order to control its spread?

   F. Hypothesis 1
   G. Hypothesis 2
   H. Hypothesis 3
   J. None of the hypotheses

3. Blackberry seeds have an impermeable seed coat that allows them to germinate after ingestion and after several years in the soil. A supporter of which of the hypotheses would be likely to claim that to ensure invasive Himalayan blackberries are eradicated, steps must be taken to reduce the spread of viable seeds?

   A. Hypothesis 3 only
   B. Hypotheses 1 and 2 only
   C. Hypotheses 1 and 3 only
   D. Hypotheses 2 and 3 only

4. In order to grow, Himalayan blackberries must capture light energy from the sun and convert it into a form of chemical energy usable by its cells. In which of the following organelles does this process occur?

   F. Cell wall

   G. Chloroplast

   H. Mitochondria

   J. Nucleus

5. Which of the following statements about the relationship between Himalayan blackberries and native species is consistent with all 3 hypotheses?

   A. Encouraging the growth of native species is necessary to reduce the spread of Himalayan blackberries.

   B. Germination rates of Himalayan blackberries outpace germination rates of native species.

   C. The spread of the Himalayan blackberry disrupts the native ecosystem in places it is found.

   D. The pollination and spread of native species is threatened when herbivores preferentially consume blackberry leaves.

6. Consider the statement, "The chemical composition of Himalayan blackberry leaves contributes to the species' ability to displace native species." Supporters of which of the hypotheses would be likely to agree with this statement?

   F. Hypothesis 1 only

   G. Hypothesis 2 only

   H. Hypotheses 1 and 2 only

   J. Hypotheses 2 and 3 only

Part 5
ACT SCIENCE

Check Your Work

1. A
Difficulty: Low
Category: Supporting Hypotheses
Getting to the Answer: Each hypothesis posits a different method of controlling the spread of the Himalayan blackberry. Hypothesis 1 states that removing leaf litter will deplete nitrogen levels in the soil, thus depriving blackberries of an essential nutrient. Choice (A) is the correct answer.

Hypothesis 2 focuses on using goats to eat the bushes and soil covers to kill the roots; it has nothing to do with soil nutrients, so B is incorrect. Hypothesis 3 states that harvesting blackberries will reduce the number of seeds available to grow into new plants. Again, there's nothing about soil nutrients, so C can be eliminated. Choice D claims that there's no hypothesis involving soil nutrients; this is incorrect since Hypothesis 1 mentions them.

2. J
Difficulty: Medium
Category: Supporting Hypotheses
Getting to the Answer: Pay careful attention to what the question is asking, which is whether any of the hypotheses claim that the fruit NEEDS to be eaten to control the spread of the blackberry. Hypothesis 1 doesn't mention the fruit at all; it only states that removing the leaf litter will stop the spread. Eliminate F. Hypothesis 2 asserts that the spread of this blackberry bush can be controlled by having goats eat the bushes. This may make G tempting, but remember that the question asks whether consumption of the fruit is necessary. Hypothesis 2 only asserts that consumption of the bush is necessary; perhaps the goats eat the bushes when there is no fruit. Eliminate G. Choice H may also be tempting, since it claims that harvesting the fruit will stop the spread of the plant. However, nothing in the hypothesis requires the fruit to be consumed once it is harvested, so H is also incorrect. The correct answer is (J).

3. D
Difficulty: Hard
Category: Supporting Hypotheses
Getting to the Answer: Hypothesis 1 does not rely on controlling the spread of seeds; rather, it focuses on making the soil conditions unfavorable for the

Himalayan blackberry. So, a supporter of that theory wouldn't think the spread of seeds needs to be reduced, since any seeds that do survive wouldn't be able to grow well in the new soil conditions. Thus, eliminate B and C. Hypothesis 2 asserts that goats will stop the spread of the bush by eating the plants; however, note that it also says that steps need to be taken to prevent seed germination. A supporter of this theory would, then, think something needs to be done to control the spread of seeds. The only remaining choice featuring Hypothesis 2 is (D), so it must be correct. Hypothesis 3 is also included in (D); this is because it also claims that stopping the spread of seeds should be part of the plan. Choice A is incorrect because it does not include Hypothesis 2.

4. G
Difficulty: Hard
Category: Applying Core Knowledge
Getting to the Answer: The question stem describes converting sunlight into usable energy; this process is known as photosynthesis. Since chloroplasts are the organelles in which photosynthesis is carried out by chlorophyll, (G) is the correct answer.

Cell walls provide structure to the cell and to the plant itself, but they are not directly involved in photosynthesis, so F can be eliminated. Mitochondria are often described as "the powerhouse of the cell" and are involved in energy production; however, they don't convert sunlight to energy, so H is incorrect. Choice J can be eliminated because the nucleus is where most of a cell's DNA is stored.

5. C
Difficulty: Medium
Category: Supporting Hypotheses
Getting to the Answer: Each hypothesis opens with facts about how the Himalayan blackberry disrupts the native ecosystem and then explains a method to counter that disruption. Thus, (C) would be consistent with each of the hypotheses and is the correct answer.

Hypotheses 1 and 3 both mention that implementation would result in better conditions for native plants. Hypothesis 2, however, does not, so A is incorrect. Choice B can be eliminated because only Hypothesis 3 mentions the rapid reproduction of the Himalayan blackberry. Choice D is incorrect because only

706 K

Hypothesis 2 mentions predation by herbivores. Even then, D gets that relationship incorrect: it's not that herbivores eat blackberries over local plants, it's that blackberries repel herbivores, allowing their spread.

6. H
Difficulty: Hard
Category: Supporting Hypotheses
Getting to the Answer: Quickly summarize each hypothesis to evaluate whether it claims that the chemical composition of the Himalayan blackberry provides it an advantage over local plants. Hypothesis 1 claims that leaf litter from the blackberry contributes nitrogen to the soil, which contributes to further blackberry growth. Thus, it's consistent with the statement in the stem. Hypothesis 2 states that a chemical compound in the leaves of the blackberry discourages predation by herbivores, which contributes to the spread of the blackberry. So, this hypothesis is also consistent. At this point, you can confidently pick (H), as it's the only choice that includes both of these hypotheses. For the record, though, Hypothesis 3 is not included in the correct choice because it does not mention the chemical composition of the blackberry as a cause of its rapid spread.

APPLYING CORE KNOWLEDGE QUESTIONS

To answer a question like this:

Human activity has increased the amount of carbon dioxide in the atmosphere; when this atmospheric carbon dioxide dissolves into the oceans, it leads to ocean acidification. Which of the following represents the change in pH of the Earth's oceans due to ocean acidification?

A.   Decreases

B.   Remains the same

C.   Increases

D.   The information given is insufficient to determine the change in pH.

You need to know this:

Advanced knowledge in Earth/space sciences, biology, chemistry, and physics is not required for ACT Science questions, but general background knowledge and a grasp of science terms in these domains may be needed to correctly answer some of the questions.

Earth and space science:

• Geology (soil, crust, mantle)
• Astronomy (star, constellation, planet, galaxy)
• Meteorology (greenhouse gases, atmosphere, climate)

Biology:

• Cell components and processes (nucleus, mitochondria, ribosomes, chloroplasts, lysosome, ATP, mitosis, meiosis, respiration, photosynthesis)
• Macromolecules (carbohydrates, lipids, proteins, DNA, RNA)
• Genetics (alleles, traits, inheritance, mutations)
• Bacterial growth

Chemistry:

• Chemical reactions (formula, reactants, products, moles)
• Atomic structure and interaction of charges (proton, electron, neutron)
• States of matter (solid, liquid, gas) and phase transitions (freezing/melting and boiling point of water)
• Properties of molecules (atomic structure, molar mass)
• pH scale (acid, base, neutral)

Physics:

- Gravity (mass *vs.* weight)
- Normal and frictional forces (and their typical directions)
- Kinetic and potential energy
- Kinematics (velocity, acceleration)
- Circuits (current, voltage, resistor, capacitor)
- Waves (period, amplitude)
- Density

You need to do this:

Review the basic concepts listed above for Earth/space sciences, biology, chemistry, and physics. Familiarize yourself with the terms and their definitions, but remember that any knowledge more detailed than that will be provided by the passage and questions.

Explanation

Identify

Without additional information, such as a figure, it's difficult to identify the passage type. However, for Applying Core Knowledge questions, your approach to Steps 2–4 will not change based on the passage type.

Analyze

The process of answering Applying Core Knowledge questions does not usually include any passage analysis because the answers to these questions are usually based on some combination of information from the question stem and your background knowledge.

Examine, predict, and answer

Question stem: The question is asking about the change in pH that has resulted from acidification.

- You need to draw from your general knowledge that acids have low pH (below 7) and bases have high pH (above 7).
- Since the ocean is becoming more acidic from the increased amounts of carbon dioxide being dissolved by the ocean, the pH of the ocean is decreasing.

Choice (A) is correct.

Try on Your Own

Directions: Take as much time as you need on these questions. Work carefully and methodically. There will be an opportunity for timed practice at the end of the chapter.

Answers are found at the end of the chapter.

Passage II

Most natural substances can occur in any of three phases (states of matter): solid, liquid, or gas. A phase diagram indicates what phase (or phases) a substance can be found in at varying temperatures and pressures. The molecular structure of a substance determines the conditions under which it will experience a phase change, such as freezing or boiling. Solid lines in a phase diagram represent these phase changes, when two phases exist in equilibrium as the substance transitions from one phase to another. Figure 1 presents a phase diagram for water (H_2O), while Figure 2 presents a phase diagram for carbon dioxide (CO_2).

Figure 1

Figure 2

1. Based on Figure 2, CO_2 exists in the liquid phase between which of the following temperatures?

    A. $-100°C$ to $-57°C$

    B. $-57°C$ to $31°C$

    C. $31°C$ to $57°C$

    D. $57°C$ to $100°C$

2. According to Figures 1 and 2, H_2O and CO_2 exist in which phase(s) at $13°C$ and 28 mm Hg and 28,000 mm Hg, respectively?

	H_2O	CO_2
F.	solid	liquid
G.	liquid	liquid
H.	gas	gas
J.	liquid	gas

3. When a substance undergoes a phase change, the behavior of the particles of that substance also change. Which of the following statements best describes the behavior of a liquid molecule?

    A. Liquid molecules are tightly packed with regular molecular arrangements.

    B. Liquid molecules move freely at high speeds.

    C. Liquid molecules are not easily compressible.

    D. Liquid molecules assume the entire shape and volume of their container.

4. Based on the data, the freezing point of CO_2 at 70,000 mm Hg is approximately:

    F. $-100°C$

    G. $-50°C$

    H. $-30°C$

    J. $0°C$

Science

5. Based on Figure 1, at a pressure greater than 5 mm Hg, H_2O can directly transition between which states of matter as the temperature decreases?

   A. From solid to liquid

   B. From solid to gas

   C. From liquid to gas

   D. From liquid to solid

6. Compared to the temperature at which CO_2 melts, the temperature at which H_2O melts is:

   F. lower.

   G. equal.

   H. higher.

   J. higher at some pressures and lower at other pressures.

7. The *triple point* is the temperature and pressure at which all three phases of a substance exist in equilibrium. According to Figure 2, the triple point of CO_2 is at approximately what temperature and pressure?

	temperature	pressure
A.	−55°C	4,000 mm Hg
B.	0°C	5 mm Hg
C.	5°C	0 mm Hg
D.	4,000°C	−55 mm Hg

CONFLICTING VIEWPOINTS PASSAGES AND SUPPORTING HYPOTHESES QUESTIONS

LEARNING OBJECTIVES

After this lesson, you will be able to:

- Identify Conflicting Viewpoints passages
- Identify the central claim of each viewpoint
- Determine how various viewpoints are connected (or not)
- Determine which hypothesis is supported given the data
- Determine how data and information from the passage or question stem relates to a particular viewpoint

To answer a question like this:

Passage III

Several plans have been proposed to get rid of space debris. Consider the following two proposals.

Proposal 1

Capture mechanisms such as nets, harpoons, and robotic arms can be used to pick up uncooperative debris that threaten other spacecraft in orbit. Orbiting at an altitude between 800 and 1,000 kilometers, large satellite hunters would use their own propulsion to steer the catch into the atmosphere, where it would burn up.

Proposal 2

Electrodynamic tethers, which generate magnetic drag, can be used to slow down the speed of space debris so that it falls closer to Earth and then burns up. Since the tethers generate thrust from the interaction with Earth's electromagnetic field, they do not need an additional power source.

Which proposal, if any, would align with the claim that space debris falling out of Earth's orbit down to Earth will burn up?

A. Proposal 1 only

B. Proposal 2 only

C. Both Proposals 1 and 2

D. Neither Proposal 1 nor 2

You need to know this:

Supporting Hypotheses questions most often appear as part of a Conflicting Viewpoints passage question set.

Conflicting Viewpoints

One of the six passages you will see on test day will be a Conflicting Viewpoints passage. In order to identify a Conflicting Viewpoints passage as part of step 1, look for these typical characteristics:

- multiple theories or hypotheses about a particular phenomenon
- an introductory paragraph(s) that defines key terms and provides background information about the phenomenon
- individually labeled viewpoints (often a "scientist" or "student") with a 1–2 paragraph theory to explain the phenomenon

Sometimes, a Conflicting Viewpoints passage will include one or more figures that illustrate the phenomenon or the theories.

The majority of questions in Conflicting Viewpoints passages require you to evaluate hypotheses. These passages will often include at least one other question type, such as an Applying Core Knowledge question.

A key skill associated with Conflicting Viewpoints passages is the ability to **identify central claims or implications of each viewpoint**.

- The central claims are the main points that sum up the theory; they are explicitly stated in the passage, whereas implications are what can be inferred from the theory.
- Questions about a theory's claims are typically straightforward because they ask about only one viewpoint, usually by referring to details of that viewpoint that are spelled out explicitly in the passage.
- To avoid trap answers, predict an answer before reading the answer choices.

Supporting Hypotheses Questions

Supporting Hypotheses questions may involve:

- Finding basic information and identifying key assumptions in theories
- Identifying strengths and weaknesses of theories
- Identifying similarities and differences among theories
- Determining which theories are supported or weakened by new information
- Determining which hypothesis, prediction, or conclusion is consistent or inconsistent with a theory or other piece of information from the passage

Some Supporting Hypotheses questions will ask you to **determine how the viewpoints are connected (or not)**. In other words, you should be comfortable noting the similarities and differences in two viewpoints.

- To find the answer, use clues in the question stem to go back to the relevant part of the passage.
- A question might ask you to identify points of agreement or disagreement among theories.
- Details mentioned in the introductory paragraph(s) or explicitly stated in multiple theories should generally be regarded as points of agreement, while details included in one theory but not in the other(s) should be treated as points of disagreement.

Other Supporting Hypotheses questions will ask you to **determine which hypothesis is supported by data**, while others will ask **how a particular viewpoint is affected by data or text from the passage**.

- A question may ask you to identify evidence, hypotheses, conclusions, or predictions that are *consistent* (or, less often, *inconsistent*) with a particular viewpoint or another piece of passage information.
- You may be asked either to determine whether new information in the question stem *strengthens/weakens* one or more of the viewpoints or to identify a piece of strengthening/weakening evidence among the answer choices.
- Information that strengthens a theory makes the theory more likely to be true, while information that weakens a theory makes it less likely to be true.
- The information does not have to prove a viewpoint true in order to strengthen it, nor does it have to prove it false to weaken it.

You need to do this:

After you have identified a Conflicting Viewpoints passage, use step 2 (analyze the passage and figures strategically) to consider each viewpoint or hypothesis individually and note, either mentally or in the margins, how the viewpoint relates to the phenomenon or issue. You should:

- examine the introductory text for the phenomenon or issue in question
- move quickly through the remaining text to identify the point of view presented by each hypothesis or scientist, paying particular attention to any similarities and differences between them
- locate units, labels, and variables in the figures, if applicable

You will be asked to consider how new information presented in the question stem relates to the given theories or hypotheses, so be sure you have a clear understanding of how the hypotheses differ from each other so that you do not confuse them.

Explanation
Identify

The introduction mentions *several plans* and there are two headings labeled *Proposal*; these clues indicate that this is a Conflicting Viewpoints passage.

Analyze

Summarize the key features of both proposals:

- **Proposal 1:** space debris would be captured with nets, harpoons, and robotic arms, then propulsion systems steer it into the atmosphere to burn up
- **Proposal 2:** electromagnetic tethers would be used to slow space debris to the point that it falls closer to Earth and burns up

Examine, predict, and answer

Summarize the information presented in the question stem: examination of each proposal as it relates to the claim will be required.

- The claim states that space debris falling out of Earth's orbit down to Earth will burn up.
- In Proposal 1, the language of *steer the catch into the atmosphere* is analogous to Proposal 2's phrase *slow down the speed of space debris so that it falls closer to Earth*, which both state will make it burn.
- Proposal 2 specifically states the debris will fall closer to Earth and burn.
- Thus, both proposals support the claim.

Choice (C) is correct.

This Conflicting Viewpoints passage only had one question, so it made sense to analyze both proposals at once. For test-like question sets, remember to divide and conquer the hypotheses.

Drills

If Supporting Hypotheses questions give you trouble, study the information above and try out these drill questions before completing the Try on Your Own questions below. Drill answers can be found in Answers and Explanations.

a. What is the central claim of Hypothesis A?

Hypothesis A

Increasing water temperature accelerates development of eel larvae by promoting larval yolk utilization and expression of targeted genes relating to development.

b.   What is the central claim of Hypothesis B?

Hypothesis B

Increased disease prevalence and transmission rates occur at warmer water temperatures, so eel larvae mortality is directly linked to increased temperature.

c.   What is the point of disagreement between Hypotheses A and B?

d.   Is Hypothesis A or B supported by Table C?

Table C		
Water temperature (°C)	Eel larvae length (mm)	Eel larvae weight (g)
14	50	0.134
18	57	0.139
22	65	0.144
26	69	0.146

e.   Is Figure D consistent with Hypothesis B?

Figure D

Try on Your Own

Directions: Take as much time as you need on these questions. Work carefully and methodically. There will be an opportunity for timed practice at the end of the chapter.

Answers are found at the end of the chapter.

Passage IV

Sweet wormwood, *Artemisia annua* L., contains many commercially useful and therapeutic compounds that can be extracted with a variety of methods. Fifty-gram plant samples were subjected to four different extraction methods in order to determine how the method used affected the amount of each compound in the oil extracted. Sample A consisted of dried plant material vacuum-sealed in a rigid chamber, Sample B of dried plant material subjected to steam distillation, Sample C of dried plant material subjected to hydrodistillation, and Sample D of plant material extracted using petroleum ether as a solvent. Table 1 lists the various compounds collected in micrograms (μg) per 100 mL of oil.

Table 1				
Compound	A	B	C	D
β-myrcene	17.1	3.7	4.2	0.9
1,8-cineole	8.5	5.3	5.4	0.3
Artemisia ketone	46.4	30.2	28.3	16.5
Artemisia alcohol	2.5	3.1	2.2	2.8
Camphor	13.2	24	16.9	20
β-caryophyllene	0.1	3.1	3.9	1.2
Monoterpene hydrocarbons (MH)	24.9	5.1	5	0.9
Oxygenated monoterpenes (MO)	70.6	69.9	60.9	42.6
Sesquiterpene hydrocarbons (SH)	0.5	13.3	13	2.6
Oxygenated diterpenes (DO)	0.6	2.2	4.6	2.3

Consider the following hypotheses that explain the varying amounts of compound obtained from each sample.

Hypothesis 1

Exposure to heat during both steam distillation and hydrodistillation leads to the loss of compounds that can be destroyed by heat.

Hypothesis 2

Exposure to heat during both steam distillation and hydrodistillation leads to an increase in compounds as more oil is able to be extracted from the plant.

Hypothesis 3

One step in the petroleum ether extraction process involves evaporation of the solvent, and some of the volatile plant compounds evaporate along with the solvent.

1. Consider the amount of β-myrcene extracted from a 50-g sample of sweet wormwood. The results obtained from the extraction processes support which of the hypotheses?

   A. Hypothesis 1 only
   B. Hypothesis 2 only
   C. Hypotheses 1 and 3 only
   D. Hypotheses 2 and 3 only

2. Consider the amount of camphor extracted from a 50-g sample of sweet wormwood. The results obtained from the extraction processes support which of the hypotheses?

   F. Hypothesis 1
   G. Hypothesis 2
   H. Hypothesis 3
   J. None of the hypotheses

3.   Based on Hypothesis 1, which of the following figures depicts the amount of compounds present in the dried plant material before steam distillation and the amount extracted in the oil after?

(Note: In each figure, "a" represents "before extraction," and "A" represents "after extraction".)

A.

B.

C.

D.

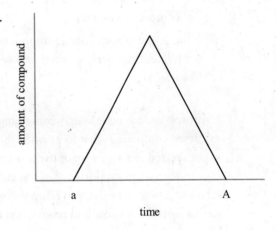

4. Which hypothesis, if any, asserts that heat-sensitive compounds of sweet wormwood can be lost during the hydrodistillation process?

    F. Hypothesis 1

    G. Hypothesis 2

    H. Hypothesis 3

    J. None of the hypotheses

5. Which of the following statements about compound extraction in *Artemisia annua* L. is consistent with all 3 hypotheses?

    A. The proportion of heat-sensitive compounds extracted does not change when using a vacuum chamber.

    B. The chemical composition of the extracted compounds varies depending upon the extraction method.

    C. The extraction method alters the quantity of compounds extracted.

    D. The proportion of volatile compounds extracted will increase when exposed to heat.

6. Hydrosols are aromatic waters containing extracted compounds that form when the vapor created during steam or hydro-distillation condenses. A supporter of which Hypothesis, 1 or 2, would be likely to claim that an herbal hydrosol will contain more aromatic compounds per unit of measurement than dry plant material?

    F. Hypothesis 1 only

    G. Hypothesis 2 only

    H. Both Hypotheses 1 and 2

    J. Neither Hypotheses 1 nor 2

Passage V

Zika virus (ZIKV) is spread by *Aedes* spp. mosquitoes. First discovered in Africa in the 1940s, ZIKV spread into Southeast Asia in the 1960s and caused explosive outbreaks in Pacific and Indian Ocean Islands in the 2000s. This led to the 2015–2016 epidemic, which caused over 500,000 cases in the Americas. Consider the following four hypotheses proposing what changes fueled the ZIKV epidemic.

Hypothesis 1

Climate change causes increased year-round temperatures, which led to a warmer environment that better supported overwinter egg survival of *Aedes* spp. mosquitoes and extended the length of ZIKV transmission, which occurs between 18°C and 34°C. Natural disasters, which contaminate water and increase the number of mosquito breeding sites, promoted transmission.

Hypothesis 2

Increased deforestation and urbanization created areas with higher human population densities, which are more suitable for the propagation of *Aedes* spp. mosquitoes and thereby led to higher rates of ZIKV incidence. Additionally, intercontinental air travel and human movement between socioeconomically distinct regions expanded the infection risk of ZIKV.

Hypothesis 3

Aggressive and unregulated use of insecticides caused widespread resistance to develop in *Aedes* spp. mosquitoes. Additionally, ZIKV persisted in animal reservoirs, which were a source for recolonization. Land use changes led to increased contact between humans and infected animals that thrive near industrialized cities, increasing ZIKV transmission.

Hypothesis 4

Economic recession created a new group of people at risk for ZIKV infection due to poor living conditions, including inadequate infrastructure for sanitary living conditions and insufficient access to readily available clean water. This resulted in increased water storage in household containers, which accounted for more than 50% of mosquito breeding sites and thus increased human exposure to ZIKV.

7. Which of the hypotheses assert that unclean drinking water leads to higher rates of ZIKV incidence?

   A. Hypothesis 2 only
   B. Hypothesis 4 only
   C. Hypotheses 1 and 4
   D. Hypotheses 1, 2, and 4

8. Consider the statement "The growth of cities resulting from industrialization increased ZIKV exposure and infection in humans." Supporters of which of the hypotheses would be likely to agree with this claim?

   F. Hypotheses 2 and 3 only
   G. Hypotheses 2 and 4 only
   H. Hypotheses 3 and 4 only
   J. Hypotheses 2, 3, and 4 only

9. The table below lists the annual temperature range (in degrees Celsius) of 4 regions.

Region	Annual Temperature Range (°C)
Region 1	−4–20
Region 2	20–35
Region 3	30–40
Region 4	40–50

Based on Hypothesis 1, the climate of which region would promote ZIKV transmission?

   A. Region 1
   B. Region 2
   C. Region 3
   D. Region 4

10. Based on Hypothesis 2, which of the following would have the highest risk for ZIKV transmission?

   F. ½ million people in 100 square kilometers
   G. 1 million people in 100 square kilometers
   H. 1 million people in 200 square kilometers
   J. 2 million people in 600 square kilometers

11. Which of the following statements about *Aedes* spp. mosquito propagation is consistent with Hypothesis 3?

   A. Water-storage containers provide breeding sites for *Aedes* spp. mosquito propagation.
   B. Urbanized areas are more suitable for the propagation of *Aedes* spp. mosquitoes.
   C. Increased year-round temperatures promote the propagation of the *Aedes* spp. mosquitoes.
   D. Insecticide resistance in *Aedes* spp. mosquitoes leads to increased propagation.

12. Suppose a sylvatic cycle (the transmission of a virus between wild hosts and vectors) between monkeys and *Aedes* spp. mosquitoes has been identified. A supporter of which hypothesis, if any, would likely claim that the establishment of sylvatic ZIKV makes elimination of ZIKV practically impossible?

   F. Hypothesis 1
   G. Hypothesis 2
   H. Hypothesis 3
   J. Hypothesis 4

How Much Have You Learned?

Directions: For test-like practice, give yourself 6 minutes to complete this question set. Be sure to study the explanations, even for questions you got right. They can be found at the end of this chapter.

Passage VI

Natural processes like tectonic deformation and Earth tides contribute to stress build-up on faults (curved fractures in the rocks of the Earth's crust). Earthquakes occur when the stress built up within the rocks is released as the rocks crack and slip past each other. Researchers propose that human activities may also modulate seismicity (the frequency of earthquakes). Three postulates are presented.

Postulate I

Earthquakes are induced by surface-mass addition, such as water impoundment behind dams. Increased seismic activity is correlated with water depth in such reservoirs. Approximately 6% of reservoirs with volumes exceeding 0.1 km³ are reported to be seismogenic (capable of generating earthquakes). A large surface load increases the shear and normal stresses and causes fluid to migrate into fault zones and increase pore pressure, which results in perturbations on faults.

Postulate 2

Extraction of mass from the Earth's subsurface via mining induces earthquakes. For instance, groundwater extraction artificially lowers the water table. This depletion of groundwater reduces normal stress that prevents slip on faults. Extraction of coal and gas is similarly linked to seismicity. Mining excavations cause stress perturbations in surrounding rocks that can exceed the strength of competent rock and cause earthquakes.

Postulate 3

Introduction of mass into the subsurface via injection induces seismicity. Disposal of waste and underground storage of gas and hydrogen into rock increases the pore pressure, which encourages rock failure. Higher frequency of earthquakes is correlated with greater volume injected. Likewise, hydraulic fracturing, or fracking, activates faults. Fracking

pumps high-pressure fluid into fractured rock to create porosity for extraction of gas and oil. The combination of fluid injection and pressure depletion produces earthquakes, releasing the stress.

1. Which of the postulates assert that fluid in rock increases pore pressure?

    A. Postulates 1 and 2 only

    B. Postulates 2 and 3 only

    C. Postulates 1 and 3 only

    D. Postulates 1, 2, and 3

2. Which of the following statements is supported by Postulate 1?

    F. Tall buildings, which increase the stress on the ground at their bases, can influence seismicity.

    G. Quarrying, which removes mass from the Earth's surface, can induce earthquakes.

    H. Substantial coastal land loss due to erosion can alter stresses at 2-km depth and trigger earthquakes.

    J. Underground nuclear tests that displace faults can generate several hundred small earthquakes.

3. Suppose that the removal of mass from the Earth's crust reduces the normal stress that prevents slip on faults. Which of the following would exert an opposite force to mitigate pressure reduction?

    A. Mass addition

    B. Mining

    C. Fracking

    D. Groundwater extraction

4. The following table lists the density of 4 fluids.

Fluid	Density (kg/m^3)
hydrocarbon	500
hydrogen	0.1
natural gas	0.5
water	1,000

Suppose that 1,000 kg of a fluid are injected into the Earth's subsurface. Based on Postulate 3, the injection of which fluid would most likely induce earthquakes?

F. Hydrocarbon

G. Hydrogen

H. Natural gas

J. Water

5. Which of the following statements about earthquakes is consistent with all three postulates?

A. Pre-existing tectonic stress is not sufficient to trigger large earthquakes.

B. Earthquakes occur in response to perturbations on faults to release tectonic stress.

C. Induced earthquakes release more stress on faults than that which is artificially loaded on them.

D. Earthquakes occur only in previously seismically inactive regions.

6. Based on Postulate 1, which of the following reservoir dimensions would be most likely to be seismogenic?

F. 0.1 km × 0.1 km × 6 km

G. 0.1 km × 0.2 km × 4 km

H. 0.1 km × 0.3 km × 4 km

J. 0.2 km × 0.1 km × 5 km

7. Suppose that excavation of tunnels for road and railway transport has been linked to earthquakes. A supporter of which of the postulates would be likely to claim, "The earthquakes resulted from an unfavorable juxtaposition of rocks, in which the rocks unable to support the large stress gradient created by the excavation activated the fault zone"?

A. Postulate 2 only

B. Postulate 3 only

C. Postulates 2 and 3 only

D. Postulates 1, 2, and 3

Science

Reflect

Directions: Take a few minutes to recall what you've learned and what you've been practicing in this chapter. Consider the following questions, jot down your best answer for each one, and then compare your reflections to the expert responses on the following page. Use your level of confidence to determine what to do next.

1. When presented with a Conflicting Viewpoints passage, what approach does an ACT expert use to go through the multiple theories and their associated questions?

    _____

    _____

    _____

2. Will two theories in a Conflicting Viewpoints passage always draw opposite conclusions about the data?

    _____

    _____

    _____

3. Will an ACT Science question potentially require an outside piece of knowledge you don't know to be able to correctly answer it?

    _____

    _____

    _____

4. What key features does an ACT expert look for when asked to identify an answer choice that would weaken a given theory?

    _____

    _____

    _____

5. How will you approach Conflicting Viewpoints passages differently as you continue to practice and improve your performance in the ACT Science section?

    _____

    _____

    _____

Responses

1. When presented with a Conflicting Viewpoints passage, what approach does an ACT expert use to go through the multiple theories and their associated questions?

First, read the introductory paragraph(s) and the first viewpoint, then search for questions that ask only about the first viewpoint and answer them. Next, read the second viewpoint, then search for questions that ask only about the second viewpoint and answer them; if there are additional viewpoints, repeat this process with each of them. Finally, answer questions that ask about multiple viewpoints and any other remaining questions.

2. Will two theories in a Conflicting Viewpoints passage always draw opposite conclusions about the data?

Of course not! Despite the name of the passage type, two theories don't necessarily have to disagree about the presented data. In fact, the data presented may support one, both, or neither of theories. There may also be more than two theories presented in a passage.

3. Will an ACT Science question potentially require an outside piece of knowledge you don't know to be able to correctly answer it?

While this is a possibility, it's important again to stress that if you've taken your high-school science courses, then these questions will be few and far between. If this happens to you on test day, do your best to eliminate any answer choices you can and make an educated guess. Most importantly, don't waste time on it; move on the massive chunk of questions that don't require outside knowledge.

4. What key features does an ACT expert look for when asked to identify an answer choice that would weaken a given theory?

Information that weakens a theory makes it less likely to be true. An answer choice does not need to definitively prove the theory false to weaken it. Rather, it just needs to detract from the theory's claims by differing with one of its statements or assumptions.

5. How will you approach Conflicting Viewpoints passages differently as you continue to practice and improve your performance in the ACT Science section?

There is no one-size-fits-all answer here. Reflect on your own habits in identifying the central claims of a theory and whether it is supported by the given data or a new piece of information, and give yourself an honest assessment of your strengths and weaknesses. Consider the strategies you've seen experts use in this chapter, and put them to work in your own practice to increase your accuracy, speed, and confidence.

Next Steps

If you answered most questions correctly in the "How Much Have You Learned?" section, and if your responses to the Reflect questions were similar to those of the ACT expert, then consider Conflicting Viewpoints passages an area of strength and move on to the next chapter. Come back to this topic periodically to prevent yourself from getting rusty.

If you don't yet feel confident, review the material in this chapter and then try the questions you missed again. As always, be sure to review the explanations closely. Then go online (**kaptest.com/login**) to use your Qbank for more practice. If you haven't already registered your book, do so at **kaptest.com/moreonline.**

GO ONLINE

kaptest.com/login

Answers and Explanations

Applying Core Knowledge Questions

1. B
Difficulty: Low
Category: Interpreting Data
Getting to the Answer: In Figure 2, carbon dioxide becomes a liquid around −57°C, when the pressure is about 4,000 mm Hg, and remains a liquid up to about 31°C, at pressures over 50,000 mm Hg. The correct answer is (B).

2. J
Difficulty: Medium
Category: Interpreting Data
Getting to the Answer: First, determine the phase of water at 13°C and 28 mm Hg. According to Figure 1, at 13°C and 28 mm Hg, H_2O exists as a liquid. Eliminate F and H. Next, determine the phase of carbon dioxide at 13°C and 28,000 mm Hg. According to Figure 2, CO_2 exists as a gas at that temperature and pressure. Thus, the correct answer is (J).

3. C
Difficulty: Low
Category: Applying Core Knowledge
Getting to the Answer: Liquids are characterized by closely packed, free-flowing molecules. There is little space between liquid molecules, so liquids are not easily compressible. The correct answer is (C).

Choice A describes a characteristic of a solid. Choice B describes a characteristic of a gas. While liquids do assume the shape of whichever part of a container their volume occupies, liquid molecules do not assume the *entire* shape and volume of a container. That is a characteristic of a gas, so D is incorrect.

4. G
Difficulty: Medium
Category: Applying Core Knowledge
Getting to the Answer: The freezing point is the point at which liquid transitions to solid at a given pressure. In Figure 2, 70,000 mm Hg is beyond the range of the graph. Extend the *y*-axis to 70,000 mm Hg and continue the solid-liquid boundary line (its slope suggests that, for every increase of 10,000 mm Hg in pressure, there is a temperature increase of a degree or two in the freezing point). Because the freezing point at a pressure of 50,000 mm Hg is just under −50°C, you can expect that

the freezing point at 70,000 mm Hg would be only a few degrees higher than that, or roughly −50°C, as in (G).

5. D
Difficulty: Medium
Category: Interpreting Data
Getting to the Answer: On Figure 1, look at the area above 5 mm Hg and ignore the area below. Above 5 mm Hg, as temperature decreases, water transitions from gas directly to liquid and then from liquid directly to solid. Since the transition from gas to liquid is not an option, the correct answer is (D), from liquid to solid.

6. H
Difficulty: Medium
Category: Synthesizing Data
Getting to the Answer: A substance melts when it transitions from solid to liquid. The solid-liquid boundary for H_2O falls along 0°C, while the solid-liquid boundary for CO_2 falls between about −57°C and −51°C. Because −51°C is less than 0°C, H_2O always melts at a higher temperature than CO_2. The correct answer is (H).

7. A
Difficulty: Medium
Category: Interpreting Data
Getting to the Answer: The triple point is the temperature and pressure at which the three phases of a substance exist in equilibrium. In Figure 2, the triple point is where the solid-liquid, liquid-gas, and solid-gas boundary lines meet. The temperature and pressure at this point are approximately −55°C and 4,000 mm Hg, respectively. The correct answer is (A).

Conflicting Viewpoints Passages and Supporting Hypotheses Questions

Drill Answers

a. Increasing water temperature increases growth rate of eel larvae.

b. Increasing water temperature increases mortality of eel larvae.

c. The effect increasing water temperature has on eels

d. Hypothesis A; at higher water temperatures, eel larvae are longer and heavier

e. Yes; at higher water temperatures, number of eel larvae alive is lower

1. C
Difficulty: Medium
Category: Supporting Hypotheses
Getting to the Answer: Consider how the data for β-myrcene relate to each hypothesis. Hypothesis 1 says that steam distillation and hydrodistillation reduce the levels of certain compounds, and Samples B and C, respectively, were the samples subject to those methods. Samples B and C do contain lower levels of β-myrcene than does Sample A, which is consistent with Hypothesis 1. Thus, you can eliminate B and D, which both leave out Hypothesis 1. The only difference between the remaining choices is that one includes Hypothesis 3 and one does not. This means that you can skip Hypothesis 2 and evaluate Hypothesis 3. This hypothesis says that in samples subject to petroleum ether extraction, as sample D was, some compounds will be lost as the ether evaporates. This is consistent with Sample D, so (C) is correct.

2. G
Difficulty: Medium
Category: Supporting Hypotheses
Getting to the Answer: According to Table 1, the levels of camphor in samples B and C, which were subject to steam distillation and hydrodistillation, respectively, were greater than the level of camphor in sample A. This is consistent with Hypothesis 2, which states that these kinds of distillation can increase the levels of certain compounds in the extracted oil. Choice (G) is correct.

3. B
Difficulty: Low
Category: Synthesizing Data
Getting to the Answer: The lines of each of these graphs represent the change in the amount of compounds in the plant matter before steam distillation and the amount of compounds in the extracted oil. According to Hypothesis 1, steam distillation leads to the loss of certain compounds, so the correct choice will have a graph with a line that slopes downward. Only (B) has such a line, so it is correct.

4. F
Difficulty: Low
Category: Supporting Hypotheses
Getting to the Answer: Only the first two hypotheses mention hydrodistillation, so you can eliminate H. Of Hypotheses 1 and 2, the first claims that

hydrodistillation decreases the amounts of some compounds, while the second claims that hydrodistillation increases the concentration of certain compounds in extracted oils. Since you're looking for a hypothesis about compounds lost during distillation, (F) must be the correct answer.

5. C
Difficulty: Medium
Category: Supporting Hypotheses
Getting to the Answer: This is an open-ended question; since you can't predict an answer, move through the choices one by one. Choice A is incorrect because none of the hypotheses make any claims about the effects of using a vacuum chamber. Be careful with B; while the levels of compounds change with each extraction method, none of the hypotheses claim that the chemical composition of the compounds changes depending on the extraction method. Choice (C) is correct; each hypothesis claims that the extraction method will affect the amount of compounds in the extracted oil. Choice D is incorrect because it is only consistent with Hypothesis 2 and is actually contradicted by Hypothesis 1.

6. G
Difficulty: Hard
Category: Supporting Hypotheses
Getting to the Answer: Hypotheses 1 and 2 both deal with the effects of steam and hydrodistillation. Hypothesis 1 claims that these methods decrease the amounts of certain compounds, while Hypothesis 2 claims that the methods increase the levels of certain compounds. Thus, only a supporter of Hypothesis 2 would claim that hydrosols have a higher proportion of certain compounds, and (G) is correct.

7. C
Difficulty: Medium
Category: Supporting Hypotheses
Getting to the Answer: Before you evaluate the choices in a question like this, scan the answer choices quickly; here, you'll notice that Hypothesis 3 is not present in any of the choices, so there's no need to consider it. Hypothesis 1 specifically mentions contaminated water, so it must be included in the correct answer; eliminate A and B. Hypothesis 2 focuses on urbanization and increased travel by humans; since there's no mention of unclean water, it won't show up in the correct choice. The only choice that includes

Hypothesis 1 and not Hypothesis 2 is (C), so it must be correct.

There's no need to evaluate Hypotheses 3 and 4, but if you do, you'll see that Hypothesis 3 focuses on pesticide resistance and animal transmission, not water, but Hypothesis 4 does mention lack of access to clean water, which is why it's included in the correct answer.

8. F
Difficulty: Hard
Category: Supporting Hypotheses
Getting to the Answer: A quick scan of the choices shows that Hypothesis 1 doesn't show up in any of the choices, so there's no need to consider it as you approach this question. Hypothesis 2 asserts that "urbanization," or the growth of cities, is one of the causes of increased ZIKV exposure, so supporters of that hypothesis would likely agree with the statement in the question stem. Thus, eliminate H, as it does not include Hypothesis 2. Hypothesis 3 mentions that conditions in industrialized cities increase the risk of ZIKV exposure, so it also must be in the correct choice; eliminate G. Hypothesis 4 asserts that poor living conditions contribute to the spread of ZIKV, but it doesn't say whether these are in urbanized areas. Thus, Hypothesis 4 should not be in the correct answer, and (F) is correct.

9. B
Difficulty: Medium
Category: Synthesizing Data
Getting to the Answer: Hypothesis 2 claims that climate change and increased temperatures have increased the risk of ZIKV exposure. Be careful, though; don't just pick the region with the warmest temperatures. The hypothesis also mentions a specific temperature range: $18°C-34°C$. Region 2 aligns most closely with this range of temperatures, so (B) is correct.

10. G
Difficulty: Hard
Category: Applying Core Knowledge
Getting to the Answer: Hypothesis 2 asserts that areas with higher population densities are at an increased risk of ZIKV transmission, so you need to be able to compare the population densities of the regions in the choices. The region in (G) has more people in the same area as the region in F, so F can be eliminated right

away. The region in H has the same number of people as that in (G), but in a larger area, so eliminate H as well. The region in J has twice as many people as the region in (G), but in six times the area, so J must have a smaller population density. (G) is correct.

11. D
Difficulty: Medium
Category: Supporting Hypotheses
Getting to the Answer: This asks for something that's consistent with Hypothesis 3, so see what it says about ZIKV: that insecticide resistance in mosquitoes leads to increased levels of ZIKV transmission. That's consistent with (D), which is the correct answer.

Choice A is consistent with Hypothesis 4, which asserts that water storage containers can provide breeding sites for mosquitoes. Choice B is consistent with Hypothesis 2, which states that urbanized areas are more suitable for mosquitoes. Increased year-round temperatures as a cause of ZIKV is a part of Hypothesis 1, so C is incorrect.

12. H
Difficulty: Hard
Category: Supporting Hypotheses
Getting to the Answer: You'll need to determine which hypothesis is consistent with a claim that transmission of ZIKV between monkeys and mosquitoes makes ZIKV nearly impossible to eliminate. Of the four hypotheses, only Hypothesis 3 deals with infected animals. It claims that the virus can persist in "animal reservoirs," such as the monkeys mentioned in the question stem. Thus, (H) is correct.

How Much Have You Learned?

1. C
Difficulty: Medium
Category: Supporting Hypotheses
Getting to the Answer: Examine the postulates to see which ones are consistent with the claim in the question stem. Postulate 1 asserts that surface load causes fluid to enter fault zones and increase pore pressure, so it needs to be included in the correct answer. Eliminate B. Postulate 2 doesn't mention pore pressure at all, so it can't be part of the correct answer. The only choice remaining that includes Postulate 1 and not Postulate 2 is (C), so it must be correct.

There's no need to consider Postulate 3 to get to the answer, but it's included because it does assert that hydrogen, a fluid, increases the pore pressure of rock.

2.   F
Difficulty: Hard
Category: Supporting Hypotheses
Getting to the Answer: Postulate 1 asserts that earthquakes can be caused by the stresses induced by the addition of mass to the surface. This supports (F), which says that the increased stress due to the weight of a building influences seismicity.

Choice G is consistent with Postulate 2, which claims that the removal of underground mass can cause earthquakes. None of the postulates deal with the effects of erosion or nuclear tests on earthquakes, so H and J are incorrect.

3.   A
Difficulty: Medium
Category: Applying Core Knowledge
Getting to the Answer: The normal force is an upward force; the removal of mass from the crust would cause stress from the force to be unbalanced, so a downward force would be needed to counteract that effect. Adding mass would create more of a downward force, so (A) is correct.

Choices B and D are incorrect because both mining and groundwater extraction would result in more mass being removed, which would exacerbate the problem. Choice C is incorrect because fracking stresses rock by injecting fluid; this would not provide an upward force to mitigate the problem.

4.   G
Difficulty: Hard
Category: Synthesizing Data
Getting to the Answer: Postulate 3 asserts that injecting fluids into subsurface rock induces earthquakes by increasing pore pressure; the greater the volume injected, the more likely an earthquake is. Since $\text{density} = \frac{\text{mass}}{\text{volume}}$, then $\text{volume} = \frac{\text{mass}}{\text{density}}$. Before you plug any numbers into this formula to figure out which fluid has the greatest volume, think critically about it first. Mass will be constant for all four fluids, so the greatest volume will be from the gas with the lowest density. That's hydrogen, which means (G) is correct.

5.   B
Difficulty: Medium
Category: Supporting Hypotheses
Getting to the Answer: This is an open-ended question; it would be hard to predict something consistent with all three postulates, so evaluate the choices one by one. Even though each postulate describes how new stresses can induce earthquakes, it's possible that pre-existing stresses can also trigger earthquakes, so A is incorrect. Choice (B) is correct because even though each postulate describes a different cause of earthquakes, each one focuses on some kind of perturbation or disturbance near a fault that triggers the earthquake. Choice C can be eliminated because none of the postulates compare the relative strengths of earthquakes and the stress loaded onto faults. Finally, D can be eliminated because none of the postulates claim that these induced earthquakes are the only types of quakes possible.

6.   H
Difficulty: Hard
Category: Applying Core Knowledge
Getting to the Answer: According to Postulate 1, reservoirs can cause earthquakes due to the increased stress from their mass, with larger reservoirs more likely to cause seismic perturbations. Thus, you'll need to calculate the volume of each of these reservoirs to see which one is largest. You can't use a calculator, but some critical thinking can help streamline the calculations. First, each one has 0.1 as one of the dimensions, so that will have no effect on the comparison. Multiply the other 2 numbers together to see which of those products is biggest: $0.1 \times 6 = 0.6$, $0.2 \times 4 = 0.8$, $0.3 \times 4 = 1.2$, and $0.2 \times 5 = 1$. Of those, 1.2 is biggest, so (H) is correct.

7.   A
Difficulty: Hard
Category: Applying Core Knowledge
Getting to the Answer: The claim being made is that tunnel excavation led to the remaining rocks being unable to support the resulting stress. This is in line with Postulate 2, which makes the same claim in regard to mining excavations. Postulates 1 and 3 make no claims about what happens during excavation, however. Postulate 1 asserts that earthquakes can be caused by extra mass on the surface, while Postulate 3 claims earthquakes are caused by fluid injected into subsurface rocks. Thus, (A) is correct, as only Postulate 2 is consistent with this claim.

CHAPTER 26

ACT SCIENCE: TIMING AND SECTION MANAGEMENT STRATEGIES

LEARNING OBJECTIVE

After completing this chapter, you will be able to:

- Triage the ACT Science section by making quick decisions about which questions to do and which to skip

Timing

You have 35 minutes to complete 6 passages with 6–8 questions each, so you need to complete each passage and accompanying questions in less than 6 minutes. Note that passages and question sets are not all the same length or difficulty, so some will take longer than others. After 17 minutes, you should have completed about three passages and question sets.

This is a brisk pace, but working through the Data Representation passages quickly will save you some extra time for Research Summaries and Conflicting Viewpoints passages. In addition, plan to triage questions and skip those that you can see at a glance will be time-consuming or difficult. Your real task is not actually to attempt all the questions in 35 minutes but to get as many points from the section as you can.

Section Management

Mark up the passages. ACT Science questions may seem to come in many varieties, but they are ultimately predictable. With enough practice and the right strategies (like those provided in chapters 23, 24, and 25), you can learn what questions to expect as you read through a passage. By marking up the passage as recommended in these chapters, you can prepare yourself to answer its questions more quickly.

Focus on getting the points. Remember: the goal is to answer as many Science questions correctly as possible. There are no points awarded simply for making your way through a tough passage or getting that one particular high-difficulty question correct. That doesn't mean you should rush through the passages as quickly as possible—that can actually cost you time when you find yourself having to reread more while working on questions—or skip every high-difficulty question, but it does mean that you should approach every passage and question set strategically using the recommendations in chapters 23, 24, and 25. In addition, know when to stop working on a question and make a strategic guess so you can spend your time getting points elsewhere.

Don't be afraid to guess. When you encounter an especially tough question that you think would take you too long to answer, it's better to make a random guess, even if you can't eliminate any choices, than to leave it blank and expect to come back later. You have a 0% chance of getting a Science question right if you leave it blank but a 25% chance of getting it right with a blind guess.

Eliminate answers that contradict the passage. If you can't figure out what to predict, narrow down the possibilities by ruling out definite incorrect answers. If an answer choice comes into conflict with scientific information from the text or with data from the passage's graphs and tables, it is almost certainly incorrect. In addition, you can sometimes eliminate answer choices that contradict a key piece of information from the question stem itself. In other cases, you can use common sense and basic logic to rule out choices that are implausible. Using process of elimination like this will either reveal the one answer that must be correct or at least increase your odds of guessing correctly among the remaining options.

Don't overthink it. Remember that the actual core knowledge on the ACT Science Test is relatively basic. Most data relationships will be relatively simple linear ones, either direct or inverse—don't strain your brain looking for something more complex when you don't need to. In addition, you'll never need to remember advanced scientific concepts or equations, and you won't need to perform elaborate calculations. If it seems like answering a question will require advanced knowledge or a complex calculation, you're most likely overthinking it.

Don't worry if you find yourself guessing on a lot of questions because you can miss quite a few questions on the Science Test and still get a great score. The median ACT test taker gets only about half of the Science questions correct!

There are three Science passage sets in the "How Much Have You Learned?" section that comes next. Use these passages to practice timing: skip questions you find too time-consuming, return to them if you have time, and keep an eye on the clock. On tougher questions, eliminate choices when you can and guess when you need to. When you are finished, check your work—and reflect on how well you managed the timing.

Keep practicing these timing strategies when you take full-length tests, both in your book and online.

How Much Have You Learned?

Directions: For test-like practice, give yourself 18 minutes to complete this question set. Be sure to study the explanations, even for questions you got right. They can be found at the end of this chapter.

Passage I

Many proteins undergo denaturation upon heating. A denatured protein is unfolded and can no longer perform its normal biological functions. Denaturation usually occurs over a temperature range. Some proteins can fold back (renature) into their original conformation when the temperature is decreased. A series of experiments was performed to determine the denaturation and renaturation behavior of 3 different proteins.

Experiment 1

Fifteen separate 15-mL samples of each of the proteins ribonuclease (RNase), carboxypeptidase (Case), and hexokinase (Hase) were heated slowly from 20°C to 160°C and cooled slowly back to 20°C. After every 5°C increase in temperature, 0.002 mL of each sample was removed and chemically analyzed to determine the temperature at which denaturation occurred. After every 5°C decrease in temperature, 0.002 mL of each sample was removed and analyzed to determine the temperature at which renaturation occurred. The results of the experiment are shown in Table 1.

Table 1			
Protein	Approximate Molecular Weight (Amu)	Denaturation Temperature Range (°C)	Renaturation Temperature Range (°C)
RNase	13,700	135–145	110–135
Case	35,000	150–155	60–140
Hase	100,000	85–95	–

Experiment 2

Solubility is also a measure of protein denaturation. A protein can be considered fully denatured when its solubility drops to zero. Each 0.002 mL sample of ribonuclease, carboxypeptidase, and hexokinase was dissolved in 10 mL of ethyl alcohol, and its solubility was measured. The solubility

measurements were taken in 5°C increments as the samples were heated from 20°C to 160°C and again as they were cooled from 160°C to 20°C. The results are shown in Figure 1 and Figure 2.

Figure 1

Figure 2

1. Suppose that protein RNase was heated from 40°C to 150°C and then cooled back to 40°C. Which of the following plots would its solubility curve most likely resemble?

A.

B.

C.

D.

2. According to Figure 1, what would most likely be the solubility of Case in 10 mL of ethyl alcohol at 0°C?

F. 0.055 g/mL

G. 0.045 g/mL

H. 0.015 g/mL

J. 0.000 g/mL

3. According to Table 1, within which temperature range, if any, did protein Hase renature?

A. 85–95°C

B. 60–140°C

C. 110–135°C

D. Hase did not renature.

4. Based on Table 1 and Figure 1, the maximum of the solubility curves for each of the three proteins corresponds to:

F. denaturation molecular weight.

G. renaturation molecular weight.

H. denaturation temperature range.

J. renaturation temperature range.

5. A student hypothesized that a higher molecular weight yields a higher average denaturation temperature. Are the results of Experiment 1 consistent with this hypothesis?

A. Yes, because RNase had the highest molecular weight and highest average denaturation temperature.

B. Yes, because Case had the highest molecular weight and the highest average denaturation temperature.

C. No, because higher molecular weights actually correspond to lower average denaturation temperatures.

D. No, because there is no correlation between molecular weight and average denaturation temperature.

6. Which of the following statements best explains why peak solubility of Case was lower after going through the process of denaturation and renaturation?

    F. Part of the renatured protein formed a precipitate.

    G. The samples before denaturation and after renaturation were taken from different parts of the solution.

    H. Only a fraction of denatured protein renatured back into its native, active form.

    J. There were contaminants in the samples that lowered solubility.

7. Suppose a fourth protein, ovalbumin, denatures between 115°C and 130°C and renatures between 70°C and 100°C. If the procedures of Experiment 2 were repeated with ovalbumin, its solubility curve would most likely peak at about:

    A. 85°C.

    B. 95°C.

    C. 105°C.

    D. 115°C.

Passage II

The rings of Saturn, the sixth planet from the sun, are less than a kilometer thick and composed of particles containing ice, rock debris, and dust. The origin of Saturn's rings, however, is not fully understood. Three hypotheses on ring origin are discussed.

Hypothesis 1

Saturn's rings were formed from collision-generated debris. Large objects such as asteroid-type bodies and/or moons passed very close to Saturn and experienced strong tidal forces, which caused collisions between the objects. When these large bodies collided, smaller fragments formed, which in turn collided and created debris. The pushing and pulling from the gravity of Saturn and its moons caused the debris to scatter and orbit, thus creating Saturn's rings.

Hypothesis 2

The particles that make up Saturn's rings were supplied by water-rich plumes venting from satellites in the south polar region of Saturn. During geological activity of the satellites, cryovolcanoes shot geyser-like jets of water vapor, molecular hydrogen, sodium chloride crystals, and ice particles up 500 km into space. Some fell back as snow, while the rest escaped and formed Saturn's rings. Over 100 geysers have been identified.

Hypothesis 3

The rings of Saturn were formed from the particles of the protoplanetary cloud around Saturn. Gravity kept dust and debris left over from the formation of Saturn in orbit. After the appearance of the magnetic field of Saturn, orbits of ice-carbon superconductive particles moved from the protoplanetary cloud to the magnetic equator plane, where magnetic energy was at a minimum. The rings resulted from the electromagnetic interaction of the particles with the planetary magnetic field.

8. Which hypothesis, if any, asserts that the materials of Saturn's rings are relics of the earliest days of Saturn's formation?

    F. Hypothesis 1

    G. Hypothesis 2

    H. Hypothesis 3

    J. None of the hypotheses

9. Assume all the outer planets, those outside the asteroid belt, have rings. Supporters of which of the hypotheses would be likely to agree with the statement, "Rings form around outer planets because the sun's heat cannot destroy superconductivity outside the asteroid belt"?

    A. Hypothesis 2 only

    B. Hypothesis 3 only

    C. Hypotheses 2 and 3

    D. Hypotheses 1, 2, and 3

10. Suppose around 200 million years ago, a moon passing too close to Saturn was ripped apart. A supporter of which of the hypotheses would be likely to claim that the moon got trapped in Saturn's gravitational pull, which tore it to shreds and circularized the orbits of the debris?

    F. Hypothesis 1 only

    G. Hypothesis 3 only

    H. Hypotheses 1 and 3 only

    J. Hypotheses 1, 2, and 3

11. As described by Hypothesis 2, which of the following is the most likely force that caused the water vapor erupted by geysers to fall back as snow?

    A. Air resistance

    B. Spring

    C. Gravitational

    D. Centrifugal

12. Which of the following statements about Saturn's rings is consistent with all 3 hypotheses?

    F. Fragments from collisions make up the rings.

    G. The rings are composed of ice particles, rock debris, and dust.

    H. The gravity of Saturn caused snow crystals to orbit and thereby form rings.

    J. The rings are a plane of solid ice and rock that is less than a kilometer thick.

13. By convention, the direction of a magnetic field goes outward from the north pole toward the south pole. Based on Hypothesis 3, which of the following figures best depicts the magnetic field around Saturn?

A.

B.

C.

D.
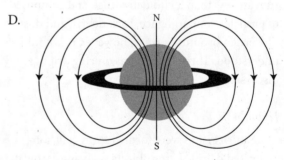

Passage III

Landfill leachate poses a threat to groundwater used for drinking, irrigation, animal feed, and industry. To assess the extent of pollution of a landfill site on the nearby water supply, 19 wells were sampled and analyzed for physicochemical properties. Wells 1, 2, and 3 were upstream of the landfill, while the remaining 10 wells were downstream. Table 1 and Table 2 show the pH, electrical conductivity (EC), and chemical oxygen demand (COD) of the groundwater in the wells during a period of low tide and high tide, respectively. Table 3 shows the landfill's impact on the level of pollution.

Table 1			
Low Tide			
Well	pH	EC (ms/cm)	COD (mg/L)
1	7.0	1.3	0
2	7.4	0.5	0
3	7.7	0.6	0
4	6.8	10.1	275
5	7.5	8.9	234
6	7.7	1.8	43
7	7.3	2.4	67
8	6.8	6.5	83
9	7.2	3.4	70
10	7.2	1.4	65
11	7.2	4.6	54
12	7.0	6.1	113
13	7.4	2.3	37

Table 2			
High Tide			
Well	pH	EC (ms/cm)	COD (mg/L)
1	6.7	1.1	0
2	6.8	0.5	0
3	6.6	0.6	0
4	6.7	11.6	290
5	7.5	8.0	324
6	6.9	1.5	56
7	6.5	5.9	89
8	6.3	6.1	112
9	6.7	3.6	74
10	6.9	1.3	82
11	7.2	4.3	66
12	7.0	6.2	154
13	7.2	1.9	53

Table 3		
Pollution level	EC (ms/cm)	COD (mg/L)
None	<1.4	0
Minimal	1.4–6.5	0
Moderate	1.4–6.5	>0 to <200
Extreme	>6.5	>200

14. According to the results of the study, what is the level of pollution for Well 13?

    F. None

    G. Hardly any

    H. Moderate

    J. Extreme

15. Based on Tables 1 and 2, the average EC, in ms/cm, for the control group data is closest to which of the following?

    A. 0.6

    B. 0.8

    C. 2.4

    D. 3.0

16. The level of *water mineralization* is proportional to the value of the water's electrical conductivity (EC). According to Table 1, which of the following wells has the strongest water mineralization?

    F. Well 4
    G. Well 6
    H. Well 11
    J. Well 12

17. Consider this statement: "The wells downstream of the landfill had greater chemical oxygen demand levels during high tide than during low tide." Do the data in the tables support this prediction?

    A. Yes; for Wells 1–3, the values for COD were higher during high tide than during low tide.

    B. Yes; for Wells 4–13, the values for COD were higher during high tide than during low tide.

    C. No; for Wells 1–3, the values for COD were lower during high tide than during low tide.

    D. No; for Wells 4–13, the values for COD were lower during high tide than during low tide.

18. The pH data for Wells 6–9 in Tables 1 and 2 is best represented by which of the following graphs?

F.

G.

H.

J.

19. Suppose the scientists sampled another well for which the values are in the following table.

pH	EC (ms/cm)	COD (mg/L)
7.7	0.5	0

Based on Tables 1 and 2, when and where was the well most likely sampled?

A. Low tide, upstream

B. Low tide, downstream

C. High tide, upstream

D. High tide, downstream

Answers and Explanations

How Much Have You Learned?

1. A
Difficulty: Low
Category: Synthesizing Data
Getting to the Answer: This question is asking you to combine parts of the graphs in Figures 1 and 2 into a single graph. Notice that Figure 1 shows the solubility of RNase increasing until it hits a peak at about 135°C, after which it rapidly drops off. Figure 2 shows RNase with no solubility at higher temperatures, but with a rapid increase just before a relatively smaller peak at about 115°C, followed by a more gradual decline as the temperature cools. Thus, the correct graph should look like two hills separated by a valley, with the larger peak coming first. This corresponds to the graph in (A), the correct answer.

Choice B is incorrect because it shows only the first peak, but not the second one as RNase renatures. Choice C is incorrect because it shows a single increase followed by a plateau, which corresponds to nothing in Figures 1 or 2. Choice D is incorrect because it doesn't capture the rise in solubility of the first peak and has it at too low of a temperature, even though it captures the second peak accurately.

2. G
Difficulty: Low
Category: Using Data
Getting to the Answer: Extend the curve representing Case until it intersects the 0°C line (the *y*-axis). The value at that intersection should be a bit less than 0.05 g/mL. Thus, the correct answer is (G).

Choice F can't be correct, because it is higher than the solubility at 20°C, and solubility clearly drops with decreasing temperature. Choices H and J would be too low.

3. D
Difficulty: Low
Category: Interpreting Data
Getting to the Answer: According to Table 1, no renaturation temperature range is listed for Hase, so you can infer Hase did not renature upon cooling after heating. The correct answer is (D).

Choice A corresponds to Hase's denaturation temperature range, and B and C correspond to the renaturation temperatures of Case and RNase, respectively.

4. H
Difficulty: Medium
Category: Synthesizing Data
Getting to the Answer: Solubility curves are found in Figure 1, where solubility is a function of temperature, so you can eliminate F and G (also, nothing in the passage suggests that molecular weight changes during denaturation or renaturation). Piecing together Table 1 with Figure 1, you can see that maximum solubility falls within the denaturation temperature range, so the correct answer is (H).

5. D
Difficulty: Medium
Category: Supporting Hypotheses
Getting to the Answer: Molecular weight and denaturation temperature can both be found in Table 1. The average denaturation temperature would fall in the middle of the denaturation temperature range. First, rank the proteins from highest to lowest molecular weight: Hase is highest, Case is in the middle, and RNase is lowest. Then match the denaturation temperature ranges to the reordered proteins: Hase is 80–95°C, Case is 150–155°C, and RNase is 135–145°C. Case has the highest temperatures in its denaturation range, but its molecular weight falls in the middle, so there is no correlation and the hypothesis is not supported. The correct answer is (D).

Choices A and B both incorrectly state that there is a correlation. Choice C is incorrect because it suggests an inverse relationship that is not supported by the data.

6. H
Difficulty: High
Category: Applying Core Knowledge
Getting to the Answer: What would best explain why the peak solubility is lower after Case denatures and then renatures? The passage states that "some proteins can fold back (renature) into their original conformation when the temperature is decreased," which suggests that not all of the molecules of a particular protein will necessarily renature after denaturing. The correct answer is (H). Choices F, G, and J are not supported by the passage.

Science

7.   D
Difficulty: High
Category: Using Data
Getting to the Answer: This question requires you to predict the results of repeating Experiment 2 with a new protein. You are given its denaturation and renaturation ranges and are asked to figure out where its solubility would peak. For the original experiments, the ranges appear in Table 1, and peak solubility can be found in Figure 1. Each protein's solubility peaks at the lower end of its denaturation range. So, you should expect that the solubility of ovalbumin will peak at the lower bound of its range at 115°C. Thus, the correct answer is (D).

8.   H
Difficulty: Medium
Category: Supporting Hypotheses
Getting to the Answer: Hypotheses 1 and 2 assert that the rings were created by collision debris and plumes of various materials, respectively, but neither makes any reference as to when the rings were created. Eliminate F and G. Hypothesis 3 asserts that the rings were formed from remnants of Saturn's protoplanetary cloud; this is the material from which Saturn itself was formed, so (H) is correct.

9.   B
Difficulty: Medium
Category: Supporting Hypotheses
Getting to the Answer: Someone making a statement such as the one in the question stem thinks that superconductivity played a role in the formation of planetary rings. Hypothesis 3 is the only one that even mentions superconductivity; it asserts that the rings resulted from interaction between superconductive particles and the planetary magnetic field. Thus, (B) is correct.

10.   F
Difficulty: Medium
Category: Supporting Hypotheses
Getting to the Answer: The scenario posited in the question stem results in a circular ring of debris around Saturn after a moon was ripped apart by Saturn's gravity. This is consistent with Hypothesis 1, which asserts that the rings were formed from moons or asteroids destroyed by tidal forces or by collisions. It is not consistent, however, with either of the other hypotheses. Hypothesis 2 claims the rings were caused by plumes ejected from Saturn's moons, while

Hypothesis 3 claims they were formed by the remnants of the protoplanetary cloud. Thus, (F) is correct.

11.   C
Difficulty: Low
Category: Applying Core Knowledge
Getting to the Answer: To answer this question, you'll need a force that would pull something back toward the surface of a moon. That's gravity, which makes (C) correct.

Choice A is incorrect because air resistance is a force that works in the opposite direction of an object as it moves through air; it wouldn't pull the water vapor back toward the surface. Spring force is the force needed to extend (or compress) a spring a particular distance; since no springs are involved in the ring-creation process, B is incorrect. Centrifugal force is an inertial force that appears to push a body outwards against the axis of rotation. Since the vapor is moving toward the planet, D is incorrect.

12.   G
Difficulty: Medium
Category: Supporting Hypotheses
Getting to the Answer: It's hard to predict a statement that would be consistent with all 3 hypotheses, so evaluate the choices one by one. Choice F is incorrect because it is only consistent with Hypothesis 1; Hypotheses 2 and 3 claim that the particles come from hydrovolcanoes and protoplanetary remnants, respectively. The passage does state that the rings are made of ice, dust, and rock; the hypotheses only differ in how the rings were formed, not what they're made out of. Thus, (G) is correct. Choice H is consistent only with Hypothesis 2, so it's incorrect. Choice J is incorrect because the rings are not a solid plane; they're composed of particles.

13.   D
Difficulty: Medium
Category: Synthesizing Data
Getting to the Answer: According to the question stem, the magnetic field originates at the north pole and moves to the south pole. Choices A and C have the field moving out of the south pole toward the north, so eliminate them. The correct answer must also be consistent with Hypothesis 3, which says the rings formed at the magnetic equator. The magnetic equator is halfway between the poles and perpendicular to them; only (D) has the rings placed correctly, so it is correct.

14. H
Difficulty: Low
Category: Synthesizing Data
Getting to the Answer: First, you'll need to look at Tables 1 and 2 to find the EC and COD for Well 13 at low and high tides. The EC ranges from 2.3 at low tide to 1.9 at high tide, and the COD ranges from 37 at low tide to 53 at high tide. All of these figures fit into the moderate range for both EC (1.4 to 6.5) and COD (0 to 200), so (H) is correct.

15. B
Difficulty: Medium
Category: Using Data
Getting to the Answer: First, look at the passage to determine which wells are the control group. Wells 1, 2, and 3 are upstream of the landfill and thus won't be contaminated by it, so they're the controls. To find the average EC, you'll need to add up the low- and high-tide values and divide by 6, the number of terms. According to Tables 1 and 2, the low-tide EC values for Wells 1, 2, and 3 are 1.3, 0.5, and 0.6, and the high-tide EC values are 1.1, 0.5, and 0.6. Since you can't use a calculator, don't waste time doing exact calculations; approximate wherever you can. Round the two 0.6 values down to 0.5; now you have four 0.5 values to add up, which is equal to 2. Round down 1.1 to 1, and now the total is 3. The final value is 1.3, so the total of the EC values is 4.3. To find the average, you'd divide this by 6. Again, though, you don't need to calculate this exactly; $\frac{4.3}{6}$ would be equal to a bit more than $\frac{2}{3}$ (which is approximately equal to 0.67), and the only choice that fits is (B), 0.8.

Choice A may be tempting because it is close to the approximated value of the average. However, remember that the estimate was that the answer would be higher than $\frac{2}{3}$, and you even rounded some numbers down to get that estimate, so the answer can't be lower than 0.67.

16. F
Difficulty: Medium
Category: Interpreting Data
Getting to the Answer: If water mineralization is proportional to EC, then the well with the highest EC will have the strongest water mineralization. The question directs you to Table 1, so look there to see which of the 4 wells in the choices has the highest EC: Well 4, at 10.1. The answer is (F).

17. B
Difficulty: Hard
Category: Synthesizing Data
Getting to the Answer: For this question, you'll need to compare COD values at low tide versus high tide for the wells downstream of the landfill, which, according to the passage, are Wells 4–13. For each of those wells, the COD value in the 4th column is higher at high tide (Table 2) than at low tide (Table 1). This supports the prediction, so (B) is correct.

Choice A is incorrect, even though it comes to the right conclusion, because it bases that conclusion on data for Wells 1–3, which are upstream, not downstream. Choices C and D are incorrect because both come to an incorrect conclusion based on incorrect interpretations of the data.

18. H
Difficulty: Hard
Category: Synthesizing Data
Getting to the Answer: First, scan the graphs in the answer choices to see what kind of trends you should look for in the data. All graphs show all low-tide pH values as higher than their corresponding high-tide values or vice versa. That means you can look at the data for just one well and eliminate half of the answer choices based on whether the high-tide pH is higher or lower than the low-tide value. Looking at Well 6, at low tide the pH is 7.7 and at high tide it's 6.9. So, you can eliminate G and J, each of which says the high tide values would be higher. Finally, to see which of the two remaining answers is correct, see which one portrays the values for Well 6 correctly. Choice (H) does so, so it's correct.

19. A
Difficulty: High
Category: Using Data
Getting to the Answer: The value of COD for the additional well sample is 0 mg/L. Based on Tables 1 and 2, COD is only 0 mg/L for Wells 1–3, which are located upstream from the landfill. Note that the EC value of 0.5 ms/cm also matches those for Wells 1–3. Eliminate B and D. Notice the pH values in Table 1 for low tide are greater than 7, while those in Table 2 for high tide are less than 7. The pH of the additional well is 7.7, which would match the pH of the wells for low tide. Choice (A) is correct.

TEST YOURSELF: ACT SCIENCE

Directions: For test-like timing, give yourself about 48 minutes to complete the following 55 questions.

Passage I

Vocalists typically produce sounds only during the exhalation phase of the breathing cycle. However, some vocalists have developed a technique that allows them to produce sounds during the inhalation phase. A study compared the differences in pitch and volume of notes sung by Vocalist A, a soprano, and Vocalist B, a bass. Each vocalist first used a traditional exhaling technique and then used an experimental inhaling technique. Table 1 compares the pitch frequency (Hz) of each note sung to a reference pitch played on an electronic keyboard and Table 2 indicates the decibel volume (dB) of each note. Figure 1 illustrates the range of pitch variation for each note sung by Vocalist A.

Table 1

Note	Reference Pitch (Hz)	Vocalist A		Vocalist B	
		Exhaling Mean Pitch (Hz)	Inhaling Mean Pitch (Hz)	Exhaling Mean Pitch (Hz)	Inhaling Mean Pitch (Hz)
C4	261.63	259.99	240.57	247.11	238.15
D4	293.66	289.53	274.79	278.51	270.81
E4	329.63	323.86	312.00	313.78	306.47
F4	349.23	340.92	334.54	334.00	326.36
G4	392.00	382.46	378.54	377.42	368.58

Table 2

Note	Vocalist A		Vocalist B	
	Exhaling Maximum Volume (dB)	Inhaling Maximum Volume (dB)	Exhaling Maximum Volume (dB)	Inhaling Maximum Volume (dB)
C4	81	64	72	66
D4	85	70	69	64
E4	91	76	66	62
F4	95	82	63	60
G4	99	88	60	58

Figure 1

Science

1. According to Figure 1, as frequency increases, the range of pitch variation for each note sung by Vocalist A:

    A. decreases using the exhaling technique.

    B. increases using the exhaling technique.

    C. decreases using the inhaling technique.

    D. increases using the inhaling technique.

2. Suppose the reference pitch for note A4 is 440 Hz. According to Tables 1 and 2, if Vocalist B sang note A4, what would the inhaled maximum volume for Vocalist B most likely be?

    F. 56 dB

    G. 70 dB

    H. 76 dB

    J. 90 dB

3. Based on Table 1, the inhaling mean pitch of Vocalist B is best represented by which of the following graphs?

    A.

    B.

    C.

    D.

4. Which of the following statements about the inhaling technique compared to the exhaling technique is consistent with the results of the study?

   F. The inhaling technique has a lower mean pitch than the exhaling technique.

   G. The inhaling technique has a lower frequency range than the exhaling technique.

   H. The inhaling technique has a higher maximum volume than the exhaling technique.

   J. The inhaling technique has a higher frequency range for each note than the exhaling technique has.

5. Lowering the *octave* of a note (such as from A4 to A3) decreases the pitch frequency by half. Based on Table 1, which of the following would most likely be the exhaling mean pitch of Vocalist A for note C3?

   A. 130 Hz

   B. 147 Hz

   C. 165 Hz

   D. 175 Hz

6. A student predicted that the inhaling mean pitch for Vocalist B would be closer to the reference pitch than the exhaling mean pitch of Vocalist B would be at higher frequencies only. Do the results of the study support this prediction?

   F. Yes; the difference between the inhaling mean pitch of Vocalist B and the reference pitch is less than the difference between the exhaling mean pitch of Vocalist B and the reference pitch only at higher frequencies.

   G. Yes; the difference between the inhaling mean pitch of Vocalist B and the reference pitch is greater than the difference between the exhaling mean pitch of Vocalist B and the reference pitch only at higher frequencies.

   H. No; the difference between the inhaling mean pitch of Vocalist B and the reference pitch is consistently less than the difference between the exhaling mean pitch of Vocalist B and the reference pitch at all frequencies.

   J. No; the difference between the inhaling mean pitch of Vocalist B and the reference pitch is consistently greater than the difference between the exhaling mean pitch of Vocalist B and the reference pitch at all frequencies.

7. A subsequent study measured the reference wavelength of each note. The corresponding results are shown in the following table.

Note	Wavelength (cm)
C4	131.87
D4	117.48
E4	104.66
F4	98.79
G4	88.01

Based on the results of the study, what is the relationship, if any, between wavelength and the maximum volume of Vocalist A?

A. As wavelength increases, the maximum volume of Vocalist A increases only.

B. As wavelength increases, the maximum volume of Vocalist A decreases only.

C. As wavelength increases, the maximum volume of Vocalist A first decreases and then increases.

D. There is no relationship between wavelength and the maximum volume of Vocalist A.

Passage II

Radiometric dating of lunar rocks indicate the Moon is 4.51 billion years old. Consider the following three hypotheses about the Moon's formation.

Hypothesis 1

The Moon originated in a glancing collision between Earth and a Mars-sized protoplanet. Most of the protoplanet's metallic elements, like iron, merged into Earth. The protoplanet's lighter debris escaped into orbit and formed the Moon, which thus has an unusually small iron core for its size. Due to the extreme heat during its violent origin, the Moon mostly lacks volatile substances (those with low boiling points), such as water. The disparity in densities between Earth and the Moon (see Table 1) refutes the idea that both bodies formed close to one another in the early solar system's accretion disk.

Table 1	
Inner Planets & the Moon	Mean Density (kg/m^3)
Mercury	5427
Venus	5243
Earth	5514
The Moon	3344
Mars	3933

Table adapted from NASA, *Planetary Fact Sheets*, last updated January 28, 2016.

Hypothesis 2

Earth and the Moon originated in the aftermath of a collision between two large protoplanets. A greater amount of the metallic elements from the collision went into forming Earth, resulting in a large iron core capable of producing a strong magnetic field. Since the Moon, unlike Earth, does not have a strong magnetic field to shield its surface, solar wind stripped the Moon of subsequently acquired water.

Hypothesis 3

Intense bombardment of the Earth by asteroids and comets created the Moon. Most of the Earth's iron and nickel had already undergone differentiation, sinking to form its core. Portions of the Earth's outermost layers, mostly composed of less dense elements, were blasted into orbit by the high-velocity impacts of asteroids and comets. That orbiting material formed multiple small moonlets. Eventually, the moonlets merged together to form the Moon.

8. Which hypothesis suggests that the Earth's core gained additional iron due to the process of the Moon's formation?

F. Hypothesis 1 only

G. Hypothesis 2 only

H. Hypotheses 1 and 2 only

J. Hypotheses 2 and 3 only

9. Which of the following statements about the Moon's formation is consistent with all three hypotheses?

   A. Extreme heat generated by the Moon's formation destroyed all but trace amounts of most volatile compounds.

   B. The Moon has fewer metallic elements, such as nickel and iron, compared to Earth.

   C. The Earth's interior had differentiated into a distinct core and outer layers prior to the Moon's formation.

   D. The high-velocity bombardment of Earth by comets and asteroids extracted the material that later formed the Moon.

10. Which hypothesis, if any, suggests that the Moon lacks water as a result of its small iron core?

    F. Hypothesis 1 only

    G. Hypothesis 2 only

    H. Hypotheses 1 and 2

    J. All of the hypotheses

11. Consider the statement "The Moon's far side features a notably thicker crust than that of the near side, which provides evidence of a smaller astronomical body absorbed into the Moon." Which of Hypotheses 1 and 3, if either, would be likely to agree with that statement?

    A. Hypothesis 1 only

    B. Hypothesis 3 only

    C. Both Hypotheses 1 and 3

    D. Neither Hypothesis 1 or 3

12. Suppose the volume of Mercury is 5.4% the volume of Earth, and the Moon is approximately 2% of Earth's volume. Will the mass of the Moon be higher or lower than Mercury's mass?

    F. Lower, because the Moon has lower density and lower volume in comparison to Mercury.

    G. Lower, because the Moon has a higher density and lower volume in comparison to Mercury.

    H. Higher, because the Moon has lower density and lower volume in comparison to Mercury.

    J. Higher, because the Moon has a higher density and lower volume in comparison to Mercury.

13. Which hypothesis, if any, suggests that the Moon's formation took place after Earth's formation?

    A. Hypothesis 1 only

    B. Hypothesis 2 only

    C. Hypotheses 1 and 3 only

    D. Hypotheses 1, 2, and 3

Passage III

When a granular material is poured onto a horizontal plane, it forms a cone-shaped mound whose curved surface forms an angle with the base known as the angle of repose. The angle of repose is the steepest angle in relation to the horizontal plane that the sides of the mound can form without slumping, as shown in the diagram.

diagram

The grain size of the material and the presence of glidants (materials that change the flowability of the grains) are two major factors that determine the angle of repose. A group of students performed the following experiments to test these factors.

Experiment 1

Three 100-gram samples of sand, each of a different grain size, plus a 100-gram sample containing a mix of all three grain sizes in equal volumes, were each poured through a funnel onto a 5-centimeter-diameter flat rubber disc as shown in the diagram. The procedure was repeated three times for each grain size of sand. The average heights and angles of repose of each of the resulting piles were measured. The results are shown in Table 1.

Experiment 2

The glidant magnesium stearate was added in varying amounts (1, 2, and 3 grams) to each 100-gram sample of sand, and the procedures in Experiment 1 were repeated. The results are shown in Table 2.

Table 1		
Particle Size (μm)	Sand	
	Average Height (cm)	Average Angle (°)
300	1.6	35
500	1.9	38
800	1.8	36
mix	2.1	41

This data is adapted from *Pharmaceutical Technology*, 2013.

Table 2						
Particle Size (μm)	Sand + 1 g Magnesium stearate		Sand + 2 g Magnesium stearate		Sand + 3 g Magnesium stearate	
	Average Height (cm)	Average Angle (°)	Average Height (cm)	Average Angle (°)	Average Height (cm)	Average Angle (°)
300	1.8	36	2.0	40	2.6	44
500	1.9	39	2.2	43	2.5	46
800	1.7	38	1.9	39	2.0	40
mix	2.0	42	2.6	47	2.9	50

This data is adapted from *Pharmaceutical Technology*, 2013.

14. Which of the following variables remained constant throughout both experiments?

F. Particle size

G. Sand height

H. Disc circumference

J. Angle of repose

15. According to Experiment 2, which of the following best describes the relationship between the amount of glidant added to a sand mixture and the angle of repose?

A. As the amount of glidant increases, the angle of repose decreases then increases.

B. As the amount of glidant increases, the angle of repose decreases.

C. As the amount of glidant increases, the angle of repose increases.

D. The amount of glidant has no effect on the angle of repose.

16. A student concludes that there is a positive correlation between the angle of repose and grain size in a grain sample of uniform size. Do the results of Experiment 1 support this conclusion?

F. No, because the sample with a mix of grain sizes had the highest average angle of repose.

G. No, because the 500 μm sand had the highest average angle of repose.

H. Yes, because the 300 μm sand had the lowest average angle of repose.

J. Yes, because the average angle of repose for each sample has a positive correlation with the average height for that sample.

17. According to Tables 1 and 2, an engineer who wanted to minimize the height of a sand pile would use:

    A. 300 μm grains with magnesium stearate.

    B. 300 μm grains without magnesium stearate.

    C. an equal mix of 300, 500, and 800 μm grains with magnesium stearate.

    D. an equal mix of 300, 500, and 800 μm grains without magnesium stearate.

18. In Experiment 1, which of the following is closest to the mass of the 800 μm sand grains in the mixed sample?

    F. 0 g

    G. 8 g

    H. 33 g

    J. 100 g

19. Which of the following statements best describes the primary effect of mixing grain sizes?

    A. Mixing grain sizes allows for more surface interaction and friction between particles, which increases the angle of repose.

    B. Mixing grain sizes reduces surface interaction and friction between particles, which increases the angle of repose.

    C. Mixing grain sizes increases the pile height, which allows for more surface interaction and friction between particles.

    D. Mixing grain sizes increases the pile height, which reduces surface interaction and friction between particles.

20. The steepest slope that a pile of a particularly sized granular material will take is known as its *talus slope*. A student claims that the talus slope of sand with a width of 500 μm is 38°. Do the results of Experiment 1 support this claim?

    F. No, because mixing 500 μm sand with other types of sand resulted in a higher average angle of repose.

    G. No, because there may have been a trial of 500 μm sand with an angle of repose greater than 38°.

    H. Yes, because when magnesium stearate was added to 500 μm sand, the average angle of repose exceeded 38° regardless of the amount of magnesium stearate added.

    J. Yes, because the average angle of repose for 500 μm sand in Experiment 1 was 38°.

Passage IV

The *greenhouse effect* is a phenomenon in which certain gases in a planet's atmosphere absorb solar radiation (up to 1,000 nm) and re-emit that energy as infrared radiation in all directions. The heat radiated back to the Earth's surface warms the surface. Figure 1 shows the concentration of carbon dioxide (CO_2), nitrous oxide (N_2O), and methane (CH_4) in the Earth's atmosphere over the past 1,000 years. Table 1 shows the global temperature anomaly (deviation from the average temperature of the past 1,000 years) over the same period. Figure 2 shows the main sources of U.S. greenhouse gas emissions over a 26-year period.

Figure 1

Table 1	
Years ago	Global Temperature Anomaly (°C)
0 (present)	0.50
200	0.22
400	0.04
600	−0.03
800	−0.18
1,000	−0.32

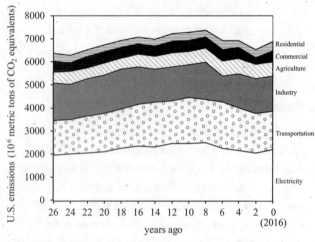

Adapted from U.S. EPA Climate Change Indicators: U.S. Greenhouse Gas Emissions, 2016.

Figure 2

21. Based on Figure 1, the concentration of CH_4 800 years ago is nearest to which of the following values?

  A. 260 ppb

  B. 285 ppb

  C. 700 ppb

  D. 950 ppb

22. According to Figure 2, which of the following U.S. sectors contributed the most to CO_2 emissions over the 26 years depicted in the graph?

  F. Residential

  G. Agriculture

  H. Transportation

  J. Electricity

23. Suppose the researchers also plotted concentration data for ozone, which was 100 ppb 1000 years ago. Based on Figure 1, if the trend in the ozone concentration matched the trend in the N_2O concentration, the ozone concentration at present would most likely be:

  A. less than 250 ppb.

  B. between 250 and 350 ppb.

  C. between 350 and 1000 ppb.

  D. greater than 1000 ppb.

24. According to the trend in Table 1, the average global temperature over the past 1,000 years would most likely fall within which interval?

  F. 0 to 200 years ago

  G. 200 to 400 years ago

  H. 400 to 600 years ago

  J. 600 to 800 years ago

25. Based on Figure 2, approximately how many 10^6 metric tons of CO_2 equivalents were produced by Industry in the U.S. from 2006 to 2016?

  A. 5,000

  B. 15,000

  C. 20,000

  D. 55,000

26. Based on Figure 1, which of the following graphs best represents a plot of CO_2, N_2O, and CH_4 concentrations 1,000 years ago?

F.

G.

H.

J.

27. Consider that electromagnetic waves, like light, obey the equation $c = f \lambda$, where c is the speed of light, f is the frequency, and λ is the wavelength. If the UV rays of sunlight striking the Earth have a higher frequency than the infrared radiation being re-emitted, which of the following statements best characterizes the energy that is absorbed and the energy that is re-emitted?

A. The wavelength of the energy absorbed is shorter than the wavelength of the energy re-emitted.

B. The wavelength of the energy absorbed is longer than the wavelength of the energy re-emitted.

C. The wavelength of the energy re-emitted is the same as the wavelength of the energy absorbed.

D. The wavelength of the energy re-emitted is the inverse of the wavelength of the energy absorbed.

Passage V

A study examined the transport of spores from moldy wood studs within walls to the surrounding air via air infiltration. Studs were inoculated with a spore solution (1×10^6 *Aspergillus niger* spores per ml) and incubated until 10% spore coverage was achieved. A total of 8 wall assemblies (2" × 6" × 8") were created, each with two moldy studs housed in its cavity.

A thin tube was inserted into the cavity and attached to a sampling chamber. These were exposed for two minutes and then examined using a compound light microscope. Spores within six fields were counted, averaged, and multiplied by 10^3 to estimate the total spore count per cubic meter. Scientists investigated air infiltration rate and path, relative humidity in the wall assemblies, and presence of insulation within the wall cavity. The results are shown in Table 1. Table 2 displays the magnification and field of view of various objective and ocular lenses of a light microscope.

Wall #	Air Infiltration Rate (lpm)					Relative Humidity (%)	Air Filtration Path	Insulation
		6.9		16.8				
		Average Spore Counts						
	Lab	Surrounding	Cavity	Surrounding	Cavity			
1	6	21	33	34.5	45	30	Direct	No
2	6	9	31.5	32	41	30	Direct	Yes
3	5	20.5	33	35.5	43.5	30	Meandering	No
4	5	13	25	30	38.5	30	Meandering	Yes
5	23	54	81.5	62	82.5	90	Direct	No
6	23	44	63	51.5	73.5	90	Direct	Yes
7	21	45	117	54	126	90	Meandering	No
8	21	38	77	45.5	82.5	90	Meandering	Yes

Table 1

This data is adapted from *Building and Environment*. Vol. 44. 2009. pp. 1568–1577.

Objective Lens Magnification	Ocular Lens Magnification (10×)	
	Total Magnification	Field of View of Microscope (mm)
1×	10×	20
2×	20×	10
3×	30×	6.7
4×	40×	5
10×	100×	2.25
20×	200×	1
40×	400×	0.45
100×	1000×	0.18

Table 2

28. Based on Table 2, which of the following combinations of lenses would give the greatest total magnification?

	objective	ocular
F.	4×	10×
G.	10×	4×
H.	10×	10×
J.	40×	4×

29. According to Table 1, the spore count from the wall cavity at 30% relative humidity, 16.8 lpm air infiltration rate, a meandering path, and no insulation is approximately which of the following values in 10^3 spore per m^3?

A. 33

B. 35.5

C. 38.5

D. 43.5

30. Suppose the study had been repeated at 60% relative humidity. The total number of spores at 60% relative humidity would most likely have been:

    F. less than the number of spores at 30% relative humidity because the relationship between relative humidity and average spore count is direct.

    G. less than the number of spores at 90% relative humidity because the relationship between relative humidity and average spore count is direct.

    H. greater than the number of spores at 30% relative humidity because the relationship between relative humidity and average spore count is inverse.

    J. greater than the number of spores at 90% relative humidity because the relationship between relative humidity and average spore count is inverse.

31. Which of the following variables remained constant throughout the study?

    A. Air infiltration rate
    B. Laboratory air spore count
    C. Duration of sampling
    D. Presence of insulation within wall assembly

32. Suppose the scientists had used a $10\times$ ocular lens and $4\times$ objective lens to count the spores in the sample of the surrounding air from Wall 7 with a 6.9 air filtration rate. If the scientists changed the objective lens to $20\times$, how many spores would they expect to see in the field of view?

    F. 2
    G. 9
    H. 45
    J. 225

33. Consider the statement "Insulation in the wall cavity decreases the number of spores transported via air infiltration." Does the data in Table 1 support this statement?

    A. Yes; the spore counts for Walls 2 and 4 are lower than those for Walls 1 and 3.

    B. Yes; the spore counts for Walls 2 and 4 are greater than those for Walls 1 and 3.

    C. No; the spore counts for Walls 2 and 4 are lower than those for Walls 1 and 3.

    D. No; the spore counts for Walls 2 and 4 are greater than those for Walls 1 and 3.

34. Suppose at $1000\times$ total magnification, scientists observed 60 *Aspergillus niger* spores arranged side by side forming a line across the center of the circular field of view. The diameter of an *Aspergillus niger* spore is closest to which of the following?

    F. $3\ \mu m$
    G. $4\ \mu m$
    H. $5\ \mu m$
    J. $6\ \mu m$

Passage VI

Nitrogen dioxide (NO_2) is a highly toxic gas that forms from the combustion of fuel. Scientists investigated the use of two types of organic films in NO_2-detecting portable gas sensors: metal-free and metal.

Experiment 1

Vapor deposition was employed to produce metal-free and metal porphyrin films for use in the gas sensors. The NO_2 gas was produced by the chemical reaction of a copper wire and concentrated nitric acid. Four different NO_2 gas concentrations were prepared: 0 ppm, 20 ppm, 40 ppm, and 80 ppm.

NO_2 gas at constant flow was introduced to a gas chamber housing the metal-free film sensor at room temperature. A UV-Vis spectrometer was then used to measure gas absorption in the metal-free film (see Figure 1). The experiment was repeated with the metal film sensor (see Figure 2).

This data is adapted from *Advances in Materials Physics and Chemistry*, Vol. 8, 2018, pp. 441-457.

Figure 1

This data is adapted from *Advances in Materials Physics and Chemistry*, Vol. 8, 2018, pp. 441-457.

Figure 3

This data is adapted from *Advances in Materials Physics and Chemistry*, Vol. 8, 2018, pp. 441-457.

Figure 2

This data is adapted from *Advances in Materials Physics and Chemistry*, Vol. 8, 2018, pp. 441-457.

Figure 4

Experiment 2

To monitor the electrical conductivity of the films in the NO_2-detecting gas sensors, a dual conductive tip was placed in contact with the film surface and connected to a power supply at a constant current of 1 mA. Voltage variation during gas exposures was obtained as a function of time. Figure 3 shows the results from the metal-free film sensor, and Figure 4 shows the results from the metal film sensor.

35. Based on Figure 3, the voltage of the metal-free sensor exposed to 80 ppm NO_2 gas after 1 minute is approximately:

A. 0.05.

B. 0.20.

C. 0.35.

D. 0.81.

36. According to Figure 1, what is the relationship, if any, between the concentration and absorption of NO_2 at approximately 700 nm as measured by the metal-free film?

    F. As concentration of NO_2 gas decreases, absorption decreases.

    G. As concentration of NO_2 gas decreases, absorption increases.

    H. As concentration of NO_2 gas decreases, absorption first increases then decreases.

    J. There is no relationship between NO_2 concentration and absorption.

37. The researchers conducting the experiments also took spectroscopic measurements of each film prior to exposing them to NO_2 gas. The researchers most likely made that decision in order to:

    A. test another variable.

    B. confirm that the spectrometer was working properly.

    C. obtain baseline absorption data.

    D. remove contaminants from the spectrometer.

38. Suppose Experiment 1 had been repeated with 60 ppm NO_2 gas using the metal film sensor. The maximum absorption peak between 650 and 850 nm for 60 ppm NO_2 would most likely have been:

    F. between 0.3 and 0.4 a.u.

    G. between 0.4 and 0.5 a.u.

    H. between 0.5 and 0.6 a.u.

    J. greater than 0.6 a.u.

39. Consider that the experiments were performed at room temperature. These conditions ensured that NO_2 was a gas because room temperature is:

    A. lower than the boiling point of NO_2.

    B. higher than the boiling point of NO_2.

    C. lower than the freezing point of NO_2.

    D. higher than the freezing point of NO_2.

40. According to the results of the experiments for 40 ppm NO_2, did the presence of metal in the film of the sensor increase or decrease the absorption at 700 nm and increase or decrease the conductivity after 41 sec?

	absorption	conductivity
F.	increase	decrease
G.	increase	increase
H.	decrease	decrease
J.	decrease	increase

41. The following table lists the wavelengths for the visible spectrum.

Color	Wavelength (nm)
blue	450–495
green	495–570
yellow	570–590
orange	590–620
red	620–750

    Based on the results of Experiment 1, is absorption in the blue wavelength region directly proportional to the concentration of NO_2 gas?

    A. No, because there is no relationship between the height of the absorption peaks and NO_2 concentration between 450 and 495 nm.

    B. No, because there is no relationship between the height of the absorption peaks and NO_2 concentration between 650 and 695 nm.

    C. Yes, because the height of the absorption peaks between 450 and 495 nm decreased as NO_2 concentration decreased.

    D. Yes, because the height of the absorption peaks between 650 and 695 nm decreased as NO_2 concentration decreased.

Passage VII

Students were given the concentration, temperature, pH, and viscosity data of 12 different salt solutions and asked to explain which properties affect a solution's conductivity, the measure of the ability to pass electrical flow (see Table 1). Each solution is composed of sodium chloride dissolved in 1 L of water at 1 atmosphere (atm) of pressure.

	Table 1			
Solution	Concentration (mol/L)	Temperature (°C)	pH	Viscosity (Pa·s)
1	0.2	25	6	1.79×10^{-4}
2	0.2	25	10	1.81×10^{-4}
3	0.2	60	6	8.80×10^{-4}
4	0.2	60	10	8.85×10^{-4}
5	0.4	25	6	1.85×10^{-3}
6	0.4	25	10	1.88×10^{-3}
7	0.4	60	6	1.89×10^{-3}
8	0.4	60	10	1.50×10^{-3}
9	0.8	25	6	1.90×10^{-3}
10	0.8	25	10	1.92×10^{-3}
11	0.8	60	6	1.94×10^{-3}
12	0.8	60	10	1.70×10^{-3}

Student 1

Increasing solution temperature and increasing concentration increases conductivity. Higher temperatures lead to greater kinetic energy, which breaks apart the intermolecular attractions between solute molecules. Higher concentrations increase the number of ions that can carry the electric current.

Student 2

Decreasing the pH of a solution and increasing the temperature increases conductivity. At a lower pH, the greater number of H^+ ions provides more charge carriers for the electric current, and at a higher temperature, the current flows at a faster rate.

Student 3

Increasing the concentration of a solution and increasing the viscosity decreases conductivity. More viscous solvents and higher concentrations of solute reduce ionic mobility, thus preventing movement of charged particles in an electric current.

Student 4

Increasing the solution temperature and increasing the viscosity decreases conductivity. At higher temperatures, kinetic energy causes intermolecular bonds to break and molecules to escape solution, which results in a lower number of current carriers. At lower viscosities, ions are more mobile and promote movement of charged particles.

42. Based on Student 2's explanation, which of the following solutions has the lowest conductivity?

   F. Solution 9
   G. Solution 10
   H. Solution 11
   J. Solution 12

43. Brine is 26% salt and possesses a viscosity four times that of tap water. The statement "The conductivity of brine is less than the conductivity of tap water" is supported by which of the student(s)?

   A. Student 3 only
   B. Student 4 only
   C. Students 3 and 4 only
   D. Students 2, 3, and 4 only

44. Suppose the properties of a 13th solution are 0.8 mol/L, 40°C, and pH of 6. Which of the following ranks Solutions 9, 11, and 13 from *least* conductive to *most* conductive, according to Student 4's viewpoint?

   F. Solution 9, Solution 11, Solution 13
   G. Solution 9, Solution 13, Solution 11
   H. Solution 13, Solution 11, Solution 9
   J. Solution 11, Solution 13, Solution 9

45. Consider the statement, "Freshwater and salt water have conductivities of approximately 5.5 μS/m and 5×10^6 μS/m, respectively, at 25°C." Which of the students' viewpoint(s) is consistent with this statement?

   A. Student 1 only
   B. Student 3 only
   C. Students 1 and 3 only
   D. Students 1 and 4 only

46. Which of the following statements would Student 3 be most likely to agree with?

   F. Solution 2 has a lower conductivity than Solution 10.
   G. Solution 3 has a lower conductivity than Solution 7.
   H. Solution 5 has a higher conductivity than Solution 1.
   J. Solution 8 has a higher conductivity than Solution 12.

47. Consider the claim, "A solution with a concentration of hydrogen ions higher than 10^7 mol/L has a greater number of ions, which increases its ability to carry electrical current." Which of the student(s) would likely agree with this claim?

   A. Student 2 only
   B. Student 3 only
   C. Students 2 and 3 only
   D. Students 3 and 4 only

48. Suppose Solution 4 is heated to a boil at 100°C. Will the kinetic energy of the particles in Solution 4 be higher or lower than it was at 60°C?

   F. Lower; molecules in the gaseous state have more kinetic energy than those in liquid state.
   G. Lower; molecules in the liquid state have more kinetic energy than those in gaseous state.
   H. Higher; molecules in the gaseous state have more kinetic energy than those in liquid state.
   J. Higher; molecules in the liquid state have more kinetic energy than those in gaseous state.

Passage VIII

When plants use sunlight to synthesize sugars from carbon dioxide and water, the process of photosynthesis occurs:

$$6CO_2 + 6H_2O \xrightarrow{\text{light}} C_6H_{12}O_6 + 6O_2$$

Experiment 1

A student created a laboratory set-up to compare the rates of photosynthesis in 3 different aquatic plants: *Egeria densa*, *Elodea canadensis*, and *Cabomba caroliniana*. The student built 3 apparatus identical to that shown in the diagram.

diagram

In each apparatus, the student filled a beaker with 350 mL of water and added 10 g of sodium bicarbonate. In the first apparatus, the student placed 4 sprigs of *E. densa*, each cut to a length of 10 cm, under a funnel and then placed an inverted test tube, filled with water, over the mouth of the funnel as shown. The student repeated this set-up with the second and third apparatus, except that instead of *E. densa*, *E. canadensis* was placed in the second funnel, and *C. caroliniana* placed in the third funnel. In each set-up, the beaker was placed 10 cm away from a fluorescent bulb.

Table 1			
Hour	Number of O_2 Bubbles Observed (Cumulative)		
	E. densa	*E. canadensis*	*C. caroliniana*
1	5	16	7
3	19	29	16
5	33	51	28
7	48	55	45
9	49	59	47

Experiment 2

The student repeated the same set-up from Experiment 1, this time using only *E. densa*. In addition, the student added 20 mL of phenol red, a pH indicator, to the test tube before placing the funnel containing *E. densa* into the water. Over a 9-hour period, the student observed the color of the solution in the test tube and measured its pH. The student's observations are summarized in Table 2.

Table 2		
Hour	Color of Solution	pH of Solution
1	yellow	6.8
3	orange	7.2
5	red	7.6
7	pink	8.0
9	pink	8.0

49. Which factor did the student intentionally vary in Experiment 1?

    A. pH

    B. Number of O_2 bubbles

    C. Species of plant

    D. Amount of light

50. A student predicted that *E. canadensis* would have the slowest rate of photosynthesis. Do the data in Table 1 support that prediction?

    F. No, because *E. canadensis* produced the highest number of O_2 bubbles in the first hour.

    G. No, because *E. canadensis* always produced more O_2 bubbles than the other plant species.

    H. Yes, because *E. canadensis* produced the highest number of O_2 bubbles in the first hour.

    J. Yes, because *E. canadensis* always produced more O_2 bubbles than the other plant species.

51. In an aqueous solution of sodium bicarbonate, the following reactions occur:

    $$NaHCO_3 + H_2O \rightarrow H_2CO_3 + NaOH$$
    $$H_2CO_3 \rightarrow H_2O + CO_2 \text{ (gas)}$$

    Which of the following statements gives the most likely reason sodium bicarbonate was added to the water in the beakers in Experiments 1 and 2?

    A. Sodium bicarbonate was added to provide the carbon dioxide that the aquatic plants needed to carry out photosynthesis.

    B. Sodium bicarbonate was added to increase the alkalinity of the water so that the aquatic plants could carry out photosynthesis.

    C. Sodium bicarbonate was added to speed up the rate at which the aquatic plants carried out the process of photosynthesis.

    D. Sodium bicarbonate was added to maintain the pH balance of the water and create an ideal environment for the aquatic plants to carry out photosynthesis.

52. Consider the statement "In an aqueous solution, CO_2 dissolves in water to form carbonic acid, which decreases the pH of that solution. One way to determine if photosynthesis is taking place is to indirectly measure the uptake of carbon dioxide by measuring the pH changes of the water near aquatic plants." According to the data in Tables 1 and 2, the student would be most likely to agree with which of the following statements?

  F. *E. canadensis* had the fastest rate of photosynthesis; the water in the test tube above *E. canadensis* would have the lowest concentration of hydrogen ions after 5 hours.

  G. *E. canadensis* had the fastest rate of photosynthesis; the water in the test tube above *E. canadensis* would have the greatest concentration of hydrogen ions after 5 hours.

  H. *E. densa* had the slowest rate of photosynthesis; the water in the test tube above *E. densa* would have the greatest concentration of hydrogen ions after 5 hours.

  J. *E. densa* had the slowest rate of photosynthesis; the water in the test tube above *E. densa* would have the lowest concentration of hydrogen ions after 5 hours.

53. According to Table 1, the cumulative number of O_2 bubbles observed for *E. densa* 4 hours after the experiment began was most likely closest to:

  A. 19
  B. 26
  C. 32
  D. 33

54. Which of the following statements about the chemical reaction would most likely explain the results of Experiment 2? After 7 hours, the pH stopped increasing because all of the:

  F. CO_2 had been converted.
  G. O_2 had been converted.
  H. $C_6H_{12}O_6$ had converted.
  J. H_2O had been converted.

55. *Respiration* is a process in which the mitochondria of animals use O_2 and glucose to produce CO_2. Suppose the student modified Experiment 2 by replacing the plant with a small fish after 9 hours. Which of the following would most likely be the pH of that solution after an additional 2 hours?

  A. 7.8
  B. 8.2
  C. 8.4
  D. 8.8

Answers and Explanations

Passage I

1.   B
Difficulty: Low
Category: Interpreting Data
Getting to the Answer: To answer this question, look for a pattern in the data. Moving from left to right as frequency increases, the shaded bars representing the exhaling technique gradually widen, indicating that the range of pitch variation is increasing as frequency increases. Thus, (B) is correct.

Choice A is incorrect because it contradicts the data in the graph; as frequency increases, the pitch variation of Vocalist A increases, not decreases. Choices C and D are incorrect because there is no single trend in pitch variation for the inhaling technique; as frequency increases, the pitch variation initially increases, but then it gradually decreases.

2.   F
Difficulty: Medium
Category: Synthesizing Data
Getting to the Answer: Because this question requires you to predict a new data point, study the tables to identify a trend in the data that you can use as a basis for your prediction. According to the data in Table 1, the frequency of A4 (440 Hz) is higher than the frequency of any note recorded in the study. According to Table 2, Vocalist B's maximum volume using the inhaling technique decreases by 2 dB as the frequency of each note increases. Thus, Vocalist B's maximum volume should be lower than any of the recorded values in Table 2. The lowest recorded volume is 58 dB, so the correct choice must be (F), the only value that is lower than 58 dB. Choices G, H, and J are all incorrect because they indicate a higher maximum volume for A4, which is inconsistent with the trends identified in Tables 1 and 2.

3.   A
Difficulty: Low
Category: Synthesizing Data
Getting to the Answer: This question asks you to select the correct visualization for a column of data reported in Table 1. Looking at the final column in Table 1, the

mean pitch frequencies recorded for Vocalist B using the inhaling technique consistently rise between C4 and G4, increasing from approximately 240 Hz to approximately 370 Hz. This trend matches the visualization in (A), making it correct. Choices B, C, and D are incorrect because they fail to accurately reflect the data reported in Table 1; each misrepresents specific data points as well as the overall data trend.

4.   F
Difficulty: Medium
Category: Interpreting Data
Getting to the Answer: To predict an answer for this question, look for trends in the data tables that reveal a difference between the exhaling and inhaling techniques. In Table 1, for every note sung by the two vocalists, the mean pitch recorded using the inhaling technique is lower than the mean pitch recorded using the exhaling technique. This trend matches (F), making it correct.

Choice H is incorrect because, according to Table 2, the maximum volume of each note is *lower* using the inhaled technique, not higher. Similarly, G and J are incorrect because it contradicts the information in Figure 1: the inhaled technique sometimes produces a larger pitch variation than that of the exhaled technique for notes C4 and D4, but the inhaled technique produces a *smaller* range of pitch variation for the notes E4, F4, and G4.

5.   A
Difficulty: Medium
Category: Using Data
Getting to the Answer: Based on the information in the question stem, you can infer that C3 would be one octave below C4. If the frequency decreases by half when the note is lowered by one octave, then Vocalist A's exhaling mean pitch for C3 should be approximately one half of Vocalist A's exhaling mean pitch for C4. According to Table 1, Vocalist A's exhaling mean pitch for C4 was 259.99 Hz, or approximately 260 Hz. Half of 260 Hz is 130 Hz, making (A) correct.

6. J
Difficulty: Low
Category: Synthesizing Data
Getting to the Answer: Because this question asks you to evaluate a student's hypothesis about mean pitch frequencies, refer to Table 1 to make your prediction. According to Table 1, Vocalist B's mean pitch was consistently closer to the reference pitch for each note when using the exhaled technique. Therefore, the data do not support the student's hypothesis that the inhaling mean pitch would be closer to the reference pitch at higher frequencies. Choice (J) is correct.

Choice F is incorrect because it misstates the data reported in Table 1; the difference between Vocalist B's inhaled mean pitch and the reference pitch was always greater than the difference between Vocalist B's exhaled mean pitch and the reference pitch. Choice G also misrepresents the data by stating that the difference between the inhaled mean pitch and the reference pitch was *only* greater at higher frequencies, when in fact it was *always* greater. In addition, G incorrectly states that the results of the study support the student's hypothesis. Finally, H is incorrect because it states that the difference between the inhaled mean pitch and the reference pitch was always *less* than the difference between the exhaled mean pitch and the reference pitch, when in fact the opposite is true.

7. B
Difficulty: High
Category: Synthesizing Data
Getting to the Answer: According to the chart in the question stem, wavelength consistently decreases between C4 and G4. To determine whether there is a relationship between wavelength and maximum volume for Vocalist A, look for patterns in Table 2. For both the exhaling and inhaling techniques, Vocalist A's maximum volume consistently increased between C4 and G4. Thus, as wavelength decreases, volume increases—or, to put it another way, as wavelength increases, volume decreases. Thus, (B) is correct.

Choice A gets the relationship backward: according to Table 2, as wavelength increases, Vocalist A's maximum volume *decreases* rather than increases. Note that as *frequency* increases Vocalist A's maximum volume increases; however, frequency and wavelength are inversely related: when one goes up, the other goes down. Choices C and D are incorrect because they

misrepresent the data in Table 2. Vocalist A's maximum volume does not decrease and then increase; instead, Vocalist A's maximum volume decreases as wavelength increases, demonstrating a clear relationship between wavelength and maximum volume.

Passage II

8. H
Difficulty: Low
Category: Supporting Hypotheses
Getting to the Answer: Hypothesis 1 states that the Moon formed after a collision between Earth and a Mars-sized protoplanet, with Earth absorbing most of the protoplanet's iron content. Hypothesis 2 suggests that the Earth inherited most of the iron of the two protoplanets that collided to form Earth and the Moon, explaining the large size of Earth's core. Thus, (H) is correct while F and G are incorrect for only being partial answers. Hypothesis 3 notes that the Earth had already formed its core by the time the formation of the Moon began, and that the Moon itself was mainly formed from the loss of lighter elements blasted out of Earth's outermost layers. J is incorrect.

9. B
Difficulty: Medium
Category: Supporting Hypotheses
Getting to the Answer: Hypothesis 1 states that most of the protoplanet's heavier elements, like iron, were deposited on Earth, while the protoplanet's lighter elements escaped into orbit and formed the Moon. Hypothesis 2 states that Earth inherited a greater share of the metallic content from the pair of protoplanets that collided to create Earth and the Moon. Hypothesis 3 states that the numerous asteroids and comets bombarding the Earth blasted lighter elements from its crust and mantle into orbit, forming the metal-poor Moon. As all three hypotheses consider the discrepancy between the amount of metallic elements like iron found on Earth and on the Moon, (B) is correct.

Only Hypothesis 1 states that the heat generated by the Moon's formation is responsible for its lack of volatiles; A is incorrect. Hypothesis 2 states that the Moon and Earth formed simultaneously; C is incorrect. While Hypothesis 3 states that the bombardment of Earth by asteroids and comets created the Moon, Hypotheses 1 and 2 involve only protoplanets. D is incorrect.

Science

10. G
Difficulty: Low
Category: Supporting Hypotheses
Getting to the Answer: Hypothesis 2 states that Earth's large iron core is capable of producing a strong magnetic field. With its smaller core and thus a weaker magnetic field, the Moon is unable to shield its surface from solar wind, which stripped the Moon of its water over time. So, (G) is correct.

Hypothesis 1 attributes the lack of lunar water to the intense heat of the Moon's formation. Hypothesis 3 describes the Moon as forming from the less dense material of Earth's outer layers, as most of Earth's denser elements like iron and nickel formed its core, but does not suggest this resulted in a lack of lunar water. Thus, F, H, and J are incorrect.

11. B
Difficulty: Medium
Category: Supporting Hypotheses
Getting to the Answer: Hypothesis 1 states that the Moon formed as a single body in the aftermath of a glancing collision between Earth and a Mars-sized protoplanet. In contrast, Hypothesis 3 states that the intense bombardment of Earth by asteroids and comets formed multiple small moonlets in Earth's orbit. These eventually merged into a single large moon. The statement in the question stem points to the crust thickness of the Moon's far side as evidence of a sizable moonlet merging with the Moon late in the process of its formation. Thus, (B) is correct.

12. F
Difficulty: High
Category: Applying Core Knowledge
Getting to the Answer: An object's density (p) is equal to its mass (m) divided by its volume (V). Thus, density is $p = \frac{m}{V}$. For this scenario, that formula must be rewritten in terms of mass: $pV = m$.

You can approximate each body's mass because the question stem gives their volumes in comparison to Earth. The volume of Mercury is $0.054 \times V_{Earth}$ and the volume of the Moon is $0.02 \times V_{Earth}$. Thus, the volume of the Moon is less than that of Mercury because 2% is less than 5.4%. Table 1 lists the mean density of

Mercury (5427 kg/m^3) and the Moon (3344 kg/m^3). Because the Moon is both less dense than Mercury and has a lower volume, the Moon would have less mass than Mercury given $pV = m$. Thus, (F) is correct, while H is incorrect. G and J can be eliminated because they state that the Moon has a higher density than Mercury, which Table 1 shows is incorrect.

13. C
Difficulty: Low
Category: Supporting Hypotheses
Getting to the Answer: Hypothesis 1 states that the primordial Earth was struck by a protoplanet, and their combined debris formed the Moon. Hypothesis 3 states that many asteroids and comets impacted the Earth. The orbiting debris coalesced into several moonlets and eventually the Moon. In both hypotheses, the Earth had already formed before it collided with one or more bodies. Thus, (C) is correct. B and D are incorrect because Hypothesis 2 states that the Moon and Earth formed simultaneously in the aftermath of a collision between two large protoplanets.

Passage III

14. H
Difficulty: Low
Category: Experimental Design
Getting to the Answer: Use process of elimination to determine the correct choice because multiple elements remained the same throughout both experiments. Three different particle sizes (300, 500, and 800 μm) were used; particle size was an independent variable, so F is incorrect. Choice G can be eliminated because the data in the table show that the sand piles did not reach the same height each time; sand height was a dependent variable. In both experiments, sand was poured through a funnel onto a flat rubber disc with a diameter of 5 centimeters. Thus, the circumference of the disc was the same in both experiments, making choice (H) correct. Choice J is incorrect because the data in the table indicate that the students measured the angle of repose throughout both experiments; the angle of repose is another dependent variable.

15. C
Difficulty: Low
Category: Using Data
Getting to the Answer: To answer this question, review the data in Table 2 and consider what happens to the average angle of repose as increasing amounts of magnesium stearate are added to each sample. For the 300 μm sample, reading the table from left to right, the average angle of repose measures 36° when 1 g of magnesium stearate is added, 40° when 2 g of magnesium stearate are added, and increases to 44° when 3 g of magnesium stearate are added. This suggests that the angle of repose increases as the amount of glidant increases. The data for the other samples follow this same trend. Thus, (C) is correct.

Choices A and B are incorrect because they misstate the relationship indicated by the data: as more glidant is added, the angle of repose consistently increases. The angle of repose does not increase and then decrease (choice A), nor does it consistently decrease (choice B). Choice D is incorrect because the data indicate that the glidant does have an effect on the angle of repose.

16. G
Difficulty: Low
Category: Interpreting Data
Getting to the Answer: This question asks you to evaluate the claim that angle of repose is positively correlated with grain size. To make a prediction, refer to the results of Experiment 1. For a positive correlation to exist, the average angle of repose must *consistently* increase as grain size increases. However, the data indicate that this is not the case. The average angle of repose increases between the 300 μm sample and the 500 μm sample, but it decreases between the 500 μm sample and the 800 μm sample. Thus, a positive correlation does *not* appear to exist, and (G) is correct.

Choice F is incorrect because the student's conclusion concerned only samples of uniform size; information about the mixed sample would not be relevant. Choice H incorrectly states that the results of Experiment 1 support the student's conclusion, when in fact the opposite is true; while the 300 μm sample did have the lowest average angle of repose, the 800 μm sample did *not* have the highest average angle of repose, so the angle of repose is not positively correlated with grain size. Similarly, J is incorrect because a positive

correlation between pile height and angle of repose does not support a conclusion about the relationship between angle of repose and grain size.

17. B
Difficulty: Medium
Category: Using Data
Getting to the Answer: Because the engineer wants to minimize the height of the sand pile, you'll want to look for the lowest height recorded in the data tables; the circumstances associated with that data point will be the ones that the engineer would most likely want to recreate. The lowest average height recorded in either experiment is 1.6 cm, which occurred in Experiment 1 when the sample grain size was 300 μm and no magnesium stearate had been added. Thus, (B) is correct.

Because the average heights recorded for 300 μm grains *with* magnesium stearate (1.8 cm, 2.0 cm, and 2.6 cm) are greater than the average height *without* magnesium stearate (1.6 cm), the data indicate that adding magnesium stearate would increase, rather than minimize, the height of the sand pile; thus, A is incorrect. Choices C and D are incorrect for similar reasons: in both experiments, the average pile heights of the mixed samples were higher than that of the 300 μm sample in Experiment 1. The engineer wants to minimize pile height, therefore, C and D are incorrect.

18. H
Difficulty: Medium
Category: Using Data
Getting to the Answer: To answer this question, review the description of Experiment 1. The passage states that "a 100-gram sample of a mix of *equal volumes* of all three grain sizes" was used. Because the three grain sizes in the mixture (300, 500, and 800 μm) were used in equal volumes, each grain size contributed approximately one third of the total mass of the mixed sample. Since the total mass of the mixed sample was 100 g, the 800 μm grains had a mass of approximately 33 g, making (H) correct.

Choice F is incorrect because the mixed sample contained some 800 μm particles, so the mass of 800 μm particles in the mixture could not have been 0 g. Similarly, J is incorrect because 100 g is the mass of the entire mixed sample; the mass of the 800 μm particles must have been less than 100 g, since the mixed sample also contained 300 μm and 500 μm particles. Choice G is incorrect because 8 g is a much smaller mass than would be expected given that the 800 μm particles represented one third of the volume of the mixed sample.

19. A
Difficulty: High
Category: Applying Core Knowledge
Getting to the Answer: To predict an answer to this question, review the data tables and analyze the results of the mixed sample compared to the three samples of uniform particle size. In both experiments, the mixed sample produced a greater average pile height and a greater average angle of repose than any of the other samples. Next, activate your core science knowledge and consider *why* this result would be observed. If the mixed sample had more surface interaction and greater friction, the sand particles would cling to each other better and slide down less, resulting in a higher sand pile and a greater angle of repose. Thus, (A) is correct.

Choice B is incorrect because *reducing* surface interaction and friction would have the opposite effect; the sand particles would slide down more easily, leading to a smaller angle of repose. Choices C and D are incorrect because they confuse the dependent and independent variables; pile height is a *result* of surface interaction and friction, rather than the other way around.

20. G
Difficulty: High
Category: Interpreting Data
Getting to the Answer: This question asks you to determine whether the results of Experiment 1 support a particular hypothesis about the maximum angle of repose for 500 μm sand particles. To predict an answer, refer back to Table 1, which reports an average angle measurement of 38° for the 500 μm sample. Initially, this may appear to support the student's hypothesis, but remember that 38° represents only the *average* measurement recorded during Experiment 1. It is certainly possible that some of the 500 μm samples might have produced an angle of repose that was greater than 38°. For example, if the angles of repose for the 500 μm samples had been 37°, 38°, and 39°, then the *average* angle of repose would have been 38°, but the *maximum* recorded angle of repose would have been 39°. Because the reported data do not indicate

whether angles greater than 38° were observed for the 500 μm sample, the data do not support (or refute) the student's hypothesis. Thus, (G) is correct.

Choice F is incorrect because it refers to the average angle of repose for the mixed sample, but the student's hypothesis is about 500 μm sand particles only. Similarly, H is incorrect because it refers to the results of Experiment 2, when magnesium stearate was added to the 500 μm sample; the question asked only whether the results of Experiment 1 would support the student's claim, so this information is irrelevant. Finally, J is incorrect because it mistakenly claims that an *average* angle of repose of 38° supports a hypothesis that the *maximum* angle of repose is 38°.

Passage IV

21. C
Difficulty: Low
Category: Interpreting Data
Getting to the Answer: This is a straightforward "data grab" question, so the most important thing is to avoid careless mistakes. In Figure 1, the units for CH_4 are on the right-hand edge, not on the left (that's CO_2 and N_2O). Check the legend carefully: CH_4 is the dotted line. Look up 800 years on the x-axis, go up to the dotted line, then look to the right. Don't worry about determining a precise value: at 800 years, the dotted line is definitely above 600 and below 800 ppb. The only choice within that range is the correct answer, (C).

22. J
Difficulty: Low
Category: Interpreting Data
Getting to the Answer: To find the value of a variable in a stacked line graph, such as Figure 2, subtract the lower boundary of the interval from the upper boundary at a given point. For example, the value of Agriculture in 2016 is roughly $5,500 - 5,000 = 500$ units.

Since the question asks for the largest contributor to CO_2 emissions, look for the variable whose boundaries are consistently the farthest apart. Electricity spans two intervals during most years, whereas no other variable consistently exceeds one and a half intervals. Thus, the answer is Electricity, choice (J).

23. A
Difficulty: Low
Category: Using Data
Getting to the Answer: First, consider what happened to the N_2O concentration over the last 1,000 years. According to Figure 1, the N_2O concentration 1,000 years ago was around 260 ppb. Today, the concentration is around 320 ppb. (Make sure you look at the N_2O axis, on the left, both times!) This means that the concentration of N_2O hasn't even doubled over the time span.

If the concentration of ozone follows the same trend, then the 100 ppb value from 1,000 years ago will have increased but not have doubled, so the concentration today should remain less than 200 ppb. The only choice that offers a concentration below 200 ppb is the correct choice, (A).

24. H
Difficulty: Medium
Category: Using Data
Getting to the Answer: According to the passage, Table 1 shows the difference between the average global temperature in one year and the average global temperature over the past 1,000 years. For example, the present-day global temperature is 0.5°C above the previous 1,000-year average, while the global temperature 800 years ago was 0.18°C below that average.

It follows logically, then, that the year in which the global temperature *matched* the previous 1,000-year average would have a value of 0°C in Table 1—that is, no difference between that year's average and the overall 1,000-year average. While there is no year with a value of 0, the value at 400 years is just above 0 and the value at 600 years is just below 0. Thus, the matching year must have been somewhere between 400 and 600 years ago, and the answer is (H).

25. B
Difficulty: Medium
Category: Using Data
Getting to the Answer: In Figure 3, the span of the Industry slice is usually around one and a half intervals. Because each interval is 1,000 units, multiply 1.5 intervals by 1,000 units by the 10 years specified in the question stem: $1.5 \times 1,000 \times 10 = 15,000$ units, so choice (B) is correct.

26. G
Difficulty: High
Category: Synthesizing Data
Getting to the Answer: Look up the concentrations of CH_4, CO_2, and N_2O for 1,000 years ago in Figure 1. Because CH_4 is measured on its own on the right side of the graph, it's the easiest to read, so start there.

The concentration of CH_4 is a little less than 700 ppb. Eliminate H and J. The next easiest concentration to read is N_2O, but don't forget to look to the left side of the graph for the measurement. It's approximately 260 ppb. The remaining graphs are both close to 260 ppb, so now look at CO_2. Note that CO_2 concentration is again on the left axis and is measured in 10^3 ppb. The reading is around 280, so the concentration is $280 \times 1,000$, or 280,000. Choice F shows CO_2 at only 280, not 280,000; eliminate. Choice (G) is correct. It shows the CO_2 reading at less than 3×10^5, or less than 300,000.

27. A
Difficulty: Medium
Category: Using Data
Getting to the Answer: The equation given in the question indicates that frequency and wavelength are inversely related. (Notice that because frequency and wavelength multiply to *c*, if you increase one of them, you must decrease the other to maintain the same product.) According to the passage, the energy is re-emitted as infrared radiation, which has a lower frequency—and therefore longer wavelength—than the ultraviolet light that makes up the solar radiation that strikes the Earth. Thus, the energy absorbed has a shorter wavelength than the energy re-emitted, and the answer is (A).

Passage V

28. J
Difficulty: Medium
Category: Using Data
Getting to the Answer: Look for a relationship between total, ocular, and objective magnification in Table 2. The ocular magnification is always $10\times$, while the total magnification is always 10 times the objective magnification. It follows logically, then, that:

Total Magnification = Ocular Magnification $\times$ Objective Magnification

Science

The question asks for the maximum total magnification, so the correct answer must be the choice whose ocular and objective magnification values multiply to the largest product. That's (J), because $40 \times 4 = 160$. Choices F and G multiply to only 40, while choice H multiplies to only 100.

29. D
Difficulty: Low
Category: Interpreting Data
Getting to the Answer: This is a straightforward "data grab" question complicated by the fact that Table 1 has a bunch of different variables. Work carefully to find the correct cell in the table. The wall with 30% relative humidity, a meandering path, 16.8 lpm air infiltration rate, and no insulation is Wall 3. The question tells you to look in the "cavity" column (rather than the "lab" or "surrounding" columns). The column that matches all of the features is the sixth column from the left, and the value for Wall 3 in that column is 43.5, choice (D).

30. G
Difficulty: Medium
Category: Using Data
Getting to the Answer: Look for a relationship between spore count and relative humidity in Table 1. Regardless of the other factors, all of the spore counts were greater at 90% humidity than at 30% humidity. This means that spore count and humidity have a direct relationship—that is, as humidity increases, so does spore count. As a result, the spore count at 60% humidity should be greater than the count at 30% humidity but less than the count at 90% humidity. The only choice that reflects this conclusion is (G). Watch out for H, which makes a correct assertion about the number of spores but incorrectly claims that spore count and humidity are inversely related.

31. C
Difficulty: Low
Category: Experimental Design
Getting to the Answer: Consider the choices one by one and eliminate the choices that changed throughout the study. Table 1 lists two different air infiltration rates, an independent variable, so A is incorrect. Spore count was what was being measured, and Table 1 also shows 40 different spore counts, so B is incorrect. Finally, Table 1 has a "yes" and a "no" for the presence of insulation, so D is incorrect. The correct answer is (C), as the

passage states that each of the cassettes was exposed for the same duration: two minutes.

32. G
Difficulty: Medium
Category: Using Data
Getting to the Answer: Look up the "surrounding" spore count for Wall 7 at a low (6.9 lpm) infiltration rate: 45. Set up a proportion. According to Table 2, a $4\times$ objective lens has a field of view of 5 mm, while a $20\times$ objective lens has a field of view of 1 mm. Thus, the $20\times$ objective lens has a field of view one-fifth the size of the $4\times$ field of view. The expected number of spores is therefore:

$$\frac{1}{5} = \frac{x}{45}$$
$$45 = 5x$$
$$9 = x$$

The answer is (G).

33. A
Difficulty: Medium
Category: Interpreting Data
Getting to the Answer: Look for a relationship between spore count and insulation. In Table 1, Walls 1 and 2 are the same except that Wall 1 doesn't have insulation and Wall 2 does. Notice that Wall 2 has fewer spores in the "cavity" column. Similarly, Walls 3 and 4 are the same except that only Wall 4 has insulation, and Wall 4 has fewer spores. Thus, there are indeed fewer spores when the wall has insulation, so the statement is correct, and C and D are incorrect. B flips the data in the table, therefore, the correct answer is (A).

34. F
Difficulty: Hard
Category: Using Data
Getting to the Answer: According to Table 2, the field of view at $1000\times$ total magnification is 0.18 mm. Divide this by the number of spores to approximate the diameter of one spore:

$$\frac{0.18 \text{ mm}}{60 \text{ spores}} \approx 0.003 \text{ mm per spore}$$

There are 1,000 μm in 1 mm, so the answer is $0.003 \times 1,000 = 3\,\mu$m, choice (F).

Passage VI

35. D
Difficulty: Low
Category: Interpreting Data
Getting to the Answer: In Figure 3, the highest dashed line is the one that represents the sensor exposed to 80 ppm NO_2. Look along the horizontal axis to find the appropriate time; note that the units are in seconds, not minutes. There's no grid line for 1 minute, but 61 seconds is close enough, especially because the data has leveled off at that point. At 61 seconds, the line is just above 0.8, which means that (D) is correct.

When looking for data in a line graph with multiple lines, make sure you look at the correct line. Choices A and C represent the voltage at 1 minute for the 20 ppm and 40 ppm sensors, respectively.

36. F
Difficulty: Low
Category: Interpreting Data
Getting to the Answer: The question directs you to Figure 1, so examine the data for the four concentrations of NO_2 at 700 nm in that graph. At 700 nm, 80 ppm has the highest absorption, followed by, in decreasing order, 40 ppm, 20 ppm, and 0 ppm. Thus, as concentration decreases, so does absorption. Choice (F) is correct.

37. C
Difficulty: Medium
Category: Experimental Design
Getting to the Answer: The experiment involved using a spectrometer to measure absorption levels. For these readings to be as accurate as possible, the researchers would need to measure the levels in the films before the experiment to get a baseline against which they could measure the effects of exposing the film to the gas. Thus, (C) is correct.

Measuring the film before the experiment started would not provide another variable; it would just provide more data on the same variable measured during the experiment, so A is incorrect. There's no indication that these scans would either confirm that the spectrometer was working or decontaminate it, so B and D are incorrect.

38. H
Difficulty: Medium
Category: Using Data
Getting to the Answer: In order to make an inference about an NO_2 concentration that wasn't tested, examine the trends in the data that do exist. Data on the metal film sensor was recorded in Figure 2, so look there. Between 650 and 850 nm, the maximum absorption peak for each sample was in the same place: approximately 725 nm. So, 60 ppm NO_2 would also have its maximum absorption peak there. Furthermore, between 650 and 850 nm, absorption increased as NO_2 concentration increased, so a line in the graph representing 60 ppm NO_2 would most likely be between the 40 ppm and 80 ppm lines. At 725 nm, the 40 ppm line is at approximately 0.5 a.u. and the 80 ppm line is at approximately 0.57 a.u., so the 40 ppm line would be between those two values. Thus, (H) is correct.

39. B
Difficulty: Medium
Category: Applying Core Knowledge
Getting to the Answer: There's no need to actually know the boiling or freezing points of NO_2 to answer this question; all you need is basic knowledge about the states of matter. A substance below its freezing point is solid, a substance above its boiling point is a gas, and a substance in between these two points is liquid. The question indicates that the researchers wanted to ensure that the NO_2 was a gas, so they must have known that room temperature is higher than the boiling point of NO_2, so (B) is correct. Note that this does mean room temperature is also higher than the freezing point of NO_2, but D is incorrect because raising the temperature of a substance above its freezing point doesn't guarantee that it will be a gas as the substance could also be a liquid.

40. F
Difficulty: Medium
Category: Synthesizing Data
Getting to the Answer: First, compare the absorption levels for 40 ppm NO_2 with and without metal. In Figure 1, which shows the results for the experiment with metal-free film, the absorption level at 700 nm is at approximately 0.35 a.u. In Figure 2, which shows the results for the experiment with metal film, the absorption level is at approximately 0.45 a.u. Because the absorption level increased with the use of the metal film, eliminate H and J, and examine the conductivity to choose between the remaining two choices.

According to Figure 3, conductivity with the metal-free film after 41 seconds was approximately 0.35 V. According to Figure 4, after 41 seconds, conductivity with the metal-free film sensor varied, but all values are below 0.2 V. Thus, the use of the metal film led to a decrease in conductivity and (F) is correct.

41. A
Difficulty: High
Category: Synthesizing Data
Getting to the Answer: Based on the new information in this table, blue light has a wavelength between 450 and 495 nm; thus, any answer to the question must provide evidence from those wavelengths. Since B and D provide evidence from wavelengths between 650 and 695 nm (which would be red light), they can be eliminated.

Now, look at Figures 1 and 2, which contain the results of Experiment 1. In each graph, for the 20, 40, and 80 ppm samples, absorption decreases as concentration increases. However, in both graphs, the lowest absorption is shown by the 0 ppm sample, which does not follow this trend. Because there is no directly proportional relationship—an increase in one variable as the other variable increases—between absorption and concentration, (A) is correct.

Passage VII

42. G
Difficulty: Medium
Category: Synthesizing Data
Getting to the Answer: Student 2 claims that conductivity is highest when pH is low and temperature is high. Because the question asks for the solution with the *lowest* conductivity, look for a solution whose pH is high and whose temperature is low. The higher of the two pH measures in the table is 10, so eliminate F and H. The lower of the two temperatures in the table is 25°C; therefore, of the solutions listed, Solution 10 has the lowest conductivity. Choice (G) is correct.

43. C
Difficulty: Medium
Category: Supporting Hypotheses
Getting to the Answer: Brine being 26% salt indicates that brine has a higher concentration of salt than tap water. Additionally, the question states the viscosity of brine is four times that of tap water. So, brine has a higher salt concentration and a higher viscosity than tap water.

Because the answer choices do not list Student 1, start with Student 2. Student 2 does not discuss the effect of salt concentration nor viscosity on conductivity, so eliminate D. Student 3 states that increasing the concentration of a solution and the viscosity decreases conductivity. Hence, Student 3 would agree that the conductivity of brine is less than that of tap water. Eliminate B. Student 4, like Student 3, states that increasing the viscosity decreases conductivity. Therefore, Student 4 would also agree that brine has a lower conductivity. Choice (C) is correct.

44. J
Difficulty: High
Category: Synthesizing Data
Getting to the Answer: Solutions 9, 11, and 13 all have a concentration of 0.8 mol/L and a pH of 6 but are at different temperatures. Solution 9 is at 25°C, Solution 11 is at 60°C, and Solution 13 is at 40°C. According to Student 4, solution temperature and conductivity are inversely related. Thus, the solution with the highest temperature would have the lowest conductivity. The solutions ranked from *least* conductive to *most* conductive is Solution 11 (60°C), Solution 13 (40°C), and Solution 9 (25°C). Choice (J) is correct.

45. A
Difficulty: Medium
Category: Supporting Hypotheses
Getting to the Answer: According to the question, salt water, which has a higher salt concentration than freshwater, has a higher conductivity than freshwater at 25°C. Look for a viewpoint that states conductivity is directly proportional to salt concentration. Student 1 states increasing salt concentration increases conductivity; this is consistent with the statement, so eliminate B. Student 3 states increasing concentration decreases conductivity, which is contrary to the statement; eliminate C. Student 4 does not discuss the effect of concentration on conductivity. Thus, (A) is correct.

46. J
Difficulty: Medium
Category: Supporting Hypotheses
Getting to the Answer: Student 3 states that increasing concentration and increasing viscosity decrease conductivity. Compare the two solutions for each answer choice to determine which statement matches Student 3's viewpoint.

Solution 2 has a lower concentration and viscosity than Solution 10, so according to Student 3, Solution 2 will have a higher conductivity than Solution 10. Eliminate F. Similarly, Solution 3 has a lower concentration and viscosity than Solution 7, so Solution 3 will have a higher conductivity than Solution 7. Eliminate G. Solution 5 has a higher concentration and viscosity than Solution 1. Thus, Solution 5 will have a lower conductivity. Eliminate H. Choice (J) is correct. Because Solution 8 has a lower concentration and viscosity than Solution 12, it will have a higher conductivity.

47. A
Difficulty: High
Category: Supporting Hypotheses
Getting to the Answer: The claim states that increasing the concentration of hydrogen ions increases the conductivity. Look for a viewpoint that would agree with this claim. Student 2 states decreasing the pH increases the number of H^+ ions and thus increases conductivity. Therefore, Student 2 would agree with the claim. Eliminate B and D. Student 3 mentions higher concentrations of solute (sodium chloride) but not of hydrogen ions; eliminate C. Choice (A) is correct.

48. H
Difficulty: High
Category: Applying Core Knowledge
Getting to the Answer: Kinetic energy is directly proportional to temperature. Hence, increasing the temperature will increase the kinetic energy. Eliminate F and G. Additionally, since the boiling point of water is 100°C, increasing the temperature of Solution 4 to 100°C will cause the molecules to transition from liquid to gaseous state. Thus, molecules in the gaseous state have more kinetic energy than those in liquid state. Choice (H) is correct.

Passage VIII

49. C
Difficulty: Low
Category: Experimental Design
Getting to the Answer: The "factor that the student intentionally varied" is another way of asking for the independent variable. Use process of elimination to determine the correct answer. The pH was measured in Experiment 2, not intentionally varied in Experiment 1,

and therefore, A is incorrect. The number of O_2 bubbles was measured in Experiment 1, making it the dependent—not independent—variable, so B can also be eliminated. In Experiment 1, the student selected 3 different species of plants, making it the independent variable. Thus, answer choice (C) is correct. Choice D is incorrect because the amount of light was neither varied nor measured in Experiment 1; this variable would be a constant.

50. G
Difficulty: Medium
Category: Synthesizing Data
Getting to the Answer: The rate of photosynthesis was observed indirectly by the presence of O_2 bubbles over a nine-hour period of time. Because O_2 is a product of the reaction, the plate with the slowest rate of photosynthesis will show the fewest number of bubbles. According to Table 1, *E. canadensis* produced the most O_2 bubbles at each time interval meaning it would have the highest rate of photosynthesis, not the slowest. Therefore, the data in Table 1 do not support the student's prediction. The correct answer is (G).

Choice F is incorrect because *E. canadensis* produced the highest number of bubbles consistently, not just during the first hour. Choice H and J are incorrect because the data do not support the student's prediction; the highest number of bubbles means that photosynthesis is happening at the fastest, not slowest, rate.

51. A
Difficulty: High
Category: Experimental Design
Getting to the Answer: According to the reaction equations provided in the question stem, sodium bicarbonate ($NaHCO_3$) reacts with water to form H_2CO_3, which then breaks down to produce water (H_2O) and carbon dioxide (CO_2). In the reaction equation for photosynthesis, provided at the beginning of the passage, the left side of the equation shows that both water and carbon dioxide are needed for photosynthesis to occur. The aquatic plants in Experiments 1 and 2 are submerged in beakers of water, but they still need a source of carbon dioxide to carry out photosynthesis. Since the sodium bicarbonate ultimately produces carbon dioxide, (A) is correct.

52. F
Difficulty: High
Category: Synthesizing Data
Getting to the Answer: First, notice that each answer choice deals with two topics: rate of photosynthesis and concentration of hydrogen ions. You can use Table 1 to compare the plants' rates of photosynthesis and narrow down the answer choices. The reaction equation for photosynthesis, provided at the beginning of the passage, shows that O_2 is produced as photosynthesis occurs. Therefore, the plant that produces the most O_2 bubbles in 5 hours will have the fastest rate of photosynthesis, and the plant that produces the fewest O_2 bubbles in 5 hours will have the slowest rate of photosynthesis. Using the hour 5 row in Table 1, you can see that *E. canadensis* produced the most O_2 bubbles (51), *E. densa* produced a medium number of bubbles (33), and *C. caroliniana* produced the fewest bubbles (28). Thus, *E. canadensis* had the fastest rate, and *C. caroliniana*, not *E. densa*, had the slowest rate, so you can eliminate H and J.

Next, you can use the photosynthesis reaction equation and the statement in the question stem to determine the relationship between photosynthesis and hydrogen ion concentration. As photosynthesis occurs within an aquatic plant, the plant takes up carbon dioxide (CO_2), thus lowering the amount of CO_2 in the water outside the plant. Because CO_2 dissolved in water forms carbonic acid and decreases the pH, having less CO_2 in the water outside the plant will increase the pH in the water, as evidenced in Table 2. The pH scale is inversely related to the concentration of hydrogen ions, so a higher pH means a more basic solution with a lower concentration of hydrogen ions. The plant with the fastest rate of photosynthesis (*E. canadensis*) will have the least CO_2 left in the water in the test tube, meaning it will have the highest pH and the lowest concentration of hydrogen ions. Therefore, (F) is the correct answer.

53. B
Difficulty: High
Category: Using Data
Getting to the Answer: Table 1 has cumulative numbers of bubbles for 3 hours and 5 hours, but not for 4 hours, so you'll have to interpolate that number based on the trend. At hour 3, 19 bubbles were

observed; by hour 5, 33 bubbles had been observed. Therefore, at hour 4, the answer must be between 19 and 33, eliminating A and D. To differentiate between choices B and C, consider the relative rate of change. Between 1 and 3 hours, the cumulative number of bubbles rose by 14, which is the same change as the one from 3 to 5 hours. Because this seems to be a linear rate, you can estimate the number of bubbles observed rose by 7 each hour. Thus, the number of bubbles observed by hour 4 would be 7 higher than the value for hour 3. Because there were 19 bubbles observed at hour 3, $19 + 7 = 26$. The answer is (B).

54. F
Difficulty: Medium
Category: Using Data
Getting to the Answer: The increasing pH level must have something to do with photosynthesis, because that's the only change happening in the test tube. The pH level would continue to rise as long as photosynthesis continued; thus, photosynthesis would have stopped when the pH stopped increasing after 7 hours. Because it stopped, the most likely explanation would be that one of the inputs to the reaction disappeared. The plant is submerged in water, so there would still be H_2O. Thus, it's most likely that it was due to lack of CO_2, and (F) is correct.

55. A
Difficulty: Medium
Category: Using Data
Getting to the Answer: According to the question stem, respiration results in the production of CO_2. Because the removal of CO_2 via photosynthesis increased the pH of the solution, returning CO_2 back to the solution should decrease the pH of the solution. Without more information, it's impossible to know how much the pH will be lowered. However, you should note that, according to Table 2, the pH was 8.0 after 9 hours. Therefore, you can infer that after 2 hours of fish respiration, the pH will be lower than 8.0, and only one choice is lower than 8, so (A) is correct.

PART 6

COUNTDOWN TO TEST DAY

CHAPTER 27

COUNTDOWN TO TEST DAY

The Week Before the Test

- Focus your additional practice on the question types and/or subject areas in which you usually score highest. Now is the time to sharpen your best skills, not cram new information.
- Make sure you are registered for the test. Remember, Kaplan cannot register you. If you missed the registration deadlines, you can request waitlist status on the test maker's website, **www.act.org.**
- Confirm the location of your test site. Never been there before? Make a practice run to make sure you know exactly how long it will take to get from your home to your test site. Build in extra time in case you hit traffic or construction on the morning of the test.
- Get a great night's sleep the two days before the test.

The Day Before the Test

- Review the methods and strategies you learned in this book.
- Put new batteries in your calculator.
- Pack your backpack or bag for test day with the following items:
  - Photo ID
  - Registration slip or printout
  - Directions to your test site location
  - Five or more sharpened no. 2 pencils (no mechanical pencils)
  - Pencil sharpener
  - Eraser
  - Calculator
  - Extra batteries
  - Non-prohibited timepiece
  - Tissues
  - Prepackaged snacks, like granola bars
  - Bottled water, juice, or sports drink
  - Sweatshirt, sweater, or jacket

The Night Before the Test

- No studying!
- Do something relaxing that will take your mind off the test, such as watching a movie or playing video games with friends.
- Set your alarm to wake up early enough so that you won't feel rushed.
- Go to bed early, but not too much earlier than you usually do. You want to fall asleep quickly, not spend hours tossing and turning.

The Morning of the Test

- Dress comfortably and in layers. You need to be prepared for any temperature.
- Eat a filling breakfast, but don't stray far from your usual routine. If you normally aren't a breakfast eater, don't eat a huge meal, but make sure you have something substantial.
- Read something over breakfast. You need to warm up your brain so you don't go into the test cold. Read a few pages of a newspaper, magazine, or novel.
- Get to your test site early. There is likely to be some confusion about where to go and how to sign in, so allow yourself plenty of time, even if you are taking the test at your own school.
- Leave your cell phone at home or in your car's glovebox. Many test sites do not allow them in the building.
- While you're waiting to sign in or be seated, read more of what you read over breakfast to stay in reading mode.

During the Test

- Be calm and confident. You're ready for this!
- Remember that while the ACT is an almost three-hour marathon (or $3\frac{1}{2}$ hours if you opt to do the Writing Test), it is also a series of shorter sections. Focus on the section you're working on at that moment; don't think about previous or upcoming sections.
- Use the methods and strategies you have learned in this book as often as you can. Allow yourself to fall into the good habits you built during your practice.
- Don't linger too long on any one question. Mark it and come back to it later.
- Can't figure out an answer? Try to eliminate some choices and take a strategic guess. Remember, there is no penalty for an incorrect answer, so even if you can't eliminate any choices, you should take a guess.
- There will be plenty of questions you CAN answer, so spend your time on those first!
- Maintain good posture throughout the test. It will help you stay alert.
- If you find yourself losing concentration, getting frustrated, or stressing about the time, stop for 30 seconds. Close your eyes, put your pencil down, take a few deep breaths, and relax your shoulders. You'll be much more productive after taking a few moments to relax.
- Use your breaks effectively. During the five-minute breaks, go to the restroom, eat your snacks, and get your energy up for the next section.

After the Test

- Congratulate yourself! Then, reward yourself by doing something fun. You've earned it!
- If you got sick during the test or if something else happened that might have negatively affected your score, request a score cancellation form from your test proctor. Visit the test maker's website for more information.
- Your scores will be available online approximately three to four weeks after your test.

PART 7

PRACTICE TESTS

How to Score Your Practice Test

The ACT is scored differently from most tests that you take at school. Your ACT score on a test section is not reported as the total number of questions you answered correctly, nor does it directly represent the percentage of questions you answered correctly. Instead, the test makers add up all of your correct answers in a section to get what's called your raw score. They then use a conversion chart, or scale, that matches up a particular raw score with what's called a scaled score. The scaled score is the number that gets reported as your score for that ACT subject test.

You gain one point for every question you answer correctly. You lose no points for answering a question incorrectly OR for leaving a question blank. This means you should ALWAYS answer EVERY question on the ACT—even if you have to guess.

You can use the instructions below to score your practice test. Most importantly, be sure to carefully review the question explanations to get the most out of your practice. Taking practice tests and analyzing your performance is one of the best ways to prepare for the ACT. Your online resources (**kaptest.com/login**) include additional practice tests in the Simulate Test Day section. When you score these online tests, Kaplan provides you with a detailed score report, which can help your review.

Score Tracker

1. **Figure out your raw score for each subject test.** Refer to the answer key to determine how many questions you answered correctly. Enter the results below:

RAW SCORES

English: [   ]

Math: [   ]

Reading: [   ]

Science: [   ]

2. **Convert your raw scores to scaled scores for each subject test.** Locate your raw score for each subject test in the following table. The score in the outside columns indicates your estimated scaled score if this were an actual ACT. Enter your scaled scores in the boxes that follow the table.

SCALED SCORE	RAW SCORES				SCALED SCORE
	Test 1 English	Test 2 Mathematics	Test 3 Reading	Test 4 Science	
36	74–75	59–60	40	40	36
35	71–73	57–58	38-39	–	35
34	70	55–56	37	39	34
33	69	54	36	38	33
32	68	53	34–35	–	32
31	67	51–52	33	37	31
30	66	49–50	32	36	30
29	64–65	47–48	31	–	29
28	63	45–46	30	35	28
27	61–62	42–44	–	34	27
26	59–60	39–41	29	32–33	26
25	56–58	37–38	28	31	25
24	53–55	34–36	26–27	29–30	24
23	50–52	32–33	25	26–28	23
22	47–49	31	23–24	24–25	22
21	44–46	29–30	22	22–23	21
20	41–43	27–28	20–21	20–21	20
19	39–40	25–26	19	18–19	19
18	37–38	22–24	18	17	18
17	35–36	19–21	16–17	15–16	17
16	32–34	16–18	15	14	16
15	29–31	13–15	14	13	15
14	26–28	10–12	12–13	11–12	14
13	24–25	8–9	11	10	13
12	22–23	7	10	9	12
11	19–21	5–6	8–9	8	11
10	16–18	4	7	7	10
9	13–15	–	6	6	9
8	11–12	3	5	5	8
7	9–10	–	–	4	7
6	7–8	2	4	3	6
5	6	–	3	–	5
4	4–5	1	2	2	4
3	3	–	–	1	3
2	2	–	1	–	2
1	0–1	0	0	0	1

SCALED SCORES

English: ☐

Math: ☐

Reading: ☐

Science: ☐

3. **Calculate your estimated composite score.** Simply add together your scaled scores for each subject test and divide by four.

ACT Practice Test 1
ANSWER SHEET

ENGLISH TEST

1. (A)(B)(C)(D)	11. (A)(B)(C)(D)	21. (A)(B)(C)(D)	31. (A)(B)(C)(D)	41. (A)(B)(C)(D)	51. (A)(B)(C)(D)	61. (A)(B)(C)(D)	71. (A)(B)(C)(D)
2. (F)(G)(H)(J)	12. (F)(G)(H)(J)	22. (F)(G)(H)(J)	32. (F)(G)(H)(J)	42. (F)(G)(H)(J)	52. (F)(G)(H)(J)	62. (F)(G)(H)(J)	72. (F)(G)(H)(J)
3. (A)(B)(C)(D)	13. (A)(B)(C)(D)	23. (A)(B)(C)(D)	33. (A)(B)(C)(D)	43. (A)(B)(C)(D)	53. (A)(B)(C)(D)	63. (A)(B)(C)(D)	73. (A)(B)(C)(D)
4. (F)(G)(H)(J)	14. (F)(G)(H)(J)	24. (F)(G)(H)(J)	34. (F)(G)(H)(J)	44. (F)(G)(H)(J)	54. (F)(G)(H)(J)	64. (F)(G)(H)(J)	74. (F)(G)(H)(J)
5. (A)(B)(C)(D)	15. (A)(B)(C)(D)	25. (A)(B)(C)(D)	35. (A)(B)(C)(D)	45. (A)(B)(C)(D)	55. (A)(B)(C)(D)	65. (A)(B)(C)(D)	75. (A)(B)(C)(D)
6. (F)(G)(H)(J)	16. (F)(G)(H)(J)	26. (F)(G)(H)(J)	36. (F)(G)(H)(J)	46. (F)(G)(H)(J)	56. (F)(G)(H)(J)	66. (F)(G)(H)(J)	
7. (A)(B)(C)(D)	17. (A)(B)(C)(D)	27. (A)(B)(C)(D)	37. (A)(B)(C)(D)	47. (A)(B)(C)(D)	57. (A)(B)(C)(D)	67. (A)(B)(C)(D)	
8. (F)(G)(H)(J)	18. (F)(G)(H)(J)	28. (F)(G)(H)(J)	38. (F)(G)(H)(J)	48. (F)(G)(H)(J)	58. (F)(G)(H)(J)	68. (F)(G)(H)(J)	
9. (A)(B)(C)(D)	19. (A)(B)(C)(D)	29. (A)(B)(C)(D)	39. (A)(B)(C)(D)	49. (A)(B)(C)(D)	59. (A)(B)(C)(D)	69. (A)(B)(C)(D)	
10. (F)(G)(H)(J)	20. (F)(G)(H)(J)	30. (F)(G)(H)(J)	40. (F)(G)(H)(J)	50. (F)(G)(H)(J)	60. (F)(G)(H)(J)	70. (F)(G)(H)(J)	

MATHEMATICS TEST

1. (A)(B)(C)(D)(E)	11. (A)(B)(C)(D)(E)	21. (A)(B)(C)(D)(E)	31. (A)(B)(C)(D)(E)	41. (A)(B)(C)(D)(E)	51. (A)(B)(C)(D)(E)
2. (F)(G)(H)(J)(K)	12. (F)(G)(H)(J)(K)	22. (F)(G)(H)(J)(K)	32. (F)(G)(H)(J)(K)	42. (F)(G)(H)(J)(K)	52. (F)(G)(H)(J)(K)
3. (A)(B)(C)(D)(E)	13. (A)(B)(C)(D)(E)	23. (A)(B)(C)(D)(E)	33. (A)(B)(C)(D)(E)	43. (A)(B)(C)(D)(E)	53. (A)(B)(C)(D)(E)
4. (F)(G)(H)(J)(K)	14. (F)(G)(H)(J)(K)	24. (F)(G)(H)(J)(K)	34. (F)(G)(H)(J)(K)	44. (F)(G)(H)(J)(K)	54. (F)(G)(H)(J)(K)
5. (A)(B)(C)(D)(E)	15. (A)(B)(C)(D)(E)	25. (A)(B)(C)(D)(E)	35. (A)(B)(C)(D)(E)	45. (A)(B)(C)(D)(E)	55. (A)(B)(C)(D)(E)
6. (F)(G)(H)(J)(K)	16. (F)(G)(H)(J)(K)	26. (F)(G)(H)(J)(K)	36. (F)(G)(H)(J)(K)	46. (F)(G)(H)(J)(K)	56. (F)(G)(H)(J)(K)
7. (A)(B)(C)(D)(E)	17. (A)(B)(C)(D)(E)	27. (A)(B)(C)(D)(E)	37. (A)(B)(C)(D)(E)	47. (A)(B)(C)(D)(E)	57. (A)(B)(C)(D)(E)
8. (F)(G)(H)(J)(K)	18. (F)(G)(H)(J)(K)	28. (F)(G)(H)(J)(K)	38. (F)(G)(H)(J)(K)	48. (F)(G)(H)(J)(K)	58. (F)(G)(H)(J)(K)
9. (A)(B)(C)(D)(E)	19. (A)(B)(C)(D)(E)	29. (A)(B)(C)(D)(E)	39. (A)(B)(C)(D)(E)	49. (A)(B)(C)(D)(E)	59. (A)(B)(C)(D)(E)
10. (F)(G)(H)(J)(K)	20. (F)(G)(H)(J)(K)	30. (F)(G)(H)(J)(K)	40. (F)(G)(H)(J)(K)	50. (F)(G)(H)(J)(K)	60. (F)(G)(H)(J)(K)

READING TEST

1. (A)(B)(C)(D)	6. (F)(G)(H)(J)	11. (A)(B)(C)(D)	16. (F)(G)(H)(J)	21. (A)(B)(C)(D)	26. (F)(G)(H)(J)	31. (A)(B)(C)(D)	36. (F)(G)(H)(J)
2. (F)(G)(H)(J)	7. (A)(B)(C)(D)	12. (F)(G)(H)(J)	17. (A)(B)(C)(D)	22. (F)(G)(H)(J)	27. (A)(B)(C)(D)	32. (F)(G)(H)(J)	37. (A)(B)(C)(D)
3. (A)(B)(C)(D)	8. (F)(G)(H)(J)	13. (A)(B)(C)(D)	18. (F)(G)(H)(J)	23. (A)(B)(C)(D)	28. (F)(G)(H)(J)	33. (A)(B)(C)(D)	38. (F)(G)(H)(J)
4. (F)(G)(H)(J)	9. (A)(B)(C)(D)	14. (F)(G)(H)(J)	19. (A)(B)(C)(D)	24. (F)(G)(H)(J)	29. (A)(B)(C)(D)	34. (F)(G)(H)(J)	39. (A)(B)(C)(D)
5. (A)(B)(C)(D)	10. (F)(G)(H)(J)	15. (A)(B)(C)(D)	20. (F)(G)(H)(J)	25. (A)(B)(C)(D)	30. (F)(G)(H)(J)	35. (A)(B)(C)(D)	40. (F)(G)(H)(J)

SCIENCE TEST

1. (A)(B)(C)(D)	6. (F)(G)(H)(J)	11. (A)(B)(C)(D)	16. (F)(G)(H)(J)	21. (A)(B)(C)(D)	26. (F)(G)(H)(J)	31. (A)(B)(C)(D)	36. (F)(G)(H)(J)
2. (F)(G)(H)(J)	7. (A)(B)(C)(D)	12. (F)(G)(H)(J)	17. (A)(B)(C)(D)	22. (F)(G)(H)(J)	27. (A)(B)(C)(D)	32. (F)(G)(H)(J)	37. (A)(B)(C)(D)
3. (A)(B)(C)(D)	8. (F)(G)(H)(J)	13. (A)(B)(C)(D)	18. (F)(G)(H)(J)	23. (A)(B)(C)(D)	28. (F)(G)(H)(J)	33. (A)(B)(C)(D)	38. (F)(G)(H)(J)
4. (F)(G)(H)(J)	9. (A)(B)(C)(D)	14. (F)(G)(H)(J)	19. (A)(B)(C)(D)	24. (F)(G)(H)(J)	29. (A)(B)(C)(D)	34. (F)(G)(H)(J)	39. (A)(B)(C)(D)
5. (A)(B)(C)(D)	10. (F)(G)(H)(J)	15. (A)(B)(C)(D)	20. (F)(G)(H)(J)	25. (A)(B)(C)(D)	30. (F)(G)(H)(J)	35. (A)(B)(C)(D)	40. (F)(G)(H)(J)

English Test

45 Minutes—75 Questions

Directions: Each passage has certain words and phrases that are underlined and numbered. The questions in the right column will provide alternatives for the underlined segments. Most questions require you to choose the answer that makes the sentence grammatically correct, concise, and relevant. If the word or phrase in the passage is already the correct, concise, and relevant choice, select NO CHANGE. Some questions will ask a question about the underlined segment. When a question is presented, choose the best answer.

Some questions will ask about part or all of the passage. These questions do not refer to a specific underlined segment. Instead, these questions will accompany a number in a box.

For each question, choose your answer and fill in the corresponding bubble on your answer sheet. Read the passage once before you answer the questions. You will often need to read several sentences beyond the underlined portion to be able to choose the correct answer. Be sure to read enough to answer each question.

Passage I

My Old-Fashioned Father

My father, though he is only in his early 50s, is stuck in his old-fashioned <u>ways. He has a</u> general mistrust of
₁
any innovation or technology that he can't immediately

1. A. NO CHANGE
    B. ways he has a
    C. ways having a
    D. ways, and still has a

grasp and he always <u>tells us, that</u> if something isn't
₂
broken, then you shouldn't fix it.

2. F. NO CHANGE
    G. tells us, that,
    H. tells us that,
    J. tells us that

He <u>has run</u> a small grocery store in town, and
₃
if you were to look at a snapshot of his back office
taken when he opened the store in 1975, you would

3. A. NO CHANGE
    B. was running
    C. runs
    D. ran

see that not much has changed since. He is the most
4

disorganized person I know and still uses a pencil

4. F. NO CHANGE
    G. not be likely to see very much that has changed since.
    H. be able to see right away that not very much has changed since.
    J. not change very much.

and paper to keep track of his inventory. His small office
5

is about to burst with all the various documents, notes,

5. Assuming that all are true, which of the following additions to the word "inventory" is most relevant in context?

    A. inventory of canned and dry goods.
    B. inventory, refusing to consider a more current method.
    C. inventory, which he writes down by hand.
    D. inventory of goods on the shelves and in the storeroom.

and receipts he has accumulated over the years, his filing
6

cabinets have long since been filled up. The centerpiece
6

of all the clutter is his ancient typewriter, which isn't

even electric. In the past few years, Father's search

for replacement typewriter ribbons has become an

increasingly difficult task, because they are no longer

being produced. He is perpetually tracking down the

few remaining places that still have these antiquated

ribbons in their dusty inventories. When people ask him

why he doesn't upgrade his equipment, he tells them,

"Electric typewriters won't work in a blackout. All I

need is a candle and some paper, and I'm fine." Little

does Father know, however, is that the "upgrade" people
7

are speaking of is not to an electric typewriter but to a

computer.

6. F. NO CHANGE
    G. years; his filing cabinets
    H. years, and besides that, his filing cabinets
    J. years and since his filing cabinets

7. A. NO CHANGE
    B. know, besides, that
    C. know, however, that
    D. know, beyond that,

CONTINUED ➡

[1] Hoping to bring Father out of the Dark Ages, <u>my sister, and I</u> bought him a brand-new computer
8
for his fiftieth birthday. [2] We offered to help him to transfer all of his records onto it and to teach him

how to use it. [3] <u>Eagerly</u>, we told him about all the
9
new spreadsheet programs that would help simplify

his recordkeeping and organize his <u>accounts; and</u>
10
emphasized the advantage of not having to completely retype any document when he found a typo. [4] Rather than offering us a look of joy for the life-changing gift we had presented him, however, he again brought up the blackout scenario. [5] To Father, this is a concrete argument, although our town hasn't had a blackout in five years, and that one only lasted an hour or two. [11] [12]

My father's state-of-the-art computer now serves as a very expensive bulletin board for the hundreds of

8. F. NO CHANGE
   G. me and my sister
   H. my sister and I
   J. my sister and I,

9. A. NO CHANGE
   B. On the other hand,
   C. In addition
   D. Rather,

10. F. NO CHANGE
    G. accounts and
    H. accounts and,
    J. accounts, we

11. The purpose of including this fact about the town's blackout history is to:
    A. make the father appear delusional.
    B. suggest that the father's reasons not to update his technology are ill-founded.
    C. add an interesting detail to set the scene.
    D. foreshadow an event that occurs later in the story.

12. The author wants to include the following statement in this paragraph:

    We expected it to save him a lot of time and effort.

    The most logical placement for this sentence would be:
    F. before Sentence 1.
    G. after Sentence 1.
    H. after Sentence 4.
    J. after Sentence 5.

CONTINUED

adhesive notes he uses to keep himself organized. <u>Sooner
than later,</u> we fully expect it will completely disappear
13
under the mounting files and papers in the back office.

<u>In the depths of that disorganized office, the computer
will join the cell phone my mom gave him a few years
ago.</u> Interestingly enough, every once in a while, that
14
completely forgotten cell phone will ring from under the

heavy clutter of the past. ⑮

13. A. NO CHANGE

    B. Sooner rather than later,

    C. Sooner or later,

    D. As soon as later,

14. F. NO CHANGE

    G. Deep in the disorganization of that office's, the computer will join the cell phone my mom gave him a few years back.

    H. In the disorganized depths of the office, the computer will soon be joined by the cell phone my mom gave him a few years ago.

    J. The computer will join the cell phone my mom gave him a few years back in the disorganized depths of that office.

15. Which of the following would provide the most appropriate conclusion for the passage?

    A. It's hard to say what else might be lost in there.

    B. We tell my father it's a reminder that he can't hide from the future forever.

    C. We have no idea who might be calling.

    D. Maybe one day I will try to find it and answer it.

CONTINUED ➤

Passage II

Breaking Baseball's Color Barrier

A quick perusal of any modern major league baseball team will reveal a roster of players of multiple ethnicities <u>from the farthest</u> reaches of the globe. Second
16
only to soccer, baseball has evolved into a global sport

and <u>a symbol among races for equality.</u>
17
Its diversity today presents a stark contrast to the state of the sport just sixty years ago. As late as the 1940s, there existed an unwritten rule in baseball that prevented all but white players <u>to participate</u> in
18
the major leagues. This rule was known as the "color barrier" or "color line." The color line in baseball actually predated the birth of the major leagues. Prior to the official formation of any league of professional baseball teams, there existed an organization of amateur baseball clubs known as the National Association of Baseball Players, <u>which was the precursor to today's</u>
19
<u>National League.</u> On December 11, 1868, the governing
19
body of this association had unanimously adopted a

16. F. NO CHANGE
    G. from the most far
    H. from the most farthest
    J. from farther

17. A. NO CHANGE
    B. among races for equality a symbol.
    C. a symbol for equality among races.
    D. for equality among races a symbol.

18. F. NO CHANGE
    G. to be able to participate
    H. from participating
    J. to participation

19. Is the underlined portion relevant here?

    A. Yes, because it helps familiarize the reader with the range of baseball associations that once existed.
    B. Yes, because it helps clarify the development the author traces.
    C. No, because the names of the organizations are not important.
    D. No, because it is inconsistent with the style of the essay to provide specific historical data.

CONTINUED

Practice Tests

rule that effectively barred any team that had, any
"colored persons" on its roster. However, when baseball

started to organize into leagues by professional teams
in the early 1880s, the National Association of Baseball
Players' decree no longer had any weight, especially in

the newly formed American Association. For a brief
period in those early years, a few African Americans
played side by side with white players on major league
diamonds.

[1] Most baseball historians believe that the first
African American to play in the major leagues was

Moses "Fleet" Walker. [2] Walker was a catcher for the
Toledo Blue Stockings of the American Association
between 1884 and 1889. [3] During that time, a few

other African Americans, including Walker's brother

20. F. NO CHANGE
G. had any, "colored persons"
H. had any "colored persons"
J. had any "colored persons,"

21. A. NO CHANGE
B. of
C. from
D. about

22. The writer is considering deleting the underlined portion. Should the writer make this deletion?

F. Yes, because the information is not relevant to the topic of the paragraph.
G. Yes, because the information contradicts the first sentence of the paragraph.
H. No, because the information shows that white players did not object to integration.
J. No, because the statement provides a smooth transition to the specific information about early African American players in the next paragraph.

23. A. NO CHANGE
B. Walker, being a catcher
C. Walker, a catcher
D. Walker who was a catcher

24. F. NO CHANGE
G. that included
H. who would include
J. including among them

CONTINUED

Weldy, <u>would be joining him</u> on the Blue Stockings.
25

[4] Unfortunately, this respite from segregation did not last for very long; as Jim Crow laws took their hold on the nation, many of the most popular white ballplayers started to refuse to take the field with their African American teammates. [5] By the 1890s, the color barrier had fully returned to baseball, where it would endure for more than half a century. [26]

Jackie Robinson would become the first African American to cross the color line <u>at the time when</u> 27 he debuted for the Brooklyn Dodgers in 1947. For Robinson's landmark achievements on and off the

diamond, he will <u>forever be recognized as</u> a hero of the 28

25. A. NO CHANGE
    B. joined him
    C. were to join him
    D. will join him

26. Upon reviewing this paragraph, the author discovers that he has neglected to include the following information:

    A handful of African Americans played for other teams as well.

    This sentence would be most logically placed after:

    F. Sentence 1.
    G. Sentence 2.
    H. Sentence 3.
    J. Sentence 4.

27. A. NO CHANGE
    B. when
    C. while
    D. when the time came that

28. F. NO CHANGE
    G. one day be recognized
    H. forever recognize
    J. be admired by a lot of people for being

CONTINUED

civil rights movement and a sports icon. His response to
                                                    29
the prejudices of American society during the 1940s and

1950s opened the door for the multi-racial and multi-

national face of modern baseball, and fans of the sport

worldwide will be forever in his debt.

29. Which choice best maintains the essay's positive tone while emphasizing the unique role that Robinson played?

A. NO CHANGE

B. The path that he blazed through

C. The stance he took against

D. His collaboration in the face of

Question 30 asks about the preceding passage as a whole.

30. Suppose the writer had been assigned to develop a brief essay on the history of baseball. Would this essay successfully fulfill that goal?

F. Yes, because it covers events in baseball over a period of more than a century.

G. Yes, because it mentions key figures in baseball history.

H. No, because people played baseball before 1868.

J. No, because the focus of this essay is on one particular aspect of baseball history.

CONTINUED

Passage III

The Bear Mountain Bridge

When the gleaming Bear Mountain Bridge officially opened to traffic on Thanksgiving Day in <u>1924</u>, it
31
was known as the Harriman Bridge, after Edward H. Harriman, a wealthy philanthropist and patriarch of the family most influential in the bridge's construction.

Before <u>they were</u> constructed, there were no bridges
32
spanning the Hudson River south of Albany. By the early 1920s, the ferry services used to transport people back and forth across the river had become woefully inadequate. In February of 1922, in an effort to alleviate some of the burden on the ferries and create a permanent link across the Hudson, the New York State Legislature <u>had authorized</u> a group of private investors,
33
led by Mary Harriman, to build a bridge. The group, known as the Bear Mountain Hudson Bridge Company (BMHBC),

was allotted thirty years to <u>build, construct, and</u>
34
<u>maintain</u> the structure, at which time the span would be
34
handed over to New York State.

The BMHBC invested almost $4,500,000 into the suspension bridge and hired the world-renowned design team <u>of Howard Baird and George Hodge</u>
35

31. A. NO CHANGE
    B. 1924; it
    C. 1924. It
    D. 1924 and it

32. F. NO CHANGE
    G. the bridges were
    H. it was
    J. it were

33. A. NO CHANGE
    B. authorized
    C. was authorized
    D. would authorize

34. F. NO CHANGE
    G. build and construct and maintain
    H. construct and maintain
    J. construct, and maintain

35. A. NO CHANGE
    B. of Howard Baird, and George Hodge
    C. of Howard Baird and, George Hodge
    D. of, Howard Baird and George Hodge

CONTINUED

as architects. [36] Baird and Hodge enlisted the help of John A. Roebling and Sons,

who were instrumental in the steel work of the
37
Brooklyn Bridge and would later work on the Golden Gate and George Washington Bridges.

Amazingly, the bridge took only twenty months and eleven days to complete, and not one life was lost. [38]

It was a technological marvel and would stand as a model for the suspension bridges of the future. At the time of the Harriman Bridge's completion, it was, at 2,257 feet, the longest single-span steel suspension

bridge in the world. Therefore, the two main cables used
39
in the suspension were 18 inches in diameter, and each contained 7,752 individual steel wires wrapped in 37 thick strands. If completely unraveled, the single wires

in both cables would be 7,377 miles longer. The bridge
40
links Bear Mountain on the western bank of the Hudson

36. The purpose of including the cost of the bridge is to:

   F. provide a piece of information critical to the point of the essay.

   G. insert a necessary transition between the second and third paragraphs.

   H. add a detail contributing to the reader's understanding of the magnitude of the project.

   J. provide an explanation of how the group raised money to invest in the bridge.

37. A. NO CHANGE

   B. who was

   C. a company

   D. a company that had been

38. If the writer were to delete the preceding sentence, the essay would primarily lose:

   F. information about how long the project had been expected to take.

   G. a warning about the dangers of large-scale construction projects.

   H. crucial information about the duration of the project.

   J. a necessary transition between Paragraphs 3 and 4.

39. A. NO CHANGE

   B. Nonetheless, the

   C. At the same time, the

   D. The

40. F. NO CHANGE

   G. long.

   H. in total length.

   J. lengthy.

CONTINUED

to Anthony's Nose on the eastern side, it lies so precisely
on an east-west plane that one can check a compass by
it. It carries Routes 6 and 202 across the Hudson and is
the point of river crossing for the Appalachian Trail.

    In an attempt to recoup some of its investment after
the bridge opened, the BMHBC charged an exorbitant
toll of eighty cents per crossing. Even with the high
toll, however, it operated at a loss for thirteen of its first
sixteen years. Finally it was acquired, more than ten
years earlier than planned, by the New York State Bridge
Authority. The bridge was renamed the Bear Mountain
Bridge. Moreover, the Bear Mountain Bridge sees
more than six million vehicles cross its concrete decks
each year.

41. A. NO CHANGE
    B. side, lies
    C. side, lying
    D. side; and it lies

42. F. NO CHANGE
    G. opened the BMHBC charged
    H. opened: the BMHBC charged
    J. opened; the BMHBC charged

43. A. NO CHANGE
    B. In contrast,
    C. Besides that fact,
    D. Today,

44. F. NO CHANGE
    G. over
    H. even more than
    J. a higher amount than

> Question 45 asks about the preceding passage
> as a whole.

45. Suppose the author had been assigned to write
a brief history of bridge building in the United
States. Would this essay successfully fulfill that
requirement?

    A. Yes, because it provides information on the
entire process from the initial funding through
the opening of the bridge.

    B. Yes, because Bear Mountain Bridge is histori-
cally significant.

    C. No, because it focuses on only one bridge.

    D. No, because the essay is primarily concerned
with the financial aspects of building and
maintaining the bridge.

CONTINUED

Passage IV

The Dream of the American West

As the sun <u>was slowly rising</u> over the Atlantic Ocean
46
and painted New York Harbor a spectacular fiery orange,
I started my old Toyota's engine. At this early hour, there
was still some semblance of the night's tranquility left on
the city sidewalks, but I knew that, as the minutes ticked
by, <u>the streets would flood with humanity.</u>
47

I smiled <u>with</u> the thought that soon all the wonderful
48
chaos of New York City would be disappearing behind

me as I <u>embarked on my trip to the other side of</u> the
49
country.

<u>As the morning sun climbed into the sky,</u>
50

46. F. NO CHANGE
    G. rising slowly
    H. rose slowly
    J. continued to rise

47. The author wants to contrast the statement about
    the quiet of the night streets with a related detail
    about the daytime activity. Assuming that all of the
    choices are true, which of the following best accom-
    plishes that goal?

    A. NO CHANGE
    B. some people might appear.
    C. everything would be different.
    D. the tranquility would be unbroken.

48. F. NO CHANGE
    G. along with
    H. at
    J. all because of

49. A. NO CHANGE
    B. embarked on this journey across
    C. traveled to the other side of
    D. traveled across

50. Which of the following alternatives to the under-
    lined portion would NOT be acceptable?

    F. At sunrise,
    G. Watching the morning sun climb into the sky,
    H. The morning sun climbed into the sky,
    J. As the sun rose,

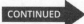

I shuddered with excitement to think that my final stop
would be in California, where the sun itself ends its
journey across America. Like the sun, however, I still
had quite a journey before me.

    I had been planning this road trip across the United
States for as long as I could remember. In my life, I had
been fortunate enough to see some of the most beautiful
countries in the world. However, it had always bothered

me that although I'd stood in the shadow of the Eiffel
Tower, marveled in the desert heat at the Pyramids
of Giza, I'd never seen any of the wonders of my own
country, except those found in my hometown of New
York City. All of that was about to change.

    As I left the city, the tall buildings began to give way
to smaller ones, then to transform into the quaint rows
of houses that clustered the crowded suburbs. Trees and
grass, then the yellow-green of cornfields and the golden

wash of wheat were slowly replacing the familiar mazes
of cement and steel. My world no longer stretched

51. The writer is considering revising this sentence by deleting the underlined portion. If she did so, the paragraph would primarily lose:

  A. information about the reasons for the writer's trip.

  B. information about the writer's destination.

  C. a description of the writer's planned route.

  D. a comparison between the sunrise in New York and the sunset in California.

52. F. NO CHANGE

  G. Eiffel Tower and had marveled in the desert heat at the Pyramids of Giza,

  H. Eiffel Tower and marveled in the desert heat at the Pyramids of Giza

  J. Eiffel Tower, and had marveled, in the desert heat, at the Pyramids of Giza

53. Given that all are true, which of the following provides the most effective transition between the third paragraph and the description of the Midwest in the fourth paragraph?

  A. NO CHANGE

  B. In fact, there were changes on the horizon almost immediately.

  C. My excitement hadn't diminished.

  D. I realized that people who lived in other areas might feel the same way about visiting New York.

54. Assuming that all are true, which of the following provides information most relevant to the main focus of the paragraph?

  F. NO CHANGE

  G. appearing before me.

  H. racing past my window.

  J. becoming monotonous.

Practice Tests

vertically toward <u>the sky, it now spread</u> horizontally
                                    55
toward eternity. For two days, I pushed through the
wind-whipped farmlands of Mid-America, hypnotized
by the beauty of the undulating yet unbroken lines. At
night, the breeze from my car would stir the wheat fields
to dance beneath the moon, and the silos hid in the
shadows, quietly imposing their <u>simply</u> serenity upon
                                      56
everything.

Then, as the <u>night's shadows</u> gave way to light,
                     57
there seemed to be a great force rising to meet the

<u>sun as it made its reappearance.</u>
              58

<u>Still,</u> I had no idea
   59

what I was looking at. Then, there was no <u>mistaking it.</u>
                                                 60
The unbroken lines of Mid-America had given way to
the jagged and majestic heights of the Rockies and the
gateway to the American West.

55. A. NO CHANGE
    B. the sky but it now spread
    C. the sky; it now spread
    D. the sky spreading

56. F. NO CHANGE
    G. simple
    H. simplest
    J. simpler

57. A. NO CHANGE
    B. nights shadows
    C. shadows from the night
    D. night shadow

58. F. NO CHANGE
    G. sun as it reappeared.
    H. reappearing sun.
    J. sun as it was also rising.

59. A. NO CHANGE
    B. Even so,
    C. At first,
    D. Eventually,

60. F. NO CHANGE
    G. mistake to be made.
    H. chance to mistake it.
    J. having made a mistake.

CONTINUED

Passage V

Traveling at the Speed of Sound

The term "supersonic" refers to anything that travels faster than the speed of sound. When the last of the supersonic Concorde passenger planes made its final trip across the Atlantic in <u>November of 2003, an interesting</u> chapter in history was finally

61
closed. The fleet of supersonic Concorde SSTs, or

"Supersonic Transports," <u>they were</u> jointly operated

62
by Air France and British Airways, had been making the intercontinental trip across the Atlantic for almost thirty years. These amazing machines cruised at Mach 2, more than twice the speed of sound. They flew <u>to a height</u> almost twice that of standard passenger

63
airplanes. The Concorde routinely made the trip from New York to London in less than three hours and was much more expensive than normal transatlantic

flights. <u>Furthermore,</u> the majority of the passengers

64
who traveled on the Concorde were celebrities or the extremely wealthy, it also attracted ordinary people who simply wanted to know how it felt to travel faster than the speed of sound. Some would save money for years just to gain that knowledge.

What is the speed of sound? Many people are surprised to learn that there is no fixed answer to this question. The speed <u>that</u> sound travels through a

65

61. A. NO CHANGE
 B. November, of 2003 an interesting
 C. November of 2003 an interesting
 D. November of 2003; an interesting

62. F. NO CHANGE
 G. those were
 H. which were
 J. which being

63. A. NO CHANGE
 B. at an altitude
 C. toward an altitude
 D. very high

64. F. NO CHANGE
 G. Despite
 H. Though
 J. Along with

65. A. NO CHANGE
 B. to which
 C. at which
 D. where

CONTINUED

given medium depends on a number of factors. To understand the speed of sound, we must first understand what a "sound" really is. 66

The standard dictionary definition of sound is "a vibration or disturbance transmitted, like waves through water, through a material medium such as a gas." Our

ears are able to pick up those sound waves and convert
            67
them into what we hear. This means that the speed at

which sound travels through gas directly depends on
                                 68
what gas it is traveling through, and the temperature and
            68
pressure of the gas. When discussing aircraft breaking
 68
the speed of sound, that gas medium, of course, is air.

As air temperature and pressure decrease with altitude,
                                          69
so does the speed of sound. An airplane flying at the speed of sound at sea level is traveling roughly at 761 mph;

however when that same plane climbs to 20,000 feet, the
 70
speed of sound is only about 707 mph. This is why the Concorde's cruising altitude was so much higher than

66. The purpose of this paragraph, as it relates to the surrounding paragraphs, is primarily to:

 F. provide an example of the main idea before continuing discussion of that idea.

 G. transition from a discussion of certain aircraft to the science behind them.

 H. present a counterargument to the main thesis before refuting that counterargument.

 J. transition from the general topic of aircraft to a story about specific airplanes.

67. Which of the following alternatives to the underlined portion would be the LEAST acceptable?

 A. change

 B. translate

 C. alter

 D. transform

68. F. NO CHANGE

 G. depends directly on the type, temperature, and pressure of the gas it is traveling through.

 H. directly depends on what gas it is, and also on the temperature and pressure of that gas.

 J. depends directly on the type, temperature, and pressure of the gas.

69. A. NO CHANGE

 B. with height,

 C. with a drop in altitude,

 D. at higher altitudes,

70. F. NO CHANGE

 G. however,

 H. and so,

 J. even so

CONTINUED →

that of a regular passenger aircraft; <u>planes can reach</u>
                                              71
<u>supersonic speeds more easily at higher altitudes.</u>
                        71

In the years since the Concorde <u>has been</u>
                                      72
decommissioned, only fighter pilots and astronauts

have been able to experience the sensation of breaking

"the sound barrier." <u>But that is all about to change very</u>
                                              73
<u>soon</u>. Newer and faster supersonic passenger planes are
 73
being developed that will be technologically superior

to the Concorde and much cheaper to operate. <u>Now,</u>
                                                  74
supersonic passenger travel will be available not only to

the rich and famous, <u>but also be for</u> the masses, so they,
                            75
too, can experience life at supersonic speeds.

71. Given that all are true, which of the following provides the most logical conclusion for this sentence?

   A. NO CHANGE
   B. they're much faster.
   C. they use much more fuel than regular aircraft.
   D. they're rarely visible because they fly above the cloud cover.

72. F. NO CHANGE
    G. came to be
    H. was
    J. had been

73. A. NO CHANGE
    B. Soon, however, that is about to change.
    C. Soon, however, that will change.
    D. That is about to change soon.

74. F. NO CHANGE
    G. Nearby,
    H. Soon,
    J. Upcoming,

75. A. NO CHANGE
    B. but also be available to
    C. but also to
    D. but for

IF YOU FINISH BEFORE TIME IS CALLED, YOU MAY CHECK YOUR WORK ON THIS SECTION ONLY. DO NOT TURN TO ANY OTHER SECTION IN THE TEST. **STOP**

Practice Tests

K 795

Mathematics Test

60 Minutes—60 Questions

Directions: Choose the correct solution to each question and fill in the corresponding bubble on your answer sheet.

Do not continue to spend time on questions if you get stuck. Solve as many questions as you can before returning to any if time permits.

You may use a calculator on this test for any question you choose. However, some questions may be better solved without a calculator.

Note: Unless otherwise stated, you can assume:

1. Figures are NOT necessarily drawn to scale.
2. Geometric figures are two dimensional.
3. The term *line* indicates a straight line.
4. The term *average* indicates arithmetic mean.

1. The eighth-grade girls' basketball team played a total of 13 games this season. If they scored a total of 364 points, what was the mean (average) score per game?

   A.   13
   B.   16
   C.   20
   D.   28
   E.   32

2. When $4\frac{3}{7}$ is written as an improper fraction in simplest form, what is the numerator of the fraction?

   F.   12
   G.   21
   H.   27
   J.   28
   K.   31

3. If $4x + 18 = 38$, then $x = ?$

   A.   3
   B.   4.5
   C.   5
   D.   12
   E.   20

4. John weighs 1.5 times as much as Ellen. If John weighs 144 pounds, how many pounds does Ellen weigh?

   F.   84
   G.   96
   H.   104
   J.   164
   K.   216

CONTINUED

5. What positive number, when divided by its reciprocal, gives a result of $\frac{9}{16}$?

   A. $\frac{3}{16}$

   B. $\frac{3}{4}$

   C. $\frac{4}{3}$

   D. $\frac{16}{9}$

   E. $\frac{16}{3}$

6. If $\sqrt[3]{x} = \frac{1}{4}$, then $x = ?$

   F. $\frac{1}{256}$

   G. $\frac{1}{64}$

   H. $\frac{1}{12}$

   J. $\frac{1}{\sqrt[3]{4}}$

   K.   64

7. If $x^2 + 14 = 63$, then x could be which of the following?

   A.   4.5

   B.   7

   C.   14

   D.   24.5

   E.   49

8. Two vectors are given by $\mathbf{v}_1 = \langle 7, -3 \rangle$ and $\mathbf{v}_2 = \langle a, b \rangle$. If $\mathbf{v}_1 + \mathbf{v}_2 = \langle 5, 5 \rangle$, then what is the value of a?

   F. -2

   G.   2

   H.   5

   J.   8

   K.   12

9. Based on past graduations, a university estimates that 6% of the graduating class will not attend the graduation ceremony. Based on this estimate, if there are 1,250 graduates, how many will not attend the ceremony?

   A.   75

   B.   140

   C.   220

   D.   350

   E.   425

10. $5.2^3 + 6.8^2 = ?$

   F.   46.24

   G.   94.872

   H.   120.534

   J.   140.608

   K.   186.848

11. Lexi uses her debit card to make a purchase totaling $40. When she records the debit in her checkbook register, she accidentally adds $40 to her balance rather than subtracting it, which results in an inaccurate total. Because of her error, Lexi's checkbook register shows:

   A. $80 less than it should.

   B. $40 less than it should.

   C. $20 more than it should.

   D. $40 more than it should.

   E. $80 more than it should.

12. $3^3 \div 9 + (6^2 - 12) \div 4 = ?$

   F.   3

   G.   6.75

   H.   9

   J.   12

   K.   15

CONTINUED

13. If bananas cost $0.24 and oranges cost $0.38, what is the total cost of x bananas and y oranges?

    A. $(x + y)(\$0.24 + \$0.38)$

    B. $\$0.24x + \$0.38y$

    C. $\$0.62(x + y)$

    D. $\dfrac{\$0.24}{x} + \dfrac{\$0.38}{y}$

    E. $\$0.38x + \$0.24y$

14. In the following figure, all of the small triangles are the same size. What percent of the entire figure is shaded?

    F.   8

    G.   24

    H. $33\frac{1}{3}$

    J.   50

    K. $66\frac{2}{3}$

15. In a high school senior class, the ratio of girls to boys is 5:3. If there are a total of 168 students in the senior class, how many girls are there?

    A.   63

    B. 100

    C. 105

    D. 147

    E. 152

16. On her first three geometry tests, Sarah scored an 89, a 93, and an 84. If there are four tests total and Sarah needs at least a 90 average for the four, what is the lowest score she can receive on the final test?

    F.   86

    G.   90

    H.   92

    J.   94

    K.   96

17. What is the solution set of $3x - 11 \geq 22$?

    A. $x \geq -11$

    B. $x < -3$

    C. $x \geq 0$

    D. $x > 3$

    E. $x \geq 11$

18. Dillon is going to randomly pick a domino from a pile of dominoes that are all facing downward. Of the dominoes in the pile, 48 have an even number of dots on them. He randomly picks a single domino. If the probability that he picks a domino with an even number of dots is $\frac{3}{4}$, how many dominoes are in the pile?

    F.   36

    G.   48

    H.   56

    J.   64

    K.   72

19. What is the value of $3x - 8y$ when $x = 4$ and $y = -\frac{1}{2}$?

    A. -4

    B.   8

    C.   12

    D.   16

    E.   28

CONTINUED

20. Court reporters type every word spoken during trials and hearings so that there is a written record of what transpired. Suppose a certain court reporter can type 3.75 words per second, and a trial transcript contains 25 pages with an average of 675 words per page. If this court reporter typed the transcript at his typical rate, how long was he actively typing?

    F. 1 hour, 15 minutes

    G. 1 hour, 40 minutes

    H. 2 hours, 10 minutes

    J. 2 hours, 30 minutes

    K. 3 hours

21. In the following figure, lines m and l are parallel and the measure of $\angle a$ is $68°$. What is the measure of $\angle f$?

    A. 22°

    B. 68°

    C. 80°

    D. 112°

    E. 292°

22. On a map, the scale is the ratio of the distance shown on the map to the actual distance. A geography teacher has a map on her wall with a scale of 1 inch:100 miles. She uses the school's copier to shrink the large wall map down to the size of a piece of paper to hand out to each of her students. To do this, she makes the map $\frac{1}{4}$ of its original size. Suppose on the students' maps, the distance between two cities is 2.5 inches. How many actual miles apart are those cities?

    F. 25

    G. 250

    H. 800

    J. 1,000

    K. 1,200

23. A piece of letter-sized paper is $8\frac{1}{2}$ inches wide and 11 inches long. Suppose you want to cut strips of paper that are $\frac{5}{8}$ of an inch wide and 11 inches long. What is the maximum number of strips of paper you could make from 1 piece of letter-sized paper?

    A. 5

    B. 6

    C. 12

    D. 13

    E. 14

24. In the following figure, $\overline{MN}$ and $\overline{PQ}$ are parallel. Point A lies on $\overline{MN}$, and points B and C lie on $\overline{PQ}$. If $AB = AC$ and $\angle MAB$ has a measure of $55°$, what is the measure of $\angle ACB$?

   F. $35°$

   G. $55°$

   H. $65°$

   J. $80°$

   K. $125°$

25. What is the slope of the line that passes through the points $(-10,0)$ and $(0,-6)$?

   A. $-\dfrac{5}{3}$

   B. $-\dfrac{3}{5}$

   C. $\dfrac{3}{5}$

   D. $\dfrac{5}{3}$

   E. 0

26. For all x, $(x+4)(x-4) + (2x+2)(x-2) = ?$

   F. $x^2 - 2x - 20$

   G. $3x^2 - 12$

   H. $3x^2 - 2x - 20$

   J. $3x^2 + 2x - 20$

   K. $3x^2 + 2x + 20$

27. What is the length of a line segment with endpoints $(3,-6)$ and $(-2,6)$?

   A.   1

   B.   5

   C.   10

   D.   13

   E.   15

28. If 60 percent of h is 80, what is 30 percent of h?

   F.   30

   G.   40

   H.   50

   J.   60

   K.   70

29. Set A contains 7 consecutive even integers. If the average of Set A's integers is 46, which of the following is the smallest integer of Set A?

   A.   36

   B.   38

   C.   40

   D.   42

   E.   44

30. Which of the following statements describes the total of the first n terms of the arithmetic sequence below?

$$1, 3, 5, 7, 9, \ldots$$

   F.   The total is always equal to 25 regardless of n.

   G.   The total is always equal to $2n$.

   H.   The total is always equal to $3n$.

   J.   The total is always equal to n^2.

   K.   There is no consistent pattern for the total.

CONTINUED ➡

31. Which of the following matrices is equal to the matrix product $\begin{bmatrix} -2 & 0 \\ 1 & -3 \end{bmatrix} \cdot \begin{bmatrix} 2 \\ 2 \end{bmatrix}$?

    A. $\begin{bmatrix} -4 & 0 \\ 2 & -6 \end{bmatrix}$

    B. $\begin{bmatrix} -4 & 2 \\ 2 & -6 \end{bmatrix}$

    C. $\begin{bmatrix} 0 & 0 \\ 0 & 0 \end{bmatrix}$

    D. $\begin{bmatrix} -4 \\ -4 \end{bmatrix}$

    E. $\begin{bmatrix} -4 \\ -6 \end{bmatrix}$

32. A playground is $(x + 7)$ units long and $(x + 3)$ units wide. If a square of side length x is sectioned off from the playground to make a sandpit, which of the following could be the remaining area of the playground?

    F. $x^2 + 10x + 21$

    G. $10x + 21$

    H. $2x + 10$

    J. $21x$

    K. 21

33. Assume m and n are nonzero integers such that $m > 0$ and $n < 0$. Which of the following *must* be negative?

    A. $-n^m$

    B. $-mn$

    C. m^n

    D. $-n - m$

    E. $n - m$

34. The point $(-3,-2)$ is the midpoint of the line segment in the standard (x,y) coordinate plane with endpoints $(1,9)$ and (m,n). Which of the following is (m,n)?

    F. $(-7,-13)$

    G. $(-2,7)$

    H. $(-1,3.5)$

    J. $(2,5.5)$

    K. $(5,20)$

35. If $f(x) = 16x^2 - 20x$, what is the value of $f(3)$?

    A. -12

    B. 36

    C. 84

    D. 144

    E. 372

36. What is the length of side $\overline{AC}$ in triangle ABC graphed on the following coordinate plane?

    F. 3

    G. 4

    H. 5

    J. 6

    K. 7

37. If $f(x) = \frac{1}{3}x + 13$ and $g(x) = 3x^2 + 6x + 12$, which expression represents $f(g(x))$?

    A. $x^2 + 12x + 4$

    B. $\frac{x^2}{3} + 2x + 194$

    C. $x^2 + 2x + 17$

    D. $x^2 + 2x + 25$

    E. $x^2 + 2x + 54$

38. What is the equation of a line that is perpendicular to the line $y = \frac{2}{3}x + 5$ and contains the point $(4, -3)$?

    F. $y = \frac{2}{3}x + 4$

    G. $y = -\frac{2}{3}x + 3$

    H. $y = -\frac{3}{2}x + 3$

    J. $y = -\frac{3}{2}x - 9$

    K. $y = -\frac{3}{2}x + 9$

39. The formula for converting a Fahrenheit temperature reading to Celsius is $C = \frac{5}{9}(F - 32)$, where C is the reading in degrees Celsius and F is the reading in degrees Fahrenheit. Which of the following is the Fahrenheit equivalent to a reading of 95° Celsius?

    A. 35°F

    B. 53°F

    C. 63°F

    D. 203°F

    E. 207°F

40. When 3 times x is increased by 5, the result is less than 11. Which of the following is a graph of the real numbers x for which the previous statement is true?

    F.

    G.

    H.

    J.

    K.

41. In the following triangle, what is the value of $\cos R$?

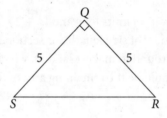

    A. $\frac{\sqrt{2}}{6}$

    B. $\frac{\sqrt{2}}{5}$

    C. $\frac{\sqrt{2}}{2}$

    D. $2\sqrt{2}$

    E. $5\sqrt{2}$

CONTINUED

42. Marvin has two saltwater fish tanks in his home. One has tangs and angelfish in a ratio of 5 to 2. The second tank has tangs and puffers in a ratio of 2 to 3. Marvin wants to put a tank in his office with angelfish and puffers using the same ratio he has at home to make it easier to buy food for them in bulk. What ratio of angelfish to puffers should he use?

   F. 2:3

   G. 2:5

   H. 5:2

   J. 5:7

   K. 4:15

43. The volume of a sphere is given by the formula $V = \frac{4}{3}\pi r^3$, where r is the radius of the sphere. What is the volume, in cubic inches, of a sphere that has a diameter of 6 inches?

   A. 3π

   B. 9π

   C. 27π

   D. 36π

   E. 288π

44. For all $x \neq -1$, which of the following is equivalent to $\dfrac{x^2 - 5x - 6}{x + 1} + x + 1$?

   F. $x - 5$

   G. $2x - 5$

   H. $x^2 - 5x - 6$

   J. $\dfrac{2x - 5}{x + 1}$

   K. $\dfrac{x^2 - 4x - 5}{x + 1}$

45. Which of the following expressions is the greatest monomial factor of $60a^3b + 45a^2b^2$?

   A. $15a^2b$

   B. $15a^3b^2$

   C. $15a^5b^3$

   D. $180a^3b^2$

   E. $180a^5b^3$

Use the following information to answer questions 46–47.

The population of fish in a certain pond from 1985 to 1995 is shown in the following graph.

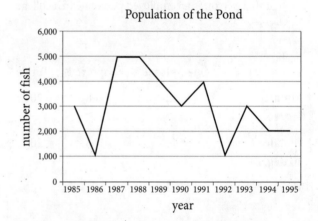

46. Which of the following best describes the percent change in the population from 1985 to 1995?

   F. 33.33% increase

   G. 33.33% decrease

   H. 50% decrease

   J. 333.33% increase

   K. 333.33% decrease

CONTINUED

47. Which of the following years contains the median population for the data?

    A. 1986

    B. 1989

    C. 1990

    D. 1991

    E. 1995

48. The following table shows the results of a study identifying the number of males and females with and without college degrees who were unemployed or employed at the time of the study. If one person from the study is chosen at random, what is the probability that that person is an employed person with a college degree?

	Unemployed	Employed	Totals
Female, degree	12	188	200
Female, no degree	44	156	200
Male, degree	23	177	200
Male, no degree	41	159	200
Totals	120	680	800

    F. $\frac{73}{160}$

    G. $\frac{10}{17}$

    H. $\frac{73}{136}$

    J. $\frac{17}{20}$

    K. $\frac{73}{80}$

49. Which of the following expressions gives the number of distinct permutations of the letters in GEOMETRY?

    A. $8!(2!)$

    B. $8!$

    C. $\frac{8!}{2!}$

    D. $\frac{8!}{6!}$

    E. $\frac{8!}{(6!)(2!)}$

50. The following graph represents the solution set to which inequality, assuming each grid line represents 1 unit?

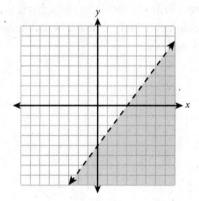

    F. $y < -\frac{4}{3}x - 4$

    G. $y > -\frac{3}{4}x - 4$

    H. $y < \frac{3}{4}x - 4$

    J. $y < \frac{4}{3}x - 4$

    K. $y > \frac{4}{3}x - 4$

51. A function h is defined by $h(x, y, z) = 4xy^2 - yz^3$. What is the value of $h(2, -1, 3)$?

    A. -35

    B. -19

    C. -1

    D. 19

    E. 35

CONTINUED ➡

52. The radius of a circle is increased so that the radius of the new circle is triple that of the original circle. How many times larger is the area of the new circle than that of the original circle?

 F. $\frac{1}{3}$

 G. 3

 H. 6

 J. 6π

 K. 9

53. The function $f(x) = 0.5\sin(2x)$ is graphed as shown over the domain $[0,2\pi]$. What is the period of the function?

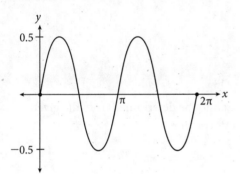

 A. $\frac{\pi}{4}$

 B. $\frac{\pi}{2}$

 C. π

 D. 2π

 E. 4π

54. For what value of x is the equation $\sqrt[3]{4x-12}+25 = 27$ true?

 F. -5

 G. -1

 H. -2.5

 J. 5

 K. 6.5

55. The chord shown in the figure is 8 units long. If the chord is 3 units from the center of the circle, what is the area of the circle?

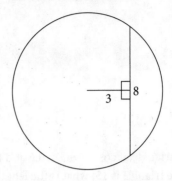

 A. 9π

 B. 16π

 C. 18π

 D. 25π

 E. 28π

56. If $f(x) = 3^{3x+3}$ and $g(x) = 27^{\left(\frac{2}{3}x-\frac{1}{3}\right)}$, for what value of x, if any, does the graph of $f(x)$ intersect the graph of $g(x)$?

 F. -4

 G. $-\frac{7}{4}$

 H. $-\frac{10}{7}$

 J. 2

 K. The graphs do not intersect.

57. What value of x satisfies the equation $\log_3(5x-40) - \log_3 5 = 2$?

 A. 17

 B. 9

 C. 1

 D. -9

 E. -17

58. A finite arithmetic sequence has five terms. The first term is 4. What is the difference between the mean and the median of the five terms?

    F. 0
    G. 1
    H. 2
    J. 4
    K. 5

59. In the following triangle, if cos ∠BAC = 0.6 and the hypotenuse of the triangle is 15, what is the length of side BC?

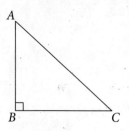

    A. 3
    B. 5
    C. 10
    D. 12
    E. 15

60. The following table several points that lie on the graph of a parabola. Based on the data in the table, what is the value of y when $x = -4$?

x	y
−2	3
0	−3
2	−5
4	−3
6	3
8	13

    F. −13
    G. −5
    H.   5
    J.   13
    K. Cannot be determined from the given information

IF YOU FINISH BEFORE TIME IS CALLED, YOU MAY CHECK YOUR WORK ON THIS SECTION ONLY. DO NOT TURN TO ANY OTHER SECTION IN THE TEST.   STOP

806

Reading Test

35 Minutes—40 Questions

Directions: The Reading Test includes multiple passages. Each passage includes multiple questions. After reading each passage, choose the best answer and fill in the corresponding bubble on your answer sheet. You may review the passages as often as necessary.

Passage I

PROSE FICTION: This passage is adapted from *The Age of Innocence*, by Edith Wharton (1920).

It was generally agreed in New York that the Countess Olenska had "lost her looks."

She had appeared there first, in Newland Archer's boyhood, as a brilliantly pretty little girl
5 of nine or ten, of whom people said that she "ought to be painted." Her parents had been continental wanderers, and after a roaming babyhood she had lost them both, and been taken in charge by her aunt, Medora Manson, also a wanderer, who was
10 herself returning to New York to "settle down."

Poor Medora, repeatedly widowed, was always coming home to settle down (each time in a less expensive house), and bringing with her a new husband or an adopted child, but after a few
15 months she invariably parted from her husband or quarrelled with her ward, and, having got rid of her house at a loss, set out again on her wanderings. As her mother had been a Rushworth, and her last unhappy marriage had linked her
20 to one of the crazy Chiverses, New York looked indulgently on her eccentricities, but when she returned with her little orphaned niece, whose parents had been popular in spite of their regrettable taste for travel, people thought it a pity
25 that the pretty child should be in such hands.

Everyone was disposed to be kind to little Ellen Mingott, though her dusky red cheeks and tight curls gave her an air of gaiety that seemed unsuitable in a child who should still have been in
30 black for her parents. It was one of the misguided Medora's many peculiarities to flout the unalterable rules that regulated American mourning, and when she stepped from the steamer her family was scandalized to see that the crepe veil she wore for

35 her own brother was seven inches shorter than those of her sisters-in-law, while little Ellen wore a crimson dress and amber beads.

But New York had so long resigned itself to Medora that only a few old ladies shook their
40 heads over Ellen's gaudy clothes, while her other relations fell under the charm of her high spirits. She was a fearless and familiar little thing, who asked disconcerting questions, made precocious comments, and possessed outlandish arts, such
45 as dancing a Spanish shawl dance and singing Neapolitan love-songs to a guitar. Under the direction of her aunt, the little girl received an expensive but incoherent education, which included "drawing from the model," a thing never dreamed
50 of before, and playing the piano in quintets with professional musicians.

Of course no good could come of this, and when, a few years later, poor Chivers finally died, his widow again pulled up stakes and departed
55 with Ellen, who had grown into a tall bony girl with conspicuous eyes. For some time no more was heard of them; then news came of Ellen's marriage to an immensely rich Polish nobleman of legendary fame. She disappeared, and when a few years later
60 Medora again came back to New York, subdued, impoverished, mourning a third husband, and in quest of a still smaller house, people wondered that her rich niece had not been able to do something for her. Then came the news that Ellen's own
65 marriage had ended in disaster, and that she was herself returning home to seek rest and oblivion among her kinsfolk.

These things passed through Newland Archer's mind a week later as he watched the Countess
70 Olenska enter the van der Luyden drawing room on the evening of the momentous dinner. In the

CONTINUED

middle of the room she paused, looking about her with a grave mouth and smiling eyes, and in that instant, Newland Archer rejected the general
75 verdict on her looks. It was true that her early radiance was gone. The red cheeks had paled; she was thin, worn, a little older-looking than her age, which must have been nearly thirty. But there was about her the mysterious authority of beauty,
80 a sureness in the carriage of the head, the movement of the eyes, which, without being in the least theatrical, struck him as highly trained and full of a conscious power. At the same time she was simpler in manner than most of the ladies present,
85 and many people (as he heard afterward) were disappointed that her appearance was not more "stylish"—for stylishness was what New York most valued. It was, perhaps, Archer reflected, because her early vivacity had disappeared; because she
90 was so quiet—quiet in her movements, her voice, and the tones of her voice. New York had expected something a good deal more resonant in a young woman with such a history.

1. The author describes which of the following practices as undesirable to New York society?

   A. Playing the piano

   B. Performing Spanish shawl dances

   C. Traveling

   D. Adopting children

2. With which of the following would the author most likely agree regarding New York society as it pertains to Medora?

   F. It is rigid and unaccepting of different behavior.

   G. It is usually whimsical, with few solid rules.

   H. It is often based on unrealistic expectations.

   J. It is snobbish but occasionally accepting of less common behavior.

3. It is most reasonable to infer that, after the death of Medora's third husband, Ellen did not help her aunt primarily because:

   A. Ellen was no longer wealthy, since her own marriage had failed.

   B. Medora had become embittered because she hadn't heard from Ellen for so long.

   C. Ellen resented the incoherent education she received from her aunt.

   D. receiving help from her niece would interfere with Medora's desire to be eccentric.

4. Based on the characterization of Newland Archer in the last paragraph, he can best be described as:

   F. thoughtful and analytical.

   G. likeable but withdrawn.

   H. harsh and unfair.

   J. stylish and gregarious.

5. In her descriptions of Medora, the author intends to give the impression that Medora is:

   A. eccentric and peripatetic.

   B. impoverished and resentful.

   C. kind and loyal.

   D. precocious and pretty.

6. As it is used in line 31, the word *flout* most nearly means:

   F. eliminate.

   G. exemplify.

   H. disregard.

   J. float.

CONTINUED ▶

7. What does the narrator suggest is a central characteristic of Medora Manson?

   A. Arrogance

   B. Immodesty

   C. Non-conformity

   D. Orthodoxy

8. Which of the following characters learns to do something otherwise unheard of by New York society?

   F. Ellen Mingott

   G. Newland Archer

   H. Medora Manson

   J. Count Olenska

9. The author includes reference to Medora's mother and Medora's marriage to "one of the crazy Chiverses" (line 20) in order to indicate that:

   A. she had an unhappy childhood.

   B. her eccentricities were not surprising.

   C. she was the perfect person to raise Ellen.

   D. she was a wanderer.

10. One can reasonably infer from the passage that on the occasion of the dinner, Newland and Ellen:

    F. had not seen each other for some time.

    G. were interested in becoming romantically involved.

    H. were both disappointed with New York society.

    J. had just met, but were immediately attracted to each other.

Passage II

SOCIAL SCIENCE: This passage discusses challenges facing Florida's two largest economic sectors due to climate change.

Every state in the U.S. relies on at least one or two industries to drive its economic growth. Boasting a top-five economy among the 50 states, Florida thrives on its tourism industry and
5 agricultural production. Recent climate change reports are a cause for concern for the policymakers who want to keep the state on its current upward economic trajectory. How serious are the threats that the state faces, and can anything be done to
10 stave off the effects of climate change before they irreparably damagethe Floridian economy?

The National Climate Assessment, a government-mandated report released every four years, references South Florida frequently as
15 a locale that is likely to experience the worsening effects of climate change sooner rather than later. In September 2017, for example, Hurricane Irma wreaked havoc on large swaths of the Florida coastline when it made landfall in the Florida Keys;
20 economists put the price tag for Irma at $50 billion, making it the costliest hurricane in Florida's history. It is estimated that if Irma had made a more direct hit on Miami, Florida's second-most popular tourist destination, the damage would have
25 been closer to $200 billion. Many scientists feel that rising sea levels are making areas like Miami and Orlando increasingly vulnerable to such catastrophic weather events.

Another top tourist attraction in Florida, the
30 Everglades, is already experiencing a reduction in size due to a combination of rising sea levels and serious weather events. Large sections of the Everglades are less than three feet above sea level, and soon many of the low-lying regions will be
35 completely submerged. This does not bode well for the over one million visitors who make the trek to the national park each year nor for the more than $20 million in revenue that the Everglades National Park generates annually. In addition, the sea level
40 rise causes salt water to push further inland and upstream, which endangers not only tourism but also the drinking water of several communities.

CONTINUED →

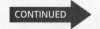

On a peninsula like Florida, it seems ironic that a lack of water could become an issue, but
45 an Environmental Protection Agency report published in 2016 pointed to a lack of irrigation due to warmer temperatures as a potential downside of a longer growing season. Florida relies on groundwater pumped from permeable underground
50 aquifers, and Florida farms consume nearly half of the state's public water supply. Citrus fruits require substantial amounts of irrigation to maintain crop size; a 2003 agriculture study found that a 20% reduction in irrigation resulted in significant losses
55 for citrus crops. The citrus fruit industry in Florida is a $10 billion industry, so any negative trends have a direct impact on Florida's overall economic health.

Climate change has an impact on the pro-
60 duce side of Florida's agriculture as well as the livestock side; although it makes up a smaller portion of Florida's $120 billion in agricultural revenue than the citrus industry, the livestock industry exports cattle, calves, milk, poultry, and
65 eggs both nationally and internationally. One problem that arises with livestock as a result of warmer temperatures is a reduction in productivity because of metabolic disruption caused by heat stress. The livestock industry also relies on the
70 extensive perennial grasslands of the region, which have degraded in quality because of the greater frequency of severe weather events. Additionally, the combination of temperature and rainfall increases have led to greater instances of livestock diseases
75 like the West Nile virus; the increase in humidity leads directly to larger mosquito populations.

With so many challenges facing their state, Floridians are taking a proactive approach to combating some of the consequences of climate
80 change. In Miami, lawmakers are considering some rather unconventional recommendations. For example, a group of Harvard students presented Miami Beach leaders with two unique options to help adapt to rising seas: concrete cisterns
85 strategically placed on roofs throughout the city to capture rainwater, and "sacrificial floors" designed to absorb excess water before it reaches the inhabited floors. Researchers are encouraging the

South Florida Water Management District to change
90 their timetable for increasing freshwater flow to the Everglades to maintain the level of freshwater higher than sea level. Farmers are investing in micro-surface and subsurface drip irrigation systems to reduce the overall volume of water
95 needed to maintain their crops and making the move to mixed crop-livestock farms, as studies have shown this farming style to be mutually beneficial to both crops and livestock.

While a complete reversal of the consequences
100 of climate change seems improbable, Floridians can be encouraged by the fact that leaders in their state are taking some pragmatic steps to cope with the changes. Furthermore, as those policymakers look to protect the sectors that have long served
105 as the foundation of Florida's economy, there is also a push to continue to diversify. International trade—Florida is already one of the largest export states—seems an ideal sector to expand with the increasingly globalized nature of economic systems.
110 Despite the challenges, Florida is preparing to weather the storm of climate change as it has weathered so many storms before.

11. The primary purpose of the passage is to:

A. describe how climate change has harmed Florida's land and industries.

B. discuss the threats climate change poses to Florida and how to address them.

C. argue for the implementation of unorthodox means of combating climate change.

D. explain the varied ways in which climate change can impact people's lives.

CONTINUED ▶

12. According to the passage, what makes Hurricane Irma significant?

   F. It cost Florida nearly $200 billion in lost revenue and infrastructure repair.

   G. It was the first hurricane to hit Florida that was significantly exacerbated by climate change.

   H. It demonstrated to scientists how damaging rising sea levels could be.

   J. It caused more economic damage to Florida than any other hurricane.

13. The second paragraph implies that South Florida:

   A. is a major source of tourism revenue for the state.

   B. is likely to be entirely submerged by rising sea levels.

   C. is more vulnerable to extreme weather than North Florida.

   D. is central to agricultural production in Florida.

14. The passage makes clear that the main threat climate change poses to the Everglades is:

   F. contamination; salt water pushed inland will poison fresh water sources.

   G. submersion; rising sea levels will put lands at low elevations under water.

   H. habitat destruction; extreme weather will degrade the park's lush vegetation.

   J. isolation; changes to the landscape will cut the park off from visitors.

15. The author references the 2016 Environmental Protection Agency report (lines 45–46) and the 2003 study (lines 53–55) primarily in order to:

   A. provide specific numerical evidence for the cost of climate change.

   B. counter an argument that contradicts the author's point.

   C. open a discussion about their long-term implications for Florida.

   D. add support for the paragraph's claims from authoritative sources.

16. The passage states that compared to the citrus industry, the livestock industry in Florida:

   F. consumes more water.

   G. creates less pollution.

   H. exports more products.

   J. generates less income.

17. According to the passage, how might climate change negatively impact the livestock industry in Florida?

   A. Decreased crop yields would mean less food for the animals.

   B. Higher temperatures would put a strain on the animals' bodies.

   C. Animals exposed to poor weather would be more likely to become ill.

   D. Water shortages would cause the animals to become dehydrated.

18. Which of the following best describes the purpose of the sixth paragraph?

   F. It outlines suggested infrastructure adaptations to be applied throughout Florida.

   G. It summarizes the primary challenges facing Florida's economy due to climate change.

   H. It explains some of the ways Floridians are planning to address problems caused by climate change.

   J. It examines how to best direct water supplies in order to compensate for imbalances in rainfall.

CONTINUED

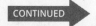

19. According to the passage, how is the agriculture industry preparing to address problems caused by climate change?

    A. Farmers are replacing microsurface and subsurface drip irrigation with more efficient systems.

    B. Industry associations are working to expand underground aquifers.

    C. Farms are integrating crops and livestock to improve production of both.

    D. Farmers are stepping up vaccinations of livestock to combat the spread of disease.

20. The detail "Florida is already one of the largest export states" (lines 107–108) most nearly serves to:

    F. identify one of the main drivers of Florida's economic expansion.

    G. compare Florida's trade balance to that of other states.

    H. explain why expanding Florida's international trade is likely to be effective.

    J. emphasize the benefits of diversifying Florida's economy.

Passage III

HUMANITIES: One of the most enjoyable ways to analyze culture is through music. By analyzing musical styles and lyrics, one can explore quintessential characteristics of particular cultures. Passage A explores the relationship between the central and southern areas of the Appalachian mountain range and country music. Passage B contrasts bluegrass and country music and culture.

Passage A

Country music has its roots in the southern portions of the United States, specifically in the remote and undeveloped backcountry of the central and southern areas of the Appalachian mountain
5   range. Recognized as a distinct cultural region since the late nineteenth century, the area became home to European settlements in the eighteenth century, primarily led by Ulster Scots from Ireland. Early inhabitants have been characterized as
10 fiercely independent, to the point of rudeness and inhospitality. It was in this area that the region's truly indigenous music, now known as country music, was born.

Rooted in spirituals as well as folk music,
15 cowboy songs, and traditional Celtic melodies, country music originated in the 1920s. The motifs are generally ballads and dance tunes, simple in form and accompanied mostly by guitar, banjo, and violin. Though today there are many genres of
20 country music, all have their roots in this mélange of sources.

The term "country" has replaced the original pejorative term "hillbilly." Hillbillies referred to Appalachian inhabitants who were considered poor,
25 uneducated, isolated, and wary; the name change reflects a more accepting characterization of these mountain dwellers.

Hank Williams put country music on the map nationally, and is credited with the movement of
30 country music from the South to more national prominence. Other early innovators include the Carter family, Ernest Tubb, Woody Guthrie, Loretta Lynn, and Bill Monroe, father of bluegrass music. More recently, Faith Hill, Reba McEntire, and
35 Shania Twain have carried on the tradition.

What might be considered the "home base" of country music is in Nashville, Tennessee, and the legendary music hall, the Grand Ole Opry. Founded

CONTINUED

in 1925 by George D. Hay, it had its genesis in the
40 pioneer radio station WSM's program *Barn Dance*.
Country singers are considered to have reached
the pinnacle of the profession if they are asked to
become members of the Opry. While noted country
music performers and acts take the stage at the Opry
45 numerous times, Elvis Presley performed there only
once, in 1954. His act was so poorly received that it
was suggested he return to his job as a truck driver.

The offshoots and relatives of country music
highlight the complexity of this genre. In a move
50 away from its mountain origins, and turning a
focus to the West, honky-tonk music became
popular in the early twentieth century. Its name is
a reference to its roots in honky-tonk bars, where
the music was played. Additionally, Western swing
55 emerged as one of the first genres to blend country
and jazz musical styles, which required a great deal
of skill and creativity. Some of the most talented
and sophisticated musicians performing in any
genre were musicians who played in bluegrass string
60 bands, another relative of country music.

Country music has always been an expression of
American identity. Its sound, lyrics, and performers
are purely American, and though the music now
has an international audience, it remains American
65 in its heart and soul.

Passage B

A style of music closely related to country is the
similarly indigenous music known as bluegrass,
which originated in the Appalachian highland
regions extending westwards to the Ozark
70 Mountains in southern Missouri and northern
Arkansas. Derived from the music brought over
by European settlers of the region, bluegrass is
a mixture of Scottish, Welsh, Irish, and English
melodic forms, infused, over time, with African-
75 American influences. Indeed, many bluegrass songs,
such as "Barbara Allen" and "House Carpenter,"
preserve their European roots, maintaining the
traditional musical style and narratives almost
intact. Story-telling ballads, often laments, are
80 common themes. Given the predominance of
coal mining in the Appalachian region, it is not
surprising that ballads relating to mining tragedies
are also common.

Unlike country music, in which musicians
85 commonly play the same melodies together,
bluegrass highlights one player at a time, with the
others providing accompaniment. This tradition of
each musician taking turns with solos, and often
improvising, can also be seen in jazz ensembles.
90 Traditional bluegrass music is typically played
on instruments such as banjo, guitar, mandolin,
bass, harmonica, and Dobro (resonator guitar).
Even household objects, including washboards and
spoons, have, from time to time, been drafted for
95 use as instruments. Vocals also differ from country
music in that, rather than featuring a single voice,
bluegrass incorporates baritone and tenor harmonies.

Initially included under the catch-all phrase "folk
music," and later referred to as "hillbilly," bluegrass
100 did not come into his own category until the late
1950s, and appeared first in the comprehensive guide
Music Index in 1965. Presumably it was named after
Bill Monroe's Blue Grass band, the seminal bluegrass
band. A rapid, almost frenetic, pace characterizes
105 bluegrass tempos. Even today, decades after their
most active performing era, The Foggy Mountain
Boys members Lester Flatt, a bluegrass guitarist and
mandolinist, and Earl Scruggs, known for his three-
finger banjo picking style, are widely considered the
110 foremost artists on their instruments.

Partially because of its pace and complexity,
bluegrass has often been recorded for movie
soundtracks. "Dueling Banjos," played in the movie
Deliverance, exemplifies the skill required by the
115 feverish tempo of the genre. The soundtrack for *O
Brother, Where Art Thou?* incorporates bluegrass and
its musical cousins folk, country, gospel, and blues.
Bluegrass festivals are held throughout the country
and as far away as the Czech Republic. Interactive,
120 often inviting audience participation, they feature
performers such as Dolly Parton and Alison Krauss.

Central to bluegrass music are the themes of the
working class—miners, railroad workers, farmers.
The phrase "high, lonesome sound" was coined to
125 represent the bluegrass undertones of intensity and
cheerlessness, symbolizing the hard-scrabble life of
the American worker. As with so much of a nation's
traditional music, and for better or worse, bluegrass
music reflects America.

CONTINUED

21. According to Passage A, country music originated from all of the following EXCEPT:

    A. Celtic melodies.

    B. spirituals.

    C. jazz.

    D. cowboy songs.

22. Based on Passage A, which of the following would be the most logical place to hear the best of country music?

    F. Honky-tonk bars

    G. Ireland

    H. The Appalachian backcountry

    J. The Grand Ole Opry

23. As it is used in line 23, the word *pejorative* most nearly means:

    A. traditional.

    B. accurate.

    C. disparaging.

    D. mountain dwelling.

24. If a song were a lament with Welsh and African-American derivation, the author of Passage B would classify it as:

    F. bluegrass.

    G. country.

    H. jazz.

    J. hillbilly.

25. According to Passage B, the instruments played in bluegrass music are:

    A. both typical and unusual.

    B. derived from African-American influences.

    C. made famous by the piece "Dueling Banjos."

    D. restricted to those used in the Ozarks.

26. According to Passage B, in addition to highlighting one player at a time, bluegrass music differs from country music in that it often:

    F. features harmonies sung by bass and tenor voices.

    G. features a single voice.

    H. is characterized by musicians commonly playing the same melodies together.

    J. is played on instruments such as the banjo and guitar.

27. It can be inferred from Passage B that laments and high, lonesome sounds both reflect:

    A. the influence of Irish music.

    B. the challenges of American life.

    C. songs sung by Shania Twain.

    D. hillbilly music.

28. As it is used in the introductory information, "quintessential" most nearly means:

    F. old-fashioned.

    G. representative.

    H. charming.

    J. unconventional.

CONTINUED

29. Passage A states that there were "talented and sophisticated" (lines 57–58) musicians playing bluegrass music. Which sentence in Passage B suggests this claim?

   A. "Central to bluegrass music are the themes of the working class—miners, railroad workers, farmers."

   B. "Partially because of its pace and complexity, bluegrass has often been recorded for movie soundtracks."

   C. "Lester Flatt, a bluegrass guitarist and mandolinist, and Earl Scruggs, known for his three-finger banjo picking style, are widely considered the foremost artists on their instruments."

   D. "A style of music closely related to country is the similarly indigenous music known as bluegrass …"

30. It can be inferred that both authors would agree that:

   F. country and bluegrass music are popular genres.

   G. both genres—country and bluegrass—are showcased at the Grand Ole Opry.

   H. music genres can evolve.

   J. country and bluegrass music are gaining in acceptance.

Passage IV

NATURAL SCIENCE: This passage is adapted from an article about the history of artificial satellites.

When the researchers at California Polytechnic university (CalPoly) and Stanford University determined the specifications of the CubeSat design back in 1999, they likely did not realize the full
5 potential of the miniature satellites. NASA's Mars Cube One (MarCO) mission has provided strong evidence that CubeSats offer many advantages for deep space exploration. The ability to build a large portion of the CubeSat with off-the-
10 shelf components means that future missions can be more cost-effective. The low cost of the satellites may also allow for more radical scientific experiments to be performed in space.

Experimental radio and antenna designs were
15 an important part of the mission. The MarCO-A and MarCO-B satellites, affectionately referred to as "Eve" and "WALL-E" by the engineering team, had softball-sized UHF and X-band radios mounted to the main unit. These allowed the satellites, which
20 were launched into space at the same time as the InSight lander, to send back photos of the landing in under eight minutes. By contrast, the lander itself took over an hour to transmit its successful landing. The same radio and antenna technology
25 also allowed for more efficient monitoring of the landing process. With only a 40% success rate as of 2017, Mars landings remain notoriously difficult. The data recorded by the MarCO satellites will help future missions.

30 Even beyond the completion of the Mars mission, engineers like Joel Krajewski, project manager for MarCO, hope to use the data sent back by the satellites to test how long technological systems can withstand the hardships of space. Both units
35 will continue to relay system data until they cease to function. The successful survival of the two modified satellites could lead to the possibility of longer explorations much deeper into the outer reaches of the universe.

40 In order to increase the success of the mission, the MarCO team fitted the satellites with some specific modifications. The cameras that MarCO-B

used to take stills of the planet as the satellite approached Mars represent a significantly more

45 economical approach. The consumer-grade cameras highlight the potential for greatly reducing the costs associated with deep space missions. Soon after receipt, images of the Red Planet, along with its moons Phobos and Deimos, were proudly

50 displayed on the NASA website. An elated Cody Colley, mission manager from JPL, happily reported, "WALL-E sent some great postcards from Mars!" It is of note that the entire MarCO project checked in at $18.5 million. Compared

55 to the price tag associated with building and sending a more traditional satellite into space, which can easily reach $100 million, CubeSats represent an unprecedented breakthrough in the financial burden of space exploration.

60   Cost reductions also mean that it is increasingly possible for science experiments that stood little chance of being greenlighted in the past to make it into deep space via a CubeSat. Several projects already exist in near-Earth orbit, including a 2009

65 study on antibacterial effectiveness in zero-g, a QuakeSat in 2003 to measure for Extremely Low Frequency (ELF) signals that some scientists believe occur before earthquakes, and the 2015 LightSail 1 mission to test propulsion systems.

70 The ability to travel greater distances into space in an economical manner will no doubt encourage researchers to propose more novel experiments for future missions.

    The possibility of linked networks of CubeSats

75 in deep space offers another intriguing proposition. The QB50 project involved the cooperation of over 30 international universities to send CubeSats into near-earth orbit to study temporal and spatial characteristics of the lower thermosphere.

80 Benefits of linked networks include increased flexibility to distribute tasks among the satellites and reduced probability of single-point failure. This kind of redundancy against failure, along with the ability to adapt in real-time, is even more

85 helpful in deep space where the satellites face an incredibly challenging environment.

    Since its inception in 1958, NASA has encouraged its researchers, scientists, and

engineers to push the limits of existing technology.

90 In building on the work of teams at CalPoly and Stanford, the engineers at NASA have proven that cost-effective CubeSat technology has the potential to exponentially increase scientific experimentation in deep space. As the MarCO team continues to

95 collect data from "Eve" and "WALL-E," the lessons learned will no doubt set a new standard for the vast array of deep space CubeSats to come.

31. Which of the following best describes the author's attitude toward the passage's main topic?

   A. Cautious optimism

   B. Dispassionate concern

   C. Disillusioned frustration

   D. Enthusiastic anticipation

32. According to the passage, the CubeSat was first designed by:

   F. Joel Krajewski

   G. Cody Colley

   H. CalPoly and Stanford researchers

   J. NASA scientists and engineers

33. As it is used in line 12, the word *radical* most nearly means:

   A. militarized and aggressive.

   B. ideologically extreme.

   C. primitive and organic.

   D. profoundly innovative.

CONTINUED

34. According to the passage, why was the MarCO satellites' experimental communication technology notable?

    F. It transmitted landing data over seven times faster than the previous technology.

    G. It took barely an hour to transmit landing data back to NASA.

    H. Its off-the-shelf components made it much less expensive than other radios.

    J. The radios were unusually space-efficient, being the size of softballs.

35. It can be inferred from the second paragraph that compared to the InSight lander, the MarCO satellites:

    A. take higher-resolution photos from greater distances.

    B. demonstrate greater efficiency by utilizing miniaturized technology.

    C. provided more helpful information to improve future Mars landings.

    D. are able to land more effectively in difficult Martian conditions.

36. The fourth paragraph primarily serves to:

    F. argue for using consumer-grade components wherever possible for future NASA projects.

    G. explain how innovative choices in technology led to significant cost reductions for the MarCO satellites.

    H. describe the many reasons why the MarCO project was less expensive than comparable satellite projects.

    J. praise the superiority of the images the MarCO satellites sent back from Mars.

37. Based on the passage, why did the scientists at NASA most likely post photos from the MarCO satellites on their website?

    A. They hoped to gain support for future missions.

    B. They wanted to prove that the new satellites were viable.

    C. They needed to satisfy public demands for information.

    D. They were pleased with the success of the mission.

38. Which of the following does the passage suggest about the experiments referenced in lines 66–69?

    F. Their creators had to wait a very long time for approval of their ideas.

    G. It is unlikely they would have been carried out using more traditional satellites.

    H. They required linked networks of satellites to effectively test different variables.

    J. They had to be conducted farther from Earth than most satellites go.

39. The passage states that the advantages of linked networks of satellites include:

   A. considerable reductions in cost from traditional satellites.

   B. increased adaptability and protection against breakdown.

   C. encouraging international cooperation due to shared ownership.

   D. the possibility of studying previously inaccessible parts of the atmosphere.

40. The comparisons in lines 19–24 and lines 53–57 are examples of how the author:

   F. juxtaposes old and new in order to systematically dismantle old methods.

   G. references prestigious institutions to increase the passage's authority.

   H. uses specific statistics in order to support points made in the passage.

   J. employs positive language to convey zeal for the passage's subject.

Science Test

35 Minutes—40 Questions

Directions: The Science Test includes multiple passages. Each passage includes multiple questions. After reading each passage, choose the best answer and fill in the corresponding bubble on your answer sheet. You may review the passages as often as necessary.

You may NOT use a calculator on this test.

Passage I

Soil, by volume, consists on average of 45% minerals, 25% water, 25% air, and 5% organic matter (including both living and nonliving organisms). Time and topography shape the composition of soil and cause it to develop into layers known as *horizons*. The soil horizons in a particular area are collectively known as the *soil profile*. The composition of soil varies in each horizon, as do the most common minerals, as can be seen in the soil profile depicted in the diagram. The diagram also shows the depth of each horizon and the overall density of the soil.

diagram

Table 1 lists the zinc and calcium contents (as percentages) in the minerals that compose soil.

Table 1		
Mineral	Zinc content (%)	Calcium content (%)
Feldspar	35–40	0–10
Hornblende	30–35	10–20
Quartz	25–30	20–30
Mica	20–25	30–40
Serpentine	15–20	40–50
Anorthite	10–15	50–60
Limestone	5–10	60–70
Shale	0–5	70–80

Table 2 shows the average percentage of minerals that compose granite and sandstone, two rock types that are commonly found in soil.

Table 2		
Mineral	Percentage of mineral in:	
	Sandstone	Granite
Feldspar	30	54
Hornblende	2	0
Quartz	50	33
Mica	10	10
Serpentine	0	0
Anorthite	0	0
Limestone	5	0
Shale	0	0
Augite	3	3

1. An analysis of an unknown mineral found in soil revealed its zinc content to be 32% and its calcium content to be 12%. Based on the data in Table 1, geologists would most likely classify this mineral as:

   A. hornblende.
   B. anorthite.
   C. serpentine.
   D. mica.

2. Geologists digging down into the A horizon would most likely find which of the following minerals?

   F. Limestone
   G. Shale
   H. Serpentine
   J. Mica

3. Based on the data presented in the diagram and Table 1, which of the following statements best describes the relationship between the zinc content of a mineral and the depth below surface level at which it is dominant? As zinc content increases:

   A. depth increases.
   B. depth decreases.
   C. depth first increases, then decreases.
   D. depth first decreases, then increases.

4. If geologists were to drill 30 feet into the Earth, which of the following minerals would they most likely encounter?

   F. Quartz, mica, and limestone
   G. Feldspar, shale, and serpentine
   H. Feldspar, quartz, and anorthite
   J. Hornblende, limestone, and serpentine

5. If augite is most commonly found in soil in close proximity to the other minerals that make up granite, then augite would most likely be found at a depth of:

   A. less than 10 feet.
   B. between 10 feet and 30 feet.
   C. between 30 feet and 60 feet.
   D. greater than 60 feet.

6. Based on the passage, how is the percentage of zinc content related to the percentage of calcium content in the minerals that make up soil?

   F. The percentage of zinc content increases as the percentage of calcium content increases.
   G. The percentage of zinc content increases as the percentage of calcium content decreases.
   H. Both the percentage of zinc content and the percentage of calcium content remain constant.
   J. There is no discernible relationship between the percentage of zinc content and the percentage of calcium content.

Passage II

Students conducted the following studies to determine the melting points of several materials. They attempted to melt the materials by submerging them in a variety of aqueous solutions that were heated to their boiling points. They used the following equation to calculate the boiling points of these solutions:

$$\Delta T_b = K_b \times m \times i,$$

where

ΔT_b = increase in boiling point above pure solvent

$K_b = 0.512 \dfrac{°C \times kg}{mol}$

$m = \text{molality} = \dfrac{\text{mol solute}}{\text{kg solvent}}$

$i = $ number of ions present per molecule of solute

CONTINUED

Study 1

In order to prepare various solutions of sodium chloride (NaCl), 100.00 g of H_2O were added to a beaker. A known quantity of NaCl was dissolved into the water, and the resulting boiling point of the solution was recorded. This procedure was repeated with different amounts of NaCl as shown in Table 1.

	Table 1		
Solution	Mass of H_2O (g)	Amount of NaCl (mol)	Boiling point (°C)
1	100.00	0	100.00
2	100.00	0.085	100.88
3	100.00	0.171	101.75
4	100.00	0.257	102.63
5	100.00	0.342	103.50

Study 2

In order to prepare various solutions of calcium chloride ($CaCl_2$), 100.00 g of H_2O were added to a beaker. A known quantity of $CaCl_2$ was dissolved into the water and the resulting boiling point of the solution was recorded. This procedure was repeated with different amounts of $CaCl_2$ as shown in Table 2.

	Table 2		
Solution	Mass of H_2O (g)	Amount of $CaCl_2$ (mol)	Boiling point (°C)
6	100.00	0.270	104.15
7	100.00	0.360	105.53
8	100.00	0.450	106.91
9	100.00	0.541	108.29
10	100.00	0.631	109.67

Study 3

Each solution from Studies 1 and 2 was brought to a boil. A small sample of a material was placed in each solution. If the material melted, a "Y" was marked in Table 3. If the material did not melt, an "N" was marked

in Table 3. This procedure was repeated for all eight materials.

	Table 3									
	Solution									
Material	1	2	3	4	5	6	7	8	9	10
1	Y	Y	Y	Y	Y	Y	Y	Y	Y	Y
2	N	Y	Y	Y	Y	Y	Y	Y	Y	Y
3	N	N	Y	Y	Y	Y	Y	Y	Y	Y
4	N	N	N	N	Y	Y	Y	Y	Y	Y
5	N	N	N	N	N	Y	Y	Y	Y	Y
6	N	N	N	N	N	N	N	Y	Y	Y
7	N	N	N	N	N	N	N	N	N	Y
8	N	N	N	N	N	N	N	N	N	N

7. Which of the following modifications to Solution 5 of Study 1 would result in an increase in its boiling point?

   I. Increasing the K_b of the solution

   II. Increasing the amount of NaCl

   III. Replacing the NaCl with an equal amount of $CaCl_2$

   A. I only
   B. I and II only
   C. II and III only
   D. I, II, and III

8. In Study 1, what was the boiling point of the solution with 0.171 mols of NaCl?

   F. 100°C
   G. 100.88°C
   H. 101.75°C
   J. 109.67°C

9. Based on the results of the studies from the passage, the boiling point of Material 5 is most likely:

   A. less than 102.63°C.

   B. between 102.63°C and 103.50°C.

   C. between 103.50°C and 104.15°C.

   D. greater than 104.15°C.

10. If a sixth solution had been prepared during Study 2 using 0.721 mol $CaCl_2$, its boiling point would most likely be closest to which of the following?

    F. 108.75°C

    G. 111.07°C

    H. 113.72°C

    J. 115.02°C

11. A ninth material was submerged in Solutions 1–6 as in Experiment 3. Which of the following is LEAST likely to be a plausible set of results for this material?

	Solution					
	1	2	3	4	5	6
A.	Y	Y	Y	Y	N	N
B.	Y	Y	Y	Y	Y	Y
C.	N	N	N	N	Y	Y
D.	N	N	N	N	N	N

A. A

B. B

C. C

D. D

12. Which of the following best explains why the students recorded data for their solutes in mol rather than g or kg?

    F. The H_2O was already measured in kg.

    G. The units for mass are less accurate.

    H. The change in boiling point depends on molality.

    J. The melting points of the various materials do not depend on the masses of the materials.

13. Would the results of Studies 1–3 support the claim that Material 7 has a lower melting point than Material 8?

    A. Yes, because in Solution 10, Material 7 melted and Material 8 did not.

    B. Yes, because in Solution 10, Material 8 melted and Material 7 did not.

    C. No, because the melting point of Material 8 cannot be determined from the data.

    D. No, because the melting point of Material 7 cannot be determined from the data.

Passage III

Engineers designing a roadway needed to test the composition of the soil that would form the roadbed. In order to determine whether their two sampling systems (System A and System B) give sufficiently accurate soil composition measurements, they first conducted a study to compare the two systems.

Soil samples were taken with varying levels of *humidity* (concentration of water). The concentrations of the compounds that form the majority of soil were measured. The results for the sampling systems were compared with data on file with the US Geological Survey (USGS), which compiles extremely accurate data. The engineers' and USGS's results are presented in Table 1.

CONTINUED ➡

Table 1					
	Level of humidity				
Concentration (mg/L) of:	10%	25%	45%	65%	80%
Nitrogen (N)					
USGS	105	236	598	781	904
System A	112	342	716	953	1,283
System B	196	408	857	1,296	1,682
Potassium oxide (K₂O)					
USGS	9.4	9.1	8.9	8.7	8.2
System A	9.4	9.0	8.7	8.5	8.0
System B	9.5	9.2	9.0	8.8	8.3
Calcium (Ca)					
USGS	39.8	24.7	11.4	5.0	44.8
System A	42.5	31.4	10.4	8.0	42.9
System B	37.1	23.2	11.6	11.1	45.1
Phosphorus oxide (P₂O₅)					
USGS	69.0	71.2	74.8	78.9	122.3
System A	67.9	69.9	72.2	76.7	123.1
System B	74.0	75.6	78.7	82.1	126.3
Zinc (Zn)					
USGS	0.41	0.52	0.64	0.74	0.70
System A	0.67	0.80	0.88	0.97	0.93
System B	0.38	0.48	0.62	0.77	0.73

Note: Each system concentration measurement is the average of 5 measurements.

14. The hypothesis that increasing humidity increases the concentration of a compound is supported by all of the following EXCEPT:

    F.   nitrogen.

    G.   potassium oxide.

    H.   phosphorus oxide.

    J.   zinc.

15. At a humidity level of 25%, it could be concluded that System B least accurately measures the concentration of which of the following compounds, relative to the data on file with the USGS?

    A.   N

    B.   Ca

    C. K_2O

    D. P_2O_5

16. The engineers hypothesized that the concentration of potassium oxide (K_2O) decreases as the level of humidity increases. This hypothesis is supported by:

    F.   the data from the USGS only.

    G.   the System A measurements only.

    H.   the data from the USGS and the System B measurements only.

    J.   the data from the USGS, the System A measurements, and the System B measurements.

17. Do the results in Table 1 support the conclusion that System B is more accurate than System A for measuring the concentration of zinc?

    A.   No, because the zinc measurements from System A are consistently higher than the zinc measurements from System B.

    B.   No, because the zinc measurements from System A are closer to the data provided by the USGS than the zinc measurements from System B.

    C.   Yes, because the zinc measurements from System B are consistently lower than the zinc measurements from System A.

    D.   Yes, because the zinc measurements from System B are closer to the data provided by the USGS than the zinc measurements from System A.

18. The relationship between humidity level and calcium concentration, as measured by System B, is best represented by which of the following graphs?

F.

G.

H.

J.

19. After conducting their comparisons, the engineers used System B to test a soil sample at the future road site. They measured the concentrations, in mg/L, of selected compounds in the sample and found that they were: potassium oxide = 9.1, calcium = 17.3, and zinc = 0.57. Based on the data in Table 1, the engineers should predict that the level of humidity is approximately:

   A.   16%.

   B.   37%.

   C.   49%.

   D.   57%.

Passage IV

Diabetes is a metabolic disorder that causes hyperglycemia (higher-than-normal blood glucose levels). The most common form is type 2 diabetes, which occurs when the body does not produce enough insulin or has a lowered level of response to insulin (insulin resistance). Insulin is a hormone produced in the pancreas that helps regulate blood glucose levels by stimulating cells to absorb and metabolize glucose. Typically occurring in adults, type 2 diabetes has developed in an increasing number of individuals over 45 years old. Three scientists offered hypotheses to explain the cause of type 2 diabetes.

Scientist 1

Studies have shown that the consumption of sugar-sweetened drinks in excess is associated with an increased risk of type 2 diabetes. Thus, the cause of type 2 diabetes is an overconsumption of sugar. When sugar intake is high, the insulin in the body is unable to normalize the increased blood glucose levels. In a study of individuals 18–25 years old who consumed more than the daily recommended amount of sugar, although their insulin levels were normal, their blood glucose levels were significantly elevated. When these individuals received small injections of supplemental insulin once a day, their blood sugar did not return to normal levels.

CONTINUED

Scientist 2

Type 2 diabetes primarily occurs as a result of obesity and lack of exercise. Experimental data have shown that diets high in fat but not high in sugar are associated with an increased risk of type 2 diabetes. In a study of healthy young men, those put on a high-fat diet had twice the blood glucose levels compared to those put on a high-carbohydrate diet. Excess fat in the bloodstream breaks down into free radicals that impair insulin action, causing cells to become insulin resistant and blood glucose levels to rise. Studies have also shown that the lack of exercise causes 7% of type 2 diabetes cases. Regular exercise can boost the body's efficiency to regulate blood glucose levels.

Scientist 3

Type 2 diabetes is not caused by lifestyle or diet but inherited. Studies have shown an increased risk of type 2 diabetes in people with a parent or sibling who has type 2 diabetes. More than 36 genes that contribute to the risk of type 2 diabetes have been found. Individuals have about a 15%–20% chance of developing type 2 diabetes if one of their parents has it and a roughly 50% chance if both parents have it. The chance of siblings having type 2 diabetes is 25%–50%.

20. The liver helps to regulate the amounts of glucose, protein, and fat in the blood. About 80% of people with diabetes have buildup of fat in the liver. This information, if true, would strengthen the viewpoint of:

    F. Scientist 1 only.

    G. Scientist 2 only.

    H. both Scientist 1 and Scientist 2.

    J. neither Scientist 1 nor Scientist 2.

21. Scientists 1 and 2 would most likely agree that the occurrence of type 2 diabetes in an individual is associated with the patient's:

    A. lifestyle.

    B. diet.

    C. genetics.

    D. age.

22. According to the passage, adults who have had their pancreas removed should exhibit:

    F. increased blood insulin levels.

    G. decreased blood sugar levels.

    H. increased blood sugar levels.

    J. decreased body fat content.

23. Suppose that an individual had an 18% chance of developing type 2 diabetes. Based on the passage, Scientist 3 would most likely predict that this individual has:

    A. a high-sugar diet.

    B. a high-fat diet.

    C. one parent with type 2 diabetes.

    D. two parents with type 2 diabetes.

24. Suppose a 50-year-old patient developed type 2 diabetes. Which of the following statements is most consistent with the information in the passage?

    F. Scientist 1 would conclude that the patient consumes excess fat daily.

    G. Scientist 2 would conclude that the patient has a high-sugar diet.

    H. Scientist 3 would conclude that the patient fails to exercise.

    J. Scientist 3 would conclude that the patient had at least one parent with type 2 diabetes.

25. Which of the following discoveries, if accurate, would support the viewpoint of Scientist 1?

    A. High intake of sugar causes insulin resistance.

    B. High intake of fat causes impaired insulin action.

    C. Low intake of sugar causes increased insulin production.

    D. Low intake of sugar causes increased free radical production.

CONTINUED

26. Which of the following arguments could Scientist 3 use as an effective counter to Scientist 2's claim that lack of exercise causes 7% of type 2 diabetes cases?

    F. The 7% that lacked exercise also have family histories of type 2 diabetes.

    G. More than 36 genes that contribute to the risk of type 2 diabetes have been found.

    H. The 7% that lacked exercise did not receive insulin injections.

    J. Scientist 2's hypothesis would suggest that more than 7% of type 2 diabetes cases should be due to lack of exercise.

Passage V

Human blood is composed of approximately 45% *formed elements*, including blood cells, and 50% plasma. The formed elements of blood are further broken down into red blood cells, white blood cells, and platelets. The mass of a particular blood sample is determined by the ratio of formed elements to plasma; the formed elements weigh approximately 1.10 grams per milliliter (g/mL) and plasma approximately 1.02 g/mL. This ratio varies according to an individual's diet, health, and genetic makeup.

The following studies were performed by a phlebotomist to determine the composition and mass of blood samples from three different individuals, each of whom was required to fast overnight before the samples were taken.

Study 1

A 10 mL blood sample was taken from each of the three patients. The densities of the blood samples were measured using the *oscillator technique*, which determines fluid densities by measuring sound velocity transmission.

Study 2

Each 10 mL blood sample was spun for 20 minutes in a centrifuge to force the heavier formed elements to separate from the plasma. The plasma was then siphoned off and its mass recorded.

Study 3

The formed elements left over from Study 2 were analyzed using the same centrifuge, except this time they were spun at a slower speed for 45 minutes so that the red blood cells, white blood cells, and platelets could separate out. The mass of each element was then recorded. The results of the three studies are shown in Table 1.

			Table 1		
Patient	Plasma (g)	Red blood cells (g)	White blood cells (g)	Platelets (g)	Total density (g/mL)
A	4.54	2.75	1.09	1.32	1.056
B	4.54	2.70	1.08	1.35	1.054
C	4.64	2.65	1.08	1.34	1.050

27. The results of the studies indicate that the blood sample with the lowest density is the sample with the most:

    A. plasma.

    B. red blood cells.

    C. white blood cells.

    D. platelets.

28. Which of the following offers the most reasonable explanation for why the phlebotomist required each patient to fast overnight before taking blood samples?

    F. It is more difficult to withdraw blood from patients who have not fasted.

    G. Fasting causes large, temporary changes in the composition of blood.

    H. Fasting ensures that blood samples are not affected by temporary changes caused by consuming different foods.

    J. Blood from patients who have not fasted will not separate when spun in a centrifuge.

CONTINUED

29. Which of the following best explains why the amount of plasma, red blood cells, white blood cells, and platelets do not add up to 10.50 g in Patient C?

    A. Some of the red blood cells might have remained in the plasma, yielding low red blood cell measurements.

    B. Some of the platelets might not have separated from the white blood cells, yielding high white blood cell counts.

    C. The centrifuge might have failed to fully separate the plasma from the formed elements.

    D. There are likely components other than plasma, red and white blood cells, and platelets in blood.

30. Based on the data collected from the studies, it is possible to determine that, as total blood density increases, the mass of red blood cells:

    F. increases only.

    G. increases, then decreases.

    H. decreases only.

    J. decreases, then increases.

31. Suppose that a 10 mL blood sample from a fourth individual contains approximately 5 mL of plasma and approximately 5 mL of formed elements. The mass of this blood sample would most likely be:

    A. less than 10.0 g.

    B. between 10.0 and 12.0 g.

    C. between 12.0 and 14.0 g.

    D. greater than 14.0 g.

32. The phlebotomist varied which of the following techniques between Study 2 and Study 3?

    F. The volume of blood taken from each patient

    G. The mass of blood taken from each patient

    H. The instrument used to separate the elements of the blood samples

    J. The amount of time the samples were left in the centrifuge

33. The patient with the greatest mass of red blood cells per sample is:

    A. Patient A.

    B. Patient B.

    C. Patient C.

    D. not possible to determine from the information given.

Passage VI

A student performed experiments to determine the relationship between the amount of electrical current carried by a material and the physical dimensions and temperature of a sample of that material. Current is measured in amperes (A) and the resistance to the flow of current is measured in ohms (Ω). Current and resistance are related to voltage, measured in volts (V), by Ohm's law: $V = A \times \Omega$. (Note that Ohm's law can also be written as $V = I \times R$, where V is voltage, I is current, and R is resistance.)

Experiment 1

The student used several lengths of an iron rod with a 1 cm diameter. The rods were heated or cooled to the specified temperatures and used to complete the circuit shown in the diagram. The circuit contains a battery and an ammeter, which measures current in milliamperes (mA). The results are presented in Table 1.

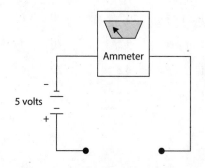

diagram

CONTINUED

Table 1

Trial	Length (cm)	Temperature (°C)	Current (mA)
1	16	80	20
2	16	20	40
3	12	80	27
4	12	20	53
5	10	80	32
6	10	20	64
7	8	80	40
8	8	20	80

Experiment 2

The student then repeated the experiment, this time using 1 cm diameter rods made from either iron or copper. The results are presented in Table 2.

Table 2

Trial	Material	Length (cm)	Temperature (°C)	Current (mA)
9	Iron	16	80	20
10	Copper	16	80	100
11	Iron	16	20	40
12	Copper	16	20	200
13	Iron	12	80	27
14	Copper	12	80	135
15	Iron	12	20	53
16	Copper	12	20	265

34. Based on the experimental results, which of the following most accurately describes the relationships between current and rod length and between current and temperature?

    F. Current is directly related to length and inversely related to temperature.

    G. Current is inversely related to both length and temperature.

    H. Current is inversely related to length and directly related to temperature.

    J. Current is directly related to both length and temperature.

35. Based on the information from the passage, which of the following rods would have the highest value for resistance?

    A. A 12 cm iron rod at 20°C

    B. A 16 cm copper rod at 20°C

    C. A 16 cm iron rod at 80°C

    D. A 12 cm copper rod at 80°C

36. The *conductivity* of a material is a measure of how readily a length of the material allows the passage of an electric current. Conductivity is represented by σ, the Greek letter sigma, with standard units of siemens per meter (*S/m*). Siemens are equivalent to inverse ohms (that is, $1/\Omega$). Based on this information, which of the following equations accurately describes the relationship between conductivity and resistance?

    F. $\Omega = \dfrac{1}{\sigma}$

    G. $\sigma = \Omega \times m$

    H. $\sigma = \dfrac{1}{\Omega + m}$

    J. $\Omega = \sigma \times m$

CONTINUED

37. If the rod used in Trial 4 of Experiment 1 were heated to a temperature of 50°C, the current it then conducts would most likely be:

    A. less than 27 mA.
    B. between 27 and 53 mA.
    C. between 53 and 80 mA.
    D. greater than 80 mA.

38. What would happen to the results of Experiment 2 if the student replaced the 5 V battery with a 10 V battery instead?

    F. The recorded current values would increase for both the copper and the iron rods.
    G. The recorded current values would increase for the copper rods but decrease for the iron rods.
    H. The recorded current values would decrease for the copper rods but increase for the iron rods.
    J. The recorded current values would decrease for both the copper and the iron rods.

39. Suppose the student took an iron rod of 8 cm and a copper rod of 8 cm, both with a 1 cm diameter, and attached them end to end, creating a composite rod with a length of 16 cm. Based on the results of Experiment 2, at a temperature of 20°C, this composite rod would most likely conduct a current of:

    A. less than 20 mA.
    B. between 20 and 40 mA.
    C. between 40 and 200 mA.
    D. greater than 200 mA.

40. Which of the following variables was NOT directly manipulated by the student in Experiment 2?

    F. Material
    G. Length
    H. Temperature
    J. Current

Writing Test

40 Minutes

Directions

The essay is used to evaluate your writing skills. You will have **40 minutes** to review the prompt and plan and write an essay in English. Before you begin, read everything in this test booklet carefully to make sure you understand the task.

Your essay will be judged based on the evidence it provides of your ability to do the following:

- Assert your own perspective on a complex issue and evaluate the relationship between your perspective and at least one other perspective
- Use reasoning and evidence to refine and justify your ideas
- Present your ideas in an organized way
- Convey your ideas effectively using standard written English

Write your essay on the lined essay pages in the answer booklet. All writing on those lined pages will be scored. Use the unlined pages in this test booklet to plan your essay. Your work on these unlined pages will not be scored.

Put your pencil down as soon as time is called.

DO NOT OPEN THIS BOOKLET UNTIL TOLD TO DO SO.

CONTINUED

Scientific Research

A great deal of pure research, undertaken without specific goals but generally to further humankind's understanding of themselves and their world, is subsidized at least partly, if not fully, by the nation's government to help drive progress and promote outcomes that improve overall quality of life for citizens. Though pure research often involves considerable time, energy, and money without any assurances of positive outcomes, it can result in economic, medical, and technological benefits. However, it can also result in negative, harmful, and perhaps irreversible outcomes, in which case taxpayer dollars can be wasted and society put at risk. Should governments fund research when the outcome is unclear? Given that taxpayers prefer that their dollars be spent efficiently and effectively, it may be unwise to allocate significant funding to endeavors that may not benefit society as a whole.

Read and carefully consider these perspectives. Each discusses government funding of scientific research.

Perspective One	Perspective Two	Perspective Three
Governments should fund as much pure research as they can afford when the intent is to benefit the mass population. Without the government's money, many research projects would have to cease unless alternative funding is secured. Even research without clear, positive consequences should be pursued because the outcome may prove beneficial, and the research can always be paused or stopped entirely if negative repercussions begin to emerge.	Governments should be very cautious and limit efforts to fund research programs with unclear consequences. Rather, these programs should demonstrate their worth and intended results when seeking government money. Governments should evaluate the merit and benefit of each program on a case-by-case basis and fund only those projects that are designed to create—and will likely achieve—clear and acceptable outcomes.	Governments should partner with private contributors to fund research. Private contributors include companies doing research and development as well as nonprofit foundations. These partnerships will distance the government from taking responsibility for any unintended or undesired consequences and relieve the burden on the taxpayer for efforts that do not prove beneficial. Additionally, this approach incentivizes research teams to provide results-based research that can generate private funding, thus increasing the chance that the research will prove useful to multiple entities, including the government.

Essay Task

Write a clear, well-reasoned essay evaluating multiple perspectives on government funding of scientific research. In your essay, be sure to:

- Assert your own perspective on the issue and evaluate the relationship between your perspective and at least one other perspective
- Use reasoning and evidence to refine and justify your ideas
- Present your ideas in an organized way
- Convey your ideas effectively using standard written English

Your perspective may be fully, somewhat, or not at all in agreement with one or more of the three perspectives in the prompt.

CONTINUED

Planning Your Essay

These pages are not scored.

Use the space below to brainstorm and plan your essay. Consider the following as you think about the prompt:

- Strengths and weaknesses of the three perspectives in the prompt
  - What observations do they offer, and what do they overlook?
  - Why are they persuasive or why are they not persuasive?
- Your own background and identity
  - What is your perspective on this issue, and what are its strengths and weaknesses?
  - What evidence will you use in your essay?

CONTINUED ▶

CONTINUED

CONTINUED

IF YOU FINISH BEFORE TIME IS CALLED, YOU MAY CHECK YOUR WORK ON THIS SECTION ONLY. DO NOT
TURN TO ANY OTHER SECTION IN THE TEST.

STOP

836 K

Answer Key

English Test

1. A	16. F	31. A	46. H	61. A
2. J	17. C	32. H	47. A	62. H
3. C	18. H	33. B	48. H	63. B
4. F	19. B	34. H	49. D	64. H
5. B	20. H	35. A	50. H	65. C
6. G	21. B	36. H	51. B	66. G
7. C	22. J	37. D	52. G	67. C
8. H	23. A	38. J	53. A	68. J
9. A	24. F	39. D	54. F	69. D
10. G	25. B	40. G	55. C	70. G
11. B	26. H	41. C	56. G	71. A
12. G	27. B	42. F	57. A	72. H
13. C	28. F	43. D	58. H	73. C
14. F	29. B	44. F	59. C	74. H
15. B	30. J	45. C	60. F	75. C

Mathematics Test

1. D	13. B	25. B	37. C	49. C
2. K	14. H	26. H	38. H	50. J
3. C	15. C	27. D	39. D	51. E
4. G	16. J	28. G	40. J	52. K
5. B	17. E	29. C	41. C	53. C
6. G	18. J	30. J	42. K	54. J
7. B	19. D	31. D	43. D	55. D
8. F	20. F	32. G	44. G	56. F
9. A	21. D	33. E	45. A	57. A
10. K	22. J	34. F	46. G	58. F
11. E	23. D	35. C	47. C	59. D
12. H	24. G	36. G	48. F	60. J

Reading Test

1. C	11. B	21. C	31. D
2. J	12. J	22. J	32. H
3. A	13. A	23. C	33. D
4. F	14. G	24. F	34. F
5. A	15. D	25. A	35. C
6. H	16. J	26. F	36. G
7. C	17. B	27. B	37. D
8. F	18. H	28. G	38. G
9. B	19. C	29. C	39. B
10. F	20. H	30. H	40. H

Science Test

1. A	11. A	21. B	31. B
2. J	12. H	22. H	32. J
3. B	13. A	23. C	33. A
4. H	14. G	24. J	34. G
5. A	15. A	25. A	35. C
6. G	16. J	26. F	36. H
7. D	17. D	27. A	37. B
8. H	18. H	28. H	38. F
9. C	19. B	29. D	39. C
10. G	20. G	30. F	40. J

Answers and Explanations

English Test

My Old-Fashioned Father

1. A
Difficulty: Low
Category: Sentence Structure
Getting to the Answer: When a period appears in the underlined portion, check to see if each sentence is complete. Here, each sentence is complete and correct; therefore (A), NO CHANGE, is correct. Choice B creates a run-on sentence. Choices C and D create sentences that are awkward and overly wordy.

2. J
Difficulty: Medium
Category: Sentence Structure
Getting to the Answer: The ACT tests very specific punctuation rules. If punctuation is used in a way not covered by these rules, it will be incorrect. No commas are required in the underlined selection; (J) is correct. Choices F, G, and H all contain unnecessary commas.

3. C
Difficulty: Medium
Category: Sentence Structure
Getting to the Answer: When a verb is underlined, make sure it places the action properly in relation to the other events in the passage. This passage is written primarily in the present tense; *runs*, (C), is the correct answer here. Choices A and B use verb tenses that do not make sense in context. The past tense verb in D is inconsistent with the rest of the passage.

4. F
Difficulty: Medium
Category: Conciseness
Getting to the Answer: Very rarely will a correct answer choice be significantly longer than the original selection. The underlined selection is grammatically and logically correct, so check the answer choices for a more concise version. You can eliminate G and H, both of which are wordier than the original. Choice J may be tempting because it's shorter than the underlined

selection, but it changes the meaning of the sentence; the back office, not the reader, is what hasn't changed. Choice (F) is correct.

5. B
Difficulty: Medium
Category: Development
Getting to the Answer: When an English Test question contains a question stem, read it carefully. More than one choice is likely to be both relevant and correct, but only one will satisfy the conditions of the stem. This paragraph deals with the author's father's refusal to give up his old-fashioned ways. Choice (B) is the most consistent choice. Choices A and D describe the items being inventoried, which is irrelevant to the point of the paragraph. Choice C is redundant; since you already know he uses paper and pencil to keep his inventory, it's understood that he's writing it by hand.

6. G
Difficulty: Medium
Category: Sentence Structure
Getting to the Answer: Commas cannot be used to combine independent clauses. Here, the comma connects two independent clauses. Choice (G) correctly replaces the comma with a semicolon. Choice H corrects the run-on error but is unnecessarily wordy. Choice J leaves the meaning of the second clause incomplete.

7. C
Difficulty: High
Category: Sentence Structure
Getting to the Answer: Beware of answer choices that make changes to parts of the selection that contain no errors; these choices will rarely be correct. As written, this sentence uses incorrect grammatical structure; the verb "is" is incorrect here, so you should eliminate A. Choice (C) eliminates it without introducing additional errors. Choices B and D correct the sentence's grammatical error, but neither uses the necessary contrast transition to relate this sentence to the one before it.

8. H

Difficulty: Low

Category: Sentence Structure

Getting to the Answer: Commas are used in a series of three or more; they are incorrect in compounds. "My sister and I" is a compound; no comma is needed, so F is incorrect. Choice (H) corrects the error without adding any new ones. Choice G uses the incorrect pronoun case; because you wouldn't say "me bought him a brand-new computer," "me" is incorrect in the compound as well. Choice J incorrectly separates the sentence's subject and its predicate verb with a comma.

9. A

Difficulty: High

Category: Organization

Getting to the Answer: When a transition word or phrase is underlined, make sure it properly relates the ideas it connects. The underlined word is the transition between the offer to help transfer records and the information about other ways the computer could be helpful. The second sentence is a continuation of the first, so you can eliminate B and D, both of which suggest a contrast. Choosing between (A) and C is a little more difficult, but remember that new errors may be introduced in answer choices. Choice C, *In addition*, would be acceptable if it were followed by a comma, but as written, it's incorrect. Choice (A) is correct.

10. G

Difficulty: Medium

Category: Sentence Structure

Getting to the Answer: Semicolons can only combine independent clauses. Here, the second clause is not independent, so the semicolon is incorrect; eliminate F. Choice (G) correctly eliminates the semicolon. Choice H incorrectly places a comma after the conjunction. Choice J creates a run-on sentence.

11. B

Difficulty: High

Category: Development

Getting to the Answer: When asked about the purpose of particular information, consider the purpose of the larger section. This paragraph describes the father's resistance to technology, which stems in part from his desire to be able to work even in blackout conditions. The information about the town's history shows that blackout

conditions seldom occur, making the father's reason a bad one. Choice (B) reflects this reasoning, and it is correct. Choice A is too extreme; the father's reason may be poor, but that does not make him delusional. Choices C and D do not relate to the purpose of the paragraph.

12. G

Difficulty: Medium

Category: Organization

Getting to the Answer: When asked to add new information, read it into the passage at the points suggested to choose its most logical placement. There are three pronouns in this new sentence; clarity requires that it be placed somewhere that these pronouns have logical antecedents. Placing it after Sentence 1, as (G) suggests, gives each pronoun a clear antecedent: *we* is the author and his sister, *him* is their father, and *it* is the computer. Choice F puts the siblings' hopes about how a computer could help their father before the information that they bought him one. Choice H's placement makes the antecedent for *it* Father's *blackout scenario*, which doesn't make sense in context. Placing the new sentence where choice J suggests gives the pronoun the antecedent *blackout*, which is also illogical.

13. C

Difficulty: Medium

Category: Development

Getting to the Answer: Idiom questions often offer more than one idiomatically correct answer choice; use context to determine which is appropriate. "Sooner than later" is idiomatically incorrect, so you should eliminate A; these are comparison words, but nothing is compared here. Both B and (C) offer proper idioms, but (C) is the one that's appropriate here. Choice D is also incorrect idiomatic usage.

14. F

Difficulty: Medium

Category: Development

Getting to the Answer: Remember to read for logic as well as for grammar and usage. The best version of this sentence is the way it is written; (F) is correct. Choice G redundantly uses the possessive *office's* where possession has already been indicated by *of.* Choice H misstates the information in the passage; the writer's father received the cell phone before the computer. Choice J incorrectly indicates that "the disorganized depths of that office" is where the writer's father received his cell phone, not where the cell phone ended up, which is opposite of the writer's intended meaning.

15. B
Difficulty: Low
Category: Organization
Getting to the Answer: When asked to add information, consider both the subject matter and the tone. This essay is about the author's father's resistance to technology. Choice (B) concludes the essay by referencing something stated at the beginning: that the writer's father tries to *hide* from the future. Choices A, C, and D, while relevant to the paragraph, do not provide strong conclusions to a passage about the father's aversion to technology.

Breaking Baseball's Color Barrier

16. F
Difficulty: Medium
Category: Agreement
Getting to the Answer: *More* or *–er* adjectives are used to compare two items; for more than two, use *most* or *–est*. This sentence is correct as written, (F); *farthest* is appropriate when comparing all areas of the globe. Choice G uses *most far*, but *most* is only correct with adjectives that don't have *–est* forms. Choice H combines *most* with the *–est* suffix, which is never correct. Choice J uses *farther*, which indicates a comparison that is not present here.

17. C
Difficulty: Medium
Category: Sentence Structure
Getting to the Answer: The fact that the underlined portion contains multiple prepositions (*among* and *for*) is a clue to look for a misplaced modifier. It makes the most sense to describe equality as being *among races*, eliminating A and B. Choice D awkwardly places the noun after its modifying phrases, so (C) is correct.

18. H
Difficulty: Medium
Category: Agreement
Getting to the Answer: Most ACT idioms questions will hinge on preposition usage. "Prevented … to participate" is idiomatically incorrect, so you can eliminate F. The proper idiom in this context is "prevented from participating," (H). Choices G and J are both idiomatically incorrect.

19. B
Difficulty: Medium
Category: Development
Getting to the Answer: When you're asked whether a piece of text is relevant, first determine the topic of the paragraph. This paragraph is about the evolution of the "*color line*" in baseball. Therefore, information that talks about the development of the industry and the shift in authority is relevant to the paragraph; (B) is correct. Choice A is incorrect because, although the text does talk about previous associations, knowing that range doesn't further the purpose of the paragraph. Choices C and D can be eliminated, since they indicate that the information is irrelevant.

20. H
Difficulty: Medium
Category: Sentence Structure
Getting to the Answer: A verb should not be separated from its object by a comma. As written, this sentence places an incorrect comma between the verb *had* and its object; eliminate F. Choice (H) eliminates the comma without introducing any additional errors. Choices G and J both add incorrect commas.

21. B
Difficulty: Medium
Category: Agreement
Getting to the Answer: When a preposition is underlined, you're most likely being tested on idioms. Select the choice that sounds the most correct when read with the following noun phrase—in this case, *professional teams*. Because the leagues are made up of professional teams, (B) is correct here. Choices A, C, and D all suggest an incorrect relationship between the leagues and the teams.

22. J
Difficulty: Medium
Category: Development
Getting to the Answer: Determining whether the underlined text should be deleted will help you quickly eliminate two answer choices. If you eliminate the underlined selection, the passage skips abruptly from the decree losing its force to a discussion of specific African-American players. The underlined text introduces those players generally, as a result of the decree losing its impact, and therefore provides a necessary transition, as indicated in (J). Choices F and G can be eliminated, since they advocate deleting the selection. The reasoning in H is not supported by the passage.

23. A
Difficulty: Medium
Category: Sentence Structure
Getting to the Answer: Expect about 25% of your English Test questions to have no error. This sentence is correct as written, (A). Choices B, C, and D all create sentence fragments.

24. F
Difficulty: Medium
Category: Sentence Structure
Getting to the Answer: The phrase "including Walker's brother Weldy" is properly used here to modify "a few other African Americans"; no change is needed, so (F) is correct. Choice G is incorrect because no comma is used to introduce a clause beginning with *that*. Choices H and J make the sentence wordier unnecessarily.

25. B
Difficulty: Medium
Category: Agreement
Getting to the Answer: Use context to determine appropriate verb tense usage. The previous sentence says that Walker *was* a catcher; the introductory phrase in this sentence refers you to the same time period. Only (B) uses a consistent tense. Choices A, C, and D all refer to future actions.

26. H
Difficulty: Medium
Category: Organization
Getting to the Answer: Since NO CHANGE is not presented as an option, you'll need to find the most logical placement for the new sentence. *Other teams* must contrast with teams already mentioned, and the only place that happens is in Sentences 2 and 3. Sentence 2 talks about one player for the Blue Stockings and Sentence 3 mentions some additional players for the same team. Sentence 4 turns to the time when segregation returned, so the information about African Americans playing for other teams must come before that, between Sentences 3 and 4, (H).

27. B
Difficulty: Low
Category: Conciseness
Getting to the Answer: When you don't spot an error in grammar or usage, check for errors of style. "At the time when" is a longer way of saying "when"; (B) is

correct here. Choice C uses *while*, which indicates a continuing period of time, but this sentence refers to a specific moment when Jackie Robinson crossed the color line. Choice D is even wordier than the original.

28. F
Difficulty: Medium
Category: Development
Getting to the Answer: Make sure your selection reflects the meaning of the sentence. The best version of this sentence is the way it is written, (F). Choice G changes the meaning of the sentence, implying that Robinson has yet to be recognized as a hero. Choice H also changes the sentence's meaning, indicating that Robinson is doing the recognizing rather than being recognized. Choice J is unnecessarily wordy.

29. B
Difficulty: High
Category: Development
Getting to the Answer: A question that asks about the essay's tone will likely include only answer choices that are grammatically correct. Be as picky as possible when determining which choice best fits the stated tone and emphasis. Choice A is too neutral, so it should be eliminated. Choice C does not emphasize the uniqueness of Robinson's role; eliminate it. Choice D mentions collaboration, which emphasizes teamwork rather than uniqueness, so it is also incorrect. Someone who blazes a path goes where no one has gone before. Thus, only (B) maintains a positive tone while showing that Robinson played a unique role.

30. J
Difficulty: Medium
Category: Development
Getting to the Answer: This question format appears frequently on the ACT; it's asking for the passage's main idea. This essay is about the color barrier in baseball; it would not fulfill an assignment to write about the history of baseball, so you can eliminate F and G. The fact that baseball was played before 1868, H, is not the reason this essay does not fulfill an assignment on baseball's history. Choice (J) correctly states the reasoning: the essay focuses only on one aspect of the game.

The Bear Mountain Bridge

31. A
Difficulty: Medium
Category: Sentence Structure
Getting to the Answer: An introductory phrase should be separated from the rest of the sentence by a comma. This introductory phrase is set off by a comma; the sentence is correct as written, (A). Choices B and C incorrectly treat the introductory phrase as an independent clause. Choice D incorrectly connects a dependent and an independent clause with the conjunction *and*.

32. H
Difficulty: Medium
Category: Agreement
Getting to the Answer: When a pronoun is underlined, check whether it matches its antecedent. The underlined portion refers to the bridge, so the correct answer will be singular; eliminate F and G. Choice J contains a subject-verb agreement error; the singular *it* requires the singular *was*. Choice (H) is correct.

33. B
Difficulty: Medium
Category: Agreement
Getting to the Answer: Make sure verb tenses make sense within the chronology of the passage. The past perfect is used in this sentence, but this tense is only correct when used to describe one past action completed before another. That is not the case here, so A is incorrect; (B) correctly replaces the verb with its past tense form. Choice C changes the meaning of the sentence (the legislature did the authorizing; it wasn't authorized by someone else) and creates a sentence that is grammatically incorrect. Choice D uses a conditional verb phrase, which is inappropriate in context.

34. H
Difficulty: Low
Category: Conciseness
Getting to the Answer: When the underlined selection contains a compound, check to see if the words mean the same thing. If so, the correct answer choice will eliminate one of them. *Build* and *construct* mean the same thing, so you can eliminate F and G right away. The only difference between (H) and J is a comma, which is incorrect in a compound; eliminate J.

35. A
Difficulty: Medium
Category: Sentence Structure
Getting to the Answer: Where the only difference among the answer choices is comma placement, remember your tested rules. This sentence needs NO CHANGE, (A). Choice B incorrectly places a comma between items in a compound. Choice C places a comma after the conjunction in a compound, which is also incorrect. Choice D incorrectly inserts a comma between a preposition and its object.

36. H
Difficulty: Medium
Category: Development
Getting to the Answer: Read the sentence without the material in question to determine what it adds to the paragraph and therefore why it was included. Looking at the paragraph as a whole, you can see that the author mentions the amount of money invested, the prominence of the architects, and the accomplishments of the firm the architects brought in to help. Removing one of these details detracts from that description; (H) is the best choice here. Choice F can be eliminated because this is not the only detail that supports the larger point; in and of itself, it's not critical. Removing this one phrase wouldn't impact the transition, as G suggests. Choice J is a trap. The segment in question does concern finances, but the text only mentions the amount of money invested, not how it was raised.

37. D
Difficulty: High
Category: Agreement
Getting to the Answer: On the ACT, "who" will only be correct when used to refer to people. Despite the fact that it's named after a person, "John A. Roebling and Sons" is the name of a company, so "who" isn't appropriate. That eliminates A and B. Choice C might be tempting because it's shorter than (D), but when C is read into the sentence, it creates a grammatical problem: "a company … and would later" requires another verb. Choice (D) is correct.

38. J

Difficulty: Medium

Category: Development

Getting to the Answer: Consider context when you're asked about the role a piece of text plays. A question that asks what would be lost if text were deleted is really just asking for the function of that text. If you read the paragraphs before and after the sentence in question, you'll see that what is missing is a clear transition; (J) is correct. Choice F distorts the meaning of the sentence, which discusses how long the project actually took, not how long it was expected to take. Choice G is out of scope; danger is only mentioned in this one sentence and then only in terms of how few lives were lost constructing the bridge. Choice H overstates the significance of the detail regarding construction time.

39. D

Difficulty: Medium

Category: Organization

Getting to the Answer: When transition words are underlined, focus on the relationship between the sentences or clauses they combine. The preceding sentence talks about the length of the bridge, and the sentence in which the underlined segment appears goes on to describe the cables in more detail. Since the second sentence isn't a result of the first sentence, you can eliminate A. Choice B inaccurately suggests an inconsistent or contradictory relationship between the sentences. Choice C is illogical; these are facts about the bridge, not events occurring simultaneously. The best choice here is no transition at all, as in (D).

40. G

Difficulty: Low

Category: Development

Getting to the Answer: When you're tested on Development: Precision, incorrect answer choices may have the wrong word in context. They may also be wordy or passive. *Longer* means a comparison: one thing is longer *than* something else. Since this sentence doesn't offer a comparison, *longer* can't be correct. Eliminate F. Choices (G) and H are both grammatically correct in context, but H is unnecessarily wordy. *Lengthy*, in J, is not correct when used to describe a specific length.

41. C

Difficulty: Medium

Category: Sentence Structure

Getting to the Answer: When the underlined portion contains a comma, check for a run-on. Because the comma separates two independent clauses, A is incorrect. Choice B eliminates the subject of the second clause, so it is incorrect. Choice D incorrectly combines a semicolon and a FANBOYS conjunction. Choice (C) makes the second clause dependent and correctly separates the clauses with a comma. Choice (C) is correct.

42. F

Difficulty: Medium

Category: Sentence Structure

Getting to the Answer: Introductory phrases and clauses should be set off from the rest of the sentence by a comma. The comma here is used correctly, so no change is needed; (F) is correct. Choice G eliminates the comma, making the sentence difficult to understand. Both the colon in H and the semicolon in J would work only if the first clause were independent, which it is not.

43. D

Difficulty: Medium

Category: Organization

Getting to the Answer: When a transition word is underlined, check to see what ideas are being connected by the transition. The previous sentence mentions that the bridge was renamed, and the sentence beginning with the underlined portion switches to the present tense to describe the number of vehicles that cross the bridge daily. There is no logical contrast between these ideas, so B and C can be eliminated. Choice A indicates a continuation of the previous thought, but that does not fit the context; eliminate it. Choice (D) is correct because it transitions from the past-tense description in the previous sentence to the present-tense description of the bridge's daily activity.

44. F

Difficulty: Medium

Category: Agreement

Getting to the Answer: Use *over* for physical location and *more than* for numbers or amounts. This sentence is correct as written, (F). Choice G replaces *more than* with *over*, which, despite its common usage, is actually a preposition that indicates location, not amount. Choice H is unnecessarily wordy. Choice J is also wordy and uses *amount*, which is incorrect for a countable noun like *vehicles*.

45. C
Difficulty: Medium
Category: Development
Getting to the Answer: As you read ACT English passages, develop a sense of the topic or *big idea*, just like you do in Reading; this question format is very common on the ACT. This passage is about one specific bridge, so it would not satisfy the requirement set out in the question stem. You can therefore eliminate A and B right away. Now turn to the reasoning. Choice D misstates the topic of the passage; (C) is correct.

The Dream of the American West

46. H
Difficulty: Medium
Category: Agreement
Getting to the Answer: Verbs in a compound should be in the same tense. The compound verb in this clause is "was … rising … and painted." Since the second verb is in the past tense, the first should be as well, so F is incorrect; (H) is correct. Choice G uses the gerund verb form without the necessary helping verb. Choice J is unnecessarily wordy.

47. A
Difficulty: Medium
Category: Development
Getting to the Answer: Read English Test question stems carefully. Often, all of the choices will be relevant and grammatically correct, but only one will fulfill the requirements of the stem. This question stem asks for a detail that shows a contrast between the quiet night streets and the daytime activity. The original text does this best. The verb in B does not convey the difference in the streets at these two times as well as *flood* in (A). Choice C is too general. Choice D does not provide the necessary contrast.

48. H
Difficulty: Medium
Category: Agreement
Getting to the Answer: Use your Kaplan resources to familiarize yourself with commonly tested idioms.

Although all four answer choices form idioms that would be correct in some contexts, one smiles *at* someone or something; (H) is correct.

49. D
Difficulty: Medium
Category: Conciseness
Getting to the Answer: When you don't spot an error in grammar or usage, look for errors in style. Choice A is a wordy way of saying *traveled across*, (D). Choices B and C are unnecessarily wordy as well.

50. H
Difficulty: Low
Category: Sentence Structure
Getting to the Answer: Read question stems carefully. This one asks which answer choice would NOT be acceptable, which means that three of the choices will be correct in context. Choices F, G, and J are appropriate introductory clauses, but (H) is an independent clause, which makes the sentence a run-on.

51. B
Difficulty: Medium
Category: Development
Getting to the Answer: Use your Reading skills for questions like this one that ask for the function of a detail. The underlined portion tells us that the writer's journey will end in California. Choice (B) is correct. The underlined selection does not mention the reasons for the writer's trip, describe her route, or make any comparisons, so A, C, and D are incorrect.

52. G
Difficulty: Medium
Category: Sentence Structure
Getting to the Answer: Use commas in a list or series only if there are three or more items. Since the writer only mentions two places she has been, the first comma here is incorrect; eliminate F. Choice (G) corrects this without introducing any additional errors. Choice H eliminates the incorrect comma but removes the one at the end of the selection, which is needed to separate the introductory clause from the rest of the sentence. Choice J does not address the error.

53. A
Difficulty: Medium
Category: Organization
Getting to the Answer: To identify the most effective transition, you'll need to read both paragraphs. Paragraph 3 is about how the author has traveled to foreign countries but, within the United States, only knows New York City. Paragraph 4 describes her drive through the Midwest. The text as written takes the reader from New York City (tall buildings) to the less populated areas, leading to the description of the cornfields. Choice (A), NO CHANGE, is the best choice here. Choice B misstates the passage; the cornfields didn't appear *almost immediately*, but gradually. Choice C and D do not provide appropriate transitions between the paragraphs.

54. F
Difficulty: Medium
Category: Development
Getting to the Answer: When you're asked to identify the *most relevant* choice, use context clues. The paragraph is about the change the author experiences as she drives from New York across the country. That contrast is clear in the passage as written; (F) is the best choice here. Choices G and H do not relate to the paragraph's topic. Choice J is opposite; the writer describes many different settings, which is the opposite of *monotonous*.

55. C
Difficulty: Medium
Category: Sentence Structure
Getting to the Answer: There are a number of ways to correct a run-on sentence, but only one answer choice will do so without introducing any additional errors. Each of the clauses in this sentence is independent; (C) corrects the run-on by replacing the comma with a semicolon. Choice B omits the comma necessary with the coordinating conjunction *but*. Choice D loses the contrast between the clauses that is present in the original.

56. G
Difficulty: Medium
Category: Agreement
Getting to the Answer: When a single adverb is underlined, you are most likely being tested on idioms. Determine what is being modified. The underlined portion modifies the noun *serenity*, so it should be an adjective.

Eliminate F. Choices H and J compare this serenity to other states of being, but there is no such comparison in the passage. Choice (G) is correct.

57. A
Difficulty: Medium
Category: Sentence Structure
Getting to the Answer: Only two apostrophe uses are tested on the ACT: possessive nouns and contractions. The noun here is possessive; the apostrophe is used correctly in (A). Choice B uses the plural *nights* instead of the possessive. Choice C is unnecessarily wordy and uses the idiomatically incorrect "shadows from the night." Choice D changes the meaning of the sentence.

58. H
Difficulty: Medium
Category: Conciseness
Getting to the Answer: If you don't spot a grammar or usage error, check for errors in style. As written, this sentence is unnecessarily wordy, so F is incorrect; (H) provides the best revision. Choices G and J are still unnecessarily wordy.

59. C
Difficulty: Medium
Category: Organization
Getting to the Answer: When a transition word or clause is underlined, determine the relationship between the ideas being connected. Look at the relationship between the sentences in this paragraph. The ideas are presented chronologically—that is, in the order in which they happened. Choice (C), *At first*, is the best transition into this series of events. Choices A and B imply contradiction or qualification, which is incorrect in context. Choice D implies that a lot went on prior to the writer's not having any idea what she was looking at, but this is presented as the first in a series of events.

60. F
Difficulty: High
Category: Conciseness
Getting to the Answer: The correct answer will rarely be longer than the original selection. This question requires no change, so (F) is correct. The pronoun's antecedent appears in the previous sentence ("what I was looking at") and the *-ing* verb form is used correctly. Choices G, H, and J are wordy; additionally, G introduces the passive voice unnecessarily.

Traveling at the Speed of Sound

61. A
Difficulty: Low
Category: Sentence Structure
Getting to the Answer: Commas are used to combine an independent and a dependent clause. This sentence is correct as written, (A), with the comma properly placed after the introductory clause. Choice B places the comma incorrectly; *of 2003* is part of the introductory clause. Choice C omits the necessary comma. Choice D incorrectly uses a semicolon between a dependent and an independent clause.

62. H
Difficulty: Medium
Category: Sentence Structure
Getting to the Answer: The underlined portion introduces nonessential information, so it should not form an independent clause. Choices F and G both make the clause an independent one; they should be eliminated. The passage is in the past tense, making the present tense verb in J incorrect. Choice (H) is correct.

63. B
Difficulty: Medium
Category: Development
Getting to the Answer: Development questions like this one require you to look at context; frequently, words will have similar meanings but be used differently. "Height" means "the distance from the top to the bottom of something"; "altitude" means "height above sea level." Since "altitude" is correct in this context, you can eliminate A. Choices (B) and C both use "altitude," but "at an altitude" is the correct idiom here; (B) is correct. Choice D creates a grammatically incorrect sentence.

64. H
Difficulty: High
Category: Organization
Getting to the Answer: When a transition word is underlined, check the logic of the transition as well as the grammar and punctuation. The sentence contrasts the famous and wealthy passengers with passengers who were ordinary people. Eliminate F and J because they do not express contrast. While G presents a contrast, it is grammatically incorrect. *Despite* creates a dependent clause requiring an *-ing* or *-ed* verb form, which is not present in the sentence. Choice (H) is correct, both logically and grammatically.

65. C
Difficulty: High
Category: Agreement
Getting to the Answer: Words like *that*, which are commonly misused in everyday speech, can make a question more challenging. Sound doesn't travel a speed, it travels *at* a speed; eliminate A. Only (C) makes the correction. Sound doesn't travel *to* a speed, as in B; *where*, D, will only be correct on the ACT when used to indicate location or direction.

66. G
Difficulty: Medium
Category: Development
Getting to the Answer: When asked about the purpose of a paragraph in relation to others, take a few seconds to summarize the paragraph in question, the one before it, and the one after it. The previous paragraph introduced the topic of supersonic aircraft. The paragraph in question transitions to questions of science, which are then discussed in the following paragraph. Choice (G) is correct. The paragraph does not provide an example or a counterargument, making F and H incorrect. The passage does not move from the general topic to a specific story, making J incorrect.

67. C
Difficulty: Medium
Category: Development
Getting to the Answer: Read English Test question stems carefully. This one asks for the LEAST acceptable alternative, which means that three of the choices will be correct in the sentence. All of the answer choices mean "change," so read each of them into the sentence. "Change them into," "translate them into," and "transform them into" are all appropriate usage, but "alter them into" is not because it changes the meaning. Choice (C) is correct here.

68. J
Difficulty: High
Category: Conciseness
Getting to the Answer: Look for constructions that repeat words unnecessarily; these will be incorrect on the ACT. The sentence tells us that the speed at which sound travels through gas depends on three things: what kind of gas it is, the temperature, and the pressure; "it is traveling through" is redundant, so F is incorrect. Choice (J) is the most concise answer, and it does

not lose any of the meaning of the underlined selection. Choices G and H do not address the error.

69. D
Difficulty: High
Category: Development
Getting to the Answer: Don't choose the shortest answer if it fails to make the writer's meaning clear. "Air temperature and pressure decrease with altitude" isn't clear; "air temperature" and "pressure" themselves do not have altitude, and we're not told to what the altitude is referring, so A is incorrect. Choice (D) makes the writer's meaning clear; when altitudes are higher, the decrease in temperature and pressure occur. Choice B does not address the error and even compounds it by replacing "altitude" with "height." Choice C contradicts the facts in the passage; higher, not lower, altitudes have this effect.

70. G
Difficulty: Medium
Category: Sentence Structure
Getting to the Answer: Beware of answer choices that make unnecessary changes to the sentence. The information provided in the two clauses contrasts, so *however* is correct, but it requires a comma to separate it from the rest of the clause. Eliminate F. Choice (G) is correct. Choice H creates an inappropriate cause-and-effect relationship between the clauses. Choice J does not address the punctuation error.

71. A
Difficulty: Medium
Category: Organization
Getting to the Answer: When you're asked to choose the most logical conclusion, first determine the sentence's function within the paragraph. The first half of this sentence previews a reason that the Concorde cruises at a higher altitude than regular planes, and it ties that reason back to the contrast between the speed of sound at two different altitudes. You need, then, a conclusion to the sentence that both explains why the planes would fly higher and does so in light of the information about altitude in the preceding sentence. The best choice here is (A); the original version of the sentence is the most logical. Choice B doesn't provide a reason; it simply repeats information that has already been stated. Choice C is out of scope; fuel consumption isn't mentioned in the

passage. Choice D is a result of the plane's higher altitude, not its cause.

72. H
Difficulty: High
Category: Agreement
Getting to the Answer: The use of *since* creates a specific marking point in the past and requires a verb that does the same. You need a simple past verb with *since*; (H) is correct. Choice F uses a tense that indicates an action that is ongoing, but the decommissioning of the Concorde has been completed. Choice G is unnecessarily wordy. The past perfect in J is only correct when used to indicate one past action completed prior to another stated past action, which is not the case here.

73. C
Difficulty: Medium
Category: Conciseness
Getting to the Answer: The phrases *about to* and *very soon* are redundant, making A, B, and D all incorrect. Furthermore, sentences beginning with coordinating (FANBOYS) conjunctions will not be correct on the ACT, which is an additional error in A. Only (C) correctly removes the redundancy.

74. H
Difficulty: Medium
Category: Organization
Getting to the Answer: When a transition word is underlined, check to see if it makes sense in the context. The sentence discusses upcoming advances to supersonic travel. Choice F places the advances in the present, which does not match the future-tense *will* later in the sentence. Choice G is about location rather than time, which does not fit the context. Choices (H) and J both refer to a future time, but only (H) makes sense in the context. The answer must be an adverb in order to describe when the advances will take place, but *Upcoming*, choice J, is an adjective. Choice (H) is therefore correct.

75. C
Difficulty: Medium
Category: Sentence Structure
Getting to the Answer: Here, the items combined by "not only ... but also" are "to the rich and famous" and "be for the masses." These items are correlated in the sentence, but they are not parallel in structure; eliminate A. Choices B and D do not address the error in parallel structure. Choice (C) corrects the error.

Mathematics Test

1. D

Difficulty: Low

Category: Statistics and Probability

Getting to the Answer: The basketball team scored 364 points in 13 games, so they scored an average of $\frac{364}{13} = 28$ points per game. Choice (D) is correct.

2. K

Difficulty: Low

Category: Number and Quantity

Getting to the Answer: To convert a mixed number to an improper fraction, you have two options:

Option 1: Rewrite the whole number part using the denominator of the fraction part, then add. Here, the result is $\frac{28}{7} + \frac{3}{7} = \frac{31}{7}$.

Option 2: Use the shortcut rule, which is: multiply the whole number by the denominator of the fraction and add the numerator, then write the result over the original denominator. Here, you get $4 \times 7 + 3 = 28 + 3 = 31$ over 7, or $\frac{31}{7}$.

Using either method, you arrive at a numerator of 31, which is (K).

3. C

Difficulty: Low

Category: Algebra

Getting to the Answer: To solve for x, you need to isolate it on one side of the equation. To do this, subtract 18 from both sides, then divide by 4. The result is:

$$4x + 18 = 38$$
$$4x = 20$$
$$x = 5$$

Choice (C) is correct. Note that you could also Backsolve to answer this question, but the algebra is quicker.

4. G

Difficulty: Low

Category: Number and Quantity

Getting to the Answer: Because John weighs *more* than Ellen, begin by eliminating J and K, as doing so will reduce the chance of a miscalculation error. According to the question, John's 144 pounds represents 1.5 times Ellen's weight. Therefore, Ellen's weight must be $\frac{144}{1.5} = 96$ pounds. Choice (G) is correct.

If you're not sure whether to multiply or divide by 1.5, you could also set up an equation and solve it. Let $J =$ John's weight and $E =$ Ellen's weight. Translating from English to math gives:

$$J = 1.5E$$
$$144 = 1.5E$$
$$\frac{144}{1.5} = E$$
$$E = 96$$

5. B

Difficulty: Medium

Category: Number and Quantity

Getting to the Answer: To find the reciprocal of a number, swap the numerator and the denominator. You could use algebra to answer the question, but Back-solving is likely to be quicker. As usual, start with C:

The reciprocal of $\frac{4}{3}$ is $\frac{3}{4}$ and $\frac{4}{3} \div \frac{3}{4} = \frac{4}{3} \times \frac{4}{3} = \frac{16}{9}$. This is too big (and it's the flip of what you're looking for), so try (B) next:

The reciprocal of $\frac{3}{4}$ is $\frac{4}{3}$ and $\frac{3}{4} \div \frac{4}{3} = \frac{3}{4} \times \frac{3}{4} = \frac{9}{16}$. Choice (B) is correct.

6. G

Difficulty: Medium

Category: Algebra

Getting to the Answer: The inverse operation of cube rooting is cubing, so cube both sides of the equation to solve for x:

$$\sqrt[3]{x} = \frac{1}{4}$$

$$x = \left(\frac{1}{4}\right)^3 = \frac{1}{4} \times \frac{1}{4} \times \frac{1}{4} = \frac{1}{64}$$

That's (G).

7. B

Difficulty: Low

Category: Algebra

Getting to the Answer: Isolate the variable, then solve for x. To do this, subtract 14 from both sides, then take the square root:

$$x^2 + 14 = 63$$
$$x^2 = 49$$
$$x = \pm 7$$

Choice (B) matches the positive value of x.

8. F

Difficulty: Medium

Category: Number and Quantity

Getting to the Answer: Don't let the vector notation scare you. Adding vectors works exactly as you would expect: to add two vectors, add the corresponding components. The question only asks about the value of a, so focus on the first entries only: $7 + a = 5$, which gives $a = 5 - 7$, or -2. Choice (F) is correct.

9. A

Difficulty: Low

Category: Number and Quantity

Getting to the Answer: The quickest way to answer this question is to estimate. While you may or may not know 6% of 1,250 off the top of your head, 10% of 1,250 is 125. Because 6% < 10%, the correct answer must be less than 125. Only (A) works.

To solve this the more traditional way, multiply 1,250 by the decimal form of 6%: $1{,}250 \times 0.06 = 75$.

10. K

Difficulty: Low

Category: Number and Quantity

Getting to the Answer: When the choices are spaced far apart, estimation is generally the quickest way to the correct answer. To estimate, round 5.2 to 5 and 6.8 to 7. Because $5^3 + 7^2 = 125 + 49 = 174$, the correct answer will be close to 174. That would be (K).

11. E

Difficulty: Low

Category: Number and Quantity

Getting to the Answer: You certainly could reason this question out logically, but it's much easier to just pick a starting balance, make the error described in the question, and see which answer choice matches. Suppose Lexi starts with a balance of $100. If she accidentally adds $40 to this amount, the incorrect new balance is $140. If she had subtracted instead, the correct balance would have been $60. Thus, the incorrect balance is $140 − $60 = $80 more than is should be. Choice (E) is correct.

12. H

Difficulty: Medium

Category: Number and Quantity

Getting to the Answer: To answer this question, you'll need to follow the order of operations (PEMDAS).

First, evaluate the parentheses:

$$3^3 \div 9 + (6^2 - 12) \div 4$$
$$= 3^3 \div 9 + (36 - 12) \div 4$$
$$= 3^3 \div 9 + 24 \div 4$$

Next, simplify the exponent:

$$3^3 \div 9 + 24 \div 4 = 27 \div 9 + 24 \div 4.$$

Then, take care of any multiplication and/or division, from left to right: $27 \div 9 + 24 \div 4 = 3 + 6$.

Finally, take care of any addition and/or subtraction, from left to right: $3 + 6 = 9$.

So (H) is correct.

13. B

Difficulty: Low

Category: Algebra

Getting to the Answer: Each banana costs $0.24, so the price of x bananas is $0.24x$. Similarly, each orange costs $0.38, so the price of y oranges is $0.38y$. Therefore, the total price of x bananas and y oranges is $0.24x + $0.38y$. That's (B).

14. H

Difficulty: Low

Category: Number and Quantity

Getting to the Answer: To find the percent shaded, divide the number of shaded triangles by the total number of triangles. There are 24 small triangles in all, and 8 of them are shaded: $\frac{8}{24} = \frac{1}{3} = 33\frac{1}{3}\%$. Choice (H) is correct.

15. C

Difficulty: Medium

Category: Number and Quantity

Getting to the Answer: The ratio of girls to boys is 5:3, so the ratio of girls to the total number of seniors is 5:(3 + 5), or 5:8. Call g the number of girls in the senior class. Set up a proportion and cross-multiply to solve for g:

$$\frac{5}{8} = \frac{g}{168}$$
$$8g = 840$$
$$g = 105$$

There are 105 girls in the senior class, which is (C).

16. J

Difficulty: Medium

Category: Statistics and Probability

Getting to the Answer: When a question about averages involves a missing value (here, the final test score), it often helps to think in terms of the sum instead. For Sarah's exam scores to average at least a 90, they must sum to at least $90 \times 4 = 360$. She already has an 89, a 93, and an 84, so she needs at least $360 - (89 + 93 + 84)$, which gives $360 - 266 = 94$ points on her final test. Choice (J) is correct.

17. E

Difficulty: Low

Category: Algebra

Getting to the Answer: Treat inequalities just as you would equations. The only exception is that if you multiply or divide by a negative number, you must flip the inequality symbol.

$$3x - 11 \geq 22$$
$$3x \geq 33$$
$$x \geq 11$$

This matches (E).

18. J

Difficulty: Medium

Category: Statistics and Probability

Getting to the Answer: Probability is the number of desired outcomes divided by the total number of possible outcomes. Here, you're given the probability $\left(\frac{3}{4}\right)$ and the number of desired outcomes (48). You're looking for the total number of possible outcomes (the number of dominos in the pile). Let d represent the number of dominos in the pile. Set up an equation using the definition of probability and the given information:

$$P(\text{even \# dots}) = \frac{\text{\# with even \# dots}}{\text{total \# dominos in pile}} = \frac{3}{4}$$
$$\frac{3}{4} = \frac{48}{d}$$
$$3d = 192$$
$$d = 64$$

Choice (J) is correct.

19. D

Difficulty: Low

Category: Algebra

Getting to the Answer: This is a straightforward substitution question, so just be careful of the negative signs. Plug in 4 for x and $-\frac{1}{2}$ for y and simplify:

$$3x - 8y$$
$$= 3(4) - 8\left(-\frac{1}{2}\right)$$
$$= 12 - (-4)$$
$$= 12 + 4$$
$$= 16$$

That's (D).

20. F

Difficulty: Medium

Category: Number and Quantity

Getting to the Answer: Whenever multiple rates are given, pay very careful attention to the units. As you read the question, decide how and when you will need to convert units. Use the factor-label method as needed. The answer choices are given in hours and minutes, so start by converting the given typing rate from words per second to words per minute:

$$\frac{3.75 \text{ words}}{1 \text{ second}} \times \frac{60 \text{ seconds}}{1 \text{ minute}} = \frac{225 \text{ words}}{1 \text{ minute}}$$

Next, find the number of words in the 25-page transcript:

$$\frac{675 \text{ words}}{1 \text{ page}} \times 25 \text{ pages} = 16{,}875 \text{ words}$$

Finally, let m be the number of minutes it takes the court reporter to type the whole transcript. Set up a proportion and solve for m:

$$\frac{225 \text{ words}}{1 \text{ minute}} = \frac{16{,}875 \text{ words}}{m \text{ minutes}}$$
$$225m = 16{,}875$$
$$m = 75$$

Because 75 minutes is not an answer choice, convert it to hours and minutes: 75 minutes = 1 hour, 15 minutes, making (F) the correct answer.

21. D

Difficulty: Low

Category: Geometry

Getting to the Answer: When two parallel lines are cut by a transversal, half of the angles will be acute and half will be obtuse. Each acute angle will have the same measure as every other acute angle. The same is true of every obtuse angle. Furthermore, the acute angles will be supplementary to the obtuse angles. Based on the information provided, $\angle a$ is an acute angle measuring 68°. Based on the figure, $\angle f$ is an obtuse angle, so $\angle a$ must be supplementary to $\angle f$. Therefore, the measure of $\angle f$ is $180° - 68° = 112°$. Choice (D) is correct.

22. J

Difficulty: Medium

Category: Number and Quantity

Getting to the Answer: If the student copy is $\frac{1}{4}$ the size of the wall map, then 2.5 inches on the student map would be $2.5 \times 4 = 10$ inches on the wall map. Now set up a proportion to find the actual distance between the cities using the scale of the wall map:

$$\frac{1}{100} = \frac{10}{x}$$
$$x = 1,000$$

The correct answer is (J).

23. D

Difficulty: Medium

Category: Number and Quantity

Getting to the Answer: The piece of paper is $8\frac{1}{2}$ inches wide. To find the number of $\frac{5}{8}$-inch wide strips of paper you can cut, divide:

$$8\frac{1}{2} \div \frac{5}{8} = \frac{17}{2} \div \frac{5}{8}$$
$$= \frac{17}{2} \times \frac{8}{5}$$
$$= \frac{136}{10} = \frac{68}{5} = 13.6$$

Thus, you can make 13 strips of paper that are $\frac{5}{8}$ of an inch wide and 11 inches long, and you will have a small, thin strip of paper left over. Choice (D) is correct.

24. G

Difficulty: Medium

Category: Geometry

Getting to the Answer: This is a pair of parallel lines cut by a transversal, but this time, there's also a triangle thrown into the mix. Begin with segment $\overline{AB}$. This is a transversal, so $\angle MAB$ and $\angle ABC$ are alternate interior angles and $m\angle MAB = m\angle ABC = 55°$. Because triangle ABC is isosceles with $\overline{AB} = \overline{AC}$, $m\angle ACB$ is also 55° (base angles of an isosceles triangle have equal measures). Choice (G) is correct.

25. B

Difficulty: Low

Category: Algebra

Getting to the Answer: Use the slope formula to find the slope of the line:

$$m = \frac{y_2 - y_1}{x_2 - x_1}$$
$$= \frac{-6 - 0}{0 - (-10)}$$
$$= -\frac{6}{10}$$
$$= -\frac{3}{5}$$

That's (B).

26. H

Difficulty: Medium

Category: Algebra

Getting to the Answer: This question seems long, but it actually isn't that complicated. FOIL the first pair of binomials, FOIL the second pair, then add the results by combining like terms:

$$(x + 4)(x - 4) = x(x) + x(-4) + 4(x) + 4(-4)$$
$$= x^2 - 4x + 4x - 16$$
$$= x^2 - 16$$

(If you noticed the difference of squares above, that will save you some time.)

$$(2x + 2)(x - 2) = 2x(x) + 2x(-2) + 2(x) + 2(-2)$$
$$= 2x^2 - 4x + 2x - 4$$
$$= 2x^2 - 2x - 4$$

Finally, add the two polynomials by combining like terms:

$$\boxed{x^2}\ominus 16 + \boxed{2x^2} - 2x \ominus 4 = 3x^2 - 2x - 20$$

Choice (H) is correct.

27. D
Difficulty: Medium
Category: Geometry
Getting to the Answer: To find the distance between two points that don't have either the same x-coordinates or the same y-coordinates, plug the points into the distance formula and evaluate:

$$\text{distance} = \sqrt{(x_2 - x_1)^2 + (y_2 - y_1)^2}$$
$$= \sqrt{(-2 - 3)^2 + (6 - (-6))^2}$$
$$= \sqrt{(-5)^2 + 12^2}$$
$$= \sqrt{25 + 144}$$
$$= \sqrt{169}$$
$$= 13$$

Choice (D) is correct.

28. G
Difficulty: Medium
Category: Number and Quantity
Getting to the Answer: Look for shortcuts; you could write an equation and solve for h, but is there a faster way? Examine the two percents: 30% is half of 60%, so 30% of h will be half of 60% of h, or half of 80, which is 40. That's (G).

29. C
Difficulty: Medium
Category: Statistics and Probability
Getting to the Answer: Because the integers in Set A are consecutive, their average must equal their middle term. In a set of 7 integers, the middle one is the fourth term. To find the smallest term, count backward from 46: 46, 44, 42, 40. That's (C). You can also answer this question by using Backsolving. Start with (C). If 40 is the smallest integer of Set A, then the next six consecutive integers must be 42, 44, 46, 48, 50, and 52. Take the average of these 7 integers:

$$\frac{40 + 42 + 44 + 46 + 48 + 50 + 52}{7} = \frac{322}{7} = 46$$

This matches the condition in the question stem: The average of these consecutive integers equals 46, so (C) must be the correct answer.

30. J
Difficulty: Medium
Category: Functions
Getting to the Answer: Test the sum for 2, then 3, then 4, then 5 terms of the sequence to see if a relationship can be determined. If $n = 2$, the sum is $1 + 3 = 4$. If $n = 3$, the sum is $1 + 3 + 5 = 9$. If $n = 4$, the sum is $1 + 3 + 5 + 7 = 16$. If $n = 5$, the sum is $1 + 3 + 5 + 7 + 9 = 25$. The sum is always equal to the square of n. Therefore, the correct answer is (J).

31. D
Difficulty: Medium
Category: Number and Quantity
Getting to the Answer: To multiply two matrices, the sizes (# of rows by # of columns) must match in a certain way. Here, the size of the first matrix is 2×2 and the size of the second is 2×1. If you multiply a 2×2 matrix by a 2×1 matrix (which is possible because the middle dimensions match), the result will be a 2×1 matrix (the outer dimensions when the sizes are written as a product). This means you can eliminate A, B, and C, which are all 2×2 matrices. To multiply the matrices, multiply each element in the first row of the first matrix by the corresponding element in the second matrix and add the products. Then repeat the process using the second row of the first matrix:

$$\begin{bmatrix} -2 & 0 \\ 1 & -3 \end{bmatrix} \cdot \begin{bmatrix} 2 \\ 2 \end{bmatrix} = \begin{bmatrix} -2(2) + 0(2) \\ 1(2) + (-3)(2) \end{bmatrix} = \begin{bmatrix} -4 \\ -4 \end{bmatrix}$$

Choice (D) is correct.

32. G
Difficulty: Medium
Category: Geometry
Getting to the Answer: This is an area question with a twist—you're cutting a piece out of the rectangle. To find the area of the remaining space, you will need to subtract the area of the sandpit from the area of the original playground. Recall that the area of a rectangle is length $\times$ width. The dimensions of the original playground are $x + 7$ and $x + 3$, so its area is $(x + 7)(x + 3)$ which FOILs to $x^2 + 10x + 21$. The sandpit is a square with side x, so its area is x^2. Remove the pit from the playground, and the remaining area is $x^2 + 10x + 21 - x^2 = 10x + 21$. Choice (G) is correct.

33. E
Difficulty: High
Category: Number and Quantity
Getting to the Answer: Because $m > 0$, m is a positive number; likewise, because $n < 0$, n is a negative number. Consider each answer choice and decide whether the expression must be positive, negative, or could be either depending on the values of m and n. Keep in mind that m and n can be even or odd integers.

A: $-n^m \rightarrow$ If m is even, n^m is positive so $-n^m$ is negative. However, when m is odd, n^m is negative, so $-n^m$ is positive. Eliminate this choice.

B: $-mn \rightarrow$ Because one number is positive and the other is negative, the product mn must be negative, so $-mn$ must be positive. Eliminate this choice.

C: $m^n \rightarrow m$ is positive, so m raised to any exponent will also be positive. A negative exponent simply means to take the reciprocal of the number, not to give the number a negative sign. Eliminate this choice.

D: $-n - m \rightarrow -n$ equals $-(-\text{number})$, which is positive, and m is positive, so $-n - m$ is a positive minus a positive. If $m > -n$, then $-n - m$ will be negative. However, if $-n > m$, then $-n - m$ will be positive. Eliminate this choice.

(E): $n - m \rightarrow n$ is negative and m is positive, so $n - m$ is a negative minus a positive. This must be negative, so (E) is the correct answer.

34. F
Difficulty: Medium
Category: Geometry
Getting to the Answer: Consider how the provided endpoint $(1,9)$ and the midpoint $(-3,-2)$ relate to each other. If the x-coordinate of the endpoint is positive 1 and the x-coordinate of the midpoint is -3, the x-coordinate of the other endpoint must be less than -3; only (F) meets this criteria and is correct. You might also notice, if you roughly sketch a graph of the points, that the endpoint (m,n) must lie in quadrant III; again, only (F) meets this criteria.

Alternatively, use the midpoint formula and the given midpoint to solve for m and n:

$$m = \left(\frac{x_1 + x_2}{2}, \frac{y_1 + y_2}{2} \right)$$

$$(-3, -2) = \left(\frac{1 + m}{2}, \frac{9 + n}{2} \right)$$

Once you have the formula set up and all the given information plugged in, separate the coordinates into two equations and solve for the variables:

$$-3 = \frac{1 + m}{2} \quad \text{and} \quad -2 = \frac{9 + n}{2}$$
$$-6 = 1 + m \qquad\qquad -4 = 9 + n$$
$$-7 = m \qquad\qquad\quad -13 = n$$

Thus $(m,n) = (-7, -13)$, which is (F).

35. C
Difficulty: Low
Category: Functions
Getting to the Answer: When given a function and a value of x, plug in the number value for each x in the equation and simplify. Make sure you follow the order of operations:

$$f(x) = 16x^2 - 20x$$
$$f(3) = 16(3)^2 - 20(3)$$
$$= 16(9) - 60$$
$$= 144 - 60 = 84$$

Choice (C) is the answer.

36. G
Difficulty: Low
Category: Geometry
Getting to the Answer: To find the length of a line segment on the coordinate plane, you would normally need to use the distance formula. This requires the coordinates of the segment's two endpoints. Because $A(1,5)$ and $C(1,1)$ have the same x-coordinate, a much faster way is to simply subtract the y-coordinate of C from the y-coordinate of A. The length of segment AC is $5 - 1$, or 4. Choice (G) is correct.

37. C
Difficulty: Medium
Category: Functions
Getting to the Answer: With nested functions, work from the inside out. To answer this question, substitute the entire rule for $g(x)$ for x in the function $f(x)$, then simplify:

$$f(g(x)) = \frac{1}{3}(3x^2 + 6x + 12) + 13$$
$$= x^2 + 2x + 4 + 13$$
$$= x^2 + 2x + 17$$

Choice (C) is correct.

38. H

Difficulty: Medium

Category: Algebra

Getting to the Answer: Perpendicular lines have negative-reciprocal slopes. Because the line in the question has a slope of $\frac{2}{3}$ (the coefficient of x), the line you are looking for must have a slope of $-\frac{3}{2}$. Eliminate F and G. The question also says that this line contains the point $(4, -3)$. Plugging all of this information into the equation of a line, $y = mx + b$, will allow you to find the final missing piece of the equation—the y-intercept:

$$y = mx + b$$
$$-3 = -\frac{3}{2}(4) + b$$
$$-3 = -6 + b$$
$$3 = b$$

With a slope of $-\frac{3}{2}$ and a y-intercept of 3, the line is $y = -\frac{3}{2}x + 3$, which matches (H).

39. D

Difficulty: Medium

Category: Algebra

Getting to the Answer: This looks like a chemistry or physics question, but in fact it's just a "plug in the number and solve for the missing quantity" question.

Be sure to plug 95 in for C (not F). To clear the fraction (rather than distributing it), multiply both sides of the equation by the reciprocal of $\frac{5}{9}$:

$$C = \frac{5}{9}(F - 32)$$
$$95 = \frac{5}{9}(F - 32)$$
$$\frac{9}{5} \times 95 = F - 32$$
$$F - 32 = 171$$
$$F = 171 + 32 = 203$$

Choice (D) is correct.

40. J

Difficulty: Medium

Category: Algebra

Getting to the Answer: First, translate from English to math: "3 times x is increased by 5" translates to $3x + 5$, and "the result is less than 11" translates to < 11. Put these together to write an inequality and then solve for x:

$$3x + 5 < 11$$
$$3x < 6$$
$$x < 2$$

This inequality is graphed with an open circle at 2 (because x cannot equal 2) and shaded to the left, where the numbers are less than 2. Your graph should look like (J).

41. C

Difficulty: Medium

Category: Geometry

Getting to the Answer: Because $\overline{QS} = \overline{QR}$, triangle QRS must be a 45°–45°–90° triangle and the hypotenuse is $5\sqrt{2}$. Remember that $\cos = \dfrac{\text{adjacent}}{\text{hypotenuse}}$. Therefore:

$$\cos R = \frac{5}{5\sqrt{2}}$$
$$= \frac{1}{\sqrt{2}}$$
$$= \frac{1}{\sqrt{2}} \times \frac{\sqrt{2}}{\sqrt{2}} = \frac{\sqrt{2}}{2}$$

Choice (C) is correct.

42. K

Difficulty: High

Category: Number and Quantity

Getting to the Answer: You need to find the ratio of angelfish to puffers. You're given two ratios: tangs to angelfish and tangs to puffers.

Both of the given ratios contain tangs, but the tang amounts (5 and 2) are not the same. To directly compare them, find a common multiple (10). Multiply each ratio by the factor that will make the number of tangs equal to 10:

tangs to angelfish: $(5{:}2) \times (2{:}2) = 10{:}4$

tangs to puffers: $(2{:}3) \times (5{:}5) = 10{:}15$

Now that the number of tangs are the same in both ratios, you can merge the two ratios to compare angelfish to puffers directly: **4**:10:**15**. So the proper ratio of angelfish to puffers is 4:15, which is (K).

43. D
Difficulty: Low
Category: Geometry
Getting to the Answer: This question is testing whether you can substitute into a formula correctly. Because you are told the diameter is 6, you know the radius, r, of the sphere is 3. Plug this value into the formula and simplify:

$$V = \frac{4}{3}\pi(3)^3 = \frac{4}{3}\pi(27) = 36\pi$$

Choice (D) is correct.

44. G
Difficulty: Medium
Category: Algebra
Getting to the Answer: To simplify the given expression, look for factors in the fraction term that will cancel. Use the denominator as a hint as to how to factor the numerator. Be careful—you cannot simply cancel the $x + 1$ in the denominator with the $x + 1$ at the end of the expression.

$$\frac{x^2 - 5x - 6}{x+1} + x + 1 = \frac{(x+1)(x-6)}{x+1} + x + 1$$
$$= x - 6 + x + 1$$
$$= 2x - 5$$

Choice (G) is correct.

45. A
Difficulty: Medium
Category: Algebra
Getting to the Answer: Don't let the language throw you—"greatest monomial factor" just means the greatest common factor. Look for the largest number that divides evenly into 60 and 45. (Use the answer choices as a hint.) The number is 15, so eliminate D and E. Next, look for the highest power of each variable that appears in *both* terms: a^2 and plain b. Thus, the greatest monomial factor is $15a^2b$, which is (A).

46. G
Difficulty: Low
Category: Statistics and Probability
Getting to the Answer: Percent change is calculated by dividing the amount of change by the original amount. In 1985, the population was 3,000; in 1995, the population was 2,000. Thus the amount of change was 1,000. Divide this by the original amount (the 1985 population) to find that the percent change was

$1,000 \div 3,000 = 0.3333$, or 33.33%. The population went *down* from 1985 to 1995, so this is a decrease of 33.33%, which is (G).

47. C
Difficulty: Medium
Category: Statistics and Probability
Getting to the Answer: This question requires brute force. You need to list the data value corresponding to each year, order the values from least to greatest, find the median (the middle value), match it to a year in the graph, and then select the correct answer.

85	86	87	88	89	90
3,000	1,000	5,000	5,000	4,000	3,000

91	92	93	94	95
4,000	1,000	3,000	2,000	2,000

Order the data, keeping the year labels:

86	92	94	95	85	90
1,000	1,000	2,000	2,000	3,000	3,000

93	89	91	87	88
3,000	4,000	4,000	5,000	5,000

The median of this group is the sixth value, or 3,000. The years 1985, 1990, and 1993 all had populations of 3,000. The only one of these years among the answer choices is 1990, which is (C).

48. F
Difficulty: Medium
Category: Statistics and Probability
Getting to the Answer: Identify which pieces of information from the table you need. The question asks for the probability that a randomly chosen person from the study is employed and has a college degree, so you need the total of both females and males with college degrees who are employed compared to all the participants in the study. There are 188 employed females with a college degree and 177 employed males with a college degree for a total of 365 employed people with a college degree out of 800 participants, so the probability is $\frac{365}{800}$, which reduces to $\frac{73}{160}$, (F).

49. C
Difficulty: High
Category: Statistics and Probability
Getting to the Answer: Distinct permutations are permutations without repetition. You need to find the number of unique orderings of the letters GEOMETRY. If all eight letters were different, the number of unique orderings would be 8!. Because the E is repeated, you must divide by 2! to account for the repeated E. The result is $\frac{8!}{2!}$, which is (C).

Note that this process is the same as using the formula for "indistinguishable" outcomes: $\frac{n!}{a! \times b! \times \ldots}$. The number of letters is 8 (so $n = 8$), and there are 2 indistinguishable E's, so $a = 2$ and there is no b.

50. J
Difficulty: Low
Category: Geometry
Getting to the Answer: To match an inequality to its graph, you need to consider three things: the equation of the line, whether the line should be solid or dashed, and the direction of the shading. You can use any, or all, of these things to eliminate choices. Here, the shading is below (or less than) the line, so the inequality symbol should be <. Eliminate G and K. The line is dashed, but all the symbols are strict inequalities, so this doesn't help. The y-intercept of the line is -4 and the line rises 4 units for each 3 units that it runs, so the slope is $\frac{4}{3}$. This means the correct inequality is $y < \frac{4}{3}x - 4$, which is (J).

51. E
Difficulty: Medium
Category: Functions
Getting to the Answer: Occasionally, you may encounter a function that is defined in terms of two or three independent variables. These functions behave just as you would expect them to. As with any function, substitute the given values for the corresponding variables and simplify. Here, $x = 2$, $y = -1$, and $z = 3$.

$$h(x, y, z) = 4xy^2 - yz^3$$
$$h(2, -1, 3) = 4(2)(-1)^2 - (-1)(3)^3$$
$$= 4(2)(1) - (-1)(27)$$
$$= 8 + 27$$
$$= 35$$

Choice (E) is correct.

52. K
Difficulty: Medium
Category: Geometry
Getting to the Answer: Write the formula for the area of a circle, using r to represent the radius of the original circle in the question: $A = \pi r^2$. This is the area of the original circle. Then write the formula for the area of the new larger circle, using $3r$ as the radius: $A = \pi(3r)^2 = \pi(9r^2) = 9\pi r^2$.

Now, divide the two areas (area of the new circle by the area of the original circle) to find out how many times larger the area of the new circle is compared to the area of the original circle.

$$\frac{\text{area of new circle}}{\text{area of original circle}} = \frac{9\pi r^2}{\pi r^2} = 9$$

Choice (K) is correct.

53. C
Difficulty: High
Category: Functions
Getting to the Answer: You don't really have to know anything about trig functions to answer this question. You just need to know the definition of *period:* the period of a repeating function is the distance along the x-axis required for the function to complete one full cycle. For a sine curve, this means one full wave (one up "bump" and one down "bump"). Here, that happens between 0 and π, which means the period is π. Choice (C) is correct.

If you happen to know the normal period of sine, which is 2π, you could also set the x term ($2x$) equal to that period and solve for x. You'll get $2x = 2\pi$, which simplifies to $x = \pi$.

54. J
Difficulty: High
Category: Algebra
Getting to the Answer: Solving equations that involve radicals may seem daunting, but they work just like other equations. In fact, they're usually easier to solve than quadratic equations because you don't have to worry about factoring. As a general rule, you need to: 1) isolate the radical part; 2) eliminate the radical by squaring both sides of the equation if the radical is a square root, cubing both sides if it's a cube root, and so on; and 3) isolate the variable. To solve the equation here, the steps are:

$$\sqrt[3]{4x - 12} + 25 = 27$$
$$\sqrt[3]{4x - 12} = 2$$
$$\left(\sqrt[3]{4x - 12}\right)^3 = 2^3$$
$$4x - 12 = 8$$
$$4x = 20$$
$$x = 5$$

Choice (J) is correct. Note that you could also use Back-solving to answer this question.

55. D
Difficulty: Medium
Category: Geometry
Getting to the Answer: The chord is perpendicular to the line segment from the center of the circle, so that line segment must be its perpendicular bisector. This allows you to add the following measures to the figure:

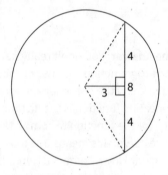

The two right triangles have legs 3 and 4, so they are both 3-4-5 right triangles with hypotenuse 5. This hypotenuse is also the radius of the circle, so plug that into the area formula to solve:

$$A = \pi r^2$$
$$= \pi (5)^2$$
$$= 25\pi$$

The correct answer is (D).

56. F
Difficulty: High
Category: Functions
Getting to the Answer: Don't let the function notation intimidate you. The graphs of two functions intersect when the function equations are equal. Therefore, you need to set the equations equal to each other and solve for x.

$$f(x) = g(x)$$
$$3^{3x + 3} = 27^{\left(\frac{2}{3}x - \frac{1}{3}\right)}$$

When the equations have variables in the exponents, you must rewrite one or both of them so that either the bases are the same or the exponents themselves are the same. In this question, the two bases seem different at first glance but, because 27 is actually 3^3, you can rewrite the equation as:

$$3^{3x + 3} = 3^{3\left(\frac{2}{3}x - \frac{1}{3}\right)}$$

This simplifies to $3^{3x + 3} = 3^{2x - 1}$. Now that the bases are equal, set the exponents equal to each other and solve for x:

$$3x + 3 = 2x - 1$$
$$x + 3 = -1$$
$$x = -4$$

Choice (F) is correct.

57. A
Difficulty: High
Category: Functions
Getting to the Answer: To solve a logarithmic equation, rewrite the equation in exponential form and solve for the variable. To rewrite the equation, use the translation $\log_b y = x$ means $b^x = y$. The left side of the given equation has two logs, so you'll need to combine them first using properties of logs before you can translate. Don't worry about the right-hand side of the equation just yet.

$$\log_b x - \log_b y = \log_b \left(\frac{x}{y}\right)$$
$$\log_3 (5x - 40) - \log_3 5 = \log_3 \left(\frac{5x - 40}{5}\right)$$
$$= \log_3 (x - 8)$$

Now the equation looks like $\log_3 (x - 8) = 2$, which can be rewritten as $3^2 = x - 8$. Simplifying yields $9 = x - 8$, or $17 = x$. Choice (A) is correct.

58. F
Difficulty: High
Category: Functions
Getting to the Answer: Fortunately, "cannot be determined" is not one of the answer choices here, because that would be very tempting. There is in fact enough information to answer this question. You just have to use what you know about arithmetic sequences—specifically, that to get from one term to the next, you

add the same number each time. Here, you don't know what that number is, so call it n. The five terms in the sequence are:

$$4$$
$$4 + n$$
$$4 + n + n$$
$$4 + n + n + n$$
$$4 + n + n + n + n$$

These terms are already listed in order, so the median is the middle term, which is $4 + n + n$, or $4 + 2n$. The mean is the sum of all the terms divided by the number of terms: $\frac{20 + 10n}{5} = 4 + 2n$. Thus, the mean and the median have the same value, making the difference between them equal to 0, which is (F).

59. D

Difficulty: High

Category: Geometry

Getting to the Answer: You are given the cosine of $\angle BAC$ and the length of the hypotenuse of the triangle, so begin by using these and SOHCAHTOA to find the length of the side adjacent to $\angle BAC$ (which is AB):

$$\cos A = \frac{\text{adjacent}}{\text{hypotenuse}}$$
$$0.6 = \frac{AB}{15}$$
$$AB = 0.6(15) = 9$$

So the adjacent side, $\overline{AB}$, is 9, and triangle ABC is a right triangle with a leg length of 9 and a hypotenuse of length 15. Triangle ABC must therefore be a 3-4-5 right triangle (scaled up by a factor of 3), and $\overline{BC}$ must have a length of 12. Choice (D) is correct.

60. J

Difficulty: High

Category: Geometry

Getting to the Answer: The question states that the points lie on the graph of a parabola (which is a nice, symmetric U shape), so use what you know about parabolas to answer the question. Notice that the x-values in the table increase by 2 each time. To find the y-value when $x = -4$, you just need to imagine adding one extra row to the top of the table. Now, think about symmetry—you can see from the points in the table that $(2,-5)$ is the vertex of the parabola. The points

$(0,-3)$ and $(4,-3)$ are equidistant from the vertex, as are the points $(-2,3)$ and $(6,3)$. This means the point whose x-value is -4 should have the same y-value as the last point in the table $(8,13)$. So, when $x = -4$, $y = 13$. Choice (J) is correct.

Reading Test

Passage I

Suggested Passage Map Notes:

¶1: Countess Olenska (CO) no longer pretty
¶2: CO 1st in NY as little girl adopted by aunt Medora (M)
¶3: M repeatedly widowed, NY accepting of M's eccentricities
¶4: all kind to Ellen (E) [aka CO], M not follow mourning rules
¶5: E was well-liked, fearless child; E's odd edu.
¶6: E married Polish nobleman, ended in disaster
¶7: NY expected CO to be more stylish and vibrant

BIG PICTURE SUMMARY:

Main idea: Ellen Mingott as a child and Countess Olenska as an adult did not fit New York society's expectations of her.

Author's purpose: To portray how a character changed from childhood to adulthood and the influences that shaped her

1. C

Difficulty: Low

Category: Detail

Getting to the Answer: Remember that the correct answer to Detail questions will be directly stated in the passage. Your notes should guide you as you locate specific references to the details in question. Line 24 mentions Ellen's parents' "regrettable taste for travel" in the context of lines describing what the people of New York thought. Predict something like "travel." Choice (C) matches this prediction. Choice A is a misused detail; Medora does teach her niece to play the piano, but nothing in the passage suggests that this was undesirable. Choice B is a misused detail; Spanish shawl dances are described as "outlandish," but this is within the context of Medora and Ellen's eccentric, but accepted, behaviors. Choice D is a misused detail; while Medora often adopted children, this is never described as undesirable.

2. J

Difficulty: High
Category: Inference
Getting to the Answer: Consider how the author writes about New York society. In lines 24–25, she writes that "people thought it a pity that the pretty child [Ellen] should be in such hands," meaning that they did not feel the eccentric Medora was a good influence on Ellen. People call Medora "misguided" (line 30), and the author notes that she scandalized her family by not adhering to the "unalterable rules" of mourning (lines 31–32). All in all, New York society seems to have some rigid and snobbish rules. On the other hand, New York society "looked indulgently on her [Medora's] eccentricities" (lines 20–21) and "resigned itself to Medora" (lines 38–39). The author's view of New York society as it pertains to Medora seems to be mixed, which matches (J). Choice F doesn't take into account New York society's acceptance of Medora's odd behavior, G is opposite, and H is not mentioned in the passage.

3. A

Difficulty: Medium
Category: Inference
Getting to the Answer: To answer Inference questions, you will have to go beyond what is directly stated in the passage. However, the correct answer choice will be supported by evidence from the passage, so make sure you make a prediction that has solid textual support. You can predict, based on lines 56–67, that Ellen was unable to help her aunt because her own marriage to the immensely rich Polish nobleman "had ended in disaster." Choice (A) matches this prediction. Choice B is a distortion; since both Medora and Ellen left New York, their communication over the years is unknown. Choice C is a distortion; while the author tells you that Ellen had an incoherent education, nothing in the passage suggests that she resented this. Choice D is a distortion; though the passage makes it clear that Medora was eccentric, this is in no way related to receiving help from her niece.

4. F

Difficulty: Medium
Category: Inference
Getting to the Answer: Predicting an answer is particularly important for Inference questions like this. Make sure you can support your prediction with information in the passage. Lines 68–70 suggest that Newland has spent time thinking about Ellen, and lines 74–93 all describe Newland's observations of Ellen. Newland is not disappointed that Ellen is not as "stylish" as others expected (lines 85–87). You can predict that Newland has thoughtfully considered Ellen, reaching conclusions that differ from those of his peers. Choice (F) matches this prediction. Choice G is out of scope; it might seem reasonable to conclude that Newland is likeable, but the passage does not provide any evidence to directly support this. Also, there is nothing to suggest that he is withdrawn. Choice H is opposite; Newland concludes that Ellen is "full of a conscious power" (lines 82–83), which is a positive rather than a "harsh" assessment, especially in contrast with others' determination that Ellen has lost her looks and is unstylish. Choice J is a distortion; Newland's observation that Ellen is not as stylish as New York society might expect says nothing about his own stylishness, nor does the author ever describe Newland's level of sociability.

5. A

Difficulty: Medium
Category: Function
Getting to the Answer: Wharton writes that Medora has "many peculiarities," (line 31), and that "New York looked indulgently on her eccentricities" (lines 20–21). This matches the first part of answer choice (A). Since you may not know what *peripatetic* means, hold on to (A) while you research the other answers. Though Wharton states that each time Medora returns to New York she looks for a less expensive house, indicating reduced circumstances, this doesn't necessarily mean that Medora is impoverished, and there is no suggestion that she is resentful. Eliminate B. Medora may be kind (she does, after all, take in orphaned Ellen), but *loyal* doesn't describe someone who "invariably parted from her husband or quarrelled with her ward" (lines 15–16), eliminating C. Choice D mixes up Medora with Ellen; these words describe Ellen as a child, so D is incorrect. Choice (A) must be correct, even if you don't know that *peripatetic* means "traveling from place to place."

6. H

Difficulty: Medium
Category: Vocab-in-Context
Getting to the Answer: The word *flout* is used in the author's description of Medora wearing a veil considered too short for acceptable mourning and dressing Ellen in "a crimson dress and amber beads"

(lines 36–37). Both of these are examples of Medora's "misguided … many peculiarities" (lines 30–31), which go against accepted New York behavior. Thus (H), disregard, is a good match. Choice F is too strong to describe Medora's behavior, as she does partially follow, rather than totally eliminate, the rules of mourning. Choice G is opposite, and while J looks close to the word *flout*, it doesn't make sense in the passage.

7.   C
Difficulty: Medium
Category: Inference
Getting to the Answer: Make sure you have good evidence for your prediction, and the correct answer choice will be easy to find. Line 21 mentions Medora's *eccentricities*, line 31 mentions her *peculiarities*, and line 44 mentions the *outlandish arts* that Medora teaches Ellen. From these descriptions, you can predict that Medora is unconventional or eccentric. Choice (C) matches this prediction. Choice A is out of scope; although Medora does not adhere to conventions, as indicated by lines 31–32, there is nothing to suggest that this is attributable to arrogance. Choice B is a distortion; the description of the short veil that Medora wore to her brother's funeral in lines 34–36 might suggest immodesty, but the author makes clear that this is evidence of Medora's willingness to flout social conventions and never mentions any immodest dress or behavior. Choice D, which means following established practice, is opposite; you are told in lines 31–32 that one of her peculiarities is to "flout the unalterable rules that regulated American mourning."

8.   F
Difficulty: Low
Category: Detail
Getting to the Answer: Detail questions like this one are straightforward, but it can sometimes be difficult to find exactly where in the passage the relevant information comes from. Make sure that you are answering the specific question being asked, so that other details don't distract you. Medora teaches Ellen "drawing from the model" (line 49), which is described as "a thing never dreamed of before," so predict Ellen or Countess Olenska. Choice (F) matches your prediction. Choice G is out of scope; Newland is not described as having learned anything at all, let alone something controversial. Choice H is a distortion; Medora teaches Ellen, but the passage does not mention Medora learning

anything herself. Choice J is a distortion; Count Olenska is only mentioned indirectly as the rich nobleman whom Medora marries. The passage makes it clear that Ellen is Countess Olenska; don't be fooled by this initially tempting, but incorrect, choice.

9.   B
Difficulty: Medium
Category: Function
Getting to the Answer: Locate where the author mentions Medora's mother and read the next few lines. The author writes that "her mother had been a Rushworth," (line 18), that Medora married "one of the crazy Chiverses" (line 20), and that because of these two conditions, "New York looked indulgently on her eccentricities" (lines 20–21). In other words, given her mother and her marriage, people were not surprised by Medora's unconventional life, which matches (B). There is no support for A, so it is out of scope. Choice C is opposite; New Yorkers "thought it a pity that the pretty child should be in such hands" (lines 24–25), and D is true but not relevant to Medora's eccentricities.

10.   F
Difficulty: High
Category: Inference
Getting to the Answer: Remember that Inference questions will have details in the incorrect answer choices that are meant to throw you off. Making a good prediction before reviewing the choices will guard against this. The beginning of the passage (line 4) implies that Newland knew Ellen when he was young. Lines 56–67 state that no one had heard from Ellen for some time, and after a few years, she came back to New York, as Medora had done before her. Predict that at the dinner, Newland and Ellen had not seen one another for an extended period of time. Choice (F) matches your prediction. Choice G is extreme; although Newland is clearly paying attention to Ellen in the last paragraph, there is nothing to suggest that either of them is interested in a romantic relationship. Choice H is extreme; while Ellen's lack of *stylishness* (lines 86–88) might suggest that she is not interested in New York society's conventions, it goes too far to say that she is disappointed. Choice J is opposite; the passage clearly portrays Ellen and Newland's encounter as a re-acquaintance.

Passage II

Suggested Passage Map Notes:

¶1: climate change threat to FL economy: tourism + agriculture

¶2: S. FL storm damage (tourism)

¶3: Everglades

¶4: not enough water for citrus farms

¶5: livestock industry

¶6: plans to deal w/ problems

¶7: more prep, diversify economy

BIG PICTURE SUMMARY:

Main idea: Potential dangers to Florida's tourism and agriculture industries from climate change and ways Floridians plan to address them.

Author's purpose: To describe how climate change is likely to impact Florida's economy

---

11. B

Difficulty: Medium

Category: Global

Getting to the Answer: This is a Global question because it asks for the purpose of the passage as a whole. Review your passage map and predict that the passage describes probable challenges to Florida's economy due to climate change and how the state is preparing to meet those challenges. The correct answer is (B).

Choice A is a distortion; while the passage does occasionally mention harm that has already occurred, it is primarily focused on future issues. Choice C is both out of scope and extreme; combating climate change itself is not addressed in the passage, and the author doesn't argue for any particular course of action. Choice D is also out of scope; the passage is focused on economic impacts, not on multiple ways climate change can impact people's lives.

12. J

Difficulty: Low

Category: Detail

Getting to the Answer: The clue "According to the passage" marks this as a Detail question. Locate where the passage discusses Hurricane Irma (in paragraph 2) and research what made it significant. The passage

states that it was "the costliest hurricane in Florida's history," so (J) is correct. It is worth noting that this is a case in which absolute language ("more…than any other") does not mark a too-extreme answer; the passage itself does make that strong a statement.

Choice F is a misused detail; Irma could hypothetically have cost that much if it had hit Miami more directly, but in reality, it cost approximately $50 billion. Choice G is a distortion; the paragraph certainly suggests that climate change increased Irma's destructiveness but not that it was the first hurricane for which that was true. Finally, H is a misused detail; while the paragraph mentions the dangers of rising sea levels, demonstrating them is not what made Irma significant.

13. A

Difficulty: Medium

Category: Inference

Getting to the Answer: The word *implies* is a clue that this is an Inference question. Research what the second paragraph says about South Florida. It lost a great deal of money as a result of a hurricane, which could have been far worse if Miami, "Florida's second-most popular tourist destination" (lines 23–24), had been directly hit. You can predict that the area generates a lot of money from tourism. Choice (A) is correct.

Choice B is extreme; while the paragraph mentions rising sea levels as a concern, it does not suggest that South Florida is likely to become submerged. Choice C is out of scope; the passage does not discuss northern Florida at all. Finally, D is incorrect because there is no evidence in the paragraph linking South Florida with agriculture.

14. G

Difficulty: Medium

Category: Detail

Getting to the Answer: "The passage makes clear" shows that this is a Detail question. Use your passage map to find where the passage discusses the Everglades and identify how climate change threatens it. Using paragraph 3, predict that the Everglades is likely to become submerged since much of it is barely above sea level. Choice (G) is correct.

Choice F is extreme; while paragraph 3 does mention salt water pushing inland, it does not say that this will poison fresh water. Choice H is a misused detail; the fifth paragraph mentions degradation of grasslands but not in reference to the Everglades. Choice J is a distortion; although paragraph 3 predicts problems for visitors, it does not suggest they will be entirely cut off from the park.

15. D
Difficulty: High
Category: Function
Getting to the Answer: The wording "author references … in order to" identifies this as a Function question. Examine the surrounding text to understand why the author includes these references. The paragraph discusses how lack of water could harm agriculture; the EPA report explains how water shortages could come about, and the study demonstrates the impact of insufficient water on citrus crops. Predict that both provide support from scientific sources for the paragraph's main idea. The correct answer is (D). This choice doesn't match the exact wording of the prediction, but correct answer choices rarely will. Look for the choice that matches the general idea of the prediction rather than its specific wording. In this case, D includes supporting the main idea, and most readers are likely to find scientific studies and reports authoritative; thus, D fits the prediction even without exactly matching it.

Choice A is true of the study but not the EPA report, while C is true of the EPA report but not the study, so both are incorrect. Nothing in the paragraph is countering an argument, so B is also incorrect.

16. J
Difficulty: Low
Category: Detail
Getting to the Answer: "The passage states" is a clue that this is a Detail question. Since the question asks for a comparison between the two industries, research toward the middle and end of the passage, after both industries have been discussed. The fifth paragraph states that livestock brings in a smaller portion of Florida's agriculture revenue. Choice (J) is correct.

Although the passage mentions both water consumption and exports, it does not compare the two industries for either, so F and H are incorrect. The passage does not discuss pollution at all, so G is out of scope.

17. B
Difficulty: Low
Category: Detail
Getting to the Answer: The phrase "According to the passage" shows that this is a Detail question. The fifth paragraph discusses issues facing the livestock industry, including heat stressing the animals, loss of grasslands, and increased insect-borne diseases. Choice (B) matches the first of these and is correct.

Choice A is a misused detail; while the passage predicts reduced crop yields, it says nothing about these crops being used to feed livestock. Choice C is a distortion; the passage says that animals are likely to get sick because of increased mosquito populations, not because of the weather itself. Choice D is a misused detail similar to A; while water shortages may occur, the passage does not discuss their impact on the livestock industry.

18. H
Difficulty: Medium
Category: Global
Getting to the Answer: This question asks for the purpose of a paragraph, which requires an understanding of both the paragraph itself and how it fits into the passage as a whole. Thus, this is a Global question. While the passage so far has described problems raised by climate change, paragraph 6 discusses some potential solutions to these problems. Choice (H) is correct.

Choice F is a misused detail; only some of the paragraph is about infrastructure adaptations. Choice G is incorrect because this paragraph has moved on from describing the problems. Finally, J is a distortion; while parts of the paragraph involve directing water supplies, it does not refer to imbalances in rainfall.

19. C
Difficulty: Medium
Category: Detail
Getting to the Answer: The phrase "According to the passage" marks this as a Detail question. Paragraph 6 describes ways to counteract climate change problems; do some research there to find what solutions are being put forward for agriculture. The last sentence of the paragraph says that farms are switching to more water-efficient subsurface irrigation and mixed crop-livestock farms. The second part matches (C), which is correct.

Choice A may be tempting, but this answer choice says that subsurface irrigation is less efficient and being replaced, the opposite of what the passage states. Choices B and D are both out of scope; neither is discussed as a solution in the passage.

20. H

Difficulty: Medium
Category: Function
Getting to the Answer: The phrase *serves to* in the question stem indicates that this is a Function question. Read around the lines in question for context to determine why the author includes this detail. The paragraph states that policymakers want to diversify Florida's economy and international trade seems like a good way to do so. Predict that the fact that Florida already exports a great deal provides a reason *why* policymakers see this as a suitable area to expand. The correct answer is (H).

Choice F is extreme; although the passage makes clear that exports are important to Florida's economy, it does not suggest that they are a primary driver of expansion. Choice G is out of scope; the passage does not compare Florida's trade balance with any other state. Finally, J is a distortion; while the paragraph does explain the importance of diversification, that is not the purpose of this detail.

Passage III

Suggested Passage Map Notes:

Passage A

¶1: country music (C) born in central & southern Appalachians
¶2: originated in 1920s from multiple sources
¶3: the term "country" replaced "hillbilly"
¶4: Hank Williams 1st to take country national; artists
¶5: Nashville, TN = country home w/ Grand Ole Opry (1925)
¶6: C relatives = honky tonk, Western Swing
¶7: C expresses Am. identity

Passage B

¶1: bluegrass (B) origin and description
¶2: B diff. from C: highlight 1 musician at a time, diff. instruments, vocal harmonies
¶3: own category in late 1950s, named after Bill Monroe's band
¶4: today: movies, festivals
¶5: B themes = working class; reflects Am.

BIG PICTURE SUMMARY:

Passage A

Main idea: Country music is an American musical genre with a rich history.

Author's purpose: To describe the origins and history of country music

Passage B

Main idea: Bluegrass music is related to but distinct from country music, with its own cultural niche.

Author's purpose: To explain what makes bluegrass music unique

21. C

Difficulty: Medium
Category: Detail
Getting to the Answer: Use your passage map to locate this detail; the second paragraph should include the necessary information. Use the list of the sources of country music ("spirituals as well as folk music, cowboy songs, and traditional Celtic melodies") to make your prediction. Choice (C) is correct because country music is not rooted in jazz. Rather, jazz was combined with country music to create Western swing. Paragraph 6 states, "Additionally, Western swing emerged as one of the first genres to blend country and jazz musical styles, which required a great deal of skill and creativity." Choice A is opposite; paragraph 2 describes the many sources of country music with the sentence, "Rooted in spirituals as well as folk music, cowboy songs, and traditional Celtic melodies, country music originated in the 1920s." Choice B is opposite; spirituals influenced the development of country music. Choice D is opposite; country music is rooted in cowboy songs.

22. J

Difficulty: Medium
Category: Inference
Getting to the Answer: The answer to an Inference question is supported by the passage. However, because all answer choices are in the passage, be

careful to assess each one in terms of the actual question asked. A look at your notes or a quick scan of the passage should provide enough information to make a prediction about where to find the best country music. Match that prediction to the correct answer. Choice (J) is correct; in paragraph 5, the author writes "Country singers are considered to have reached the pinnacle of the profession if they are asked to become members of the Opry." To hear the best music, it makes sense to go to the place where those at the pinnacle, or top of their field, perform. Choice F is a misused detail; one would hear honky-tonk music, a derivative of country, but not country music itself, in these bars. Choice G is a misused detail; Ireland is the original home of the Ulster Scots, many of whom settled in Appalachia. Choice H is a misused detail; though country music had its origins in the mixture of music created in Appalachia, the author does not state that it is the place to hear the best music.

23. C

Difficulty: High
Category: Vocab-in-Context
Getting to the Answer: As with all Vocab-in-Context questions, use the surrounding clues to define the word in question. The word appears in paragraph three, where the original term "hillbillies" is used to describe "Appalachian inhabitants who were considered poor, uneducated, isolated, and wary." The more accepting word "country" has replaced "hillbillies," indicating that pejorative is a negative word, an adjective used to highlight the negative characteristics described in the paragraph. This matches (C), since disparaging means belittling, or bad. Choice A is a synonym for *original* rather than a word that means *negative*. Choice B is out of scope, as the author never expresses that the negative view is accurate, and D refers to where the people live rather than fitting the context of describing the term (i.e., it is not a "mountain-dwelling term").

24. F

Difficulty: Low
Category: Inference
Getting to the Answer: Both passages introduce several genres of American music, but this question refers to Passage B, so research the passage carefully. In the first paragraph, the author introduces bluegrass music and writes that it is "a mixture of Scottish, Welsh, Irish, and English melodic forms, infused, over

time, with African-American influences." (lines 73–75), and that laments "are common themes." (lines 79–80). These are exactly the components of the song in the question, making (F) correct. The other answers refer to Passage A and are described as having different derivations.

25. A

Difficulty: Medium
Category: Detail
Getting to the Answer: Locate the paragraph in which bluegrass instruments are described, and match those descriptions with the correct answer choice. Your notes point to only one paragraph in which musical instruments are mentioned. Scan the answer choices, then reread the information in that paragraph to determine which answer choice characterizes the information given. Choice (A) is correct; musical instruments are described in the second paragraph and include typical ones such as "banjo, guitar, mandolin, bass, harmonica, and Dobro (resonator guitar)." But the paragraph goes on to include far less typical ones, such as "household objects, including washboards and spoons," which are not usually considered musical instruments, but are sometimes included in a bluegrass band. Choice B is a misused detail; African-American influences are provided as one more source of the bluegrass genre but instrumentation is not referenced. Choice C is a misused detail; this is an example of a bluegrass piece used in a movie soundtrack. Choice D is out of scope; the reference to the Ozark mountains concerns the origin of bluegrass and has nothing to do with a description of musical instruments.

26. F

Difficulty: High
Category: Detail
Getting to the Answer: The answer to a Detail question is stated in the passage. Locate the paragraph in which the differences between country and bluegrass music are discussed. Paragraph 2 includes the information you need to answer the question. Be sure to keep straight which details describe each genre of music. Choice (F) is correct. Paragraph 2 details two characteristics of bluegrass music: first, that "bluegrass highlights one player at a time, with the others providing accompaniment," and second, that "bluegrass incorporates baritone and tenor harmonies." Choice G is opposite; country music features a single voice. Choice

H is opposite; country musicians commonly play the same melodies together. Choice J is a distortion; which instruments are used is not cited as a difference between the music styles.

27. B

Difficulty: Medium
Category: Inference
Getting to the Answer: Locate the paragraphs that mention *laments* and "high, lonesome sound," and consider what the author means by including these two details. The reference to *laments* is in the first paragraph and the reference to "high, lonesome sound" in the last paragraph are examples of "the hard-scrabble life of the American worker," which matches (B). Choice A is out of scope; the elements mentioned in the question stem do not necessarily reflect Irish music; bluegrass has multiple sources. Choice C is a misused detail; Shania Twain is an example of a country singer and is mentioned in Passage A only. Choice D is a misused detail; though bluegrass was originally called "hillbilly," this is the name for the genre, not the theme.

28. G

Difficulty: Medium
Category: Vocab-in-Context
Getting to the Answer: Vocab-in-Context questions require that you understand the context of a cited word or phrase. Locate the reference and focus your research on the text immediately preceding and immediately following the word or phrase in question. The introductory paragraph states, "One of the most enjoyable ways to analyze culture is through music." Look for an answer choice that indicates that music can provide specific insight about a culture as a whole. Choice (G) matches this prediction. Choices F, H, and J are a distortion; *quintessential* does not mean "old-fashioned," "charming," or "conventional or typical."

29. C

Difficulty: Medium
Category: Inference
Getting to the Answer: When asked to use a quote to find support in one paragraph for information in another, be sure to read the quote in the context of the paragraph. First find the paragraph in which the quote from Passage A appears, then match the

quote to one in Passage B. Choice (C) is correct; Flatt and Scruggs are mentioned in Passage B, paragraph 3, in which they are characterized as "the foremost artists on their instruments." The best artists are certainly "talented and sophisticated." Choice A is a misused detail; this quote refers to bluegrass themes, whereas the question asks for one that supports talented and sophisticated musicians. Choice B is out of scope; the "pace and complexity" of the music does not necessarily relate to the skill of the musicians themselves. Choice D is out of scope; the relation between bluegrass and country music refers to the kinship of the genres, not the musicians.

30. H

Difficulty: Medium
Category: Global
Getting to the Answer: When looking for something on which both authors would agree, first determine what each one actually states in the passage, then consider what must be true based on those statements. The evolution, or gradual change, in music, as with anything else, must start from somewhere, so look to the parts of each passage that detail the genesis of the music genres, then consider the progression from there. Choice (H) is correct; both authors detail the various music sources that became either country or bluegrass. In the first passage, the author mentions "folk music, cowboy songs, and traditional Celtic melodies," and in the second passage, the author refers to "Scottish, Welsh, Irish, and English melodic forms, infused, over time, with African-American influences." Both authors affirm that the two music genres are "indigenous." Thus, it must be true that both country and bluegrass music have evolved from their various roots to become American music, supporting agreement on the fact that music can evolve. Choice F is out of scope; each passage mentions how its particular music genre is popular (as explained in the next sentence in the explanation—the Czech festivals and international growth), but both authors don't describe why *both* genres are popular, only their own. Choice G is a misused detail; the Grand Ole Opry showcases country music only, not bluegrass. Choice J is out of scope; the passages don't each discuss both genres, only their own.

Passage IV

Suggested Passage Map Notes:

¶1: CubeSats good for space exploration
¶2: improved radios
¶3: testing for longer missions
¶4: consumer cameras → less expensive
¶5: less expensive → more experiments possible
¶6: plans to deal w/ problems
¶7: CubeSats improve future space exploration

BIG PICTURE SUMMARY:

Main idea: CubeSats offer many advantages for exploration and experimentation in deep space.

Author's purpose: To explore the benefits of using CubeSats

---

31. D

Difficulty: Medium
Category: Global
Getting to the Answer: The clues *author's attitude* and *main topic* identify this as a Global question. Review your notes to determine the author's tone and predict that the author is positive about the CubeSats and looking forward to their future. This matches (D).

Choice A is a distortion; the author is optimistic, but not cautious. Choice B is too neutral, and C is too negative.

32. H

Difficulty: Low
Category: Detail
Getting to the Answer: The phrase "According to the passage" marks this as a Detail question. Think about where in the passage you might find the original designers of the CubeSat and use your notes to help. The first sentence states that researchers at California Polytechnic and Stanford Universities "determined the specifications of the CubeSat design." This matches (H).

Choices F, G, and J all refer to other people in the passage who made use of the CubeSats, but who were not the original designers. NASA used the design for the MarCO mission, for which Joel Krajewski was a project manager and Cody Colley was a mission manager.

33. D

Difficulty: Medium
Category: Vocab-in-Context
Getting to the Answer: The clue words "most nearly means" show that this is a Vocab-in-Context question. Refer to the passage to see how *radical* is used in the sentence. It describes scientific experiments, so predict that it means ground breaking. Choice (D) is correct.

Choices A and B refer to alternate meanings of *radical* that are not supported by the passage; there is no evidence that the experiments are ideologically motivated or involve militarization or aggression. Choice C, "primitive and organic," is the exact opposite of a scientific experiment in space.

34. F

Difficulty: Medium
Category: Detail
Getting to the Answer: The words "According to the passage" identify this as a Detail question. Use your notes to find where the passage discusses communication technology. Research paragraph 2 and predict that the satellites' radios and antennae were faster and more efficient. The correct answer is (F).

Choice G is incorrect because it describes the InSight lander's communication technology. Choice H is incorrect because it describes the MarCO satellites' cameras, not their radios. Choice J is incorrect because, although the passage mentions that the MarCO radios are the size of softballs, it does not discuss whether the radios were unusually small.

35. C

Difficulty: High
Category: Inference
Getting to the Answer: You can easily tell that this is an Inference question because of the word *inferred* in the question stem. Research the second paragraph to determine how the MarCO satellites compared to the InSight lander. The passage says that their communications are faster, but the answers to Inference questions are never explicitly stated in the passage. The paragraph goes on to say that they offered "more efficient monitoring of the landing process" and that their data would "help engineers design better landing technology for future missions." Since these sentences draw comparisons, you can

predict that the MarCO satellites accomplished these tasks more effectively than the InSight lander itself. The correct answer is (C).

You may have had difficulty predicting for this question. If so, remember that you can eliminate incorrect answers to find the correct one. Choice A is out of scope; the passage does not discuss the resolution of photos or their distances. Choice B is incorrect because the passage does not mention miniaturized technology. Finally, choice D is incorrect because the satellites themselves do not land.

36. G
Difficulty: Medium
Category: Function
Getting to the Answer: The phrase *serves to* in the question stem indicates that this is a Function question. Review your notes to identify the purpose of the fourth paragraph and predict that it describes how using commercially available cameras made the satellites less expensive. Choice (G) is correct.

Choice F is extreme; the author is not arguing for anything in this paragraph, much less for using off-the-shelf components wherever possible. Choice H is too broad; the paragraph describes only one reason why the project was less costly. Choice J is a misused detail; although the paragraph does briefly praise the images, that is not its main purpose.

37. D
Difficulty: Medium
Category: Inference
Getting to the Answer: The words "Based on the passage" are a clue that this is an Inference question. In the fourth paragraph, where the passage discusses posting mission photos, it describes the scientists as proud and elated. You can predict that they were happy about how well the satellites did. This matches choice (D).

Choices A, B, and C are all out of scope; there is no evidence to suggest that the scientists had anything to prove or any demands to satisfy, and while they may have hoped to gain support, this is not stated in the passage.

38. G
Difficulty: Medium
Category: Inference
Getting to the Answer: The clue words "the passage suggest" show that this is an Inference question. The paragraph discusses how the CubeSats allow for an increased number and variety of scientific experiments than were previously feasible, so you can predict that these experiments were made possible because of the CubeSats. This fits with (G). Remember that correct answers will not always match the exact wording of your prediction, so you must be alert for equivalent meanings.

Choice F is out of scope; the paragraph does not discuss the experiments' creators at all. Choice H is incorrect because, while the passage does describe an experiment using linked satellites later on, it is not in these lines. Finally, J is opposite; the paragraph states that these experiments are in near-Earth orbit.

39. B
Difficulty: Medium
Category: Detail
Getting to the Answer: "The passage states" wording marks this as a Detail question. Consult your notes to find that the passage discusses linked satellite networks and their advantages in the sixth paragraph. You can predict that these networks are flexible and less likely to fail. Choice (B) is correct.

Choice A is a misused detail; while the passage does say that CubeSats are less expensive, that is not an advantage of linked networks specifically. Choice C is incorrect because there is no evidence that the international cooperation mentioned was a result of the satellite network. Choice J is incorrect because the passage does not suggest that the thermosphere was previously inaccessible or that linked networks of satellites were necessary to study it.

40. H
Difficulty: High
Category: Function
Getting to the Answer: The phrase "how the author" shows that this is a Function question, since it is about something the author does in the text. Review the lines in the question stem and determine what they have in common. In both, the author uses concrete numbers in order to drive home a point. The correct answer is (H).

Choice F is a distortion; while the author does juxtapose old and new, it is not for the purpose of dismantling old methods. Choice G is incorrect because not only does the author not use NASA or Stanford to increase the passage's authority, these institutions are not even mentioned in these lines. Finally, J is extreme; the language the author uses in the comparisons in the cited lines is neutral.

Science Test

Passage I

1.   A
Difficulty: Low
Category: Using Data
Getting to the Answer: The question stem tells you that you're looking for a mineral composed of 32% zinc and 12% calcium. Table 1 lists the percentages of calcium and zinc in a variety of minerals, so look there for an answer. According to Table 1, hornblende is composed of 30%–35% zinc and 10%–20% calcium. Choice (A) is thus correct.

2.   J
Difficulty: Low
Category: Interpreting Data
Getting to the Answer: Diagram 1 presents the most common minerals in each soil horizon. A geologist digging down into the A horizon would encounter mostly quartz and mica. Quartz isn't included as a possible answer, but mica is. Choice (J) is thus correct. Choice F is incorrect because limestone isn't commonly found until the C horizon. Choice G is incorrect because shale isn't common until the final horizon. Choice H is incorrect because serpentine is commonly found in the B horizon.

3.   B
Difficulty: Medium
Category: Interpreting Data
Getting to the Answer: Based on Diagram 1, you can see that the minerals are arranged in Table 1 so that the shallowest are at the top of the table and the deepest are at the bottom. However, as you move down the table, you'll notice that zinc content decreases, which indicates an inverse relationship between depth and zinc content. In other words, as zinc content *increases*, depth *decreases*. Choice (B) is thus correct.

4.   H
Difficulty: Low
Category: Interpreting Data
Getting to the Answer: Based on Diagram 1, the only minerals geologists wouldn't commonly find at a depth of 30 feet or lower (to the bottom of the B Horizon) are limestone and shale. You can eliminate F, G, and J because each contains one of these minerals. Choice (H), then, is correct.

5.   A
Difficulty: Medium
Category: Using Data
Getting to the Answer: The mineral content of granite is located in Table 2, so start there. Table 2 shows that granite is composed of feldspar, quartz, mica, and augite. If augite is found close to the other minerals in granite, then it should be located at roughly the same depth as feldspar, quartz, and mica. Now use Diagram 1 to find the depths at which those three minerals are most commonly found. Feldspar is found in the O horizon, at a depth of 2 feet or less, while quartz and mica are found in the A horizon, at a depth of 2 to 10 feet. So you should definitely expect to find augite at depths of less than 10 feet, as in (A).

6.   G
Difficulty: Low
Category: Interpreting Data
Getting to the Answer: Zinc content percentage and calcium content percentage are found in Table 1, so examine it for an answer. Moving down the table, zinc content steadily decreases as calcium content steadily increases. The two quantities are inversely related, making (G) correct.

Passage II

7.   D
Difficulty: Medium
Category: Using Data
Getting to the Answer: To answer this question, examine the formula that is provided at the beginning of the passage: $\Delta T_b = K_b \times m \times i$. This equation indicates that the boiling point will increase more if K_b, m, or i is increased. Item I would increase K_b, item II would increase m, and item III would increase i (because $CaCl_2$ splits into 3 ions, while NaCl only splits into 2 ions). Because all three items would increase the boiling point of Solution 5, (D) is correct.

8. H

Difficulty: Low

Category: Interpreting Data

Getting to the Answer: The results for Study 1 are presented in Table 1. Table 1 shows that for 0.171 mol of NaCl, the boiling point is increased to 101.75°C. Choice (H) is thus correct.

9. C

Difficulty: Medium

Category: Synthesizing Data

Getting to the Answer: This question asks about the melting point of Material 5. Table 3 provides data about when Material 5 melted, indicating that it did not melt in Solution 5, but that it did melt in Solution 6. Therefore, its melting point will be somewhere between the boiling points of those solutions. Table 1 shows that Solution 5 has a boiling point of 103.50°C and Table 2 shows that Solution 6 has a boiling point of 104.15°C, so Material 5's melting point must fall somewhere in between those values. Choice (C) is thus correct.

10. G

Difficulty: Medium

Category: Using Data

Getting to the Answer: Table 2 provides the boiling points for solutions consisting of various amounts of $CaCl_2$ added to water. The trend seems linear: for each increase of roughly 0.9 mol $CaCl_2$, the boiling point increases by roughly 1.4 degrees Celsius. The highest amount of $CaCl_2$ on the table is 0.631 mol, roughly 0.9 less than the amount in the question stem. Therefore, the increase will be roughly 1.4 degrees higher than 109.67°C, or 111.07°C. Choice (G) is thus correct. Choice F is between the boiling points for Solutions 9 and 10, which is too low. Choices H and J are too high.

11. A

Difficulty: Medium

Category: Synthesizing Data

Getting to the Answer: Table 3 gives an indication of the points at which each material begins to melt. Based on the information from Tables 1 and 2, a higher-numbered solution corresponds to a higher boiling point. It would be highly implausible for a material to melt at a low temperature but not at a

higher temperature, which is the trend depicted in (A). The other choices are incorrect because they are all possibilities already revealed in Study 3's results: B corresponds to the results for Material 1, C to the results for Material 4, and D to the results for Materials 6, 7, and 8.

12. H

Difficulty: High

Category: Experimental Design

Getting to the Answer: The equation for boiling point elevation given in the passage indicates that the increase in temperature depends upon the molality of the solution. As noted in the explanation of the equation, molality is defined as moles (mol) of solute over kilograms (kg) of solvent. Thus, the students recorded the moles of a solute, rather than its mass, in order to make the calculation of molality—and the subsequent calculation of change in boiling point—easier. Choice (H) is correct. Choice F makes little sense; measuring the solvent's mass does nothing to prevent measuring the solute's mass. Choice G is a false statement; moles are usually calculated on the basis of mass, so if anything mass measurements are more accurate. Choice J is true but irrelevant to the question.

13. A

Difficulty: Medium

Category: Synthesizing Data

Getting to the Answer: Table 3 shows that Material 7 melted in Solution 10, whereas Material 8 did not. That means that Material 7 must have a melting point of no more than 109.67°C (the boiling point of Solution 10), while Material 8 must have a melting point higher than that temperature. Thus, the results do support the claim that Material 7 has the lower melting point, making (A) correct. Choice B is incorrect because it reverses the results for the materials. Choice C is incorrect because the exact melting point of Material 8 does not need to be determined to support the claim—it only has to be shown to have a higher melting point than Material 7. Choice D is incorrect because the approximate melting point of Material 7 can be determined: it must be between the boiling point temperatures of Solutions 9 and 10.

Passage III

14. G

Difficulty: Medium

Category: Supporting Hypotheses

Getting to the Answer: According to Table 1, the concentrations of nitrogen, phosphorus oxide, and zinc all tend to increase as humidity level increases, regardless of which of the three data sources is considered. For potassium oxide, however, the trend is reversed: the concentration decreases as humidity increases. Choice (G) is thus correct.

15. A

Difficulty: Low

Category: Interpreting Data

Getting to the Answer: To answer this question, compare the System B data to the USGS data at 25% humidity for the 4 compounds given as answer choices. For nitrogen (N), the USGS concentration is 236 mg/L, while System B measures it as 408 mg/L, which is close to double. For calcium (Ca), USGS has 24.7 mg/L and System B has 23.2 mg/L, a much smaller difference, meaning B can be eliminated. For potassium oxide (K_2O), USGS has 9.2 mg/L and System B has 9.1 mg/L, a very small difference, allowing you to eliminate C too. Finally, for phosphorus oxide (P_2O_5), USGS has 71.2 mg/L and System B has 75.6 mg/L, still smaller than the difference seen in nitrogen, meaning D can also be eliminated. Nitrogen shows by far the biggest difference, whether this is calculated in absolute or relative terms, so (A) is correct.

16. J

Difficulty: Low

Category: Supporting Hypotheses

Getting to the Answer: From Table 1, you can see that the potassium oxide concentration continually decreases from 9.4 mg/L to 8.2 mg/L as humidity increases from 10% to 80% in the USGS data, continually decreases from 9.4 to 8.0 in System A, and continually decreases from 9.5 to 8.3 in System B. Because the data from all 3 sources supports the hypothesis that potassium oxide levels decrease with increasing humidity, (J) is correct.

17. D

Difficulty: Medium

Category: Synthesizing Data

Getting to the Answer: The question asks you to determine which system is more accurate, so ultimately you're trying to find the one that is closer to the USGS data, which is described in the passage as "extremely accurate." Looking at the data for zinc, you can see that the measurements from System B are always closer to the data from the USGS than are the measurements from System A. Therefore, you know the answer to the question is yes, allowing you to eliminate A and B. Choice C, though, is incorrect because it gives incorrect reasoning: System B does give lower measurements than System A, but that alone doesn't make it more accurate. The measurements from System B are more accurate because they are closer to the data from the USGS than are the measurements from System A. Choice (D) is thus correct.

18. H

Difficulty: Medium

Category: Synthesizing Data

Getting to the Answer: To answer this question, look at the row in the table that represents calcium concentrations for System B. You can see that the numbers gradually decrease from 10% humidity to 65% humidity, then increase quickly from 65% to 85% humidity. The only graph that shows values decreasing and then rapidly increasing is (H).

19. B

Difficulty: High

Category: Using Data

Getting to the Answer: Examine the System B data in Table 1 to answer this question. According to the table, a potassium oxide level of 9.1 mg/L falls between the values for 25% humidity (9.2) and 45% humidity (9.0), a calcium level of 17.3 mg/L also falls between the values for 25% (23.2) and 45% (11.6), and a zinc level of 0.57 mg/L likewise falls between the values for 25% (0.48) and 45% (0.62). Therefore, the level of humidity for this sample should almost certainly be some value between 25% and 45%. Only (B) falls within this range.

Passage IV

20. G

Difficulty: Low

Category: Supporting Hypotheses

Getting to the Answer: What are Scientist 1's and Scientist 2's viewpoints? Scientist 1 believes that type 2 diabetes is caused by excess sugar consumption, and Scientist 2 says that type 2 diabetes is caused by obesity as a result of a high-fat diet and lack of exercise. If new research suggested that 80% of people with diabetes have buildup of fat in the liver, this information would support the view of Scientist 2 only. The correct answer is (G).

21. B

Difficulty: Low

Category: Supporting Hypotheses

Getting to the Answer: Scientist 1 states that "the cause of type 2 diabetes is an overconsumption of sugar," while Scientist 2 states that "diets high in fat but not high in sugar are associated with an increased risk of type 2 diabetes." Thus, both scientists would mostly likely agree that the occurrence of type 2 diabetes in an individual is associated with the patient's diet. The correct answer is (B). Choice A is only mentioned by Scientist 2, and C is only mentioned by Scientist 3. Age is mentioned in the introductory text, but even though type 2 diabetes is more prevalent in adults, the passage does not suggest that age causes type 2 diabetes, so D is also incorrect.

22. H

Difficulty: Medium

Category: Supporting Hypotheses

Getting to the Answer: The passage states that type 2 diabetes occurs "when the body does not produce enough insulin," and explains that "insulin is a hormone produced in the pancreas that helps regulate blood glucose levels." If the pancreas is removed, the body would not produce insulin, and would thus be unable to regulate blood glucose levels, thereby causing type 2 diabetes to develop. None of the answer choices state this explicitly, but (H) gives the major symptom of diabetes that was stated in the introductory paragraph: elevated blood glucose levels (hyperglycemia). Choices F and G are incorrect because they state the opposite of what you should expect. You can also eliminate J because you're given no reason

to suspect a link between the pancreas and body fat content.

23. C

Difficulty: Medium

Category: Supporting Hypotheses

Getting to the Answer: According to Scientist 3, type 2 diabetes is inherited. Eliminate A and B, which correspond to the hypotheses of Scientists 1 and 2, respectively. Scientist 3 states "individuals have about a 15%–20% chance of developing type 2 diabetes if one of their parents has it and a roughly 50% chance if both parents have it." 18% falls within the 15%–20% range. Therefore, Scientist 3 would probably predict that an individual with an 18% chance of developing type 2 diabetes has one parent with type 2 diabetes. The correct answer is (C).

24. J

Difficulty: Medium

Category: Supporting Hypotheses

Getting to the Answer: Remember to keep straight who said what. If a 50-year-old developed type 2 diabetes, Scientist 1 would likely conclude the patient has a high-sugar diet, Scientist 2 would likely conclude the patient has a high-fat diet and/or lacks exercise, and Scientist 3 would likely conclude the patient inherited it from one or more parents. The only answer choice that correctly matches one of these predictions is (J).

25. A

Difficulty: High

Category: Supporting Hypotheses

Getting to the Answer: According to Scientist 1, the elevated blood glucose levels in individuals with normal insulin levels did not return to normal when they received small injections of supplemental insulin. It can thus be inferred that although insulin levels were normal, the body had a lowered response to insulin, indicating insulin resistance. Look for a choice that supports the idea that a high-sugar diet is caused by or otherwise related to lowered response to insulin. Choice (A) does just that. Choices B and D are incorrect because they mention fat intake and free radical production, respectively, which were only discussed by Scientist 2. Choice C is incorrect because Scientist 1 discussed the effects of a high-sugar diet, not a low-sugar one.

26. F
Difficulty: High
Category: Supporting Hypotheses
Getting to the Answer: Scientist 3 believes that "type 2 diabetes is not caused by lifestyle or diet but inherited." To challenge Scientist 2's claim that the lack of exercise causes 7% of type 2 diabetes cases, Scientist 3 would have to explain how the actual cause of the occurrence of type 2 diabetes in these individuals is due to inheritance, rather than lifestyle. Choice (F) does precisely that: if the individuals who didn't exercise also had family histories of diabetes, then Scientist 3 could claim that the patients actually developed diabetes because of their genetics, not their lifestyles. Even though Scientist 3 actually states the information in G, it does not directly address Scientist 2's claim from the question stem. Choice H is incorrect because insulin injections are only discussed by Scientist 1. Choice J is incorrect because Scientist 2 does not suggest that type 2 diabetes solely results from lack of exercise, but also blames diets high in fat.

Passage V

27. A
Difficulty: Low
Category: Interpreting Data
Getting to the Answer: To answer this question, turn to the results of the studies in Table 1. According to the table, the lowest-density blood sample is 1.050 g/mL, that of Patient C. Looking at each column, you can see that Patient C has more platelets than Patient A but fewer than Patient B, fewer white blood cells than Patient A, the fewest red blood cells, but the most plasma. Choice (A), then, is correct.

28. H
Difficulty: Medium
Category: Experimental Design
Getting to the Answer: According to the passage, the purpose of the studies was "to determine the composition and mass of blood samples." Thus, the phlebotomist has an interest in avoiding anything that could alter the composition or mass of the blood on a temporary basis because it would skew the results of the studies. The passage also states that diet can affect the composition of blood, so it would make sense that the phlebotomist would try to control this factor by requiring the patients to fast. Choice (H) is thus

correct. Choice F is incorrect because you're given no reason to suspect that taking blood is easier if a patient has fasted. Choice G is incorrect because if fasting could greatly change the composition of blood, then the phlebotomist would likely have made sure the patients avoided it by eating something beforehand. Choice J is incorrect because you're given no indication in the passage that anything the patient does can affect the ability of blood to separate in a centrifuge.

29. D
Difficulty: High
Category: Applying Core Knowledge
Getting to the Answer: According to Table 1, Patient C had a density of 1.050 g/mL, which amounts to a 10.50 g mass for a 10 mL sample. However, if you add up the masses of the components listed in Table 1, you get a total of less than 10.50 g (9.71 g, to be specific). The question is asking you to explain this discrepancy. To find the best explanation, consider each of the possibilities offered in the answer choices. Choice A does not offer an adequate explanation, because if some red blood cells remained in the plasma, then they would have been weighed along with the plasma, which means their mass would have been included. Choice B also falls short; the mass of the platelets would have been included when the white blood cells were weighed. Choice C suffers from a similar problem: if some of the formed elements remained in the plasma, their masses would simply be included when the plasma was weighed. By process of elimination, (D) must be correct. And this makes sense because the only components that were weighed were plasma, red blood cells, white blood cells, and platelets. If there were additional components, their masses would not be included in Table 1. This is also consistent with the opening of the passage, which claims that blood is 45% formed elements and 50% plasma, leaving 5% of the blood unaccounted for.

30. F
Difficulty: Low
Category: Interpreting Data
Getting to the Answer: Go back to Table 1 and look at the columns for total density and red blood cell mass. (Circle each column if you tend to get distracted by the other information.) Reading the table from the bottom up, you can see that, as total density increases, the mass of the red blood cells also increases, (F).

31. B

Difficulty: Medium

Category: Using Data

Getting to the Answer: The introduction to the passage states that "formed elements weigh approximately 1.10 grams per milliliter (g/mL) and plasma approximately 1.02 g/mL." Here, you have about 5 mL of plasma, so the total mass of plasma is roughly 5 mL $\times$ 1.02 g/mL = 5.1 g. You also have about 5 mL of formed elements, so the total mass of formed elements is about 5 mL $\times$ 1.10 g/mL = 5.5 g. The total mass of the sample would then be around 5.1 g + 5.5 g = 10.6 g. It may be a bit higher due to elements other than the plasma and formed elements, but the total mass is still likely to be between 10.0 and 12.0 g, as in (B).

32. J

Difficulty: Low

Category: Experimental Design

Getting to the Answer: The passage explains that the phlebotomist placed the blood samples in a centrifuge for 20 minutes in Study 2 and at a slower speed for 45 minutes in Study 3. Only (J) captures any element of this difference. Choice F is incorrect because you're told at the beginning of the passage that 10 mL of blood were taken from each patient. Choice G is incorrect because, while the mass of the blood samples did vary from patient to patient, the masses weren't intentionally varied by the phlebotomist from Study 2 to Study 3. Choice H is incorrect because a centrifuge was used in both Studies 2 and 3.

33. A

Difficulty: Low

Category: Interpreting Data

Getting to the Answer: To answer this question, simply compare the masses in the red blood cell column of Table 1. According to the table, Patient A has a red blood cell mass of 2.75 g, Patient B a mass of 2.70 g, and Patient C a mass of 2.65 g. Because Patient A has the greatest mass of red blood cells, (A) is correct.

Passage VI

34. G

Difficulty: Medium

Category: Interpreting Data

Getting to the Answer: Since the question asks about length and temperature, the simplest data set to consider is Table 1, because Table 2 includes

another variable, type of material. Comparing the odd numbered trials (all conducted at 80°C) or the even numbered trials (all conducted at 20°C) shows that the shorter the rod, the higher the current, which is an inverse relationship. Choices F and J can be eliminated. Comparing any trials which hold length of the rod constant while changing the temperature, such as Trials 1 and 2, show that as temperature goes down, current through the rod goes up, which is another inverse relationship. Because both length and temperature are inversely related to current, (G) is correct.

35. C

Difficulty: Medium

Category: Using Data

Getting to the Answer: The passage states that voltage, current, and resistance are related through Ohm's law, $V = A \times \Omega$, where Ω stands for resistance in ohms and A stands for current in amperes. In the circuit used for these experiments, the voltage is held constant at 5 V, as indicated by the battery in Figure 1. This means that if current goes up, resistance must have gone down. Conversely, the lowest current will result from the highest resistance. Because each of the rods featured in the answer choices were tested in Experiment 2, to find the rod with the highest resistance, you merely need to find the one with the lowest recorded current in Table 2. The rod in Trial 9 conducted a current of only 20 mA, less than any of the others, so it must have the highest resistance. Choice (C) is thus correct.

36. H

Difficulty: High

Category: Using Data

Getting to the Answer: According to the question stem, conductivity uses the units of siemens per meter ($\sigma = S/m$) and siemens are equal to inverse ohms ($S = 1/\Omega$). Putting these two equations together, you can see that the units of conductivity are equivalent to inverse ohms divided by meters ($\sigma = [1/\Omega]/m$), which simplifies to $\sigma = 1/(\Omega \times m)$. Choice (H) is thus correct.

37. B

Difficulty: Low

Category: Using Data

Getting to the Answer: According to Table 1, the rod in Trial 4 conducted 53 mA of electricity at 20°C. A rod of the same length was used in Trial 3, but it was heated to 80°C and conducted only 27 mA.

Because 50°C is in between these two values, it is reasonable to assume that the current conducted will fall somewhere between 27 and 53 mA. Choice (B) is therefore correct.

38. F
Difficulty: Medium
Category: Using Data
Getting to the Answer: The introduction to the passage mentions Ohm's law, $V = I \times R$, which shows that voltage and current are directly related. Because the resistance values wouldn't change (the same rods would be used), the increase in voltage with the 10 V battery would lead to higher recorded values for current, regardless of the material of the rods. Thus, since both the copper and iron rods would conduct larger currents with a 10 V battery, (F) is correct.

39. C
Difficulty: Medium
Category: Using Data
Getting to the Answer: According to the results of Experiment 2, copper conducts electricity more effectively than iron. Thus, a 16 cm composite rod that was half-copper and half-iron would be expected to conduct electricity better than a 16 cm iron rod but worse than a 16 cm copper rod. According to Table 2, a 16 cm iron rod at 20°C conducts 40 mA, while a 16 cm copper rod at that temperature conducts 200 mA. Thus, the composite rod should conduct a current of somewhere between 40 and 200 mA, as in (C).

40. J
Difficulty: Low
Category: Experimental Design
Getting to the Answer: The variables that are directly manipulated in an experiment are the independent variables, so this question is asking for the one variable that is not an independent variable. In both experiments, the dependent variable—in other words, the variable that was observed and measured—was the current recorded by the ammeter. Thus, current was not directly manipulated by the student, so (J) is correct.

Writing Test

Level 6 Essay

I fully agree that pure scientific research is vital to increase our understanding of ourselves and our world, and that this research, even without specific goals, can result in important benefits to society. To fund this research, a consortium of government, pharmaceutical companies, and non-profit agencies should be formed, pooling money but giving no one group entire oversight or responsibility.

Many life-changing discoveries have been found without purposely looking for them. Alexander Fleming did not set out to discover penicilin, but in doing so accidentally saved millions of people from death. Putting a man on the moon did not help people on Earth, but it certainly taught us a lot about our universe. This kind of pure research must continue, and the cost should be shared by the government, drug companies, and non-profit groups. This type of research can be prohibitively expensive; thus, monies must be drawn from various sources, each contributing as much as possible. No single organization can completely fund ongoing research, especially if there is no stated goal other than to hopefully discover something beneficial. Tax payers, pharmaceutical company investors, and non-profit group members expect results, which may be long in coming, or, indeed, continually elusive. However, efforts must continue. As Thomas Edison said, "Just because something doesn't do what you planned it to do doesn't mean it's useless."

Consider also that pharmaceutical companies are always searching for new therapeutic drugs. They send scientists out into the field to come back with anything interesting, which is then researched and, if promising, developed into a new drug. Such is the relation between blood sugar and diabetes, leading to the insulin that my diabetic cousin takes; without insulin, he would not survive. If a drug company develops an important drug, it can make millions of dollars from the sale of it, leading to funding more research. Non-profit organizations also have a stake in pure research, since another accidental discovery could prove to be financially beneficial. Finally, if the government shares the burden of underwriting research, it is not at risk for being fully blamed if the research does not produce positive results. Taxpayers would be more liable to accept a minimal lose in a good cause rather than a major loss in an unsure endeavor. A partnership would ensure continued funding and the funders, as well as all citizens, would benefit from discoveries.

On the other hand, people who say the government should fund only research which has demonstrated its worth do not understand the function of pure research. It is not possible for researchers to say with certainty that they are going to find a cure for cancer. Researchers have to be able to say they are searching for something as yet unknown with the hope that it will be beneficial. And what is a clear and acceptable outcome? If cancer researchers find a cure for diabetes, but not cancer, is that acceptable if it is not the stated intention? A great deal of science is luck and perserverance. According to this perspective, if a researcher wanted government funding to work in the Amazonian rain forest with the general intent of exploring indigenous plants, the government would be unable to fund the project because there is no clearly beneficial objective. But that is exactly how quinine, a now widely used treatment for malaria, was found, and the general exploration was certainly worth funding. Finally, it is unlikely that pure research, no matter who funds it, will result in disaster. Researchers are very careful to prevent this, and even if a disaster did happen, it would not be the fault of whom is funding the research.

It is quite clear that pure research is invaluable, as the examples of penicilin, quinine, and insulin support. It cannot be dependent on the whims, finances, and oversight of any one group but must be a concerted effort among all and for all who may benefit.

Score Explanation (6 in all domains)

This essay is clearly focused on the prompt, shows complete understanding of the issue, logically assesses the implications of all three perspectives, and puts forth the author's point of view in both the first and fifth paragraphs. This is a cohesive, critical analysis of the perspectives, with a solid, well-supported thesis.

Ideas and Analysis (6)

The argument is driven by strong and clear analysis of each perspective, with good examination of implications. The writer's consistent focus on the benefits of pure research makes the essay cohesive and precise: pure research is worth pursuing and, for economic and oversight reasons, must be funded by a consortium of groups. Keeping this focus, the writer is able to explore each perspective, identify pros and cons, and provide strong support for her point of view. Critical, logical thinking is clearly displayed.

Development and Support (6)

The writer introduces her argument with a strong statement supporting pure research in general, and she immediately follows up with her perspective. That perspective is developed through reference to "life-changing discoveries," the cost of research, specific discussion of drug company research and benefits, and what may constitute acceptable risk. Support is strong, referencing Alexander Fleming, penicillin, space exploration, quinine, and insulin, and inserting a relevant quote from Thomas Edison. Reasoning and support are well integrated, and the author never loses sight of the thesis. Both alternatives are discussed. One alternative is discussed in detail, while the other is given only passing, but still strong consideration ("And what is a clear and acceptable outcome?," "Finally, it is unlikely that pure research, no matter who funds it, will result in disaster."). Development moves from the general to the specific, with excellent support for each point, and a clear and consistent perspective.

Organization (6)

There is a clear and strong introduction and a summary conclusion, both of which enlarge the specifics of the prompt to the larger issues involved. Each paragraph begins with a topic sentence, and the contrasting view is signaled with the phrase "On the other hand," while the third paragraph is introduced with the creative transition phrase "Consider also." The essay is cohesive and flows well, ideas are well-connected, and support is explicit, relevant, and well-positioned to enhance the argument.

Language Use (6)

The writing is mostly high-level, with the use of a rhetorical question and words such as "perseverance," "accountable," "consortium," and "pharmaceutical." Several sentences are varied and complex. The grammar and punctuation are mostly correct, though there are some spelling errors ("penicilin," "perserverance"). The writer's style is appropriately formal, even with a personal example, and her word choice is effective in characterizing the perspectives and writing a persuasive argument.

Level 4 Essay

Pure research is done for the purpose of discovery without a specific goal in mind. Even so, it has produced important breakthroughs such as treatment for Alzheimer's disease, and even the development of the GPS. Though scientific research is vitally important, people disagree about who should pay for it. Some people think that the government should fund the research if the goal is a good one. Others think that the government should only give money to research that can be shown will be helpful. Still others believe that the government and private companies should work together to give scientists the money they need, which is the best way to do it, and the perspective I agree with.

I know the importance of research because my little brother has asthma and requires daily medication. Though I don't know who paid for the research that helped make his meds, I'm quite sure that the research behind it took a long time and cost a great deal of money. Though the government may have enough money to fully fund research like this, it has other responsibilities as well and can't afford to fund research alone, especially if the outcome is unsure. However, with other money from drug companies and non-profit agencies, research can continue to be funded without any one entity eating into their finances earmarked for other purposes. Even if the research doesn't show results for many years, a group of funders can provide enough money so that scientists can keep working until they discover something helpful and then continue to develop it.

The government can't do everything on its own and companies shouldn't have to work by themselves either. If they team up, lots of research can get done. Asthma is now manageable, but there are plenty of other illnesses that are very deadly. Everybody is hoping for a cure for cancer one day, and scientists need time and money to find one. Groups working together can give those scientists the time and money they need, since no one group is responsible for an immediate, beneficial result from the research it funds. The government and companies should pick an amount of money they want to spend each year on scientific research and give it to a variety of research groups. Then, if any of the groups make a major discovery, they can earn more money and invest it back into ongoing research.

On the other hand, some people think that scientists should have to show the government that their projects will be helpful in order to get money. That would exclude a lot of past and future research that was done purely in the hopes of discovery but without assurances. Louis Pasture wouldn't have gotten money from his government to make penicillin since it was a total accident. Being able to pinpoint the exact purpose and result of pure research is precisely the opposite of what pure research aims to do.

Like all important things, research requires time, effort and money. The best way to fund it is to gather a group of government, private, and non-profit agencies who can pool their resources to let scientists keep working. Some research may fail miserably, but some may change the course of the world. That possibility is surely worth funding.

Score Explanation (4 in all domains)

The writer provides a minimal discussion of all three perspectives, but fails to fully consider the implications of the other perspectives. He doesn't fully consider counterarguments, but he does provide relevant support for his opinion.

Ideas and Analysis (4)

Ideas are clearly stated, if redundant. The argument centers around "time, effort, and money," with discussion of each taking up most of the essay. His perspective is analyzed primarily through a personal anecdote about his brother, which is more related to research in general than to pure research. However, the author is consistent in his argument and able to critique another perspective while returning to his own point of view.

Development and Support (4)

The writer begins with a good statement defining pure research, immediately bringing in the examples of Alzheimer's and the GPS, though a brief explanation of their relevance would enhance the support. The first paragraph also introduces all perspectives. However, when the writer states his own opinion at the end of the introduction, he does not do so forcefully. The argument is developed with a personal statement about his brother's asthma, which leads into further discussion of funding. The writer continues this argument in the next paragraph, again referencing asthma and mentioning cancer, though both statements are fleeting and do not offer strong support. One other alternative is discussed in the fourth paragraph, nicely harking back to the definition of pure research (the incorrect reference to Pasteur and penicillin does not affect the support).

Organization (4)

The writer provides a clear introductory paragraph and a good conclusion, and he is able to tie the essay together by harking back to the initial definition of pure research at the end of the fourth paragraph with "Being able to pinpoint the exact purpose and result of pure research is precisely the opposite of what pure research aims to do." The first paragraph shows good connection between perspectives ("Some," "Others," "Still others"). However, there are few transitions other than the one introducing paragraph four; better use of transitions would make the essay flow more smoothly. The essay is nonetheless cohesive in its perspective.

Language Use (4)

The writing style is adequate, with some spelling and grammar errors. Word choice could be improved by avoiding very informal words and phrases ("eating into their finances," "total accident," "meds," "plenty of other diseases") and expressing ideas with more high-level vocabulary and complex sentence structure. Less use of contractions would also raise the language to a more appropriately formal essay level.

Level 2 Essay

Working with a real goal in mind is the best way to do a project and the goverment has lots of money, so I think the government should pay for research projects but only those which will succeed. I did a school sience project with too other kids but we ended up fighting and not finishing it, which is what would happen if lots of groups got together to fund something.

When my teacher assigns a sience project even though I get to choose which one to do she expects results. The goverment should think the same way because if they don't they will be spending money for something which could be useless. Just like my teacher does when she decides what grade to give my project, the goverment should think about how successful the research might be and save their money for research that will really come up with something important.

Like it says, "to many cooks spoil the broth" which means that when theres a whole group of people, chances are the end result is bad. That goes for the govement partnering with other groups also they should pay for research by themselves but only if it looks like the research will come up with something good.

Score Explanation (2 in all domains)

Though the author addresses the prompt and takes a side, this essay is very poorly written and supported, and ideas and analysis are weak with little clarity.

Ideas and Analysis (2)

This essay indicates a lack of understanding of the prompt and task, and poor reasoning and writing skills. The author has focused primarily on the issues of money and the negative effects of working with partners, likening the latter to working with others on a science project. She has not analyzed any perspective in depth; instead, ideas are repetitive, with shallow support. The author has not looked beyond her own school experience, thus her argument is weak and analysis of the prompt is superficial.

Development and Support (2)

The author fails to develop her thesis beyond general, poorly supported statements which repeat her two ideas that working together is detrimental to a project, and government money should be spent on projects with demonstrated success. Her support is weak and irrelevant, focusing on a school project, equating it with pure research, and suggesting that the government should determine its funding in the same way that a teacher determines a grade. The phrase which opens the third sentence is a trite platitude, again lacking any real thought and analysis. The author's reasoning is inadequate and confused, and she fails to examine the argument logically.

Organization (2)

Though there are three separate paragraphs and the conclusion echoes the first paragraph's perspective, each paragraph is weak and disjointed, with no transition phrases to tie the essay together. Ideas are poorly grouped together; the author repeatedly compares a school project to governmental pure research funding.

Language Use (2)

There are numerous spelling and punctuation errors, word choice is simplistic, and the writing fails to be persuasive. "Government" and "science" are consistently misspelled, and there are several instances of improper pronoun/antecedent agreement. The author misuses the word "too," omits the apostrophe from "there's," and follows the missed apostrophe with a run-on sentence. Word choice and sentence structure are rudimentary, and the essay lacks the strength and style of writing which would make it persuasive and engaging.

You can evaluate your essay and the model essay based on the following criteria, which are covered in chapter 27:

- Does the author discuss all three perspectives provided in the prompt?
- Is the author's own perspective clearly stated?
- Does the body of the essay assess and analyze each perspective?
- Is the relevance of each paragraph clear?
- Does the author start a new paragraph for each new idea?
- Is each sentence in a paragraph relevant to the point made in that paragraph?
- Are transitions clear?
- Is the essay easy to read? Is it engaging?
- Are sentences varied?
- Is vocabulary used effectively? Is college-level vocabulary used?

ACT Practice Test 2
ANSWER SHEET

ENGLISH TEST

1. Ⓐ Ⓑ Ⓒ Ⓓ   11. Ⓐ Ⓑ Ⓒ Ⓓ   21. Ⓐ Ⓑ Ⓒ Ⓓ   31. Ⓐ Ⓑ Ⓒ Ⓓ   41. Ⓐ Ⓑ Ⓒ Ⓓ   51. Ⓐ Ⓑ Ⓒ Ⓓ   61. Ⓐ Ⓑ Ⓒ Ⓓ   71. Ⓐ Ⓑ Ⓒ Ⓓ
2. Ⓕ Ⓖ Ⓗ Ⓙ   12. Ⓕ Ⓖ Ⓗ Ⓙ   22. Ⓕ Ⓖ Ⓗ Ⓙ   32. Ⓕ Ⓖ Ⓗ Ⓙ   42. Ⓕ Ⓖ Ⓗ Ⓙ   52. Ⓕ Ⓖ Ⓗ Ⓙ   62. Ⓕ Ⓖ Ⓗ Ⓙ   72. Ⓕ Ⓖ Ⓗ Ⓙ
3. Ⓐ Ⓑ Ⓒ Ⓓ   13. Ⓐ Ⓑ Ⓒ Ⓓ   23. Ⓐ Ⓑ Ⓒ Ⓓ   33. Ⓐ Ⓑ Ⓒ Ⓓ   43. Ⓐ Ⓑ Ⓒ Ⓓ   53. Ⓐ Ⓑ Ⓒ Ⓓ   63. Ⓐ Ⓑ Ⓒ Ⓓ   73. Ⓐ Ⓑ Ⓒ Ⓓ
4. Ⓕ Ⓖ Ⓗ Ⓙ   14. Ⓕ Ⓖ Ⓗ Ⓙ   24. Ⓕ Ⓖ Ⓗ Ⓙ   34. Ⓕ Ⓖ Ⓗ Ⓙ   44. Ⓕ Ⓖ Ⓗ Ⓙ   54. Ⓕ Ⓖ Ⓗ Ⓙ   64. Ⓕ Ⓖ Ⓗ Ⓙ   74. Ⓕ Ⓖ Ⓗ Ⓙ
5. Ⓐ Ⓑ Ⓒ Ⓓ   15. Ⓐ Ⓑ Ⓒ Ⓓ   25. Ⓐ Ⓑ Ⓒ Ⓓ   35. Ⓐ Ⓑ Ⓒ Ⓓ   45. Ⓐ Ⓑ Ⓒ Ⓓ   55. Ⓐ Ⓑ Ⓒ Ⓓ   65. Ⓐ Ⓑ Ⓒ Ⓓ   75. Ⓐ Ⓑ Ⓒ Ⓓ
6. Ⓕ Ⓖ Ⓗ Ⓙ   16. Ⓕ Ⓖ Ⓗ Ⓙ   26. Ⓕ Ⓖ Ⓗ Ⓙ   36. Ⓕ Ⓖ Ⓗ Ⓙ   46. Ⓕ Ⓖ Ⓗ Ⓙ   56. Ⓕ Ⓖ Ⓗ Ⓙ   66. Ⓕ Ⓖ Ⓗ Ⓙ
7. Ⓐ Ⓑ Ⓒ Ⓓ   17. Ⓐ Ⓑ Ⓒ Ⓓ   27. Ⓐ Ⓑ Ⓒ Ⓓ   37. Ⓐ Ⓑ Ⓒ Ⓓ   47. Ⓐ Ⓑ Ⓒ Ⓓ   57. Ⓐ Ⓑ Ⓒ Ⓓ   67. Ⓐ Ⓑ Ⓒ Ⓓ
8. Ⓕ Ⓖ Ⓗ Ⓙ   18. Ⓕ Ⓖ Ⓗ Ⓙ   28. Ⓕ Ⓖ Ⓗ Ⓙ   38. Ⓕ Ⓖ Ⓗ Ⓙ   48. Ⓕ Ⓖ Ⓗ Ⓙ   58. Ⓕ Ⓖ Ⓗ Ⓙ   68. Ⓕ Ⓖ Ⓗ Ⓙ
9. Ⓐ Ⓑ Ⓒ Ⓓ   19. Ⓐ Ⓑ Ⓒ Ⓓ   29. Ⓐ Ⓑ Ⓒ Ⓓ   39. Ⓐ Ⓑ Ⓒ Ⓓ   49. Ⓐ Ⓑ Ⓒ Ⓓ   59. Ⓐ Ⓑ Ⓒ Ⓓ   69. Ⓐ Ⓑ Ⓒ Ⓓ
10. Ⓕ Ⓖ Ⓗ Ⓙ   20. Ⓕ Ⓖ Ⓗ Ⓙ   30. Ⓕ Ⓖ Ⓗ Ⓙ   40. Ⓕ Ⓖ Ⓗ Ⓙ   50. Ⓕ Ⓖ Ⓗ Ⓙ   60. Ⓕ Ⓖ Ⓗ Ⓙ   70. Ⓕ Ⓖ Ⓗ Ⓙ

MATHEMATICS TEST

1. Ⓐ Ⓑ Ⓒ Ⓓ Ⓔ   11. Ⓐ Ⓑ Ⓒ Ⓓ Ⓔ   21. Ⓐ Ⓑ Ⓒ Ⓓ Ⓔ   31. Ⓐ Ⓑ Ⓒ Ⓓ Ⓔ   41. Ⓐ Ⓑ Ⓒ Ⓓ Ⓔ   51. Ⓐ Ⓑ Ⓒ Ⓓ Ⓔ
2. Ⓕ Ⓖ Ⓗ Ⓙ Ⓚ   12. Ⓕ Ⓖ Ⓗ Ⓙ Ⓚ   22. Ⓕ Ⓖ Ⓗ Ⓙ Ⓚ   32. Ⓕ Ⓖ Ⓗ Ⓙ Ⓚ   42. Ⓕ Ⓖ Ⓗ Ⓙ Ⓚ   52. Ⓕ Ⓖ Ⓗ Ⓙ Ⓚ
3. Ⓐ Ⓑ Ⓒ Ⓓ Ⓔ   13. Ⓐ Ⓑ Ⓒ Ⓓ Ⓔ   23. Ⓐ Ⓑ Ⓒ Ⓓ Ⓔ   33. Ⓐ Ⓑ Ⓒ Ⓓ Ⓔ   43. Ⓐ Ⓑ Ⓒ Ⓓ Ⓔ   53. Ⓐ Ⓑ Ⓒ Ⓓ Ⓔ
4. Ⓕ Ⓖ Ⓗ Ⓙ Ⓚ   14. Ⓕ Ⓖ Ⓗ Ⓙ Ⓚ   24. Ⓕ Ⓖ Ⓗ Ⓙ Ⓚ   34. Ⓕ Ⓖ Ⓗ Ⓙ Ⓚ   44. Ⓕ Ⓖ Ⓗ Ⓙ Ⓚ   54. Ⓕ Ⓖ Ⓗ Ⓙ Ⓚ
5. Ⓐ Ⓑ Ⓒ Ⓓ Ⓔ   15. Ⓐ Ⓑ Ⓒ Ⓓ Ⓔ   25. Ⓐ Ⓑ Ⓒ Ⓓ Ⓔ   35. Ⓐ Ⓑ Ⓒ Ⓓ Ⓔ   45. Ⓐ Ⓑ Ⓒ Ⓓ Ⓔ   55. Ⓐ Ⓑ Ⓒ Ⓓ Ⓔ
6. Ⓕ Ⓖ Ⓗ Ⓙ Ⓚ   16. Ⓕ Ⓖ Ⓗ Ⓙ Ⓚ   26. Ⓕ Ⓖ Ⓗ Ⓙ Ⓚ   36. Ⓕ Ⓖ Ⓗ Ⓙ Ⓚ   46. Ⓕ Ⓖ Ⓗ Ⓙ Ⓚ   56. Ⓕ Ⓖ Ⓗ Ⓙ Ⓚ
7. Ⓐ Ⓑ Ⓒ Ⓓ Ⓔ   17. Ⓐ Ⓑ Ⓒ Ⓓ Ⓔ   27. Ⓐ Ⓑ Ⓒ Ⓓ Ⓔ   37. Ⓐ Ⓑ Ⓒ Ⓓ Ⓔ   47. Ⓐ Ⓑ Ⓒ Ⓓ Ⓔ   57. Ⓐ Ⓑ Ⓒ Ⓓ Ⓔ
8. Ⓕ Ⓖ Ⓗ Ⓙ Ⓚ   18. Ⓕ Ⓖ Ⓗ Ⓙ Ⓚ   28. Ⓕ Ⓖ Ⓗ Ⓙ Ⓚ   38. Ⓕ Ⓖ Ⓗ Ⓙ Ⓚ   48. Ⓕ Ⓖ Ⓗ Ⓙ Ⓚ   58. Ⓕ Ⓖ Ⓗ Ⓙ Ⓚ
9. Ⓐ Ⓑ Ⓒ Ⓓ Ⓔ   19. Ⓐ Ⓑ Ⓒ Ⓓ Ⓔ   29. Ⓐ Ⓑ Ⓒ Ⓓ Ⓔ   39. Ⓐ Ⓑ Ⓒ Ⓓ Ⓔ   49. Ⓐ Ⓑ Ⓒ Ⓓ Ⓔ   59. Ⓐ Ⓑ Ⓒ Ⓓ Ⓔ
10. Ⓕ Ⓖ Ⓗ Ⓙ Ⓚ   20. Ⓕ Ⓖ Ⓗ Ⓙ Ⓚ   30. Ⓕ Ⓖ Ⓗ Ⓙ Ⓚ   40. Ⓕ Ⓖ Ⓗ Ⓙ Ⓚ   50. Ⓕ Ⓖ Ⓗ Ⓙ Ⓚ   60. Ⓕ Ⓖ Ⓗ Ⓙ Ⓚ

READING TEST

1. Ⓐ Ⓑ Ⓒ Ⓓ   6. Ⓕ Ⓖ Ⓗ Ⓙ   11. Ⓐ Ⓑ Ⓒ Ⓓ   16. Ⓕ Ⓖ Ⓗ Ⓙ   21. Ⓐ Ⓑ Ⓒ Ⓓ   26. Ⓕ Ⓖ Ⓗ Ⓙ   31. Ⓐ Ⓑ Ⓒ Ⓓ   36. Ⓕ Ⓖ Ⓗ Ⓙ
2. Ⓕ Ⓖ Ⓗ Ⓙ   7. Ⓐ Ⓑ Ⓒ Ⓓ   12. Ⓕ Ⓖ Ⓗ Ⓙ   17. Ⓐ Ⓑ Ⓒ Ⓓ   22. Ⓕ Ⓖ Ⓗ Ⓙ   27. Ⓐ Ⓑ Ⓒ Ⓓ   32. Ⓕ Ⓖ Ⓗ Ⓙ   37. Ⓐ Ⓑ Ⓒ Ⓓ
3. Ⓐ Ⓑ Ⓒ Ⓓ   8. Ⓕ Ⓖ Ⓗ Ⓙ   13. Ⓐ Ⓑ Ⓒ Ⓓ   18. Ⓕ Ⓖ Ⓗ Ⓙ   23. Ⓐ Ⓑ Ⓒ Ⓓ   28. Ⓕ Ⓖ Ⓗ Ⓙ   33. Ⓐ Ⓑ Ⓒ Ⓓ   38. Ⓕ Ⓖ Ⓗ Ⓙ
4. Ⓕ Ⓖ Ⓗ Ⓙ   9. Ⓐ Ⓑ Ⓒ Ⓓ   14. Ⓕ Ⓖ Ⓗ Ⓙ   19. Ⓐ Ⓑ Ⓒ Ⓓ   24. Ⓕ Ⓖ Ⓗ Ⓙ   29. Ⓐ Ⓑ Ⓒ Ⓓ   34. Ⓕ Ⓖ Ⓗ Ⓙ   39. Ⓐ Ⓑ Ⓒ Ⓓ
5. Ⓐ Ⓑ Ⓒ Ⓓ   10. Ⓕ Ⓖ Ⓗ Ⓙ   15. Ⓐ Ⓑ Ⓒ Ⓓ   20. Ⓕ Ⓖ Ⓗ Ⓙ   25. Ⓐ Ⓑ Ⓒ Ⓓ   30. Ⓕ Ⓖ Ⓗ Ⓙ   35. Ⓐ Ⓑ Ⓒ Ⓓ   40. Ⓕ Ⓖ Ⓗ Ⓙ

SCIENCE TEST

1. Ⓐ Ⓑ Ⓒ Ⓓ   6. Ⓕ Ⓖ Ⓗ Ⓙ   11. Ⓐ Ⓑ Ⓒ Ⓓ   16. Ⓕ Ⓖ Ⓗ Ⓙ   21. Ⓐ Ⓑ Ⓒ Ⓓ   26. Ⓕ Ⓖ Ⓗ Ⓙ   31. Ⓐ Ⓑ Ⓒ Ⓓ   36. Ⓕ Ⓖ Ⓗ Ⓙ
2. Ⓕ Ⓖ Ⓗ Ⓙ   7. Ⓐ Ⓑ Ⓒ Ⓓ   12. Ⓕ Ⓖ Ⓗ Ⓙ   17. Ⓐ Ⓑ Ⓒ Ⓓ   22. Ⓕ Ⓖ Ⓗ Ⓙ   27. Ⓐ Ⓑ Ⓒ Ⓓ   32. Ⓕ Ⓖ Ⓗ Ⓙ   37. Ⓐ Ⓑ Ⓒ Ⓓ
3. Ⓐ Ⓑ Ⓒ Ⓓ   8. Ⓕ Ⓖ Ⓗ Ⓙ   13. Ⓐ Ⓑ Ⓒ Ⓓ   18. Ⓕ Ⓖ Ⓗ Ⓙ   23. Ⓐ Ⓑ Ⓒ Ⓓ   28. Ⓕ Ⓖ Ⓗ Ⓙ   33. Ⓐ Ⓑ Ⓒ Ⓓ   38. Ⓕ Ⓖ Ⓗ Ⓙ
4. Ⓕ Ⓖ Ⓗ Ⓙ   9. Ⓐ Ⓑ Ⓒ Ⓓ   14. Ⓕ Ⓖ Ⓗ Ⓙ   19. Ⓐ Ⓑ Ⓒ Ⓓ   24. Ⓕ Ⓖ Ⓗ Ⓙ   29. Ⓐ Ⓑ Ⓒ Ⓓ   34. Ⓕ Ⓖ Ⓗ Ⓙ   39. Ⓐ Ⓑ Ⓒ Ⓓ
5. Ⓐ Ⓑ Ⓒ Ⓓ   10. Ⓕ Ⓖ Ⓗ Ⓙ   15. Ⓐ Ⓑ Ⓒ Ⓓ   20. Ⓕ Ⓖ Ⓗ Ⓙ   25. Ⓐ Ⓑ Ⓒ Ⓓ   30. Ⓕ Ⓖ Ⓗ Ⓙ   35. Ⓐ Ⓑ Ⓒ Ⓓ   40. Ⓕ Ⓖ Ⓗ Ⓙ

English Test

45 Minutes—75 Questions

Directions: Each passage has certain words and phrases that are underlined and numbered. The questions in the right column will provide alternatives for the underlined segments. Most questions require you to choose the answer that makes the sentence grammatically correct, concise, and relevant. If the word or phrase in the passage is already the correct, concise, and relevant choice, select NO CHANGE. Some questions will ask a question about the underlined segment. When a question is presented, choose the best answer.

Some questions will ask about part or all of the passage. These questions do not refer to a specific underlined segment. Instead, these questions will accompany a number in a box.

For each question, choose your answer and fill in the corresponding bubble on your answer sheet. Read the passage once before you answer the questions. You will often need to read several sentences beyond the underlined portion to be able to choose the correct answer. Be sure to read enough to answer each question.

Passage I

My Cousin Nicola

My father and his two younger brothers emigrated from Italy to New York in the early 1970s. Only their older sister Lucia, <u>which</u> was already married, remained

1. A. NO CHANGE
   B. whom
   C. who
   D. she who

behind in their small home <u>town, this village</u> lies in the shadow of Mount Vesuvius. Growing up in America, my cousins and I were as close as brothers and sisters, but

2. F. NO CHANGE
   G. town, it can be seen where it
   H. town it
   J. town that

we hardly <u>known</u> our family across the Atlantic. When I was a young child, my parents and I went to Italy to visit Aunt Lucia and her family for a week. I first met my

3. A. NO CHANGE
   B. knew
   C. had knew
   D. been known

cousin <u>Nicola however</u>, I remember that we were not
₄

4. F. NO CHANGE
   G. Nicola, so then
   H. Nicola because
   J. Nicola then.

only about the same age, <u>and</u> we also got along well. But
₅

5. A. NO CHANGE
   B. so
   C. but
   D. then

because <u>I being</u> so young, I remember little else. I hadn't
₆
seen him again up until this last summer.

   Nicola decided that he wanted to join the Italian

Air Force after finishing high school. Before beginning

his service, though, he wanted to travel for a bit.

<u>He had never been to America, even though so many of</u>
₇
<u>his relatives live here, but he had been to England already.</u>
₇
When the rest of the cousins heard the news, they were

6. F. NO CHANGE
   G. I, who was
   H. I was
   J. I,

7. Assuming that each choice is true, which one provides the most relevant information about Nicola's travel plans?

   A. NO CHANGE
   B. He had never been to America, so he called my father and asked if he could come spend the summer with us in New York.
   C. He had never been to America, which is most easily reached from Italy by plane.
   D. Because it was expensive for his whole family to travel overseas, Nicola had never been to America before.

<u>ecstatic</u>. Most of them had never met Nicola or, like me,
₈

8. Three of these choices indicate that the cousins looked forward to meeting Nicola. Which choice does NOT do so?

   F. NO CHANGE
   G. excited.
   H. apprehensive.
   J. thrilled.

CONTINUED ➡

hadn't seen him, since we were kids; they were eager to
    9
get to know him.

Two weeks later, we picked Nicola up at JFK Airport. Right away, I was surprised by his height. I am the tallest of all the cousins in America, and Nicola was easily a couple of inches taller than me. In addition to our height, he and I had another similarity: we were both musicians. The moment I saw the acoustic guitar slung over his shoulder, I knew he and I would get along just fine. None of them plays an instrument, and I always
            10
thought that I was the only musician

in the family (even though some relatives have lovely
    11
singing voices). I was happy to find out I was wrong.
    11
Throughout that summer, Nicola and I shared the gift of music. We would sing and play our guitars long into the night, only stopping when my mother came downstairs and forced us to quit. We liked many of the same bands, and we taught each other to play our favorite songs. Taught to him as a child before she
                    12
passed away in Italy, I was taught by him the Italian
    12
folk songs of our grandmother more importantly. It
    12
was through those songs that I truly connected to the beauty

9.   A.   NO CHANGE
     B.   hadn't seen him since we were kids
     C.   hadn't seen him since we were kids;
     D.   hadn't seen, him since we were kids,

10.   F.   NO CHANGE
      G.   us
      H.   the Americans
      J.   my American cousins

11.   A.   NO CHANGE
      B.   in the family, which has at least 20 members that I know of.
      C.   in the family.
      D.   DELETE the underlined portion (ending the sentence with a period).

12.   F.   NO CHANGE
      G.   Teaching him as a child before she passed away, our grandmother in Italy more importantly taught to me many of the Italian folk songs.
      H.   Teaching him as a child, more importantly, by our grandmother in Italy, I was taught by him many Italian folk songs.
      J.   More importantly, however, he taught me many of the Italian folk songs our grandmother in Italy had taught him as a child before she passed away.

CONTINUED

of our ancestry. On the night before Nicola returned to

Italy, my father <u>would have thrown</u> a big party for all of
                          13

the relatives.

Nicola and I played the folk songs of <u>our grandmothers</u>
                                              14

country for the American side of our family. When we were

done, my Uncle Vittorio had a tear in his eye. Since coming

to America so long ago, he had never been able to return to

Italy. In the music and our singing, Nicola and I brought

the beautiful country back to Uncle Vittorio.

13. A. NO CHANGE
    B. will have thrown
    C. threw
    D. throws

14. F. NO CHANGE
    G. our grandmother's
    H. our grandmothers'
    J. are grandmother's

| Question 15 asks about the preceding passage as a whole. |

15. Suppose the writer's goal had been to write a
    personal narrative that emphasizes the value
    of family. Would this passage accomplish this
    purpose?

    A. Yes, because it shows how connecting with
        distant family can be meaningful.

    B. Yes, because it shows how much closer the
        narrator is to Nicola than to his American
        cousins.

    C. No, because the narrator and Nicola are not
        closely related.

    D. No, because the passage does not mention any
        family members besides Nicola.

CONTINUED ▶

Passage II

The Handsome Bean

On the ground floor of the apartment <u>building</u>
<u>where, I live</u>, the Handsome Bean coffee shop is almost
always bustling with customers. During the warm
months, the shop sets up outdoor tables on the sidewalk,
and the chatter of conversation mixed with the aroma
of coffee often floats in through my window to wake me
in the mornings. Next to the Handsome Bean is a used
bookstore, and the two shops share many of the same
customers. People come to find a book and stay to enjoy
a cup of coffee. Across the street from the building is the
neighborhood Little League field. ☐17 The Handsome

Bean often <u>sponsors</u> a local team. During the games, the
coffee shop offers a discount to parents whose children

16. F. NO CHANGE
    G. building where I live,
    H. building, where I live
    J. building where I live

17. The purpose of including the location of the Little
    League field is to:

    A. introduce the kind of team the Handsome
       Bean sponsors.
    B. transition from a discussion of the Handsome
       Bean to a discussion of baseball.
    C. add a detail that helps the reader picture
       the scene.
    D. downplay the importance of the Handsome
       Bean.

18. F. NO CHANGE
    G. had sponsored
    H. was a sponsor of
    J. supported

are competing across the street. [19] It is a pleasure to

19. At this point, the writer wants to add a sentence that provides additional detail about the customers who come to the Handsome Bean. Which of the following sentences would best achieve the writer's purpose?

A. In addition to this discount, the shop offers all patrons a punch card to receive a tenth coffee for free.

B. The shop also sells ice cream, so it often gets very crowded with children and parents after the Little League games are over.

C. The Handsome Bean also provides uniforms for an elementary school soccer team.

D. The Little League field doesn't have a concession stand, so the coffee shop doesn't have much competition for the parents' business.

have as a neighbor a business that <u>children. And adults</u>
enjoy so much.

20. F. NO CHANGE

G. children and adults

H. children and that adults

J. children. Adults

<u>Over the past few years, I have become friends with</u>
<u>Mary, the owner of the shop</u>. The store's main counter is a
century-old antique that Mary bought and restored to

21. Which choice most effectively leads the reader into the topic of this paragraph?

A. NO CHANGE

B. Mary, the shop's owner, has a great appreciation for history.

C. The Handsome Bean has only been open for a couple of years, but the owner, Mary, has taken great care to make it look like it has been there for decades.

D. Before Mary, the shop's owner, opened the Handsome Bean, the space had been unoccupied for six months.

Practice Tests

CONTINUED ➡

its <u>originally conditional</u>, and the photos that adorn the
22

back wall <u>depicts</u> our town during the 1920s and 1930s.
23
My favorite detail of the shop, however, is the original
tin ceiling. One afternoon, while staring at the intricate
patterns etched into the tin tiles, I noticed a name
camouflaged within the ornate design: Harvey. I pointed
it out to Mary, and she said the original owner of the
building was named Harvey Wallaby. Her guess was
that he had probably written it there more than 70 years
ago. [24] That night after the coffee shop had closed,
Mary and I etched our names into the ceiling right next
to Harvey's, hoping that our names would similarly be
discovered in the far-off future.

On Friday nights, the Handsome Bean has live
entertainment, usually in the <u>form of, a</u> band or a poetry
25
reading. For a small-town coffee shop, the Handsome

Bean attracts a <u>good amount</u> of talented musicians and
26

22. F. NO CHANGE
G. original conditional,
H. original condition,
J. conditionally original,

23. A. NO CHANGE
B. depict
C. has depicted
D. shows

24. The writer is considering deleting the sentence below from the passage:

Her guess was that he had probably written it there more than 70 years ago.

If the writer were to delete this sentence, the essay would primarily lose:

F. an additional detail about the building that houses the coffee shop.
G. a depiction of the action taken by Mary and the writer.
H. an emphasis on the original owner's influence.
J. a description of the shop's interior.

25. A. NO CHANGE
B. form; of a
C. form, of a
D. form of a

26. F. NO CHANGE
G. better amount
H. better number
J. good number

CONTINUED

poets. <u>It being that I am amazed by the performances,</u>
²⁷
<u>they</u> transpire within its cozy walls.
²⁷

[1] The clientele of the coffee shop is as varied as the selection of flavored brews. [2] In the mornings, the Handsome Bean is abuzz with the 9-to-5 crowd stopping in for some java before heading off to work. [3] During the day, the tables are home to local artists lost in their thoughts and cappuccinos. [4] The evening finds the Handsome Bean filled with bleary-eyed college students loading up on caffeine so they can cram all night for their upcoming exams or <u>finishing</u> their research papers
²⁸
with looming due dates. [5] Then there's me, sitting in the corner, maybe talking to Mary or reading the paper, smiling at the thought that the best cup of coffee in town is found right beneath my bedroom window. [6] In the afternoons, a group of high school <u>students who</u> stops
²⁹

by to have an ice cream cone or an egg cream. [30]

27. A. NO CHANGE
    B. Amazing the performances, it is that I know they
    C. I am amazed by the performances that
    D. Amazing the performances, they

28. F. NO CHANGE
    G. finish
    H. finishes
    J. finalizing

29. A. NO CHANGE
    B. students that
    C. students, and they
    D. students

30. For the sake of logic and coherence, Sentence 6 should be placed:

    F. where it is now.
    G. before Sentence 2.
    H. before Sentence 4.
    J. before Sentence 5.

CONTINUED

Passage III

Mr. Midshipman Marryat

The paragraphs below may or may not be in the most logical order. A number in brackets appears above each paragraph. At the end of the passage, Question 45 will ask you to determine the most logical place for Paragraph 1.

[1]

Born to an upper-class English family in 1792, Marryat had a thirst for <u>naval adventure</u> and exploration
31
very early in his childhood. As a young boy at private school, he tried to run away to sea a number of times.

<u>Finally, his exasperated parents</u> at last granted him
32

his wish in 1806; <u>they were</u> enlisted in the British Royal
33
Navy as a midshipman. Marryat had the luck to be assigned to sail upon the frigate *HMS Imperieuse* under

the command of Lord Cochrane. Cochrane, <u>that's</u> naval
34

31. A. NO CHANGE
    B. naval, adventure,
    C. naval, adventure
    D. naval adventure;

32. F. NO CHANGE
    G. His exasperated parents
    H. In the end, his exasperated parents
    J. Ultimately, the result was that his exasperated parents

33. A. NO CHANGE
    B. they
    C. he
    D. and he

34. F. NO CHANGE
    G. who's
    H. whose
    J. who the

exploits are legendary, would later serve as the inspiration

for <u>a number of</u> Marryat's fictional characters. 36
                35

35. The writer is considering deleting the phrase "a number of." If the writer decided to delete the phrase, would the meaning of the sentence change?

   A. Yes, because without this phrase, the reader would think that all of Marryat's fictional characters were based on Cochrane.

   B. Yes, because without this phrase, the reader would not understand that Marryat used Cochrane as a model for more than one fictional character.

   C. No, because this phrase is an example of wordiness that should be eliminated from the sentence.

   D. No; although the phrase adds a detail about Marryat's character, this detail is not essential to the meaning of the sentence.

36. At this point, the writer is considering adding the sentence below:

   The well-known writer Patrick O'Brian also modeled his Captain Jack Aubrey after Cochrane.

   Should the writer make this addition?

   F. Yes, because if readers know that other writers were inspired by Cochrane, they will better understand that Cochrane was an impressive person.

   G. Yes, because the added detail provides information about a writer who used a style similar to Marryat's.

   H. No, because the essay doesn't reveal the relationship between O'Brian and Marryat.

   J. No, because the detail distracts from the main focus of the essay.

CONTINUED

[2]

Unlike most of the other <u>famous</u> authors who have
37
spun tales of brave British naval officers fighting for
king and country on the high seas, Frederick Marryat
actually served as a captain in the British navy. While
others could only use their imagination and accounts
to describe what life must have been like for a young
man rising through the ranks from lowly midshipman
to all-powerful captain <u>from historical records</u>, Marryat
38
needed only to dip into the vast library of adventure
stored in his memory.

[3]

Marryat's three years aboard the *Imperieuse* were
filled with experiences that would later serve him well
in his writing career. The *Imperieuse* saw much action
off the coast of Spain, where Marryat took part in
capturing a Spanish castle and numerous vessels in the
Mediterranean. Marryat willingly accepted any chance to
distinguish himself in the eyes of his revered <u>captain
39
and literary inspiration, Cochrane</u>. In fact, Marryat once
39
jumped into the turbulent sea to save the life of another

midshipman who <u>had fallen</u> overboard. Not only did
40
Marryat have the privilege of knowing first-hand a
character as illustrious as Cochrane, but his own bold
experiences as a midshipman would also be the basis for
his most famous novel, *Mr. Midshipman Easy.*

37. Which of the following would NOT be an equiva-
    lent replacement for the underlined portion?

    A. prominent
    B. beloved
    C. well-known
    D. noteworthy

38. The best placement for the underlined portion is:

    F. where it is now.
    G. after the word *accounts.*
    H. after the word *others.*
    J. after the word *adventure.*

39. A. NO CHANGE
    B. captain, and literary inspiration Cochrane.
    C. captain and literary inspiration Cochrane.
    D. captain and, literary inspiration, Cochrane.

40. F. NO CHANGE
    G. would have fallen
    H. had been falling
    J. falls

[4]

As Marryat quickly climbed through the ranks of the British navy, <u>many feats were accomplished by him</u>. These included single-handedly saving his ship during a horrific storm and fighting in a number of sea battles against the United States Navy during the War of 1812. He <u>therefore</u> earned a medal from the Royal Humane Society for inventing a special lifeboat.

[5]

<u>Marryat earned his greatest acclaim for his novels and short stories during this time</u>, which were published in England while he was at sea. He retired from the navy shortly after being awarded the rank of post captain

in 1825 to concentrate <u>for writing</u> full-time. Marryat's thrilling stories of sea adventure still live today because, as the old cliché goes, the best stories are the ones that are true.

41. A. NO CHANGE
    B. his accomplishment of many feats occurred.
    C. his many feats were accomplished.
    D. he accomplished many feats.

42. F. NO CHANGE
    G. also
    H. again
    J. thirdly

43. A. NO CHANGE
    B. During this time, Marryat earned his greatest acclaim for his novels and short stories,
    C. His greatest acclaim was earned by him, for his novels and short stories during this time,
    D. During this time for his novels and short stories, earned him his greatest acclaim,

44. F. NO CHANGE
    G. at writing
    H. on writing
    J. with writing of

Question 45 asks about the preceding passage as a whole.

45. The most logical placement of Paragraph 1 is:

    A. where it is now.
    B. after Paragraph 2.
    C. after Paragraph 3.
    D. after Paragraph 4.

CONTINUED ▶

Passage IV

The Toughest Task in Sports

[1]

I've often heard others make the comment that
the hardest single act in all of sports is to hit a major
league fastball. I'm not going to deny that hitting a ball
traveling at upwards of 95 miles per hour is a daunting
task, but I can think of something even tougher than
taking a major league at-bat: stopping a crank shot
in lacrosse. <u>Football quarterbacks facing oncoming</u>
<u>defensive linemen are also in a difficult position</u>.
46

46. F. NO CHANGE
G. Also in a challenging position are football
quarterbacks facing oncoming defensive
linemen.
H. (Football quarterbacks also face a daunting task when they are rushed by defensive
linemen.)
J. DELETE the underlined portion.

[2]

Lacrosse <u>that is</u> often referred to as "the fastest
47
sport on two feet," and with good reason. The game is

47. A. NO CHANGE
B. which has been
C. is
D. DELETE the underlined portion.

often <u>brutally</u>, and the best players normally possess
48

48. F. NO CHANGE
G. brutal
H. brute
J. brutality

a bit of <u>toughness and</u> a bit of finesse. Using sticks
49
known as "crosses" to pass a hard rubber ball back and
forth through the air, players on two teams sprint

49. A. NO CHANGE
B. toughness; and
C. toughness
D. toughness, and,

CONTINUED

around a field; <u>they then attempted</u> to set up a shot on
                       50
the opposing team's goal. As in hockey or soccer, the

only thing that stands between the ball and the goal is

the goalkeeper. Using just his body and his crosse, the

goalie must protect the six-foot by six-foot goal from

being penetrated by a ball that is less than eight inches in

circumference.

[3]

This brings me to the heart of my argument. A

regulation lacrosse ball is almost an inch narrower than

a regulation baseball, with an unstitched, smooth rubber

surface. The fastest baseball pitch on record was clocked

at 105.1 mph, <u>because</u> the average pitching speed is in
                 51
the low nineties. In men's lacrosse, because the crosse acts

as a lever, the

fastest crank shots on <u>goal, can</u> reach more than
                          52
110 mph. Even at the high school level, crank shots of

more than 90 mph

<u>made by high school players</u> are not uncommon. Unlike
            53
a baseball pitcher throwing his fastball from a fixed

position on the mound, a lacrosse player may shoot

50. F. NO CHANGE
    G. they must attempt
    H. we must attempt
    J. we then attempted

51. A. NO CHANGE
    B. before
    C. though
    D. moreover,

52. F. NO CHANGE
    G. goal, can,
    H. goal can
    J. goal can,

53. A. NO CHANGE
    B. made by these high school players
    C. shot by high school players
    D. DELETE the underlined portion.

CONTINUED

from anywhere on the field. ⏹54 This means that a lacrosse goalie may be asked to stop a crank shot from only six

feet away! To make the goalie's job even more <u>absurd</u>, a
                                               55
lacrosse player may shoot from over his shoulder, from his side, or drop his stick down and wind up from the

ground. <u>On top of that</u>, the best players often employ a
         56
variety of fakes, and most have the ability to shoot left-handed or right-handed, depending upon their angle to the goal.

54. The writer is considering adding a comma and the following information to the end of the preceding sentence:

    which is usually grass.

    Should the writer make this addition?

    F. Yes, because it allows the reader to picture the field.
    G. Yes, because it adds a detail that supports the rest of the sentence.
    H. No, because it distracts from the focus on the game.
    J. No, because it weakens the claim in the following sentence.

55. A. NO CHANGE
    B. insurmountable,
    C. harrowing,
    D. difficult,

56. Of the following possible replacements for the underlined portion, which would be LEAST acceptable?

    F. In addition,
    G. On the other hand,
    H. Furthermore,
    J. What's more,

CONTINUED

[4]

<u>Like hitting a major league fastball, stopping a</u>
                                    57
<u>crank shot in lacrosse is tough</u>. Both of these endeavors,
     57

57. Which choice is the most effective and logical transition from the topic of Paragraph 3 to the topic of Paragraph 4?

   A. NO CHANGE

   B. The combination of these unknown variables makes stopping a crank shot in lacrosse tougher than hitting a major league fastball.

   C. Though baseball is less challenging than lacrosse, both sports require tremendous skill and dedication from athletes.

   D. There is little question that stopping a crank shot in lacrosse is among the toughest tasks an athlete can face.

however, <u>require</u> the same set of skills. One must possess
                58
superlative athleticism, great hand-eye coordination,

58.   F. NO CHANGE

   G. requires

   H. required

   J. would have required

and catlike quickness. Above all, <u>you must be</u> fearless.
                                        59

59.   A. NO CHANGE

   B. one must be

   C. they must be

   D. he must have been

CONTINUED

Question 60 asks about the preceding passage
as a whole.

60. Suppose that the writer had wanted to write an
essay comparing the strategies used by baseball
pitchers and lacrosse goalies. Would this essay fulfill
the writer's goal?

    F. Yes, because the writer compares both sports
throughout the essay.

    G. Yes, because the writer details the challenges
that lacrosse goalies face.

    H. No, because the writer does not provide any
specific details about baseball pitchers.

    J. No, because the writer focuses on comparing
the difficulty of hitting a ball pitched by a
major league pitcher to the difficulty of blocking a crank shot in men's lacrosse.

Passage V

Thomas Edison, Tinfoil Cylinders, and MP3 Players

[1]

Thomas Edison first recorded sounds on tinfoil cylinders in the 1870s, and since then, <u>formats for recording music have come and gone</u> at a breakneck pace. Innovation in recording music has been constant, and the popularity and lifespan of the newest format have always been transitory at best. Those first tinfoil cylinders, which were hailed as a miracle in their day, quickly progressed to wax cylinders, then hard plastic cylinders and, within a decade, were completely replaced by the next "miracle," the gramophone disc record.

[2]

The vinyl phonograph record, which sounded, soon <u>better</u> supplanted the gramophone in the 1940s. This new-fangled format dominated the music landscape for the next 30 years, but like its predecessors, it would eventually fall into obsolescence. The vinyl <u>record being</u> no longer mass-marketed to the public. For that matter, neither is its successor, the 8-track cartridge of the 1970s.

61. A. NO CHANGE
    B. formats for recording music have come and gone,
    C. formats for recording music, have come and gone
    D. formats, for recording music have come and gone

62. The most logical placement for the underlined word would be:
    F. where it is now.
    G. before the word *vinyl*.
    H. after the word *sounded*.
    J. before the word *gramophone*.

63. A. NO CHANGE
    B. record, having been
    C. record is
    D. record,

CONTINUED

[3]

It may seem curious to a 60-year-old man today that a high school student could be well acquainted with the older vinyl record format <u>so</u> has never even
64
heard of an 8-track cartridge. DJs and those who mix

popular music still <u>uses and appreciates</u> the vinyl
65

<u>record format cherished by them</u>. They have kept
66

records from disappearing into oblivion. [67]

[4]

That same 60-year-old man witnessed the rise and fall of the cassette tape, so he may not be surprised that the compact disc experienced a similar spiral toward its

64. F. NO CHANGE
G. yet
H. thus
J. or

65. A. NO CHANGE
B. use and appreciates
C. uses and appreciate
D. use and appreciate

66. F. NO CHANGE
G. record format that they cherish.
H. format for records they play on turntables.
J. record format.

67. The writer is considering adding a comma and the following information to the end of the preceding sentence:

along with the 8-track and the more recent recording format, the cassette tape.

Should the writer make this addition?

A. Yes, because it adds details relevant to the focus of the passage.
B. Yes, because it reinforces the passage's main argument.
C. No, because it distracts from the passage's main topic of vinyl records.
D. No, because it weakens the passage's main argument.

own doom. For the first <u>time, though</u> it was not the
68
sound quality of the recording that is ushering in the

change. This time, the driving force was something

<u>different</u> the quality of the player itself.
69

[5]

A standard audio compact disc can store only about

700 megabytes worth of digital data, which equates

to only about an hour's worth of songs. <u>Moreover,</u>
70
modern technological devices, such as smartphones and

tablets, can have up to an impressive 1 terabyte worth

of storage space. For those who are music lovers, this

has completely changed the experience of listening to

their favorite songs. <u>Contrasting by</u> the one hour's worth
71
of songs stored on a single CD, a 1-terabyte device can

store two years' worth of uninterrupted music on

a gadget about the size of an old cassette tape. <u>It's no</u>
72
<u>wonder that smartphones are among the most popular</u>
72
<u>technology purchases for people of all ages.</u>
72

68. F. NO CHANGE
 G. time; though
 H. time, though,
 J. time though,

69. A. NO CHANGE
 B. different;
 C. different:
 D. different,

70. F. NO CHANGE
 G. In contrast,
 H. Despite,
 J. Subsequently,

71. A. NO CHANGE
 B. Compared to
 C. While
 D. In contrast of

72. In this paragraph, the writer wants to help readers understand the storage capacity and size of modern devices. Which true statement would best help the writer accomplish this goal?

 F. NO CHANGE
 G. It is not unreasonable to expect that techno-logical improvements will soon allow these devices to store twice as many songs.
 H. Experts in the music industry predict that these devices will quickly be replaced by something new, just as compact disc players replaced cassette players.
 J. Entire music libraries that were once confined to the living room wall can now fit into a music lover's pocket and be taken and listened to anywhere.

CONTINUED ▶

[6]

Has the apex in the climb toward better and better ways to play recorded music been reached? Indeed, the incredible storage capacity of the latest developments in music recording devices must be the pinnacle of this technology.
73

73. Which choice best concludes the sentence and essay by responding to the question asked in the previous sentence with the ideas raised in the first paragraph of the essay?

A. NO CHANGE

B. For those who believe it has, history hints that they are wrong; such a proclamation will surely prove to be shortsighted when the next "miracle" in music arrives.

C. The tinfoil cylinder, the vinyl phonograph record, the 8-track cartridge, and the cassette tape are all examples of successes in music recording media.

D. Recording technologies have certainly come a long way since the first sound recordings made by Thomas Edison.

Questions 74 and 75 ask about the preceding passage as a whole.

---

74. After reading the essay, the writer realized that some information had been left out. The writer then composed the sentence below to convey that information:

> Though the gramophone record's disc shape proved to have longevity, the gramophone record itself did not.

The most effective and logical placement of this sentence would be before the first sentence of Paragraph:

F. 2.

G. 3.

H. 4.

J. 5.

75. Suppose the writer had set out to write an essay explaining the process of recording sounds in a variety of formats. Does this essay meet that purpose?

A. Yes, because the essay describes the different recording formats used since the 1870s.

B. Yes, because the writer provides specifics about how each new recording format has improved upon earlier formats.

C. No, because the essay discusses a limited number of recording formats.

D. No, because the essay does not discuss the mechanics of how sounds are recorded and played back in different formats.

Mathematics Test

60 Minutes—60 Questions

Directions: Choose the correct solution to each question and fill in the corresponding bubble on your answer sheet.

Do not continue to spend time on questions if you get stuck. Solve as many questions as you can before returning to any if time permits.

You may use a calculator on this test for any question you choose. However, some questions may be better solved without a calculator.

Note: Unless otherwise stated, you can assume:

1. Figures are NOT necessarily drawn to scale.
2. Geometric figures are two dimensional.
3. The term *line* indicates a straight line.
4. The term *average* indicates arithmetic mean.

1. Khristina walked $1\frac{2}{3}$ miles on Sunday and $2\frac{3}{4}$ miles on Monday. What was the total distance, in miles, that she walked over those two days?

    A. $3\frac{1}{2}$

    B. $3\frac{5}{7}$

    C. $3\frac{11}{12}$

    D. $4\frac{1}{4}$

    E. $4\frac{5}{12}$

2. The expression $2y^3 \cdot 3xy^2 \cdot 6xy^2$ is equivalent to which of the following?

    F. $11x^2y^7$

    G. $11x^2y^{12}$

    H. $36x^2y^7$

    J. $36xy^{12}$

    K. $36x^2y^{12}$

3. Ms. Ruppin is a machinist who works 245 days a year and earns a salary of \$51,940. She recently took an unpaid day off from work to attend a bridge tournament. The company pays temporary replacements \$140 a day. How much less did the company have to pay in salary by paying the replacement instead of Ms. Ruppin that day?

    A. \$ 72

    B. \$113

    C. \$140

    D. \$196

    E. \$212

CONTINUED ➤

4. On his first four 100-point tests this quarter, a student has earned the following scores: 52, 70, 76, 79. What score must the student earn on the fifth 100-point test in order to earn an average test grade of 75 for all five tests?

F. 69

G. 70

H. 71

J. 98

K. The student cannot earn an average of 75.

5. Relative humidity is found by dividing the grams of water vapor per cubic meter of air by the maximum possible grams of water vapor per cubic meter of air, then converting to a percentage. If on a given day the air has 6.7 grams of water vapor per cubic meter, and the maximum possible at that temperature is 19.2 grams of water vapor per cubic meter, what is the relative humidity, to the nearest percent?

A. 19%

B. 30%

C. 35%

D. 67%

E. 87%

6. A fence completely surrounds a pool that is 30 feet by 10 feet. What is the approximate length, in feet, of the fence?

F. 20 feet

G. 40 feet

H. 60 feet

J. 80 feet

K. 160 feet

7. A film that is 3 hours, 40 minutes long must be cut into two equal parts. What will be the duration of each part?

A. 1 hour, 10 minutes

B. 1 hour, 30 minutes

C. 1 hour, 50 minutes

D. 1 hour, 55 minutes

E. 2 hours, 20 minutes

8. If $2x - 5 = 7x + 3$, then $x = $?

F. $-\dfrac{8}{5}$

G. $-\dfrac{5}{8}$

H. $-\dfrac{2}{5}$

J. $\dfrac{2}{5}$

K. $\dfrac{8}{9}$

9. What two numbers should be placed in the blanks below so that each pair of consecutive numbers has the same difference?

13, ____, ____, 49

A. 22, 31

B. 23, 39

C. 24, 38

D. 25, 37

E. 26, 39

10. If x is a real number such that $x^3 = 729$, then $\sqrt{x} + x^2 = $?

F. 9

G. 21

H. 53

J. 84

K. 90

11. Which of the following is the decimal equivalent of $\frac{1}{11}$? (Note that a bar indicates a numerical pattern that is repeated.)

    A. $0.\overline{09}$

    B. 0.090909

    C. $0.0\overline{909}$

    D. 0.09090909

    E. $0.090909\overline{9}$

12. If a ball is randomly chosen from a bag with exactly 10 purple balls, 10 yellow balls, and 8 green balls, what is the probability that the ball chosen will NOT be green?

    F. $\frac{2}{7}$

    G. $\frac{2}{5}$

    H. $\frac{1}{2}$

    J. $\frac{9}{14}$

    K. $\frac{5}{7}$

13. In the following figure, lines l and m are parallel and $a = 110$. Which of the following is equal to the sum of b, c, and d?

    A. 250

    B. 260

    C. 270

    D. 280

    E. 290

Use the following information to answer questions 14–15.

Erin hiked a small mountain over the course of a day. She began at 7 a.m. at an altitude of 4,000 feet. As she climbed the mountain, Erin climbed at a constant speed during each one-hour interval. She finished her hike back at 4,000 feet at 1 p.m. Erin's altitude, as a function of time, is shown in the following graph.

14. For how long, in hours and minutes, was Erin at or above 4,500 feet?

    F. 1 hour, 20 minutes

    G. 3 hours

    H. 4 hours

    J. 4 hours, 20 minutes

    K. 5 hours

CONTINUED ▶

15. Which graph best represents the absolute value of the velocity that Erin traveled, in vertical feet per hour?

(Note: Ignore acceleration and deceleration at the beginning and end of each one-hour interval.)

A.

B.

C.

D.

E.

16. What expression must be in the center cell of the following table so that the sums of each row, each column, and each diagonal are equivalent?

$-3x$	$4x$	$-7x$
$-6x$	?	$2x$
$3x$	$-8x$	$-x$

F. $-6x$

G. $-4x$

H. $-2x$

J. $2x$

K. $4x$

17. If an object travels at a speed of 3 feet per second, how many feet does it travel in half an hour?

A. 1,800

B. 2,400

C. 3,600

D. 4,200

E. 5,400

18. Leila has 5 necklaces, 8 pairs of earrings, and 3 hair clips. How many distinct sets of accessories, each consisting of a necklace, a pair of earrings, and a hair clip, can Leila choose?

F. 16

G. 55

H. 64

J. 120

K. 360

CONTINUED

19. At a factory, 90,000 tons of grain are required to make 150,000 tons of bread. How many tons of grain are required to produce 6,000 tons of bread?

    A.   3,600

    B.   10,000

    C.   25,000

    D.   36,000

    E.   60,000

20. In a certain set of integers, the ratio of even numbers to odd numbers is 2:3. What percent of the numbers in the set are even?

    F.   20%

    G. $33\frac{1}{3}$%

    H.   40%

    J.   60%

    K. $66\frac{2}{3}$%

21. For all positive integers a, b, and c, which of the following is FALSE?

    A. $\dfrac{a \cdot b}{c \cdot b} = \dfrac{a}{c}$

    B. $\dfrac{a \cdot a}{b \cdot b} = \dfrac{a^2}{b^2}$

    C. $\dfrac{a \cdot b}{b \cdot a} = 1$

    D. $\dfrac{a + b}{b} = \dfrac{a}{b} + 1$

    E. $\dfrac{a + b}{c + b} = \dfrac{a}{c} + 1$

22. What is the slope-intercept form of $-3x - y + 7 = 0$?

    F. $y = 3x - 7$

    G. $y = 3x + 7$

    H. $y = -7x + 3$

    J. $y = -3x - 7$

    K. $y = -3x + 7$

23. Which of the following is a solution to the equation $x^2 - 8x = 8x$?

    A.   32

    B.   16

    C.   8

    D.   4

    E.   −4

24. Which of the following expressions describes the indicated values on the number line shown here?

    F. $x \le 1$

    G. $x \ge 1$

    H. $|x| \le 1$

    J. $|x| \ge 1$

    K. $x \ge |1|$

25. A chord 30 centimeters long is 8 centimeters from the center of a circle, as shown. What is the radius of the circle, to the nearest tenth of a centimeter?

    A.   38.0

    B.   34.0

    C.   31.2

    D.   22.8

    E.   17.0

CONTINUED

26. The velocity, in meters per second, of an object is given by the equation $V = \frac{5}{3}t + 0.05$, where t is the amount of time that has passed, in seconds. After how many seconds will the object be traveling at 0.575 meters per second?

    F. 0.28
    G. 0.315
    H. 0.365
    J. 0.525
    K. 0.57

27. A city has decided to store an estimated 15,000 cubic yards of sand for later distribution to the city's beaches. If this sand were spread evenly over the entire soccer field shown, about how many yards deep would the sand be?

    A. Less than 1
    B. Between 1 and 2
    C. Between 2 and 3
    D. Between 3 and 4
    E. More than 4

28. The hypotenuse of right $\triangle ABC$ shown below is 18 feet long. The cosine of $\angle A$ is $\frac{4}{5}$. About how many feet long is $\overline{AC}$?

    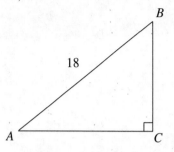

    F. 15.2
    G. 14.4
    H. 13.9
    J. 12.6
    K. 10.8

29. The pictograph that follows shows the number of beds in each of several hotels, rounded to the nearest 50 beds. According to the graph, what fraction of the beds in these four hotels are at the Bedtime Hotel?

    A. $\frac{1}{4}$
    B. $\frac{1}{3}$
    C. $\frac{2}{5}$
    D. $\frac{5}{11}$
    E. $\frac{1}{2}$

CONTINUED

30. Points B and C lie on $\overline{AD}$ as shown. The length of $\overline{AD}$ is 38 units, $\overline{AC}$ is 26 units long, and $\overline{BD}$ is 20 units long. If it can be determined, how many units long is $\overline{BC}$?

A ———— B — C — D

F.   6
G.   8
H.   12
J.   18
K.   Cannot be determined from the given information

31. What is the x-coordinate of the point in the standard (x,y) coordinate plane at which the two lines $y = 4x + 10$ and $y = 5x + 7$ intersect?

A.   3
B.   4
C.   7
D.   10
E.   22

32. Meri read 96 pages in 2 hours and 40 minutes. What was Meri's average rate in pages per hour?

F.   24
G.   30
H.   36
J.   42
K.   48

33. If an integer is randomly chosen from the first 50 positive integers, what is the probability that an integer with a digit of 3 is selected?

A. $\dfrac{1}{10}$
B. $\dfrac{7}{25}$
C. $\dfrac{3}{10}$
D. $\dfrac{2}{5}$
E. $\dfrac{3}{5}$

34. If $s = 4 + t$, then $(t - s)^3 = ?$

F. -64
G. -12
H. -1
J.   12
K.   64

35. A zoo has the shape and dimensions, in yards, in the given figure. The viewing point for the giraffes is halfway between points B and F. Which of the following is the location of the viewing point from the entrance at point A?

(Note: The zoo's borders run east/west or north/south.)

A.   400 yards east and 350 yards north
B.   400 yards east and 500 yards north
C.   600 yards east and 350 yards north
D.   750 yards east and 300 yards north
E.   750 yards east and 350 yards north

CONTINUED

36. In a contest, the weight of a first-place watermelon is 15 pounds less than 3 times the weight of the second-place watermelon. If w is the weight of the second-place watermelon, which of the following expresses the weight, in pounds, of the first-place watermelon?

    F.　$w - 5$

    G.　$w + 15$

    H.　$w - 15$

    J.　$3w + 15$

    K.　$3w - 15$

37. If xy is negative, which of the following CANNOT be negative?

    A.　$y - x$

    B.　$x - y$

    C.　x^2y

    D.　xy^2

    E.　x^2y^2

38. Which of the following sets of numbers has the property that the sum of any two numbers in the set is also a number in the set?

    I.　The set of even integers

    II.　The set of odd integers

    III.　The set of prime numbers

    F.　I only

    G.　III only

    H.　I and II only

    J.　I and III only

    K.　I, II, and III

39. The sides of a triangle are in the ratio of exactly 15:17:20. A second triangle, similar to the first, has a longest side of length 12. To the nearest tenth of a unit, what is the length of the shortest side of the second triangle?

    A.　15.9

    B.　10.2

    C.　9.0

    D.　7.0

    E.　Cannot be determined from the given information

40. In the figure shown, $WXZY$ is a trapezoid, point X lies on $\overline{WT}$, and the angle measures are as marked. What is the measure of $\angle ZXT$?

    F.　$20°$

    G.　$30°$

    H.　$40°$

    J.　$55°$

    K.　$65°$

41. What are the values of θ, between $0°$ and $360°$, when $\sin \theta = \dfrac{\sqrt{3}}{2}$?

    A.　$30°$ and $150°$ only

    B.　$60°$ and $120°$ only

    C.　$45°$ and $135°$ only

    D.　$60°$ and $150°$ only

    E.　$60°$ only

CONTINUED

42. Of 896 seniors at a certain university, approximately $\frac{1}{3}$ are continuing their studies after graduation, and approximately $\frac{2}{5}$ of those continuing their studies are going to law school. Which of the following is the best estimate of how many seniors are going to law school?

    F.   120
    G.   180
    H.   240
    J.   300
    K.   360

43. If $a = -2$, $b = 4$, and $c = 7$, then $(a + b)(c - a) = ?$

    A. -30
    B. -10
    C. 10
    D. 18
    E. 30

44. If $\log_7 7^{\sqrt{7}} = x$, then x is between which of the following pairs of consecutive integers?

    F.   0 and 1
    G.   2 and 3
    H.   4 and 5
    J.   6 and 7
    K.   7 and 8

45. The following chart shows the distribution of employees at a company into different teams in different departments. According to the chart, how many total employees are there?

Department	Number of Teams	Employees per Team
Development	1	4
Marketing	2	3
Accounting	3	2
Public Relations	5	5

    A.   14
    B.   25
    C.   41
    D.   84
    E.   154

46. The percent increase from 6 to 16 is equal to the percent increase from 12 to what number?

    F.   16
    G.   22
    H.   23
    J.   32
    K.   36

47. A circle in the standard (x,y) coordinate plane is tangent to the x-axis at 4 and tangent to the y-axis at 4. Which of the following is an equation of the circle?

    A. $x^2 + y^2 = 4$
    B. $x^2 + y^2 = 16$
    C. $(x - 4)^2 + (y - 4)^2 = 4$
    D. $(x - 4)^2 + (y - 4)^2 = 16$
    E. $(x + 4)^2 + (y + 4)^2 = 16$

CONTINUED

48. Liza drove at an average speed of 40 miles per hour for 2 hours and then increased her average speed by 25% for the next 3 hours. Her average speed for the 5 hours was r miles per hour. What is the value of r?

    F. 44
    G. 45
    H. 46
    J. 47
    K. 48

49. The number of executives at a large company, by division, can be modeled using the following matrix.

Marketing	Human Resources	Operations	Legal
[20	12	40	10]

    The company is downsizing and the head of Human Resources estimates the proportion of current executives who will be laid off within the next year. The estimates are shown in the following matrix.

    $$\begin{array}{r} \text{Marketing} \\ \text{Human Resources} \\ \text{Operations} \\ \text{Legal} \end{array} \begin{bmatrix} 0.3 \\ 0.5 \\ 0.2 \\ 0.4 \end{bmatrix}$$

    Given these matrices, what is the head of Human Resources' estimate of the number of current executives in these departments who will be laid off within the next year?

    A. 24
    B. 27
    C. 30
    D. 32
    E. 36

50. The probability distribution of the discrete random variable X is shown in the following table. Based on the probability distribution, what is the expected value of X?

X	Probability $P(X = x)$
10	$\frac{1}{5}$
11	$\frac{1}{10}$
12	$\frac{3}{10}$
13	$\frac{3}{20}$
14	$\frac{1}{4}$

    F. $10\frac{4}{5}$
    G. 11
    H. 12
    J. $12\frac{3}{20}$
    K. $13\frac{1}{20}$

51. Which of the following is the solution set for all real numbers x such that $x - 2 < x - 5$?

    A. The empty set
    B. The set containing all real numbers
    C. The set containing all negative real numbers
    D. The set containing all nonnegative real numbers
    E. The set containing only zero

52. The figure shown here represents the function $g(x) = \sqrt{x}$

Suppose $h(x)$ is a transformation of $g(x)$ and is given by the equation $h(x) = \sqrt{x+1} + 3$. Which of the following correctly states the domain and range of $h(x)$?

F.   Domain: $x \geq -1$; Range: $y \geq 0$

G.   Domain: $x \geq -1$; Range: $y \geq 3$

H.   Domain: $x \geq 0$; Range: $y \geq 0$

J.   Domain: $x \geq 1$; Range: $y \geq -3$

K.   Domain: $x \geq 1$; Range: $y \geq 3$

53. Diane wants to draw a circle graph showing the favorite teachers at her school. When she polled her classmates, 25% said Mr. Green, 15% said Ms. Brown, 35% said Mrs. White, 5% said Mr. Blue, and the remaining classmates said teachers other than Mr. Green, Ms. Brown, Mrs. White, or Mr. Blue. The teachers other than Mr. Green, Ms. Brown, Mrs. White, or Mr. Blue will be grouped together in an Other sector. What will be the degree measure of the sector that represents Other?

A.   144°

B.   72°

C.   36°

D.   20°

E.   15°

54. The first and seventh terms in a sequence are 1 and 365, respectively. If each term after the first in the sequence is formed by multiplying the preceding term by 3 and subtracting 1, what is the sixth term?

F.   40

G.   41

H.   121

J.   122

K.   123

55. A portion of which of the following systems of inequalities is represented by the shaded region of the given graph?

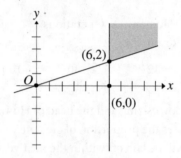

A. $y \geq \frac{1}{3}x$ and $x \geq 6$

B. $y \geq 3x$ and $x \geq 6$

C. $y \leq \frac{1}{3}x$ and $x \geq 6$

D. $y \leq 3x$ and $x \geq 6$

E. $y \leq \frac{1}{3}x$ and $x \leq 6$

56. If $f(x) = 2(x+7)$, then $f(x+c) = ?$

F. $2(x+7) + c$

G. $2x + c + 7$

H. $2x + c + 14$

J. $2x + 2c + 7$

K. $2x + 2c + 14$

CONTINUED

57. A formula for the volume, V, of a right circular cylinder is $V = \pi r^2 h$, where r is the radius and h is the height. The cylindrical swimming pool shown here is filled completely with water and has a radius of 6 feet and a depth of 4 feet.

If 1 cubic foot of water weighs approximately 62.4 pounds, then the weight, in pounds, of the water in the swimming pool is:

A. less than 20,000.

B. between 20,000 and 25,000.

C. between 25,000 and 30,000.

D. between 30,000 and 35,000.

J. more than 35,000.

58. A triangle, $\triangle ABC$, is reflected across the y-axis to create the image $\triangle A'B'C'$ in the standard (x,y) coordinate plane (for example, A reflects to A'). If the coordinates of point A are (v,w), what are the coordinates of point A'?

F. $(v,-w)$

G. $(-v,w)$

H. $(-v,-w)$

J. (w,v)

K. Cannot be determined from the given information

59. If $a = 6c + 7$ and $b = 3 - 2c$, which of the following expresses a in terms of b?

A. $a = \dfrac{16 - b}{3}$

B. $a = \dfrac{17 - b}{2}$

C. $a = 16 - 3b$

D. $a = 25 - 12b$

E. $a = 6b + 7$

60. In complex numbers, where $i^2 = -1$, what is the simplified form of the expression $\dfrac{(2i + 2)^2}{(2i - 2)^2}$?

F. $\dfrac{i + 1}{i - 1}$

G. $\dfrac{i}{4}$

H. $\dfrac{4}{i}$

J. 1

K. -1

IF YOU FINISH BEFORE TIME IS CALLED, YOU MAY CHECK YOUR WORK ON THIS SECTION ONLY. DO NOT TURN TO ANY OTHER SECTION IN THE TEST.

STOP

K 915

Reading Test

35 Minutes—40 Questions

Directions: The Reading Test includes multiple passages. Each passage includes multiple questions. After reading each passage, choose the best answer and fill in the corresponding bubble on your answer sheet. You may review the passages as often as necessary.

Passage I

LITERARY NARRATIVE: This passage is adapted from the novel *My Doggie and I* by R.M. Ballantyne.

I possess a doggie—not a dog, observe, but a doggie. If he had been a dog I would not have presumed to intrude him on your notice. A dog is all very well in his way—one of the noblest of
5 animals, I admit, and preeminently fitted to be the companion of man, for he has an affectionate nature, which man demands, and a forgiving disposition, which man needs—but a dog, with all his noble qualities, is not to be compared to a
10 doggie.

Freely admit that you don't at once perceive the finer qualities, either mental or physical, of my doggie, partly owing to the circumstance that he is shapeless and hairy. The former quality is not
15 attractive, while the latter tends to veil the amiable expression of his countenance and the luster of his speaking eyes. But as you come to know him he grows upon you; your feelings are touched, your affections stirred, and your love is finally evoked.
20 As he resembles a doormat, or rather a scrap of a very ragged doormat, and has an amiable spirit, I have called him "Dumps." I should not be surprised if you did not perceive any connection here. You are not the first who has failed to see it; I never saw it
25 myself.

When I first met Dumps, he was scurrying towards me along a sequestered country lane. It was in the Dog Days. Dust lay thick on the road; the creature's legs were remarkably short though
30 active, and his hair being long he swept up the dust in clouds as he ran. He was yelping, and I observed that one or two stones appeared to be racing with, or after, him. The voice of an angry man also

seemed to chase him, but the owner of the voice
35 was at the moment concealed by a turn in the lane, which was bordered by high stone walls.

Rabies, of course, flashed into my mind. I grasped my stick and drew close to the wall. The hairy whirlwind, if I may so call it, came wildly on,
40 but instead of passing me, or snapping at my legs as I had expected, it stopped and crawled towards me in a piteous, supplicating manner that at once disarmed me. If the creature had lain still, I should have been unable to distinguish its head from its
45 tail; but as one end of him whined, and the other wagged, I had no difficulty.

Stooping down with caution, I patted the end that whined, whereupon the end that wagged became violently demonstrative. Just then the owner
50 of the voice came round the corner. He was a big, rough fellow, in ragged garments, and armed with a thick stick, which he seemed about to fling at the little dog, when I checked him with a shout—

"You'd better not, my man, unless you want your
55 own head broken!"

You see, I am a pretty well-sized man myself, and, as I felt confidence in my strength, my stick, and the goodness of my cause, I was bold.

"What d'you mean by ill-treating the little dog?"
60 I demanded sternly, as I stepped up to the man.

"A man may do as he likes with his own, mayn't he?" answered the man, with a sulky scowl.

"A 'man' may do nothing of the sort," said I indignantly, for cruelty to dumb animals always
65 has the effect of inclining me to fight, though I am naturally of a peaceable disposition. "There is an Act of Parliament," I continued, "which goes by the honored name of Martin, and if you venture to infringe that Act I'll have you taken up and
70 prosecuted."

CONTINUED

While I was speaking I observed a peculiar leer
on the man's face, which I could not account for.
He appeared, however, to have been affected by
my threats, for he ceased to scowl, and assumed a
75 deferential air as he replied, "Well, sir, it do seem
rather hard that a man's head should be broken for
kindness."

"Kindness!" I exclaimed, in surprise.

"Ay, kindness, sir. That there animal loves me,
80 it do, like a brother, and the love is mutual. We've
lived together now—off an' on—for the matter of
six months. Well, I get employment in a factory
about fifteen miles from here, in which no dogs is
allowed. Of course, I can't give up that employment,
85 sir, can I? Neither can my doggie give up his master
that he's so fond of, so I'm obliged to leave him in
the charge of a friend, with strict orders to keep
him locked up till I'm fairly gone. Well, off I goes,
but he manages to escape and runs after me. Now,
90 what can a feller do but drive him home with sticks
an' stones, though it do get to my heart to do it?
But if he goes to the factory, he's sure to be shot, or
dragged, or drowned, or something; so you see, sir,
it's out of pure kindness I'm chasing him."

95 I confess that I felt somewhat doubtful of the
truth of this story; but, in order to prevent any
expression of my face betraying me, I stooped and
patted the dog while the man spoke. It received my
attentions with evident delight. A thought suddenly
100 flashed on me:

"Will you sell your little dog?" I asked.

1. The narrator implies that his "doggie" differs from a
   "dog" in that his "doggie":

   A. may be less impressive at first sight.

   B. is older than a puppy but not a dog.

   C. is forgiving of humans, no matter what.

   D. is a majestic creature, both handsome and
      good-natured.

2. According to paragraph 2, which of the following
   accurately describes Dumps?

   F. His eyes are dull, and his body is shapeless.

   G. Observers are quickly struck by his wise
      demeanor.

   H. He has kind-looking eyes that are often hidden
      behind his hair.

   J. His abundant hair gives him the appearance of
      a well-groomed carpet.

3. The description in paragraphs 3–4 suggests that
   Dumps was running:

   A. at a leisurely pace, stopping to sniff the grass.

   B. in a desperate manner, looking for help.

   C. as though compelled by immobilizing terror.

   D. to fetch a stick as part of his favorite game.

4. As it is used in line 53, *checked* most nearly means:

   F. prevented.

   G. square patterned.

   H. verified.

   J. assaulted.

5. The author places the word *man* in quotes (line 63)
   in order to:

   A. compare the narrator's recognition of the dog
      owner's large size to his own stature.

   B. indicate that the narrator is ironically agreeing
      with the dog owner's assertion.

   C. signal that the narrator is attempting to start
      a violent fight with the dog owner despite his
      typical peaceful nature.

   D. imply that the narrator considers the dog
      owner inhumane regarding his treatment of
      animals.

6. According to lines 66–77, the dog's owner stops scowling at the narrator because:

    F. after listening to the narrator, he decides that the dog is unlikely to bite the narrator.

    G. he shifts his concern away from his dog's behavior to anxiety about being late for his job at the factory.

    H. he is concerned about the narrator's mention of breaking the law and wants to make a better impression.

    J. the narrator has stopped threatening to hit the dog with a stick and is offering to help.

7. Throughout the passage, the narrator's attitude toward the reader is best described as:

    A. considerate and wanting the reader to think well of him.

    B. argumentative about how pets are commonly perceived.

    C. fearful that the reader will disagree with his unorthodox views.

    D. deceptive in order to gain a favorable opinion from the reader.

8. Which choice best reflects the dog owner's explanation as to why chasing the dog with a stick is actually a demonstration of kindness?

    F. The dog belongs to the owner, so the owner is entitled to treat the dog as he chooses.

    G. The owner cannot take the dog to his factory job, but the dog escapes and runs after him so he must drive the dog back.

    H. Dogs love running after thrown sticks, and this activity will provide the dog with exercise before the owner goes to work at the factory.

    J. The men who work at the factory have a record of mistreating animals, especially dogs.

9. The narrator most likely doubts the dog owner's story (lines 79–94) because:

    A. the owner is so eager to sell the dog that the narrator doubts he really cares for it.

    B. the narrator cannot believe that a man with his temperament could hold down a job.

    C. it seems unlikely that the dog would actually be harmed as the owner claims.

    D. the owner seems to claim he loves the dog only after being threatened with legal prosecution.

10. The passage implies that the narrator wants to buy the dog primarily because:

    F. he believes the dog will make the great companion he's been looking for.

    G. he cares for animals and suspects that the dog's owner is treating it badly.

    H. he fears the dog's owner and hopes to appease him by offering him money.

    J. the dog's owner wishes that the dog didn't have to be alone while he's at work.

CONTINUED ➡

Passage II

SOCIAL STUDIES: The following two passages were written in the early 1990s and present two viewpoints about the ways that the public responds to the results of scientific research.

Passage A

The way that people in present-day industrial societies think about science in the modern world actually tends to cultivate the very unscientific perception that science supplies

5 us with unquestionable facts. If there is one unquestionable fact about science, it is that science is inherently uncertain. Research consists not so much of a search for truth as a search for some degree of certainty in an uncertain world. Every

10 research study, every experiment, and every survey incorporates an extensive statistical analysis that is meant to be taken as qualifying the probability that the results are consistent and reproducible. Yet policy makers, public relations interests, and

15 so-called experts in the popular media continue to treat the results of every latest study as if they were surefire truths.

History is filled with examples of the fallibility of scientific certainties. From the medieval monks

20 who believed the sun orbited around Earth and the world was only 4,000 years old, to the early twentieth-century scientists who thought that X-rays were a hoax and that exploding a nuclear bomb would set off a chain reaction that would destroy

25 all matter in the universe, it has been demonstrated repeatedly that science deals primarily with possibilities and is subject to the same prejudices as other kinds of opinions and beliefs. Yet statistics are complicated, and in our need to feel that we live in

30 a universe of predictable certainties, it is tempting to place our faith in the oversimplified generalities of headlines and sound bites rather than the rigorous application of probabilities. Ironically, even though the intent of science is to expand the realm

35 of human knowledge, an unfounded prejudice stemming from a desire for scientific constancy can actually discourage inquiry.

Science serves an important practical function; predictability and reproducibility are vital to

40 making sure that our bridges remain standing, our nuclear power plants run smoothly, and our cars start in the morning so we can drive to work. When these practicalities become everyday occurrences, they tend to encourage a complacent

45 faith in the reliability and consistency of science. Yet faced with so many simple conveniences, it is important to remember that we depend on the advance of science for our very survival. With progress expanding into those gray areas at the

50 boundaries of scientific exploration, caution and prudence are just as important as open-mindedness and imagination. As technological advances engage increasingly complex moral questions within fields such as pharmaceutical developments, indefinite

55 extension of life, and the potential for inconceivably potent weapons, an understanding of the limitations of science becomes just as important as an understanding of its strengths.

Passage B

While it is important that scientific knowledge

60 be taken into consideration in significant matters of public interest, such consideration must be tempered with critical rigor. In the early days during the ascendance of science as a practical discipline, the public was inclined to view every

65 new advance and discovery with a healthy skepticism. In the late 19th century, when Italian astronomer Giovanni Schiaparelli first detected seas and continents on the planet Mars, many people balked at the idea of Earth-like topography on the

70 Red Planet. Just a few decades later, when fellow Italian astronomer Vincenzo Cerulli provided evidence that the seas and continents Schiaparelli observed were merely optical illusions, public disbelief proved to be entirely appropriate.

75 Since then, the historic tendency of the public to question scientific findings has unfortunately been lost. Yet in present-day industrial societies, and especially where public policy is at issue, response to scientific research needs more than

80 ever to pursue an informed, critical viewpoint. Who performs a research study, what kind of study it is, what kinds of review and scrutiny it comes

under, and what interests support it are every bit as important as a study's conclusions.

85   Studies of mass media and public policy reveal that, all too often, scientific findings presented to the public as objective and conclusive are actually funded at two or three degrees of removal by corporate or political interests with a specific
90   agenda related to the outcome of those findings. For example, some critics question the issue of whether a study of the effectiveness of a new drug is more likely to produce favorable results when the study is funded by the pharmaceutical company
95   that owns the drug patent. In cases where such findings conflict with the interests of the funding parties, analysts sometimes wonder if information was repressed, altered, or given a favorable public relations slant in order to de-emphasize dangerous
100   side effects. Some critics of company-funded studies argue that the level of misrepresentation included in such studies borders on immoral.

Part of the problem grows from the public's willingness to place blind faith in the authority of
105   science without an awareness of the interests that lie behind the research. Public officials then, in turn, may sometimes be too willing to bend in the face of public or private political pressure rather than pursuing the best interests of the constituency.
110   Issues such as genetics, reproductive health, and preventative care are particularly fraught with political angst. Where the safety of individuals is at stake, a precautionary principle of allowing for unpredictable, unforeseen negative effects of
115   technological advances should be pursued. It is the duty of active citizens in a free society to educate themselves about the real-world application of risk-assessment and statistical analysis, and to resist passive acceptance of the reassurances of self-styled
120   scientific authorities. The most favorable approach to policy decisions based on realistic assessments finds a middle ground between the alarmism of political "Chicken Littles" and the recklessness of profit-seeking risk takers.

11. According to Passage A, policy makers consider the results of studies:

    A.   with concern.

    B.   as unquestioned truth.

    C.   as debatable.

    D.   as false.

12. The word "probabilities" in line 33 is used to express the author's belief that:

    F.   scientific theories will eventually be proven true.

    G.   current scientific findings will be regarded as outdated by future scientists.

    H.   viewing scientific results as possibly wrong is a wise approach.

    J.   refusing to question science is unavoidable because people prefer certainty.

13. As it is used in line 44, the word *complacent* most nearly means:

    A.   conceited.

    B.   dangerous.

    C.   unquestioned.

    D.   dissatisfied.

14. According to Passage B, which of the following is an example of a scientific discovery greeted with skepticism by the public?

    F.   A pharmaceutical study funded by the drug patent holder

    G.   Schiaparelli's detection of continents on Mars

    H.   The statement that X-rays are a hoax

    J.   Darwin's theory of evolution

CONTINUED ▶

15. The author of Passage B uses the first paragraph to explain:

    A. a new scientific hypothesis.

    B. a historical contrast.

    C. a public policy generality.

    D. the underlying cause of an issue.

16. With which of the following statements would the author of Passage B most likely agree?

    F. People should not unquestioningly accept the results of scientific studies.

    G. More government control and regulation are needed to ensure that science serves the best interests of the public.

    H. Society should place less emphasis on modern conveniences and more on understanding the limitations of science.

    J. The results that scientists derive from research are less reliable now than they were in former times.

17. What does the author of Passage A believe is the biggest obstacle to reaching the solution described by the author of Passage B in lines 115–120 ("It is the duty…authorities")?

    A. Policy makers are too willing to bend to public pressure when it comes to regulating scientific research.

    B. The interests that fund research are the same interests that stand to profit by favorable results, making impartiality impossible.

    C. Statistics are too abstract when compared with the concrete evidence of technological conveniences.

    D. Unanswered ethical questions are increasingly coming under scrutiny at the forefront of our most advanced scientific research.

18. Both passages refer to which of the following?

    F. Present-day industrial societies

    G. Early twentieth-century scientists

    H. Critics of company-funded studies

    J. Significant matters of public interest

19. According to Passage B, which of the following is an example of the "fallibility of scientific certainties" (lines 18–19) mentioned in Passage A?

    A. Medieval monks who believed the sun orbited around Earth

    B. People who balked at the idea of Earth-like topography on Mars

    C. Issues such as genetics, reproductive health, and preventative care

    D. Early twentieth-century scientists who thought that X-rays were a hoax

20. The authors of both passages mention the term "pharmaceutical" in order to:

    F. highlight a particular scientific field in which moral questions may arise.

    G. point out an example of the recklessness of profit-seeking risk takers.

    H. identify unfounded prejudice stemming from a desire for scientific constancy.

    J. cite the usefulness of the current approach regarding drug testing and analysis.

Passage III

HUMANITIES: This passage is adapted from a Wikipedia article titled "Walter Scott."

Born in Edinburgh in 1771, the young Walter Scott survived a childhood bout of polio that would leave him lame in his right leg for the rest of his life. After studying law at Edinburgh University,

5 he followed in his father's footsteps and became a lawyer in his native Scotland. Beginning at age 25, he started dabbling in writing, first translating works from German, then moving on to poetry. In between these two phases of his literary career, he

10 published a three-volume set of collected Scottish ballads, *The Minstrelsy of the Scottish Border*. This was the first sign of his interest in Scotland and history in his writings.

After Scott had founded a printing press, his

15 poetry, beginning with *The Lay of the Last Minstrel* in 1805, brought him great fame. He published a number of other poems over the next ten years, including in 1810 the popular *Lady of the Lake*, portions of which (translated into German) were

20 set to music by Franz Schubert. Another work from this time period, *Marmion*, produced some of his most quoted (and most often misattributed) lines, such as

Oh! what a tangled web we weave

25 *When first we practise to deceive!*

When Scott's press became embroiled in financial difficulties, Scott set out, in 1814, to write a successful (and profitable) work. The result was *Waverley*, a novel that did not name its author. It

30 was a tale of the last Jacobite rebellion in the United Kingdom, the "Forty-Five," and the novel met with considerable success. There followed a large number of novels in the next five years, each in the same general vein. Mindful of his reputation as a poet,

35 he maintained the anonymity he had begun with *Waverley*, always publishing the novels under a name such as "Author of Waverley" or attributed as "Tales of…" with no author. Even when it was clear that there would be no harm in coming out into

40 the open, he maintained the façade, apparently out of a sense of fun. During this time, the nickname "The Wizard of the North" was popularly applied

to the mysterious best-selling writer. His identity as the author of the novels was widely rumored, and

45 in 1815, Scott was given the honour of dining with George, Prince Regent, who wanted to meet "the author of Waverley."

In 1820, Scott broke away from writing about Scotland with *Ivanhoe*, a historical romance set in

50 twelfth-century England. It, too, was a runaway success and, as he did with his first novel, he unleashed a slew of books along the same lines. As his fame grew during this phase of his career, he was granted the title of Baronet, becoming Sir

55 Walter Scott. At this time, he organized the visit of King George IV to Scotland, and when the King visited Edinburgh in 1822, the spectacular pageantry Scott had concocted to portray the King as a rather tubby reincarnation of Bonnie Prince

60 Charlie made tartans and kilts fashionable and turned them into symbols of national identity.

Beginning in 1825, Scott fell into dire financial straits again, and his company nearly collapsed. That he was the author of his novels became general

65 knowledge at this time as well. Rather than declare bankruptcy he placed his home, Abbotsford House, and income into a trust belonging to his creditors, and proceeded to write his way out of debt. He kept up his prodigious output of fiction (as well

70 as producing a biography of Napoleon Bonaparte) through 1831. By then his health was failing, and he died at Abbotsford in 1832. Though not in the clear by then, his novels continued to sell, and he made good on his debts from beyond the grave. He was

75 buried in Dryburgh Abbey; nearby, fittingly, a large statue can be found of William Wallace—one of Scotland's great historical figures.

Scott was responsible for two major trends that carry on to this day. First, he popularized the

80 historical novel; an enormous number of imitators (and imitators of imitators) would appear in the nineteenth century. It is a measure of Scott's influence that Edinburgh's central railway station, opened in 1854, is called Waverley Station. Second,

85 his Scottish novels rehabilitated Highland culture after years in the shadows following the Jacobite rebellions.

CONTINUED ▶

Scott was also responsible, through a series of pseudonymous letters published in the *Edinburgh Weekly News* in *1826*, for retaining the right of Scottish banks to issue their own banknotes, which is reflected to this day by his continued appearance on the front of all notes issued by the Bank of Scotland.

90

21. The main idea of the passage is that:

    A.   historical novels can be very successful in rehabilitating a country's culture.

    B.   Sir Walter Scott's writings achieved both financial success and cultural impact.

    C.   Scott became known more for his financial failures than for his literary talents.

    D.   the success of Scott's novels was largely due to the anonymity of the author.

22. According to the passage, Walter Scott turned to writing novels because:

    F.   his childhood bout with polio made it difficult for him to continue working as a lawyer.

    G.   his printing press business was being sued over copyright violations.

    H.   his three-volume set of Scottish ballads did not sell well.

    J.   his printing press business was losing money.

23. According to the author, Scott published *Waverly* anonymously because:

    A.   he didn't want to damage his reputation as a lawyer.

    B.   he had fun watching people try to determine who the author was.

    C.   his novels sold faster without an author's name on them.

    D.   he was afraid writing fiction would take away from his reputation as a poet.

24. The author would most likely describe Scott's effect on how Scotland was viewed as:

    F.   damaging, since Scott degraded Scottish culture by popularizing tartans and kilts.

    G.   unimportant, since Scott's novels were no more than popular fiction.

    H.   ground-breaking, since Scott was the first to write serious analyses of Scottish history.

    J.   positive, since Scott made Scottish culture acceptable again after years of neglect.

25. Based on the passage, it is reasonable to assume that Scott's reputation after his death:

    A.   remained favorable.

    B.   waned because there were no more of his novels being published.

    C.   declined because he died without paying all of his debts.

    D.   was debased because of all his imitators.

26. As it is used in line 40, the word *façade* most nearly means:

    F.   pretense.

    G.   building front.

    H.   bluff.

    J.   character.

27. The author most likely uses "fittingly" (line 75) when describing the presence of a statue of William Wallace near Scott's grave in Dryburgh Abbey because:

    A.   Scott's first major novel was about the achievements of William Wallace.

    B.   Scott wrote novels about Scottish history and Wallace is a famous historical figure from Scotland.

    C.   Scott was a very religious man and deserved to be buried in an abbey.

    D.   Wallace was an avid fan of Scott's poetry.

CONTINUED

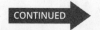

28. The passage suggests that the author's attitude toward Sir Walter Scott is:

F. restrained and skeptical.

G. derisive and contemptuous.

H. interested and appreciative.

J. passionate and envious.

29. Based on the fifth paragraph (lines 62–77), it is reasonable to infer that Sir Walter Scott's attitude toward his debts was:

A. irresponsible, since he left them to be taken care of after his death.

B. resentful, for he believed that they were caused by his partners.

C. impatient, because he became annoyed that his creditors hounded him so.

D. accepting, since he acknowledged his responsibility and tried to pay them back.

30. The author's use of "dabbling" in line 7 suggests that:

F. Scott sought to establish himself in a field in which he had little experience.

G. the financial losses eventually suffered by Scott's printing press began with this activity.

H. Scott's inexperience led to the poor quality of his literary work.

J. Scott's initial work led to his interest in Scottish history.

Passage IV

NATURAL SCIENCE: The following is adapted from Wikipedia articles titled "Lemur" and "Ring-tailed Lemur."

Lemurs are part of a suborder of primates known as prosimians, and make up the infraorder Lemuriformes. This type of primate was the evolutionary predecessor of monkeys and apes
5 (simians). The term "lemur" is derived from the Latin word *lemures*, which means "spirits of the night." This likely refers to many lemurs' nocturnal behavior and their large, reflective eyes. It is generically used for the members of the four
10 lemuriform families, but it is also the genus of one of the lemuriform species. The two flying lemur species are not lemurs, nor are they even primates.

Lemurs are found naturally only on the island of Madagascar and some smaller surrounding islands,
15 including the Comoros (where it is likely they were introduced by humans). While they were displaced in the rest of the world by monkeys, apes, and other primates, the lemurs were safe from competition on Madagascar and differentiated into a number of
20 species. These range in size from the tiny 30-gram pygmy mouse lemur to the 10-kilogram indri. The larger species have all become extinct since humans settled on Madagascar, and since the early twentieth century the largest lemurs reach about seven
25 kilograms. Typically, the smaller lemurs are active at night (nocturnal), while the larger ones are active during the day (diurnal).

All lemurs are endangered species, due mainly to habitat destruction (deforestation) and hunting.
30 Although conservation efforts are underway, options are limited because of the lemurs' limited range and because Madagascar is desperately poor. Currently, there are approximately 32 living lemur species.

35 The ring-tailed lemur is a relatively large prosimian, belonging to the family Lemuridae. Ring-tailed lemurs are the only species within the genus *Lemur* and are found only on the island of Madagascar. Although threatened by habitat
40 destruction and therefore listed as vulnerable by the IUCN Red List, ring-tailed lemurs are the most

CONTINUED →

populous lemurs in zoos worldwide; they reproduce readily in captivity.

Mostly grey with white underparts, ring-tailed
45 lemurs have slender frames; their narrow faces are white with black lozenge-shaped patches around the eyes and black vulpine muzzles. The lemurs' trademark, their long, bushy tails, are ringed in black and white. Like all lemurs, ring-tailed lemurs
50 have hind limbs longer than their forelimbs; their palms and soles are padded with soft, leathery skin and their fingers are slender and dexterous. On the second toe of their hind limbs, ring-tailed lemurs have claws specialized for grooming purposes.

55 The very young animals have blue eyes while the eyes of all adults are a striking yellow. Adults may reach a body length of 46 centimeters (18 inches) and a weight of 5.5 kilograms (12 pounds). Their tails are longer than their bodies, at up to 56
60 centimeters (22 inches) in length.

Found in the southwest of Madagascar and ranging farther into highland areas than any other lemur, ring-tailed lemurs inhabit deciduous forests with grass floors or forests along riverbanks
65 (gallery forests); some may also inhabit dry, open brush where few trees grow. Ring-tailed lemurs are thought to require primary forest (that is, forests that have remained undisturbed by human activity) in order to survive; such forests are now being
70 cleared at a troubling rate.

While primarily frugivores (fruit-eating), ring-tailed lemurs will also eat leaves, seeds, and the odd insect. Ring-tailed lemurs are diurnal and primarily arboreal animals, forming troops of up
75 to 25 individuals. Social hierarchies are determined by sex, with a distinct hierarchy for each gender; females tend to dominate the troop, while males will alternate between troops. Lemurs claim a sizable territory, which does not overlap with those
80 of other troops; up to 5.6 kilometers (3.5 miles) of this territory may be covered in a single day's foraging.

Both vocal and olfactory signals are important to ring-tailed lemurs' communication: 15 distinct
85 vocalizations are used. A fatty substance is exuded from the lemurs' glands, which the lemurs run their tails through; this scent is used by both sexes to mark territory and to challenge would-be rivals amongst males. The males vigorously wave their
90 tails high in the air in an attempt to overpower the scent of others.

The breeding season runs from April to June, with the female fertile period lasting for only a day. Gestation lasts for about 146 days, resulting in a
95 litter of either one or two. The young lemurs begin to eat solid food after two months and are fully weaned after five months.

31. According to the passage, lemurs survived on the island of Madagascar because:

A. their large, reflective eyes allowed them to move around at night when predators were asleep.

B. their ability to mark their territory by scent gave them adequate territory for foraging.

C. monkeys, apes, and other primates were not a threat to them on Madagascar.

D. their strong social hierarchy allowed them to band together for safety.

32. According to the passage, the social organization of the ring-tailed lemur:

F. places females at the top of the hierarchy.

G. functions to ensure adequate food supplies.

H. has followed the same structure since antiquity.

J. is notable for its equality of the sexes.

33. As it is used in line 73, the word *odd* most nearly means:

A. strange.

B. unusual.

C. eerie.

D. occasional.

34. According to the passage, why are ring-tails the most populous species of lemurs in zoos?

    F. They inhabit deciduous forests, which make the lemurs' capture relatively easy.

    G. They have no difficulty giving birth in a zoo environment.

    H. Their attractive appearance makes them popular with patrons.

    J. Their eating preferences are easily accommodated.

35. The passage suggests that the rate at which primary forests are being cleared is "troubling" (line 70) because:

    A. it is causing significant soil erosion in the lemurs' primary habitat.

    B. valuable hardwoods are being destroyed.

    C. lemurs' predators inhabit the cleared area.

    D. lemurs need to live in primary forests to survive.

36. All of the following are given as ways in which ring-tailed lemurs use olfactory signals EXCEPT:

    F. to put male challengers on notice.

    G. to mask the scent of other lemurs.

    H. to signify group identification.

    J. to mark their territory.

37. According to the passage, which of the following describes a characteristic of the infraorder Lemuriformes?

    A. They are nocturnal.

    B. They evolved before monkeys and apes did.

    C. They include two species of flying lemurs.

    D. They are found only on Madagascar.

38. Which of the following can reasonably be inferred from information in the second paragraph (lines 13–27)?

    F. The pygmy mouse lemur is diurnal.

    G. The larger species of lemur were hunted for their fur.

    H. The indri lemur is extinct.

    J. Lemurs are descended from monkeys.

39. When ring-tailed lemurs grow from young animals to adults:

    A. they become less aggressive.

    B. they no longer need primary forests.

    C. their eye color changes.

    D. they become known as flying lemurs.

40. Which of the following questions is NOT answered by the passage?

    F. Will conservationists be able to prevent the extinction of lemurs?

    G. Why did lemurs survive on Madagascar?

    H. How many offspring can a female lemur produce per year?

    J. What makes up the lemur's diet?

IF YOU FINISH BEFORE TIME IS CALLED, YOU MAY CHECK YOUR WORK ON THIS SECTION ONLY. DO NOT TURN TO ANY OTHER SECTION IN THE TEST.

STOP

Science Test

35 Minutes—40 Questions

Directions: The Science Test includes multiple passages. Each passage includes multiple questions. After reading each passage, choose the best answer and fill in the corresponding bubble on your answer sheet. You may review the passages as often as necessary.

You may NOT use a calculator on this test.

Passage I

In the 1920s, scientists developed numerous models of the atom, most of which posited a central nucleus surrounded by electrons (see Figure 1).

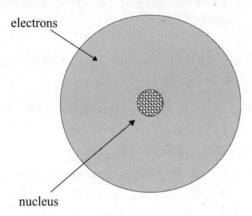

Figure 1

The protons and neutrons in the atom's nucleus have positive and neutral charges, respectively, whereas electrons have a negative charge. In the process of becoming ionized, an atom gains or loses electrons, thereby obtaining an overall positive or negative charge. Additionally, after atoms have become energized, they release such energy in the form of light. Electrons are thought to be responsible for this process.

In the 1920s, two scientists debated the way in which electrons surround an atom's nucleus.

Scientist 1: Bohr model

Electrons move around an atom's nucleus in precise co-planar, concentric circular orbits. Any given orbit can only hold a certain number of electrons. Once the orbit is filled with electrons, the next level orbit must be used. For this reason, some atoms will be larger (have a larger radius) than others.

Additionally, if electrons become energized, they will "jump" from one orbit to the next. When they return to their normal energy level, they emit energy in the form of light. This accounts for the fact that excited atoms emit very specific and well-defined colors of light. If the position of electrons is not specified, the precise wavelengths of light that are emitted cannot be explained.

Scientist 2: Electron cloud model

The precise location of electrons cannot be detected. Electrons move around a nucleus in a cloud. In this cloud, certain regions have a higher probability of containing electrons than others. The cloud extends all around the nucleus in 3 dimensions. The uncertainty of any one electron's position and the nature of its existence as a charged particle contribute to an understanding of the wave-particle nature of matter and energy.

Though this model is seemingly at odds with a number of assumptions about the stability of matter in larger-scale reality, it is anchored to a concept called the *wave function*. The wave function helps to specify the distinct shape of the probability clouds surrounding a nucleus. This explains how the position of the electrons can be random and yet localized.

CONTINUED ▶ **K**

1. Which of the following statements is most consistent with the electron cloud model?

    A. Electrons orbit the nucleus of an atom in fixed paths.

    B. Electrons are found in the nucleus of an atom.

    C. Electrons exhibit almost random patterns of movement around a nucleus.

    D. Electrons have a fixed position outside the nucleus.

2. By suggesting that the position of an electron follows the wave function, Scientist 2 supports which of the following claims?

    F. The probability of an electron's position depends on its orbit.

    G. The color of emitted light depends on the charge of an atom.

    H. Protons and neutrons are also subject to the wave-particle duality.

    J. Electron configuration affects an atom's shape and corresponding properties.

3. According to the passage, a similarity between the Bohr model and the electron cloud model is that:

    A. electrons do not have a fixed position.

    B. the charge of electrons is based on probability.

    C. protons and neutrons are composed of many smaller particles.

    D. the atom is indivisible.

4. According to Scientist 1, which of the following observations provides the strongest evidence that electrons do NOT lie in a probability cloud surrounding the nucleus?

    F. Electrons have a fixed position around the nucleus.

    G. The light emitted by energized electrons is specific and predictable.

    H. Electrons behave according to the wave function.

    J. The charge of electrons is constant.

5. After the 1920s, it was observed that a single electron will exhibit patterns of motion that imply both that it is a distinct particle and also that the path it takes correlates to a probability. Which model does this observation strengthen?

    A. The electron cloud model, because the observation supports wave-particle duality.

    B. The electron cloud model, because the observation shows that an electron travels in a distinct path.

    C. The Bohr model, because the observation indicates that electrons travel in orbits.

    D. The Bohr model, because the observation confirms that electrons behave according to probability.

6. Scientist 2 implies that the Bohr model is *weakened* by observing that:

    F. electrons have a greater chance of lying in specific areas around the nucleus than others.

    G. electrons behave like photons.

    H. the precise position of electrons cannot be known.

    J. the orbits of electrons are not circular.

CONTINUED →

7. Which of the following diagrams is most consistent with the Bohr model of the atom?

A.

protons, neutrons, electrons

B.

nucleus

electrons

C.

nucleus

electrons

D.

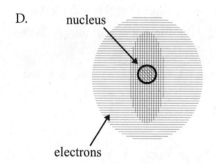

nucleus

electrons

Passage II

Scientists noted an increase in acid rainfall and reports of respiratory ailments in a certain community. They suspected that both of these outcomes were due to increased levels of airborne pollutants, such as carbon monoxide and sulfur dioxide, entering the atmosphere in that community. Common sources of gaseous pollutants are factories, motor vehicles, or industrial processes that burn fossil fuels and release byproducts of their reactions into the air. To determine the sources of these pollutants, scientists conducted the following studies.

Study 1

The scientists found that one likely source of pollutant gases was a network of highways located near the community. Sampling stations at ground level were set up near two major highways so that air samples could be measured and analyzed daily. The results of these analyses, with pollutant levels in parts per million (ppm), are shown in Table 1.

Table 1		
Date	Carbon monoxide level (ppm)	Sulfur dioxide level (ppm)
Highway 1		
January 6	2.3	0.002
January 7	3.2	0.002
January 8	2.9	0.003
January 9	2.6	0.002
January 10	2.1	0.004
Highway 2		
January 6	3.4	0.004
January 7	3.8	0.006
January 8	4.9	0.004
January 9	3.4	0.003
January 10	3.2	0.002

CONTINUED

Study 2

Scientists also suspected that another source of pollutants was from the community's power plant, an older coal-burning plant. Air samples were recorded from the tops of two different monitoring towers near the power plant's two main smokestacks, which emit most of the byproducts created in the electricity-generating process. The results are shown in Table 2.

Table 2

Date	Ozone level (ppm)	Carbon monoxide level (ppm)	Sulfur dioxide level (ppm)
Tower 1			
January 6	0.05	3.3	0.005
January 7	0.06	3.2	0.006
January 8	0.11	3.3	0.009
January 9	0.15	4.3	0.013
January 10	0.10	4.2	0.009
Tower 2			
January 6	0.04	2.0	0.004
January 7	0.05	2.9	0.005
January 8	0.06	3.0	0.008
January 9	0.05	2.8	0.006
January 10	0.04	2.1	0.004

8. How is the design of Study 1 different from the design of Study 2, in terms of sampling methods?

   F. In Study 1, sampling was done weekly, while in Study 2, sampling was done every day.

   G. In Study 1, air was sampled at ground level, while in Study 2, air was sampled at the tops of two towers.

   H. In Study 1, ozone levels were sampled, while in Study 2, ozone levels were not sampled.

   J. In Study 1, only carbon monoxide was sampled, while in Study 2, only sulfur dioxide was sampled.

9. In order to obtain more information about the relationship between carbon monoxide, sulfur dioxide, and respiratory ailments, which of the following studies should be carried out next?

   A. Studying how asthma is affected by changes in temperature throughout the year.

   B. Assessing the rates of respiratory illness in communities with different average levels of carbon monoxide and sulfur dioxide.

   C. Adding large amounts of carbon monoxide and sulfur dioxide to the air surrounding Highway 1.

   D. Encouraging carpools to decrease traffic levels in the highways around this community.

10. Scientists suspected that sulfur dioxide emissions from the power plant were contributing to acid rain, which in turn was affecting the acidity of lakes in the surrounding countryside. In order to test this hypothesis, which of the following should the scientists do next?

   F. Sample sulfur dioxide levels near the power plant's smaller smokestacks.

   G. Measure the number of respiratory ailments suffered by people living near the lakes.

   H. Increase the amount of coal burned by the power plant.

   J. Measure the acidity of the water at a number of lakes with varying levels of atmospheric sulfur dioxide.

11. What hypothesis concerning respiratory ailments were the scientists hoping to test in Study 1?

   A. Pollutants from vehicular highway traffic cause an increase in respiratory ailments.

   B. Emissions from coal-burning power plants cause a decrease in respiratory ailments.

   C. Rainfall in the communities located near the highways causes a decrease in respiratory ailments.

   D. Acid rain tends to deposit pollutants into areas where highway traffic is least frequent.

12. Assuming that a neutral air level for both carbon monoxide and sulfur dioxide is 0 ppm and given the results of Studies 1 and 2, all of the following actions would be likely to contribute to reductions in levels of airborne pollutants EXCEPT:

   F. building more highways in the areas surrounding the community.

   G. placing limits on the amount of highway traffic near the community.

   H. reducing the amount of coal burned at the power plant.

   J. installing filters in the power plant's smokestacks that remove sulfur dioxide from the plant's emissions.

13. As carbon monoxide emissions are carried away from their sources, they tend to diffuse (become less concentrated). Which of the following would be the most likely approximate carbon monoxide level near Highway 1 on January 7 if the sampling station were set up closer to the roadway?

   A. 1.0 ppm

   B. 2.0 ppm

   C. 3.0 ppm

   D. 4.0 ppm

14. Which of the following accurately describe(s) the results of Study 2?

   I. Ozone levels and sulfur dioxide levels increased then decreased in both towers.

   II. Carbon monoxide levels in Tower 2 were always greater than those in Tower 1.

   III. January 9 showed the highest emissions for all pollutants at both towers.

   F. I only

   G. II only

   H. I and II only

   J. I, II, and III

Passage III

Conductivity is the ability of a sample of a material to transmit electricity. All materials have electrical properties that divide them into three broad categories: *conductors*, *insulators*, and *semiconductors*. A conductor is a substance that allows an electric charge to travel from one object to another. An insulator is a substance that prevents an electric charge from traveling between objects. Substances with levels of conductivity between that of a conductor and that of an insulator are called semi-conductors. The unit of current is the ampere (A), and an *ammeter* is an instrument used to measure the current flowing in a circuit, as can be seen in Diagram 1.

Diagram 1

A scientist carried out three studies to determine the validity of the hypothesis that a wire conducts more current when the diameter of the wire increases or when the temperature of the wire decreases.

Study 1

Wires were made from five different materials. Each strand of wire had a diameter of exactly 4 millimeters (mm). The strands of wire connecting the battery, light bulb and ammeter were a total of 0.5 meters (m) long and were kept at a temperature of 50°C. Table 1 displays the current, in milliamps (mA) recorded by the ammeter.

Table 1	
Material	Current (mA)
Silicon carbide (SiC)	4.6
Copper (Cu)	9.4
Rubber	0.0
Zinc telluride (ZnTe)	5.2
Steel	3.5

Study 2

The conditions in Study 1 were repeated, except the diameter of the wires was increased to 6 mm. The length between the battery and the light bulb and the ammeter was held constant at 0.5 m and the wires were kept at 50°C. Table 2 displays the findings.

Table 2	
Material	Current (mA)
Silicon carbide (SiC)	6.5
Copper (Cu)	11.3
Rubber	0.0
Zinc telluride (ZnTe)	7.1
Steel	5.4

Study 3

Study 2 was repeated at 30°C. Table 3 displays the findings.

Table 3	
Material	Current (mA)
Silicon carbide (SiC)	7.3
Copper (Cu)	12.1
Rubber	0.0
Zinc telluride (ZnTe)	8.9
Steel	6.6

15. Which of the following ranges represents the amperage of all five wires with diameters of 6 mm at 30°C?

   A. 5.4 mA to 11.3 mA
   B. 0.0 mA to 9.4 mA
   C. 0.0 mA to 11.3 mA
   D. 0.0 mA to 12.1 mA

16. The scientist hypothesized that increasing the diameter of a wire increases the amount of current it conducts. The results from the studies for each of the following materials support the scientist's hypothesis EXCEPT the results for:

   F. silicon carbide.
   G. rubber.
   H. copper.
   J. steel.

17. According to the results of the studies, a wire made from ZnTe would conduct the most current under which of the following conditions?

   A. 1 mm diameter, 0.5 m length at 40°C
   B. 4 mm diameter, 0.5 m length at 40°C
   C. 4 mm diameter, 0.5 m length at 20°C
   D. 8 mm diameter, 0.5 m length at 20°C

18. What would the ammeter read if the scientist used wires of 4 mm diameter at 30°C and a total length of 0.5 m, but if the material for the wire from the battery to the ammeter was copper, the wire from the ammeter to the light bulb was rubber, and the light bulb back to the battery was steel?

   F. 0.0 mA
   G. 3.5 mA
   H. 9.4 mA
   J. 12.9 mA

CONTINUED ▶

19. How would the current conducted by the materials most likely be affected if Study 3 was repeated and the temperature of the wires was increased to 100°C?

    A. The current would decrease with the exception of rubber.

    B. The current would remain unchanged.

    C. The current would either increase or decrease, depending on the type of material.

    D. The current would increase with the exception of rubber.

20. Based on the results of the studies, which of the following best describes the properties of rubber?

    F. Rubber's capacity as a conductor increases with temperature.

    G. Rubber's capacity as an insulator increases with temperature.

    H. Rubber's capacity as an insulator increases with diameter.

    J. Rubber's capacity as an insulator is unaffected by temperature or diameter.

21. Which of the following effects would be the most appropriate for the scientist to investigate next in order to learn more about the ability of wires to conduct current?

    A. The effect of temperature on conductivity

    B. The effect of diameter on conducted current

    C. The effect of choice of material on conductivity

    D. The effect of wire length on conducted current

Passage IV

The climate (long-term meteorological conditions) of a region consists of the average weather (short-term meteorological conditions) in that region over a period of years. Climate is measured by monitoring the variation in temperature, humidity, atmospheric pressure, wind, and precipitation. A microclimate is a smaller area within a climate region that has its own unique climate. Scientists performed the following studies to investigate the microclimates of neighboring rural and urban (population greater than 50,000 people) areas.

Study 1

Monthly average air temperatures and relative humidity for neighboring rural and urban areas were collected over a period of 11 years. Results indicated that, compared to the relative humidity of the rural area, the relative humidity of the urban area was 2% lower in the winter and 6% lower in the summer. Figure 1 shows the average temperature for August (summer) and February (winter) for the rural and urban areas.

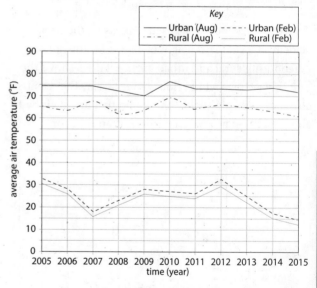

Figure 1

CONTINUED

Study 2

Annual precipitation and cloud cover were recorded for the same neighboring rural and urban areas over the same period of 11 years. Results showed that the rural area had on average 5% fewer cloudy or hazy days than the urban area for each year. Figure 2 shows the total accumulated precipitation for each year.

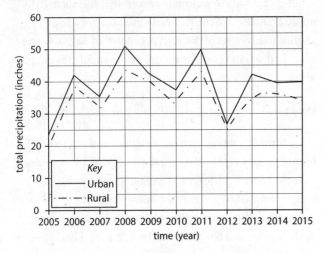

Figure 2

Study 3

An anemometer was used to measure the wind velocity at a standard height of 33 feet for the same neighboring rural and urban areas. Figure 3 shows the monthly average wind velocity over a year. The scientists also measured air quality and found that urban air had about 10 times more dust particles than rural air.

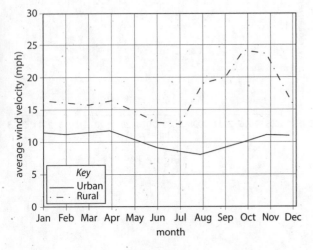

Figure 3

22. According to Study 1, the greatest difference in average air temperature during the summer between the urban and rural areas occurred in which year?

F. 2007

G. 2010

H. 2012

J. 2014

23. According to Study 3, average wind velocities in the rural area were closest for which of the following pairs of months?

A. January and April

B. April and July

C. July and September

D. September and November

24. Suppose new evidence showed that buildings increase frictional drag on air flowing over built-up terrain. Based on Study 3, would it be justified to conclude that the rural area has more buildings than the urban area?

F. Yes, because the average wind velocity is lower for the rural area than for the urban area.

G. Yes, because the average air temperature is lower for the rural area than for the urban area.

H. No, because the average wind velocity is higher for the rural area than for the urban area.

J. No, because the average air temperature is higher for the rural area than for the urban area.

CONTINUED ➤

25. Based on Study 1, what conclusion can be drawn from the fact that the difference in relative humidity between the urban and rural areas is less in the winter than in the summer?

    A. The relative humidity is higher for the urban area than for the rural area.

    B. The average winter air temperature is higher for the urban area than for the rural area.

    C. Relative humidity differences correlate with average air temperature differences.

    D. Relative humidity differences correlate with average wind velocity differences.

26. Scientists hypothesized that building materials and road surfaces in urban areas absorb heat during the day and release it at night, increasing the air temperature. Do the results of Study 1 support this hypothesis?

    F. Yes; the recorded summer temperatures in the urban area were lower than those in the rural area.

    G. Yes; the recorded summer temperatures in the urban area were higher than those in the rural area.

    H. No; the recorded humidity in the urban area was lower than that in the rural area.

    J. No; the recorded humidity in the urban area was higher than that in the rural area.

27. Given that dust particles act as hygroscopic nuclei, encouraging rain production, which of the following best explains why the rural area received less rain than the urban area in Study 2?

    A. The wind velocity was higher in the urban area than the rural area.

    B. There were more dust particles in the air at the urban area to become nuclei.

    C. There were fewer cloudy days in the urban area.

    D. Higher relative humidity in the urban area allowed the air to hold more moisture.

28. At a third area located near the other two, the scientists determined the average summer air temperature to be 75°F and the average annual precipitation to be 40 inches. Based on the data from the studies, the scientists should predict that the average wind velocity is most likely:

    F. between 8 and 12 mph.

    G. between 12 and 15 mph.

    H. between 15 and 20 mph.

    J. between 20 and 25 mph.

Passage V

The movement of planets and other celestial bodies in the solar system is governed by the force of gravity. Gravitational effects are determined by considering many factors, such as a body's mass and the distance between bodies. Table 1 lists the masses and radii for several planets.

Table 1		
Planet	Mass (kg)	Radius (km)
Saturn	5.68×10^{26}	58,232
Jupiter	1.90×10^{27}	69,911
Earth	5.97×10^{24}	6,371
Venus	4.87×10^{24}	6,052
Mercury	3.29×10^{23}	2,440

Figure 1 shows the acceleration due to gravity of an object at various distances from the center of 3 planets.

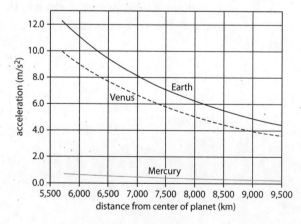

Figure 1

CONTINUED

Perihelion is the point in a planet's orbit at which it is closest to the sun. Figure 2 shows how the orbital velocity of the same 3 planets varies as each planet approaches and recedes from perihelion (a negative distance means the planet is approaching perihelion, positive means the planet is receding).

Figure 2

29. According to Figure 2, as Mercury approaches perihelion and then recedes from it, its orbital velocity:

    A.   increases, then decreases.

    B.   decreases, then increases.

    C.   decreases only.

    D.   increases only.

30. Suppose that a planet was found to have a mass between that of Saturn and Jupiter. Based on Table 1 and assuming a similar density, which of the following would be the most likely radius for the planet?

    F.   2,240 km

    G.   6,197 km

    H.   63,452 km

    J.   87,128 km

31. Which of the planets listed in Table 1 has the greatest mass?

    A.   Saturn

    B.   Jupiter

    C.   Earth

    D.   Mercury

32. According to Figure 2, the orbital velocity of Mercury 75×10^6 km away from perihelion, approaching, is closest to the orbital velocity of which of the following?

    F.   The orbital velocity of Mercury 100×10^6 km away from perihelion, approaching.

    G.   The orbital velocity of Mercury 75×10^6 km away from perihelion, receding.

    H.   The orbital velocity of Mercury 50×10^6 km away from perihelion, receding.

    J.   The orbital velocity of Mercury 50×10^6 km away from perihelion, approaching.

33. According to Figure 1, does an object fall faster toward Earth or toward Venus from a distance of 8,000 km?

    A.   Venus, because the acceleration due to gravity from Venus is higher.

    B.   Venus, because the acceleration due to gravity from Venus is lower.

    C.   Earth, because the acceleration due to gravity from Earth is higher.

    D.   Earth, because the acceleration due to gravity from Earth is lower.

34. Based on Table 1 and Figure 1, it would be most reasonable to predict that the object with the highest acceleration due to gravity would be an object at a distance of:

    F.   7,000 km from the center of Venus.

    G.   7,500 km from the center of Saturn.

    H.   8,500 km from the center of Earth.

    J.   9,000 km from the center of Mercury.

CONTINUED ➤

Passage VI

The following chemical equation represents a typical acid-base neutralization reaction:

$$HCl + NaOH \rightarrow H_2O + NaCl$$

Table 1 lists common pH indicators and the pH ranges over which a distinct color change occurs.

Table 1

Indicator	pH range
Methyl yellow	2.9–4.0
Bromocresol green	3.8–5.4
Methyl red	4.4–6.2
Phenol red	6.8–8.4
Phenolphthalein	8.3–10.0
Alizarine	10.1–12.0

In the process of acid-base titration, the *equivalence point* is the point at which equal concentrations of an acid and base are present. When an acid or base is added to a solution at its equivalence point, changes in pH are typically much more drastic than they are at other points in the titration process. Figure 1 shows the pH of Solution A and Solution B versus the amount of an NaOH solution added.

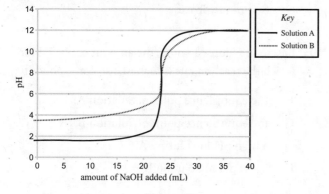

Figure 1

Figure 2 shows the reaction rate for Solutions A and B (as a percentage of the reaction rate at their equivalence point) versus the amount of NaOH solution added.

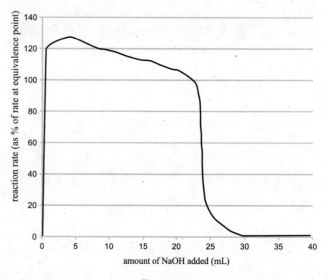

Figure 2

CONTINUED

35. If the experimental setup were reversed and Solution A were titrated into a beaker of NaOH, which of the following graphs would best represent the corresponding titration curve?

    A.

    B. pH

    volume of acid added

    C. pH

    volume of acid added

    D. pH

    volume of acid added

36. Based on Table 1 and Figure 1, which indicator changes color in a pH range that includes the equivalence point of Solution A ?

    F. Bromocresol green

    G. Methyl red

    H. Phenol red

    J. Alizarine

37. If the chemical reaction associated with the chemical equation shown in the passage takes place completely (with negligible unused reactants), the pH of the resulting solution should be approximately:

    A. 0.

    B. 2.

    C. 7.

    D. 14.

38. According to Figure 2, for which of the following volumes of NaOH does the reaction rate exceed the reaction rate at the equivalence point?

    F. 0 mL

    G. 5 mL

    H. 25 mL

    J. 30 mL

39. In the chemical equation shown in the passage, the sodium in NaOH becomes part of which of the following compounds?

    A. Water

    B. Table salt

    C. Hydrochloric acid

    D. Sodium hydroxide

40. Based on Figures 1 and 2, the amount of NaOH for which the reaction rate is highest also corresponds to:

    F. the equivalence point of Solution A.

    G. the equivalence point of Solution B.

    H. a high pH in Solution A.

    J. a low pH in Solution B.

Writing Test

40 Minutes

Directions

The essay is used to evaluate your writing skills. You will have **40 minutes** to review the prompt and plan and write an essay in English. Before you begin, read everything in this test booklet carefully to make sure you understand the task.

Your essay will be judged based on the evidence it provides of your ability to do the following:

- Assert your own perspective on a complex issue and evaluate the relationship between your perspective and at least one other perspective
- Use reasoning and evidence to refine and justify your ideas
- Present your ideas in an organized way
- Convey your ideas effectively using standard written English

Write your essay on the lined essay pages in the answer booklet. All writing on those lined pages will be scored. Use the unlined pages in this test booklet to plan your essay. Your work on these unlined pages will not be scored.

Put your pencil down as soon as time is called.

DO NOT OPEN THIS BOOKLET UNTIL TOLD TO DO SO.

Student Loans

Despite the rising cost of higher education, financial experts agree that a college diploma is worth the investment. As students enroll in college to increase their lifetime earning potential, broaden their opportunities, and pursue careers, many worry about the challenge of paying off student loans once they graduate. Student loan repayment includes both the original amount borrowed as well as interest accrued over time, which often takes students years to repay. Should colleges and financial institutions be expected to develop programs and policies to address student concern regarding loans? Given the fact that affording college is a primary factor in deciding whether or not to pursue higher education, it is prudent for institutions to develop practices to better assist students in financing their degrees.

Perspective One	Perspective Two	Perspective Three
Student loans should not be subject to interest rates if a student is able to pay off the loan within a reasonable amount of time. Financial lenders, including the United States government, should not be making a profit on loans that students need to complete their degrees. Should a student request additional time to repay the loan beyond the agreed-upon repayment schedule, interest or a penalty fee can then be applied to the remaining balance.	Higher education is a commodity and is subject to supply and demand principles inherent in a capitalist market. Colleges, financial institutions, and the United States government should not make special accommodations for college students. All loans should be held to the same standard and should not differ according to a borrower's intended use.	The amount of money students can borrow should be proportional to the annual salary they are projected to earn once they graduate. Students should not be allowed to borrow more money than they can pay back in a reasonable amount of time. Reducing or eliminating interest rates does not address the more concerning issue of disproportionate debt and future earning potential.

CONTINUED

Read and carefully consider these perspectives. Each suggests a particular way of thinking about student loans.

Essay Task

Write a clear, well-reasoned essay evaluating multiple perspectives on student loans. In your essay, be sure to:

- Assert your own perspective on the issue and evaluate the relationship between your perspective and at least one other perspective
- Use reasoning and evidence to refine and justify your ideas
- Present your ideas in an organized way
- Convey your ideas effectively using standard written English

Your perspective may be fully, somewhat, or not at all in agreement with one or more of the three perspectives in the prompt.

Planning Your Essay

These pages are not scored.

Use the space below to brainstorm and plan your essay. Consider the following as you think about the prompt:

- Strengths and weaknesses of the three perspectives in the prompt
  - What observations do they offer, and what do they overlook?
  - Why are they persuasive or why are they not persuasive?
- Your own background and identity
  - What is your perspective on this issue, and what are its strengths and weaknesses?
  - What evidence will you use in your essay?

CONTINUED ➜

CONTINUED ➤

CONTINUED

IF YOU FINISH BEFORE TIME IS CALLED, YOU MAY CHECK YOUR WORK ON THIS SECTION ONLY. DO NOT TURN
TO ANY OTHER SECTION IN THE TEST.

STOP

944 K

Answer Key

English Test

1. C	16. G	31. A	46. J	61. A
2. J	17. A	32. G	47. C	62. H
3. B	18. F	33. C	48. G	63. C
4. J	19. B	34. H	49. A	64. G
5. C	20. G	35. A	50. G	65. D
6. H	21. C	36. J	51. C	66. J
7. B	22. H	37. B	52. H	67. A
8. H	23. B	38. G	53. D	68. H
9. C	24. F	39. A	54. H	69. C
10. J	25. D	40. F	55. D	70. G
11. C	26. J	41. D	56. G	71. B
12. J	27. C	42. G	57. B	72. J
13. C	28. G	43. B	58. F	73. B
14. G	29. D	44. H	59. B	74. F
15. A	30. H	45. B	60. J	75. D

Mathematics Test

1. E	13. A	25. E	37. E	49. A
2. H	14. J	26. G	38. F	50. J
3. A	15. A	27. B	39. C	51. A
4. J	16. H	28. G	40. K	52. G
5. C	17. E	29. A	41. B	53. B
6. J	18. J	30. G	42. F	54. J
7. C	19. A	31. A	43. D	55. A
8. F	20. H	32. H	44. G	56. K
9. D	21. E	33. B	45. C	57. C
10. J	22. K	34. F	46. J	58. G
11. A	23. B	35. D	47. D	59. C
12. K	24. J	36. K	48. H	60. K

Reading Test

1. A	11. B	21. B	31. C
2. H	12. H	22. J	32. F
3. B	13. C	23. D	33. D
4. F	14. G	24. J	34. G
5. D	15. B	25. A	35. D
6. H	16. F	26. F	36. H
7. A	17. C	27. B	37. B
8. G	18. F	28. H	38. H
9. D	19. B	29. D	39. C
10. G	20. F	30. F	40. F

Science Test

1. C	11. A	21. D	31. B
2. J	12. F	22. J	32. G
3. A	13. D	23. A	33. C
4. G	14. F	24. H	34. G
5. A	15. D	25. C	35. A
6. H	16. G	26. G	36. H
7. C	17. D	27. B	37. C
8. G	18. F	28. F	38. G
9. B	19. A	29. A	39. B
10. J	20. J	30. H	40. J

Answers and Explanations

English Test

My Cousin Nicola

1.   C
Difficulty: Medium
Category: Agreement
Getting to the Answer: Use *who* or *whom* to refer to a person. The underlined word begins a description of Lucia; the correct pronoun is *who*, because Lucia is a person. Choice (C) is correct. *Which*, in A, is incorrect when used to refer to a person. Choice B uses the objective case *whom*; you wouldn't say "*her* was already married," so "*whom* was already married" is incorrect. *She who*, in D, makes the sentence unnecessarily wordy and awkward.

2.   J
Difficulty: Medium
Category: Sentence Structure
Getting to the Answer: Independent clauses should either be joined by a semicolon or connected with a coordinating conjunction; otherwise, one of the clauses must be made subordinate. As written, the sentence is a run-on. None of the answer choices offers a semicolon or a comma and a coordinating conjunction, but (J) makes the second clause dependent by using *that*. Choices G and H do not address the run-on error.

3.   B
Difficulty: Medium
Category: Agreement
Getting to the Answer: Use context to determine appropriate verb tenses. This sentence uses the simple past tense *were* and doesn't indicate any time shift, so the simple past tense *knew* makes the most sense. Choice (B) is correct. Choice A uses the past participle *known* without the necessary helping verb *had*. Choice C incorrectly uses *had knew*; the past participle of *know* is *known*. Choice D uses *been known* without the necessary helping verb *had*; it also creates a sentence that is grammatically incorrect.

4.   J
Difficulty: Medium
Category: Organization
Getting to the Answer: Remember to read for logic, as well as grammar and usage. This sentence inappropriately uses the contrast word *however*. Choice (J) correctly uses *then*, a transition word indicating time. Choices G and H use cause-and-effect transitions, which are inappropriate in context.

5.   C
Difficulty: Medium
Category: Agreement
Getting to the Answer: When an idiomatic construction begins with *not only*, it must conclude with *but also*. Only (C) correctly completes the idiom. *And*, A, *so*, B, and *then*, D, all fail to correctly complete the idiom.

6.   H
Difficulty: Medium
Category: Sentence Structure
Getting to the Answer: The *-ing* form can serve several functions; when used as a verb, it requires a helping verb to be correct. *I being* here is grammatically incorrect; (H) substitutes the correct verb form *was*. Choice G creates a grammatically incorrect sentence, and J omits the verb.

7.   B
Difficulty: Medium
Category: Development
Getting to the Answer: With Writer's Purpose questions like this one, you need to identify the choice that matches the purpose stated in the question stem. The question asks you to select the sentence that gives the most relevant information about Nicola's travel plans. Only (B) tells you about Nicola's plans; he intends to spend the summer with his family in New York. Choice A mentions Nicola's trip to England, which is out of scope for the passage. Choice C provides general information about the easiest way to travel from Italy to America, but it doesn't tell you anything about Nicola's specific plans to visit America. Choice D also focuses on the past, explaining why Nicola had not previously come to America; this doesn't match the question stem's call for information about Nicola's travel plans.

8. H
Difficulty: Medium
Category: Development
Getting to the Answer: Always read question stems carefully; it's easy to miss an important word like NOT or EXCEPT. The question asks for the word that does NOT show that the cousins looked forward to meeting Nicola. The only negatively charged word here is *apprehensive*, which suggests that the cousins feared Nicola's arrival. Choice (H) is correct. Choices F, G, and J all use positively charged words that indicate the cousins were looking forward to Nicola's visit.

9. C
Difficulty: Medium
Category: Sentence Structure
Getting to the Answer: A phrase set off between commas must be nonessential: the sentence must still make sense without it. As written, this sentence treats the phrase "hadn't seen him" as nonessential, but "like me, since they were kids" does not make sense—this phrase must remain in the sentence. Choice (C) eliminates the incorrect comma without introducing any additional errors. Choices B and D create run-on sentences; additionally, D incorrectly inserts a comma between a verb and its object.

10. J
Difficulty: High
Category: Agreement
Getting to the Answer: When a pronoun is underlined, first determine to what or whom it refers. In this case, the reference is unclear. The last plural noun is *musicians*, but that refers to the narrator and Nicola, who do play instruments. Eliminate F. Choice G clearly refers to the narrator and Nicola, so it should also be eliminated. Choice H is ambiguous: to which Americans does the sentence refer? Choice (J) correctly identifies the group mentioned earlier in the paragraph: the narrator's American cousins.

11. C
Difficulty: Medium
Category: Conciseness
Getting to the Answer: The shortest answer isn't always correct—D omits a phrase necessary for the sentence to make sense. Choices A and B include information irrelevant to the topic of the writer meeting Nicola. That leaves (C), which eliminates the irrelevant information without losing the logic of the sentence.

12. J
Difficulty: Medium
Category: Sentence Structure
Getting to the Answer: As a general rule, descriptive phrases modify the nouns that immediately follow them. As written, this sentence tells us that *I* was "Taught to him . . . before she passed away in Italy." Choice (J) is the most concise and logical version of this sentence. Choice G incorrectly indicates that the grandmother, not Nicola, taught the songs to the writer. Choice H gives the introductory phrase no logical noun to modify, making its grammatical structure incorrect.

13. C
Difficulty: Low
Category: Agreement
Getting to the Answer: A verb is underlined, so start by checking to see if the tense is correct. The simple past tense is used in this paragraph: *shared* and *connected*. The correct tense here is the simple past *threw*, as in (C). Choice A uses the conditional tense "would have thrown," but the sentence describes something the writer's father actually did, not something hypothetical. Choice B uses the future perfect tense, but the sentence describes something that happened in the past, not an upcoming event. Choice D uses the present tense, but the action happened in the past.

14. G
Difficulty: Low
Category: Sentence Structure
Getting to the Answer: "Possessive versus plural" questions can often be answered quickly: does the sentence refer to more than one grandmother or something belonging to a grandmother? This sentence is discussing the country that *belongs* to the grandmother, so an apostrophe is needed to make *grandmother* possessive. Only (G) does this without introducing an additional error. Choice F is missing the necessary apostrophe; *grandmothers* is plural, not possessive. Choice H uses the plural possessive *grandmothers'*, but only one grandmother is discussed in the paragraph. Choice J corrects the punctuation error but substitutes the homophone *are* for the plural possessive pronoun *our*.

15. A
Difficulty: Medium
Category: Development
Getting to the Answer: When asked about the purpose of the passage as a whole, consider its topic and tone. The narrator describes a personal experience getting to know his cousin from Italy. The tone is positive, emphasizing their similarities and ending with a scene in which family members are touched emotionally by the singing of family folk songs. Thus, the passage accomplishes the stated purpose; eliminate C and D. Choice B is a distortion; the differences between Nicola and the narrator's American cousins are not the reason the essay accomplishes the stated purpose. Thus, (A) is correct.

The Handsome Bean

16. G
Difficulty: Medium
Category: Sentence Structure
Getting to the Answer: When the only difference in the answer choices is the use of commas, focus on sentence structure. Are there items in a list that need to be separated by commas? A nonessential phrase that needs to be set off from the rest of the sentence with a pair of commas? An introductory phrase or clause that needs to be separated from the rest of the sentence? This sentence treats the phrase *I live* as nonessential, but removing it creates a sentence fragment. Choice (G) properly places a comma between the introductory phrase describing the location of the Handsome Bean coffee shop and the sentence's independent clause. Choice H creates an introductory clause with no noun to modify, which is grammatically incorrect. Choice J fails to set off the introductory phrase from the body of the sentence, making the sentence difficult to understand.

17. A
Difficulty: Medium
Category: Development
Getting to the Answer: When you're asked the purpose of including a detail, read around that detail for context. By describing the proximity of the Little League field, the writer provides a context for the teams the Handsome Bean often sponsors. Without this information, the following sentence would not fit well in the context. Thus, (A) is correct. There is no change of topic, so B is incorrect. While the information helps

the reader picture the scene, C misses the function of introducing the sponsored team in the following sentence. Choice D does not match the tone of the passage, which portrays the Handsome Bean positively.

18. F
Difficulty: Low
Category: Agreement
Getting to the Answer: Use context to determine the answers to questions with underlined verbs. The verbs in this paragraph are in the present tense: *come, stay, is,* and *offers.* The present tense *sponsors* is correct, so no change is needed, and (F) is correct. Choice G uses the past perfect *had sponsored,* incorrectly suggesting that the coffee shop sponsored the Little League team before another past event. Choices H and J use the past tense, which is inconsistent with the rest of the paragraph.

19. B
Difficulty: Medium
Category: Development
Getting to the Answer: Read question stems carefully. Note that all four answer choices may be relevant to the passage, but only one will fulfill the specific requirements of the question. The question asks for additional detail about the customers who come to the coffee shop. Only (B) focuses on customers—the parents and children who come for ice cream after the Little League games. Choice A focuses on an additional discount provided by the coffee shop, not on the customers of the shop. Choice C provides a detail about another sport supported by the coffee shop; this doesn't match the purpose stated in the question stem. Choice D provides more information about the Little League field, not about the coffee shop's customers.

20. G
Difficulty: Medium
Category: Sentence Structure
Getting to the Answer: When the end of one sentence and the beginning of the next are underlined, consider whether one or both are sentence fragments. As written, both of these sentences are fragments, since neither expresses a complete thought. Choice (G) correctly combines the two fragments into a single sentence. Choice H is unnecessarily wordy. Choice J does not address the error.

21. C
Difficulty: Medium
Category: Development
Getting to the Answer: Remember the first step in the Kaplan Method: read the passage and identify the issue. Here, you need to select the sentence that best introduces the topic of the paragraph, so you'll need to read the paragraph. The paragraph describes the antique décor of the coffee shop—its "century-old" counter, the photos from the 1920s and 1930s, and the "original tin ceiling." Choice (C) effectively leads into this description by explaining that the owner wants the shop to "look like it has been there for decades." Choice A focuses on the friendship between the writer and Mary; this doesn't connect with the details of the antique counter, old photos, and original tin ceiling. Choice B is too general; (C) provides a more specific reason for the decorating decisions Mary has made. Choice D explains that the space was vacant before the Handsome Bean opened, but this doesn't introduce the description of the décor.

22. H
Difficulty: Low
Category: Agreement
Getting to the Answer: The object of a preposition must be a noun, pronoun, or gerund (-ing verb form functioning as a noun). For this sentence to make sense, the noun *condition* is required as the object of *to*. Since nouns can only be modified by adjectives, (H) is correct. Choices F and G use the adjective *conditional* as the object of the preposition, which is grammatically incorrect. Although *original* can function as a noun, it could not then be modified by an adverb, so J is incorrect.

23. B
Difficulty: Medium
Category: Agreement
Getting to the Answer: The ACT will often separate a tested verb from its subject with an intervening phrase or clause. Make sure that you've correctly identified the subject with which an underlined verb must agree. As in many sentences on the ACT, a description separates the subject and verb here; the subject of the verb *depicts* is the plural *photos*. The plural form *depict* is needed; (B) is correct. Choices C and D do not address the error; additionally, C introduces an unwarranted verb tense change.

24. F
Difficulty: High
Category: Development
Getting to the Answer: To answer this type of question, focus on the function of the sentence. What purpose does it serve in the paragraph? The sentence provides the reader with the information that the building is at least 70 years old. Therefore, if the sentence were deleted, you would lose information about the age of the building. Choice (F) is correct. Choice G refers to Mary and the writer etching their names in the ceiling, but the sentence does not describe this action. Choice H relates the sentence to the influence of the original owner; however, the time at which Harvey etched his name has little to do with his influence on Mary, the writer, or anyone else. Choice J treats the sentence as a description of the interior of the coffee shop, but no description of the ceiling is given in this sentence.

25. D
Difficulty: Medium
Category: Sentence Structure
Getting to the Answer: A comma should not be inserted between a preposition and its object. This sentence requires no comma; (D) is correct. Choice B uses a semicolon, which is only correct when used to connect two independent clauses. Choice C treats "usually in the form" as a nonessential phrase. However, deleting this phrase does not leave a logical sentence, so C is incorrect.

26. J
Difficulty: Medium
Category: Agreement
Getting to the Answer: Use *number* for items that are countable and *amount* for quantities that are not. The talented musicians and poets are countable, so *number* should be used instead of *amount*. Since the number of talented performers isn't compared to anything, *good* is the correct adjective. The answer is (J). Choices F and G use *amount* where *number* would be correct; additionally, Choice G uses the comparative adjective *better*, but nothing is compared here. Choice H also uses *better*, which is correct only in a comparison.

27. C
Difficulty: Medium
Category: Conciseness
Getting to the Answer: Be aware of phrases like "It being that"; they add no real meaning to the sentence and provide no clear antecedent for the pronoun. "It being that" is unnecessary here, but eliminating it creates a run-on sentence. Choice (C) eliminates the unnecessary language and makes the second clause subordinate. Choices B and D both use incorrect grammatical structure.

28. G
Difficulty: Medium
Category: Agreement
Getting to the Answer: Elements in a compound must be parallel in structure. The conjunction *or* creates a compound: students load up on caffeine "so they can cram all night . . . or finishing their research papers." Choice (G) makes the two verbs, *cram* and *finish*, parallel. Choices H and J do not address the parallelism error.

29. D
Difficulty: Medium
Category: Sentence Structure
Getting to the Answer: A sentence may have multiple nouns and verbs and still be a fragment. A complete sentence requires a subject and a verb in an independent clause that expresses a complete thought. The subject here is "a group of high school students," but the clause "who stops by to have an ice cream cone or an egg cream" describes the students without providing a predicate verb. Choice (D) eliminates the pronoun, making *stops* the predicate verb. Choice B does not address the error and incorrectly uses *that* to refer to people. Choice C creates an error in subject-verb agreement; the plural pronoun *they* does not agree with the verb *stops.*

30. H
Difficulty: Medium
Category: Organization
Getting to the Answer: When you need to add or move information, read the new information into the passage at the suggested points to determine its logical placement. The paragraph describes different customers at the coffee shop throughout a typical day, starting in the morning and ending in the evening. This sentence talks about customers who come to the coffee shop in the afternoon, so it should be placed between Sentence 3, which talks about daytime customers, and Sentence 4, which describes customers in the evening. Choice (H) is correct. Choices F and J both place the information about customers in the afternoon after information about customers in the evening. Choice G places the information about afternoon customers before the information about morning customers.

Mr. Midshipman Marryat

31. A
Difficulty: Low
Category: Sentence Structure
Getting to the Answer: Remember your tested comma rules. If a sentence doesn't satisfy a tested condition, the comma will be incorrect. No change is needed here, so (A) is correct. Choice B treats *naval, adventure,* and *exploration* as three items in a list, but *naval* is an adjective, not a noun. Choice C places a comma between the adjective *naval* and *adventure*, the noun it describes. Choice D adds a semicolon, but the second clause is not independent.

32. G
Difficulty: Low
Category: Conciseness
Getting to the Answer: Always read until you have enough information to identify the issue. A problem that isn't apparent in the underlined portion may be clear when you consider the whole sentence. The sentence is grammatically correct, but it uses redundant language: *Finally* and *at last* mean the same thing. Choice (G) is the most concise and is therefore correct. Choice H changes *Finally* to *In the end*, but this doesn't correct the redundancy problem. Choice J makes the redundancy problem worse by using both *Ultimately* and *the result.*

33. C
Difficulty: Medium
Category: Agreement
Getting to the Answer: Every pronoun must have a clear and logical antecedent. Marryat, not his parents, enlisted in the British navy, so the pronoun here should be *he*, not *they*. Both (C) and D correct the pronoun, but D introduces a new error; a comma, not a semicolon, is used with a coordinating conjunction (*and*). Choice B does not address the error.

34. H
Difficulty: Low
Category: Agreement
Getting to the Answer: Remember the difference between *who's* and *whose*. *Who's* always stands for *who is* or *who has*, while *whose* shows possession. The *naval exploits* were Cochrane's, so the pronoun *whose* is correct here, as in (H). Choice F uses *that's*, which is a contraction for *that is*; "that is naval exploits are legendary" doesn't make sense in context. Choice G uses *who's*, a contraction for *who is* or *who has*; "who is (or has) naval exploits are legendary" doesn't make sense. Choice J creates a grammatically incorrect sentence.

35. A
Difficulty: Medium
Category: Development
Getting to the Answer: Use your elimination skills here. Once you've answered the question *yes* or *no*, you can immediately eliminate two choices and focus your attention on the remaining two. The question asks you if the phrase "a number of" adds meaning to the sentence, so take a look at the sentence without the phrase. Omitting the phrase leaves you with Cochrane "as the inspiration for Marryat's fictional characters." A reader could easily assume that this means that Cochrane was the inspiration for all of Marryat's characters, which definitely changes the meaning of the sentence. Choice (A) provides the correct answer. Choice B is incorrect because *characters* is plural, which indicates that Cochrane was a model for more than one character. Choices C and D incorrectly state that omitting the phrase would not change the meaning of the sentence.

36. J
Difficulty: Medium
Category: Development
Getting to the Answer: When you're asked about adding a new phrase or sentence, consider both relevance and tone. The focus of this essay is Marryat and how his adventures at sea influenced his writing. The description of Cochrane as an inspiration for Marryat is directly related to the essay's focus, but the information that Cochrane inspired another writer is irrelevant. The sentence should not be added because it is not connected to the main idea of the essay, so (J) is correct. Choices F and G would both incorrectly add the sentence to the essay. Choice H is incorrect

because even adding an explanation of the relationship between O'Brian and Marryat would not make this detail relevant to the topic of the essay.

37. B
Difficulty: Medium
Category: Development
Getting to the Answer: The question asks which choice would NOT be equivalent, so determine which answer choice stands out from the rest. Choices A, C, and D all convey that the authors are widely known. Choice (B) has a different sense. *Beloved* means *well-loved*, which is not the same as being widely known. Thus, (B) is correct.

38. G
Difficulty: Medium
Category: Organization
Getting to the Answer: The question asks you to correctly place the prepositional phrase in the sentence, so start by determining what came "from historical records." The sentence explains that Marryat had vast experiences at sea, while other writers had only "their imaginations and accounts." It makes sense that these accounts came "from historical records," so the placement in (G) is correct. Choice F indicates that the captain himself, not stories about him, came "from historical records." Choice H indicates that the other writers came "from historical records," which doesn't make sense. Choice J indicates that Marryat's memories of adventures came "from historical records"; this contradicts the information in the passage.

39. A
Difficulty: Medium
Category: Sentence Structure
Getting to the Answer: Not every underlined portion will contain an error; about 25% of English Test questions will require no change. In this sentence, "captain and literary inspiration" describes Cochrane; (A) correctly sets "Cochrane" off from the rest of the sentence. Choices B and D incorrectly place commas within a compound; commas are used to set off items in a series of three or more. Choice C omits the comma necessary to set off "Cochrane" from the rest of the sentence.

40. F
Difficulty: Medium
Category: Agreement
Getting to the Answer: Verb tenses must make sense in the context of the sentence, so consider whether one action logically occurs before another. This sentence tells you about two past events—a midshipman falling overboard and Marryat jumping into the sea to save him. The first event was the midshipman falling, so the past perfect "had fallen" in (F) is correct. Choice G uses the conditional "would have fallen," but Marryat didn't prevent the midshipman from falling into the sea; he jumped in after the midshipman. Choice H illogically suggests that the midshipman was still in the process of falling overboard when Marryat jumped in to save him. Choice J incorrectly uses the present tense; all of the actions in this sentence took place in the past.

41. D
Difficulty: Low
Category: Conciseness
Getting to the Answer: The passive voice is not always incorrect, but it is generally wordier than the active. If a passive construction can be easily made active, the correct answer choice will do so. Marryat is the one who accomplished the feats, so an active sentence will focus on him, rather than his actions. Choice (D) makes *he* the subject and uses the active verb *accomplished*. Choices A and C make *feats*, not Marryat, the subject, requiring passive and unnecessarily wordy constructions. Choice B is also unnecessarily wordy.

42. G
Difficulty: Medium
Category: Organization
Getting to the Answer: When a transition word is underlined, check both the grammar and the logic of the transition. The underlined word connects Marryat's successes at sea with his earning a medal for inventing a special lifeboat. The second idea does not follow from the first, making F incorrect. Choice H suggests that Marryat won medals for his earlier feats, which is not supported by the paragraph. Choice J inappropriately begins a list with its third item. Choice (G) is correct; the best transition is simply to add the final item to Marryat's list of successes.

43. B
Difficulty: Medium
Category: Sentence Structure
Getting to the Answer: Modifying words and phrases should be as close as possible to the person, thing, or action they describe. Marryat's "novels and short stories" were published in England while he was at sea; (B) makes this clear. In A, "during this time" seems to be what was published in England, which is illogical. Choice C is awkwardly worded, and "by him" is redundant with "His greatest acclaim." The sentence created by D is grammatically incorrect.

44. H
Difficulty: Medium
Category: Agreement
Getting to the Answer: Many ACT Usage questions hinge on preposition choice. The correct idiom here is "concentrate on writing," as in (H). Choice F uses "concentrate for"; you might concentrate for a period of time, but you don't concentrate *for* writing. Choice G uses "concentrate at"; you might concentrate at a place, such as school, but you don't concentrate *at* writing. Choice J uses two prepositions that are inappropriate in context. You don't concentrate *with* writing; additionally, "writing of full-time" suggests that Marryat was writing about the topic of full-time.

45. B
Difficulty: Medium
Category: Organization
Getting to the Answer: The first paragraph in a passage typically introduces the passage's topic. Only Paragraph 2 uses Marryat's full name: *Frederick Marryat*. This paragraph also introduces the topic: Marryat wrote about the adventures he had at sea. This makes Paragraph 2 a better opening paragraph than Paragraph 1; (B) is correct. Choice C interrupts the chronology by placing information about Marryat's enlistment in the navy after details about his first few years in the navy. Choice D similarly disrupts the chronological order by placing information about Marryat's enlistment in the navy after all of the details about his experiences in the navy.

The Toughest Task in Sports

46. J
Difficulty: Low
Category: Conciseness
Getting to the Answer: When DELETE is an option, read the underlined selection for relevance. The first paragraph compares the challenge of hitting a major league fastball to that of stopping a crank shot in lacrosse. The rest of the passage focuses on lacrosse, returning to the comparison to baseball in the third and fourth paragraphs. The description of quarterbacks is out of scope, so it should be deleted, (J). Choices G and H also concern the challenges faced by quarterbacks.

47. C
Difficulty: Medium
Category: Sentence Structure
Getting to the Answer: The words *that* and *which* often begin dependent clauses; when one of these words is included in an underlined portion, make sure it doesn't create a sentence fragment. As written, this sentence has no predicate verb. *Lacrosse* is the subject, but "is often referred to" is the verb for the clause that begins with *that* and describes *Lacrosse*. Removing *that* makes "is often referred to" the main verb; (C) is correct. Choices B and D do not correct the fragment error.

48. G
Difficulty: Medium
Category: Agreement
Getting to the Answer: An adverb can modify a verb, adjective, or another adverb; it cannot be used to modify a noun. Here, the adverb *brutally* is used to modify the noun *game*. The adjective form *brutal* in (G) is correct. Although *brute*, H, can be used as an adjective, it is incorrect in this context. Choice J uses *brutality*, which is a noun, where the adjective form is needed.

49. A
Difficulty: Medium
Category: Sentence Structure
Getting to the Answer: When the main difference in the answer choices is punctuation, remember your tested rules. A comma is not needed to separate two items connected with *and*. No change is needed, making (A) correct. Choice B uses a semicolon, which would only be correct if an independent clause

followed it. Choice C omits the conjunction, making the meaning of the sentence unclear. Choice D inserts a comma after *and*; commas are incorrect after the conjunctions in compounds.

50. G
Difficulty: High
Category: Agreement
Getting to the Answer: A pronoun and a verb are underlined, so you have several things to check. Make sure that the pronoun has a clear antecedent and is used consistently. Then make sure that the verb agrees with its subject and is in the correct tense. The pronoun *they* correctly refers to the *players*, but this paragraph is written in the present tense (*is, possess, stands, sprint*). The present tense *attempt* in (G) is correct. Choice F incorrectly uses the past tense. In the context of the paragraph, the author is not included among those playing lacrosse, so the pronoun *we* in choices H and J is incorrect.

51. C
Difficulty: Medium
Category: Organization
Getting to the Answer: The underlined portion is a transition word, so check whether the sentence is logically and grammatically correct. The transition connects the fastest recorded pitch speed with the fact that few pitchers can pitch at speeds in the upper nineties. The first idea is not the result of the second, so A is incorrect. The passage is citing statistics where no temporal relationship is implied; eliminate B. Choice D turns the sentence into a run-on. Choice (C) correctly contrasts the fastest recorded pitch with the idea that few pitchers come close to that record.

52. H
Difficulty: High
Category: Sentence Structure
Getting to the Answer: If you're not sure how to approach a tough Punctuation question, try boiling the sentence down to its basics. Identify the subject and verb in each clause. Remember that a single comma should not separate a subject from its verb. Eliminate the introductory phrase and dependent clause from this sentence, and you're left with "the fastest crank shots on goal, can reach 110 mph." The subject is "crank shots," and the verb is "can reach." There should be no comma separating them, so (H) is correct. Choice F treats "the fastest crank shots on goal" as a

nonessential phrase, but the sentence does not make sense without it. Choice G inserts two commas, treating "can" as nonessential. However, "can" is a necessary part of the verb phrase "can reach." Choice J places the comma between the two verbs in the verb phrase, which will never be correct.

53. D
Difficulty: Medium
Category: Conciseness
Getting to the Answer: Always consider redundancy when DELETE is an answer choice. "By high school players" is redundant in a sentence that begins "Even at the high school level." Choice (D) removes the redundant language. Choices B and C both contain redundancies.

54. H
Difficulty: Low
Category: Development
Getting to the Answer: When asked whether to add new information, first consider whether it is relevant. The information about the composition of the field is not relevant to the point about the difficulty of stopping a lacrosse shot. Eliminate F and G. Choice (H) accurately describes the irrelevance of the new information, so it is correct.

55. D
Difficulty: High
Category: Development
Getting to the Answer: When the answer choices are all single words with similar meanings, you are likely being tested on Precision. Choose the word that best describes the challenging job of the goalie. Choice A does not fit; to be absurd is to be ridiculous or meaningless, which does not apply to the goalie's job. Choice B is incorrect because a task cannot be *more* insurmountable; if it is insurmountable, the task cannot be done, and there is no way to have a higher degree of that failure. A harrowing event is deeply disturbing. While the goalie's job is challenging, we do not get a sense that the narrator is disturbed by the job. Rather, the narrator seems in awe of lacrosse goalies. Thus, C is incorrect. Choice (D), *difficult*, accurately describes the goalie's job.

56. G
Difficulty: Low
Category: Organization
Getting to the Answer: Think about what relationships these transitions depict. The preceding sentence gives an explanation of why a lacrosse goalie has a difficult task. This sentence adds to that explanation, telling you that players can make fake moves to trick the goalie. Choices F, H, and J all use transitions that indicate one idea is being added to another. Only (G) indicates a different relationship; "On the other hand" suggests a contrast between the ideas in the two sentences.

57. B
Difficulty: Medium
Category: Organization
Getting to the Answer: When asked to connect paragraphs, be sure you read through them, considering both subject matter and tone. The keyword *however* in the second sentence of Paragraph 4 tells you that there must be some sort of contrast between the first and second sentences. The second sentence also refers to "Both of these endeavors," so the sentence in question should discuss both hitting a major league pitch and blocking a crank shot. Only (B) meets both of these requirements. Choices A and C do not provide the contrast indicated by "however"; additionally, the slang phrase "is tough" in A is inconsistent with the tone of the rest of the passage. Choice D does not mention hitting a major league pitch, making "Both of these endeavors" in the second sentence illogical.

58. F
Difficulty: Medium
Category: Agreement
Getting to the Answer: Get in the habit of *matching* verbs with their subject nouns. Since the subject of the underlined verb is the plural *Both*, this sentence needs no change, (F). Choice G is singular and does not agree with the plural subject *Both*. Choice H changes the verb to the past tense, but the passage is in the present tense. Choice J uses the conditional *would have*, but there is nothing conditional or hypothetical about the writer's opinion.

59. B
Difficulty: Medium
Category: Agreement
Getting to the Answer: A pronoun is underlined, so the issue may be pronoun-antecedent agreement, ambiguity, or a pronoun shift. Check context clues. The preceding sentence uses the third-person pronoun *One*. Because the underlined sentence adds a thought to the preceding sentence, the pronouns should be consistent. This makes (B) correct. Choice A uses the second-person pronoun *you*. Choice C shifts to the third-person plural *they*. Choice D shifts from *one* to *he*; it also illogically changes the verb tense.

60. J
Difficulty: Medium
Category: Development
Getting to the Answer: This type of question requires you to determine the main idea of the passage. In the first paragraph, the writer argues that "stopping a crank shot in men's lacrosse" is "even tougher than taking a major league at-bat." All of the following details support this position. Choice (J) correctly identifies the main idea of the passage. Choices F and G are both automatically out, because the passage does not go into any depth about the strategies employed by baseball pitchers. Choice H is incorrect because the passage provides details in Paragraph 3 about the speeds achieved by baseball pitchers.

Thomas Edison, Tinfoil Cylinders, and MP3 Players

61. A
Difficulty: Medium
Category: Sentence Structure
Getting to the Answer: If you're not sure whether a phrase or clause should be set off from the sentence by commas, try reading the sentence without it. If the sentence no longer makes sense, then the commas are incorrect. The sentence is correct as written, (A). Choice B incorrectly separates the prepositional phrase "at a breakneck pace" from the verb it describes. Choices C and D both incorrectly insert a comma between the subject "formats" and the verb phrase "have come and gone."

62. H
Difficulty: High
Category: Organization
Getting to the Answer: More than one placement may create a grammatically correct sentence, so make sure that the sentence is also logical. What word in this sentence does *better* most logically describe? The main idea of the sentence is that the vinyl record replaced the gramophone, so something about the vinyl record must have been better than the gramophone. It makes the most sense to describe the vinyl record as sounding better, as in (H). Choice F places *better* before *supplanted*, which means *replaced*, but the sentence isn't comparing the way the vinyl record replaced the gramophone to the way another technology replaced the gramophone. Choice G puts *better* before *vinyl*, but *vinyl* isn't being compared to anything in the sentence that results. Choice J creates an illogical sentence, indicating that the gramophone was the better recording format even though it was replaced by the vinyl record.

63. C
Difficulty: Medium
Category: Sentence Structure
Getting to the Answer: The *-ing* verb form cannot be the predicate (main) verb in a sentence. As written, this sentence is a fragment. Choice (C) corrects this by providing a predicate verb without introducing any additional errors. Choices B and D do not address the error.

64. G
Difficulty: High
Category: Organization
Getting to the Answer: With Organization questions, focus on the relationship between ideas. The two ideas here are contrasted—a high school student might know about one older type of recording device but not the other. Choice (G) has the only contrasting transition word. Choices F and H incorrectly indicate a cause-and-effect relationship; it doesn't make sense that familiarity with the vinyl record would lead to unfamiliarity with the 8-track. Choice J uses *or*, which doesn't make sense in context. It wouldn't seem *curious* that younger people had either heard of one of these recording techniques or not heard of the other; what's *curious* is that they are familiar with the older one but not the more recent.

65. D
Difficulty: Medium
Category: Agreement
Getting to the Answer: A compound subject joined with *and* requires a plural verb form. The subject here is *DJs and those*, so the two verbs need to be in the plural form. Choice (D) is correct. Choices B and C change one verb but not the other.

66. J
Difficulty: Medium
Category: Conciseness
Getting to the Answer: Redundant information may be contained within the underlined selection, or the underlined information may be redundant because of information elsewhere in the sentence or paragraph. Since we already know that DJs and music-mixers *appreciate* vinyl recordings, it is redundant to also say that they *cherish* them; (J) is correct. Choice G does not address the error. Choice H is unnecessarily wordy.

67. A
Difficulty: Medium
Category: Development
Getting to the Answer: When asked whether to add new information, note the context surrounding the proposed addition. The passage focuses on changes in music-playing technology, so the new information is relevant, adding an interesting detail. Eliminate C and D. The passage does not make an argument, so B is incorrect. Choice (A) correctly states the reason for making the addition.

68. H
Difficulty: Medium
Category: Sentence Structure
Getting to the Answer: *Aside* words like *though*, *for example*, and *however* should be set off with commas since the sentence would still make sense without them. Choice (H) places the commas correctly. Choices F and J only use one of the necessary commas to separate *though* from the rest of the sentence. Choice G uses a semicolon, which is correct only when used to combine independent clauses.

69. C
Difficulty: High
Category: Sentence Structure
Getting to the Answer: Colons are used to introduce or emphasize a brief definition, explanation, or list.

The information after the underlined selection serves as an explanation of the *something different* to which the writer refers. Choice (C) correctly places a colon before this information. Choice A uses no punctuation, which makes the sentence hard to understand. Choice B incorrectly uses a semicolon between an independent clause and an explanatory phrase. Choice D uses a comma, which doesn't set off the explanation as well as the colon does.

70. G
Difficulty: Medium
Category: Organization
Getting to the Answer: When a transition word is underlined, check whether it makes sense logically and grammatically. The transition connects the fact that older technologies could not hold much music to the fact that newer technologies can hold more. These ideas stand in contrast to each other. Eliminate F and J because they lack contrast. Choice H is a contrast transition, but it makes the sentence ungrammatical. *Despite* cannot be a modifying phrase on its own, so eliminate H. Choice (G) is correct.

71. B
Difficulty: Medium
Category: Agreement
Getting to the Answer: Read idioms for both proper construction and logic in context. *Contrasting by* is idiomatically incorrect; the best choice here is (B), *Compared to*. Choice C uses incorrect grammatical structure. Choice D is idiomatically incorrect.

72. J
Difficulty: Medium
Category: Development
Getting to the Answer: Read all question stems carefully. The correct answer choice will maintain the passage's tone and satisfy the stated purpose. The question stem asks for a choice that will "help readers understand the [modern device's] storage capacity and size," so you can immediately eliminate choices F and H, which address the device's popularity, not its storage capacity. Both G and (J) discuss the modern device's storage capacity, but (J)'s information is more specific and better satisfies the requirement of the question stem by focusing on the current technology rather than future improvements.

73. B
Difficulty: High
Category: Development
Getting to the Answer: Note that the question stem indicates that the correct answer must achieve several goals: conclude the essay, respond to the question, and connect to the first paragraph. The question in the previous sentence asks the reader whether the "apex" in music recording has been achieved. The first paragraph introduces the idea that "Innovation in recording music has been constant." The remainder of the essay chronicles the history of developments in recording technology. Putting all these ideas together, an appropriate conclusion for this essay would likely answer that we haven't reached the "apex"; rather, history suggests that there will continue to be new technologies in music recording. This matches (B), which further evokes the first paragraph by referring to new developments as "miracles." Choice A is incorrect because it is the opposite of the author's claim in the essay; the author thinks recording technology has and will continue to improve. Although choice C lists examples from the essay and choice D refers to a detail from the first paragraph, they are incorrect because they do not address the question from the previous sentence by affirming that the history of music recording suggests that the technology will continue to improve.

74. F
Difficulty: Medium
Category: Organization
Getting to the Answer: The first sentence of a paragraph typically introduces the topic of the paragraph, so look for the paragraph that contains details related to this sentence. Paragraph 2 explains how the gramophone record was replaced by the vinyl phonograph record. The new sentence introduces the idea that the gramophone record's popularity did not last, so the beginning of Paragraph 2 is the most logical placement. Choice (F) is correct. The gramophone is not mentioned in Paragraphs 3, 4, or 5.

75. D
Difficulty: Medium
Category: Development
Getting to the Answer: This is a question about the main idea of the essay. By determining the main idea, you can quickly eliminate two answer choices. The main idea of the essay is that recording formats have

changed and improved rapidly since the 1870s and are likely to continue changing rapidly. This main idea does not include any technical explanation of how sounds are recorded, so you can immediately eliminate A and B. Choice C can also be ruled out since, far from discussing "a limited number of recording formats," this essay mentions nearly all of them; (D) is correct.

Mathematics Test

1. E
Difficulty: Low
Category: Number and Quantity
Getting to the Answer: To add or subtract fractions, you must first write them over the same denominator.

$$1\frac{2}{3}+2\frac{3}{4}=\frac{5}{3}+\frac{11}{4}=\frac{20}{12}+\frac{33}{12}=\frac{53}{12}=4\frac{5}{12}$$

Or, alternatively, plug the numbers into your calculator: $1.6667+2.75=4.4167$. When you enter (E) into your calculator, you get the same result.

2. H
Difficulty: Low
Category: Algebra
Getting to the Answer: The signs (multiplication dots) between these terms say to *multiply*—keep that in mind as you apply the rules for exponents. Be careful not to leave any parts out or multiply by any part more than once. First, multiply the number parts together: $2\cdot3\cdot6=36$, which immediately eliminates F and G. Then, x times x is x^2, which eliminates J. Now multiply the y's to get $y^3\cdot y^2\cdot y^2=y^{3+2+2}=y^7$, so (H) is correct. Remember that you're counting the number of y's that are being multiplied, so add the exponents.

3. A
Difficulty: Low
Category: Number and Quantity
Getting to the Answer: Make sure you solve for what the question is asking. Incorrect answer choices will often be other parts of the question or steps along the way. Ms. Ruppin earns $\frac{\$51,940}{245}=\$212$ per day. The company will save $\$212-\$140=\$72$ by paying the replacement instead, which is (A). Note that E is Ms. Ruppin's pay and C is the replacement's pay. Don't fall for the traditional traps.

4. J
Difficulty: Medium
Category: Statistics and Probability
Getting to the Answer: Answering questions about averages always starts the same way: set up the formula using the given information. The average is equal to the sum of the terms divided by the number of terms. Let x be the fifth test score. Then the equation for this question is:

$$\frac{52 + 70 + 76 + 79 + x}{5} = 75$$

$$\frac{277 + x}{5} = 75$$

$$277 + x = 375$$

$$x = 98$$

Choice (J) is correct.

5. C
Difficulty: Low
Category: Number and Quantity
Getting to the Answer: This may seem like a complicated question, but the first sentence tells you everything you need to answer the question. Divide the amount of water vapor per cubic meter, 6.7 grams, by the maximum, 19.2 grams:

$$\frac{6.7}{19.2} \approx 0.34896 = 34.896\% \approx 35\%$$

Choice (C) is correct.

6. J
Difficulty: Low
Category: Geometry
Getting to the Answer: Try to translate what you're asked for into concepts that you know. This question asks for the distance around the pool, also known as the perimeter. To find the perimeter of a rectangle, add up all the sides, keeping in mind that opposite sides have the same lengths: $2(30) + 2(10) = 80$ feet, which is (J).

7. C
Difficulty: Low
Category: Number and Quantity
Getting to the Answer: Keep careful track of units. A film that is 3 hours, 40 minutes long will be a total of $(3 \times 60) + 40 = 220$ minutes long. Half that is $\frac{220}{2} = 110$ minutes, or 1 hour, 50 minutes, making (C) the correct answer.

8. F
Difficulty: Low
Category: Algebra
Getting to the Answer: Watching your positives and negatives is key! Subtracting when you mean to add (or vice versa) will lead you straight to an incorrect answer choice.

$$2x - 5 = 7x + 3$$

$$-5 = 5x + 3$$

$$-8 = 5x$$

$$-\frac{8}{5} = x$$

Choice (F) is correct.

9. D
Difficulty: Low
Category: Functions
Getting to the Answer: Sometimes Backsolving will be much easier than trying to work out the algebra. You're not going to be able to tell whether you need a larger or smaller number here, so start with A and work your way down until you have the answer.

A: $22 - 13 = 9$ and $49 - 31 = 18$. The difference between the first pair and the last pair is not the same. Eliminate.

B: $23 - 13 = 10$ and $49 - 39 = 10$. So far so good, but what about going from the second to the third number? $39 - 23 = 16$, which is not the same as the difference between the other pairs. Eliminate.

C: $24 - 13 = 11$ and $49 - 38 = 11$. However, $38 - 24$ is 14, not 11. Eliminate.

(D): $25 - 13 = 12$, $49 - 37 = 12$, and $37 - 25 = 12$. With a difference of 12, the sequence 13, 25, 37, 49 works. Choice (D) is correct.

If you would rather approach the question algebraically, imagine that you're adding the same thing three times in order to get from 13 to 49 (since you always add the same amount to get the next number). This means that:

$$13 + 3x = 49$$

$$3x = 36$$

$$x = 12$$

The difference is 12, which means the next two numbers are $13 + 12 = 25$ and $25 + 12 = 37$. You can check that $37 + 12 = 49$. Choice (D) is correct.

10. J
Difficulty: Medium
Category: Algebra
Getting to the Answer: Keeping the values for $\sqrt{x}$, x, and x^2 straight is important. It's easy to quit a step too soon and confuse x with $\sqrt{x}$.

$$x = \sqrt[3]{729} = 729^{\frac{1}{3}} = 9$$

$$\sqrt{x} + x^2 = \sqrt{9} + 9^2 = 3 + 81 = 84$$

Choice (J) is correct.

11. A
Difficulty: Low
Category: Number and Quantity
Getting to the Answer: If you divide 1 by 11 on your calculator, it will most likely stop after 8 or 10 digits. This should be enough for you to see which numbers repeat. Here, the 09 repeats again and again, so write the bar over 09. Choice (A) is correct. The other answer choices repeat the wrong digits or fail to show that the digits repeat.

12. K
Difficulty: Medium
Category: Statistics and Probability
Getting to the Answer: Pay close attention to words like *not* and *except*—these will make all the difference in a question. Probability is defined as the ratio of the number of desired outcomes to the total number of possible outcomes. The total number of balls in the bag is $10 + 10 + 8 = 28$. The number of non-green balls is $10 + 10 = 20$. The probability of choosing a ball that isn't green is $\frac{20}{28} = \frac{5}{7}$, which is (K).

13. A
Difficulty: Low
Category: Geometry
Getting to the Answer: Remember the rules for parallel lines and transversals. All acute angles are equal, and all obtuse angles are equal. If a is 110, then the corresponding angle below it has the same measure. If you also remember that the angle measure of a straight line is 180°, you're in good shape.

$$110 + d = 180 \rightarrow d = 70$$
$$b + c = 180 \text{ (because the two angles form a straight line)}$$
$$b + c + d = 180 + 70 = 250$$

Choice (A) is correct.

14. J
Difficulty: Medium
Category: Functions
Getting to the Answer: When a question includes a graph, be sure to fully understand it before trying to answer the question. Erin reached an altitude of 4,500 feet at 8 a.m. She stayed at or above 4,500 feet until the final hour of her hike. This suggests that she was at or above 4,500 feet for at least 4 full hours. She descended the final 750 feet at a constant speed in one hour. More specifically, she descended the 250 feet from 4,750 feet to 4,500 feet in 20 minutes. Therefore, she was at or above 4,500 feet for 4 hours 20 minutes, which is (J).

15. A
Difficulty: High
Category: Functions
Getting to the Answer: The question states that during each one-hour interval, Erin traveled at a constant speed. Therefore, a graph showing her speed should remain constant (horizontal on the graph) within each one-hour interval. The only graph that does this is graph (A). All other graphs show a change in speed during each interval, which suggests an acceleration or deceleration and, ultimately, movement at speeds that are not constant.

16. H
Difficulty: Low
Category: Algebra
Getting to the Answer: You don't need to calculate every row, column, and diagonal—because they should all be equal, you just need to look at one row or column that doesn't contain the middle square and one row, column, or diagonal that does contain the middle square. The first column sums to $-3x - 6x + 3x = -6x$. The second column should have the same sum. Call the missing square m:

$$4x + m - 8x = -6x$$
$$m - 4x = -6x$$
$$m = -2x$$

Choice (H) is correct.

17. E

Difficulty: Medium

Category: Number and Quantity

Getting to the Answer: Sometimes, part of the challenge of questions involving units of measurement is making such units—here, seconds and hours—consistent. To keep the units organized, consider using the factor-label method:

$$\frac{3\text{ ft}}{1\text{ sec}} \times \frac{60\text{ sec}}{1\text{ min}} \times 30\text{ min} = 5{,}400\text{ ft}$$

Choice (E) is correct.

18. J

Difficulty: Low

Category: Statistics and Probability

Getting to the Answer: Once you know the rule, all questions like this are straightforward. Simply multiply the number of possibilities for each type to arrive at $5 \times 8 \times 3 = 120$, or (J).

19. A

Difficulty: Medium

Category: Number and Quantity

Getting to the Answer: Blindly doing calculations is not a good way to approach a question like this—many incorrect answers involve doing the incorrect calculations with the given numbers. Make a plan before you start manipulating numbers. Set up a proportion using the ratio of grain to bread. Be sure to keep track of the zeroes.

$$\frac{90{,}000}{150{,}000} = \frac{x}{6{,}000}$$

$$\frac{9}{15} = \frac{x}{6{,}000}$$

$$54{,}000 = 15x$$

$$3{,}600 = x$$

Choice (A) is the answer.

20. H

Difficulty: Medium

Category: Number and Quantity

Getting to the Answer: When you know that the given parts add up to the whole, then you can turn a part-to-part ratio into two part-to-whole ratios—put each term

of the ratio over the sum of the terms. Here, because all the numbers in the set must be either even or odd, the parts do add up to the whole. The sum of the terms in the ratio 2:3 is 5, so the part-to-whole ratio for even numbers in the set to all the numbers in the set is 2:5. Use this to find the percent:

$$\frac{\text{Even numbers}}{\text{All the numbers}} = \frac{2}{5} \times 100\% = \frac{200\%}{5} = 40\%$$

That's (H).

21. E

Difficulty: Medium

Category: Algebra

Getting to the Answer: If you're not comfortable simplifying the expressions on the left to see if they match the expressions on the right, you can Pick Numbers for a, b, and c, although this is likely to take more time. Algebraically, choice A is true because you can cancel the factor b in the numerator and denominator of the expression on the left. Choice B is true based on rules of exponents: $a^1 \cdot a^1 = a^{1+1} = a^2$, and the same for b. Choice C is true because both the numerator and the denominator equal ab, and anything divided by itself equals 1 (except for zero, but that's not relevant here). Choice D is true: $\frac{a+b}{b} = \frac{a}{b} + \frac{b}{b} = \frac{a}{b} + 1$. Choice (E) is false because you cannot divide the first terms and the second terms separately. When you divide, you can only divide out factors (things that are multiplied in both the numerator and denominator), not terms (things that are added or subtracted in the numerator and denominator).

22. K

Difficulty: Medium

Category: Algebra

Getting to the Answer: Even if you forgot what the slope-intercept form looks like, the answer choices tell you to solve for y. Before you start moving the x term and the constant, notice that if you add y to both sides of the equation, your work is done. The result is $-3x + 7 = y$, which matches (K).

23. B
Difficulty: Medium
Category: Algebra
Getting to the Answer: Before you factor a quadratic equation, make sure one side is equal to zero. Here, $x^2 - 8x = 8x$ becomes $x^2 - 16x = 0$.

$$x^2 - 16x = 0$$
$$x(x - 16) = 0$$
$$x = 0 \quad \text{or} \quad x - 16 = 0$$
$$x = 0 \quad \text{or} \quad x = 16$$

The latter answer is (B).

24. J
Difficulty: Medium
Category: Number and Quantity
Getting to the Answer: Be sure not to be tempted by answers that are partly right. The inequality $x \geq 1$ describes the right half of the values on the number line but leaves out the left half. The selected values on the number line consist of 1, everything greater than 1, -1, and everything less than -1. The easiest way to describe this set is that the absolute value of x, or its distance from zero on the number line, is greater than or equal to 1. This can be written in mathematical notation as $|x| \geq 1$. Thus, (J) is correct.

25. E
Difficulty: Medium
Category: Geometry
Getting to the Answer: Even if a question talks about rounding, the correct answer may require no rounding whatsoever. The distance from a point to a line is measured perpendicularly, so you can be sure that the triangle is a right triangle. Because this distance is perpendicular and measured from the radius, it bisects the chord, which means the base of the triangle is 15. Use the Pythagorean theorem (or your knowledge of common Pythagorean triplets) to find the length of the hypotenuse, r:

$$8^2 + 15^2 = r^2$$
$$r = \sqrt{8^2 + 15^2}$$
$$= \sqrt{64 + 225}$$
$$= \sqrt{289} = 17$$

That's (E).

26. G
Difficulty: Medium
Category: Algebra
Getting to the Answer: Don't confuse your variables—here you're given V and you need to solve for t:

$$V = \frac{5}{3}t + 0.05$$
$$0.575 = \frac{5}{3}t + 0.05$$
$$0.525 = \frac{5}{3}t$$
$$t = \left(\frac{3}{5}\right)0.525 = 0.315$$

Choice (G) is correct.

27. B
Difficulty: Medium
Category: Geometry
Getting to the Answer: If a question seems confusing, try rewording it in simpler terms. The sand over the soccer field will make a rectangular prism, and you're looking for the height if the volume is 15,000 cubic yards. The volume of a rectangular prism is length times width times height. The length of this soccer field is $100 + 18 + 18 = 136$ yards, the width is 60.5 yards, and the height is unknown. Put this information into an equation with the volume of sand:

$$l \cdot w \cdot h = V$$
$$136 \cdot 60.5 \cdot h = 15,000$$
$$8,228h = 15,000$$
$$h \approx 1.82$$

The value of h is between 1 and 2, making (B) the correct answer.

28. G
Difficulty: Medium
Category: Geometry
Getting to the Answer: Most of the trigonometry on the ACT simply tests whether you know the definitions of sine, cosine, and tangent. Remember the method for finding the three basic trigonometric functions: SOHCAHTOA tells you that cosine is calculated by

dividing the adjacent side by the hypotenuse. Let x be the length of $\overline{AC}$.

$$\cos A = \frac{\text{adjacent}}{\text{hypotenuse}}$$

$$\frac{4}{5} = \frac{x}{18}$$

$$5x = 4(18)$$

$$5x = 72$$

$$x = 14.4$$

Choice (G) is correct.

29. A
Difficulty: Medium
Category: Statistics and Probability
Getting to the Answer: Don't automatically start calculating the actual numbers of beds—the graph is already sufficient to answer this question. Bedtime has 2.5 pictures of beds (each representing 100 actual beds). There's a total of $1.5 + 2 + 4 + 2.5 = 10$ pictures of beds. So the fraction of the total beds that are at Bedtime is $\frac{2.5}{10} = \frac{25}{100} = \frac{1}{4}$, which is (A).

30. G
Difficulty: Medium
Category: Geometry
Getting to the Answer: Sometimes drawing a good diagram (or strategically using the one given) will be key to answering a question. Here, you should add the given measures to the figure to get started:

Because $26 + 20 = 46$, the overlapping part, BC, must be $46 - 38 = 8$, which is (G). If you didn't see that right away, you can always calculate from one piece to another. If $AC = 26$ and $AD = 38$, CD must be 12. If $CD = 12$ and $BD = 20$, BC must be 8, which again is (G).

31. A
Difficulty: Medium
Category: Algebra
Getting to the Answer: The intersection of two lines is simply the one (x,y) point that makes both equations true. You can solve this like any system of equations.

$$4x + 10 = 5x + 7$$

$$10 = x + 7$$

$$3 = x$$

Choice (A) is correct. If you had accidentally solved for the y-coordinate, you would have gotten E. Look out for traps like this in coordinate geometry questions.

32. H
Difficulty: Medium
Category: Number and Quantity
Getting to the Answer: To get Meri's rate in pages per hour, take the 96 pages and divide by the time in hours. The time is given as "2 hours and 40 minutes." Forty minutes is $\frac{2}{3}$ of an hour, so you can express Meri's time as $2\frac{2}{3}$ hours, or $\frac{8}{3}$ hours:

$$\text{Pages per hour} = \frac{96 \text{ pages}}{\frac{8}{3} \text{ hours}}$$

$$= 96 \times \frac{3}{8} = 36 \text{ pg/hr}$$

This matches (H).

33. B
Difficulty: High
Category: Statistics and Probability
Getting to the Answer: If an integer is chosen randomly from the first 50 integers, the probability of choosing any particular number is $\frac{1}{50}$, and the probability of choosing an integer with a digit of 3 is the number of integers with a digit of 3 divided by 50. The integers 3, 13, 23, 30, 31, 32, 33, 34, 35, 36, 37, 38, 39, and 43 are the only integers with 3s in them, for a total of 14 different integers, so the probability is $\frac{14}{50}$ or $\frac{7}{25}$, which is (B).

34. F
Difficulty: Medium
Category: Algebra
Getting to the Answer: This question is much easier than it looks. Plug the expression given for *s* into the cubed expression and see what happens:

$$(t - \boxed{s})^3 = (t - (\boxed{4 + t}))^3$$
$$= (t - 4 - t)^3$$
$$= (-4)^3 = (-4)(-4)(-4) = -64$$

That's (F).

35. D
Difficulty: High
Category: Geometry
Getting to the Answer: Feel free to draw all over your test booklet—that's what it's there for. This question tests your ability to read coordinates and to find a midpoint (although you may not realize this at first glance). Set up a coordinate system to compare points *B* and *F*. Because you're trying to find the distance relative to *A*, make *A* (0,0). Then *B* is at (800,0). Use the labeled distances to find the *x*-value of *F*, which is 700 (*AB − DC − FE*), and the *y*-value, which is 600 (*CB − DE*). This means *F* is at (700,600). The lookout point is at the midpoint of *B* and *F*, so you can use the midpoint formula:

$$\left(\frac{800 + 700}{2}, \frac{0 + 600}{2}\right) = (750,300)$$

Using these coordinates, the lookout is 750 yards to the right (east) of point *A* and 300 yards up (north), which is (D).

36. K
Difficulty: Low
Category: Algebra
Getting to the Answer: Carefully translate potentially intimidating word problems. "Fifteen pounds less than" tells you to subtract 15 from some quantity.

That quantity is three times the weight of the second-place watermelon, or 3*w*, so 3*w* − 15 is the correct expression. Choice (K) is correct. Picking Numbers can also help if you have difficulty translating. Pick *w* = 10. Three times this quantity is 30 and 15 less than 30 is 15. Substitute 10 for *w* in each of the answer choices, eliminating any choice that does not equal 15:

F: 10 − 5 = 5 Eliminate.
G: 10 + 15 = 25 Eliminate.
H: 10 − 15 = −5 Eliminate
J: 3(10) − 15 = 15 Eliminate.
(K): 3(10) − 15 = 15 Keep.

The only expression that works is (K).

37. E
Difficulty: Medium
Category: Number and Quantity
Getting to the Answer: If you remembered that any number squared is positive, a quick look at the answer choices would tell you that (E), x^2y^2, will be positive for any nonzero values of *x* and *y*, and is therefore the correct answer. If you didn't remember that, you should make a note of it, because it's a very important concept. You can also solve this one by Picking Numbers. If *xy* is negative, then either *x* or *y* is negative and the other is positive because a negative times a positive equals a negative. Picking a couple of pairs of numbers for *x* and *y* will tell you that both *x − y* and *y − x* can be either positive or negative depending on the exact values of *x* and *y*; x^2y will be negative if *y* is negative, and xy^2 will be negative if *x* is negative. However, any values you pick for *x* and *y* will give you a positive number for x^2y^2, so again, (E) is correct.

38. F
Difficulty: High
Category: Number and Quantity
Getting to the Answer: Picking Numbers is the easiest, fastest way to answer this question. Choose a pair of numbers from each set and add them together. If you are unable to prove immediately that a set does not have the property described in the question stem, you may want to choose another pair. In set I, if you add 2 and 4, you get 6. Adding 12 and 8 gives you 20. Adding −2 and 8 gives you 6. Because each sum is a member of the set of even integers, set I seems to be true. For set II, adding 3 and 5 yields 8, which is not an odd integer. Therefore, set II is not true. Finally, if you

add two primes, say 2 and 3, you get 5. That example is true. If you add 3 and 5, however, you get 8, and 8 is not a prime number. Therefore, only set I has the property, and the answer is (F).

39. C
Difficulty: Medium
Category: Geometry
Getting to the Answer: Similar triangles have equal angles and proportional sides. Be sure to keep track of which side is proportional to which—the longest side of one triangle goes with the longest side of the other triangle and so on. Use the given ratio and the fact that the longest side of the second triangle has length 12 to set up a proportion comparing the longest sides of both triangles and the shortest sides of both triangles:

$$\frac{12}{20} = \frac{x}{15}$$

$$20x = 12(15)$$

$$20x = 180$$

$$x = 9$$

Choice (C) is correct.

40. K
Difficulty: Medium
Category: Geometry
Getting to the Answer: The angles of triangle YXZ sum to 180°, so:

$$m\angle YZX + 20° + 95° = 180°$$

$$m\angle YZX = 65°$$

The bases of the trapezoid, $\overline{WX}$ and $\overline{YZ}$, are parallel, making $\angle YZX$ and $\angle TXZ$ alternate interior angles relative to transversal XZ. This means $m\angle TXZ = 65°$, which is (K).

41. B
Difficulty: High
Category: Functions
Getting to the Answer: Knowing the basic trig values for benchmark angles (multiples of 30° and 45°) would certainly help here. However, Backsolving also works because there are numbers in the answer choices. Use

your calculator to find the sine of each angle (make sure your calculator is in "degree" mode first). Note that $\frac{\sqrt{3}}{2}$ is approximately equal to 0.866.

sin 30° = 0.5
sin 45° ≈ 0.7071
sin 60° ≈ 0.866
sin 120° ≈ 0.866
sin 135° ≈ 0.7071
sin 150° = 0.5

Choice (B) is correct.

42. F
Difficulty: Medium
Category: Number and Quantity
Getting to the Answer: When given two ratios, make sure you check whether the second one is a fraction of the first group or a fraction of the total. The number of students continuing their studies = $\frac{1}{3}(896) \approx 299$. Of that 299, the number of students going to law school is $\frac{2}{5}(299) \approx 120$, which is (F).

43. D
Difficulty: Medium
Category: Number and Quantity
Getting to the Answer: Knowing what each letter in the mnemonic "PEMDAS" represents will make simple number operations questions a breeze on test day. Substitute the values for a, b, and c, and evaluate the expression following the order of operations: $(a+b)(c-a) = (-2+4)[7-(-2)] = (2)(9) = 18$. Choice (D) is the correct answer.

44. G
Difficulty: High
Category: Functions
Getting to the Answer: If you remember your properties of logs, this question is very straightforward. Because $\log_b b^x = x$, the value of x is $\sqrt{7} \approx 2.65$, which lies between 2 and 3. Choice (G) is correct.

If you don't remember this property, you'll have to rewrite the logarithmic equation as an exponential equation and solve: $\log_7 7^{\sqrt{7}} = x$ is equivalent to the exponential form $7^x = 7^{\sqrt{7}}$. The bases are the same (7), so the exponents must be equal. This means $x = \sqrt{7} \approx 2.65$, which lies between 2 and 3.

45. C
Difficulty: Low
Category: Statistics and Probability
Getting to the Answer: If a question that involves reading a table or chart seems easy, it probably is. All you have to do is be careful that you don't make an arithmetic error. Carefully calculate the number of employees by division, then add to find the total:

Development = $1 \times 4 = 4$
Marketing = $2 \times 3 = 6$
Accounting = $3 \times 2 = 6$
Public Relations = $5 \times 5 = 25$

Total: $4 + 6 + 6 + 25 = 41$

That's (C).

46. J
Difficulty: Medium
Category: Number and Quantity
Getting to the Answer: Even though this question uses the word *percent*, you are never asked to find the actual percent itself. Set this question up as a proportion to get the answer more quickly. Use the definition: percent change equals amount of change divided by original amount.

$$\frac{16 - 6}{6} = \frac{x - 12}{12}$$
$$\frac{10}{6} = \frac{x - 12}{12}$$
$$120 = 6(x - 12)$$
$$120 = 6x - 72$$
$$192 = 6x$$
$$32 = x$$

Choice (J) is correct.

47. D
Difficulty: High
Category: Geometry
Getting to the Answer: Concepts such as "tangent to" are less scary if you work on becoming more comfortable with math vocabulary. It also helps to draw a sketch like the one below:

As you can see in the sketch, the center of the circle is at $(4,4)$, and the radius is 4. In the equation of a circle, $(x - h)^2 + (y - k)^2 = r^2$, the center is at (h,k), and the radius is r. Plug in the information you know to get $(x - 4)^2 + (y - 4)^2 = 4^2$, which is (D). If you're stuck, try plugging in a few points. For example, using either $(4,0)$ or $(0,4)$ eliminates all answers except B and (D), and $(4,8)$ eliminates B.

48. H
Difficulty: High
Category: Number and Quantity
Getting to the Answer: The average speed is the total distance traveled divided by the total hours traveled. Liza drove at 40 miles per hour for 2 hours, for a total of 40×2, or 80 miles. If she increased her speed by 25%, then she increased her speed by $0.25(40) = 10$, so her new speed was $40 + 10 = 50$ miles per hour. So she drove at 50 miles per hour for the next 3 hours, for a total of $50 \times 3 = 150$ miles. She went 80 miles and then 150 miles, for a total of 230 miles, and she drove for 2 hours and then for 3 hours, for a total of 5 hours. Liza's average rate for the trip was 230 miles divided by 5 hours, or 46 miles per hour, making (H) the correct answer.

49. A
Difficulty: Medium
Category: Number and Quantity
Getting to the Answer: Even if you're not sure how to perform operations on matrices, you can probably reason out the answer. The number of people who will leave Marketing is $0.3(20) = 6$. You can compute the number for each department, then add them all together. This will give you the same result as multiplying the matrices.

$$[20 \quad 12 \quad 40 \quad 10] \begin{bmatrix} 0.3 \\ 0.5 \\ 0.2 \\ 0.4 \end{bmatrix}$$

$$= 20(0.3) + 12(0.5) + 40(0.2) + 10(0.4)$$
$$= 6 + 6 + 8 + 4 = 24$$

Choice (A) is correct.

50. J
Difficulty: Medium
Category: Statistics and Probability
Getting to the Answer: The expected value of a random discrete variable is the weighted average of all possible values that the variable can take on. The weights are determined by the probability distribution. To find the expected value, multiply each possible value by its given probability and then add the products:

$$E(X) = \frac{1}{5}(10) + \frac{1}{10}(11) + \frac{3}{10}(12) + \frac{3}{20}(13) + \frac{1}{4}(14)$$

$$= 2 + \frac{11}{10} + \frac{36}{10} + \frac{39}{20} + \frac{14}{4}$$

$$= \frac{40}{20} + \frac{22}{20} + \frac{72}{20} + \frac{39}{20} + \frac{70}{20}$$

$$= \frac{243}{20} = 12\frac{3}{20}$$

Choice (J) is correct.

51. A
Difficulty: Medium
Category: Algebra
Getting to the Answer: Don't get too caught up in the language—figure out what the solution is, then think about which answer choice means that. Subtract x from both sides: $-2 < -5$. When is -2 less than -5? Never. What set has nothing in it? The empty set, which is (A).

52. G
Difficulty: High
Category: Functions
Getting to the Answer: The fastest route to the correct answer here (because you're given a graph of the parent square root function) is to write the domain and range of $g(x)$ and then adjust the values based on the transformation. The x-values of the curve shown in the graph begin at 0 and extend to the right indefinitely, so the domain is $x \geq 0$. The transformation $(x + 1)$ shifts the graph to the left 1 unit, so the domain of $h(x)$ is $x \geq -1$. Eliminate H, J, and K. Likewise, the y-values of the curve shown in the graph begin at 0 and extend upward indefinitely, so the range is $y \geq 0$. The transformation $(+3)$ shifts the graph up 3 units, so the range of $h(x)$ is $y \geq 3$. This means (G) is correct.

Note that you could also quickly sketch the graph of $h(x)$ to find its domain and range. The graph would look like the dashed curve below:

53. B
Difficulty: High
Category: Geometry
Getting to the Answer: Once you're strong on the basics, combining two concepts on seemingly complex questions like this one will be a breeze! The percent who chose one of the four named teachers is 25% + 15% + 35% + 5% = 80%. This means that 20% of the answers were grouped under "Other." A circle has 360 degrees, so the measure of the Other sector will be 20% of 360, or 0.2(360) = 72°, which is (B).

54. J
Difficulty: Medium
Category: Functions
Getting to the Answer: Because you're looking for the sixth term of the sequence, call the sixth term x. Every term in this sequence is formed by multiplying the previous term by 3 and then subtracting 1, so the seventh term must be formed by multiplying the sixth term, x, by 3, and then subtracting 1; in other words, the seventh term is equal to $3x - 1$. Because the seventh term is 365, you have $365 = 3x - 1$. You can solve for x by adding 1 to both sides of the equation and then dividing by 3. The result is $x = 122$, which is (J).

55. A
Difficulty: Medium
Category: Geometry
Getting to the Answer: A great way to test inequalities is to plug in a point or two. All the points in the shaded region of the graph should work in *both* inequalities. However, a more algebraic approach may save some time. Because only values of x greater than 6 are shaded, $x \geq 6$ should be one of the inequalities, eliminating E. Because the area *above* the slanted line is shaded, the other inequality should have a $\geq$ symbol,

eliminating C and D. To choose between (A) and B, examine the slanted line more closely. From the dot at the origin to the dot at (6,2), the line rises 2 units and runs 6 units, so the slope of the line is $\frac{1}{3}$, making (A) the correct answer.

56. K
Difficulty: High
Category: Functions
Getting to the Answer: The question asks you to evaluate the function $f(x)$, replacing x with $(x+c)$. Replace any instance of x in the function definition with $x+c$. This means that $2(x+7)$ will be $2(x+c+7)$. Use the distributive property and multiply each term in parentheses by 2 to get $2x+2c+2(7)$, or $2x+2c+14$, which is (K).

57. C
Difficulty: Medium
Category: Geometry
Getting to the Answer: If the answer choices are ranges of numbers, you might be able to save time by rounding numbers and estimating values. Start by finding the volume of the swimming pool: $V = \pi r^2 h = \pi(6)^2(4) = \pi(36)(4) = 144\pi$ cubic feet. To find the weight of the water in the pool, multiply the pool's volume in cubic meters by the weight of 1 cubic foot: 144π cubic feet $\times$ 62 pounds per cubic feet $= 8,928\pi$ pounds. Because the answer choices consist of large ranges of numbers, you can estimate the volume by rounding π to the nearest whole number, which is 3. Using 3 as an estimate for π, $8,928\pi$ pounds is approximately 26,784 pounds, making (C) correct.

58. G
Difficulty: Medium
Category: Geometry
Getting to the Answer: Drawing a triangle and flipping it over the y-axis will help you visualize this situation and others like it. Choose nice coordinates to represent A and see what happens to those coordinates:

Based on the diagram, the y-coordinate stays the same, and the x-coordinate goes from positive to negative. This means that (v,w) will become $(-v,w)$, which is (G).

59. C
Difficulty: High
Category: Algebra
Getting to the Answer: To get a in terms of b, you'll first need to get c in terms of b, because c is the variable the two equations have in common.

$$b = 3 - 2c$$
$$b + 2c = 3$$
$$2c = 3 - b$$
$$c = \frac{3 - b}{2}$$
$$a = 6c + 7$$
$$a = 6\left(\frac{3-b}{2}\right) + 7$$
$$a = 3(3 - b) + 7$$
$$a = 9 - 3b + 7$$
$$a = 16 - 3b$$

A perfect match for (C)!

60. K
Difficulty: High
Category: Number and Quantity
Getting to the Answer: You don't have to know anything about complex numbers ahead of time. All the information you need is in the question stem. Treat i as a variable, write the squared binomials as repeated multiplication, FOIL, and replace i^2 with -1 whenever it appears:

$$\frac{(2i+2)^2}{(2i-2)^2} = \frac{(2i+2)(2i+2)}{(2i-2)(2i-2)}$$
$$= \frac{4i^2 + 4i + 4i + 4}{4i^2 - 4i - 4i + 4}$$
$$= \frac{4(-1) + 8i + 4}{4(-1) - 8i + 4}$$
$$= \frac{8i}{-8i} = -1$$

Choice (K) is correct.

Reading Test

Passage I

Suggested Passage Map Notes:

¶1: dog vs. doggie

¶2: describes doggie look; doggie grows on you; called "Dumps"

¶3: meeting Dumps: dog running; angry man

¶4: afraid of dog, but dog whines

¶5: owner wants to hurt dog

¶6–9: argue about dog

¶10: narrator threatens owner

¶11–12: owner changes and claims kindness to dog

¶13: owner story: loves dog, got new job, dog escapes, must drive dog back

¶14–15: narrator doubts story, offers to buy dog

BIG PICTURE SUMMARY:

Main idea: Despite his rough appearance, Dumps the doggie evokes affection. The author met Dumps when the dog was running from his possibly abusive former owner.

Author's purpose: To describe his dog, his affection for his dog, and the circumstances under which he first met his dog

1. A
Difficulty: High
Category: Inference
Getting to the Answer: Review the narrator's discussion of dogs in paragraph 1. In paragraph 2, the narrator notes that people may not initially notice his doggie's "finer qualities," but they will see his "amiable spirit" after getting to know him. Predict that while both dogs and the narrator's doggie are companionable, the main distinction is that his doggie must be less initially appealing; this matches (A). Choice B is incorrect because the narrator never discusses the relative ages of any dog or doggie. Choice C cannot be correct because a "forgiving disposition" (lines 7–8) is attributed to dogs, while

the correct answer must reflect a trait of his doggie. Likewise, D reflects the narrator's description of dogs in paragraph 1.

2. H
Difficulty: Medium
Category: Detail
Getting to the Answer: List the characteristics of Dumps before looking at the answer choices. The narrator states that his "finer qualities" are not obvious but goes on to describe his other features in lines 11–25. Predict: Dumps is mangy-looking, but friendly. This matches (H). Choice F is incorrect because his eyes are described as having a "luster" rather than being "dull." Choice G is the opposite; the narrator claims "you don't at once perceive" his mental qualities. Choice J is a distortion because while the dog is certainly hairy, he resembles a "ragged doormat" rather than something "well-groomed."

3. B
Difficulty: Medium
Category: Inference
Getting to the Answer: Consider the scene in paragraphs 3–4. Dumps is described as "active," "yelping," and running so quickly that he was kicking up stones. The narrator also notes hearing "the voice of an angry man." Though the narrator expects the dog to "snap" at him, the dog instead approaches him in a "piteous" manner. This matches (B). Choice A does not match the description of a dog running "wildly." Choice C is too extreme; the dog is trying to escape the "angry man," but he is running away, so he is clearly not so upset that he is "immobilized." Choice D is a distortion: the narrator states in the next paragraph that the owner "seemed about to fling" a "thick stick" at the dog (lines 52–53), not toss a stick in a playful manner.

4. F
Difficulty: Low
Category: Vocab-in-Context
Getting to the Answer: The dog's owner is ready to throw a stick at the dog, so the narrator "checks" him by shouting a threat. The narrator is trying to stop the owner from hurting the dog, so predict "checked" means stopped. This matches (F), "prevented." The scene has nothing to do with a square design, G, and

the narrator is not merely "verifying" something, H, but shouting to prevent an act of violence. "Assaulted," J, is too extreme for a verbal response and lacks the necessary connotation of preventing the throw.

5.   D
Difficulty: High
Category: Function
Getting to the Answer: When stopped, the owner scowls and claims that "A man may do as he likes with his own." The narrator responds with indignation, showing the owner and the reader that animal welfare is important to him. The word "man" is emphasized to indicate that the narrator is using it sarcastically; he does not think the owner is acting like a "man" at all, which matches (D). Choice A is a misused detail; the narrator does refer to the other man as "big" in paragraph 5, but he is not using the word "man" to describe the other man's size. Instead, he is using it to question his humanity. Choice B is opposite, as the narrator does not agree with the owner, answering him "indignantly." Choice C is a distortion. Although the narrator states that "cruelty" to animals "has the effect of inclining me to fight," his actions are not physical.

6.   H
Difficulty: Low
Category: Detail
Getting to the Answer: In lines 61–62, the owner initially responded to the narrator's words with a "sulky scowl." In response, the narrator mentions an Act of Parliament and makes a threat. At this, the owner stops scowling, seeming "to have been affected by my threats." The owner was worried about the narrator's threats of prosecution, (H). Choice F is out of scope; the owner never seems worried that the dog will bite, and the dog has been behaving kindly toward the narrator since running up to him. Choice G is incorrect because the owner does not discuss his factory job until a later paragraph and never mentions being late to work. Choice J distorts the passage: the owner, not the narrator, was about to throw a stick at the dog.

7.   A
Difficulty: High
Category: Inference
Getting to the Answer: Consider the narrator's tone and comments directed toward the reader. Although the introduction might appear to be argumentative, the narrator includes comments to the reader in lines

2–3 and lines 22–25 that display a thoughtful attitude. He will later explain his behavior in lines 65–66: "I am naturally of a peaceable disposition." Clearly, the narrator doesn't want the reader to think him a brute. This tone matches (A). Choice B is opposite; the narrator is mindful of the reader, though he argues with the dog owner in the passage. Choice C is extreme; the narrator never expresses fear that anyone will disagree with his views about dogs, doggies, or animal welfare. Choice D is also extreme. The narrator seems to desire the reader to have a favorable opinion of him, but nothing suggests that he is so concerned that he's misrepresenting the events.

8.   G
Difficulty: Medium
Category: Inference
Getting to the Answer: Locate the paragraph that contains the owner's explanation about "kindness" (lines 79–94) and review his story. To prevent the dog from following him to the factory, the owner chases him home "out of pure kindness." This matches (G). Choice F is a misused detail; the owner does make this claim in lines 61–62, but this is before he's trying to explain his behavior toward the dog as kindness. Choice H is out of scope, as no mention is made of playing fetch, and the owner even admits that the throwing of "sticks an' stones" is meant to drive the dog home. Choice J is a distortion. While the owner does claim that the dog might be harmed at the factory, he does not claim that the men at the factory "have a record" of these types of actions in the past.

9.   D
Difficulty: High
Category: Inference
Getting to the Answer: In lines 79–94, the owner explains his motivation for his treatment of the dog. After hearing this, the narrator is "somewhat doubtful of the truth of this story." The narrator had just seen the owner mistreating his dog, despite his claims, and his initial "scowl" morphs to a "deferential air" (line 75) as soon as the narrator threatens to have him arrested for his behavior. It seems that the owner is putting on an act to avoid prosecution, (D). Choice A is out of scope; the passage concludes before the purchase of the dog is discussed, so we don't know anything about the owner's eagerness. The narrator calls the owner "big" and "rough" (lines 50–51) but never questions his employability, B, only his treatment of animals.

Choice C is a distortion; the narrator's suspicion of the story stems from the owner's contradictory actions and behaviors, not his assumptions about conditions at the owner's workplace.

10. G
Difficulty: Medium
Category: Inference
Getting to the Answer: Keep in mind both the characters' actions and motivations as well as the timing. Immediately after the owner's story about why chasing the dog with sticks is "kindness," the narrator doubts this explanation and has the sudden thought of buying the dog (lines 95–101). The narrator has considered everything that's happened thus far and realizes that the win-win-win scenario for himself, the owner, and the dog is for him to buy the dog, which matches (G). Choice F is a distortion. The first paragraphs do establish that the dog is "amiable," but the narrator is immediately motivated by his concern for the dog's welfare. Choice H is opposite; rather, he acts assertively toward the owner, as in lines 57–58: "as I felt confidence in my strength, my stick, and the goodness of my cause, I was bold." Choice J is also a distortion, as the narrator believes the owner is just pretending to have concern for the dog's welfare.

Passage II

Suggested Passage Map Notes:

Passage A

¶1: Present-day people think science is unquestionable

¶2: History shows that science is not always correct

¶3: People think science remains constant, but questioning leads to progress

Passage B

¶1: Historically people were skeptical about science

¶2: Scientific research should be questioned

¶3: Pharma. company studies should be scrutinized

¶4: Policy decisions should be based on balance of faith and doubt

BIG PICTURE SUMMARY:
Passage A

Main idea: The public misunderstands scientific research as supplying unquestionable certainties rather than probabilities because science seems predictable in everyday life.

Author's purpose: To argue that science research is subject to uncertainties, possibilities, and limitations

Passage B

Main idea: The current public is not critical enough of scientific research, especially as it is applied to public policy.

Author's purpose: To argue for better public knowledge about the background of scientific studies and a middle-of-the-road approach to applying research to public policy

11. B
Difficulty: Low
Category: Detail
Getting to the Answer: The first mention of policy makers is in paragraph 1, line 14, where the author writes that they "treat the results of every latest study as if they were surefire truths." In other words, they accept the results without question, which matches (B). Choices A, C, and D are opposites.

12. H
Difficulty: Low
Category: Inference
Getting to the Answer: Because the question cites a specific part of the passage, reread the relevant text to make a prediction. In line 33, the author uses the word "probabilities" to refer to the scientific discipline that studies the comparative chances of events taking place, which matches (H). Choice F is opposite; the author believes that science is uncertain, so theories will not necessarily be proven true. Choice G is out of scope; the author does not include information about how future scientists will impact current data. Choice J is a distortion; the author does state that "an unfounded prejudice stemming from a desire for scientific constancy can actually discourage inquiry," but that is not related to the idea that science is an implementation of probabilities.

13. C
Difficulty: Medium
Category: Vocab-in-Context
Getting to the Answer: The word *complacent* follows examples of predictable events, including a car starting and a power plant running without problems. Since we assume these events will always be the same, we become used to them and don't question them at all. In the same way, we have a "a complacent faith in the reliability and consistency of science" and assume that study results are always correct. Choice (C), unquestioned, is a synonym for *complacent*. All other choices are incorrect definitions based on the context provided.

14. G
Difficulty: Medium
Category: Detail
Getting to the Answer: Lines 68–69 state that "many people balked" at Schiaparelli's ideas about features on Mars; (G) matches this prediction and is correct. Alternatively, you could scan through the passage looking for each of the answer choices and eliminate those which were accepted by the public. Choice F is questioned by "some critics," who we cannot assume are the general public. Choice H is in Passage A, not Passage B, and J isn't in the passage at all. That leaves (G) as the correct answer.

15. B
Difficulty: Medium
Category: Function
Getting to the Answer: Use your passage notes to help predict an answer for a Function question that refers to an entire paragraph. The first paragraph of Passage B outlines the way that skepticism toward science has changed over time. Choice (B) matches the function of paragraph 1. Choice A is out of scope; no new hypothesis is introduced in this paragraph. Choice C is a misused detail; paragraph 2 introduces the issue of public policy, but this question asks specifically about paragraph 1. Choice D is a misused detail; underlying causes are discussed in the third paragraph, not the first.

16. F
Difficulty: High
Category: Inference
Getting to the Answer: Remember not to make too big a logical leap; the correct inference will not stray

far from the text. The author believes that people are too ready to believe the results of scientific studies. Choice (F) fits well with the text and represents a logical, supportable inference. Choice G is out of scope; neither author supports the idea of government control and regulation. Choice H is a misused detail; this idea applies to Passage A. Choice J is out of scope; the belief that the reliability of science has decreased isn't discussed in the passage.

17. C
Difficulty: High
Category: Inference
Getting to the Answer: Keeping track of each author's primary viewpoints or beliefs can help you to more quickly evaluate and eliminate answer choices. Passage B describes a solution in which people understand enough about science to assess its reliability for themselves, but Passage A claims that people don't do this because they desire a world of certainties. The contrast between striving for more knowledge and clinging to easy beliefs is captured in (C). Choice A is a distortion; the actions and attitudes of policymakers don't prevent people from becoming better educated. Choice B is a misused detail; Passage B discusses the difficulties of obtaining impartial results, but this is not relevant to the question. Choice D is out of scope; the author of Passage A discusses ethical questions, but this is not related to the solution specified in Passage B.

18. F
Difficulty: Low
Category: Detail
Getting to the Answer: Remember that the answers to Detail questions are always stated directly. By turning first to the passages, you can accurately predict the correct answer and not be misled by misused details. Passage A includes the phrase "present-day industrial societies" in the first sentence, and Passage B mentions "present-day industrial societies" in the second paragraph. Choice (F) matches your research. Choice G is a misused detail; this phrase is from paragraph 2 in Passage A. Choice H is a misused detail; this is included in paragraph 3 in Passage B. Choice J is a misused detail; this is mentioned in the first paragraph of Passage B only.

19. B
Category: Detail
Difficulty: Medium
Getting to the Answer: Prediction is key in Detail questions. Incorrect answer choices will often reference other details erroneously. In paragraph 2, the passage directly states "In the late 19th century, when Italian astronomer Giovanni Schiaparelli first detected seas and continents on the planet Mars, many people balked at the idea of Earth-like topography on the Red Planet," which shows the fallibility, or inaccuracy, of a scientific certainty. Use this as a prediction. Choice (B) matches the prediction. Choice A is a misused detail; this example is mentioned in Passage A, not Passage B. Choice C is a distortion; the author of Passage B discusses this in paragraph 4, but these are not examples of the fallibility of scientific certainties. Choice D is a misused detail; this example is mentioned in Passage A, not Passage B.

20. F
Difficulty: Medium
Category: Function
Getting to the Answer: When a question stem includes a specific line reference, you usually need to read a little before and a little after those particular lines in order to understand the full context of the quoted portion. The word cited in the question stem comes from the third paragraphs of Passage A and Passage B. Passage A says, "technological advances engage increasingly complex moral questions within fields such as pharmaceutical developments" and Passage B states that "Some critics of company-funded studies argue that the level of misrepresentation included in such studies borders on immoral." Choice (F) matches with the references to moral questions in both passages. Choice G is a misused detail; this is mentioned in Passage B only, in the last paragraph. Choice H is a misused detail; this is mentioned in Passage A only, in the third paragraph. Choice J is a misused detail; drug testing and analysis is discussed in paragraph 3 of Passage A but not in paragraph 3 of Passage B.

Passage III

Suggested Passage Map Notes:

¶1: Walter Scott (S) born in Scotland in 1771, wrote Scottish ballads

¶2: S poetry brought fame

¶3: 1814, S started writing novels anonymously for $

¶4: 1820 S wrote *Ivanhoe* set in England, became Baronet

¶5: wrote for $ until his death in 1832

¶6: S (1) popularized historical novel, (2) rehabilitated Highland culture

¶7: S responsible for Scottish banks retaining right to issue own banknotes

BIG PICTURE SUMMARY:

Main idea: Scott faced highs and lows through his writing career, which included writing poetry and historical fiction about his native Scotland.

Author's purpose: To describe the career and influence of author Sir Walter Scott

21. B
Difficulty: Medium
Category: Global
Getting to the Answer: This question focuses on the big picture. You should be predicting the purpose and main idea of every passage so you can deal with questions like this quickly. Your notes should tell you that the author is writing more about Scott's achievements than about his weaknesses. You can predict that the answer will be favorable overall. Choice A is out of scope; this choice lacks a sufficient focus on Scott. Choice (B) matches your prediction. Scott's success is stressed throughout and the last two paragraphs point out Scott's impact in several areas. Choice C is a distortion; although you read that Scott had financial difficulties, the financial aspect is much less important than is the success of his writing. Choice D is a distortion; the passage offers no support for this claim.

22. J
Difficulty: Medium
Category: Detail
Getting to the Answer: On Detail questions, first find the appropriate section in the passage. Read the question carefully; sometimes a single word can make a major difference in selecting the correct answer. Note that the question asks about why Scott started writing novels, not poetry, so look to paragraph 3, where the author first talks about Scott's novels. The first line tells you that financial difficulties led Scott to write a novel, which met with great success. Look for a choice that matches this idea. Choice F is out of scope; the author doesn't list this outcome as a result of Scott's polio. Choice G is out of scope; nothing in the passage mentions "copyright violations." Choice H is out of scope; the author doesn't reference whether the ballads sold well or not. Choice (J) fits the prediction.

23. D
Difficulty: Low
Category: Detail
Getting to the Answer: If your notes don't help, titles, whether italicized or capitalized, are easier to spot when skimming. In the third paragraph, you see that the author references *Waverly* to mention that Scott left his name off it because he was "mindful of his reputation as a poet." Use this as your prediction. Choice A is a distortion; your research tells you that it was his reputation as a poet, not as a lawyer, that concerned Scott. Choice B is a misused detail; the author tells you that Scott found writing anonymously "fun" only after he believed that it would not damage his reputation as a poet. Choice C is out of scope; although the fact that Scott was "widely rumored" to be the author indicates that there was public interest in the novels' author, there is nothing to suggest that interest spurred sales. Choice (D) matches the prediction.

24. J
Difficulty: Medium
Category: Inference
Getting to the Answer: Use the passage to help you understand the author's view of this concept. First find where the author refers to Scott and Scottish history, and then focus on the tone of that discussion. Consider the author's overall attitude toward Scott, which is positive. In paragraph 4, the author mentions Scott's popularization of the tartan and kilt and writes that he turned them into symbols of national identity. Also, in paragraph 6, you see in lines 85–87 that Scott's novels "rehabilitated Highland culture after years in the shadows." Choice F is opposite; the author's tone is more admiring than this. Choice G is opposite; to say that Scott "rehabilitated Highland culture" sounds important. Choice H is a distortion; Scott wrote novels, not "serious analyses of Scottish history." Choice (J) matches the research above.

25. A
Difficulty: Medium
Category: Inference
Getting to the Answer: When in doubt, keep in mind the overall tone that the author takes in the passage. This question asks about Scott's reputation after his death. Since the overall structure of the passage is chronological, it is likely that the answer will come toward the end. The last three paragraphs give evidence of Scott's continued popularity: you read that his novels continued to sell after his death, eventually covering his debts; that Edinburgh's central railroad station was named after his first successful novel; and that his picture is on Scottish currency today. You can predict that his reputation has only grown or is still positive. Choice (A) matches the prediction, and a quick check of the other choices shows that this is the only one with a positive description. Choice B is opposite; the passage clearly states that Scott's novels continued to sell well after his death. Choice C is a distortion; his debts were unpaid, but this did not affect Scott's reputation. Choice D is a distortion; the passage does mention such imitators (lines 80–82), but the author doesn't suggest that they damaged Scott's reputation.

26. F
Difficulty: High
Category: Vocab-in-Context
Getting to the Answer: Sir Walter Scott never put his own name to his novels, but instead attributed them to "the author of *Waverley*," or to no author at all. He continued to do this even when his novels became so popular that it would not have hurt his reputation to reveal his name. Nevertheless he "maintained the façade," meaning that he continued to hide his own authorship under the pretense that he was not the author of the novels, a match for (F). Choice G is another definition of façade, but it doesn't make sense in the context of the passage. Choice H has a negative connotation, while the author says Scott maintained

the pretense "out of a sense of fun." Choice J also doesn't make sense in the sentence.

27. B
Difficulty: Low
Category: Function
Getting to the Answer: To understand the function of a word in context, reading the entire sentence it appears in should be enough. Ask yourself why the placement of this statue would be fitting—the author has not referred to Wallace before this point. The author has, however, previously stressed Scott's affinity for his native land, Scotland, for which Wallace is a great historical figure. Look for a connection with Scotland among the choices. Choice A is out of scope; nothing in the passage suggests that Scott ever wrote a novel about Wallace. Choice (B) fits your prediction. Choice C is out of scope; this fails to address the choice of Wallace. Choice D is out of scope; the passage doesn't support this.

28. H
Difficulty: Medium
Category: Inference
Getting to the Answer: You will need to answer this question from your overall impression of the passage rather than any specific paragraph. First you need to decide whether the author's attitude is positive or negative. Look to the close of the passage; you know that the author believes Scott was responsible for two major trends. The focus on Scott's achievements indicates that the author admires Scott's work. Choice F is a distortion; nothing indicates that the author is skeptical toward Scott's achievements. Choice G is opposite; both of these adjectives are too negative. Choice (H) matches your prediction. Choice J is out of scope; the passage gives no such indication of jealousy.

29. D
Difficulty: Low
Category: Inference
Getting to the Answer: Paragraph references focus your research. Use your notes and reference the passage as needed. The author writes that Sir Walter refused to declare bankruptcy, insisting on putting his home and income into a trust that would eventually pay back his creditors completely. Predict that he was committed to paying his debts back. Choice A is opposite; the passage clearly contradicts this. Choice B is out of scope; the author never discusses the cause

of Scott's debts. Choice C is out of scope; the author doesn't mention such annoyance on Scott's part. Choice (D) matches the prediction.

30. F
Difficulty: Low
Category: Inference
Getting to the Answer: Read the complete sentence for context. You may need to read the ones before and after as well. The prior sentence states that Scott was working as a lawyer, after which you read the first mention of Scott's writings. The subsequent sentences make clear that the emphasis has shifted to Scott's literary career. So the sentence including "dabbling" deals with Scott's first forays into writing. Look for a choice that captures that idea. Choice (F) matches the thrust of the prediction. Choice G is a misused detail; Scott's printing press is not mentioned until paragraph 3, and the author draws no connection between his "dabbling" and his financial troubles. Choice H is a distortion; he was certainly inexperienced, but there is no evidence that his work was inferior. Choice J is a distortion; "dabbling" refers to Scott's writing, not to his interest in history.

Passage IV

Suggested Passage Map Notes:

¶1: Lemur (L) part of suborder of primates, nocturnal; flying lemurs not primates

¶2: L found on Madagascar, larger are nocturnal, smaller are diurnal

¶3: All L species are endangered b/c deforestation and hunting

¶4: Ring-tailed lemur (RTL) most populous L in zoos

¶5: RTL physical characteristics

¶6: RTL baby v. adult characteristics

¶7: RTL live in forests or open brush, require primary forests

¶8: RTL behavior, territory

¶9: RTL communication

¶10: RTL breeding

BIG PICTURE SUMMARY:

Main idea: Several species of lemurs inhabit Madagascar and are endangered. The characteristics of ring-tailed lemurs in particular are described.

Author's purpose: To describe the classification, location, status, and characteristics of lemurs, particularly the ring-tailed lemur

31. C
Difficulty: Low
Category: Detail
Getting to the Answer: Incorrect answers on Detail questions often include material relevant to other sections of the passage. Be sure you research the passage carefully to interpret the context correctly. You are looking for a factor that is responsible for the lemurs' survival. Your notes should help you find your way to paragraph 2, where the author first discusses Madagascar. The author says the lemurs "were safe from competition" on the island. That should factor into the correct choice. Choice A is a misused detail; the author does mention that lemurs have large reflective eyes, but doesn't relate this to survival. Choice B is a misused detail; scent marking is related to their social organization, not their survival. Choice (C) paraphrases the relevant sentence in paragraph 2 and is correct. Choice D is a misused detail; the author mentions "hierarchy" later, but not as an explanation for the lemurs' survival.

32. F
Difficulty: Medium
Category: Detail
Getting to the Answer: Taking good notes and marking the passage will help you on Detail questions that lack line references. From your notes, you should see that social organization is discussed in paragraph 8. The writer states that there are separate hierarchies for each gender and that "females tend to dominate the troop." Look for this among the choices. Choice (F) matches your prediction. Choice G is a distortion; the author does reference "foraging," but not in the context of social organization. Choice H is out of scope; the author doesn't offer support for such a sweeping statement. Choice J is opposite; the author writes that females tend to dominate the troop.

33. D
Difficulty: Medium
Category: Vocab-in-Context
Getting to the Answer: Since *odd* is a common word, it's important to think about it in the specific context of what the author has written. The author uses the word when describing what ring-tailed lemurs usually eat—fruit, leaves, and seeds, plus an insect every now and then. Thus, *odd* refers to *occasional*, as (D) says. All other answer choices are possible definitions of *odd*, but none makes sense in the sentence.

34. G
Difficulty: Medium
Category: Detail
Getting to the Answer: The answers to Detail questions are stated directly in the passage—you can find the answer with research. This point is fairly obscure, and may not be reflected in your notes. If you have to, skim for *zoo*, which appears in paragraph 4. The author states that ring-tailed lemurs are the most populous lemurs in zoos and follows that by writing "they reproduce readily in captivity." Use that as your prediction. Choice F is out of scope; the author doesn't make such a contention. Choice (G) is a good paraphrase of the text referenced above. Choice H is out of scope; the author does not make this point. Choice J is a distortion; the author addresses "foraging," but not in connection with zoos.

35. D
Difficulty: Medium
Category: Inference
Getting to the Answer: When given a line reference, move quickly and read at least that entire sentence to discern context. The author indicates that lemurs need to live in primary forest to survive. The clearing will likely endanger the lemurs' continued survival. Look for a match to this idea. Choice A is out of scope; the author does not refer to this. Choice B is out of scope; the author does not refer to this. Choice C is out of scope; the author doesn't reference such predators here. Choice (D) matches the research above.

36. H
Difficulty: Low
Category: Detail
Getting to the Answer: This is an EXCEPT question. That means you need to find three choices that are mentioned in the text and one that is not. Don't

confuse the two. Your notes can help you to locate "olfactory signals"; they appear in paragraph 9. Work through the paragraph, crossing off the three choices that do appear. Choice F is opposite; this appears in lines 88–89. Choice G is opposite; this appears in lines 90–91. The author does not reference (H), which makes it the correct answer. Choice J is opposite; this appears in line 88.

37. B
Difficulty: Medium
Category: Detail
Getting to the Answer: Detail questions are answered directly in the passage. Referencing it before making a prediction will help you avoid misused details. Note that the question concerns all lemurs (Lemuriformes), not only ring-tailed lemurs. This leads you to the first paragraph, which discusses lemurs in general. You may be unsure exactly which characteristic to predict, so compare this paragraph to the choices. Choice A is a distortion; many lemurs are nocturnal, but not all lemurs are. Choice (B) makes sense. Paragraph 1 states that lemurs represent the "evolutionary predecessor" of monkeys and apes, a paraphrase of what you see here. Choice C is opposite; at the end of paragraph 1, the author clearly states that these species are not actually lemurs. Choice D is opposite; the first sentence in paragraph 2 states that lemurs are found on Madagascar "and some smaller surrounding islands."

38. H
Difficulty: Medium
Category: Inference
Getting to the Answer: You need to "read between the lines" to find the correct answer. But don't make too great a logical leap. Check your notes for the second paragraph, and read it again if necessary. The question is very open-ended, so work through the choices and compare them to the information in the paragraph. Choice F is opposite; the author states that the pygmy mouse lemur is the smallest species and that smaller species are typically nocturnal, not diurnal. Choice G is out of scope; the author does not discuss why certain species of lemur have become extinct. Choice (H) works. The author writes that the indri was the largest lemur. The next sentence states that "the larger

species" are all extinct. Therefore, you can infer that the indri is extinct. Choice J is opposite; in paragraph 1, you learn that lemurs are described as evolutionary *predecessors* of monkeys, meaning monkeys are descended from them.

39. C
Difficulty: Medium
Category: Detail
Getting to the Answer: You map should note that paragraphs 5 and 6 describe the physical attributes of ring-tailed lemurs, and paragraph 6 states that "the very young animals have blue eyes while the eyes of all adults are a striking yellow." Since there's no other reference to anything else that changes when ring-tailed lemurs become adults, (C) has to be the correct answer. Choice A is out of scope; there's nothing in the passage that supports this. Choice B is contradicted by the sentence "Ring-tailed lemurs are thought to require primary forest" (lines 66–67), and D is opposite; flying lemurs are not lemurs at all, as lines 11–12 state.

40. F
Difficulty: Medium
Category: Detail
Getting to the Answer: Because this question asks which question is not answered, it functions as an EXCEPT question. Find the issue that is not addressed in the passage. The answers to these questions could fall anywhere in the passage. Your notes, though, should help you find the information you need. The author touches on (F) in paragraph 3, saying that "options are limited." This implies that the question of survival has not been fully answered. If you're unsure at this point, work through the others to see that they are answered. Choice G is opposite; this is answered in the second sentence of paragraph 2. Lemurs survived because they did not have to compete with monkeys and apes. Choice H is opposite; looking at the last paragraph, you see that the female is fertile for only one day a year, and that gestation lasts 146 days. So the female can have only one litter, and the author states that a litter consists of one or two babies. Choice J is opposite; this is answered in paragraph 8. The author states lemurs eat fruit, "leaves, seeds, and the odd insect."

Science Test

Passage I

1. C
Difficulty: Medium
Category: Thinking Like a Scientist—Evaluating Hypotheses
Getting to the Answer: According to Scientist 2, the positions of electrons are "random and yet localized" as they move around the nucleus. They don't follow fixed orbits, but they are more likely to be in some places than others. Thus, one way to describe the movement of electrons would be to say that it's "almost random," as in (C). Choice A is incorrect because it better describes the Bohr model. Choices B and D are incorrect because they contradict both models; both models suggest that electrons move around the nucleus in some way.

2. J
Difficulty: High
Category: Thinking Like a Scientist—Evaluating Hypotheses
Getting to the Answer: Scientist 2 mentions the wave function in order to explain the way in which an electron's possible position is given boundaries. These boundaries determine the shape of an atom, which in turn helps to define many of its properties. Choice (J) is thus correct. Choice F conflates the two models, but only the Bohr model describes orbits and only the electron cloud model deals with probabilities. Choice G is incorrect because neither scientist suggests a dependence between charge and the color of light emitted by an atom. Choice H is incorrect because Scientist 2 only discusses the wave-particle duality with respect to electrons.

3. A
Difficulty: Low
Category: Thinking Like a Scientist—Evaluating Hypotheses
Getting to the Answer: Although the two models offer differing accounts of how electrons move around the nucleus, both agree that electrons move rather than remaining in a fixed position. Choice (A) is thus correct. Choice B is incorrect because neither view suggests that charge is based on probability; only the electron cloud model discusses probability, but there it is applied only to position, not charge. Choice

C is incorrect because neither scientist discusses the composition of protons and neutrons. Choice D is incorrect because both views discuss the components of atoms, suggesting that atoms can in fact be divided into smaller parts.

4. G
Difficulty: Medium
Category: Thinking Like a Scientist—Evaluating Hypotheses
Getting to the Answer: Scientist 1 cites the fact that excited electrons emit very specific wavelengths of light when reverting to lower energy orbits, and makes the following argument in favor of the Bohr model: "If the position of electrons is not specified, the precise wavelengths of light that are emitted cannot be explained." This poses a direct challenge to the view of Scientist 2, so (G) is correct. Choice F is incorrect because it contradicts the views of both scientists. Choice H is incorrect because it's cited by Scientist 2 as support for the probability cloud idea. Choice J is incorrect because it's a fact agreed to by both scientists.

5. A
Difficulty: High
Category: Thinking Like a Scientist—Evaluating Hypotheses
Getting to the Answer: According to Scientist 2, "[t]he uncertainty of any one electron's position and the nature of its existence as a charged particle contribute to an understanding of the wave-particle nature of matter and energy." The findings mentioned in the question stem further support this wave-particle duality. Therefore, (A) is correct. Choice B is incorrect because traveling in distinct paths is part of the Bohr model. Choices C and D are incorrect because they suggest the observation supports the Bohr model. Choice D also incorrectly supplies reasoning in favor of the electron cloud model rather than the Bohr model.

6. H
Difficulty: Medium
Category: Thinking Like a Scientist—Evaluating Hypotheses
Getting to the Answer: Scientist 2 begins by stating that "[t]he precise location of electrons cannot be detected." This challenges the idea from the Bohr

model that electrons travel in fixed paths, which would allow their locations to be identified precisely. Choice (H) is therefore correct. Choice F is incorrect because it is not inconsistent with the Bohr model (Scientist 1 would say that electrons have a 100% chance of occupying one of the fixed orbit paths, and a 0% chance of being elsewhere). Choices G and J are incorrect because they are not discussed by either scientist.

7.   C
Difficulty: Medium
Category: Experiments—Synthesizing Data
Getting to the Answer: According to Scientist 1's account of the Bohr model, "[e]lectrons move around an atom's nucleus in precise co-planar, concentric circular orbits." Choice (C) is the only option that reflects this. Choice A in incorrect because it shows an atom without a nucleus. Choice B shows an atom with orbiting electrons, but the electrons do not orbit in co-planar, concentric circles. Choice D would be a better representation of the electron cloud model.

Passage II

8.   G
Difficulty: Low
Category: Experiments—Design & Methodology
Getting to the Answer: This question simply requires you to find the answer choice that reflects differences in sampling between the two studies. The passage notes that sampling was conducted "at ground level" for Study 1 but "from the tops of two different monitoring towers" for Study 2. Choice (G) is thus correct. Choice F contradicts the passage—in both experiments, sampling was done on a daily basis. Choice H is tempting, but it switches the studies, making the statement untrue. Choice J does not work either—both pollutants mentioned were sampled in each experiment.

9.   B
Difficulty: Medium
Category: Experiments—Design & Methodology
Getting to the Answer: Although several of these procedures might be worthwhile, only (B) correctly proposes studying all three variables mentioned in the question stem (carbon monoxide, sulfur dioxide, and respiratory ailments). Choice A includes a respiratory ailment (asthma), but it is incorrect because temperature was not one of the variables mentioned.

Choices C and D are incorrect because they describe procedures that would not provide any information about respiratory ailments.

10.   J
Difficulty: Medium
Category: Experiments—Design & Methodology
Getting to the Answer: To test the hypothesis from the question stem, you'd need an experiment that relates sulfur dioxide and the acidity of lakes. Only (J) connects sulfur dioxide to the acidity of lake water, so it is correct. Choice F is incorrect because it doesn't provide a link between sulfur dioxide and lake acidity. Choice G might be tempting because the passage does mention respiratory ailments, but G also fails to provide a direct link between sulfur emissions and lake acidity. Choice H is also incorrect: while the amount of coal burned might increase the amount of sulfur dioxide emitted by the plant, doing this alone won't tell you anything about the link between sulfur dioxide and the acidity of the lake.

11.   A
Difficulty: Medium
Category: Experiments—Design & Methodology
Getting to the Answer: The first paragraph describes the motivation behind the studies: "Scientists noted an increase in acid rainfall and reports of respiratory ailments in a certain community. They suspected that both of these outcomes were due to increased levels of airborne pollutants, such as carbon monoxide and sulfur dioxide, entering the atmosphere in that community." Because Study 1 involved measuring the levels of these pollutants near two highways, it is reasonable to conclude that the scientists were trying to determine if pollution from traffic was the source of these respiratory problems. This fits well with the hypothesis expressed in (A). Choice B is incorrect because the power plant is only a factor in Study 2, not Study 1. Choice C incorrectly states that Study 1 was concerned with measuring rainfall. Choice D is incorrect because it fails to involve respiratory ailments.

12.   F
Difficulty: Medium
Category: Experiments—Synthesizing Data
Getting to the Answer: The studies in this passage suggest that emissions from highway traffic and from power plants contribute to airborne pollutant levels that are above 0 ppm. Building more highways, as in

Practice Tests

(F), would consequently be likely to increase, rather than reduce, highway traffic and subsequent pollution, making (F) the correct answer. Choice G is incorrect because it would be likely to help: highway traffic is indicated as a source of pollutants, so traffic limits would help reduce pollution due to highway vehicles. Choice H would also be likely to help: burning coal is the source of the power plant's pollutant emissions, so reducing coal burning would reduce emission levels. Choice J is incorrect for a similar reason: filters would decrease the amount of sulfur dioxide reaching the outside air, thereby reducing nearby levels of this airborne pollutant.

13. D
Difficulty: Medium
Category: Data—Inference & Calculation
Getting to the Answer: If emissions become less concentrated farther away from their sources, what would you expect to happen if you moved closer to the source? You could expect emissions measured closer to a source (the roadway, in this case) to be more concentrated. Thus, the correct answer will be larger than the data point for Highway 1 on January 7 in Table 1, which is 3.2 ppm. Choice (D) is the only option larger than 3.2 ppm, so it is correct. Choices A, B, and C are all smaller than 3.2 ppm.

14. F
Difficulty: Medium
Category: Data—Detail & Interpretation
Getting to the Answer: Look carefully at Table 2, which compiles the results of Study 2. According to the table, ozone and sulfur dioxide levels both show an increase followed by a decrease in both towers, supporting statement I. Because I is true, G can be eliminated. Carbon monoxide levels were always greater in Tower 1, not Tower 2, so statement II is false, meaning that H and J can also be eliminated. Choice (F) must therefore be correct. This can be confirmed by determining that statement III is false: Tower 2 had the highest level of emissions on January 8, not January 9.

Passage III

15. D
Difficulty: Medium
Category: Data—Inference & Calculation
Getting to the Answer: Each of the tables includes rubber, which always produces an amperage of 0.0 mA.

This means A can be eliminated. Study 2 and Study 3 both use 6 mm wire, but only Study 3 was conducted at 30°C, so use Table 3 to find the range. The highest value is 12.1 mA, so the range is 0.0 mA to 12.1 mA. Choice (D) matches this range. Choices B and C give the ranges for Study 1 and Study 2, respectively.

16. G
Difficulty: Low
Category: Experiments—Synthesizing Data
Getting to the Answer: Comparing the data in Tables 1 and 2 shows that for most of the materials tested in these experiments, the current carried by the wire increases as the diameter of the wire increases. The exception is rubber, which does not carry current in any of these trials, so it is the only material that does not support the hypothesis that a larger diameter results in more current carried. Choice (G) is thus correct.

17. D
Difficulty: Medium
Category: Experiments—Synthesizing Data
Getting to the Answer: Start by looking at what happens to current when the diameter of a zinc telluride (ZnTe) wire increases. Tables 1 and 2 show that when the diameter increases, the amount of current conducted increases. For temperature, comparing Tables 2 and 3 shows that when temperature decreases, current increases. Thus, to find the wire that would carry the largest current, you want the wire with the largest diameter and the lowest temperature. Choice (D) is thus correct.

18. F
Difficulty: Medium
Category: Data—Inference & Calculation
Getting to the Answer: The conditions described in the question stem differ from the setup of any of the studies conducted in the passage, but the key is to focus on the most important information. The materials of the wires are copper, rubber, and steel. According to the results of the 3 studies, rubber always yields an ammeter reading of 0.0 mA. This makes it an insulator, according to the definition provided in the introductory paragraph, that is, "a substance that prevents an electric charge from traveling between objects." Because the rubber wire interrupts the flow of charge in the circuit, no current will be conducted, so the ammeter will read 0.0 mA. Choice (F) is thus correct.

19. A
Difficulty: Medium
Category: Data—Inference & Calculation
Getting to the Answer: The scientist hypothesized that decreasing the temperature increases the amount of current a wire will carry, and this hypothesis was generally supported by a comparison of the results in Tables 2 and 3, with the exception of rubber, which never conducted a current. Consequently, if the temperature of a wire were instead *increased*, the amount of current carried would *decrease*, except for rubber, which would remain unchanged at 0.0 mA. Choice (A) is thus correct. Choice B is incorrect because only the current for rubber would remain unchanged. Choice C is incorrect because the current would never increase at a higher temperature; it would only decrease or remain unchanged. Choice D is incorrect because the current would decrease for most of the materials.

20. J
Difficulty: Medium
Category: Data—Inference & Calculation
Getting to the Answer: You can see by looking at the tables that rubber conducts 0.0 mA of electricity throughout all three studies. Because it prevents the flow of current, this makes it an insulator, based on the definition provided in the passage. However, because the results of all three studies are the same for rubber, it does not appear that its capacity as an insulator is affected by changes to its diameter or temperature. Choice (J) is thus correct.

21. D
Difficulty: Low
Category: Experiments—Design & Methodology
Getting to the Answer: The question asks you to identify which effect the scientist should investigate next to learn more. Choice A, however, was revealed by comparing the results of Studies 2 and 3, while B was revealed by comparing Studies 1 and 2. Choice C was investigated in all of the studies. That leaves (D), which is correct because wire length was held constant throughout all of the studies, so it would be an appropriate choice to manipulate in a future study to determine its effect on current conducted.

Passage IV

22. J
Difficulty: Low
Category: Data—Detail & Interpretation
Getting to the Answer: The question stem points you to the top two curves in Figure 1. To find the greatest difference, determine the average air temperature in August for the urban area (the solid line) and rural area (the dash-dot line) for each of the years listed in the answer choices. The respective August urban and rural temperatures were approximately 75°F and 68°F in 2007; 77°F and 70°F in 2010; 73°F and 66°F in 2012, and 74°F and 63°F in 2014. The differences in temperature between urban and rural are 7°F in 2007, 2010, and 2012, and 11°F in 2014. Therefore, the correct answer is (J). Alternatively, rather than calculate the exact differences, you could eyeball the graph and estimate; it shouldn't be too hard to see that the gap between the top two curves is wider for 2014 than for the other years.

23. A
Difficulty: Low
Category: Data—Detail & Interpretation
Getting to the Answer: Look at Figure 3 to find out which pair of months had the closest average wind velocities. According to Figure 3, the average wind velocity for the rural area was approximately 16 mph for January, 16 mph for April, 13 mph for July, 20 mph for September, and 23 mph for November. Since the average wind velocities for January and April are about the same, the correct answer is (A).

24. H
Difficulty: Medium
Category: Data—Inference & Calculation
Getting to the Answer: The question stem mentions Study 3, in which the scientists studied wind velocity and air quality. Eliminate G and J, which mention average air temperature (the focus of Study 1). The new evidence states that buildings increase frictional drag on air flowing over built-up terrain. An increase in frictional drag would lead to lower wind velocity, which means that having more buildings lowers wind velocity. According to Figure 3, the average wind velocity is lower for the urban area than for the rural area, which suggests that there are more buildings in the urban area. Thus, the conclusion in the question stem that the rural area has more buildings than the urban

area would NOT be justified based on the results. The correct answer is (H). Even if you were unaware of what effect frictional drag would have on wind velocity, you could still eliminate F because it provides the reasoning that wind velocity is lower for the rural area, which is directly contradicted by Figure 3.

25. C
Difficulty: Medium
Category: Data—Inference & Calculation
Getting to the Answer: According to Study 1, "compared to the relative humidity of the rural area, the relative humidity of the urban area was 2% lower in the winter and 6% lower in the summer." Figure 1 shows a similar relationship for average air temperature differences. The difference in the average summer air temperatures between the urban and rural areas is greater than the difference in the average winter air temperatures. Thus, because they follow similar trends, you can conclude that relative humidity differences and average air temperature differences are correlated. The correct answer is (C). Choice A is not true according to the passage: the relative humidity is lower for the urban area. Choice B is true but does not answer the question, which concerns both winter and summer temperature differences. Choice D is incorrect because it mentions wind velocity, which was measured in Study 3 and not Study 1.

26. G
Difficulty: Medium
Category: Experiments—Synthesizing Data
Getting to the Answer: The hypothesis from the question stem suggests that since building materials and road surfaces increase the air temperature of urban areas, urban areas would have higher air temperature than rural areas. According to Figure 1, the summer temperatures of the urban area during August are higher than those of the rural area during August. Therefore, yes, the results do support the hypothesis. Eliminate H and J. Choice (G) correctly states summer temperatures in the urban area were higher than those in the rural area, making (G) the correct answer.

27. B
Difficulty: Medium
Category: Data—Inference & Calculation
Getting to the Answer: Make sure your response draws from the information given in the passage and question stem. According to Study 3, there are about

10 times more dust particles in the air of the urban area than of the rural area. Given that dust particles act as hygroscopic nuclei, it is likely that the urban areas will have more rain because of the higher level of dust in the air at those areas. And, indeed, Figure 2 shows that the urban area received more precipitation than the rural area. Thus, the correct answer is (B). Choices A, C, and D are not true statements. According to the passage, compared to the urban area, the rural area had higher wind velocity, fewer clouds, and higher relative humidity.

28. F
Difficulty: Medium
Category: Experiments—Synthesizing Data
Getting to the Answer: Based on Figure 1, 75°F is approximately the average air temperature for the urban area in the summer, while Figure 2 suggests that the average annual precipitation for the urban area is about 40 inches. Therefore, this third area is likely also an urban area, which could be expected to have a similar wind velocity to the urban area that was studied. According to Figure 3, the wind velocity for the urban area varied between about 8 and 12 mph. Thus, it is reasonable to expect that this third area will have an average wind velocity of somewhere between 8 and 12 mph, as in (F).

Passage V

29. A
Difficulty: Medium
Category: Data—Detail & Interpretation
Getting to the Answer: Based on Figure 2, Mercury speeds up as it approaches perihelion and slows down as it moves away. Choice (A) is thus correct. Choice B suggests the opposite trend. Choice C suggests that orbital velocity decreases, but that happens only as the planet moves away from perihelion. Choice D suggests that orbital velocity increases, but that happens only as the planet moves toward perihelion.

30. H
Difficulty: Low
Category: Data—Inference & Calculation
Getting to the Answer: A planet with a mass in between that of Jupiter and Saturn, assuming a similar density, would have a radius that lies between the radii of Jupiter and Saturn, that is, between 58,232 and 69,911 km. Only (H) falls into this range. Choice

F suggests a radius less than that of Mercury. Choice G suggests a radius between that of Earth and Venus. Choice J suggests a radius larger than that of Jupiter.

31. B
Difficulty: Low
Category: Data—Detail & Interpretation
Getting to the Answer: According to Table 1, Saturn has a mass of 5.68×10^{26} kg, Jupiter a mass of 1.90×10^{27} kg, Earth a mass of 5.97×10^{24} kg, and Mercury a mass of 3.29×10^{23} kg. Of these, Jupiter has the greatest mass, so (B) is correct.

32. G
Difficulty: Medium
Category: Data—Detail & Interpretation
Getting to the Answer: Based on Figure 2, Mercury's orbital velocity at 75×10^6 km away from perihelion is roughly 53 m/s. The next point at which it has this orbital velocity is 75×10^6 km as it recedes from perihelion. Choice (G) is thus correct. This can also be seen from the symmetry of Mercury's curve in Figure 2: the velocity at a particular distance while approaching is always equal to the velocity at that same distance while receding. Choice F is incorrect because it corresponds to a velocity of about 50 m/s. Choices H and J are incorrect because both correspond to a velocity of about 56 m/s.

33. C
Difficulty: Medium
Category: Thinking Like a Scientist—Applying Core Knowledge
Getting to the Answer: Acceleration is simply the change in velocity per unit of time, so a larger acceleration due to gravity will cause a falling object to reach a given velocity more quickly—in other words, it will cause the object to fall faster. Because Earth has a higher acceleration due to gravity than does Venus, objects on Earth fall faster than objects on Venus. Choice (C) is thus correct.

34. G
Difficulty: Medium
Category: Data—Inference & Calculation
Getting to the Answer: Figure 1 provides an object's acceleration due to gravity at various distances from the center of planets, so compare each answer choice

to this graph to find the one that would have the highest acceleration. For choice F, Figure 1 shows that an object 7,000 km from the center of Venus would have an acceleration of a little less than 7.0 m/s^2.

For choice (G), Figure 1 does not include Saturn. However, the question stem also directs you to Table 1, which provides the mass of planets, including Saturn, and the passage indicates that mass is one factor that impacts gravitational effects. The masses of the three planets included in Figure 1—Earth, Venus, and Mercury—follow the trend that the greater the planet's mass, the higher an object's acceleration due to gravity at any distance from the planet's center. Saturn's mass (5.68×10^{26} kg) in Table 1 is much greater than any of the planets included in Figure 1 (the highest, Earth, is 5.97×10^{24} kg). So you can predict that an object's acceleration at 7,500 km from the center of Saturn would be considerably greater than that of an object at 7,500 km from the center of Earth. In other words, it would be *greater than* 7.0 m/s^2, so eliminate F and keep (G).

For H, an object 8,500 km from the center of Earth would have an acceleration of about 5.5 m/s^2 according to Figure 1. And for J, an object 9,000 km from the center of Mercury would have an acceleration of less than 1.0 m/s^2. Both of these are less than the prediction of *greater than* 7.0 m/s^2 for (G), which is the correct answer.

Passage VI

35. A
Difficulty: Medium
Category: Experiments—Synthesizing Data
Getting to the Answer: As can be seen in Figure 1, titration of a strong base into a strong acid generates a curve that starts with an acidic pH (a value considerably less than 7), followed by a sharp increase to a basic pH (a value considerably greater than 7). Titration of a strong acid into a strong base would show the reverse behavior, starting well above pH 7 and finishing well below pH 7. Choice (A) is thus correct. Choice B has an appropriate appearance, but it is incorrect because it bottoms out near a neutral pH (near 7) instead of an acidic pH. Choices C and D are incorrect because their curves do not match the general shape seen in Figure 1.

Practice Tests

36. H
Difficulty: Medium
Category: Experiments—Synthesizing Data
Getting to the Answer: This question asks about the equivalence point, which is defined in the passage as "the point at which equal concentrations of an acid and base are present." The passage also notes that the change in pH immediately after and immediately before the equivalence point will be drastic, so you should look for the point in the middle of the sharp increase for Solution A in Figure 1. Based on the figure, the equivalence point for Solution A is found at a pH of about 7 (after approximately 24 mL of NaOH have been added). According to Table 1, phenol red has a pH range of 6.8—8.4, making it the only indicator that includes pH 7 in its range. Choice (H) is thus correct. Choices F and G are incorrect because they change colors at too low of a pH, while J is incorrect because it changes colors at too high of a pH.

37. C
Difficulty: Low
Category: Thinking Like a Scientist—Applying Core Knowledge
Getting to the Answer: This question is easier to answer if you remember from high school chemistry that 7 is a neutral pH. The passage describes the chemical equation as "a typical acid-base neutralization reaction." Thus, if it goes to completion without excess reactants, the resulting solution should have a neutral pH of 7. Choice (C) is correct. Choices A and B present acidic pH values, while D presents a basic pH.

38. G
Difficulty: Medium
Category: Data—Detail & Interpretation
Getting to the Answer: Figure 2 presents the reaction rate as a percentage of the rate at the equivalence point. Thus, any percentage value greater than 100% corresponds to a reaction rate that is faster than the rate at the equivalence point. The curve in Figure 2 is above 100% between approximately 1 mL and 24 mL. Choice (G) is correct because it is the only option with a volume in this range.

39. B
Difficulty: Medium
Category: Thinking Like a Scientist—Applying Core Knowledge
Getting to the Answer: Familiarity with the names of elements and simple compounds will help to answer this question. According to the reaction presented in the passage, sodium (Na) moves from NaOH to NaCl as the reaction proceeds forward. NaCl is sodium chloride, commonly known as table salt. Choice (B) is correct. Choices A and C are incorrect because water (H_2O) and hydrochloric acid (HCl) do not contain sodium. Choice D is incorrect because sodium hydroxide (NaOH) is where the sodium is found before the reaction, not after it.

40. J
Difficulty: Medium
Category: Experiments—Synthesizing Data
Getting to the Answer: Because the question asks about a reaction rate, look at Figure 2 first. The highest reaction rate (with a value of over 125%) is found after about 5 mL of NaOH have been added. Figure 1 shows low pH values for both solutions at 5 mL of NaOH. Choice (J) is correct because it is the only option that features a low pH. Choices F and G are incorrect because both points are found after about 24 mL of NaOH have been added, when the reaction rate is only 100%. Choice H is incorrect because a high pH in Solution A is only found after about 25 mL or more of NaOH have been added, when the reaction rate drops below 100%.

Writing Test

Level 6 Essay

In today's world the truth of the matter is that a high school diploma no longer makes a job applicant competitive; a college degree is now required for most high-paying jobs which also offer advancement opportunities. Given the high cost of a college education—and even community college fees may be beyond the reach of some students—taking out a student loan is almost a given for the college student. The question is, however, how these loans should be structured. Several options are offered, but the fairest and most workable is that of no-interest government and bank loans.

Firstly, as the issue states, student loans can take years to repay, even when the former students earn good salaries and repay the loan month by month. This is simply because the cost of a college education is so high. The average cost of a four-year college ranges from almost $10,000 per year to over $35,000. For all but the wealthiest of students, paying for college without a loan is prohibitive. My cousin spent years trying to pay off her student loans and, in the long run, defaulted and had to declare bankruptcy. Surely this is not the intention of either the government, other lending institutions, or colleges.

Loans are not special entitlements; they are fundamental to allow students of all economic backgrounds to attend college. As such, the government should not be making money from student loans. Interest is essentially a fee charged for borrowing money, with some sort of collateral insuring repayment. In the case of a college loan, that collateral is the student's future earning capacity. Granted, the principal must be repaid, but beyond that, taking money out of earnings cuts into the former student's ability to use that money for other purchases, including housing, which are so vital in driving the country's economy. Charging only the principal needed to pay for college insures that students can not only pay the yearly tuition, but are also more likely to be able to settle the entire loan and after graduation, contribute to the economy as a whole. In the special circumstance that some students need more time, it is then fair to add some further amount of payment as recognition that the original agreement was not fulfilled. This is the fairest solution and one that provides the greatest opportunity for students to go to college and pay off their loans.

The second option defines a college education as a commodity, which is something that can be bought and sold and also implies choice. Although it can be argued that a college education can be bought, it is not the same as oil or wheat. It is not used for the moment but for the future and it cannot be compared to loans for items that people choose to buy, such as cars or refrigerators. Loans to support an educated populace as the backbone of our society are not the same as car loans and should not be treated as such. If we truly believe in education, we must make allowances for the loans required to fund it. As we have all learned, college is an investment in the future. It has become less and less a personal choice and more of a requirement for job consideration. When considered on a supply and demand basis, it is even more important, since studies show that jobs requiring a college degree are in more and more demand. A capitalist market requires the ability to be competitive and creative; this is exactly what a college education provides. Educated students are far more important than almost anything else a loan can support, and any accommodations, including making college loans less expensive than other loans, is for the benefit of society and the future, and should be promoted, not prohibited.

Finally, the third point of view is simply ridiculous. There is absolutely no way to determine how much money a person will earn in the future. We can make considered guesses—lawyers will earn more than waiters—but there is no guarantee that the lawyer will not be fired and the waiter will not become a restaurant owner. Basing the loan amount on future earnings can also mean that the graduate has no opportunity to change his career from a high-earning one, such as a lawyer, to one that may truly be his heart's desire, such as being an artist. Furthermore, even if one were to train to be a lawyer, it is possible that he will not find a job that pays him the same amount of money the loan projected him to earn. At one time, investment counselors were earning a lot of money, and therefore would have been low-risk borrowers, but after the investment scandal several years ago, many investment counselors are doing other jobs, have no job, or may even be in jail. College graduates are just starting their careers; how well they do, what they earn, and whether they stay in their original jobs are unknown and cannot be used to determine a loan amount.

College loans should be as accessible and easy to repay as possible. There is nothing more important than an educated and far-sighted generation of college graduates. They are the ones who will run the government, captain business, and teach children. To deprive them of their college opportunity by making it too hard for them to either get or repay adequate loans is to deprive this country of those who will steer its future.

Score Explanation (6 in all domains)

This essay exhibits strong and consistent writing skills. The introduction summarizes the arguments to come and heralds the author's point of view. Each following paragraph then discusses one perspective and its implications, using specific and appropriate examples. The conclusion reiterates the writer's opinion and moves it from specific to general, connecting it to a wider concept.

Ideas and Analysis (6)

The author's ideas are clearly, logically, and persuasively stated: a college-educated populace is the backbone of the country, and since paying for college is difficult, student loans should be granted without adding the financial burden of interest. Ideas are cohesive, build on each other, and are well-developed. Insight and analysis are excellent, examining the issue from both the perspective of the student still in college and the college-educated worker, with implications about the cost of education, the importance of a college education, and the ability of the earner to contribute to the national economy. The conclusion that to make tuition borrowing a heavy burden "is to deprive this country of those who will steer its future" provides both a succinct ending as well as additional insight.

Development and Support (6)

The line of reasoning throughout the essay is clear, consistent, and forceful. Starting out with a general statement about the importance of a college education in today's workplace, the author then enlarges on this idea with specifics about the cost of education (with supporting numbers) that requires most students to take out loans, the argument that college loans are not "special entitlements," cogent reasons why these loans should be interest-free, and well-argued critique of the other two options. Support is excellent, including the example of the writer's cousin and comment that "Surely this [default] is not the intention of either the government or colleges," and reference to a capitalist economy and consumer spending which drives it. The examples of lawyers and investment counselors are highly relevant to the author's critique of the other two perspectives, and show his ability to connect actual events to his thinking.

Organization (6)

The organization is excellent, with good transitions ("Firstly," "The second option," "Finally"). The writer's perspective is firmly introduced in the opening paragraph and reiterated in the conclusion, and all body paragraphs are in logical and persuasive order. The three paragraphs supporting the writer's point of view are persuasive in their individual perspectives on the issue, and contrast well with the two paragraphs critiquing the other viewpoints. There is a central idea, maintained throughout both in direct support and in contrast to other perspectives, and the essay is coherent, flows well, and makes a strong and effective argument.

Language Use (6)

Word choice, writing style, and vocabulary all enhance the argument. High-level vocabulary with words such as "concomitant," "entitlements," and "prohibited" raise the argument to a sophisticated level. There are no grammar mistakes or punctuation errors, and only one spelling error ("insures" for "ensures"). Sentence structure is somewhat varied, particularly with the use of dashes in paragraph five. The phrase "the third point of view is simply ridiculous" begs for more temperate wording, but it does illustrate the author's commitment to his ideas. The tone is appropriately firm and formal for a persuasive essay.

Level 4 Essay

Throughout our school lives, parents and teachers emphasize the importance of going to college. Consequently almost all my friends in my high school are planning on going to college. Some will even be the first in their families to have a higher education, or perhaps even finish high school. They will be better educated than their parents, have more opportunities for better and higher-paying jobs, and perhaps be able to contribute something unique to society. However, the cost of a college education, and the need for loans, means that most students will take out loans. Because the loans are for a good cause, and the end result may benefit all of society, these loans should be readily available and interest free.

I know from the home loan my parents have that it's hard to pay loans back every month, so the less money a borrower has to pay every month, the more likely that the loan will eventually be paid in full. When applying that to college loans, the best way to structure them is to not add anything extra, including interest. The added cost of interest means that students will have to pay more, it will take longer and be harder, and some may not be able to do it at all. The education for a doctor, for example, takes many years, each one involving the cost of schooling. Though a doctor may make a great deal of money over time, this won't happen right away, but the loan payments will and it will all add up to perhaps an unpayable debt. The government makes a great deal of money off taxes, and banks make plenty of money from credit cards; it should not be allowed for them to also make money from student loans.

Those who want to base school loans on future earnings are going to run into a lot of problems. As freshmen and sophomores, how can we be sure of what we will do when we graduate from college, so how can loans for the first two years of college be based on future earnings? And what if a person can't find a job right after school or decides to change his career? Holding a person captive in a career because it's the only way he can make enough money to repay his student loans is unfair to the person and could deprive him from the opportunity to do something else which would benefit society.

Since financial institutions, and the government when it works as one, can get their money back if people actually pay their monthly installments, it makes sense to do what they can to make it easy. Students are borrowing money for something that actually benefits society as a whole. They are not asking for college to be free (although that would be great) but just a fair chance at paying the money they owe without the burden being so much that they can't pay for the necessities of life. If the government and the banks want to get their money back they definitely should make the loans cheaper by not charging interest.

Score Explanation (4 in all domains)

The writer of this essay remains focused on the issue throughout and develops a clear opinion in the first paragraph. Support is varied, showing some recognition of the complexity of the issue. One alternative perspective is critiqued, followed by reiteration of the author's conclusion. The rhetorical questions in the second paragraph add to the writing quality.

Ideas and Analysis (4)

The author's thesis—loans should be interest-free to enable borrowers to repay them, and banks and the government have no need to add interest—is consistent throughout the essay. The argument recognizes several contexts in which this applies, including children better educated than their parents, the cost of a college education, the burden on the borrower, and not restricting workers to a job simply because they can make enough money to repay the loan. The author analyzes the issue more broadly when discussing the job market, career changes, and possible benefits to society. The author's thoughts are clearly expressed and contribute to a generally persuasive essay.

Development and Support (4)

Though couched primarily in personal terms ("almost all my friends in my high school are planning on going to college"), the author's reasoning moves from the opening statement, to her perspective, the reasons supporting it (including benefits to society), critique of an alternative, and her conclusion, showing clear and logical development. She expands on her thesis, emphasizing how interest-free loans make it more likely that the borrower can repay with undue burden, and supports this with reference to her parents' home loan, the length and cost of a doctor's education, taxes, and credit cards. Her critique of the third perspective, though somewhat simplistic, is relevant to the thesis.

Organization (4)

The author's thesis is clear and supported by the introductory comments regarding many students planning on going to college. The organizational strategy is clear in the progression of the essay, and ideas are grouped logically. The second paragraph expands on the thesis and is cohesive in its development. The writer then reflects on an alternative perspective, but returns to her thesis in the final paragraph, reiterating the benefit of no-interest loans both to the borrower and possibly to society. There are some internal transition words ("consequently," "however") and paragraph transition words to help the essay flow better. For the most part, the organization is adequate for a persuasive essay.

Language Use (4)

Word choice is correct but simple, with phrases such as "plenty of money," "run into lots of problems," and "make the loans cheaper." Though overall the grammar and spelling are correct, some sentences are awkwardly phrased ("it should not be allowed for them to also make money from student loans") and the phrase "end result" is redundant. Rhetorical questions are well-placed and make good points. Overall, word choice is adequate and occasionally above-average with words such as "burden," "captive," and "unique." Tone and style are generally appropriate.

Level 2 Essay

Everybody knows that the cheaper something is, the more people can afford to buy it. Getting a loan for college isn't exactly buying something but it ends up being the same thing because it means you have to pay for something. With a loan you don't pay the full price rite away but you do in the long run so its better to have to pay less than more which is what happens if theres no interest on the loan. If you have to get a loan, getting a goverment one without interest is best, but you still have to make a lot of money so you can pay your loan and also have money to live.

Even though its not a choice for the essay, I think a better way to get money for college is to get a scholarship because you dont have to pay that back. People who are good at something like sports, like I am, should be rewarded with a college scholarship. I hope I will get a football scholarship because Im the quarterback on the varsity football team and were one of the top three teams in the high school division. If I get a football scholaship I can go to college and still play football and I won't have to pay any money for a loan. It doesnt matter if loans have extra money to pay back like interest because all that money is hard to pay back no matter how much it is. So a scholarship is better and thats what I want so I can go to college.

Score Explanation (2 in all domains)

Though the essay provides some support for the first perspective, the author then goes off-topic and neglects to consider the prompt from any perspective but his own. Though scholarships are available for college tuition, they are irrelevant to the task, thus the writer has neither understood the tasks nor fulfilled them in any way. This essay does not show coherent thinking, writing, or attention to the task.

Ideas and Analysis (2)

The writer gives a passing nod to the prompt with a weak response, which is then abandoned in favor of an off-topic thesis. The majority of the essay is irrelevant and even the argument in favor of scholarships lacks any analysis or support. Logic is garbled or non-existent, and no attempt is made to address any alternative perspective for the prompt, though the author does recognize that his perspective is not one of the three given.

Development and Support (2)

There is minimal response to the prompt with no development of ideas. Support is given only in terms of "the cheaper something is." Even the author's own claim is weak, consisting of personal opinion only with no support. But for the brief and somewhat incoherent response to the first perspective, this essay would merit a score of 1.

Organization (2)

The entire essay is contained in two paragraphs with no clear introduction or conclusion. The second paragraph is introduced with a contrast transition ("Even though,") and an argument proceeds from there, but since the argument is irrelevant to the prompt, the entire organization of the paragraph is off-topic. The second-to last sentence somewhat references the task but simply echoes the first paragraph's contention that it is difficult to pay back a loan. This essay does not show appropriate thinking, writing, or attention to the task.

Language Use (2)

Sentence structure and word choice are simplistic, and there are multiple spelling and punctuation errors ("goverment" for "government," "scholaship" for "scholarship," "rite" for "write"). There is a noticeable lack of commas within sentences, and apostrophes are missing from several words. The third sentence is unnecessarily long and should be broken up. The personal and somewhat antagonistic tone and voice are inappropriate for the purpose.

You can evaluate your essay and the model essay based on the following criteria, which are covered in the Practice Makes Perfect section of this book:

- Does the author discuss all three perspectives provided in the prompt?
- Is the author's own perspective clearly stated?
- Does the body of the essay assess and analyze each perspective?
- Is the relevance of each paragraph clear?
- Does the author start a new paragraph for each new idea?
- Is each sentence in a paragraph relevant to the point made in that paragraph?
- Are transitions clear?
- Is the essay easy to read? Is it engaging?
- Are sentences varied?
- Is vocabulary used effectively? Is college-level vocabulary used?